EYEWITNESS TRAVEL

EUROPE

D0003094

DK

LONDON, NEW YORK,
MELBOURNE, MUNICH AND DELHI
www.dk.com

PROJECT EDITOR Ferdie McDonald, Claire Marsden
ART EDITOR Paul Jackson
EDITORS Sam Atkinson, Simon Hall, Andrew Szudek
DESIGNERS Anthony Limerick, Sue Metcalfe-Megginson,
Rebecca Milner
PICTURE RESEARCHERS Katherine Mesquita, Alex Pepper, Lily Sellar
MAP CO-ORDINATOR Casper Morris
DTP DESIGNER Maite Lantaron

MAPS
Ben Bowles, Rob Clynes, James Macdonald
(Colourmap Scanning Ltd)

PHOTOGRAPHERS
Max Alexander, Demetrio Carrasco, Kim Sayer, Linda Whitwam

Reproduced by Colourscan, Singapore
Printed and bound by South China Printing Co. Ltd., China

First published in Great Britain in 2001
by Dorling Kindersley Limited
80 Strand, London WC2R 0RL

Reprinted with revisions 2002, 2003, 2004, 2006, 2008

Copyright © 2001, 2008 Dorling Kindersley Limited, London
A Penguin Company

Front cover main image: the 12th-century Alcázar in Segovia, Spain

---

**The information in this
DK Eyewitness Travel Guide is checked regularly.**
Every effort has been made to ensure that this book is as up-to-date
as possible at the time of going to press. Some details, however,
such as telephone numbers, opening hours, prices, gallery hanging
arrangements and travel information are liable to change. The
publishers cannot accept responsibility for any consequences arising
from the use of this book, nor for any material on third party
websites, and cannot guarantee that any website address in this
book will be a suitable source of travel information. We value the
views and suggestions of our readers very highly. Please write to:
Publisher, DK Eyewitness Travel Guides,
Dorling Kindersley, 80 Strand, London WC2R 0RL, Great Britain.

◁ **The Hôtel de Ville, Brussels' magnificent town hall** *(see pp224–5)*

**Enjoying the evening sunshine in a
café overlooking a Greek harbour**

CONTENTS

HOW TO USE
THIS GUIDE **6**

VISITING EUROPE

PUTTING EUROPE ON
THE MAP **10**

PRACTICAL & TRAVEL
INFORMATION **12**

EUROPE AT A
GLANCE

THE LANDSCAPES OF
EUROPE **22**

GREAT MUSEUMS AND
GALLERIES **24**

THE HISTORY OF
EUROPE **26**

THE BRITISH
ISLES

GREAT BRITAIN **36**

IRELAND **108**

**Punting on the Cam beside Queens'
College, Cambridge** *(see p73)*

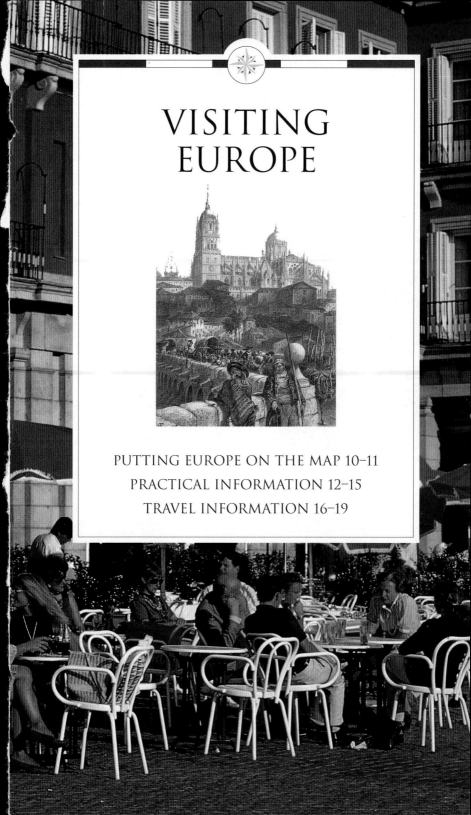

VISITING
EUROPE

PUTTING EUROPE ON THE MAP 10–11

PRACTICAL INFORMATION 12–15

TRAVEL INFORMATION 16–19

Putting Europe on the Map

The continent of Europe stretches as far east as Russia's Ural Mountains, a total surface area of 10.4 million sq km (4 million sq miles). However, the 20 countries covered in this guide occupy a much smaller area, being concentrated in the northwestern and central parts of the continent and along the Mediterranean coast in the south. These countries are shown on this map in dark green. They include 18 of the nations that make up the European Union, the political association of European states based in Brussels *(see p228)*. The map also shows the principal international airports and the major road links. Europe's rail network is shown on the map on the inside back cover.

Satellite Photograph of Europe
This image shows the range of landscapes on the European continent, from the frozen coast of northern Scandinavia, through fertile plains on either side of the Alps and Pyrenees, to the balmy regions of the Mediterranean.

0 kilometers 250

0 miles 250

KEY

✈ International airport

— Highway

— Major road

--- Ferry route

▪▪▪ International boundary

ATLANTIC OCEAN

Faroe Islands

Shetland Islands

Orkney Islands

NORTH SEA

Bergen
Stavanger
Kristiansand

Inverness
Aberdeen
Glasgow   Edinburgh
NORTHERN IRELAND   Belfast   Newcastle
Galway   DUBLIN   GREAT
IRELAND   BRITAIN
Cork
Birmingham
Cardiff   Harwich   AMSTERDAM
LONDON   NETHERLANDS
Southampton   Dover   BRUSSELS   Düsseldorf
Calais   BELGIUM
Le Havre   Luxembourg   LUX.
St-Malo   PARIS   Metz
Rennes
Nantes   Tours   Dijon   Zürich
FRANCE   BERN
SWITZ.
Lyon   Geneva   Milan
A Coruña   Bordeaux   Turin   Genoa
Bay of   Toulouse   Marseille   Nice
Biscay   Bilbao
Oporto   Corsica
Ajaccio
SPAIN   Zaragoza
PORTUGAL   MADRID   Barcelona   Sardinia
LISBON
Valencia   Palma   Menorca
Faro   Granada   Alicante   Mallorca   Cágliari
Seville   Ibiza
Gibraltar   Málaga   MEDITERRANEAN
Tangier
Melilla   Algiers
MOROCCO   ALGERIA

◁ **Café life in Plaza Mayor, Madrid**

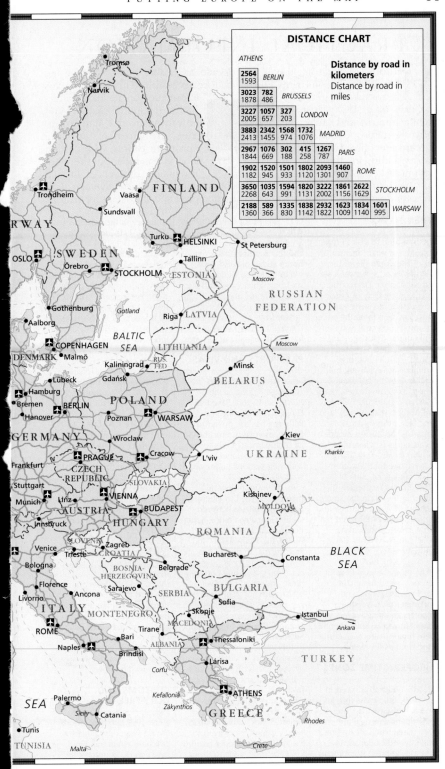

DISTANCE CHART

Distance by road in kilometers
Distance by road in miles

ATHENS								
2564 1593	BERLIN							
3023 1878	**782** 486	BRUSSELS						
3227 2005	**1057** 657	**327** 203	LONDON					
3883 2413	**2342** 1455	**1568** 974	**1732** 1076	MADRID				
2967 1844	**1076** 669	**302** 188	**415** 258	**1267** 787	PARIS			
1902 1182	**1520** 945	**1501** 933	**1802** 1120	**2093** 1301	**1460** 907	ROME		
3650 2268	**1035** 643	**1594** 991	**1820** 1131	**3222** 2002	**1861** 1156	**2622** 1629	STOCKHOLM	
2188 1360	**589** 366	**1335** 830	**1838** 1142	**2932** 1822	**1623** 1009	**1834** 1140	**1601** 995	WARSAW

PRACTICAL INFORMATION

Millions of visitors travel to Europe for reasons many Europeans take for granted – the rich diversity of history, architecture, art, and landscape. In Western Europe tourist facilities are generally of a high standard, while in the former Communist countries of Eastern Europe their scope and quality have improved significantly over the past decade. As a result, the whole of Europe is more accessible. This section gives information on practical matters such as passport formalities and how to get around. Many countries are members of the European Union, with certain laws in common, but there are also notable differences. In each country chapter a *Practical Information* section gives specific details for visitors.

The European Union Flag

WHEN TO GO

The best time to visit Europe depends on your itinerary, but most people prefer the summer months, between May and September. Due to the diverse geography of Europe, the weather has wide variations. Summers in northwestern Europe can be cool and rainy, while in the east they can be unbearably hot. The Mediterranean, with its hot, dry summers and relatively mild winters, has the balmiest climate, but crowds are a major drawback, particularly in July and August, making May and June better times to visit. August is the busiest month because this is when most French, Italian, and Spanish citizens take their vacations.

The climate of parts of Scandinavia is extreme: in winter in the north the sun rises only for a few hours and the roads can be blocked by snow, while summertime attracts many visitors, drawn by the prospect of enjoying the "midnight sun".

The mountainous areas of Europe have unique climates. The Pyrenees, Alps, and Apennines all have short summers and long winters with heavy snowfall. Consequently, these regions offer wonderful opportunities for skiing.

EUROPEAN TIME ZONES

The 20 countries covered in this guide fall across three time zones. Great Britain, Ireland, and Portugal are on GMT (Greenwich Mean Time), while the other European countries are one hour ahead (+1), except for Greece, which is two hours ahead (+2). So, for example, London, Dublin, and Lisbon are five hours ahead of New York, while Paris and Budapest are six hours ahead, and Athens is seven hours ahead.

In Europe the clocks go forward by one hour in March (Daylight Saving), and go back in the fall, usually in October.

PASSPORTS AND VISAS

Most western European countries belong to the European Union. Based in Brussels, this European authority has the power to pass certain laws affecting all member states. There are currently 27 member states, with negotiations underway with other states.

In 1999, the following EU members agreed to eliminate passport controls between them: Germany, France, Spain, Portugal, Belgium, Luxembourg, the Netherlands, Italy, and Austria. In theory it is sufficient to carry an identity card when traveling between these countries, but it is worth carrying your passport just in case. The other EU countries (Britain, Denmark, Finland, Greece, Ireland, and Sweden) have yet to sign up to this agreement, and so passports are needed by everyone entering or leaving.

If you are arriving in Europe from a non-EU country, a passport is required. However, since 1999 visitors from the United States, Canada, Japan, New Zealand, Norway, and Switzerland no longer require visas for short visits to those countries in the agreement (Germany, France, Spain, Portugal, Belgium, Luxembourg, the Netherlands, Italy, and Austria). Instead, you should receive an official entry stamp on your passport when entering the country (or from a police station within 72 hours). For longer stays, a visa may be required. Check this with the embassy of the country you plan to visit.

Some countries require a visa regardless of your length of stay; refer to the individual *Practical Information* sections in each chapter for full details.

STUDENT CARDS

As well as various bus and rail tickets that offer discounts on European travel *(see p18)*, students with a recognized student card may be eligible for a wider range of discounts. The best card is the International Student Identity Card (ISIC), which gives discounts on all kinds of goods and transport, as well as cheap admission to many museums, galleries, and other sights. Most students can obtain this card from their educational establishment at home but it can also be obtained abroad from an ISIC issuing office or from branches of STA Travel *(see p17)*. For US students, this card also includes some medical cover.

CUSTOMS AND DUTY-FREE

Since 1999 duty-free goods are no longer available for purchase when traveling between EU countries; these

FRANCE AND THE LOW COUNTRIES

FRANCE 144

BELGIUM AND LUXEMBOURG 218

THE NETHERLANDS 244

THE IBERIAN PENINSULA

SPAIN 276

PORTUGAL 352

ITALY AND GREECE

ITALY 386

GREECE 468

Field of sunflowers, a common crop in central and southern France

GERMANY, AUSTRIA, AND SWITZERLAND

GERMANY 522

AUSTRIA 586

SWITZERLAND 612

SCANDINAVIA

SWEDEN 638

NORWAY 656

DENMARK 672

FINLAND 688

SIDE TRIP TO ST. PETERSBURG 696

CENTRAL AND EASTERN EUROPE

CZECH REPUBLIC 706

HUNGARY 728

POLAND 744

GENERAL INDEX 762

ACKNOWLEDGMENTS 794

RAIL MAP OF EUROPE
Inside back cover

Leaning Tower of Pisa rising behind the Baptistry *(see p411)*

The spectacular hilltop Monestir de Montserrat in Catalonia *(see pp316–17)*

HOW TO USE THIS GUIDE

This Dorling Kindersley travel guide helps you to get the most from your visit to Europe. *Visiting Europe* maps the continent, and gives tips on practical considerations and travel. *Europe at a Glance* gives an overview of some of the main attractions and a brief history. The book is divided into seven sections, each covering a group of two, three, or four countries. The chapter on each country starts with a historical portrait and a map of the country. The main sight-seeing section then follows, with maps of the major cities. For each country there is a section of practical and travel information, followed by listings of recommended hotels and restaurants.

EUROPE MAP
The colored areas shown on the map on the inside front cover indicate the 19 country chapters in this guide.

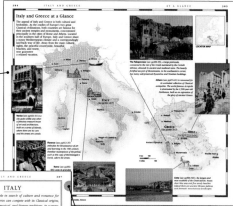

1 At a Glance
The map here highlights the most interesting cities, towns, and regions in the countries covered in the section (in this example Italy and Greece).

Each country chapter has color-coded thumb tabs.

2 Introduction to a Country
This section gives the reader an insight into the country's geography, historical background, politics, and the character of the people. A chart lists the key dates and events in the country's history.

3 Country Map
For easy reference, sights in each country are numbered and plotted on a map. The black bullet numbers (e.g. ❸) also indicate the order in which the sights are covered in the chapter.

Sights at a Glance lists the numbered sights in alphabetical order.

For the larger countries there is an index of the practical and listings pages at the end of the chapter.

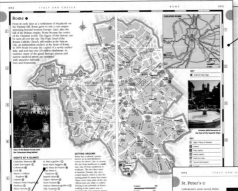

4 City Map
This plots individual sights within the most important cities. The sights within a city such as Rome are indicated with clear bullet numbers (e.g. ③), in contrast to the black bullets used on the country maps.

Visitors' Checklist gives all the practical information needed to plan your visit.

Sights at a Glance lists the numbered sights within the city.

5 Major Sights
Historic buildings are dissected to reveal their interiors, while museums and galleries have color-coded floor plans to help you find the most important exhibits.

Stars indicate the features that no visitor should miss.

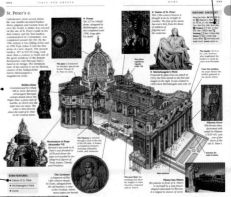

6 Detailed Information
Cities, towns and other sights are described individually. Their entries appear in the same order as the numbering on the country map at the beginning of the section.

Each entry begins with essential practical information, including the address and telephone number of the local tourist information office. Opening times are given for major sights and museums.

7 Practical Information
This section covers subjects such as visas, security, travel, shopping, and entertainment. The larger countries are covered in greater detail.

Directory boxes give contact information for the services and venues mentioned in the text.

Climate charts *(see p13)* are provided for each country.

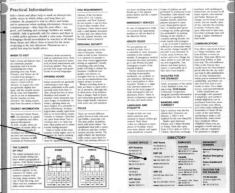

planes or blocks of seats in advance, then resell the tickets at more competitive rates. The main drawback with these tickets is that they are usually non-refundable. They also tend to land at remote airports and at wildly unsocial hours. The level of in-flight service and comfort is usually lower, too.

PACKAGE DEALS

One of the easiest ways to arrange your visit to Europe is to book a package vacation. These are offered by all the major airlines, as well as various reputable independent companies, such as **Central Holidays** and **American Express**. They normally include flights, transfers, and accommodations, and sometimes side trips and food, and the cost is sometimes far less than if you were to buy these separately. While an excellent way of reducing the strain of organizing your vacation, the downside with a package tour is that it usually involves traveling in large numbers on specific flights to a hotel which, because the price has been pared to the bone, may not offer a high standard of food or facilities. On the other hand, there are specialist package tour operators that do offer top quality hotels and use scheduled flights.

FLY-DRIVE

Many airlines, as well as numerous travel companies, offer fly-drive packages, which combine air fares and car rental. These deals are often worth considering, as they give you flexibility and offer a saving over arranging the two parts separately.

INTERNET BOOKING

The internet is becoming a popular way of booking tickets. Two of the best sites for this are **Expedia and Opodo**. Expedia has a system called a "Fare Tracker" whereby you fill in a form online and they e-mail you information when tickets become available. The US company **Europebyair** also provides excellent deals on flights to Europe. It offers a FlightPass for non-European citizens, valid for 62 European cities and one-way flights between these destinations for a very reasonable price.

FLIGHTS WITHIN EUROPE

There is an extensive flight network serving most major cities, making it quick and easy to fly within Europe. If you are traveling some distance, and especially between Great Britain and other parts of Europe, flying can be the least expensive way to go. Indeed, if you want to get to destinations such as Portugal or Greece quickly, flying is almost the only option. However, between major cities, such as Berlin and Paris, you could go by train, which is almost as quick and cheap, and saves the trouble of getting to an airport *(see p18)*.

It is best to avoid flying between major cities on Friday evenings and early Monday mornings because these flights can be crowded with European commuters.

As with transatlantic flights, you can get cheaper tickets by booking early. The best cities for finding good deals from "bucket shops" are London, Athens, and Amsterdam.

LOW-COST AIRLINES

Recent years have seen the emergence of so-called "no frills" airlines in Europe, such as **Ryanair, easyJet, Air Berlin** and **Eurowings**, which offer very competitive prices. A return flight from London to Berlin, for example, can cost as little as £50 ($70). To keep prices down, there is usually less legroom, on-board catering is minimal or costs extra, and outlying airports may be used, but unless you must have these benefits, the price justifies the inconvenience.

DIRECTORY

EUROPEAN NATIONAL AIRLINES

Air France
Tel 800-237 2747 (US).
Tel 1-300 39 01 90 (Aus).
www.airfrance.com

Alitalia
Tel 800-223 5730 (US).
www.alitalia.com

British Airways
Tel 800-AIRWAYS (US).
Tel 1-300 767 177 (Aus).
www.british-airways.com

Iberia
Tel 800-772 4642 (US).
www.iberia.com

KLM
Tel 800-447 4747 (US).
Tel 1-300 303 747 (Aus).
www.klm.com

Lufthansa
Tel 800-645 3880 (US).
Tel 1-300 655 727 (Aus).
www.lufthansa.com

SAS
Tel 800-221 2350 (US).
Tel 300 727 707 (Aus).
www.flysas.com

TRAVEL AGENTS

STA Travel
10 Downing St, New York, NY 10014, US.
Tel 800-781 4040.
www.statravel.com

Trailfinders
215 Kensington High St, London W8, UK.
Tel 020-7938 3939
(for long-haul travel).
Tel 020-7937 1234
(for European travel).
www.trailfinders.com

PACKAGE DEALS

American Express
Tel 800-297 2977.
www.americanexpress.com/travel

Central Holidays
Tel 800-935 5000.
www.centralholidays.com

INTERNET BOOKING

Europebyair
www.europebyair.com

Expedia
www.expedia.com

Opodo
www.opodo.com

LOW-COST AIRLINES

Air Berlin
www.airberlin.com

easyJet
www.easyjet.com

Eurowings
www.eurowings.com

Ryanair
www.ryanair.com

Europe by Train

Trains are generally a popular, reliable, and comfortable means of travel, which also gives visitors the chance to enjoy the passing countryside. With the Channel Tunnel in operation between Britain and France, it is now possible to travel all the way from Scotland to mainland Greece by rail, and the number of passes and discounts on offer ensure that costs need not be high.

TYPES OF TRAIN

All kinds of train serve the rail network in Europe, from the slow local lines of remote regions, to fast diesel-powered intercity expresses. For the latter, such as the French TGV (Train à Grande Vitesse), the Spanish AVE (Alta Velocidad Española), and the German ICE (InterCity Express), you usually need to reserve a seat in advance, and they are more expensive.

A pan-European rail system is still a dream of the European Union, but there has been some progress. The French operate TGV trains to Zürich, Bern, Turin, and Milan, where they link up with Italy's Pendolino trains; Brussels is connected to Paris, Amsterdam, Cologne, and Geneva by the high-speed Thalys network, while Germany's ICE system also runs to Bern, Switzerland.

Overnight trains are popular, offering couchettes, or bunks (usually four or six per compartment), or the more desirable sleepers (usually two or three beds per compartment). The price of a sleeper tends to be higher (three times the couchette price), but it is worth it if comfort is important.

RAIL PASSES FOR NON-EUROPEANS

The cheapest way of seeing Europe by rail is to buy one of the many passes available. For non-Europeans the most popular of these is the Eurailpass from **Eurail**, or if you are under 26, the Eurail Youthpass. It is best to buy these tickets in the US or Australia before traveling because they can be 10 percent cheaper than if you wait and buy them in Europe. You can also buy these on the Internet through Eurail and **Rail Europe**. These passes do not include the supplements payable on many of the faster trains: the EC (EuroCity), IC (InterCity), and EN (EuroNight) trains. You must pay these before boarding – if you don't and are caught by a conductor you will then have to pay the supplement plus a fine.

The Eurailpass offers unlimited travel in 17 European countries. These include Austria, Belgium, Denmark, Finland, France, Germany, Greece, Hungary, Ireland, Italy, Luxembourg, the Netherlands, Norway, Portugal, Spain, Sweden, and Switzerland. It is available as a consecutive-day pass if you want to make frequent short hops by train, or as a flexipass if you are on a trip with extended stop-overs. It is also valid for some ferries.

Other variations on the Eurailpass include the Saver Flexipass, which gives at least a 15 percent reduction per person when two or more people are traveling together. The Youth Flexipass is an option for those under 26 years of age, and applies whether you are traveling in a group or alone.

For further information on national train services and passes in individual countries see the *Travel Information* section for each country.

PASSES FOR EUROPEANS

For Europeans the best pass is the Inter-Rail, which is also available from Rail Europe or from main train operators in individual countries. The Inter-Rail pass divides 28 countries in Europe into eight zones and is for anyone under 26 years old who has been resident in a European country for at least six months. For those over 26 years, there is the Inter-Rail 26-Plus. What you pay depends on the number of zones you want to travel in and the length of your stay.

EUROSTAR/EUROTUNNEL

Connecting London's Waterloo Station to Lille and the Gare du Nord in Paris the **Eurostar** foot passenger train service provides the fastest link between the two capitals. It also operates to Brussels' Gare du Midi. These journeys only take three hours.

The **Eurotunnel** company operates a service between Folkestone in Great Britain and Calais in France that has drive-in compartments for vehicles. For a day trip it costs a set price per car with passengers (the more passengers, the cheaper the cost per person). Daytime journeys are more expensive than those departing after 10 o'clock at night.

DIRECTORY

RAIL PASSES

Eurail
www.eurail.com
Official US website.
www.railpass.com
Tel 877-RAILPASS (US).
Booking and information.

Rail Europe
178/9 Piccadilly,
London W1V 0BA.
Tel 0870-837 1371.
🕐 *10am–6pm Mon–Fri,*
10am–5pm Sat.
www.raileurope.com
For Eurailpasses.
www.raileurope.co.uk
For Inter-Rail passes.

EUROSTAR/EUROTUNNEL

Eurostar
Tel 0870-518 6186 (UK).
Tel 0892-35 35 39 (France).
www.eurostar.com
For foot passengers.

Eurotunnel
Tel 0870-535 3535 (UK).
Tel 0810-63 03 04 (France).
www.eurotunnel.com
For cars & buses.

Europe by Road and Ferry

While many prefer the ease of traveling by train when they want to get somewhere fast, traveling by car gives you the chance to stop at will and explore many areas of Europe on the way. Car ferries and the Channel Tunnel have extended Europe's boundaries into the Scottish Hebrides and down to the Aegean.

DRIVING PERMITS

Many non-European licenses can be used in Europe, but an international driving permit is worth having, if only to make life easier when renting or leasing a vehicle (you have to be at least 21 years of age when renting). Be aware that it is mandatory to have an international permit in parts of Eastern Europe. The permit lasts for one year.

DRIVING IN EUROPE

In Great Britain, Northern Ireland, the Republic of Ireland, Cyprus, Malta, and Gibraltar people drive on the left-hand side of the road. The rest of Europe drives on the right. Remember that in most of Europe distances are measured in kilometers (1 km equals 0.6 miles). The exceptions are Great Britain and Ireland, which work in both metric and Imperial measurements. Most highways have a speed limit of around 100–135 km/h (60–80 mph). The fastest roads are in Germany where the speed limit is 210 km/h (130 mph) on the *Autobahnen*. Roads are very congested during August, the vacation month, especially during the first and last weekends and on routes to the coast.

The cost of driving in Europe varies from country to country. Italian *autostrade*, French *autoroutes*, and Spanish *autopistas* are regularly punctuated by toll booths, while a one-time fee must be paid on entering Switzerland and Austria. However, the vast majority of roads are free in the Netherlands, Great Britain, and Germany, although tolls are charged on certain bridges.

Fuel prices vary enormously across Europe. Gibraltar, Andorra, and Luxembourg are by far the cheapest, while France, Italy, and the Netherlands are the most expensive, with Spain, Great Britain, and Switzerland somewhere in between. The difference in price can be up to 30 percent. Unleaded gas is used almost exclusively in Scandinavia and Western Europe, but it is rarely available in the east.

CAR RENTAL

Car rental is a competitive business in Europe, so prices are generally quite affordable. The biggest car rental companies in Europe are Europcar, Avis, Hertz, Sixt, and Budget, all of which offer an excellent level of service. Local contact details are given in the *Travel Information* section for each country. There are also US companies that specialize in European car rentals. These include firms such as **Europcar, Kemwel, Europe by Car**, and **Auto Europe**.

TRAVELING BY BUS

Domestic bus services provide an alternative to the rail network throughout Europe, and while these are cheaper, they are generally much slower and offer less in terms of comfort and amenities. The exceptions are Portugal, Greece, and parts of Spain, where buses have superseded trains, and Hungary, which has a bus system that is as good as the rail network. In most European countries, buses are best used as extensions of the railway, affording access to villages and remoter regions. Advance bookings for these are rarely needed.

International buses are also a second-best to express trains, but the tour options are worth considering. One example, **Eurolines,** offers passes that allow you to visit 31 European capitals over a 15-, 30- or 60-day period.

TRAVELING BY FERRY

Once in Europe you may need to go by boat to get to the more outlying areas. Many of the islands of Greece and Scotland, for example, are only accessible by sea. Or, if you start your trip to Europe by flying into Great Britain, it is possible to continue by ferry, catamaran, or hydrofoil to Ireland, France, Belgium, the Netherlands, and Spain. Companies operating regular ferries from Great Britain are **P&O** and **Sea France**.

It can also be easier and cheaper to travel by sea than by air from Spain to the Balearic Islands, from Italy to Sardinia and Sicily, and to Greece from Italy. For further details, see the *Travel Information* section of the individual countries.

DIRECTORY

CAR RENTAL

Auto Europe
Tel 888-223 5555 (US).
www.autoeurope.com

Europcar
Tel 877-940 6900 (US).
www.europcar.com

Europe by Car
Tel 800-223 1516 (US).
www.europebycar.com

Kemwel
Tel 877-820 0668 (US).
www.kemwel.com

TRAVELING BY BUS

Eurolines
Tel 08705-808 080 (UK).
www.eurolines.co.uk

FERRY SERVICES

P&O
Tel 08705-980 333 (UK).
www.poferries.com

Sea France
Tel 08704-431 653 (UK).
www.seafrance.com

EUROPE AT
A GLANCE

THE LANDSCAPES OF EUROPE 22–23
GREAT MUSEUMS AND GALLERIES 24–25
THE HISTORY OF EUROPE 26–31

The Landscapes of Europe

A wide range of climatic and geological conditions has forged an impressive variety of landscapes in Europe. Although the appearance of much of the land has changed dramatically since mankind began to cultivate it around 7,000 years ago, there are still many remote and wild regions, such as the spectacular peaks of the Alps and the Pyrenees. As well as being simply beautiful in their own right, Europe's diverse landscapes offer endless opportunities for outdoor activities.

Norway
Indenting the country's west coast, the wild and rugged Norwegian fjords are a truly spectacular sight, offering some of the most breathtaking scenery in Scandinavia.

Great Britain
Dartmoor in southwest England is a wilderness of great natural beauty. The windswept open moorland at the area's bleak and isolated heart has inspired many romantic tales.

ATLANTIC
OCEAN

NORTH
SEA

IRELAND

GREAT
BRITAIN

NETHERLAND

BELGIUM &
LUXEMBOURG

France
The wine-producing regions of France, such as Champagne, boast lush, fertile vegetation, with row upon row of neatly planted vines.

Bay
of
Biscay

FRANCE

SWITZ

PORTUGAL

SPAIN

MEDITERRANEAN SEA

Portugal
The interior of southern Portugal is largely characterized by parched plains, dotted with cork oaks and olive trees, and vast dusty wheat fields stretching uninterrupted to the horizon.

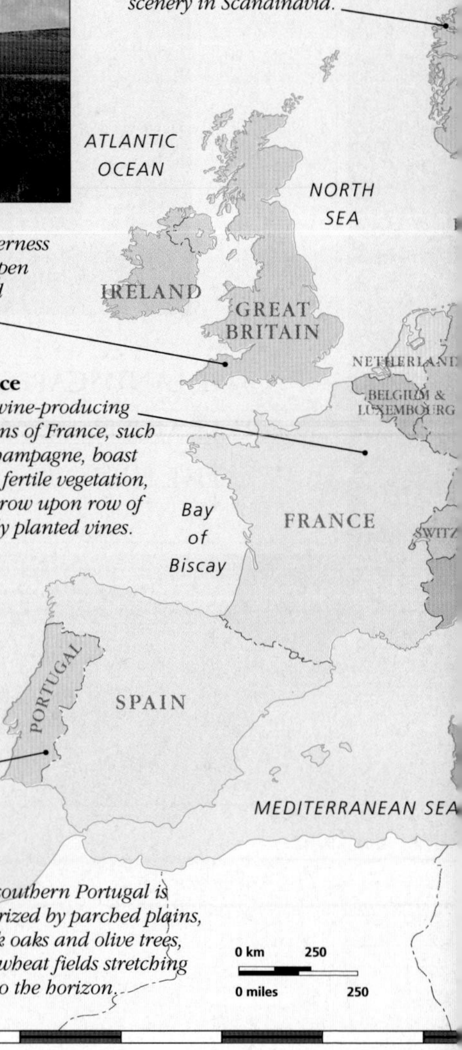

0 km   250

0 miles   250

◁ The many islands of Stockholm, capital of Sweden

Hungary
North of the Hungarian capital, the Danube flows through a verdant landscape of vineyards, orchards, and thickly wooded hills. Known as the Danube Bend, this is one of the river's most beautiful stretches.

Switzerland
Switzerland's landscape is dominated by the Alps, Europe's highest mountain range. Dramatic, snow-covered peaks, stunning vistas, and a range of first-class winter sports facilities draw millions of visitors to this part of Europe every year.

Greece
The Greek mainland and islands have some of Europe's finest coastal scenery. There are thousands of beaches, ranging from small rocky coves backed by pine-clad cliffs to broad swathes of golden sand.

Great Museums and Galleries

The museums and galleries of Europe include national collections, the former collections of Europe's royal and noble families, and a whole host of smaller local institutions. The museums highlighted here are those with the largest and richest collections, which ought to be included in the itinerary of every visitor to Europe. Between them they contain many of the world's best-known and best-loved artistic treasures. These range from archaeological finds from the early civilizations of the Middle East, through pieces from Egyptian, Greek, and Roman times, to masterpieces of the Renaissance and other great periods of European art.

Rijksmuseum, Amsterdam
The Rijksmuseum (see pp256–8) is known for its Rembrandts and other great Dutch paintings of the 17th century. Frans Hals' Wedding Portrait *is a joyful celebration of Dutch life.*

British Museum, London
A vast collection of antiquities and other artifacts from all over the world is is housed inside Britain's national museum (see pp52–3). There is a fascinating display of mummies and other exhibits from Ancient Egypt.

Louvre, Paris
The celebrated home of the Mona Lisa *and the* Venus de Milo, *the Louvre also houses Jean Watteau's melancholy study* Gilles or Pierrot *(c.1717), one of many French works on display (see pp158–60).*

ATLANTIC
OCEAN

NORTH
SEA

IRELAND

GREAT
BRITAIN

NETHERLA

BELGIUM &
LUXEMBOU

Bay
of
Biscay

FRANCE

PORTUGAL

SPAIN

MEDITERRANEAN

Prado, Madrid
The former royal collection in Madrid (see pp288–90) contains the finest assembly of Spanish paintings in the world. Of many highly individual works, Goya's Saturn Devouring His Son *is one of the most powerful.*

0 km   250

0 miles   250

Pergamon Museum, Berlin
This fabulous collection of antiquities includes the famous blue-tiled Ishtar Gate from Babylon, dating from the 6th century BC (see p532).

Kunsthistorisches Museum, Vienna
Based on the imperial collections of the Habsburgs, the museum (see p596) houses archaeology, paintings, and sculpture, such as this woodcarving of the Madonna (c.1495) by Tilman Riemenschneider.

Uffizi, Florence
The Uffizi (see pp422–4) was built originally as the "offices" of the Medici rulers of Florence. Transformed into a gallery in 1581, the building now displays such masterpieces as The Annunciation by da Vinci.

Vatican Museums, Rome
Classical and Early Christian statues excavated in Rome over the centuries include this charming Good Shepherd (4th century AD). The vast papal museum (see pp396–8) also holds great paintings by Michelangelo and Raphael commissioned during the Renaissance.

NORWAY

SWEDEN

FINLAND

DENMARK

Baltic Sea

POLAND

GERMANY

CZECH REPUBLIC

AUSTRIA HUNGARY

ITALY

GREECE

SEA

The History of Europe

In this timeline of European history, important political and social events appear on the upper half of the page, while the lower half charts contemporary developments in art and architecture. In the art and architecture section the emphasis is on structures and works of art that both illustrate major historical trends and can still be seen today. They are described in more detail in the main sightseeing section of the book.

451–429 BC The great general Perikles presides as uncrowned king of Athens. He establishes democracy in the city and commissions great buildings such as the Parthenon (see pp478–80). However, he also involves Athens in Peloponnesian Wars (431–404), in which Sparta and its allies defeat Athens

FROM PREHISTORY TO THE EARLY MIDDLE AGES

From prehistoric times Europe saw a succession of civilizations that flourished then collapsed. Much of our knowledge of the period comes only from archaeological remains, although the Mycenaeans did leave written inscriptions. Later periods are chronicled in Greek and Roman histories. However, many of these were written long after the events they describe and tend to be a blend of legend and fact.

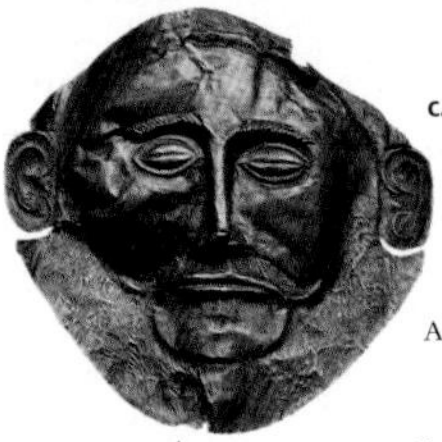

c.1500 BC Mycenaean culture dominates mainland Greece This gold death mask from Mycenae, known as the "Mask of Agamemnon," is on display at the National Museum of Archaeology in Athens (see p476)

750–600 BC Greek colonists spread to Sicily, southern Italy, Marseille, and Spain

c.800 BC Rise of Etruscans in Italy

509 BC Romans expel Etruscan kings and found republic

c.2300 BC Start of Bronze Age in Europe

2000–1100 BC Series of Minoan civilizations in Crete

c.1000 BC Iron-working reaches central Europe from the Near East

	PREHISTORY				CLASSICAL
2500 BC	2000 BC	1500 BC	1000 BC	500 BC	
	MINOAN AND MYCENAEAN			GREEK AND ETRUSCAN	

c.1200 BC Collapse of Mycenaean culture

447 BC Work begins on the Parthenon, the great temple dedicated to Athena on the Acropolis in Athens (see pp478–80)

6th century BC Etruscan sarcophagi topped with lifelike terra-cotta sculptures of the deceased (see p405)

c.1450 BC Mycenaeans (see p491) take over palace of Knossos. Palaces in mainland Greece start to exhibit pillared, frescoed halls, ideas borrowed from the Minoans

4th century BC Magnificent Greek theater built at Epidaurus (see p491)

c.1700 BC First Minoan palace at Knossos on Crete destroyed. A new palace was immediately built to replace it. This colorful scene is one of many fine Minoan frescoes in the Irákleio Archaeological Museum in Crete (see p500)

6th century BC Greek vases of the red-figure type start to appear. The figures are left in the color of the clay, silhouetted against a black glaze. They often show scenes of myth and legend, such as the Trojan War

ART AND ARCHITECTURE

Artistic styles in prehistoric Minoan and Mycenaean cultures were strongly influenced by Egyptian and Middle Eastern models. However, during the Hellenistic period the trend was reversed. Following Alexander the Great's conquests, Greek styles of sculpture, temple architecture, and ceramics were exported to Egypt and as far east as Afghanistan. The Romans were great admirers of the Greeks and the growth of the Roman Empire helped spread the Greek aesthetic throughout western Europe.

27 BC Augustus becomes first Roman emperor. This sculpture in the Vatican Museums (*see pp396–8*) shows him in a traditional Greek heroic pose

201 BC Rome defeats Carthaginians and expands rapidly to dominate Mediterranean

5th century AD Visigoths take control of Iberian Peninsula. The Roman aqueduct at Segovia (*see p294*) survived both the Visigothic and the subsequent Moorish invasion of Spain

AD 476 Fall of Western Roman Empire

338 BC Philip II defeats Greeks, making Macedon great power

c.AD 481–511 Franks under Clovis conquer much of present-day France

AD 117 Roman Empire at greatest extent on death of Emperor Trajan

AD 493–526 Kingdom of Italy ruled by Theodoric the Ostrogoth from Ravenna

323 BC Death of Alexander the Great. His empire stretches from Macedon to northern India

AD 395 Division of Roman Empire into eastern and western halves

6th century AD Byzantines reconquer much of Italy, but then lose most of their gains to the Lombards

AD 313 Edict of Milan: Christianity favored by Roman emperor Constantine

AD 711 Moorish invasion of Spain

GREECE	ROMAN EMPIRE		AFTER THE FALL OF ROME	
250 BC	AD 1	AD 250	500	750
HELLENISTIC AND ROMAN			BYZANTINE	

AD 30 Amphitheater built at Verona (*see p430*)

AD 118 Building of magnificent domed temple, the Pantheon in Rome (*see p400*)

8th–10th centuries AD Churches in distinctive pre-Romanesque style built in Asturias, part of northern Spain never conquered by the Moors. Examples survive in Oviedo (*see p303*)

AD 72 Work starts on the Colosseum in Rome (*see p403*)

4th century AD Christian motifs start to appear in Roman art; building of St. Peter's and other Christian basilicas in Rome

7th century AD Sutton Hoo ship burial. Over much of Europe relics from this era are rare. One exception is the treasure found buried with an Anglo-Saxon leader, who died c.625. The hoard can be seen at the British Museum (*see p52*)

AD 81 Arch of Titus (*see p402*) erected in Rome to commemorate crushing of Jewish Revolt in AD 70. It served as a model for later triumphal arches

5th century AD Apse mosaics in church of Santa Maria Maggiore, Rome (*see p404*)

c.330 BC Start of Hellenistic period. *The Dying Galatian* was a famous Greek sculpture dating from the 3rd century BC. It was frequently copied in the Hellenistic period. This Roman copy is in the Capitoline Museums in Rome (*see p401*)

6th century AD Byzantine mosaics in church of Sant'Apollinare Nuovo in Ravenna (*see p443*). Ravenna remained an outpost of the Byzantine Empire until AD 752

FROM THE MIDDLE AGES TO THE 18TH CENTURY

During this period many of the states of present-day Europe gradually took shape, with powerful centralized kingdoms, notably Spain, Portugal, France, and England, emerging from the medieval feudal system. The Middle Ages were marked by wars between kings and nobles and even between popes and emperors. The Catholic church owned extensive lands and was a powerful political force. However, its influence over much of northern Europe was lost in the Reformation of the 16th century with the emergence of Protestantism.

9th century Vikings terrorize Europe, gaining control of much of England, Scotland, Ireland, and northern France. The Isle of Lewis chessmen (11th century) give a striking picture of the members of a Viking court. Carved of walrus ivory, they can be seen in the British Museum *(see pp52–3)*

800 The Frankish king, Charlemagne, is crowned Holy Roman Emperor

896 Magyars reach eastern Europe, laying foundation of present-day Hungary

1066 Norman conquest of England

1054 East-West Schism: Roman Church splits definitively with Eastern Orthodox Church

955 Saxon king Otto defeats Magyars

1096–9 First Crusade; knights of northern Europe capture Jerusalem

12th and 13th centuries Emperors and popes fight for control of Germany and Italy. Frederick I Barbarossa, Holy Roman Emperor, quarreled frequently with the pope but set off on the Third Crusade, only to drown in 1190 before he reached the Holy Land

12th and 13th centuries Gradual reconquest of Spain and Portugal from the Moors

12th century Venice grows rich supplying the crusades and trading with the east

EARLY MIDDLE AGES			MIDDLE AGES	
800	900	1000	1100	1200
BYZANTINE AND ROMANESQUE				GOTHIC

c.800 *Book of Kells*, the greatest of the Irish illuminated copies of the Bible *(see p125)*

1064 Work begins on Pisa's Duomo *(see p411)*, a magnificent example of Italian Romanesque

1071 Completion of St. Mark's, Venice's great Byzantine basilica *(see pp434–5)*

10th century Beginnings of Romanesque architecture, characterized by rounded Roman arches, delicate arcades, and tall bell towers

9th and 10th centuries Irish High Crosses *(see p125)*

11th century Christianity reaches Norway – building of striking wooden "stave" churches *(see p656)*

c.785 Start of building of the Mezquita in Córdoba, capital of the Moorish Caliphate in Spain *(see pp326–7)*. The *mihrab* (prayer niche) is framed by a beautiful horseshoe arch. Spanish buildings retained Moorish features like this even after the completion of the reconquest of Spain in 1492

late 11th century Building of Durham Cathedral *(see p77)*, England's finest Norman (Romanesque) church

c.1194 Chartres Cathedral, France *(see pp180–81)* rebuilt in new Gothic style. Pointed arches and ribbed vaulting create possibility of soaring height in church design

ART AND ARCHITECTURE

The Middle Ages in Europe produced remarkable ecclesiastical architecture: first in the Romanesque style, then the even more spectacular Gothic. The Renaissance turned its back on the Gothic with the rediscovery of Classical principles, while Renaissance art was based on scientific understanding of perspective and anatomy, and also on the idealism of Classical sculpture.

c.1267–1336 Life of Giotto, who introduces a new realism to Italian painting. *St. Francis appears to the Monks at Arles* is one of a series of magnificent frescoes he painted for the Basilica di San Francesco in Assisi *(see pp406–7)*

1618–48 Thirty Years' War: religious differences and territorial ambitions embroil most of northern Europe

1386 Union of crowns of Poland and Lithuania, which together form largest state in Europe

1517 Martin Luther condemns church in his 95 Theses, sparking Reformation. Protestantism sweeps across much of northern Europe

1347–51 Black Death kills perhaps a third of the population of Europe

1492 Spanish expel Moors from Granada; Columbus's first voyage to America

1520s Charles V, Holy Roman Emperor, defeats François I of France in war for control of Italy

1683 Defeat of Turks at siege of Vienna allows expansion of Austrian Habsburg empire

1715 Death of Louis XIV. The "Sun King" made France the most powerful state in Europe and presided over the great age of French Classical culture. However, his expansionist policies were largely thwarted by the British, Austrians, and Dutch

1337–1453 Hundred Years' War between England and France

1458–90 Hungary at its height in reign of Matthias Corvinus

1453 Collapse of Byzantine Empire increases Turkish threat to eastern Europe

1609 Dutch gain effective independence from Spain

1622 Battle of Mohács; Kingdom of Hungary falls to Turks

1740–86 Rise of Prussia under Frederick II "the Great"

LATE MIDDLE AGES		REFORMATION		AGE OF ENLIGHTENMENT
1300	1400	1500	1600	1700
		RENAISSANCE	BAROQUE	ROCOCO

1436 Completion of dome of Florence Cathedral *(see pp416–17)*

1519 Château de Chambord, François I's magnificent Renaissance château in the Loire Valley *(see p179)*

1730s Light decorative Rococo style, most popular in France, southern Germany, and Austria

1441 Death of great Flemish painter Van Eyck, who perfected oil-painting technique

1483–1520 Life of Raphael, painter of the Raphael Rooms in the Vatican *(see p398)*

1704 Start of building of Blenheim Palace, grandest of the stately homes of 18th-century Britain *(see pp74–5)*

1598–1680 Life of Gian Lorenzo Bernini, leading architect and sculptor of the Roman Baroque

1606–69 Life of Rembrandt, greatest of the 17th-century Dutch masters

1452–1519 Life of Leonardo da Vinci, multi-talented Renaissance genius. There are two versions of his *Virgin of the Rocks*, one in the Louvre, Paris *(see pp158–60)*, and one in the British Museum, London *(see pp52–3)*

1661 Enlargement of French royal palace at Versailles *(see pp168–9)* begins

1675–1710 Building of Christopher Wren's St. Paul's Cathedral in London *(see p58)*

1475–1564 Life of painter, sculptor, and architect Michelangelo

THE FRENCH REVOLUTION TO THE PRESENT
The French Revolution established a supposedly democratic republic, but the need for a central authority allowed the brilliant general Napoleon to take power and proclaim himself Emperor. The Old Regime died hard and after Napoleon's defeat, many of the old rulers of Europe were restored to their thrones. In time, however, birthright and tradition had to give way to technological progress, the growth of capitalism, the rising power of the bourgeoisie, and the spread of workers' movements. Greater democracy gave the vote to more and more of the population, but wherever democracy broke down, there was the danger it would be replaced by a totalitarian regime, such as the Nazis in Germany and the Communist regimes of the old Soviet Bloc.

1830–40 George Stephenson's *Rocket* becomes the prototype for steam locomotives. Following the success of the Liverpool–Manchester line, opened in 1930, the spread of railroads speeds the Industrial Revolution in Britain

1805 Napoleon defeats Austrians at Austerlitz; by 1807 he controls most of western and central Europe

1804 Napoleon crowns himself Emperor of the French

1789 French Revolution leads to execution by guillotine of Louis XVI and reign of terror in 1793. In 1794 more moderate elements take over

1812 Defeats in Peninsular War and Russia weaken French hold on Europe

1831 Creation of Kingdom of Belgium

1815 Napoleon defeated at Waterloo; Congress of Vienna more or less restores status quo in Europe

1838–1901 Reign of Queen Victoria: apogee of British Empire

1848 Year of revolutions throughout Europe

1852 Napoleon III becomes Emperor of France

1860 Unification of most of Italy

1870 Franco-Prussian War; German victory allows Bismarck to achieve unification of Germany

AGE OF ENLIGHTENMENT	INDUSTRIAL REVOLUTION	AGE
1775	1800	1825	1850	1875
NEOCLASSICAL	EMPIRE	REGENCY	REALISM	IMPRESSIONISM

1785 *The Oath of the Horatii* by Jacques Louis David, French Neoclassical painter. This incident from early Roman history extols the republican spirit that would inspire the French Revolution. The painting hangs in the Louvre, Paris (*see pp158–60*)

c.1814 Goya's powerful paintings recording French atrocities in the Peninsular War, *May 2, 1808* and *May 3, 1808*. They hang in the Prado, Madrid (*see pp288–90*)

1841–1919 Life of Pierre Auguste Renoir, one of the greatest of the artists associated with the Impressionist movement

c.1800 Empire style in fashion and furnishings. Many aspects of design in Europe influenced by Napoleon's Egyptian expedition

1852–70 Second Empire style; rebuilding of Paris by Haussmann (*see p164*)

1874 Claude Monet uses the word "Impression" in title of a painting, giving rise to the term Impressionism

1883 Gaudí begins work on la Sagrada Família cathedral in Barcelona (*see pp312–13*)

1890 Suicide of Dutch painter Van Gogh, unrecognized in his lifetime, now the most sought-after of Post-Impressionist painters (*see p259*)

ART AND ARCHITECTURE
Revivalist styles dominated 19th-century architecture, with imitations of Classical, Gothic, and Renaissance buildings. In contrast, painting evolved radically following the example of the French Impressionists. In the 20th century new building materials – steel, concrete, and glass – were the inspiration of Modernism. Modern art meanwhile experimented with every conceivable form of expression from Surrealism to Conceptual Art.

1857–65 The Ringstrasse built in Vienna, an example of grand 19th-century city planning. This photograph (c.1880) shows horse-drawn trams passing in front of the Staatsoper (*see p595*)

1914 Outbreak of World War I. Millions die as trench warfare along Western Front reaches stalemate

1944 Normandy Landings. Allied forces create second front, which leads to eventual defeat of Germany in 1945

1949 Berlin Air Lift stops Russian blockade of West Berlin

1939 Outbreak of World War II. Germany overruns Poland, then, in 1940, France

1956 Hungarian uprising against Communist rule crushed by Russian tanks

1989 Collapse of Communism in Eastern Europe. Poland, Hungary, Czechoslovakia, and other countries oust Communist rulers. Reopening of Berlin Wall leads to reunification of Germany in 1990

1918 Defeat of Germany, following American entry into war in 1917

1957 Treaty of Rome: European Economic Community marks beginning of European Union

1995 Membership of European Union reaches 15, with entry of Sweden, Finland, and Austria

1901 First award of Nobel prizes in Sweden and Norway

1936–9 Spanish Civil War

1933 Hitler comes to power in Germany

1968 Student protests in France and many other parts of Europe

2002 Introduction of common currency, the euro, in 12 countries of the European Union

2004 Ten more countries join the European Union

1919 Treaty of Versailles (1919) creates new states, including Poland, Czechoslovakia, Hungary, and Finland

1973 Carnation Revolution in Portugal

2007 Bulgaria and Romania join the European Union

OF IMPERIALISM | THE EUROPEAN UNION

| 1900 | 1925 | 1950 | 1975 | 2000 |

ART NOUVEAU | ART DECO AND MODERNISM | POST-MODERNISM

1999 Sir Norman Foster's striking additions to the old Reichstag building in Berlin *(see p530)*

1907 First exhibition of Cubist works by Picasso and others

1919 Foundation of Bauhaus in Weimar *(see p543)*, which exerts worldwide influence on architecture

1937 *Guernica* painted by Pablo Picasso in reaction to bombing of Basque civilians in Spanish Civil War. The painting is currently on show at the Centro de Arte Reina Sofía, Madrid *(see p291)*

1997 Astonishing sculptural forms used by American architect Frank Gehry for new Guggenheim Museum in Bilbao *(see p304)*

1920s and 1930s The term Art Deco is given to design and architecture using modern materials and clean, geometrical shapes

1992 Barcelona Olympics. The city's glorious 20th-century buildings by Gaudí and others are restored and the old port is transformed *(see pp306–15)*

1890s Era of Art Nouveau. The posters of Czech-born Alfons Mucha typify the style, also known as Jugendstil or Secession. Many artists break away from the official academy of their country, notably in Vienna and Berlin

1977 Opening of the Centre Pompidou in Paris *(see p153)*. The design by Renzo Piano, Richard Rogers, and Gianfranco Franchini places service ducts and escalators on the outside of the building

THE
BRITISH ISLES

THE BRITISH ISLES AT A GLANCE 34–35

GREAT BRITAIN 36–107

IRELAND 108–139

The British Isles at a Glance

The islands of Great Britain and Ireland lie to the northwest of continental Europe and have remained relatively isolated throughout their history. Great Britain consists of three countries, England, Scotland, and Wales, each with a distinctive way of life and traditions. These three, together with Northern Ireland, form the United Kingdom. In the south of Ireland, the Republic of Ireland is a separate country. London, one of Europe's liveliest cities, offers the greatest range of cultural attractions. The islands have a rich variety of land-scapes, from rolling green hills to windswept moors and craggy mountains in the Scottish Highlands.

The Highlands (see p87) *is an area prized for its beauty and diversity of wildlife. This region of mountains and glens is home to many animal species rarely found living wild elsewhere in the British Isles.*

Dublin (see pp112–21), *Ireland's capital, has a lively atmosphere. Many of its finest public buildings, such as the Custom House, date from the 18th century.*

Killarney (see p127) *is a typical friendly Irish town in County Kerry. The surrounding area is renowned for its spectacular scenery, with three huge lakes, waterfalls, and some of the country's highest mountains.*

IRELAND
(See pp108–39)

Inverness

Fort William

Glasgow

Belfast

Galway

DUBLIN

Caernarfon

Killarney

Cork

Plymouth

◁ **A tranquil corner of England's Lake District**

Edinburgh
(see pp82–6) *is
the administrative
and cultural cap-
ital of Scotland. Its
castle, which dates
back to the 12th
century, gives
spectacular views
of the entire city.*

LOCATOR MAP

York (see pp78–9) *is a city of
historical treasures, with many
relics from the Roman and Viking
ages. Its magnificent minster has
the largest collection of medieval
stained glass in Britain, and the
city walls are well preserved.*

EDINBURGH

Aberdeen

Carlisle

London (see pp42–63) *was
founded by the Romans in the
1st century AD. The oldest part
of the capital is the City, where Sir
Christopher Wren's masterpiece,
St. Paul's Cathedral, stands.*

York

Manchester
Liverpool

GREAT BRITAIN
(See pp32–107)

Birmingham

Cambridge

Oxford

ardiff
Bristol
Bath

LONDON

Bath (see pp70–71)
*is named after the
Roman baths that stand
at the heart of the old
town, next to the splendid
medieval abbey. The city is
full of elegant Georgian
terraces, built in local
honey-colored limestone.*

Brighton

Exeter

| 0 km | 75 |
| 0 miles | 75 |

GREAT BRITAIN

Separated from the rest of Europe by the English Channel, Britain has been assiduous in preserving its traditions. However, the island can offer the visitor much more than stately castles and pretty villages. A diversity of landscape, culture, literature, art, and architecture, as well as a unique heritage, results in a nation balancing the needs of the present with those of the past.

Britain's character has been shaped by its geographical position as an island. Never successfully invaded since 1066, its people have developed their own distinctive traditions, and although today a member of the European Union, Britain continues to delight in its nonconformity. Britain's heritage can be seen in its ancient castles, cathedrals, and stately homes with their gardens and parklands. It is also evident in the many age-old customs played out across the nation throughout the year.

For a small island, Great Britain encompasses a surprising variety in its regions, whose inhabitants maintain distinct identities. Scotland and Wales are separate countries from England with their own legislative assemblies. They also have their own surviving Gaelic languages and unique traditions.

The landscape is varied, too, from the mountains of Wales, Scotland, and the north, through the flat expanses of the Midlands and eastern England, to the soft, rolling hills of the south and west. The long, broad beaches of East Anglia contrast with the rocky inlets along much of the west coast.

Despite the spread of towns and cities over the last two centuries, rural Britain still flourishes. The countryside is dotted with farms and charming villages, with picturesque cottages and lovingly tended gardens. The most prosperous and densely populated part of the nation is the Southeast, close to London, where modern office buildings bear witness to the growth of service and high-tech industries.

HISTORY

Britain began to assume a cohesive character as early as the 7th century AD, as Anglo-Saxon tribes migrating from the continent absorbed existing Celtic and Roman influences and finally achieved supremacy in England.

Punting on the River Cherwell, Oxford

◁ **St. Martin-in-the-Fields church and the fountains of London's Trafalgar Square**

However, they suffered repeated Viking incursions and were overcome by the Normans at the Battle of Hastings in 1066, when William the Conqueror founded the royal lineage which still rules the country today. The disparate cultures of the Normans and Anglo-Saxons combined to form the English nation, a process nurtured by Britain's position as an island. Scotland's four divided kingdoms had also unified under one monarch by this time, with the crowning of Duncan I in 1034.

The next 400 years saw English kings extend their domain at home as well as abroad. Wales was conquered in 1282, and by 1296 control was also gained over Scotland. The Scots rose up again, however, winning back their independence under Robert the Bruce in 1314. The Tudor monarchs consolidated England's strength and laid the foundations for Britain's future

Queen Elizabeth I
(reigned 1558–1603)

commercial success. Henry VIII recognized the importance of sea power and, under his daughter, Elizabeth I, English sailors ranged far across the world. The total defeat of the Spanish Armada in 1588 confirmed Britain's position as a major maritime power.

The Stuart period saw the English and Scottish crowns unite, but internal struggles eventually led to the Civil War in 1642. By the time of the Act of Union with Scotland in 1707, however, the whole island was united and the foundations for representative government had been laid. The combination of internal security and maritime strength allowed Britain to seek wealth overseas. By the end of the Napoleonic Wars in 1815, Britain was the world's leading trading nation. The opportunities offered by industrialization were seized, and by the reign of Queen Victoria (1837–1901), a colossal empire had been established across the globe. Challenged by Europe and the rise of the US, and drained by its role in two world wars, Britain's influence waned after 1945. By the 1970s almost all its former colonies had become independent Commonwealth nations.

KEY DATES IN BRITISH HISTORY

AD 43–410 Roman occupation of Britain

440–50 Start of Angle, Saxon, and Jute invasions

1034 Duncan I becomes first king of all Scotland

1066 William the Conqueror defeats King Harold and becomes the first Norman king of England

1256 First Parliament to include ordinary citizens

1533–4 Henry VIII forms Church of England

1535 Act of Union with Wales

1558–1603 Reign of Elizabeth I

1603 Union of English and Scottish crowns; James VI of Scotland becomes James I of England

1642 Civil War breaks out

1649 Charles I executed. Commonwealth declared by Parliament

1707 Act of Union with Scotland

1721 Robert Walpole becomes Britain's first Prime Minister

1837–1901 Reign of Queen Victoria. Industrial Revolution leads to growth of British Empire

1924 First Labour government

1948 National Health Service introduced

1973 Britain joins European Community

1999 Formation of Scottish Parliament and Welsh Assembly

2005 52 killed and hundreds injured in terrorist bomb attacks on public transport in London

SOCIETY AND POLITICS

British cities are melting-pots for people not just from different parts of the country but also from overseas. Irish immigration has long ensured a flow of labor into the country, and since the 1950s hundreds of thousands have

The colorful costumes of Notting Hill Carnival, an annual multicultural celebration held in London

The Eden Project, Cornwall, an entertaining educational center devoted to mankind's relationship with plants

come from former colonies in Africa, Asia, and the Caribbean, many of which are members of the Commonwealth. Nearly five percent of Britain's 58 million inhabitants are from non-white ethnic groups – and about half of these were born in Britain. The result is a multicultural society that can boast a wide range of music, art, food, and religions.

Britain's class structure is based on a subtle mixture of heredity and wealth. Even though many of the great inherited fortunes no longer exist, some old landed families still live on their estates, and many now open them to the public. The monarchy's position highlights the dilemma of a people seeking to preserve its most potent symbol of national unity in an age suspicious of inherited privilege. Without real political power, although still head of the Church of England, the Queen and her family are subject to increasing public scrutiny.

Democracy has deep foundations in Britain. With the exception of the 17th-century Civil War, power has passed gradually from the Crown to the people's elected representatives. During the 20th and 21st centuries, the Labour (left wing) and Conservative (right wing) parties have, during their periods in office, favored a mix of public and private ownership for industry and ample funding for the state health and welfare systems.

CULTURE AND THE ARTS

Britain has a famous theatrical tradition stretching back to the 16th century and William Shakespeare. His plays have been performed on stage almost continuously since they were written, and the works of 17th- and 18th-century writers are also frequently revived. Modern British playwrights, such as Tom Stoppard, draw on this long tradition with their vivid language and by using comedy to illustrate serious themes.

In the visual arts, Britain has a strong tradition in portraiture, caricature, landscape, and watercolor. In modern times David Hockney and Francis Bacon, and sculptors Henry Moore and Barbara Hepworth have enjoyed worldwide recognition. Britain has also become famous for its innovative fashion designers, such as Vivienne Westwood and Alexander McQueen.

The indigenous film industry produces occasional international hits such as *Four Weddings and a Funeral* and *The Full Monty*. British television is famous for the high quality of its news, current affairs, and nature programs, as well as for its drama.

The British are great sports fans. Soccer, rugby, cricket, and golf are popular both to watch and to take part in. An instantly recognizable English image is that of the cricket match on a village green. The British also make use of their national parks as enthusiastic walkers and hikers.

The BAT and BALL

A cricketing pub sign showing the 18th-century version of the game

Exploring Great Britain

Britain's main attraction is its capital, London, but there are many other noteworthy towns to explore throughout the country. Highlights include the university cities of Cambridge and Oxford, the historic centers of York and Bath, and Edinburgh, the capital of Scotland. In the sparsely populated regions of Northern England, Wales, and Scotland, the land itself becomes the center of attention – the Lake District, Snowdonia, and the Isle of Skye are all areas of outstanding natural beauty.

SIGHTS AT A GLANCE

Aberdeen **28**
Bath pp70–71 **9**
Blenheim Palace pp74–5 **15**
Brighton **3**
Bristol **10**
Caernarfon **13**
Cairngorms **29**
Cambridge **17**
Canterbury **2**
Cardiff **11**
Chester **18**
Devon and Cornwall **8**
Durham **23**
Edinburgh pp82–6 **24**
Glasgow **25**
Inverness **30**

Isle of Skye **31**
Lake District **22**
Liverpool **19**
LONDON pp42–63 **1**
Manchester **20**
Oxford **14**
St. Andrews **27**
Salisbury **6**
Snowdonia **12**
Stirling **26**
Stonehenge **7**
Stratford-upon-Avon **16**
Winchester **5**
Windsor Castle pp66–7 **4**
York pp78–9 **21**

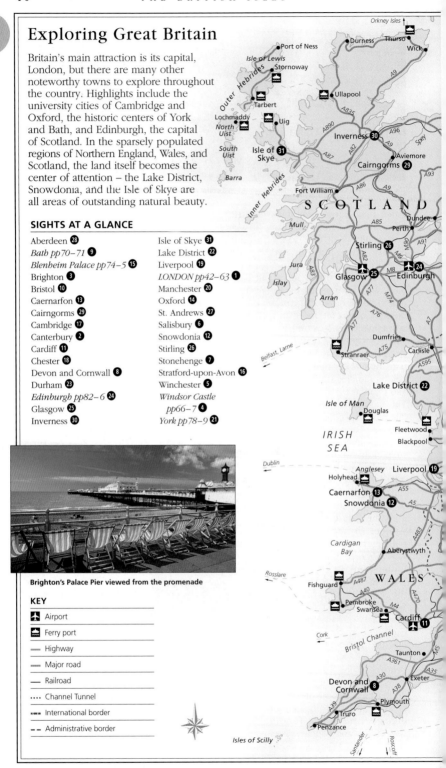

Brighton's Palace Pier viewed from the promenade

KEY

- ✈ Airport
- ⛴ Ferry port
- ─ Highway
- ─ Major road
- ─ Railroad
- ···· Channel Tunnel
- ▬▬ International border
- ▬ ▬ Administrative border

For additional map symbols *see back flap*

SEE ALSO

- *Practical Information* pp88–9
- *Travel Information* pp90–91
- *Shopping* pp92–3
- *Entertainment* pp94–5
- *Where to Stay* pp96–101
- *Where to Eat* pp102–7

DISTANCE CHART

LONDON								
179 111	*BIRMINGHAM*	**Distance in kilometers**						
241 150	**164** 102	*CARDIFF*	Distance in miles					
599 372	**466** 290	**600** 373	*EDINBURGH*					
626 389	**470** 292	**602** 374	**72** 45	*GLASGOW*				
851 529	**721** 448	**853** 530	**254** 158	**269** 167	*INVERNESS*			
296 184	**130** 81	**278** 173	**343** 213	**344** 214	**597** 371	*MANCHESTER*		
341 212	**332** 206	**261** 152	**784** 427	**785** 426	**1038** 545	**451** 250	*PLYMOUTH*	
333 207	**208** 129	**381** 237	**301** 187	**344** 214	**550** 342	**106** 66	**532** 331	*YORK*

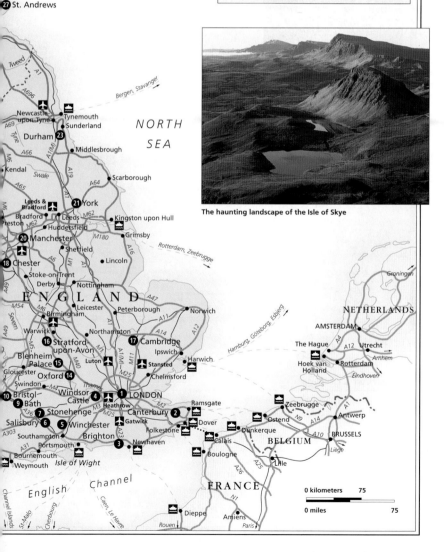

The haunting landscape of the Isle of Skye

(Map of Great Britain and surrounding regions)

A98 · A96 · Orkney Isles, Shetland Isles · **28** Aberdeen · A94 · **27** St. Andrews

Tweed · A1 · A696 · Bergen, Stavanger

Newcastle upon Tyne · Tynemouth · Sunderland · A69 · Tyne · Durham **23** · A1(M) · A66 · Middlesbrough · Kendal · Swale · A19 · Scarborough · A65 · A64 · A1 · Leeds & Bradford · **21** York · Bradford · Leeds · M62 · Kingston upon Hull · Preston · M62 · Huddersfield · **20** Manchester · M180 · Grimsby · Sheffield · A16 · Chester **18** · A6 · M1 · Lincoln · Stoke-on-Trent · Derby · Nottingham · M54 · E N G L A N D · A47 · Leicester · Peterborough · Norwich · Birmingham · A11 · A14 · A12 · Warwick · Northampton · **16** Stratford-upon-Avon · M1 · **17** Cambridge · Blenheim Palace **15** · M40 · Luton · A1(M) · M11 · Ipswich · Harwich · Gloucester · Oxford **14** · M25 · Stansted · Swindon · Thames · Chelmsford · **10** Bristol · **9** Windsor Castle · **4** **1** LONDON · Bath · M3 · Heathrow · M2 · Ramsgate · **7** Stonehenge · M25 · Canterbury **2** · Salisbury **6** · Gatwick · Dover · A303 · **5** Winchester · A23 · Folkestone · Southampton · Brighton **3** · Newhaven · Calais · Portsmouth · Bournemouth · Weymouth · Isle of Wight · Boulogne

NORTH SEA

Rotterdam, Zeebrugge · Hamburg, Göteborg, Esbjerg · NETHERLANDS · Groningen · AMSTERDAM · The Hague · A12 · Utrecht · Arnhem · Hoek van Holland · Rotterdam · Eindhoven · Zeebrugge · A1 · Antwerp · Ostend · A14 · BRUSSELS · Dunkerque · BELGIUM · Liège · Lille · A26 · A25

English Channel · FRANCE · N1 · Dieppe · Amiens · Paris · Caen, Le Havre · Cherbourg · Channel Islands · St-Malo · Rouen

| 0 kilometers | 75 |
| 0 miles | 75 |

London ❶

The largest city in Europe, London is home to about seven million people. Founded by the Romans in the first century AD as an administrative center and trading port, the capital is the principal residence of British monarchs, as well as the center of government and business, and is rich in historic buildings. In addition to its many museums and galleries, London is an exciting city, with a vast array of entertainments. Developments completed for the millennium, such as the Tate Modern art gallery and London Eye ferris wheel (the highest in the world), have added to the city's range of attractions.

Millennium Foot Bridge leading to the Tate Modern on Bankside

Summer relaxation along the banks of the Thames at Richmond

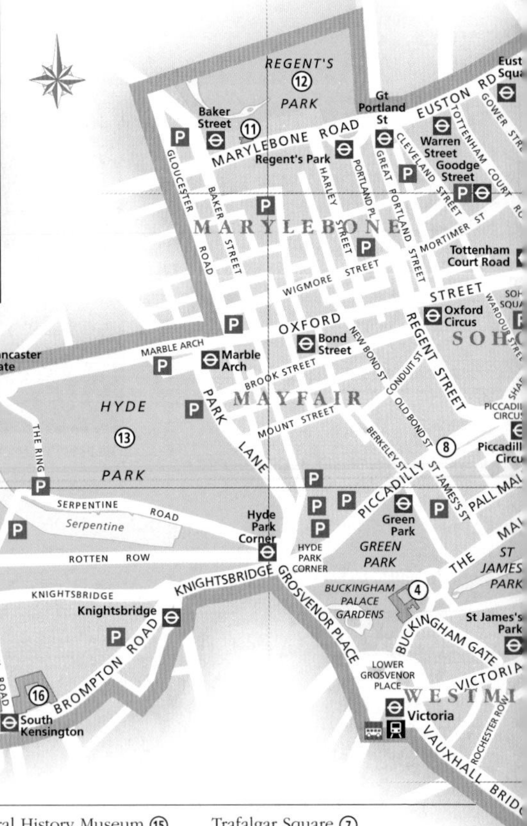

SIGHTS AT A GLANCE

British Museum pp52–3 ⑩
Buckingham Palace ④
Covent Garden ⑨
Houses of Parliament ②
Hyde Park ⑬
London Eye ③
Madame Tussaud's and the London Planetarium ⑪
Museum of London ⑱
National Gallery ⑥

Natural History Museum ⑮
Piccadilly ⑧
Regent's Park ⑫
St. Paul's Cathedral ⑰
Science Museum ⑭
Shakespeare's Globe ⑳
Tate Britain ⑤
Tate Modern ⑲
Tower Bridge ㉒
Tower of London pp60–61 ㉑

Trafalgar Square ⑦
Victoria and Albert Museum ⑯
Westminster Abbey pp46–7 ①

Greater London *(see inset map)*
Greenwich ㉓
Hampton Court ㉖
Notting Hill and Portobello Road ㉔
Richmond and Kew ㉕

GETTING AROUND

London's subway system – the "tube" or "underground" – runs from about 5:30am until just after midnight. Overground rail services are useful for trips farther afield. London's buses are now much quicker, since the introduction of the Congestion Charge (£8 a day) to enter central London with a car. The well-known black cabs are a safe and convenient way to travel from door to door.

SEE ALSO

- *Where to Stay* pp96–8
- *Where to Eat* pp102–4

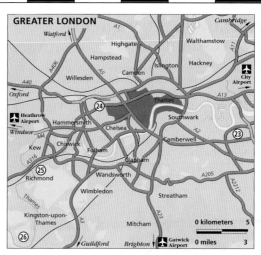

GREATER LONDON

KEY

Area of main map

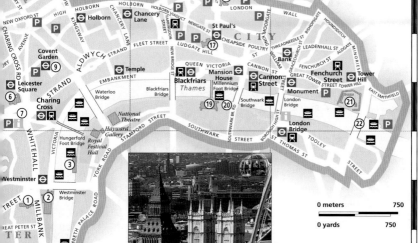

KEY

▨	Sight / Place of interest
✈	Airport
🚉	Train station
⊖	Underground station
🚌	Bus station
⛴	Riverboat boarding point
P	Parking
ℹ	Tourist information
⋯	Pedestrian street

Viewing Big Ben and Westminster Abbey from the capsules of the London Eye

Street-by-Street: Whitehall and Westminster

Westminster has been at the center of political and religious power in England since the 11th century, when King Canute built a palace here and Edward the Confessor founded Westminster Abbey. Whitehall is synonymous with the ministries concentrated around it. On weekdays the streets are crowded with civil servants going about their business, replaced at weekends by a steady flow of tourists.

Downing Street
No. 10 has been the prime minister's official residence since 1732, when Sir Robert Walpole was given the house by George II.

The Cabinet War Rooms, now open to the public, were Winston Churchill's World War II headquarters.

St. Margaret's Church is a favorite venue for political and society weddings.

★ **Westminster Abbey**
The abbey (see pp46–7) is London's oldest and most important church. The north façade is a Victorian addition.

Central Hall was built in 1911 as a Methodist meeting hall. In 1946 it hosted the first General Assembly of the United Nations.

Dean's Yard
This secluded grassy square is surrounded by picturesque buildings from different periods, many used by Westminster School.

Statue of Richard the Lion-Heart (1860)

The Burghers of Calais is a cast of Auguste Rodin's 1886 original sculpture in France.

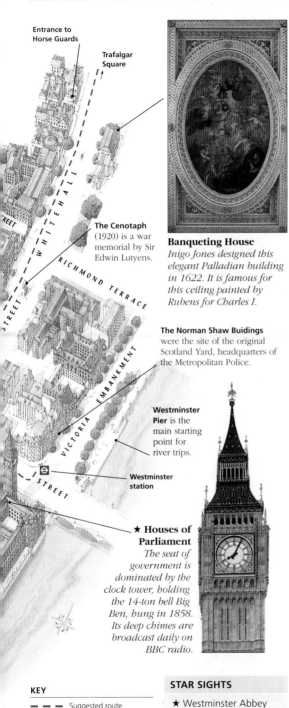

Entrance to
Horse Guards

Trafalgar
Square

The Cenotaph
(1920) is a war
memorial by Sir
Edwin Lutyens.

Banqueting House
*Inigo Jones designed this
elegant Palladian building
in 1622. It is famous for
this ceiling painted by
Rubens for Charles I.*

The Norman Shaw Buidings
were the site of the original
Scotland Yard, headquarters of
the Metropolitan Police.

**Westminster
Pier** is the
main starting
point for
river trips.

**Westminster
station**

**★ Houses of
Parliament**
*The seat of
government is
dominated by the
clock tower, holding
the 14-ton bell Big
Ben, hung in 1858.
Its deep chimes are
broadcast daily on
BBC radio.*

KEY

– – – Suggested route

0 meters   100

0 yards   100

STAR SIGHTS

★ Westminster Abbey

★ Houses of
  Parliament

Westminster
Abbey ①

See pp46–7.

Houses of
Parliament ②

SW1. **Tel** 020-7219 3000. ⊖ Westminster. ⊟ 3, 11, 12, 24, 53, 88,
148, 159, 211, 453. ⬚ call 0870-
906 3773 to book tour tickets
(Aug–Sep only for overseas visitors).
www.parliament.uk

Since the 16th century this
site has been the seat of the
two Houses of Parliament:
the House of Commons,
made up of elected Members
of Parliament (MPs) and the
upper house, the House of
Lords. The latter, formerly
filled with hereditary peers,
bishops, and life peers, was
reformed in 2000.

The present Neo-Gothic
building by Sir Charles Barry
replaced the original palace,
which was destroyed by fire
in 1834. Westminster Hall
survived the fire, and still has
a magnificent 14th-century
hammerbeam roof.

To hear debates in either of
the houses from the visitors'
galleries, you can stand in
line on the day. Debates start
at 2:30pm. To attend the popular Prime Minister's Question
Time, apply for tickets to your
local MP or to your embassy.

London Eye ③

South Bank SE1. **Tel** 0870-5000 600.
⊖ Waterloo, Westminster. ⊟ 77,
RV1, 381. ◯ daily. ● Dec 25, Jan
10–17. 🎫 (pick up tickets at County
Hall, next to the Eye, at least 30 mins
before boarding time). ⬚ ♿
www.londoneye.co.uk

Reaching to a height of
135 m (443 ft) above the
Thames river, this is the
world's highest Ferris wheel,
and was installed to mark the
Millennium. Its capsules offer
a gentle, 30-minute ride as
the wheel makes a full turn,
with breathtaking views over
the city and for up to 42 km
(26 miles) around. "Flights"
are on the hour or half-hour
and need to be booked as
the wheel is very popular.

Westminster Abbey ①

Westminster Abbey has been the burial place of
Britain's monarchs since the 11th century and the
setting for many coronations and royal weddings. It
is one of the most beautiful buildings in London, with
an exceptionally diverse array of architectural styles,
ranging from the austere French Gothic of the nave to
the astonishing complexity of Henry VII's chapel. Half
national church, half national museum, the abbey is
crammed with an extraordinary collection of tombs
and monuments honoring some of Britain's greatest
public figures, from politicians to poets.

North/Main Entrance
The mock-medieval stonework, like this carved dragon, is Victorian.

Statesmen's Aisle contains monuments to some of the country's greatest political leaders.

The Cloisters, built mainly in the 13th and 14th centuries, link the Abbey church with the other buildings.

★ **Nave**
Built under the direction of master mason Henry Yevele, the nave reaches to a height of 31 m (102 ft), and is the highest in England. The ratio of height to width is 3:1.

CORONATION

The coronation ceremony is over 1,000 years old and since 1066, with the crowning of William the Conqueror on Christmas Day, the abbey has been its sumptuous setting. The coronation of Queen Elizabeth II in 1953 was the first to be televised.

Flying Buttresses
The massive flying buttresses help transfer the great weight of the 31-m (102-ft) high nave.

STAR FEATURES

★ Nave
★ Henry VII Chapel
★ Chapter House

★ **Henry VII Chapel**
*The Chapel, built in
1503–19, has superb late
Perpendicular vaultings
and choir stalls dating
from 1512.*

The Sanctuary, built by
Henry III, has been the
scene of 38 coronations.

Poets' Corner
*Among the great
poets honored here
are Shakespeare
(above), Chaucer,
and T.S. Eliot.*

VISITORS' CHECKLIST

Broad Sanctuary SW1.
Tel 020-7222 5152. St.
James's Park, Westminster.
3, 11, 12, 24, 53, 88, 148,
159, 211, 453.
Westminster Pier.
Cloisters 8am–6pm daily.
**Royal Chapels, Poets' Corner,
Chapter House, Choir,
Statesmen's Aisle & Nave**
9:30am–3:45pm Mon–Fri
(until 6pm Wed), 9:30am–
1:45pm Sat. **Museum**
10:30am–4pm daily. for
Royal Chapels, Poets' Corner,
Chapter House, Museum,
Statesmen's Aisle, Nave.
limited. Evensong: 5pm
Mon–Fri, 3pm Sat & Sun.
www.westminster-abbey.org.uk

★ **Chapter House**
*This beautiful octagonal
room, remarkable for its
13th-century tiled floor, is
lit by six huge stained-glass
windows showing scenes
from the abbey's history.*

The museum
has many of
the abbey's
treasures,
including
wood, plaster,
and wax
effigies of
monarchs.

The Pyx Chamber is
where the coinage was
tested in medieval times.

HISTORICAL PLAN OF THE ABBEY

The first abbey church was established as early as the 10th
century, but the present French-influenced Gothic structure
was begun in 1245 at the behest of Henry III. Because of its
unique role as the coronation church, the abbey escaped
Henry VIII's dissolution of Britain's
monastic buildings (1536–9) during
the Protestant Reformation.

KEY

	Built before 1400
	Built in 1503–19
	Completed by 1745
	Completed after 1850

St. Edward's Chapel
*The Coronation Chair is
housed here, along with
the tombs of many
medieval monarchs.*

The Victoria Monument, Buckingham Palace

Buckingham Palace ④

SW1. *Tel* 020-7321 2233. 🚇 St. James's Park, Victoria, Green Park. 🚌 C1, 8, C10, 11, 16, 36, 38, 52, 73, 211. **State Rooms** ◯ Aug–end Sep: daily. 🖼 🔲 🔲 phone first. **Queen's Gallery** 🖼 *Changing of the Guard* 11:30am on alternate days (subject to change). *Tel* 020-7321 2233. **www**.royal.gov.uk

The Queen's official London home is a very popular attraction. Conversion of the 18th-century Buckingham House was begun for George IV in 1826, but the first monarch to occupy the palace was Queen Victoria, in 1837. When the monarch is in residence the Royal Standard flag is flown.

The palace tour takes visitors up the grand staircase and through the splendor of the state rooms. The royal family's private apartments are not open to the public.

In the Music Room royal babies are christened, and state guests presented. The Queen carries out many formal ceremonies in the richly gilded Throne Room, and the Ballroom is used for state banquets and investitures.

Valuable works of art, such as *The Music Lesson* (c.1660) by Dutch master Jan Vermeer, are on display in the Picture Gallery. A selection of works from the monarch's art collection, one of the finest and most valuable in the world, is displayed in the **Queen's Gallery**, a small building located to one side of the palace. The famous Changing of the Guard takes place on the palace forecourt. Crowds gather to watch the colorful half-hour parade of guards, dressed in red jackets and tall, furry hats called bearskins, exchanging the palace keys.

State coaches and other official vehicles may be viewed at the Royal Mews nearby. The star exhibit is the gold state coach built for George III in 1761, with fine panels by Giovanni Cipriani.

Overlooking the forecourt, the East Wing façade of the palace was redesigned by Aston Webb in 1913. He also created the spacious, tree-lined avenue known as the Mall, which leads from the palace to Trafalgar Square. Used for royal processions on special occasions, the Mall is closed to traffic on Sundays. The national flags of foreign heads of state fly from its flagpoles during official visits.

The avenue follows the edge of St. James's Park, a reserve for wildfowl, and popular picnic spot in the heart of the city. Originally a marsh, the park was drained by Henry VIII and incorporated into his hunting grounds. Later, Charles II redesigned it as a fashionable promenade, with an aviary along its southern edge (from which Birdcage Walk takes its name). In summer, concerts are held on the park bandstand.

Tate Britain ⑤

Millbank SW1. *Tel* 020-7887 8000. 🚇 Pimlico. 🚌 3, 77a, 88, 507, C10. 🚤 between Tate Britain and Tate Modern. ◯ daily. ⬤ Dec 24–26. 🖼 for major exhibitions. ♿ 🔲 🔳 🔲 🔲 **www**.tate.org.uk

Founded in 1897, the Tate Gallery, now called Tate Britain, focuses primarily on British art. Many of the modern works formerly kept here have been moved to the Tate Modern *(see p59)*, further down the Thames river.

Recently expanded, Tate Britain shows the world's largest display of British art, ranging from Tudor times to the present day, in line with the original intention of the gallery's sponsor, sugar magnate Sir Henry Tate.

One of the most exquisite early works is a portrait of a bejeweled Elizabeth I (c.1575), by Nicholas Hilliard. The influence of the 17th-century Flemish artist Sir Anthony van Dyck on English painters can be seen in William Dobson's *Endymion Porter* (1642–5) and the works of Thomas Gainsborough (1727–88).

Among the collection are some fine examples of William Hogarth's sharply satirical pictures, which remain popular today. The famed horse paintings of George Stubbs include *Mares and Foals in a Landscape* (1760).

Tate Britain holds a large number of paintings by the visionary poet and artist

The portico of the Tate Britain building, dating from 1897

The Trafalgar Square façade of the National Gallery

William Blake (1757–1827). His work was imbued with a mystical intensity, a typical example being *Satan Smiting Job with Sore Boils* (c.1826). England's great 19th-century landscape artists, Constable and Turner, are also well represented. John Constable's famous *Flatford Mill*, painted in 1816–17, is one of his many depictions of the Essex countryside. The Clore Galleries, open since 1987, house the works of J.M.W. Turner (1775–1851), whose paintings were left to the nation some years after his death on condition that they were kept together. His watercolor *A City on a River at Sunset* (1832) is a highlight. The Tate also holds many works by the 19th-century Pre-Raphaelites, including J.E. Millais' *Ophelia* (1851–2), as well as the works of several modern and contemporary artists, such as Henry Moore and David Hockney. The Tate's exhibitions change frequently to explore as much of the collection as possible.

National Gallery ⑥

Trafalgar Sq WC2. *Tel 020-7747 2885.* ⊖ *Charing Cross, Leicester Sq, Piccadilly Circus.* 🚌 *3, 6, 9, 11 & many others.* ◻ *daily.* ● *Jan 1, Dec 24–26.* ♿ *via Sainsbury Wing entrance.* ▣ **www**.nationalgallery.org.uk

London's leading art museum, the National Gallery has over 2,300 paintings, most on permanent display. The collection was started in 1824 when George IV persuaded a reluctant government to purchase 38 major paintings. These became the core of a national collection of European art that now ranges from Giotto in the 13th century to the 19th-century Impressionists. The gallery's particular strengths are in Dutch, Italian Renaissance, and 17th-century Spanish painting.

The gallery's paintings are hung in chronological order. In 1991 the modern Sainsbury Wing was added to the main Neoclassical building (1834–8) to house the impressive Early Renaissance collection (1260–1510). *The Leonardo Cartoon* (c.1500), a chalk drawing by Leonardo da Vinci of the Virgin and Child, St. Anne, and John the Baptist, has been moved from here to a more prominent position near the Trafalgar Square entrance. Other Italian painters represented include Masaccio, Piero della Francesca, and Botticelli.

Perhaps the most famous of the Northern European works is *The Arnolfini Marriage* by Jan van Eyck (1434).

Most of the gallery's other exhibits are housed on the first floor of the main building. Among the 16th-century paintings, *The Adoration of the Kings* (1564) by Flemish artist Pieter Brueghel the Elder is notable. *Christ Mocked* (1490–1500) by Hieronymus Bosch is included in the Netherlandish and German section. The superb Dutch collection gives two rooms to Rembrandt. Annibale Carracci and Caravaggio are strongly represented among Italian painters. Spanish artist Diego Velázquez's only surviving female nude, the *Rokeby Venus* (1647–51), is one of the most popular and well-known of the 17th-century works of art. The great age of 19th-century landscape painting is perhaps best represented by Constable's *The Hay Wain* (1821), a masterpiece of changing light and shadow.

In the Impressionist section, Renoir's *Boating on the Seine* (1879–80) demonstrates the free, flickering touch used by the movement's artists to capture the fleeting moment. Other 19th-century highlights include Van Gogh's *Sunflowers*, Monet's *Waterlilies*, Rousseau's *Tropical Storm with Tiger*, and Seurat's *Bathers at Asnières*.

Lesser paintings of all periods are displayed on the lower floor of the main building. The better of the gallery's two restaurants is located in the Sainsbury Wing.

Bathers at Asnières (1884) by Georges Seurat, in the National Gallery

The West End

The West End is the city's social and cultural center, right next to the London home of the royal family. Stretching from the edge of Hyde Park to Covent Garden, the district bustles all day and late into the night. Whether you are looking for art, history, street- or café-life, it is the most rewarding area in which to begin an exploration of the city. Monuments, shops, cinemas, and restaurants radiate out from Trafalgar Square, and the entertainment scene is at its liveliest in the busy streets around Chinatown, Soho, and Leicester Square. From the garish lights of boisterous Piccadilly Circus to genteel St. James's Square, the West End embraces all aspects of London life, and caters to every budget.

Trafalgar Square by night with Nelson's Column in the foreground

Trafalgar Square ⑦

WC2. ⊖ *Charing Cross.* 🚌 *3, 6, 9, 11, 12, 13, 15, 23, 24, 29, 53, 88, 91, 139, 159, 176, 453.*

London's main venue for rallies and outdoor public meetings, Trafalgar Square was conceived by John Nash and mostly constructed during the 1830s. The 50-m (165-ft) tall column commemorates Admiral Lord Nelson, Britain's most famous sea lord, and dates from 1842. Edwin Landseer's four lions were added 25 years later. Today the square is very popular with tourists.
Admiralty Arch, designed in 1911, separates courtly London from the hurly-burly of Trafalgar Square. The central gate is opened only for royal processions. The restored buildings on the square's south side were built in 1880 as the Grand Hotel. The north side is now taken up by the National Gallery

and its Sainsbury Wing *(see p49)*. In the northeast corner stands **St. Martin-in-the-Fields**. This 18th-century church by James Gibbs became a model for the Colonial style of church-building in the US.
    Adjoining the National Gallery, the **National Portrait Gallery** depicts Britain's history through portraits, photographs, and sculptures. Subjects range from Elizabeth I to photographs of politicians, actors, and rock stars.
    Further north, Leicester Square is at the heart of the West End entertainment district with the city's leading cinemas and lively nightclubs, while London's Chinatown attracts a steady throng of diners and shoppers. Bordering it, Shaftesbury Avenue is the main artery of London's theaterland.

🏛 **National Portrait Gallery**
2 St. Martin's Place WC2. **Tel** 020-7306 0055. ◯ *daily.* ● *Dec 24–26.* 🖼 *for special exhibitions.* ♿ 🖥 📷 📱 *audio guide.* **www**.npg.org.uk

Piccadilly ⑧

W1. ⊖ *Piccadilly Circus, Green Park.* 🚌 *9, 14, 19, 22, 38.*

The thoroughfare called Piccadilly links Hyde Park Corner with Piccadilly Circus, but the name also refers to the surrounding area. Today Piccadilly has two contrasting faces: a bustling commercial district full of shopping arcades, eateries, and cinemas; and St. James's, to the south, which still focuses on a wealthy, glamorous clientele.
    Piccadilly Circus, with its dazzling neon lights, is a focal point of the West End. It began as an early 19th-century crossroads between Piccadilly and John Nash's Regent Street. Briefly an elegant space, edged by curving stucco façades, by 1910 the first electric advertisements had been installed.
    Crowds congregate beneath the delicately poised figure of Eros, the Greek god of love. Erected in 1892 as a memorial to the Earl of Shaftesbury, a Victorian philanthropist, the statue was originally intended to represent an angel of mercy.
    Among the many notable sights along Piccadilly, the **Royal Academy**, founded in 1768, houses a permanent art collection, including a Michelangelo relief of the *Madonna and Child* (1505). Its annual summer exhibition is renowned for clever juxtaposition of new and established works.
    The tranquil **St. James's Church** was designed by Sir Christopher Wren in 1684,

Alfred Gilbert's 1892 statue of Eros in Piccadilly Circus

A street performer in front of crowds at Covent Garden's Piazza

and the recently restored 18th-century **Spencer House** contains fine period furniture and paintings. This Palladian palace was built for an ancestor of Princess Diana.

Shopping in and around Piccadilly is very expensive, especially in Bond Street, where many famous designer labels have stores, and in the Burlington Arcade, which is patrolled by beadles. On Piccadilly itself, Fortnum and Mason, founded in 1707, is one of London's most prestigious food stores, while the grand Ritz hotel is a popular afternoon tea venue for the suitably dressed. Jermyn Street is renowned for high quality men's clothing.

South of Piccadilly is St. James's Square, laid out in the 1670s and dominated by a statue of William III. It has long been the most fashionable address in London. Pall Mall, named after the 17th-century game of *palle-maille* (a cross between croquet and golf) once played here, is lined with gentlemen's clubs, which admit only members and their guests. It leads to the 16th-century **St. James's Palace**, built for Henry VIII. The palace is still the official headquarters of the Court of St. James. Opposite is the **Queen's Chapel**, the first Classical church in England.

🏛 Royal Academy
Burlington House, Piccadilly W1.
Tel 020-7300 8000. ⬭ daily. ⬤
Dec 24–25. 🎟 for exhibitions.
🎫 reserve in advance. ♿
www.royalacademy.org.uk

🏛 Spencer House
27 St. James's Pl SW1. *Tel* 020-7499
8620. ⬭ Sun. ⬤ Jan & Aug.
🎟 🎫 compulsory. ♿
www.spencerhouse.co.uk

Covent Garden ⑨

WC2. ⬇ *Covent Garden.* 🚌 *1, 6,
9, 13, 15, 23, 59, 68, 87, 91, 168,
171, 176.* ⬇ *daily.*

Open-air cafés, street entertainers, stylish shops, and markets make Covent Garden a magnet for visitors. The name derives from a medieval convent garden which supplied Westminster Abbey with produce.

At its center is the Piazza, designed by 17th-century architect Inigo Jones as an elegant residential square, after an example from the Tuscan town of Livorno. For a time, houses around the Piazza were highly sought-after, but decline accelerated when a fruit and vegetable market developed. In 1973 the market moved to a

new site and Covent Garden was revamped. Today only **St. Paul's Church** remains of Inigo Jones's buildings. Samuel Pepys saw a Punch and Judy show under the portico in 1662, and street entertainment has been a tradition here ever since.

The **Royal Opera House** *(see p95)*, designed in 1858 by E.M. Barry, but totally renovated in 1997–9, is home to the Royal Opera and Royal Ballet Companies. Many of the world's greatest dance performers have appeared on its stage.

Covent Garden has many theatrical associations. The site of the **Theatre Royal**, completed in 1812, has been occupied by a theater since 1663. **St. Martin's Theatre** is home to the world's longest running play, *The Mousetrap*.

Other attractions include the **London Transport Museum** and an area of "alternative" shops around Neal Street and Neal's Yard. The **Lamb and Flag** (1623) in Rose Street is one of London's oldest pubs.

🏛 London Transport Museum
Covent Garden WC2. *Tel* 020-7379
6344. ⬭ daily. ⬤ Dec 24–26. 🎟
♿ www.ltmuseum.co.uk

Statue of a resting ballerina, facing the Royal Opera House

British Museum ⑩

The oldest public museum in the world, the British Museum was established in 1753 to house the collections of the physician Sir Hans Sloane (1660–1753). Sloane's artifacts have been added to by gifts and purchases from all over the world, and the museum now contains innumerable items stretching from the present day to prehistory. Robert Smirke designed the main part of the building (1823–50), but the architectural highlight is the modern Great Court, with the world-famous Reading Room at its center, opened by the Queen in 2000. The 94 galleries which run for more than 2 miles (4 km), cover civilizations from ancient Assyria to modern Japan.

PREHISTORIC AND ROMAN BRITAIN

Relics of prehistoric Britain are on display in six separate galleries. The most impressive items include the Mold gold cape made from a sheet of decorated gold; an antlered headdress worn by hunter-gatherers some 9,000 years ago; and "Lindow Man," a 1st-century AD sacrificial victim who lay preserved in a bog until 1984. Some superb Celtic metalwork is also on show, alongside the silver Mildenhall Treasure and other notable Roman pieces. The Hinton St. Mary mosaic (4th century AD) features a roundel containing the earliest known British depiction of Christ.

Reconstruction of the ceremonial helmet found at Sutton Hoo

MEDIEVAL, RENAISSANCE, AND MODERN OBJECTS

The spectacular Sutton Hoo ship treasure, the burial hoard of a 7th-century Anglo-Saxon king, is on display in Room 41. This superb find, made in 1939, revolutionized scholars' understanding of Anglo-Saxon life and ritual. The artifacts uncovered include a helmet and shield, Celtic hanging bowls, the remains of a lyre, and gold and garnet jewelry.

Adjacent galleries contain a collection of clocks, watches, and scientific instruments. Some exquisite timepieces are on view, including a 400-year-old clock from Prague, designed as a model galleon; in its day it pitched, played

music, and even fired a cannon. Also nearby are the famous 12th-century Lewis chessmen, and a gallery housing Baron Ferdinand Rothschild's (1839–98) remarkably varied treasures. The most spectacular of these is a gold enameled reliquary of the Holy Thorn (Christ's Crown of Thorns), dating from the 15th century.

The museum's modern collection includes Wedgwood pottery, illustrated books, glassware, and a series of Russian revolutionary plates.

WESTERN ASIA

Numerous galleries at the museum are devoted to the Western Asian collections, covering 7,000 years of history. The most famous items are the 7th-century BC Assyrian reliefs from King Ashurbanipal's palace at Nineveh, but of equal interest are two large human-headed bulls from 7th-century BC Khorsabad, and an inscribed Black Obelisk of Assyrian King Shalmaneser III. Rooms 51–59 on the upper floor contain pieces from ancient Sumeria, part of the Oxus Treasure (which lay buried for over 2,000 years), and the museum's collection of clay cuneiform tablets. The earliest of these are inscribed with the oldest known pictographs (c.3300 BC).

ANCIENT EGYPT

Egyptian sculptures can be found in Room 4 on the main floor. These include a fine red granite head of a king, thought to be Amenophis III, and a colossal statue of king Ramses II. Also on show is the Rosetta Stone, which was used by Jean-François Champollion (1790–1832) as a primer for deciphering Egyptian hieroglyphs. An extraordinary array of mummies, jewelry, and Coptic art can also be found in rooms 61–66 upstairs, including a famous bronze cat with a gold nose-ring. The various instruments used by embalmers to preserve bodies before entombment are all displayed.

Ancient Egyptian tomb painting, *The Festival of Sekhtet* (1410 BC)

The Portland Vase, depicting the betrothal of Peleus and Thetis

GREECE AND ROME

The Greek and Roman collections include the museum's most famous treasure, the Elgin Marbles. These 5th-century BC reliefs from the Parthenon once comprised a marble frieze which decorated Athena's temple at the Acropolis in Athens. Much of it was ruined in battle in 1687, and most of what survived was removed between 1801 and 1804 by the British diplomat Lord Elgin, and sold to the British nation. Other highlights include the Nereid Monument, and sculptures and friezes from the Mausoleum at Halicarnassus. The beautiful 1st-century BC cameo-glass Portland Vase is located in the Roman Empire section.

ORIENTAL ART

Fine porcelain and ancient Shang bronzes (c.1500–1050 BC) are highlights of the museum's Chinese collection. Particularly impressive are the ceremonial ancient Chinese bronze vessels, with their enigmatic animal-head shapes. The fine Chinese ceramics range from delicate tea bowls to a model pond which is almost a thousand years old. Adjacent to these is one of the finest collections of Asian religious sculpture outside India. These include an assortment of sculpted

The Young Prince with his Parents (c.1600), an Indian miniature

reliefs which once covered the walls of the Buddhist temple at Amarati, and which recount stories from the life of the Buddha. A Korean section contains some gigantic works of Buddhist art.

Islamic art, including a stunning jade terrapin found in a water tank, can be found in Room 34. Rooms 90–94 house temporary exhibitions for prints and drawings from Asia and Japan.

AFRICA

An interesting collection of African sculptures, textiles, and graphic art can be found in Room 25, located in the basement. Famous bronzes from the Kingdom of Benin stand alongside modern African prints, paintings, and drawings, plus an array of colorful fabrics.

VISITORS' CHECKLIST

Great Russell St WC1.
Tel 020-7323 8000.
🔵 Tottenham Court Road,
Holborn, Russell Square. 🚌 7,
8, 10, 14, 19, 24, 25, 29, 30,
38, 55, 68, 134, 188. ⏱ 10am–
5:30pm Sat–Wed,10am–8:30pm
Thu–Fri. 🔴 Jan 1, Good Fri,
Dec 24–26. 🎫 ♿
www.thebritishmuseum.ac.uk

THE GREAT COURT AND THE OLD READING ROOM

Surrounding the Reading Room of the former British Library, the £100-million Great Court opened to coincide with the new millennium. Designed by Sir Norman Foster, the Court is covered by a wide-span, lightweight roof, creating London's first ever indoor public square. The Reading Room itself has been restored to its original design, so visitors can sample the atmosphere which Karl Marx, Mahatma Gandhi, and George Bernard Shaw found so agreeable. From the outside, however, it is scarcely recognizable; it is housed in a multi-level construction which partly supports the roof, and which also contains a Center for Education, temporary exhibition galleries, bookshops, cafés, and restaurants. Part of the Reading Room also serves as a study suite where those wishing to learn more about the Museum's collections have access to information.

The Great Court and Reading Room of the British Museum

Madame Tussaud's and the London Planetarium ⑪

Marylebone Rd NW1. **Tel** 0870-400 3000. ⊖ Baker St. ◻ daily. ⬤ Dec 25. 📷 🎫 📱 🖥 ♿ **www**.madame-tussauds.com & **www**.london-planetarium.com

Madame Tussaud began her wax-modeling career making death masks of victims of the French Revolution. In 1835, after moving to England, she set up an exhibition of her work in Baker Street, near the museum's present site.

Traditional techniques are still used to create the figures of royalty, politicians, actors, pop stars, and sporting heroes. In the renowned Chamber of Horrors some of the original French Revolution death masks are displayed, and vivid scenes of murders are recreated. Visitors travel in stylized taxi-cabs in the final section "witnessing" momentous events in the city's history, from the Great Fire of 1666 to the Swinging Sixties.

The London Planetarium was amalgamated into Madame Tussaud's in 2006. It now features an animated show based on extra-terrestrials.

Making a model of singer Luciano Pavarotti at Madame Tussaud's

Regent's Park ⑫

NW1. **Tel** 020-7486 7905. ⊖ Regent's Park, Great Portland St, Camden Town. ◻ daily. ♿ **London Zoo Tel** 020-7722 3333. ◻ daily. ⬤ Dec 25. 📷

This area of land was enclosed as a park in 1812. John Nash designed the scheme and originally envisaged a kind of

Wooden rowboats available to rent on Regent's Park boating lake

garden suburb, dotted with 56 villas in a variety of Classical styles. Eight villas were eventually built inside the park (three survive round the edge of the Inner Circle).

The boating lake boasts many varieties of water birds. In summer Queen Mary's Gardens are full of flowers and Shakespeare productions are staged at the Open Air Theater nearby. Musical performances are also held at the bandstand on the weekend. Broad Walk provides a picturesque stroll north from Park Square towards Primrose Hill.

London Zoo, with its vast animal enclosures, borders the park, and is also an important center of wildlife research and conservation work.

Statue of Peter Pan in Kensington Gardens

Hyde Park ⑬

W2. **Tel** 020-7298 2100. ⊖ Hyde Park Corner, Knightsbridge, Lancaster Gate, Marble Arch. ◻ dawn–11pm daily. ♿

The ancient manor of Hyde was part of the lands of Westminster Abbey seized by Henry VIII at the Dissolution of the Monasteries in 1536. James I opened the park to the public in the early 17th century, and it was soon one of the city's most fashionable public spaces. Unfortunately it also became popular with duelists and highwaymen, prompting William III to have 300 lights hung along Rotten Row, the first street in England to be lit at night. Today Rotten Row is used for horseback riding.

In 1730 the Westbourne River was dammed by Queen Caroline to create an artificial lake – the Serpentine. Today cafés, restaurants, and the Serpentine Gallery, which has exhibitions of modern art, dot the fringes of the lake, which is a popular venue for boating and swimming.

At the southeast corner of Hyde Park stands Apsley House, the grand former home of the Duke of Wellington. Now a museum of memorabilia to the great politician and soldier, the lavish interiors designed by Robert Adam are also worth seeing.

A law passed in 1872 made it legal to assemble an audience and address it on whatever topic you chose. Since then, Speaker's Corner, at the northeast corner of the park, has been the established venue for budding orators. Crowds gather on Sundays to listen to lively speeches.

Adjoining Hyde Park are Kensington Gardens, the former grounds of Kensington Palace, which were opened to the public in 1841. A royal residence for centuries, the palace was Princess Diana's home until her untimely death.

Attractions in the gardens include the bronze statue of J. M. Barrie's fictional Peter Pan (1912), by George Frampton, and the Round Pond where model boats are sailed. The dignified Orangery (1704) is now an upscale café.

Street-by-Street: South Kensington

The numerous museums and colleges created in the wake of the Great Exhibition of 1851 *(see pp56–7)* continue to give this neighbourhood its dignified character. Visited as much by Londoners as tourists, the museum area is liveliest on Sundays and on summer evenings during the Royal Albert Hall's famous season of classical "Prom" concerts *(see p126)*.

The Royal Albert Hall
Opened in 1870 and modeled on a Roman amphitheater, this magnificent concert hall hosts a range of events.

to Kensington Gardens

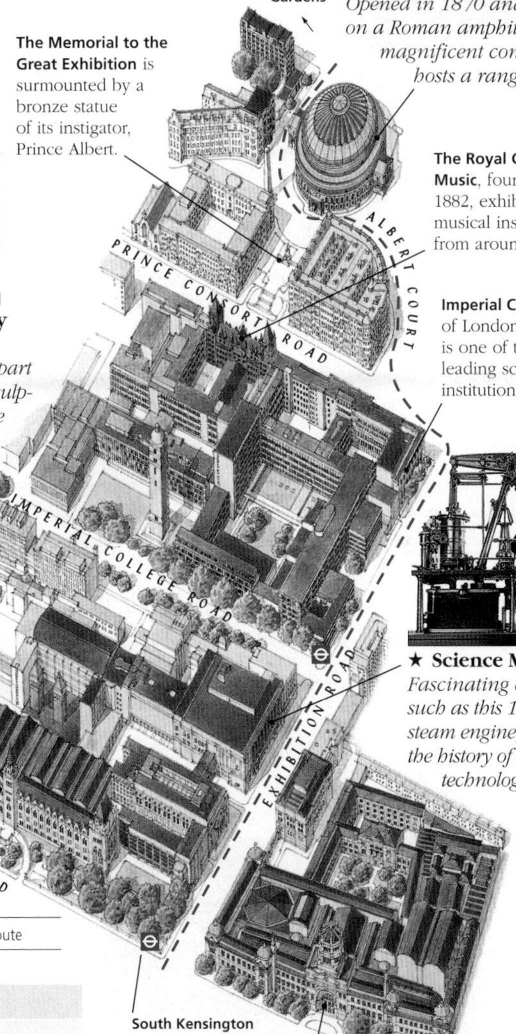

The Memorial to the Great Exhibition is surmounted by a bronze statue of its instigator, Prince Albert.

The Royal College of Music, founded in 1882, exhibits historic musical instruments from around the world.

Imperial College, part of London University, is one of the country's leading scientific institutions.

PRINCE CONSORT ROAD

ALBERT COURT

★ **Natural History Museum**
This pterodactyl is part of a menagerie of sculptures that adorn the façade of the great museum (see p56).

IMPERIAL COLLEGE ROAD

★ **Science Museum**
Fascinating exhibits, such as this 18th-century steam engine, celebrate the history of science and technology (see p56).

EXHIBITION ROAD

CROMWELL ROAD

KEY

– – – Suggested route

STAR SIGHTS

★ Science Museum

★ Natural History Museum

★ Victoria and Albert Museum

South Kensington station (two entrances on Exhibition Road)

0 meters	100
0 yards	100

★ **Victoria and Albert Museum**
The museum has a fine collection of decorative arts from around the world (see p57).

Children exploring the "Pattern Pod" at the Science Museum

Science Museum ⑭

Exhibition Rd SW7. 🄴 *South Kensington.* 🚌 *9, 10, 14, 52, C1.* **Tel** *0870-870 4868.* ◯ *daily.* ⬤ *Dec 24– 26.* 🈂 *for special exhibitions only.* 🄴 www.sciencemuseum.org.uk

Centuries of scientific and technological development are illustrated and explained at the Science Museum – from Ancient Greek and Roman medicine to space exploration and nuclear fission.

The massive and impressive collection, exhibited on five floors, includes steam engines, spacecraft, and early mechanical computers. The museum aims to bring entertainment to the process of learning, with numerous interactive displays for children and staff on hand to provide explanations. Of equal importance is the social context of science: how inventions have transformed day-to-day life, and the process of discovery itself.

The best of the displays are "Flight," which gives visitors the opportunity to experiment with aeronautical concepts, and "Launch Pad," designed to give 7- to 13-year-olds a knowledge of basic scientific principles. A plasma ball is one of many hands-on exhibits.

"The Exploration of Space" exhibits the scarred Apollo 10 spacecraft which carried three astronauts to the moon and back in May 1969. There is also a video of the Apollo 11 moon landing a few weeks later.

More down-to-earth, but just as absorbing, is "Food for Thought," which reveals the impact of science and technology on every aspect of diet, explored through demonstrations and historic reconstructions, such as an 18th-century kitchen.

Other popular sections include "Optics," which has holograms, lasers, and color-mixing experiments, and "Power and Land Transport," which displays working steam engines, vintage trains, cars, and motorbikes.

The Wellcome Wing is devoted to contemporary science and technology. "Antenna" is a constantly updated exhibition devoted to the latest scientific breakthroughs. "Pattern Pod" introduces younger children to the patterns of science in a fun and colorful way. "Digitopolis" explores our relationship with digital technology, including virtual reality. "In Future" is a multi-user game in which partici-

Triceratops skull, Natural History Museum

pants decide how current scientific research could affect the future. Our imagination of human identity is the subject of "Who Am I?", where visitors can learn about genetics and current biomedical discoveries. The wing also contains an IMAX® cinema, a SimEx simulator ride, and a café.

Natural History Museum ⑮

Cromwell Rd SW7. 🄴 *South Kensington.* 🚌 *14, 49, 70, 74, 345, C1.* **Tel** *020-7942 5000.* ◯ *daily.* ⬤ *Dec 24, 25, 26.* 🈂 🄴 www.nhm.ac.uk

This vast cathedral-like building, designed by Alfred Waterhouse, is the most architecturally flamboyant of the South Kensington museums. Its richly sculpted stonework conceals an iron and steel frame. This building technique was revolutionary when the museum first opened in 1881. The imaginative displays tackle fundamental issues such as the ecology and evolution of the planet, the origin of species, and the development of human beings – all explained through a dynamic combination of the latest technology, interactive displays, and traditional exhibits.

The museum is divided into three sections: the Life and Earth Galleries and the Darwin Centre. In the Life Galleries, the Ecology exhibition begins its exploration of the complex web of the natural world, and man's role in it, through a convincing replica of a moon-lit rainforest buzzing with the sounds of insects. The most popular exhibits are in the Dinosaur section which has real dinosaur skeletons and life-like animatronics. "Creepy Crawlies," with specimens from the insect and spider world, and the Mammals exhibition, enable visitors to see endangered and danger-ous creatures close-up. The

The colorful "Antenna" section in the Science Museum Wellcome Wing

For hotels and restaurants in this region see pp96–8 and pp102–4

extinct dodo is among the many species displayed in the Bird Gallery.

The Earth Galleries explore the history of Earth and its wealth of natural resources, and offer the opportunity to experience the rumblings of an earthquake. The Darwin Centre gives the chance to go behind the scenes to observe zoological specimens and to find out more about the museum's scientific research.

Victoria and Albert Museum ⑯

Cromwell Rd SW7. ⊖ *South Kensington.* 🚌 *14, 74, C1.* **Tel** *020-7942 2000.* ◯ *daily.* ⬤ *Dec 24–26.* 🎫 *for special exhibitions.* 🎫 ♿ **www**.vam.ac.uk

Originally founded in 1852 as a Museum of Manufacturing – to inspire and raise standards among students of design – the V&A, as it is popularly known, has 11 km (7 miles) of galleries on four floors. The museum was renamed by Queen Victoria in 1899, in memory of her late husband, and contains one of the world's richest collections of fine and applied arts.

Since 1909 the museum has been housed in a building designed by Sir Aston Webb. The museum is undergoing a dramatic restructuring of much of its collection and gallery spaces, alongside a grand development of the central Pirelli Garden.

Donatello's marble relief of *The Ascension* is included in the sculpture collection along with sculptures from India and the Middle and Far East. Craftsmanship in porcelain, glass, and pottery is displayed on levels 4 and 6, with rare pieces by Picasso and Bernard Leach, intricate Near Eastern tiles, and a wide selection of Chinese pieces.

The most celebrated item in the vast array of furniture is

Façade of the Victoria and Albert Museum

the *Great Bed of Ware*, made around 1590. The Victorian designers who decorated the plush Morris, Gamble, and Poynter Rooms recreated historic styles with newer industrial materials. The fully furnished interiors offer a vivid picture of social life through their displays of furniture and other domestic objects. Among exhibits in the 20th-Century Gallery is Daniel Weil's painting *Radio in a Bag* (1983). The V&A has a wide collection of musical instruments and metalwork, including a 16th-century salt cellar, the *Burghley Nef*. The Silver gallery also explores the history and techniques of silvermaking. Gallery III is devoted to the making of sculpture, ranging from medieval ivories to modern bronzes.

18th-century wooden doll, Victoria and Albert Museum

Among the textiles, weapons, jewelry, metalwork, glass, and paintings of the South Asia gallery is the automated *Tippoo's Tiger* (c.1790), which mauls a European soldier when activated. Eight galleries, devoted to the arts of the Far East, display rare jade and ceramics, a giant Buddha's head from AD 700–900, and a Ming canopied bed. Among exhibits in the China gallery is a watercolor on silk from the Qing Dynasty (1644–1912). The Toshiba Gallery focuses on Japanese art, including Samurai armor and woodblock prints. The world-renowned Fashion Court is displayed on level 1. It is devoted to fashionable clothing from the mid-1500s to the present day. The figures here are fully dressed, complete with contemporary accessories.

The museum also houses valuable illustrated documents in the National Art Library and the national collection of photographs with images from 1856 to the present.

The City and Southwark

Dominated by gleaming office blocks, befitting its status as London's financial and business center, the City is also the oldest part of the capital. The Great Fire of 1666 obliterated many of its buildings, and much of the reconstruction was undertaken by Sir Christopher Wren. St. Paul's Cathedral is the most magnificent of his surviving works. Humming with activity in business hours, the City empties at night. Southwark, on the south bank of the Thames, was a refuge for prostitutes and gamblers in the Middle Ages. Theaters, including the Globe, where many of Shakespeare's plays were performed, and other places of entertainment were built along the waterfront in the second half of the 16th century.

Spacious interior of St. Paul's Cathedral in the City

St. Paul's Cathedral ⑰

Ludgate Hill EC4. **Tel** 020-7246 4128. ⊖ St. Paul's, Mansion House. 🚌 4, 11, 15, 17 & others. 🕐 8:30am–4pm Mon–Sat; for services only Sun, Dec 25 & Good Fri. 📷 📹 www.stpauls.co.uk

Rebuilt on the site of a medieval cathedral after the Great Fire of 1666, this magnificent Baroque building, designed by Sir Christopher Wren, was completed in 1710.

St. Paul's has been the setting for great ceremonial events, including the funeral of Sir Winston Churchill in 1965 and the wedding of Prince Charles and Lady Diana in 1981.

At 110 m (360 ft) high, the dome is the second largest in the world, after that of St. Peter's in Rome. Supported by a brick cone, the lantern weighs a massive 850 tonnes. The dome's gallery affords a splendid view over London.

Modifications to Wren's original plan include the towers of the west front, the double colonnade of the west portico, and the balustrade – added against his wishes in 1718. Pediment carvings on the west portico show the Conversion of St. Paul.

Wren created a cool and majestic interior. The nave, transepts, and choir are arranged in the traditional shape of a cross. Its climax is in the great open space of the crossing, below the main dome, which is decorated with monochrome frescoes by Sir James Thornhill, a leading architectural painter of the time. From the south aisle, 259 steps ascend to the Whispering Gallery, so-called because of the unusual acoustics. The north aisle is vaulted with small domes like those of the nave ceiling.

Much of the fine wrought ironwork was created by Jean Tijou, a Huguenot refugee. The intricate carvings of cherubs, fruits, and garlands on the choir stalls are the work of Grinling Gibbons.

Memorials to famous figures, such as Lawrence of Arabia and Lord Nelson, can be seen in the crypt. The inscription on Wren's tomb is fitting: "Reader, if you seek his memorial look all around you."

Museum of London ⑱

London Wall EC2. **Tel** 0870-444 3851. ⊖ Barbican, St. Paul's. 🕐 Mon–Sat & public hols, Sun pm (lower galleries closed until 2009 for refurbishment). 🕐 Jan 1, Dec 24–26. ♿ www.museumoflondon.org.uk

This museum traces life in London from prehistoric times to the 20th century.

Objects from Roman London include a brightly colored 2nd-century fresco, while from the Tudor city an example of an early English delft plate, made in 1602 at Aldgate, bears an inscription praising Elizabeth I.

The 17th-century section contains the shirt Charles I wore on the scaffold, and an audio-visual display recreating the Great Fire of 1666. A dress in Spitalfields silk, dating from 1753, is among the many fine costumes on display.

One of the most popular exhibits is the lavishly gilded Lord Mayor's State Coach, built in 1757 and still used for the Lord Mayor's Show held in November each year. The Victorian Walk takes visitors back to the time of Charles Dickens, recreating the atmosphere of 19th-century London with authentic shop interiors.

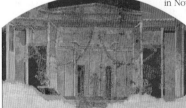

Roman wall painting in the Museum of London

Sculpture from inaugural exhibition in the vast Turbine Hall, Tate Modern

Tate Modern ⑲

Bankside SE1. **Tel** 020-7887 8000.
🚇 Southwark, Blackfriars, Waterloo.
🚌 45, 63, 100, 381, 344, RV1. ◯
daily. ⬤ Dec 24–26. 🎟 special exhibitions. 🏷 🗗 www.tate.org.uk

One of the world's most
important collections of 20th-
century art now has a worthy
home in this imposing former
power station with its vast,
cathedral-like spaces.

Originally designed by
Sir Giles Gilbert Scott, the
architect of London's red
telephone kiosks, the huge
Bankside building had been
disused since 1981, when it
was acquired by the Tate
Gallery in 2000. Swiss architects were responsible for the
building's redesign, which
allows the works of art to be
displayed in a dynamic style
suited to their innovative spirit.

Unusually, the permanent
collection is exhibited in four
themed groups: poetry and
dream, idea and object, states
of flux and material gestures.
The paintings and sculptures
embrace Surrealism, Abstract
Expressionism, Pop Art,
Minimal and Conceptual Art.

Major works include
Picasso's *The Three Dancers*,
Dalí's *The Metamorphosis of
Narcissus*, and Andy Warhol's
Marilyn Diptych. There are
also regular temporary
exhibitions of works by lesser-
known artists, and by more
controversial newcomers. At
the top of the building are
two new floors, enclosed in
glass. One is a restaurant with
superb views. Natural light
from these floors filters down
to the upper galleries.

Shakespeare's Globe ⑳

New Globe Walk SE1. **Tel** 020-7902
1400. 🚇 London Bridge, Mansion
House. ◯ daily. ⬤ Dec 24, 25.
Performances May–Oct.
🎟 🗗 every 30 mins.
www.shakespeares-globe.org

A detailed reproduction of
an Elizabethan theater has
been built on the riverside
close to the site of the original
Globe, Shakespeare's
"wooden O" where many of
his plays were first performed.
Open to the elements, the
theater operates only in the
summer. Seeing a play here
can be a lively experience,
with "groundlings" (those
with cheap standing-room
tickets) in front of the stage
encouraged to cheer or jeer.
An informative tour of the
theater is offered by "resting"
Globe actors, and visitors can
enjoy being center stage
among them. Beneath the
theater is the Underglobe,
where every aspect of
Shakespeare's work is vividly
brought to life through the
use of modern technology
and traditional crafts.

Tower of London ㉑

See pp60–61.

Tower Bridge ㉒

SE1. **Tel** 020-7403 3761. 🚇 Tower
Hill, London Bridge. **The Tower
Bridge Exhibition** ◯ daily.
⬤ Dec 24–26. 🎟 🏷 🔼
www.towerbridge.org.uk

This flamboyant piece of
Victorian engineering,
completed in 1894, soon
became a symbol of London.
Its two Gothic towers contain
the mechanism for raising the
roadway to permit large ships
to pass through. The towers
are made of a supporting
steel framework clad in stone.
When raised, the roadway
creates a space 40 m (135 ft)
high and 60 m (200 ft) wide.
In its heyday it was raised
and lowered five times a day.

The bridge now houses **The
Tower Bridge Exhibition**, with
displays which bring its
history to life. There are fine
river views from the walkways
between the towers, and the
steam engine room which was
in use until 1976 can be visited.

Tower Bridge, a symbol of
Victorian London

Tower of London ㉑

Soon after he became king in 1066, William the Conqueror built a fortress here to guard the entrance to London from the Thames Estuary. In 1097 the White Tower, which today occupies the center of the complex, was completed in stone; other fine buildings have been added over the centuries. The Tower has served as a royal residence, armory, treasury, and most famously as a prison for enemies of the Crown. Some were tortured and among those who met their death here were the "Princes in the Tower," the sons and heirs of Edward IV. Today the Tower is a popular attraction, housing the Crown Jewels and other fine exhibits. Thirty seven Yeoman Warders, known as "Beefeaters," guard the complex and live here. Its most celebrated residents are seven ravens. Legend claims that the kingdom will fall if they desert the Tower.

Tower of London raven

Beauchamp Tower
Many high-ranking prisoners were held here, often with their own servants. The tower was built by Edward I around 1281.

Tower Green was the execution site for aristocratic prisoners, away from crowds on Tower Hill, where many had to submit to public execution. Seven people died here, including two of Henry VIII's six wives, Anne Boleyn and Catherine Howard.

Two 13th-century curtain walls protect the tower.

Queen's House
This Tudor building is the sovereign's official residence at the Tower.

Main entrance from Tower Hill (Middle Tower)

THE CROWN JEWELS

The world's best-known collection of precious objects, now displayed in a splendid exhibition room, includes the gorgeous regalia of crowns, scepters, orbs, and swords used at coronations and other state occasions. Most date from 1661, when Charles II commissioned replacements for regalia destroyed by Parliament after the execution of Charles I. Only a few older pieces survived, hidden by royalist clergymen until the Restoration. These included Edward the Confessor's sapphire ring, now incorporated into the Imperial State Crown. The crown was made for Queen Victoria in 1837 and has been used at the coronation of every monarch since.

The Sovereign's Ring (1831)

The Sovereign's Orb (1661), a hollow gold sphere encrusted with jewels

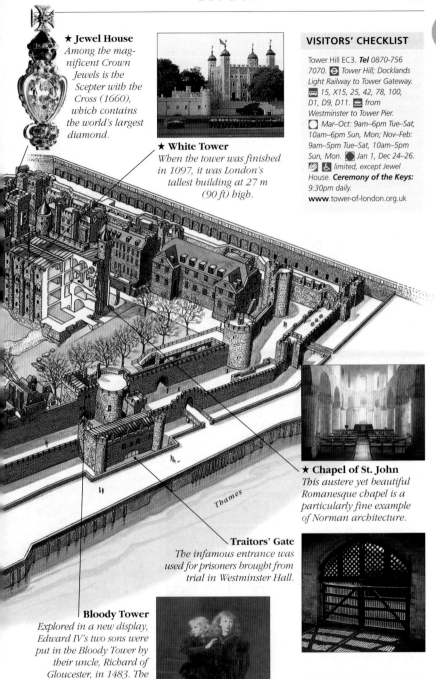

★ Jewel House
Among the magnificent Crown Jewels is the Scepter with the Cross (1660), which contains the world's largest diamond.

★ White Tower
When the tower was finished in 1097, it was London's tallest building at 27 m (90 ft) high.

★ Chapel of St. John
This austere yet beautiful Romanesque chapel is a particularly fine example of Norman architecture.

Thames

Traitors' Gate
The infamous entrance was used for prisoners brought from trial in Westminster Hall.

Bloody Tower
Explored in a new display, Edward IV's two sons were put in the Bloody Tower by their uncle, Richard of Gloucester, in 1483. The princes, depicted here by John Millais (1829–96), disappeared mysteriously and their uncle became King Richard III later that year. In 1674 the skeletons of two children were found nearby.

VISITORS' CHECKLIST

Tower Hill EC3. **Tel** 0870-756 7070. 🚇 Tower Hill; Docklands Light Railway to Tower Gateway. 🚌 15, X15, 25, 42, 78, 100, D1, D9, D11. 🚢 from Westminster to Tower Pier. 🕐 Mar–Oct: 9am–6pm Tue–Sat, 10am–6pm Sun, Mon; Nov–Feb: 9am–5pm Tue–Sat, 10am–5pm Sun, Mon. 🔴 Jan 1, Dec 24–26. 🎦 ♿ limited, except Jewel House. **Ceremony of the Keys:** 9:30pm daily.
www.tower-of-london.org.uk

STAR SIGHTS

★ Jewel House

★ White Tower

★ Chapel of St. John

London: Farther Afield

Over the centuries, London has steadily expanded to embrace the scores of villages that surrounded it. Although now linked in an almost unbroken urban sprawl, many of these areas have managed to retain a strong individual character. Portobello Road has hosted a market since 1837, while Notting Hill, once farmland, is now covered with townhouses. Greenwich and Richmond recall the days when the Thames was an important artery for transport and commerce. The riverside around Richmond and Kew to the southwest of London was a favorite site for the great country retreats of the aristocracy. Perhaps the grandest riverside residence of all is the royal palace of Hampton Court, set in elaborate, luxuriant gardens.

View from the hill at Greenwich of the 17th-century Queen's House

Greenwich ㉓

SE10. 🚉 *Greenwich, Maze Hill, & Docklands Light Railway to Cutty Sark, Greenwich.* 🚢 *from Westminster.*

Best known as the place from which the world's time is measured, Greenwich also marks the historic eastern approach to London by land and water. The area is steeped in maritime and royal history.

The meridian line that divides the earth's eastern and western hemispheres passes through the **Royal Observatory Greenwich** (now housing a museum) and millions of visitors have been photographed standing with one foot on either side of it. Designed by Christopher Wren, the building is topped by a ball on a rod, dropped at 1pm every day since 1833 so that ships' chronometers could be set by it.

Because of its historic links with time, Greenwich was chosen as the site for Britain's year 2000 exhibition – the **Millennium Dome**.

The exquisite **Queen's House,** designed by Inigo Jones, has been restored to how it looked in the late 17th century. Highlights are the unusually-shaped main hall and the intriguing spiral "tulip staircase."

The adjoining **National Maritime Museum** has exhibits ranging from primitive canoes, through Elizabethan galleons, to modern ships. Nearby, the **Old Royal Naval College** was designed by Christopher Wren in two halves so the Queen's House could retain its river view. The chapel and the Painted Hall are open to the public.

Also worth visiting is the **Cutty Sark**, a 19th-century clipper ship. The ship is undergoing restoration, due

Clock tower of the Old Royal Observatory, Greenwich

for completion in 2009. The visitor centre remains open.

A colorful antique shop on London's Portobello Road

Notting Hill and Portobello Road ㉔

W11. 🚇 *Notting Hill Gate, Ladbroke Grove.* 🏪 *Fri & Sat.*

Notting Hill and Portobello Road have been a focus for the Caribbean community since the peak years of immigration in the 1950s and '60s. Today this is a trendy residential district, whose vibrant cosmopolitan spirit is captured in the 1999 film starring Julia Roberts and Hugh Grant.

The West Indian flavor is best experienced during Europe's largest street carnival. First held in 1966, it takes over the entire area on the August bank holiday weekend. For three days costumed parades flood through the crowded streets.

Portobello Road market has a bustling atmosphere with hundreds of stands and shops selling a variety of collectables. The southern end consists almost exclusively of stands selling antiques, jewelry, and souvenirs popular with tourists.

Richmond and Kew ㉕

SW15. 🔁 *Kew Gardens, Richmond.* 🚆 *to Kew Bridge, Richmond.*

The attractive village of Richmond took its name from a palace built in 1500 by Henry VII (formerly the Earl of Richmond), the remains of which can be seen off the green. The vast **Richmond Park** was once Charles I's royal hunting ground. In summer, boats sail from central London to Richmond and Kew.

The nobility continued to favor Richmond after royalty had left, and some of their mansions have survived. The Palladian villa, **Marble Hill House**, was completed in 1729 for the mistress of George II.

On the opposite side of the Thames, **Ham House**, built in 1610, had its heyday later that century when the aristocratic Lauderdale family moved in.

Syon House has been inhabited by the Dukes and Earls of Northumberland for over 400 years. Attractions include lavish Neoclassical interiors, remodelled by Robert Adam in the 1760s, landscaped parkland by Capability Brown, and a spectacular conservatory.

On the riverbank to the south, **Kew Gardens**, the most complete botanic gardens in the world, is flawlessly maintained, with examples of nearly every plant that can be grown in Britain. Highlights are the Palm House, with thousands of exotic tropical blooms, and the delicate plants of the Temperate House. The Gardens became a UNESCO World Heritage Site in 2003. Near the river, **Kew Bridge Steam Museum** is housed in an old water pumping station.

An aerial view of the impressive Hampton Court Palace

🏛 Syon House
London Rd, Brentford. **Tel** 020-8560 0881. **House** ⬜ mid-Apr–Oct: Wed, Thu, Sun. **Gardens** ⬜ daily (Nov–Feb: Sat, Sun). ⬤ Dec 25–26. 🔖

🌿 Kew Gardens
Kew. **Tel** 020-8332 5655. 🔁 Kew Gardens. 🚌 65, 237, 267, 391, 419. ⬜ daily. ⬤ Dec 24, 25. 🔖

Deer grazing in Richmond Park, a former royal hunting ground

Hampton Court ㉖

East Molesey, Surrey. **Tel** 0870-752 7777. 🚆 🚆 Hampton Court. 🚌 111, 216, 411, 451, 461, R68. ⬜ daily. ⬤ Dec 24–26. 🔖 📷 ♿

Cardinal Wolsey, chief minister to Henry VIII, began building Hampton Court as his country residence in 1514. A few years later, in the hope of retaining royal favor, he gave it to the king. The palace was extended first by Henry, and again at the end of the 17th century by William III and Mary II, with the help of Christopher Wren.

From the outside the palace is a harmonious blend of Tudor and English Baroque. A remarkable feature is the Astronomical Clock, created for Henry VIII in 1540.

Inside, Wren's Classical royal rooms, such as the King's Apartments, contrast with Tudor architecture, such as the Great Hall. The stained-glass window here shows Henry VIII flanked by the coats of arms of his six wives. Superb woodwork in the Chapel Royal, including the massive reredos by Grinling Gibbons, dates from a major refurbishment by Queen Anne (c.1711). In the Queen's Gallery, where entertainments were often staged, the marble chimneypiece is by John Nost. Many of the state apartments are decorated with furniture, paintings, and tapestries from the Royal Collection. The King's Staircase has wall paintings by Antonio Verrio. Nine canvases depicting the Triumph of Julius Caesar (1490) are housed in the Mantegna Gallery.

The restored Baroque privy garden, originally created for William and Mary, features radiating avenues of majestic limes and formal flowerbeds. The Fountain Garden still has a few yews planted during their reign. Other attractions are the maze and the Great Vine, planted in 1768.

The distinctive Palm House at London's famous Kew Gardens

Canterbury ❷

Kent. 🏘 *50,000.* 🚊 🚌
ℹ️ *The Buttermarket, Sun Street
(01227-378 100).* 🖼 *Wed & Fri.*

Canterbury was an important Roman town even before St. Augustine arrived in 597, sent by the pope to convert the Anglo-Saxons to Christianity. The town rose in importance, soon becoming the center of Christianity in England.

Under the Normans, the city maintained its position as the country's leading archbishopric. A new cathedral was built on the ruins of the Anglo-Saxon cathedral in 1070. It was enlarged and rebuilt many times; as a result it embraces examples of all styles of medieval architecture.

The most poignant moment in the cathedral's history came in 1170 when Thomas Becket, the Archbishop of Canterbury and enemy of King Henry II, was murdered here. **Trinity Chapel** was built to house Becket's remains.

Until the Dissolution the cathedral was one of the chief places of pilgrimage in all Christendom. The *Canterbury Tales* by Geoffrey Chaucer (c.1345–1400), one of the greatest works of early English literature, tells of a group of pilgrims who are traveling from London to Becket's shrine in 1387.

Adjacent to the ruins of **St. Augustine's Abbey** is **St. Martin's Church**, one of the oldest in England.

The domes and minarets of the Royal Pavilion, Brighton

Beneath Canterbury's streets lies the **Roman Museum**, the highlight of which are the foundations of a Roman house.

🏰 Cathedral
Christ Church Gate. *Tel 01227-762 862.* ⬜ *daily.* ⬤ *during services and concerts, Dec 25.* 📷 ♿ 🎫
www.canterbury-cathedral.org

Brighton ❸

🏘 *249,000.* 🚊 🚌 ℹ️ *5 Pavilion Bldgs (0906-711 2255).* 🖼 *Mon–Sat.* 🎭 *International Arts Festival (May).*

As the nearest south coast city to London, Brighton is perennially popular.

The spirit of the Prince Regent (later George IV) lives on in the magnificence of the **Royal Pavilion**, originally a farmhouse where the prince resided with the Catholic widow Mrs. Fitzherbert after their secret marriage. As his

parties became more lavish, George needed a suitably extravagant setting. In 1815 he employed architect John Nash to transform the house into the fantastic Oriental palace that we see today. Completed in 1822, the exterior remains largely unaltered.

Traditional seaside fun is centered around Brighton's pebble beach. **Brighton Pier**, a late-Victorian pleasure ground, is now filled with amusement arcades. Also worth visiting is the maze of shops and winding alleys from the original village of Brighthelmstone, called **The Lanes**.

🏛 Royal Pavilion
Old Steine. *Tel 01273-290 900.*
⬜ *daily.* ⬤ *Dec 25, 26.* 📷 🎫
♿ *limited.* **www**.royalpavilion.org.uk

Windsor Castle ❹

See pp66–7.

Winchester ❺

Hampshire. 🏘 *36,000.* 🚊 🚌
ℹ️ *Guildhall, The Broadway
(01962-840 500).* 🖼 *Wed–Sat.*

The capital of the ancient kingdom of Wessex, the city of Winchester was also the headquarters of England's Anglo-Saxon kings.

William the Conqueror built one of his first English castles here. The only surviving part is the **Great Hall**, erected in 1235 to replace the original. It is now home to the legendary Round Table of King Arthur,

Canterbury Cathedral dominating the skyline

said to have been built by the wizard Merlin but actually made in the 13th century.

The **Westgate Museum** is one of two surviving 12th-century gatehouses in the city wall. The room (once a prison) above the gate has a glorious 16th-century painted ceiling.

Winchester has been an ecclesiastical center for many centuries. Its fine **cathedral** was begun in 1079. Originally a Benedictine monastery, it has preserved much of its Norman architecture despite numerous modifications. The writer Jane Austin is buried here. Built around 1110, **Wolvesey Castle**, once home of the bishops of Winchester, now lies in ruins.

⚔ Great Hall
Castle Ave. **Tel** 01962-846 476.
◯ daily. ● Dec 25, 26. ♿

The 13th-century Round Table in the Great Hall, Winchester

Salisbury ●

Wiltshire. 🏰 40,000. 🚉 🚌
ℹ Fish Row (01722-334 956).
🛍 Tue & Sat. 🎭 Salisbury Festival
(end May–mid-Jun).

Salisbury was founded in 1220, when the Norman hilltop settlement of Old Sarum was abandoned in favor of a site amid lush water meadows, where the Nadder, Bourne, Avon, Ebble, and Wylye meet.

A **cathedral** was built here in the early 13th century. It is a fine example of the Early English style of Gothic architecture, typified by tall, pointed lancet windows. The magnificent landmark spire is the tallest in England.

The spacious and tranquil **Close**, with its schools, alms-

The awe-inspiring megaliths of Stonehenge, Salisbury Plain

houses, and clergy housing, makes a fine setting for Salisbury's cathedral. In the medieval King's House, the **Salisbury and South Wiltshire Museum** has displays on early man, Stonehenge, and Old Sarum.

Beyond the walls of the Cathedral Close, Salisbury developed its chessboard layout, with areas devoted to different trades, perpetuated in street names such as Fish Row and Butcher Row.

The busy High Street leads to the 13th-century **Church of St. Thomas**, which has a lovely carved timber roof (1450). Nearby on Silver Street, **Poultry Cross** was built in the 15th century as a covered poultry market. In the bustling **Market Place** many of the brick and tile-hung Georgian façades conceal medieval houses.

🔒 Cathedral
The Close. **Tel** 01722-555 120.
◯ daily. 📷 donation. 📷 ♿

🏛 Salisbury and South Wiltshire Museum
The Close. **Tel** 01722-332 151.
◯ Mon–Sat (Jul–Aug: Sun pm).
● Dec 23–31. 📷 ♿ limited

Stonehenge ●

Off A303, Wiltshire. **Tel** 0870-333 1181. 🚌 3 from Salisbury. ◯ daily.
● Jan 1, Dec 24–26. 📷 📷 ♿

Built in several stages from about 3000 BC onward, Stonehenge is Europe's most famous prehistoric monument. We can only guess at the rituals that took place here, but the alignment of the stones leaves little doubt that the circle reflects the changing trajectory of the sun through the sky and the passing of the seasons.

Stonehenge's monumental scale is all the more impressive given that the only available tools were made of stone, wood, and bone. To quarry, transport, and erect the huge stones, its builders must have had the command of immense resources and pools of labor. Stonehenge was completed in about 1250 BC; despite popular belief, it was not built by the Druids, who flourished in Britain 1,000 years later.

A collection of ceremonial bronze weapons, jewelry, and other finds excavated at Stonehenge can be seen in the museum in Salisbury.

Sculpture by Elisabeth Frink (1930–93) in Cathedral Close, Salisbury

Windsor Castle ❹

The oldest continuously inhabited royal residence in Britain, the castle, originally made of wood, was built by William the Conqueror in 1080 to guard the western approaches to London. He chose the site because it was on high ground and just a day's journey from his base in the Tower of London. Successive monarchs have made alterations that render it a remarkable monument to royalty's changing tastes. King George V's affection for it was shown when he chose Windsor for his family surname in 1917. The castle is an official residence of the present queen, who often stays here at weekends.

Albert Memorial Chapel
First built in 1240, it was rebuilt in 1485 and finally converted into a memorial for Prince Albert in 1863.

King Henry VIII Gate

Castle Hill and main entrance

★ St. George's Chapel
The architectural high-light of the castle, this chapel was built between 1475 and 1528 and is an out-standing Late Gothic work. Ten monarchs are buried here.

The Round Tower
was first built in wood by William the Conqueror. In 1170 it was rebuilt in stone by Henry II. It now houses the Royal Archives and Photographic Collection, but is not open to the public.

Statue of Charles II

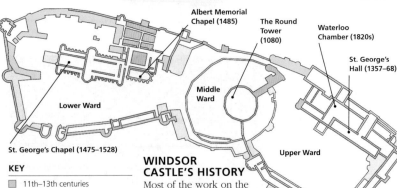

Albert Memorial Chapel (1485)

The Round Tower (1080)

Waterloo Chamber (1820s)

St. George's Hall (1357–68)

Middle Ward

Lower Ward

St. George's Chapel (1475–1528)

Upper Ward

KEY

	11th–13th centuries
	14th century
	15th–18th centuries
	19th–20th centuries

WINDSOR CASTLE'S HISTORY

Most of the work on the castle – founded in 1080 as a motte and bailey – was carried out by Henry II and Edward III, before it was remodeled by George IV in 1823.

Drawing Gallery
*This chalk etching
of Christ by
Michelangelo is part
of the Resurrection
Series. It belongs to
the Royal Collection,
a small selection of
which is shown here
at any one time.*

VISITORS' CHECKLIST

Castle Hill. **Tel** 020-7766 7304.
⬤ 9:45am–5:15pm (Nov–Feb:
4:15pm) daily (last adm: 1 hr 15
mins before closing). ⬤ Good
Fri, Dec 25–26. 🎟 ♿ ✝ **St.
George's Chapel** 5:15pm Mon–
Sat; Sun (for worshippers only).

**The Audience
Chamber** is where
the Queen greets
her guests.

**The Queen's
Ballroom**

Queen Mary's Dolls' House was
designed by Sir Edwin Lutyens in
1924. Every item was built on a
1:12 ratio. The wine cellar
contains genuine vintage wine.

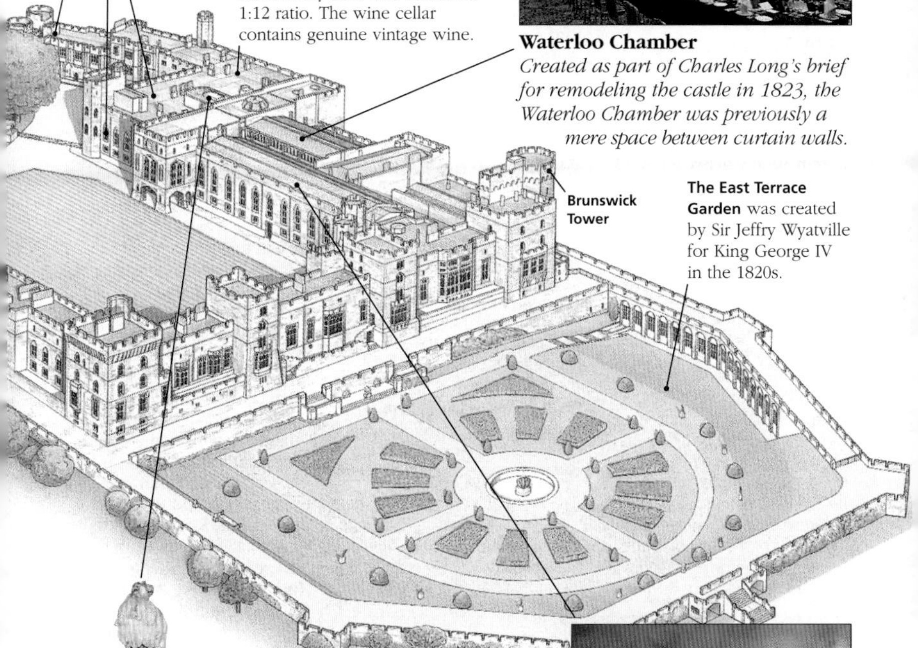

Waterloo Chamber
*Created as part of Charles Long's brief
for remodeling the castle in 1823, the
Waterloo Chamber was previously a
mere space between curtain walls.*

**Brunswick
Tower**

**The East Terrace
Garden** was created
by Sir Jeffry Wyatville
for King George IV
in the 1820s.

★ State Apartments
*These rooms hold many treasures,
including this late 18th-century
state bed in the King's State
Bedchamber, used for the
visit in 1855 of Napoleon III.*

STAR FEATURES

★ St. George's Chapel
_____

★ State Apartments

The Fire of 1992
*A devastating blaze began during
maintenance work on the State
Apartments. St. George's Hall was
destroyed but has been rebuilt.*

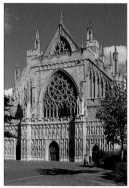

West front of the Cathedral Church of St. Peter in Exeter, Devon

Devon and Cornwall ❽

🚉 🚌 *Truro (Cornwall), Exeter (Devon).* ℹ️ *Boscawen Street, Truro (01872-274 555); Paris Street, Exeter (01392-265700).*

Miles of stunning coastline dominate this magical corner of Britain. Busy seaside resorts alternate with secluded coves and fishing villages rich in maritime history. Inland, lush pastures contrast with stark and treeless moorland.

Britain's most westerly point, **Land's End**, is noted for its remote and wild landscape. Nearby, the former Benedictine monastery of **St. Michael's Mount** rises dramatically from the waters of Mount Bay off Cornwall's southern coast. On the north coast, **St. Ives**, with its crescent of golden sands, is internationally renowned for its two art museums, the Barbara Hepworth Museum and the Tate Gallery St. Ives.

The **Eden Project** in St. Austell was built in 1998–2000 in an old Cornish china clay pit. The aim of this vast educational and research center is to teach visitors about the vital relationship between plants, people, and resources in an informative and fun way. Two bulbous "greenhouses," huge segmented geodesic domes known as biomes, dominate the site, which holds some 4,500 species of plants.

The administrative capital of Cornwall is **Truro**, a city of gracious Georgian buildings and cobbled streets. Here, the Royal Cornwall Museum has displays on mining, smuggling, and Methodism.

Devon's capital is **Exeter**, a lively city with fine Roman and medieval relics. The mainly 14th-century Cathedral Church of St. Peter is one of the most superbly ornamented cathedrals in Britain.

Devon's most popular recreation area is **Dartmoor National Park**. At its heart is a bleak and windswept landscape, dotted with tors – outcrops of granite rock – and grazed by herds of wild ponies.

🍴 **Eden Project**
St. Austell. **Tel** 01726-811 911.
🚉 St. Austell, then local bus.
🕐 daily. 🔴 Dec 24–25. 🎫 ♿
www.edenproject.com

🍴 **Dartmoor National Park**
Devon. 🚉 🚌 to Exeter, Plymouth, Totnes then local bus. ℹ️ Visitor Centre, Princetown (01822-890414).

Bath ❾

See pp70–71.

A wild Dartmoor pony, a familiar sight in Devon's national park

Bristol ❿

Avon. 👥 450,000. ✈️ 🚉 🚌
ℹ️ The Annex, Wildscreen Walk, Harbourside (0906-711 2191). 🚢 daily. 🎭 Harbor Festival (Jul–Aug), International Balloon Fiesta (Aug).

The city of Bristol, at the mouth of the Avon, was once the main British port for transatlantic trade, pioneering the era of the steam liner. The city grew rich on the transportation of wine, tobacco, and, in the 17th century, slaves.

There is a covered market in the city center, part of which occupies the **Corn Exchange**, built by John Wood the Elder in 1743. **St. John's Gate** has colorful statues of Bristol's mythical founders, King Brennus and King Benilus.

Bristol's **cathedral** took an unusually long time to build. The choir was begun in 1298, the transepts and tower were finished in 1515, but the nave took another 350 years to build.

Designed by Isambard Kingdom Brunel, the **SS Great Britain** was the world's first large iron passenger ship. Launched in 1843, it traveled 32 times round the world. The ship now stands in the dock where it was originally built, undergoing restoration.

The **British Empire and Commonwealth Museum**, in the 19th-century rail station at Temple Meads, is the first major museum to chart the 500-year history of the British Empire.

The **Arnolfini Gallery** is a showcase for contemporary art, dance, drama, and film. It is on the harborside, which is lined with cafés, bars, and galleries.

Cornwall's wild and rugged southern coastline

For hotels and restaurants in this region see pp96–101 and pp102–7

Wales

Wales is a country of outstanding natural beauty, with varied landscapes. Visitors come to climb dramatic mountain peaks, walk in the forests, fish in the broad rivers, and enjoy the miles of untainted coastline. The country's many seaside towns have long been popular with British vacationers. As well as outdoor pursuits, there is the vibrancy of Welsh culture, with its strong Celtic roots, to be experienced. The Welsh have their own language, which has survived despite the pervasive use of the English tongue.

Cardiff Castle's clock tower, a 19th-century addition by Burges

Cardiff ⓫

Glamorgan. 🏠 310,000. ✈ 🚆 🚌
ℹ The Hayes (0870-121 1258).
🎭 Cardiff Festival (Jul/Aug).

Cardiff was first occupied by the Romans, who built a fort here in AD 75. In the 1830s the town began to develop as a port, and by 1913 it was the world's leading coal exporter. Confirmed as the Welsh capital in 1955, it is now devoted to commerce and administration.
    Cardiff Castle began as a Roman fort. It was renovated in the 19th century by William Burges, who created an ornate mansion rich in medieval images and romantic detail.
    Cardiff's civic center is set around Alexandra Gardens. The Neoclassical **City Hall** (1905) is dominated by its huge dome and clock tower. The **Crown Building** now houses the Welsh Office, responsible for Welsh government affairs.
    To the south of the center, the docklands are being transformed by the creation of a marina and waterfront. Here, the **Pier Head Building**, constructed in 1896, is a reminder of the city's heyday.

⚓ **Cardiff Castle**
Castle St. **Tel** 029-2087 8100. ◯ daily.
● Jan 1, Dec 25–26. 🎫 🎥 ♿
grounds only. **www**.cardiffcastle.com

Snowdonia ⓬

Gwynedd. 🚆 Betws-y-Coed.
ℹ The Royal Oak Stables, Betws-y-Coed (01690-710 426).

The scenery of Snowdonia National Park ranges from rugged mountain country to moors and beaches. The area is well known as a destination for hikers, and villages such as **Betws-y-Coed** and **Llanberis** are busy hill-walking centers.
    The main focus of this vast area is **Snowdon**, which at 1,085 m (3,560 ft) is the highest peak in Wales. Hikers wishing to explore Snowdonia's peaks should be wary of sudden weather changes. In summer, less intrepid visitors can take the Snowdon Mountain Railway from Llanberis to Snowdon's summit.

Snowdonia, famous for dangerous peaks and popular with climbers

Caernarfon ⓭

Gwynedd. 🏠 10,000. 🚌 ℹ Castle St (01286-672 232). 🛍 Sat.

One of the most famous castles in Wales looms over this busy town, created after Edward I's defeat of the last native Welsh prince, Llywelyn ap Gruffydd, in 1283. The town walls merge with modern streets that spread beyond the medieval center and open into a market square.
    Caernarfon Castle was built as a seat of government for North Wales. It contains several interesting displays, including the **Royal Welsh Fusiliers Museum** and an exhibition tracing the history of the Princes of Wales.
    On the hill above the town are the ruins of **Segontium**, a Roman fort built around AD 78.

⚓ **Caernarfon Castle**
Y Maes. **Tel** 01286-677 617.
◯ daily. ● Jan 1, Dec 24–26. 🎫 🎥

Caernarfon Castle, one of the forbidding fortresses built by Edward I

Street-by-Street: Bath ❾

Bath owes its magnificent Georgian townscape to the bubbling pool of water at the heart of the Roman baths. The Romans transformed Bath into England's first spa resort and it regained fame as a spa town in the 18th century. At this time the two brilliant John Woods (Elder and Younger) designed the city's fine Palladian-style buildings. Today, the traffic-free heart of this lively town is full of street musicians, museums, and enticing shops.

The Circus
This is a daring departure from the typical Georgian square, by John Wood the Elder (1705–54).

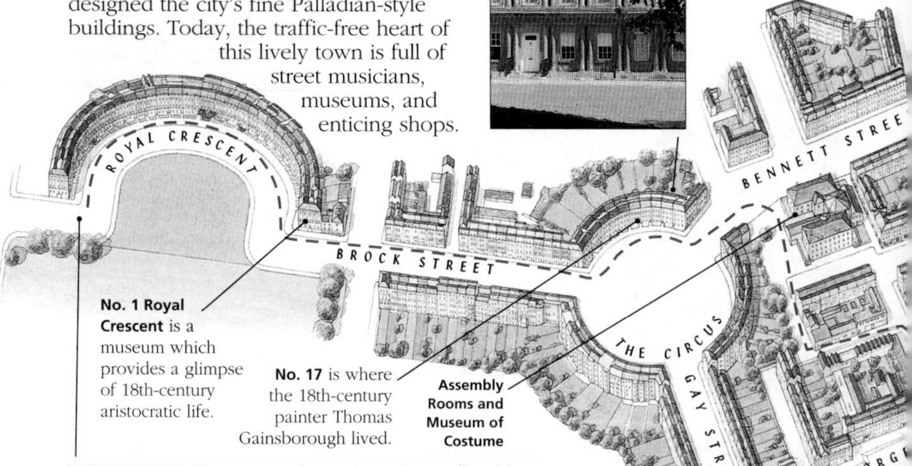

ROYAL CRESCENT

BROCK STREET

BENNETT STREET

THE CIRCUS

GAY STREET

GEORGE

No. 1 Royal Crescent is a museum which provides a glimpse of 18th-century aristocratic life.

No. 17 is where the 18th-century painter Thomas Gainsborough lived.

Assembly Rooms and Museum of Costume

★ Royal Crescent
Hailed as the most majestic street in Britain, this graceful arc of 30 houses (1767–74) is the masterpiece of John Wood the Younger. West of Royal Crescent, Royal Victoria Park (1830) is the city's largest open space.

QUEEN SQUARE

BARTON STREET

BEAUFORT SQ

Jane Austen (1775–1817), the writer, stayed at No. 13 Queen Square on one of many visits to Bath in her youth.

Milsom Street and New Bond Street contain some of Bath's most elegant shops.

Theatre Royal (1805)

KEY

- – – – Suggested route

| 0 meters | 100 |
| 0 yards | 100 |

THE KING'S SPRING

STAR SIGHTS

★ Royal Crescent

★ Roman Baths

★ Bath Abbey

Pump Rooms
These tearooms once formed the social hub of the 18th-century spa community. They contain this decorative drinking fountain.

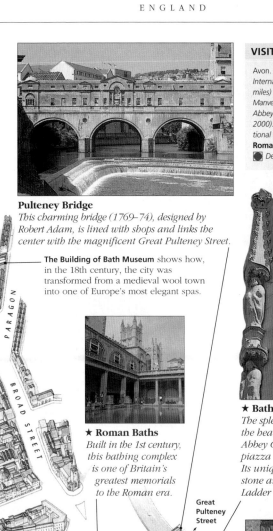

Pulteney Bridge
This charming bridge (1769–74), designed by Robert Adam, is lined with shops and links the center with the magnificent Great Pulteney Street.

The Building of Bath Museum shows how, in the 18th century, the city was transformed from a medieval wool town into one of Europe's most elegant spas.

★ Roman Baths
Built in the 1st century, this bathing complex is one of Britain's greatest memorials to the Roman era.

VISITORS' CHECKLIST

Avon. 🏘 85,000. ✈ Bristol International Airport, 32 km (20 miles) W. 🚉 Dorchester St. 🚌 Manvers St. ℹ Abbey Chambers, Abbey Church Yard (0906-711 2000). 🎪 daily. 🎵 International Music Festival (May–Jun). **Roman Baths Museum** 🕐 daily. 🔴 Dec 25–26. 📷 ♿ limited.

★ Bath Abbey
The splendid abbey stands at the heart of the old city in the Abbey Church Yard, a paved piazza enlivened by buskers. Its unique façade features stone angels climbing Jacob's Ladder to heaven.

Great Pulteney Street

Parade Gardens
Courting couples came to this pretty riverside park for secret liaisons in the 18th century.

Sally Lunn's House (1482) is one of Bath's oldest houses.

Train station

The massive dining hall at Christ Church College, Oxford University

Oxford ⑭

Oxfordshire. 🏛 *134,000.* 🚇 🚌
ℹ *15–16 Broad St (01865-726 871).*
📅 *Wed, Thu.* 🎪 *St. Giles Fair (Sep).*

Oxford has long been a strategic point on the western routes into London – its name describes its position as a convenient spot for crossing the river (a ford for oxen).

English students expelled from Paris founded the university in 1167. The development of England's first university created the spectacular skyline of tall towers and "dreaming spires."

Many of the 36 colleges that make up **Oxford University** were founded between the 13th and 16th centuries and cluster around the city center. The colleges were designed along the lines of monastic buildings but were surrounded by gardens.

Christ Church, the largest of the Oxford colleges, dates from 1525 when Cardinal Wolsey founded it as an ecclesiastical college. It has produced 16 British prime ministers in the last 200 years. Other colleges worth visiting are **All Souls**, **Magdalen**, **Merton**, **Lincoln**, and **Corpus Christi**.

The university's library, the **Bodleian**, was founded in 1320. One of its most famous rooms is the Divinity School (1488), which has a beautiful Gothic vaulted ceiling. The Baroque rotunda named the **Radcliffe Camera** (1748) is a reading room.

Oxford is more than just a university town and there is a wealth of interesting sights aside from the colleges.

One of the best British museums outside London, the **Ashmolean Museum** was opened in 1683. Its exceptional art collection includes works by Bellini, Raphael, Turner, Rembrandt, Michelangelo, Picasso, and a large group of Pre-Raphaelites. There are also fine Greek and Roman

Radcliffe Camera, Bodleian Library, Oxford

carvings, a collection of stringed musical instruments, and the Alfred Jewel, a gold enameled ring that is more than 1,000 years old.

Carfax Tower is all that remains of the 14th-century Church of St. Martin, demolished in 1896. Watch the clock strike the quarter hours, and climb to the top for a panoramic view of the city.

The **Martyrs' Memorial** commemorates the three Protestants burned at the stake on Broad Street – Bishops Latimer and Ridley in 1555, and Archbishop Cranmer in 1556 – during the reign of Catholic Queen Mary.

St. Mary the Virgin Church is the official church of the university, and is said to be the most visited parish church in England.

Two of Oxford's most interesting museums adjoin each other. The **University Museum of Natural History** contains relics of dinosaurs as well as a stuffed dodo. The **Pitt Rivers Museum** has one of the world's most extensive ethnographic collections – masks and tribal totems from Africa and the Far East – and archaeological displays.

Completed in 1669, the **Sheldonian Theatre** was the first building designed by Christopher Wren and was built as a place to hold university degree ceremonies. The ceiling depicts the triumph of religion, art, and science over envy, hatred, and malice.

🏛 **Ashmolean Museum**
Beaumont St. **Tel** *01865-278 000.*
🕐 *Tue–Sat, Sun pm & public hols.*
⬤ *Jan 1, Good Fri, Dec 25–28.*
📷 *Sat.* ♿

🏛 **University Museum and Pitt Rivers Museum**
Parks Rd. **Tel** *01865-272 950 /270 927*
🕐 *University: daily; Pitt Rivers: pm daily.* ⬤ *Easter, Dec 24–26.*
♿ *limited*

Blenheim Palace ⑮

See pp74–5.

The Great Quadrangle of All Souls College, Oxford University

Stratford-upon-Avon ⑯

Warwickshire. 🚶 22,000. 🚉 🚌 ℹ️ Bridge Foot (0870-160 7930). 🔄 Fri. 🎭 Shakespeare's Birthday (late Apr).

Situated on the west bank of the River Avon, Stratford-upon-Avon attracts hordes of tourists eager to see buildings connected with William Shakespeare, born here in 1564. The town is also the provincial home of the Royal Shakespeare Company, whose performances are staged at the **Royal Shakespeare Theatre**.

The High Street turns into Chapel Street, the site of **New Place**. Shakespeare died here in 1616, and it is now a herb garden. The playwright is buried at **Holy Trinity Church**. Bought for the nation in 1847, **Shakespeare's Birthplace** was restored to Elizabethan style. A new attraction, "Shakespearience", provides an entertaining view of the life of the Bard.

Shakespeare monument at Holy Trinity Church, Stratford

Another Stratford native, John Harvard, emigrated to America and in 1638 left his estate to a new college, later renamed Harvard University. **Harvard House** displays family mementos.

No tour of Stratford would be complete without a visit to **Anne Hathaway's Cottage**. Before her marriage to Shakespeare Anne lived here, 1 mile (1.5 km) from the town. Despite fire damage, the cottage is still impressive, with some original 16th-century furniture.

Cambridge ⑰

Cambridgeshire. 🚶 120,000. 🚉 🚌 ℹ️ Wheeler St (0871-226 8006). 🔄 daily. 🎭 Folk Festival (July).

Cambridge has been an important town since Roman times, being located at the first navigable point on the River Cam. When, in 1209, a group of religious scholars broke away from Oxford University after academic and religious disputes, they came here. Student life dominates the city, but it is also a thriving market center serving a rich agricultural region.

Cambridge University has 31 colleges, the oldest being **Peterhouse** (1284) and the newest **Robinson** (1979). Many of the older colleges have peaceful gardens backing onto the River Cam, which are known as "Backs." An enjoyable way to view these is to rent a punt (a long narrow boat propelled by using a pole) from one of the boatyards along the river – with a "chauffeur" if required. The layout of the older colleges, as at Oxford, derives from their early connections with religious institutions, although few escaped heavy-handed alterations in the Victorian era.

Henry VI founded **King's College** in 1441. Work on the chapel – one of the most important examples of late medieval English architecture – began five years later, and took 90 years to complete. Henry himself decided that the building should dominate the city and gave specific instructions about its dimensions. He also stipulated that a choir of six lay clerks and 16 boy choristers – educated at the College school – should sing daily at services.

The awe-inspiring choir of King's College Chapel, Cambridge

This still happens in term time but today the choir also gives concerts all over the world.

St. John's College, whose alumni include the Romantic poet William Wordsworth, spans the Cam and boasts one of the town's most beautiful bridges. Known as the Bridge of Sighs, it was named after its Venetian counterpart.

One of Britain's oldest public museums, the **Fitzwilliam Museum** has works of exceptional quality and rarity, especially antiquities, ceramics, paintings, and manuscripts. These include paintings by Titian and the 17th-century Dutch masters, an impressive collection of works by the French Impressionists, and most of the important British artists of the past 300 years.

🏛 **Fitzwilliam Museum**
Trumpington St. **Tel** 01223-332 900. 🕐 Tue–Sun & public hols. Jan 1, Good Fri, Dec 24–27, 31. 💷 donation. ♿ limited

Bridge of Sighs, St. John's College, Cambridge University

Blenheim Palace ⑮

After John Churchill, the 1st Duke of Marlborough, defeated the French at the Battle of Blenheim in 1704, Queen Anne gave him the manor of Woodstock and had this palatial house built for him in gratitude. Designed by Nicholas Hawksmoor and Sir John Vanbrugh, it is one of the country's most outstanding examples of English Baroque. The magnificent palace grounds, at the center of which is a huge lake, owe their present appearance to the great 18th-century landscape designer, Lancelot (Capability) Brown. Blenheim Palace was the birthplace, in 1874, of the wartime British prime minister, Winston Churchill. Today the palace is the home of the 11th Duke of Marlborough, John George.

★ Long Library
This 55-m (183-ft) long room was designed by Vanbrugh as a picture gallery. The stucco work on the ceiling is by Isaac Mansfield (1725).

The Grand Bridge was built in 1708. It has a 31-m (101-ft) main span and contains rooms within its structure.

The Chapel holds a marble monument to the 1st Duke of Marlborough, sculpted in 1733.

★ Water Terrace Gardens
These splendid gardens were laid out in the 1920s by French architect Achille Duchêne in 17th-century style, with detailed patterned beds and fountains.

STAR SIGHTS

- ★ Long Library
- ★ Saloon
- ★ Water Terrace Gardens

Great Hall
The hall's magnificent ceiling, painted by Sir James Thornhill in 1716, shows Marlborough presenting his plan for the Battle of Blenheim to Britannia.

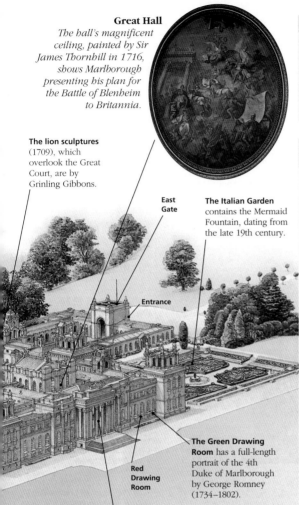

The lion sculptures (1709), which overlook the Great Court, are by Grinling Gibbons.

East Gate

The Italian Garden contains the Mermaid Fountain, dating from the late 19th century.

Entrance

The Green Drawing Room has a full-length portrait of the 4th Duke of Marlborough by George Romney (1734–1802).

Red Drawing Room

VISITORS' CHECKLIST

Woodstock, Oxfordshire. **Tel** 0870-602 080. 🚉 Oxford, then bus. **Palace & Gardens** ◯ mid-Feb–mid-Dec: 10:30am–5:30pm daily. ● Nov & Dec: Mon & Tue. 🦽 📷 **Park** ◯ 9am–5pm daily. www.blenheimpalace.com

OTHER NOTABLE STATELY HOMES

Burghley House
Lincolnshire. **Tel** 01780-752 451. 🚉 Stamford. ◯ Apr–Oct: daily. 🦽 📷 Built by Queen Elizabeth I's adviser, William Cecil, 1st Lord Burghley (1520–98).

Castle Howard
Yorkshire. **Tel** 01653-648 333. 🚉 York, then bus. ◯ Mar–Nov: daily. 🦽 📷 Baroque mansion (1699–1712) by John Vanbrugh and Nicholas Hawksmoor.

Chatsworth House
Derbyshire. **Tel** 01246-582 204. 🚉 Chesterfield. ◯ mid-Mar–Dec: daily. 🦽 limited. Splendid Baroque palace built in 1687–1707 by the 4th Earl of Devonshire.

Hardwick Hall
Derbyshire. **Tel** 01246-850 430. 🚉 Chesterfield. ◯ Apr–Oct: Wed, Thu, Sat, Sun. 🦽 limited. Fine Tudor mansion begun in 1591 by Bess of Hardwick, Countess of Shrewsbury.

★ Saloon
The murals and painted ceiling of the state dining room are by French artist Louis Laguerre (1663–1721). The room is used once a year on Christmas Day.

EIGHTEENTH-CENTURY GARDENS

Styles of gardening in Britain expanded alongside architecture and other fashions. The 18th century brought a taste for large-scale "natural" landscapes, characterized by woods, lakes, and a seeming lack of boundaries. The pioneer of this new style was the famous landscape designer Lancelot (Capability) Brown (1715–83). His nickname came from his habit of telling clients that their land had "great capabilities." In 1764 he re-landscaped the grounds of Blenheim Palace, creating the magnificent, huge lake. Today his reputation is controversial, because in creating his idyllic landscapes he swept away many of the beautiful formal gardens previously in vogue.

Capability Brown (1715–83)

Detail of a carving on the façade of Bishop Lloyd's House, Chester

Chester ⑱

Cheshire. 🏙 125,000. 🚃 🚌
ℹ️ Town Hall, Northgate St (01244-402 111). 🗓 Mon–Sat.

First settled by the Romans in AD 79, the main streets of Chester are now lined with timber buildings, many dating from the 13th and 14th centuries. These are the **Chester Rows**, which, with their two tiers of stores and continuous upper gallery, anticipate today's multistory shops by several centuries. Their oriel windows and decorative timber-work are mostly 19th century. The façade of the 16th-century **Bishop Lloyd's House** in Watergate Street is the most richly carved in Chester. The Rows are at their most attractive where Eastgate Street meets Bridge Street.

A town crier calls the hour and announces news from the Cross – a reconstruction of a 15th-century stone crucifix. South of here, the **Grosvenor Museum** explains Chester's history. To the north is the **cathedral**. The choir stalls have splendid misericords and delicate spirelets on the canopies. The cathedral is surrounded on two sides by high city walls, originally Roman but rebuilt at intervals. Also worth seeing is the **Roman amphitheater** just outside town, built in AD 100.

🏛 **Grosvenor Museum**
Grosvenor St. **Tel** 01244-402 008.
⬤ Mon–Sat, Sun pm. ⬤ Jan 1, Good Fri, Dec 24–26. ♿ limited.

Liverpool ⑲

Liverpool. 🏙 450,000. ✈ 11 km (7 miles) SE. 🚢 🚃 🚌 ℹ️ 08 Place (0151-233 2008). 🗓 Sun.

During the 17th and 18th centuries, Liverpool's westerly seaboard gave it a leading role in the Caribbean slave trade. After the city's first ocean steamer set sail from here in 1840, would-be emigrants to the New World poured into the city, including a large number of Irish refugees of the potato famine.

Liverpool's waterfront is overlooked by the well-known **Royal Liver Building**. The 19th-century warehouses around Albert Dock have been redeveloped as museums, galleries, restaurants, and shops. Among these, the **Maritime Museum** and the **Tate Liverpool**, which houses one of the best collections of contemporary art in England outside of London, are well worth visiting.

Liverpool is famous as the home town of the phenomenally successful Beatles. The **Beatles Story** is a walk-through exhibition which charts their meteoric rise to fame in the 1960s.

Clock tower of the Royal Liver Building, Liverpool

One of the most prestigious art galleries in the city is **The Walker**. Paintings range from early Italian and Flemish works to 20th-century art.

Liverpool's Gothic-style **Anglican Cathedral**, completed in 1978 by Sir Giles Gilbert Scott, is the world's largest. The Roman Catholic **Metropolitan Cathedral of Christ the King** (1962–7) is a striking circular building surmounted by a stylized crown of thorns 88 m (290 ft) high.

🏛 **Tate Liverpool**
Albert Dock. **Tel** 0151-702 7400.
⬤ Tue–Sun. ⬤ Dec 24–26, Jan 1, Good Friday. 📷 ♿

🏛 **The Walker**
William Brown St. **Tel** 0151-478 4199. ⬤ Mon–Sat, Sun pm. ⬤ Jan 1, Dec 25. 📷 by appt. ♿

Manchester ⑳

Manchester. 🏙 2.5 million. ✈ 18 km (11 miles) S. 🚃 🚌 ℹ️ Lloyd St (0871-222 8223). 🗓 daily.

Manchester is famous as a pioneer of the industrial age, with its cotton spinning machines and early railways.

Among the city's many fine 19th-century buildings are the Neo-Gothic **cathedral**, the **Royal Exchange**, now a theater and restaurant, and the **Free Trade Hall**, now the Radisson Edwardian Hotel, with only the original façade remaining. The **Manchester Ship Canal**, opened in 1894, is a magnificent engineering feat.

The **Museum of Science and Industry in Manchester** captures the city's spirit of industrial might with a display of working steam engines and

Modern city blocks on the banks of the Manchester Ship Canal

Lush, green fields below the Skiddaw fells in the Lake District

an exhibition on the Liverpool and Manchester Railway. Another museum of note is the **Whitworth Art Gallery**, with its splendid collection of contemporary art, textiles, and prints. The Turner watercolors are a highlight. Housed in a 19th-century porticoed building, the **City Art Galleries** contain an excellent selection of British art, as well as early Italian, Flemish, and French paintings.

The Lakeland poet William Wordsworth

🏛 **Whitworth Art Gallery**
University of Manchester, Oxford Rd. **Tel** 0161-275 7450. ⬜ Mon–Sat & Sun pm. ⬤ Dec 24–Jan 2, Good Fri. ♿

York ㉑

See pp78–9.

Lake District ㉒

Cumbria. 🚉 Kendal; Windermere. 🚌 Kendal; Keswick; Windermere. 🛈 Town Hall, Highgate, Kendal (01539-725 758); Moot Hall, Market Sq, Keswick (01768-772 645).

The Lake District boasts some of the country's most spectacular scenery, with high peaks, lonely fells, and beautiful lakes. The area constitutes Britain's largest national park and offers a range of outdoor activities, from hill walking to boating.

Kendal is the southern gateway to the Lake District. Of interest here is the Museum of Lakeland Life and Industry, housed in the stable block of

the 18th-century Abbot Hall. The nearest lake to Kendal is Windermere, over 16 km (10 miles) long. A year-round car ferry connects the lake's east and west shores, and summer steamers link the main towns on the north-south axis. Among these, one of the most popular is **Bowness**, where the Windermere Steamboat Museum has a collection of superbly restored watercraft.

Ambleside, another attractive lakeside town, is a good base for walkers and climbers. Nearby is Hill Top, the 17th-century farmhouse where the author Beatrix Potter wrote many of her famous children's stories.

The Lake District's most famous son, the Romantic poet William Wordsworth (1770–1850), lived for a while at **Grasmere**, on the shores of the lake of the same name, north of Ambleside. His home, Dove Cottage, contains a museum dedicated to his life.

To the west of Windermere lie Coniston Water and picturesque **Duddon Valley**, popular walking country.

In the northern part of the Lake District **Keswick**, with its lake, Derwent Water, has been a busy vacation destination since Victorian days. The Keswick Museum and Art Gallery holds original manuscripts of

Lakeland writers such as Robert Southey (1774–1843) and Wordsworth. To the east of the town lies the ancient stone circle of Castlerigg. North of Keswick is Skiddaw, England's fourth highest peak and a straightforward climb for anyone reasonably fit.

Durham ㉓

County Durham. 🚉 🚌 🛈 Millenium Place (0191-384 3720). 🛍 Sat.

Durham was built on a rocky peninsula in 995. The site was chosen as the last resting place for the remains of St. Cuthbert. The relics of the Venerable Bede were brought here 27 years later, adding to the town's attraction to pilgrims.

Durham's **cathedral**, built between 1093 and 1274, is a striking Norman structure. The vast dimensions of the 900-year-old columns, piers, and vaults, and the lozenge, chevron, and dogtooth patterns carved into them, are its main innovative features. The exotic Galilee Chapel, begun in 1170, was inspired by the mosque at Córdoba, Spain (see pp326–7).

The Norman **castle**, begun in 1072, served as an Episcopal Palace until 1832, when Bishop William van Mildert gave it away to found Britain's third university here. In the castle grounds, Tunstal's Chapel was built around 1542 and has some particularly fine woodwork, including a unicorn misericord. The castle keep, sited on a mound, is now part of the university.

⛪ **Durham Castle**
Tel 0191-334 3800. ⬜ univ hols: daily; term: Mon, Wed, Sat (pm), Sun. 📷

Moorish-style arches in the 12th-century Galilee Chapel, Durham Cathedral

Street-by-Street: York ㉑

The city of York has retained so much of its medieval structure that walking into its center is like
entering a living museum. Many of the ancient timbered houses, which overhang narrow, winding
streets such as the Shambles, are protected by a
conservation order. Cars are banned from the
center, so there are always student bikes
bouncing over cobbled streets. The chief glory
of York is its cathedral, the Minster. The city
also has 18 medieval churches, 5 km
(3 miles) of medieval city walls, and many
elegant Jacobean and Georgian buildings.

York's medieval city walls
still encircle the old city. It is
possible to walk round them,
although there are large gaps.
The gates are known as "bars."

At Monk Bar the
gatehouse retains
a working portcullis.

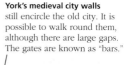

★ **York Minster**
*The 15th-century choir
screen is lined with
statues of the kings
of England from
William I to Henry VI.*

Thirsk

HIGH PETERGATE

LOW PETERGATE

MINSTER YARD

GOODRAMGATE

DEANGATE

ST LEONARDS PLACE

DUNCOMBE PLACE

BLAKE STREET

STONEGATE

DAVYGATE

PARL

St. Mary's Abbey

**The Yorkshire
Museum** contains a
fine collection of
fossils, discovered
at Whitby in the
19th century.

MUSEUM STREET

LENDAL STREET

CONEY STREET

OUSE

OUSE B

SPURRIERG

Lendal Bridge

**Train station,
bus station,
National Rail-
way Museum,
and Leeds**

**Ye Old Starre
Inne** is one of
the oldest
pubs in York.

In Coffee Yard,
look out for the
carved figure of
a red devil, relic
of a medieval
print shop.

St. Olave's Church
*The 11th-century church, next to the gate-
house of St. Mary's Abbey, was founded by
the Earl of Northumbria in memory of
St. Olaf, King of Norway. To the left is the
Chapel of St. Mary on the Walls.*

Guildhall
*This two-headed
medieval roof boss
is on the 15th-
century Guildhall,
situated beside the
River Ouse and
restored after bomb
damage during
World War II.*

For hotels and restaurants in this region see pp96–101 and pp102–7

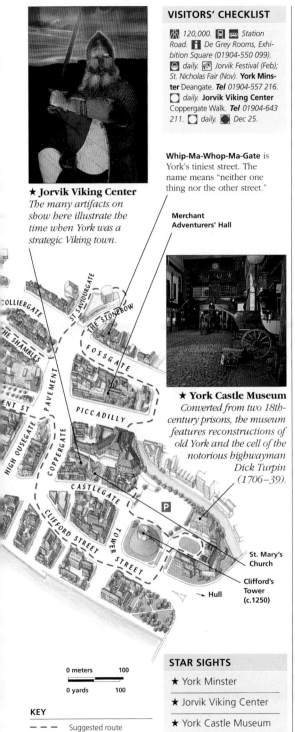

★ Jorvik Viking Center
The many artifacts on show here illustrate the time when York was a strategic Viking town.

Whip-Ma-Whop-Ma-Gate is York's tiniest street. The name means "neither one thing nor the other street."

Merchant Adventurers' Hall

★ York Castle Museum
Converted from two 18th-century prisons, the museum features reconstructions of old York and the cell of the notorious highwayman Dick Turpin (1706–39).

St. Mary's Church

Clifford's Tower (c.1250)

Hull

0 meters 100
0 yards 100

KEY

– – – Suggested route

STAR SIGHTS

★ York Minster

★ Jorvik Viking Center

★ York Castle Museum

Exploring York

To the Romans the city of York was Eboracum, to the Saxons it was Eoforwic, and to the Vikings Jorvik. Danish street names are a reminder that from 867 York was a major Viking settlement. **Jorvik Viking Center**, the Viking museum, is built underground on an archaeological site excavated at Coppergate. The latest technology brings the sights and smells of 10th-century York dramatically to life.

Between 1100 and 1500 York was England's second city. **York Minster**, the largest Gothic church in northern Europe, was begun in 1220. It has a remarkable collection of medieval stained glass. The vast Great East Window (1405–8) depicts the Creation. In 1984 a disastrous fire in the south transept destroyed the roof and shattered its magnificent rose window. This has since been restored.

Much of York's wealth in the late Middle Ages came from the cloth trade. The **Merchant Adventurers' Hall**, the headquarters of a powerful guild of traders, is a beautifully preserved timber-framed building that dates from the mid-14th century.

In the 19th century York's position on the route to Scotland made it a major rail center. Train enthusiasts should head for the **National Railway Museum**, the largest of its kind in the world, where the rolling stock on show includes Queen Victoria's royal carriage.

National Railway Museum
Leeman Rd. **Tel** 01904-621261. daily. Dec 24–26.

The square central tower of York Minster rising above the city

Scotland

Scotland's landscape is breathtaking, with sparkling lochs, awesome mountains, and windswept isles. The ruggedness of its climate and natural environment has helped to forge a tough, self-reliant nation, whose history has been characterized by resistance to English domination. Castles, many in ruins, are found all over the country – a legacy of its turbulent past. Culturally, Edinburgh has always been the country's chief attraction, but the rival city of Glasgow, despite the collapse of its traditional heavy industries, has much to offer too.

The imposing City Chambers in George Square, Glasgow

Edinburgh ㉔

See pp82–6.

Glasgow ㉕

🏛 *735,000.* ✈ 🚉 🚌 ℹ *11 George Square (0141-204 4400).* 🛍 *Sat, Sun.* 🎭 *Jazz Festival (Jul).* **www**.seeglasgow.com

Glasgow's era of great prosperity was the industrial 19th century. Coal seams in Lanarkshire fueled the city's cotton mills and ironworks, belying its Celtic name, *Glas cu*, meaning "dear green place." Relics of this manufacturing past contrast starkly with the glossy image of modern Glasgow, renowned for its galleries and museums. The deprived East End stands side by side with the restored 18th-century Merchant City and Victorian George Square.

Glasgow's **cathedral** was one of the few to escape destruction during the Scottish Reformation and is a rare example of an almost complete 13th-century church. The crypt holds the tomb of St. Mungo. In the cathedral precinct, the **St. Mungo Museum of Religious Life and Art** is the first of its kind in the world, illustrating religious themes with a superb range of artifacts.

It is in the more affluent West End, to where merchants retreated from industrial Clydeside, that Glasgow's most important galleries and museums can be found. The **Kelvingrove Art Gallery and Museum**, housed in a striking red sandstone building dating to 1901, is home to a splendid collection of art, with works by Botticelli, Giorgione, Rembrandt, Degas, Millet, and Monet, while the Scottish Gallery contains the famous *Massacre of Glencoe* by James Hamilton (1853–94). Other highlights include dinosaur skeletons, Egyptian artifacts and a real spitfire suspended in the main hall.

The **Hunterian Art Gallery** houses Scotland's largest print collection and paintings by major European artists from the 16th century to the present. A display of works by Glasgow's most celebrated designer, Charles Rennie Mackintosh (1868–1928), is supplemented by a reconstruction of No. 6 Florentine Terrace, where he lived from 1906 to 1914.

South of the river, the Pollok Country Park is the site of the **Burrell Collection**, star of Glasgow's renaissance. Highlights include examples of 15th-century stained glass and tapestries, a bronze bull's head (7th century BC) from Turkey, Matthijs Maris' *The Sisters* (1875), and a self-portrait by Rembrandt (1632). On the same site, Pollok House is an attractive Georgian building. It holds one of Britain's best collections of 16th- to 19th-century Spanish paintings.

Stained glass by Charles Rennie Mackintosh

Other sights worth visiting are the **Tenement House**, a modest apartment in a tenement block preserved from Edwardian times, and **Provand's Lordship** (1471), the city's oldest surviving house. The **House for an Art Lover** is a showcase for the work of Charles Rennie Mackintosh. For a social history of the city from the 12th to the 20th century, visit the **People's Palace**, a cultural museum located in the city's East End.

🏛 **Kelvingrove Art Gallery and Museum**
Argyle St, Kelvingrove. *Tel 0141-276 9599.* ◯ *daily.* 🎫 ♿

🏛 **Hunterian Art Gallery**
82 Hillhead St. *Tel 0141-330 5431.* ◯ *Mon–Sat.* ● *Dec 24–Jan 5 & public hols.* ♿ *restricted.*

🏛 **Burrell Collection**
Pollok Country Park. *Tel 0141-287 2550.* ◯ *daily.* ● *Jan 1–2, Dec 25–26.* 🎫 ♿

The Burrell Collection in Pollok Country Park on Glasgow's outskirts

The 15th-century Stirling Castle, atop its rocky crag

Stirling 🖲

🏠 28,000. 🚊 🚌 ℹ 41 Dunbarton Rd (0870-720 0620). www.visitscottishheartlands.org

Located between the Ochil Hills and the Campsie Fells, Stirling grew up around its castle, historically one of Scotland's most important fortresses. **Stirling Castle** is one of the finest examples of Renaissance architecture in the country. Dating from the 15th century, it was last defended, against the Jacobites, in 1746, and stands within sight of no fewer than seven battlefields. One of these – Bannockburn – was where Robert the Bruce defeated the English in 1314.

Stirling's Old Town is still protected by the original 16th-century walls, built to keep out Henry VIII. Two buildings stand out among a number of historic monuments in the town: the medieval **Church of the Holy Rude** and **Mar's Wark**, with its ornate façade.

🔱 **Stirling Castle**
Castle Wynd. **Tel** 01786-450 000. ⬤ daily. ⬤ Dec 25–26. 🏛 📷 ⬤ limited.

St. Andrews 🖲

Fife. 🏠 14,000. 🚊 Leuchars. 🚌 ℹ 70 Market St (01334-472 021). www.standrews.co.uk

Scotland's oldest university town and one-time ecclesias-tical capital, St. Andrews is now a shrine for golfers from all over the world. Its main streets and cobbled alleys, lined with university buildings and medieval churches, converge on the ruined 12th-

century **cathedral**. Once the largest in Scotland, it was later pillaged for stones to build the town. **St. Andrew's Castle** was built for the bishops of the town in 1200.

The Royal and Ancient Golf Club, founded in 1754, has a magnificent links course and is the ruling arbiter of the game. The city has other golf courses, open to the public for a modest fee, and is home to the **British Golf Museum**.

🏛 **British Golf Museum**
Bruce Embankment. **Tel** 01334-460 046. ⬤ 9:30am–5:30pm daily (Nov–Mar: 10am–4pm daily). 📷 ♿

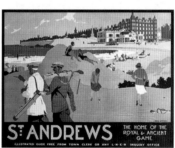
An old railway poster illustrating the lure of St. Andrews for golfing enthusiasts

Aberdeen 🖲

🏠 220,000. ✈ 13 km (8 miles) NW. 🚊 🚌 ℹ 23 Union St (01224-288 828). 🛒 Thu, Fri, Sat.

Europe's offshore oil capital, Aberdeen is also one of Britain's most important fishing ports, and hosts Scotland's largest fish market.

Among its fine buildings is the 16th-century home of a former provost (mayor) of the city. Period rooms inside **Provost Skene's House** span 200 years of design and include the 17th-century Great Hall, a Regency Room, and a Georgian Dining Room. The Painted Gallery holds one of Scotland's most important cycles of religious art, dating from the 17th century.

Founded in 1495, **King's College** was the city's first university. The chapel has stained-glass windows by Douglas Strachan.

St. Andrew's Cathedral is the Mother Church of the Episcopal Communion in the United States. Coats of arms on the ceiling depict the American states.

Housed in a historic building overlooking the harbor, **Aberdeen Maritime Museum** traces the city's long seafaring tradition.

🏠 **Provost Skene's House**
Guestrow. **Tel** 01224-641 086. ⬤ daily. ⬤ Jan 1–2, Dec 25–31. www.aagm.co.uk

GOLF

Scotland's national game was pioneered on the sandy links around St. Andrews. The earliest record dates from 1457, when golf was banned by James II on the grounds that it was interfering with his subjects' archery practice. Mary, Queen of Scots enjoyed the game and was berated in 1568 for playing straight after the murder of her husband Darnley. Scotland has several other world-class golf courses, including Royal Troon, Gleneagles, and Carnoustie.

Victorian engraving of Mary, Queen of Scots at St. Andrews

Edinburgh 24

It was not until the reign of James IV (1488–1513) that Edinburgh gained the status of Scotland's capital. Overcrowding made the Old Town a difficult place to live, and led to the construction of a Georgian New Town in the late 1700s. Today, Edinburgh is second only to London as a financial center in the British Isles, and houses the new Scottish parliament building, situated next to the old Palace of Holyroodhouse. Edinburgh hosts a celebrated annual International Festival every August. One of the world's premier arts jamborees, it features drama, dance, opera, music, and ballet. The more eclectic "Fringe" developed in parallel with the official event, but has now exceeded it in terms of size. It is estimated that the population of the city doubles from 400,000 to 800,000 every August.

View of Princes Street from the top of Calton Hill

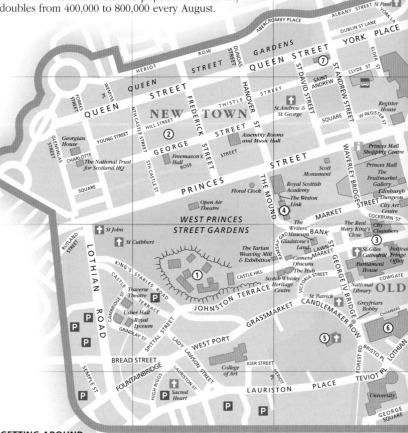

GETTING AROUND

Central Edinburgh is compact, so walking or cycling is an excellent way to explore the city. Other options include a comprehensive bus service and a multitude of black taxis. Avoid exploring the center by car, because the streets tend to be congested with traffic, and parking may be difficult. Car use has been actively discouraged in recent years.

SEE ALSO

- *Where to Stay* p101
- *Where to Eat* p107

SIGHTS AT A GLANCE

Calton Hill ⑧
Edinburgh Castle ①
Greyfriars Kirk ⑤
Palace of Holyroodhouse ⑨
National Gallery of Scotland ④
New Town ②
Royal Mile ③
Royal Museum and
    Museum of Scotland ⑥
Scottish National Portrait
    Gallery ⑦

An audience of thousands at the Military Tattoo in Edinburgh
Castle, held during August each year

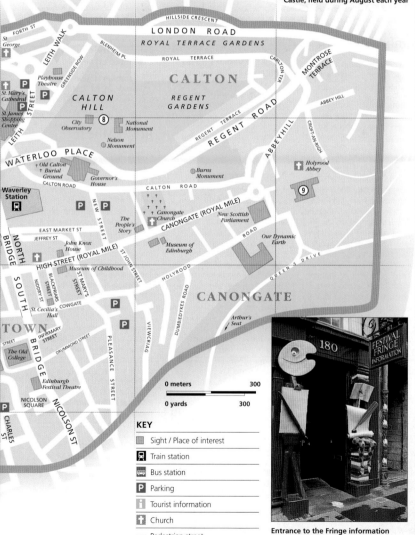

KEY

▢	Sight / Place of interest
🚊	Train station
🚌	Bus station
P	Parking
i	Tourist information
✝	Church
▬	Pedestrian street

0 meters   300
0 yards   300

Entrance to the Fringe information
office, located on the Royal Mile

The battlements of Edinburgh Castle rising above Princes Street Gardens

Edinburgh Castle ①

Castle Hill. **Tel** *0131-225 9846.* ⭘ *daily.* 🌑 *Dec 25–26.* 🈳 ☑ 🚾 **www**.historic-scotland.gov.uk

Standing on the basalt core of an extinct volcano, the castle is an assemblage of buildings dating from the 12th to the 20th centuries, reflecting its changing role as fortress, palace, military garrison, and state prison. The castle was a favorite royal residence until the Union of 1603, after which monarchs resided in England.

The Scottish regalia are displayed in the 15th-century **palace** where Mary, Queen of Scots gave birth to James VI. The castle also holds the Stone of Destiny, a relic of ancient Scottish kings seized by the English, and returned in 1996. The castle's oldest existing building is the 12th-century **St. Margaret's Chapel.** A stained-glass window depicts the queen of Malcolm III, after whom it is named.

Other important buildings include the 15th-century **Great**

Hall, meeting place of the Scottish parliament until 1639, and the **Governor's House** (1742), which has Flemish-style crow-stepped gables. A 15th-century Burgundian siege gun, known as Mons Meg, is kept in the castle vaults, where French graffiti recall the prisoners held here during the 18th- and 19th-century wars.

New Town ②

The first phase of the "New Town," to the north of Princes Street, was built in the 18th century to relieve the congested and unsanitary conditions of the old town. **Charlotte Square,** with its lavish town houses, was the climax of this phase. On the north side, the **Georgian House,** owned by the National Trust of Scotland, has been furnished to show the lifestyle of its 18th-century residents.

The most magnificent of the later developments is the **Moray Estate,** by James Gillespie Graham, where a

linked series of large houses forms a crescent, an oval, and a twelve-sided circus.

🏛 **Georgian House**
7 Charlotte Sq. **Tel** *0131-226 3318.* ⭘ *Mar–Dec: daily.* 🈳 🚾 *limited.*

Royal Mile ③

Composed of four ancient streets which formed the main thoroughfare of medieval Edinburgh, the Royal Mile linked the castle to Holyrood Palace. A walk starting from the castle takes you past many of the city's oldest buildings and a number of interesting museums.

The lower floors of the **Tartan Weaving Mill & Exhibition** date from the early 17th century and were once the home of the Laird of Cockpen. Its 19th-century **Camera Obscura** remains a popular attraction. A little further on, **Gladstone's Land** is a carefully restored 17th-century merchant's house. Another fine mansion, built in 1622, has been converted into a **Writers' Museum,** housing memorabilia of Robert Burns, Sir Walter Scott, and Robert Louis Stevenson.

St. Giles Cathedral, properly known as the High Kirk of Edinburgh, was the base from which Protestant minister John Knox led the Scottish Reformation. His house, also on the Royal Mile, is open to the public. The cathedral's Thistle Chapel has impressive rib-vaulting and carved heraldic canopies. It honors the knights of the Most Ancient and Most

Charlotte Square in the New Town

For hotels and restaurants in this region see pp96–101 and pp102–7

Noble Order of the Thistle. Just past St. Giles, the Italianate **Parliament House**, built in the 1630s, has housed the Scottish Courts since the 1707 Act of Union with England and Wales.

Farther east, opposite **John Knox's House** (1450), there is a good **Museum of Childhood**, while **The People's Story** (1591) tells the social history of Edinburgh – from plagues to punk rock.

Thistle Chapel, St. Giles Cathedral, Royal Mile

🏠 **Gladstone's Land**
477B Lawnmarket. *Tel 0131-226 5856.* ◯ *Apr–Oct: Mon–Sat, Sun pm.* 📷

National Gallery of Scotland ④

The Mound. *Tel 0131-624 6200.* ◯ *daily.* 📷 *by appt.* ♿ www.nationalgalleries.org

One of Scotland's finest art galleries, the National Gallery of Scotland has an impressive collection of British and European paintings. Designed by William Henry Playfair, it was opened in 1859. Many of the works of art are still exhibited as they were in the 19th century. Serried ranks of paintings hang on deep red walls behind a profusion of statues and period furniture.

Some of the highlights among the Scottish works are the society portraits by Allan Ramsay and Henry Raeburn, including the latter's *Reverend Robert Walker Skating on Duddingston Loch* (c.1800), an image reproduced annually on thousands of Christmas cards.

German works include Gerard David's almost comic-strip treatment of the *Three Legends of St. Nicholas*, dating from the early 16th century. Italian paintings include a fine *Madonna* by Raphael, as well as works by Titian and Tintoretto. From Spain there is a delightful genre painting of *An Old Woman Cooking Eggs* by Velázquez (c.1620).

An entire room is devoted to *The Seven Sacraments* by Nicholas Poussin, dating from around 1640. Dutch and Flemish painters represented include Rembrandt, Van Dyck, and Rubens, while among the British offerings are important works by Reynolds and Gainsborough.

An Old Woman Cooking Eggs by Velázquez, National Gallery of Scotland

Greyfriars Kirk ⑤

Greyfriars Place. *Tel 0131-226 5429.* ◯ *Apr–Oct: Mon–Sat; Nov–Mar: Thu pm.* 📷 ♿

Greyfriars Kirk played a key role in Scotland's history. In 1638 the National Covenant was signed here, marking the Protestant stand against Charles I's imposition of an episcopal church. Throughout the wars of the 17th century, the kirkyard was used as a mass grave for executed Covenanters. The Martyrs' Monument is a sobering reminder of the many Scots who lost their lives. Greyfriars is also known for its association with a faithful dog, Bobby, who lived beside his master's grave from 1858 to 1872. Greyfriars Bobby's statue stands outside Greyfriars Kirk.

Greyfriars Bobby

Royal Museum and Museum of Scotland ⑥

Chambers St. *Tel 0131-247 4422.* ◯ *Mon–Sat, Sun pm.* 📷 ♿ www.nms.ac.uk

A great Victorian glass palace, completed in 1888, houses the **Royal Museum of Scotland**. It started life as an industrial museum, but over time acquired an eclectic array of exhibits, ranging from stuffed animals to ethnographic artifacts.

In 1993 work began on a site next door, to display Scotland's impressive array of antiquities. The resulting **Museum of Scotland**, opened in 1998, tells the story of the country, starting with its geology and natural history, through to later industrial developments. Among its many stunning exhibits is St. Fillan's Crozier, said to have been carried at the head of the Scottish army at Bannockburn in 1314.

The view from Duncan's Monument at the top of Calton Hill, Edinburgh

Scottish National Portrait Gallery ⑦

1 Queen St. **Tel** 0131-624 6200. ⬜ daily. 📷 by appt. ♿
www.nationalgalleries.org

An informative exhibition on the royal house of Stuart is just one of the attractions at the Scottish National Portrait Gallery. The displays detail the history of 12 generations of Stuarts, from the time of Robert the Bruce to Queen Anne. Memorabilia include Mary, Queen of Scots' jewelry and a silver traveling canteen left by Bonnie Prince Charlie at the Battle of Culloden. The upper gallery has portraits of famous Scots, including one of the country's best-loved poet Robert Burns (1759–96) by Alexander Nasmyth. Others portrayed include Flora MacDonald, who helped Bonnie Prince Charlie escape after his defeat by the English in 1745, philosopher David Hume (1711–76), novelist Sir Walter Scott (1771–1832), and Ramsay MacDonald, who became Britain's first Labour prime minister in 1924.

Calton Hill ⑧

City center east, via Waterloo Pl.

Calton Hill, at the east end of Princes Street, is a large open space dotted with Neo-classical monuments. It has one of Edinburgh's more memorable landmarks – a half-finished "Parthenon".

Conceived as the National Monument to the dead of the Napoleonic Wars, building began in 1822 but funds ran out and it was never finished. Nearby, the **Nelson Monument** commemorates the British victory at Trafalgar, providing a fine vantage point over the city. The Classical theme continues with Duncan's Monument and the old **City Observatory**, designed by William Playfair in 1818 and based on Athens' Tower of the Winds. Tours and free lectures are arranged here by the Astronomical Society of Edinburgh.

Palace of Holyroodhouse ⑨

East end of the Royal Mile. **Tel** 0131-556 1096. ⬜ daily. ● check for seasonal closures. 📷 ♿ limited.
www.royal.gov.uk

Queen Elizabeth II's official Scottish residence, the palace was built by James IV in the grounds of an abbey in 1498. It was later the home of James V and his wife, Mary of Guise, and was remodeled in the 1670s for Charles II. The Royal Apartments (including the Throne Room and Royal Dining Room) are used for investitures and for banquets whenever the Queen visits. A chamber in the so-called James V tower is believed to have been the scene of David Rizzio's murder in 1566. He was the Italian secretary of Mary, Queen of Scots. She witnessed the grisly act, which was authorized by her jealous husband, Lord Darnley. Bonnie Prince Charlie, last of the Stuart pretenders to the English throne, also held court at Holyrood Palace, in 1745.

The adjacent Holyrood Park, a former royal hunting ground, is home to three lochs, a large number of wildfowl, and the Salisbury Crags. Its high point is the hill known as Arthur's Seat, an extinct volcano and well-known Edinburgh landmark. The name is probably a corruption of Archer's Seat.

The grand 17th-century façade of Holyrood Palace

The Highlands

Stock images of Scottishness – clans and tartans, whisky and porridge, bagpipes and heather – originate in the Highlands. Gaelic-speaking Celts arrived from Ireland before the 7th century, establishing small fishing and cattle-raising communities. Nowadays the region has oil and tourist industries. Inverness, the Highland capital, makes a good starting point for exploring Loch Ness and the Cairngorms. The Isle of Skye has some of Britain's most dramatic scenery.

Sea lochs on the Isle of Skye, dominated by the Cuillin peaks

Snow-covered peaks of the Cairngorms, viewed from Aviemore

Cairngorms ㉙

🚉 🚌 *Aviemore.* 🛈 *Grampian Rd, Aviemore (0845-225 5121).*

Rising to a height of 1,309 m (4,296 ft), the Cairngorm mountains form the highest landmass in Britain.

Cairn Gorm itself is the site of one of Britain's first ski centers. Transportation to the 28 ski runs is provided daily from **Aviemore**. The chairlift that climbs Cairn Gorm affords superb views over the Spey Valley. **Rothiemurchus Estate** has a visitor center offering guided walks.

The **Cairngorm Reindeer Center** organizes walks in the hills among Britain's only herd of reindeer, and ospreys can be observed at the **Loch Garten Nature Reserve**.

Drivers can see bison, bears, wolves, and boar in the **Kincraig Highland Wildlife Park**.

Inverness ㉚

🏛 *60,000.* 🚉 🚌 🛈 *Castle Wynd (0845-225 5121).* **www**.visithighlands.com

Inverness is the center of communication, commerce, and administration for the Highlands. Dominating the

high ground above the town is **Inverness Castle**, a Victorian building of red sandstone. Below the castle, the **Inverness Museum and Art Gallery** provides a good introduction to the region's history. Its exhibits include a fine collection of Inverness silver. The **Scottish Kiltmaker Visitor Centre** offers an insight into the history, culture, and tradition of the kilt.

In summer **Jacobite Cruises** (call 01463-233 999 for information) runs regular boat trips along the Caledonian Canal and on the famous **Loch Ness**, southwest of Inverness. The Loch is 39 km (24 miles) long and up to 305 m (1,000 ft) deep. On the western shore, the ruins of the 16th-century **Urquhart Castle** can be seen. The **Official Loch Ness Exhibition Centre** provides information about the Loch and its mythical monster.

🏛 **Museum and Art Gallery**
1 Castle Wynd. *Tel* 01463-237 114.
⭘ *Mon–Sat.* ⬤ *Jan 1–2, Dec 25–26.* ♿

Isle of Skye ㉛

🏛 *11,500.* ⛴ *from Mallaig or Glenelg.* 🚌 🛈 *Bayfield House, Portree (0845-225 5121).*

Skye, the largest of the Inner Hebrides, can be reached by the bridge linking Kyle of Lochalsh and Kyleakin. The coast is shaped by a series of dramatic sea lochs, while the landscape, from Quiraing, a plateau of volcanic towers and spikes in the north, to the Cuillins, one of Britain's most spectacular mountain ranges, is majestic. Bonnie Prince Charlie (1720–88) escaped here from the mainland disguised as a maidservant following the defeat of his army at Culloden.

Skye's main settlement is **Portree**, with its colorful harbor. **Dunvegan Castle** on the island's northwest coast has been the seat of the Clan MacLeod chiefs for over seven centuries. South of here, the **Talisker distillery** produces one of the best Highland malts.

The ruins of Urquhart Castle on the western shore of Loch Ness

Practical Information

Colorful pageantry, ancient history, and a varied countryside attract millions of tourists to Britain each year. Facilities for visitors have improved considerably in recent years, with major urban centers offering a good variety of restaurants and hotels. The affluent southern region is more expensive than the rest of Britain. Telephone and postal systems are efficient, and violent crime is uncommon.

WHEN TO VISIT

Britain's temperate maritime climate does not produce extremes of heat or cold, but weather patterns shift constantly, and the climate can differ widely in places only a short distance apart. The southeast is generally drier than elsewhere. Be sure to pack a mix of warm and light clothing and an umbrella. Walkers can be surprised by bad weather.

Britain's towns and cities are all-year destinations, but many attractions open only between Easter and October. Some hotels are crammed at Christmas and New Year. The main family holiday months, July and August, and public holidays, are always busy. Spring and fall offer a good compromise: fewer crowds and relatively fine weather.

TOURIST INFORMATION

The **British Tourist Authority (BTA)** has offices in a number of major cities worldwide. In Britain, tourist information is available in many towns and public places, including airports, main train and bus stations, and at some sites of historical interest. These bureaus offer general tourist advice and will also reserve accommodations.

Both the regional and national tourist boards have comprehensive lists of local attractions and registered accommodations. The monthly magazine of **VisitBritain**, *In Britain*, available in tourist offices, contains articles about worthwhile places to visit and also includes an events diary. A charge may be made for more detailed maps and books.

For route planning, road atlases and local maps and guidebooks are available in most bookstores.

OPENING HOURS

Many businesses and shops are closed on Sundays, though trading is now legal. Museums and galleries are generally open from 10am to 5 or 6pm, with many opening later in the day on Sundays. Those outside the capital are normally closed for one day or one afternoon a week. On public holidays, known as bank holidays in Britain, banks, offices, most shops, and some restaurants will be closed.

VISA REQUIREMENTS AND CUSTOMS

A valid passport is needed to enter Britain. Visitors from the European Union (EU), the United States, Canada, New Zealand, and Australia do not require a visa to enter the country. Anyone who arrives in Britain from a member country of the EU can pass through a special channel at customs, but random checks are still made to detect any prohibited goods.

When entering from outside the EU go through the green customs channel if you have nothing to declare, and the red channel if you have goods which exceed allowances.

PERSONAL SECURITY

Britain is not a dangerous place for visitors, and it is most unlikely that your stay will be blighted by crime. Due to past terrorist attacks, there are occasional security alerts, notably on the underground, but these are mainly false alarms, often due to people accidentally leaving a bag or parcel lying around.

POLICE

The sight of a traditional British "bobby" patrolling the streets in a tall hat is now less common than the police patrol car with flashing lights and sirens. However, policemen on foot can still be found, and are courteous and helpful. If you have anything stolen, you should report the theft at the nearest police station.

THE CLIMATE OF GREAT BRITAIN

The moderate British climate rarely sees winter nights colder than -15 °C (5 °F), even in the far north, or summer days warmer than 30 °C (86 °F) in the south. Despite the country's reputation, annual rainfall is quite low – less than 100 cm (40 in) – and heavy rain is rare. The Atlantic coast, warmed by the Gulf Stream, gives the west a warmer, wetter climate than the east.

LONDON

°C/F			
	22/72		
	13/55	14/58	16/60
	7/44		10/50	7/45
0°C				3/38
32°F			

☀	5 hrs	6 hrs	3.5 hrs	1.5 hrs
☂	39 mm	45 mm	50 mm	44 mm
month	Apr	Jul	Oct	Jan

EDINBURGH

°C/F			
	18/62		
	11/52	11/52	13/56
	4/39		7/44	16/61
0°C				0/32
32°F			

☀	2.5 hrs	5.5 hrs	3 hrs	1.5 hrs
☂	38 mm	70 mm	58 mm	47 mm
month	Apr	Jul	Oct	Jan

EMERGENCY SERVICES

In an emergency, dial 999 to reach police, fire, and ambulance services, which are on call 24-hours a day. Calls are free from any public or private phone. In coastal areas this number also applies for calls to the voluntary coastguard rescue service. You can also turn up at a hospital emergency room at any time. Emergency medical treatment in a British National Health Service (NHS) emergency room is free, but any kind of additional medical care could prove to be very expensive.

HEALTH ISSUES

You can buy a wide range of medicines from pharmacies, which in Britain are known as chemists. Boots is the best-known chain store. If you are likely to need prescription drugs, either bring your own or get your doctor to write out the generic name of the drug (as opposed to the brand name). Some pharmacies are open until midnight, whilst doctors' offices (known as surgeries) are normally open during the day only.

FACILITIES FOR THE DISABLED

The facilities on offer for disabled visitors to Britain are steadily improving: new buildings offer elevators and ramps for wheelchair access, and adapted toilets. Many banks, theaters, and museums provide aids for the visually or hearing impaired. Given advance notice, rail, ferry, and bus personnel will help disabled passengers. The Disabled Person's Railcard provides discounted rail fares. Hertz offers hand-controlled vehicles for rental at no extra cost. For more general information about services contact **RADAR, Holiday Care Service**, or **Mobility International**.

BANKING AND CURRENCY

Britain's currency is the pound sterling (£), which is divided into 100 pence (p). Scottish banknotes are also legal tender in England and Wales, but you may find that not all stores will take them.

Banking hours vary, but most are open from 9am to 5pm, Monday to Friday. Most banks cash traveler's checks, and have cash machines

(ATMs) that accept most cards. You can also change money at private bureaux de change, which are located in major tourist areas and operate longer hours than banks. Exchange rates and commission charges can vary considerably.

Although credit cards are widely accepted in Britain, smaller stores, guesthouses, and cafés may not have the facilities for card transactions.

COMMUNICATIONS

Public telephone booths are available throughout Britain and may be card- or coin-operated. In major towns and public places, some booths are equipped with facilities to accept credit cards and offer internet access. It is less costly to telephone in the evenings and at weekends.

Post offices are usually open from 9am to 5:30pm Monday to Friday, and until 12:30pm on Saturday. Sub-post offices are located in local stores. Stamps can be purchased from any outlet which displays the sign "Stamps sold here." Mail boxes come in several shapes, but are always painted red.

DIRECTORY

Travel Information

Since it is an international gateway for air and sea traffic, traveling to Britain poses few problems. By air, visitors have a large choice of carriers serving Europe, Australasia, and North America. Bus travel is an inexpensive form of transportation from Europe, while traveling by train has been transformed by the advent of the Channel Tunnel. Traveling within Britain itself is fairly easy. There is an extensive road network reaching all parts of the country. The national rail network is improving and services to the smaller towns are good. Bus travel is the least expensive option; it serves most areas but can be slow.

FLYING TO GREAT BRITAIN

Britain has about 130 airports but only a handful of these are equipped for long-distance travel. The largest is London's Heathrow, which is served by many of the world's leading airlines, with direct flights from most major cities. Other international airports include London Gatwick, London Stansted, Manchester, Birmingham, Newcastle, Glasgow, and Edinburgh.

British Airways has flights to destinations across the world. Other British airlines include **Virgin Atlantic**, with routes to the US and Far East, and **bmi british midland international**, which flies to the US and Western Europe. Several no-frills airlines, such as Ryanair and easyJet, offer low-cost flights to destinations all over Europe.

American airlines offering services to Britain include **American Airlines, Delta Air Lines**, and United, while from Canada, the main carrier is **Air Canada**. From Australasia, **Qantas** and **Air New Zealand** vie for passengers with many Far Eastern rivals.

CHARTERS AND PACKAGE DEALS

Charter flights offer relatively inexpensive seats, but have less flexible departure times than standard scheduled flights. Packages are also worth considering, as airlines and tour operators can put together a great range of flexible deals to suit your needs. These can include car rental or rail travel.

DOMESTIC FLIGHTS

Britain's size means that internal air travel only makes sense over long distances, such as from London to Scotland, or to one of the many offshore islands.

The **British Airways** shuttle flights between London and cities such as Glasgow, Edinburgh, and Manchester are extremely popular with business travelers. At peak times of the day, flights leave every hour, while at other times there is usually a flight every two hours.

TRAVELING IN LONDON

In London, daily, weekly, and monthly tickets called Travelcards are valid on all public transportation. However, if you are only using buses, it is better to buy a daily or weekly bus pass. Both types of pass are available at most newsagents and train or underground stations.

Fares in London are based on six train zones and two bus zones; there is a standard charge for travel within each zone and between zones, regardless of the distance traveled. The area covered by each zone varies slightly between buses and trains.

London also has express train services to Britain's two busiest airports, Heathrow and Gatwick, which leave from Paddington and Victoria stations respectively at regular intervals. The journey time is 15 minutes to Heathrow, and 30 minutes to Gatwick.

When traveling by bus, you pay the driver as you enter, or the conductor (if there is one) during your journey. The sightseeing buses that drive past many of London's historic sights are often run by private companies and will not accept bus passes or Travelcards.

All-night bus services are available in London from about 11pm until early morning. You can use Travelcards and bus passes on these. Night buses carry the letter N before the route number, and most pass through Trafalgar Square.

Taxis are available at every major train station, as well as at ranks near hotels and all over central London. All licensed cabs must carry a "For Hire" sign, which is lit up whenever they are free. The famous black cabs are the safest taxis to use in London since all the drivers are licensed and they also know where they are going. Most cab drivers expect a tip.

Sometimes, the best way to see London is on foot, but however you choose to get around, try to avoid the rush hours from 8 to 9:30am, and 4:30 to 6:30pm.

LONDON UNDERGROUND

The underground in London, known as the tube, is one of the largest systems of its kind in the world. London tube trains run every day, except December 25, from about 5:30am until after midnight. Fewer trains run on Sundays. The 12 tube lines are color-coded and maps are available at every station, while maps of the central section are displayed on each train. If you are making multiple journeys by tube, it is best to buy a daily or weekly Travelcard (see above).

RAIL TRAVEL

Britain has a privatized rail network that covers the whole of the country. It consists of several regional services, such as Great North Eastern Railways and Great Western Trains. **Virgin Trains**, which runs many cross-country routes, operates two other networks – West Coast Trains and Cross Country Trains. The system is generally quite reliable.

The main stations in London all serve different areas of the country; Euston serves the Midlands and northwest, King's Cross serves the northeast and Scotland, Liverpool Street serves East Anglia, Waterloo and Paddington serve the West Country and Wales, and Victoria and Charing Cross serve the South Coast.

First-class tickets for most journeys are available, and roundtrip fares are less costly than two one-way tickets. There are four discount fare types for adults: Apex and Superapex tickets must be booked at least a week or 14 days in advance; Savers and Supersavers cannot be used during peak hours.

If you plan to do much traveling by train around Britain, buy a rail pass. These can be bought from BR agents abroad, such as **Rail Europe** and **CIE Tours International**. The All Line Rail Rover allows unlimited travel within Great Britain. Passes are available for families and young persons.

LONG-DISTANCE BUSES

In Britain, long-distance express buses and ones used for sightseeing excursions are usually referred to as coaches. Coach services are generally less expensive than rail travel. Journey times, however, are longer and much less predictable on crowded roads. Tickets can be purchased at major international airports, **Victoria Coach Station** – the main terminal for journeys into and out of London – and most large travel agents. The largest British coach operator is **National Express**. Another major operator is **Scottish Citylink**, with services between London, the North, and Scotland.

TRAVELING BY ROAD

The most startling difference for most foreign motorists in Britain is that one drives on the left, with corresponding adjustments at traffic circles and junctions. Distances are measured in miles. Traffic density in towns and at busy holiday times can cause long delays. Parking is a particular problem in towns and cities.

Renting a car in Britain can be expensive. One of the most competitive national companies is **Autos Abroad**, but small local firms may undercut even these rates. International car rental companies such as **Avis**, **Budget**, and **Hertz** also operate in Britain. You need a valid driver's license and a passport when you rent. Most companies will not rent to novice drivers, and set age limits (usually 21–70).

FERRY SERVICES

About 20 car and passenger services travel regularly across the Channel and the North and Irish seas, the major ones including **P&O** and **Sea France**. Fares vary greatly according to the season, time of travel, and duration of stay.

Brittany Ferries run longer (often overnight) services between Plymouth, Poole and Portsmouth to the west coast of France as well as one 20-hour service outside the winter months between Plymouth and Santander in Spain.

CHANNEL TUNNEL

The Channel Tunnel offers a nonstop rail link between Britain and Europe. **Eurostar** services (for foot passengers) run from St. Pancras station in London to Lille and Paris in France, and Brussels in Belgium. Traveling from London direct to Paris or Brussels takes about 3 hours.

The **Eurotunnel** service (commonly known as the Shuttle) transports vehicles between Folkestone and Calais in about half an hour.

DIRECTORY

AIRLINES

Air Canada
Tel 0871-220 1111 (UK).
Tel 888-247 2262 (US and Canada).

Air New Zealand
Tel 0800-028 4149 (UK).
Tel 0800-737 000 (NZ).

American Airlines
Tel 08457-789 789 (UK).
Tel 800-433 7300 (US).

bmi british midland international
Tel 0870-607 0555 (UK).

British Airways
Tel 0870-850 9850 (UK).
Tel 800-403 0882 (US).

Delta Air Lines
Tel 0845-600 0950 (UK).
Tel 800-241 4141 (US).

Qantas
Tel 0800-0014 0014 (UK).
Tel 13 13 13 (Australia).

Virgin Atlantic
Tel 08705-747 747 (UK).
Tel 800-821 5438 (US).

RAIL TRAVEL

CIE Tours International
Tel 201-292 3438 (US).

National Rail Inquiries
Tel 0845-748 49 50.

Rail Europe
Tel 0870-837 1371.
www.raileurope.co.uk

Virgin Trains
Tel 08457-222 333.

BUS COMPANIES

National Express
Tel 0870-580 8080.
www.nationalexpress.com

Scottish Citylink
Tel 0870-550 5050.

CAR RENTAL

Autos Abroad
Tel 0870-066 7788.

Avis
Tel 0870-010 0287.
www.avis.co.uk

Budget
Tel 0871-565 656.
www.budget.com

Hertz
Tel 0870-844 8844.
www.hertz.com

FERRY SERVICES

Brittany Ferries
Tel 08709-076 103.

P&O
Tel 0870-600 0600.

Sea France
Tel 0870-443 1653.
www.seafrance.com

CHANNEL TUNNEL SERVICES

Eurostar
Tel 0870-518 6186.
www.eurostar.com
(for foot passengers).

Eurotunnel
Tel 0870-535 3535.
(for cars & buses).

Shopping

While the West End of London is undeniably Britain's most exciting place to shop, many regional centers offer nearly as wide a range of goods. Moreover, regional shopping can be less stressful, less expensive, and remarkably varied, with craft studios, farm shops, street markets, and factory showrooms adding to the enjoyment of bargain-hunting. Britain is famous for its country clothing: wool, tartan, waxed cotton, and tweed are all popular, along with classic prints such as Liberty or Laura Ashley. Other particularly British goods include antiques, floral soaps and scents, porcelain, glass, and local crafts.

OPENING HOURS

In general, you can assume most stores in Britain will open during the week from 9am or 10am until 5pm or 6pm. Hours on Saturdays may be shorter. Some town-center stores now open on Sundays, but more often when it is near Christmas. Some stores open late for one evening a week – usually Thursday – while in villages the shops may close at lunchtime for an hour, or for one afternoon each week. Market days vary from town to town; some markets are held on Sundays.

OUT-OF-TOWN SHOPPING CENTERS

These large complexes, similar to American malls, are rapidly increasing around Britain. The advantages of car access and easy, cheap parking are undeniable, and most centers are accessible by public transportation. The centers usually feature clusters of popular upscale stores, with many services offered, such as toilets, cafés, nurseries, restaurants, and movies.

DEPARTMENT STORES

Certain big department stores are only found in London, but others have provincial branches. **John Lewis**, for example, has shops in 22 locations. It sells a huge range of fabrics, clothing, and household items, combining quality service with good value. **Marks & Spencer**, with 303 branches through-out Britain, is even more of a

household name, famed for its good-value clothing and prepared food. The sizes of all chain stores, and the range of stock they carry, will differ from region to region.

The most famous of London's many department stores is **Harrods**, with 300 departments, 4,000 employees, and a spectacular Edwardian food hall. Nearby, **Harvey Nichols** stocks designer clothing and boasts the city's most stylish food hall. Gourmets should make a pilgrimage to **Fortnum and Mason**, which has stocked high-quality food for nearly 300 years. **Selfridges** sells virtually everything, from fine cashmeres to household gadgets. **Liberty**, the West End's last privately owned department store, still sells the hand-blocked silks and Oriental goods for which it was famous when it first opened in 1875.

CLOTHING STORES

Once again, London has the widest range, from *haute couture* to cheap and cheerful ready-made items. Shopping for clothing in the regions, however, can often be less tiring. Many towns popular with tourists – Oxford, Bath, and York for instance – have independently-owned clothing stores where you receive more personal service. Or you could try one of the chain stores found throughout the country for stylish, reasonably priced clothes, as well as younger and less expensive fashions.

Traditional British clothing – waxed Barbour jackets and Burberry trench coats – are

found in outlets such as **The Scotch House, Burberry,** and **Gieves and Hawkes**, while **Laura Ashley** is renowned for its floral print dresses. For kilts and tartans, the best place is **Hector Russell**, found in both Edinburgh and Glasgow.

London is the place for designer fashions, however, as many designers have specialized outlets here. **Vivienne Westwood**, doyenne of the punkish avant-garde, uses London as her British base.

MARKETS

Large towns and cities usually have a central covered market that operates most weekdays, selling everything from fresh produce to pots and pans. Many towns hold weekly markets in the main square.

The fashionable markets of London are **Covent Garden, Portobello Road**, and **Camden Lock**, where you can find an assortment of secondhand clothes, handmade crafts, and antiques. **Spitalfields** is a burgeoning East End market.

FOOD AND DRINK

Supermarkets are a good way to shop for food. The range and quality of items in stock is usually excellent. Several large chains compete for market share and as a result, prices are generally lower than smaller shops. However, the smaller town-center stores such as local bakeries, greengrocers, or markets, may give you a more interesting choice of fresh regional produce, and more personal service.

Alcoholic beverages are available in a huge variety of shops around Britain, many of them wine merchants, such as the chain store **Oddbins**. For whisky, Scotland is the place to go; **Cadenheads** and **The Whisky Shop** both have a wide variety of rare scotches.

BOOKS AND MAGAZINES

The capital is the hub of Britain's book trade, as many of the country's leading publishers are located within central London. Charing Cross

Road is the focal point for those searching for new, antiquarian, and secondhand volumes, and it is the home of **Foyle's**, with its massive but notoriously badly organized stock. Large branches of such chains as **Waterstone's** and **Borders** (which also sells magazines) are here, although they can also be found in most cities and major towns.

GIFTS AND SOUVENIRS

Most reputable large stores can arrange to ship expensive items back home for you. If you want to buy things that you can carry in a suitcase, the choice is wide. You can purchase attractive, well-made, portable craft items all over the country, especially in those areas that are popular with tourists. For slightly more unusual presents, have a look in museum shops and at the range of items available in National Trust and English Heritage properties.

Some chain stores are very convenient places to pick up attractive gifts and souvenirs. **The Body Shop** sells natural cosmetics and toiletries in recyclable plastic packaging, while **Past Times** sells modern reproductions of ancient British jewelry designs, including Celtic, Roman, and Tudor pieces. For designer gifts, try the **Conran Shop** in London, which sells stylish accessories for the home.

ART AND ANTIQUES

Britain's long history means there are many interesting artifacts to be found. Many towns, such as Brighton, have dozens of antique shops. You might also like to visit a jumble or flea market in the hope of picking up a bargain.

The largest collection of original photographs for sale in the country is at the **Photographers' Gallery** in London. For paintings, **Maas Gallery** in London's Mayfair district excels in Victorian masters. In Scotland, **The Scottish Gallery** has everything from jewelry to pieces by well-known Scottish artists, while **Finnie Antiques** is a treasure trove of antiques.

DIRECTORY

DEPARTMENT STORES

Fortnum and Mason
181 Piccadilly,
London W1.
Tel 020-7734 8040.

Harrods
87–135 Brompton Rd,
London SW1.
Tel 020-7730 1234.

Harvey Nichols
109–125 Knightsbridge,
London SW1.
Tel 020-7235 5000.

John Lewis
69 St. James Centre,
Edinburgh EH1.
Tel 0131-556 9121.
One of many branches.

Liberty
210–220 Regent St,
London W1.
Tel 020-7734 1234.

Marks & Spencer
173 & 458 Oxford St,
London W1.
Tel 020-7935 7954.
Two of many branches.

Selfridges
400 Oxford St,
London W1.
Tel 0870-837 7377.

CLOTHING STORES

Burberry
165 Regent Street,
London W1.
Tel 020-7806 1328.

2 Brompton Rd,
London SW1.
Tel 020-7968 0000.

Gieves & Hawkes
1 Savile Row,
London W1.
Tel 020-7434 2001.

Hector Russell
110 Buchanan St,
Glasgow G1.
Tel 0141-221 0217.

Laura Ashley
451 Oxford St,
London W1.
Tel 0871-223 1425.
One of many branches.

Vivienne Westwood
6 Davies St, London W1.
Tel 020-7629 3757.

MARKETS

Camden Lock
Chalk Farm Rd,
London NW1.
⏰ 9:30am–5:30pm Mon–Fri, 10am–6pm Sat–Sun.

Covent Garden
The Piazza, London WC2.
⏰ 9am–5pm daily.

Portobello Road
Portobello Rd,
London W10.
⏰ 7am–5:30pm Sat.

Spitalfields
Commercial St,
London E1.
⏰ 9am–5pm daily.

FOOD AND DRINK

Cadenheads
172 Canongate,
Edinburgh EH8.
Tel 0131-556 5864.

Oddbins
395 Strand, London WC2.
Tel 020-7240 3008.
One of many branches.

The Whisky Shop
Unit L2/O2, Buchanan Galleries, 220 Buchanan Street, Glasgow G1.
Tel 0141-331 0022.

BOOKS AND MAGAZINES

Borders
120 Charing Cross Rd,
London WC2.
Tel 020-7379 8877.
One of many branches.

Foyle's
113–119 Charing Cross Rd, London WC2.
Tel 020-7437 5660.

Waterstone's
128 Princes St, Edinburgh.
Tel 0131-226 2666.
One of many branches.

GIFTS AND SOUVENIRS

The Body Shop
374 Oxford St,
London W1.
Tel 020-7409 7868.
One of many branches.

Conran Shop
Michelin House, 81 Fulham Rd, London SW3.
Tel 020-7589 7401.

Past Times
47 Merchant Rd,
Bristol BS1.
Tel 0845-070 7421.
One of many branches.

ART AND ANTIQUES

Finnie Antiques
103 Niddrie Rd,
Glasgow G48.
Tel 0141-357 5812.

Maas Gallery
15a Clifford St,
London W1.
Tel 020-7734 2302.

Photographers' Gallery
5 & 8 Great Newport St,
London WC2.
Tel 020-7831 1772.

The Scottish Gallery
16 Dundas St, Edinburgh.
Tel 0131-558 1200.

Entertainment

London is the entertainment capital of Britain, with an array of world-class cultural and sporting events. Around the country, theaters, opera houses, concert halls, and other venues host a wide range of performing and dramatic arts programs. The summer months also see numerous open-air arts festivals. Ticket prices are often less expensive outside the capital. Britain offers hundreds of special interest holidays for those wanting to acquire a new skill or learn a new sport. Walking, sailing, skiing, pony-trekking, and golfing holidays are popular. Soccer, rugby, and cricket are favorite sports.

ENTERTAINMENT LISTINGS

For information about what's on in London, check the *Evening Standard* or the listings magazine *Time Out* (published every Wednesday). All the quality broadsheet newspapers have detailed arts reviews and listings of cultural events in London and throughout the country. Local newspapers, libraries, and tourist offices can supply details of regional events.

TICKETS

Ticket availability varies from show to show. You may be able to buy a ticket at the door, especially for a mid-week matinee, but for the more popular West End shows seats may have to be reserved weeks or even months in advance through agencies – ubiquitous in central London – or by telephone or in person at theater box offices. Half-price tickets for some same-day shows can be obtained from Leicester Square. Beware of counterfeit tickets offered by touts.

THEATER

Britain has an enduring theatrical tradition dating back to Shakespeare. London is the place to enjoy theater at its most varied and glamorous. The West End alone has more than 50 theaters. The **Barbican** and the **National Theatre** stage a mixture of classics and challenging new productions. The major commercial theaters, showing more

popular plays and musicals, are located along Shaftesbury Avenue and the Haymarket, and around Covent Garden and Charing Cross Road.

Outside the capital, at Stratford-upon-Avon, the **Royal Shakespeare Theatre** presents a year-round program of the great bard's works. Bristol's **Theatre Royal** is the oldest working theater in Britain. Good productions are staged at the Manchester **Royal Exchange**, and the **Traverse** in Edinburgh.

Open-air theater is a feature of city life in the summer with street entertainers at London's Covent Garden and other urban centers. London's Globe theater *(see pp58–59)* stages performances of Shakespeare's plays, and open-air theaters at Regent's Park and Holland Park also have a summer program.

Perhaps the liveliest theatrical festival in Britain is the two-week **Edinburgh Festival** held in late summer. Many seaside resorts also have a summer theater season.

MUSIC

A diverse musical repertoire can be found in a variety of venues across Great Britain. London, in particular, is one of the world's great centers for music, and home to several world-class orchestras and chamber groups. As well as classical concerts, there are dozens of rock, reggae, soul, folk, country, jazz, and Latin concerts taking place on every day of the week. There are also numerous nightclubs that play everything from 70s disco to the very latest house-music beats.

Major pop-concert venues in the capital include **Wembley Arena** and **Carling Apollo**. The **Royal Albert Hall** hosts a range of concerts, including the popular classical Proms. The **Wigmore Hall**, the **Barbican Concert Hall**, and the **Royal Festival Hall** are also notable classical venues. The **Royal Opera House** is a world-class venue, and home to the Royal Opera. English National Opera performs at the **London Coliseum**. Classical open-air concerts are also held at Marble Hill House and **Kenwood House** during the summer.

A wide range of musical events is staged in towns and cities across Great Britain. Liverpool and Manchester have excellent orchestras and are also centers for modern music, while **Glyndebourne** hosts an annual opera festival. Wales has a very strong choral tradition, while northern England is renowned for booming brass bands. Scotland, of course, is famous for its bagpipers.

DANCE

Classical ballet is performed at the **Royal Opera House**, home of the Royal Ballet, and the **London Coliseum** where the English National Ballet usually performs. The **Place Theatre, Sadler's Wells**, and the **Institute for Contemporary Art** (**ICA**) are major venues for contemporary dance.

Birmingham is home to the Birmingham Royal Ballet and is the best place to see performances outside London. Traditional English Morris dancing or the Scottish Highland fling and Celtic dancing *(ceilidhs)* can be enjoyed at local festivals.

CINEMA

The latest movies can be seen in any large town. Premieres with international film stars are usually held at London's Leicester Square cinemas. The capital now has a 3D cinema, the **BFI London IMAX**. Young children may see films graded U (universal) or PG (parental guidance). Cinema prices vary widely; some are less expensive at off-peak times, such as Mondays or afternoons. For first nights of new releases it is advisable to book in advance.

SPECIAL INTEREST VACATIONS

Hundreds of options are available from any kind of sport, to arts and crafts, such as painting, calligraphy, and jewelry-making, and a wide range of educational courses to suit all levels.

Reservations can be made with organizers or through a travel agent. The English and Scottish Tourist Boards have pamphlets on some of these activities.

OUTDOOR ACTIVITIES

Britain has an extensive network of long-distance footpaths and shorter trail routes for walkers, together with designated cycle routes and bridle paths.

There are 2,000 golf courses in Britain and many clubs welcome visiting players (bring confirmation of your handicap). Green fees vary widely. Tennis courts can be found in every town and many hotels.

Sailing is popular in the Lake District, and the south coast resorts have plenty of pleasure craft. Boating on the Thames and on Britain's network of canals is a common summer pursuit. Surfers and windsurfers head for the West Country and South Wales.

The best game fishing (trout and salmon) is in the West Country, Wales, and Scotland. Soccer, rugby, cricket, and horse-racing are all popular sports in Britain. Details of matches and meetings can be found in national newspapers. During the last week of June and the first week of July, the Wimbledon tournament attracts many visitors to the **All England Lawn Tennis and Croquet Club**.

Among adventure sport options are rock-climbing and mountaineering, aeronautical sports and gliding. Skiing and other winter sports are possible in Scotland. Ice-skating rinks are located in major cities and horse-riding centers are found throughout the country, with pony-trekking in tourist areas.

DIRECTORY

THEATER

Barbican
Silk St, London EC2.
Tel 020-7638 4141.

Bristol Old Vic
King St
Bristol BS1.
Tel 0117-987 7877.

Edinburgh Festival
The Hub, Castlehill,
Edinburgh EH1.
Tel 0131-473 2015.

National Theatre
South Bank Centre,
London SE1.
Tel 020-7452 3000.

Royal Exchange
St. Anne's Square,
Manchester M2.
Tel 0161-833 9833.

Royal Shakespeare Theatre
Stratford-upon-Avon
CV37.
Tel 01789-403 444

Traverse
Cambridge St,
Edinburgh EH1.
Tel 0131-228 1404.

MUSIC

Glyndebourne
Lewes, East Sussex BN8.
Tel 01273-812 321.

Kenwood House
Hampstead Lane,
London NW3.
Tel 020-8348 1286.

Carling Apollo
Queen Caroline St,
London W6.
Tel 0870-380 0017.

London Coliseum
St. Martin's Lane,
London WC2.
Tel 0870-145 0200.

Philharmonic Hall
Hope St, Liverpool L1 9BP.
Tel 0151-210 2895.

Royal Albert Hall
Kensington Gore,
London SW7.
Tel 020-7589 8212.

Royal Festival Hall
South Bank Centre,
London SE1.
Tel 020-7960 0600.

Royal Opera House
Bow St, London WC2.
Tel 020-7304 4000.

Symphony Hall
International Convention
Centre, Broad St,
Birmingham B1 2EA.
Tel 0121-780 3333.

Wembley Arena
Empire Way, Wembley,
Middlesex HA9.
Tel 0870-060 0870.

Wigmore Hall
36 Wigmore St,
London W1.
Tel 020-7935 2141.

DANCE

ICA
Nash House, Carlton
House Terrace,
The Mall, London SW1.
Tel 020-7930 3647.

Place Theatre
17 Duke's Road,
London WC1.
Tel 020-7121 1100.

Sadler's Wells
Rosebery Ave,
London EC1.
Tel 0870-737 7737.

CINEMA

BFI London IMAX
Waterloo Rd,
London SE1.
Tel 0870-787 2525.

OUTDOOR ACTIVITIES

All England Lawn Tennis and Croquet Club
Church Road, Wimbledon,
London SW19.
Tel 020-8944 1066.

Association of Pleasure Craft Operators
Marine House,
Thorpe Lea Rd, Egham,
Surrey.
Tel 0844-800 9575.

British Activity Holiday Association
The Hollies, Oak Bank
Lane, Hoole Village,
Chester CH1.
Tel 01244-301 342.
www.baha.org.uk

British Mountaineering Council
177–179 Burton Rd,
Manchester M20.
Tel 0870 010 4878.

British Waterways
Willow Grange, Church Rd,
Watford, WD1.
Tel 01923-201 120.

English Golf Union
National Golf Centre,
The Broadway,
Woodhall Spa, Lincs LN10.
Tel 01526-354 500.

Outward Bound
Watermillock, Nr Penrith,
Cumbria CA11.
Tel 08705-134 227.

Ski Club of Great Britain
57–63 Church Road,
London SW19.
Tel 020-8410 2000.

Where to Stay in Great Britain

The range of accommodations available in Britain is extensive, and whatever your budget you should find something to suit you. London is much more expensive than the rest of the country, but even here there are affordable yet comfortable hotels. Out in the country, B&Bs (offering bed and breakfast) are economical.

PRICE CATEGORIES
For a standard double room per night, inclusive of service charge and any additional taxes such as VAT:

ⓔ under £65
ⓔⓔ £65–£100
ⓔⓔⓔ £100–£150
ⓔⓔⓔⓔ £150–£200
ⓔⓔⓔⓔⓔ over £200

LONDON

WEST END AND WESTMINSTER Dover Hotel
ⓔⓔ

42–44 Belgrave Rd, SW1 **Tel** *020-7821 9085* **Fax** *020-7834 6425* **Rooms** *34* **Map** *C4*

This well-maintained hotel is terrific value for money. It may not be luxurious once past the grand stucco façade, but the decor is refreshingly modern and every room has satellite TV and pristine en suite shower and WC. It's handy for Victoria Station and Pimlico's many pubs and cafés. **www.dover-hotel.co.uk**

WEST END AND WESTMINSTER Citadines Covent Garden/Holborn
ⓔⓔⓔ

94–99 High Holborn, WC1 **Tel** *020-7395 8800* **Fax** *020-7395 8799* **Rooms** *192* **Map** *D3*

This centrally located branch of the French apart'hotel chain offers pleasant, good-value accommodations for up to four people. Studios or one-bedroom apartments have kitchenettes, dining tables, satellite TVs, and hi-fis. There are also handy business facilities and an on-site breakfast room. **www.citadines.com**

WEST END AND WESTMINSTER Elizabeth Hotel and Apartments
ⓔⓔⓔ

37 Eccleston Square, SW1 **Tel** *020-7828 6812* **Fax** *020-7828 6814* **Rooms** *37 & 5 apartments* **Map** *C4*

The rates are surprisingly reasonable in this elegant town house hotel on a grand garden square. Winston Churchill used to live a couple of doors down. Rooms are simple yet tastefully furnished and guests have access to the private gardens and stately drawing room with newspapers, tea, coffee, and biscuits. **www.elizabethhotel.com**

WEST END AND WESTMINSTER Claridges
ⓔⓔⓔⓔⓔ

Brook St, W1 **Tel** *020-7629 8860* **Fax** *020-7499 2210* **Rooms** *203* **Map** *C3*

Favored by the European aristocracy in the 19th century, Empress Eugénie wintered here. Nowadays it attracts show business *glitterati* and business clients alike. Rooms range from Victorian to contemporary by way of fabulous Art Deco suites. Gordon Ramsay's fêted restaurant and a smart bar are further draws. **www.claridges.co.uk**

WEST END AND WESTMINSTER Covent Garden Hotel
ⓔⓔⓔⓔⓔ

10 Monmouth St, WC2 **Tel** *020-7806 1000* **Fax** *020-7806 1100* **Rooms** *58* **Map** *D3*

This exquisite hotel's Covent Garden location is one reason why it is popular with thespians. Part of the Firmdale chain, it is decorated in contemporary-English style with antiques and fresh fabrics. Brasserie Max is a popular meeting spot and films are shown in the luxurious screening room at weekends. **www.firmdalehotels.com**

WEST END AND WESTMINSTER One Aldwych
ⓔⓔⓔⓔⓔ

1 Aldwych, WC2 **Tel** *020-7300 1000* **Fax** *020-7300 1001* **Rooms** *105* **Map** *D3*

A grand modern hotel in former Edwardian newspaper offices. Impressive details include original art and tarazzo-stone bathrooms with heated floors and mini TVs. There is a spacious health club with a swimming pool, several trendy restaurants, and the buzzing, high-ceilinged Lobby Bar. **www.onealdwych.com**

WEST END AND WESTMINSTER Ritz
ⓔⓔⓔⓔⓔ

150 Piccadilly, W1 **Tel** *020-7493 8181* **Fax** *020-7493 2687* **Rooms** *133* **Map** *C3*

There are two staff for every room in this famous grand hotel on the edge of Green Park. You can even have your luggage unpacked for you. Rooms are in lavish Louis XVI style with antique furnishings and gold leaf, plus all modern conveniences. The Rivoli Bar has been restored to its Art Deco splendor. **www.theritzlondon.com**

WEST END AND WESTMINSTER Savoy
ⓔⓔⓔⓔⓔ

Strand, WC2 **Tel** *020-7836 4343* **Fax** *020-7240 6040* **Rooms** *263* **Map** *D3*

This legendary hotel was an afterthought, Richard D'Oyly Carte capitalized on the success of his Savoy Theatre by providing a place to stay. The rest is history. Monet painted the Thames view from his window, Elton John flooded a bathroom, and the dry martini was made popular in the bar. There's a rooftop pool as well. **www.fairmont.com/savoy**

WEST END AND WESTMINSTER The Connaught
ⓔⓔⓔⓔⓔ

Carlos Place, W1 **Tel** *020-7499 7070* **Fax** *020-7495 3262* **Rooms** *92* **Map** *C3*

The Connaught maintains its traditional charm while moving with the times. Facilities include butler service and a state-of-the-art gym. The interior feels less stuffy since many of the public rooms, including the Grill and the Connaught Bar, were restyled by renowned designer Nina Campbell. **www.theconnaught.com**

Key to Symbols *see back cover flap*

WEST END AND WESTMINSTER The Dorchester

Park Lane, W1 **Tel** *020-7629 8888* **Fax** *020-7409 0114* **Rooms** *250* **Map** *B3*

The epitome of the glamorous luxury hotel, with an outrageously lavish lobby and a star-studded history, the Dorchester has recently been revamped but maintains its tasteful floral bedrooms. The Art Deco-style marble bathtubs are probably the deepest in London. For even more pampering, pop down to the fabulous Art Deco spa. **www.thedorchester.com**

SOUTH KENSINGTON AND HYDE PARK Edward Lear

28–30 Seymour St, W1 **Tel** *020-7402 5401* **Fax** *020-7706 3766* **Rooms** *31* **Map** *B3*

This characterful small hotel is in the former home of Victorian poet and artist Edward Lear. Rooms are tidy and spacious with satellite TVs. Opt for en suite or shared facilities to keep the cost down. There's a computer with free internet access and leather seating in the pleasant guests' lounge. **www.edlear.com**

SOUTH KENSINGTON AND HYDE PARK Knightsbridge Green Hotel

159 Knightsbridge, SW1 **Tel** *020-7584 6274* **Fax** *020-7225 1635* **Rooms** *28* **Map** *B4*

A shopaholic's dream, this well-kept hotel is right on Knightsbridge and rates are reasonable for more spending power in Harrods and Harvey Nichols. The tidy, modern rooms are regularly upgraded and feature air conditioning, satellite TVs, and wireless internet access. There's also a small business center on-site. **www.thekghotel.com**

SOUTH KENSINGTON AND HYDE PARK Blakes Hotel

33 Roland Gardens, SW7 **Tel** *020-7370 6701* **Fax** *020-7373 0442* **Rooms** *45* **Map** *B4*

Blakes is the original "boutique hotel", created by designer Anouska Hempel over two decades ago. Rooms range in style from baronial manor to opulent Oriental and contain pieces collected on her travels. The discreet residential location has made it a favorite celebrity hideaway. Only some suites are air conditioned. **www.blakeshotels.com**

SOUTH KENSINGTON AND HYDE PARK The Capital Hotel

22–24 Basil St, SW3 **Tel** *020-7589 5171* **Fax** *020-7225 0011* **Rooms** *49* **Map** *B4*

Situated between Harrods and Harvey Nichols, this service-oriented hotel even offers personal shoppers and jogging partners. Its Michelin two-starred restaurant has been refurbished in 1940s-influenced style. Bedrooms feature king-size beds, designer fabrics, and the latest technology. **www.capitalhotel.co.uk**

SOUTH KENSINGTON AND HYDE PARK The Gore

190 Queen's Gate, SW7 **Tel** *020-7584 6601* **Fax** *020-7589 8127* **Rooms** *50* **Map** *A4*

The Gore has been in operation for more than 110 years and, while it has recently been refurbished, it preserves the atmosphere of a bygone age. Rooms feature four-poster beds, framed pictures, luxurious draperies, and opulent fabrics. There's a paneled bar and casual bistro as well. **www.gorehotel.co.uk**

SOUTH KENSINGTON AND HYDE PARK The Halkin

Halkin St, SW1 **Tel** *020-7333 1000* **Fax** *020-7333 1100* **Rooms** *41* **Map** *B4*

Modern comforts meet Eastern serenity at this gracious luxury hotel. Warm wood tones, curved lines, and creamy bed linen are accented by southeast Asian art handpicked by the Singaporean owner. Be sure to have a meal at Nahm, it is the only Michelin-starred Thai restaurant outside Thailand. **www.halkin.como.bz**

REGENT'S PARK AND BLOOMSBURY Hotel Cavendish

75 Gower St, WC1 **Tel** *020-7636 9079* **Fax** *020-7580 3609* **Rooms** *31* **Map** *C2*

This characterful B&B near London University has a fascinating history, D.H. Lawrence and the Beatles have stayed here. Rooms are simple yet comfortably furnished, and some have original fireplaces. Original artworks brighten up the breakfast room and there's a pretty garden as well. Shared facilities available. **www.hotelcavendish.com**

REGENT'S PARK AND BLOOMSBURY Crescent Hotel

49–50 Cartwright Gardens, WC1 **Tel** *020-7387 1515* **Fax** *020-7383 2054* **Rooms** *27* **Map** *D2*

One of several hotels in this striking Regency Street, the Crescent has been run by the same family since the 1950s. Most of the well-kept bedrooms have en suite facilities. Soft drinks and snacks are served in the lounge, and guests can use the tennis courts in the private gardens. **www.crescenthoteloflondon.com**

REGENT'S PARK AND BLOOMSBURY 22 York Street

22–24 York St, W1 **Tel** *020-7224 2990* **Fax** *020-7224 1990* **Rooms** *20* **Map** *B3*

This beautiful property is a cut above most B&Bs. Liz and Michael Callis ensure that rooms in these two immaculately preserved Georgian houses are spotless and stylishly furnished with antiques and French quilts. A gourmet continental breakfast is served in the rustic kitchen. Non-smoking throughout. **www.22yorkstreet.co.uk**

REGENT'S PARK AND BLOOMSBURY The Langham

1C Portland Place, W1 **Tel** *020-7636 1000* **Fax** *020-7323 2340* **Rooms** *425* **Map** *C2*

The Langham was Europe's first grand hotel when it opened in 1865 and still offers an ultra-luxurious experience behind its sprawling Victorian façade. Rooms achieve a tasteful middle ground between modern and traditional and there are extensive spa facilities including a swimming pool. Near Regent's Park. **www.langhamhotels.com**

REGENT'S PARK AND BLOOMSBURY Charlotte Street Hotel

15–17 Charlotte St, W1 **Tel** *020-7806 2000* **Fax** *020-7806 2002* **Rooms** *52* **Map** *C2*

The ground floor bar is always buzzing with local workers as well as guests in this exquisitely designed hotel in a street full of restaurants. Reflecting the area's history, its decor nods to the Bloomsbury Set period with original artworks by Vanessa Bell and others. Weekend films in the screening room. **www.charlottestreethotel.com**

Map References *see map of London pp42–3*

REGENT'S PARK AND BLOOMSBURY Sanderson   🖼️ P 🍴 🏃 📺 🖥️ & £££££

50 Berners St, W1 **Tel** *020-7300 1400* **Fax** *020-7300 1401* **Rooms** *150*   **Map** *C3*

The Sanderson's witty decor, including a red lips sofa and framed portrait that seems to hang in mid-air, is like a surreal stage set. Rooms have every comfort, and the Malaysian restaurant, Suki, and two sophisticated cocktail bars are destinations in their own right. The Agua spa offers holistic pampering. **www.morganshotelgroup.com**

THE CITY AND SOUTHWARK The Zetter   🖼️ 🍴 🏃 &   £££

86–88 Clerkenwell Rd, EC1 **Tel** *020-7324 4444* **Fax** *020-7324 4445* **Rooms** *59*   **Map** *E3*

In an area known for its loft apartments, this is a loft hotel in a 19th-century warehouse. Rooms have exposed brick, quirky 1970s furniture, old Penguin books, hot-water bottles, and high-tech extras, while vending machines on each floor dispense necessities. Hip-Italian restaurant at street level. **www.thezetter.com**

THE CITY AND SOUTHWARK Great Eastern   🖼️ P 🍴 🏃 📺 🖥️ & £££££

40 Liverpool St, EC2 **Tel** *020-7618 5000* **Fax** *020-7618 5001* **Rooms** *267*   **Map** *F3*

This magnificent 19th-century railway hotel was given a makeover by design guru Terence Conran, juxtaposing dramatic modern elements with the original Victorian features. Cutting-edge art is displayed throughout, bedrooms are furnished with Eames and Jacobson pieces, and there are five fabulous eateries. **www.great-eastern-hotel.co.uk**

NOTTING HILL The Portobello Hotel   🖼️ 🏃   ££££

22 Stanley Gardens, W11 **Tel** *020-7727 2777* **Fax** *020-7792 9641* **Rooms** *24*

This divinely decadent Notting Hill mansion has lured rock royalty for over 30 years with its hip location and extravagantly decorated rooms. Choose from such exotic retreats as the serene Japanese room with private grotto garden and the notorious "Round Bed Room", with its freestanding Victorian bath. **www.portobello-hotel.co.uk**

SOUTHERN ENGLAND

BRIGHTON De Vere Grand Brighton   🖼️ 🍴 ♨️ 🏃 🖥️   £££

Kings Rd, Brighton, East Sussex, BN1 2FW **Tel** *01273-224300* **Fax** *01273-720 613* **Rooms** *200*

Brighton's only five-star hotel, this is arguably the nation's finest big seaside hotel. There's a hair and beauty salon, an indoor swimming and spa pool, sauna, solarium, steam bath, and gymnasium. The hotel's nightclub, Midnight Blues, opens on Friday and Saturday. Price includes breakfast. **www.grandbrighton.co.uk**

BRIGHTON Hotel Du Vin Brighton   🍴 🏃   £££

2–6 Ship St, Brighton, East Sussex, BN1 1AD **Tel** *01273-718588* **Fax** *01273-718599* **Rooms** *37*

Set in the Lanes conservation area, a stone's throw from the seafront, this cutting-edge hotel and bistro is housed in a collection of eccentric, Gothic Revival and mock-Tudor buildings. All the bedrooms are elegantly decorated with Egyptian linen and handsprung mattresses. **www.hotelduvin.com**

CANTERBURY The Falstaff   🍴 🏃   £££

8–10 St Dunstans St., Canterbury, Kent, CT2 8AF **Tel** *01227-462138* **Fax** *01227-463525* **Rooms** *46*

The Falstaff, at the heart of one of England's most historic cities, celebrated its 600th year in 2005. The one-time coaching inn has been extended into a recently-restored wood mill. All rooms are en suite, and have TV and hot drink facilities. It stands next to the imposing Westgate Tower. **www.foliohotels.com/falstaff**

CANTERBURY The Abode   🖼️ 🍴 🖥️   ££££

High St, Canterbury, Kent, CT1 2RX **Tel** *01227-766266* **Fax** *01227-451512* **Rooms** *72*

Located on the pedestrianized High Street in Canterbury, The Abode dates from the 16th century and has many original features. All the bedrooms, some furnished in Tudor or Georgian style, have satellite TV. Enjoy food and drinks at the Sully's Restaurant or Jacobs Brasserie. Price includes breakfast. **www.abodehotels.co.uk**

WINCHESTER Lainston House   🍴 🏃 🖥️ &   ££££

Sparsholt, Winchester, Hampshire, SO21 2LT **Tel** *01962-863588* **Fax** *01962-776672* **Rooms** *50*

One of England's most handsome hotels, Lainston House has country style yet is just minutes from the center of Winchester. Behind the imposing Queen Anne red-brick frontage is a friendly welcome. There are 63 acres to wander in, a gourmet restaurant, and you can always order a DVD from room service. **www.exclusivehotels.co.uk**

THE WEST COUNTRY AND WALES

BATH Royal Crescent   🖼️ 🍴 ♨️ 🏃 🖥️   £££££

16 Royal Crescent, Bath, Somerset, BA1 2LS **Tel** *01225-823333* **Fax** *01225-339401* **Rooms** *45*

Located at the center of Bath's glorious semi-circle of Georgian grandiosity. The simple but imposing Bath stone façade is the first glimpse of one of Britain's great hotels. Rooms brim with antiques, beds are luxuriant, there's a spa, and the restaurant is elegance personified. **www.royalcrescent.co.uk**

Key to Price Guide *see p96* **Map References** *see map of London pp42–3*

BEDDGELERT Sygun Fawr Country House

Beddgelert, Gwynedd, LL55 4NE **Tel** *01766-890258* **Rooms** *11*

Set in a truly rural setting, this four-star, country-house hotel sits amid a vast expanse of mountains and gardens. The rooms at this former 17th-century manor feature exposed stone work, oak beams, and inglenook fireplaces. The dining room, located in the oldest part of the building, has antique furniture. **www.sygunfawr.co.uk**

BRECON Castle of Brecon

The Castle Square, Brecon, Powys, LD3 9DB **Tel** *01874-624611* **Fax** *01874-623737* **Rooms** *30*

The oldest hotel in Wales and located in the town center, this outstanding family-run establishment occupies the remains of Brecon castle. The rooms are spacious, with en suite facilities; the south-facing rooms have breathtaking views over Brecon Beacons National Park. Ideally located for walking and horse riding. **www.breconcastle.co.uk**

BRISTOL Westbourne

40–44 St Pauls Rd, Clifton, Bristol, Somerset, BS8 1LR **Tel** *0117-973 4214* **Fax** *0117-974 3552* **Rooms** *31*

The well-located Westbourne Hotel provides superb accommodations for business travellers and families alike, within easy reach of the city centre and all its attractions. The cuisine and levels of service are exemplary, though there are plenty of good restaurants within walking distance. Price includes breakfast. **www.westbournehotel-bristol.co.uk**

CARDIFF St David's Hotel & Spa

Havannah St, Cardiff, CF10 5SD **Tel** *02920-454045* **Fax** *02920-313075* **Rooms** *132*

Overlooking Cardiff's trendy waterfront bay, this five-star hotel and spa is one of Wales's most luxurious hotels. Offers plush rooms and state-of-the-art leisure amenities. Each room has a private, deck-style balcony with views across the bay. Tailormade spa packages are available, as are conference facilities. **www.thestdavidshotel.com**

EXETER Barcelona

Magdalen St, Exeter, Devon, EX2 4HY **Tel** *01392-281000* **Fax** *01392-281001* **Rooms** *46*

This brilliantly converted former eye hospital gives the wink to inspired 1950s style with all the convenience of a modern hotel. The rooms are stylishly furnished with comforts such as satellite TV, video players, and internet. Business facilities are available, and Café Paradiso prepares Mediterranean cuisine. **www.aliashotels.com**

PENZANCE Summer House

Cornwall Terrace, Penzance, Cornwall, TR18 4HL **Tel** *01736-363744* **Fax** *01736-360959* **Rooms** *5*

This charming Grade II listed Regency house has been converted into a delightfully intimate hotel and lies very close to the sea. Tropical walled garden, fresh-cut flowers, polished wooden floors and inventive Mediterranean inspired cuisine await. All the bedrooms are individually styled. Price includes breakfast. **www.summerhouse-cornwall.com**

PORTHKERRY Egerton Grey

Porthkerry, Barry, South Glamorgan, CF62 3BZ **Tel** *01446-711666* **Fax** *01446-711690* **Rooms** *10*

Refined Victorian country-house hotel boasting a vast collection of antiques. The rooms are furnished with a wealth of period furnishings, original brasswork, open fireplaces, ornate mouldings, and oak paneling – even the food in the restaurant is served on antique china. The huge grounds include a croquet lawn. **www.egertongrey.co.uk**

PORTMEIRION Portmeirion

Portmeirion, Gwynedd, LL48 6ET **Tel** *01766-770000* **Fax** *01766-771331* **Rooms** *68*

This village-like complex, built initially by Clough Williams-Ellis as a private peninsula, is now a holiday retreat with a popular hotel, self-catering cottages, shops, and restaurants. The lavish rooms and suites are furnished in a contemporary style, and are well-equipped with modern facilities. **www.portmeirion-village.com**

ST IVES The Garrack Hotel

Burthallam Lane, St Ives, Cornwall, TR26 3AA **Tel** *01736-796199* **Fax** *01736-798955* **Rooms** *20*

Unusually for the busy little artists' haunt of St Ives, the Garrack has its own on-site car parking, as well as delightfully themed subtropical gardens. All rooms have private bathrooms and TV while some have jacuzzi or spa baths. Dine on seafood, meat, and vegetarian specialties. Includes breakfast. **www.garrack.com**

CENTRAL ENGLAND

BIRMINGHAM Malmaison

1 Wharfside St, Birmingham, B1 1RD **Tel** *0121-2465000* **Fax** *0121-2465002* **Rooms** *189*

A stylish, award-winning hotel in a former 1960s Royal Mail sorting office, Malmaison sits amid designer stores and within walking distance of the city center. The rooms are furnished in chocolate and cream tones, with soft lighting, and CD libraries. Also has a spa with sauna, Jacuzzi, and choice of treatments. **www.malmaison-birmingham.com**

CAMBRIDGE Cambridge Fourwentways

A11/A1307 Fourwentways, Cambridgeshire, CB8 6AP **Tel** *08700-1911519* **Fax** *01223-839479* **Rooms** *71*

Convenient for both the M11 and the A14, this branch of the nationwide budget hotel chain is ideally located close to the Imperial War Museum's aviation displays at Duxford as well as the equestrian museums and training gallops of Newmarket. A Little Chef eatery is on the same site. Offers good online deals. **www.travellodge.co.uk**

Key to Symbols *see back cover flap*

CAMBRIDGE Arundel House Hotel
Chesterton Rd, Cambridge, Cambridgeshire, CB4 3AN **Tel** *01223-367701* **Fax** *01223-367721* **Rooms** *105*

This hotel, created from a terrace of late 19th-century Victorian houses, overlooks the River Cam and is a short walk from the city center. The historic façade and gracefully decorated rooms have been retained while providing all the latest amenities. Parking is available. Price includes continental breakfast. **www.arundelhousehotels.co.uk**

OXFORD Macdonald Randolph Hotel
Beaumont St, Oxford, Oxfordshire, OX1 2LN **Tel** *0870-400 8200* **Fax** *01865-791678* **Rooms** *151*

The refined Randolph has starred in the TV series *Inspector Morse* and numerous movies, including *Shadowlands*. It's the veritable heart of Oxford, and a favorite for students' parents, American tourists, and the business community. Rooms are tastefully decorated. Dining is in classical silver-service mode. **www.macdonaldhotels.co.uk**

OXFORD The Old Parsonage Hotel
1 Banbury Rd, Oxford, Oxfordshire, OX2 6NN **Tel** *01865-310210* **Fax** *01865-311262* **Rooms** *30*

Walls of Cotswold stone screen the Old Parsonage from Oxford's passing hubbub, creating the pleasing illusion of a country retreat. The luxurious bedrooms are air conditioned and have broadband internet. Fresh Jersey lobsters are served in the restaurant from May through September. Price includes breakfast. **www.oldparsonage-hotel.co.uk**

STRATFORD-UPON-AVON Victoria Spa Lodge
Bishopton Lane, Bishopton, Stratford-upon-Avon, Warwickshire, CV37 9QY **Tel** *01789-267985* **Rooms** *7*

Built in 1837, this non-smoking Victorian spa hotel was visited by Queen Victoria, hence its name and the appearance of her coat of arms in the hotel gables. The bedrooms face forward onto the hotel grounds; some overlook Stratford-upon-Avon's canal. Serves a generous breakfast, and has a helpful staff. **www.stratford-uopn-avon.co.uk/victoriaspa**

WILMCOTE Pear Tree Cottage
7 Church Rd, Wilmcote, Stratford-upon-Avon, CV37 9UX **Tel** *01789-205889* **Fax** *01789-262862* **Rooms** *3*

Perfectly located for exploring Shakespeare country, this cosy B&B is just a short walk from Mary Arden's House – the home of Shakespeare's mother. Offers rooms as well as self-catering apartments. Guests are free to make use of the owners' comfortable lounge. **www.peartreecot.co.uk**

NORTHERN ENGLAND

DURHAM Whitworth Hall Country Park Hotel
Near Spennymoor, Durham, County Durham, DL16 7OX **Tel** *01388-811772* **Fax** *01388-818669* **Rooms** *29*

A Grade II listed building set amid several acres of lovely gardens. Offers stately en suite rooms; some with great views. The deer grazing in the surrounding grounds enhance the hotel's tranquil and relaxing ambiance. An idyllic location for weddings. Also provides conference facilities. **www.whitworthhall.co.uk**

GRASMERE Howfoot Lodge
Town End, Grasmere, Cumbria, LA22 9SQ **Tel** *015394-35366* **Fax** *015394-35268* **Rooms** *7*

This Victorian guesthouse is owned by the Wordsworth Trust. It stands in landscaped gardens and is furnished with period antiques in keeping with the house. Has pleasant and cheerful rooms, two of which are deluxe standard. An excellent place for outdoor activities such as walks and bicycling. **www.howfoot.co.uk**

LEEDS 42 The Calls
42 The Call, Leeds, West Yorkshire, LS2 7EW **Tel** *0113-2440099* **Fax** *0113-2344100* **Rooms** *41*

A refreshingly different town-house hotel that manages to be trendy without becoming a cliché. This converted cornmill, set beside River Nidd, features beamed ceilings, original mill mechanisms, modern handmade beds, and a collection of original works of art. Offers luxurious rooms. **www.42thecalls.co.uk**

LIVERPOOL Hope Street Hotel
Selside, Kendal, Cumbria, LA8 9LE **Tel** *01539-823259* **Fax** *01539-823259* **Rooms** *4*

Built in 1860 in the style of a Venetian palazzo, Liverpool's first boutique hotel is set in the city's beautiful Georgian quarter. The contemporary rooms are individually designed and feature solid wood floors, large beds, and Egyptian cotton sheets. A good base from which to explore this World Heritage city. **www.hopestreethotel.co.uk**

MANCHESTER The Midland Hotel
Peter St, Manchester, Lancashire, M60 2DS **Tel** *0161-2363333* **Fax** *0161-9324100* **Rooms** *312*

This imposing, red sandstone hotel has been one of Manchester's most familiar landmarks since it opened in 1903. Elegance, luxury, and high standards of service, comfort, and cuisine are on offer. Also has an indoor pool and a spa. Price includes breakfast. **www.qhotels.co.uk**

PENRITH North Lakes Hotel & Spa
Ullswater Rd, Penrith, Cumbria, CA11 8QT **Tel** *01768-868111* **Fax** *01768-868291* **Rooms** *84*

The use of local stone, natural wood, and open log fires create a genuine "away from it all" mood at this delightful family resort. Features a children's activity program, massive indoor pool, and a spa. This contemporary hotel is a Shire Hotels property. Price includes breakfast. **www.northlakeshotel.com**

Key to Price Guide *see p96* **Key to Symbols** *see back cover flap*

WINDERMERE Holbeck Ghyll

Holbeck Lane, Windermere, Cumbria, LA23 1LU **Tel** *01539-432375* **Fax** *01539-434743* **Rooms** *23*

An oasis of calm, perfect for relaxing on the terrace and soaking up fantastic views across Lake Windermere to the rugged fells beyond. Food is mouthwateringly good, and the plush armchairs and open fire of the lounge encourage relaxation. Also has a spa and sauna. **www.holbeckghyll.com**

YORK Middlethorpe Hall

Bishopthorpe Rd, York, Yorkshire, YO23 2GB **Tel** *01904-641241* **Fax** *01904-620176* **Rooms** *29*

One of the selective Historic House Hotels chain and, arguably, its finest. Set on 20 acres of outstanding gardens and parkland, this country-house hotel is filled with antiques and works of art. Built in 1699, it offers elegant accommodations in the main house and the adjacent mews cottages. **www.middlethorpe.com**

SCOTLAND

ABERDEEN Ardoe House Hotel

S Deeside Rd, Aberdeen, Aberdeenshire, AB12 5YP **Tel** *08701-942104* **Fax** *01224-861283* **Rooms** *109*

Located 5 km (3 miles) from the city center, this is one of Aberdeen's best hotels. The rooms at this luxurious retreat are lavish and tastefully decorated. The suites have four-poster beds. All rooms offer striking views of the countryside. Also has amenities such as Jacuzzi, tennis courts, and beauty salons. **www.ardoehouse.com**

EDINBURGH 7 Danube Street

7 Danube St, Edinburgh, EH4 1NN **Tel** *0131-3322755* **Fax** *0131-3433648* **Rooms** *3*

A delightful B&B, housed in a Georgian town house, in a quiet, but central part of Edinburgh. The comfortable, non-smoking rooms have attached bathrooms, and provide modern amenities such as computer points and a personal key and entrance. Within easy reach of many attractions and eateries. **www.aboutedinburgh.com/danube.html**

EDINBURGH The Scotsman

20 N Bridge, Edinburgh, EH1 1YT **Tel** *0131-5565565* **Fax** *0131-6523652* **Rooms** *69*

This stylish hotel is housed in the converted former offices of *The Scotsman* newspaper, and offers great views of the city. The luxurious rooms and suites are decorated with authentic Scottish estate tweeds, and feature amenities such as DVD and CD players, TVs, internet access, coffee makers, and more. **www.thescotsmanhotel.co.uk**

EDINBURGH The Balmoral

1 Princes St, Edinburgh, EH2 2EQ **Tel** *0131-5562414* **Fax** *0131-5573747* **Rooms** *188*

Boasting the best known address in Edinburgh, The Balmoral is favored by those who are accustomed to the very best in life. This elegant hotel has luxurious, tastefully furnished suites and rooms, with internet access, fax machines, TVs, and more. Also offers conference facilities, a spa, and excellent eateries. **www.thebalmoralhotel.com**

GLASGOW Tulip Inn

80 Ballater St, Glasgow, G5 0TW **Tel** *0141-4294233* **Fax** *0141-4294244* **Rooms** *114*

This city-center budget hotel offers modern, spacious, and well-equipped rooms with facilities such as satellite TV, walk-in shower rooms, and trouser presses. Families are well catered for here, and children under 16 stay for free. Full Scottish breakfast is served in the trendy hotel bistro. **www.tulipinnglasgow.co.uk**

GLASGOW Radisson SAS

301 Argyle St, Glasgow, G2 8DL **Tel** *0141-2043333* **Fax** *0141-2043344* **Rooms** *250*

This contemporary, award-winning hotel is mainly recognized for its innovative design. Boasts lavishly furnished rooms, suites, and an apartment, well-equipped with many innovative features. Also has conference rooms, a popular bar, and a good restaurant. A definite choice for those who appreciate modern surroundings. **www.radisson.com**

INVERNESS Glenmoriston Town House

20 Ness Bank, Inverness, Inverness-shire, IV2 4SF **Tel** *01463-223777* **Fax** *01463-712378* **Rooms** *30*

A traditional town-house hotel that has been tastefully and luxuriously upgraded. The hotel overlooks the River Ness and is only minutes from the town center. The rooms are furnished in a contemporary style, with modern amenities. Boasts an award-winning French restaurant. **www.glenmoriston.com**

ISLE OF SKYE Duisdale

Sleat, Isle Ornsay, Isle of Skye, Inverness-shire, IV43 8QW **Tel** *01471-833202* **Fax** *01471-833404* **Rooms** *17*

Friendly Victorian house set on a hill, with magnificent views of the Sound of Sleat. This small hotel has been flamboyantly decorated and has lots of character. The rooms are spacious and comfortably furnished. Also offers delicious food and lovely gardens. **www.duisdale.com**

ISLE OF SKYE Three Chimneys

Colbost, Dunvegan, Isle of Skye, Inverness-shire, IV55 8ZT **Tel** *01470-511258* **Fax** *01470-511358* **Rooms** *6*

Arguably the finest restaurant-with-rooms in Scotland, this intimate hotel is recognized for the excellence of its cooking and hospitality of the owners. Features modern and luxurious accommodations. The spectacular location makes for a memorable visit. **www.threechimneys.co.uk**

Where to Eat in Great Britain

The British restaurant scene has moved far from its once dismal reputation. This is partly due to an influx of foreign chefs and cooking styles, but home-grown restaurateurs have risen to the challenge of redeeming British food, too, and the indigenous cooking has improved out of all recognition since the early 1990s.

PRICE CATEGORIES
Include a three-course meal for one, half a bottle of house wine, and all unavoidable extra charges such as cover, service, and VAT:
ⓔ under £20
ⓔⓔ £20–£35
ⓔⓔⓔ £35–£45
ⓔⓔⓔⓔ £45–£55
ⓔⓔⓔⓔⓔ over £55

LONDON

WEST END AND WESTMINSTER Gay Hussar
ⓔⓔ
2 Greek St, W1D 4NB **Tel** *020-7437 0973*   **Map** *D3*

Once the place of choice for old journalists to meet, gossip, and enjoy second-rate food that reminded them of their private schools. Now, however, it provides a proper insight into authentic Hungarian cuisine, wines, and spirits. Good value for money.

WEST END AND WESTMINSTER Belgo Centraal
ⓔⓔⓔ
50 Earlham St, WC2H 9HP **Tel** *020-7813 2233*   **Map** *D3*

Nice and handy for Neal Street, Belgo Centraal remains popular every night. The cool young staff whip up a great variety of Belgian cuisine, from *moules marinières* to more exotic creations featuring Belgium's famous beers. Meat-eaters are also catered for. Eat at the long refectory tables and enjoy the fun.

WEST END AND WESTMINSTER Bertorelli
ⓔⓔⓔ
44A Floral St, WC2E 9DA **Tel** *020-7836 3969*   **Map** *D3*

An Italian institution in Covent Garden, Bertorelli's Roman empire now extends farther afield. This is the flagship, though not the one you may have seen in the film *Sliding Doors*. Freshly prepared and flavorful home cooking is served in a friendly ambiance. Sensible prices are an extra bonus. Closed Sundays.

WEST END AND WESTMINSTER Elena's L'Etoile
ⓔⓔⓔ
30 Charlotte St, W1T 2NA **Tel** *020-7636 7189*   **Map** *C2*

This long-standing local eatery is extremely busy at lunchtime, with media people from surrounding ad agencies and TV companies. The time-tested menu delivers classic French bistro food under the gaze of celebrity pictures that cover the walls. It's not cheap but guarantees quality and that indefinable extra – real atmosphere.

WEST END AND WESTMINSTER Langan's Brasserie
ⓔⓔⓔ
Stratton St, W1J 8LB **Tel** *020-7491 8822*   **Map** *C3*

The original and perhaps still the best in this chain of restaurants, Langan's faithfully adheres to the style of its late eponymous owner. Service is discreetly attentive and the staff are friendly. Try the house specialty, Langan's bangers and mash with white onion sauce, or the fabulous soufflé with anchovy sauce.

WEST END AND WESTMINSTER L'Escargot Marco Pierre White
ⓔⓔⓔ
48 Greek St, W1D 4EF **Tel** *020-7437 6828*   **Map** *D3*

Another Soho institution, this restaurant is now run by Marco Pierre White, a legendary chef. Expect high standards but be surprised by the very reasonable prices. In the Picasso Room you can look at some of the master's works while eating artistically crafted fine food. Try the parfait of foie gras *en gelée* with toasted Poilâne bread. Closed on Sun.

WEST END AND WESTMINSTER Loch Fyne
ⓔⓔⓔ
2–4 Catherine St, WC2B 5JS **Tel** *020-7240 4999*   **Map** *D3*

At Loch Fyne, a seafood restaurant, the fish and shellfish are brought in fresh from Scotland. The wine list is suitably chosen to match the crustaceans and other edible sea creatures on offer. Portions are generous whether you choose a platter of oysters or a large plate of poached smoked haddock.

WEST END AND WESTMINSTER Porter's English Restaurant
ⓔⓔⓔ
17 Henrietta St, WC2E 8QH **Tel** *020-7836 6466*   **Map** *D3*

A great place for proper fish and chips, Porter's is known for serving hearty British "grub" with tasty pie dishes such as steak and Guinness, cod, salmon, and prawn. Desserts are equally large and not for those on a diet. Prices are good for the location. Cheerful staff.

WEST END AND WESTMINSTER Sofra
ⓔⓔⓔ
36 Tavistock St, WC2E 7PB **Tel** *020-7240 3773*   **Map** *D3*

A reputed London institution, Sofra has been serving superior Turkish food for many years. The specialty is the healthy option involving a variety of little dishes to share. Bread and olives come free throughout the meal, while dips such as hummous and *tzatziki* always taste fresh and clean.

Key to Symbols *see back cover flap*

WEST END AND WESTMINSTER The Gaucho Grill

125–126 Chancery Lane, WC2A 1PU **Tel** *020-7242 7727* **Map** *D3*

There are a few branches of the Gaucho around London and they remain of consistent value. The star attraction is still its delicious steak. A large wine list helps wash down an enormous meal and the cocktails are good too. Ideal for pleasant, no-frills dining, it's a well-priced place in a reasonably expensive area. Closed Sundays.

WEST END AND WESTMINSTER Hakkasan

8 Hanway Place, W1T 14B **Tel** *020-7927 7000* **Map** *C3*

An expensive Chinese restaurant, Hakkasan has maintained a consistently high turnover. The decor is superb, and the food even more so. No windows mean you can't peer in to check it out before entering. Although busy, it's a great choice for gourmets who can afford it. Don't miss the dim sum.

WEST END AND WESTMINSTER Umu

14–16 Bruton Place, W1J 6L **Tel** *020-7499 8881* **Map** *C3*

Seriously expensive but extremely stylish, Umu has a futuristic front door that will make you gasp. The beautiful interior and friendly service by great staff are impressive too. With a remarkable sake list, this is one of the few places in London where you can find genuine Japanese *kaiseki*. There's also a good tasting menu.

SOUTH KENSINGTON AND HYDE PARK Racine

239 Brompton Rd, SW3 2EP **Tel** *020-7584 4477* **Map** *B4*

Racine sets out to showcase French cuisine and succeeds very well. Genuine French food, French waiters, and great atmosphere all combine to keep locals coming back for more. The venison, when in season, is excellent and the menu changes regularly. The service is good.

SOUTH KENSINGTON AND HYDE PARK Nahm

The Halkin, 5 Halkin St, SW1X 7DJ **Tel** *020-7333 1234* **Map** *C4*

This remarkable Thai restaurant has a Michelin star so you can arrive with high expectations. The set menu doesn't disappoint. A recommended appetizer is *ma hor* (minced prawns and chicken simmered in palm sugar with deep fried shallots, garlic, and peanuts, served on pineapple and mandarin orange). Not cheap but worth the price.

SOUTH KENSINGTON AND HYDE PARK Zafferano

5 Lowndes St, SW1X 9EY **Tel** *020-7235 5800* **Map** *B4*

Zafferano has long been recognized as one of the capital's premier Italian restaurants. It's a discreet place, where the emphasis is firmly on the quality of the food. Dishes such as risotto with white truffle and char-grilled lamb with aubergine (eggplant) allow the quality of the ingredients to shine through.

SOUTH KENSINGTON AND HYDE PARK Restaurant Gordon Ramsay

68 Royal Hospital Rd, SW3 4HP **Tel** *020-7352 4441* **Map** *B4*

Awarded with three Michelin stars, this restaurant strives for perfection in everything from place settings to service. Expensive, yet reputedly the best restaurant in London, this dining experience promises to be unforgettable. As a souvenir of London, meal memories here will last a lifetime.

SOUTH KENSINGTON AND HYDE PARK Tom Aikens

43 Elystan St, SW3 3NT **Tel** *020-7584 2003* **Map** *B4*

Top chef, Tom Aikens is often praised by other chefs for his lovingly constructed and beautifully plated dishes. A practitioner of classic cuisine, his flavors are finely balanced and the overall eating experience is highly memorable. A very popular restaurant, so book ahead.

REGENT'S PARK AND BLOOMSBURY Michael Moore

19 Blandford St, W1U 3DH **Tel** *020-7224 1898* **Map** *C3*

This perennially popular restaurant mixes excellent food with a genuinely friendly ambiance. Michael Moore (no relation to the American film-maker) is there virtually every night and tours the tables for a chat. A very accomplished chef, he changes his delightful menu regularly and keeps his regulars flocking back for more.

REGENT'S PARK AND BLOOMSBURY Orrery

55 Marylebone High Street, W1U 5RB **Tel** *020-7616 8000* **Map** *C2*

Housed in an old stable block, the dining room is a calm oasis offering stylish dining and contemporary French cuisine. Head for the summer roof terrace for al fresco dining and choose from the *menu du jour* or the à la carte. The intimate bar area is a good place to sample fine Cuban cigars.

THE CITY AND SOUTHWARK Bengal Cuisine

12 Brick Lane, E1 6RF **Tel** *020-7377 8405*

Just about every building in Brick Lane is an Indian restaurant, but the quality varies. Bengal Cuisine is certainly a lot more modern than most of them. The food is very good value and the cook goes easy on the chilli to suit the Western palate. Staff are happy to advise on dishes if asked. There's a good Sunday buffet as well.

THE CITY AND SOUTHWARK Baltic

74 Blackfriars Rd, SE1 8HA **Tel** *020-7928 1111* **Map** *D4*

Located inside a former coach house with high ceilings, Baltic exudes charm. The eastern European influence is noticeable in Baltic's beetroot and vodka cured salmon. There's a massive range of vodkas and the food constantly surprises with dishes such as roast saddle of wild boar. The kitchen is on show and there's often live jazz.

Map References *see map of London pp42–3*

THE CITY AND SOUTHWARK Silka

6–8 Southwark St, London Bridge, SE1 1RQ **Tel** 020-7378 6161 **Map** E4

Ayurvedic food is a specialty here, which is essentially food balanced for body and soul, and is particularly good for vegetarians. Of course, there are also all the usual Indian dishes too. There is some reluctance on the staff's part to write down your order so do check that what arrives is actually what you asked for. Closed Sundays.

THE CITY AND SOUTHWARK The Spitz

109 Commercial St, E1 6BG **Tel** 020-7392 9032

The Spitz is a friendly place, with live background music setting the ideal tone. The location near Spitalfields Market attracts a mixed crowd. Food is diverse and imaginative: goat's cheese and walnut salad is a specialty. The live jazz is only on Fridays and Saturdays.

THE CITY AND SOUTHWARK Moro

34–36 Exmouth Market, EC1R 4QE **Tel** 020-7833 8336

Moro is well known for its Spanish-Moroccan cuisine and serves up consistently good food to regulars. Courgette (zucchini) and mint tortilla is an example of light, flavorsome food and there are some very good breads. Buy ingredients next door and take their famous cookbook home with you.

GREENWICH Rivington Grill

178 Greenwich High Rd, Greenwich, SE10 8NN **Tel** 020-8293 9270

Located next to the cinema, Rivington is a great spot for lunch, dinner, or drinks before or after a movie or tour around historic Greenwich. Hearty British cuisine including regional dishes is served in a modern dining room with exposed brickwork, crisp white linen tablecloths, and low lighting. The Market Breakfast is good.

SOUTHERN ENGLAND

BRIGHTON Seven Dials

1, Buckingham Place, Seven Dials, Brighton, East Sussex, BN1 3TD **Tel** 01273-885555

A bustling eatery much beloved by Brighton's Sunday supplement set, Seven Dials is housed in a converted bank. The menu makes good use of local organic produce. Private dining is provided in the downstairs Vault, while a summer terrace offers the perfect spot for al fresco people-watching.

BRIGHTON La Fourchette

105 Western Rd, Brighton, East Sussex, BN1 2AA **Tel** 01273-722556

Lauded as one of Brighton's best restaurants, this handsome bistro is a relaxed showcase for regional and classic French cooking. The odd Moroccan twist spices up proceedings. An excellent wine list to match, while the choice of desserts will test the strongest resolve.

CANTERBURY The Goods Shed

Station Road West, Canterbury, Kent, CT2 8AN **Tel** 01227-459153

At this farmers' market diner-cum-café, there's a blackboard menu offering well-constructed treats. The simple home cooking uses the best of the day's produce from the myriad of stalls. As it is increasingly popular with local foodies, seating can be a problem during peak times. Closed Mondays; lunch only Sundays.

SALISBURY Café Med

68 Castle St, Salisbury, Wiltshire, SP1 3TS **Tel** 01722-328402

Renowned for its wine list, this lively restaurant-cum-wine bar has a simple but effective menu featuring satisfying dishes such as grilled salmon. The service is efficient, with an emphasis on ensuring you enjoy your night. Early bird specials are available.

WINDSOR Amalfi

9 Datchet Rd, Windsor, Berkshire, SL4 1QB **Tel** 01753-855576

With views across to Windsor Castle, this long-established, cozy little Italian restaurant serves all the usual favorites, as well as a variety of continental and vegetarian dishes. Starters come in very generous portions, and the fish dishes are highly recommended. Friendly service and a relaxed atmosphere make this place a favorite among locals.

THE WEST COUNTRY AND WALES

BATH Moon and Sixpence

6A Broad St, Bath, Somerset, BA1 5LJ **Tel** 01225-460962

A well-kept secret, Moon and Sixpence is a favorite with locals and discerning visitors. Slightly hidden up a cobbled path, it offers quiet dining right in the bustling city center. The reasonably priced food is loosely termed modern nternational. Particularly pleasant in summer when table service is provided in the downstairs conservatory.

Key to Price Guide see p102 **Map References** see map of London pp42–3

BATH The Bath Priory

Weston Road, Bath, Somerset, BA1 2XT **Tel** *01225-331922*

Not the original Priory, this top-notch establishment stands in a vast 19th-century Bath property, surrounded by four acres of award-winning gardens. The views are outstanding, and the food is pretty spectacular too. French and English Michelin-star cuisine includes a glorious sautéed escalope of salmon in lobster sauce.

BRISTOL Riverstation

The Grove, Bristol, BS1 4RB **Tel** *0117-9144434*

Formerly a harborside police station left in decline, Riverstation has fully exploited its potential to become one of the city's top restaurants offering modern European cuisine. Of its two floors, the dock floor has a bar and kitchen which is busy all day long. The other floor is a light and airy restaurant.

CARDIFF The Armless Dragon

97 Wyeverne Road, Cathays, Cardiff, CF24 4BG **Tel** *02920-382357*

At the Armless Dragon, one of Cardiff's most popular dining venues, contemporary Welsh cuisine is served in a smart, but laid-back setting. The menu is arranged by theme, using local produce from Wales, such as chicken from Monmouthshire, ham from Carmarthen, spider crab from Pembrokeshire, and lamb from Brecon.

CHAGFORD Gidleigh Park

Gidleigh Park, Chagford Devon, TQ13 8HH **Tel** *01647-432367*

Officially one of the best restaurants this country has to offer, Gidleigh Park has won several awards and accolades. The attention to detail is what sets it apart. Menus change according to the season, but expect fine quality whatever the month. The wine choice is also among the nation's best. Perfect for special occasions.

DARTMOUTH The New AngeL

2 South Embankment, Dartmouth, Devon, TQ6 9BH **Tel** *01803-839425*

Formerly called Carved Angel, this restaurant takes its new name from its present Michelin-starred owner. Unlike formal, old-fashioned dining rooms, it welcomes the entire family, except dogs, in an unpretentious environment. No fixed-price menus, just individually priced dishes. Get there early for 8:30am coffee, croissants, and cooked breakfast.

EXETER Thai Orchid

5 Cathedral Yard, Exeter, Devon, EX1 1HJ **Tel** *01392-214215*

Very friendly and welcoming service greets you as soon as you step inside this pleasing Oriental establishment. Authentic Thai cuisine is on offer in the 16th-century building, where the stone-masons who built Exeter's glorious cathedral originally boarded. Fresh orchids on each table are a thoughtful finishing touch.

LLANBERIS The Gwynedd Hotel & Restaurant

Llanberis, Snowdonia, Gwynedd, LL55 4SU **Tel** *01286-870203*

Fabulously situated at the foot of Mount Snowdon, this restaurant prides itself on the varied menu of local and seasonal cuisine. The owners, Mark and Dita Bartlett, pay meticulous attention to every detail. Dinner and lunch come complete with sightseeing information.

PENZANCE Harris's

46 New St, Penzance, Cornwall, TR18 2LZ **Tel** *01736-364408*

Run by the Harris family for over 30 years, this small restaurant wins acclaim for freshly made dishes served with local produce and fish from nearby Newlyn market. There are excellent-value fixed-price menus for both lunch and dinner, where you can choose one, two, or three courses. The crab Florentine comes highly recommended.

ST IVES Alba

Old Lifeboat House, Wharf Rd, St Ives, Cornwall, TR26 1LF **Tel** *01736-797222*

With spectacular views of the bay, mesmerizing Alba is housed in the old lifeboat building. Equally breathtaking is the double AA Rosette cuisine, predominantly seafood, all sourced locally. The accompanying wine list is as impressive. The restaurant is split between two floors.

CENTRAL ENGLAND

BIRMINGHAM La Toque d'Or

27 Warstone Lane, Hockley, Birmingham, B18 6JQ **Tel** *0121-2333655*

Elegant dining in a tiny alleyway in Birmingham's Jewelry Quarter. The Parisian-style cuisine is based on the vision of AA Rosette-winning chef, Didier Philipot. Food is traditionally French, but with a British twist, using ham from Cumbria, scallops from the Isle of Skye, and organic eggs from the Cotswolds. Advance reservations are advised.

CAMBRIDGE Restaurant 22

22 Chesterton Rd, Cambridge, Cambridgeshire, CB4 3AX **Tel** *01223-351880*

Small but perfectly formed, Restaurant 22 is set in a smart Victorian town house that serves British and French favorites, with the odd Asian twist added for extra interest. The decent wine list is predominantly French, but does travel farther afield to good effect.

Key to Symbols *see back cover flap*

CAMBRIDGE Midsummer House

Midsummer Common, Cambridge, Cambridgeshire, CB4 1HA **Tel** *01223-369299*

On the banks of the River Cam, Midsummer House is a plush restaurant that boasts an array of awards. The elegant ambiance is well-served by a kitchen with a heavy French accent. A recent face-lift adds to the charm, with a slate floor and warm shades giving a distinctly Mediterranean feel to proceedings.

OXFORD Browns

5–11 Woodstock Rd, Oxford, Oxfordshire, OX2 6HA **Tel** *01865-511995*

A branch of the booming brasserie chain, Browns is a firm favorite with business folk and weekend lunchers. The menu has recently been polished with more contemporary dishes, such as asparagus and wild mushroom risotto, to complement snacks and salads, sandwiches, and steaks. Pretty seating spills out onto the sidewalk in summer.

OXFORD Cherwell Boathouse

Bardwell Rd, Oxford, Oxfordshire, OX2 6SR **Tel** *01865-552746*

With a riverfront location at a punting station, Cherwell Boathouse is a favorite with wine buffs and romantics. Simple, but flawless, modern European cooking is enhanced by a well-priced and famously good wine selection. Try the honed-to-perfection goat's cheese or adventurous dishes such as pan-fried pollock.

STRATFORD-UPON-AVON Marlowe's Restaurant

18 High St, Stratford-upon-Avon, Warwickshire, CV37 6AU **Tel** *01789-204999*

Two restaurants housed in an Elizabethan town house, in the heart of Stratford. Serves both as a silver-service formal restaurant, perfect for business clients and posh events, and as a more informal and lower priced bistro with patio dining. Autographed pictures of visiting glitterati such as Vanessa Redgrave and Sir Alec Guinness line the bar.

NORTHERN ENGLAND

AMBLESIDE The Samling

Ambleside Rd, Ambleside, Cumbria, LA23 1LR **Tel** *01539-431922*

This delightful, award-winning restaurant offers dining in unashamed comfort. Line-caught sea bass, hand-dived scallops, and succulent Herdwick lamb are some of the dishes on the gourmet menu. The well-stocked cellar holds choice wines from across the world, plus some fine old whiskies.

COCKERMOUTH Quince and Medlar

11–13 Castlegate, Cockermouth, Cumbria, CA13 9EU **Tel** *01900-823579*

A historic, Georgian building near Cockermouth Castle is home to this family-run, vegetarian restaurant. The stylish surroundings enhance the intimate candlelit dinners. For 18 years, this eatery has been serving imaginative dishes, exploiting modern vegetarian cuisine to the full and drawing inspiration from around the world.

DURHAM Bistro 21

Aykley Heads House, Aykley Heads, Durham, County Durham, DH1 5TS **Tel** *0191-3844354*

Set within an early 18th-century building, originally a farmhouse, this popular bistro retains a distinct bucolic feel and, in summer, tables appear in the courtyard for al fresco dining. The cuisine is modern British with overtones of the Mediterranean and there's an ever-changing list of special dishes exploiting seasonal fresh produce.

KENDAL One Bridge Street

Bridge St, Kendal, Cumbria, LA9 7DD **Tel** *01539-738855*

Photographs of old Kendal decorate the walls of this fine historic house, where the small dining rooms create an intimate setting. Chef Julian Ankers exploits the flavors of traditional English fare and local produce to create exciting and tasty dishes.

LIVERPOOL 60 Hope Street

60 Hope St, Liverpool, Merseyside, L1 9BZ **Tel** *0151-7076060*

Ideal for a casual meal, the Café Bar in the basement serves a range of light meals, from sandwiches and salads to more substantial dishes. For a formal setting, choose the restaurant, which offers modern European cuisine within relaxed and unpretentious surroundings. The wine selection complements the food.

MANCHESTER Le Mont

Le Mont at Urbis, Levels 5 & 6, Cathedral Gardens, Manchester, Lancashire, M3 4BG **Tel** *0161-6058282*

From its lofty location above Urbis, this stylish restaurant treats diners to a spectacular panorama of the Manchester skyline. Serves excellent modern French cuisine, which has an unexpected Manchester flavor. Features fresh regional produce that includes seafood, poultry, and game.

WINDERMERE Holbeck Ghyll Country House Hotel

Holbeck Lane, Windermere, Cumbria, LA23 1LU **Tel** *01539-432375*

Set in a 19th-century hunting lodge, this intimate, Michelin-star restaurant (voted Cumbrian Restaurant of the Year) has good views across the lake. Serves English cuisine which reflects just a hint of France. The set dinner offers a tempting range of choices at each course, such as scallops or langoustine followed by beef, pigeon, or venison with a port-based sauce.

Key to Price Guide *see p102* **Key to Symbols** *see back cover flap*

YORK Melton's Too
25 Walmgate, York, North Yorkshire, YO1 9TX **Tel** *01904-629222*

Located in a former saddler's, this open plan bistro retains many original features, but has a distinctively modern feel. While losing nothing of the original Melton's dedication to good cooking, this place has a more informal appeal; an ideal venue whether you want just a light bite or a full dinner. The bar has a good range of specialty beers.

YORK The Blue Bicycle Restaurant
34 Fossgate, York, North Yorkshire, YO1 9TA **Tel** *01904-673990*

Seafood and modern European dishes are the specialties at this atmospheric restaurant. Situated beside River Foss, in a building that housed a 19th-century brothel, it still retains some of the original booths in the cellar. A guitarist provides an added attraction on Saturday evenings.

SCOTLAND

ABERDEEN The Silver Darling
Pocra Quay, Footdee, N Pier, Aberdeen, Aberdeenshire, AB11 5DQ **Tel** *01224-576229*

A superb seafood bistro restaurant located on the north side of Aberdeen harbor. This well-established venue is one of the best places to enjoy the daily catch, which has been carefully cooked and presented. Try and get a table by the window to make the most of the splendid coastline views.

EDINBURGH Waterfront Wine Bar
1c Dock Place, Edinburgh, EH6 6LU **Tel** *0131-5547427*

One of the best original Leith bar-restaurants, located on the water's edge, and offering a cozy place to relax.Friendly, knowledgeable staff and contemporary dishes ensure a good experience all round. Seafood plays a large part in the menu. The café is extremely popular and usually packed with locals and visitors to the area.

EDINBURGH Atrium and Blue Bar Café
10 Cambridge St, Edinburgh, EH1 2ED **Tel** *0131-2288882*

Two restaurants run by consummate professionals: the more formal Atrium is open for lunch and dinner, and offers a fine, contemporary dining experience, while the informal Blue Bar Café is open all day for snacks, coffee, drinks, lunch, and dinner. The cuisine is modern British with a Mediterranean twist. Superb quality in both places.

EDINBURGH Restaurant Martin Wishart
54 The Shore, Edinburgh, EH6 6RA **Tel** *0131-5533557*

Possibly the finest dining experience in all of Scotland. Chef Martin Wishart's creative and innovative cuisine is in great demand by lovers of fine food, and justifiably so. Serves modern French fare, using the best produce available. The service is excellent, the ambiance welcoming, and the experience truly memorable.

GLASGOW Brian Maule at Chardon d'Or
176 W Regent St, Glasgow, G2 4RL **Tel** *0141-2483801*

One of the finest restaurants in the city. Highly acclaimed chef Brian Maule provides an innovative menu of French cuisine, using locally sourced Scottish ingredients. Serves a variety of fish, poultry, and game. The stylish, yet unpretentious, ambiance and the friendly and efficient staff complete the experience.

GLASGOW Ubiquitous Chip
12 Ashton Lane, Glasgow, G12 8SJ **Tel** *0141-3345007*

A Glasgow West End institution, this prestigious restaurant serves traditional Scottish cuisine, made with fresh local ingredients, and has been a home of culinary excellence for over 30 years. Great atmosphere and a friendly staff make this a notable dining spot.

INVERNESS Culloden House
Culloden, Inverness, Inverness-shire, IV2 7BZ **Tel** *01463-790461*

A historic building with loads of character, set in lovely grounds, close to the Culloden Visitor Center. Offers Scottish country house-style food, with sauces, jellies, sorbets, and mousses interspersing a wide variety of hearty and appetizing meat, game, and fish dishes. Accommodations are also available.

OBAN The Knipoch Hotel
On A816, nr Oban, Argyll, PA34 4QT **Tel** *01852-316251*

Situated on the outskirts of Oban, this traditional country hotel has been a popular stopping place for many years. The bar meals here are excellent, while the dinners range from three to five courses. In addition, the huge array of vegetables and flamboyant puddings are as eyecatching as they are tasty.

ST. ANDREWS The Peat Inn
On B940, Cupar, nr St Andrews, Fife, KY15 5LH **Tel** *01334-840206*

Highly accomplished modern cooking, using regional produce and seasonal vegetables, has established this smart hotel-restaurant as one of the best in Britain. The innovative cuisine is prepared by renowned chef David Wilson, whose passion for good Scottish fare is evident in his creations. Lunch is particularly good value.

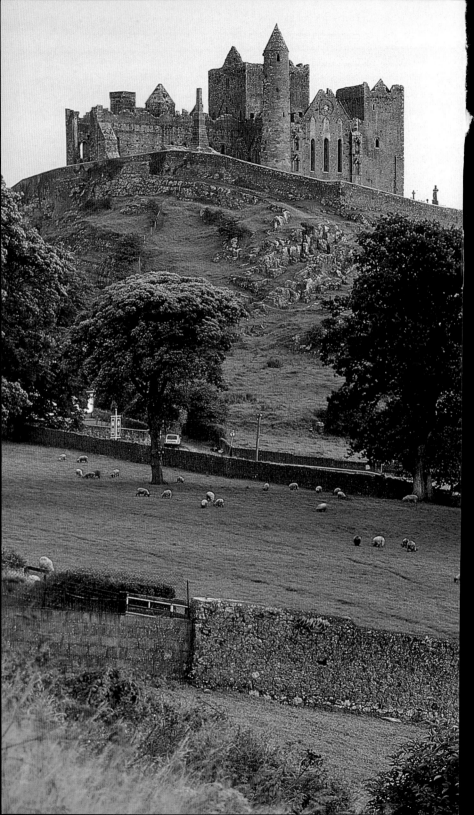

IRELAND

*I*t is easy to see Ireland as a lush, green island dotted with quaint, thatched cottages and friendly pubs filled with music, wit, and poetry. Despite the contrasting reality of rapid economic growth and fundamental political change, the tourist industry helps sustain this image of rural bliss, and the genuine good humor of the people invariably makes Ireland a most welcoming place to visit.

History and religion have created two communities in Ireland, with the Protestant majority in the North determined to remain part of the United Kingdom. Bombings and shootings in Northern Ireland have tarnished the world's view of the country, but the Good Friday Agreement of 1998 has brought new hopes for peace.

Despite the Troubles, the Irish retain a positive attitude that is both easy-going and forward-looking. Both parts of the island have young, highly educated populations. The Republic of Ireland, formerly among the poorer countries of the European Union, has become one of its success stories. EU subsidies have improved the transport infrastructure and many multinationals, especially computing, chemical, and telecommunications companies, have established subsidiaries in Ireland. Since 1990, the economy has seen annual economic growth of between 7 and 11 percent. Young people are not only staying in Ireland, but actually returning from abroad. Despite this high-tech revolution, agriculture remains a mainstay of the economy, with dairy cattle feeding on rich meadowlands and sheep grazing on the poorer upland pastures. The traditional Irish talent for breeding and training racehorses is undiminished. Tourism thrives with more than 5.5 million visitors to the Republic each year and Dublin is one of Europe's hotspots for a weekend break.

HISTORY

In the past Ireland's isolation cut it off from many of the major events of European history. Roman legions never invaded and the country's early history is shrouded in myths of warring gods and heroic High Kings.

Dingle, a lively, friendly fishing harbor in southwest Ireland

◁ The ruined Rock of Cashel, once a fortress of the kings of Munster, then seat of a medieval bishopric

O'Connell Street in Dublin just after the Easter Rising of 1916

The bellicose Celtic tribes were quick to embrace Christianity in the 5th century AD. Until the Viking invasions of the 9th century, Ireland enjoyed an era of relative peace. Huge monasteries were founded, where scholarship and the arts flourished. The Vikings never succeeded in gaining control of the island, but in 1169 the English arrived with greater ambitions. Many Irish chiefs submitted to Henry II of England, and his Anglo-Norman knights carved out large fiefdoms for themselves.

Direct English control was usually limited to the "Pale", the well-defended area around Dublin. Matters changed when in 1532 Henry VIII broke with the Catholic church. Ireland became a battleground between Irish Catholics and English armies dispatched to crush resistance. Irish lands were confiscated and granted to Protestants from England and Scotland. England's conquest was completed with William of Orange's victory over James II in 1690. During the English Ascendancy, repressive Penal Laws denied Irish Catholics the most basic freedoms, but opposition to English rule was never totally quashed.

The Famine of 1845–8 was the bleakest period of Irish history. Over two million either died or were forced to emigrate. A campaign for Home Rule gathered strength, but it took the war of 1919–21 to force the issue. The Treaty of 1921 divided the island in two. The South became the Irish Free State, gaining full independence in 1937. The Catholic minority in Northern Ireland suffered under Protestant rule and in the late 1960s began to stage civil rights protests. The situation quickly got out of hand. The British sent in troops and acts of terrorism and sectarian violence took the place of reasoned dialogue.

KEY DATES IN IRISH HISTORY

8th century BC Humans first inhabit Ireland

600 BC Arrival of Celts from Europe and Britain

AD 432 St. Patrick brings Christianity to Ireland

795 First Viking invasion

999 Viking king of Dublin defeated by Irish High King, Brian Boru

1169 Anglo-Norman invasion; Henry II of England proclaims himself overlord of Ireland

1541 Henry VIII declared King of Ireland

1690 William of Orange defeats James II at Battle of the Boyne

1695 Penal Laws restrict civil rights of Catholics

1801 Act of Union with Britain

1828 Catholic Emancipation Act

1845–8 Potato Famine leaves one million dead

1921 Anglo-Irish treaty divides Ireland into the Irish Free State and Northern Ireland

1937 The Irish Free State becomes entirely independent of Britain and is renamed Éire

1969 British troops sent to Northern Ireland

1998 Good Friday Agreement sets out framework for self-government in Northern Ireland

2002 The euro replaces the punt

2006 Plans laid for bilingual Irish-English society

LANGUAGE AND CULTURE

Ireland was a Gaelic-speaking nation until the 16th century, when English rule sent the language into decline. The Republic today is officially bilingual and 35 percent of adults claim to know some Gaelic. Many speak it fluently, but perhaps only 3 percent use it regularly. Some degree of knowledge is needed for university entrance and careers in the public sector. Irish culture, on the other hand, is in no danger of being eroded. The people have a genuine love of legends, literature, and songs, and festivals play an important part in community life. Traditional and modern music flourishes, whether at well-attended concerts or impromptu sessions in the local pub.

Traditional Irish dance

Exploring Ireland

Dublin is Ireland's chief attraction, a small, friendly capital with most of its sights and lively nightlife concentrated in the center. Elsewhere the pace of life is slow and the country's great appeal is in its landscape: from the lush green pastures, bogs, and lakes of the center of the island to dramatic mountains and bleak, rocky headlands in the southwest. Touring by car is the most convenient way to explore Ireland. In Northern Ireland roads are generally good; in the Republic they can be agreeably empty, but vary enormously in quality.

Jaunting car for hire in Killarney

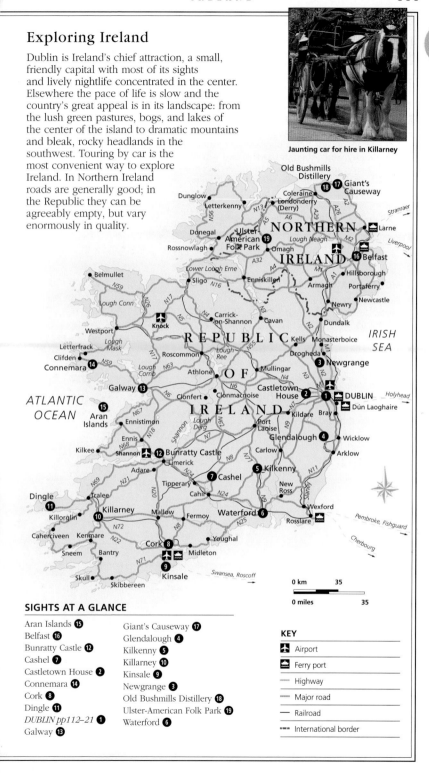

SIGHTS AT A GLANCE

Aran Islands ⑮

Belfast ⑯

Bunratty Castle ⑫

Cashel ⑦

Castletown House ②

Connemara ⑭

Cork ⑧

Dingle ⑪

DUBLIN pp112–21 ①

Galway ⑬

Giant's Causeway ⑰

Glendalough ④

Kilkenny ⑤

Killarney ⑩

Kinsale ⑨

Newgrange ③

Old Bushmills Distillery ⑱

Ulster-American Folk Park ⑲

Waterford ⑥

KEY

✈	Airport
⛴	Ferry port
—	Highway
—	Major road
—	Railroad
▪▪▪	International border

0 km   35

0 miles   35

Dublin ❶

Although it is a fairly small city, Ireland's capital is famous for its many pubs, and its rich cultural heritage attracts millions of visitors each year. The Liffey river runs through the middle of the city, and is the original source of its prosperity. The first harbor in Dublin was established in the early 9th century, when Vikings founded one of their largest settlements outside Scandinavia on the site of the present city. Since then, it has suffered wars and conflict over many centuries. In the 20th century Dublin established its own identity and today it is a thriving, modern city, rich in history and proud of its past. Dublin and its surrounding county have a population of just over one million.

SIGHTS AT A GLANCE

Christ Church Cathedral ⑨
Dublin Castle ⑦
Dublinia ⑩
Grafton Street ⑤
The Liffey ⑪
Merrion Square ②
National Gallery ③
National Museum ④
O'Connell Street ⑫
Parnell Square ⑬
St. Patrick's Cathedral ⑧
Temple Bar ⑥
Trinity College ①

Greater Dublin
(see inset map)
Guinness Store House ⑭
Phoenix Park ⑮

KEY

■ Sight / Place of interest
✈ International airport
⛴ Ferry port
🚆 Train station
🚌 Bus station
P Parking
ℹ Tourist information
✝ Church
⸱⸱⸱ Pedestrian street

SEE ALSO

- *Where to Stay* p136
- *Where to Eat* p138

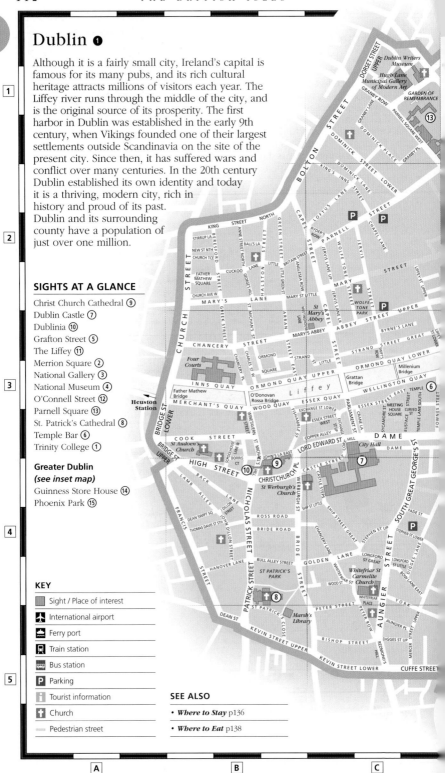

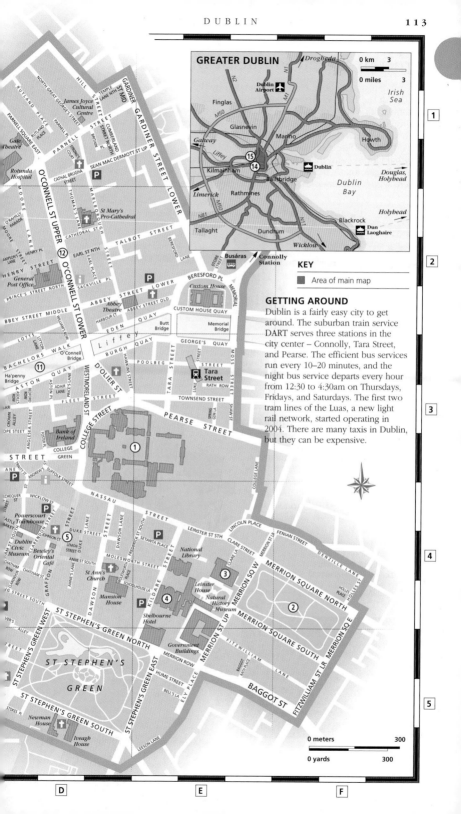

GREATER DUBLIN

0 km 3
0 miles 3

Drogheda

N1

M1

Dublin Airport

N2

Finglas

M50

Galway

Liffey

Glasnevin

Marino

Howth

Irish Sea

Kilmainham

15
14

Ballsbridge

Dublin

Douglas, Holyhead

Limerick

Rathmines

Dublin Bay

N81

M50

N11

Holyhead

Tallaght

Dundrum

Wicklow

Blackrock

Dun Laoghaire

KEY

◼ Area of main map

GETTING AROUND

Dublin is a fairly easy city to get around. The suburban train service DART serves three stations in the city center – Connolly, Tara Street, and Pearse. The efficient bus services run every 10–20 minutes, and the night bus service departs every hour from 12:30 to 4:30am on Thursdays, Fridays, and Saturdays. The first two tram lines of the Luas, a new light rail network, started operating in 2004. There are many taxis in Dublin, but they can be expensive.

0 meters 300
0 yards 300

Street-by-Street: Southeast Dublin

The area around College Green, dominated by the
façades of the Bank of Ireland and Trinity College, is
very much the heart of Dublin. The alleys and malls
cutting across busy pedestrianized Grafton Street boast
many of Dublin's better stores, hotels, and restaurants.
Just off Kildare Street are the Irish Parliament, the
National Library, and the National Museum. To escape
the city bustle many head for sanctuary in St. Stephen's
Green, which is overlooked by fine Georgian buildings.

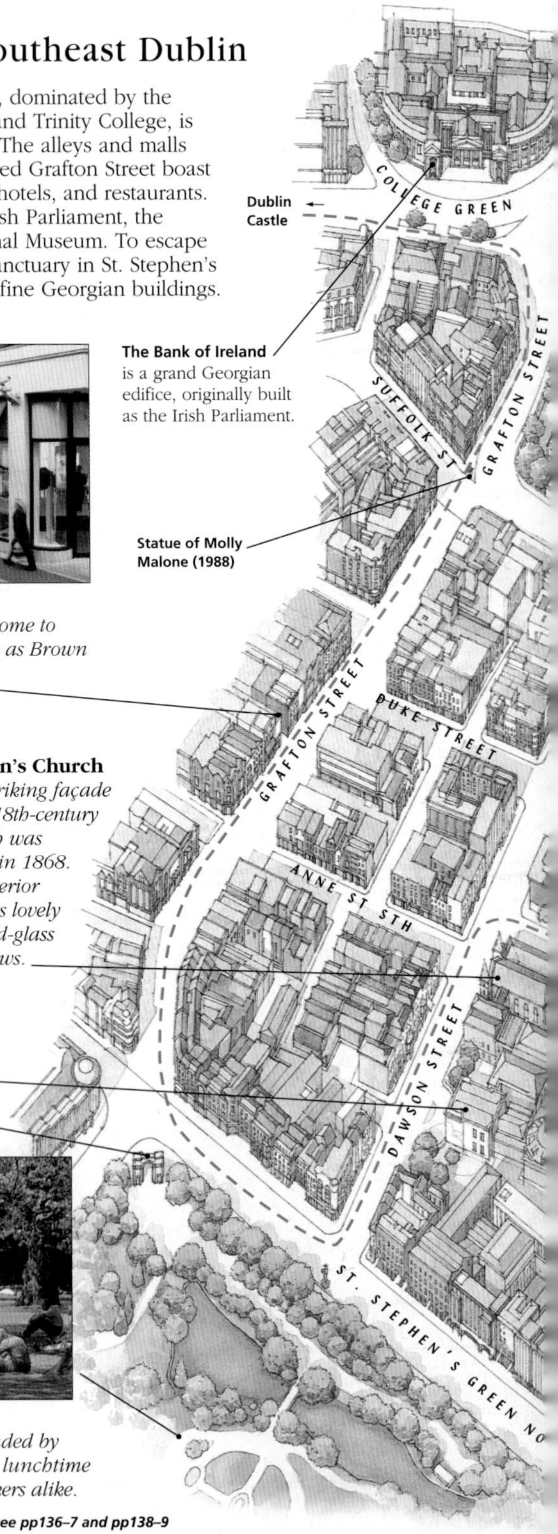

The Bank of Ireland
is a grand Georgian
edifice, originally built
as the Irish Parliament.

**Statue of Molly
Malone (1988)**

Grafton Street
*This popular pedestrian street is home to
many of Dublin's best shops, such as Brown
Thomas (see p117).*

St. Ann's Church
*This striking façade
of the 18th-century
church was
added in 1868.
The interior
features lovely
stained-glass
windows.*

The Mansion House has
been the offical
residence of Dublin's
Lord Mayor since 1715.

Fusiliers' Arch (1907)

St. Stephen's Green
*This relaxing city park is surrounded by
many fine buildings. In summer, lunchtime
concerts attract tourists and workers alike.*

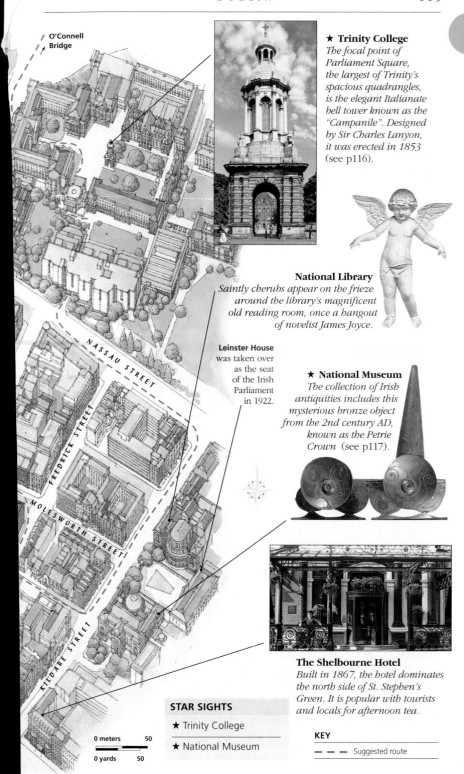

O'Connell
Bridge

★ Trinity College
*The focal point of
Parliament Square,
the largest of Trinity's
spacious quadrangles,
is the elegant Italianate
bell tower known as the
"Campanile". Designed
by Sir Charles Lanyon,
it was erected in 1853
(see p116).*

National Library
*Saintly cherubs appear on the frieze
around the library's magnificent
old reading room, once a hangout
of novelist James Joyce.*

Leinster House
was taken over
as the seat
of the Irish
Parliament
in 1922.

★ National Museum
*The collection of Irish
antiquities includes this
mysterious bronze object
from the 2nd century AD,
known as the Petrie
Crown (see p117).*

NASSAU STREET

FREDRICK STREET

MOLESWORTH STREET

KILDARE STREET

The Shelbourne Hotel
*Built in 1867, the hotel dominates
the north side of St. Stephen's
Green. It is popular with tourists
and locals for afternoon tea.*

STAR SIGHTS

★ Trinity College

★ National Museum

0 meters 50

0 yards 50

KEY

– – – Suggested route

View down the central aisle of Trinity College's Old Library

Trinity College ①

College Green. *Tel* 01-608 1724.
DART to Pearse. 10, 14, 15, 45,
46, 48 & many others. **Old Library
and Treasury** daily (Oct–May: pm
only Sun). 10 days at Christmas.
www.tcd.ie/library

Trinity was founded in 1592
by Elizabeth I on the site of
an Augustinian monastery as
a bastion of Protestantism. It
was not until the 1970s that
Catholics started entering the
university. Its cobbled quads
and lawns still have a monastic
feel, providing a pleasant
haven in the heart of the city.
In front of the main entrance
on College Green are statues
of two of Trinity's most famous
18th-century students, playwright Oliver Goldsmith and

political writer Edmund Burke.
Literary alumni of more recent
times include the playwrights
Oscar Wilde (1854–1900) and
Samuel Beckett (1906–89).

The oldest surviving part of
the college is the red-brick
building (the Rubrics) on the
east side of Library Square,
built around 1700. The Old
Library itself dates from 1732.
Its spectacular Long Room
measures 64 m (210 ft) from
end to end. It houses 200,000
antiquarian texts,
marble busts of
scholars and the
oldest harp in
Ireland. Below
the Library is the
Treasury, where
the college's
most precious
volumes – the
beautifully
illuminated
manuscripts
produced in
Ireland from the
7th to the 9th
century – are
kept. The most
famous, the *Book of Kells (see
p125)*, may have been created
by monks from Iona, who fled
to Kells in 806 after a Viking
raid. The scribes embellished
the text with intricate patterns
as well as human figures and
animals. Almost as fine is the
Book of Durrow, which dates
from the late 7th century.

**Portrait of St. Matthew
from the Book of Kells**

Merrion Square ②

DART to Pearse. 5, 7A, 8, 10,
45 & many others.

Merrion Square is one of
Dublin's largest and grandest
Georgian squares. Covering
about 5 ha (12 acres), the
square was laid out by John
Ensor around 1762.

On the west side are the
impressive façades of the
Natural History Museum, the
National Gallery
and the front
garden of
Leinster House,
seat of the Dáil
and the Seanad
(the two houses
of the Irish
Parliament). The
other three sides
of the square are
lined with lovely
Georgian town
houses. Many
have brightly
painted doors
and original
features such as
wrought-iron balconies,
ornate doorknockers and fan-
lights. The oldest and finest
houses are on the north side.

Many of the houses – now
predominantly used as office
space – have plaques detailing
famous former occupants,
such as Catholic emancipation
leader Daniel O'Connell, who

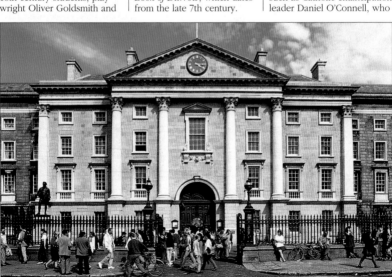

Façade of Trinity College, Dublin, the Republic's most prestigious university

For hotels and restaurants in this region see pp136–7 and pp138–9

Georgian town houses overlooking Merrion Square gardens

lived at No. 58, and poet W.B. Yeats (No. 82). Oscar Wilde spent his childhood at No. 1.

The attractive central park has colorful flower and shrub beds. In the 1840s it served a grim function as a soup kitchen, feeding the hungry during the Great Famine.

National Gallery ③

Merrion Square West. **Tel** 01-661 5133. ☒ DART to Pearse. ▥ 5, 7, 45 & 48A. ☐ daily (pm only Sun). ◉ Good Fri & Dec 24–26. ☑ ☒ ☓ ☒ ☐ ☐ ⅱ www.nationalgallery.ie

This purpose-built gallery was opened to the public in 1864. More than 700 works are on display and, although there is a strong emphasis on Irish landscapes and portraits, all major schools of European painting are represented. The ground-floor rooms show Irish and British art, including a whole section dedicated to the works of Jack B. Yeats (1871–1957). There are also paintings by his father and sisters.

Over the years the gallery has benefited from many generous bequests. Playwright George Bernard Shaw left a third of his estate to it. The Shaw Fund Gallery is an elegant hall, lined with full-length portraits, dating from the 17th century onward, and lit by magnificent Waterford Crystal chandeliers.

On the first floor works are hung in broadly chronological order according to nation. The Italian, French, Flemish and Dutch collections

account for most of the space. Caravaggio's *The Taking of Christ,* a major attraction, hung unrecognized for years in the Dublin Jesuit House of Study, until rediscovered in 1990.

National Museum ④

Kildare St. **Tel** 01-677 7444. ☒ DART to Pearse. ▥ 10, 11, 13 and many others. ☐ Tue–Sat & 2–5pm Sun. ◉ Good Fri & Dec 25. ☑ ☒ ☓ ☒ � ground floor only. www.museum.ie

The National Museum of Ireland (Archaeology and History) was built in the 1880s to the design of Sir Thomas Deane. Its splendid domed rotunda features marble pillars and a zodiac mosaic floor. The ground floor holds *Ór– Ireland's Gold*, a collection of Bronze Age finds, including many beautiful pieces of jewelry. Objects from the later Iron Age Celtic period are on display in the Treasury. There are also many well-known treasures from the era of Irish Christianity *(see pp124–5).*

The Road to Independence exhibition covers events between 1900 and 1921. The objects associated with the 1916 Easter Rising include the

The Taking of Christ by Caravaggio (1602), one of the highlights of the National Gallery

Republican flag that flew briefly over Dublin's General Post Office in O'Connell Street *(see p120).*

The first floor houses Viking artifacts and the Ancient Egypt gallery. The Viking exhibition features coins, pottery, and swords excavated in the 1970s from the Viking settlement, discovered beside the Liffey at Wood Quay near Christ Church Cathedral *(see p119).*

The Museum has another branch at Benburb Street, west of the city center. Housed in the vast Collins Barracks, established in 1700 by William III, this annex is gradually being extended to fill all four barrack blocks. The principal exhibits are the museum's collections of furniture, silver, and scientific instruments.

7th-century plaque depicting the Crucifixion, National Museum

Grafton Street ⑤

▥ 14, 15, 46 & many others.

The spine of Dublin's most stylish shopping district runs south from College Green to the glass St. Stephen's Green Shopping Centre. This busy pedestrianized strip, with its energetic buskers and talented street theater artists, boasts one of Dublin's best department stores, Brown Thomas, and popular traditional pubs hidden along the side streets.

At the junction with Nassau Street is a statue by Jean Rynhart of *Molly Malone* (1988), the celebrated "cockles and mussels" street trader of the well-known Irish folk song.

Shoppers in Temple Bar

Temple Bar ⑥

🚌 *11, 16A, 16B, 19A.* 🚏 *St. Andrews church (01-605 7700).* **Project** *39 East Essex Street.* **Tel** *01-881 9613.* ⏲ *11am–7pm Mon–Sat; shows nightly.* 📺 ♿

The area of cobbled streets between Dame Street and the Liffey are named after Sir William Temple who acquired the land in the early 1600s. The term "bar" meant a riverside path. In the 1800s it was home to small businesses, but over the years went into decline. In the early 1960s the land was bought up with plans for redevelopment. Artists and retailers took short-term leases but stayed on when the plans were scrapped and Temple Bar prospered. Today it is an exciting place, with restaurants, bars, clubs, shops, and galleries. Organizations based here include the **Irish Film Institute**, which has two screens, as well as a bookshop and café, **Project**, a contemporary arts center for theater, dance, music, film, and visual art, and the **Gallery of Photography**, the only Irish art gallery to be devoted solely to photographs.

St. Patrick's Cathedral ⑧

St. Patrick's Close. **Tel** *01-475 4817.* 🚌 *49A, 49B, 54A, 65A, 65B, 123.* ⏲ *daily.* 📷 ♿

Ireland's largest church was founded beside a sacred well where St. Patrick is said to have baptized converts around AD 450. It was originally just a wooden chapel, but in 1192 Archbishop John Comyn commissioned a magnificent new stone structure.

Jonathan Swift, Dean of St. Patrick's from 1713

The cathedral is 91 m (300 ft) long; at the western end is a 43-m (141-ft) tower, restored by Archbishop Minot in 1370 and now known as Minot's Tower. Much of the present building dates back to work completed between 1254 and 1270. Thanks to the generosity of Sir Benjamin

Dublin Castle ⑦

For seven centuries Dublin Castle was a symbol of English rule, ever since the Anglo-Normans built a fortress here in the 13th century. Nothing remains of the original structure except the much-modified Record Tower and the butt of the Powder Tower. After a fire in 1684, the Surveyor-General, Sir William Robinson, laid down the plans for the Upper and Lower Castle Yards in their present form. On the first floor of the south side of the Upper Yard are the luxurious State Apartments, formerly home to the British-appointed Viceroys of Ireland. They are still used for state occasions.

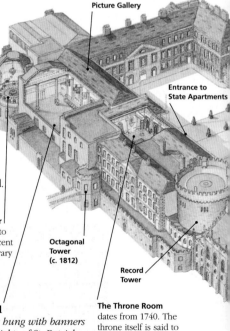

Picture Gallery

Entrance to State Apartments

Octagonal Tower (c. 1812)

Record Tower

Bermingham Tower has been adapted to house the magnificent Chester Beatty Library and Gallery of Oriental Art.

St. Patrick's Hall
This grand hall is hung with banners of the defunct Knights of St. Patrick. The 18th-century ceiling paintings are allegories of the relationship between Britain and Ireland.

The Throne Room dates from 1740. The throne itself is said to have been presented to William of Orange after his victory at the Battle of the Boyne *(see p110).*

For hotels and restaurants in this region see pp136–7 and pp138–9

Guinness, the cathedral underwent extensive restoration during the 1860s.

The interior is dotted with memorials. The most elaborate is the one erected in 1632 by Richard Boyle, Earl of Cork, in memory of his second wife Katherine. It is decorated with painted carvings of members of the Boyle family. Others remembered in the church include the harpist Turlough O'Carolan (1670–1738) and Douglas Hyde (1860–1949), Ireland's first President.

Many visitors come to see the memorials associated with Jonathan Swift (1667–1745), Dean of St. Patrick's and a scathing satirist, best known as the author of *Gulliver's Travels*. In the north transept is "Swift's Corner," which has various memorabilia such as an altar table and a bookcase holding his death mask. On the southwest side of the nave, two brass plates mark his grave and that of his beloved "Stella", Ester Johnson.

Christ Church Cathedral ⑨

Christchurch Place. **Tel** *01-677 8099.* 🚌 *49A, 49B, 50, 54A, 65A, 65B, 66, 77, 123.* ◯ *daily.* 📷 ♿ *limited.* **www.cccdub.ie**

The cathedral was commissioned in 1172 by Richard de Clare, known as Strongbow, the Anglo-Norman conqueror of Dublin, and by Archbishop Laurence O'Toole. It replaced an earlier wooden church built by the Vikings. At the Reformation, the cathedral passed to the Protestant Church of Ireland. By the middle of the 19th century it was in very bad repair, but was completely remodeled by architect George Street in the 1870s. Even so, the north wall, the one closest to the river, still leans out alarmingly as a result of subsidence. As part

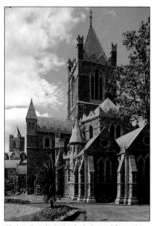

Christ Church Cathedral viewed from the east, with the Old Synod Hall behind

of the remodeling, the Old Synod Hall was built and linked to the cathedral by an attractive covered bridge.

In the dark, dusty crypt are fragments removed from the cathedral during its restoration. There are also the mummified bodies of a cat and a rat found in an organ pipe in the 1860s. The nave has some fine early Gothic arches. At the west end is a memorial known as the Strongbow Monument. The large effigy in chain armor is probably not Strongbow, but the curious half-figure beside it may be part of his original tomb. The Chapel of St. Laud houses a casket containing the heart of St. Laurence O'Toole.

Dublinia ⑩

St. Michael's Hill. **Tel** *01-679 4611.* 🚌 *49A, 49B, 54A, 123.* ◯ *daily.* ● *Mar 17, Dec 23–26.* 📷 ♿ **www.dublinia.ie**

Housed in the Neo-Gothic Synod Hall, which is linked by a bridge to Christ Church Cathedral, the Dublinia covers the period of Dublin's history from the arrival of the Anglo-Normans in 1170 to the closure of the monasteries in the 1540s. An audiotape-guided tour takes visitors through lifesize reconstructions of the medieval city. Up until 1983, the Synod Hall was home to the ruling body of the Church of Ireland.

Bedford Tower (1760)

Entrance to Upper Yard

Lower Yard

Church of the Most Holy Trinity (1814)

Government offices

VISITORS' CHECKLIST

Off Dame St. **Tel** *01-645 8812.* 🚌 *49, 56A, 77, 77A, 123.* **State Apartments** ◯ *daily.* ● *Jan 1, Good Fri, Dec 24–27.* 📷 📹 *obligatory.* **Library and Gallery of Oriental Art** Bermingham Tower. **Tel** *01- 407 0750.* ◯ *May–Sep: daily; Oct–Apr: Tue–Sun.* ● *Jan 1, Dec 24–26.* ♿

Figure of Justice
Cynical Dubliners have joked that this statue above the castle entrance appears to be turning her back on the city.

James Gandon's Four Courts overlooking the River Liffey

The Liffey ⑪

🚌 25, 25A, 51, 66, 66A, 67, 67A, 68, 69 and many others.

Though modest in size compared with the rivers of other capital cities, the Liffey features strongly in Dubliners' everyday lives and holds a special place in their affections. The handiest pedestrian link between Temple Bar (see p118) and the north of the city is **Ha'penny Bridge**. This attractive, cast-iron bridge, originally called Wellington Bridge, was opened in 1816. Its official name now is the Liffey Bridge. Its better-known nickname comes from the toll of a halfpenny levied on it up until 1919.

The two most impressive buildings on the Liffey are the **Custom House** and the **Four Courts**, both designed by

Carved head representing the River Liffey on the Custom House

James Gandon at the end of the 18th century. In 1921, supporters of Sinn Fein celebrated their election victory by setting light to the Custom House, seen as a symbol of British imperialism. The building was not fully restored until 1991, when it reopened as government offices. A series of 14 magnificent heads by Edward Smyth, personifying Ireland's rivers and the Atlantic Ocean, form the keystones of arches and entrances.

The Four Courts suffered a similar fate during the Irish Civil War of 1921–2, when it was bombarded by government troops after being seized by anti-Treaty rebels. Here too, the buildings were restored to their original design. A copper-covered lantern dome rises above a Corinthian portico crowned with the figures of Moses, Justice and Mercy.

The monument to Daniel O'Connell

O'Connell Street ⑫

🚌 3, 10, 11, 13, 16A, 22A, 22B, 120 and many others.

Dublin's main thoroughfare, formerly called Sackville Street, was renamed in 1922 after Daniel O'Connell, who was known as the "Liberator"

for his tireless campaigns for Catholic rights in the 19th century. The street was laid out in the 18th century as an elegant residential parade, but the construction of Carlisle (now O'Connell) Bridge in 1790 turned it into the city's principal north-south route. As a result, little remains of its intended grandeur.

A few venerable buildings survive, including the **General Post Office**. Built in 1818, the GPO became a symbol of the 1916 Easter Rising. Members of the Irish Volunteers and Irish Citizen Army seized the building on Easter Monday, and Patrick Pearse read out the Proclamation of the Irish Republic from its steps. The rebels remained inside for a week, but shelling from the British eventually forced them out. During the following weeks, 14 of the leaders were caught and shot. Inside the building is a sculpture of the mythical Irish hero Cuchulainn, dedicated to those who died.

A walk up the central mall is the best way to inspect the series of sculptures lining the route. At the south end stands a massive memorial to Daniel O'Connell, unveiled in 1882. In the middle is the Monument of Light, an elegant stainless steel spire erected in 2003. At the north end is the obelisk-shaped monument to Charles Stewart Parnell (1846–91).

Parnell Square ⑬

🚌 *3, 10, 11A, 13, 16A, 16B, 19A, 22A, 22B.* **Dublin Writers Museum** 18 Parnell Sq North. *Tel 01-872 2077.* ⏺ *daily.* ⬤ *Dec 25–26.* 🏛 **Dublin City Gallery, The Hugh Lane** Charlemont House. *Tel 01-222 5565.* ⏺ *Tue–Sun.* ⬤ *Dec 23–28.*

The square at the top of O'Connell Street looks sadly neglected. Even so, it contains a number of noteworthy sights, including the **Rotunda Hospital**, Europe's first purpose-built maternity hospital, founded in 1745. Its chapel has some fine Rococo stuccowork. The former grand supper room of the hospital is now the **Gate Theatre**, famous for producing new plays.

On the north side of the square, two grand 18th-century townhouses have been converted into museums: the **Dublin Writers Museum**, devoted to Irish literature, and the **Dublin City Gallery, The Hugh Lane**. The latter houses the Impressionist paintings bequeathed to Dublin Corporation by Sir Hugh Lane, who died on the torpedoed liner *Lusitania* in 1915. The square also contains a **Garden of Remembrance** opened in 1966 on the 50th anniversary of the Easter Rising.

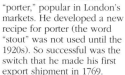

Arthur Guinness

Guinness Storehouse ⑭

St. James's Gate, Dublin 8. *Tel 01-408 4800.* 🚌 *51B, 78A, 123.* ⏺ *daily.* ⬤ *Good Fri, Dec 24–26, Jan 1.* 🏛♿🅿🍴🛍 www.guinness-storehouse.com

Guinness is a black beer, known as "stout," renowned for its distinctive malty flavor and smooth creamy head. The Guinness brewery site at St James's Gate is the largest brewery in Europe and exports beers to more than 120 countries.

The World of Guinness exhibition is housed in a 19th-century warehouse, used for hop storage until the 1950s. It chronicles 200 years of brewing at St James's Gate. The tour starts in a Victorian kieve (or mash filter), and goes on to examine all other stages of the brewing process. Displays show how production methods have changed over the years since 1759, when Arthur Guinness took over the backstreet brewery. Guinness started brewing ale, but was aware of a black beer called "porter," popular in London's markets. He developed a new recipe for porter (the word "stout" was not used until the 1920s). So successful was the switch that he made his first export shipment in 1769.

The tour ends with an audiovisual show, followed by a visit to the sampling bar where you can enjoy a couple of glasses of draft Guinness.

The Phoenix Column

Phoenix Park ⑮

Park Gate, Conyngham Rd, Dublin 8. 🚌 *10, 25, 26, 37, 38, 39.* ⏺ *daily.* **Visitor Center** *Tel 01-677 0095.* ⏺ *mid-Mar–Oct: daily; Nov–mid-Mar: Sat –Wed.* ♿ *limited.* **Zoo** *Tel 01-474 8900.* ⏺ *daily.* 🏛🅿🍴♿

Just to the west of the city center, ringed by an 11-km (7-mile) wall, is Europe's largest enclosed city park. The name "Phoenix" is said to be a corruption of the Gaelic Fionn Uisce, or "clear water." The Phoenix Column is crowned by a statue of the mythical bird. The park originated in 1662, when the Duke of Ormonde turned the land into a deer park. It was opened to the public in 1745.

Near Park Gate is the lake-side People's Garden. A little further on are the Zoological Gardens, which are renowned for the breeding of lions, including the one that introduces MGM movies.

The park has two very conspicuous monuments. The Wellington Testimonial is a 63-m (204-ft) obelisk, begun in 1817 and completed in 1861. Its bronze bas-reliefs were made from captured French cannons. The 27-m (90-ft) steel Papal Cross marks the spot where the pope said Mass in front of one million people in 1979. Buildings within the park include two 18th-century houses: Áras an Uachtaráin, the Irish President's official residence, for which 525 tickets are issued every Saturday for a free guided tour, and Deerfield, home of the US ambassador. Ashtown Castle is a restored 17th-century tower house, now the Phoenix Park Visitor Centre.

The Gallery of Writers at the Dublin Writers Museum, Parnell Square

Southeast Ireland

Enjoying the warmest climate in Ireland, the Southeast has always presented an attractive prospect for invaders and settlers. Its highlights include the Neolithic tombs in the Valley of the Boyne, early Christian monastic sites, and towns such as Waterford that grew from Viking settlements. It is also the setting for many great 18th-century houses built by the ruling English aristocracy. The wildest landscapes of the region are to be found in the forested hills and desolate moorland of the Wicklow Mountains south of Dublin.

Elegant stuccoed hall and staircase in Castletown House

Castletown House ❷

Celbridge, Co. Kildare. **Tel** 01-628 8252. 🚌 67, 67A from Dublin. ◯ Easter Sun–Sep: daily (pm only Sat, Sun & public hols); Oct: Mon–Fri & Sun. 🎟 obligatory. 🚫 🖥 ♿

Built in 1722–32 for William Conolly, Speaker of the Irish Parliament, Castletown was Ireland's first grand Palladian-style country house. Most of the interiors were commissioned by Lady Louisa Lennox, wife of Conolly's great-nephew, Tom, who lived here in the late 18th century. It was she who added the magnificent long gallery at the top of the house, with its Pompeiian-style friezes, cobalt-blue walls and niches framing Classical statuary. From the long gallery visitors can admire the curious obelisk-topped memorial to Speaker Conolly erected by his widow in 1740.

A portrait of Lady Louisa is incorporated in the superb Rococo stuccowork by the Francini brothers in the staircase hall. Another personal reminder of Lady Louisa is the print room, the last surviving, intact example of its kind. In the 18th century, ladies pasted prints directly on to the wall and framed them with elaborate festoons. Castletown remained in the family until 1965.

Newgrange ❸

8 km (5 miles) E of Slane, Co. Meath. 🚆 to Drogheda. 🚌 to visitor centre via Drogheda. **Brú na Bóinne Interpretive Centre Tel** 041-988 0300. ◯ daily. ● Dec 24–27. 🎟 obligatory. 🚫 in tomb. 🖥 🏫

The origins of Newgrange, one of the most important passage graves in Europe, are steeped in mystery. Built around 3200 BC, the grave was rediscovered in 1699. When it was excavated in the 1960s, archaeologists realized that at dawn on the winter solstice (December 21) a beam of sunlight shines through the roof box, a rectangular opening above the entrance to the tomb and a feature unique to Newgrange. The light travels along the 19-m (62-ft) passage and hits the central recess in the burial chamber. It is thus the world's oldest solar observatory.

Between 1962 and 1975 the grave and the mound, or cairn, covering it were restored. The retaining wall at the front of the cairn was rebuilt using white quartz and granite stones found scattered around the site. It is estimated that the original tomb, created by people who had neither the wheel nor metal tools, may have taken up to 70 years to build. About 200,000 tons of loose stones were transported to build the cairn. Larger slabs were used to make the circle around the cairn and the retaining kerb. Many of the kerbstones and the slabs lining the passage and chamber are decorated with zigzags, spirals, and other geometric motifs.

Each of the three recesses in the central chamber contained a chiseled "basin stone" that held funerary offerings and the bones of the dead. The chamber's corbeled ceiling has proved completely water-proof for 5,000 years.

Newgrange is very popular, especially in summer, so visits are by tour only and you have to wait your turn at the **Brú na Bóinne Interpretive Centre**. This has displays on the area's Stone Age heritage. The tour includes the nearby tomb at Knowth. The last one starts at 3:15pm in winter and at 5:15pm in midsummer.

Aerial view of Newgrange, showing the cairn and circle of standing stones

Round tower at Glendalough

Glendalough ④

Co. Wicklow. St. Kevin's Bus from Dublin. **Ruins** ◯ daily. in summer. **Visitors' Center Tel** 0404-45352. ◯ daily. ● Dec 24–27. limited.

The steep, wooded slopes of Glendalough, the "valley of the two lakes," harbor one of Ireland's most atmospheric ruined monasteries. Founded by St. Kevin in the 6th century, it functioned as a monastic center until the Dissolution of the Monasteries in 1539.

Most of the buildings date from the 8th to 12th centuries. The reconstruction (see pp124–5) shows how the monastery may have looked in its heyday. The main ruins lie near the smaller Lower Lake. You enter the monastery through the double stone arch of the gatehouse, from where a short walk leads to a graveyard with a restored round tower in one corner. Other ruins include the roofless cathedral, the tiny Priest's House and the 12th-century St. Kevin's Cross. Below, nestled in the lush valley, stands a small oratory. It is popularly known as St. Kevin's Kitchen, because its belfry resembles a chimney.

A path along the south bank of the river leads to the Upper Lake and some of the other buildings associated with St. Kevin. Here, the scenery is wilder and you are better able to enjoy the tranquillity of Glendalough.

Kilkenny ⑤

Co. Kilkenny. 20,000. Shee Almshouse, Rose Inn St (056-775 1500). Kilkenny Arts Week (Aug).

In a lovely setting beside the River Nore, Kilkenny is Ireland's most attractive inland city. Many of its houses feature the local black limestone, known as Kilkenny marble. The city is proud of its heritage and hosts a major arts festival. It is also a brewery city, filled with atmospheric old pubs.

Built in the 1190s, **Kilkenny Castle** was the seat of the Anglo-Norman Butler family from the late 14th century up until 1967. With its drum towers and solid walls, the castle retains its medieval form, but has undergone many alterations. The Long Gallery, rebuilt in the 1820s to house the Butler art collection, has a striking hammerbeam and glass roof. The painted ceiling has a strong Pre-Raphaelite feel, with motifs inspired by the Book of Kells (see p125).

The area known, in the days of segregation, as Englishtown boasts the city's grandest buildings, such as Rothe House, a fine Tudor merchant's house, built around two courtyards. The area of narrow alleyways or "slips" is part of Kilkenny's medieval heritage.

The Irishtown district is dominated by **St. Canice's Cathedral** and a round tower that you can climb for a good view of the city. The Gothic cathedral dates from the 13th century. It has a finely sculpted west door and an array of 16th-century tombs with beautiful effigies of the Butler family in the south transept.

Waterford ⑥

Co. Waterford. 44,000. The Granary, Merchant's Quay (051-875 823). Sat. International Festival of Light Opera (Oct).

Ireland's oldest city, Waterford was founded by the Vikings in 914, and later extended by the Anglo-Normans. Its commanding position on the Suir estuary made it southeast Ireland's main port. The 18th century saw the establishment of local industries, including the world-famous glassworks.

The remains of the city walls define the area fortified by the Normans. The largest surviving structure is **Reginald's Tower**, overlooking the river. Although the city retains its medieval layout, most of the finest buildings are Georgian, including **Christchurch Cathedral**, designed in the 1770s by local architect John Roberts. From June to August you can admire the waterfront by taking a pleasure cruise on the river.

Waterford Crystal decanter

The **Waterford Crystal Factory** lies 2.5 km (1.5 miles) south of the center. The original factory was founded in 1783, but closed in 1851. A new factory opened in 1947.

Tomb of 2nd Marquess of Ormonde in St. Canice's Cathedral, Kilkenny

Early Celtic Christianity

Ireland became Christian in the 5th century, following the missions of St. Patrick and others. The situation was soon reversed, with many Irish missionaries, such as St. Columba and St. Columbanus, sailing to Great Britain, France, and beyond. The Irish church developed more or less free from the control of Rome, but nevertheless had strong links with the east. As in Egypt, the Christian faith inspired a proliferation of hermitages and remote monasteries. Decorative motifs in illuminated manuscripts reflect Egyptian Christian imagery, and materials used in making the inks came from the Middle East. The advent of the Vikings in the 9th century forced the monasteries to take defensive measures, but they continued to flourish despite frequent raids.

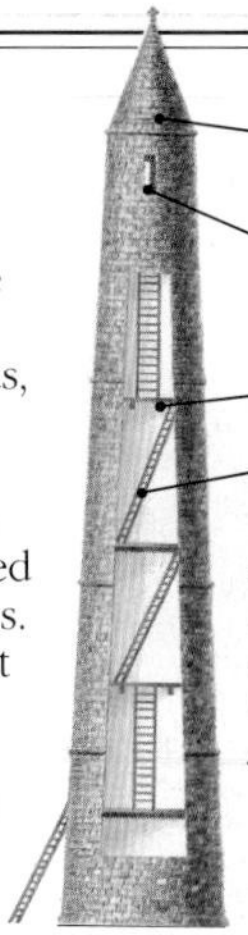

Conical roof

Lookout window

Wooden floor

Movable ladder

Round towers, *first built in the 10th century, were bell towers and refuges from Viking raids. The entrance could be 4 m (13 ft) above ground and was reached by a ladder.*

CELTIC MONASTERY

This reconstruction shows Glendalough in about 1100. Monasteries were probably the largest centers of population in Ireland before the Vikings started to found towns.

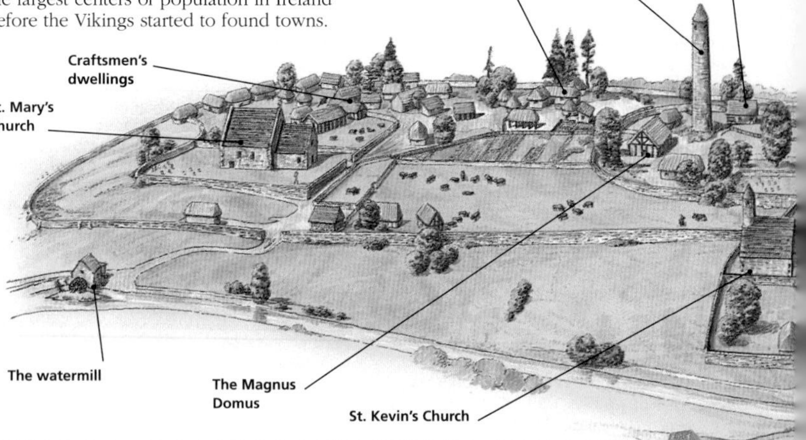

Refectory and kitchen

Abbot's house

Craftsmen's dwellings

St. Mary's Church

The watermill

The Magnus Domus

St. Kevin's Church

IRELAND'S HIGH CROSSES

High Crosses are found in parts of Britain as well as Ireland, yet in their profusion and craftsmanship, Irish crosses are exceptional. The ringed cross has become a symbol of Irish Christianity and is still imitated today. The medieval High Crosses were carved between the 8th and 12th centuries. Early ones, such as the 8th-century cross at Ahenny, bore spirals and interlacing patterns, but in the 9th and 10th centuries a new style emerged with sculpted scenes from the bible, "sermons in stone," aimed at educating a largely illiterate population.

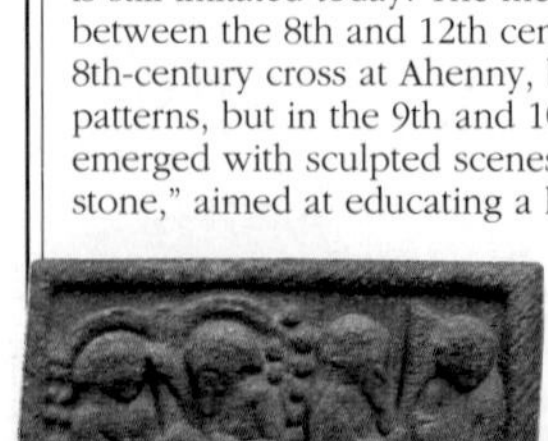

Muiredach's Cross at Monasterboice is the finest surviving example of a cross carved with biblical scenes. This panel shows the Fall of Man: Eve offering Adam the apple in the Garden of Eden and Cain slaying Abel.

Ornamental High Cross at Ahenny

Cross of the Scriptures, Clonmacnoise

THE BOOK OF KELLS

The most richly decorated of all the Irish illuminated manuscripts dating from the 8th–10th centuries, the Book of Kells contains the four gospels in Latin, copied onto leaves of high-quality vellum. It is remarkable both for the beauty of the script and for the inspired fantasy of the illumination. There is no record of its existence before the early 11th century, but it was probably created in about 800. It would have taken many years of work by the

Page of the Genealogy of Christ from the Book of Kells

scriptorium of a monastery. It may have been brought to Kells by monks from Iona who fled to Ireland after a Viking raid in 806. The manuscript was moved to Trinity College *(see p116)* in the 17th century for safe-keeping.

WHERE TO SEE EARLY CHRISTIAN SITES IN IRELAND

Important early Christian sites besides Glendalough include Clonmacnoise, the Rock of Cashel *(see p126)*, Clonfert, Kells, and Devenish Island. Though most of the monastic buildings are ruins, they have usually continued to be used as cemeteries right up to modern times. Monasteries were built on the Aran Islands *(see p129)* and even on the remote rocky Skellig Michael off the Dingle Peninsula. Round towers and High Crosses are preserved all over Ireland, often standing beside churches of much more recent construction.

Clonmacnoise *was founded in the 6th century. The monastery was noted for its piety and scholarship. Now it is an atmospheric collection of ruins in a remote spot on the Shannon. This carved Romanesque doorway is part of the Nun's Church.*

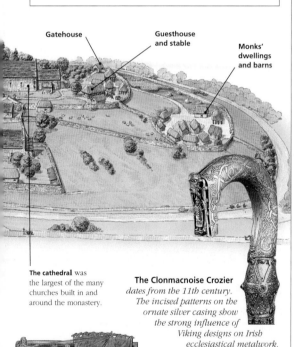

Gatehouse — Guesthouse and stable — Monks' dwellings and barns

The cathedral was the largest of the many churches built in and around the monastery.

The Clonmacnoise Crozier *dates from the 11th century. The incised patterns on the ornate silver casing show the strong influence of Viking designs on Irish ecclesiastical metalwork.*

The Voyage of St. Brendan *is a fantastic legend of early medieval Irish Christianity. The 6th-century saint and his followers set sail into the Atlantic in a small boat, sighting volcanic islands, ice floes, whales, and even, some say, America.*

Devenish Island *has a fine restored round tower and enjoys a peaceful setting on Lower Lough Erne. Lake islands were popular as monastic sites.*

Southwest Ireland

Magnificent scenery has attracted visitors to this region since Victorian times. Killarney and its romantic lakes are a powerful magnet for tourists, as is the attractive coastline of Cork and Kerry, where rocky headlands jut out into the Atlantic and colorful fishing villages nestle in the bays. Yet much of the southwest remains unspoiled, with a friendly atmosphere and authentic culture still alive in Irish-speaking pockets.

The Rock of Cashel

Cashel ❼

Co. Tipperary. 🏛 2,500. 🚌 ⓘ
Heritage Centre, Main St (062- 62511).
Rock Tel 062-61437. ⭘ daily. ◉
Dec 24–26. 📷 ✔ ♿ limited.

The town's great attraction is the magnificent medieval Rock of Cashel. Many people stay overnight to enjoy eerie floodlit views of the rocky stronghold rising dramatically out of the Tipperary plain. The Rock was a symbol of royal and ecclesiastical power for more than a thousand years. From the 5th century AD it was the seat of the Kings of Munster, rulers of southwest Ireland. In 1101, they handed

Cashel over to the Church, and it flourished as a religious center until a siege by a Cromwellian army in 1647 ended in the massacre of its 3,000 occupants.

A good proportion of the medieval complex still stands, though the main building, the Gothic cathedral, is roofless. The earlier Cormac's Chapel is an outstanding example of Romanesque architecture. Other prominent features of the Rock are a restored round tower and the weatherbeaten St. Patrick's Cross. The carved figure on the east face of the cross is said to be St. Patrick.

Cork ❽

Co. Cork. 🏛 136,000. 🚉 🚌
ⓘ Tourist House, Grand Parade
(0214-255 100). 🎷 Jazz Festival
(Oct); Film Festival (Oct).

Cork city derives its name from the marshy banks of the River Lee – its Irish name Corcaigh means marsh – where St. Finbarr founded a monastery around AD 650. The center of Cork today occupies an island between two arms of the river. Its waterways,

bridges, and narrow alleys, combined with the Georgian architecture of the old Quays, give Cork a continental feel. In the 18th century many of today's streets were waterways lined with warehouses and merchants' residences.

Noted for its chic bars, ethnic restaurants, bookshops, and boutiques, Paul Street is the hub of the liveliest district in town. The nearby **Crawford Art Gallery** has some fine Irish works of art.

A prominent landmark is the steeple of **St. Anne Shandon** on a hill in the north of the city. It is topped by a weather vane in the shape of a salmon. Visitors can climb up and ring the famous Shandon bells.

🏛 **Crawford Art Gallery**
Emmet Place. **Tel** 0214-907 855.
⭘ 10am–5pm Mon–Sat. ◉ public
hols, Dec 24–Jan 3. ⦿ ▭ ▯ ♿

The battlemented keep and other ruined towers of Blarney Castle

Environs
Beautiful countryside surrounds Cork, especially along the valley of the Lee river. Popular outings include a tour of the whiskey-making **Old Midleton Distillery**, and a trip to **Blarney Castle** and the legendary stone that bestows magical eloquence on all who kiss it. There are also plenty of opportunities for walking and fishing.

🏛 **Old Midleton Distillery**
Midleton, Co. Cork. **Tel** 0214-613
594. ⭘ daily. ◉ Dec 24–26,
Dec 31–Jan 1. 📷 ⦿ ▭ ▯ ♿

♣ **Blarney Castle**
Blarney, Co. Cork. **Tel** 0214-
385252. ⭘ daily. ◉ Dec 24–25.
ⓘ ♿ grounds only.

South channel of the Lee river flowing through the city of Cork

For hotels and restaurants in this region see pp136–7 and pp138–9

Newman's Mall in the quaint village of Kinsale

Kinsale ❾

Co. Cork. ⚇ *3,400*. ▭ ❶ *Pier Road (0214-772 234)*. ⚑ *Regatta (Aug); Festival of Fine Food (Oct)*.

For many visitors to Ireland, Kinsale heads the list of places to see. One of the prettiest small towns in Ireland, it has had a long and checkered history. The defeat of the Irish forces and their Spanish allies at the Battle of Kinsale in 1601 signalled the end of the old Gaelic order.

An important naval base in the 17th and 18th centuries, Kinsale today is a popular yachting center. It is also famous for the quality of its cuisine and has a popular annual Festival of Fine Food.

Charles Fort, a fine example of a star-shaped bastion fort, was built by the English in the 1670s to protect Kinsale against foreign naval forces. To reach it take the signposted coastal walk from the quayside.

♣ Charles Fort
3 km (2 miles) E of Kinsale.
Tel 0214-772 263. ☐ *mid-Mar–Oct: 10am–6pm daily; Nov–mid-Mar: 10am–5pm daily. Last adm: 1 hr before closing*. ● *Christmas week*. ▨ ▧ ▣ ⚇ *limited*.

Killarney ❿

Co. Kerry. ⚇ *9,500*. ▯ ▭
❶ *Beech Road (064-31633)*.

Killarney is often derided as "a tourist town" but this does not detract from its cheer- ful atmosphere. The infectious Kerry humor is personified by the wise-cracking "jarveys," whose families have run jaunting cars (pony and trap

rides) here for generations. The town does get very crowded in the summer but this is inevitable, given the lure of the **Lakes of Killarney**. The three lakes and many of the heather-covered hills surrounding them lie within **Killarney National Park**. Although the landscape is dotted with ruined castles and abbeys, the lakes are the focus of attention: the moody watery scenery is subject to subtle shifts of light and color. Well-known beauty spots include the Meeting of the Waters, the Ladies' View, so called because it delighted Queen Victoria's ladies-in-waiting in 1861, and the Gap of Dunloe, a dramatic mountain pass. The largest of the lakes, Lough Leane, is dotted with uninhabited islands. Boat trips across the lake run from Ross Castle on the shore nearest Killarney.

Overlooking the lakes is **Muckross House**, an imposing mansion built in 1843 in Elizabethan style, set in beautiful landscaped gardens. It houses a museum of Kerry Life, with displays on the history of southwest Ireland, and a craft center.

The town is also the starting point for the popular **Ring of Kerry** tour around the Iveragh Peninsula. Allow a day's drive to enjoy its captivating mountain and coastal scenery.

🏛 Muckross House
4 km (2.5 miles) S of Killarney. *Tel 064-31440*. ☐ *daily*. ● *Christmas week*. ▨ ▧ ▣ ▢ ⚇

Dingle ⓫

Co. Kerry. ⚇ *2,100*. ▭ ❶ *Mar–Oct: Main St (06691-51188)*. ⊟ *Fri*.

This once remote Irish-speaking town is today a thriving fishing port and popular tourist center. Brightly painted – often fairly hippy – craft shops and cafés abound. Along the quayside are lively bars offering music and sea-food. The harbor is home to Dingle's biggest star, Fungie the dolphin, who has been a permanent resident since 1983 and can be visited by boat or on swimming trips.

Gallarus Oratory, a tiny dry-stone Early Christian church

Environs
Dingle is a good base for exploring the scattered archaeological remains of the Dingle Peninsula. The most fascinating is the **Gallarus Oratory**, northwest of Dingle. This miniature dry-stone church, shaped like an upturned boat, was built from the 6th to the 9th centuries. West of Dingle, along the coast road, are the Iron Age fort of Dunbeg and Early Christian beehive huts.

The Upper Lake, smallest and most remote of the Lakes of Killarney

Bunratty Castle ⑫

This formidable 15th-century castle is one of Ireland's major tourist attractions. Its most important residents were the O'Briens, Earls of Thomond, who lived here from around 1500 until the 1640s. The interior has been restored to look as it did under the so-called "Great Earl," who died in 1624. The adjacent Folk Park and the mock medieval banquets held in the castle attract busloads of visitors, but despite its commercialization, Bunratty is well worth a visit. The Folk Park recreates rural life at the end of the 19th century, with a whole village, complete with stores, a school, and dwellings ranging from a laborer's cottage to an elegant Georgian house.

VISITORS' CHECKLIST

Bunratty, Co. Clare. *Tel 061-360 788.* 🚌 *from Limerick, Ennis & Shannon Airport.* **Bunratty Castle** ⬜ *9:30am–5:30pm daily (Jul–Aug: 9am–6pm).* **Folk Park** ⬜ *9:30am–5:30pm (Jun–Aug: 9am–6pm) daily.* ⬤ *Good Fri, Dec 24–26.* 🎫 🍴 ♿ *to Folk Park.* www.shannonheritage.com

Great Hall
The castle's grandest room served as banqueting hall and audience chamber. Among the furnishings bought by the owner, Lord Gort, when he set about restoring the castle in the 1950s was this Tudor standard.

South Solar
This richly paneled "solar," or upper chamber, was a guest apartment.

Anteroom

The North Solar was the Great Earl's private apartment.

The Murder Hole was designed for pouring boiling water or pitch onto the heads of attackers.

Entrance

The Earl's Robing Room also served as a private audience chamber.

North Front
The entrance, raised well above ground level to deter invaders, is typical of castles of the period.

Main Guard
This was where the castle's soldiers ate, slept, and listened to music from the Minstrels' Gallery.

For hotels and restaurants in this region see pp136–7 and pp138–9

The imposing Kylemore Abbey on the shores of Kylemore Lough, Connemara

Galway ⓭

Co. Galway. 👥 56,000. 🚉 🚌
ℹ The Fairgreen, Foster St (091-537
700). 🚢 Sat. 🎨 Arts Festival (mid-
Jul); Galway Races (late Jul/Aug);
Oyster Festival (late Sep).

Galway is the center for the
Irish-speaking regions in the
West of Ireland and a lively
university city. In the 15th and
16th centuries it was a prosperous trading port, controlled
by 14 merchant families, or
"tribes." Its allegiance to the
English Crown cost the city
dear when, in 1652, it was
sacked by Cromwell's forces.
In the 18th century Galway
fell into decline, but in recent
years, its fortunes have revived
through high-tech industries.
    The city stands on the banks
of the Corrib river. Many of
the best stores, pubs, theaters,
and historic sights are packed
into the narrow lanes of the
"Latin Quarter" around Quay
Street. Nearby is the Collegiate
Church of St. Nicholas, the
city's finest medieval building.
To the south stands the 16th-
century Spanish Arch, where
ships from Spain unloaded
their cargoes. Across the
Corrib, facing the arch, is the
Claddagh. The only remnants
of this once close-knit, Gaelic-
speaking community are its
friendly pubs and Claddagh
rings – betrothal rings that are
traditionally handed down
from mother to daughter.

Connemara ⓮

Co. Galway. 🚌 to Clifden or
Letterfrack. ℹ Mar–Oct: Galway
Road, Clifden (095-21163). **National
Park Visitors' Center Tel** 095-41
054. ⏰ Mar–Oct: daily. 🎨 🖥 ♿

This wild region to the west
of Galway encompasses bogs,
mountains, and rugged
Atlantic coastline. The small
market town of Clifden is
a convenient and popular
base for exploring.
Starting from Clifden, the
Sky Road is an 11-km (7-
mile) circular route with
spectacular ocean views.
South of Clifden, the
coast road to Roundstone
skirts a massive bog,
impromptu landing site
of the first transatlantic
flight made by Alcock
and Brown in 1919.
    **Connemara National
Park** near Letterfrack
includes some spectacular
scenery, dominated by the
mountains known as the
Twelve Bens. Here visitors
have a chance to spot
red deer and the famous
Connemara ponies.

Nearby **Kylemore Abbey** is a
19th-century romantic, battlemented fantasy. It became
an abbey when Benedictine
nuns, fleeing from Belgium
during World War I, sought
refuge here. The building is
now a select girls' boarding
school, but its gardens, with
restaurant, shop, and
spectacular lakeside setting
make it a popular destination.

Aran Islands ⓯

Co. Galway. 👥 900. ✈ from Inverin
(091-593 034). ⛴ from Rossaveal
(091-568 903); from Doolin (Easter–
Oct: 065-707 4189). ℹ Kilronan,
Inishmore (099-61263). **Heritage
Center** ⏰ daily. 🎫 🎨 ♿

Inishmore, Inishmaan, and
Inisheer, the three Aran
Islands, are formed from a
limestone ridge. The largest,
Inishmore, is 13 km (8 miles)
long and 3 km (2 miles) wide.
The attractions of the islands
include the austere landscape
crisscrossed with dry-stone
walls, stunning coastal views,
and prehistoric stone forts.
The islands are a bastion of
traditional Irish culture with
most of the islanders engaged
in fishing, farming, or tourism.
Ferries sail at least once a day
in winter and several times
daily in summer. Cars cannot
be taken to the islands.
    At Kilronan on Inishmore,
jaunting cars (ponies and traps)
and minibuses wait by the pier
to give tours; bicycles can also
be hired. Nearby, the **Aran
Heritage Center** is dedicated
to the disappearing Aran way
of life. The islands are famous
for their distinctive knitwear
and traditional costumes.

Colorful shopfronts lining Quay Street
in Galway's "Latin Quarter"

Northern Ireland

The province of Northern Ireland was created after the partition of the island in 1921. Its six counties (plus Donegal, Monaghan, and Cavan, which became part of the Republic) were part of Ulster, one of Ireland's four traditional kingdoms. Though densely populated and industrialized around Belfast, away from the capital the region is primarily agricultural. It also has areas of outstanding natural beauty, notably the rugged Antrim coastline around the Giant's Causeway.

Mosaic of St. Patrick's journey to Ireland in Belfast Cathedral

Belfast ⓰

Co. Antrim. 🔂 500,000. ✈ 🚇 🚌
🛈 47 Donegall Place (028-9024 6609).
🎟 Royal Ulster Agricultural Show & Lord Mayor's Show (May); Belfast Festival at Queen's (late Oct–Nov).

Belfast was the only city in Ireland to experience the full force of the Industrial Revolution. Its shipbuilding, linen, rope-making, and tobacco industries caused the population to rise to almost 400,000 by the end of World War I. The wealth it enjoyed is still evident in its imposing banks, churches, and other public buildings. The Troubles and the decline of traditional industries have since damaged economic life, but Belfast remains a handsome city and most visitors are agreeably surprised by the genuine friendliness of the people.

Most of Belfast's main streets (and bus routes) radiate out from the hub of Donegall Square. In its center stands the vast Portland stone bulk of the 1906 **City Hall** with its huge central copper dome. Statues around the building include Queen Victoria at the front and, on the east side, Sir Edward Harland, founder of the Harland and Wolff shipyard, which built the *Titanic*. A memorial to those who died when the ship sank in 1912 stands close by.

Sights in and around the square include the **Linen Hall Library**, the late-Victorian **Grand Opera House** in Great Victoria Street, and Belfast's most famous pub, the **Crown Liquor Saloon**, which dates back to the 1880s.

The Neo-Romanesque **Belfast Cathedral** in Donegall Street is the Protestant cathedral, consecrated in 1904. The interior is remarkable for the vast mosaics added by the two Misses Martin in the 1920s. Lord Carson (1854–1935), implacable opponent of Home Rule, is buried in the south aisle.

Away from the center, Belfast has pleasant suburbs unaffected by the civil strife of recent times. The area around **Queen's University** to the south of the city has two major attractions in the **Ulster Museum** and the **Botanic Gardens**. The

Detail of Titanic Memorial outside Belfast City Hall

museum covers all aspects of Ulster, from archaeology to technology. Its treasures include jewelry from the *Girona*, a Spanish Armada ship that sank off the Giant's Causeway in 1588.

🏛 **Ulster Museum**
Botanic Gardens. **Tel** 028-9038 3000. ● for refurbishment until 2009. 🅿 ▢ ▢ ♿
www.ulstermuseum.org.uk

Giant's Causeway ⓱

Co. Antrim. 🚇 to Portrush. 🚌 from Portrush, Bushmills, or Coleraine.
Visitors' Center (028-2073 1855). ◯ daily. ▢ 🅿 on request. ♿ limited.

The sheer strangeness of the Giant's Causeway and the bizarre regularity of its basalt columns has made it the subject of numerous legends. The most popular tells how the giant, Finn MacCool, laid the causeway to provide a path across the sea to his lady love, who lived on the island of Staffa in Scotland, where there are similar rock formations. The geological explanation is that 61 million years ago, in a series of volcanic eruptions, molten lava poured from narrow fissures in the ground, filling in the valleys and

The ornate Victorian interior of the Crown Liquor Saloon

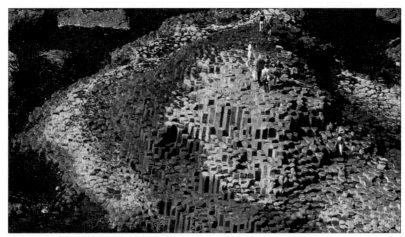

The extraordinarily regular columns of the Giant's Causeway exposed at low tide

burning the vegetation that grew here. The basalt lava cooled rapidly. In the process it shrank and cracked evenly into polygonal blocks. Towards the end of the Ice Age, erosion by sea ice exposed the rocks and shaped the Causeway. Most of the columns are hexagonal, but some have four, five, eight, or even ten sides. They are generally about 30 cm (12 in) across. There are in fact three causeways, the Grand, Middle, and Little. Distinctive features have been given poetic names, such as the "Honeycomb" and the "Wishing Chair."

Tourists arrive by the busload from the visitors' center. Nothing, however, can destroy the magic of the place, and it is easy to escape the crowds by taking one of the coastal paths.

Old Bushmills Distillery ⓲

Bushmills, Co. Antrim. *Tel* 028-2073 3218. 🚌 from Giant's Causeway & Coleraine. ☐ Apr–Oct: daily; Nov–Mar: daily (pm Sat & Sun). ● 2 weeks at Christmas. 🏷 🚻 🛒 obligatory. 🍴 🚹 limited.

Bushmills has an attractive square and an excellent river for salmon and trout fishing,

but its main claim to fame is whiskey. The Old Bushmills plant prides itself on being the oldest distillery in the world, its "Grant to Distil" dating from 1608.

In 1974 Bushmills joined the Irish Distillers Group based at the Midleton plant near Cork *(see p126)*, but its brands have retained their distinctive character. "Old Bushmills" is unusual in that it is made from a blend of single malt and a single grain. The tour of the distillery, which features audio-visual displays, ends with a sampling session in the "1608 Bar," which is housed in the former malt kilns.

Whiskey barrel at Old Bushmills

Ulster-American Folk Park ⓳

Co. Tyrone. *Tel* 028-8224 3292. 🚌 from Omagh. ☐ Apr–Sep: daily; Oct–Mar: Mon–Fri. 📷 🚹 🚻 🛒

One of the best open-air museums of its kind, the Folk Park grew up around the restored boyhood home of Judge Thomas Mellon (founder of the Pittsburgh banking dynasty). The park's permanent exhibition, called "Emigrants," examines why two million people left Ulster for America during the 18th and 19th centuries. It also

shows what became of them, following stories of both fortune and failure.

The park has more than 30 historic buildings, some of them original, some replicas. There are settler homesteads (including that of John Joseph Hughes, the first Catholic Archbishop of New York), churches, a schoolhouse, and a forge, some with craft displays, all with costumed interpretative guides. There's also an Ulster streetscape, a reconstructed emigrant ship, and a Pennsylvania farmstead, complete with log barn, corn crib, and smokehouse. The six-roomed farmhouse is based on one built by Thomas Mellon and his father in the early years of their new life in America.

A fully stocked library and database allow the descendants of emigrants to trace their family roots. Popular American festivals, such as Halloween and Independence Day, are celebrated at the park.

Pennsylvania log farmhouse at the Ulster-American Folk Park

Practical & Travel Information

Ireland's capital cities compare favorably to any in
Europe for ease of transportation and communications,
but in remoter areas the pace of life is much slower.
Banks may open only two days a week and public
transportation can be infrequent. The division of Ireland
into the Republic and Northern Ireland, with separate
currencies and communication systems, complicates
matters further. Travel in Ireland is best enjoyed if you
adopt the Irish approach and just take your time.

TOURIST INFORMATION

Before leaving for Ireland you
can get information from **Bord
Fáilte** (Irish Tourist Board) or
Northern Ireland Tourist Board
(NITB) offices. Regional
tourist offices provide more
detailed information,
including accommodations.

In summer, all the sights are
open but crowds are naturally
at their biggest. In winter many
sights keep shorter hours or
open only at the weekend and
some close down completely.

VISA REQUIREMENTS

Visitors from EU member
states, the US, Canada,
Australia, and New Zealand
need a valid passport but
not a visa for entry into the
Republic or Northern Ireland.
UK nationals do not need a
passport to enter the
Republic, but may find one
useful as proof of identity.

SAFETY AND EMERGENCIES

Ireland is one of the safest
places to travel in Europe.
Petty theft, such as pickpocketing, is seldom a problem

outside certain parts of Dublin
and a few other large towns.
Tourist offices and hoteliers
will gladly point out the areas
to be avoided. In Northern
Ireland, the main security risk
in the recent past has been
the threat of bombings,
though even at the height of
the Troubles this hardly ever
affected tourists. Visitors may
find, on the rare occasion, they
are confronted by a police
checkpoint. If you see a sign
indicating a checkpoint ahead,
slow down and use low
beams. Have your passport
handy as proof of identity.

Travel insurance for the UK
will not cover you for the
Republic, so make sure you
have an adequate policy.

The police are called the
Gardaí in the Republic and
the Police Service of Northern
Ireland (PSNI) in the north.

BANKING AND CURRENCY

The unit of currency in the
Republic prior to 2002
was the punt, or Irish pound
(IR£). However, on January 1,
2002, the punt was replaced by
the euro *(see p15)*.

Northern Ireland uses
British currency – pounds

sterling (£). These currencies
are not inter-changeable.
Alongside the Bank of
England currency in the
North, four provincial banks
issue their own notes, for use
only in the province.

Banking hours are from
10am to 4pm, although some
banks close for lunch from
12:30 to 1:30pm. In the
smaller towns in the Republic,
banks are often open only one
or two days a week.

COMMUNICATIONS

Main post offices in the
Republic and Northern
Ireland are usually open from
9am to 5:30pm during the
week and from 9am to 1pm
on Saturdays. The postal
service in Northern Ireland is
much faster than that in the
Republic, where it can take at
least six days for a letter to
reach the United States.

Most phones in the Republic
are operated by EIRCOM, and
in Northern Ireland by British
Telecom. Both offer efficient,
up-to-date card- and coin-
operated public phones.

FLYING TO IRELAND

Flights from most large
European cities arrive at
Dublin Airport. The major
airline operating between
Britain and the Republic is
Aer Lingus, although rival
Ryanair has grown fast. Aer
Lingus and **Continental
Airlines** fly direct from the US
to Shannon Airport, 16 km (10
miles) outside Limerick, as well
as to Dublin Airport. Aeroflot
flies from Shannon to Moscow
via Amsterdam or via Dublin.

There are flights for pilgrims
to Knock International Airport
from Dublin, London Stansted,
and Manchester Airport.

Cork airport is served by
flights from London (Heathrow
and Stansted), Paris,
Birmingham, Manchester, and
Bristol airports amongst others.

British Airways and **bmi
British Midland** fly to Belfast
International Airport from
London Heathrow; British
Airways also flies from Man-
chester and Glasgow. There
are two easyJet flights every
day from Amsterdam to Belfast.

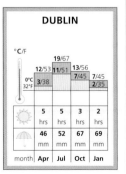

THE CLIMATE OF IRELAND

Rain can be the scourge of a
holiday in Ireland, especially
on the west coast. However,
strong winds off the Atlantic
mean that the weather often
changes with astonishing
speed. Though the rainfall is
heavy, winters are mild and
there is little snowfall except
on the higher mountains.
Dublin and the sheltered
east coast have the warmest
climate and least rainfall.

DUBLIN

month	Apr	Jul	Oct	Jan
°C/F	12/53	19/67 11/51	13/56 7/45	7/45
	3/38			2/35
☀ hrs	5	5	3	2
☔ mm	46	52	67	69

0°C / 32°F

ARRIVING BY SEA

Ferries from ports in Britain and France are a popular way of getting to Ireland, especially with groups or families intending to tour the country by car. There are large seasonal variations in fares.

Irish Ferries and **Stena Line** operate regular daily crossings from Holyhead, Pembroke, and Fishguard in Wales to Dublin Port, Dun Laoghaire, and Rosslare. The fastest routes take about 1 hour 40 minutes. There are also Irish Ferries services from Holyhead to Dublin and to Rosslare from Cherbourg and Roscoff. Brittany Ferries go from Roscoff to Cork.

The fastest crossing to Belfast is the 1 hour 45 minute Stena Line service from Stranraer in Scotland. **P&O Irish Sea** cross to Larne (north of Belfast) from Cairnryan in Scotland, and **Norse Merchant** runs a regular service from Liverpool to Dublin and Belfast.

You can buy combined coach/ferry and rail/ferry tickets from coach offices or train stations all over Britain.

RAIL TRAVEL

Although the more rural areas in the Republic are not served by rail, **Irish Rail** (Iarnród Éireann) operates a service to most large towns. Dublin has two main train stations: Connolly serves the north and the line south along the coast to Rosslare; Heuston serves Cork and the southwest, and Galway and the west. Dublin's local rail service, the DART (Dublin Area Rapid Transit), links towns between Malahide (County Dublin) and Greystones (County Wicklow) with the center of Dublin.

There are two main routes out of Belfast: a line westward to Londonderry, and Ireland's only cross-border service, a high-speed service linking Belfast and Dublin.

BUSES AND TAXIS

The Republic's national bus company, **Bus Éireann**, operates routes to all cities and most of the towns. **Ulsterbus** runs an excellent service in Northern Ireland, with express links between all major towns.

A "Rambler" ticket allows passengers a period of unlimited bus travel in the Republic. In the North, a "Freedom of Northern Ireland" ticket offers the same benefits.

Taxis in Ireland range from saloon cars to people carriers. Cruising taxis are rare. The most likely places to find taxis are at train and bus stations, hotels, and taxi stands.

CAR RENTAL

Car rental firms do good business, so in summer it is wise to book ahead. Car rental – particularly in the Republic – can be expensive and the best rates are often obtained by reserving in advance. Broker companies, such as **Holiday Autos** in the UK, will shop around to get the best deal. If you intend to cross the border in either direction, you must inform the rental company, as there may be an additional insurance premium.

In both the Republic and in Northern Ireland, motorists drive on the left as in Great Britain (*see p91*).

DIRECTORY

TOURIST BOARDS

Bord Fáilte
In Ireland:
Baggot St Bridge,
Dublin 2.
Tel 01-602 4000.
www.ireland.ie
In the US:
345 Park Avenue,
New York,
NY 10154.
Tel 800-223 6470.

**Northern Ireland
Tourist Board**
In Northern Ireland:
St. Anne's Court,
59 North St, Belfast BT1.
Tel 028-9024 6609.
www.discovernorthern
ireland.com
In the UK:
103 Wigmore St,
London W1U 1QS.
Tel 0800-039 700.
www.tourismireland.com

EMBASSIES

Australia
7th Floor, Fitzwilton
House, Wilton Terrace,
Dublin 2.
Tel 01-664 5300.

Canada
65–68 St. Stephen's
Green,
Dublin 2.
Tel 01-417 4100.

UK
Merrion Rd,
Dublin 4.
Tel 01-205 3700.

US
42 Elgin Rd,
Ballsbridge,
Dublin 4.
Tel 01-668 7122.

EMERGENCY
SERVICES

**Police, Ambulance,
and Fire services**
Tel 999 (Republic and NI).

AIRLINES

Aer Lingus
Tel 01-886 8841 (Dublin).
Tel 0845-084 4444 (UK).
Tel 1800-474 7424 (US).
www.aerlingus.com

bmi British Midland
Tel 01-407 3036 (Dublin).
Tel 0870-607 0555 (UK).
www.flybmi.com

Continental Airlines
Tel 01-672 7070 (Dublin).
Tel 1800-523 3273 (US).
www.continental.com

Ryanair
Tel 01-609 7800 (Dublin).
Tel 0870-333 1250 (UK).
www.ryanair.com

FERRY COMPANIES

Irish Ferries
Tel 0818-300 400 (Dublin).
Tel 0870-517 1717 (UK).

Norse Merchant
Tel 0181-92999 (NI).
Tel 0870-600 4321 (UK).

P&O Irish Sea
Tel 0140-73434 (Dublin).
Tel 0870-242 4777 (UK).

Stena Line
*Tel 08705-204 204
(Dublin).*
Tel 08705-707 070 (UK).

RAIL TRAVEL

**Irish Rail (Iarnród
Éireann)**
Tel 01-836 6222.
www.irishrail.ie

**Northern Ireland
Railways**
Tel 028-9066 6630.
www.translink.co.uk

BUS COMPANIES

Bus Éireann
Tel 01-836 6111.

Ulsterbus/Translink
Tel 028-9066 6630.

CAR RENTAL

Holiday Autos
Tel 0870-400 0000 (UK).

Shopping & Entertainment

Ireland offers a wide range of quality handmade goods, including Aran sweaters, Waterford crystal, fine Irish linen, and Donegal tweed. As with its produce, the best entertainment is local and highly individual. Ireland's cities are well served by theaters, cinemas, and concert venues, but there are many other local events including arts festivals with traditional music and dance. Not to be overlooked is the entertainment provided by a night in an Irish pub. Finally, the beautiful countryside offers the chance to unwind by walking, riding, fishing, or playing a round of golf.

WHERE TO SHOP

The choice of places to shop in Ireland ranges from tiny workshops to large factory outlets, and from chic boutiques to high-street chain stores.

In Dublin, the Temple Bar area contains a number of fashionable craft shops. One of the largest shopping centers in the city is St. Stephen's Green Shopping Centre, full of clothes and craft shops. Near Grafton Street is the Powerscourt Townhouse Shopping Centre.

CRAFTS

Crafts are a flourishing way of life in rural Ireland. The Crafts Council of Ireland, which has branches in Kilkenny and Dublin, can recommend good small-scale specialist stores. Outlets particularly worth visiting include the **Kilkenny Design Centre** and **Bricín**, which sell a wide selection of items.

Established in 19th-century Ulster, the **Belleek Pottery** produces creamy china with intricately worked decorative motifs, such as shamrocks and flowers. **Royal Tara China**, in Galway, is Ireland's leading fine bone china manufacturer, with designs inspired by Celtic themes.

Waterford Crystal is undoubtedly the most famous name in Irish glass-making but there are many other names of similar quality. **Galway Irish Crystal** is an excellent make, available as elegant ornaments and gifts. Jerpoint Abbey in County Kilkenny inspires stylish local designs by **Jerpoint Glass**. With a tradition that dates

back to Celtic times, distinctive jewelry is produced all over Ireland. The Claddagh ring of Galway is the most famous – a lovers' symbol with two hands cradling a crowned heart.

Aran sweaters are sold all over Ireland, but particularly in County Galway and on the Aran Islands. A well-known outlet for these and other knitwear products is **Blarney Woollen Mills**. Donegal tweed is a byword for quality, noted for its texture and subtle colors. It can be bought at **Magee and Co** in Donegal.

Damask linen was brought to Northern Ireland in the late 17th century by Huguenot refugees. The North is still the place for linen, with sheets and table linen on sale in Belfast at **Smyth's Irish Linen**.

Smoked salmon, farmhouse cheeses, handmade preserves, and, of course, Irish whiskey make perfect last-minute gifts.

ENTERTAINMENT LISTINGS AND TICKETS

The tourist board for the Republic, **Bord Fáilte**, and the **Northern Ireland Tourist Board** *(see p133)* both publish a yearly *Calendar of Events* that lists major fixtures and events around the country. The regional tourist offices also provide local information.

Tickets are often available on the night but it is safer to book in advance. Most venues will accept credit card bookings. Try the main listings magazine *In Dublin* – available from all newsagents – for information about the city's nightlife. The free *Dublin Event Guide* is available from pubs and cafés.

ENTERTAINMENT VENUES

In many Irish cities, the main theaters host a wide range of concerts, events, and plays. In central Belfast, the **Grand Opera House** and **Lyric Theatre** put on an interesting program. Dublin's two most famous theaters are the **Abbey** and the **Gate Theatre** are renowned for their productions of Irish and international plays, as is the **Cork Opera House**.

Keep an eye out for smaller theater groups around the country. The **Druid Theatre** in Galway puts on an original repertoire and Waterford boasts a resident drama company at the **Garter Lane Theatre**.

Other venues for classical music include Dublin's great auditorium, the **National Concert Hall**, the **Crawford Art Gallery** in Cork, and the **Ulster Hall** in Belfast.

The **Waterford Festival of Light Opera** and the **Wexford Festival of Opera** attract opera lovers from around the world. Wexford revives neglected operas while Waterford puts on more mainstream operas and musicals. Dublin's opera venue is the **Point Theatre**.

A lack of large-capacity rock venues has led to concerts in Ireland being staged at outdoor sites during the summer. Die-hard rock and jazz fans should search out the musical pubs for Irish bands.

IRISH MUSIC AND DANCE

The Irish pub has helped keep traditional music alive and provided the setting for the musical revival that began in the 1960s. Nights of Irish music and song are scheduled in pubs such as An Phoenix and The Lobby in Cork, and The Laurels in Killarney. However, sessions of informal or impromptu music are commonplace. Wherever you are, the locals will advise you of the nearest musical pubs.

Popular dance spectaculars have raised the profile, if not the understanding, of real Irish country dance. Visit **Comhaltas Ceoltóirí Éireann**, in Monkstown near Dublin, or any of its branches around the country for genuine traditional music and dance nights all year.

IRISH FESTIVALS

The Irish are expert festival organizers, staging a week of street entertainment, theater, music, and dance to celebrate almost everything under the sun *(see Directory for listings)*.

IRISH PUBS

The Irish pub is known for its convivial atmosphere and the "crack" – the Irish expression for fun. Wit is washed down with the national drinks of whiskey or Guinness.

City pubs often have grand interiors, a testament to the importance of the brewing and distilling industries in Victorian times. In the countryside, pubs provide an important focus for far-flung rural communities and some even double as shops.

Pubs vary greatly throughout the country, so be sure to try out a few wherever you visit. Dublin is famed for its literary pubs; the Dublin Literary Pub Crawl is an entertaining way to get a feel for the city's booze-fuelled literary heritage. Spontaneous music sessions are common in the many pubs of Kilkenny and County Clare. Some of the most picturesque establishments are in Cork and Kerry. Galway's tourists and student population guarantee a lively pub atmosphere.

OUTDOOR ACTIVITES

No matter where you are in Ireland, the countryside is never far away. Horses thrive on the green turf and racing is a national passion. A day at the track during Galway Race Week in July is a great social event. Those who want to do more than just watch should try horse riding through the unspoiled countryside.

Another way to experience the countryside is to take a river or canal cruise. **Emerald Star** has a fleet of cruisers for use on the waterways. Alternatively you may want to play golf at one of Ireland's beautiful golf courses, or try some fishing. Maps and locations for fishing are available from the **Central Fisheries Board**. The **Golfing Union of Ireland** can advise on golf courses.

Detailed information on a wide range of outdoor activities is available from **Bord Fáilte** *(see p133)*, and local tourist offices.

DIRECTORY

CRAFTS

Belleek Pottery
Belleek, Co. Fermanagh.
Tel 028-6865 8501.

Blarney Woollen Mills
Blarney, Co. Cork.
Tel 021-451 6111.

Bricín
26 High Street, Killarney,
Co. Kerry.
Tel 064-34902.

Galway Irish Crystal
Merlin Park, Galway.
Tel 091-757 311.

Jerpoint Glass
Stoneyford, Co. Kilkenny.
Tel 056-772 4350.

Kilkenny Design Centre
Castle Yard, Kilkenny.
Tel 056-22118.

Magee and Co
The Diamond, Donegal.
Tel 073-22660.

Royal Tara China
Tara Hall, Mervue,
Galway.
Tel 091-705 602.

Smyth's Irish Linen
65 Royal Ave, Belfast.
Tel 028-9024 2232.

Waterford Crystal
Kilbarry, Waterford.
Tel 051-373 311.

ENTERTAINMENT VENUES

Abbey Theatre
Abbey St Lower, Dublin 1.
Tel 01-878 7222.

Cork Opera House
Emmet Place, Cork.
Tel 021-427 4308.

Crawford Art Gallery
Emmet Place, Cork.
Tel 0214-273 377.

Druid Theatre
Chapel Lane, Galway.
Tel 091-568 660.

Garter Lane Theatre
22A O'Connell St,
Waterford.
Tel 051-855 038.

Gate Theatre
Cavendish Row,
Dublin 1.
Tel 01-874 4045.

Grand Opera House
Great Victoria St,
Belfast.
Tel 028-9024 1919.

Lyric Theatre
55 Ridgeway St, Belfast.
Tel 028-9038 1081.

National Concert Hall
Earlsfort Terrace, Dublin 2.
Tel 01-417 0000.

Point Theatre
East Link Bridge, North
Wall Quay, Dublin 1.
Tel 01-836 6777.

Ulster Hall
Bedford St, Belfast.
Tel 028-9032 3900.

MUSIC, DANCE, AND FESTIVALS

Comhaltas Ceoltóirí Éireann
32 Belgrave Sq,
Monkstown, Co. Dublin.
Tel 01-280 0295.

Dublin Theatre Festival
Assorted drama (Oct).
47 Nassau St, Dublin 2.
Tel 01-667 8439.

Galway Arts Festival
Theater, traditional music, and dance (late Jul–Aug).
Black Box Theatre, Dyke
Rd, Terryland, Galway.
Tel 091-509 700.

Kilkenny Arts Week
Crafts, poetry, classical music, and films (Aug).
9–10 Abbey Business
Centre, Kilkenny.
Tel 056-775 2175.

Waterford Festival of Light Opera
*Light opera
(late Sep–Oct).*
For information contact
the Theatre Royal.
Tel 051-874 402.

Wexford Festival of Opera
Opera (Oct–Nov).
Theatre Royal, High St,
Wexford.
Tel 053-912 2144.

IRISH PUBS

Dublin Literary Pub Crawl
37 Exchequer St.
Tel 01-670 5602.

OUTDOOR ACTIVITIES

Central Fisheries Board
Mobhi Boreen, Glasnevin,
Dublin 9.
Tel 01-837 9206.

Emerald Star
The Marina,
Carrick-on-Shannon,
Co. Leitrim.
Tel 071-962 7633.

Golfing Union of Ireland
www.gui.ie

Where to Stay in Ireland

The choice of accommodations in Ireland is enormous: you can stay in an elegant 18th-century country house, a luxurious (or slightly run-down) castle, a Victorian town house, an old-fashioned commercial hotel, or a cozy village inn. Whichever you choose, you can be certain you'll receive a warm welcome.

PRICE CATEGORIES
Price categories for a standard double room per night, including tax, service and breakfast. Prices for Belfast are in pounds sterling.

€ under 65 euros (£50)
€€ 65–130 euros (£50–£100)
€€€ 130–190 euros (£100–£150)
€€€€ 190–260 euros (£150–£200)
€€€€€ over 260 euros (£200)

DUBLIN

SOUTHEAST DUBLIN Georgian Hotel
€€€   Map F5

18–22 Baggot St Lower, Dublin 2 **Tel** *01-634 5000* **Fax** *01-634 5100* **Rooms** *20*

Warm and friendly, this three-star hotel consists of three Georgian houses with a modern extension and is well located, just a short stroll from St. Stephen's Green. Comfortably done-up bedrooms are neat and well equipped. Complimentary guest parking is available. There's a traditional Irish bar, Maguires. **www.georgianhotel.ie**

SOUTHEAST DUBLIN Number 31
€€€   Map E5

31 Leeson Close, Leeson St Lower, Dublin 2 **Tel** *01-676 5011* **Fax** *01-676 2929* **Rooms** *20*

Reputedly the most stylish guesthouse in the city, this elegant Georgian house is more of a boutique hotel than a B&B, with individually decorated, luxurious bedrooms. The Coach House features a collection of original art and a sunken seating area. Delicious breakfasts are served in the plant-filled conservatory. **www.number31.ie**

SOUTHEAST DUBLIN Buswells
€€€€   Map E4

25 Molesworth St, Dublin 2 **Tel** *01-614 6500* **Fax** *01-676 2090* **Rooms** *67*

Comprising five Georgian town houses, this slightly old-fashioned hotel has been in operation since 1882. It has a central location beside government buildings and on a street renowned for high-level commercial art galleries. The sophisticated interior is done in warm colors. Frequented by political figures. **www.quinnhotels.com**

SOUTHEAST DUBLIN Davenport
€€€€€   Map F4

Merrion Square, Dublin 2 **Tel** *01-607 3500* **Fax** *01-661 5663* **Rooms** *115*

Close to the National Gallery, this hotel lies in the heart of Georgian Dublin. The Neo-Classical facade dates from 1863. Mahogany, brass and marble furnishings give it the feel of a gentleman's club. Ample bedrooms are well appointed with warmly colored decor. There's a fitness suite and a business center. **www.ocallaghanhotels.ie**

SOUTHWEST DUBLIN Avalon House
€   Map C4

55 Aungier St, Dublin 2 **Tel** *01-475 0001* **Fax** *01-475 0303* **Rooms** *70*

One of the longest established hostels in the city, the centrally located Avalon House provides cheap and cheerful accommodations in a restored redbrick Victorian building. Rooms are clean, with pine and tile floors, high ceilings, and an open fire. Popular with young, independent travelers. There's a café in the front. **www.avalon-house.ie**

SOUTHWEST DUBLIN Jury's Christchurch inn
€€   Map B4

Christ Church Place, Dublin 8 **Tel** *01-454 0000* **Fax** *01-454 0012* **Rooms** *182*

Opposite Christ Church Cathedral, in the old Viking center of Dublin, this modern hotel lies within walking distance of Temple Bar and the city centre. Rooms are neat and well equipped. Bathrooms are adequate, if a little on the small side. Prices charged per room prove particularly good value for families. **www.jurysdoyle.com**

SOUTHWEST DUBLIN Clarence Hotel
€€€€€   Map C3

6–8 Wellington Quay, Dublin 2 **Tel** *01-407 0800* **Fax** *01-407 0820* **Rooms** *49*

Overlooking the River Liffey, this 1852 Dublin landmark was bought by the rock band U2 in 1992. Extensively refurbished, it has acquired cult status. With original wood-paneling in Arts and Crafts style, and luxuriously furnished rooms, this old establishment successfully combines contemporary cool and comfort. **www.theclarence.ie**

NORTH OF THE LIFFEY Gresham Hotel
€€€€€   Map D2

23 O'Connell St Upper, Dublin 1 **Tel** *01-874 6881* **Fax** *01-878 7175* **Rooms** *288*

One of Dublin's oldest and best-known hotels, the Gresham is a popular rendezvous spot with ever-lively public areas. It has been recently refurbished, with pleasant furnishings that combine classic and contemporary styles. Well-equipped bedrooms are cheerfully decorated. A good business hotel. **www.gresham-hotels.com**

FARTHER AFIELD Glenogra Guesthouse
€€

64 Merrion Road, Ballsbridge, Dublin 4 **Tel** *01-668 3661* **Fax** *01-668 3698* **Rooms** *12*

This stylish and award-winning guesthouse provides pleasant and good-value B&B accommodations in this leafy, up-market area of Dublin. The owners create a welcoming atmosphere for their guests. Bedrooms are well-appointed and the breakfast is good. **www.glenogra.com**

Map References *see map of Dublin pp112–3*

REST OF IRELAND

BELFAST Europa Hotel   €€€€
Great Victoria St, Co Antrim, BT2 7AP **Tel** *028-9027 1066* **Fax** *028-9032 7800* **Rooms** *240*

An imposing building in the heart of the Golden Mile, Europa is one of Belfast's best hotels, ideal for business people and tourists. Bill Clinton stayed here during his visits to the city. Standard rooms offer en-suite facilities and all other expected amenities. The Grand Opera House and Waterfront Hall are nearby. **www.hastingshotels.com**

CASHEL Cashel Palace Hotel   €€€€
Main St, Co Tipperary **Tel** *062-62707* **Fax** *062-61521* **Rooms** *23*

Originally a bishop's palace, this beautiful Queen Anne-style house, dating from 1730, is set in its own grounds in the centre of Cashel town. The large, elegant rooms overlook tranquil gardens to the rear and the famed Rock of Cashel. The Bishop's Buttery restaurant serves lunch and dinner. A peaceful retreat. **www.cashel-palace.ie**

CLIFDEN Dolphin Beach Country House   €€€
Lower Sky Rd, Co Galway **Tel** *095-21204* **Fax** *095-22935* **Rooms** *9*

This charming beachside house, with its own private cove, is bright and stylish, with a friendly atmosphere. Bedrooms are spacious, with antique furniture and crisp bed linen and there is delicious home cooking in the dining room overlooking the bay. **www.connemara.net/DolphinBeachHouse/**

CORK Hayfield Manor Hotel   €€€€€€
Perrott Ave, College Rd, Co Cork **Tel** *021-484 5900* **Fax** *021-431 6839* **Rooms** *88*

A member of the Small Luxury Hotels of the World, this delightful place is set amid gardens. Though opened in 1996, it has the feel of a fine period house. Elegant furnishings are of a high standard. Generously proportioned and thoughtfully designed bedrooms come with good bathrooms. Excellent leisure facilities. **www.hayfieldmanor.ie**

DINGLE Emlagh House   €€€
Dingle, Co Kerry **Tel** *066-915 2345* **Fax** *066-915 2369* **Rooms** *10*

A few minutes' walk from the heart of Dingle, this luxurious guesthouse is set in peaceful landscaped gardens. It is furnished in a tasteful country-house style with Irish art, though a contemporary feel prevails. Bedrooms are cosy, ample and decorated with flowers. Most of them have harbor views. **www.emlaghhouse.com**

GALWAY Killeen House   €€€
Bushy Park, Co Galway **Tel** *091-524 179* **Fax** *091-528 065* **Rooms** *6*

Set amid gardens sweeping down to Lough Corrib, this charming 1840 house reflects the host's love for antiques and flair for design. Each bedroom is decorated in a different style – Victorian, Edwardian, Regency and Art Nouveau – and furnished impressively with well-appointed bathrooms. Delicious breakfasts. **www.killeenhousegalway.com**

KILKENNY Butler House   €€
16 Patrick St, Co Kilkenny **Tel** *056-776 5707* **Fax** *056-776 5626* **Rooms** *13*

This gracious Georgian town house is an integral part of the Kilkenny Castle estate. Decor is contemporary, with period features such as marble fireplaces and plasterwork ceilings. Bedrooms are large and relatively snug. Excellent breakfasts in the refurbished stables of the castle, which now houses the Kilkenny Design Centre. **www.butler.ie**

KILLARNEY Hotel Dunloe Castle   €€€
Killarney, Co Kerry **Tel** *064-44111* **Fax** *064-44583* **Rooms** *110*

This modern hotel stands in lovely subtropical gardens, with its award-winning collection of rare plants and flowers, by the ruins of the 13th-century castle. Rooms are large and well appointed. Facilities feature an on-site equestrian centre, indoor tennis courts and fishing on the River Laune. **www.killarneyhotels.ie**

KINSALE Old Bank House   €€€€
11 Pearse St, Co Cork **Tel** *021-477 4075* **Fax** *021-477 4296* **Rooms** *17*

Situated right in the center of town, this used to be a working branch of the Munster and Leinster Bank. Now it is a well-run guesthouse, offering excellent accommodations. Bedrooms are spacious and decorated in a country-house style with good bathrooms. Some enjoy picturesque views of the town. **www.oldbankhousekinsale.com**

LETTERFRACK Rosleague Manor House Hotel   €€€
Letterfrack, Co Galway **Tel** *095-41101* **Fax** *095-41168* **Rooms** *20*

This wonderful, 200-year-old Regency Manor is a tranquil retreat appealing to all sensibilities. Gardens planted with exotic plants and shrubs sweep down to Ballinakill Bay. Elegantly furnished, it holds great charm and character and provides relaxed luxury and panoramic views. Country house cuisine is superbly executed. **www.rosleague.com**

WATERFORD Waterford Castle   €€€€€
The Island, Ballinakill, Co Waterford **Tel** *051-878 203* **Fax** *051-879 316* **Rooms** *19*

Dating from the 15th century, this luxury hotel lies on a private 310-acre island, 5 km (3 miles) outside Waterford city. Reached by a private car ferry, the Castle mixes old-world elegance with modern comfort. Good fine-dining choices as well as an 18-hole golf course and tennis. Non-smoking property. **www.waterfordcastle.com**

Key to Symbols *see back cover flap*

Where to Eat in Ireland

Thanks to the island's high-quality fish and other fresh produce, Irish cooking now ranks among the best in Europe; the town of Kinsale in County Cork has established itself as "Gourmet Capital of Ireland." If your budget is small, it is still possible to eat well, with a wealth of options in both city and rural locations.

PRICE CATEGORIES
Price categories for a three-course meal for one, including half a bottle of house wine, and all extra charges. Prices for Belfast are in pounds sterling:

€ under 25 euros (£15)
€€ 25–35 euros (£15–£25)
€€€ 35–50 euros (£25–£35)
€€€€ 50–70 euros (£35–£50)
€€€€€ over 70 euros (£50)

DUBLIN

SOUTHEAST DUBLIN Kilkenny Restaurant & Café   €€

5–6 Nassau St, Dublin 2 **Tel** *01-677 7075*   **Map** *E4*

Situated on the first floor of a high-quality craft shop, the Kilkenny overlooks the grounds of Trinity College. Wholesome, freshly-prepared soups, sandwiches, panini, salads, quiches, hot casseroles, and pies are available in this self-service restaurant. Lovely desserts include baked cheesecake, carrot cake, and fruit tarts.

SOUTHEAST DUBLIN Bang Café   €€€

11 Merrion Row, Dublin 2 **Tel** *01-676 0898*   **Map** *E5*

Across the road from the Shelbourne Hotel, this hip restaurant is the essence of stylish minimalism, reflected in its food as well as the decor of natural tones and dark wood furnishings. Contemporary cuisine includes good fish dishes, mouthwatering scallops, and excellent sausages and mash. Service is professional.

SOUTHEAST DUBLIN Trocadero   €€€

3–4 Andrew St, Dublin 2 **Tel** *01-677 5545*   **Map** *D3*

This much-loved restaurant has been in operation since 1956. A haunt of actors and the literati, it has deep-red walls lined with black-and-white images of the notables who have passed through its doors. Traditional classics include rack of lamb, steak, and Dublin Bay prawns, and tempting desserts. Service is intimate and welcoming.

SOUTHEAST DUBLIN L'Ecrivain   €€€€€

109a Lower Baggot St, Dublin 2 **Tel** *01-661 1919*   **Map** *F5*

One of the best restaurants in the city, L'Ecrivain combines classic formality with contemporary cool. Authentic French cuisine with an Irish flavor includes delicacies such as Galway Bay oysters and caviar. Seasonal game and seafood as well as tasty desserts and cheeses also figure on the menu. Service is great.

SOUTHWEST DUBLIN Leo Burdock's   €

2 Werburgh St, Dublin 8 **Tel** *01-454 0306*   **Map** *B4*

The patrons of Leo Burdock's, the oldest fish-and-chip takeaway in Dublin, include the ordinary folk of Dublin and the stars. Fresh fish and chips made from top-grade Irish potatoes. There's a wide choice of fish including scampi, smoked cod, haddock, and lemon sole goujon. Service is efficient. There's another branch on Liffey Street.

SOUTHWEST DUBLIN Lord Edward   €€€

23 Christchurch Place, Dublin 8 **Tel** *01-454 2420*   **Map** *B4*

The oldest seafood restaurant in the city, Lord Edward is located above a cosy and traditional pub, which serves lunch downstairs. It has changed little over the years and maintains an old-fashioned feel. Long-established waiters are known for their charming service.

SOUTHWEST DUBLIN The Tea Room   €€€€€

The Clarence Hotel, 6–8 Wellington Quay, Dublin 2 **Tel** *01-407 0800*   **Map** *C3*

The Clarence Hotel is owned by rock band U2. Come in by the Essex Street entrance, opposite the Project Theatre, and savor excellent cuisine served in this stylish dining room. High ceilings and large windows create a bright and airy atmosphere. Menus are innovative and seasonal. The lunch menu is particularly good value.

NORTH OF THE LIFFEY Chapter One   €€€€

18–19 Parnell Sq, Dublin 1 **Tel** *01-873 2266*   **Map** *C1*

In the cellar of the Dublin Writers' Museum, Chapter One is often cited by critics as the best restaurant north of the Liffey. Relish the imaginative European cuisine, with an Irish twist, in a dining room of character and comfort. The pre-theater menu is a favorite among regulars who frequent the nearby Gate theater.

FARTHER AFIELD The Lobster Pot   €€€€

9 Ballsbridge Terrace, Ballsbridge, Dublin 4 **Tel** *01-660 9170*

This long-established upstairs restaurant deservedly commands a loyal following. High-quality food is well presented by professional, charming waiters. Specialities feature dressed Kilmore crab, Dublin Bay prawns in Provençal sauce, generously-sized sole on the bone, delicious steaks, chicken, and game dishes.

Map References *see map of Dublin pp138–9*

REST OF IRELAND

BELFAST Cayenne   🔊🏃   €€€€
7 Lesley House, Shaftesbury Sq, Co Antrim, BT2 7DB **Tel** *028-90331532*

Celebrity chefs Paul and Jeanne Rankin opened this restaurant in 1999, and serve a delicious mix of Thai, Japanese, and other Asian-influenced dishes. Exotic and innovative mains, such as spiced breast of duck with Shanghai noodles, sprouting broccoli, oyster mushrooms, and black bean sauce are typical.

BLARNEY Blair's Inn   🔊🏃🎴🎵   €€€
Cloghroe, Co Cork **Tel** *021-4381470*

Immaculately maintained and very inviting, this pretty whitewashed riverside pub has hanging flower baskets and a lovely garden outside. Inside, open fires and a charming interior are complemented by reliably good food. Traditional dishes include casserole of beef and stout, and baked lemon sole stuffed with crab meat in a white butter sauce.

CASHEL Chez Hans Restaurant   🔊🏃   €€€€
Moore Lane, Co Tipperary **Tel** *062-61177*

Since 1968, patrons have been traveling from all over the county to savor the excellent cooking here. Housed in a converted church, it has become a veritable temple for food-lovers. Dishes showcase succulent Tipperary beef and lamb. Sole on the bone is particularly good. The early-bird dinner is good value. Reservations advised.

CLIFDEN Ardagh Hotel & Restaurant   🔊   €€€
Ballyconneely Rd, Co Galway **Tel** *095-21384*

This award-winning restaurant, situated on the first floor of the hotel, has lovely views of the sea, particularly at sunset. The modern dining room is pleasantly furnished and welcoming, with linen tablecloths, candles, fresh flowers, and an open fire. On the menu are lobsters from the on-site sea tank, locally caught seafood, and prime meats.

CORK Jacobs on the Mall   🔊🏃   €€€€
30a South Mall, Co Cork **Tel** *021-4251530*

This highly acclaimed restaurant, with one of the country's leading chefs, is set in the former Turkish baths. Decorated in a charming contemporary style, it has a unique ambience. Creative and colorful dishes include scallops and crab cakes with mango salad, and a hot-and-sour dressing. Home-made ice creams are irresistible.

DINGLE Lord Baker's Restaurant & Bar   🔊🏃   €€€
Main St, Co Kerry **Tel** *066-9151277*

Believed to be the oldest bar in Dingle, this welcoming hostelry, with an open fire, serves delicious bar food such as home-made soups, crab claws in garlic butter, and smoked salmon with capers. The restaurant is more formal. Specialties include classic seafood mornay and monkfish wrapped in bacon.

GALWAY The Park Room Restaurant   🔊🏃   €€€
Park House Hotel, Co Galway **Tel** *091-564924*

Located within the pleasant Park House hotel, this restaurant offers Irish and international cuisine of a very good standard. Linen-clad tablecloths and fresh flowers create a relaxed, welcoming atmosphere. Sample dishes include pan-fried fillet of John Dory and ostrich fillet with garlic potato and grilled shallots. Just off Eyre Square.

KILKENNY Zuni   🔊🏃🎴   €€€
26 Patrick St, Co Kilkenny **Tel** *056-7723999*

Also offering stylish accommodations, Zuni has become a by-word for contemporary chic and superb food in this delightful medieval town. The cuisine is worldly in style, with influences from Morocco to southeast Asia. A well-designed restaurant, it has a great atmosphere and tasteful furnishings. Try the tasty risotto, salads, and pasta.

KILLARNEY Gaby's Seafood Restaurant   🔊🏃   €€€€
27 High St, Co Kerry **Tel** *064-32519*

A member of the World Master Chefs Society and one of Ireland's longest established seafood restaurants, Gaby's reputedly offers the best seafood in town. Cooking is imaginative and of a high standard with a carefully chosen wine list. A real treat is the lobster "Gaby" with cognac and cream. Desserts are exquisite.

KINSALE Man Friday   🏃🎴   €€€
Scilly, Co Cork **Tel** *021-4772260*

The oldest restaurant in Kinsale, Man Friday is nationally regarded for its excellent cuisine, unique atmosphere, and friendly service. A recipient of numerous awards, it comprises a number of adjoining rooms of character and a garden terrace, lovely on a summer's evening. There's a great choice of comfort food and a superb seafood platter.

WATERFORD Fitzpatrick's Restaurant   🔊🏃🎵   €€€€
Manor Court Lodge, Cork Rd, Co Waterford **Tel** *051-378851*

In a listed stone building on the outskirts of the city, this bright and colorful fine-dining restaurant is reputed for its classical cuisine with a French influence. Linen-clad tables with fresh flowers and candles create a welcoming atmosphere. Try the roasted sea bass. Staff are courteous and attentive. Reservations are recommended.

Key to Symbols *see back cover flap*

FRANCE AND THE LOW COUNTRIES

FRANCE AND THE LOW COUNTRIES
AT A GLANCE 142–143

FRANCE 144–217

BELGIUM AND LUXEMBOURG 218–243

THE NETHERLANDS 244–271

France and the Low Countries at a Glance

France dominates the northwest of continental Europe. To the northeast of France lie Belgium and the Netherlands, known as the Low Countries because they occupy flat plains and land reclaimed from the sea. South of Belgium is the tiny state of Luxembourg. France has some of Europe's greatest attractions, notably the culture and nightlife of Paris. Visitors often choose to tour just one or two of the country's regions: the mountains of the Alps or the Pyrenees, one of the historic wine-growing areas, or the warm south. Belgium and the Netherlands have many historic cities full of fine museums and art galleries. Visiting these countries can be rewarding because all the major sights lie within easy reach of each other.

Paris (see pp150–71), *France's capital, is a city of distinctive districts. Montmartre, the hilltop artists' quarter, is dominated by the Sacré Coeur.*

The Loire Valley (see pp176–9) *is one of France's most popular regions for touring. It is dotted with magnificent châteaux, built by kings and nobles during the Renaissance. One of the finest is Chenonceau.*

Southwest France (see pp188–9) *has a huge variety of attractions, from the peaks of the Pyrenees to Atlantic seaside resorts such as Biarritz and the world-famous vineyards of Bordeaux (see p186).*

• Cherbourg

St. Malo •

• Rennes

Nantes

PARIS

Chartres

Orléans

FRANCE
(See pp144–217)

• Limoges

Bordeaux

• Biarritz

Toulouse

0 km   75

0 miles   75

◁ A field of poppies in northeast France, where the battles of World War I were fought

NETHERLANDS
(See pp244–271)

● AMSTERDAM

● BRUSSELS

**BELGIUM AND
LUXEMBOURG**
(See pp218–243)

le ●

● LUXEMBOURG CITY

● Reims

Nancy ●
Strasbourg ●

● Troyes

● Dijon
● Besançon

lermont-
errand ●
● Lyon

● Grenoble

● Cannes
● Marseille

LOCATOR MAP

Amsterdam (see pp248–59)
is a unique city, criss-crossed
by canals, its relaxed atmosphere a refreshing change
from Europe's other traffic-
clogged capital cities.

Brussels (see pp222–9),
the capital of Belgium,
thrives as the head-
quarters of the European
Union. The Grand Place,
with its soaring Gothic
town hall, is one of
Europe's most
spectacular squares.

Dijon (see pp184–5) flourished in the Middle
Ages under the powerful dukes of Burgundy. The
former palace where the dukes held court now
houses the prestigious Musée des Beaux Arts,
with its rich collection of art and sculpture.

The South of France
(see pp190–97) is one
of the traditional
playgrounds of
Europe's rich and
famous, where grand
hotels, luxury yachts,
and pristine beaches
contrast with picturesque
old fishing ports.

FRANCE

*T**he best advocates for visiting France are the French themselves, convinced as they are that their way of life is best, and their country the most civilized on earth. The food and wine are justly celebrated, while French literature, art, cinema, and architecture can be both profound and provocative. France is a country that stimulates the intellect and gratifies the senses.***

France belongs to both northern and southern Europe, encompassing regions ranging from Brittany, with its Celtic maritime heritage, and Germanic Alsace-Lorraine, to the Mediterranean sunbelt and the peaks of the Alps and Pyrenees. The capital, Paris, is the country's linchpin, with its intellectual excitement, intense tempo of life, and notoriously brusque citizens.

Strangely, as life in France becomes more city-based and industrialized, so the desire grows to safeguard the old, traditional ways and to value rural life. The idea of life in the country – *douceur de vivre* (the Good Life), long tables set in the sun for the wine and anecdotes to flow – is as seductive as ever for residents and visitors alike. Nevertheless, the rural way of life has been changing. Whereas in 1945 one person in three worked in farming, today it is only one in 16. France's main exports used to be luxury goods such as perfumes, Champagne, and Cognac; today, these have been overtaken by cars, telecommunications equipment, and fighter aircraft. The French remain firmly committed to their roots, however, and often keep a place in the country for vacations or their retirement.

HISTORY
Though famous for the rootedness of its peasant population, France has also been a European melting pot, from the arrival of the Celtic Gauls in the 1st millennium BC, through to the Mediterranean immigrations of the 20th century. Roman conquest by Julius Caesar had an enduring impact but, from the 4th and 5th centuries AD, Germanic invaders destroyed much of the Roman legacy. The Franks provided political leadership in the following centuries, but when their line died out in the late 10th century, France was politically fragmented.

The traditional game of *boules or pétanque*, still a popular pastime – especially in the south

◁ The Château de Saumur, one of the many fairy-tale castles of the Loire Valley

The Capetian dynasty gradually pieced France together over the Middle Ages, a period of economic prosperity and cultural vitality. The Black Death and the Hundred Years' War brought setbacks, and French power was seriously threatened by the dukes of Burgundy and the English crown. In the Renaissance period, François I (reigned 1515–47) dreamt of making France a major power, but was thwarted by the Habsburg Emperor Charles V. The Reformation then plunged the country into religious conflict. However, the 17th century saw France, under Louis XIV, rise to dominate Europe militarily and intellectually.

Napoleon, the brilliant general who rose to be Emperor of France

In the Age of Enlightenment French culture and institutions were the envy of Europe. The ideas of Voltaire and Rousseau undermined the authority of the Church and the state, nowhere more than in France itself. The Revolution of 1789 ended the absolute monarchy and introduced major social and institutional reforms, many of which were endorsed by Napoleon, whose empire dominated Europe at the start of the 19th century. Yet the Revolution also inaugurated the instability that has remained a hallmark of French politics: since 1789, France has seen three forms of monarchy, two empires, and five republics.

Throughout the political turmoil of the 19th century, France remained a leading source of literary and artistic movements. In painting, the French Impressionists were the inspiration for the development of modern art and would-be painters began to flock to Paris instead of Rome. France also retained its position as the arbiter of taste in fashion, food, wine, and good manners.

Rivalry with Germany dominated French politics for most of the late 19th and early 20th centuries. The population losses in World War I were traumatic for France, while during 1940–44 the country was occupied by Germany. Yet since 1955, the two countries have proved the backbone of the developing European Union.

MODERN POLITICS

For much of the 20th century, domestic politics was marked by confrontations between Left and Right. In 1958 the problems of governing the country led to the introduction of a new constitution – the Fifth Republic – with Charles de Gaulle as president.

KEY DATES IN FRENCH HISTORY

1200–700 BC Arrival of the Celts during Bronze and Iron Ages

51 BC Romans complete conquest of Gaul

AD 481 Frankish leader Clovis becomes first Merovingian king

800 Coronation of Charlemagne, greatest of the Carolingians, as Holy Roman Emperor

1180–1223 Reign of Philip Augustus

1337–1453 Hundred Years' War with England

1562–93 Wars of Religion

1660–1715 Reign of Louis XIV

1789 French Revolution

1804 Napoleon crowned emperor

1815 Defeat of Napoleon: monarchy restored

1848 Revolution; short-lived Second Republic

1852–70 Second Empire under Napoleon III

1919 Treaty of Versailles after World War I

1940 Germans overrun France

1958 Fifth Republic with Charles de Gaulle as president

1968 Student uprising and de Gaulle's downfall

1994 Channel Tunnel opens

2002 Euro replaces Franc as legal tender

2005 Referendum goes against proposed EU constitution

The student uprising of May 1968, which challenged all the old assumptions of the French ruling elite

Relaxing in the sun at a traditional French café

However, in 1968 protesting students and striking workers combined to paralyse the country and de Gaulle resigned the following year.

The old divide between Left and Right has given way to a more center-focused consensus fostered by François Mitterrand, Socialist President from 1981 to 1995, and forced on the Conservative Jacques Chirac, who succeeded him, by the election of Socialist Lionel Jospin as Prime Minister in 1997. In 2002, however, a landslide victory for the center-right coalition ousted Jospin. The Republican spirit lives on in strikes and mass demonstrations. Unemployment – France's worst social problem – has led to growing racism against Arab immigrants.

Tempting display of *charcuterie* and cheeses on a Lyon market stall

LANGUAGE AND CULTURE
Culture is taken seriously in France: writers, intellectuals, artists, and fashion designers are held in high esteem. The French remain justly proud of their cinema, and are determined to defend it against pressures from Hollywood. Other activities – from the music industry to the French language itself – are subject to the same protectionist attitudes.

Avant-garde art and literature and modern architecture enjoy strong patronage in France. Exciting architectural projects range from new buildings in Paris – the Louvre pyramid and La Grande Arche at La Défense – to the post-modern housing projects of Nîmes and Marseille in the south.

CONTEMPORARY SOCIETY
Social change has resulted from the decline in the influence of the Catholic Church. Parental authoritarianism has waned and there is a much freer ambience in schools – two trends resulting from the May 1968 uprising.

French social life, except between close friends, has always been marked by formality – handshaking, and the use of titles and the formal *vous* rather than the intimate *tu*. However, this is changing, especially among the young, who now call you by your first name, and use *tu* even in an office context. Standards of dress have become more informal too, though the French are still very concerned to dress well.

France is a country where tradition and progress are found side by side. The Euro has taken over, yet some people still calculate in old Francs, replaced back in 1960. France's agribusiness is one of the most modern in the world, but the peasant farmer is deeply revered. France has Europe's largest hypermarkets, which have been ousting local grocers. Although American in inspiration, they are French in what they sell, with wonderful displays of cheeses and a huge range of fresh vegetables, fruit, and herbs.

The TGV, France's impressive high-speed train

Exploring France

France is a large country and, although it has over 60 million inhabitants, is less densely populated than most of its western European neighbors. Paris belongs to northern Europe, while the south is Mediterranean in climate and lifestyle. Distances limit the amount of the country you can visit, though train services are good and there is an extensive network of highways. Popular tourist destinations include the châteaux of the Loire, the mountains of the Alps and Pyrenees, historic wine-growing regions *(see pp186–7)*, and the resorts of the Côte d'Azur.

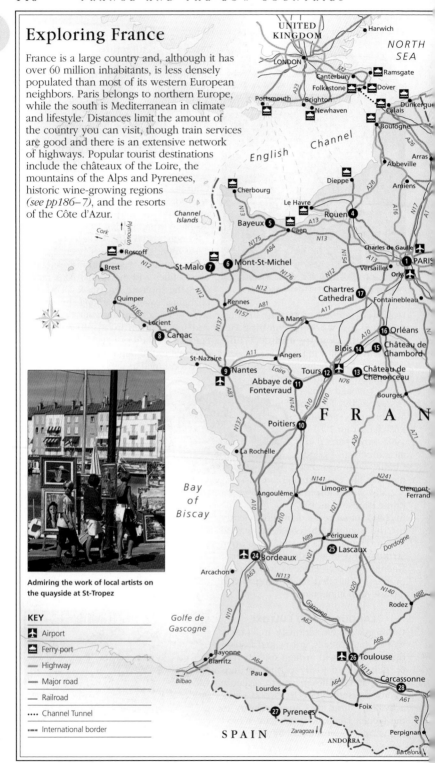

Admiring the work of local artists on the quayside at St-Tropez

KEY

✈	Airport
⛴	Ferry port
—	Highway
—	Major road
—	Railroad
••••	Channel Tunnel
▪▪▪	International border

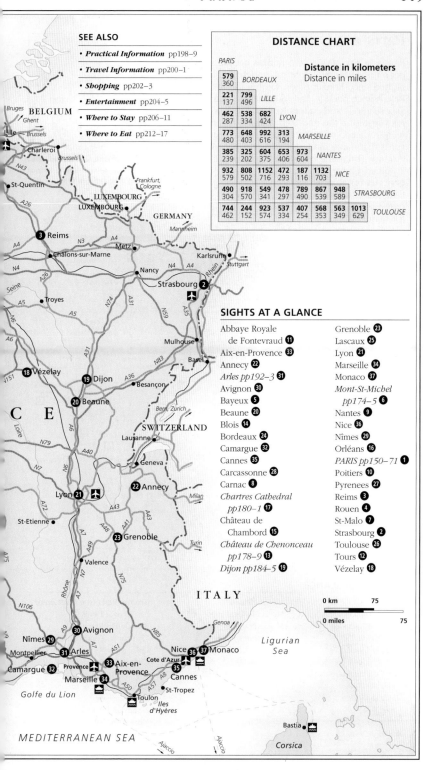

SEE ALSO

- *Practical Information* pp198–9
- *Travel Information* pp200–1
- *Shopping* pp202–3
- *Entertainment* pp204–5
- *Where to Stay* pp206–11
- *Where to Eat* pp212–17

DISTANCE CHART

Distance in kilometers
Distance in miles

PARIS								
579 / 360	BORDEAUX							
221 / 137	**799** / 496	LILLE						
462 / 287	**538** / 334	**682** / 424	LYON					
773 / 480	**648** / 403	**992** / 616	**313** / 194	MARSEILLE				
385 / 239	**325** / 202	**604** / 375	**653** / 406	**973** / 604	NANTES			
932 / 579	**808** / 502	**1152** / 716	**472** / 293	**187** / 116	**1132** / 703	NICE		
490 / 304	**918** / 570	**549** / 341	**478** / 297	**789** / 490	**867** / 539	**948** / 589	STRASBOURG	
744 / 462	**244** / 152	**923** / 574	**537** / 334	**407** / 254	**568** / 353	**563** / 349	**1013** / 629	TOULOUSE

SIGHTS AT A GLANCE

Abbaye Royale de Fontevraud ⑪
Aix-en-Provence ㉝
Annecy ㉒
Arles pp192–3 ㉛
Avignon ㉚
Bayeux ⑤
Beaune ⑳
Blois ⑭
Bordeaux ㉔
Camargue ㉜
Cannes ㉟
Carcassonne ㉘
Carnac ⑧
Chartres Cathedral pp180–1 ⑰
Château de Chambord ⑮
Château de Chenonceau pp178–9 ⑬
Dijon pp184–5 ⑲

Grenoble ㉓
Lascaux ㉕
Lyon ㉑
Marseille ㉞
Monaco ㊲
Mont-St-Michel pp174–5 ⑥
Nantes ⑨
Nice ㊱
Nîmes ㉙
Orléans ⑯
PARIS pp150–71 ①
Poitiers ⑩
Pyrenees ㉗
Reims ③
Rouen ④
St-Malo ⑦
Strasbourg ②
Toulouse ㉖
Tours ⑫
Vézelay ⑱

0 km — 75
0 miles — 75

Paris ❶

Paris is a city of over two million people, and has been the economic, political, and artistic hub of France since Roman times. During the medieval and Renaissance periods, Paris dominated northern Europe as a religious and cultural center. The city was rejuvenated in the mid-19th century, when its slums were replaced with the elegant avenues and boulevards that make modern Paris a delight to stroll around. Today the city strives to be at the heart of a unified Europe. Chic cafés, gourmet restaurants, and fashionable shopping are the major attractions for many visitors.

Notre-Dame viewed from the tranquil setting of Square Jean XXIII

SEE ALSO

- *Where to Stay* pp206–8
- *Where to Eat* pp212–13

SIGHTS AT A GLANCE

Arc de Triomphe ㉑
Centre Pompidou ④
Champs-Elysées ㉒
Eiffel Tower ⑱
Ile de la Cité ①
Jardin du Luxembourg ⑨
Jardin des Tuileries ⑫
Musée du Louvre pp158–60 ⑪
Musée de l'Orangerie ⑬
Musée d'Orsay ⑮

Musée Picasso ⑤
Musée du Quai Branly ⑲
Musée Rodin ⑯
Notre-Dame pp154–5 ②
Palais de Chaillot ⑳
Panthéon ⑧
Place de la Bastille ⑦
Place de la Concorde ⑭
Place des Vosges ⑥
St-Germain-des-Prés ⑩
Sainte-Chapelle ③

Greater Paris *(see inset map)*
Basilique St-Denis ㉙
Bois de Boulogne ㉗
Château de Fontainebleau ㉜
Château de Vaux-le-Vicomte ㉛
Château de Versailles pp168–9 ㉘
Cimetière du Père Lachaise ㉕
La Défense ㉖
Disneyland Paris ㉚
Montmartre ㉓
Parc de la Villette ㉔

GETTING AROUND

The Parisian subway consists of 14 metro lines, referred to by their number and terminus names. This is often the least expensive way to get around the capital. In central Paris, these lines overlap the routes of the RER commuter trains, which reach outlying areas. Buses are often the fastest way to travel short distances. The city's night buses are called Noctambuses. Taxis are expensive, but handy after the metro shuts down.

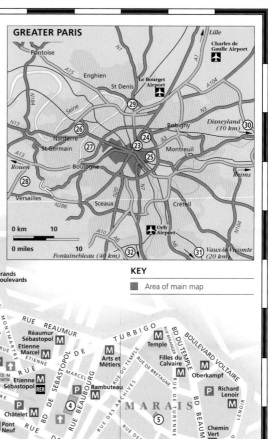

GREATER PARIS

| 0 km | 10 |
| 0 miles | 10 |

KEY

Area of main map

KEY

Sight / Place of interest

✈ Airport

Ⓜ Metro station

RER RER station

Ⓟ Parking

🛈 Tourist information

✝ Church

✡ Synagogue

| 0 meters | 750 |
| 0 yards | 750 |

Western end of the Ile de la Cité, where the island is crossed by the Pont Neuf

Ile de la Cité ①

Ⓜ *Châtelet, Cité.* **Conciergerie** 2 Blvd du Palais. *Tel 01-53 40 60 97.* ◯ *daily.* ● *Jan 1, May 1, Dec 25.* 🖼 🖼 *(phone to check).* **www**.monum.fr

This boat-shaped island on the Seine is the nucleus of Paris. The capital's name derives from the Parisii, one of the Celtic tribes who lived here in the 3rd century BC. The settlement was later expanded by the Romans, the Franks, and the Capetian kings.

Remains of the earliest buildings can be seen in the **Crypte Archéologique**, below the square in front of the mighty Notre-Dame cathedral, which stands at one end of the island. At the other end is another Gothic masterpiece: the Sainte-Chapelle church, surrounded by the huge complex of buildings forming the **Palais de Justice**. One of these, the sinister-looking **Conciergerie**, was a prison from 1391 until 1914. During the French Revolution the prison filled to overflowing, and Marie-Antoinette was held in a tiny cell here until her execution in 1793. The Conciergerie has a superb Gothic Hall and a 14th-century clock tower.

Crossing the western end of the island is the oldest bridge in Paris, the oddly named **Pont Neuf** (new bridge), which dates back to 1578.

The colorful Marché aux Fleurs et Oiseaux takes place daily in the Place Louis Lépine and is the city's most famous flower market. On Sundays caged birds are also sold.

Notre-Dame ②

See pp154–5.

Sainte-Chapelle ③

4 Boulevard du Palais. *Tel 01-53 40 60 80.* Ⓜ *Cité.* ◯ *daily.* ● *Jan 1, May 1, Nov 1 & 11, Dec 25.* 🖼 🖼

Hailed as one of the great architectural masterpieces of the Western world, in the Middle Ages this church was likened to "a gateway to heaven." Sainte-Chapelle was built in 1248 to house sacred relics, including Christ's Crown of Thorns, purchased from the Byzantine emperor at great expense by the devout King Louis IX.

The church consists of two chapels. The lower chapel was used by servants and minor officials, while the exquisite upper chapel, reached by means of a narrow, spiral staircase, was reserved for the royal family and courtiers. This chapel has many glorious stained-glass windows, separated by pencil-like columns soaring 15 m (50 ft) to the star-studded roof. Over 1,100 biblical scenes from the Old and New Testaments are depicted, as well as the story of how the relics were brought to Sainte-Chapelle. The 86 panels of the circular Rose Window, which are best seen at sunset, tell the story of the Apocalypse.

Badly damaged during the Revolution, and converted into a flour warehouse, the church was renovated a century later by architect Viollet-le-Duc. The spire, erected in 1853, rises 75 m (245 ft) into the air.

The Gothic Sainte-Chapelle church

Centre Pompidou ④

Pl G Pompidou. **Tel** 01-44 78 12 33.
Ⓜ Rambuteau, Châtelet, Hôtel de
Ville. ⓇⒺⓇ Châtelet-Les-Halles.
🚌 21, 29, 38, 47 & many others.
Musée National d'Art Moderne.
⭕ 11am–9pm Wed–Mon.
⬤ May 1. 📷 💳 ♿
www.centrepompidou.fr

With its skeleton of struts,
ducts, and elevators scaling
the outside of the building,
and offering fine views of the
city, this famous cultural
center has room for a vast
exhibition area inside.

Among the artists featured
in the Musée National d'Art
Moderne are Matisse, Picasso,
Miró, and Pollock, representing such schools as Fauvism,
Cubism, and Surrealism. Star
attractions are *Sorrow of the
King* (1952) by Matisse, and
Georges Braque's *The Duo*
(1937). A library is housed
on the first, second, and
third floors, while temporary
exhibitions are held on the
first and sixth floors.

Outside, the Piazza is
usually full of crowds watching
the street performers. On one
side of the square, the Atelier
Brancusi is a reconstruction of
the workshop of Romanian-
born artist Constantin Brancusi
(1876–1957), who left his
entire *oeuvre* to the nation.

Musée Picasso ⑤

Hôtel Salé, 5 Rue de Thorigny.
Tel 01-42 71 25 21. Ⓜ St-Sébastien
Froissart, St-Paul. ⭕ Wed–Mon.
⬤ Jan 1, Dec 25. 📷 💳 🖥 ♿
www.museepicasso.fr

The Spanish-born artist Pablo
Picasso (1881–1973) spent
most of his life in France. On
his death, the French state
inherited many of his works
in lieu of death duties, opening
a museum to display them in
1986. Housed in a 17th-
century mansion originally
built for a salt tax collector,
the collection comprises over
200 paintings, 158 sculptures,
100 ceramic works, and some
3,000 sketches and engravings.
The full extent of Picasso's
artistic development is
presented, from the somber

**Pipes and ducts on the outside of
the Centre Pompidou**

Blue period *Self-Portrait*
(1901) to Cubist collages and
Neoclassical works such as
Pipes of Pan. Highlights
include *The Two Brothers*
(1906), *The Kiss* (1969), and
*Two Women Running on the
Beach* (1922). The museum
also features a sculpture
garden. Exhibitions change
regularly and not all paintings
are on show at any one time.

Place des Vosges ⑥

Ⓜ Bastille, St-Paul.

This perfectly symmetrical
square, laid out in 1605 by
Henri IV, and known as Place
Royale, was once the residence
of the aristocracy. Considered
among the most beautiful in
the world by Parisians and
visitors alike, the square is
surrounded by 36 houses, nine

on each side. Built of brick and
stone, with dormer windows
over arcades, they have
survived intact for almost 400
years. Today, the historic
houses accommodate antiques
shops and fashionable cafés.

The square has been the
scene of many historical
events over the centuries,
including a three-day
tournament in celebration of
the marriage of Louis XIII to
Anne of Austria in 1615.
Among the square's famous
former residents are the
literary hostess, Madame de
Sévigné, born here in 1626,
Cardinal Richelieu, pillar of
the monarchy, and Victor
Hugo, who lived in one of
the houses for 16 years.

Place de la Bastille ⑦

Ⓜ Bastille.

Nothing remains of the
infamous prison stormed
by the revolutionary mob on
July 14, 1789, the event that
sparked the French Revolution.
A row of paving stones from
No. 5 to No. 49 Boulevard
Henri IV traces the line of
former fortifications.

The 52-m (170-ft) hollow
bronze Colonne de Juillet
stands in the middle of the
traffic-clogged square to
honor the victims of the July
Revolution of 1830. On the
south side of the square (at
120 Rue de Lyon) is the 2,700-
seat **Opéra Bastille**, completed
in 1989, the bicentennial of
the French Revolution.

Central fountain and fine Renaissance houses in the Place des Vosges

Notre-Dame ②

No other building embodies the history of Paris more than Notre-Dame. It stands majestically on the Ile de la Cité, cradle of the city. Built on the site of a Roman temple, the cathedral was commissioned by Bishop de Sully in 1159. The first stone was laid in 1163, marking the start of two centuries of toil by armies of medieval architects and craftsmen. It has been witness to great events of French history ever since, including the coronation of Napoleon Bonaparte (1804) and the state funeral of Charles de Gaulle (1970). During the Revolution, the building was desecrated and rechristened the Temple of Reason. Extensive renovations (including the addition of the spire and gargoyles) were carried out in the 19th century by architect Viollet-le-Duc.

★ West Front
Three main portals with superb statuary, a central rose window, and an openwork gallery are the outstanding features of the cathedral's façade.

The South Tower houses Emmanuel, the cathedral's most sonorous bell.

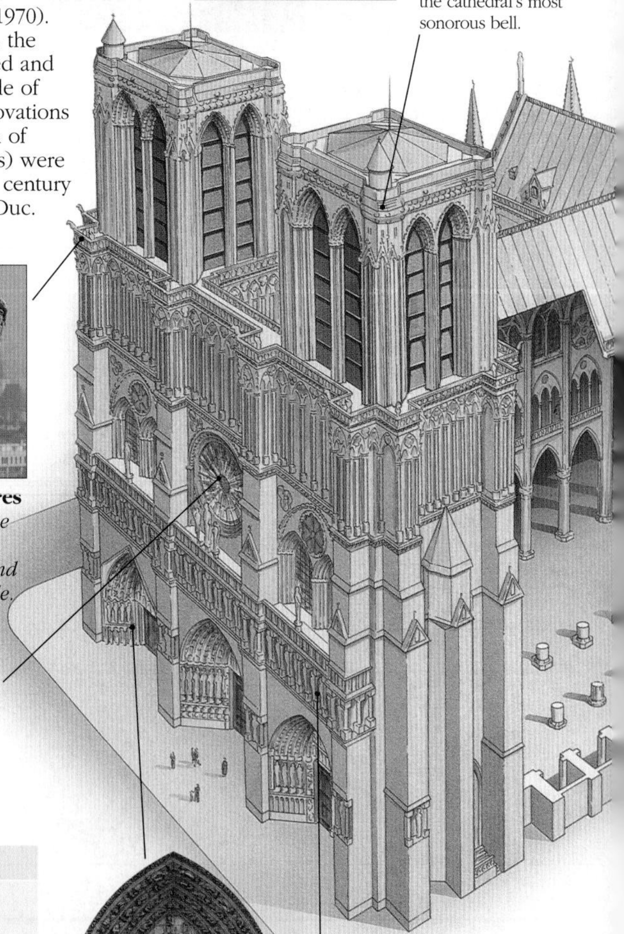

★ Galerie des Chimières
The cathedral's grotesque gargoyles (chimières) perch menacingly around ledges high on the façade.

The West Rose Window depicts the Virgin in a medallion of rich reds and blues.

STAR FEATURES

- ★ West Front and Portals
- ★ Flying Buttresses
- ★ Rose Windows
- ★ Galerie des Chimières

The Kings' Gallery features 28 kings of Judah gazing down from above the main door.

★ Portal of the Virgin
A statue of the Virgin surrounded by saints and kings decorates this massive 13th-century portal.

★ Flying Buttresses
Jean Ravy's spectacular flying buttresses at the east end of the cathedral have a span of 15 m (50 ft).

The Spire, designed by Viollet-le-Duc, soars to a height of 90 m (295 ft).

VISITORS' CHECKLIST

6 Place du Parvis-Notre-Dame. **Tel** 01-42 34 56 10. M Cité. 🚌 21, 38, 85, 96 to Ile de la Cité. ○ 7:45am–7pm daily (Treasury: 10am–6:45pm daily; towers: from 9:30am daily.) 🕇 8am, 9am, noon, 6:15pm Mon–Fri; 8am, 9am, noon, 6:30pm Sat; 8:30am, 10am, 11:30am, 12:45pm, 6:30pm Sun. 🔗 for Treasury and towers. 🔗 www.cathedraledeparis.com

★ South Rose Window
The south façade window, with its central depiction of Christ, is an impressive 13 m (43 ft) in diameter.

The Treasury houses the cathedral's religious treasures, including ancient manuscripts and reliquaries.

The transept was completed during the reign of Louis IX, in the 13th century.

Statue of Virgin and Child
Against the southeast pillar of the crossing stands the 14th-century statue of the Virgin and Child. It was brought to the cathedral from the chapel of St. Aignan and is known as Notre-Dame de Paris (Our Lady of Paris).

The Cathedral from the Left Bank
Notre-Dame's spectacular island setting is enhanced by the trees of Square Jean XXIII, a formal garden laid out at the eastern end of the Ile de la Cité.

Street-by-Street: Latin Quarter

Since the Middle Ages this riverside quarter has been dominated by the Sorbonne – it acquired its name from early Latin-speaking students. The area is generally associated with artists, intellectuals, and a bohemian way of life, and has a history of political unrest. In 1871 the Place St-Michel became the center of the Paris Commune, and in May 1968 it was one of the sites of the student uprisings that briefly engulfed the city.

St-Séverin
Begun in the 13th century, this beautiful church took three centuries to build and is a fine example of the Flamboyant Gothic style.

★ **Boulevard St-Michel**
The northern end of the Boul'Mich, as it is affectionately known, is a lively mélange of cafés, bookshops, and clothes stores, with nightclubs and experimental film houses nearby.

Cluny-La Sorbonne

Little Athens
takes its name from the many Greek restaurants situated in its picturesque streets.

St-Michel

★ **Musée National du Moyen Age**
The museum holds a fine collection of medieval art, with many beautiful tapestries. This detail is from the late 15th-century series of tapestries The Lady with the Unicorn.

0 meters		100
0 yards		100

For hotels and restaurants in this region see pp206–8 and pp212–13

LA SORBONNE

Seat of the University of Paris until 1969, the Sorbonne was established in 1257 by Robert de Sorbon, confessor to Louis IX, to enable poor scholars to study theology. It achieved fame as a center of learning in the late Middle Ages. The first printing house in France was founded here in 1469. Suppressed during the Revolution for opposition to liberal, 18th-century philosophical ideas, and re-established by Napoleon in 1806, the Sorbonne split into 13 separate universities in 1971. Lectures are still held on the original site.

St-Julien-le-Pauvre, one of the oldest churches in Paris, dates back to the 12th century.

Maubert-Mutualité

View of the Panthéon from the Jardin du Luxembourg

Panthéon ⑧

Place du Panthéon. **Tel** 01-44 32 18 00. Ⓜ Place Monge, Cardinal-Lemoine. ◯ daily. ● Jan 1, May 1, Nov 11, Dec 25.

Famous as the last resting place of some of France's greatest citizens, this magnificent church was built between 1764 and 1790 to honor Sainte Geneviève, patron saint of Paris. During the Revolution it was turned into a pantheon, to house the tombs of the illustrious.

Based on Rome's pantheon, the temple portico has 22 Corinthian columns, while the tall dome was inspired by that of St. Paul's in London (see p58). Geneviève's life is celebrated in a series of 19th-century nave murals. Many French notables rest in the crypt, including Voltaire, Rousseau, and Victor Hugo. The ashes of Pierre and Marie Curie are also held here.

Jardin du Luxembourg ⑨

Ⓜ Odéon. RER Luxembourg. ◯ daily.

This graceful and historic area offers a peaceful haven in the heart of Paris. The gardens, which cover 25 ha (60 acres), were opened to the public in the 19th century by their then owner, the Comte de Provence. They are centered around the Luxembourg Palace, which was built for Marie de Médicis, the widow of Henri IV, and is now the home of the French Senate. Dominating the gardens is an octagonal lake surrounded by formal terraces, where sunbathers gather on fine summer days.

St-Germain-des-Prés ⑩

3 Place St-Germain-des-Prés. **Tel** 01-55 42 81 33. Ⓜ St-Germain-des-Prés. ◯ daily.

Originating in 558 as a basilica to house holy relics, this is the oldest church in Paris. St-Germain had become a powerful Benedictine abbey by the Middle Ages, but was largely destroyed by fire in 1794. Major restoration took place in the 19th century. A single tower survives from the original three, housing one of the most ancient belfries in France. Famous tombs include that of 17th-century philosopher, René Descartes.

After World War II, the area attracted writers and artists, including one of the leading figures of the Existentialist movement, Jean-Paul Sartre, and writer Simone de Beauvoir. Bars and cafés, such as *Les Deux Magots* and the *Café de Flore*, which were their daily haunts, are now popular with tourists.

De Médicis fountain in the Jardin du Luxembourg

Ⓜ

KEY

− − − Suggested route

STAR SIGHTS

★ Musée National du Moyen Age

★ Boulevard St-Michel

Musée du Louvre ⑪

The Musée du Louvre, containing one of the world's most important art collections, has a history dating back to medieval times. First built as a fortress in 1190 by King Philippe-Auguste, it lost its dungeon and keep in the reign of François I, who commissioned a Renaissance-style building. Thereafter, four centuries of kings and emperors improved and enlarged the palace. It was first opened as a museum in 1793 under the First Republic. Major renovations were completed in 1998.

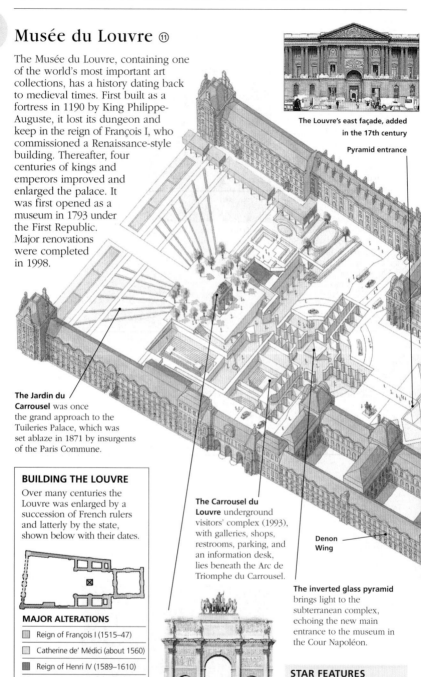

The Louvre's east façade, added in the 17th century

Pyramid entrance

The Jardin du Carrousel was once the grand approach to the Tuileries Palace, which was set ablaze in 1871 by insurgents of the Paris Commune.

BUILDING THE LOUVRE

Over many centuries the Louvre was enlarged by a succession of French rulers and latterly by the state, shown below with their dates.

MAJOR ALTERATIONS

- ☐ Reign of François I (1515–47)
- ☐ Catherine de' Médici (about 1560)
- ■ Reign of Henri IV (1589–1610)
- ☐ Reign of Louis XIII (1610–43)
- ☐ Reign of Louis XIV (1643–1715)
- ■ Reign of Napoleon I (1804–15)
- ■ Reign of Napoleon III (1852–70)
- ☐ François Mitterrand (1981–95)

The Carrousel du Louvre underground visitors' complex (1993), with galleries, shops, restrooms, parking, and an information desk, lies beneath the Arc de Triomphe du Carrousel.

Denon Wing

The inverted glass pyramid brings light to the subterranean complex, echoing the new main entrance to the museum in the Cour Napoléon.

★ **Arc de Triomphe du Carrousel**
This triumphal arch was built to celebrate Napoleon's military victories in 1806.

STAR FEATURES

★ Perrault Colonnade

★ Medieval Moats

★ Arc de Triomphe du Carrousel

For hotels and restaurants in this region see pp206–8 and pp212–13

THE GLASS PYRAMID

Plans for the modernization and expansion of the Louvre were first conceived in 1981. These included the transfer of the Ministry of Finance from the Richelieu wing to offices elsewhere and a new main entrance.

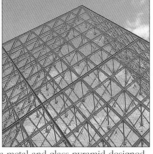

This took the form of a metal and glass pyramid designed by architect I.M. Pei. Opened in 1989, the pyramid enables the visitor to see the surrounding buildings, while allowing light down into the underground visitors' reception area.

VISITORS' CHECKLIST

Entrance through Pyramid or directly from metro. **Tel** *01 40 20 53 17.* M *Palais-Royal, Louvre Rivoli, Musée de Louvre.* 🚌 *21, 27, 39, 48, 68, 69, 72, 95.* RER *Châtelet-les-Halles.* P *Carrousel du Louvre (entrance via Ave du Général Lemmonnier); Place du Louvre, Rue St-Honoré.* **Museum** ◻ *9am–5:30pm Wed–Sun.* ● *Jan 1, May 1, Aug 15, Dec 25.* **Hall Napoléon** *(including History of the Louvre, Medieval Louvre, temporary exhibitions, restaurants, bookshop.)* ◻ *9am–10pm (6pm for exhibitions) Wed–Mon.* ● *same as museum.* 🎟️ *(reduced after 6pm and free for under-26s after 6pm Fri.)* ♿ *partial.* 📷 *phone 01 40 20 55 55.* **www**.louvre.fr

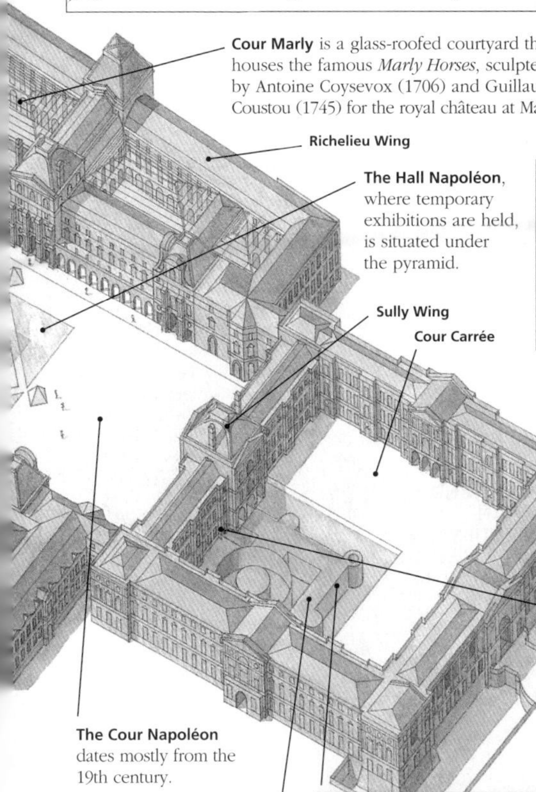

Cour Marly is a glass-roofed courtyard that houses the famous *Marly Horses*, sculpted by Antoine Coysevox (1706) and Guillaume Coustou (1745) for the royal château at Marly.

Richelieu Wing

The Hall Napoléon, where temporary exhibitions are held, is situated under the pyramid.

Sully Wing

Cour Carrée

★ **Perrault's Colonnade**
The east façade, with its majestic rows of columns, was built by Claude Perrault, who worked on the Louvre with Louis Le Vau in the mid-17th century.

The Salle des Caryatides is named after the four monumental statues created by Jean Goujon in 1550 to support the upper gallery. Built for Henri II, it is the oldest room in the palace.

The Cour Napoléon dates mostly from the 19th century.

Philippe-Auguste's old fortress, with its distinctive tower and keep, was transformed into a royal residence by Charles V in about 1365.

★ **Medieval Moats**
The base of the twin towers and the drawbridge support of Philippe-Auguste's fortress can be seen in the excavated area.

Exploring the Louvre's Collection

Owing to the vast size of the Louvre's collection, it is useful to set a few viewing priorities before starting. The collection of European paintings (1400–1848) is comprehensive, with over half the works by French artists. The extensively renovated departments of Oriental, Egyptian, Greek, Etruscan, and Roman antiquities are of world renown and feature numerous new acquisitions and rare treasures. The hugely varied display of *objets d'art* includes furniture, jewelry, scientific instruments, and armor.

The famously enigmatic *Mona Lisa* (c.1504) by Leonardo da Vinci

EUROPEAN PAINTING: 1400 TO 1848

Notable Flemish paintings include Jan van Eyck's *Madonna of the Chancellor Rolin* (c.1435). The fine Dutch collection features *Self-portrait* and *Bathsheba* (1654), both by Rembrandt. Among important German works are a *Venus* (1529) by Lucas Cranach and a portrait of Erasmus by Hans Holbein.

Italian paintings are arranged chronologically, and include Fra Angelico's *Coronation of the Virgin* (1435) and the celebrated *Mona Lisa* (1504) by Leonardo da Vinci.

Outstanding French works are represented by Enguerrand Quarton's *Villeneuve-lès-Avignon Pietà* (1455) and the delightfully frivolous *The Bathers* (1770) by Fragonard.

Among English artists featured are Gainsborough, Reynolds, and Turner, while the Spanish collection has portraits by Goya and works by El Greco and Zurbarán.

EUROPEAN SCULPTURE: 1100 TO 1848

The French section opens with a 12th-century figure of Christ and a head of St. Peter. Several works by French sculptor Pierre Puget (1620–94) are assembled in a glass-covered courtyard. Other masterpieces of French sculpture, including Jean-Antoine Houdon's busts of Diderot and Voltaire, stand in the Cour Marly. A notable Flemish sculpture is Adrian de Vries's long-limbed *Mercury and Psyche* (1593). Michelangelo's *Slaves* and Benvenuto Cellini's *Fontainebleau Nymph* are among the many splendid Italian works.

ORIENTAL AND EGYPTIAN ANTIQUITIES

Important works of Mesopotamian art include one of the world's oldest documents, a basalt block, bearing a proclamation of laws by Babylonian King Hammurabi, from about 1750 BC.

The warlike Assyrians are represented by delicate carvings, and a fine example of Persian art is the enameled brickwork depicting the king's archers (5th century BC).

Egyptian art on display, dating from between 2500 and 1400 BC, and mostly produced for the dead, includes lifelike funeral portraits, such as the *Squatting Scribe*, and several sculptures of married couples.

GREEK, ETRUSCAN, AND ROMAN ANTIQUITIES

The famous Greek marble statues here, the *Winged Victory of Samothrace* and the *Venus de Milo*, both date from the Hellenistic period (late 3rd to 2nd century BC). A highlight of the Roman section is a 2nd-century AD bronze head of the Emperor Hadrian. Other fine pieces include a bust of Agrippa and a basalt head of Livia. The star of the Etruscan collection is the terra-cotta sarcophagus of a married couple. Among the vast array of earlier fragments, a geometric head from the Cyclades (2700 BC) and a swan-necked bowl hammered out of a gold sheet (2500 BC) are noteworthy.

OBJETS D'ART

Venus de Milo

More than 8,000 items feature in this collection, many of which came from the Abbey of St-Denis, where the kings of France were crowned. Treasures include a serpentine plate from the 1st century AD and a golden scepter made for King Charles V in about 1380. The French crown jewels include the splendid coronation crowns of Louis XV and Napoleon, scepters, and swords. The Regent, one of the purest diamonds in the world, worn by Louis XV at his coronation in 1722, is also on show.

An entire room is taken up with a series of tapestries, the *Hunts of Maximilian*, executed for Emperor Charles V in 1530. The large collection of French furniture ranges from the 16th to the 19th centuries, and includes pieces by exceptional furniture-maker André Charles Boulle. He is particularly noted for his technique of inlaying copper and tortoiseshell. Among more unusual items is Marie-Antoinette's inlaid steel and bronze writing desk.

For hotels and restaurants in this region see pp206–8 and pp212–13

Neoclassical statues and urns in the Jardin des Tuileries

Jardin des Tuileries ⑫

Ⓜ *Tuileries, Concorde.* ☐ *7:30am–7pm daily.*

These gardens once belonged to the Palais des Tuileries, a palace which was razed to the ground during the time of the Paris Commune in 1871.

The gardens were laid out in the 17th century by André Le Nôtre, royal gardener to Louis XIV. He created a Neoclassical garden with a broad central avenue, regularly spaced terraces, and topiary arranged in geometric designs. Recent restoration has created a new garden with lime and chestnut trees and striking modern sculptures. Also in the gardens, two royal

tennis courts built in 1851 and known as the *Jeu de Paume* – literally "game of the palm" – now host exhibitions of contemporary art.

Musée de l'Orangerie ⑬

Jardin des Tuileries, Place de la Concorde. *Tel 01-44 77 80 07.* Ⓜ *Concorde.* 🚍 *24, 42, 52, 72, 73, 84, 94.* ☐ *12:30–7pm Wed–Mon.* ● *May 1, Dec 25.* 🕮 🗂 🎁 ♿
www.musee-orangerie.fr

The museum reopened in 2006 following a long closure for restructuring. Claude Monet's crowning work, his celebrated water lily series, still takes pride of place here. Known as the *Nymphéas*, most of the canvases were painted between 1899 and 1921 in the garden at Giverny, Normandy, where Monet lived from 1883 until his death at the age of 86.

This superb work is complemented by the Walter-Guillaume collection of artists of the Ecole de Paris, from the late Impressionist era to the inter-war period. Among a number of paintings by Cézanne are still lifes, portraits such as *Madame Cézanne*, and landscapes. The collection also features *The Red Rock*. There are 24 canvases by Renoir, one the most notable of which is *Les Fillettes au Piano*. Picasso is represented by early works such as *The Female Bathers*. Henri Rousseau has nine paintings, including *The Wedding and Le Carriole du Père Junier*. Among outstanding portraits is that of by Modigliano. Works by Sisley, Derain, and Utrillo are also featured. All the works are bathed in the natural light that filters through the windows of the museum.

Place de la Concorde ⑭

Ⓜ *Concorde.*

One of Europe's most magnificent and historic squares, covering over 8 ha (20 acres), the Place de la Concorde was a swamp until the mid-18th century. It became the Place Louis XV in 1763 when royal architect Jacques-Ange Gabriel was asked by the king to design a suitable setting for an equestrian statue of himself. He created an open octagon, with only the north side containing mansions.

The statue, which lasted here less than 20 years, was replaced by the guillotine (the Black Widow, as it came to be known), and the square was renamed Place de la Révolution. On January 21, 1793, Louis XVI was beheaded here, followed by over 1,300 other victims, including Marie Antoinette, Madame du Barry, Charlotte Corday (Marat's assassin), and revolutionary leaders Danton and Robespierre. The blood-soaked square was optimistically renamed Place de la Concorde after the Reign of Terror finally came to an end in 1794.

The grandeur of the square was enhanced a few decades later when the 3,200-year-old Luxor obelisk was presented to King Louis-Philippe as a gift from the viceroy of Egypt (who also donated Cleopatra's Needle in London). Two fountains and eight statues personifying French cities were also installed.

Flanking the Rue Royale on the north side of the square are two of Gabriel's Neoclassical mansions, the Hôtel de la Marine and the exclusive Hôtel Crillon.

Obelisk in Place de la Concorde

Entrance to the great collection of Impressionist and other paintings at the Musée de l'Orangerie

Interior of the Musée d'Orsay, showing original station architecture

Musée d'Orsay ⑮

Rue de la Légion d'Honneur. **Tel** 01-40 49 49 78. **M** Solférino. **RER** Musée d'Orsay. ⬜ 24, 68, 69, 84 & many others. ⬜ Tue–Sun. ⬜ Jan 1, May 1, Dec 25. 📷 ⬜ ♿ **www**.musee-orsay.fr

Originally built as a rail terminus in the heart of Paris, Victor Laloux's superb building, completed in 1900, narrowly avoided demolition in the 1970s. In 1986 it reopened as the Musée d'Orsay, with much of the original architecture preserved. The majority of the exhibits are paintings and sculptures dating from between 1848 and 1914, but there are also displays of furniture, the decorative arts, and cinema. The social, political, and technological context in which these diverse visual arts were created is explained.

Paintings from before 1870 are on the ground floor, presided over by Thomas Couture's massive *Romans in the Age of Decadence* (1847). Neoclassical masterpieces, such as Ingres' *La Source*, hang near Romantic works like Delacroix's turbulent *Tiger Hunt* (1854), and canvases by Degas and Manet, including the latter's *Le Déjeuner sur l'Herbe* and *Olympia* (1863).

The museum's central aisle overflows with sculpture, from Daumier's satirical busts of members of parliament to Carpeaux's exuberant *The Dance* (1868). Decorative arts and architecture are on the middle level, where there is

also a display of Art Nouveau, including Lalique jewelry and glassware. Impressionist works on the upper level include Renoir's *Moulin de la Galette* (1876). Matisse's *Luxe, Calme et Volupté* is among highlights of the post-1900 collection.

Musée Rodin ⑯

79 Rue de Varenne. **Tel** 01-44 18 61 10. **M** Varenne. **RER** Invalides. ⬜ 6, 9, 82, 87, 92. ⬜ Tue–Sun. ⬜ Jan 1, May 1, Dec 25. 📷 ♿ restricted. **www**.musee-rodin.fr

Auguste Rodin (1840–1917), widely regarded as one of France's greatest sculptors, lived and worked here in the Hôtel Biron, an elegant 18th-century mansion, from 1908 until his death. In return for a state-owned flat and studio, Rodin left his work to the nation, and it is now exhibited here. Some of his most celebrated sculptures are on display in the attractive garden and include *The Burghers of Calais, The Thinker, The Gates of Hell,* and *Balzac.*

The indoor exhibits are arranged in chronological order, spanning the whole of Rodin's career. Major works in the collection include *The Kiss* and *Eve.*

Rodin's *The Kiss* (1886) at the Musée Rodin

Les Invalides ⑰

M La Tour-Maubourg, Varenne. **RER** Invalides. ⬜ 28, 49, 63, 69 & many others. **Hôtel des Invalides Tel** 01-44 42 37 72. ⬜ daily. ⬜ Jan 1, May 1, Nov 1, Dec 25. **St-Louis-des-Invalides Tel** 01-44 42 37 65. ⬜ daily. **Dôme Church Tel** 01-44 42 37 72. ⬜ daily. ⬜ Jan 1, May 1, Jun 17, Nov 1, Dec 25. 📷 ⬜ ♿ restricted.

This vast ensemble of monumental buildings is one of the most impressive architectural sights in Paris. The imposing **Hôtel des Invalides**, from which the area takes its name, was commissioned by Louis XIV in 1671 for his wounded and homeless veterans. Designed by Libéral Bruand, it was completed in 1676 by Jules Hardouin-Mansart. Nearly 6,000 soldiers once resided here; today there are fewer than 100. Behind the Hôtel's harmonious Classical façade – a masterpiece of French 17th-century architecture – are several museums.

The **Musée de l'Armée** is one of the most comprehensive museums of military history in the world, with exhibits covering all periods from the Stone Age to World War II. Among items on display are François I's ivory hunting horns and a selection of arms from China, Japan, and India. The **Musée de l'Ordre de la Libération** was set up to honor feats of heroism during World War II, while the **Musée des Plans-Reliefs** has an extensive collection of detailed models of French forts and fortified towns, considered top secret until as late as the 1950s.

St-Louis-des-Invalides, the chapel of the Hôtel des Invalides, is also known as the "soldiers' church." It was built from 1679 to 1708 by Jules Hardouin-Mansart, to Bruand's design. The stark, Classical interior is designed in the shape of a Greek cross and has a fine 17th-century organ by Alexandre Thierry.

The **Dôme Church** was begun in 1676 to complement the existing buildings of Les Invalides, and to reflect the splendor of Louis XIV's reign. Reserved for the exclusive use of the Sun King himself, the resulting masterpiece is one of the greatest examples of *grand siècle* architecture and a monument to Bourbon glory. The crypt houses the tomb of Napoleon – six coffins with an enormous red sarcophagus on a pedestal of green granite. Marshal Foch, the World War I hero, is also buried here.

Façade of the Hôtel des Invalides, showing the splendid gilded dome

Eiffel Tower ⑱

Built for the Universal Exhibition of 1889, and to commemorate the centennial of the Revolution, the 324-m (1,063-ft) Eiffel Tower (Tour Eiffel) was meant to be a temporary addition to the Paris skyline. Designed by Gustave Eiffel, it was fiercely decried by 19th-century aesthetes. It was the world's tallest building until 1931, when New York's Empire State Building was completed. A number of crazy stunts have been attempted here. In 1912 a local tailor launched himself from the tower using a cape as wings. He plunged to his death.

VISITORS' CHECKLIST

Champ-de-Mars. **Tel** 01-44 11 23 23. **M** Bir Hakeim. **RER** Champ-de-Mars, Trocadéro. 🚌 42, 69, 82, 87. ⭘ daily. 🎫 🔁 limited. 📷 🍴 www.tour-eiffel.fr

The third level, 276 m (905 ft) above the ground, offers superb views. On a clear day it is possible to see for 72 km (45 miles) – as far as Chartres Cathedral *(see pp180–81)*.

The second level, at 115 m (376 ft), is reached either by elevator or by 359 steps from the first level.

Double-decker elevators take visitors to the top level, which can hold up to 400 people at a time.

The Jules Verne Restaurant is one of the best in Paris, offering excellent food and panoramic views.

THE EIFFEL TOWER IN FIGURES

• There are a total of 1,665 steps from bottom to top
• The tower is held together by a total of 2.5 million rivets
• It never sways more than 7 cm (2.5 in)
• The tower weighs 10,100 tons
• 50 tons of paint are used every seven years

The Eiffel Tower at night

The first level, at 57 m (187 ft), can be reached by elevator or by 345 steps. There is a post office here.

Trocadéro fountains in front of the Palais de Chaillot

Musée du Quai Branly ⑲

22 Rue de l'Université. **Tel** 01-56 61 70 00. Ⓜ Alma-Marceau. RER Pont de l'Alma. ⏱ Tue–Sun. 🏛 🔢 🎞 🛒 🚻 www.quaibranly.fr

Built to give the arts of Africa, Asia, Oceania, and the Americas a platform as shining as that reserved for Western art, this museum boasts a collection of more than 3,000 objects. It is particularly strong on Africa, with stone, wooden, and ivory masks, as well as

ceremonial tools. The Jean Nouvel-designed building, raised on stilts, is a sight in itself: the ingenious use of glass allows the surrounding greenery to act as a natural backdrop for the collection.

Palais de Chaillot ⑳

Place du Trocadéro 17. **Tel** 01-44 05 39 10. Ⓜ Trocadéro. RER Trocadéro. 🚌 27, 30, 32, 63, 72, 82. **Museums** ⏱ Wed–Mon. 🏛 🎞

With its curved colonnaded wings, each culminating in a

vast pavilion, this palace was designed in Neoclassical style for the 1937 Paris Exhibition by Azéma, Louis-Hippolyte Boileau, and Jacques Carlu. It is adorned with sculptures and bas-reliefs, and the pavilion walls are inscribed in gold with words composed by the poet Paul Valéry. The square between the two pavilions is highly decorated with bronze sculptures, ornamental pools, and shooting fountains. Steps lead down from here to the **Théâtre National de Chaillot**, famous for its avant-garde productions.

The **Cité de l'Architecture et du Patrimoine** is a vast new complex and information center incorporating Viollet-le-Duc's original Musée des Monuments Français (1882).

The **Musée de l'Homme** in the west wing traces human evolution through a series of anthropological, archaeological, and ethnological displays. Next door is the **Musée de la Marine**, devoted to French naval history.

The centerpiece of the lovely Jardins de Trocadéro is a long rectangular ornamental pool, bordered by statues. The gardens themselves are perfect for a quiet evening stroll.

BARON HAUSSMANN

A lawyer by training and civil servant by profession, Georges-Eugène Haussmann (1809–91) was appointed Prefect of the Seine in 1853 by Napoleon III. For 17 years Haussmann was responsible for the urban modernization of Paris. With a team of the best architects and engineers, he demolished the chaotic, insanitary streets of the medieval city and created a well-ventilated and ordered capital in a geometrical grid. He also increased the number of street-lights and sidewalks, giving rise to the cafés that enliven modern Parisian street life. The plan involved redesigning the area at one end of the Champs-Elysées and creating a star of 12 avenues centered around the new Arc de Triomphe.

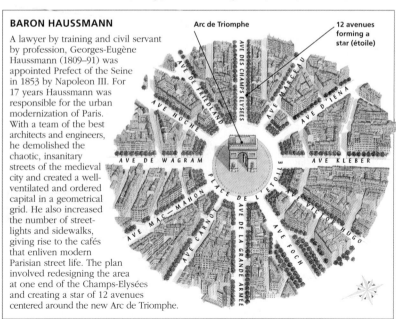

The east façade of the Arc de Triomphe

Arc de Triomphe ㉑

Place Charles de Gaulle. **Tel** 01-55 37 73 77. **M** Charles de Gaulle–Etoile. 🚌 22, 30, 31, 73, 92. 🕐 daily. 🔴 Jan 1, May 1, Dec 25. 🈂️ 🔲 🚹 **www**.monum.fr

After his greatest victory, the Battle of Austerlitz in 1805, Napoleon promised his men they would "go home beneath triumphal arches." The first stone of what was to become the world's most famous triumphal arch was laid the following year. But disruptions to architect Jean Chalgrin's plans – combined with the demise of Napoleonic power – delayed completion of this monumental structure until 1836. Standing 50 m (164 ft) high, the Arc is encrusted with flamboyant reliefs, shields, and sculptures, depicting military scenes such as the Napoleonic battles of Austerlitz and Aboukir.

On Armistice Day, 1921, the body of the Unknown Soldier was placed beneath the arch to commemorate the dead of World War I. The flame of remembrance which burns above the tomb is rekindled by various veterans organizations each evening. Today, the Arc

de Triomphe is the customary rallying point for many victory celebrations and parades.

The viewing platform on top of the Arc overlooks the length of the Champs-Elysées. On the other side, a fine view stretches as far as La Défense.

Champs-Elysées ㉒

M Franklin D. Roosevelt, George V, Champs-Elysées Clemenceau. **Grand Palais** Porte A, Ave Eisenhower. **Tel** 01-44 97 78 00. 🕐 Tue–Sun. 🈂️ 🔲 🚹 **Petit Palais** Ave Winston Churchill. **Tel** 01-42 65 12 73. 🕐 Tue–Sun. 🔴 public hols. 🚹 🔲 for exhibitions.

Paris's most famous and popular thoroughfare had its beginnings in about 1667, when landscape gardener André Le Nôtre extended the royal view from the Tuileries by creating a tree-lined avenue. The Champs-Elysées (Elysian Fields) has also been known as the "triumphal way" since the homecoming of Napoleon's body from St. Helena in 1840. With the addition of cafés and restaurants in the late 19th century, the Champs-Elysées became the most fashionable boulevard in Paris.

The formal gardens that line the Champs-Elysées from Place de la Concorde to the Rond-Point have changed little since they were laid out by architect Jacques Hittorff in 1838, and were used as the setting for the 1855 World's Fair. The Grand Palais and the Petit Palais were also built here for the Universal Exhibition of 1900.

The exterior of the massive **Grand Palais** combines an imposing Neoclassical façade with a riot of Art Nouveau ironwork. A splendid glass roof is decorated with colossal bronze statues of flying horses and chariots at its four corners. Inside is a science exhibition (Le Palais de la Découverte) and the Galeries Nationales du Grand Palais, which holds frequent temporary exhibitions.

Facing the Grand Palais, the recently renovated **Petit Palais** houses the Musée des Beaux-Arts de la Ville de Paris. Arranged around a pretty semicircular courtyard and garden, the palace is similar in style to the Grand Palais, with Ionic columns, a grand porch, and a dome echoing that of the Invalides across the river. The exhibits are divided into medieval and Renaissance objets d'art, paintings, and drawings; 18th-century furniture and objets d'art; and works by the French artists Gustave Courbet, Jean Ingres, and Eugène Delacroix.

Musée des Beaux-Arts de la Ville de Paris, in the Petit Palais

The deceptively rustic exterior of Au Lapin Agile, one of the best known nightspots in Paris

Montmartre ㉓

 Abbesses, Anvers. 🚌 30, 54, 80, 85. **Sacré-Coeur** 35 Rue du Chevalier de la Barre. **Tel** 01-53 41 89 00. ☐ daily. 🔲 for crypt and dome. ♿ restricted. **www**.sacre-coeur.montmartre.com

The steep hill of Montmartre has been associated with artists for 200 years. Théodore Géricault and Camille Corot came here at the start of the 19th century, and in the early 20th century Maurice Utrillo immortalized the streets in his works. Today, street artists of varying talents exhibit their work in the Place du Tertre, and thrive on the tourist trade. Exhibitions at the **Musée de Montmartre** usually feature works of artists associated with the area, while the **Musée d'Art Naïf Max Fourny** houses almost 600 examples of naive art. The **Espace Montmartre Salvador Dalí** displays over 300 works by the Surrealist painter and sculptor. Much of the area

still preserves its rather louche, prewar atmosphere. Former literary haunt **Au Lapin Agile**, or "Agile Rabbit," is now a club. The celebrated **Moulin Rouge** nightclub is also in the vicinity.

The name Montmartre, thought to derive from martyrs tortured and killed here around AD 250, is also associated with the grandiose **Sacré-Coeur**. Dedicated to the Sacred Heart of Christ, the basilica was built as a result of a vow made at the outbreak of the Franco-Prussian War in 1870. Businessmen Alexandre

Façade of the Romano-Byzantine Sacré-Coeur

Legentil and Hubert Rohault de Fleury promised to finance its construction should France be spared from the impending Prussian onslaught. Despite the war and the Siege of Paris, invasion was averted and work began in 1876 to Paul Abadie's designs. The basilica, completed in 1914, is one of France's most important Roman Catholic shrines. It contains many treasures, including a figure of the *Virgin Mary and Child* (1896) by Brunet.

Below the forecourt, Square Willette is laid out on the side of a hill in a series of descending terraces. A funicular railway takes visitors up from the bottom of the gardens to the foot of the steps of the basilica.

Parc de la Villette ㉔

30 Ave Corentin-Cariou. Ⓜ Porte de la Villette. 🚌 75, 139, 150, 152, 250A. **Cité des Sciences Tel** 01-40 05 80 00. ☐ Tue–Sun. 🔲 ♿

The old slaughterhouses and livestock market of Paris have been transformed into this massive urban park, designed by Bernard Tschumi. The major attraction of the site is the **Cité des Sciences et de l'Industrie**, a hugely popular science and technology museum. Architect Adrien Fainsilber has created an imaginative interplay of light, vegetation, and water in the high-tech, five-floor building, which soars to a height of 40 m (133 ft). At the museum's heart is the Explora exhibit, a fascinating guide to the worlds of science and technology. The Géode, a giant entertainment sphere, houses a huge hemispherical cinema screen. In the auditorium of the Planetarium, special effects projectors create exciting images of the stars and planets.

Also in the park, the **Grande Halle** was the old cattle hall, and has been turned into a huge exhibition space. The **Cité de la Musique** is a quirky but elegant complex that holds a music conservatory – home of the world-famous Paris *conservatoire* since 1990 – and a concert hall. Built as a venue for pop concerts, the **Zénith theater** seats over 6,000 spectators.

Cimetière du Père Lachaise ㉕

16 Rue du Repos. Ⓜ *Père-Lachaise, A Dumas.* **Tel** *01-55 25 82 10.* ◯ *Mon–Fri.*

Paris's most prestigious cemetery is set on a wooded hill overlooking the city. The land was once owned by Père de la Chaise, Louis XIV's confessor, but it was bought by order of Napoleon in 1803 to create a completely new cemetery. This became so popular with the Parisian bourgeoisie that its boundaries were extended six times during the 19th century. Here are buried celebrities such as the writer Honoré de Balzac, the famous playwright Molière, the composer Frédéric Chopin, singer Edith Piaf, and actors Simone Signoret and Yves Montand. Famous foreigners interred in the cemetery include Oscar Wilde and the singer Jim Morrison. The Columbarium, built at the end of the 19th century, houses the ashes of American dancer Isadora

Monument to Oscar Wilde in the Père Lachaise Cemetery

Duncan, among others. The equally charismatic Sarah Bernhardt, famous for her portrayal of Racine heroines, also reposes at Père Lachaise. Striking funerary sculpture and famous graves make this a pleasant place for a leisurely, nostalgic stroll.

La Défense ㉖

Ⓡ *La Défense.* **La Grande Arche** **Tel** *01-49 07 27 57.* ◯ *daily.* 🎫 ♿

This skyscraper business city on the western edge of Paris is the largest office development in Europe and covers 80 ha (198 acres). It was launched in 1957 to create a new home for leading French and foreign companies. **La Grande Arche** is an

enormous hollow cube, spacious enough to contain Notre-Dame cathedral. Designed by Danish architect Otto von Spreckelsen in the late 1980s, the arch houses an exhibition gallery and offers superb views over the city.

Bois de Boulogne ㉗

Ⓜ *Porte Maillot, Porte Dauphine, Porte d'Auteuil, Sablons.* ◯ *24 hrs daily.* 🎫 *to specialist gardens and museum.* ♿

Located between the river Seine and the western edges of Paris, this 865-ha (2,137-acre) park offers a vast belt of greenery for strolling, cycling, riding, boating, picnicking, or spending a day at the races. The Bois de Boulogne was once part of the immense Forêt du Rouvre. In the mid-19th century Napoleon III had the area redesigned and landscaped by Baron Haussmann along the lines of Hyde Park in London (*see p54*). A number of self-contained parks include the Pré Catelan, which has the widest beech tree in Paris, and the Bagatelle gardens, with architectural follies and an 18th-century villa famous for its rose garden. The villa was built in just 64 days as the result of a bet between the Comte d'Artois and Marie-Antoinette.

By day the Bois is busy with families, joggers, and walkers, but after dark it is notoriously seedy – and best avoided.

Kiosque de l'Empereur, on an island in the Grand Lac, Bois de Boulogne

Château de Versailles ㉘

Visitors passing through the dazzling state rooms of this colossal palace, or strolling in its vast gardens, will soon understand why it was the glory of the Sun King's reign. Started by Louis XIV in 1668, the palace grew from a modest hunting lodge built for his father, Louis XIII, to become the largest palace in Europe, housing some 20,000 people. Architect Louis Le Vau built the first section, which expanded into an enlarged courtyard. From 1678, Jules Hardouin-Mansart added the north and south wings and the superb Hall of Mirrors. He also designed the chapel, completed in 1710. The interiors were largely the work of Charles Le Brun, and the great landscape gardener, André Le Nôtre, redesigned the gardens with their monumental fountains.

★ Hall of Mirrors
This magnificent room, 70 m (233 ft) long, was the settting for great state occasions. It was here that the Treaty of Versailles was ratified at the end of World War I.

Marble Courtyard
The courtyard is decorated with marble paving, urns, and busts. Above the gilded central balcony, the figures of Hercules and Mars flank the clock on the pediment.

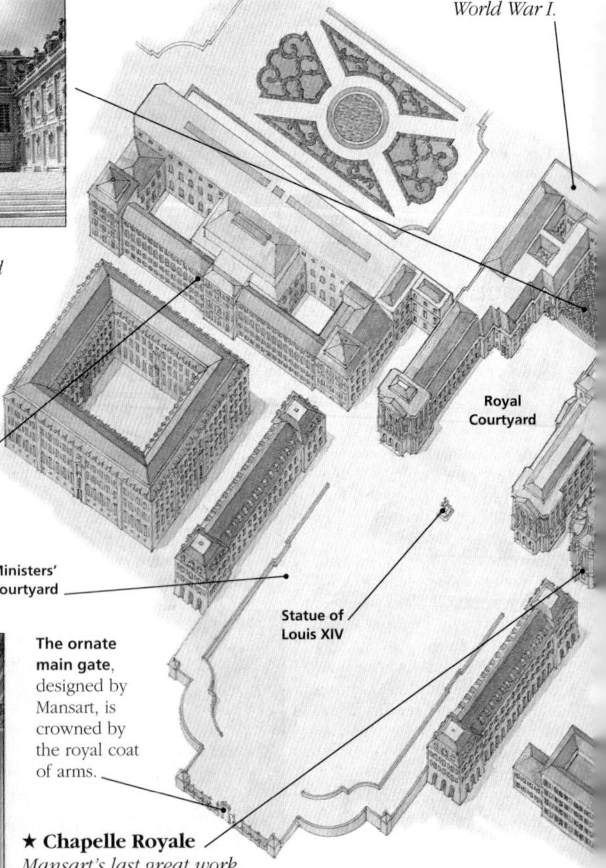

The South Wing
originally housed the apartments of great nobles. It is now a history museum.

Ministers' Courtyard

Royal Courtyard

The ornate main gate, designed by Mansart, is crowned by the royal coat of arms.

Statue of Louis XIV

★ Chapelle Royale
Mansart's last great work, this Baroque chapel was Louis XIV's final addition to Versailles. The beautiful interior is decorated with Corinthian columns and superb Baroque murals.

STAR FEATURES

★ Chapelle Royale

★ Hall of Mirrors

VISITORS' CHECKLIST

Versailles, Yvelines. **Tel** 01-30 83
76 20. 🚇 Versailles Chantiers,
Versailles Rive Droite. 🚊 Versailles
Rive Gauche. 🚌 171 from Paris.
Château ⬤ 9am–6:30pm Tue–
Sun (5:30pm in winter). ⬤ some
public hols. 📷 **Grand & Petit
Trianon** ⬤ pm daily. ⬤ Jan 1,
Dec 25. 📷 🎫 ♿ **Musée des
Carrosses** ⬤ pm Sat & Sun. 📷
🎆 Les Fêtes de Nuit (Aug–Sep).
www.chateauversailles.fr

The 17th-century Fountain of Neptune by Le Nôtre and Mansart

North Wing

*The chapel, Opera House,
and picture galleries occupy
this wing, which originally
housed royal apartments.*

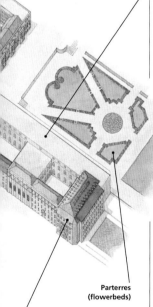

Parterres
(flowerbeds)

The Opera House in the
North Wing was completed
for the 1770 marriage of
the future Louis XVI and
Marie-Antoinette.

Exploring the Palace

The main rooms of the palace
are on the first floor. Around
the Marble Courtyard are the
private apartments of the king
and queen. Visitors can see
the King's Bedroom, where
Louis XIV died, aged 77, in
1715. The room next door, the
Cabinet du Conseil, was where
the monarch would receive
ministers and family members.

On the garden side, the state
apartments are richly decorated
with colored marbles, carvings
in stone and wood, murals,
and gilded furniture. Each is
dedicated to an Olympian
deity. Louis XIV's throne room,
the Salon d'Apollon, designed
by Le Brun, is dedicated to
the god Apollo. A copy
of the famous portrait of
Louis by Hyacinthe
Rigaud hangs above the
fireplace. The war theme
of the Salon de la Guerre
is reinforced by a stucco
relief of Louis XIV riding
to victory. The high point
of the tour is the Hall of
Mirrors, with its 17 great
mirrors reflecting the light
from tall arched windows.

Marie-Antoinette's beloved Petit Trianon

Among the other major
attractions are the Chapelle
Royale and the **Musée des
Carrosses** (coach museum)
opposite the palace.

The Gardens of Versailles

The gardens are a fitting
counterpart to the colossal
palace. Immediately in front
of the palace is the Water
Parterre, decorated with superb
bronze statues. Paths lead
through the formal gardens,
with their regularly patterned
flowerbeds and hedges, to
groves, lakes, fountains, and
architectural features such as
the Colonnade (1685), a circle
of marble arches designed by
Mansart. The largest stretch
of water is the Grand Canal,
where Louis XIV held
spectacular boating parties.

The gardens contain two
smaller palaces. The **Grand
Trianon**, built of stone and
pink marble, was designed by
Mansart in 1687 as a discreet
hideaway for Louis XIV and
his mistress, Madame de
Maintenon. The nearby **Petit
Trianon** (1762) was built for
Madame de Pompadour,
Louis XV's
mistress. It later
became a favorite
retreat for Marie-
Antoinette.
Behind it is the
Hameau, a mini-
village where the
queen would
dress up as a
shepherdess and
play with a flock
of groomed and
perfumed lambs.

Basilique St-Denis ㉙

1 Rue de la Légion d'Honneur. **M**
St-Denis-Basilique. RER *St-Denis.* **Tel**
01-48 09 83 54. ◯ *daily.* ● *Jan 1,*
May 1, Dec 25. 🎟 📷 ♿ *restricted.*

Constructed between 1137 and 1281, the basilica is on the site of the tomb of St. Denis, the first bishop of Paris, who was beheaded in Montmartre in AD 250. According to legend, his decapitated figure, clutching his head, was seen here, and an abbey was erected to commemorate the martyred bishop. The basilica was the first church to be built in the Gothic style of architecture.

From as early as the 7th century St-Denis was a burial place for French rulers, and all the queens of France were crowned here. During the Revolution many tombs were desecrated and scattered, but the best were stored, and now represent a fine collection of

funerary art. Memorials include those of Dagobert (died 638), François I (died 1547), Henri II (died 1559) and Catherine de' Medici (died 1589), and Louis XVI and Marie-Antoinette (died 1793).

Of the medieval effigies, the most impressive are of Charles V (1364) and a 12th-century likeness in enameled copper of Blanche de France with her dog. Their mask-like serenity contrasts with the realistic Renaissance portrayal of agony in the sculptures of the mausoleum of Louis XII and Anne de Bretagne.

Disneyland Paris ㉚

Marne-la-Vallée, Seine-et-Marne. 🚆
TGV from Lille or Lyon. RER *Marne-la-Vallée-Chessy.* 🚌 *from CDG & Orly airports.* **Tel** *08-25 30 60 30.* ◯ *daily.*
🎟 ♿ www.disneylandparis.fr

The theme park, which lies 32 km (20 miles) east of Paris, covers 60 ha (150 acres). It is divided into five themed

areas. Although these rely heavily on Hollywood nostalgia, Disneyland Paris has tried to give the park a European touch.

"Frontierland," inspired by the Wild West of 19th-century America, can be explored on paddlewheel steamboats. A roller coaster trundles through mountain scenery.

In "Adventureland" visitors encounter characters and tales from adventure fiction, including Caribbean pirates and the Swiss Family Robinson.

Small-town America at the turn of the century is evoked in "Main Street." Authentic details include horse-drawn vehicles and a traditional barber's shop.

Young children will enjoy "Fantasyland," devoted to Disney characters and tales, where they can fly with Peter Pan or search the Alice in Wonderland maze for the Queen of Hearts' castle.

"Discoveryland" has futuristic architecture and sophisticated technology. Here, visitors can choose to be miniaturized by a hapless inventor or sent on a thrilling space trip.

Château de Vaux-le-Vicomte ㉛

Maincy, Seine-et-Marne. 🚗 RER
Melun, then taxi. **Tel** *01-64 14 41 90.*
◯ *late Mar–mid-Oct: daily.* 🎟 ♿

Located 64 km (40 miles) southeast of Paris, just north of Melun, the château enjoys a peaceful rural setting. Nicolas Fouquet, a powerful court financier to Louis XIV, challenged architect Le Vau and decorator Le Brun to create the most sumptuous palace of the day. The result was one of the greatest 17th-century French châteaux. However, it also led to his downfall. Louis was so enraged – because its luxury cast the royal palaces into the shade – that he had Fouquet arrested and confiscated all his estates.

As befits Fouquet's grand tastes, the interior is a gilded banquet of frescoes, stucco, caryatids, and giant busts. The Salon des Muses boasts Le Brun's magnificent frescoed

The tomb of Louis XII and Anne de Bretagne in the Basilique St-Denis

Château de Vaux-le-Vicomte seen across the formal gardens designed by Le Nôtre

ceiling of dancing nymphs and poetic sphinxes. La Grande Chambre Carrée is decorated in Louis XIII style with paneled walls and an impressive triumphal frieze, evoking Rome.

Much of Vaux-le-Vicomte's fame is due to French landscape gardener André Le Nôtre (1613–1700). At Vaux he perfected the concept of the *jardin à la française*: avenues framed by statues and box hedges, water gardens with ornate pools, and geometrical parterres "embroidered" with floral motifs.

Château de Fontainebleau ㉜

Seine-et-Marne. 🚈 **Tel** *01-60 71 50 60.* 🕐 *Wed–Mon.* 📷 📷 ♿
www.musee-chateau-fontainebleau.fr

Fontainebleau was a favorite royal residence from the 12th to the mid-19th century. Its charm lies in its relative informality and its spectacular setting in a forest 65 km (40 miles) south of Paris. The present château dates back to François I. Drawn to the area by the local hunting, the Renaissance king created a decorative château modeled on Florentine and Roman styles. Subsequent rulers enlarged and embellished the château, creating a cluster of buildings

in various styles from different periods. During the Revolution the apartments were looted by a mob, and remained bare until the 1800s when Napoleon refurbished the whole interior.

The Cour du Cheval Blanc, once a simple enclosed courtyard, was transformed by Napoleon into the main approach to the château. At one end is the Escalier du Fer-à-Cheval (1634), an imposing horseshoe-shaped staircase.

The interior suites showcase the château's history as a royal residence. The Galerie François I has a superb collection of Renaissance art. The Salle de Bal, a Renaissance ballroom designed by Primaticcio (1552), features emblems of Henri II on the walnut coffered ceiling

and reflected in the parquet floor. The apartments of Napoleon I house his grandiose throne, in the former Chambre du Roi. The complex of buildings also contains the Musée Napoléon, in which eight rooms recreate different scenes from the Emperor's life.

Nearby is the Chapelle de la Sainte Trinité, designed for Henri II in 1550. The chapel acquired its vaulted and frescoed ceiling under Henri IV, and was completed during the reign of Louis XIII.

The gardens are also worth exploring. The Jardin Anglais is a romantic "English" garden planted with cypresses and exotic species. The Jardin de Diana features a bronze fountain of Diana the huntress.

The Salle de Bal of Henri II, Château de Fontainebleau

Northern France

Northern France's main sights span thousands of years of history, from the awesome megaliths of Carnac, through the 18th-century grandeur of Nancy's town architecture, to Strasbourg's futuristic Palais de l'Europe, seat of the European Parliament. Its cities boast some of the country's greatest cathedrals, such as those of Reims and Rouen. The region's most famous religious monument is Mont-St-Michel, whose evocative silhouette has welcomed pilgrims since the 11th century.

Strasbourg's fine Gothic cathedral surrounded by historic buildings

Strasbourg ❷

Bas Rhin. 🏘 450,000. 🛬 15 km (8 miles) SW. 🚆 🚌 🅸 17 Place de la Cathédrale (03-88 52 28 22). 🎷 International Music Festival (Jun). www.ot-strasbourg.fr

Located halfway between Paris and Prague, this cosmopolitan city is often known as "the crossroads of Europe." It is also home to the European Parliament.

A boat trip along the waterways that encircle Strasbourg's Old Town takes in the **Ponts-Couverts** – bridges with medieval watchtowers – and the old tanners' district, dotted with attractive half-timbered houses.

Dating from the late 11th century, the **Cathédrale Notre-Dame** dominates the city. There are wonderful views from the top of its spire.

The grand Classical **Palais Rohan** houses three museums: the Musée des Beaux Arts, the Musée Archéologique, and the Musée des Arts Décoratifs, which has one of the finest displays of ceramics in France.

Also worth visiting is the **Musée d'Art Moderne et Contemporain**, **Le Vaisseau**, a scientific discovery center for children aged 3–15, and the **Musée Alsacien**, which contains exhibits on local traditions, arts, and crafts.

Reims ❸

Marne. 🏘 200,000. 🚆 🚌 🅸 2 Rue Guillaume de Machault (03-26 77 45 25). www.reims-tourisme.com

Renowned throughout the world from countless champagne labels, Reims has a rich historical legacy.

The city's most famous monument is the magnificent Gothic **Cathédrale Notre-Dame**, begun in 1211. For several centuries the cathedral was the setting for the coronation of French kings. Highlights are the 13th-century Great Rose Window and the west façade, decorated with over 2,300 statues.

On the eve of a coronation, the future king spent the night in the **Palais du Tau** (1690), the archbishops' palace adjoining the cathedral. Its

15th-century banqueting hall, the Salle du Tau, with its barrel-vaulted ceiling and Arras tapestries, is a star attraction.

Among other fine historic buildings are the 17th-century **Ancien Collège des Jésuites**, with its Baroque interior, and the **Basilique St-Remi**, the oldest church in Reims.

Relics of the town's Roman past include the **Crypto-portique**, part of the former forum, and the **Porte Mars**, a triumphal Augustan arch.

The **Musée de la Reddition** occupies the building that served as Eisenhower's French headquarters during World War II. It was here, in 1945, that the general received the Germans' surrender, which ended the war.

Environs
A short drive south of Reims is **Epernay**. Here you can visit the cellars of a number of distinguished champagne "houses," including those of Moët et Chandon.

🅷 **Cathédrale Notre-Dame**
3 Rue Guillaume de Machault. **Tel** 03-26 47 55 34. ☐ daily. ☑ by appt. ♿

Rouen ❹

Seine Maritime. 🏘 138,000. 🛬 11 km (7 miles) SE. 🚆 🚌 🅸 25 Place de la Cathédrale (02-32 08 32 40). www.rouentourisme.com

Formerly a Celtic trading post, Roman garrison, and Viking colony, Rouen became the capital of the Norman Duchy in 911. Today it is a rich and cultured city that boasts a wealth of splendid

Statuary on the west façade of Reims' Cathédrale Notre-Dame

Detail from the 11th-century Bayeux Tapestry

historical monuments. Rouen's Gothic cathedral, the **Cathédrale Notre-Dame**, has an impressive west façade, made famous by the great Impressionist painter Claude Monet (1840–1926), who made almost 30 paintings of it. A number of these can be seen in the city's excellent **Musée des Beaux Arts**.

From the cathedral, the Rue du Gros Horloge leads west, passing under the city's Great Clock, to the Place du Vieux Marché, where Joan of Arc was burnt at the stake in 1431.

The Flamboyant Gothic **Eglise St-Maclou** and the Gothic **Eglise St-Ouen** are two of Rouen's finest churches. The Eglise St-Ouen is noted for its restored 14th-century stained-glass windows.

The **Musée de la Céramique** displays around 1,000 pieces of Rouen faïence – colorful glazed earthenware – as well as other pieces of French and foreign china.

The former family home of Gustave Flaubert (1821–80) has been converted into a museum containing memorabilia from this famous French novelist's life.

🏛 **Musée des Beaux Arts**
Square Verdrel. *Tel* 02-35 71 28 40.
◯ Wed–Mon. ● public hols. 🗟 🕭

Bayeux ❺

Calvados. 🏠 15,000. 🚇 🚌 🛈
Pont-St-Jean (02-31 51 28 28).

The main reason for making a stop at this small town in Normandy is to see the world-renowned Bayeux Tapestry. This incredible work of art depicts William the Conqueror's invasion of England and the Battle of

Hastings in the 11th century from the Norman perspective. It was probably commissioned by Bishop Odo of Bayeux, William's half-brother. The 70-m (230-ft) long embroidered hanging is displayed in a renovated seminary, the **Centre Guillaume-le-Conquérant**, which also gives a detailed audio-visual account of the events leading up to the Norman conquest.

Apart from its tapestry, a cluster of 15th–19th-century buildings and the Gothic **Cathédrale Notre-Dame** are Bayeux's principal attractions.

Bayeux was the first town in Nazi-occupied France to be liberated by the Allies following the D-Day landings in 1944. On the southwest side of the town's ring road, the **Musée Mémorial de la Bataille de Normandie** traces the events of the Battle of Normandy in World War II.

🏛 **Centre Guillaume-le-Conquérant**
Rue de Nesmond. *Tel* 02-31 51 25 50.
◯ daily. ● Jan 1–2, Dec 25–26.
🗟 🕭

Mont-St-Michel ❻

See pp174–5.

St-Malo ❼

Ille-et-Vilaine. 🏠 53,000. ✈ 🚉
🚌 🛈 Esplanade St-Vincent (02-99 56 64 43). 🛒 Mon–Sat.

Once a fortified island, St-Malo stands in a commanding position at the mouth of the river Rance. In the 16th–19th centuries the port won prosperity and power through the exploits of its seafaring population.

Intra-muros, the old walled city, is encircled by ramparts that provide fine views of St-Malo and its offshore islands. Within the city walls is a web of narrow, cobbled streets with tall 18th-century buildings housing many souvenir shops, seafood restaurants, and creperies.

St-Malo's castle, the **Château de St-Malo** dates from the 14th and 15th centuries. The great keep today houses an interesting museum charting the city's history. In the three-towered fortification known as the **Tour Solidor**, to the west of St-Malo, is a museum devoted to the ships and sailors that rounded Cape Horn.

Carnac ❽

Morbihan. 🏠 4,600. 🚌 🛈 74 Avenue des Druides (02-97 52 13 52).

This popular town is probably most famous as one of the world's great prehistoric sites. As long ago as 4000 BC thousands of ancient granite rocks were arranged in mysterious lines and patterns in the country-side around Carnac by Mega-lithic tribes. Their original purpose is uncertain, though they are thought to have religious significance or to be related to an early astronomical calendar. Celts, Romans, and Christians have since adapted them to their own beliefs.

You can see some of the menhirs at the Kermario site, on the town outskirts, while in the center, the **Musée de Préhistoire** gives an insight into the area's ancient history.

Menhirs (prehistoric standing stones) in a field near Carnac

Mont-St-Michel ⑥

Shrouded by mist, engulfed by sea, soaring proud above glistening sands – the silhouette of Mont-St-Michel is one of the most enchanting sights in France. Now linked to the mainland by a causeway, the island of Mont-Tombe (Tomb on the Hill) stands at the mouth of the river Couesnon, crowned by a fortified abbey that almost doubles its height. Lying strategically on the frontier between Normandy and Brittany, Mont-St-Michel grew from a humble 8th-century oratory to become a Benedictine monastery that had its greatest influence in the 12th and 13th centuries. Pilgrims known as *miquelots* journeyed from afar to honor the cult of St. Michael, and the monastery was a renowned center of medieval learning. After the French Revolution the abbey became a prison. It is now a national monument that draws some 850,000 visitors a year.

★ **Abbey Church**
Four bays of the Romanesque nave in the abbey church survive. Three were pulled down in 1776, creating the West Terrace.

St. Aubert's Chapel, built on an outcrop of rock, dates from the 15th-century and is dedicated to Aubert, the founder of Mont-St-Michel.

Gabriel Tower

Gautier's Leap
Situated at the top of the Inner Staircase, this terrace is named after a prisoner who leaped to his death here.

The ramparts – a series of fortified walls with imposing towers – were built following attacks by the English during the Hundred Years' War.

Entrance

VISITING THE ABBEY

The abbey is built on three levels, which reflect the monastic hierarchy. The monks lived on the highest level *(shown here)*, in an enclosed world of church, cloister, and refectory. The abbot entertained his noble guests on the middle level. Soldiers and pilgrims further down on the social scale were received at the lowest level. Guided tours begin at the West Terrace at the church (highest) level and end on the lowest level in the almonry, where alms were distributed to the poor.

La Merveille is the name given to the buildings on the north side of the church.

Abbey Church

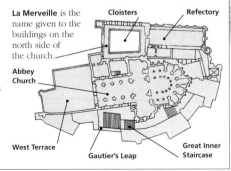

Cloisters

Refectory

West Terrace

Gautier's Leap

Great Inner Staircase

★ **Cloisters**
With their elegant English Purbeck marble columns, the cloisters are a beautiful example of early 13th-century Anglo-Norman style.

★ **La Merveille**
The main three-story monastic complex, added to the church's north side in the early 13th century, is known as La Merveille (The Miracle). The Knights' Room, on the middle floor, has magnificent Gothic rib-vaulting and finely decorated capitals.

Eglise St-Pierre

Liberty Tower

King's Tower

The Arcade Tower
provided lodgings for the abbot's soldiers.

VISITORS' CHECKLIST

to Pontorson, then bus.
Boulevard de l'Avancée
(02-33 60 14 30). St-Michel de Printemps (May).
Abbey Tel 02-33 89 80 00.
May–Sep: 9am–5pm;
Oct–Apr: 9:30am–6pm.
Night visits during summer.
Jan 1, May 1, Dec 25.
12:15pm Tue–Sun.
www.ot-montsaintmichel.com

STAR FEATURES

★ Abbey Church

★ La Merveille

★ Cloisters

★ Grande Rue

★ **Grande Rue**
Now crowded with tourists and souvenir shops, the pilgrims' route, followed since the 12th century, climbs up past the Eglise St-Pierre to the abbey gates.

The Loire Valley

Renowned for its sumptuous chateaux, the relics of royal days gone by, the glorious valley of the Loire is rich in both history and architecture. As the Loire runs through the heart of France, so the region embodies the essence of the French way of life. Its sophisticated cities, luxuriant landscape, and magnificent food and wine add up to a modern paradise. The Loire has long been described as exemplifying *la douceur de vivre*: it combines a leisurely pace of life, a mild climate, and the gentle ways of its inhabitants. The overall impression is one of an unostentatious taste for the good things in life.

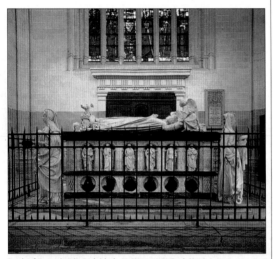

Tomb of François II in Cathédrale St-Pierre et St-Paul, Nantes

Nantes ❾

Loire-Atlantique. 🏘 *270,000.* ✈ 🚇
🚌 ℹ *2 Place St-Pierre (08-92 46 40 44).* 🏪 *Tue–Sun.* www.nantes-tourisme.com

The ancient port of Nantes was the ducal capital of Brittany for 600 years, but is now considered a part of the Pays de la Loire. Many of its fine 18th- and 19th-century buildings were built on profits from maritime trade. Modern-day Nantes is a lively city, with good museums, chic bars and shops, and wide open spaces.

The **Cathédrale St-Pierre et St-Paul** was begun in 1434, but not completed until 1893. It is notable for its sculpted Gothic portals and Renaissance tomb of François II (1435–88), the last duke of Brittany.

The **Château des Ducs de Bretagne**, now with a

museum documenting the town's history, was the birthplace of Anne of Brittany, who irrevocably joined her fiercely independent duchy to France by her successive marriages to Charles VIII and Louis XII. A smaller royal lodging lies to the west of it. It was here, in Brittany's Catholic bastion, that Henri IV signed the 1598 Edict of Nantes, which granted all Protestants freedom of worship.

The **Musée des Beaux-Arts** has a splendid array of paintings representing key movements from the 15th to the 20th centuries. Packed with mementos, books, and maps, the **Musée Jules Verne** is dedicated to the life and works of the famous writer (1828–1905).

🏛 **Musée des Beaux-Arts**
10 Rue Georges Clemenceau.
Tel 02-51 17 45 00. ⬤ *Wed–Mon.*
⬤ *public hols.* 📷 ♿

Poitiers ❿

Vienne. 🏘 *85,000.* ✈ 🚇 🚌
ℹ *45 Place Charles de Gaulle (05-49 41 21 24).* 🏪 *Tue–Sun.* www.ot-poitiers.fr

Three of the greatest battles in French history were fought around Poitiers, the most famous in 732 when Charles Martel halted the Arab invasion. Today the town is a dynamic regional capital with a rich architectural heritage.

Behind the Renaissance façade of the **Palais de Justice** is the 12th-century great hall of the palace of Henry II and Richard the Lion-Heart. This is thought to be the scene of Joan of Arc's examination by a council of theologians in 1429.

Notre-Dame-la-Grande, whose west front is covered with superb 12th-century Poitevin sculpture, stands out among the city's churches, as does the 4th-century **Baptistère St-Jean**, one of the oldest Christian buildings in France. The latter contains Romanesque frescoes.

The **Musée Sainte-Croix** has archaeological exhibits, as well as paintings and sculpture.

Environs
Just 7 km (4.5 miles) north of Poitiers, **Futuroscope** is a theme park dedicated to state-of-the-art visual technology, including the largest cinema screen in Europe.

🏛 **Futuroscope**
Jaunay-Clan. **Tel** 05-49 49 30 80.
⬤ *daily.* ⬤ *Jan.* 📷 ♿
www.futuroscope.com

The high-tech Kinemax cinema at Futuroscope, near Poitiers

Abbaye Royale de Fontevraud ⓫

Maine-et-Loire. 🚌 **Tel** 02-41 51 71 41. ◯ daily. ● Jan 1, May 1, Nov 1 & 11, Dec 25. 🎫 📷 ♿ restricted. **www**.abbaye-fontevraud.com

Fontevraud Royal Abbey, founded in 1101, was the largest of its kind in France. It now hosts concerts and exhibitions. The abbey's nuns lived around the Renaissance Grand Moûtier cloisters, and the leper colony's nurses were housed in the St-Lazare priory, now the abbey's hotel. Little remains of the monastic quarters, but the St-Benoît hospital survives. Most impressive is the octagonal kitchen in the Tour Evraud, a rare example of secular Romanesque architecture.

In the nave of the abbey church, the painted effigy of Henry Plantagenet (1133–1189), Count of Anjou and King of England, lies by those of his wife Eleanor of Aquitaine, who died here in 1204, and their son, Richard the Lion-Heart (1157–1199).

Tours ⓬

Indre-et-Loire. 🏛 140,000. ✈ 🚉 🚌 🛈 78 Rue Bernard Palissy (02-47 70 37 37). 🛒 Tue–Sun.

The pleasant cathedral city of Tours is built on the site of a Roman town, and became an important center of Christianity in the 4th century under St. Martin. In 1461 Louis XI made the city the French capital. However, during Henri IV's reign, the city lost favor with the monarchy and the capital left Tours for Paris.

The medieval old town, Le Vieux Tours, is full of narrow streets lined with beautiful half-timbered houses. St. Martin's tomb lies in the crypt of the New Basilica, built on the site of the medieval Old Basilica. Two towers, the **Tour Charlemagne** and the **Tour de l'Horloge**, survive from the earlier building.

Nearby, the vaulted cellars of the 13th-century **Eglise St-Julien** now form the **Musée des Vins de Touraine**, where

exhibits include a Renaissance winepress and displays on early viticultural history.

The foundation stone of the **Cathédrale St-Gatien** was laid in the early 13th century. Building work continued until the mid-16th century, and the cathedral provides an illustration of how the Gothic style developed over time.

The **Château Royal de Tours**, a royal residence between the 13th and 15th centuries, houses the Historial de Touraine, which illustrates the region's history in waxworks.

Château de Chenonceau ⓭

See pp178–9.

Blois ⓮

Loir-et-Cher. 🏛 60,000. 🚉 🚌 🛈 Place du Château (02-54 90 41 41). 🛒 Tue–Thu & Sat–Sun

A powerful feudal stronghold in the 12th century, Blois rose to glory under Louis XII, who established his court here in 1498. The town remained at the center of French royal and political life for much of the next century. Today, Blois is the quintessential Loire town. The partly pedestrianized old quarter is full of romantic courtyards and fine mansions.

François I's staircase, Château de Blois

Home to kings Louis XII, François I, and Henri III, no other Loire château has such a sensational history as the **Château de Blois**. It was here, in 1588, that the ambitious Duc de Guise, leader of the Catholic Holy League, was murdered on the orders of Henri III. The building itself juxtaposes four distinct architectural styles, reflecting its varied history.

Among Blois' most impressive religious monuments are the beautiful three-spired **Eglise St-Nicolas**, formerly part of a 12th-century Benedictine abbey, and the **Cathédrale St-Louis**, which dominates the eastern half of the city. The cathedral is a 17th-century reconstruction of a Gothic church that was almost destroyed in 1678.

⚜ **Château de Blois**
Place du Château. **Tel** 02-54 90 33 33. ◯ daily. ● Jan 1, Dec 25. 🎫 📷

The historic town of Blois, viewed from across the Loire

Château de Chenonceau ⑬

Chenonceau, stretching romantically across the River Cher, is considered by many to be the loveliest of the Loire châteaux. Surrounded by elegant formal gardens and wooded grounds, this pure Renaissance building began life as a modest manor and water mill. Over the centuries it was transformed by the wives and mistresses of its successive owners into a palace designed solely for pleasure. The story of these ladies is told in the château's *son et lumière* (literally "sound and light") shows, held nightly during the summer months.

Chambre de Catherine de' Medici
Henri II's wife Catherine made her own mark on Chenonceau's design, with this sumptuous bedchamber.

Formal Gardens
The current designs of the formal gardens created by Diane de Poitiers and Catherine de' Medici date from the 19th century.

Louise de Lorraine's room
was painted black and decorated with monograms, tears, and knots in white after the assassination of her husband, Henri III.

The Cabinet Vert was originally covered with green velvet.

The Tour des Marques survives from the 15th-century castle of the Marques family.

Chapel
The chapel has a vaulted ceiling and sculpted pilasters. The stained glass, destroyed by a bomb in 1944, was replaced in 1953.

Grande Galerie
The elegant gallery is Florentine in style. It was created by Catherine de' Medici in 1570–76 as an addition to the bridge built for Diane de Poitiers.

VISITORS' CHECKLIST

Indre-et-Loire. 🚉 🚌 *from Tours.* **Tel** *02-47 23 44 01.* ⭕ *daily; opening times vary – call for details.* 📷 ♿ *limited.* **www**.chenonceau.com

The arched bridge over the Cher was designed by Philibert de l'Orme in 1559 for Diane de Poitiers. It was built on the site of the old water mill.

The Château de Chambord on the banks of the Closson

DIANE DE POITIERS

Diane de Poitiers was Henry II's lifelong mistress, holding court as queen of France in all but name. Her beauty inspired many French artists, who often depicted her in the role of Diana, the Classical goddess of the hunt.

In 1547 Henry offered the Château de Chenonceau to Diane, who improved the palace by creating stunning formal gardens and an arched bridge over the River Cher.

After Henry's accidental death in 1559, Diane was forced to leave Chenonceau by his widow Catherine de' Medici, in exchange for the fortress-like Château de Chaumont. Diane retired to Anet, and remained there until her death in 1566.

Château de Chambord ⑮

Loir-et-Cher. 🚌 *to Blois, then taxi or bus.* **Tel** *02-54 50 40 00.* ⭕ *daily.* ⬛ *Jan 1, May 1, Dec 25.* 📷 ☑

The brainchild of the extravagant François I, the château began as a hunting lodge in the Forêt de Boulogne. In 1519 the original building was razed and Chambord begun, to a design probably initiated by Leonardo da Vinci. By 1537 the keep, with its towers and terraces, had been completed by 1,800 men and three master masons. The following year, François I began building a private royal pavilion on the northeast corner, with a connecting two-story gallery. His son, Henri II, continued the west wing with the chapel, and Louis XIV completed the 440-roomed edifice in 1685.

The innovative double-helix Grand Staircase was supposedly designed by Leonardo da Vinci. The two flights of stairs ensure that the person going up and the person going down cannot meet.

Orléans ⑯

Loiret. 🏛 *113,000.* ✈ 🚉 🚌 ℹ *2 Place de l'Etape (02-38 24 05 05).* 🛒 *Tue–Sun.* **www**.tourisme-orleans.com

Orléans was the capital of medieval France, and it was here that Joan of Arc battled the English in 1429, during the Hundred Years' War. Later captured by the enemy and accused of witch-craft, she was burned at the stake in Rouen at the age of 19. Since her martyrdom, Joan has become a pervasive presence in Orléans.

A faded grandeur lingers in Vieil Orléans, the old quarter bounded by the imposing **Cathédrale Sainte-Croix**, the Loire, and the Place du Martroi. The **Maison de Jeanne d'Arc** was rebuilt in 1961 on the site where Joan lodged in 1429. Inside, audiovisual exhibits recreate her life.

A selection of European art of the 16th to early 20th centuries is on display at the **Musée des Beaux-Arts**.

🏛 **Maison de Jeanne d'Arc** 3 Place du Général de Gaulle. **Tel** 02-38 52 99 89. ⭕ Tue–Sun (Nov–Apr: pm only). ⬛ public hols 📷

The lofty interior of the Cathédrale Sainte-Croix, Orléans

Chartres Cathedral ⑰

According to art historian Emile Male, "Chartres is the mind of the Middle Ages manifest." Begun in 1020, the Romanesque cathedral was destroyed by a devastating fire in 1194. Only the north and south towers, south steeple, west portal, and crypt remained. Inside, the sacred *Veil of the Virgin* relic was the sole treasure to survive. Peasant and lord alike labored to rebuild the church in just 25 years. Few alterations were made after 1250 and, fortunately, Chartres was left unscathed by the Wars of Religion and the French Revolution. The result is an authentic Gothic cathedral with a true "Bible in stone and glass" reputation.

Elongated Statues
These statues on the Royal Portal repre-sent Old Testa-ment figures.

The taller of the two spires dates from the start of the 16th century. Flamboyant Gothic in style, it contrasts sharply with the solemnity of its Romanesque counterpart.

Gothic Nave
As wide as the Romanesque crypt below it – the largest in France – the Gothic nave reaches a lofty height of 37 m (121 ft).

★ Stained-Glass Windows
The three 12th-century lancet windows on the west front, celebrated for their rare blue color, are among the oldest of their kind in the world.

★ Royal Portal
The Royal Portal (1145–55) and part of the west front survive from the original Romanesque church. The central tympanum has a carving of Christ in Majesty.

STAR FEATURES

★ South Porch

★ Royal Portal

★ Stained-Glass Windows

The Labyrinth is inlaid in the nave floor. Pilgrims used to follow the tortuous route by crawling on their knees, echoing the Way of the Cross.

CHARTRES' STAINED GLASS

Over 150 stained-glass windows in the cathedral illustrate biblical stories and daily life in the 13th century (bring binoculars if you can). During both World Wars the windows were dismantled piece by piece and removed for safety. Some windows were restored and releaded in the 1970s, but much more remains to be done. Each window is divided into panels, which are usually read from left to right, bottom to top (earth to heaven). The number of figures or abstract shapes used is symbolic: three stands for the Church; squares and the number four symbolize the material world or the four elements; circles represent eternal life.

VISITORS' CHECKLIST

Place de la Cathédrale, Chartres, Eure-et-Loir. 🚉 🚌 from Paris. **Tel** 02-37 18 26 26. ⬤ 8:30am–7:30pm daily. ✝ 11:45am & 6:15pm Mon–Fri (9am Tue, Fri); 6pm Sat; 9:15 & 11am Sun. ♿
📧 www.chartres-tourisme.com

The vaulted ceiling is supported by a network of ribs.

Apsidal Chapel
This chapel houses the oldest cathedral treasure, the Veil of the Virgin *relic. Supposedly worn by the Virgin Mary, the artifact brought many pilgrims to Chartres during the Middle Ages.*

The St. Piat Chapel, built between 1324 and 1353, contains many artifacts, relics, and treasures.

South Rose Window
The cathedral has three massive rose windows. That on the south front (c.1225) illustrates the Apocalypse, *with* Christ in Majesty.

★ South Porch
Sculpture on the massive South Porch (1197–1209) reflects a selection of New Testament teaching.

Burgundy and the French Alps

Burgundy is France's richest province, historically, culturally, and gastronomically. The region's fine wines have inspired awe for centuries, and every year the historic town of Beaune hosts one of the most famous wine auctions in the world. Dijon is a splendid city, filled with the great palaces of the old Burgundian nobility. The majestic French Alps attract visitors for winter sports, and, in summer, walking and a host of water sports on the glittering mountain lakes.

Tympanum sculpture showing Christ and the apostles at Basilique Ste-Madeleine, Vézelay

Vézelay ⑱

Yonne. 🕍 *400.* 🚌 **Basilique Ste-Madeleine** *Tel 03-86 33 39 50.* 🚆 *Sermizelles, then bus.* ◯ *daily.* ✔

Tourists come to Vézelay to visit the picturesque **Basilique Ste-Madeleine**. In the 12th century, at the height of its glory, the abbey claimed to house the relics of Mary Magdalene, and it was a starting point for the pilgrimage to Santiago de Compostela in Spain *(see p302).*
The star attractions of the Romanesque church are the tympanum sculpture (1120–35) above the central doorway, the exquisitely carved capitals in the nave and narthex, and the immense Gothic choir.

Dijon ⑲

See pp184–5.

Beaune ⑳

Côte D'Or. 🕍 *23,000.* 🚆 🚌 ℹ *Boulevard Pepreuil (03-80 26 21 30).* 🎵 *Baroque Music (Jul).*

The indisputable highlight of the old center of Beaune is the **Hôtel-Dieu**. The hospice was founded in 1443 for the town's inhabitants, many of whom were left poverty-stricken after the Hundred Years' War. Today it is considered a medieval jewel, with its superb multicolored Burgundian roof tiles. It houses many treasures, including the religious masterpiece, Rogier van der Weyden's *Last Judgement* polyptych.
The Hôtel des Ducs de Bourgogne, built in the 14th–16th centuries, houses the **Musée du Vin de Bourgogne**, with displays of traditional winemaking equipment.
Further to the north is the 12th-century Romanesque church, the **Collégiale Notre-Dame**, which has a collection of fine 15th-century tapestries.

🏥 **Hôtel-Dieu**
Rue de l'Hôtel-Dieu. *Tel 03-80 24 45 00.* ◯ *daily.* ● *Dec–Mar: 11:30am–2pm daily.* ✔ ✔ ♿

Lyon ㉑

Rhône. 🕍 *453,000.* ✈ *25 km (16 miles) E.* 🚆 🚌 ℹ *Place Bellecour (04-72 77 69 69).* ◯ *daily.* **www.**lyon-france.com

Dramatically situated on the banks of the Rhône and Saône rivers, Lyon has been a vital gateway between the north and south since ancient times. Vieux Lyon, the oldest part of the city, is the site of the Roman settlement of Lugdunum, the commercial and military capital of Gaul founded by Julius Caesar in 44 BC. Vestiges of this prosperous city can be seen in the superb **Musée de la Civilisation Gallo-Romaine**. There are also two excavated Roman amphitheaters: the **Grand Théâtre**, built in 15 BC to seat 30,000 spectators, and the smaller **Odéon**.
Other major sights are the 19th-century mock-Byzantine **Basilique Notre-Dame de Fourvière**, and the **Cathédrale St-Jean**, begun in the 12th century. Vieux Lyon's fine Renaissance mansions are the former homes of bankers and silk merchants.

THE DUKES OF BURGUNDY

In the 14th and 15th centuries the dukes of Burgundy built up one of the most powerful states in Europe, which included Flanders and parts of Holland. From the time of Philip the Bold (1342–1404) the ducal court became a center of art, chivalry, and immense wealth. The duchy's demise came with the death of Charles the Bold in 1477.

Tomb of Philip the Bold in Dijon's Musée des Beaux Arts (see p184)

Cathédrale St-Jean at the foot of the slopes of Vieux Lyon

The excellent **Musée des Beaux Arts** showcases the country's largest and most important collection of fine arts after the Louvre. The modern works, dating from after the mid-1900s, have found a new home in the **Musée d'Art Contemporain** in the north of the city. An exquisite display of silks and tapestries, some dating back to early Christian times, can be seen in the **Musée Historique des Tissus**.

🏛 **Musée de la Civilisation Gallo-Romaine**
17 Rue Cléberg. **Tel** 04-72 38 81 90. ⬜ Tue–Sun. ⬤ public hols. 🈲 ♿

Annecy 🌕

Annecy. 🏘 51,000. 🚉 🚌 🛈 1 Rue Jean Jaurès (04-50 45 00 33). ⬤ Tue, Fri–Sun. **www**.lac-annecy.com

Annecy is one of the most beautiful towns in the Alps, set at the northern tip of Lac d'Annecy and surrounded by snow-capped mountains.

A stroll around the town's small medieval quarter, with its canals, flower-covered bridges, and arcaded streets,

is one of the main attractions of a stay here. Look out for the formidable **Palais de l'Isle**, a 12th-century prison in the middle of the Thiou canal.

The turreted **Château d'Annecy**, perched high on a hill, affords fine panoramic views. The clear waters of the lake are perfect for swimming and water sports. Boat trips leave from the Quai Thiou.

Environs
One way to enjoy the area's spectacular scenery is to take a boat to **Talloires**, a tiny lakeside village, noted for its hotels and restaurants.

Grenoble 🌕

Isère. 🏘 165,000. ✈ 🚉 🚌
🛈 14 Rue de la République
(04-76 42 41 41). ⬤ Tue–Sun.

Ancient capital of Dauphiné, Grenoble is a busy and thriving city, attractively located at the confluence of the Drac and Isère rivers, in the shadow of the mighty Vercors and Chartreuse massifs.

A cable car from the Quai Stéphane-Jay on the north bank of the Isère takes you up to the 16th-century **Fort de la Bastille**, where you are rewarded with magnificent views of the city and surrounding mountains. From here, paths lead down through pretty gardens to the excellent **Musée Dauphinois** at the foot of the hill. Housed in a 17th-century convent, the museum contains displays on local history, arts, and crafts.

On the other side of the river, the focus of life is the Place Grenette, a lively square lined with sidewalk cafés. Nearby, the Place St-André is the heart of the medieval city, overlooked by Grenoble's oldest buildings, including the 13th-century **Eglise St-André** and the 15th-century **Palais de Justice**.

Also worth visiting is the **Musée de Grenoble**, the city's principal art museum. With works by Chagall, Picasso, and Matisse, the modern collection is especially good.

🏛 **Musée de Grenoble**
5 Place de Lavalette. **Tel** 04-76 63 44 44. ⬜ Wed–Mon. ⬤ Jan 1, May 1, Dec 25. 🈲 🎫 ♿

Annecy's 12th-century Palais de l'Isle on the Thiou canal

Street by Street: Dijon ⑲

The center of Dijon is noted for its
architectural splendor – a legacy from
the dukes of Burgundy *(see p182)*.
Wealthy parliament members also had
elegant *hôtels particuliers* (private mansions) built in the 17th and 18th centuries.
The capital of Burgundy, Dijon today has
a rich cultural life and a renowned
university. The city's great art treasures
are housed in the Palais des Ducs. Dijon
is also famous for its mustard and *pain
d'épice* (gingerbread), a reminder of the
town's position on the medieval spice
route. A major rail hub during the 19th
century, it now has a TGV link to Paris.

Hôtel de Voguë
*This elegant 17th-century mansion is
decorated with Burgundian cabbages
and fruit garlands by Hugues Sambin.*

★ Notre-Dame
*This magnificent 13th-
century Gothic church
is best known for its
many gargoyles,
the Jacquemart
clock, and, on the
north wall, the
sculpted owl
(chouette), said
to bring good
luck when
touched.*

Train
and bus
stations

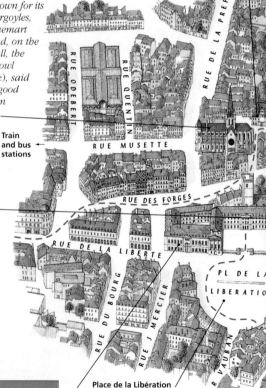

RUE ODEBERT
RUE QUENTIN
RUE DE LA PREFECTURE
RUE MUSETTE
RUE DES FORGES
RUE DE LA LIBERTÉ
RUE DU BOURG
RUE J. MERCIER
R. VAUBAN
PL DE LA
LIBERATION

Musée des Beaux Arts
*The collection of Flemish masters
here includes this 14th-century
triptych by Jacques de Baerze
and Melchior Broederlam.*

Place de la Libération
was created by Mansart
in the 17th century.

★ Palais des Ducs
*The dukes of Burgundy held court here, but
the building seen today was mainly built
in the 17th century for the parliament. It
now houses the Musée des Beaux Arts.*

Rue Verrerie
This cobbled street in the old merchants' quarter is lined with medieval half-timbered houses. Some, such as Nos. 8, 10, and 12, have fine wood carvings.

VISITORS' CHECKLIST

Côte d'Or. 🏘 153,000. 🛫 5 km (3 miles) SSE. 🚉 🚌 Cours de la Gare. 🛈 Pavillon Place Darcy (08-92 70 05 58). 🛒 Tue, Thu– Sat. 🎭 Festival de Musique (Jun); Fêtes de la Vigne (Sep). **Musée des Beaux Arts Tel** 03-80 74 52 70. ◻ Wed–Mon. ● main public hols. 📷 ♿ **Musée Magnin Tel** 03-80 67 11 10. ◻ Tue–Sun. ● some public hols. 📷 ♿ limited.

★ St-Michel
Begun in the 15th century and completed in the 17th century, St-Michel's façade combines Flamboyant Gothic with Renaissance details. On the richly carved porch, angels and biblical motifs mingle with mythological themes.

Musée Magnin
A collection of French and foreign 16th–19th-century paintings is displayed among period furniture in this 17th-century mansion.

The Eglise St-Etienne
dates from the 11th century but has been rebuilt many times. Its characteristic lantern was added in 1686.

STAR SIGHTS

★ Palais des Ducs

★ Notre-Dame

★ St-Michel

KEY

– – – Suggested route

0 meters   100

0 yards   100

The Wines of France

Winemaking in France dates back to pre-Roman times, although it was the Romans who disseminated the culture of the vine and the practise of winemaking throughout the country. The range, quality, and reputation of the fine wines of Bordeaux, Burgundy, and Champagne in particular have made them role models the world over. France's everyday wines can be highly enjoyable too, with plenty of good-value *vins de pays* and *vins de table* now emerging from the southern regions. Many wine producers offer tours and have their own tasting rooms, where visitors can try a selection of wines without feeling pressurized to buy.

Château Cos d'Estournel, *in the Bordeaux region, produces a rich and fruity Cabernet Sauvignon. The grandeur of its exotic design is typical of château architecture.*

THE WINE REGIONS OF FRANCE

Each of the 10 principal wine-producing regions has its own identity, based on grape varieties, climate and soil, and local culture. Around 40 percent of all French wines are included in the *appellation d'origine contrôlée* system, which guarantees their style and geographic origin, though not their quality.

BORDEAUX WINES

Bordeaux is the world's largest fine wine region, and, for its red wines, certainly the most familiar outside France. The great wine-producing areas lie close to the banks of the rivers Gironde, Garonne, and Dordogne. These rivers, and the river port of Bordeaux itself, have been crucial to the region's wine trade; some of the prettiest châteaux line the river banks, enabling easy transportation. Grape varieties used include

Château Pitray   **Château Thieuley**

Cabernet Sauvignon, Merlot, and Petit Verdot (red); Sémillon and Sauvignon Blanc (white).

HOW TO READ A WINE LABEL

Even the simplest label will provide a key to the wine's flavor and quality. It will bear the name of the wine and its producer, its vintage if there is one, and whether it comes from a strictly defined area (*appellation contrôlée* or VDQS) or is a more general *vin de pays* or *vin de table*. It may also have a regional grading, as with the *crus classés* in Bordeaux. The shape and color of the bottle are also guides. Most good-quality wine is bottled in green glass, which helps to protect it from light.

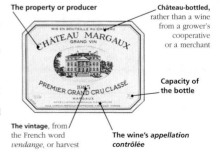

The property or producer

Château-bottled, rather than a wine from a grower's cooperative or a merchant

Capacity of the bottle

The vintage, from the French word *vendange*, or harvest

The wine's *appellation contrôlée*

BURGUNDY WINES

The tiny vineyards in each of Burgundy's wine-producing regions, from Chablis in the north to Beaujolais in the south, can produce wines that, at their best, are unequalled anywhere else. This is unmissable territory for the "serious" wine-lover, with its time-honored traditions and dazzling *grands crus*. Grape varieties used include Pinot Noir, Gamay, and César (red); Pinot Blanc and Chardonnay (white).

Domaine François Raveneau

Domaine Michel Lafarge

TOURS OF MAJOR WINERIES

Winemakers are usually happy to welcome tourists in summer, but try not to visit at harvest time (Sep–Oct). Whatever time of year you visit, be sure to make an appointment in advance.

Bordeaux
Château Cheval Blanc
Saint Emilion. *Tel* 05-57 55 55 55.
Fax 05-57 55 55 50.

Château Haut-Brion
Pessac. *Tel* 05-56 00 29 30.
Fax 05-56 98 75 14.

Château Margaux
Margaux. *Tel* 05-57 88 83 83.
Fax 05-57 88 31 32.

Château Lafite Rothschild
Pauillac. *Tel* 05-53 89 78 00.
Fax 05-56 59 26 83.

Burgundy
Clos de la Barre
Meursault. *Tel* 03-80 21 22 17.
Fax 03-80 21 61 64.

Maison Louis Latour
18 Rue des Tonneliers, Beaune.
Tel 03-80 24 81 10.
Fax 03-80 22 36 21.

Champagne
Krug
5 Rue Coquebert, Reims.
Tel 03-26 84 44 20.
Fax 03-26 84 44 49.

Moët & Chandon
20 Avenue de Champagne,
Epernay. *Tel* 03-26 51 20 00.
Fax 03-26 51 20 21.

Piper Heidsieck
51 Boulevard Henry Vasnier,
Reims. *Tel* 03-26 84 43 44.
Fax 03-26 84 43 84.

Champagne *is a region synonymous with the finest sparkling wines. The skill of the blenders, using reserves of older wines, creates consistency and excellence year on year. Champagne bubbles are produced by fermenting yeast inside the bottle – traditional methods are still used all over the region. In a process called* remuage, *bottles are gradually rotated in order to loosen the sediment, which is ultimately removed from the wine.*

KEY

- Alsace and Lorraine
- Bordeaux
- Burgundy
- Champagne
- Jura and Savoie
- Languedoc-Roussillon
- The Loire Valley
- Provence
- The Rhône Valley
- Southwest France

Chardonnay vines *in the* grand cru *vineyard of Corton-Charlemagne produce some of the greatest white Burgundies of all. The Chardonnay grape is now cultivated not only in Burgundy and Champagne, but all over the world. In the Loire valley and southern France, it is used for* vins de pays.

Southwest France

The southwest is farming France, a green and peaceful land nurturing crops from sunflowers to walnuts. Other key country products include forest timber, Bordeaux wines, and wild mushrooms. Major modern industries, including aerospace, are focused on the two chief cities, Bordeaux and Toulouse. Visitors are mainly drawn to the wine chateaux, the ski slopes of the Pyrenees, and the prehistoric caves of the Dordogne. The major sights of this favored region include some of France's most celebrated Romanesque buildings.

Monument aux Girondins, Place des Quinconces, Bordeaux

Bordeaux ㉔

Gironde. 🏛 220,000. ✈ 🚉 🚌 ❙ 12 Cours du 30 Juillet (05-56 00 66 00). 🍽 daily. 🍷 Fête du Vin Nouveau (Oct). **www**.bordeaux-tourisme.com

Built on a curve of the Garonne river, Bordeaux has been a major port since pre-Roman times and for centuries a focus and crossroads of European trade. The export of wine has always been the basis of the city's prosperity, and today the Bordeaux region produces over 44 million cases of wine per year.

Along the waterfront, a long sweep of Classical façades is broken by the Esplanade des Quinconces, with its statues and fountains. At one end, the Monument aux Girondins (1804–1902) commemorates the Girondists sent to the guillotine by Robespierre

during the Terror (1793–5). Buildings of architectural interest include the massive **Basilique St-Michel**, begun in 1350, which took 200 years to complete, and the 18th-century **Grand Théâtre**, a magnificent example of the French Neoclassical style. The **Musée des Beaux Arts** holds an excellent collection of paintings, ranging from the Renaissance to our time.

> 🏛 **Musée des Beaux Arts**
> 20 Cours d'Albret. **Tel** 05-56 10 20 56. ◯ Wed–Mon. ⬤ public hols.
> 📷

Environs
The tourist office in Bordeaux organizes tours to various wine châteaux (see pp186–7).

Lascaux ㉕

Montignac. **Tel** 05-53 51 95 03. ◯ Feb–Mar & Nov–Dec: Tue–Sun; Apr–Oct: daily. ⬤ Jan, Dec 25. 📷 📷

Lascaux is the most famous of the prehistoric sites in the Dordogne region. Four young boys and their dog came across the caves and their astounding Palaeolithic paintings in 1940, and the importance of their discovery was swiftly recognized.

Lascaux has been closed to the public since 1963 because of deterioration due to carbon dioxide caused by breathing. An exact copy, Lascaux II, has been created a few minutes' walk down the hillside, using the same materials. The replica is beautiful and should not be spurned: high-antlered elk, bison, and plump horses cover the walls, moving in herds or files, surrounded by arrows and geometric symbols thought to have had ritual significance.

Toulouse ㉖

Haute-Garonne. 🏛 390,000. ✈ 🚉 🚌 ❙ Donjon du Capitole (05-61 11 02 22). 🍽 Tue–Sun. 🎹 Piano (Sep), Jazz (Oct). **www**.ot-toulouse.fr

Toulouse, the most important town in southwest France, is the country's fourth largest metropolis, and a major industrial and university city.

The area is also famous for its aerospace industry; Concorde, Airbus, and the Ariane space rocket all originated here. Airbus tours can be booked at www.taxiway.fr. **Cité de l'Espace** has a planetarium and interactive exhibits on space exploration.

The church known as **Les Jacobins** was begun in 1229 and took over two centuries to finish. The Gothic masterpiece features a soaring, 22-branched palm tree vault in the apse. The belltower (1294) is much

Palm vaulting in the apse of Les Jacobins, Toulouse

A picturesque village set in a lush valley among the foothills of the Pyrenees mountains

imitated in southwest France. Toulouse became a center of Romanesque art in Europe due to its position on the route to Santiago de Compostela *(see p302)*. The largest Romanesque basilica in Europe, the **Basilique de St-Sernin**, was built in the 11th–12th centuries to accommodate pilgrims. The **Musée des Augustins** has sculptures from the period, and incorporates cloisters from a 14th-century Augustinian priory. Also featured are French, Italian, and Flemish paintings.

The 16th-century palace known as the **Hôtel d'Assézat** now houses the Fondation Bemberg, named after local art lover Georges Bemberg, with Renaissance art and 19th- and 20th-century French work.

🏛 **Musée des Augustins**
21 Rue de Metz. **Tel** 05-61 22 21
82. ◯ *daily.* ⬤ *Jan 1, May 1, Dec 25.* 🖼 📷 ♿ **www.**augustins.org

Pyrenees ㉗

✈ *Pau.* 🚉 🚌 *Bayonne & Pau.*
ℹ *Place des Basques, Bayonne (05-59 46 01 46); Place Royale, Pau (05-59 27 27 08).*

The mountains dominate life in the French Pyrenees. A region in many ways closer to Spain than France, over the centuries its remote terrain and

tenacious people have given heretics a hiding place and refugees an escape route.

The **Parc National des Pyrénées** extends 100 km (62 miles) along the French–Spanish frontier. It boasts some of the most splendid alpine scenery in Europe, and is rich in flora and fauna. Within the park are 350 km (217 miles) of footpaths.

The region's oldest inhabitants, the Basque people, have maintained their own language and culture. **Bayonne** on the Atlantic coast is the capital of the French Basque country, and has been an important town since Roman times. **Biarritz**, west of Bayonne, has

two casinos and three good beaches, with the best surfing in Europe. A short distance south, **St-Jean-de-Luz** is a sleepy fishing village that explodes into life in summer. A main attraction is the Eglise St-Jean Baptiste, where Louis XIV married the Infanta Maria Teresa of Spain in 1660.

A lively university town with elegant architecture, **Pau** is the most interesting large town in the central Pyrenees. It has long been a favorite resort of affluent foreigners.

Other places of interest include the many mountain ski resorts, the shrine at **Lourdes**, and the pretty hilltop town of **St-Bertrand-de-Comminges**.

THE MIRACLE OF LOURDES

In 1858, a 14-year-old girl named Bernadette Soubirous experienced 18 visions of the Virgin at the Grotte Massabielle near the town of Lourdes. Despite being told to keep away from the cave by her mother – and the local magistrate – she was guided to a spring with miraculous healing powers. The church endorsed the miracles in the 1860s, and since then many people claim to have been cured by the holy water. A huge city of shrines, churches, and hospices has since grown up around the spring, with a dynamic tourist industry to match.

Pilgrims at an open-air mass in Lourdes

The South of France

The south is France's most popular holiday region, drawing millions of visitors each year to the resorts of the Riviera and the Côte d'Azur, and to the vivid landscape and historic villages of Provence. Painters such as Cézanne, van Gogh, and Picasso, have been inspired by the luminous light and brilliant colors of the region. Agriculture is still a mainstay of the economy, but the new high-tech industries of Nice now make a significant contribution to the region's prosperity.

Château Comtal in the restored citadel of Carcassonne

Carcassonne ㉘

Aude. 🏠 46,000. 🚉 🚌 ✈
🛈 28 Rue de Verdun (04-68 10 24 30). 🛒 Tue, Thu & Sat. 🎪 Festival de la Cité (all of Jul), Medieval fête (Aug) www.carcassonne.com

The citadel of Carcassonne is a perfectly restored medieval town. It crowns a steep bank above the Aude river, a fairytale sight of turrets and ramparts overlooking the Basse Ville below.

The strategic position of the citadel between the Atlantic and the Mediterranean led to its original settlement, consolidated by the Romans in the 2nd century BC.

At its zenith in the 12th century the town was ruled by the Trencavels, who built the château and cathedral. The Cathars, a persecuted Christian sect, were given sanctuary here in 1209 but, after a two-week siege, the town fell to the Crusaders sent to eradicate them. The attentions of architectural historian Viollet-le-Duc led to Carcassonne's restoration in the 19th century.

Flanked by sandstone towers, the defenses of the **Porte Narbonnaise** included two portcullises, two iron doors, a moat, and a drawbridge. A fortress within a fortress, the **Château Comtal** has a surrounding moat and five defensive towers.

Within the Romanesque and Gothic **Basilique St-Nazaire** is the famous Siege Stone, inscribed with scenes said to depict the siege of 1209.

Nîmes ㉙

Gard. 🏠 145,000. ✈ 🚉 🚌
🛈 6 Rue Auguste (04-66 58 38 00). 🛒 daily. www.ot-nimes.fr

An important crossroads in the ancient world, Nîmes is well known for its bullfights and Roman antiquities. The city has had a turbulent history, and suffered particularly in the 16th-century Wars of Religion, when the Romanesque **Cathédrale Notre-Dame et St-Castor** was badly damaged. In the 17th and 18th centuries the town prospered from textile manufacturing, one of the most enduring products being denim or *serge de Nîmes*.

All roads in the city lead to the amphitheater, **Les Arènes**. Built at the end of the 1st century AD, it is still in use today as a venue for concerts, sporting events, and bullfights.

The **Maison Carrée** is an elegant Roman temple, the pride of Nîmes. Built by Augustus' son-in-law Marcus Agrippa, it is one of the best preserved in the world, with finely fluted Corinthian columns and a sculpted frieze.

Set in the Roman wall is the **Porte d'Auguste**, a gateway built for travelers on the Domitian Way, which passed through the center of Nîmes. Nearby is the **Castellum**, a tower used for storing water brought in by aqueduct. The water was distributed around the town by a canal system. A display of Roman statues and mosaics can be seen at the **Musée Archéologique**.

Five floors of Nîmes' controversial arts complex, the **Carré d'Art**, which stands opposite the Maison Carrée, lie underground. The complex incorporates a library, a roof-terrace restaurant around a huge glass atrium, and the Musée d'Art Contemporain.

🏛 **Musée Archéologique**
13 bis Boulevard Amiral Courbet. *Tel* 04-66 76 74 80. 🕐 Tue–Sun.
Jan 1, May 1, Nov 11, Dec 25. 🗟

Environs
To the northeast of the city lies the **Pont du Gard**, a 2,000-year-old aqueduct. The Romans considered this to be the best testimony to the greatness of their empire, and at 49 m (160 ft) it was the highest bridge they ever built.

The Pont du Gard, outside Nîmes, a major feat of Roman engineering

For hotels and restaurants in this region see pp206–11 and pp212–17

Avignon ⑳

Vaucluse. 🏙 *100,000.* ✈ 🚆 🚌
ℹ *41 Cours Jean Jaurès (04-32 74
32 74).* 🛍 *Tue–Sun.* 🎭 *Le Festival
d'Avignon (mid-Jul–mid-Aug).*
www.avignon-tourisme.com

Massive ramparts enclose this
fascinating town. The huge
Palais des Papes is the
dominant feature, but
Avignon contains other riches.
To the north of the Palais is
the 13th-century **Musée du
Petit Palais**, once the Archbishop of Avignon's residence.
It has received such notorious
guests as Cesare Borgia and
Louis XIV. Now a museum,
it displays Romanesque
and Gothic sculpture and
paintings of the Avignon and
Italian Schools, with works by
Botticelli and Carpaccio.

Avignon boasts some fine
churches, such as the 12th-
century **Cathédrale de Notre-**

**Open-air performance at
the annual Avignon Festival**

Dame-des-Doms, with its
Romanesque cupola and
papal tombs, and the 14th-
century **Eglise St-Didier**.

The **Musée Lapidaire**
contains statues, mosaics,
and carvings from pre-Roman
Provence. The **Musée Calvet**
features a superb array of
exhibits, including Roman
finds. It also gives an overview
of French art during the past
500 years, with works by

Rodin, Manet, and Dufy.
The Place de l'Horloge is the
center of Avignon's social life.
Under the town hall's Gothic
clock tower stands a merry-
go-round from 1900. Until the
19th century, brightly-patterned
calicoes called *indiennes* were
printed nearby. These inspired
today's Provençal patterns.

From mid-July until mid-
August, the Avignon Festival
takes place at the Palais des
Papes. France's largest festival,
it includes ballet, drama, and
classical concerts. The "Off"
festival has street theater and
music from folk to jazz.

The **Pont St-Bénézet**, built
from 1171–1185, once had 22
arches, but most were destroyed by floods in 1668. One
of the remaining arches bears
the tiny Chapelle St-Nicolas.

⛪ **Palais des Papes**
Place du Palais-des-Papes. **Tel** 04-90
27 50 00. ⬜ *daily.* 🏛 🎫

PALAIS DES PAPES

Pope Clement V moved the papal court to
Avignon in 1309. Here it remained until 1377,
during which time his successors transformed
the modest episcopal building into the present
magnificent palace.

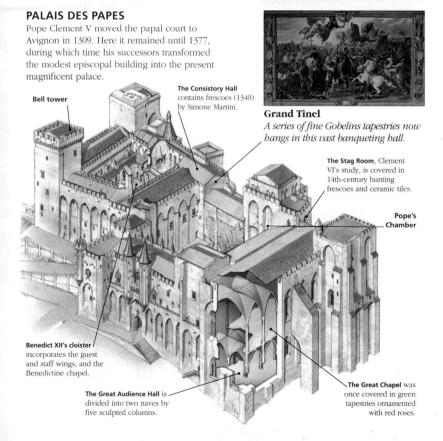

The Consistory Hall
contains frescoes (1340)
by Simone Martini.

Bell tower

Grand Tinel
*A series of fine Gobelins tapestries now
hangs in this vast banqueting hall.*

The Stag Room, Clement
VI's study, is covered in
14th-century hunting
frescoes and ceramic tiles.

**Pope's
Chamber**

Benedict XII's cloister
incorporates the guest
and staff wings, and the
Benedictine chapel.

The Great Audience Hall is
divided into two naves by
five sculpted columns.

The Great Chapel was
once covered in green
tapestries ornamented
with red roses.

Street-by-Street: Arles ③

Few other towns in Provence combine all the region's charms so well as Arles. Its position on the Rhône makes it a natural gateway to the Camargue *(see p195)*. Its Roman remains, such as Constantine's baths and the amphitheater, are complemented by the ocher walls and Roman-tiled roofs of later buildings. Van Gogh spent time here in 1888–9, but Arles is no longer the industrial town he painted. Visitors are now its main business, and entertainment ranges from the Arles Festival to bullfights. A bastion of Provençal tradition and culture, its museums are among the best in the region. For enthusiasts, an inclusive ticket is available giving access to all museums. All the tourist sites in Arles are within comfortable walking distance of the central Place de la République.

The Musée Réattu houses 18th-century and modern art, including witty Picasso sketches, paintings by the local artist Jacques Réattu (1760–1833), and sculptures by Russian-born Ossip Zadkine (1890–1967).

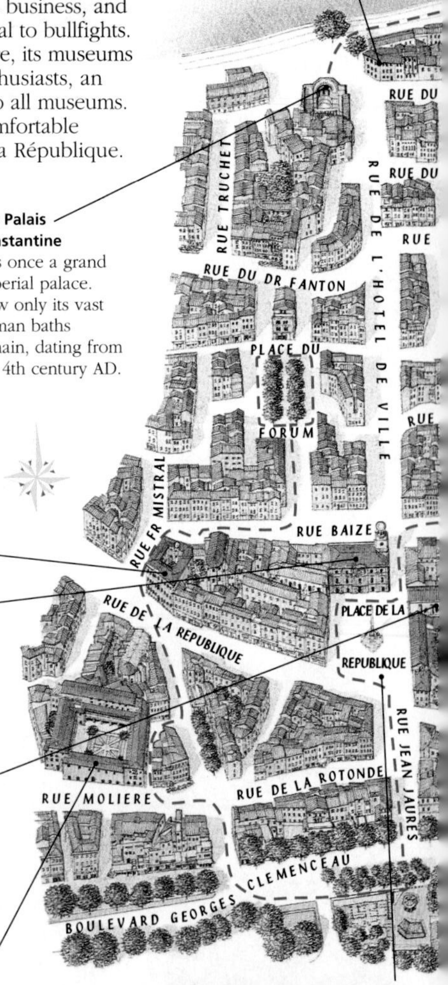

The Palais Constantine was once a grand imperial palace. Now only its vast Roman baths remain, dating from the 4th century AD.

View of Arles from the opposite bank of the Rhône

The Museon Arlaten was founded in 1904 by the Provençal poet Frédéric Mistral with his Nobel Prize money, and is devoted to the culture and customs of his beloved Provence.

The Hôtel de Ville, the town hall, has an impressive vaulted ceiling.

★ **Eglise St-Trophime**
This fine Romanesque church has an ornate 12th-century portal carved with saints and apostles.

L'Espace Van Gogh is dedicated to the famous artist's life and works.

STAR SIGHTS

- ★ Les Arènes
- ★ Théâtre Antique
- ★ Eglise St-Trophime

Egyptian Obelisk
This ancient obelisk with fountains at its base (one of which is shown here) came from the Roman circus across the Rhône.

★ **Les Arènes**
The amphitheater is one of the best-preserved Roman sites in Provence. The top tier provides an excellent panoramic view of Arles.

VISITORS' CHECKLIST

Bouches-du-Rhône. 52,000.
25 km (15 miles) NW.
Boulevard des Lices (04-90 18 41 20). Wed, Sat.
Fête des Gardians (May 1);
Féria des Fêtes d'Arles (early Jul).
Féria des Prémices du Riz (early Sep). www.arlestourisme.com

★ **Théâtre Antique**
Once a Roman theater, its stones were later used for other buildings. These last remaining columns are called the "two widows."

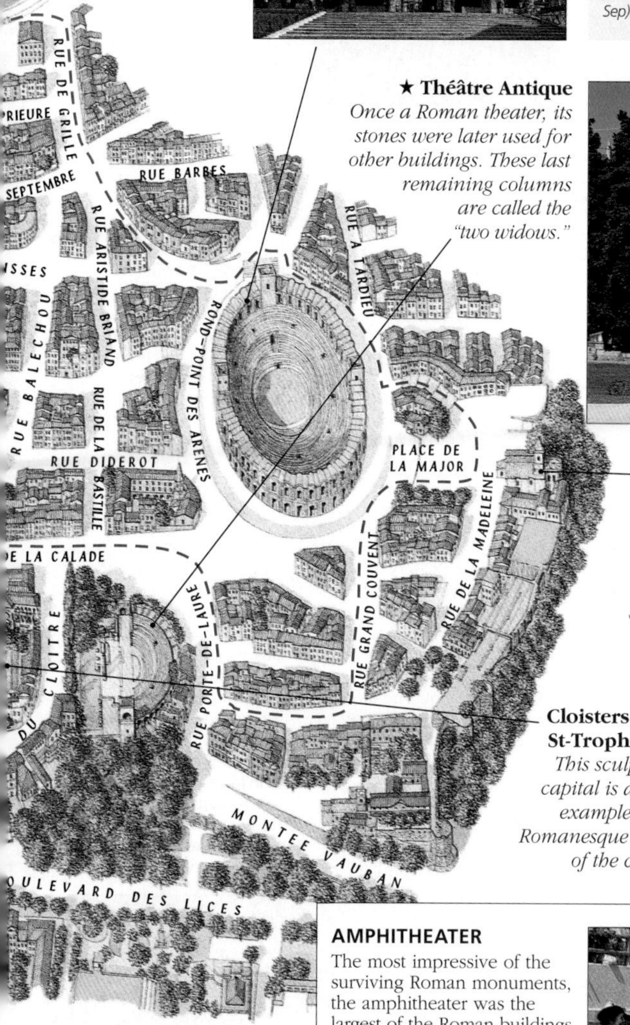

Notre-Dame-de-la-Major is dedicated to St. George, patron saint of the Camargue *gardians* (cowboys).

PLACE DE LA MAJOR

RUE DE GRILLE
RUE BARBES
RIEURE
SEPTEMBRE
ISSES
RUE ARISTIDE BRIAND
RUE BALECHOU
RUE DE LA BASTILLE
RUE DIDEROT
DE LA CALADE
ROND-POINT DES ARÈNES
RUE A TARDIEU
RUE DE LA MADELEINE
RUE GRAND COUVENT
RUE PORTE-DE-LAURE
DU CLOITRE
MONTEE VAUBAN
OULEVARD DES LICES

Cloisters of St-Trophime
This sculpted capital is a fine example of the Romanesque beauty of the cloisters.

KEY

– – – Suggested route

0 meters 100
0 yards 100

AMPHITHEATER

The most impressive of the surviving Roman monuments, the amphitheater was the largest of the Roman buildings in Gaul. Slightly oval, it measures 136 m (446 ft) by 107 m (351 ft) and could seat 21,000. The floors of some of the internal rooms were decorated with mosaics, the better to wash down after bloody affrays. Today bullfights and other games are held regularly in the arena.

Rodeo-style games in the arena

Camargue 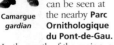 ❷

Bouches-du-Rhône. 🚉 🚌 ℹ️ 5
Ave Van Gogh, Stes-Maries-de-la-Mer
(04-90 97 82 55). 🎭 Pèlerinage des
Gitans (end May & end Oct).
www.saintesmaries.com

This flat, sparsely populated
land is one of Europe's
major wetland regions and
natural history sites. Extensive
areas of salt marsh, lakes,
pastures, and sand dunes
cover a vast 140,000 ha
(346,000 acres). The native
white horses and black bulls
are tended by the region's
cowboys, or *gardians*. Numerous seabirds and wildfowl
also occupy the region.

Bullfights are advertised in
Saintes-Maries-de-la-Mer, the
region's main tourist center,
which has a sandy beach with
water sports and boat trips.

A few kilometers inland,
the information center at
Pont-de-Gau offers
wonderful views over the
flat lagoon. Photo-
graphs and
documents chron-
icle the history
of the Camargue
and its diverse
flora and fauna.
Most of the
birds that live in
or migrate within
the region, inclu-
ding thousands
of flamingoes
which come
here to breed,
can be seen at
the nearby **Parc
Ornithologique
du Pont-de-Gau.**

Camargue
gardian

In the north of the region, a
traditional Provençal *mas* or
farmhouse, Mas du Pont de
Rousty, has been converted to
accommodate the fascinating
Musée Camarguais. Displays
here provide an introduction to
the customs and traditions of
the Camargue.

🦩 **Parc Ornithologique
du Pont-de-Gau**
Pont-de-Gau. **Tel** 04-90 97 82 62.
⬜ daily. 📷 ♿

🏛 **Musée Camarguais**
Parc Naturel Régional de Camargue,
Mas du Pont de Rousty. **Tel** 04-90 97
10 82. ⬜ Apr–Sep: daily; Oct–Mar:
Wed–Mon. ⬛ public hols. 📷 ♿

Impressionist painter Cézanne's
studio in Aix-en-Provence

Aix-en-Provence ❸

Bouches-du-Rhône. 🏘 140,000. 🚉
🚌 ℹ️ 2 Place Général de Gaulle
(04-42 16 11 61). ⬛ daily.
www.aixenprovencetourisme.com

Provence's former capital is
an international students' town,
with a university that dates
back to 1409. The city was
transformed in the 17th
century, when ramparts, first
raised by the Romans in their
town of Aquae Sextiae, were
pulled down, and the mansion-
lined Cours Mirabeau was built.

North of the Cours Mirabeau
lies the town's old quarter.
Cathédrale St-Sauveur creaks
with history. The jewel of the
church is the triptych of *The
Burning Bush* (1476) by
Nicolas Froment. The modest
Atelier Paul Cézanne, a studio
designed by Cézanne himself,
is much as he left it when he
died in 1906.

The main museum is the
Musée Granet. François
Granet (1775–1849) left his
collection of French, Italian,

and Flemish paintings to Aix.
Work by Provençal artists is
also shown, some by Granet.

🏛 **Musée Granet**
13 Rue Cardinale. **Tel** 04-42 38 14
70. ⬜ Tue–Sun. 📷 ♿

Marseille ❸

Bouches-du-Rhône. 🏘 1,000,000.
✈ 25 km NW. 🚢 🚉 🚌 ℹ️ 4 La
Canebière (04-91 13 89 00). ⬛
daily. www.marseille-tourisme.com

France's most important port
and oldest major city is
centered on the surprisingly
attractive Vieux Port. On the
north side are the commercial
docks and the old town, rebuilt
after World War II.

The old town's finest building
is the **Vieille Charité**, a large,
well-restored 17th-century
hospice. The first floor has a
small but rich collection of
ancient Egyptian artifacts.

The Neo-Byzantine **Notre-
Dame-de-la-Garde** dominates
the city but Marseille's finest
piece of religious architecture
is the **Abbaye de St-Victor**,
founded in the 5th century,
with crypts containing catacombs, sarcophagi, and the
cave of the martyr St. Victor.

During postwar rebuilding
the Roman docks were
uncovered. The **Musée des
Docks Romains** mainly
displays large storage urns
once used for wine, grain,
and oil. In the Centre Bourse
shopping center is the **Musée
d'Histoire de Marseille**.
Reconstructions of the city at
the height of the Greek
period make this a good
starting point for a tour.

Old harbor of Marseille, looking towards the Quai de Rive Neuve

For hotels and restaurants in this region see pp206–11 and pp212–17

Flavors of the South of France

It's a heady experience just to stand, look, and sniff in a Provençal market. Tables sag under piles of braided pink garlic, colorful fresh peppers, tomatoes, eggplants, zucchini, and asparagus. In the fall and winter an earthy scent fills the air, with wild mushrooms, Swiss chard, walnuts, and quinces crowding the stalls. The waters of Coastal Provence provide a

Rosemary

bountiful sea harvest, including plump mussels, oysters, and *tellines* (tiny clams). The area is especially famous for its fish dishes, notably *bouillabaisse*. Lamb is the most common meat in Provence; the best comes from the Camargue, where lambs graze on herbs and salt-marsh grass. The South supplies France with the first of the season's peaches, cherries, and apricots.

Fish liquor

Red snapper

Bouillabaisse, *a fish soup originating in Marseille, is a luxury today. It consists of an assortment of local seafood including monkfish, mullet, snapper, scorpion fish, and conger eel, flavoured with tomatoes, saffron, and olive oil. Traditionally, the fish liquor is served first with croutons spread with rouille, a spicy mayonnaise. The fish is eaten afterwards.*

Croutons

Rouille (meaning "rust"), a mayonnaise with chillies and garlic

Monkfish

Conger eel   Red mullet

OLIVES AND OLIVE OIL

Most of the olive crop is crushed for oil. Ripe olives are black and the unripe ones are green; both can be preserved in brine or oil. At the end of the olive harvest *tapenade* is popular, a paste of black olives, capers, anchovies, and olive oil eaten with bread.

Fougasse *is a flattish, lattice-like bread variously studded with black olives, anchovies, onions, and spices. The sweet version is flavoured with almonds.*

Black olives   Tapenade   Olive oil

Aïoli *is a sauce made of egg yolks, garlic, and olive oil. It is served with salt cod, boiled eggs, snails, or raw vegetables.*

Ratatouille *is a stew of onions, eggplants, zucchini, tomatoes, and peppers, cooked in olive oil and garlic.*

Salade Niçoise *comes in many versions but always includes lettuce, green beans, tomatoes, black olives, eggs, and anchovies.*

The Côte d'Azur

The Côte d'Azur is, without doubt, the most celebrated seaside in Europe. Almost everybody who has been anybody for the past 100 years has succumbed to its glittering allure. Today the Côte d'Azur is busy all year round; expect heavy traffic around Cannes and St-Tropez in summer. Between Cannes and Menton, the coast forms the glamorous French Riviera, playground of the rich and famous. The bustling city of Nice lies at the area's heart, richly deserving the title "capital of the Côte d'Azur."

BEACHES OF THE COTE D'AZUR

The sun-drenched coastline of the Côte d'Azur is one of the busiest in Europe. To the east lie the Riviera's big, traditional resorts, while to the west are smaller towns in coves and bays. Beaches are sandy west of Antibes, and more shingly to the east.

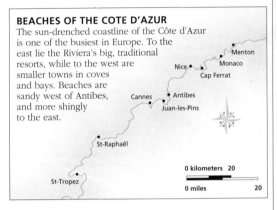

0 kilometers 20

0 miles 20

Exploring the Côte d'Azur

The Côte d'Azur is the most popular destination in France for sun-worshipers, with its seaside vacation towns and long, golden beaches. **St-Tropez** is currently the trendiest resort; Tahini-Plage is the coast's showcase for fun, sun, fashion, and glamor. By contrast, the family resort of **St-Raphaël** is peaceful, with excellent tourist facilities.

East of **Cannes**, at the western edge of the Riviera, **Juan-les-Pins** is a lively resort. Its all-night bars, nightclubs, and cafés make it popular with teenagers and young adults.

Founded by the Greeks, **Antibes** is one of the oldest towns along this stretch of coast, and home to a large museum of Picasso's work, donated by the artist himself.

Clifftop walks replace seafront promenades around the wooded peninsula of **Cap Ferrat**, where grand villas and private beaches can be glimpsed between the trees.

At the eastern edge of the Riviera, past the glitz of the casinos and hotels of **Monaco**, the beaches of **Menton** are the warmest along the coast; sunbathers enjoy a beach climate all year round.

Harborside at St-Tropez on the Côte d'Azur

For hotels and restaurants in this region see pp206–11 and pp212–17

Uma Thurman arriving at the Cannes Film Festival

Cannes ㉟

Alpes-Maritimes. 70,000. 🚌 🚆 ℹ️ Palais des Festivals, 1 La Croisette (04-93 39 24 53). 🛒 daily.

The first thing that most people associate with Cannes is its many festivals, especially the International Film Festival held each May. The first Cannes Film Festival took place in 1946 and, for a while, it remained a small and exclusive affair. The mid-1950s marked the change from artistic event to media circus, but Cannes remains the international marketplace for moviemakers and distributors. The annual festival is held in the huge **Palais des Festivals**.

There is, however, more to the city than this glittering event. The Old Town is centered in the Le Suquet district, which is dominated by the church of **Notre-Dame de l'Espérance**, built in the 16th and 17th centuries in the Provençal Gothic style. The famed **Boulevard de la Croisette** is lined with palm trees. Luxury stores and hotels look out over fine sandy beaches.

Nice ㊱

Alpes-Maritimes. 346,000. 🛫 🚢 🚆 🚌 ℹ️ 5 Promenade des Anglais (08-92 70 74 07). 🛒 Tue–Sun. 🎭 Carnival (Feb). **www**.nicetourisme.com

The largest resort on the Mediterranean coast, Nice has the second busiest airport in France. Its temperate winter climate and verdant subtropical vegetation have long attracted visitors, and today it is also a center for business conferences and package travelers.

There are many art museums in Nice, two of which devote themselves to the works of particular artists. The **Musée Matisse** displays drawings, paintings, bronzes, fabrics, and artifacts. The **Musée Chagall** holds the largest collection of works by Marc Chagall, with paintings, drawings, sculpture, stained glass, and mosaics.

A strikingly original complex of four marble-faced towers linked by glass passageways houses the **Musée d'Art Contemporain**. The collection is particularly strong in Neo-Realism and Pop Art. The **Musée des Beaux Arts** displays works by Dufy, Monet, Renoir, and Sisley.

A 19th-century palace, the **Palais Masséna** is filled with paintings of the Nice school, works by the Impressionists, Provençal ceramics, folk art, and a gold cloak once worn by Napoleon's beloved Josephine.

The onion domes of the **Cathédrale Orthodoxe Russe St-Nicolas**, completed in 1912, make this Nice's most distinctive landmark.

🏛 **Musée Matisse**
164 Ave des Arènes de Cimiez.
Tel 04-93 81 08 08. ☐ Wed–Mon.
⬤ some public hols. 🖼 ♿

🏛 **Musée Chagall**
36 Ave du Docteur Ménard. **Tel** 04-93 53 87 20. ☐ Wed–Mon. ⬤
Jan 1, May 1, Dec 25. 🖼 ♿

Skyscrapers and apartment blocks of modern Monte Carlo in Monaco

Monaco ㊲

Monaco. 🏠 34,000. ✈ (Nice).
🚉 🅸 2a Boulevard des Moulins
(092-16 61 16). 🍴 daily. 🎪
International Circus Festival (Jan–Feb).
www.visitemonaco.com

Arriving among the towering skyscrapers of Monaco today, it is hard to envisage the turbulence of its history. At first a Greek settlement, later taken by the Romans, it was bought from the Genoese in 1297 by the Grimaldis who, in spite of bitter family feuds, still rule as the world's oldest monarchy. Monaco covers 1.9 sq km (0.74 sq miles) and, although its size has increased by one-third in the form of landfills, it still occupies an area smaller than New York's Central Park.

The best-known section of Monaco is Monte Carlo. People flock to the annual car rally held here in January, but the area owes its renown mainly to its **Grand Casino**. Source of countless legends, it was instituted by Charles III to save himself from bankruptcy in 1856. So successful was this money-making venture that, by 1870, he was able to abolish taxation for his people. Designed in 1878 and set in formal gardens, the casino gives a splendid view over Monaco. Even the most exclusive of the gaming rooms can be visited.

Across the harbor lies Monaco-Ville, the seat of government. The interior of the 13th-century **Palais Princier**, with its priceless furniture and magnificent frescoes, is open to the public from April to September.

The aquarium of the **Musée Océanographique** holds rare species of marine plants and animals. Marine explorer Jacques Cousteau established his research center here.

A quiet stretch along Nice's 5 km (3 miles) of beachfront

The lavish surroundings of the Belle Epoque Grand Casino

Practical Information

France is justifiably proud of its many attractions, for which it has good tourist information facilities. Both in France and abroad, French Government Tourist Offices are an invaluable source of reference for practical aspects of your stay, especially for those with special needs. If you are unfortunate enough to need medical or emergency assistance, France has excellent hospitals, ambulance, fire, and police services. The country also has a modern communications network, making it easy to keep in touch by telephone, post, or e-mail.

VISA REQUIREMENTS AND CUSTOMS

Currently there are no visa requirements for EU nationals or visitors from the United States, Canada, Australia or New Zealand who plan to stay in France for under three months. Visitors from most other countries require a tourist visa. Non-EU visitors can, with some exceptions, reclaim the French sales tax (TVA) on goods if they spend over a certain amount in one shop and get a *détaxe* receipt.

TOURIST INFORMATION

All major cities and large towns have *offices de tourisme*. Small towns and even villages have *syndicats d'initiative*. Both will give you town plans, advice on accommodations, and information on regional recreational and cultural activities.

You can also get information before you leave for France from **French Government Tourist Offices**, or by contacting local tourist offices (see individual town headings in this guide) or the appropriate CRT (Comité Régional de Tourisme) – ask the FGTO for the address.

PERSONAL SECURITY

Violent crime is rare in France – even a major city such as Paris is surprisingly safe. However, muggings and brawls do occur, so avoid isolated or poorly lit places, especially at night. Women should take extra care, especially when traveling alone. Also beware of pickpockets, who are active in large cities.

POLICE

There are two types of police in France. The *Police Nationale* look after large towns and cities. If you need to contact them, find the *Commissariat de Police* (police headquarters). Small towns, villages, and country areas are policed by the *Gendarmerie Nationale*. If you need to report a crime in these places, go to the nearest local *gendarmerie*.

OPENING HOURS

Generally, opening hours for tourist sights are from 10am–5:40pm with one late evening per week. Most close on public holidays.

National museums and sights are normally closed on Tuesdays, with a few exceptions which close on Mondays. Municipal museums normally close on Mondays. Churches are open every day but sometimes shut at lunchtime.

FACILITIES FOR THE DISABLED

Facilities for the disabled vary in France. Details of services in most towns can be obtained from the **GIHP** (Groupement pour l'Insertion des Personnes Handicapées Physiques). The **Association des Paralysés de France** provides information on wheelchair access.

MEDICAL TREATMENT

All European Union Nationals are entitled to French social security coverage. However, treatment must be paid for at the time, and hospital rates vary widely. Reimbursements may be obtained if you have the correct documents before you travel, but the process is long and complicated.

All travelers, particularly non-EU nationals, should, therefore, consider purchasing travel insurance before they arrive. In the case of a medical emergency call **SAMU** (*Service d'Aide Médicale Urgence*). However, it is often faster to call **Sapeurs Pompiers** (the fire

THE CLIMATE OF FRANCE

Set on Europe's western edge, France has a varied, temperate climate. An Atlantic influence prevails in the northwest, with westerly sea winds bringing humidity and warm winters. The east experiences Continental temperature extremes with frosty, clear winters and often stormy summers. The south enjoys a Mediterranean climate, with hot, dry summers and mild winters.

PARIS

°C/F	Apr	Jul	Oct	Jan
	14/58	24/75	16/61	
	7/44	15/59	9/49	7/44
				2/35
☀ hrs	6	8	4.5	2
☂ mm	50	58	55	55
month	Apr	Jul	Oct	Jan

0°C 32°F

NICE

°C/F	Apr	Jul	Oct	Jan
	17/63	27/80	21/70	
	10/50	19/67	13/55	13/55
				5/41
☀ hrs	7.5	11	6.5	5
☂ mm	62	16	108	83
month	Apr	Jul	Oct	Jan

0°C 32°F

service), who offer a first aid and ambulance service. This is particularly true in rural areas.

Casualty departments (service des urgences) in public hospitals can deal with most medical problems. Your consulate should be able to provide you with details of an English-speaking doctor in the area. Pharmacists can also suggest treatments for many health problems. Look for the green cross sign outside pharmacies.

BANKING AND CURRENCY

The French unit of currency is the euro. This replaced the French franc and was introduced into general circulation in January 2002. The best way to take currency when traveling is often as traveler's checks, as, in the case of theft, they are replaceable. These can be obtained from **American Express**, **Thomas Cook**, or your bank.

Most credit cards are widely accepted in France, but, because of the high commissions charged, American Express is often not. The most commonly used credit card is Carte Bleue/Visa. Eurocard/MasterCard (Access in UK) is also often accepted. Credit cards issued in France contain a microchip and are

called "smart cards", but many machines can also read cards with magnetic strips. If you find your conventional card cannot be read in the smart card slot get the cashier to swipe the card through the magnetic reader. You may be asked to tap in your PIN code (code confidentiel) on a small keypad.

You can also use credit cards in most banks to withdraw cash; either from an ATM (automatic teller machine), which should have an English language option, or from a cash desk. Banks are usually open Mon–Fri, from 9am–4:30 or 5:15pm, with some also open on Saturday morning. Many close for lunch, and many, especially in the south, are closed on Monday.

COMMUNICATIONS

Payphones in France take coins or plastic telephone cards (télécartes). Cards are cheaper and more convenient to use than coins. They are sold in either 50 or 120 units and can be bought at post offices, tobacconists (tabacs), and newsagents. For local calls, a unit lasts up to six minutes. Many phones now also accept credit cards (with a PIN number). Post offices have telephone booths (cab-

ines) where you can telephone first and pay after the call. This is cheaper than making long-distance calls from hotels. The Minitel electronic phone directory, shopping, and information service can also be used in most post offices.

La Poste (the Post Office) used to be called the P.T.T. (postes, télégraphes, téléphones), and some road signs still give directions to the P.T.T. The postal service in France is fast and reliable. However, it is not cheap, especially when sending a parcel abroad.

At La Poste, postage stamps (timbres) are sold singly or in carnets of seven or ten. They are also sold at tabacs, although you need to go to the post office for international stamps. At post offices you can also use telephone directories (annuaires), buy phonecards, cash or buy money orders (mandats), and make international calls.

Post offices usually open from 9am–5pm Mon–Fri, often with a break for lunch, and 9am–noon on Saturdays. Mail boxes are yellow, and often have separate slots for the town you are in, the département, and other destinations (autres destinations).

Internet cafés are slowly making an appearance, especially in major towns.

DIRECTORY

EMBASSIES

Australia
4 Rue Jean Rey,
75015 Paris.
Tel 01-40 59 33 00.

Canada
35 Ave Montaigne,
75008 Paris.
Tel 01-44 43 29 00.

UK
Consulate:
18bis Rue d'Anjou,
75008 Paris.
Tel 01-44 51 31 00.

US
2 Ave Gabriel,
75008 Paris.
Tel 01-43 12 22 22.

TOURIST INFORMATION

French Government Tourist Office
25–27 Rue des Pyramides,
75001 Paris.
Tel 0892-683 000.
www.franceguide.com

In Australia:
French Tourist Bureau,
Level 22,
25 Bligh Street,
Sydney, NSW 2000.
Tel 612-9321 5244.

In Canada:
1981 Ave McGill College,
Suite 490,
Montréal,
Québec H3A 2W9.
Tel 514-288 4264.

In the UK:
178 Piccadilly,
London W1V 0AL.
Tel 09068-244 123.

In the US:
444 Madison Ave, 16th
Floor, New York, NY 10022.
Tel 212-838 7800.

FACILITIES FOR THE DISABLED

Association des Paralysés de France
17 Bld August Blanqui,
75013 Paris.
Tel 01-40 78 69 00.

GIHP
10 Rue Georges de
Porto-Riche, 75014 Paris.
Tel 01-43 95 66 36.

EMERGENCY NUMBERS

Ambulance (SAMU)
Tel 15 or 18 (Sapeurs Pompiers).

Fire (Sapeurs Pompiers)
Tel 18.

Police and Gendarmerie
Tel 17.

BANKING

American Express
11 Rue Scribe, 75009 Paris.
Tel 01-47 14 50 00.

Thomas Cook
25 Bld des Capucines,
75002 Paris.
Tel 08-26 82 67 77.

Travel Information

France has highly advanced transportation systems, with Paris at the hub of its air, rail, and road networks. Paris's two main airports have direct flights to North America, Africa, Japan, and the rest of Europe. The city's six major railway stations connect it to some 6,000 destinations in France, and provide links to the whole of Europe. An extensive, well-developed road network makes it easy to reach all parts of the country by car or bus. France is also well connected by sea, with frequent ferry crossings from the UK to ports on the Channel.

FLYING TO FRANCE

France is served by nearly all international airlines. Paris is the major airline destination in France, but there are a number of other international airports across the country. Some airports near the border, such as Geneva, Basle, and Luxembourg, can also be used for destinations in France.

The main French airline is **Air France**, which has services to major cities across the world. The main British airlines with regular flights to France are **British Airways** and **British Midland**. Inexpensive flights from the UK to various French destinations are available from carriers such as **easyJet** and **Ryanair**. Major airlines including **American Airlines**, **Delta**, and **United** operate flights from the United States. **Air Canada** flies from several cities in Canada, and **Qantas** provides flights from Australia and New Zealand.

AIR FARES

Airline fares are at their highest during the peak summer season in France, usually from July to September. Fierce competition between airlines, however, means there are often discounts on offer.

APEX fares are booked in advance. They cannot be changed or cancelled without penalty and there are also minimum and maximum stay requirements. Packages are also worth considering, as airlines and tour operators can put together a great range of flexible deals to suit your needs. These can include car rental and rail travel, enabling you to continue overland.

DOMESTIC FLIGHTS

There are a number of domestic airlines that fly between the cities of France, some of which only operate within one region; others also fly to French-speaking countries, with Air France offering the largest number of routes. However, unless you are eligible for discounts, you may find it cheaper and faster to travel on the high-speed trains, given the time it can take to reach the airports.

FERRY SERVICES

There are several crossings between the UK and French ports. **P&O Ferries** operates between Dover and Calais, with frequent crossings (75-90 minutes). P&O also operates between Portsmouth and Le Havre (5 hrs 30 mins) or Cherbourg (5 hrs). There is also an express catamaran service from Portsmouth to Cherbourg (2 hrs 45 mins).

Brittany Ferries runs a nine-hour service from Portsmouth to St-Malo, a six-hour service from Portsmouth to Caen, and a six-hour service from Plymouth to Roscoff. **Sea France** has a fleet of six ships and has been operating up to 15 crossings daily each way between Calais and Dover since 1996. Crossings take 1 hr 15 minutes. You need to check in 30 minutes before departure.

CHANNEL TUNNEL

The Channel Tunnel (Tunnel sous La Manche) was inaugurated in 1994. A car-carrying shuttle service, which is operated by **Eurotunnel**,

runs between Folkestone and Calais. The passenger service, **Eurostar**, links London and Paris (2.5 hrs).

GETTING AROUND PARIS

Central Paris is compact, and the best way to get around is often to walk. Public transportation in the city is good, however, with an efficient metro (subway) system, frequent buses, and a commuter train service (RER). These are all operated by the Paris transportation company, RATP.

There are many types of ticket available, sold at metro and RER stations, and most can be used on any RATP service, including buses. Single bus tickets can also be bought from the driver when boarding. All tickets used on buses must be stamped in the machine on board.

Single RATP tickets are valid in metro/RER zones 1 or 2, or for any bus journey. *Carnets* (books of ten single tickets), are more economical if you plan to make a number of journeys. Various passes are also available, which entitle you to unlimited travel in certain zones for a set number of days.

RAIL TRAVEL

France has always been known for the punctuality of its trains. The French state railway, the **Société Nationale des Chemins de Fer (SNCF)**, provides an excellent rail network which covers nearly all of France. The fastest services are provided by the high-speed TGV (*Trains à Grande Vitesse*) trains, which link most major cities.

Overnight services are popular in France, and most long-distance trains have *couchettes* (bunks), which you must reserve for a fee. Reservations are also compulsory for all TGV services, trains on public holidays, and for a *siège inclinable* (reclinable seat). Information on the various rail services and fares is available from the **Rail Europe** office in London. In France, leaflets are available at most stations. There are a number of special tickets available, including ones for over 60s, families, and under 26s. There are also special tickets for those doing a lot of train travel.

Automatic ticket and reservation machines *(billetterie automatique)* are found at main stations. They take credit cards or coins. You can also check train times, fares, and make reservations by phoning **SNCF**. Both reservations and tickets must be validated in one of the orange *composteur* machines near the platforms before boarding the train.

TRAVELING BY ROAD

France has one of the densest road networks in Europe, with modern motorways which allow quick and easy access to all parts of the country. However, you can save money on tolls and explore France in a more leisurely way by using some of the other high-quality roads, such as RN *(route nationale)* and D *(départementale)* routes.

Most motorways in France have a toll system *(autoroutes à péage)*, which can be quite expensive, especially over

long distances. There are some short sections which are free, however, usually close to major centers. Tolls can be paid with either credit cards or cash. Where only small sums are involved, you throw coins into a large receptacle and the change is given automatically.

Speed limits in France are shown in km/h. The limit in all towns, unless shown otherwise, is 50 km/h (30 mph). On major roads, higher limits are usually shown. On the *autoroutes* the usual limit is 130 km/h (80 mph), but this is reduced to 110 km/h (70 mph) when it is raining. On-the-spot fines may be demanded for speeding offences, and there are severe penalties for drink-driving.

Sunday is usually a good time to travel in France, as there are very few trucks on the road. Try to avoid traveling at the French holiday rush periods known as the *grands départs*. The worst times are weekends in July, and at the beginning and end of August.

All the main international car-rental companies operate in France. It is worth ringing around before you leave for

France as there are many special offers for rentals booked and prepaid in the UK or US. Good deals are often available from **Autos Abroad**, brokers who use cars owned by other car rental companies, such as Budget and National Citer. Booking in this way may work out at half the price of the standard rental.

BUSES

Long-distance buses generally operate only where there is not a good train service in operation (for example, between Geneva and Nice). SNCF (the state railway) operates some bus routes and issues regional TER *(Transports Express Régionaux)* timetables and tickets. **Eurolines** serves a wider range of destinations within France, as well as providing services to hundreds of major cities across Europe. They also offer excursions and arrange accommodations.

There are also many local buses, which run from the town's *Gare Routière*.

DIRECTORY

AIRLINES

Air Canada
Tel 08-20 87 08 71.
Tel 800-247 2262 (Can).
www.aircanada.ca

Air France
Tel 3654.
Tel 0870-1424 343 (UK).
Tel 800-237 2747 (US).
www.airfrance.fr

American Airlines
Tel 08-10 87 28 72.
Tel 800-433 7300 (US).
www.aa.com

British Airways
Tel 08-25 82 54 00.
Tel 0870-850 9850 (UK).
www.britishairways.com

British Midland
Tel 01-41 91 87 04.
Tel 0870-607 0555 (UK).
www.flybmi.com

Delta Air Lines
Tel 08-00 35 40 80.
Tel 800-241 4141 (US).
www.delta.com

easyJet
Tel 0870-600 0000 (UK).
Tel 0826-102 611.
www.easyjet.com

Qantas
Tel 020-8846 0466 (UK).
Tel 800-0014 0014 (Aus).
www.qantas.com

Ryanair
Tel 0871-246 0000 (UK).
Tel 0892-232 375 (France).
www.ryanair.com

United Airlines
Tel 08-10 72 72 72.
Tel 800-241 6522 (US).
www.united.com

FERRY SERVICES

Brittany Ferries
Tel 08-25 82 88 28.
Tel 0870-9000 389 (UK).
www.brittanyferries.com

P&O Ferries
Tel 0870-520 2020 (UK).
www.poferries.com

Sea France
Tel 0870-443 1653 (UK).
www.seafrance.com

CHANNEL TUNNEL

Eurostar
Tel 08-92 35 35 39.
Tel 0870-518 6186 (UK).
www.eurostar.com

Eurotunnel
Tel 810-630 304.
Tel 0870-535 3535 (UK).
www.eurotunnel.com

RAIL TRAVEL

Rail Europe
Tel 0870-5848 848.
Tel 020-7647 4900 (UK).
www.raileurope.co.uk

SNCF, Paris
Tel 08-92 35 35 39.
www.sncf.com

CAR RENTAL

Autos Abroad
Tel 0870-066 7788 (UK).
www.autosabroad.com

Avis
Tel 0220-050 505 (UK).
Tel 01-44 18 10 50 (Paris).
www.avis.fr

Europcar
Tel 0870-607 5000 (UK).
Tel 08-25 35 23 52 (Paris).
www.europcar.com

Hertz
Tel 020-8684 7743 (UK).
Tel 01-39 38 38 38 (Paris).
www.hertz.com

BUSES

Eurolines
Tel 08-92 89 90 91.
www.eurolines.fr

Shopping

Shopping in France is a delight. Whether you go to the hypermarkets and department stores, or seek out the many small specialist stores and markets, you will be tempted by the stylish presentation and high quality of the goods on offer. France is especially renowned for its wine, with a vast selection available, from cheap table wines to classic vintages. French food is also excellent, in particular the cheeses, cured meats, patés, cakes, and pastries. France also offers world-famous fashion, pottery and porcelain, crystal, and fine-quality antiques.

OPENING HOURS

Food shops open at about 7am and close around noon for lunch. After lunch most are open until 7pm or later. Bakeries often stay open until 1pm or later.

Shops that do not close at lunchtime include some supermarkets, department stores, and most hypermarkets.

General opening hours for non-food shops are around 9am–7pm Mon–Sat, often with a break for lunch. Many are closed on Mondays.

Food shops (and newsagents) are open on Sunday mornings. Virtually every shop in France is closed on Sunday afternoon, except for the last weeks before Christmas when hypermarkets remain open all day. Smaller shops may be closed one day of the week, usually Monday. However, those in tourist regions are often open every day in the high season.

LARGER SHOPS

Hypermarkets (*hypermarchés* or *grandes surfaces*) can be found on the outskirts of every sizeable town: look for signs indicating *centre commercial*. Among the biggest are Carrefour, Casino, Auchan, and Continent. Discount petrol is often sold and, most, but not all, now have pumps which take credit cards.

Department stores (*grands magasins*), such as the cheap and cheerful Monoprix and Prisunic, are often found in town centers. Others, like the more upscale **Au Printemps** and **Galeries Lafayette**, can be found both in town and out-of-town centers.

SPECIALIST SHOPS

One of the pleasures of shopping in France is that specialist shops for food still flourish despite the new large supermarkets. The *boulangerie*, for bread, is frequently combined with a *pâtisserie* selling cakes and pastries. The *traiteur* sells prepared foods. Cheese shops (*fromagerie*) and other shops specializing in dairy products (*laiterie*) may also be combined, while the *boucherie* (butcher's) and *charcuterie* (pork butcher's/delicatessen) are often separate shops. For general groceries go to an *épicerie*. An *épicerie fine* is a delicatessen.

MARKETS

Markets are found in towns and villages all over France. To find out where the market is, ask a passerby for *le marché*. Markets usually finish promptly at noon and do not reopen in the afternoon.

Look for local producers, including those with only one or two special items to sell, as their goods are often cheaper and of better quality.

By law, price tags include the origin of all produce: *pays* means local. Chickens from Bresse are marketed wearing a red, white, and blue badge giving the name of the producer as proof of authenticity. If you are visiting markets over several weeks, look for items just coming into season, such as fresh walnuts, the first wild asparagus, truffles, early artichokes, or wild strawberries. The special seasonal markets held throughout France are the best places to find these items, and there are often *foires artisanales* held at the same time, which sell local produce, arts, and crafts.

REGIONAL PRODUCE

French regional specialties can be bought outside their area of origin, although it is interesting to buy them locally. Provence, in the south, prides itself on the quality of its olive oil, while the southwest is notable for its patés. Central France is famous for snails, cured meats, and Roquefort cheese. Cheese is also an important product of the temperate north, the best-known varieties being Brie and Camembert.

Popular drinks are also associated with particular regions. Pastis, made from aniseed, is popular in the south, while Calvados, made from apples, is from the north.

Location also determines quality. Lyon's culinary importance stems from the many locally produced cheeses, the proximity of Bresse for chickens, Charolais for beef, and the Alsace region for sausages.

WINE

In wine-producing areas, follow the *dégustation* (tasting) signs to vineyards (*domaines*) where you can taste the wine. You will be expected to buy at least one bottle. Wine cooperatives sell the wine of small producers. Here you can buy wine in five- and ten-liter containers (*en vrac*), as well as in bottles. The wine is often rated AOC, *appellation d'origine contrôlée*, selling at less than 2 euros a liter. As wine sold *en vrac* is "duty-free," customers receive a *laissez-passer* (permit) indicating their destination. Bottled wine sold by co-ops is duty-paid.

CLOTHING

France is famous for its fashion, and elegant clothes can be found even in quite small towns. Paris, however, is the home of *haute couture*. There are 23 couture houses listed with the Fédération

Française de la Couture, and most of these are concentrated on the Right Bank around Rue du Faubourg-St-Honoré and Avenue Montaigne. Famous names include **Yves Saint Laurent**, **Chanel**, **Guy Laroche**, **Christian Lacroix**, **Nina Ricci**, and **Christian Dior**. Other top designers include **Hermès** and **Giorgio Armani**.

Men don't have the luxury of *haute couture* dressing: their choice is limited to ready-to-wear, but most of the big name womenswear designers also produce a range for men. A good example is **Gianni Versace**, with his classic Italian clothes for men. On the Right Bank, the household name designers include **Giorgio Armani**, the stylish **Pierre Cardin**, **Yves Saint Laurent**, and **Lanvin**, who is particularly popular for his beautifully made leather accessories. If time is short and you want to make all your purchases under one roof, try the *grands magasins*. These stores offer a wide choice of fashions, and prices will be more within most people's budgets. **Au Printemps**, for example, is huge, with separate buildings for menswear, household goods, and womens' and children's clothes. The beauty department, with its vast perfume selection, is definitely worth a visit. **Le Bon Marché**, on the Left Bank, was the first department store in Paris, and is the most chic, with an excellent food hall. **Galeries Lafayette** has a wide range of clothes at all price levels. Closed for renovation until 2010, **La Samaritaine** is one of the oldest shops in Paris.

ART AND ANTIQUES

You can buy fabulous art and antiques from stores, galleries, and flea-markets all over France. The best places to visit in Paris are **Le Louvre des Antiquaires**, a huge building containing around 250 antique dealers, and the famous **Marché aux Puces de St-Ouen** flea market (open Saturday to Monday). To avoid paying duty, you will need a certificate of authenticity when exporting objets d'art over 20 years old and any goods over a century old that are worth more than €150,000. Seek professional advice and declare them at customs if in doubt.

TAX-FREE SHOPPING

Visitors resident outside the European Union can reclaim the sales tax, TVA, on French goods if they spend more than €305 in one shop, get a *détaxe* receipt, and take the goods out of the country within six months. The form should be handed in at customs when leaving the country, and the reimbursement will be sent to you.

Exceptions for *détaxe* rebates are food and drink, medicines, tobacco, cars, and motorbikes. More information is available from the **Centre des Renseignements des Douanes**, but this is usually in French.

DIRECTORY

CLOTHING

Chanel
42 Ave Montaigne, 75008 Paris.
Tel 01-47 23 61 00.

5 Bld de la Croisette, 06400 Cannes.
Tel 04-93 38 55 05.

Christian Dior
30 Ave Montaigne, 75008 Paris.
Tel 01-40 73 73 73.

38 Bld de la Croisette, 06400 Cannes.
Tel 04-92 98 98 00.

Christian Lacroix
73 Rue du Faubourg St-Honoré, 75008 Paris.
Tel 01-42 68 79 04.

Gianni Versace
62 Rue du Faubourg St-Honoré, 75008 Paris.
Tel 01-47 42 88 02.

Giorgio Armani
6 Place Vendôme, 75001 Paris.
Tel 01-42 86 64 90.

Guy Laroche
20 Rue de la Trémaille, 75008 Paris.
Tel 01-40 69 68 00.

Hermès
24 Rue du Faubourg St-Honoré, 75008 Paris.
Tel 01-40 17 47 17.

Lanvin
22 Rue de Faubourg St-Honoré, 75008 Paris.
Tel 01-40 68 10 40.

15 Rue de Faubourg St-Honoré, 75008 Paris.
Tel 01-44 71 33 33.

Nina Ricci
39 Ave Montaigne, 75008 Paris.
Tel 01-40 88 67 60.

Pierre Cardin
27 Ave Marigny, 75008 Paris.
Tel 01-42 66 92 25.

Yves Saint Laurent
7 Ave George V, 75008 Paris.
Tel 01-56 62 64 00.

44 Bld Croisette, 06400 Cannes.
Tel 04-93 38 39 15.

DEPARTMENT STORES

Le Bon Marché
24 Rue de Sèvres, 75007 Paris.
Tel 01-44 39 80 00.

Galeries Lafayette
40 Bld Haussmann, 75009 Paris.
Tel 01-42 82 34 56.

11 Rue Ste Catherine, 33000 Bordeaux.
Tel 05-56 90 92 71.

6 Rue Maréchal Foch, 06400 Cannes.
Tel 04-97 06 25 00.

Au Printemps
64 Bld Haussman, 75009 Paris.
Tel 01-42 82 50 00.

La Samaritaine
19 Rue de la Monnaie, 75001 Paris.
Tel 01-40 41 20 20.

ART AND ANTIQUES

Le Louvre des Antiquaires
2 Place du Palais-Royal, 75001 Paris.
Tel 01-42 97 27 27.

Marché aux Puces de St-Ouen
Av Porte de Clignancourt, 75018 Paris.

TAX-FREE SHOPPING

Centre des Renseignements des Douanes
84 Rue d'Hauteville, 75010 Paris.
Tel 08-25 30 82 63.
Fax 01-53 24 68 30.

Entertainment

The entertainment center of France is Paris. Whether your preference is for drama, ballet, opera, jazz, cinema, or dancing the night away, Paris has it all. Across the rest of the country the arts are also well represented, and there are a number of internationally renowned arts festivals throughout the year. With a varied physical, as well as cultural, landscape, there are also many possibilities for outdoor sports and activities, including golf, tennis, walking, and skiing. Specialist holidays cater to those interested in French language, food, and wine.

ENTERTAINMENT LISTINGS

Two of the best listings magazines in Paris are *Pariscope* and *L'Officiel des Spectacles*. Published every Wednesday, you can pick them up at any newsstand. Local newspapers and *offices de tourisme* are the best places to find entertainment listings for the regions.

BOOKING TICKETS

Depending on the event, tickets can often be bought at the door, but for popular events it is wiser to purchase tickets in advance, at the box office or at **FNAC** chains. Theater box offices open daily from about 11am–7pm. Most accept credit card bookings by telephone. You can also purchase tickets from **Virgin Megastore** and other commercial centers in large towns.

THEATER

From the grandeur of the **Comédie Française** to slapstick farce and avant-garde drama, theater is flourishing in Paris. Founded in 1680 by royal decree, the Comédie Française is the bastion of French theater, aiming to keep classical drama in the public eye. In an underground auditorium in the Art Deco Palais de Chaillot, the **Théâtre National de Chaillot** stages lively productions of mainstream European classics. The **Théâtre National de la Colline** specializes in contemporary drama. Among the most important of the independents is the **Comédie des Champs-Elysées**, while for

over 100 years the **Palais Royal** has been the temple of risqué farce.

Excellent theaters and productions are also to be found in major cities across France, and there are big theater festivals held in Nancy (June) and Avignon (July; *see p191*).

MUSIC

The music scene in Paris has never been so busy, especially with the emergence of many internationally successful contemporary French groups. There are numerous first-class venues in the city, with excellent jazz, opera, contemporary, and classical music concerts.

Opened in 1989, the ultramodern 2,700-seat **Opéra de Paris Bastille** stages classic and modern operas. Productions from outside France are staged at the **Opéra Comique**.

The **Salle Pleyel** is Paris's principal concert hall and home of the Orchestre de Paris. Paris's newest venue is the **Cité de la Musique** in the Parc de la Villette.

Top international and pop acts are usually to be found at huge arenas such as the **Palais Omnisports de Paris-Bercy** or the **Zénith**. A more intimate atmosphere is found at the legendary **Olympia**.

Paris is, perhaps, most renowned for its jazz, and the best talent in the world can be heard here on any evening, especially throughout October during the jazz festival. All the great jazz musicians have performed at **New Morning**, which also hosts African, Brazilian, and other sounds. For Dixieland go to **Le Petit Journal St-Michel**.

Jazz is also popular across France, and big international jazz festivals are held right through the year, in Cannes (February; *see p196*), Antibes and Juan-le-Pins (July), and Le Mans (April). Opera and classical music are also widely performed, notably at the Aix festival during July (*see p195*).

CLUBS AND CABARET

Music in Paris nightclubs tends to follow the trends set in the US and Britain, although home-grown groups, especially those playing garage, are popular and influential both here and abroad.

Balajo, once frequented by Edith Piaf, and the ultra-hip **Folies Clubbing**, once a strip joint, are particularly up-to-the-minute with their music. **La Locomotive** attracts a mixed crowd to its three-level mainstream house nights. For a more Latin touch, try **La Java**. The dance floor of this club, where Edith Piaf once performed, now sways to Cuban and Brazilian sounds.

When it comes to picking a cabaret, the rule of thumb is simple: the better-known places are best. The **Folies-Bergère** is the oldest music hall in Paris and probably the most famous in the world. It is rivaled by the **Moulin Rouge**, birthplace of the cancan.

CINEMA

Paris is the world's capital of film appreciation. There are now more than 300 screens within the city limits, distributed among 100 cinemas. Most are concentrated in cinema belts, which enjoy the added appeal of nearby restaurants and shops. The Champs-Elysées has the densest cinema strip in town, where you can see the latest Hollywood smash or French *auteur* triumph, as well as some classic re-issues.

The cinemas on the Grands Boulevards include two notable architectural landmarks: the 2,800-seat **Le Grand Rex**, with its Baroque decor, and the **Max Linder Panorama**, which was refurbished in the 1980s.

The largest screen in France is the **La Géode** flagship in the 19th *arrondissement*. On the Left Bank, the area around Odéon-St-Germain-des-Prés has taken over from the Latin Quarter as the city's heartland for art and repertory cinemas.

OUTDOOR ACTIVITIES

A country as richly diverse in culture and geography as France offers an amazing variety of sport and leisure activities. Information on current leisure and sporting activities in a particular region is available from the tourist offices listed for each town in this guide.

Golf is popular in France, especially along the north and south coasts and in Aquitaine. You will need to take your handicap certificate with you if you want to play. Tennis is also a favorite sport, and there are courts to rent in almost every town.

More than 30,000 km (19,000 miles) of *Grandes Randonneés* (long distance tracks) and shorter *Petites Randonneés* cover France. The routes are clearly way-marked, and vary in difficulty, including long pilgrim routes, alpine crossings, and tracks through national parks. Some routes are open to mountain bikes and horses.

The mountains provide for excellent skiing and mountaineering. The Atlantic coast around Biarritz offers some of the best surfing and windsurfing in Europe. Sailing and waterskiing are popular all round France, and swimming facilities are generally good, although beaches in the south can be crowded in August.

SPECIALIST VACATIONS

French government Tourist Offices *(see p199)* have extensive information on travel companies offering special interest vacations. Send off

for *The Traveller in France Reference Guide*. Vacations are based on subjects such as the French language, wine appreciation, and cooking, as well as craft activities and organized nature trips.

SPECTATOR SPORT

The main sporting action in France revolves largely around soccer, rugby, tennis, and horse racing. There are various stadia and circuits all over the country; the best are near major cities, particularly Paris. Here, the **Stade de France** and the **Palais Omnisports de Paris-Bercy** host all the major events. **Parc des Princes** is home to the top Paris soccer team Paris St-Germain.

Cycling is also a very popular sport in France, and there is racing action across the country. The most famous event is the annual Tour de France held during July.

DIRECTORY

BOOKING TICKETS

FNAC
Forum Les Halles,
1 Rue Pierre Lescot,
75001 Paris.
Tel 01-40 41 40 00.

Virgin Megastore
52–60 Av des Champs-
Elysées, 75008 Paris.

THEATER

**Comédie des
Champs-Elysées**
15 Ave Montaigne,
75008 Paris.
Tel 01-53 23 99 19.

Comédie Française
1 Pl Colette,
75001 Paris.
Tel 08-25 10 16 80.

Palais Royal
38 Rue Montpensier,
75001 Paris.
Tel 01-42 97 59 81.

**Théâtre National de
Chaillot**
Place du Trocadéro,
75016 Paris.
Tel 01-53 65 30 00.

**Théâtre National de
la Colline**
15 Rue Malte-Brun, 75020
Paris. *Tel* 01-44 62 52 52.

MUSIC

Cité de la Musique
221 Ave Jean-Jaurès,
75019 Paris.
Tel 01-44 84 44 84.

Opéra Comique
(Salle Favart) 5 Rue Favart,
75002 Paris.
Tel 01-42 44 45 46.

**Opéra de Paris
Bastille**
120 Rue de Lyon, 75012
Paris. *Tel* 08-92 69 78 68.

Salle Pleyel
252 Rue du Faubourg St-
Honoré, 75008 Paris.
Tel 01-42 56 13 13.

New Morning
7–9 Rue des Petites-
Ecuries, 75010 Paris.
Tel 01-45 23 51 41.

Olympia
28 Bld des Capucines,
75009 Paris.
Tel 08-92 68 33 68.

**Palais Omnisports de
Paris-Bercy**
8 Bld de Bercy 75012.
Tel 08-92 69 23 00.

**Le Petit Journal
St-Michel**
71 Bld St-Michel, 75005
Paris. *Tel* 01-43 26 28 59.

Zénith
211 Ave Jean-Jaurès,
75019 Paris.
Tel 01-42 08 60 00.

CLUBS AND
CABARET

Balajo
9 Rue de Lappe, 75011
Paris. *Tel* 01-47 00 07 87.

Folies-Bergère
32 Rue Richer, 75009
Paris. *Tel* 01-44 79 98 90.

Folies Clubbing
11 Pl Pigalle, 75009 Paris.
Tel 01-48 78 55 25.

La Java
105 Rue du Faubourg-du-
Temple, 75010 Paris.
Tel 01-42 02 20 52.

La Locomotive
90 Bld de Clichy, 75018
Paris. *Tel* 01534-118 888.

Moulin Rouge
82 Bld de Clichy, 75018
Paris. *Tel* 01-53 09 82 82.

CINEMA

La Géode
26 Ave Corentin-Cariou,
75019 Paris.
Tel 08-92 68 45 40.

Le Grand Rex
1 Bld Poissonnière, 75002
Paris. *Tel* 01-42 36 83 96.

**Max Linder
Panorama**
24 Bld Poissonnière,
75009 Paris.
Tel 01-40 30 20 10.

SPECTATOR SPORT

**Palais Omnisports de
Paris-Bercy**
8 Bld de Bercy, 75012
Paris. *Tel* 08-92 69 23 00.

Parc des Princes
24 Rue du Commandant-
Guilbaud, 75016 Paris.
Tel 08-25 07 50 77.

Stade de France
La Plaine St-Denis,
93210 Paris.
Tel 01-55 93 00 00.

Where to Stay in France

French hotels are graded from nought to a maximum of four stars. They range from historic châteaux with magnificent furnishings and food to informal family-run hotels. In high season some will offer only full *pension* (all meals) or *demi-pension* (breakfast and dinner). A popular option for a self-catering vacation is a rural *gîte*.

PRICE CATEGORIES
Price categories for a standard double room per night during the high season, including tax and service. Breakfast is not included, unless specified:
€ under 80 euros
€€ 80–130 euros
€€€ 130–180 euros
€€€€ 180–250 euros
€€€€€ over 260 euros

PARIS

BEAUBOURG AND LES HALLES Hôtel Roubaix   €€
6 rue Greneta, 75003 **Tel** *01-42 72 89 91* **Fax** *01-42 72 58 79* **Rooms** *53*   **Map** *E3*

In an area with few good places to stay, Hôtel Roubaix is a pleasantly old-fashioned and inexpensive choice. The owners are exceptionally friendly and the rooms are clean, if a little shabby. The hotel is popular with repeat guests, so be sure to book a room in advance. **www.hotel-de-roubaix.com**

CHAILLOT QUARTER Hôtel Keppler   €€
12 rue Keppler, 75016 **Tel** *01-47 20 65 05* **Fax** *01-47 23 02 23* **Rooms** *49*   **Map** *B2*

This is an excellent budget hotel, a rare commodity in an expensive part of the city. Set on a quiet street, the rooms here are simple but clean, spacious and comfortable. High ceilings throughout add to the sense of space. **www.hotel-keppler-paris.federal-hotel.com**

CHAILLOT QUARTER Hôtel du Bois   €€€
11 rue du Dôme, 75016 **Tel** *01-45 00 31 96* **Fax** *01-45 00 90 05* **Rooms** *41*   **Map** *B2*

Two minutes from the Arc de Triomphe and the Champs Elysées, Hôtel du Bois is ideal for haute-couture boutique lovers. Behind a typically Parisian façade is an interior exuding British charm – Georgian furniture in the lounge, thick patterned carpets, and fine prints in the guest rooms. **www.hoteldubois.com**

CHAILLOT QUARTER Raphaël   €€€€€
17 av Kléber, 75016 **Tel** *01-53 64 32 00* **Fax** *01-53 64 32 01* **Rooms** *85*   **Map** *B2*

This hotel is the epitome of discreet elegance, where film stars come to be sheltered from the paparazzi. The decor is opulent, and the roof terrace bar is the loveliest in Paris, popular with the jet set. There are amazing views of the city, especially at night when the monuments are illuminated. **www.raphael-hotel.com**

CHAMPS-ELYSEES Résidence Lord Byron   €€€€
5 rue Chateaubriand, 75008 **Tel** *01-43 59 89 98* **Fax** *01-42 89 46 04* **Rooms** *31*   **Map** *B2*

Close to the Etoile, the Résidence Lord Byron is a small, discreet hotel with a courtyard garden for breakfast. Its bright guest rooms are quiet but small; if you want more space, ask for a salon room or a ground-floor room. **www.escapade-paris.com**

CHAMPS-ELYSEES Four Seasons George V   €€€€€
31 av George V, 75008 **Tel** *01-49 52 70 00* **Fax** *01-49 52 71 10* **Rooms** *246*   **Map** *B2*

This legendary hotel, dotted with salons, old furniture, and art, lost a little of its charm when it was renovated. But it gained a stunning restaurant, Le Cinq, which boasts the world's top sommelier and an award-winning chef. There is also a great spa. Sheer opulence. **www.fourseasons.com/paris**

CHAMPS-ELYSEES Le Bristol   €€€€€
112 rue du Faubourg-St-Honoré, 75008 **Tel** *01-53 43 43 00* **Fax** *01-53 43 43 01* **Rooms** *180*   **Map** *B2*

One of Paris's finest hotels, the Bristol's large rooms are sumptuously decorated with antiques and magnificent marble bathrooms. The period dining room, with its Flemish tapestries and glittering crystal chandeliers, has been given rave reviews. There is a wonderful swimming pool. **www.hotel-bristol.com**

INVALIDES AND EIFFEL TOWER QUARTER Grand Hôtel Levêque   €€
29 rue Cler, 75007 **Tel** *01-47 05 49 15* **Fax** *01-45 50 49 36* **Rooms** *50*   **Map** *B3*

The Levêque lies between the Eiffel Tower and the Invalides on a pedestrianized street with a quaint fruit-and-vegetable market. The great location isn't the only attraction – guest rooms are well kept and the hotel also provides internet access. **www.hotel-leveque.com**

INVALIDES AND EIFFEL TOWER QUARTER Hôtel de Suède St-Germain   €€€€
31 rue Vaneau, 75007 **Tel** *01-47 05 00 08* **Fax** *01-47 05 69 27* **Rooms** *40*   **Map** *C4*

Located near the Orsay and Rodin museums, Hôtel de Suède St-Germain offers elegant rooms, decorated in late 18th-century style with pale colors. Guests receive an exceptionally warm welcome. The deluxe rooms offer a view over the park. A lovely little garden to breakfast in completes the picture. **www.hoteldesuede.com**

Key to Symbols *see back cover flap*

LATIN QUARTER Hôtel Esmeralda €

4 rue St-Julien-le-Pauvre, 75005 **Tel** *01-43 54 19 20* **Fax** *01-40 51 00 68* **Rooms** *19* **Map** *E4*

The much-loved bohemian Hôtel Esmeralda lies in the heart of the Latin Quarter. With old stone walls and beamed ceilings, its charm has seduced the likes of Terence Stamp and Serge Gainsbourg. The best rooms overlook Notre-Dame cathedral. Breakfast is not provided here.

LATIN QUARTER Hôtel des Grandes Ecolse €€

75 rue Cardinal Lemoine, 75005 **Tel** *01-43 26 79 23* **Fax** *01-43 25 28 15* **Rooms** *51* **Map** *D4*

This hotel is a cluster of three small houses around a beautiful garden, where you can breakfast in good weather. The rooms are all comfortable and furnished with traditional 18th-century-style floral wallpaper; some open on to the courtyard. Internet access is available. **www.hotel-grandes-ecoles.com**

LATIN QUARTER Hôtel des Grands Hommes €€€

17 pl du Panthéon, 75005 **Tel** *01-46 34 19 60* **Fax** *01-43 26 67 32* **Rooms** *31* **Map** *E4*

Teachers at the Sorbonne frequent this quiet family hotel close to the Jardin du Luxembourg. It boasts a great view of the Panthéon from the attic rooms on the upper floor. The guest rooms are comfortable. Wi-Fi service is available. **www.hoteldesgrandshommes.com**

LUXEMBOURG QUARTER Hôtel Récamier €€

3 bis pl St-Sulpice, 75006 **Tel** *01-43 26 04 89* **Fax** *01-46 33 27 73* **Rooms** *30* **Map** *D4*

Situated on the place St-Sulpice, the mid-sized Hôtel Récamier is a family hotel that exudes an air of old-fashioned charm. The Récamier is a favorite spot with both writers and Left Bank tourists. The guest rooms overlooking the square have lovely views.

MONTMARTRE Regyn's Montmartre €

18 pl des Abbesses, 75018 **Tel** *01-42 54 45 21* **Fax** *01-42 23 76 69* **Rooms** *22*

Near Sacré-Cœur, this is an impeccably kept budget hotel. The top-floor guest rooms have views of the Eiffel Tower. Around the corner is Tabac des Deux Moulins at 15 rue le Pic, where Amélie worked in the film *Amélie*. **www.regynsmontmartre.com**

MONTMARTRE Terrass Hôtel €€€€€

12–14 rue Joseph-de-Maistre, 75018 **Tel** *01-44 92 34 14* **Fax** *01-42 52 29 11* **Rooms** *100*

Montmartre's most luxurious hotel, the rooms here are comfortably, if unremarkably, furnished. A few rooms retain the original Art-Deco woodwork. The big draw is the rooftop restaurant, where in the summer fashionable Parisians take in a world-class view. **www.terrass-hotel.com**

MONTPARNASSE Villa des Artistes €€€

9 rue de la Grande Chaumière, 75006 **Tel** *01-43 26 60 86* **Fax** *01-43 54 73 70* **Rooms** *59*

The Villa des Artistes aims to recreate Montparnasse's artistic heyday when Modigliani, Beckett, and Fitzgerald were all visitors here. The guest rooms are clean, but the main draw is the large patio garden and fountain, where you can breakfast in peace. **www.villa-artistes.com**

OPERA QUARTER Ambassador €€€€€

16 bd Haussmann, 75009 **Tel** *01-44 83 40 40* **Fax** *01-42 46 19 84* **Rooms** *300* **Map** *D2*

One of Paris's best Art Deco hotels, the Ambassador has been restored to its former glory with plush carpeting and antique furniture. The ground floor has pink marble columns, Baccarat crystal chandeliers, and Aubusson tapestries. The restaurant, "16 Haussmann", is popular with Parisian gourmets. **www.hotelambassador-paris.com**

ST-GERMAIN-DES-PRES Grand Hôtel des Balcons €€

3 rue Casimir Delavigne, 75006 **Tel** *01-46 34 78 50* **Fax** *01-46 34 06 27* **Rooms** *50* **Map** *D4*

Embellished with Art Nouveau features, this hotel has a beautiful hall with stained-glass windows and striking 19th-century-style lamps and wood paneling. Most guest rooms, quiet and well-decorated, enjoy a balcony. High-speed internet access with Wi-Fi is available. **www.balcons.com**

ST-GERMAIN-DES-PRES Hôtel du Quai Voltaire €€

19 quai Voltaire, 75007 **Tel** *01-42 61 50 91* **Fax** *01-42 61 62 26* **Rooms** *33* **Map** *D3*

Overlooking the river, this hotel was once the favorite of Blondin, Baudelaire, and Pissarro, and has featured in several films. It is best to avoid the rooms facing the quay, as they suffer from traffic noise. Higher floors are quieter, though, and the views are superb. **www.quaivoltaire.fr**

ST-GERMAIN-DES-PRES Hôtel de l'Abbaye St-Germain €€€€

10 rue Cassette, 75006 **Tel** *01-45 44 38 11* **Fax** *01-45 48 07 86* **Rooms** *44* **Map** *D4*

A 17th-century abbey, just steps from the Jardin du Luxembourg, this charming hotel has a history as a preferred hideout for artists and writers. Its finely furnished guest rooms and apartments have been tastefully done up and provided with modern facilities. **www.hotel-abbaye.com**

ST-GERMAIN-DES-PRES Relais Christine €€€€€

3 rue Christine, 75006 **Tel** *01-40 51 60 80* **Fax** *01-40 51 60 81* **Rooms** *51* **Map** *D4*

Always full, the Relais Christine is the epitome of the hôtel de charme. Part of a cloister from a 16th-century abbey, the hotel is a romantic, peaceful haven. The guest rooms, especially the deluxe rooms, are bright and spacious. Wi-Fi facilities are available. Reserve in advance. **www.relais-christine.com**

Map References *see map of Paris pp150–51*

THE MARAIS Hôtel de la Bretonnerie
22 rue Ste-Croix de la Bretonnerie, 75004 **Tel** *01-48 87 77 63* **Fax** *01-42 77 26 78* **Rooms** *29*   **Map** *D3*

Carved stone walls and an arched dining room in the basement are some of the charming features of Hôtel de la Bretonnerie, housed in a 17th-century mansion. Its spacious rooms, with beams and antique furniture, are each decorated differently. Service is warm and friendly. **www.bretonnerie.com**

THE MARAIS Pavillon de la Reine
28 pl des Vosges, 75003 **Tel** *01-40 29 19 19* **Fax** *01-40 29 19 20* **Rooms** *56*   **Map** *F4*

Set back from the marvelous place des Vosges, the Pavillon de la Reine is the best hotel in the Marais. Incredibly romantic, the hotel has a peaceful courtyard and sumptuous guest rooms, furnished with excellent reproduction antiques. **www.pavillon-de-la-reine.com**

TUILERIES QUARTER Brighton
218 rue de Rivoli, 75001 **Tel** *01-47 03 61 61* **Fax** *01-42 60 41 78* **Rooms** *65*   **Map** *D3*

A real insiders' location, the Brighton provides a much-sought-after Rivoli address without the sky-high prices. The guest rooms have beautiful, high ceilings and large windows that look out either over the Jardin des Tuileries or over the courtyard. **www.esprit-de-france.com**

TUILERIES QUARTER Ritz
15 pl Vendôme, 75001 **Tel** *01-43 16 30 70* **Fax** *01-43 16 45 38* **Rooms** *162*   **Map** *D3*

A legendary address, the Ritz still lives up to its reputation, combining elegance and decadence. The Louis XVI furniture and chandeliers are all original, and the floral arrangements are works of art. The Hemingway Bar is home to the glitterati. **www.ritzparis.com**

VERSAILLES Hôtel de Clagny
6 impasse de Clagny, 78000 **Tel** *01-39 50 18 09* **Fax** *01-39 50 85 17* **Rooms** *21*

The welcome in this quiet hotel near the train station is genuinely friendly. The rooms are simply furnished and clean, but unremarkable. There are numerous restaurants in the vicinity, and the owners of the Hôtel de Clagny are only too pleased to offer guidance.

FONTAINEBLEAU Grand Hôtel de l'Aigle Noir
27 pl de Napoléon Bonaparte, 77300 **Tel** *01-60 74 60 00* **Fax** *01-60 74 60 01* **Rooms** *18*

This prestigious mansion overlooks Fontainebleau château and its vast park. The elegant rooms are decorated in styles ranging from Louis XIII to Napoléon III. The conciergerie can organize a host of activities in the area and the bar serves snacks all day. **www.hotelaiglenoir.com**

NORTHERN FRANCE

CARNAC Lann Roz
36 av de la Poste, 56340 **Tel** *02-97 52 10 48* **Fax** *02-97 52 24 36* **Rooms** *13*

A friendly hotel with a pretty garden ten minutes' walk from the beach. The rooms are fresh and bright, decorated in pale blues and pinks. The typical Breton dining room with oak beams and open fireplaces serves local specialties. There is a terrace and garden. **www.lannroz.com**

REIMS Château Les Crayères
64 bd Henry Vasnier, 51100 **Tel** *03-26 82 80 80* **Fax** *03-26 82 65 52* **Rooms** *20*

Superbly aristocratic château with every luxury set in an English-style park next to the Roman crayères – the wine cellars of the Champagne houses which have been cut into the chalk. There is a superb restaurant, one of the best in France. **www.lescrayeres.com**

ROUEN Le Vieux Carré
34 rue Ganterie, 76000 **Tel** *02-35 71 67 70* **Fax** *02-35 71 19 17* **Rooms** *13*

City-center hotel near the Musée des Beaux Arts and a short walk from the cathedral. This charming timbered 18th-century building hides prettily decorated, intimate guest rooms. Cozy atmosphere and attentive service. There is a shaded cobbled courtyard and tearoom. **www.vieux-carre.fr**

ST MALO Hôtel Elizabeth
2 rue des Cordiers, 35400 **Tel** *02-99 56 24 98* **Fax** *02-99 56 39 24* **Rooms** *17*

This hotel is located within the ramparts of the old town, just 2 minutes' drive from the ferry terminal. The building has a 16th-century stone façade. The interior is classic in style, if a little somber. Rooms are comfortable and well equipped. Friendly owners, and private garage. **www.st-malo-hotel-elizabeth.com**

STRASBOURG Au Cerf d'Or
6 pl de l'Hôpital, 67000 **Tel** *03-88 36 20 05* **Fax** *03-88 36 68 67* **Rooms** *43*

An inexpensive base for visiting the sights of old Strasbourg, this old-style half-timbered Alsace hotel has refurbished rooms throughout. The main hotel has more charming rooms, but the annex has a small pool and a sauna. There are several restaurants on the nearby waterfront. **www.cerf-dor.com**

Key to Price Guide *see p206* **Map References** *see map of Paris pp150–51*

THE LOIRE VALLEY

AZAY LE RIDEAU Manoir de la Rémonière
La Chapelle St Blaise, 37190 **Tel** *02-47 45 24 88* **Fax** *02-47 45 45 69* **Rooms** *9*

This 15th-century manor house in romantic grounds faces the château at Azay le Rideau. The guest rooms are spacious; some traditional, others modern. The interior has been beautifully restored. Outdoor activities include hot-air ballooning, archery, and fishing. Perfect for children. **www.manoirdelaremoniere.com**

CHARTRES Le Grand Monarque
22 place des Epars, 28005 **Tel** *02-37 18 15 15* **Fax** *02-37 36 34 18* **Rooms** *50*

This converted 16th-century staging post, with massively thick stone walls, has been managed by the same family since the 1960s; part of the Best Western network. The rooms are simple. There is a pleasant bistro, and a gastronomic restaurant, "Le Georges". **www.bw-grand-monarque.com**

CHENONCEAUX Hostel du Roy
9 rue du Dr Bretonneau, 37150 **Tel** *02-47 23 90 17* **Fax** *02-47 23 89 81* **Rooms** *32*

A sprawling hotel-restaurant, with a 16th-century fireplace and a dining room hung with hunting trophies. The well-equipped rooms are simple and appealing, and the atmosphere relaxing. There is a garden and pretty terrace. The restaurant serves classic dishes, including game in season. **www.hostelduroy.com**

CHINON Château de Marçay
Le Château, 37500 **Tel** *02-47 93 03 47* **Fax** *02-47 93 45 33* **Rooms** *34*

Elegant hotel in this restored 15th-century fortified château. Enjoy the lovely views over the surrounding parkland and vineyards from the well-appointed bedrooms. Refined and aristocratic atmosphere, impeccable service and cuisine. **www.chateaudemarcay.com**

FONTEVRAUD-L'ABBAYE Le Prieuré St-Lazare
38 rte St Jean de l'Habit, 49590 **Tel** *02-41 51 73 16* **Fax** *02-41 51 75 50* **Rooms** *52*

The surroundings of this hotel, housed in the former St-Lazare priory within the famous royal abbey complex, are stunning. The rooms are elegantly decorated in a modern, contemporary style. The restaurant, in the ancient cloister, is a gourmet's delight. Closed mid-Nov–Mar. **www.hotelfp-fontevraud.com**

NANTES Hôtel La Pérouse
3 allée Duquesne, 44000 **Tel** *02-40 89 75 00* **Fax** *02-40 89 76 00* **Rooms** *46*

Named after a French navigator, this chic hotel with its zen atmosphere opened in 1993. The rooms have glossy wooden flooring and crisp, contemporary furniture. Reasonably quiet. The breakfast buffet is good. Free access to nearby gym for guests. **www.hotel-laperouse.fr**

TOURS Hôtel de l'Univers
5 bd Heurteloup, 37000 **Tel** *02-47 05 37 12* **Fax** *02-47 61 51 80* **Rooms** *85*

Statesmen and royals have stayed at this luxurious hotel. A picture gallery depicts the famous guests since 1846. Elegant architecture, right in the city center, with large, prettily furnished bedrooms. The restaurant serves classic gourmet cuisine. Private garage. **www.hotel-univers.fr**

BURGUNDY AND THE FRENCH ALPS

ANNECY Hôtel de l'Abbaye
15 chemin de l'Abbaye, 74940 **Tel** *04-50 23 61 08* **Fax** *04-50 23 61 71* **Rooms** *18*

A hotel, full of character, occupying a 15th-century abbey set in its own gardens. A stone archway leads to a cobbled courtyard surrounded by a wooden gallery with access to the bedrooms. Charming rooms, some with jacuzzi. Quiet, comfortable atmosphere. Buffet breakfast. **www.hotelabbaye-annecy.com**

BEAUNE Hôtel Le Cep
27 rue Maufoux, 21200 **Tel** *03-80 22 35 48* **Fax** *03-80 22 76 80* **Rooms** *62*

In the heart of the old town is this elegant hotel, renovated in a Renaissance style. Legend has it that Louis XIV preferred to stay here rather than at the hospice. The rooms, some with Baroque decor, are ornately furnished with antiques. Each is named after a local wine. **www.hotel-cep-beaune.com**

DIJON Hostellerie le Sauvage
64 rue Monge, 21000 **Tel** *03-80 41 31 21* **Fax** *03-80 42 06 07* **Rooms** *22*

This attractive half-timbered hotel was a staging post in the 15th century. Located in the city center near the historic sites, it can be noisy – the quietest rooms overlook a lovely interior cobbled courtyard, where meals can be taken in fine weather. Excellent service. Good breakfast. **www.hotellesauvage.com**

Key to Symbols *see back cover flap*

GEVREY-CHAMBERTIN Hôtel les Grands Crus   ▤ P   €€

Route des Grands Crus, 21220 **Tel** *03-80 34 34 15* **Fax** *03-80 51 89 07* **Rooms** *24*

A light, airy hotel with wonderful views over the *grands crus* vineyards. Located in the heart of the Côte de Nuits, this country house built in a typical Burgundian style has traditionally furnished rooms that overlook the garden. The comfy lounge centers around an open fireplace. **www.hoteldesgrandscrus.com**

GRENOBLE Splendid Hôtel   ▦ ✿ ▤ P   €

22 rue Thiers, 38000 **Tel** *04-76 46 33 12* **Fax** *04-76 46 35 24* **Rooms** *45*

Smart, centrally located hotel in a quiet location, with a walled garden. The guest rooms range from classical to modern, with gaily painted frescoes. Efficient service and amenities. Continental and à la carte breakfast served in the dining room, or garden terrace. **www.splendid-hotel.com**

VEZELAY L'Espérance   ▥ ♨ ✿ ▤ P   €€€€

St-Père-sous-Vézelay, 89450 **Tel** *03-86 33 39 10* **Fax** *03-86 33 26 15* **Rooms** *30*

The guest rooms here are in three buildings: the main building has classic furnishings, Moulin has rustic charm, and Pré des Marguerites is contemporary, with terraces overlooking the garden. Wonderful restaurant, excellent but expensive wines, and impeccable service. **www.marc-meneau-esperance.com**

SOUTHWEST FRANCE

BIARRITZ Hôtel du Palais   ▥ ♨ ✿ ▩ ▤ P   €€€€€

1 av de l'Impératrice, 64200 **Tel** *05-59 41 64 00* **Fax** *05-59 41 67 99* **Rooms** *132*

The grande dame of Biarritz's hotel scene, with an ambiance harking back to the resort's Belle Epoque heyday. A magnificent heated seawater pool, direct beach access, a putting green, a playground, and kids' pool complement the lovely rooms and outstanding restaurants. **www.hotel-du-palais.com**

BORDEAUX Best Western Bayonne Etche-Ona   ▦ ▤   €€

4 rue Martignac, 33000 **Tel** *05-56 48 00 88* **Fax** *05-56 48 41 60* **Rooms** *63*

This is two hotels in one: the contemporary Bayonne and (just round the corner) the more atmospheric Etche-Ona with its Basque-inspired decor. Both occupy elegant 18th-century mansions in the heart of the Golden Triangle and offer comfortable rooms and top-notch service. **www.bordeaux-hotel.com**

MARGAUX Le Pavillon de Margaux   ▥ ♨ P   €€

3 rue Georges-Mandel, 33460 **Tel** *05-57 88 77 54* **Fax** *05-57 88 77 73* **Rooms** *14*

In the center of Margaux village, this handsome hotel provides a comfortable base for exploring the Médoc vineyards. Guest rooms, which are "sponsored" by local wine châteaux, are individually styled. Some have antiques and four-posters, others rattan and floral fabrics. **www.pavillondemargaux.com**

PAU Hôtel du Parc Beaumont   ▥ ♨ ▤ P   €€

1 av Edouard VII, 64000 **Tel** *05-59 11 84 00* **Fax** *05-59 11 85 00* **Rooms** *72*

This luxurious modern hotel, part of the Concorde group, stands in beautiful grounds next to Pau's casino and palm-lined boulevard with great views of the Pyrenees. Rooms are lavishly furnished, and there is a heated pool, whirlpool, sauna, and hammam (Turkish bath). **www.hotel-parc-beaumont.com**

ST JEAN-DE-LUZ La Devinière   P   €€€

5 rue Loquin, 64500 **Tel** *05-59 26 05 51* **Fax** *05-59 51 26 38* **Rooms** *10*

The bedrooms in this charming 18th-century building are all different, prettily decorated and furnished with antiques, artworks, and rare books. There is a cozy lounge-library with an open fireplace and a grand piano, and a breakfast-tea room. Tiny garden. No restaurant. **www.hotel-la-deviniere.com**

TOULOUSE Hôtel des Beaux Arts   ▦ ▥ ▤ P   €€

1 pl du Pont Neuf, 31000 **Tel** *05-34 45 42 42* **Fax** *05-34 45 42 43* **Rooms** *19*

Behind a beautiful Belle Epoque façade, beside the Pont Neuf, lies a chic hotel with modern comforts. The less expensive rooms are on the small side – better to upgrade for river views and more space. For a special occasion, opt for room 42 with its own tiny terrace among the roof tiles. **www.hoteldesbeauxarts.com**

THE SOUTH OF FRANCE

AIGUES-MORTES Hôtel St Louis   ▥ P   €€

10 rue Amiral Courbet, 30220 **Tel** *04-66 53 72 68* **Fax** *04-66 53 75 92* **Rooms** *22*

Spacious rooms with modern comforts and a location next to the famous Constant Tower make this friendly hotel in an 18th-century building one of the better places to stay in Aigues-Mortes. Good restaurant, pretty patio, and garage parking available for a fee. **www.lesaintlouis.fr**

Key to Price Guide *see p206* **Key to Symbols** *see back cover flap*

AIX EN PROVENCE Hôtel des Augustins

3 rue Masse, 13100 **Tel** *04-42 27 28 59* **Fax** *04-42 26 74 87* **Rooms** *29*

In a converted 12th-century convent, with the reception housed in a 15th-century chapel, the Hôtel des Augustins offers a haven of peace in the heart of bustling Aix. The rooms are large and comfortable in traditional Provençal style. No restaurant, but places to eat nearby. **www.hotel-augustins.com**

ANTIBES Mas Djoliba

29 av Provence, 06600 **Tel** *04-93 34 02 48* **Fax** *04-93 34 05 81* **Rooms** *13*

Mas Djoliba is a big, old-fashioned farmhouse set among lots of greenery, with palm trees surrounding the pool terrace. Convenient for old Antibes and the beaches nearby, it is perfect for a romantic weekend or a longer stay. Closed end October–early February. **www.hotel-djoliba.com**

ARLES Hôtel d'Arlatan

26 rue du Sauvage, 13200 **Tel** *04-90 93 56 66* **Fax** *04-90 49 68 45* **Rooms** *47*

The former 15th-century town residence of the Comtes d'Arlatan, this is one of the most beautiful historic hotels in the region. The rooms are furnished with antiques. Glass panels in the salon floor reveal 4th-century Roman foundations. Walled garden and stone terrace. **www.hotel-arlatan.fr**

CANNES Hôtel Molière

5-7 rue Molière, 06400 **Tel** *04-93 38 16 16* **Fax** *04-93 68 29 57* **Rooms** *24*

This 19th-century building is very close to la Croisette, Cannes' sea-front esplanade, with bright and comfortable rooms and balconies overlooking an attractive garden where breakfast is served. Good value and very much in demand – book well in advance. **www.hotel-moliere.com**

CANNES Carlton Inter-Continental

58 la Croisette, 06400 **Tel** *04-93 06 40 06* **Fax** *04-93 06 40 25* **Rooms** *338*

The grandest of the grand, this is where the stars come to stay. During the film festival, there is a long waiting list for reservations. Art Deco surroundings, with discreetly luxurious facilities in the rooms and public areas, and a private beach with loungers and parasols. **www.intercontinental.com/cannes**

CARCASSONNE Hôtel de la Cité

Pl August-Pierre Pont, 11000 **Tel** *04-68 71 98 71* **Fax** *04-68 71 50 15* **Rooms** *53*

The finest hotel in the Languedoc-Roussillon region, with immaculate service, opulent rooms, a glorious pool, formal gardens, superb restaurants, and an unbeatable location within Carcassonne's medieval town, La Cité. Golf, canoeing, and white-water rafting are available nearby. **www.hoteldelacite.com**

NICE Windsor

11 rue Dalpozzo, 06000 **Tel** *04-93 88 59 35* **Fax** *04-93 88 94 57* **Rooms** *57*

The Hôtel Windsor provides a wide array of services and facilities, including a pool in an exotic palm garden, a children's play area, and a health and beauty center offering massage and a sauna. Some rooms are individually decorated by local artists. Snack bar and restaurant. **www.hotelwindsornice.com**

NICE Le Negresco

37 promenade des Anglais, 6000 **Tel** *04-93 16 64 00* **Fax** *04-93 88 35 68* **Rooms** *121*

The Negresco is the grande dame of Riviera hotels and has been a landmark on the promenade des Anglais since it opened in 1913, with a seemingly endless list of rich and famous guests. Superbly decorated and furnished with works of art, flawless service, and modern facilities. **www.hotel-negresco-nice.com**

NIMES New Hôtel la Baume

21 rue Nationale, 30000 **Tel** *04-66 76 28 42* **Fax** *04-66 76 28 45* **Rooms** *34*

Housed in an elegant 17th-century townhouse, la Baume is one of the most pleasant places to stay in Nîmes. A short step from the sights, it blends old-world charm with modern facilities. Some rooms are even listed as historic monuments. No restaurant, but a welcoming café-bar. **www.new-hotel.com**

ST JEAN CAP FERRAT Clair Logis

12 av Prince Rainier de Monaco, 06230 **Tel** *04-93 76 11 85* **Fax** *04-93 76 51 82* **Rooms** *18*

This old-fashioned villa set in a large, lush garden has attracted a list of famous guests including Général de Gaulle. The rooms are comfortable in a slightly old-fashioned way, with smaller, more modern rooms in the annex. There is no pool, but the beach is not far away. **www.hotel-clair-logis.fr**

ST JEAN CAP FERRAT La Voile d'Or

Port de St-Jean, 06230 **Tel** *04-93 01 13 13* **Fax** *04-93 76 11 17* **Rooms** *45*

Not quite the most expensive hotel in St-Jean but not far off, La Voile d'Or is worth every cent – service is superb and the rooms are immaculate. Two pools, views of the yacht harbour and the coast, and beach pavilions. Excellent restaurant in classic French culinary tradition. **www.lavoiledor.fr**

ST TROPEZ La Ponche

Port des Pêcheurs, 83990 **Tel** *04-94 97 02 53* **Fax** *04-94 97 78 61* **Rooms** *18*

For those looking for a boutique hideaway in St-Tropez, this cluster of one-time fishermen's cottages may fit the bill. The bedrooms are large and artfully chic, and include two family-size rooms. Among the famous guests have been Pablo Picasso and 1950s film star Romy Schneider. **www.laponche.com**

Where to Eat in France

The variety of places to eat in France is enormous. Throughout the day, the ubiquitous café is ideal for a snack, while bistros and brasseries offer full menus. Restaurants are usually only open in the evening, but encompass the whole gamut of French cooking, from simple and rustic to the very finest *haute cuisine*.

PRICE CATEGORIES
Price categories are for a three-course meal for one, including a half-bottle of house wine, tax and service:
€ under 30 euros
€€ 30–45 euros
€€€ 45–60 euros
€€€€ 60–90 euros
€€€€€ over 90 euros

PARIS

BEAUBOURG AND LES HALLES Au Pied du Cochon   €€€
6 rue Coquillière, 75004 **Tel** *01-40 13 77 00*   **Map** *D3*

This colorfully restored brasserie was once popular with high society, who came to observe the workers in the old market and to savor the onion soup. Although touristy, this huge place is fun, and its menu has something for everyone (including excellent shellfish). Still one of the best places after a night out.

BEAUBOURG AND LES HALLES Georges   €€€€
19 rue Beaubourg, 75004 **Tel** *01-44 78 47 99*   **Map** *E3*

On the top floor of the Centre Pompidou, the Georges offers stunning views. Light and inspired cuisine, such as cherry tomato and goat's cheese cake, sole meunière, lamb with chutney, and macaroons. Roasted scallops with lemon butter is a hit. Minimalist decor, with lots of steel and aluminium.

CHAILLOT AND PORTE MAILLOT La Butte Chaillot   €€€€
110 bis av Kléber, 75016 **Tel** *01-47 27 88 88*   **Map** *A3*

This is the boutique restaurant of the renowned, not to say deified, chef Guy Savoy. The bistro cuisine includes snail salad, oysters with a cream mousse, roast breast of veal with rosemary, and apple tart. The clientele are smartly attired, so make sure you dress up.

CHAILLOT AND PORTE MAILLOT Le Relais du Parc   €€€€€
55–57 av Raymond Poincaré, 75016 **Tel** *01-47 27 59 59*   **Map** *A3*

In this historic townhouse, Alain Ducasse and Joel Robuchon create France's great "classic" dishes. Each culinary region is featured, and dishes include *turbot de Bretagne*, *chevreuil d'Alsace* (venison) and *foie gras de canard des Landes*. Enviable wine list highlights the Bordeaux region. Michelin starred.

CHAMPS-ELYSEES Le Bœuf sur le Toit   €€
34 rue du Colisée, 75008 **Tel** *01-53 93 65 55*   **Map** *B2*

Highly inspired by the 1930s Les Années Folles, this building was formerly a cabaret venue (The Ox on the Roof). Exemplifying the classic Paris Art Deco brasserie, its changing menu can include sole meunière, snails, *foie gras* and crème brûlée. The specialty is crêpes Suzette.

CHAMPS-ELYSEES Guy Savoy   €€€€
18 rue Troyon, 75017 **Tel** *01-43 80 40 61*   **Map** *B2*

A handsome dining room and professional service further complement the remarkable cuisine of Guy Savoy. The three Michelin-starred menu includes oysters in aspic, Bresse chicken with a sherry vinegar glaze, poached or grilled pigeon with lentils, and an extraordinary dessert list.

FONTAINEBLEAU Le Caveau des Ducs   €€€
24 rue de Ferrare, 77300 **Tel** *01-64 22 05 05*

Near the château de Fontainebleau, this restaurant has a carved staircase leading to the magnificent 17th-century cellars that house the dining room, decorated with tapestries and chandeliers. Classic cuisine, such as snails in puff pastry. Good lunch menu of main course salad and a glass of wine.

ILE DE LA CITE AND ILE SAINT-LOUIS La Rose de France   €€
24 pl Dauphine, 75001 **Tel** *01-43 54 10 12*   **Map** *E4*

Majestic setting overlooking a 17th-century square. Updated French classics, with specialties like John Dory with rhubarb, ginger, and Basmati rice. More traditional is the duck fillet in ratatouille. A *cuisine du marché* restaurant, La Rose uses the freshest produce from the day's market.

INVALIDES AND EIFFEL TOWER QUARTER L'Arpège   €€€€€
84 rue de Varenne, 75007 **Tel** *01-47 05 09 06*   **Map** *C4*

Alain Passard's three-star restaurant near the Musée Rodin is one of the most highly regarded in Paris. It has striking pale-wood decor and sprightly young service as well as excellent food. The lobster and turnip vinaigrette and duck Louise Passard are classics. Don't miss the apple tart.

Key to Symbols *see back cover flap*

JARDIN DES PLANTES QUARTER Marty Restaurant 🛗🚹🏠🅿 €€

20 av des Gobelins, 75005 **Tel** *01-43 31 39 51* **Map** *E5*

The Marty was established by E. Marty in 1913 and is still family-run. The interior is authentic Art Deco in style, but the cuisine steals the show. The menu features hearty fare, such as roast duck or rabbit casserole, and seasonal dishes, such as gazpacho. Excellent crème brûlée.

LATIN QUARTER Le Balzar 🚹🏠 €€

49 rue des Ecoles, 75005 **Tel** *01-43 54 13 67* **Map** *E4*

There's a fair choice of brasserie food here but the main attraction is the Left Bank ambiance. Traditionally dressed waiters weave their way among the hustle and bustle, providing express service, with archetypal brasserie decor to match: there are large mirrors and comfortable leather seats.

LATIN QUARTER L'Atelier Maître Albert 🛗🚹📋🍷🍴 €€€€

1 rue Maître Albert, 75005 **Tel** *01-56 81 30 01* **Map** *D4*

Dishes from the rôtisserie are this restaurant's specialty. Traditional fare such as veal kidneys and mouthwatering chocolate cake are the chief attractions. Other specialties include veal, mixed salad *du moment*, and chicken livers. The antique fireplace is a nice touch. This is another Guy Savoy restaurant.

MONTMARTRE Beauvilliers 🏠🍴 €€€€

52 rue Lamarck, 75018 **Tel** *01-42 54 54 42*

Montmartre's best restaurant and one of the most festive in Paris, this is where effusive chef Edouard Carlier delves into old cookbooks to create favorites such as *escabèche* of red mullet (specially marinated), veal *rognonnade* (loin of veal with kidney) and a very lemony lemon tart.

MONTPARNASSE La Coupole 📋🍴 €€

102 bd du Montparnasse, 75014 **Tel** *01-43 20 14 20*

This famous brasserie has been popular with the fashionistas, artists, and thinkers since its creation in 1927. Under the same ownership as Brasserie Flo, it has a similar menu: shellfish, smoked salmon, and good desserts. Lamb curry is a specialty. Open from breakfast until 2am.

OPERA QUARTER La Vaudeville 🚹🏠🍴 €€

29 rue Vivienne, 75002 **Tel** *01-40 20 04 62* **Map** *D2*

This is one of seven brasseries owned by Paris's reigning brasserie king, Jean-Paul Bucher. Good shellfish, Bucher's famous smoked salmon, many fish dishes as well as classic brasserie standbys like pig's trotters and *andouillette* (tripe sausage). Quick, friendly service and a noisy ambiance make it fun.

OPERA QUARTER La Fontaine Gaillon 🚹🏠📋🅿🍴 €€€€

1 rue de la Michodière, 75002 **Tel** *01-47 42 63 22* **Map** *D2*

Housed in a 17th-century mansion, Fontaine Gaillon is partly owned by legendary film actor Gérard Depardieu. The menu showcases sautéed John Dory, Merlan Colbert with sorrel purée, confit de canard, and lamb chops. The interiors are comfortable, and there is a good wine list.

SAINT-GERMAIN-DES-PRES Procope 🍴 €€€

13 rue de l'Ancienne Comédie, 75006 **Tel** *01-40 46 79 00* **Map** *D4*

Opened in 1686, Paris's oldest café welcomed literary and political figures such as Voltaire and Diderot. Nowadays, it's still a hub for the intelligentsia, who sit alongside those curious about this historical place. Coq-au-vin (chicken cooked in wine) is the specialty. Shellfish platters, too.

THE MARAIS Auberge Nicolas Flamel 🚹🍴 €€€

51 rue de Montmorency, 75003 **Tel** *01-42 71 77 78* **Map** *E3*

Located in Paris's oldest house (1407) and named after the famous alchemist who lived here, this restaurant's specialties include *tatin de foie gras poellé* (pan-fried *foie gras*) and *gala au pain d'épices* (gingerbread pudding). The tour de force here, however, is *gigot de sept heures* (lamb, slow roasted for 7 hours), from a medieval recipe.

THE MARAIS L'Ambroisie 🛗🚹🏠📋🍷🍴 €€€€€

9 pl des Vosges, 75004 **Tel** *01-42 78 51 45* **Map** *F4*

In a former jewelry shop restored by Chef Bernard Pacaud, this is one of only seven Michelin three-star restaurants in Paris. The cuisine includes a mousse of sweet red peppers, truffle *feuilleté* (layered pastry) and langoustines. Reservations accepted one month in advance.

TUILERIES QUARTER Le Grand Véfour 🛗🚹📋🍷🅿🍴 €€€€€

17 rue de Beaujolais, 75001 **Tel** *01-42 96 56 27* **Map** *D3*

This 18th-century restaurant is considered by many to be Paris's most attractive. The chef Guy Martin effortlessly maintains his third Michelin star with dishes such as scallops with Beaufort cheese, cabbage ravioli with a truffle cream, and *endive galette* (pancake).

VERSAILLES Le Valmont 🚹🏠📋🍴 €€€

20 rue au Pain, 78000 **Tel** *01-39 51 39 00*

Refined cuisine is served at this bistro tucked behind the market hall. Chef Philippe Mathieu presents an ambitious menu with dishes such as mille feuille of haddock and celery, St-Pierre with pleurote mushrooms, and chocolate dessert with Kirsch-infused cherries. Good wines by the glass.

Map References *see map of Paris pp150–51*

NORTHERN FRANCE

BAYEUX La Table du Terroir

€€

42 rue St Jean, 14400 **Tel** *02-31 92 05 53*

In summer, dining on the terrace is a treat; in winter the rustic dining-room is welcoming, with large convivial wooden tables and old hewn stone walls. La Table du Terroir specializes in meat dishes, home-made pâtés, and terrines. The desserts are delicious, too.

CARNAC La Bavolette

€€

9 allée du Parc, 56340 **Tel** *02-97 52 19 69*

One of the classier eating places at the popular seaside resort of Carnac-Plage. Fish brochettes and sardine terrine are among the favorites. La Bavolette's specialties include fish soup served with a rich garlicky *aioli* and croutons, and flambéed langoustines.

EPERNAY La Table Kobus

€

3 rue Dr Rousseau, 51200 **Tel** *03-26 51 53 53*

An original brasserie near the center of this town that is all about champagne. Uniquely, you can bring your own bottle of champagne to drink with your meal. The menu is classic French cuisine. The home-made terrine of *foie gras* is particularly recommended.

MONT-ST-MICHEL Auberge St Pierre

€€

Grande rue, 50170 **Tel** *02-33 60 14 03*

Lamb grazed on the surrounding salt marshes, known as *agneau pré-salé*, features on the menu in this charming timbered 15th-century building. Seafood is also a house specialty. Try the favorites such as crab or salmon. Fresh local produce is used in the preparation of traditional dishes.

MONT-ST-MICHEL La Mère Poulard

€€€€

Grande rue, 50170 **Tel** *02-33 89 68 68*

A deluxe brasserie on the famous Mont St-Michel, where visitors come from all over the world to sample the famous omelette Mère Poulard, cooked in a long-handled pan over a fire. Also delicious are the *pré-salé* lamb (lamb fed on the surrounding salt marshes), and spit-roasted pig.

REIMS La Brasserie Boulingrin

€

48 rue Mars, 51100 **Tel** *03-26 40 96 22*

This famous Reims brasserie and a regular meeting place for locals has kept its Art Deco mosaics of jolly grape harvesters known as "Vendangeurs en Champagne". Good value and a lively place to dine, near the covered market. Oysters and steak tartare are specialties. There is also a large selection of champagnes.

REIMS Château les Crayères

€€€€€

64 bd Vasnier, 51100 **Tel** *03-26 82 80 80*

In the former home of the Pommery Champagne family, this gourmet retreat allows visitors to relax in sumptuous guest rooms and savor superb cuisine. The dining room is grand, with huge windows and tapestries. Try the lobster, veal and ham spaghetti, or almond biscuit with lemon and raspberry cream.

ROUEN La Couronne

€€€

31 pl Vieux Marché, 76000 **Tel** *02-35 71 40 90*

In the oldest auberge in France, dating from 1345, the experienced, talented chef ensures that you pass a memorable moment here with classic gourmet dishes such as *foie gras* with chestnuts, veal with fried beetroot and duck à la Rouennaise. Great Normandy cheeses.

ROUEN Restaurant Gill

€€€€

8–9 quai de la Bourse, 76000 **Tel** *02-35 71 16 14*

A highly recommended restaurant on the Seine quays. For nearly 20 years chef Gilles Tournadre has been creating sophisticated dishes in this elegant dining room. Specialities include crayfish salad, Pigeon *à la rouennaise* and fillet of bass with asparagus. Remarkable wine list.

ST-MALO Le Chalut

€€€€

8 rue de la Corne de Cerf, 35400 **Tel** *02-99 56 71 58*

Map

One of St. Malo's best restaurants, the chef excels in fish dishes and well-chosen produce simply prepared. Monkfish and artichokes with sherry butter, and St-Pierre and white asparagus with langoustine sauce are examples of the delicious dishes on offer. Good selection of cheese, too.

STRASBOURG Au Crocodile

€€€€€

10 rue Outre, 67000 **Tel** *03-88 32 13 02*

Map

One of the finest restaurants in France's other capital. Splendid polished woodwork, elegant decor, and the famous crocodile brought back from a campaign in Egypt by an Alsatian Captain in the French army. Super service and light original cuisine. A truly great wine list that covers the world.

Key to Price Guide *see p212* **Key to Symbols** *see back cover flap*

THE LOIRE VALLEY

BLOIS Au Rendez-vous des Pêcheurs
27 rue du Foix, 41000 **Tel** *02-54 74 67 48*

Well known regionally, this restaurant is famed for its menu focusing on seafood and fish creations like Loire pike-perch with leek salad, stuffed courgette flowers, and roast sea bass. There is also Sologne game, in season, and a good selection of wines from Cheverny and Montlouis. Book ahead.

CHARTRES Le Grand Monarque
22 pl des Epars, 28000 **Tel** *02-37 18 15 15*

Within this magnificent 17th-century staging post are both a gourmet "le Georges" restaurant, and a brasserie serving traditional food. The cuisine is ambitious and flavorful, with dishes such as red mullet and Loire eel in vinaigrette, and bass cooked in a clay crust. First-rate wine cellar.

CHENONCEAU Auberge de Bon Laboureur
6 rue de Docteur Bretonneau, 37150 **Tel** *02-47 23 90 02*

Refined classic cuisine is served in this former coaching inn just a few minutes from the château. The produce is seasonal and vegetables come from their own vegetable patch. A typical menu could include langoustine bisque, bass with green and white asparagus, and shortbread biscuit topped with lemon and citrus-flavored cream.

FONTEVRAUD-L'ABBAYE La Licorne
Allée Sainte-Catherine, 49590 **Tel** *02-41 51 72 49*

Next to the splendid abbey, this popular restaurant has a pretty courtyard terrace and elegant dining room. The menu includes creations such as prawns and basil ravioli in morel sauce and, for dessert, strawberries flavored with roses. Good Saumur wines. Book ahead.

NANTES La Cigale
4 pl Graslin, 44000 **Tel** *02-51 84 94 94*

This ornate Belle Epoque brasserie dates from 1895 when it was frequented by celebrated writers and the Nantes elite. The quality of the cuisine matches the exceptional interior. Oysters, carpaccio of salmon, and beef *à la plancha* (cooked on a hot plate). Open all day. Extensive wine list.

ORLEANS Les Antiquaires
2 rue Au lin, 45000 **Tel** *02-38 53 52 35*

Popular with locals for its inventive cuisine, the well-known chef Philippe Bardau prepares contemporary dishes such as pan-fried asparagus with a morel sauce, and roast pigeon with a smoked aubergine mousse. The dining room is decorated in warm tones. Great selection of local wines.

TOURS L'Atelier Gourmand
37 rue Etienne Marcel, 37000 **Tel** *02-47 38 59 87*

A charming small restaurant in a 15th-century building in the old part of Tours. Fabrice Bironneau presents a competitively priced, interesting menu. Fresh dishes include succulent rabbit terrine accompanied by red fruits, ragoût of lamb, and a fondant of chocolate. Warm, homely ambiance.

TOURS Jean Bardet
57 rue Groison, 57 rue Groison, **Tel** *02-47 41 41 11*

In a Napoléon III mansion house with an opulent dining room, this gastronomic temple of the Loire serves inspired dishes, including lightly smoked Racan pigeon with licorice-flavored sauce, and pineapple glazed with dark rum accompanied by gingerbread ice-cream. Jean Bardet has a great wine list.

BURGUNDY AND THE FRENCH ALPS

BEAUNE La Ciboulette
69 rue Lorraine, 21200 **Tel** *03-80 24 70 72*

A delightful little bistro frequented by locals; always a good sign. The basic decor is in contrast with the high standard of cooking. Hearty dishes, such as steak with pungent Epoisses cheese feature on the menu. The best value in town. Local wine merchants come here to choose from the excellent wine list.

BEAUNE Hostellerie de Levernois
Route de Cobertault, Levernois, 21200 **Tel** *03-80 24 73 58*

This beautiful old mansion with formal gardens occupies an idyllic country setting. The classic restaurant serves up "serious" cuisine, such as snails with garlic, lightly smoked pigeon and foie gras with caramelized turnips in blackcurrant sauce, or salmon smoked over vine cuttings. Vast wine list. Faultless service.

DIJON Le Bistrot des Halles   🅰🔲▤🅿   €

10 rue Bannelier, 21000 **Tel** *03-80 49 94 15*

At lunchtime this 1900s-style bistro is roaring. Located next to the market, it attracts food merchants and local business people with its meat pie, *jambon persillé* (ham with a parsley sauce) and *bœuf bourguignon*. Well-known Dijon chef Jean-Pierre Billoux, who has an up-market restaurant in Dijon center, oversees this bistro.

DIJON Le Pré aux Clercs   🚹🔲🍷   €€€

13 pl de la Libération, 21000 **Tel** *03-80 38 05 05*

Run by Jean-Pierre Billoux, one of the most renowned chefs in Dijon. Traditional rustic ingredients with a novel modern twist result in unique dishes, such as caramelized lamb. The fixed-price menus offer classic dishes, such as a *foie gras* terrine. Charming dining area and good choice of Burgundy wines.

GRENOBLE Le Chasse-Spleen   🅰▤🍷   €€

6 pl Lavalette, 38000 **Tel** *04-38 37 03 52*

Well situated in central Grenoble, Le Chasse-Spleen is known for the quality of its cooking. Dishes are inventive, such as the *parmentier* of minced oxtail with *foie gras* specialty and the regional dessert baba with Chartreuse. Inside, walnut-drying racks hang from the ceiling, and Baudelaire's poems decorate the walls.

LYON Le Mercière   🅰🔲🍷   €€

56 rue Mercière, 69002 **Tel** *04-78 37 67 35*

Chic, lively Lyonnais brasserie with its own *traboule* (medieval passageway) crossing the dining room. Frequented by both tourists and locals, the menu includes regional specialties such as ravioli served in a truffle stock, Bobosse *andouillette* (tripe sausage), and a mouthwatering chocolate mousse. Good Rhône wines.

LYON Léon de Lyon   🅰🚹▤🆃🅿🍷   €€€€€

1 rue Pléney, 69001 **Tel** *04-72 10 11 12*

The expert chef and owner serves classic produce with a modern twist in the heart of the city. Intimate dining area. Seasonal menus offering artichoke and *foie gras*, carp with Nantua sauce, roast venison, wild strawberry tart, and stewed rhubarb.

SOUTHWEST FRANCE

BAYONNE Auberge du Cheval Blanc   🅰🚹▤🅿   €€€

68 rue Bourgneuf, 64100 **Tel** *05-59 59 01 33*

Stray from the set menu to eat à la carte at this well-regarded hotel in the riverside Petit Bayonne quarter. The menu changes with the seasons, with local dishes, such as *xamano* (ham and mashed potatoes), fine Atlantic seafood, interesting soups and casseroles, and delicious desserts. Respectable wine list. Closed Feb.

BIARRITZ Chez Albert   🚹🔲🅿   €€

Port des Pêcheurs, 64200 **Tel** *05-59 24 43 84*

From the terrace there are superb views of Biarritz's picturesque fishing harbor and surrounding cliffs and beaches, making this fine seafood restaurant popular. Arrive early for the best tables. Piled platters of seafood, freshly caught lobster, sole, sea bream, tuna, and sardines are among the treats here.

BIARRITZ Le Sissinou   🚹▤🍷   €€€

5 av Maréchal Foch, 64200 **Tel** *05-59 22 51 50*

Managed by chef Michel Cassou-Debat – a veteran of some of France's top establishments – Sissinou is one of Biarritz's most talked-about restaurants. Elegant in a minimalist way. Wonderful food such as tuna carpaccio and a fricassée of veal sweetbreads served with carrots flavored with balsamic vinegar, and desserts that invite indulgence.

BORDEAUX La Tupina   🚹🔲🆃🍷   €€€

6 rue Porte de la Monnaie, 33800 **Tel** *05-56 91 56 37*

The heart of La Tupina is the open fire over which succulent meats are grilled and in winter a cauldron of soup bubbles away. This is an excellent place to try bordelais specialties such as lamprey in wine, grilled shad, or baby eels cooked in olive oil with garlic and hot pepper. Simple, old-fashioned desserts.

PAU Chez Pierre   🚹▤🅿🍷   €€

16 rue Louis Barthou, 64000 **Tel** *05-59 27 76 86*

Chez Pierre exudes 19th-century elegance and prides itself on the old-fashioned, club-like atmosphere that harks back to Pau's heyday as a British expatriate's hideaway. Classic French regional cooking along with some surprises, such as cod with espelette peppers, and an extensive wine list.

TOULOUSE Brasserie Flo Les Beaux Arts   🚹🔲▤   €€

1 quai de la Daurade, 31000 **Tel** *05-61 21 12 12*

An authentic and bustling brasserie serving a broad range of dishes, from salads and seafood to southwestern favorites. To start, you could opt for a flavorsome dish of scallops baked with chanterelle mushrooms, followed by a seafood *pot-au-feu*, and prune-and-armagnac ice cream. The menu changes regularly.

Key to Price Guide *see p212* **Key to Symbols** *see back cover flap*

TOULOUSE Les Jardins de l'Opéra (Dominique Toulousy) ★▤🍴🖤 €€€€
*1 pl du Capitole, 31000 **Tel** 05-61 23 07 76*

Gourmet dining at its most refined in the restaurant of the Grand Hôtel de l'Opéra. Hushed tones and widely spaced tables create a suitably reverent atmosphere for dishes such as whole lobster garnished with a seaweed crust, or figs cooked in Banyuls wine and filled with vanilla ice cream. Impeccable service.

THE SOUTH OF FRANCE

AIX-EN-PROVENCE L'Aixquis ▤🖤 €€€
*22 rue Victor Leydet, 13100 **Tel** 04-42 27 76 16*

An up-to-date array of dishes and a good wine list have made this one of Aix's most popular eating places. L'Aixquis is located in a narrow lane in central Aix. Chef Benoît Strohm is known for excellent Provençal cooking, such as rabbit marinated in herbs. Closed Sun, Mon lunch.

AIX-EN-PROVENCE Le Clos de la Violette ▦▤🖤 €€€€€
*10 av Violette, 13100 **Tel** 04-42 23 30 71*

This is an elegant address in a chic mansion standing in its own gardens: tranquil, intimate, and perfect for a romantic evening. People do dress up a little to eat here. The wine list is extensive (and very strong on local and Provençal wines) and the menu is Provençal with a modern edge. Closed Sun, Mon.

ARLES Lou Marques ★▦▤🖤 €€€
*Bd Lices, 13200 **Tel** 04-90 52 52 52*

Lou Marques – the restaurant of the venerable Hôtel Jules César – is one of the best places to eat in Arles, with a central location, pleasant terrace with tables under white umbrellas, and a bill of fare that concentrates on classic Provençal dishes. Dignified surroundings. Closed Nov–Apr; Sat, Sun.

AVIGNON Hiély-Lucullus ★▤🖤 €€€
*5 rue de la République, 84000 **Tel** 04-90 86 17 07*

Old-fashioned provincial restaurant with a long history of catering to the gourmands of Avignon. Decorated in Belle Epoque style, the restaurant has a menu concentrating on the classics, such as foie gras flan with morels. On the first floor of a medieval building.

CANNES La Palme d'Or ♿▤🍴🅿🖤 €€€€€
*73 la Croisette, 06400 **Tel** 04-92 98 74 14*

Children are not actually barred from this restaurant of the stars, nor is it essential to wear a tie – but diners who are not dressed to impress may feel self-conscious here. The food is imaginative and superb, with an impressive, costly wine list. Reservations required. Closed Sun, Mon.

CARCASSONNE L'Ecurie ★▦🅿 €
*43 boulevard Barbes, 11000 **Tel** 04-68 72 04 04*

Housed in 18th-century stable buildings, "The Stables" is worth a visit just to sit in these elegant old-fashioned surroundings. A favorite with local people, its restaurant tends towards meat dishes, traditionally presented. There is a pretty inner courtyard with tables in the shade or in the sun.

MARSEILLE Restaurant Michel ♿★▦▤🖤 €€€€
*6 rue des Catalans, 13000 **Tel** 04-91 52 64 22*

Bouillabaisse is the specialty of the house at this fine, busy brasserie. Other fish dishes include bourride, sardines, and the always reliable catch of the day, fresh and simply grilled. Popular with locals – get there early to be sure of a table. Wine list includes names from Bandol and Cassis.

MONACO Zebra Square ♿★▦▤🅿🖤 €€€€
*10 av Princesse Grace, 98000 **Tel** 00 377 99 99 25 50*

This trendy restaurant is an offshoot of one of Paris's smartest hotel-restaurants and lives up to its name with zebra stripes everywhere. The menu is multi-cultural and features good grills, seafood, and fusion recipes. Great location, with terrace tables right on the sea. The best choice in Monaco for lunch or dinner.

NICE Le Boccaccio ▦▤🖤 €€€
*7 rue Massena, 06000 **Tel** 04-93 87 71 76*

One of the best places for seafood in Nice, the central Boccaccio is on a bustling car-free street. The interior design is imaginative, with stained-glass windows and tables spread over several floors, and the bill of fare features the best fish dishes – fresh, simply prepared, and with attentive service.

NIMES Lisita ★▦▤🖤 €€€
*2 bd des Arènes, 30000 **Tel** 04-66 67 29 15*

Map

Lisita is not to be missed. This is one of the most popular restaurants in Nîmes, serving cutting-edge food and an outstanding wine list. The surroundings are attractive too, with modern design set off by old stone walls in two rooms, plus an attractive terrace. Closed Sun, Mon.

BELGIUM AND LUXEMBOURG

amed for its magnificent Flemish art and Gothic architecture, Belgium, like neighboring Luxembourg, is a melting pot of various influences including Dutch, French, and German. The histories of the two countries have long been interlinked, but culturally and linguistically they are distinct. Luxembourg, a major financial center, is one of the smallest states in Europe.

In recent times, both Belgium and Luxembourg have largely avoided the limelight, but it was here, in the Middle Ages, that the first great towns of Northern Europe were born, and where the first experiments with oil paintings were made. Today, Brussels, as the center of government for the European Union, is theoretically the capital of Europe, but its reputation remains overshadowed by those of the larger European capitals.

Perhaps more than any other country in Europe, Belgium is most aptly defined by contrasts. The division between the Flemish inhabitants of the north and the French-speaking Walloons in the south is mirrored by a geographical divide; the estuarial plains of Brabant and Flanders give way to the rolling hill-country of the Ardennes, which stretches south and east through the castle-dotted woods of Luxembourg.

HISTORY

At the start of the 12th century, commerce became the guiding force in Europe, and the centers of trade quickly grew into powerful cities. Rivers and canals were keys to the growth of the area's towns; Brussels, Ghent, Ypres, Antwerp, and Bruges became the focus of a cloth trade between Belgium, France, Germany, Italy, and England.

In 1369 Philip, Duke of Burgundy, married the daughter of the Count of Flanders, and a few years later the Low Countries and eastern France came under the couple's Burgundian rule. A century later, the death of Mary of Burgundy left her husband, the Habsburg Emperor Maximilian, ruler of Belgium. In 1488 Brussels and the rest of Flanders rebelled against this new power, but the Austrians prevailed, largely because of a plague which decimated the population in 1490.

European Parliament building rising above the trees of Parc Léopold, Brussels

◁ **Detail of the façade of the Hôtel de Ville in the Grand Place, Brussels**

By 1555 the Low Countries had passed into the hands of the Spanish Habsburgs, whose Catholic repression of the Protestants sparked the Dutch Revolt. In the course of the wars that led to Dutch independence (1568–1648), the predominantly Catholic southern part of the Low Countries remained under Spanish rule. In 1700 the Spanish Habsburg dynasty died out, and England, Austria, and other powers united to oppose French designs on the region in the War of the Spanish Succession. When the war came to an end in 1713,

King Leopold I, the first king of the Belgians, crowned in 1830

the Treaty of Utrecht transferred Belgium and Luxembourg to the Austrian Habsburgs.

Belgium was again ruled by foreign powers between 1794 and 1830. First, by the French Republicans, and then, after Napoleon's defeat, by the Dutch. William I of Orange was appointed King of the Netherlands at the Congress of Vienna in 1815, and his autocratic style, together with a series of anti-Catholic measures, bred considerable discontent, especially among the French-speaking Walloons. An 1830 uprising ousted the Dutch and made Leopold I king of a newly independent Belgium. Nine years later Luxembourg, a Grand-Duchy since 1815, also gained independence.

Both countries' economies flourished throughout the 19th century, but all was eclipsed with the start of World War I. In 1940 the Germans invaded again, this time under Hitler's command.

Belgium's history in the latter half of the 20th century was dominated by the ongoing language debate between the Flemings and the Walloons. The constitution was redrawn, creating a federal state with three separate regions: Flanders, Wallonia, and Brussels.

KEY DATES IN THE HISTORY OF BELGIUM AND LUXEMBOURG

56 BC Julius Caesar conquers the Low Countries

963 AD Count Siegfried establishes Luxembourg

1229 Brussels granted its first charter

1430 Under Burgundian rule, Brussels becomes the major administrative center of the region

1482 The region falls under Austrian sovereignty

1519 Charles V, ruler of Burgundy, becomes Holy Roman Emperor.

1555–1794 Spanish and Austrian rule

1794 French Republican armies take over

1815 Belgium and Luxembourg pass to William I of Orange, King of the Netherlands

1830 Belgium gains independence

1839 Luxembourg gains independence

1914 Both countries invaded by Germany

1940 Nazi troops occupy both countries

1958 EEC headquarters set up in Brussels

1962 Act of Parliament divides Belgium into Dutch- and French-speaking regions

1967 NATO headquarters move to Brussels

1988 Flemish and Walloon regions of Belgium granted fiscal autonomy

2000 Grand Duke of Luxembourg abdicates in favor of his eldest son, Henri

LANGUAGE AND CULTURE

In the north of Belgium, the Flemish have their roots in the Netherlands and Germany, while the Walloons of the south are related to the French. French is one of the official languages of Luxembourg, as is German, but the indigenous language is Letzeburgesch, a dialect of German spoken by all.

Artistically, Belgium is best known for its 17th-century painters (including Rubens, van Dyck, and Jordaans) and more recently for its Art Nouveau style of architecture and Surrealist artists such as Magritte. Today the country is one of the world's most popular producers of chocolate and beer.

A glass of Chimay, a popular Belgian beer

Exploring Belgium and Luxembourg

Brussels is not only the capital of Belgium but also of Europe, as the center of government for the European Union. The city lies in the center of the country on the flat, fertile Brabant plain. Today, its excellent communications make it an ideal place from which to explore the historic towns of Antwerp, Ghent, and Bruges. Toll-free motorways compare favorably with any in France, train travel is swift and competitively priced, and there are good bus services in the areas not covered by trains. Transport in Luxembourg is equally good, with the hub of communications in Luxembourg City itself.

The medieval market square, seen from the Belfort tower, Bruges

SIGHTS AT A GLANCE

Antwerp ❷
Bruges pp232–4 ❸
BRUSSELS pp222–9 ❶

Ghent ❹
Luxembourg ❻
Waterloo ❺

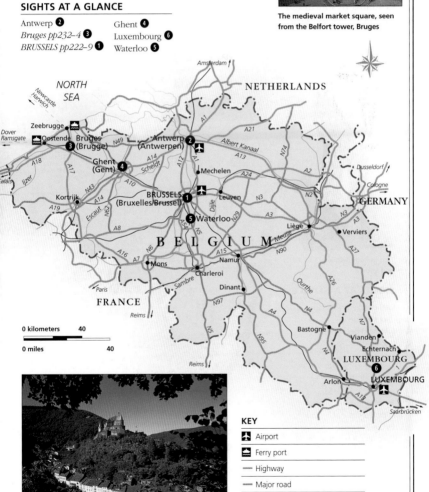

KEY

✈	Airport
⛴	Ferry port
━	Highway
━	Major road
━	Railroad
▪▪▪	International border

Picturesque Château de Vianden, Luxembourg

Brussels ❶

With over one million inhabitants, the Brussels-Capital Region is made up of nineteen districts. The actual city of Brussels is much smaller and divided into two main areas. Historically the poorer area, where workers and immigrants lived, the Lower Town is centered around the splendid 17th-century Grand Place. The Upper Town, traditional home of the aristocracy, is an elegant area that encircles the city's green oasis, the Parc de Bruxelles. Some of the most striking buildings in this part of the city are the shiny postmodern structures of European institutions.

SEE ALSO

- *Where to Stay* p240
- *Where to Eat* p242

Two famous Belgians: Tintin and Snowy

SIGHTS AT A GLANCE

Cathédrale Sts-Michel
   et Gudule ⑤
Centre Belge de la
   Bande Dessinée ④
Grand Place ①
Manneken Pis ③
Musée du Costume et
   de la Dentelle ②
Musées Royaux des
   Beaux-Arts ⑥
Palais Royal ⑦
Parc du Cinquantenaire ⑩
Parliament Quarter ⑨
Place du Grand Sablon ⑧

Greater Brussels
(see inset map)
Bruparck ⑫
Musée Horta ⑪

| 0 meters | 500 |
| 0 yards | 500 |

GETTING AROUND

Brussels' Lower Town is well served by trams. However, many streets are pedestrianized, and usually the quickest way of getting around is on foot. In the Upper Town, the best option is to take one of the buses that run through the district. Brussels' metro stations are well placed for the main sights of interest, and the system offers a fast and efficient way of reaching the suburbs.

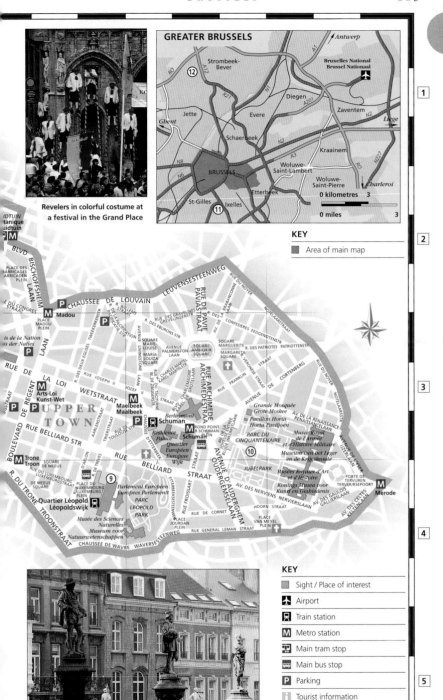

Revelers in colorful costume at a festival in the Grand Place

GREATER BRUSSELS

Antwerp

Strombeek-Bever

Bruxelles National
Brussel Nationaal

Diegen

Jette

Evere

Zaventem

Liege

Ghent

Schaerbeek

Kraainem

BRUSSELS

Woluwe-
Saint-Lambert

St-Gilles   Ixelles

Etterbeek

Woluwe-
Saint-Pierre

Charleroi

0 kilometres   3

0 miles   3

KEY

Area of main map

IDTUIN
tanique
uidtuin

BLVD   BISCHOFFSHEIM

PLACE DES
BARRICADES
ARRICADEN
PLEIN

RUE DU CONGRES STRAAT

CHAUSSEE DE LOUVAIN

LEUVENSESTEENWEG

RUE DU NOTER

Madou

PLACE
MADOU
PLEIN

is de la Nation
is der Naties

SQUARE
MARIE-
LOUISE
MARIA-
LOUIZA
SQUARE

SQUARE
AMBIORIX
SQUARE

SQUARE
MARGUERITE
MARGARETA
SQUARE

RUE DE
LA LOI

WETSTRAAT

RUE ARCHIMEDE
ARCHIMEDESTRAAT

AVENUE DE CORTENBERG

Arts-Loi
Kunst-Wet

U P P E R
T O W N

Maelbeek
Maalbeek

Schuman

ROND POINT
SCHUMAN

Schuman

Grande Mosquée
Grote Moskee

Pavillon Horta
Horta Paviljoen

PARC DU
CINQUANTENAIRE

Musée Royal
de l'Armée
et d'Histoire Militaire
Museum van het Leger
en de Krijgskunde

Trone
Troon

SQUARE
DE MEEUS

Résidence
Palace

Quartier
Européen
Europese
Wijk

Berlaymont

AVENUE D'AUDERGHEM
OUDERGEMSELAAN

JUBELPARK

Musées Royaux d'Art
et d'Histoire
Koninklijke Musea voor
Kunst en Geschiedenis

PORTE DE
TERVUREN
TERVURENPOORT

Merode

Quartier Léopold
Léopoldswijk

Parlement Européen
Europees Parlement

PARC
LEOPOLD
PARK

Musée des Sciences
Naturelles
Museum voor
Natuurwetenschappen

CHAUSSEE DE WAVRE   WAVERSESTEENWEG

KEY

Sight / Place of interest

Airport

Train station

Metro station

Main tram stop

Main bus stop

Parking

Tourist information

Church

Pedestrian street

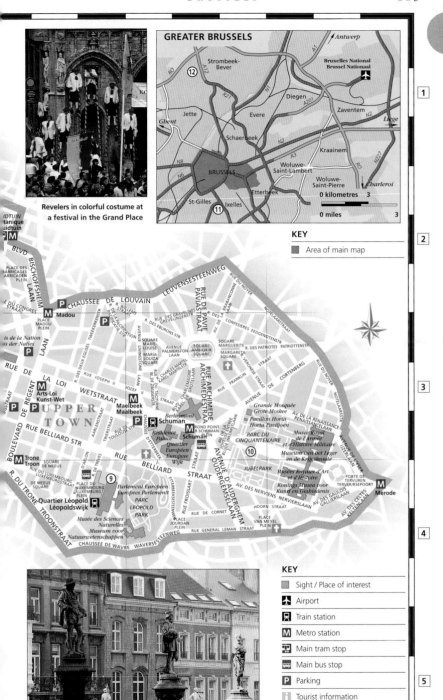

Bronze statues in the Place du Petit Sablon in the Upper Town

Grand Place, Brussels' historic main square

Grand Place ①

Ⓜ *Bourse, Gare Centrale.* 🚌 *29,*
34, 47, 48, 71 & many others. 🚊 *3,*
52, 55, 56, 81. **Musée de la Ville**
Maison du Roi. **Tel** *02-279 4350.*
◯ *10am–5pm Tue–Sun.* ◉ *Jan 1,*
May 1, Nov 1 & 11, Dec 25. 🌀 🎥
by prior arrangement.

The geographical, historical,
and commercial heart of the
city, the Grand Place is the
first port of call for most
visitors to Brussels. A market
was held on this site as early
as the 11th century. During
the first half of the 15th
century, Brussels' town hall,
the Hôtel de Ville, was built,
and city traders began to add
individual guildhalls in a
medley of styles. In 1695,
however, two days of cannon
fire by the French destroyed
all but the town hall and two
façades. Trade guilds were
urged to rebuild their halls to

La Maison du Roi, built on the site
of old bread, meat, and cloth halls

designs approved by the
town council, resulting in the
splendid Baroque ensemble
that can be seen today.

Occupying the entire southwest side of the square, the
Gothic **Hôtel de Ville** *(see
p225)* is the architectural
masterpiece of the Grand
Place. Opposite it stands
La Maison du Roi (1536).
Despite its name, no king
ever lived here; the building
was used as a temporary jail
and a tax office. Redesigned
in Gothic style in the late
19th century, it is now
home to the Musée de la
Ville, which contains
16th-century paintings
and tapestries, and a
collection of around
650 costumes created
for the Manneken Pis.

On the square's eastern
flank, the vast Neoclassical
edifice known as **La Maison
des Ducs de Brabant**
was designed by
Guillaume de Bruyn
and consists of six
former guildhalls. Facing
it are **Le Renard**, built in the
1690s for the guild of haber-
dashers, and **Le Cornet**
(1697), the boatmen's guildhall, whose gable resembles a
17th-century frigate's bow. **Le
Roi d'Espagne**, also known as
La Maison des Boulangers,
was built in the late 17th
century by the wealthy bakers'
guild. The gilt bust over the
entrance represents St. Aubert,
patron saint of bakers. Today,
the building houses one of the
Grand Place's best-loved bars,
whose first floor offers fine
views of the bustling square.

Musée du Costume et de la Dentelle ②

Rue de Violette 12. **Tel** *02-213 4450.*
Ⓜ *Gare Centrale.* 🚌 *34, 48, 95, 96.*
◯ *10am–12:30pm, 1:30–5pm*
Mon–Fri; 2–5pm Sat & Sun. ◉ *Wed.*
🌀 *on request.* ♿ *restricted.*

Housed in two 18th-century
gabled houses, this museum
is dedicated to one of
Brussels' most successful
exports, Belgian lace, which
has been made here since
the 12th century. The ground
floor has a display of costumes
showing how lace has
adorned fashions of every era.
Upstairs is a fine collection of
antique lace from France,
Flanders, and Italy.

Manneken Pis ③

Rues de l'Etuve & du Chêne.
Ⓜ *Gare Centrale.* 🚌 *34, 48, 95, 96.*
🚊 *3, 52, 55, 56, 81.*

The tiny statue of a young
boy relieving himself is
Brussels' most unusual sight.

The original bronze statue
by Jérôme Duquesnoy the
Elder was first placed on
the site in 1619. After it
was stolen and damaged
by a former convict in
1817, a replica was
made and returned to
its revered site. The
inspiration for the statue
is unknown, the
mystery only lends itself
to rumor and fable
and increases the little
boy's charm. One
theory claims that in
the 12th century the
son of a duke was caught
urinating against a tree in the
midst of a battle, and was
thus commemorated in
bronze as a symbol of the
country's military courage.
When, in 1698, a city governor
provided a set of clothes with
which to dress the statue, he
began a tradition that is still
observed today. Visiting heads
of state donate miniature
versions of their national
costume for the boy, and now
a collection of 650 outfits,
including an Elvis suit, can be
seen in the Musée de la Ville.

**Manneken Pis
statue**

Hôtel de Ville

The idea of erecting a town hall to reflect Brussels' growth as a major European trading center had been under consideration since the end of the 13th century, but it was not until 1401 that the first foundation stone was laid. Completed in 1459, the Hôtel de Ville emerged as the finest civic building in the country, a stature it still enjoys. Jacques van Thienen was commissioned to design the left wing, where he used ornate columns, sculptures, turrets, and arcades. Jan van Ruysbroeck's elegant spire helped seal the building's reputation. Tours are available of the interior, which contains 15th-century tapestries and works of art.

VISITORS' CHECKLIST

Grand Place. **Tel** 02-279 4365.
M Bourse, Gare Centrale.
many routes. 3, 52, 55, 56, 81.
(for guided tours) 3:15pm
Tue & Wed (all year); 10:45am,
12:15pm Sun (Apr–Sep). public hols & election days.

★ Maximilian Room
This lavish hall, used today by the city council, takes its name from the portrait of Maximilian I of Austria over the fireplace. It contains 18th-century tapestries depicting the history of 6th-century King Clovis.

★ Council Chamber
This room was where the ruling council of Brabant used to meet. Ancient tapestries and gilt mirrors line the walls above an inlaid floor.

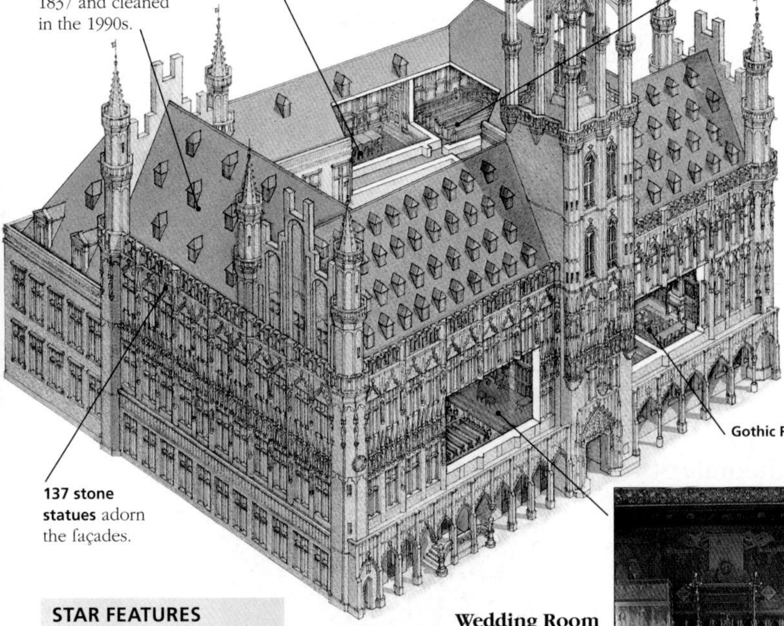

The tower, begun in 1449, is 96 m (315 ft) high. It is topped by a statue of St. Michael, patron saint of Brussels.

The gabled roof, like much of the town hall, was fully restored in 1837 and cleaned in the 1990s.

Gothic Room

137 stone statues adorn the façades.

STAR FEATURES

★ Council Chamber

★ Maximilian Room

Wedding Room
A Neo-Gothic style dominates this civil marriage office. Its ornate carved timbers include mahogany inlaid with ebony.

Art Nouveau entrance hall of the Centre Belge de la Bande Dessinée

Centre Belge de la Bande Dessinée ④

20 Rue des Sables. **Tel** 02-219 1980.
🚌 38, 58, 61. 🚊 56, 81, 90.
Ⓜ Botanique, Rogier, Centrale.
◯ 10am–6pm Tue–Sun. ● Jan 1, Dec 25. 🎫 🗯 ⑪ 🚻 ⑪ ♿

This unique museum pays tribute to the Belgian passion for comic strips, or *bandes dessinées*, and to world-famous comic strip artists from Belgium and abroad.

One of the exhibitions shows the great comic strip heroes, from Hergé's Tintin – who made his debut in 1929 – to the Smurfs and the Flemish comic strip characters Suske and Wiske. Other displays explain the stages of putting together a comic strip. There is also a series of life-size cartoon sets, of special appeal to children. The museum holds 6,000 original plates, and a valuable archive of photographs and artifacts.

The collection is housed in a beautiful building, built in 1903–6 to the design of the Belgian Art Nouveau architect Victor Horta (*see p229*).

Cathédrale Sts-Michel et Gudule ⑤

Parvis Ste-Gudule. **Tel** 02-217 8345.
🚌 29, 60, 63, 65, 66, 71. 🚊 92,
93, 94. Ⓜ Centrale. ◯ daily. 🗯 to crypt and treasury. ♿ call in advance.
www.cathedralestmichel.be

Belgium's finest surviving example of Brabant Gothic architecture, the Cathédrale

Sts-Michel et Gudule is the national church of Belgium. There has been a church on this site since at least the 11th century. Work began on the Gothic cathedral in 1225 under Henry I, Duke of Brabant, and continued over a period of 300 years.

The cathedral interior is relatively bare, due to Protestant ransacking in 1579 and thefts during the French Revolution. Over the west door, however, is a magnificent 16th-century stained-glass window of the Last Judgment. Another splendid feature is the flamboyantly carved Baroque pulpit in the central aisle, by an Antwerp sculptor, Hendrik Frans Verbruggen. In the crypt are the remains of the original Romanesque church, which dates back to 1047.

Musées Royaux des Beaux-Arts ⑥

Rue de la Régence 3. **Tel** 02-508
3211. 🚌 25, 27, 38, 60, 71, 95, 96.
🚊 92, 93, 94. Ⓜ Parc, Centrale ◯
10am–5pm Tue–Sun. ● public hols.
🗯 🎫 call in advance. ⑪ 🖥 ⑪ ♿
www.fine-arts-museum.be

Six centuries of art, both Belgian and international, are displayed in the two museums that make up the Musées Royaux des Beaux-

The Assumption of the Virgin (c.1615) by Rubens at the Musées royaux des Beaux Arts

The white limestone façade of the Cathédrale Sts-Michel et Gudule

Arts, the Musée d'Art Ancien (15th–18th centuries) and the Musée d'Art Moderne (19th century–present day). Both museums have colored "routes," which guide the visitor through galleries representing the different schools and periods of art.

The Musée d'Art Ancien holds one of the world's finest collections of works by the Flemish Primitive School. A work of particular note is *The Annunciation* (c.1415–25) by the Master of Flémalle. The trademarks of the Flemish Primitives are a lifelike vitality and a clarity of light. The greatest exponent of the style was Rogier van der Weyden (c.1400–64), the official city painter to Brussels, who has several splendid works on display at the museum.

Peter Brueghel the Elder (c.1525–69), one of the most outstanding Flemish artists, settled in Brussels in 1563. His earthy scenes of peasant life remain his best known works, and are represented here by paintings such as *The Bird Trap* (1565).

Another highlight of the Musée d'Art Ancien is the world-famous collection of works by Peter Paul Rubens (1577–1640).

The Assumption of the Virgin stands out among his religious canvases. Other notable paintings include van Dyck's *Portrait of Porzia Imperial with her daughter Maria Francesca* (1620s) and *Three Children with Goatcart* by Frans Hals (c.1582–1666).

Opened in 1984, the Musée d'Art Moderne is situated in a unique setting: eight levels of the building are underground. Works in the 19th-century section vary greatly in style and subject matter, from Neoclassicism, exemplified by David, to Realism, Impressionism, and Symbolism.

The Fauvist painter Rik Wouters' *Woman in a Blue Dress in front of a Mirror* (1914) is one of many works by leading Belgian artists of the 20th century. Foreign artists include Matisse, Paul Klee, and Chagall. The biggest attraction of this part of the museum, however, is the collection of paintings by the Belgian Surrealists, including René Magritte (1898–1967). Surrealism had its roots back in the 16th century, with the phantasmagoria of Bosch and Peter Brueghel the Elder. One of Magritte's most famous works, on show here, is *The Domain of Arnheim* (1962) – an eerie composition showing an eagle-mountain rearing over a small bird's nest.

Palais Royal ⑦

Place des Palais. **Tel** 02-551 2020.
▦ 21, 27, 38, 60, 71, 95, 96.
▯ 92, 93, 94. Ⓜ *Trône, Parc.*
◯ *10:30am– 4:30pm Tue–Sun.*
◉ *mid-Sep–mid-Jul.* 🄳 ♿
www.monarchie.be

The official home of the Belgian monarchy, this is one of the finest 19th-century buildings in the Upper Town. Construction began in the 1820s on the site of the old Coudenberg Palace. Work continued under Léopold II (reigned 1865– 1909), when much of the exterior was completed. The most lavish state reception rooms include the Throne Room, with 28 wall-mounted chandeliers, and the Hall of Mirrors. The latter,

The recently restored, 19th-century Palais Royal

similar to the Hall of Mirrors at Versailles *(see pp168–9)*, is where ceremonial occasions are held, and guests presented to the king and queen.

Place du Grand Sablon ⑧

▦ 27, 48, 95, 96. ▯ 91, 92, 93, 94.
Ⓜ *Centrale, Louise.*

Located on the slope of the escarpment that divides Brussels in two, the Place du Grand Sablon is like a stepping stone between the upper and lower towns. The name "sablon" derives from the French "sable" (sand), and the square is so called because this old route down to the city center once passed through sandy marshes.

Terrace café in the upscale Place du Grand Sablon

Today this is an area of upscale antiques dealers, fashionable restaurants, and trendy bars, where you can stay drinking until the early hours of the morning.

At the far end of the square stands the lovely church of **Notre-Dame du Sablon**, built in the Brabant Gothic style, and boasting some glorious stained-glass windows. On the opposite side of the road to the church is the **Place du Petit Sablon**. In contrast to the busy café scene of the larger square, these pretty formal gardens are a peaceful spot to stop for a rest. Sit and admire the 48 bronze statues by Art Nouveau artist Paul Hankar, each representing a different medieval guild of the city. At the back of the gardens is a fountain, built to commemorate Counts Egmont and Hoorn, the martyrs who led a Dutch uprising against the tyrannical rule of the Spanish under Philip II. On either side of the fountain are 12 further statues of prominent 15th- and 16th-century figures, including Gerhard Mercator, the Flemish geographer and mapmaker.

Notre-Dame du Sablon window

The triumphal central archway and surrounding colonnades of the Parc du Cinquantenaire

Parliament Quarter ⑨

🚌 21, 27, 34, 38, 54, 60, 80, 95, 96.
Ⓜ Maelbeek, Trône, Schuman.

The vast, modern steel and glass complex, located just behind the Quartier Léopold train station, is one of three homes of the European

Postmodern building known as "Les Caprices des Dieux" in Brussels' Parliament Quarter

Parliament (the other two are Strasbourg and Luxembourg). This gleaming building has its critics: the huge structure housing the hemicycle that seats the 600-plus MEPs has been dubbed "Les Caprices des Dieux" ("Whims of the Gods"), which refers both to the shape of the building, similar to a French cheese of the same name, and to its lofty aspirations. Many people also regret that to make way for the building, a large part of the once-lively Quartier Léopold has been lost. Though there are still plenty of bars and restaurants here, a lot of the charm has gone.

Parc du Cinquantenaire ⑩

Avenue de Tervuren. 🚌 27, 28, 36, 67.
🚊 81, 82. Ⓜ Schuman, Mérode.
Musées Royaux d'Art et d'Histoire
Tel 02-741 7211. ◯ Tue–Sun. ●
public hols. ♿ 🖭 www.kmkg-mrah.be **Musée Royal de l'Armée et d'Histoire Militaire Tel** 02-737 7811.
◯ Tue–Sun. ● Jan 1, Dec 25. 📷
♿ www.klm-mra.be **Autoworld**
Tel 02-736 4165. ◯ 10am–6pm daily (5pm in winter). ● Jan 1, Dec 25.

The finest of Léopold II's grand projects, the Parc and Palais du Cinquantenaire were built for the Golden Jubilee celebrations of Belgian independence in 1880. The park was laid out on unused marshland. The palace, at its entrance, was to comprise a triumphal arch, based on the Arc de

---

BRUSSELS AND THE EUROPEAN UNION

In 1958, following the signing of the Treaty of Rome in the previous year, the European Economic Community (EEC), now the European Union (EU), was born, and Brussels became its headquarters. Today, the city remains home to most of the EU's institutions. The European Commission, the EU body that formulates policies, is based in the tricorn-shaped Berlaymont Building. The city is also one of the seats of the European Parliament, which currently has around 732 members, known as MEPs (Members of the European Parliament). The most powerful institution is the Council of Ministers, composed of representatives of each member state. Each nation has a certain number of votes, according to its size. The Council must approve all legislation for the EU, often a difficult task to accomplish given that most Europe-wide legislation will not be to the liking of every state.

The signing of the Treaty of Rome, 1957

Triomphe in Paris *(see p165)*, and two large exhibition areas. By the time of the 1880 Art and Industry Exposition, however, only the two side exhibition areas had been completed. Further funds were found, and work continued for 50 years. The arch was completed in 1905. Until 1935, the large halls on either side of the central archway were used to hold trade fairs, before being converted into museums.

Also known as the Musée du Cinquantenaire, the excellent **Musées Royaux d'Art et d'Histoire** contain a vast array of exhibits. Sections on ancient civilizations cover Egypt, Greece, Persia, and the Near East. Other displays feature Byzantium and Islam, China and the Indian subcontinent, and the Pre-Columbian civilizations of the Americas. Decorative arts from all ages include glassware, silverware, porcelain, lace, and tapestries. There are also religious sculptures and stained glass.

The **Musée Royal de l'Armée et d'Histoire Militaire** deals with all aspects of Belgium's military history. There are new sections on both World Wars, as well as a separate hall containing historic aircraft.

Housed in the south wing of the Cinquantenaire Palace, **Autoworld** has one of the best collections of automobiles in the world.

Part formal gardens, part tree-lined walks, the park is popular with Brussels' Eurocrats and families at lunchtimes and weekends.

Musée Horta ⑪

Rue Américaine 23–25. *Tel* 02-543 0490. 54. 81, 82, 91, 92. Albert, Louise. 2–5:30pm Tue–Sun. public hols. **www**.hortamuseum.be

Architect Victor Horta (1861–1947) is considered the father of Art Nouveau, and his impact on Brussels architecture is unrivaled by any other designer of his time. A museum dedicated to

Elegant Art Nouveau staircase at the Musée Horta

his unique style is today housed in his restored family home, in the fashionable Ixelles district. Horta himself designed the house, between 1898 and 1901. The airy interior of the building displays trademarks of the architect's style – iron, glass, and curves – in every detail, while retaining a functional approach. Most impressive are the dining room, with its ornate ceiling featuring scrolled metalwork, and the central staircase. Decorated with curved wrought iron, the stairs are enhanced further by mirrors and glass, bringing natural light into the house.

Bruparck ⑫

Boulevard du Centenaire. *Tel* 02-474 8377. 84, 89. 23, 81. M Heysel. **Mini-Europe** *Tel* 02-478 0550. daily. Jan–Mar. **Océade** *Tel* 02-478 4944. daily. **Kinepolis** *Tel* 02-474 2600. for performances only. **Atomium** *Tel* 02-475 4777. daily. **www**.bruparck.com

Located on the outskirts of the city, this theme park is popular with families. The most visited attraction is **Mini-Europe**, which has over 300 miniature reconstructions (built at a scale of 1:25) of Europe's major sights, from Athens' Acropolis to London's Houses of Parliament.

For film fans, **Kinepolis** has 29 cinemas, including an IMAX cinema with a semi-circular 600-sq m (6,456-sq ft) screen.

If warmth and relaxation are what you are looking for, **Océade** is a tropically heated water park that features giant slides, wave machines, and even artificial sandy beaches.

Towering over Bruparck is Brussels' most distinctive landmark, the **Atomium**. Designed by André Waterkeyn for the 1958 World's Fair, represents an atom of iron magnified 165 billion times, the structure has a viewing platform at the top.

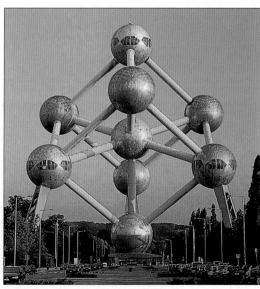

The Atomium, rising 100 m (325 ft) over the Bruparck

Bronze statue of Silvius Brabo in Antwerp's Grote Markt

Antwerp **❷**

🏛 *500,000.* 🚹 🚆 🚍
ℹ️ *15 Grote Markt (03-232 0103).*
www.visitantwerpen.be

In the Middle Ages Antwerp was a thriving hub of the European cloth trade, and the principal port of the Duchy of Brabant. Today, it is the main city of Flemish-speaking Belgium, and the center of the international diamond trade.

At the heart of the city's old medieval district is the Grote Markt. The Brabo Fountain, at its center, has a statue of the soldier Silvius Brabo, said to be the nephew of Julius Caesar. The square is overlooked by the ornately gabled **Stadhuis** (Town Hall), built in 1564, and the Gothic **Onze Lieve Vrouwe Kathedraal** (Cathedral of Our Lady), which dates back to 1352.

Among the paintings inside the cathedral are two triptychs by Antwerp's most famous son, Peter Paul Rubens (1577–1640).

The narrow, winding streets of the old town are lined with fine medieval guildhalls, such as the **Vleeshuis**, or Meat Hall, once occupied by the Butchers' Guild. Dating from the early 16th century, it is built in alternate stripes of stone and brick, giving it a streaky bacon-like appearance.

When Rubens died in 1640, he was buried in the family's chapel at the lovely sandstone **Sint Jacobskerk** (1491–1656), also located in the old town.

One of the most prestigious of Antwerp's many museums is the **Koninklijk Museum voor Schone Kunsten**, which houses an impressive collection of ancient and modern art. Works from the 17th century include masterpieces by the "Antwerp Trio" of van Dyck (1599–1641), Jordaens (1593–1678), and Rubens. More modern exhibits include works by the Surrealist René Magritte (1898–1967) and Rik Wouters (1882–1916).

Other museums catering to special interests are the **Diamond Museum**, recently updated and now housed in a large building near to the central station, and the **Museum Plantin-Moretus**, which is devoted to the early years of printing and celebrates the achievements of Antwerp's most successful printer, Christopher Plantin.

Rubenshuis was Rubens' home and studio for the last 30 years of his life. A tour takes you round his living quarters, equiped with period furniture, as well as his studio and the *kunst-kamer*, or art gallery, where he exhibited both his own and other artists' work, and entertained friends and wealthy patrons.

🏛 **Koninklijk Museum voor Schone Kunsten**
Leopold de Waelplaats 1–9. *Tel 03-238 7809.* 🚆 *8.* ⏰ *10am–5pm Tue–Sun.* ⬛ *public hols.* 🚫 ♿

🏛 **Rubenshuis**
Wapper 9–11. *Tel 03-201 1555.* 🚍 *1, 23, 290.* 🚆 *4, 8.* ⏰ *10am–5pm Tue–Sun.* ⬛ *public hols.* 🚫 ♿

Bruges **❸**

See pp232–4.

Stone gatehouse of Ghent's medieval Het Gravensteen

Ghent **❹**

🏛 *228,000.* 🚆 🚍 🚤
ℹ️ *Botermarkt 17A, (09-266 5232).*
www.gent.be

The heart of Ghent's historic center was built in the 13th and 14th centuries when the city prospered as a result of the cloth trade. The closure of vital canal links in 1648, however, led to a decline in the town's fortunes. In the 18th and 19th centuries Ghent flourished again as a major industrial center.

Dominating the old medieval quarter is the imposing **Het Gravensteen**, or Castle of the Counts. Parts of the castle, once the seat of the Counts of

Jacob Jordaens' joyous *As the Old Sang, the Young Play Pipes* (1638) in the Koninklijk Museum voor Schone Kunsten, Antwerp

The Pacification Hall in Ghent's Stadhuis, with its impressive tiled floor

Flanders, date back to the 12th century, although most parts, including the gatehouse, were built later.

Many of Ghent's finest historic buildings are found on Graslei, a picturesque street that borders the river Leie. The street is lined with well-preserved guildhalls dating from the Middle Ages.

The magnificent **St Baafskathedraal** has features representing every phase of the Gothic style. In a small side chapel is one of Europe's most remarkable paintings, Jan van Eyck's *Adoration of the Mystic Lamb* (1432). Opposite the cathedral stands the huge 14th-century **Belfort** (belfry). From the top of the tower you can enjoy splendid views of the city. From here it is a short walk to the **Stadhuis** (Town Hall), whose Pacification Hall was the site of the signing of the Pacification of Ghent (a declaration of the Low Countries' repudiation of Spanish rule) in 1576.

Ghent's largest collection of fine art, covering all periods up to the 20th century, is in the **Museum voor Schone Kunsten**, some 20 minutes' walk southeast of the center. There are works by Rubens and his contemporaries Jacob Jordaens and Anthony van Dyck. Occupying an elegant 18th-century townhouse, the **Museum voor Sierkunst** is a decorative arts museum, with lavishly furnished 17th-, 18th-, and 19th-century period rooms. An extension covers modern design, from Art Nouveau to contemporary works.

⚓ **Het Gravensteen**
Sint-Veerleplein. *Tel* 09-225 9306.
◯ 9am–5pm daily. 🖼

🏛 **Museum voor Schone Kunsten**
Citadelpark. *Tel* 09-240 0700. ◯ 10am–6pm Tue–Sun. 🖼 🎫 ♿

Waterloo ❺

🏚 30,000. 🚉 🚌 ℹ *Chaussée de Bruxelles 218 (02-354 9910).*
www.waterloo.be

This small town is most famous for its association with the Battle of Waterloo, which saw Napoleon and his French army defeated by the Duke of Wellington's troops on June 18, 1815. The best place to start a visit here is the **Musée Wellington**, which occupies the inn where

Wellington stayed the night before the battle. Its narrow rooms are packed with curios alongside plans and models of the battlefield.

The **Musée de Cires** (Waxwork Museum) has models of soldiers dressed in period uniforms, while the **Eglise St-Joseph** contains dozens of memorial plaques to the British soldiers who died at Waterloo.

For an excellent view over the battlefield, head for the **Butte de Lion**, a 45-m (148-ft) high earthen mound, 3 km (2 miles) south of the town. Next to it is a gallery where Louis Demoulin's fascinating circular painting *Panorama de la Bataille* is displayed.

🏛 **Musée Wellington**
Chaussée de Bruxelles 147. *Tel* 02-354 7806. ◯ 10am–5pm daily. 🖼

The Butte de Lion viewed from the battlefield of Waterloo

THE BATTLEFIELDS OF BELGIUM

Belgium's strategic position between France and Germany has long made it the battleground or "cockpit" of Europe. Napoleon's defeat at Waterloo was just one of many major conflicts resolved on Belgian soil. In the early 18th century French expansion under Louis XIV was thwarted here, and more recently Belgium witnessed some of the bloodiest trench warfare of World War I, including the introduction of poison gas at Ypres (Ieper). Today there are several vast graveyards, where the tens of thousands of soldiers who died on the Western Front lie buried.

Aftermath of Passchendaele (Third Battle of Ypres), 1917

Street-by-Street: Bruges ❸

Traditional organ grinder

With good reason, Bruges is one of the most popular tourist destinations in Belgium. The city owes its pre-eminent position to the beauty of its historic center, whose winding lanes and picturesque canals are lined with splendid medieval buildings. These are mostly the legacy of the town's heyday as a center of the international cloth trade, which flourished for 200 years from the 13th century. During this golden age, Bruges' merchants lavished their fortunes on fine mansions, churches, and a set of civic buildings of such extravagance that they were the wonder of northern Europe. Today, the streets are well maintained: there are no billboards or high-rises, and traffic is heavily regulated.

View of the River Dijver
A charming introduction to Bruges is provided by the boat trips along the city's canals.

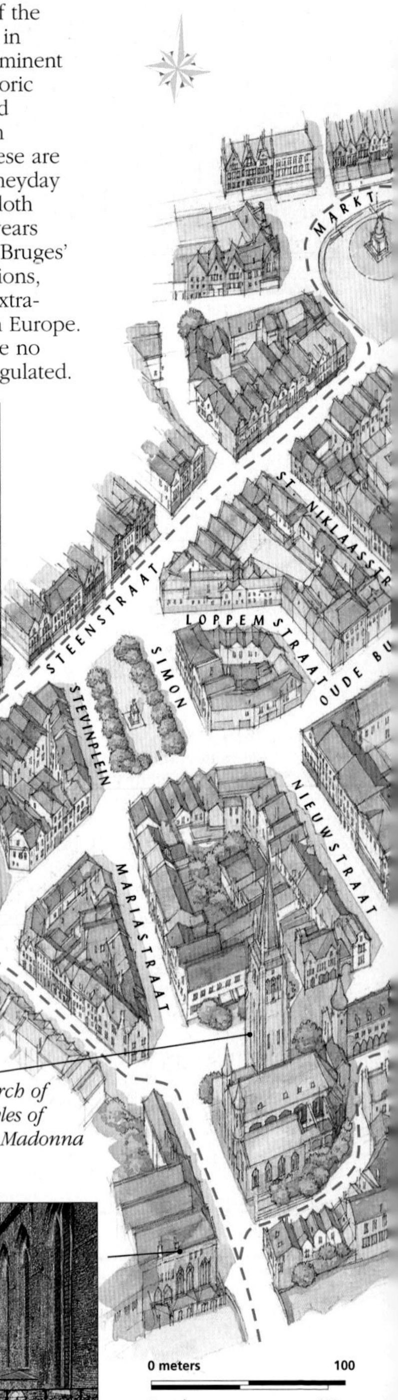

Bus and train stations

Onze Lieve Vrouwekerk
Dating from 1220, the Church of Our Lady employs many styles of architecture and contains a Madonna and Child by Michelangelo.

Hans Memling Museum and St. Janshospitaal
This 12th-century hospital operated until 1976. It contains a well-preserved 15th-century dispensary.

| 0 meters | 100 |
| 0 yards | 100 |

★ The Markt
Medieval gabled houses line this 13th-century market square at the heart of Bruges, which still holds a market each Saturday.

Oude Griffie, or Old Recorder's House

Blind Donkey Alley
This tiny alley leads from the Burg to the 18th-century Vis-markt (Fish Market).

Heilig Bloed Basiliek
(see p234)

Groeninge Museum
(see p234)

The Arentshuis Museum has a display of antique lace, and paintings by Frank Brangwyn (1867–1956).

Gruuthuse Museum
(see p234)

The Belfort
Built in the 13th century, the Belfort, or Belfry, is a stunning octagonal tower where the city's medieval charter of rights is held.

★ Stadhuis
One of the oldest and finest town halls in Belgium, this was built between 1376 and 1420. Inside, the beautifully restored Gothic hall is noted for its 1385 vaulted ceiling.

KEY

– – – Suggested route

STAR SIGHTS

★ The Markt

★ Stadhuis

For hotels and restaurants in this region see pp240–41 and pp242–3

🏛 Groeninge Museum

Dijver 12. **Tel** 050-44 8711.
⏲ 9:30am–5pm Tue–Sun.
⬤ Jan 1, Dec 25. 🖼

Bruges' premier fine art museum holds a superb collection of early Flemish and Dutch masters. Artists featured include Rogier van der Weyden (c.1400–1464), Jan van Eyck (d.1441), and Hans Memling (c.1430–94). Van Eyck's *Virgin and Child with Canon* (1436), a richly detailed painting noted for its realism, and Memling's *Moreel* triptych (1484) are among the museum's most outstanding exhibits. Painted in the early 16th century, the *Last Judgment* triptych is one of a number of works at the museum by Hieronymous Bosch (c.1450–1516). Peter Brueghel the Younger (1564–1638) is also well represented. Later Belgian works include paintings by Surrealists Paul Delvaux (1897–1994) and René Magritte (1898–1967).

Fifteenth-century oak-paneled chapel in the Gruuthuse Museum

🏛 Gruuthuse Museum

Dijver 17. **Tel** 050-44 8762.
⏲ 9:30am–5pm Tue–Sat (to 4pm Sat); 1:30–5pm Sun. ⬤ Jan 1, Dec 25. 🖼

This museum occupies a large medieval mansion close to the Dijver Canal. In the 15th century it was inhabited by a merchant (the Lord of the Gruuthuse), who had the right to levy a tax on "gruit," an imported mixture of herbs added to barley during the beer-brewing process. The mansion's labyrinthine rooms, with their ancient chimney-pieces and wooden beams, have survived intact, and

Panel of Hans Memling's *Moreel* triptych in the Groeninge Museum

today contain a collection of fine and applied arts. The exhibits range from wood carvings, tapestries, porcelain, and ceramics, to medical instruments and weaponry. The authentic kitchen and beautiful oak-paneled chapel (1472) transport visitors back to medieval times.

🔒 Heilig Bloed Basiliek

Burg 10. **Tel** 050-33 6792. ⏲ daily.
Museum ⬤ Mon, Wed pm (in winter).

The Basilica of the Holy Blood is Bruges' holiest church, holding one of the most sacred relics in Europe. In the upper chapel, rebuilt after it was destroyed by the French in the 1790s, is a 17th-century tabernacle, which houses a phial said to contain a few drops of blood and water washed from the body of Christ by Joseph of Arimathea.

🏛 Begijnhof

Wijngaardplein 1. **Tel** 050-33 0011.
⏲ daily.

Béguines were members of a lay sisterhood founded in 1245, who did not take vows, but led a devout life. The *begijnhof*, or *béguinage*, is the walled complex in a town that housed the Béguines. In Bruges this is an area of quiet tree-lined canals edged by white, gabled houses. Visitors can enjoy a stroll here and visit the simple church, built in 1602. One of the houses, now occupied by Benedictine nuns, is open to the public.

🏛 Houishbrouwerij de Halve Maan

Walplein 26. **Tel** 050-33 2697.
⏲ 11am–4pm daily (Nov–Mar: to 3pm). 🎫 compulsory. 🖼
www.halvemaan.be

Before World War I there were 31 breweries in Bruges. This one has been producing Straffe Hendrik since 1856. Here you can follow the beer-making process, from the first hops to a taste of the finished product in the small bar. There are also good views of Bruges from the oast room at the top of the building.

🏛 Museum voor Volkskunde

Balstraat 43. **Tel** 050-33 0044.
⏲ 9:30am–5pm Tue–Sun.

This excellent folk museum occupies an attractive terrace of brick almshouses in the northeast of the town. Each of the houses is dedicated to a different aspect of traditional Flemish life. Several crafts are represented, and visitors are shown a series of typical historical domestic interiors.

Pretty 17th-century almshouses, home to the Museum voor Volkskunde

Luxembourg

One of Europe's smallest sovereign states, the Grand Duchy of Luxembourg is often overlooked by travelers in Europe. The capital, Luxembourg City, is well known as a world center of international finance, but behind the modern face of the city lies a rich history stretching back over 1,000 years. The northern half of the country boasts some spectacular scenery, especially the Ardennes, a region of dense forests, deep valleys, and hilltop castles. Historic towns such as Vianden and Echternach are good bases for exploring the countryside and offer plenty of opportunities for outdoor activities.

View of Luxembourg City with its aqueduct and hilltop historic center

Luxembourg City

🏛 82,000. ✈ 6 km (4 miles) E. 🚉 🚌 🛈 30 Place Guillaume II (22 28 09). www.lcto.lu

Luxembourg City enjoys a dramatic location, set atop hills and cliffs rising above the Alzette and Pétrusse valleys. The town grew up around a castle, built on a rocky promontory known as the Rocher du Bock in AD 963. The castle was destroyed in the late 19th century by the city's inhabitants, but some of the fortifications have been preserved, most famously the Bock and Pétrusse **Casemates**. These huge networks of underground defensive galleries, which date back to the 17th century, not only provided shelter for thousands of soldiers, but also housed workshops, kitchens, bakeries, and slaughterhouses. The **Crypte Archéologique du Bock**, currently closed for renovation, has displays on the history of the city's fortifications.

Luxembourg City's **Palais Grand Ducal** has been the official royal residence since 1890. The oldest parts of the building, which used to be the town hall, date from the latter half of the 16th century. Nearby, the **Cathédrale Notre-Dame** was begun in 1613. Inside is a fine Baroque organ gallery by Daniel Muller.

Two museums worth visiting are the **Musée National d'Art et d'Histoire**, which has a good archaeological section and a collection of ancient and modern sculpture and paintings, and the **Musée de l'Histoire de la Ville de Luxembourg**, which focuses on the city's historical past.

♣ **Casemates**
Bock Casemates Montée de Clausen. ⏰ Mar–Oct: 10am–5pm.
🏛 **Pétrusse Casemates** Place de la Constitution. ⏰ Easter, Whitsun, & Jul–Sep: 11am–4pm. 🏛

🏛 **Musée National d'Art et d'Histoire**
Place Marché aux Poissons. Tel 47 93 301. ⏰ 10am–5pm Tue–Sun (8pm Thu). 🏛 🏛 🏛

Vianden

🏛 1,600. 🚌 🛈 1a Rue du Vieux Marché (83 42 57). **Château de Vianden** Tel 83 41 08. ⏰ Apr–Sep: 10am–6pm; Oct, Mar: 10am–5pm; Nov–Feb: 10am–4pm. ⬤ Sat in winter. 🏛 🏛

Surrounded by medieval ramparts, Vianden, in the Luxembourg Ardennes, is a popular tourist destination. The main attraction is the 11th-century **Château de Vianden**. Its rooms feature a range of architectural styles, from the Romanesque to the Renaissance. A cable car takes visitors to the top of a nearby hill, giving superb views of the castle.

Echternach

🏛 4,000. 🚌 🛈 9–10 Parvis de la Basilique (72 02 30). **Abbey Basilica** ⏰ daily. **Abbey Museum** ⏰ Apr–Oct: 10am–noon, 2–5pm daily. 🏛 www.mullerthal.lu

Located in Petite Suisse (Little Switzerland), a picturesque region of wooded hills northeast of the capital, Echternach is dotted with fine medieval buildings, including the 15th-century turreted **Town Hall**. The star sight, however, is the **Benedictine abbey**, founded by St. Willibrord in the 7th century. The crypt of the abbey basilica (c.900) contains some glorious frescoes. There are excellent walks and cycle routes in the surrounding countryside.

Medieval Town Hall in the Place du Marché, Echternach

Practical & Travel Information

Visitors to Belgium and Luxembourg can expect high levels of service and comfort in all aspects of their stay. Public transportation is clean and efficient, and there are abundant tourist information facilities, in add-ition to all the other modern conveniences one expects of a highly developed country. Brussels and Luxembourg City are among the safest capital cities in Europe and, due to their small size, can be easily explored on foot.

TOURIST INFORMATION

In Belgium, the **Tourist and Information Office of Brussels** publishes maps and guides, and also offers a Brussels Card. This "tourist passport" includes a three-day pass to all public transport in the Brussels region, combined with unlimited access to 30 museums.

Luxembourg's **National Tourist Office** is located in the train station in the capital. It sells the Luxembourg Card, which gives unlimited travel on public transport nation-wide, as well as admission to over 30 sites of interest, and reductions on many others. The card, which is valid for one, two, or three days between Easter and October, can also be bought at hotels, campsites, youth hostels, and train and bus stations.

Local tourist information offices can be found in most towns and villages throughout Belgium and Luxembourg.

OPENING HOURS

Most shops and businesses in Belgium and Luxem-bourg are open from 10am until 5 or 6pm Monday to Saturday, with some local shops closing for an hour at lunch. Some stores open at noon on Mondays. In the major cities and towns many shops are open on Sundays and until later in the evening.

In both countries most museums are closed on Mondays. Outside the high season (April to September), be prepared to find many sights of interest closed.

VISA REQUIREMENTS

Citizens of the EU, US, Australia, New Zealand, and Canada do not require a visa to enter either Belgium or Luxembourg, but must present a valid passport and hold proof of onward passage. Bear in mind that in Belgium it is a legal requirement to carry ID on one's person at all times.

SAFETY AND EMERGENCIES

Belgium and Luxembourg are safe countries, with street crime against visitors a relatively rare occurrence. However, in Brussels it is inadvisable to wander alone at night in the poorer areas to the west and north of the city center, and in the city's parks, especially at Botanique.

In case of emergencies, the numbers to call are listed in the Directory opposite.

LANGUAGE

The two principal languages of Belgium are Dutch, spoken in Flanders, and French, the language of the Wallonians. There is also a German-speaking enclave in the far east of the country. In the capital both languages are used on all street signs and in place names.

Luxembourg has three official languages: French, German, and Letzeburgesch, or Luxembourgeois. In both Belgium and Luxembourg, especially in the capital cities, many people speak English.

BANKING AND CURRENCY

Both Belgium and Luxem-bourg have replaced their traditional currencies, the Belgian franc and the Luxembourg franc, with the Euro. On January 1, 2002, Euro notes and coins came into general circulation and these can be used anywhere inside the participating member states (*see p15*).

Banking hours are from 9am to 4pm in Belgium and 9am to 4:30pm in Luxembourg. In both countries most of the banks close for an hour at lunch-time, and some of the city branches open on Saturday mornings.

COMMUNICATIONS

Belgian post offices are open from 9am to 5pm Monday to Friday. In Luxembourg the hours are 9am to noon and 1:30pm to 5pm Monday to Friday. Some larger branches open on Saturday mornings.

Many public payphones in Belgium and Luxembourg accept only phonecards, available at newsagents and post offices. In Brussels you can use cash in the phone booths in metro stations. There are no local area codes in Luxembourg.

THE CLIMATE OF BELGIUM AND LUXEMBOURG

Belgium and Luxembourg have a temperate climate, characterized by constant low rainfall throughout the year. Winters are usually chilly and damp, and rain may turn to snow or sleet. Summers are warmer and much brighter, but the evenings can still be cool. Spring is the driest season.

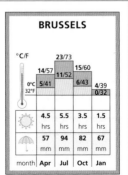

BRUSSELS			
°C/F	23/73		
	14/57	15/60	
	11/52		
0°C 5/41		6/43	4/39
32°F			0/32
4.5 hrs	5.5 hrs	3.5 hrs	1.5 hrs
57 mm	94 mm	82 mm	67 mm
month	Apr	Jul	Oct	Jan

ARRIVING BY AIR

Belgium's principal airport is Brussels National Airport, known locally as Zaventem. Flights into Luxembourg arrive at Findel Airport, which is 6 km (4 miles) east of Luxembourg City.

Airlines flying to Belgium and Luxembourg include **SN Brussels Airlines** (Belgium) and **Luxair** (Luxembourg), British Airways, American Airlines, KLM, and Lufthansa. Brussels is also served by Air Canada and Delta Air Lines. Most flights from Canada and the US go via another European city. Virgin Express and Ryanair have low-cost flights between Brussels and various European cities.

ARRIVING BY SEA

Belgium can be easily reached by ferry from Britain several times daily. **Norfolkline** has a number of crossings every day between Dover and Dunkirk. **P&O Ferries** also operates regular ferry crossings from Dover to Calais (France) and from Hull to Zeebrugge.

RAIL TRAVEL

Belgium is at the heart of Europe's high-speed train networks. **Eurostar** services between Brussels' Gare du Midi and London's Waterloo station take just under three hours. The **Thalys** network links Brussels with Amsterdam, Paris, Cologne, and Geneva.

Within Belgium train services are operated by **Belgian National Railways** (Société Nationale de Chemins de Fer Belges/Belgische Spoorwegen). The network is modern and efficient, and usually the best way to travel between major cities and towns. Luxembourg's rail system is run by **Chemins de Fer Luxembourgeois (CFL)**. In both countries a variety of rail passes is available. The Benelux Tourrail pass allows unlimited travel on any five days within a month's period in Belgium, Luxem- bourg, and the Netherlands.

TRAVELING BY BUS

In Belgium the two main long-distance bus operators are **De Lijn**, which covers routes in Flanders, and **TEC**, which provides services in Wallonia. Bus terminuses are usually close to train stations.

Luxembourg benefits from an extensive bus network, which compensates for the more limited rail system. One-day passes are available, and can be used on both long-distance and inner-city buses from the time of purchase until 8am the next day. Benelux Tourrail passes are valid on buses operated by Chemins de Fer Luxembourgeois.

TRAVELING BY CAR

Drivers from the UK can reach mainland Europe by the car train service offered by Eurotunnel. Within Belgium and Luxembourg the freeways and main roads are well-maintained and fast. Variations between the French and Flemish spellings of town names can be confusing for visitor drivers in Belgium; it is advisable to find out both names of your destination before beginning your journey. All the major car rental firms are represented in Belgium and Luxembourg, but renting a vehicle is fairly expensive.

DIRECTORY

TOURIST OFFICES

Belgium
Grand Place 1,
1000 Brussels.
Tel 02-513 8940.
www.visitbelgium.com

Luxembourg
Gare Centrale,
Luxembourg City.
Tel 42 82 82 20.
www.ont.lu

UK
Belgian Tourist Office,
217 March Wall,
London E14 9FJ.
Tel 0207 537 1132.
Tel 0800 954 5245.
www.belgium
theplaceto.be

Luxembourg Tourist Office,
122–124 Regent Street,
London W1B 5SA.
Tel 020-7434 2800.
www.luxembourg.co.uk

US

Belgian Tourist Office,
220 East 42nd St,
Suite 3402, New York, NY
10017. *Tel 212-758 8130.*
Luxembourg Tourist Office,
17 Beekman Place, New
York, NY 10022.
Tel 212-935 8888.
www.visitluxembourg.com

EMBASSIES

UK (Belgium)
Rue Arlon 85, B-1040
Brussels. *Tel 02-287 6211.*

UK (Luxembourg)
14 Blvd Roosevelt,
L-2450 Luxembourg City.
Tel 22 98 64.

US (Belgium)
Blvd du Régent 27, B-1000
Brussels. *Tel 02-508 2111.*

US (Luxembourg)
22 Blvd Emmanuel Serva
is, L-2535 Luxembourg
City.
Tel 46 01 23.

EMERGENCY NUMBERS

Belgium
Police *Tel 101.*
Ambulance and
fire services *Tel 100.*

Luxembourg
Police *Tel 113.*
All other services *Tel 112.*

AIRLINES

SN Brussels Airlines
Tel 070-35 1111 (Belgium).
Tel 0870-735 2345 (UK).
Tel 151-6740 5200 (US).
www.flysn.fr

Luxair
Tel 4798 4242
(Luxembourg).
www.luxair.lu

FERRY COMPANIES

Norfolkline
Tel 0870-870 1020 (UK).
www.norfolkline.com

P&O Ferries
Tel 08705-980 333 (UK).
www.poferries.com

RAIL TRAVEL

Belgian National Railways
Tel 02-528 2828.
www.b-rail.be

Chemins de Fer Luxembourgeois
Tel 49 90 49 90.
www.cfl.lu

Eurostar
Tel 0870-518 6186 (UK).
Tel 02-528 2828 (Belgium).
www.eurostar.com

Thalys
Tel 070-66 7788 (Belgium).
www.thalys.com

BUSES

De Lijn
Tel 01-544 0711.

TEC
Tel 01-023 5353.

Shopping & Entertainment

Belgium is an ideal place to shop for luxury goods, from fine chocolates and cutting-edge fashion to mounted diamonds. As a virtually duty-free zone, Luxembourg attracts tourists in search of cheap cigarettes and alcohol. For relatively small cities, Brussels and Luxembourg City offer a wide range of cultural events. Those who prefer outdoor activities will find plenty to entertain them. The flat Flanders region in Belgium is ideal cycling country, while the hilly Ardennes and the Petite Suisse area of Luxembourg are popular with hikers.

WHERE TO SHOP

For luxury items and gifts, one of Brussels' best shopping arcades is the **Galéries Saint-Hubert**. It houses several jewelry stores, the Belgian leather bag maker Delvaux, fine chocolate shops, and smart boutiques, including women's fashion designer Kaat Tilley. The **Galéries d'Ixelles** is full of tiny ethnic shops and cafés, while the quaint **Galérie Bortier** is the place to shop for antiquarian books and maps.

Top fashion designers are well represented in Brussels. Their outlets can be found on Avenue Louise and Boulevard de Waterloo. For the original creations of the Antwerp Six and of new wave designers, try Rue Antoine Dansaert.

Less expensive, mainstream stores, including Belgium's only department store Inno, are located in the Rue Neuve. Inno is not spectacular by British or American standards.

The principal shopping areas in Luxembourg City are the Grand Rue and its side streets, and the Auchan shopping center which is found on Kirchberg.

WHAT TO BUY

Belgian chocolate is considered by many to be the finest in the world. Among the internationally renowned *"grandes maisons de chocolat"* with stores in Brussels are **Godiva** and **Wittamer**. The sweet-toothed will also be tempted by the edible chocolate sculptures produced by **Pierre Marcolini** and by the wares of fine biscuit specialist **Dandoy**.

Another famous Belgian export is lace, though a fall in the number of people entering the trade in recent years has resulted in a shortage of authentic, handmade goods. Before purchasing an item, make sure it has not been manufactured in the Far East. Places to shop for authentic Belgian lace include **Maison F. Rubbrecht** in Brussels and the **Kant Centrum** in Bruges. The latter also has a museum of lace-making.

Specialty Belgian beers can be bought at Brussels' **Beer Mania**, while **Little Nemo** and **La Bande des Six Nez** specialize in comic-strip memorabilia. If you plan to invest in diamonds, or simply wish to gaze and admire, **Diamondland** in Antwerp is a good place to start.

Among the best buys in Luxembourg are fuel, tobacco, and alcohol, due to the low rate of duty imposed on such goods. One of the country's most famous manufacturing names is **Villeroy & Boch**, makers of fine porcelain and tableware. Their flagship store is in the Rue du Fossé in the capital. There is also a factory outlet northwest of the city center where you can buy seconds at 20 percent discount.

MARKETS

From 9am on Saturdays and Sundays, Brussels' Place du Grand Sablon is the site of a fine antiques market. Also worth visiting is the huge, vibrant market around the Gare du Midi (Sundays, 6am to 1pm), with its mix of North African and home-grown delicacies, including oils, spices, and exotic herbs.

BOOKSTORES

In Brussels, **Waterstone's** sells English-language magazines and books. For international newspapers, go to the **Librairie de Rome**.

English-language books and newspapers can be bought in Luxembourg City at the **Magasin Anglais**.

ENTERTAINMENT LISTINGS

The principal source of entertainment information in Belgium is *The Bulletin*, published weekly in English, and available from newsstands throughout the country. The magazine's listings section, *What's On*, is distributed free to hotels in the capital.

Details of events in Luxembourg are published in the "Culture" section of *L'Agenda du Luxembourg*, available from the National Tourist Office.

OPERA, CLASSICAL MUSIC, AND DANCE

Brussels' Opera House, **La Monnaie**, is among Europe's finest venues for opera. The season runs from September through to June, and most productions are sold out many months in advance.

Designed by Victor Horta in 1928, the **Palais des Beaux-Arts** is home to the Belgian National Orchestra and boasts the city's largest auditorium for classical music. The main concert season lasts from September to June.

Regular performances of contemporary dance by several leading Belgian companies take place at the Art Deco **Kaaitheater** and the **Halles de Schaerbeek**.

Luxembourg's Printemps Musical is a festival of classical music concerts and ballet that takes place in the capital throughout April and May. Principal venues include the **Conservatoire de Musique de la Ville de Luxembourg** and the **Théâtre Municipal**. The City Tourist Information Office on the Place d'Armes is able to provide more information and assist with ticket reservations.

JAZZ, ROCK, AND BLUES

One of the best places to catch good jazz acts in Brussels is **Sounds**, a large venue featuring some of Belgium's top artists. The club also has Blues nights. On Saturday and Sunday afternoons, it is worth stopping at **L'Archiduc**, a refurbished Art Deco bar in the center of town, where you can listen to jazz in a relaxed atmosphere. **Ancienne Belgique** hosts up-and-coming guitar bands, folk, Latin, and techno acts.

CINEMA

At Brussels' Bruparck *(see p229)*, the 29-screen Kinepolis cinema complex shows Hollywood block-busters and major British and French releases. Real movie fans should not miss a visit to the Musée du Cinéma in the Palais des Beaux-Arts complex. The museum shows classic films, from Chaplin to Taran-tino, with nightly programs of silent movies sometimes with a live piano accompaniment.

OUTDOOR ACTIVITIES

Belgium and Luxembourg have extensive networks of cycle tracks, and you can rent bicycles easily from a number of outlets, including many train stations. For route details the best source of information is the local tourist information office. The US-based **CBT Tours** organizes cycle tours in Belgium.

Tourist offices throughout Belgium and Luxembourg also offer walking guides and maps. To arrange hiking tours in the popular Ardennes area, contact Belgium-based **BCD**.

In Luxembourg, the lake at Echternach offers plenty of opportunities for swimming, sailing, and windsurfing, while the rivers of the Ardennes region are fine territory for canoeing and kayaking. To obtain further information on the latter, contact the **Fédération Luxembourge-oise de Canoë-Kayak**. For information on the whole range of sporting activities available contact the **City Tourist Office**.

DIRECTORY

SHOPPING ARCADES

Galérie Bortier
Rue de la Madeleine 17–19, Brussels.

Galéries d'Ixelles
Chaussée d'Ixelles, Brussels.

Galéries Saint-Hubert
Rue des Bouchers, Brussels.

SPECIALTY ITEMS

La Bande des Six Nez
Chaussée de Wavre 179, Brussels.
Tel 02-513 7258.

Beer Mania
Chaussée de Wavre 174–176, Brussels.
Tel 02-512 1788.

Dandoy
Rue au Beurre 31, Brussels.
Tel 02-511 0326.

Diamondland
Appelmansstraat 33A, Antwerp.
Tel 03-229 2990.

Godiva
Grand Place 21, Brussels.
Tel 02-511 2537.

Kant Centrum
Peperstraat 3A, Bruges.
Tel 050-33 00 72.

Little Nemo
Boulevard Lemmonier 25, Brussels.
Tel 02-514 6804.

Maison F. Rubbrecht
Grand Place 23, Brussels.
Tel 02-512 0218.

Pierre Marcolini
Rue des Minimes 1, Brussels.
Tel 02-514 1206.

Villeroy & Boch
2 Rue du Fossé, Luxembourg City.
Tel 46 33 43.

330 Rue Rollingergrund, Luxembourg City.
Tel 46 82 11.

Wittamer
Place du Grand Sablon 6–12, Brussels.
Tel 02-512 3742.
www.wittamer.com

BOOKSTORES

Librairie de Rome
16A Rue Jean Stas, Brussels.
Tel 02-511 7937.

Magasin Anglais
16 Avenue Victor Hugo, Luxembourg City.
Tel 22 49 25.

Waterstone's
Boulevard Adolphe Max 71, Brussels.
Tel 02-219 2708.

OPERA, CLASSICAL MUSIC & DANCE

Conservatoire de Musique de la Ville de Luxembourg
33 Rue Charles Martel, Luxembourg City.
Tel 47 96 55 55.

Halles de Schaerbeek
Rue Royale Sainte-Marie 22, Brussels.
Tel 02-218 2107.
www.halles.be

Kaaitheater
Square Sainteclette 20, Brussels. *Tel 01-201 5959.*
www.kaaitheater.be

La Monnaie
Place de la Monnaie, Brussels.
Tel 07-023 3939.
www.lamonnaie.be

Palais des Beaux-Arts
Rue Ravenstein 23, Brussels.
Tel 02-507 8200.
www.bozar.be

Théâtre Municipal
1 Rond-Point Robert Schuman, Luxembourg City.
Tel 47 08 95.

JAZZ, ROCK & BLUES

Ancienne Belgique
Boulevard Anspach 110, Brussels.
Tel 02-548 2424.
www.abconcerts.be

L'Archiduc
Rue Antoine Dansaert 6, Brussels.
Tel 02-512 0652.
www.archiduc.net

Sounds
Rue de la Tulipe 28, Brussels.
Tel 02-512 9250.
www.soundsjazzclub.be

OUTDOOR ACTIVITIES

CBT Tours
Tel 800-736 2453 (US).

Fédération Luxembourgeoise de Canoë-Kayak
6 Rue de Pulvermühl, L-2356, Luxembourg.
Tel 75 03 79.

Luxembourg City Tourist Office
Tel 22 28 09.
www.lcto.lu

BCD
Tel 01-571 6011 (Belgium).
www.BCDtravel.be

Where to Stay in Belgium & Luxembourg

In both countries, top end hotels offer exceptional standards of comfort to their largely corporate clients, and their prices reflect this. However, some offer substantial weekend or summer discounts, and there are also plenty of mid-range and lower budget hotel options.

PRICE CATEGORIES:
Price categories are for a standard double room per night, including tax and service. Breakfast is not included unless specified.

€ Under 80 euros
€€ 80–130 euros
€€€ 130–180 euros
€€€€ 180–260 euros
€€€€€ Over 260 euros

BRUSSELS

LOWER TOWN Aristote
€€ Map B3
Avenue de Stalingrad 7, 1000 Brussels **Tel** *02-513 1310* **Fax** *02-513 8070* **Rooms** *25*

Located in a striking-looking building between the Grand Place and the central station, Hotel Aristote occupies a renovated 19th-century townhouse with small, but elegant bedrooms and a popular pizzeria (decorated in medieval style). Staff are friendly and offer plenty of sightseeing tips and advice. **www.aristote-hotel.be**

LOWER TOWN Mozart
€€ Map C3
Rue du Marché-aux-Fromages 23, 1000 Brussels **Tel** *02-502 6661* **Fax** *02-502 7758* **Rooms** *47*

A three-star budget hotel in a fabulous location, Hotel Mozart is a great choice for young travelers looking to stay in the thick of the action. The hotel is fantastically decorated with a luxurious reception and plenty of personal touches in each of the 47 rooms. Book early to avoid disappointment. **www.hotel-mozart.be**

LOWER TOWN Hotel Metropole
€€€ Map C2
Place de Brouckère 31, 1000 Brussels **Tel** *02-217 2300* **Fax** *02-218 0220* **Rooms** *305*

Built in 1895, this plush hotel boasts striking architecture and a mix of French Renaissance, Empire, and Art Deco styles. Most rooms are decorated in period style and there are high ceilings, stained-glass, and crystal chandeliers in the lobby, bar, and gourmet restaurant. Complimentary breakfast. **www.metropolehotel.be**

LOWER TOWN Amigo
€€€€ Map C3
Rue de l'Amigo 1–3, 1000 Brussels **Tel** *02-547 4747* **Fax** *02-513 5277* **Rooms** *174*

This newly-restored five-star hotel in the Rocco Forte Hotel chain provides an elegant setting and great location just near the Grand Place. Rooms have king-size beds and marble bathrooms. Family suites are available and there is an award-winning restaurant. Meeting room, spa, and fitness facilities. **www.hotelamigo.com**

LOWER TOWN Radisson SAS Royal Hotel
€€€€ Map C2
Rue du Fosse-aux-Loups 47, 1000 Brussels **Tel** *02-219 2828* **Fax** *02-219 6262* **Rooms** *281*

A fabulous five-star hotel behind a glorious Art Deco façade (designed by famed Belgian designer, Michel Haspers), Radisson is one of the best places to stay in the city. Stunning garden and gourmet 2-star Michelin hotel restaurant. The hotel will organize city tours. **www.radisson.com**

LOWER TOWN Le Plaza
€€€€€ Map C2
Boulevard Adolphe Maxlaan 118–126, 1000 Brussels **Tel** *02-278 0100* **Fax** *02-278 0101* **Rooms** *193*

An opulent five-star hotel which regularly provides accommodation to visiting stars and gentry, Le Plaza even has its own theater. The building itself dates back to 1930 when it was built to model Paris' famous George V hotel. Rooms were renovated in 1996 to provide modern facilities. Business- and tourist-friendly. **www.leplaza-brussels.be**

UPPER TOWN Les Bluets
€€ Map C4
Rue Berckmans 124, 1060 Brussels **Tel** *02-534 3983* **Fax** *02-543 0970* **Rooms** *10*

Charming, family-run, non-smoking hotel in a 19th-century bourgeois townhouse. The 10 rooms are decorated with a laidback mix of antique furnishings, objets d'art, and modern facilities. An interesting place to stay for its characterful approach to hotellery. Small plant-covered annex. **www.bluets.be**

UPPER TOWN Hotel Le Sablon
€€€ Map C3
Rue de la Paille 2–8, 1000 Brussels **Tel** *02-513 6040* **Fax** *02-511 8141* **Rooms** *32*

A friendly boutique hotel with sauna and relaxation center, the Sablon boasts a fantastic location beside the city's main art galleries and is within walking distance of the characterful cafés on Place du Grand Sablon. Rooms are large with split-level suites and plenty of facilities. The staff are particularly helpful. **www.hesperia-sablon.com**

UPPER TOWN Stanhope
€€€€€ Map D3
Rue du Commerce 9, 1000 Brussels **Tel** *02-506 9111* **Fax** *02-512 1708* **Rooms** *96*

Providing deluxe Belgian hospitality in three converted townhouses, the five-star boutique Hotel Stanhope is decorated in English country style and delivers old-fashioned service that even stretches to chauffeur-driven cars. Elegant rooms, beautiful interior garden, and gourmet restaurant. Conference facilities. **www.stanhope.be**

Key to Symbols *see back cover flap* **Map References** *see map of Brussels pp222–3*

REST OF BELGIUM

ANTWERP 't Sandt ▤ Ⓟ €€€
Zand 13–19, 2000 Antwerp **Tel** *03-232 9390* **Fax** *03-232 5613* **Rooms** *14*

A cosy hotel in Antwerp's historical center, 't Sandt occupies a protected Neo-Rococo building from the mid-19th century that was the site of the city's first customs duty office. The 12 rooms and two apartments are individually decorated. The Cathedral Penthouse has one of the city's best views. **www.hotel-sandt.be**

ANTWERP Antwerp Hilton ⚏ ⅠⅠ �📺 Ⓟ €€€€
Groenplaats, 2000 Antwerp **Tel** *03-204 1212* **Fax** *03-204 8688* **Rooms** *211*

Well-located next to the historical cathedral, the Antwerp Hilton has some great views over the city's sights. An architectural landmark (it sits behind a listed Baroque façade), the hotel occupies part of the former Grand Bazar department store. Rooms are business-friendly with fax machines and wi-fi internet connections. **www.hilton.com**

BRUGES Bourgoensch Hof ⚏ ⅠⅠ Ⓟ €€
Wollestraat 39, 8000 Bruges **Tel** *050-33 1645* **Fax** *050-34 6378* **Rooms** *17*

Situated in Bruges' historical center near the central market, the three-star Hotel Bourgoensch Hof boasts some fabulous canal-side views. Rooms are simple, but well presented; most visitors to both the hotel and its bistro come for the views. Hotel bistro with outdoor terrace. Paid parking available on request. **www.bourgoensch-hof.be**

BRUGES Hotel de Tuilerieën ▤ Ⓟ €€€€€
Dyver 7, 8000 Bruges **Tel** *050-34 3691* **Fax** *050-34 0400* **Rooms** *45*

A luxurious four-star hotel with indoor pool, the Hotel de Tuilerieën offers a deluxe break in the heart of Bruges' medieval center. Rooms are spacious and elegantly decorated with four-poster beds and antique furnishings. Stately breakfast dining room with banquet tables and crystal chandeliers. **www.ilachateau.com/tuilerie/index.htm**

GHENT The Boatel ▤ Ⓟ €€
Voorhoutkaai 44, 9000 Ghent **Tel** *09-267 1030* **Fax** *09-267 1039* **Rooms** *7*

The two-star Boatel is a floating hotel constructed from a converted canal boat. Moored in Portus Ganda, a short walk from the center of town, its seven cosy rooms (five standard and two luxury) are carefully-decorated in various styles. Great river views! **www.theboatel.com**

GHENT Ghent River Hotel ⚏ 📺 €€€
Waaistraat 5+, 9000 Ghent **Tel** *09-266 1010* **Fax** *09-266 1015* **Rooms** *77*

This four-star riverside hotel occupies a mid-19th century rice mill on the banks of the River Leie. Although the entrance is modern, the rooms are more in keeping with the building's rich history, including wood-beamed ceilings and wooden floors. Fitness room with sauna. Bicycles for rent. **www.ghent-river-hotel.be**

LUXEMBOURG

LUXEMBOURG CITY Hotel Français ⚏ ⅠⅠ ▤ ▤ ♿ €€
14, pl d'Armes, L-1136 Luxembourg **Tel** *47 45 34* **Fax** *46 42 74* **Rooms** *25*

Friendly hotel in a fantastic location on the pedestrianized Place d'Armes in the heart of Luxembourg's old city (no access by car, but two garages nearby). Large rooms with modern bathrooms. Ask for a room on a high floor to avoid crowd noise on weekends. Gourmet restaurant with great views over the city. **www.hotelfrancais.lu**

LUXEMBOURG CITY Hôtel Le Châtelet ⅠⅠ 📺 ▤ Ⓟ €€
2, bd de la Pétrusse, L-2320 Luxembourg **Tel** *40 21 01* **Fax** *40 36 66* **Rooms** *42*

Small and welcoming three-star hotel in a peaceful location at the entrance to Petrusse Valley, within walking distance of the old city and the financial district. Rooms are split between two traditional old Luxembourg houses. All are cosy and clean. Small, rustic restaurant. Excellent breakfast. Free internet corner. **www.chatelet.lu**

LUXEMBOURG CITY Parc Beaux-Arts Hotel Luxembourg ⅠⅠ ▤ Ⓟ ♿ €€€€
1, rue Sigefroi, L-2536 Luxembourg **Tel** *26 86 76 1* **Fax** *26 86 76 36* **Rooms** *10*

First-class hotel in a fantastic location in the heart of the old city, the Parc Beaux-Arts occupies a beautifully-restored and stylishly-decorated 250-year-old building. Spacious and well-appointed rooms with views over the Grand-Ducal Palace. Generous breakfast. Children under 12 stay for free. **www.parcbeauxarts.lu**

LUXEMBOURG CITY Hotel Le Royal Luxembourg ⚏ ⅠⅠ ▤ 📺 ▤ Ⓟ ♿ €€€€€
12, bd Royal, L-2449 Luxembourg **Tel** *241 61 61* **Fax** *22 59 48* **Rooms** *210*

Elegant hotel in a fabulous location, the five-star Le Royal is one of Luxembourg's most exclusive hotels; particularly its 'Royal Club Wing' with superior rooms and suites. There is wi-fi in public areas and two top restaurants with outside dining. Ask for a room overlooking the park. Rated as one of the world's leading hotels. **www.hotelroyal.lu**

Where to Eat in Belgium & Luxembourg

Belgians love food, and their cooking reflects this. Choose from the plethora of top gastronomic restaurants concentrated in Brussels or opt for one of the many unpretentious eateries serving local specialties. Luxembourg has its fair share of haute-cuisine restaurants with good value set lunches available.

PRICE CATEGORIES:
Price categories are for a three-course meal for one, including a half-bottle of house wine, tax, and service:
€ Under 25 euros
€€ 25–40 euros
€€€ 40–50 euros
€€€€ 50–65 euros
€€€€€ Over 65 euros

BRUSSELS

LOWER TOWN 't Kelderke   €€
Grand Place 15, 1000 **Tel** *02-513 7344*   **Map** *B3*

On the Grand Place, this cellar restaurant is as busy as you may expect but the feel is decidedly genuine. Moules-frites (mussels and French fries) are served in their traditional, huge black pails at a fast and furious pace. Expect to wait for a table, but not for too long.

LOWER TOWN L'Achepot   €€
Place Ste-Catherine 1, 1000 **Tel** *02-511 6221*   **Map** *B2*

This small, family-run Brussels tavern off the Vismarkt (fish market) serves fish simply but very well. Apart from the seafood, try the traditional *stoemp* (a coarse mash with vegetables and sausages) and *chèvre* (goat's cheese) salad; if you're feeling more adventurous, there is a wide range of offal dishes, including kidneys, brain, tripe, and liver.

LOWER TOWN In 't Spinnekopke   ♿🖼   €€€
Place du Jardin aux Fleurs, 1000 **Tel** *02-511 8695*   **Map** *B3*

A superb example of quality Belgian food can be found in this intimate former 17th-century coaching inn. In 't Spinnekopke (In the Spider's Head) has a strong range of unusual local beers and items on the menu that are cooked in them. Friendly service and a wonderful terrace in an area that's off the beaten track.

LOWER TOWN L'Ogenblik   🖼   €€€€
Galeries des Princes 1, 1000 **Tel** *02-511 6151*   **Map** *C3*

In the center of the stunning Saint Hubert's Galleries, this thirty-year-old Parisian-style bistro with a relaxed ambience is a gastronomic wonder. Dishes such as duck magret carpaccio with parmesan cuttings, or sea bass fillet with aubergine (eggplant) caviar are a gourmand's delight.

LOWER TOWN Aux Arcades   ♿🖼   €€€€€
Rue des Bouchers 36, 1000 **Tel** *02-514 0819*   **Map** *C3*

One of the better establishments in the often-busy restaurant alley next to the Grand Place, Aux Arcades is decorated in the style of 17th-century Flemish art and is famous for its bouillabaisse. As with most places along Rue des Bouchers, stick to the fixed menu and you will get yourself a relative bargain.

LOWER TOWN Comme Chez Soi   ♿👥   €€€€€
Place Rouppe 23, 1000 **Tel** *02-512 2921*   **Map** *B3*

Widely regarded as the city's best restaurant, Comme Chez Soi, with its three Michelin stars, is particularly strong in the game department. A mahogany bar and over-stuffed leather couches all feature in the lounge area. Not to be missed is the signature *Mi-cuit au Chocolat Belge Grand Cru*, a hot chocolate dessert. Book well in advance.

UPPER TOWN De Ultieme Hallucinatie   ♿👥   €€€
Rue Royale 316, 1000 **Tel** *02-217 0614*   **Map** *D2*

Constructed in 1850 and transformed in 1904, this is the city's only remaining restaurant with an original Art Nouveau interior. Recommended specialties include the pike in Cantillon *gueuze* beer. The venue hosts a trilingual "Afterwork Party" from 5pm on the first Thursday of every month.

UPPER TOWN L'Idiot du Village   ♿   €€€€
Rue Notre-Seigneur 19, 1000 **Tel** *02-502 5582*   **Map** *B4*

The fifteen-year-old Village Idiot is reportedly a favored establishment of foreign ministers and even Belgian royalty. No wonder, with such intriguing concoctions as the escalope of hot *foie gras*, pepper and vanilla, served on earthy crockery of a more rustic era. Reservations are recommended at this extremely popular eatery.

UPPER TOWN La Tortue du Zoute   ♿👥🖼   €€€€
Rue de Rollebeek 31, 1000 **Tel** *02-513 1062*   **Map** *C3*

While the menu at the Tortue is solidly based around the lobster – for which the chefs offer ten different preparations – other wonders of the sea receive no less consideration. The bistro is located on a delightful, descending cobbled pedestrian street filled with boutiques and other restaurants.

Key to Symbols *see back cover flap* **Map References** *see map of Brussels pp222–3*

REST OF BELGIUM

ANTWERP Rooden Hoed
€€€

Oude Koornmarkt 25, 2000 **Tel** *03-233 2844*

As the oldest restaurant in Antwerp – it first served food back in 1750 – the Rooden Hoed is one of the city's most renowned eateries. It specializes in seafood, especially mussels, of which there are at least half a dozen ways of having them cooked. You can have a pre-dinner drink in the restaurant's medieval cellar.

ANTWERP P. Preud'Homme
€€€€

Suikerrui 28, 2000 **Tel** *03-233 4200*

Providing a memorable dining experience in the grand surroundings of a beautiful Art Nouveau building, P. Preud'Homme is one of Antwerp's finest restaurants. Its menu includes fine fare such as lobster, game, terrine, and scallops, and the wine list to accompany it is of suitably high quality.

BRUGES De Stove
€€

Kleine Sint-Amandsstraat 4, 8000 **Tel** *050-337835*

The very intimate De Stove has room for just 20 patrons, so with its simple furnishings and eponymous iron stove, is the perfect place for a romantic evening. The *foie gras* and duck are exceptional, but be sure not to miss the fresh North Sea fish, supplied daily – particularly the breaded cod in butter sauce.

BRUGES De Visscherie
€€€€

Vismarkt 8, 8000 **Tel** *050-330212*

Thirty years ago, Mr and Mrs Tillo Declercq opened De Visscherie, a seafood restaurant overlooking the centuries-old Vismarkt (fish market). The house's signature dish is the monkfish waterzooi with saffron, but try any of the turbot variations. The establishment is a popular destination for locals, so book ahead.

BRUGES De Karmeliet
€€€€€

Langestraat 19, 8000 **Tel** *050-338259*

Regarded as the best restaurant in Bruges. In 1996 chef Geert Van Hecke became the first Flemish chef to be awarded three Michelin stars. The servings are substantial, as is common in Flanders. Many dishes are made with Belgian genever (a type of schnapps). The potato bouillon with shrimp and cod, despite sounding rather humble, is a favorite.

GHENT Coeur d'Artichaut
€€€

Onderbergen 6, 9000 **Tel** *09-225 3318*

A renowned restaurant in the centre of Ghent, Coeur d'Artichaut has a menu that changes every month. Featuring classic European dishes with a twist in addition to inventive Asian selections, it is housed in an impressive mansion building that also incorporates a patio area. A lunch menu is also available. Closed on Sundays and Mondays.

GHENT Georges
€€€€

Donkersteeg 23–27, 9000 **Tel** *09-225 1918*

A Ghent institution, this friendly seafood restaurant is now over eighty years old, having remained in the same family the whole time. Georges, a father-and-son operation, is one of Ghent's pricier addresses, but offers superior, far from indifferent service. The oysters, crab and mussels of Lélande are the main attraction here.

LUXEMBOURG

LUXEMBOURG CITY Le Bouquet Garni
€€€€

32, rue de l'Eau, L-1449 Luxembourg **Tel** *26 20 06 20*

Charming French restaurant in a beautifully restored 18th-century mansion in heart of the old city. Chefs Lysiane and Thierry Duhr delight customers with delicious, but well-priced set menus and original one-off mains using locally-caught game. Sister bistro, Salon Saint-Michel, can be found on the ground floor.

LUXEMBOURG CITY Clairefontaine
€€€€€

Place de Clairefontaine 9, L-1341 Luxembourg **Tel** *46 22 11*

Elegant French restaurant decorated with old wood paneling and expensive silverware. Meet on the private terrace for pre-meal aperitifs to enjoy views of Place Clairefontaine and the cathedral. Impressive set 'temptation', 'champagne' or 'gourmet' menus, as well as mouthwatering à la carte dining. Advance booking recommended.

LUXEMBOURG CITY Restaurant Speltz
€€€€€

8, rue Chimay, L-1333 Luxembourg **Tel** *47 49 50*

Stylish and welcoming Michelin-starred restaurant located a stone's throw from the Grand-Ducal Palace, Speltz has built its reputation on its contemporary blend of local produce from France and Luxembourg. Popular mains include roast saddle of veal in Savoy cabbage and pike-perch fillet with potato scales. Good choice of vegetarian dishes.

THE NETHERLANDS

*S*ituated at the mouth of the River Rhine, the Netherlands is a man-made country that owes its life to the sea: much of the land once lay under water, and a maritime trading tradition was the principal source of the nation's wealth, most notably in the 17th century. The Netherlands is also one of the world's most liberal countries, with a long history of cultural and racial tolerance.

The shape of the Netherlands (or Holland, as it is also known) has changed dramatically over the last 2,000 years. Medieval maps show nearly half of the country under water, but since then large areas have been reclaimed from the sea; the current shoreline is maintained by a drainage system of windmills, dykes, and canals.

With some 16 million people in just 41,547 sq km (16,041 sq miles) of land, it is the third most densely populated country in Europe (after Monaco and Malta), but this is barely perceptible to the visitor. Only when arriving by plane do you see how much of the area is still covered with water, and how little precious land remains. The orderly Dutch cities and towns never seem overcrowded, but homes are often small, with steep, narrow staircases and modest gardens. Given the fragility of their environment, it is understandable that the Dutch are so good at preserving it.

The three biggest cities – Amsterdam, the capital, Rotterdam, the industrial hub, and the Hague, the seat of government – are all in the west of the country, part of the urban conglomeration known as the Randstad.

HISTORY

Between the 4th and 8th centuries AD, after the collapse of the Roman Empire, the area corresponding to present-day Holland was conquered by the Franks. As with all the Low Countries, it was later ruled by the House of Burgundy, before passing into the hands of the Habsburgs. When the Habsburg Empire was divided in 1555, the region came under the control of the Spanish branch of the family, which caused the Dutch Revolt of 1568, led by William I of Orange. The Dutch Republic was finally established in 1579, with the Treaty of Utrecht, but it took until 1648 for the Spanish officially to recognize its sovereignty.

Skating on a frozen Dutch river, flanked by drainage windmills

◁ Boats anchored at the canalside in Amsterdam

The battle for independence and the need for wealth to fight the Spanish armies stimulated trading success overseas. The Dutch colonized much of Indonesia and established a profitable empire based on spice. The Dutch East India Company thrived, and in the New World Holland briefly ruled over large parts of Brazil. Tulip bulbs were imported from Turkey and cultivated behind the dunes, thus beginning a lucrative flower industry that still flourishes today. However, war with England radically trimmed Dutch sea-power by the end of

William I of Orange (1533–84), leader of the Dutch Revolt

the 17th century, and from then on the country's fortunes waned. In 1795 French troops ousted William V of Orange, and in 1813, with the retreat of Napoleon, the Netherlands united with Belgium, its neighbor, an arrangement which lasted for 17 years.

KEY DATES IN DUTCH HISTORY

300–700 Region ruled by the Franks

1419 Philip the Good of Burgundy begins to unify the Low Countries

1482 The Netherlands pass by marriage to the Austrian Habsburgs

1555 Philip II of Spain inherits the Netherlands

1568 The Dutch Revolt ends Spanish rule

1579 The northern districts unite, forming the Republic of the United Netherlands

1602 The Dutch East India Company founded

1634 Tulip mania begins

1606–69 Life of Rembrandt

1648 Spain recognizes Dutch independence

1794–1813 The Napoleonic era brings the Netherlands under French control

1914–18 Holland is neutral during World War I

1940–45 The country is occupied by Germany throughout most of World War II

1949 The Dutch East Indies gain independence, becoming Indonesia

1957 The Netherlands signs the Treaty of Rome, and joins European Community

1981 Amsterdam is recognized as the cultural capital of the Netherlands

2000 Parliament legalizes controlled euthanasia

2002 The euro replaces the Dutch guilder

The Netherlands remained neutral in both World Wars, and although it escaped occupation in 1914, the Nazi invasion of 1940 left lasting scars on the nation. In the 1960s the country became a haven for the hippy counter-culture, an influence which is still visible today.

LANGUAGE AND CULTURE

Dutch, or Netherlandic, is a Germanic language which derives from the speech of the Western Franks. A number of dialects are spoken, and in Friesland the dialect (Fries) shows Celtic influences. Nevertheless, as in so many European countries, the dialects are disappearing due to the popularity of national television stations on which a standardized version of Dutch is usually spoken.

Culturally, Holland has a huge amount to offer. Its rich history is reflected in countless old buildings and its large number of fine museum collections. The compact size of the city centers makes it easy to stroll along a canal admiring gabled houses, and step into a museum for an hour or two, before ending the day at a nearby café or pub. The Dutch also have much to boast in the realm of the performing arts, so visitors should find time to enjoy one of the world-famous orchestras or modern dance companies, or attend an organ concert in an old church, or simply spend an evening in one of Amsterdam's jazz clubs.

A fiercely independent people, the Dutch have long been champions of freedom, and have a traditional tolerance of minorities. Jews have been welcome for centuries, and although Catholicism was banned after independence, the authorities turned a blind eye to its practice. Today that tolerance is extended to asylum seekers, gays and lesbians, and people of different backgrounds. A respect for the right to live one's own life underlies the liberal laws on prostitution and drugs.

Exploring the Netherlands

Although the Netherlands' seat of government is at The Hague, Amsterdam is the nominal capital, and it is here that the main cultural attractions can be found. The folkloric villages of Marken and Volendam are only a short drive away, as are the towns of Alkmaar, famous for its traditional cheese market, Haarlem, with its nearby bulbfields, and Utrecht, with its medieval churches. The port of Rotterdam, the pottery center of Delft, and the university town of Leiden lie to the south and west.

SIGHTS AT A GLANCE

Alkmaar ❸
AMSTERDAM pp248–259 ❶
Delft ❾
Haarlem ❹
The Hague ❽
Leiden ❼

Marken and Volendam ❷
Paleis Het Loo ❺
Rotterdam ❿
Utrecht ❻

THE NETHERLANDS

See main map

Groningen
NETHERLANDS
AMSTERDAM
Enschede
The Hague
Rotterdam
GERMANY
Eindhoven
Antwerp
Cologne
BELGIUM

0 km 90
0 miles 90

Typical Dutch rural scene, with children wearing traditional dress

KEY

✈ Airport
⛴ Ferry port
— Highway
═ Major road
— Railroad
▪▪▪ International border

0 kilometers 20
0 miles 20

Ameland
Terschelling
Vlieland
W a d d e n z e e
A31
Leeuwarden
Harlingen
Groningen
Texel
A7
A7
Heerenveen
A32
Den Helder
Meppel
N9
N242
IJsselmeer
A50
Emmerloord
Enkhuizen
A6
N50
N302
Kampen
Zwolle
❸ Alkmaar • Hoorn
Markermeer
Lelystad
N247
❷ Marken and Volendam
A28
Haarlem ❹ AMSTERDAM
A6
Harderwijk
❶
N302
Schiphol ✈ N E T H E R L A N D S
N201 Hilversum
Paleis Het Loo ❺
A4
Amersfoort
A1
Enschede
❼ Leiden
A50
N11
❻ Utrecht
Duisburg
NORTH SEA
The Hague ❽ (Den Haag)
A12
A12
Arnhem
Hoek van Holland
Delft ❾ ✈
Gouda
Lek
A2
A15
Tiel
A52
Hull, Harwich
Leerdam
Waal
Vlaardingen
❿ Rotterdam
Lek
A27
Nijmegen
A15
A50
Antwerp • Dordrecht
Eindhoven
Eindhoven

Amsterdam ❶

Amsterdam was founded around 1200 as a small fishing village on marshland at the mouth of the Amstel river. The young township grew to become the chief trading city of northern Europe, and, in the 17th century, the center of a massive empire. With a population of almost 800,000, today Amsterdam is a place where beauty and serenity coexist happily with a slightly seamy side. From the seedy nightspots of the Red Light District, to the grace and elegance of the city's 17th-century canal houses and the rich cultural heritage of its museums, Amsterdam boasts a variety of attractions.

SIGHTS AT A GLANCE

Amsterdams Historisch
 Museum ⑨
Anne Frank Huis ⑩
Begijnhof ⑧
Golden Bend ⑫
Joods Historisch Museum ⑤
Jordaan ⑪
Koninklijk Paleis ⑦
Museum Amstelkring ②
Museum Het Rembrandthuis ④
Nederlands
 Scheepvaartmuseum ⑭
Nemo ⑬
Nieuwe Kerk ⑥
Oude Kerk ①
Plantage ⑮
Red Light District ③
Rijksmuseum pp256–7 ⑯
Stedelijk Museum ⑱
Van Gogh Museum ⑰

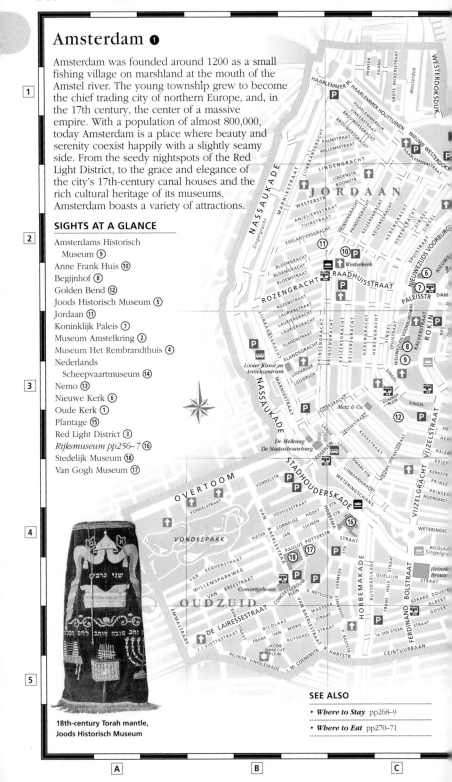

**18th-century Torah mantle,
Joods Historisch Museum**

SEE ALSO

• *Where to Stay* pp268–9

• *Where to Eat* pp270–71

GETTING AROUND

The most useful tram routes for tourists are lines 1, 2, 4, 5, 7, 9, 14, and 16, which go south from Centraal Station and branch out to all the main sights. Lines 13, 14, and 17 lead west to Jordaan. Buses 22 and 32 serve Nemo and the Scheepvaartmuseum, which you cannot reach by tram. A canalbus service runs from the Singelgracht to Centraal Station, stopping at the city's major landmarks.

17th-century clandestine Catholic church, at the Museum Amstelkring

KEY

▨	Sight / Place of interest
🚉	Train station
🚌	Bus station
🚊	Main tram stop
⛴	Canalbus boarding point
⛴	Tour boat boarding point
P	Parking
ℹ	Tourist information
✝	Church
✡	Synagogue
	Pedestrian street

0 meters 500

0 yards 500

Houseboats on Prinsengracht, in Amsterdam's western canal ring

The Oude Kerk, a calm and peaceful haven at the heart of the Red Light District

Oude Kerk ①

Oudekerksplein 23. **Tel** 020-625 8284. ▣ 4, 9, 16, 24, 25. ◻ daily (Sun: pm only). ● Jan 1, Apr 30, Dec 25. ✝ 11am Sun. ▨ ♿ www.oudekerk.nl

The origins of the Oude Kerk (Old Church) go back to the early 13th century, when a wooden church was built on a burial ground on a sand bank. The present Gothic structure is 14th century, and has grown from a single-aisled church into a basilica. As it expanded, the building became a gathering place for traders and a refuge for the poor. Though many of its paintings and statues were destroyed following the Alteration in 1578, the delicate 15th-century vault paintings on the gilded ceiling escaped damage. In 1755 the paintings were hidden with layers of blue paint and were not revealed until 200 years later in 1955. The Oude Kerk's beautiful stained-glass windows were also undamaged in the ransackings of the late 16th century. The Lady Chapel, which dates from 1552, contains some of the best stained glass. The magnificent oak-encased Great Organ, the work of Jan Westerman, was added to the church in 1724.

Museum Amstelkring ②

Oudezijds Voorburgwal 40. **Tel** 020-624 6604. ▣ 4, 9, 16, 24, 25. ◻ daily (Sun and public hols: pm only). ● Jan 1, Apr 30. ▨ ♿ www.museumamstelkring.nl

Tucked away on the edge of the Red Light District is a restored 17th-century canal house, with two smaller houses to the rear. The combined upper floors conceal a Catholic church,

The opulent 17th-century parlor at the Museum Amstelkring

known as Ons' Lieve Heer op Solder (Our Lord in the Attic). After the Alteration, when Amsterdam officially became Protestant, many such clandestine churches sprang up around the city. Built in 1663, the one here served the Catholic community until 1887, when the nearby St. Nicolaaskerk was completed. Above the mock marble altar is Jacob de Wit's glorious painting *The Baptism of Christ* (1716). The tiny box bedroom where the resident priest slept is hidden off a bend in the stairs.

The lower floors of the building became a museum in 1888, and today contain elegantly refurbished rooms, as well as a fine collection of church silver, religious arti-facts, and paintings. Restored to its former opulence, the parlor is a splendid example of a living room in the Dutch Classical style of the 17th century.

Red Light District ③

▣ 4, 9, 14, 16, 24, 25.

Prostitution in Amsterdam dates back to the city's emergence as a port in the 13th century. By 1478 it had become so widespread that attempts were made to contain it. Prostitutes straying outside their designated area were marched back to the sound of pipe and drum. A century later the Calvinists tried to outlaw the practice,

The Death of the Virgin Mary by Dirk Crabeth, one of three restored stained-glass windows in the Oude Kerk's Lady Chapel

For hotels and restaurants in this region see pp268–9 and pp270–71

but their attempts were half-hearted, and by the mid-17th century prostitution was openly tolerated. In 1850 Amsterdam had a population of 200,000 and a total of 200 brothels, most of which catered for rich clients.

Today, Amsterdam's Red Light District, known locally as de Walletjes (the little walls), is centered around the Oude Kerk. The area is criss-crossed by a network of tiny lanes lined with garish sex shops and seedy clubs. At night the little alleys assume a somewhat sinister aspect, and it is not wise to wander around alone, but by day hordes of visitors generate a festive atmosphere, and among the sleaze there are interesting restaurants, bars, and cafés, and beautiful canalside houses to be discovered.

Museum Het Rembrandthuis ④

Jodenbreestraat 4. *Tel* 020-520 0400.
Ⓜ *Nieuwmarkt.* 🚊 *9, 14.* ⭘ *daily.*
⬤ *Jan 1.* 🈚 ◩ ◪ ▢
www.rembrandthuis.nl

Born in Leyden, Rembrandt (1606–69) worked and taught in this house from 1639 until 1656. He lived in the ground-floor rooms with his wife, Saskia, who died here in 1642, leaving the artist with a baby son, Titus. Many of the artist's most famous paintings were created in the first-floor studio, which, along with the other rooms in the house, has been restored and refurbished to show exactly how it looked in the 17th century. On display is an excellent selection of Rembrandt's etchings and drawings, including various self-portraits showing the artist in different moods and guises. There are also landscapes, nude studies, and religious pieces, as well as temporary exhibitions of other artists' works.

Interior of the Grote Synagoge, part of the Joods Historisch Museum

Joods Historisch Museum ⑤

Nieuwe Amstelstraat 1. *Tel* 020-531 0310. Ⓜ *Waterlooplein.* 🚊 *9, 14.*
🚊 *Muziektheater.* ⭘ *daily.*
⬤ *Yom Kippur.* 🈚 ◪ *on request.*
🈯 www.jhm.nl

This complex of four synagogues was built in the 17th and 18th centuries by the Ashkenazi Jews, who arrived in Amsterdam from eastern Europe in the 1630s.

At first restricted to working in certain trades, the Ashkenazi Jews were granted full civil equality in 1796. Their synagogues were central to Jewish life in Amsterdam until the devastation caused by the Nazi occupation of World War II, which left them empty. The buildings were restored in the 1980s and connected by internal walkways. In 1987 they opened as a museum dedicated to Jewish culture and the history of Judaism in the Netherlands.

The impressive Grote Synagoge, with its bright and airy interior, was designed by Elias Bouman and first opened in 1671. Next door is the Nieuwe Synagoge (New Synagogue), built in 1752. It is dominated by the wooden Holy Ark (1791), which came from a synagogue in Enkhuizen in northern Holland.

Religious art and artifacts on display include Hanukah lamps, Torah mantles, and scroll finials. The buildings were renovated in 2006; a print room was created in the basement and a children's museum on the top floor.

18th-century Torah scroll finial

The house where Rembrandt lived and worked in the mid-17th century

Nieuwe Kerk ⑥

Dam. **Tel** *020-638 6909.* 🚊 *1, 2, 4, 5 & many others.* ⏰ *during exhibitions only.* 🖼 ♿ 🖥 🏪
www.nieuwekerk.nl

Dating from the late 14th century, Amsterdam's second parish church was built as the population outgrew the Oude Kerk *(see p250)*. During its turbulent history, the Nieuwe Kerk (New Church) has been destroyed by fire, rebuilt, and then stripped of its treasures after the Alteration of 1578, when the Calvinists took civil power.

Albert Vinckenbrinck's flamboyant carved pulpit (1664) is the focal point of the church interior, reflecting the Protestant belief that the sermon is central to worship. Other notable features include Jacob van Campen's ornate Great Organ (1645) and, in the apse, the tomb of the famous 17th-century commander-in-chief of the Dutch Navy, Admiral de Ruyter (1607–76), by Rombout Verhulst.

The splendid Classical façade of the 17th-century Koninklijk Paleis

Rombout Verhulst's memorial to Michiel de Ruyter in the apse of the Nieuwe Kerk

Koninklijk Paleis ⑦

Dam. **Tel** *020-624 8698.* 🚊 *1, 2, 4, 5 & many others.* ⏰ *phone for details or consult website.* ⚫ *public hols and when Queen in residence.* 🖼 🎥 *2pm Wed & Sun.* ♿
www.koninklijkhuis.nl

The Koninklijk Paleis, still used occasionally by the Dutch royal family for official functions, was built as the Stadhuis (Town Hall). Work began on this vast sandstone edifice in 1648, after the end of the 80 Years' War with Spain. It dominated its surroundings, and more than 13,600 piles were driven into the ground for the foundations.

The Classically inspired design by Jacob van Campen (1595–1657) reflects the city's mood of confidence after the Dutch victory. Civic pride is also shown in the allegorical sculptures by Artus Quellin (1609–68), which decorate the pediments, and in François Hemony's statues and carillon.

Inside, the full magnificence of the architecture is best appreciated in the huge Burgerzaal (Citizens' Hall). Based on the assembly halls of ancient Rome, this 29-m (95-ft) high room runs the length of the building, and boasts a superb marble floor inlaid with maps of the eastern and western hemispheres, as well as epic sculptures by Quellien. Most of the furniture on display, including the chairs, clocks, and chandeliers, dates from 1808, when Louis Bonaparte took over the building as his royal palace.

Amsterdams Historisch Museum ⑧

Kalverstraat 92, Nieuwezijds Voorburgwal 357, St. Luciensteeg 27. **Tel** *020-523 1822.* 🚊 *1, 2, 4, 5, 9 & many others.* ⏰ *daily.* ⚫ *Jan 1, Apr 30, Dec 25.* 🖼 🎥 ♿ 🖥 🏪
www.ahm.nl

The convent of St. Lucien was turned into a civic orphanage in the latter half of the 16th century. The original red-brick convent was enlarged over the years, and in 1975 it opened as the city's historical museum.

The permanent exhibitions are housed around the inner courtyard of the complex. Clear signposting allows the visitor either to concentrate on a specific period – *The Young City, The Mighty City*, or *The Modern City* – or to take a grand tour through the entire history of Amsterdam.

The museum's largest section, *The Mighty City*, focuses on trade, commerce, and culture during the period of Amsterdam's Golden Age. Items on display range from a globe belonging to the famous cartographer Willem Blaeu to a late 18th-century model of an East Indiaman.

Amsterdam's wealth from trade attracted great artists, who chronicled the era in extraordinary detail. There are views of the city and the port, and portraits of prominent and ordinary citizens. Some works, such as Jacob de Wit's *Maid of Amsterdam* (1741), celebrate the glory of the city in heroic, allegorical style. Others give a realistic picture of the life of the paupers and orphans. The paintings of anatomy lessons include one by Rembrandt, *The Anatomy Lesson of Dr. Jan Deijman* (1656). This shows the dissection of "Black Jan," a convicted criminal who had been hanged.

In the Civic Guards' Gallery hangs a series of group portraits of the various militia companies charged with defending law and order in the city in the 16th and 17th centuries. Paintings by Rembrandt and Cornelis Anthonisz stand out among lesser-known works.

One of the museum's most extraordinary exhibits is the 17th-century 5.30-m (17-ft) statue of Goliath that stands in the restaurant.

Statue of Goliath (c.1650) in the Amsterdams Historisch Museum

Begijnhof ⑨

Spui. 🚊 1, 2, 5, 9, 14, 16, 24, 25. **Tel** 020-623 3565. ⭕ daily

The Begijnhof was built in 1346 as a sanctuary for the Begijntjes, a lay Catholic sisterhood who lived like nuns, although they took no monastic vows. In return for

lodgings within the complex, these worthy women undertook to educate the poor and look after the sick. Although none of the earliest dwellings survives, the rows of beautiful houses that overlook the Begijnhof's well-kept green include Amsterdam's oldest surviving house, Het Houten Huis, at No. 34. Dating from around 1420, it is one of only two wooden-fronted houses in the city, since timber buildings were banned in 1521 after a series of catastrophic fires. On a wall directly behind No. 34 is a collection of fascinating stone plaques, illustrating biblical themes.

The southern side of the square is dominated by the Engelse Kerk (English Church), which dates from the 15th century and retains its original medieval tower. The church was confiscated after the Alteration and rented to a group of English and Scottish Presbyterians in 1607. Directly opposite is the Begijnhof Chapel (Nos. 29–30), a well-preserved clandestine church, where the Begijntjes worshipped in secret until religious tolerance was restored in 1795. It once housed relics of the 1345 Miracle of Amsterdam. Four stained-glass windows depict scenes of the Miracle.

Anne Frank Huis ⑩

Prinsengracht 267. **Tel** 020-556 7100. 🚊 13, 14, 17. ⛴ Prinsengracht. ⭕ daily (Jan 1 & Dec 25: pm only). ⬤ Yom Kippur. 📷 **www**.annefrank.org

For two years during World War II, the Frank and Van Daan families, both Jewish, hid here until their betrayal to the Nazis. The 13-year-old Anne began her famous diary in July 1942. First published in 1947 as *Het Achterhuis (The Annex)*, and since translated into dozens of languages, the journal gives a moving account of growing up under persecution, and of life in confinement. Anne made her last entry in August 1944, three days before her family was arrested.

Visitors to the Anne Frank Huis climb to the second floor where an introductory video is shown. You then enter the annex where the families hid via the revolving bookcase that concealed its entrance. The rooms are now empty, except for the posters in Anne's room and Otto Frank's model of the annex as it was during the occupation. The house also has exhibitions on World War II and anti-Semitism. Try to arrive early – with 900,000 visitors a year, the museum gets very crowded.

Family photograph of Anne Frank (1929–45)

Attractive gabled houses and central green of Amsterdam's Begijnhof, which is still occupied by single women

The Westerkerk, designed by Hendrick de Keyser, overlooking Prinsengracht in Jordaan

Jordaan ⑪

🚋 13, 14, 17.

The Jordaan grew up at the same time that Amsterdam's Grachtengordel (Canal Ring) was being developed in the first half of the 17th century. The marshy area to the west of the more fashionable canals was set aside as an area for workers whose industries were banned from the town center. Its network of narrow streets and waterways followed the course of old paths and drainage ditches. Immigrants fleeing religious persecution also settled here. It is thought that Huguenot refugees called the district *jardin* (garden), later corrupted to "Jordaan."

Flowing through the heart of the district are the tranquil tree-lined canals known as the Egelantiersgracht and the Bloemgracht. The canalside residences of the Egelantiersgracht were originally settled by artisans, while the Bloemgracht was a center for dye and paint manufacture. One of the most charming spots along the Egelantiersgracht is **St. Andrieshofje** at Nos. 107–114. This *hofje* (almshouse) was built in 1617 and the passage that leads to its courtyard is decorated with splendid blue and white tiles.

The 85-m (272-ft) high tower of the **Westerkerk** soars above Jordaan's streets, and gives panoramic views of the city. Begun in 1620, the church has the largest nave of any Dutch Protestant church.

Historically a poor area, recently Jordaan has taken on a bohemian air. Among the old workers' houses are quirky shops selling anything from designer clothes to old sinks, and lively brown cafés and bars, which spill onto the sidewalks in summer.

Golden Bend ⑫

🚋 1, 2, 4, 5, 9, 14 & many others.
Kattenkabinet *Tel* 020-626 5378.
🕐 10am–2pm Tue–Fri; pm Sat & Sun. ⬤ public hols.

The most impressive canal-side architecture in the city can be seen along the section of the Herengracht between Leidestraat and Vijzelstraat.

This stretch of canal is known as the Golden Bend because of the great wealth of the shipbuilders, merchants, and politicians who began building houses here in the 1660s. Most of the opulent mansions have been turned into offices or banks, but their elegance gives an insight into the lifestyle of the earliest residents.

Two of the finest and best-preserved buildings are No. 412, designed by Philips Vingboons in 1664, and No. 475, with its two sculpted female figures over the front door. Built in 1730, the latter is an example of the Louis XIV style, which became popular in the 18th century. The **Kattenkabinet** (Cat Museum), at No. 497, is one of the few houses on the Golden Bend accessible to the public. It is well worth visiting for its rather unusual collection of feline artifacts. Also on view here are some splendid paintings by Jacob de Wit (1695–1754) and an attractive formal garden.

Ornate capital from the façade of a building on the Golden Bend

THE GRACHTENGORDEL

Faced with a rapidly growing population, at the beginning of the 17th century Amsterdam's town planner, Hendrick Staets, formed an ambitious project to quadruple the size of

the city. In 1614, work began on cutting three new residential canals, collectively known as the Grachtengordel (Canal Ring), to encircle the existing city. Built for the wealthiest citizens, the grand houses along the Keizersgracht (Emperor's Canal), Herengracht (Gentleman's Canal), and Prinsengracht (Prince's Canal) represent Amsterdam's finest architecture, and are a testimony to the city's Golden Age.

Seeing the world through a soap bubble at Nemo

Nemo ⑬

Oosterdok 2. **Tel** 0900-91 91 100.
🚋 22, 32. ⏰ 10am–5pm Tue–Sun.
⬤ Jan 1, Apr 30, Dec 25. 📷 ♿
www.e-nemo.nl

In June 1997 Holland's national science center moved to this curved building that protrudes 30 m (99 ft) over the water. Divided into five themed zones (Inter-activity, Technology, Energy, Science, and Humanity), which are updated every three years, the center presents techno-logical innovations in a way that allows visitors' creativity full expression. You can inter-act with virtual reality, operate the latest industrial equipment under expert supervision, harness science to produce a work of art, participate in countless games, experiments, demonstrations, and work-shops, and take in a variety of lectures and films.

Nederlands Scheep-vaartmuseum ⑭

Kattenburgerplein 1. **Tel** 020-523 2222. 🚌 22, 32. ⬤ Oosterdok, Kattenburgergracht. ⏰ Tue–Sun (mid-Jun–mid-Sep: daily).
⬤ Jan 1, Apr 30, Dec 25. 📷 ♿
www.scheepvaartmuseum.nl

Once the arsenal of the Dutch Navy, this vast Classical sand-stone edifice was built in 1656. It is supported by 18,000 piles driven into the bed of the Oosterdok. The Navy stayed in residence here until 1973, when the building was converted into the National Maritime Museum, holding the largest collection of boats in the world. Displays of real ships, models, and maps give a survey of the country's seafaring tradition.

One of the museum's finest original exhibits is a 17-m (54-ft) long gilded barge, made in 1818 for King William I. The vessel was last used in 1962 for Queen Juliana's 25th wedding anniversary celebra-tions. Another major attraction is a full-size model of a Dutch East Indiaman, the *Amsterdam*. During the 16th century the Dutch East India Company used such vessels to sail as far as China, Japan, and Indonesia in the development of the spice trade. The museum is currently being renovated. The *Amsterdam* remains open and part of the collection is on show at other locations (visit the website for up-to-date information).

Seals basking in a pool at the Artis zoological complex in Plantage

Plantage ⑮

🚋 6, 9, 14. **Artis** Plantage Kerklaan 30–40. **Tel** 020-523 3400. ⏰ daily.
📷 🍴 ♿ **Hortus Botanicus Amsterdam** Plantage Middenlaan 2. **Tel** 020-625 8411. ⏰ daily. ⬤ Jan 1, Dec 25. 📷 🍴 ♿ **Hollandse Schouwburg** Plantage Middenlaan 24. **Tel** 020-531 0340. ⏰ daily. ⬤ Yom Kippur. ♿

Plantage is a part of the city that is often overlooked by tourists. Its name dates from the time when it was an area of green parkland beyond the city wall, where 17th-century Amsterdammers spent their leisure time. Though much of the greenery has gone, there is still a lot to see and do here.

The area is dominated by **Artis**, a zoological complex founded in 1838, which has more than 5,000 animal species. There are also three greenhouses, a planetarium, a geological museum, an excellent aquarium, and a modest zoological museum.

Nearby, the **Hortus Botanicus Amsterdam** began as a small apothecaries' herb garden in 1682 and now contains one of the world's largest botanical collections.

Plantage has a strong Jewish tradition, and many monu-ments commemorate Jewish history in Amsterdam. Formerly a theater, the **Hollandse Schouwburg** is now a somber memorial to the 104,000 Dutch Jewish victims of World War II. More than 60,000 Jews were held here before being de-ported to concentration camps.

William I's royal barge on display at the Nederlands Scheepvaartmuseum

Rijksmuseum ⑯

The Rijksmuseum is a familiar Amsterdam landmark and possesses an unrivaled collection of Dutch art, begun in the early 19th century. The huge museum opened in 1885 to bitter criticism from Amsterdam's Protestant community for its Neo-Gothic style. The main building will undergo extensive renovation until 2009, during which time the most famous treasures will be on view in the south wing (Philips Wing).

Second floor

Winter Landscape with Skaters *(1618)*
Mute painter Hendrick Avercamp specialized in intricate icy winter scenes.

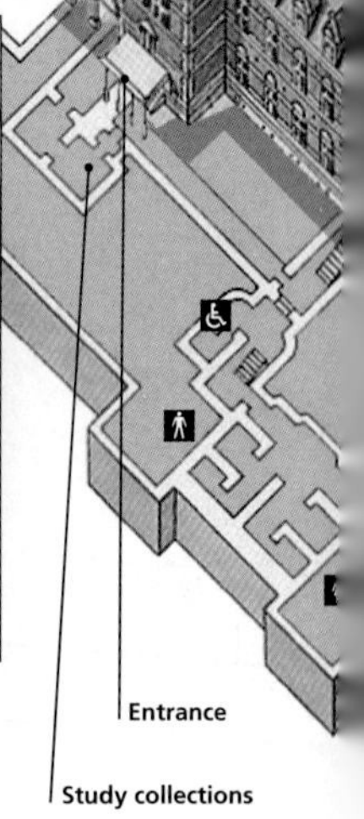

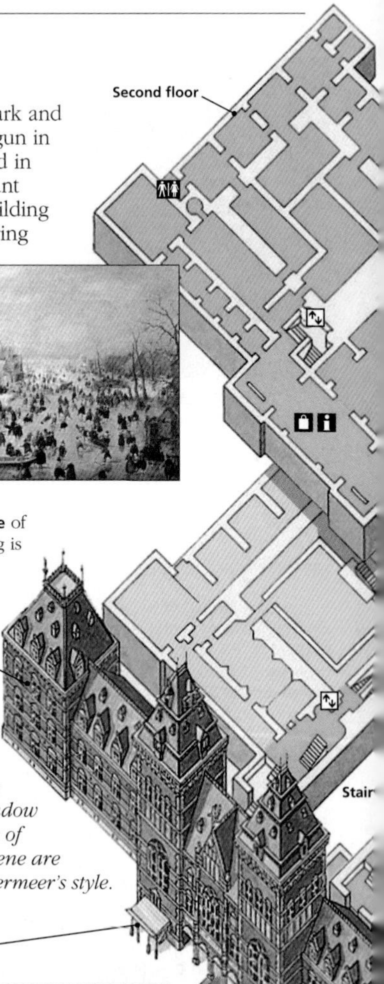

The Gothic façade of Cuypers' building is red brick with elaborate decoration, including colored tiles.

★ The Kitchen Maid *(1658)*
The light falling through the window and the stillness of this domestic scene are typical of Jan Vermeer's style.

Stair

Entrance

KEY TO FLOORPLAN

- Dutch history
- Dutch painting
- European painting
- Sculpture and decorative art
- Prints and drawings
- Asiatic art
- Temporary exhibitions
- Non-exhibition space

STAR PAINTINGS

- ★ The Night Watch by Rembrandt
- ★ St. Elizabeth's Day Flood
- ★ The Kitchen Maid by Vermeer

★ St. Elizabeth's Day Flood *(1500)*
An unknown artist painted this altarpiece, which shows a disastrous flood in 1421. The dykes protecting Dordrecht were breached, and 22 villages were swept away by the flood water.

Entrance

Study collections

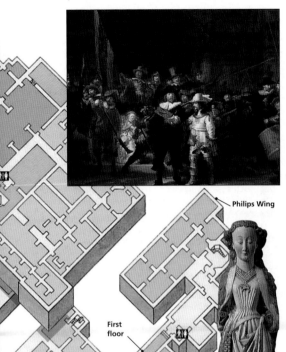

VISITORS' CHECKLIST

Stadhouderskade 42. **Tel** 020-674 7047. 🚋 2, 5, 6, 7, 10. 🚌 Stadhouderskade. ⬜ 9am–6pm daily (Philips Wing only). ⬤ Jan 1. 🎫 📷 ♿ www.rijksmuseum.nl

★ **The Night Watch** *(1642)*
The showpiece of Dutch 17th-century art, this vast canvas by Rembrandt was commissioned as a group portrait of an Amsterdam militia company.

Philips Wing

GALLERY GUIDE

There are entrances on either side of the driveway under the building – the left leads into the Dutch history section, the right to prints and drawings, sculpture and applied art, and then continues on up the stairs. On the first floor is a huge ante-chamber, with a shop and information desk. The entrance on the left begins with early Dutch painting, leading to the acclaimed 17th-century collection. Some disruption can be expected until 2008 due to major renovation work.

First floor

St. Catherine *(c.1465)*
This sculpture by the Master of Koudewater shows the saint stamping on Emperor Maxentius, who allegedly killed her with his sword.

Philips Wing

GENRE PAINTING

For the contemporaries of Jan Steen (1625–79), this cosy everyday scene was full of symbols that are obscure to the modern viewer. The dog on the pillow may represent fidelity, and the red stockings the woman's sexuality; she is probably a prostitute. Such genre paintings were often raunchy, but nearly always had a moral twist – domestic scenes by artists such as ter Borch and Honthorst were symbolic of brothels, while other works illustrated proverbs. Symbols like candles or skulls indicated mortality.

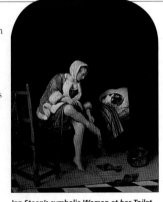

Jan Steen's symbolic *Woman at her Toilet*, painted in about 1660

Ground Floor

Exploring the Rijksmuseum

The Rijksmuseum is too vast to be seen in a single visit, though the key pieces can be seen in the Philips Wing. If time is short, start with the incomparable 17th-century Dutch paintings, taking in Rembrandt, Frans Hals, Vermeer, and many other Old Masters. The collection of Asiatic artifacts and the sculpture and applied arts departments are equally wonderful, while the Dutch history section also provides a rewarding experience.

The heavily ornamented Neo-Gothic façade of the Rijksmuseum

EARLY PAINTING AND FOREIGN SCHOOLS

Alongside Flemish and Italian art are religious works by Netherlandish painters, such as *The Seven Works of Charity* (1504) by the Master of Alkmaar, Jan van Scorel's *Mary Magdalene* (1528), and Lucas van Leyden's triptych, *Adoration of the Golden Calf* (1530).

DUTCH PAINTING OF THE GOLDEN AGE

The 17th century was a golden age for Dutch art. By this time, religious themes had been replaced by secular subjects, such as realistic portraiture, landscapes, still lifes, seascapes, domestic interiors, and animal portraits.

The most famous artist of this era is Rembrandt, whose works here include *Portrait of Titus in a Monk's Habit* (1660), *Self-Portrait as the Apostle Paul* (1661), and *The Jewish Bride* (1663), as well as the brilliant *The Night Watch (see p257).*

Also not to be missed are Jan Vermeer's (1632–75) serenely light-filled interiors, such as *The Kitchen Maid (see p257)* and *The Woman Reading a Letter* (1662). Of several portraits by Frans Hals (1580–1666) the best-known are *The Wedding Portrait* and *The Merry Drinker* (1630). *The Windmill at Wijk* by Jacob van Ruisdael (1628–82) is a great landscape by an artist at the height of his career. Other artists whose works contribute to this unforgettable collection include Pieter Saenredam (1597–1665), Jan van de Capelle (c.1624–79), and Jan Steen *(see p257).*

LATER DUTCH PAINTING

Portraiture and still lifes continued to dominate 18th-century Dutch painting. The evocative *Still Life with Flowers and Fruit* by Jan van Huysum (1682–1749) stands out among works on display

here. Other 18th-century artists represented are Adriaan van der Werff (1659–1722) and Cornelis Troost (1696–1750).

The 19th-century collection features works by the Hague School, a group of Dutch artists who came together around 1870 in Den Haag. Their landscape work captures the atmospheric quality of subdued Dutch sunlight. Look out for Anton Mauve's *Morning Ride on the Beach* (1876) and the beautiful Polder landscape, *View near the Geestbrug,* by Hendrik Weissenbruch (1824–1903).

SCULPTURE AND APPLIED ARTS

Exhibits in this section span several centuries, ranging from religious medieval sculpture to Art Nouveau glass. Highlights that capture the wealth of the Golden Age include an exquisite display of glassware, Delftware, and diamond-encrusted jewelry.

ASIATIC ART

Rewards of the Dutch imperial trading past are on show in this section. Some of the earliest artifacts are the most unusual: tiny bronze Tang-dynasty figurines from 7th-century China, and granite rock carvings from Java (c.8th century). Later exhibits include Chinese parchment paintings, inlaid Korean boxes, and decorative Vietnamese dishes.

The Jewish Bride by Dutch Master, Rembrandt (1606–69)

The Bedroom at Arles, painted during van Gogh's stay in France

Van Gogh Museum ⑰

Paulus Potterstraat 7.
Tel 020-570 5200. 🚃 2, 3, 5, 12, 16. ◯ daily. ● Jan 1. 📷 ♿ 🎧
www.vangoghmuseum.nl

Vincent Van Gogh (1853–90), born in Zundert, began painting in 1880. He worked in the Netherlands for five years, before moving to Paris, and then settling at Arles *(see pp192–3)* in the south of France in February 1888. There he painted over 200 canvases in 15 months. During his time in France, however, van Gogh suffered recurrent nervous crises, hallucinations, and depression. After a fierce argument with his contemporary, French artist Gauguin, he cut off part of his own ear and his mental instability forced him into an asylum. Van Gogh's final years were characterized by tremendous bursts of activity. During the last 70 days of his life he painted 70 canvases. In July 1890 he finally shot himself and died two days later. At the time of his death he was on the verge of being acclaimed.

Van Gogh's younger brother Theo, an art dealer, amassed a collection of 200 of his paintings and 500 drawings.

Vincent van Gogh in 1871

These, together with around 850 letters written by the artist to Theo, form the core of the museum's outstanding collection. Famous works on display include *The Potato Eaters* (1885), from the artist's Dutch period, *The Bedroom at Arles* (1888), painted to celebrate his achievement of domestic stability in the Yellow House in Arles, and *Vase with Sunflowers* (1889). One of van Gogh's last paintings is the dramatic *Wheatfield and Crows* (1890). The menacing crows and violence of the sky show the depth of the artist's mental anguish in the last few weeks before his death. Also on show are selected works by van Gogh's friends and contemporaries, as well as temporary exhibitions.

Stedelijk Museum ⑱

TPG Building, near Centraal Station (temporarily). **Tel** 020-573 2911. 🚃 2, 3, 5, 12. ◯ 10am–6pm daily (but check website for up-to-date information). ● Jan 1. 📷 ♿
www.stedelijk.nl

The Stedelijk Museum was designed to hold a personal collection bequeathed to the city in 1890 by art connoisseur Sophia de Bruyn. It is housed in a late 19th-century Neo-

classical building, adorned with statues of famous artists and architects. In 1938, the museum became the national museum of modern art, showing works by well-known names such as Picasso, Matisse, Chagall, and Monet. Constantly changing exhibitions reflect the latest developments not only in painting and sculpture, but also in printing, drawing, photography, video, and industrial design.

Among the museum's best collections are works by the Dutch painter Mondriaan (1872–1944). One of the founding members of De Stijl (The Style) – an artistic movement which espoused clarity and simplicity – Mondriaan went on to produce many abstract geometrical compositions, such as *Composition in Red, Black, Blue, Yellow, and Grey*.

Other artists represented in the exhibitions include the American photographer Man Ray (1890–1977), the Russian Kazimir Malevich (1878–1935), founder of the abstract movement Suprematism, and the Swiss sculptor Jean Tinguely (1925–91), who created humorous sculptures from junk and recycled metal.

The museum is currently being renovated (until 2009) and some of the collection is on display in the TPG Building. The Stedelijk website gives details of the changing exhibitions.

Statue of 16th-century artist Pieter Aertsen on the Stedelijk's façade

A typical 17th-century gabled timber house in Marken

Marken and Volendam ❷

Marken 👥 *2,000.* 🚌 🚲
Volendam 👥 *18,000.* 🚌 ℹ️
Zeestraat 37 (0299-363747). 🅿️ *Sat.*

Located on the shores of the Marker Meer, and less than an hour's drive from Amsterdam, Marken and Volendam are extremely popular with tourists, who are drawn to these picturesque towns by their old-world character. In spite of the crowds, it is worth spending a few hours exploring their narrow streets and canals, lined, as they are, with attractive 17th-century gabled timber houses. You may even spot the local inhabitants wearing traditional dress.

Places to look out for in particular include the **Marker Museum** in Marken, an old fisherman's dwelling that now houses a heritage center, and

Volendam's **Spaander Hotel** situated at No. 15 Haven. The walls of the hotel's café are covered with works by late 19th-century artists who came here to paint the pretty town.

Alkmaar ❸

🏙️ *93,000.* 🚉 ℹ️ *Waaggebouw, Waagplein 2–3 (072-5114 284).* 🧀 *cheese market: Apr–Sep: 10am–12:30pm Fri.*

Alkmaar is one of the few Dutch towns to maintain its traditional cheese market, which has been held here since medieval times. Every Friday morning in summer local producers lay out Gouda and Edam cheeses in the Waagplein, and from here porters sporting colorful straw hats take them off on sledges for weighing at the **Waaggebouw** (Weigh House). This imposing building, altered in 1582 from a 14th-century chapel, also houses the **Het Hollands Kaasmuseum**, where local cheese-making techniques are explained.

Alkmaar's massive Gothic church, the **Grote Kerk**, was completed in 1520 and contains the tomb of Floris V, Count of Holland. The nave is dominated by the 17th-century organ, built by Jacob van Campen and painted by Cesar van Everdingen.

🏛️ **Het Hollands Kaasmuseum**
Waaggebouw, Waagplein 2.
Tel *072-5114 284.* ⏰ *Apr–Oct: Mon–Sat.* 📷 ♿

The soaring pipes of the famous organ in Haarlem's Grote Kerk

Haarlem ❹

🏙️ *153,000.* 🚉 ℹ️ *Stationsplein 1 (0900-616 1600).* 🅿️ *Mon, Fri & Sat.* 🎷 *Haarlem Jazz Festival (mid-Aug).*

Haarlem is the center of the Dutch printing, pharmaceutical, and bulb-growing industries. Most of the city's main attractions are within easy walking distance of the Grote Markt, a lively square overlooked by the Gothic **Grote Kerk**. Also known as Sint Bavo's, this huge church was built between 1400 and 1550. Its highly decorative organ (1735) has been played by both Handel and Mozart. Also on the Grote Markt, the **Stadhuis** (Town Hall) dates from 1250 and displays a mixture of architectural styles. The oldest part of the building is the beamed medieval banqueting hall of the counts of Holland.

The **Amsterdamse Poort**, the medieval gateway that once formed part of the city's defenses, was built in 1355.

Haarlem is well known for its *hofjes* (almshouses), which began to appear in the 16th century. Established in 1610, **St. Elisabeth's Gasthuis** now houses a historical museum. The **Frans Hals Museum** occupies the almshouse where the famous artist (1582–1666) supposedly lived out his last years. In addition to a superb collection of paintings by Hals himself, there is a selection of

Porters carrying cheeses on sledges at Alkmaar's traditional market

Dutch paintings and applied art dating from the 16th and 17th centuries.

Frans Hals Museum
Groot Heiligland 62. *Tel* 023-5115 775. ○ Tue–Sat, pm Sun. ● Jan 1, Dec 25.

Paleis Het Loo ❺

Koninklijk Park 1, Apeldoorn. *Tel* 055-577 2400. 🚉 *to Apeldoorn, then bus.* ○ Tue–Sun. ● Jan 1.

Stadholder William III built Het Loo in 1686 as a royal hunting lodge. Generations of the House of Orange used the lodge as a summer palace, which came to be regarded as the "Versailles of the Netherlands." The building's Classical façade belies the opulence of the interior. Among the most lavish apartments are the Royal Bedroom of William III (1713), with its wall coverings and draperies of rich orange damask and blue silk, and the Old Dining Room (1686). In the latter half of the 20th century, old prints, records, and plans were used to carefully recreate Het Loo's beautiful formal gardens.

The sumptuously decorated Royal Bedroom of Stadholder William III

Utrecht ❻

🏙 234,000. 🚉 🚌 🛈 *Vinkenburgstraat 19 (0900-128 8732).*

Utrecht was founded by the Romans in AD 47 to protect a strategic river crossing on the Rhine. The town was one of

BULBFIELDS OF THE NETHERLANDS

Bulb species cultivated in the Netherlands include lilies, gladioli, daffodils, hyacinths, irises, crocuses, and dahlias. The most famous bulb of all, however, is the tulip. Originally from Turkey, it was first grown in Dutch soil by Carolus Clusius in 1593. Occupying a 30-km (19-mile) strip between Haarlem and Leiden, the Bloembollenstreek is the most important bulb-growing area in the country. From late January the polders bloom with a succession of brightly colored bulbs, building to a climax in mid-April when the tulips flower. If you do not have a car, there are plenty of organized tours that visit the bulbfields, or you can rent a bicycle from Haarlem train station.

A blanket of color formed by tulips in the Bloembollenstreek

the first places in the Netherlands to embrace Christianity, and in the Middle Ages it grew into an important religious center. The city retains many of its medieval churches and monasteries. The **Domkerk**, Utrecht's cathedral, was begun in 1254. Today, only the north and south transepts, two chapels, and the choir remain, along with the 15th-century cloisters and a chapterhouse. The **Domtoren**, which stands apart from the cathedral, is one of the tallest towers in the Netherlands, at 112 m (367 ft). Completed in 1382, on the site of the small 8th-century church of St. Willibrord, it affords magnificent views of the city.

Among Utrecht's many museums are the **Museum Catharijneconvent**, which deals with the troubled history of religion in the Netherlands and owns an award-winning collection of medieval art, and the **Nederlands Spoorweg-museum**, a superb railway museum, housed in the fully restored 19th-century Maliebaan station. At the heart of the collection at the **Centraal Museum** is a series of portraits by artist Jan van Scorel (1495–1562), known as the "Utrecht Caravaggisti". There is also an impressive collection of modern and contemporary

art, with works by Van Gogh, Courbet and Damien Hirst, as well as sculpture, costume and furniture collections.

Museum Catharijneconvent
Lange Nieuwstraat 38. *Tel* 030-2313 835. ○ Tue–Sun. ● Jan 1, Apr 30. www.catharijneconvent.nl

Centraal Museum
Nicolaaskerkhof 10. *Tel* 030-2362 362. ○ Tue–Sun. ● Jan 1, Apr 30, Dec 25. www.centraalmuseum.nl

Utrecht's massive Gothic Domtoren, which dominates the city

Leiden ❼

🏃 *115,000.* 🚍 🚌 ℹ️ *Stationsweg 2d (0900-222 2333).* 🛒 *Wed, Sat.*

Leiden is a prosperous town that dates back to Roman times. Its famous university is the oldest in the Netherlands, founded in 1575 by William of Orange. Created in 1587, the university's botanical garden, the **Hortus Botanicus der Rijksuniversiteit Leiden**, is still open to the public.

One of Leiden's biggest attractions is the **Rijksmuseum van Oudheden** (National Museum of Antiquities). Established in 1818, the museum houses an outstanding collection of Egyptian artifacts, including the 1st-century AD Temple of Taffeh. There are also displays of textiles, musical instruments, Etruscan bronzework, and fragments of Roman mosaics and frescoes.

The magnificent Gothic **Pieterskerk** was built in the 15th century. Its interior is rather austere, but there is a splendid organ (1642), enclosed in gilded woodwork.

Dating back to 1640, the old Lakenhal (Cloth Hall) now houses the **Stedelijk Museum**, with exhibitions of art and furniture from the 16th century onward. The pride of the collection is Lucas van Leyden's Renaissance triptych, *The Last Judgment* (1526–7). Leiden also has an excellent ethnological museum, the **Rijksmuseum voor Volkenkunde**, which reopened in April 2001 after undergoing an extensive restoration program.

Hortus Botanicus, the tranquil botanical gardens of Leiden University

🏛 **Rijksmuseum van Oudheden**
Rapenburg 28. *Tel 0900-6600 600.*
⬜ *Tue–Sun.* ⚫ *Jan 1, Oct 3, Dec 25.* 🈳 🚻 🔲

🏛 **Rijksmuseum voor Volkenkunde**
Steenstraat 1. *Tel 071-5168 800.*
⬜ *Tue–Sun.* ⚫ *Jan 1, Dec 25.*
🈳 🔲 🚻 www.rmv.nl

The Hague ❽

🏃 *446,000.* 🚍 🚌 ℹ️ *Koningin Julianaplein 30 (0900-340 3505).* 🛒 *Mon, Wed, Fri, Sat.*

The political capital of the Netherlands, The Hague (Den Haag or 's-Gravenhage) is home to prestigious institutions, such as the Dutch parliament and the International Court of Justice.

When The Hague became the seat of government in 1586, it was a small town built around the castle of the counts of Holland. That same castle, much rebuilt, stands at the heart of the city, and forms part of the Binnenhof, where today's parliament sits.

The fairy-tale, double-turreted Gothic **Ridderzaal** (Hall of the Knights), the 13th-century dining hall of Count Floris V, is open to the public when parliament is not in session.

An outstanding collection of works by Dutch Masters Rembrandt, Jan Vermeer, and Jan Steen is assembled in the Royal Picture Gallery at the **Mauritshuis**. More Dutch Golden Age paintings are on view at the **Museum Bredius** and the **Galerij Prins Willem V**.

The **Haags Gemeentemuseum** has an applied arts section that includes the world's largest collection of paintings by De Stijl (see p259) artist Piet Mondrian.

Formerly called Het Oude Hof (the Old Court), the **Paleis Noordeinde** is a splendid 17th-century palace built in the Classical style. It is used as a temporary residence by Queen Beatrix.

🏰 **Ridderzaal**
Binnenhof 8a. *Tel 070-364 6144.*
⬜ *Mon–Sat (call in advance).*
⚫ *public hols.* 🈳 🔲 *obligatory.*

🏛 **Mauritshuis**
Korte Vijverberg 8. *Tel 070-302 3456.* ⬜ *Tue–Sun.* ⚫ *Jan 1, Dec 25.* 🈳 🔲 🚻

🏛 **Galerij Prins Willem V**
Buitenhof 35. *Tel 070-302 3456.*
⚫ *until 2008.* 🈳

Environs
Only a 15-minute tram ride from the center of Den Haag, **Scheveningen** has clean, sandy beaches and several good seafood restaurants. The resort also has a Sea Life Center and a small marine biology center, the Zee Museum.

The Binnenhof, home of the Dutch parliament, in The Hague

For hotels and restaurants in this region see pp268–9 and pp270–71

Delft 9

🏛 95,000. 🚉 🚌 ℹ️ *Hippolytus-buurt 4 (0900-5151 555).* ⛴ *Thu, Sat.*

The charming town of Delft is most famous for its blue-and-white pottery, known as Delftware, which was introduced to the Netherlands by immigrant Italian potters in the 16th century. **De Porceleyne Fles** is one of two Delftware potteries still in operation, and is open for guided tours.

Delft is also the resting place of William of Orange (1533–84), who commanded the Dutch Revolt against Spanish rule from his headquarters in the town. His richly-decorated tomb lies in the **Nieuwe Kerk**, built between 1383 and 1510, but subsequently restored

Hand-painted
17th-century
Delft tiles

following damage caused by fire and explosion. The former convent that William used as his military headquarters, and where he was assassinated by order of Philip II of Spain, is now home to the **Stedelijk Museum Het Prinsenhof**.

The museum contains a rare collection of antique Delftware, as well as tapestries, silverware, medieval sculpture, and portraits of the Dutch royal family.

Other sites of interest are the **Volkenkundig Museum Nusantara**, an ethnological museum, whose exhibits were brought back from Indonesia by traders working for the Dutch East India Company, and the **Oude Kerk**, which dates from the 13th century. The church holds the tomb of one of the town's most famous sons, the artist Jan Vermeer (1632–75).

🔒 **Nieuwe Kerk**
Markt. *Tel 015-2123 025.*
⭕ *Mon–Sat.* 🖼

🏛 **Stedelijk Museum Het Prinsenhof**
St. Agathaplein 1. *Tel 015-2602 358.*
⭕ *Tue–Sat, Sun pm.* ● *Jan 1, Dec 25.* 🖼 🛈

Delft's Nieuwe Kerk, with its soaring 100-m (328-ft) high tower

Rotterdam 10

🏛 602,000. ✈ *6 km (4 miles) NW.*
🚉 🚌 ℹ️ *Coolsingel 5 (0900-403 4065).* ⛴ *Tue, Fri, Sat, Sun.*

Rotterdam occupies a strategic position where the Rhine meets the North Sea. Barges from the city transport goods deep into the continent, and ocean-going ships carry European exports around the world.

Following damage during World War II, the Oudehaven, Rotterdam's old harbor area, has been rebuilt in daring and avant-garde styles. The pyramid-shaped **Gemeente Bibliotheek** (Public Library) is similar to the Pompidou Center in Paris *(see p153),* while Piet Blom's **Kijk-Kubus** (Cube Houses) of 1982 are

extraordinary apartments set on a series of concrete stilts and tilted at angles.

The excellent **Museum Boijmans-van Beuningen** holds Netherlandish and Dutch art, from the medieval paintings of Jan van Eyck to modern works using laser technology. Among its most famous exhibits are a number of paintings by Peter Brueghel and Rembrandt.

Other museums of note are the **Historisch Museum Rotterdam**, the city's main historical museum, the **Wereldmuseum Rotterdam**, with its superb ethnological collection, and the **Maritiem Museum Rotterdam**, whose highlight is an iron-clad warship, *De Buffel,* built in 1868.

For a spectacular view of the city, take the elevator up the 185-m (600-ft) high **Euromast**. Built in 1960, it is the tallest construction in the country, and has a restaurant and an exhibition area.

🏛 **Museum Boijmans-van Beuningen**
Museumpark 18–20. *Tel 010-441 9400.* ⭕ *Tue–Sun.* ● *Jan 1, Apr 30, Dec 25.* 🖼 ♿

🏛 **Historisch Museum Rotterdam**
Korte Hoogstraat 31. *Tel 010-217 6717.* ⭕ *Tue–Sun.* ● *Jan 1, Apr 30, Dec 25.* 🖼 ♿

🏛 **Wereldmuseum Rotterdam**
Willemskade 25. *Tel 010-270 7172.*
⭕ *Tue–Sun.* 🖼 🛈 🖥 ♿

Peter Brueghel the Elder's *The Tower of Babel* (c.1553) in the Museum Boijmans-van Beuningen in Rotterdam

Practical & Travel Information

The Netherlands is a straightforward country to travel in, and visitors should find its citizens, who are often multilingual, helpful and friendly. One of the joys of a visit to Amsterdam is the relatively car-free environment. Trams, bicycles, and pedestrians are given a higher priority in the center than motor vehicles. Outside the capital, the Dutch public transportation network is one of the most highly developed in Europe.

TOURIST INFORMATION

The NBT (**Netherlands Board of Tourism**) has offices in many cities world-wide. Within the Netherlands, the state-run tourist information organization is the Vereniging Voor Vreemdelingenverkeer, known as the **VVV**. They have around 450 offices throughout the country. Courteous and friendly staff provide information on sights, transportation, and events, and will also change money and reserve hotel rooms.

The Museum Card (*Museum-jaarkaart*), available from branches of the VVV, is valid for a year, and allows admission to over 400 museums and galleries throughout the country.

VISA REQUIREMENTS AND CUSTOMS

Citizens of the EU, Australia, New Zealand, the US, and Canada need only a valid passport to enter the Netherlands. Those visitors coming from non-EU states can reclaim VAT on certain goods. Call the freephone customs information line (0800-0143) for further details.

SAFETY AND EMERGENCIES

After a recent cleanup by the authorities, Amsterdam is much safer than many North American and European cities. Drugs-related crime is still a problem, but tourists should not be affected by this, as long as they act sensibly, and avoid certain areas after dark, in particular the Zeedijk district.

In case of emergencies, the appropriate number to call is listed in the directory opposite.

HEALTH ISSUES

Minor health problems can be dealt with by a chemist (*drogist*), who stocks non-prescription drugs. If you need prescription medicines, go to a pharmacy (*apotheek*), open from 8:30am to 5:30pm Monday to Friday.

Attracted by the canals, mosquitoes can be an irritant in Amsterdam, so bring plenty of repellent sprays and anti-histamine creams with you.

MUSEUM OPENING TIMES

Many state-run museums are closed on Mondays, and open from 10am to 5pm, Tuesday to Saturday, and from 1 to 5pm on Sunday. Most museums adopt Sunday hours for national holidays, apart from New Year's Day, when they are always closed.

BANKING AND CURRENCY

On January 1, 2002, the Dutch unit of currency, the guilder, was replaced by the euro (*see p15*).

Banks open from 9 or 10am to 4 or 5pm, Monday to Friday. Some city branches close at 7pm on Thursdays and open on Saturday mornings. Banks are usually the best place to change money, but official bureaux de change, the GWK (*grenswissel-kantoor-bureaus*), also have reasonable exchange rates. Credit cards are not as widely accepted in the Netherlands as in other European countries.

COMMUNICATIONS

Public telephones are identifiable by the green and white logo of the PTT and KPN, the Dutch state-run telecoms companies. Few phone booths still take coins. You can buy phonecards at post offices, newsstands, and train stations.

Most post offices are open Monday to Friday from 9am to 5pm. Apart from normal postal services, they also change currency and traveler's checks, and have telephone and fax services. Stamps can also be bought at tobacconists or souvenir stores.

FLYING TO THE NETHERLANDS

Carriers operating non-stop flights from the US to the Netherlands include charter operator **Martinair**, **Delta Air Lines**, **United Airlines**, and **Northwest Airlines/KLM**. Seven airlines fly direct from the UK to the Netherlands, among them **British Airways** and low-cost airlines including **Ryanair** and **easyJet**. The least expensive way to get from Amsterdam's Schiphol Airport to the city center is by the airport rail service. Trains leave for

---

THE CLIMATE OF THE NETHERLANDS

The Netherlands has a temperate climate. Winters are frequently freezing, and spring and autumn can be chilly. July and August are the warmest months, but North Sea winds often make it seem cooler. You should expect rainfall all year round, but spring is generally the driest season. The heaviest rainfall occurs in the autumn, especially in November.

AMSTERDAM

°C/F	Apr	Jul	Oct	Jan
high	13/55	22/72	14/58	5/51
low	4/39	12/54	7/45	1/34
sun	5 hrs	6.5 hrs	3 hrs	1.5 hrs
rain	35 mm	57 mm	70 mm	56 mm

0°C / 32°F

Centraal Station seven times each hour between 5:40am and 1am, after which they run hourly. The journey takes 20 minutes. Schiphol Airport station is also connected to other cities in the Netherlands.

ARRIVING BY SEA

Ferry companies offering car and passenger services from the UK to the Nether-lands include **P&O North Sea Ferries**, with daily sailings from Hull to Rotterdam.

Sea France operates daily services between Dover and Calais in France, while P&O also operates regular crossings from Hull to Zeebrugge in Belgium.

RAIL TRAVEL

International rail routes provide a fast and efficient link between Amsterdam and many other European cities. From Centraal Station high-speed **Thalys** trains run to Brussels in 2 hours 30 minutes, and to Paris in just over 4 hours. In both Paris and

Brussels, passengers can change to the Eurostar for an onward connection to London.

The Dutch rail system, operated by Nederlandse Spoorwegen, is one of the most modern and efficient in Europe, with an extensive route network. The **OVR** (Openbaar Vervoer Reisinformatie) has information on rail trips for tourists, plus details of special fares. It does not, however, issue tickets, which you buy at the ticket office. If you need to arrange rail travel abroad, visit the offices of **Nederlandse Spoorwegen Internationaal**, located in Amsterdam's Centraal Station.

TRAVELING BY BUS

Long-distance bus travel is an inexpensive, if tiring, way to reach the Netherlands. **Eurolines** and **Hoverspeed City Sprint** have at least two daily services from the UK to Amsterdam, crossing the English Channel by ferry and hovercraft respectively.

Buses in the Netherlands are reliable and efficient. The *strippenkaart* (ticket strip),

available in multiples of 15, allows you to travel on buses all over the Netherlands, as well as on trams and the metro in city centers. The city is divided into zones, and each unit, or strip, covers one zone, even when changing between bus, tram, and metro. You can buy a *strippenkaart* at VVV offices, newsstands, or train and bus stations.

TRAVELING BY CAR

An ever-expanding highway system makes it easy to travel to the Netherlands from anywhere in Europe. Major roads in the Netherlands (marked N) are generally well-maintained, but Dutch highways (labeled A) have narrow lanes, traffic lights, and sometimes no hard shoulder. When driving in towns, especially in Amsterdam, be careful of cyclists and trams.

Most of the principal international car rental firms have offices in Amsterdam and at Schiphol Airport, but local Dutch companies are significantly less expensive.

DIRECTORY

NETHERLANDS BOARD OF TOURISM (NBT)

UK
Imperial House, 7th Floor, 15–19 Kingsway, London, WC2B 6UN.
Tel 020-7539 7950.
Fax 020-7539 7953.
www.holland.com/uk

US
355 Lexington Avenue, New York, NY 10017.
Tel 888-Go Holland.
Fax 212-370 9507
www.holland.com/us

TOURIST OFFICES IN THE NETHERLANDS

VVV Centraal Station
Centraal Station, Stationsplein, Amsterdam.
Tel 0900-400 4040.

EMBASSIES

Australia
Carnegielaan 4, 2517 KH Den Haag.
Tel 070-310 8200.

Canada
Sophialaan 7, 2514 JP Den Haag.
Tel 070-311 1600.

Ireland
Dr. Kuyperstraat 9, 2514 BA Den Haag.
Tel 070-363 0993.

UK
Lange Voorhout 10, 2514 ED Den Haag.
Tel 070-427 0427.

US
Lange Voorhout 102, 2514 EJ Den Haag.
Tel 070-310 9209.

EMERGENCIES

Ambulance, Fire, and Police
Tel 112.

AIRLINES

British Airways
Tel 0870 850 9850 (UK).
Tel 020-346 9559 (Netherlands).

Delta Air Lines
Tel 800-241 4141 (US).

easyJet
Tel 0871-750 0100 (UK).
Tel 023 568 4880 (Netherlands).
www.easyjet.com

KLM
Tel 0870-507 4074 (UK).
Tel 800-374 7747 (US).
Tel 020-474 7747 (Netherlands).

Martinair
Tel 800-627 8462 (US).

Northwest Airlines
Tel 800-225 2525 (US).

Ryanair
Tel 0871-246 0000 (UK).
www.ryanair.com

United Airlines
Tel 800-538 2929 (US).

FERRY COMPANIES

P&O European
Tel 0870-520 2020 (UK).

Sea France
Tel 0870-443 1653 (UK).

RAIL TRAVEL

Nederlandse Spoorwegen Internationaal
Tel 0900-9296.

OVR
Tel 0900-9292.

Thalys
Tel 0900-9296.

BUSES

Eurolines UK Ltd
Tel 01582-404 511.

Hoverspeed City Sprint
Tel 0870-524 0241 (UK).

Shopping & Entertainment

The Netherlands is justly famous for its cheeses, beers, and flowers, available at specialist stores and super-markets across the country. Amsterdam is a cosmopolitan city, so it is also easy to find a selection of foreign and ethnic goods, from Indonesian beads to French designer wear. The famous brown cafés and coffee shops are an important part of Dutch social life, and visitors to the Netherlands should not miss the chance to try one.

OPENING HOURS

Stores in the Netherlands are usually open from 9 or 10am to 6pm Tuesday to Saturday, and from 1 to 6pm on Monday. In the larger cities, many shops stay open until 9pm on Thursdays.

WHERE TO SHOP

Most of Amsterdam's large department and clothing stores are located in the Nieuwe Zijde, especially along Kalverstraat. The city's best-known department stores are **De Bijenkorf**, often described as the Dutch Harrods, **Metz & Co**, and **Maison de Bonneterie**. Less expensive ones include Vroom & Dreesman and Hema. For luxury fashion, the classy PC Hooftstraat and Van Baerlestraat are lined with chic designer boutiques, such as MEXX and The People of the Labyrinths.

The streets crossing Amster-dam's Canal Ring, such as Herenstraat and Hartenstraat, contain many specialist stores, selling everything from ethnic fabrics to handmade dolls.

WHAT TO BUY

One famous Dutch export is Delftware, the blue-and-white pottery from Delft *(see p263)*. Only two factories still make it, though imitation pieces are found in tourist stores all over the country. A certification stamp indicates that an article is genuine. In Amsterdam, the **Galleria d'Arte Rinascimento** and **Holland Gallery de Munt** stock authentic Delftware.

The Dutch are keen beer drinkers. As well as brand names like Heineken, Grolsch, and Amstel, there are many local specialties, such as Zatte, a rare, bottle-fermented beer, and Wieckse Witte, a white beer. Specialist store **De Bierkoning** offers the widest choice and best advice.

You can usually buy a good selection of Dutch cheeses at supermarkets, including any branch of **Albert Heijn**, street markets, or specialist food stores. Instead of buying the ubiquitous Edam, try one of the many varieties of Gouda. Mature Gouda has a rich, salty taste and crumbly texture, while young Gouda is fresh and curdy.

Other items for which the Netherlands is famous are flowers, which you can buy at Amsterdam's **Rivièra Maison**, among many other places, and diamonds. For the latter, visit the diamond-cutting center **Stoeltie Diamonds**.

MARKETS

The Dutch love street trading and almost every town has at least one open-air market. In Amsterdam, the best-known are the Albert Cuypmarkt in Albert Cuyp-straat, with an assortment of Dutch and ethnic food, cheap clothes, and flowers, and the Waterlooplein flea market, in Oude Zijde. The Looier Kunst en Antiekcentrum, at No. 109 Elandsgracht, is a covered market boasting the largest collection of art and antiques in the Netherlands.

ENTERTAINMENT LISTINGS AND TICKETS

The monthly magazine, *Day by Day*, is available from VVV offices *(see pp264–5)* for a small fee; free issues can be found in some hotels and restaurants. The free monthly *Uitkrant* also has entertainment listings for the capital, and is easy to follow for non-Dutch speakers.

The main reservations office for entertainment and cultural activities in Amsterdam is the **AUB** (Amsterdam Uitburo). The VVV and Dutch Tourist Information Office will also book tickets for some venues.

ENTERTAINMENT VENUES

Among Amsterdam's many theater venues are the **Theater Bellevue**, the **Stads-schouwburg**, and the **Felix Meritis**. For experimental theater, head for **De Brakke Grond** and other venues located along the street known as the Nes. The **Koninklijk Theater Carré** hosts long-running international musicals.

Dance is an important aspect of cultural life in the Netherlands. The Dutch National Ballet is housed in Amsterdam's large-capacity **Muziektheater**, while experimental dance can be enjoyed at **De Meervaart** and the Stadsschouwburg. The Muziektheater is also home to the Dutch National Opera.

The focus for Amsterdam's classical music scene is the **Concertgebouw**, home to the celebrated Royal Concertgebouw Orchestra.

The Netherlands has a huge number of jazz venues. In Amsterdam the internationally renowned **Bimhuis**, the **Muziekgebouw aan 't IJ**, and the **Alto Jazz Café** are worth visiting. The North Sea Jazz Festival, held in Den Haag in July, attracts some of the biggest names in the industry, while Rotterdam's **Dizzy** is another top venue.

Amsterdammers equate rock and pop with two venues, **Paradiso** and **De Melkweg**, which offer a varied program. Big-name bands also play at Rotterdam's Ahoy and Utrecht's Vredenburg stadiums.

BROWN CAFES AND COFFEE SHOPS

The traditional Dutch "local pub," the brown café, is characterized by dark wooden furnishings, low ceilings, dim lights, and a fog of tobacco smoke. It is a warm and friendly place, and often a social focus for the local neighborhood. There are hundreds in Amsterdam, but one of the best is the tiny and characterful **'t Doktertje**.

For many visitors, a stay in the Netherlands is incomplete without a trip to a smoking coffee shop. At this type of establishment cannabis is openly sold and smoked. Though technically illegal, the sale of soft drugs is tolerated by the Dutch authorities if it remains discreet. **Siberië** is one of the smaller, more relaxed places in Amsterdam, while **The Bulldog** is more commercial and tourist-filled.

CANAL TOURS

There are many operators in Amsterdam offering canal tours. In addition to the daytime sightseeing trips, there are night cruises, which often feature cheese-and-wine refreshments, a stop at a pub, or a romantic candlelit dinner. **Lovers** cruises are the most reasonably-priced, while **P. Kooij** are more upscale.

CYCLING

It is claimed that there are more bicycles in the Netherlands than inhabitants. The endlessly flat landscape and thousands of miles of well-maintained cycle tracks make cycling an extremely popular activity, even within cities. **Yellow Bike** organizes excursions in and around Amsterdam between April and October, while the US-based **Euro-Bike and Walking Tours** arranges week-long tours around the whole country. **Cycletours Holland** has a number of "bike-and-boat" itineraries covering the main regions of interest. For those who wish to do things independently, bicycles can be rented easily from many outlets across the country, and at over 100 train stations. The VVV are able to supply detailed route maps.

DIRECTORY

DEPARTMENT STORES

De Bijenkorf
Dam 1, Amsterdam.
Tel 0900 0919.
Wagenstraat 32, Den Haag.
Tel 0900 0919.

Maison de Bonneterie
Rokin 140–142,
Amsterdam.
Tel 020-531 3400.

Metz & Co
Leidsestraat 34–36,
Amsterdam.
Tel 020-520 7020.

SPECIALIST ITEMS

Albert Heijn
Jodenbreestraat 21,
Amsterdam.
Tel 020-624 1249.

De Bierkoning
Paleisstraat 125,
Amsterdam.
Tel 020-625 2336.

Galleria d'Arte Rinascimento
Prinsengracht 170,
Amsterdam.
Tel 020-622 7509.

Holland Gallery de Munt
Muntplein 12, Amsterdam.
Tel 020-623 2271.

Rivièra Maison
Gelderlandplein 185–199,
Amsterdam.
Tel 020-644 0047.

Stoeltie Diamonds
Wagenstraat 13–17,
Amsterdam.
Tel 020-623 7601.

ENTERTAINMENT TICKETS

AUB
Leidseplein 26, Amsterdam.
Tel 0900-0191.

ENTERTAINMENT VENUES

Alto Jazz Café
Korte Leidsedwarsstraat
115, Amsterdam.
Tel 020-626 3249.

Bimhuis
Piet Heinkade 1,
Amsterdam.
Tel 020-788 2188.

De Brakke Grond
Vlaams Cultureel Centrum,
Nes 45, Amsterdam.
Tel 020-626 6866.

Concertgebouw
Concertgebouwplein 2–6,
Amsterdam.
Tel 020-671 8345.

Dizzy
's-Gravendijkwal 127,
Rotterdam.
Tel 010-477 3014.

Felix Meritis
Keizersgracht 324,
Amsterdam.
Tel 020-623 2321.

Koninklijk Theater Carré
Amstel 115–125,
Amsterdam.
Tel 020-524 9494.

De Meervaart
Meer en Vaart 300,
Amsterdam.
Tel 020-410 7700.

De Melkweg
Lijnbaansgracht 234a,
Amsterdam.
Tel 020-531 8181.

Muziekgebouw aan 't IJ
Piet Heinkade 1,
Amsterdam.
Tel 020-788 2000.

Het Muziektheater
Amstel 3, Amsterdam.
Tel 020-625 5455.

Paradiso
Weteringschans 6–8,
Amsterdam.
Tel 020-626 4521.

Stadsschouwburg
Leidseplein 26, Amsterdam.
Tel 020-624 2311.

Theater Bellevue
Leidsekade 90,
Amsterdam.
Tel 020-530 5301.

BROWN CAFES & COFFEE SHOPS

't Doktertje
Rozenboomsteeg 4,
Amsterdam.
Tel 020-626 4427.

Siberië
Brouwersgracht 11,
Amsterdam.
Tel 020-623 5909.

The Bulldog
Leidseplein 15,
Amsterdam.
Tel 020-625 6278.

CANAL TOURS

Lovers
Opposite Prins Hendrikkade
26, Amsterdam.
Tel 020-530 1090.

P. Kooij
Opposite Rokin 125,
Amsterdam.
Tel 020-623 3810.

CYCLING

Cycletours Holland
Buiksloterweg 7a,
Amsterdam.
Tel 020-521 8490.

Euro-Bike and Walking Tours
PO Box 990, Dekalb,
IL 60115, USA.
Tel 1-800-321 6060.

Yellow Bike
Nieuwezijds Kolk 29,
Amsterdam.
Tel 020-620 6940.

Where to Stay in the Netherlands

Accommodations in Amsterdam range from luxurious
five-star hotels to cheap hostels for those on a budget.
In between are scores of B&Bs (bed and breakfasts),
many in pretty canal houses, whose interiors are often
maintained in period style. Elsewhere in the Netherlands,
standards of accommodations are generally high.

PRICE CATEGORIES
The following prices are
for a standard double room per
night, including breakfast,
tax and service.
€ Under 120 euros
€€ 120–170 euros
€€€ 170–220 euros
€€€€ 220–270 euros
€€€€€ Over 270 euros

AMSTERDAM

CENTRAL CANAL RING Dikker & Thijs Fenice Hotel   €€
Prinsengracht 444, 1017 KE **Tel** *020-620 1212* **Fax** *020-625 8986* **Rooms** *42*   **Map** *C4*

Owned by a publisher, this hotel is proud of its literary connections and the authors who stay here. The 18th-century
warehouse building is magnificent, and the décor is smart. Although just moments from Leidseplein, the atmosphere
here is resolutely upmarket. All the sights are within walking distance. **www.dtfh.nl**

CENTRAL CANAL RING Ambassade Hotel   €€€€
Herengracht 341, 1016 AZ **Tel** *020-555 0222* **Fax** *020-555 0277* **Rooms** *59*   **Map** *C3*

With its long literary associations, this is the bookworm's choice of lodgings: the library is lined with signed copies
from the numerous authors who have stayed here. Arranged across ten buildings, rooms are furnished in an unfussy,
classic way, and bathrooms, though small, are marbled. Staff are discreet and attentive. **www.ambassade-hotel.nl**

EASTERN CANAL RING NH Schiller   €€
Rembrandtplein 26–36, 1017 CV **Tel** *020-554 0700* **Fax** *020-554 4400* **Rooms** *92*   **Map** *D4*

Fun-seekers should look no further than this hotel, with its commanding view over Rembrandtplein. The rooms at
the back are not so noisy, and all are decorated with smart furnishings. Brasserie Schiller is very cosy, while the
eponymous next-door bar has Art Deco fittings and attracts a media crowd. **www.nh-hotels.com**

MUSEUM QUARTER Stayokay City Hostel Vondelpark   €
Zandpad 5, 1054 GA **Tel** *020-589 8996* **Fax** *020-589 8955* **Rooms** *105*   **Map** *B4*

The second Amsterdam outpost of a worthy organization, this hostel on the edge of the Vondelpark is ideal for
families and nature lovers. Accommodations range from double rooms to 20-bed dorms, and it is all non-smoking.
There is a TV room, and Brasserie Backpackers has a lovely terrace looking onto the park. **www.stayokay.com**

MUSEUM QUARTER De Filosoof   €€
Anna van der Vondelstraat 6, 1054 GZ **Tel** *020-683 3013* **Fax** *020-685 3750* **Rooms** *38*   **Map** *B4*

A much-loved hotel on a street off the Vondelpark. Every room here is individually decorated according to a different
philosopher or treatise. There is Passion, Wittgenstein or local boy Spinoza, for example. It is a favourite of brooding
intellectuals, who make use of the lovely garden and, of course, the library. **www.hotelfilosoof.nl**

NIEUWE ZIJDE Rho Hotel   €€
Nes 5–23, 1012 KC **Tel** *020-620 7371* **Fax** *020-620 7826* **Rooms** *170*   **Map** *C3*

Just steps from bustling Dam Square, though tucked down a backstreet bristling with interesting bars, restaurants,
and theaters, this hotel is well placed and good value. Its glory days as a gold merchants' office are visible in the
beautiful Art Nouveau lobby. Though plain, the rooms are neat and tidy. **www.rhohotel.nl**

NIEUWE ZIJDE NH Barbizon Palace   €€€
Prins Hendrikkade 59–72, 1012 AD **Tel** *020-556 4564* **Fax** *020-624 3353* **Rooms** *270*   **Map** *D2*

The jewel in the NH crown, this hotel's public area has sleek black-and-white décor. Facilities are outstanding and
include excellent breakfasts, the Michelin-starred Restaurant Vermeer, and a 14th-century chapel serving as one of
eight conference rooms. **www.nh-hotels.com**

NIEUWE ZIJDE Grand Hotel Krasnapolsky   €€€
Dam 9, 1012 JS **Tel** *020-554 9111* **Fax** *020-622 8607* **Rooms** *468*   **Map** *C2*

The location of this hotel – on Dam Square, overlooking the Koninklijk Paleis – is great. Accommodations range from
utter luxury in the Tower Suite to compact rooms at the back. Facilities are top-notch and include restaurants, a café,
and a cocktail bar. The Winter Garden is where weekend brunches are enjoyed. **www.nh-hotels.com**

OUDE ZIJDE Grand Hôtel Amrâth Amsterdam   €€€€€
Prins Hendrikkade 108–114, 1011 AK **Tel** *020-552 0000* **Fax** *020-552 0900* **Rooms** *173*   **Map** *D2*

Overlooking the old harbor, this luxury hotel occupies the 1913 Sheepvaarthuis, one of the landmark Amsterdam
School buildings. The hotel opened in summer 2007 and offers spacious rooms equipped with every comfort. The
Seven Seas restaurant serves fine French/international cuisine. **www.amrathamsterdam.com**

Key to Symbols *see back cover flap*

PLANTAGE Rembrandt

Plantage Middenlaan 17, 1018 DA **Tel** *020-627 2714* **Fax** *020-638 0293* **Rooms** *17* **Map** *D4*

One of the few cheaper options in this area, this hotel is good for families intent on visiting nearby Artis zoo. Public spaces are covered in flamboyant murals that recall the hotel's namesake, and have dark, wooden furniture. The bedrooms, meanwhile, are brighter and more modern, and all are en-suite. **www.hotelrembrandt.nl**

WESTERN CANAL RING Truelove Antiek and Guesthouse

Prinsenstraat 4, 1015 DC **Tel** *020-320 2500* **Fax** *020-320 2500* **Rooms** *2* **Map** *C2*

A small, two-roomed, romantic bolt hole in the heart of Amsterdam's most interesting shopping area. It is non-smoking, simple and stylish; although there is no breakfast (you are spoiled for choice nearby), there are considerate touches like wine, water, and fresh flowers in the rooms. **www.truelove.be**

WESTERN CANAL RING Hotel Toren

Keizersgracht 164, 1015 CZ **Tel** *020-622 6352* **Fax** *020-626 9705* **Rooms** *96* **Map** *C2*

A stylish place decorated in tasteful pastel hues and stripes, Hotel Toren boasts a fascinating history: it has been a merchant's house and a university, and it was also used to hide Jews during World War II. On the downside, standard rooms are small, so spend a little extra on a superior: you get extra leg room and a spa bath. **www.hoteltoren.nl**

REST OF THE NETHERLANDS

APELDOORN Bilderberg Hotel De Keizerskroon

Koningstraat 7, 7315 HR **Tel** *055-521 7744* **Fax** *055-521 4737* **Rooms** *94*

A large, popular hotel with good facilities, pleasingly situated on the edge of a park near the Royal Palace. Rooms are spacious, and decorated in trendy citrus and brown shades, with big comfortable beds; the largest rooms have sofas. There's a smart restaurant, a snug bar, and a small swimming pool. **www.bilderberg.nl**

DELFT Hotel de Ark

Koornmarkt 65, 2611 EC **Tel** *015-215 7999* **Fax** *015-214 4997* **Rooms** *38*

Arranged across three houses beside a bustling canal, De Ark is convenient for the station and city center. Rooms, in bright, fresh colors are well-sized (as are bathrooms), with lovely touches like Delft-tiled fireplaces. The bridal suites boast two-person baths and saunas, and there are also apartments for longer stays. **www.deark.nl**

THE HAGUE Le Meridien Hotel des Indes

Lange Voorhout 54-56, 2514 EG **Tel** *070-361 2345* **Fax** *070-361 2350* **Rooms** *92*

One of the most famous – and best – in the whole country, this monumental hotel is a luxurious base for exploring the city. Décor references the colonial period with dark heavy wood, swathes of marble and potted palms. Rooms are spacious and well-equipped. One minus point: staff could be more gracious. **www.hoteldesindes.nl**

HAARLEM Haarlem Hotelsuites

Kleine Houtstraat 13, 2011 DD **Tel** *023-540 7146* **Fax** *023-551 8923* **Rooms** *5*

On a restaurant-lined street at the heart of the city, the apartments here are spacious and stylish. They have large living rooms with squashy sofas and bedrooms have comfy big beds; some apartments have private roof terraces. Breakfast is served in the nearby Boulangerie café, or delivered to the apartment. **www.haarlem-hotelsuites.nl**

LEIDEN Pension De Witte Singel

Witte Singel 80, 2311 BP **Tel** *071-512 4592* **Fax** *0182-514 2890* **Rooms** *6*

This simple, unpretentious little guesthouse occupies a lovely town house overlooking a canal. There are just six rooms; the ones at the back have views over the chestnut trees in the garden, while the front-facing ones overlook the water. Rooms are clean and tidy, with either private or shared facilities. **www.pension-ws.demon.nl**

ROTTERDAM Hotel New York

Koninginnenhoofd 1, 3072 AD **Tel** *010-439 0500* **Fax** *010-484 2701* **Rooms** *72*

This monumental hotel in a former shipping-line HQ feels gloriously isolated, though it's near the center. Most rooms are decorated in bold modern designs with lovely bathrooms; the more expensive ones, in the directors' boardrooms, remain untouched, with wood-paneling and chandeliers. **www.hotelnewyork.nl**

UTRECHT Grand Hotel Karel V

Geertebolwerk 1, 3511 XA **Tel** *030-233 7555* **Fax** *030-233 7500* **Rooms** *121*

The best hotel in the city is housed in a former military building filled with historical detail. The luxurious rooms and suites have great bathrooms, and are arranged across different wings. A new wing opened in 2007. Amenities are tip-top: a Michelin-starred restaurant, a brasserie, a wine bar, and huge gardens. Breakfasts are excellent. **www.karelv.nl**

VOLENDAM Hotel Restaurant Van den Hogen

Haven 106, 1131 EV **Tel** *0299-363 775* **Fax** *0299-369 498* **Rooms** *5*

This small hotel is right on the waterfront, close to all the fishing boats, and near the bars and restaurants. Most rooms have views over the IJsselmeer, and are clean and tidy, though decorated in plain, functional style, and all are en-suite. There's a cosy, traditional fish restaurant downstairs. **www.hogen.nl**

Map References *see map of Amsterdam pp248–9*

Where to Eat in the Netherlands

Although the Netherlands does not boast the gastronomic reputation of France or Italy, the chance of finding good food at a reasonable price is high. As well as Dutch restaurants, there are plenty of other establishments serving culinary delights from around the world. Amsterdam, in particular, is full of ethnic restaurants.

PRICE CATEGORIES
The following price ranges are for a three-course meal for one, including half a bottle of wine, plus all unavoidable extra charges, such as cover, service and tax.

€ Under 30 euros
€€ 30–40 euros
€€€ 40–50 euros
€€€€ Over 50 euros

AMSTERDAM

CENTRAL CANAL RING Los Pilones
€€   Map C3

Kerkstraat 63, 1017 GC **Tel** *020-320 4651*

A small cantina run by two Mexican brothers who serve authentic dishes. Los Pilones offers some of the best Mexican food in the whole of Amsterdam. Expect the occasional unusual combination such as *enchiladas* with a chocolate sauce. The pièce de résistance is their huge range of tequilas (around 35). Closed lunch; Mon.

CENTRAL CANAL RING Proeverij 274
€€€   Map C4

Prinsengracht 274, 1016 HH **Tel** *020-421 1848*

Popular with both locals and visitors to the city, this warm and romantic two-floored restaurant serves classic international dishes made with organic ingredients. Book the round table by the door for a delightful view over the canal. Groups of up to 25 people can be catered for in the downstairs basement. Closed lunch.

EASTERN CANAL RING SSK
€€   Map D4

Falckstraat 3, 1017 VV **Tel** *020-330 1128*

You will feel like you are having dinner at a friend's house at SSK. Hostess-chef Hanneke van den Bergh creates a fixed three-course meal using produce she has bought fresh from the market and specialist shops. The cuisine is traditional, but with a twist. Organic wines are chosen to match the food. Closed lunch; Sun–Tue.

EASTERN CANAL RING Beddington's
€€€€   Map D4

Utrechtsedwarsstraat 141, 1017 WE **Tel** *020-620 7393*

One for discerning taste buds and those in search of slow-paced dining in sober, stylish surroundings. From the open kitchen, British owner/chef Jean Beddington produces seamless French and Asian fusion, with a sprinkling of British sensibility. Delightful desserts and friendly service. Closed lunch; Mon, Sun.

MUSEUM QUARTER Brasserie van Baerle
€€€€   Map B4

Van Baerlestraat 158, 1071 BG **Tel** *020-679 1532*

This French-style brasserie is particularly popular with Dutch celebrities, especially for lunch and Sunday brunch (when it opens at 10am). Mouth-watering dishes include grilled sea bass with home-made crab mayonnaise and a roast-pepper dressing. Exceptional wine list and gorgeous garden terrace. Booking recommended. Closed Sat lunch.

NIEUWE ZIJDE Brasserie Harkema
€€   Map C3

Nes 67, 1012 KD **Tel** *020-428 2222*

A classic Parisian brasserie with a stylish New York sensibility, Harkema serves haute cuisine at affordable prices. It is immensely popular, especially in the evenings, so it is wise to book ahead. Feast on delights such as sautéed venison steak on toast with fried chanterelle mushrooms, followed by chocolate tart with a Bastogne biscuit base.

NIEUWE ZIJDE Green Planet
€€   Map C3/D2

Spuistraat 122, 1012 VA **Tel** *020-625 8280*

This vegetarian restaurant uses organic ingredients to create healthy, tasty dishes, including soups, huge salads, freshly baked breads, and homemade dips. The chef will also oblige any special dietary needs. Try Green Planet's renowned vegan tofu-lemon cheesecake. Closed lunch; Sun.

NIEUWE ZIJDE Kapitein Zeppos
€€€   Map C3

Gebed Zonder End 5, 1012 HS **Tel** *020-624 2057*

Tucked down a tiny alley, lit by fairy-lights, this bar-restaurant (with Belgian ceramic-tile tables and eclectic ornaments) was once a coach stable, then a cigar factory. The kitchen turns out delicious French-Mediterranean cuisine, with Italian, Moroccan and Spanish influences. Ideal for a romantic evening. Closed Mon.

NIEUWE ZIJDE Supperclub
€€€€   Map C3

Jonge Roelensteeg 21, 1012 PL **Tel** *020-344 6400*

Remove your shoes and recline on cushioned beds at this restaurant-club. DJs spin upbeat lounge music as you graze on culinary delights from the open kitchen – all spread out over five courses. Fine wines, video art, massage, and offbeat performances complete this assault on the senses. There is also a lounge bar downstairs. Closed lunch.

Key to Symbols *see back cover flap*

OUDE ZIJDE Café Roux (The Grand Hotel)

♿ 🖼 🎐 €€€€

Oudezijds Voorburgwal 197, 1012 EX **Tel** *020-555 3560*

***Map** C3/D2*

This informal Art Deco restaurant affords a unique opportunity to try dishes created by master chef Albert Roux at a reasonable price, especially the set menu. The wonderful French and British dishes are made using the best-quality local products. The wine selection is excellent. Breakfast is served 6:30–10:30am.

PLANTAGE La Rive (Amstel Hotel)

♿ €€€€

Professor Tulpplein 1, 1018 GX **Tel** *020-520 3264*

***Map** D4*

This Michelin-starred restaurant within the Amstel Hotel is one for connoisseurs. Outstanding cuisine from its modern French-Mediterranean kitchen is matched by an excellent wine list. Reserve the chef's table in the kitchen (four to eight people) for an unusual twist to your dining experience. Dress code is elegant. Closed Sat lunch, Sun.

REST OF THE NETHERLANDS

ALKMAAR Rose's

€

Fnidsen 107, 1811 NE **Tel** *072-515 2606*

Brightly colored Mexican restaurant that offers a reasonably priced and filling menu full of the classics. Alongside favourites like *tacos*, *enchiladas* and *fajitas*, there are burgers and more refined dishes such as blackened fish and duck breast with tamarind. To accompany, there is a varied menu of cocktails and Mexican beers. Closed lunch.

DELFT Le Vieux Jean

🚶 €€€€

Heilige Geestkerkhof 3, 2611 HP **Tel** *015-213 0433*

This lovely, understated little place near the Nieuwe Kerk looks – and tastes – like a real French restaurant. Polished wood, white linen table cloths, and fine crockery are a fitting setting to show off classics like *coquilles St. Jacques* and lamb chops in butter, rounded off with cheese and a glass of 20-year-old port. Closed Sat lunch; Mon, Sun.

HAARLEM Lambermons

♿ €€

Spaarne 96, 2011 CL **Tel** *023-542 7804*

Housed in an old brewery building, Lambermons dispenses with the usual formula of choosing three courses from a printed menu. Instead, diners in this "cooking theater" are presented with a dish every half hour, and can choose as many (or as few) as they wish. Dishes change daily: French-inspired meat and fish dominates. Closed lunch; Mon.

THE HAGUE Dayang

🍽 €

Prinsestraat 65, 2513CB **Tel** *070-364 9979*

This tiny "toko" is thought by many to have some of the best Indonesian food in the The Hague – a real accolade, as the city is famed for that country's cuisine. The authentic food is cheap, but nothing is sacrificed to quality: meat and fish are juicy, and anything served with the spicy peanut sauce is recommended. Closed Mon.

THE HAGUE Bistro Mer

🖼 €€€€

Javastraat 9, 2585 AB **Tel** *070-360 7389*

Fish, lobster and oysters are the specialty at this restaurant in The Hague's refined embassy district. An abundance of mirrors and the airy conservatory overlooking the courtyard (with outside seating) enhance the experience of the French-influenced food. For dessert, the *crêpes suzettes* with ginger are recommended.

LEIDEN City Hall

🚶 ♿ 🖼 €

Stadshuisplein 3, 2311 EJ **Tel** *071-514 4055*

A well-priced staple in the basement of the town hall, attracting a cross-section of Leiden's population, from students to businesspeople. The interior is slick, white and space age, and food imaginative Mediterranean: swordfish carpaccio, *mesclun* and goat's cheese salad, giant profiterole with nutty ice cream. Also popular for breakfast and lunch.

ROTTERDAM Kade 4

🚶 🖼 €

Spaansekade 4, 3011 ML **Tel** *010-270 9001*

On the water's edge in the beautiful Old Harbour in the shadow of the expressionist cube houses, "Quay 4" comes into its own in summer when diners can eat on the water's edge (and it's also pleasant inside). Lunch offers light wraps and salads, while evening meals include Dutch favourites such as mustard soup and North Sea shrimps.

UTRECHT Le Bibelot

🚶 🖼 €€

Oudegracht 181, 3511 NE **Tel** *030-231 3353*

Traditional French food served in the unpretentious surroundings of a friendly, cosy restaurant with canal views in the city center. All the favorites are present, from onion soup to delicious *crêpes suzettes*, and unusually for this kind of restaurant, there is a good choice for vegetarians. The three-course set dinner is excellent value. Closed lunch; Mon.

UTRECHT Goesting

♿ 🖼 €€€€

Veeartsenijpad 150, 3572 DH **Tel** *030-273 3346*

This building was a stable, but is now an upmarket restaurant, with low ceilings and tables nestled in arches. The short menu shows off the kitchen's skills in innovating around formal dishes, using the best ingredients: air-dried ham from Ruurlo served with rhubarb jam, tournedos with Fryske Hynder whisky from Bolsward. Closed lunch; Mon, Sun.

Map References *see map of Amsterdam pp248–9*

THE IBERIAN PENINSULA

THE IBERIAN PENINSULA
AT A GLANCE 274–275

SPAIN 276–351

PORTUGAL 352–381

The Iberian Peninsula at a Glance

A wonderful, warm climate and superb beaches have made the Iberian Peninsula a popular package-tour destination, drawing millions of visitors to well-known areas such as the Algarve in Portugal, and the Costa del Sol in Spain. But there are also tranquil fishing villages, first-class museums and galleries, and a wealth of splendid architecture, from the grand monuments left by the region's Moorish rulers to ultramodern, 20th-century designs. The Catholic faith has deep roots in Portugal and Spain. As well as spectacular cathedrals, there are many colorful religious festivals that take place all year round, making a visit all the more enjoyable.

0 km 75

0 miles 75

Santander

Oviedo

Lugo

Santiago de Compostela

León

Valladolid

Oporto

Salamanca

PORTUGAL
(See pp352–381)

Toledo

Toledo (see pp296–8) *has one of the largest cathedrals in Christendom, a massive Gothic structure that soars above the rooftops of the perfectly preserved medieval town.*

LISBON

Ciudad

Córdoba

Seville

Lisbon (see pp356–65) *rises above the estuary of the Tagus on a series of a hills. The oldest part of the city is crowned by the restored battlements of the Castelo de São Jorge.*

Málaga

Seville (see pp328–31) *is regarded as the soul of Andalusia. The city's famous bullring is arguably the finest in the whole of Spain and a perfect venue for a first experience of the* corrida, *or bullfight.*

◁ **The rocky coast of Galicia, northwestern Spain**

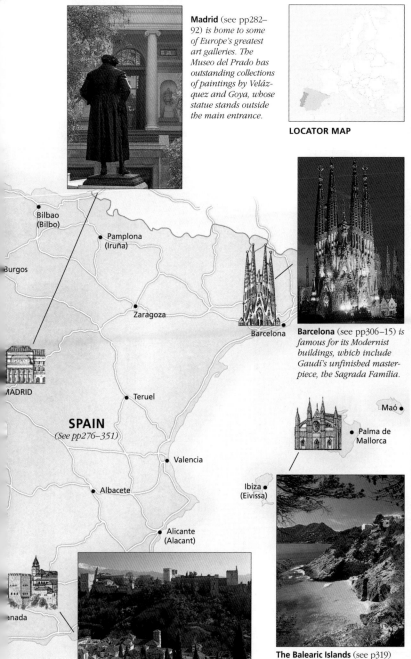

Madrid (see pp282–92) *is home to some of Europe's greatest art galleries. The Museo del Prado has outstanding collections of paintings by Veláz-quez and Goya, whose statue stands outside the main entrance.*

LOCATOR MAP

Bilbao
(Bilbo)

Pamplona
(Iruña)

Burgos

Zaragoza

Barcelona

Barcelona (see pp306–15) *is famous for its Modernist buildings, which include Gaudí's unfinished master-piece, the Sagrada Família.*

MADRID

Teruel

SPAIN
(See pp276–351)

Maó

Palma de
Mallorca

Valencia

Albacete

Ibiza
(Eivissa)

Alicante
(Alacant)

nada

Granada (see pp320 and 322–3), *in the foothills of the snowcapped Sierra Nevada, is unmissable for its Moorish heritage. Its greatest monument is the stunning Alhambra palace.*

The Balearic Islands (see p319) *are often associated with mass tourism, but away from the busy resorts, there are hundreds of unspoiled coastal villages and beautiful coves to be discovered.*

SPAIN

The familiar images of Spain – flamenco dancing, bullfighting, tapas bars, and solemn Easter processions – do no more than hint at the diversity of this country. Spain has four official languages, two major cities of almost equal importance, and a greater range of landscapes than any other European country. These contrasts make Spain an endlessly fascinating place to visit.

Separated from the rest of Europe by the Pyrenees, Spain reaches south to the coast of North Africa, and has both Atlantic and Mediterranean coastlines. The country's climate and scenery vary dramatically, from the snow-capped peaks of the Pyrenees, through the green meadows of Galicia and the orange groves of Valencia, to the dry, barren regions in the south.

Madrid, Spain's capital, lies geographically in the center of the country. The *madrileños* – as the city's inhabitants are known – have an individualistic spirit and a sardonic sense of humor that set them apart from other Spaniards. Madrid may be the nominal capital, but it is rivaled in commerce, sport, and the arts by Barcelona, the main city of Catalonia.

In the last 50 years Spain has undergone more social change than anywhere else in western Europe. In the first half of the 20th century, it was largely a poor, rural country. Gradually people flooded into the cities, leaving the rural areas depopulated. The 1960s saw the beginning of spectacular economic growth, partly due to a burgeoning tourist industry. Since then Spain has become a major player in European and world affairs.

HISTORY

From the 11th century BC the coastal regions of the Iberian Peninsula were colonized by sophisticated eastern Mediterranean civilizations, starting with the Phoenicians, then the Greeks and the Carthaginians. Celts mixed with native Iberian tribes, forming the Celtiberians. The Romans arrived in 218 BC to take possession of the peninsula's huge mineral wealth. The fall of the Roman Empire in the 5th century AD left Spain in the hands of the Visigoths, invaders from the north. Their poor political organization,

The colorful art of bullfighting, still a strong tradition all over Spain

◁ View from a typical hilltop Castilian town across the vast plains of central Spain

The Moor Boabdil surrendering Granada to the Catholic Monarchs

however, meant they were easily conquered by the Moors, who arrived from North Africa around 711.

Within a few years the Moors controlled almost the entire peninsula. Europe's only major Muslim territory, the civilization of Al Andalus excelled in mathematics, geography, astronomy, and poetry, and by the 9th century Córdoba was Europe's leading city.

In the 11th century, northern Christian kingdoms initiated a military reconquest of Al Andalus. The marriage, in 1469, of Fernando of Aragón and Isabel of

Castile – the so-called Catholic Monarchs – led to Spanish unity. They took Granada, the last Moorish stronghold, in 1492. In the same year Columbus discovered the Americas, and the conquistadors began plundering the civilizations of the New World.

The 17th century was a golden age for Spain – a time of outstanding artistic and literary output. This brilliance occurred, however, against a backdrop of economic deterioration and ruinous wars with France and the Low Countries. Spain's misfortunes continued in the 19th century, with an invasion by Napoleon's troops, leading to the War of Independence (Peninsular War). In the course of this century, Spain also lost all her South and Central American colonies.

The late 19th century was a time of national decline, with anarchism developing as a response to rampant political corruption. Political instability led to dictatorship in the 1920s and, a decade later, the Spanish Civil War. The victor, the Nationalist General Franco, ruled by repression until his death in 1975. Since then Spain has been a democratic state.

General Franco, Nationalist leader in the Spanish Civil War

KEY DATES IN SPANISH HISTORY

1100 BC Arrival of Phoenicians, first in a wave of settlers from across the Mediterranean

218–202 BC Romans oust Carthaginians from southeastern Spain

5th century AD Visigoths take control of Spain

711 Moors invade Spain and defeat Visigoths

756 Independent emirate established at Córdoba; Moorish civilization flourishes

11th century Christian kingdoms begin reconquest of Moorish territories

1492 Catholic Monarchs capture Granada, last Moorish stronghold. Columbus reaches America

1561 Madrid becomes capital of Spain

17th century Spain's Golden Age

1808–14 Spanish War of Independence

1898 Spain loses her last American colony, Cuba

1936–9 Spanish Civil War; Nationalist General Franco emerges victor

1975 Death of Franco; restoration of Bourbon monarchy as Juan Carlos I is proclaimed king

1986 Spain joins the EC (now EU)

1992 Barcelona hosts the Olympic Games

2000 Spain celebrates 25 years of democracy

2004 Nearly 200 people die in terrorist bomb attacks on trains in Madrid

DEVELOPMENT AND DIPLOMACY

After the death of the dictator General Franco in 1975, Spain became a constitutional monarchy under King Juan Carlos I. The post-Franco era, up until the mid-1990s, was dominated by the Socialist Prime Minister Felipe González, whose party, PSOE, was responsible for major improvements in roads, education, and health services. Spain's entry to the European Community in 1986 triggered a spectacular increase in the country's prosperity. Its international reputation was given a further boost in 1992 when Barcelona hosted the Olympic Games and Seville was the site of Expo '92.

With the establishment of democracy, the 17 autonomous regions of Spain have acquired considerable powers. A significant number of Basques favor independence for the Basque Country. The Basque terrorist group ETA, and its campaign of violence, is one of the major problems facing the government, headed by José Luis Rodríguez Zapatero of the Socialist Workers' Party.

RELIGION, LANGUAGE, AND CULTURE

Following the Christian Reconquest in the Middle Ages, a succession of rulers tried to impose a common culture, but today Spain remains a culturally diverse nation. Several regions have maintained a strong sense of their own identities. Catalonia, the Basque Country, Valencia, the Balearic Islands, and Galicia have their own languages, which are in everyday use, and, in some cases, have supplanted Castilian as the first language of the region.

During the Middle Ages Spain gained a reputation for religious intolerance. The Inquisition, established by the Catholic Monarchs, saw thousands of non-Catholics tortured, executed, or expelled from the country. Today, Spain enjoys complete religious freedom. Nevertheless, Catholicism is still a powerful influence in society. Saints' days and other important events in the Christian calendar are marked by many traditional ceremonies, enthusiastically maintained in towns and villages throughout modern Spain.

Religious procession in a Seville street during *Semana Santa* (Holy Week)

THE SPANISH WAY OF LIFE

The Spanish are known for their natural sociability and zest for living. They commonly put as much energy into enjoying life as they do into their work. The stereotypical "mañana" ("leave it until tomorrow") is a myth, but many people fit their work around the demands of their social life, rather than be ruled by the clock. The day is long in Spain, and the Spanish have a word, *madrugada*, for the time between midnight and dawn, when city streets are often still full of revelers enjoying themselves. Eating out is an important social activity, with friends and family often meeting up in a pavement café or restaurant for a chat and a meal.

Underpinning Spanish society is the extended family. In the past, a lack of efficient public services has forced the Spanish to rely on close relatives, rather than institutions, to find work or seek assistance in a crisis. It is not uncommon for three generations to live under one roof, and even life-long city dwellers refer fondly to their *pueblo* – the town or village where their family comes from, and which they return to as often as they can.

Spaniards socializing over drinks and a meal at a sidewalk café

Exploring Spain

Although many visitors to Spain come for the beaches alone, increasingly tourists are drawn by the country's rich cultural heritage. The most popular destinations are Madrid and Barcelona, which boast world-class museums and a wealth of medieval and modern architecture. For those with time to travel further afield, Seville, Granada, and Córdoba in the far south are the best places to see relics of Spain's Moorish past. Spain is Europe's third largest country, so getting around can be time-consuming. However, there is a reliable network of trains, as well as good highways and bus services.

Ciutadella harbor, on the island of Menorca, at twilight

SIGHTS AT A GLANCE

Ávila **5**
Barcelona pp306–15 **18**
Bilbao **14**
Burgos pp299–301 **7**
Cádiz **34**
Córdoba pp324, 326–7 **30**
Costa Blanca **24**
Costa del Sol **28**
El Escorial **2**
Granada pp320, 322–3 **26**
Jerez de la Frontera **33**
León **8**
MADRID pp282–92 **1**
Málaga **27**
Mallorca and the
  Balearic Islands **25**
*Monestir de Montserrat
pp316–7* **19**
Oviedo **11**
Pamplona **16**
Parc Nacional
  d'Aigüestortes **17**
Parque Nacional
  de Doñana **32**
Picos de Europa **12**
Poblet **20**
Rías Baixas **10**
Ronda **29**
Salamanca **6**
San Sebastián **15**
Santander **13**
Santiago de
  Compostela **9**
Segovia **4**
Seville pp328–31 **31**
Tarragona **21**
Toledo pp296–8 **3**
Valencia **23**
Zaragoza **22**

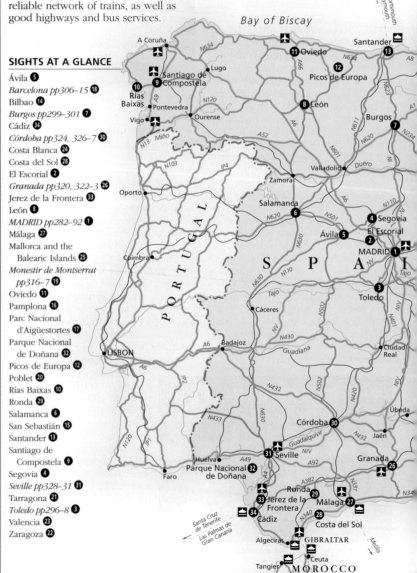

SEE ALSO

- *Practical Information* pp332–3
- *Travel Information* pp334–5
- *Shopping* pp336–7
- *Entertainment* pp338–9
- *Where to Stay* pp340–45
- *Where to Eat* pp346–51

DISTANCE CHART

Distance in kilometers
Distance in miles

MADRID								
621 / 388	BARCELONA							
397 / 248	620 / 388	BILBAO						
400 / 250	908 / 568	795 / 497	CÓRDOBA					
544 / 340	997 / 623	939 / 587	187 / 117	MALAGA				
623 / 389	1129 / 706	707 / 442	977 / 611	1153 / 721	PONTEVEDRA			
538 / 336	1046 / 654	933 / 583	138 / 86	219 / 137	922 / 576	SEVILLE		
352 / 220	349 / 218	633 / 396	545 / 341	648 / 405	975 / 609	697 / 436	VALENCIA	
325 / 203	296 / 185	324 / 203	725 / 453	869 / 543	833 / 521	863 / 539	326 / 204	ZARAGOZA

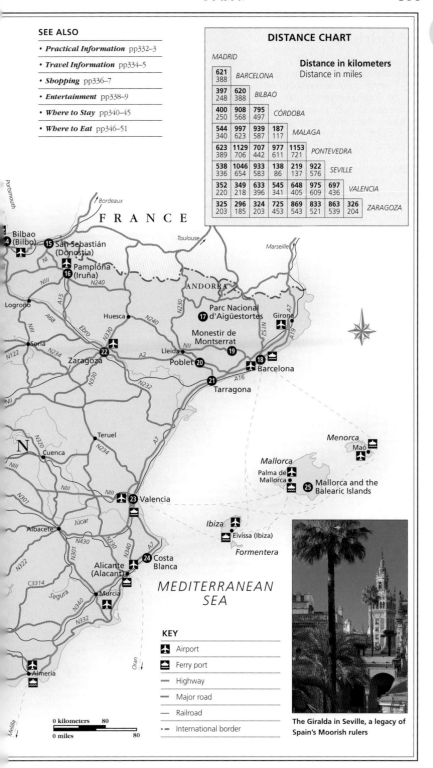

KEY

✈	Airport
⛴	Ferry port
—	Highway
—	Major road
—	Railroad
–·–	International border

0 kilometers 80

0 miles 80

The Giralda in Seville, a legacy of Spain's Moorish rulers

Madrid ❶

Spain's capital, a city of over three million people, is situated close to the geographical center of the country, at the hub of both road and rail networks. The origins of the city date back to AD 852, when the Moors built a fortress near the Manzanares river and a small community grew up around it. It was not until 1561, however, that the city became the capital of a newly formed nation-state. In the following centuries, under the Habsburgs and then the Bourbons, the city acquired some of its most notable landmarks, including the splendid Plaza Mayor and the Palacio Real. At the same time, the blossoming city attracted some of Spain's most outstanding artists, such as court painters Velázquez and Goya, whose works can be admired in the world-famous Museo del Prado.

19th-century *taberna* (taverna), one of the few left in Madrid today

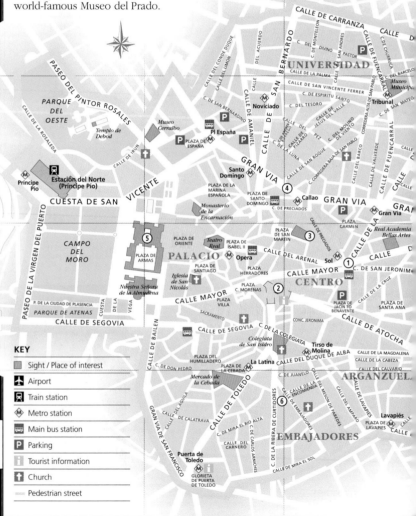

KEY

- 🟦 Sight / Place of interest
- ✈ Airport
- 🚆 Train station
- Ⓜ Metro station
- 🚌 Main bus station
- 🅿 Parking
- ℹ Tourist information
- ✝ Church
- --- Pedestrian street

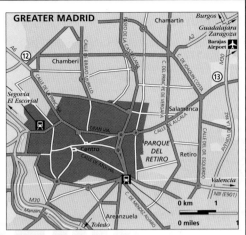

GETTING AROUND

The Metro is the most efficient way of getting around Madrid. Lines 1, 2, 3, 5, and 10 serve all the main sights; lines 1 and 2 are good for getting to the museums around the Paseo del Prado. Useful buses include the 51, 52, 150, and 153 to the Puerta del Sol, and 2, 8, 14, 15, 27, 74, and 146 to the Plaza de Cibeles. Buses to Madrid's Barajas airport leave from the terminal below Plaza de Colón.

SEE ALSO

• *Where to Stay* pp340–41

• *Where to Eat* pp346–7

GREATER MADRID

KEY

■ Area of main map

SIGHTS AT A GLANCE

Centro de Arte
 Reina Sofía ⑨
Gran Vía ④
Monasterio de las
 Descalzas Reales ③
Museo Arqueológico
 Nacional ⑪
*Museo del Prado
 pp288–90* ⑦
Museo Thyssen-
 Bornemisza ⑧
Palacio Real ⑤
Parque del Retiro ⑩
Plaza Mayor ②
Puerta del Sol ①
El Rastro ⑥

Greater Madrid
(see inset map)
Museo de América ⑫
Plaza de Toros de
 las Ventas ⑬

The beautiful 17th-century Plaza Mayor, at the heart of Old Madrid

Old Madrid

When Felipe II chose Madrid as his capital in 1561, it was a small Castilian town of little importance. In the following years, it was to grow into the nerve center of a mighty empire. During the reign of the Habsburg dynasty, many royal monasteries, churches, and private palaces were built. In the 17th century the Plaza Mayor was added, and the Puerta del Sol became the spiritual and geographical heart not only of Madrid but of all Spain. Old Madrid's splendid Bourbon palace, the Palacio Real, was built under Felipe V in the first half of the 18th century.

Bear and strawberry tree, the symbol of Madrid, Puerta del Sol

Puerta del Sol ①

Ⓜ Sol.

With its many shops and cafés, the Puerta del Sol ("Gateway of the Sun") is one of Madrid's liveliest areas. The square marks the site of the original eastern entrance to the city, once occupied by a gatehouse and a castle.

A statue of Carlos III (reigned 1759–88) stands at the center of the square. On its southern edge is the austere Casa de Correos, dating from the 1760s. Originally the city's post office, it later became the headquarters of the Ministry of the Interior. During the Franco regime, the police cells below the building were the site of human rights abuses. Outside the building, a symbol on the ground marks Kilometer Zero, considered the center of Spain's road network.

On the opposite side of the square is a bronze statue of the symbol of Madrid – a bear reaching for the fruit of a *madroño* (strawberry tree). The Puerta del Sol has witnessed many important historical events. On May 2,

1808 the uprising against the occupying French forces began in the square, and in 1912 the liberal prime minister José Canalejas was assassinated here.

Ongoing repair works, due to be completed in 2007, may cause some disruption.

Plaza Mayor ②

Ⓜ Sol.

For hundreds of years this beautiful 17th-century square was a center of activity, with bullfights, executions, pageants, and trials by the Inquisition taking place here.

The first great public event was the beatification of the city's patron, St. Isidore, in 1621. Perhaps the greatest occasion, however, was the arrival from Italy of Carlos III (Carlos VII of Naples) in 1760. He became king of Spain after his half-brother, Fernando VI, died without an heir.

Façade of the Casa de la Panadería on the Plaza Mayor

Designed by architect Juan Gómez de Mora, the square was started in 1617 and built in just two years. At its center is an equestrian statue of Felipe III, who ordered the square's construction.

The elegant arcades that line the Plaza Mayor are today filled with cafés and craft shops. One of the more interesting buildings is the Casa de la Panadería, whose façade is decorated with splendid allegorical paintings.

On Sundays the square is the venue for a collectors' market, with stalls selling coins, stamps, books, and other items.

Decorated chapel, Monasterio de las Descalzas Reales

Monasterio de las Descalzas Reales ③

Plaza de las Descalzas 3. **Tel** 91- 454 88 00. Ⓜ Sol, Callao. ◯ 10:30am–12:45pm, 4–5:45pm Tue–Thu & Sat, 10:30am–12:45pm Fri, 11am–1:45pm Sun & public hols. ● Jan 1 & 6, 3 days after Easter, May 1 & 15, Sep 9, Nov 9, Dec 24–25, 31. 📷 (except Wed for EU residents). 🎫 **www**.patrimonionacional.es

This religious building is a rare surviving example of 16th-century architecture in Madrid. Around 1560, Felipe II's sister, Doña Juana, decided to convert a medieval palace on this site into a convent.

Doña Juana's rank accounts for the massive store of art amassed by the Descalzas Reales (Royal Barefoot Sisters), which includes a fresco of

The vast Palacio Real, Madrid's 18th-century Bourbon palace

Felipe IV's family and, above the main staircase, a ceiling by Claudio Coello. The Sala de Tapices contains stunning tapestries, while paintings on display include works by Brueghel the Elder, Titian, Zurbarán, Murillo, and Ribera.

Gran Vía ④

M *Plaza de España, Santo Domingo, Callao, Gran Vía.*

A main traffic artery of the modern city, the Gran Vía was inaugurated in 1910.

Lined with cinemas, tourist shops, hotels, and restaurants, this grand avenue also has many buildings of architectural interest. At the Alcalá end of the street, the French-inspired Edificio Metrópolis and the Edificio la Estrella (No. 10) are both worth seeing. The latter is a good example of the eclectic mix of Neoclassical design and ornamental detail

One of the many 1930s Art Deco buildings lining the Gran Vía

that was fashionable when the street was first developed. Look out for some interesting carved stone decoration, such as the striking gargoyle-like caryatids at No. 12.

Further along the Gran Vía, around the Plaza del Callao, are a number of Art Deco buildings, including the well-known Capitol cinema and bingo hall, built in the 1930s.

Palacio Real ⑤

Calle de Bailén. **Tel** *91-454 88 00.* **www**.*patrimonionacional.es* M *Ópera, Plaza de España.* 🚌 *3, 25, 33, 39, 148.* ◯ *Apr–Sep: 9am–6pm Mon–Sat, 9am–3pm Sun & hols; Oct–Mar: 9:30am–5pm Mon–Sat, 9am–2pm Sun & hols.* ◗ *Jan 1 & 6, May 1 & 15, Oct 12, Nov 9, Dec 24, 25 & 31.* 🎟 *(except Wed for EU residents).* 🖼 🎒 ♿ 🚹

Madrid's vast and lavish Palacio Real (Royal Palace) was commissioned by Felipe V after the royal fortress that had occupied the site for centuries was ravaged by fire in 1734. The palace was the home of Spanish royalty until the abdication of Alfonso XIII in 1931. Today it is used by the present king for state occasions only.

The exuberant decor of the interior reflects the tastes of the Bourbon kings, Carlos III and Carlos IV. The walls and ceiling of the Porcelain Room, commissioned by the former, are covered in green and white royal porcelain, which is embossed with cherubs and wreaths. Named after its Neapolitan designer, the

Gasparini Room is equally lavishly decorated. In the adjacent antechamber hangs a portrait of Carlos IV by Goya. Other star attractions are the Dining Room, with its fine ceiling paintings and superb Flemish tapestries, and the 18th-century Throne Room.

Shoppers browsing around the Rastro flea market

El Rastro ⑥

Calle de la Ribera de Curtidores. M *La Latina, Embajadores.* ◯ *10am–2pm Sun & public hols.*

Madrid's famous flea market was established in the Middle Ages. Its heyday came in the 19th century, but today there are still plenty of locals, as well as tourists, who come to the Calle de la Ribera de Curtidores to browse around the many stalls selling a huge range of wares – from new furniture to second-hand clothes. The market's other main street is the Calle de Embajadores, which runs down past the dusty Baroque façade of the Iglesia de San Cayetano.

Street-by-Street: Paseo del Prado

Banco de España sculpture

In the late 18th century, before the museums and lavish hotels of Bourbon Madrid took shape, the Paseo del Prado was laid out and soon became a fashionable spot for strolling. Today the Paseo's main attraction lies in its museums and art galleries. Most notable are the Museo del Prado (just south of the Plaza Cánovas del Castillo) and the Museo Thyssen-Bornemisza, both displaying world-famous collections of paintings. Among the monuments built under Carlos III are the Puerta de Alcalá, the Fuente de Neptuno, and the Fuente de Cibeles, which stand in the middle of busy roundabouts.

Paseo del Prado
Based on the Piazza Navona in Rome, the Paseo was built by Carlos III as a center for the arts and sciences in Madrid.

Banco de España
Spain's central reserve bank is housed in this massive building with three façades at the Plaza de Cibeles.

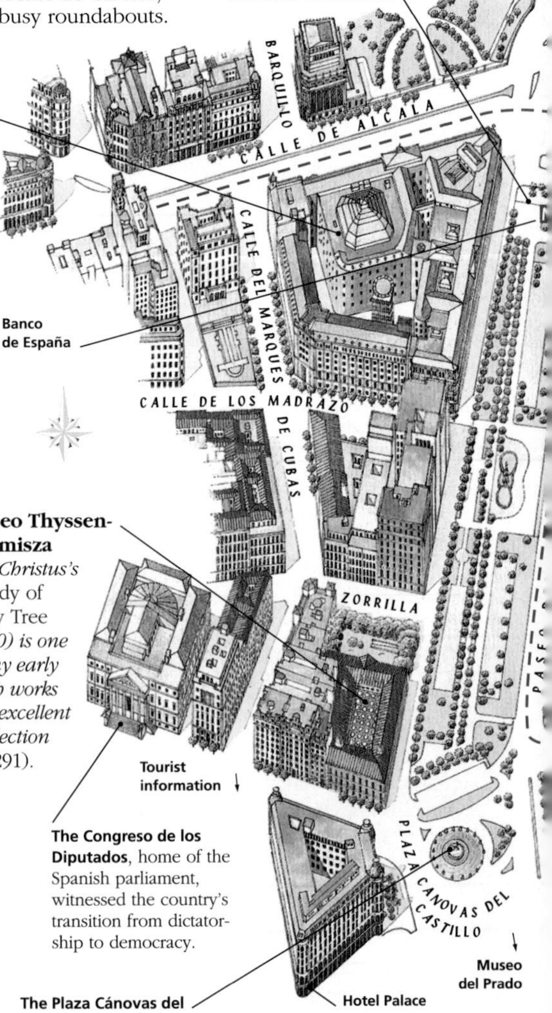

Banco de España

★ Museo Thyssen-Bornemisza
Petrus Christus's Our Lady of the Dry Tree *(c.1450) is one of many early Flemish works in this excellent art collection (see p291).*

Tourist information

The Congreso de los Diputados, home of the Spanish parliament, witnessed the country's transition from dictatorship to democracy.

The Plaza Cánovas del Castillo is dominated by a sculpted fountain of the god Neptune in his chariot.

Hotel Palace

Museo del Prado

STAR SIGHTS

* ★ Museo Thyssen-Bornemisza
* ★ Puerta de Alcalá
* ★ Plaza de Cibeles

| 0 meters | 100 |
| 0 yards | 100 |

Palacio de Linares
This grandly decorated late 19th-century palace now houses the Casa de América, an organization that promotes Latin American culture.

Palacio de Comunicaciones

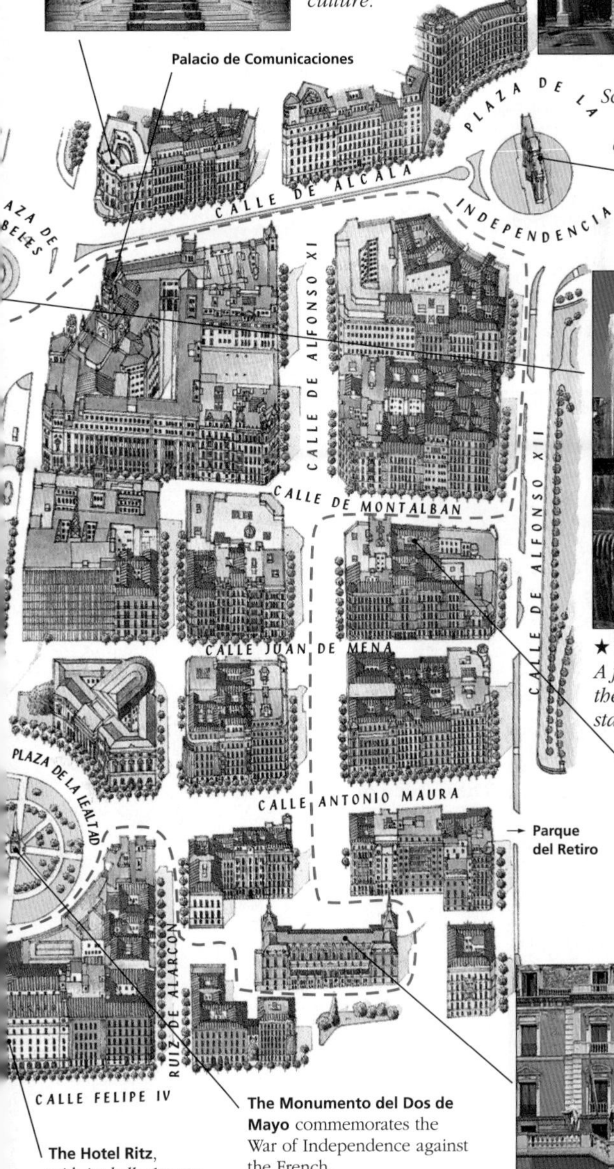

★ Puerta de Alcalá
Sculpted from granite, this former gateway into the city is especially beautiful when floodlit at night.

PLAZA DE LA INDEPENDENCIA

CALLE DE ALCALÁ

AZA DE BELES

CALLE DE ALFONSO XI

CALLE DE MONTALBAN

CALLE DE ALFONSO XII

CALLE JUAN DE MENA

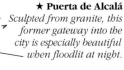

★ Plaza de Cibeles
A fountain with a statue of the Roman goddess Cybele stands in this square.

PLAZA DE LA LEALTAD

CALLE ANTONIO MAURA

→ Parque del Retiro

The Museo Nacional de Artes Decorativas was founded in 1912 as a showcase for Spanish ceramics and interior design.

RUIZ DE ALARCON

CALLE FELIPE IV

The Monumento del Dos de Mayo commemorates the War of Independence against the French.

The Hotel Ritz, with its *belle-époque* interior, is one of the most elegant hotels in the whole of Spain.

KEY

– – – Suggested route

Salón de Reinos
The former army museum (and part of the old Retiro Palace) will become part of the Prado Museum from 2009.

Museo del Prado ⑦

The Prado Museum houses the world's greatest assembly of Spanish paintings from the 12th to the 19th centuries, including major works by Velázquez and Goya. It also houses impressive foreign collections, particularly of Italian and Flemish works. The Neoclassical building was designed in 1785 by Juan de Villanueva on the orders of Carlos III. From early 2006, a fully refurbished Casón del Buen Retiro and a new building in the cloisters on San Jéronimo's church will be open to the public. In 2009 the former army museum (Salón de Reinos) will also become part of the Prado.

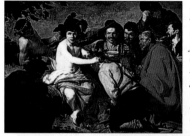

★ Velázquez Collection
The Triumph of Bacchus *(1629), Velázquez's first portrayal of a mythological subject, shows the god of wine (Bacchus) with a group of drunkards.*

The Three Graces *(c.1635)*
This was one of the last paintings by the Flemish master Rubens, and was part of his personal collection. The three women dancing in a ring – the Graces – are the daughters of Zeus, and represent Love, Joy, and Revelry.

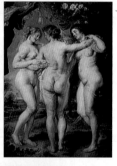

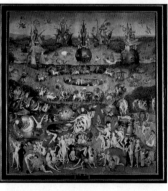

The Garden of Delights *(c.1505)*
Hieronymus Bosch, known as El Bosco in Spanish, was one of Felipe II's favorite artists, and is especially well represented in the Prado. This enigmatic painting is part of a triptych depicting paradise and hell.

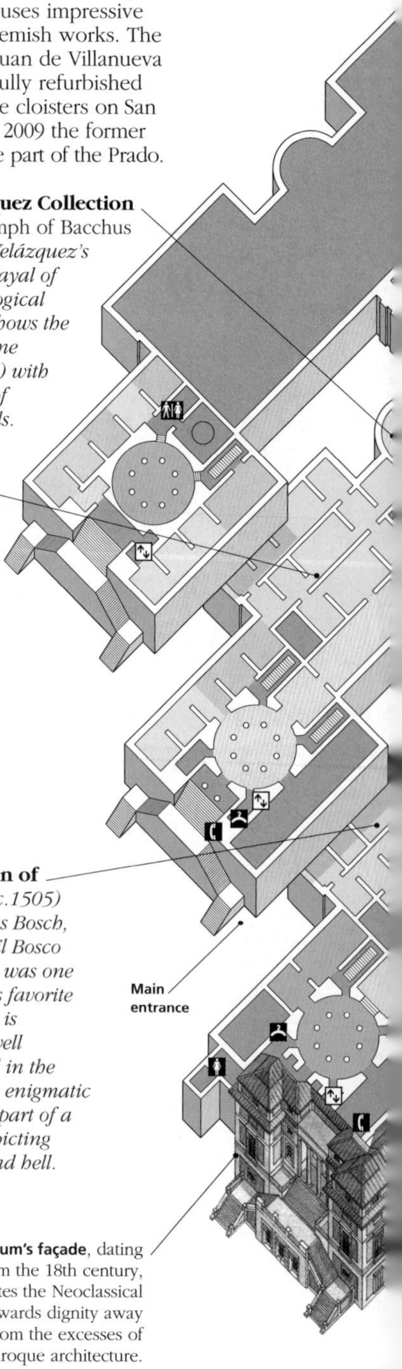

Main entrance

The museum's façade, dating from the 18th century, illustrates the Neoclassical move towards dignity away from the excesses of Baroque architecture.

STAR EXHIBITS

- ★ Velázquez Collection
- ★ Goya Collection

For hotels and restaurants in this region see pp340–41 and pp346–7

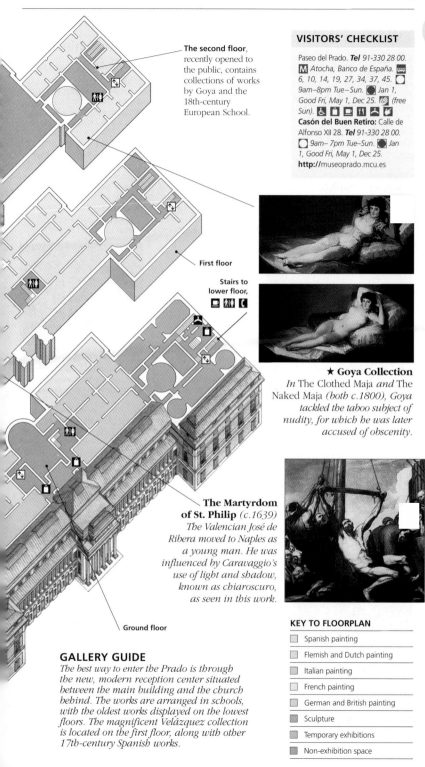

The second floor, recently opened to the public, contains collections of works by Goya and the 18th-century European School.

First floor

Stairs to lower floor,

VISITORS' CHECKLIST

Paseo del Prado. *Tel* 91-330 28 00.
Ⓜ Atocha, Banco de España.
6, 10, 14, 19, 27, 34, 37, 45.
9am–8pm Tue–Sun. Jan 1,
Good Fri, May 1, Dec 25. (free
Sun).
Casón del Buen Retiro: Calle de
Alfonso XII 28. *Tel* 91-330 28 00.
9am–7pm Tue–Sun. Jan
1, Good Fri, May 1, Dec 25.
http://museoprado.mcu.es

★ **Goya Collection**
In The Clothed Maja *and* The Naked Maja *(both c.1800), Goya tackled the taboo subject of nudity, for which he was later accused of obscenity.*

The Martyrdom of St. Philip *(c.1639)*
The Valencian José de Ribera moved to Naples as a young man. He was influenced by Caravaggio's use of light and shadow, known as chiaroscuro, as seen in this work.

Ground floor

GALLERY GUIDE
The best way to enter the Prado is through the new, modern reception center situated between the main building and the church behind. The works are arranged in schools, with the oldest works displayed on the lowest floors. The magnificent Velázquez collection is located on the first floor, along with other 17th-century Spanish works.

KEY TO FLOORPLAN

☐	Spanish painting
☐	Flemish and Dutch painting
☐	Italian painting
☐	French painting
☐	German and British painting
■	Sculpture
■	Temporary exhibitions
■	Non-exhibition space

Exploring the Prado's Collection

The importance of the Prado is founded on its royal collections. The wealth of foreign art, including many of Europe's finest works, reflects the historical power of the Spanish crown. The Low Countries and parts of Italy were under Spanish rule for hundreds of years. The 18th century was an era of French influence, following the Bourbon accession to the Spanish throne. The Prado is worthy of repeated visits, but if you go only once, see the Spanish works of the 17th century.

SPANISH PAINTING

Right up to the 19th century, Spanish painting focused on religious and royal themes. There are a few examples of Spain's early medieval art in the Prado, such as the anonymous mural paintings from the Holy Cross hermitage in Maderuelo. Spanish Gothic art can be seen in the works of Bartolomé Bermejo and Fernando Gallego.

Renaissance features began to emerge in the paintings of Pedro de Berruguete and Fernando Yáñez de la Almedina, whose work shows the influence of Leonardo da Vinci. Among examples of 16th-century Mannerism are paintings by Pedro Machuca and Luis de Morales "the Divine". One of the great masters of this period was the Cretan-born artist El Greco, who made his home in Toledo. The distortion of the human figure, typical of the Mannerist style, is carried to extreme in his painting *The Adoration of the Shepherds* (1612–14).

The Golden Age of the 17th century produced such great artists as José de Ribera and Francisco de Zurbarán. Works by both are on display in the Prado. This period, however, is best represented by the work of Diego Velázquez, Spain's leading court painter. Examples of his royal portraits and religious and mythological paintings are displayed, including his masterpiece *Las Meninas* (1656), a portrait of the Infanta Margarita surrounded by her courtiers.

Another great Spanish painter, Francisco de Goya, revived Spanish art in the 18th century. His later work embraces the horrors of war, as seen in *The 3rd of May* (1814), and culminated in a somber series known as *The Black Paintings*.

FLEMISH AND DUTCH PAINTING

Exceptional Flemish works of art include Rogier van der Weyden's masterpiece, *The Deposition* (c.1430), and some of Hieronymus Bosch's major paintings, such as the *Temptation of St. Anthony* (c.1500) and *The Haywain* (c.1485–90). Among the 16th-century paintings is the superb *Triumph of Death* (1562) by Brueghel the Elder. There are nearly 100 canvases by the 17th-century Flemish painter Peter Paul Rubens, of which the greatest is *The Adoration of the Magi*. The two most notable Dutch paintings on display are both by Rembrandt: *Artemisia* (c.1500) and a fine self-portrait.

The Adoration of the Shepherds (1612–14) by El Greco

ITALIAN PAINTING

The most remarkable Italian paintings are Botticelli's dramatic wooden panels that depict *The Story of Nastagio degli Onesti*, Raphael's *Christ Falls on the Way to Calvary* (1516), and *Christ Washing the Disciples' Feet* (c.1547) by Tintoretto. Venetian masters Titian – Charles V's court painter – and Veronese are equally well represented. Also on display are works by Giordano, Fra Angelico, Caravaggio, and Tiepolo, master of Italian Rococo.

Fra Angelico's The Annunciation (c.1430), from the Early Renaissance

FRENCH AND GERMAN PAINTING

Marriages between French and Spanish royalty in the 17th century brought French art to Spain. This section contains a selection of works by Poussin, Jean Ranc, Claude Lorrain, and Antoine Watteau.

German art is represented by Albrecht Dürer's lively *Self-Portrait* (1498), as well as by the works of Lucas Cranach and the late 18th-century court painter Anton Raffael Mengs.

CASÓN DEL BUEN RETIRO

Reopened in early 2006, the Casón is a study center, housing restoration studios, a specialist school, and a library. The former ballroom serves as the main gallery until the new Salón de Reinos (the former army museum) opens in 2009. After this, the Casón will cease its exhibitions.

Spacious interior of the Museo Thyssen-Bornemisza

Museo Thyssen-Bornemisza ⑧

Paseo del Prado 8. *Tel* 91-369 01 51. Ⓜ *Banco de España, Sevilla.* 🚌 *1, 2, 5, 9, 14, 15, 20.* 🕐 *10am–7pm Tue–Sun (Jul–Aug: 10am–11pm Tue–Sat).* 🈺 📷 ♿ 🏛 🖥 🍴 ♨ **www.**museothyssen.org

This magnificent museum houses a collection of art assembled by Baron Heinrich Thyssen-Bornemisza and his son, Hans Heinrich. From its beginnings in the 1920s, the collection was intended to illustrate the history of Western art, from the 14th to the 20th century. Among the museum's exhibits are masterpieces by Titian, Goya, and Van Gogh.

The series of Dutch and Flemish works is a strong point of the collection. Highlights include Jan van Eyck's *The Annunciation* (c.1435–41), Petrus Christus's *Our Lady of the Dry Tree* (c.1450), and *The Toilet of Venus* (c.1629) by Peter Paul Rubens.

On the ground floor are two temporary exhibition galleries, with free access. There is also a new café/restaurant with views of the garden.

The new extension has joined the museum to two adjacent buildings in order to better display its collection of Impressionist works, mainly from the 19th century.

Centro de Arte Reina Sofía ⑨

Calle Santa Isabel 52. *Tel* 91-467 50 62. Ⓜ *Atocha.* 🚌 *6, 14, 18, 19, 27, 45, 55, 68.* 🕐 *10am–9pm (2:30pm Sun) Wed–Mon.* ⬤ *main public hols.* 🈺 *(free Sat pm & Sun).* 📷 ♿ 🏛 **www.**museoreinasofia.mcu.es

Housed in an 18th-century former general hospital, this superb museum traces art through the 20th-century, with major works by such influential artists as Picasso, Salvador Dalí, Joan Miró, and Eduardo Chillida. There is also space dedicated to post-World War II

movements, such as Abstract, Pop, and Minimal Art.

The highlight of the collection is Picasso's *Guernica* (1937). This Civil War protest painting was inspired by the mass air attack in 1937 on the Basque village of Gernika by German pilots flying for the Nationalist air force.

The museum has recently seen the addition of three new glass buildings, which allows the permanent collection to extend over three floors.

Parque del Retiro ⑩

Tel 91-409 23 36. Ⓜ *Retiro, Ibiza, Atocha.* 🕐 *daily.* ♿

The Retiro Park formed part of Felipe IV's royal palace complex. All that remains of the palace is the Casón del Buen Retiro (now part of the Prado museum) and the Salón de Reinos (the former army museum). In 2005 the latter is due to move to the Alcázar in Toledo (*see p298*).

First fully opened to the public in 1869, the Retiro remains a popular place for relaxing in Madrid. The park has a pleasure lake, where rowing boats can be hired. On one side of the lake, in front of a half-moon colonnade, stands an equestrian statue of Alfonso XII.

To the south of the lake are two attractive palaces. The Neoclassical Palacio de Velázquez and the Palacio de Cristal (Crystal Palace) were built by Velázquez Bosco in 1887 as exhibition venues.

Colonnade and statue of Alfonso XII (1901) overlooking the Parque del Retiro's boating lake

For hotels and restaurants in this region see pp340–41 and pp346–7

Roman floor mosaic in the Museo Arqueológico Nacional

Museo Arqueológico Nacional ⑪

Calle Serrano 13. *Tel 91-577 79 12.*
Ⓜ *Serrano, Retiro.* 🚌 *1, 9, 19, 51, 74.*
◯ *9:30am–8pm (6:30pm Jul & Aug)*
Tue–Sat, 9:30am–3pm Sun. ◯ *main*
public hols. 🖼 *(free Sat pm & Sun).*
📷 ♿ **www**.man.es

Founded by Isabel II in 1867, Madrid's National Archaeological Museum has hundreds of fascinating exhibits, ranging from the pre-historic era to the 19th century.

One of the highlights of the prehistoric section is the exhibition on the ancient civilization of El Argar (1800–1100 BC) – an advanced agrarian society that flourished in southeast Spain. There is also a display of jewelry uncovered at the Roman settle-ment of Numantia, near Soria, and a 5th-century BC bust of a wealthy Iberian woman known as *La Dama de Elche*.

The museum's ground floor is largely devoted to the period between Roman and Mudéjar Spain, and contains some impressive Roman mosaics.

Outstanding pieces from the Visigothic period include a collection of 7th-century gold votive crowns from Toledo province, known as the Treasure of Guarrazar.

Also on show are examples of Andalusian pottery from the Islamic era and various Romanesque exhibits, among them an ivory crucifix carved in 1063 for King Fernando I.

Steps outside the museum's entrance lead underground to an exact replica of the Altamira caves in Cantabria – complete with their Paleolithic paintings – some of the world's finest prehistoric art. The earliest engravings and drawings date back to around 18,000 BC. The boldly colored bison paintings date from around 13,000 BC.

Museo de América ⑫

Avenida de los Reyes Católicos 6.
Tel 91-549 26 41. Ⓜ *Moncloa.* ◯
9:30am–3pm Tue–Sat, 10am–3pm Sun.
◯ *some public hols.* 🖼 *(free on Sun).*
♿ **www**.museodeamerica.mcu.es

This fine museum houses a collection of artifacts relating to Spain's colonization of the Americas. Many of the exhibits, which date back to prehistoric times, were brought to Europe by the early explorers of the New World.

The collection is arranged thematically, with individual rooms on, for example, society, religion, and communication. One of the highlights of the museum is the rare Mayan *Códice Tro-cortesiano* (AD 1250–1500) from Mexico – a hieroglyphic parchment illustrated with scenes of everyday life. Also worth seeing are the Treasure of the Quimbayas, pre-Columbian gold and silver items dating from AD 500–1000, and the display of contemporary folk art from some of Spain's former American colonies.

Plaza de Toros de las Ventas ⑬

Calle Alcalá 237. *Tel 91-356 22 00.*
Ⓜ *Ventas.* ◯ *for bullfights only.*
Museo Taurino *Tel 91-725 18 57.*
◯ *9:30am–2:30pm Mon–Fri, 10am–*
1pm Sun. 🖼 *daily (91-556 9237).*
♿ **www**.las-ventas.com

Las Ventas is undoubtedly one of the most beautiful bullrings in Spain. Built in 1929 in Neo-Mudéjar style, it replaced the city's original bullring which stood near the Puerta de Alcalá. Outside the bullring are monuments to two famous bullfighters: Antonio Bienvenida and José Cubero.

Adjoining the bullring, the **Museo Taurino** contains bullfighting memorabilia, such as portraits and sculptures of famous matadors. There is also a display of the tools of the bullfighter's trade, including capes and *banderillas* – sharp darts used to wound the bull *(see opposite).*

Plaza de Toros de Las Ventas, Madrid's magnificent bullring

For hotels and restaurants in this region see pp340–41 and pp346–7

The Art of Bullfighting

Bullfighting is a sacrificial ritual in which men (and a few women) pit themselves against an animal bred for the ring. In this "authentic religious drama," as the poet Federico García Lorca described it, the spectator experiences the same intensity of fear and exaltation as the matador. There are three stages, or *tercios*, in the *corrida* (bullfight). The first two, which involve a team of men both on horseback and

Poster for a bullfight

on foot, are aimed at progressively weakening the bull. In the third, the matador moves in for the kill. Despite opposition on the grounds of cruelty, bullfighting is still very popular. For many Spaniards, the *toreo*, the art of bullfighting, is a noble part of their heritage. However, fights today are often debased by practises designed to disadvantage the bull, in particular shaving its horns to make them blunt.

The *toro bravo* (fighting bull), *bred for courage and aggression, enjoys a full life prior to its time in the ring. Bulls must be at least four years old before they can fight.*

Manolete *is regarded by most followers of bullfighting as one of Spain's greatest matadors ever. He was finally gored to death by the bull Islero at Linares, Jaén, in 1947.*

The matador wears a *traje de luces* (suit of lights), a colorful silk outfit embroidered with gold sequins.

Joselito *was a leading matador, famous for his purist style. He displayed superb skill with the* capote *(red cape) and the* muleta *(matador's stick). Following a short retirement, he has returned to the ruedos (bullring).*

Banderillas, barbed darts, are thrust into the bull's back muscles to weaken them.

THE BULLRING

The audience at a bullfight is seated in the *tendidos* (stalls) or in the *palcos* (balcony), where the *presidencia* (president's box) is situated. Opposite are the *puerta de cuadrillas*, through which the matador and team arrive, and the *arrastre de toros* (exit for bulls). Before entering the ring, the matadors wait in a *callejón* (corridor) behind *barreras* and *burladeros* (barriers). Horses are kept in the *patio de caballos* and the bulls in the *corrales*.

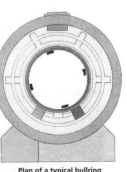

Plan of a typical bullring

KEY

- Tendidos
- Palcos
- Presidencia
- Puerta de cuadrillas
- Arrastre de toros
- Callejón
- Barreras
- Burladeros
- Patio de caballos
- Corrales

Central Spain

Much of Spain's vast central plateau, the *meseta*, is covered with wheat fields or dry, dusty plains, but there are many attractive places to explore. Spain's largest region, Castilla y León, has a rich history. It boasts some of the country's most splendid architecture, from Segovia's famous Roman aqueduct, to the Gothic cathedrals of Burgos and Léon and the Renaissance grandeur of Salamanca's monuments. Ávila's medieval city walls are a legacy of the long struggles between the Christians and the Moors. Dotted with windmills and medieval castles, Castilla-La Mancha is home to the historic town of Toledo, another popular destination.

The Library at El Escorial, with its 16th-century frescoed ceiling

El Escorial ❷

El Escorial. **Tel** 91-890 59 04. 🚇
from Atocha or Chamartín, Madrid.
🚌 *661, 664 from Moncloa, Madrid.*
⭕ *Tue–Sun.* ⬤ *public hols.* 📷
(except Wed for EU residents). ♿

Felipe II's imposing palace of San Lorenzo de El Escorial was built in 1563–84 in honor of St. Lawrence. The austere, unornamented building set a new architectural style – known as "Herreriano" after the palace's architect, Juan de Herrera. Its interior was conceived as a mausoleum and contemplative retreat rather than a splendid residence.

Among the most impressive parts of the palace is the **Library**, with a collection of over 40,000 books and manuscripts. Its ceiling is decorated with 16th-century frescoes by Tibaldi. The **Royal Pantheon**, a huge mausoleum made in marble, contains the funerary urns of Spanish monarchs.

Some of the most important works of the royal Habsburg collections, including Flemish, Italian, and Spanish paintings, are housed in the **Museum of Art**, located on the first floor. Other fine works of art can be found in the chapter houses, with their fresco-adorned ceilings, and in the basilica.

In contrast to the artistic wealth of other parts of the palace, the royal apartments are remarkably humble.

Toledo ❸

See pp296–8.

Segovia ❹

Segovia. 👥 *60,000.* 🚉 🚌 🛈
Plaza Mayor 10 (921-46 03 34).

Segovia is one of the most spectacularly sited cities in Spain. The old town is set high on a rocky spur, surrounded by the Eresma and Clamores rivers. With its cathedral, aqueduct, and castle dominating the skyline, the view of the town from the valley below at sunset is magical.

Perched on a rocky outcrop at the city's western end is the **Alcázar**, a fairytale castle with gabled roofs, turrets, and crenellations. Begun in the 12th century, the castle assumed its present form between 1410 and 1455, though it had to be largely rebuilt following a fire in 1862. The castle contains a museum of weaponry and several sumptuous apartments.

Dating from 1525, Segovia's **cathedral** was the last great Gothic church to be built in Spain. It replaced the old cathedral, destroyed in 1520 when the Castilian towns revolted against King Carlos I. Other churches in the old town include the Romanesque **San Juan de los Caballeros**, which has an outstanding sculpted portico, **San Esteban**, and **San Martín**.

Segovia's Roman **aqueduct** was built in the 1st century AD and remained in use until the late 19th century.

♟ Alcázar
Plaza de la Reina Victoria Eugenia. **Tel**
921-46 07 59. ⭕ *daily.* ⬤ *Jan 1 & 6,*
Dec 25. 📷 *(free Tue for EU residents).*
📷 *(by appt and for a fee).* ♿

Environs
The palace of **Riofrío**, 11 km (7 miles) southwest of the city, was built as a hunting lodge for Felipe V's widow, Isabel Farnese, in 1752. Today, it houses a hunting museum.

Segovia's distinctive Alcázar, perched high above the city

Section of Ávila's 12th-century city walls

Ávila ❺

Ávila. 🏠 57,000. 🚉 🚌 🛈 Plaza Pedro Davila 4 (920-21 13 87).

The perfectly preserved medieval walls that encircle this historic city were built in the 12th century by Christian forces as a defense against the Moors. Of the nine gate-ways in the walls, the most impressive is the **Puerta de San Vicente**. Ávila's **cathedral**, whose unusual exterior is carved with beasts and scaly wild men, also forms part of the city walls.

Ávila is the birthplace of St. Teresa (1515–82), one of the Catholic Church's greatest mystics and reformers. The **Convento de Santa Teresa** occupies the site of the home of this saint, who also lived for many years in the **Monasterio de la Encarnación**.

Among the city's finest churches are the 12th-century **Iglesia de San Vicente** and the Romanesque-Gothic **Iglesia de San Pedro**.

Beyond the town center, the beautiful **Real Monasterio de Santo Tomás** contains the tomb of Tomás de Torquemada (1420–98), the notorious head of the Spanish Inquisition.

Salamanca ❻

Salamanca. 🏠 160,000. ✈ 15 km (9 miles) E. 🚉 🚌 🛈 Plaza Mayor 14 (923-21 83 42). www.salamanca.es

Home to one of the oldest universities in Europe, Salamanca is also Spain's best showcase of Renaissance and Plateresque architecture.

The city's famous **university** was founded by Alfonso IX of León in 1218. The 16th-century façade of the main building on the Patio de las Escuelas is a splendid example of the Plateresque style. This form of early Spanish Renaissance architecture is so called because of its fine detail, which resembles ornate silverwork – *platero* in Spanish means silversmith.

The 16th-century, mainly Gothic **new cathedral** and the 12th- to 13th-century, Romanesque **old cathedral** stand side by side. A high-light of the old cathedral is the richly colored altarpiece (1445) by Nicolás Florentino.

The magnificent **Plaza Mayor** was built by Felipe V in the 18th century to thank the city for its support during the War of the Spanish Succession. Among the arcaded buildings lining the square are the Baroque town hall and the Royal Pavilion, from where the royal family used to watch events in the square.

Other fine monuments located in the heart of the city include the 16th-century **Iglesia-Convento de San Esteban**, with its lovely ornamented façade, and the **Convento de las Dueñas**, which preserves Moorish and Renaissance features.

The **Museo Art Nouveau y Art Deco** holds an important collection of 19th- and 20th-century paintings, jewelry, ceramics, and stained glass.

On the city outskirts, the 1st-century AD Roman bridge, the **Puente Romano**, offers a good view over the entire city.

🏫 **Universidad**
Patio de las Escuelas 1. *Tel* 923-29 44 00. ⬜ daily. ⬤ Dec 25. 🎟 (except Mon am).

🏛 **Museo Art Nouveau y Art Deco**
Calle Gibraltar 14. *Tel* 923-12 14 25. ⬜ Tue–Sun. 🎟 (free Thu am). ♿ 📷

View of Salamanca's twin cathedrals from the Puente Romano

Street-by-Street: Toledo ❸

Picturesquely sited on a hill above the River Tagus is the historic center of Toledo. Behind the old walls lies much evidence of the city's rich history. The Romans built a fortress on the site of the present-day Alcázar. In the 6th century AD the Visigoths made Toledo their capital, and left behind many churches. After it was captured from the Moors by Alfonso VI in 1085, the city became the capital of the Christian kingdom of Castile. During the Middle Ages, Toledo was a melting pot of Christian, Muslim, and Jewish cultures, and it was during this period that the city's most outstanding monument – its cathedral – was built. In the 16th century the painter El Greco came to live in Toledo, and today the city is home to many of his works.

Iglesia de San Román
This church contains a museum relating the city's past under the Visigoths.

Puerta de Valmardón

| 0 meters | 100 |
| 0 yards | 100 |

CÁRDENAL LORENZANA

CALLE DE ALFONSO X

CALLE DE SAN ROMÁN

CALLE DE ALFONSO XII

CALLE DE ALFONSO XII

CALLE DE LA TRINIDAD

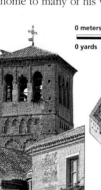

★ Iglesia de Santo Tomé
This church, with a beautiful Mudéjar tower, houses El Greco's masterpiece, The Burial of the Count of Orgaz.

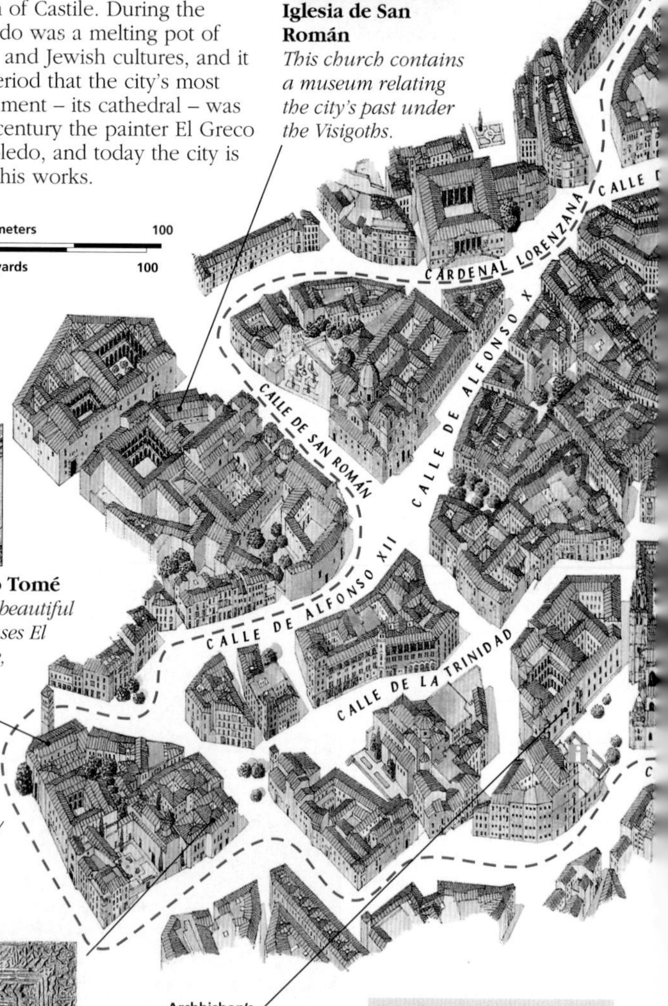

Sinagoga del Tránsito and Casa-Museo de El Greco

Archbishop's Palace

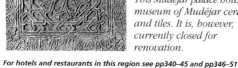

Taller del Moro
This Mudéjar palace houses a museum of Mudéjar ceramics and tiles. It is, however, currently closed for renovation.

STAR SIGHTS

★ Iglesia de Santo Tomé

★ Museo de Santa Cruz

★ Cathedral

The Puerta del Sol has a double Moorish arch and two towers.

Ermita del Cristo de la Luz
This small mosque, the city's only remaining Muslim building, dates from around AD 1000.

Tourist information, bus and train stations

PLAZA DE ZOCODOVER

ALFILERITOS

CALLE DEL COMERCIO

CUESTA DE CARLOS V

SIXTO RAMÓN PARRO

CARDENAL CISNEROS

KEY

– – – Suggested route

VISITORS' CHECKLIST

Toledo. 🚶 75,500. 🚆 Paseo de la Rosa (902-24 02 02). 🚌 Avenida de Castilla-La Mancha (925-21 58 50). 🛈 Plaza del Ayuntamiento 1 (925-25 40 30). 🛒 Tue. 🎉 Corpus Christi (May/Jun), Virgen del Sagrario, (Aug 15). **Iglesia de San Román** ⬤ Tue–Sun. 📷 **Taller del Moro** ⬤ Tue–Sun. 📷

The **Plaza de Zocodover** is named after the market which was held here in Moorish times. It is still the city's main square, with many cafés and shops.

★ Museo de Santa Cruz
The city's main fine arts collection includes several tapestries from Flanders. Among them is this 15th-century zodiac tapestry, with well-preserved rich colors.

★ Cathedral
Built on the site of a Visigothic cathedral and a mosque, this impressive structure is one of the largest cathedrals in Christendom (see p298). The beautiful Gothic high altar reredos (1504) is the work of several artists.

Alcázar
In the central patio of the fortress is a replica of the statue Carlos V y el Furor. The original is housed in Madrid's Museo del Prado.

Exploring Toledo

Easily reached from Madrid by rail, bus or car, Toledo is best explored on foot. To visit all the main sights you need at least two days, but it is possible to walk around the medieval and Jewish quarters in a long morning. To avoid the heavy crowds, go midweek and stay for a night, when the city is at its most atmospheric.

Toledo cathedral rising above the rooftops of the medieval quarter

🏠 Cathedral

Calle Cardenal Cisneros 1. **Tel** 925-22 22 41. **Choir, Treasury, Chapterhouse, and Sacristy** ○ Mon–Sat, pm Sun. 📷 📷 ♿.

The splendor of Toledo's cathedral reflects its history as the spiritual heart of the Spanish church and the seat of the Primate of all Spain. The present cathedral stands on the site of a 7th-century church. Work began in 1226, but the last vaults were not completed until 1493. This long period of construction explains the cathedral's mixture of styles: the exterior is pure French Gothic, while inside, Spanish decorative styles, such as Mudéjar – a hybrid Christian-Islamic style – and Plateresque, are used.

Among the cathedral's most outstanding features are the polychrome reredos of the high altar (1504), and the choir. In the treasury is a 16th-century Spanish silver monstrance, over 3 m (10 ft) high. The monstrance is carried through the streets of Toledo during the Corpus Christi celebrations. Standing out from the mainly Gothic interior, the Transparente is a stunning Baroque altarpiece of marble, jasper, and bronze, sculpted by Narciso Tomé.

🏛 Museo de Santa Cruz

Calle Cervantes 3. **Tel** 925-22 10 36. ○ daily. ● Jan 1, May 1, Dec 25. 📷 (free Sat pm & Sun).

Recently refurbished, this museum of fine arts has a superb collection of medieval and Renaissance tapestries, paintings, and sculptures. There are also works by the Cretan artist El Greco, as well as examples of two typical Toledan crafts: armor and damascened swords, the latter made by inlaying blackened steel with gold wire. The museum is housed in a fine Renaissance building.

The Assumption (1613) by El Greco, in the Museo de Santa Cruz

🏠 Iglesia de Santo Tomé

Plaza del Conde 4. **Tel** 925-25 60 98. ○ daily. 📷 except Wed pm for EU residents.

Visitors come to this church mainly to admire El Greco's masterpiece, *The Burial of the Count of Orgaz*. The church is thought to date back to the 12th century, and its tower is one of the best examples of Mudéjar architecture in the city.

♣ Alcázar

Cuesta de Carlos V. **Tel** 925-22 16 73. ● for expansion until 2008.

Charles V's fortified palace stands on the site of former Roman, Visigothic, and Muslim fortresses. In 1936 it was almost completely destroyed during a 70-day siege by the Republicans. The restored building houses an army museum and a private library, which holds a valuable collection of books and manuscripts dating back to the 11th century.

🏠 Sinagoga del Tránsito

Calle Samuel Leví. **Tel** 925-22 36 65. ○ Tue–Sun. 📷 (free Sat pm & Sun).

A wonderfully elaborate Mudéjar interior is hidden behind the humble façade of this 14th-century former synagogue. Next to the synagogue is an interesting museum dedicated to the Sephardic (Spanish Jewish) culture.

🏛 Casa-Museo de El Greco

Calle Samuel Leví. **Tel** 925-22 40 46. ○ Tue–Sun. 📷 (free Sat pm & Sun).

It is uncertain whether El Greco actually lived in or simply near to this house, now a museum containing a collection of his works. Canvases on display include the superb series *Christ and the Apostles*. Below the museum, on the ground floor, is a chapel with a fine Mudéjar ceiling and works of art by painters of the Toledan School, such as Luis Tristán, a student of El Greco.

♦ Puerta Antigua de Bisagra

When Alfonso VI of Castile conquered Toledo in 1085, he entered it through this gateway – the only one in the city to have kept its original 10th-century military architecture. The towers are topped by a 12th-century Arab gatehouse.

For hotels and restaurants in this region see pp340–45 and pp346–51

The Arco de Santa María in Burgos, adorned with statues and turrets

Burgos **7**

Burgos. 168,000. 🗐 🚌 **i** Plaza de Alonso Martínez 7 (947-20 31 25).

Founded in 884, Burgos was the capital of the united kingdoms of Castile and León from 1073 until 1492. A few hundred years later, Franco chose Burgos as his headquarters during the Civil War.

Approaching the city via the bridge called the Puente de Santa María, you enter the old town through the grand **Arco de Santa María**. The other main route into Burgos is the Puente de San Pablo, where a statue commemorates local hero El Cid (1043–99). Born Rodrigo Díaz de Vivar, this great warrior fought for both the Moors and the Christians in the Reconquest, and for his heroism was named El Cid, from the Arabic *Sidi* (Lord). He is immortalized in the anonymous poem, *El Cantar del Mío Cid* (1180).

Not far from the statue of El Cid stands the **Casa del Cordón**, a 15th-century former palace (now a bank). It was here that the Catholic

Monarchs welcomed Columbus on his return, in 1497, from the second of his voyages to the Americas.

Burgos's **cathedral** *(see pp300–301)* is a UNESCO World Heritage site and the city's most prominent landmark. Nearby, the **Iglesia de San Nicolás** boasts a fine 16th-century altarpiece, while the **Iglesia de San Lorenzo** has a splendid Baroque ceiling. The **Museo de Burgos** contains archaeological and fine art collections.

West of the city is the 12th-century **Real Monasterio de Huelgas**, a former convent that houses a textile museum.

🏛 **Museo de Burgos**
Calle Calera 25. **Tel** 947-26 58 75. ⏲ Tue–Sun. 🌐 (except Sat & Sun). 🚻

🕍 **Real Monasterio de Huelgas**
Calle de los Compases. **Tel** 947-20 16 30. ⏲ 10am–1pm & 3:45–5:30pm Tue–Sat, 10:30am–2pm Sun & public hols. 🚫 Jan 1 & 6, Apr 18, May 1, Jun 20 & 30, Dec 8, 24, 25, 31. 🌐 🚻 (except Wed for EU residents).

León **8**

León. 147,000. 🗐 🚌 **i** Plaza de la Regla 4 (987-23 70 82).

Founded as a camp for the Romans' Seventh Legion, León became the capital of

Statue of El Cid, Burgos's most famous son

the kingdom of León in the Middle Ages and played a central role in the early years of the Reconquest.

The city's Gothic **cathedral**, on Plaza de la Regla, dates from the mid-13th century. As well as some glorious stained glass, it has a splendid west front, decorated with a series of 13th-century carvings.

The **Colegiata de San Isidoro** is built into the Roman walls encircling the city. The Romanesque **Panteón Real** (Royal Pantheon) is decorated with carved capitals and 12th-century frescoes. León's old quarter is a maze of narrow alleyways, lined with bars, cafés, churches, and old mansions. The **Hostal de San Marcos** was founded in the 12th century as a monastery for pilgrims on route to Santiago *(see p302)*. A gem of Spanish Renaissance architecture, the present building was begun in 1513 for the Knights of Santiago. Today it houses a luxurious hotel and the **Museo de León**.

🏛 **Museo de León**
Plaza Santo Domingo. **Tel** 987-24 50 61. ⏲ Tue–Sun. 🚫 main public hols. 🌐 (except Sat & Sun).

Environs
To the east of León, the 10th-century **Iglesia de San Miguel de Escalada** is one of the finest surviving churches built by the Mozarabs – Christians influenced by the Moors.

Detail from a 13th-century carving decorating the west front of León's cathedral

Burgos Cathedral

Christ at the Column, by Diego de Siloé

Spain's third-largest cathedral was founded in 1221 under Fernando III and was named a UNESCO World Heritage site in 1984. The groundplan – a Latin cross – measures 84 m (276 ft) by 59 m (194 ft). Its construction was carried out in several stages over three centuries, involving artists and architects from across Europe. The style is almost entirely Gothic, with influences from Germany, France, and the Low Countries. In the Middle Ages the cathedral was a main stopping point for pilgrims on the road to Santiago *(see p302)*. Burgos's most celebrated son, the medieval hero of the Reconquest, El Cid, is buried in the cathedral, as is his wife.

West Front
The lacy, steel-grey spires soar above a sculpted balustrade depicting Castile's early kings.

★ Golden Staircase
Diego de Siloé's elegant Renaissance staircase (1519–22) links the nave with the Gothic Coroneria Gate (kept locked) at street level.

STAR FEATURES

★ Golden Staircase

★ Constable's Chapel

★ Crossing

Lantern

Tomb of El Cid

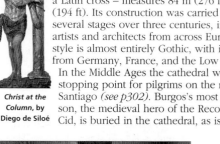

Capilla de Santa Tecla

Puerta de Santa María (main entrance)

Capilla de Santa Ana
The altarpiece (1490) in this chapel is by the sculptor Gil de Siloé. The central panel shows the Virgin with St. Joachim.

The Capilla de la Presentación (1519–24) is a funerary chapel with a star-shaped, traceried vault.

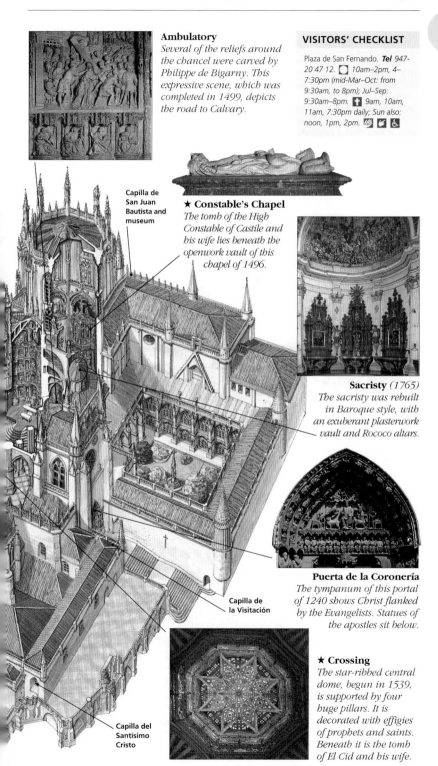

Ambulatory
Several of the reliefs around the chancel were carved by Philippe de Bigarny. This expressive scene, which was completed in 1499, depicts the road to Calvary.

VISITORS' CHECKLIST

Plaza de San Fernando. *Tel* 947-20 47 12. ☐ 10am–2pm, 4–7:30pm (mid-Mar–Oct: from 9:30am, to 8pm); Jul–Sep: 9:30am–8pm. ✝ 9am, 10am, 11am, 7:30pm daily; Sun also: noon, 1pm, 2pm. 🗺 📷 ♿

Capilla de San Juan Bautista and museum

★ Constable's Chapel
The tomb of the High Constable of Castile and his wife lies beneath the openwork vault of this chapel of 1496.

Sacristy (1765)
The sacristy was rebuilt in Baroque style, with an exuberant plasterwork vault and Rococo altars.

Puerta de la Coronería
The tympanum of this portal of 1240 shows Christ flanked by the Evangelists. Statues of the apostles sit below.

Capilla de la Visitación

★ Crossing
The star-ribbed central dome, begun in 1539, is supported by four huge pillars. It is decorated with effigies of prophets and saints. Beneath it is the tomb of El Cid and his wife.

Capilla del Santísimo Cristo

Northern Spain

Northern Spain encompasses a variety of landscapes and cultures. In the far northwest of the peninsula, the Galicians are fiercely proud of their customs and language. Spain's greenest region, Galicia boasts some of the most attractive stretches of Atlantic coast, as well as the beautiful city of Santiago de Compostela. Popular with hikers and naturalists, the spectacular Picos de Europa massif sits astride the border between Asturias and Cantabria. The Basque Country is a unique part of Spain whose main attractions include superb cuisine, fashionable seaside resorts, and the cultural center of Bilbao, with its famous Guggenheim Museum.

Santiago de Compostela's grand cathedral towering over the city

Santiago de Compostela ❾

A Coruña. 🎿 100,000. ✈ 10 km (6 miles) N. 🚉 🚌 🛈 Calle Rúa do Villar 63 (981-55 51 29). 🎭 Fiesta (Jul 25). **www**.santiagoturismo.com

In the Middle Ages this fine city was Christendom's third most important place of pilgrimage after Jerusalem and Rome. In 813 the body of Christ's apostle James was supposedly discovered here, and in the following centuries pilgrims from all over Europe flocked to the city.

On the Praza do Obradoiro stands the city's **cathedral**, built in honor of St. James. The present structure dates from the 11th–13th centuries, but the Baroque west façade was added in the 18th century. The square's northern edge is flanked by the grand **Hostal de los Reyes Católicos**, built by the Catholic Monarchs (see p278) as a resting place for

sick pilgrims. It is now a hotel. Nearby are the 9th-century **Convento de San Paio de Antealtares**, one of the city's oldest monasteries, and the **Convento de San Martiño Pinario**, whose Baroque church has a wonderfully ornate Plateresque façade.

The **Convento de Santo Domingo de Bonaval**, east of the center, is also worth visiting. Part of the monastery now houses a Galician folk museum. There is also the

Centro Gallego de Arte Contemporáneo, with works by leading Galician artists.

🏛 **Centro Gallego de Arte Contemporáneo**
Calle Valle Inclán s/n. *Tel* 981-54 66 29. ☐ Tue–Sun. 🎫 by prior appointment (call 981-54 66 31). ♿

Rías Baixas ❿

Pontevedra. 🚉 🚌 Pontevedra. 🛈 Calle General Gutierrez Mellado 1, Pontevedra (986-85 08 14).

The southern part of Galicia's west coast consists of four large *rías*, or inlets, between pine-covered hills. Known as the Rías Baixas (Rías Bajas), they offer fine beaches, safe bathing, and lovely scenery.

The main town on the coast is lively **Pontevedra**, which has many historic monuments, such as the Gothic Convento de Santo Domingo, and an excellent provincial museum.

Many areas along the coast have become popular holiday resorts, such as **Sanxenxo**, west of Pontevedra. To the south, **Baiona** and **Panxón** both have good beaches, as well as sailing and a variety of water sports. In spite of tourism, much of the coastline, particularly the quieter northernmost part, remains unspoiled. Here you can visit many small fishing ports and watch the locals harvesting mussels and clams.

While in Rías Baixas look out for *hórreos* – traditional stone-built granaries raised on stilts. The waterfront of picturesque **Combarro** is lined with these buildings, typical of the whole of Galicia.

The tranquil fishing village of Combarro in the Rías Baixas

For hotels and restaurants in this region see pp340–45 and pp346–51

Santa María del Naranco, a Pre-Romanesque church in Oviedo

Oviedo ⓫

Asturias. 🏛 200,000. 🚏 🚌
🛈 *Marqués de Santa Cruz 1 (985-22 75 86).* **www**.ayto-oviedo.es

Oviedo, the cultural and commercial capital of Asturias, is best known for its Pre-Romanesque buildings. This style flourished in the 8th–10th centuries and was confined to a small area of the kingdom of Asturias, one of the few areas of Spain that escaped invasion by the Moors.

With its huge barrel-vaulted hall and arcaded galleries, the church of **Santa María del Naranco**, in the north of the city, was built as a summer palace for Ramiro I in the 9th century. Equally impressive are the church of **San Miguel de Lillo** and the 9th-century church of **San Julián de los Prados**, with its frescoes.

In the center of Oviedo, the Flamboyant Gothic **cathedral** and the 9th-century **Iglesia de San Tirso** are both worth taking some time to see.

The city has two museums of note: the **Museo Arqueológico**, which contains local prehistoric, Roman, and Romanesque treasures, and the **Museo de Bellas Artes** (Museum of Fine Arts).

🏛 **Museo Arqueológico**
Calle San Vicente 5. **Tel** *985-21 54 05.* ◯ *phone for details.*
🏛 **Museo de Bellas Artes**
Calle Santa Ana 1. **Tel** *985-21 30 61.* ◯ *Tue–Sun.* ♿

Picos de Europa ⓬

Asturias, Cantabria, and Castilla y León. 🚌 *Oviedo to Cangas de Onís.*
🛈 *Cangas de Onís (985-84 86 14).*
Fuente Dé cable car Tel *942-73 66 10.* ◯ *daily.* ⬤ *Jan 6–Mar 1.*

This beautiful mountain range– christened "Peaks of Europe" by returning sailors as this was often the first sight of their homeland – offers superb upland hiking and supports a diversity of wildlife.

The two main gateways to the Picos are **Cangas de Onís**, northwest of the park, and **Potes**, on the eastern side. About 8 km (5 miles) southeast of the former, **Covadonga** is where, in 722, the Visigoth Pelayo is said to have defeated a Moorish army, inspiring Christians to reconquer the peninsula. The road south from Cangas de Onís follows the spectacular gorge known as the Desfiladero de los Beyes.

The Fuente Dé cable car, in the heart of the park, climbs 900 m (2,950 ft) to a rocky plateau, offering magnificent panoramic views.

Santander ⓭

Cantabria. 🏛 180,000. ✈ ⛴ 🚏 🚌
🛈 *Jardines de Pereda (942-220 30 00).* 🎭 *International Festival (Jul–Aug).*

Cantabria's capital, Santander, is a busy port that enjoys a splendid site on a deep bay on Spain's north Atlantic coast.

The early 20th-century Palacio de la Magdalena in Santander

The **cathedral** was rebuilt in Gothic style, following a fire in 1941 that destroyed the entire town. The 12th-century crypt has been preserved. Nearby, the **Museo de Bellas Artes** has works by Goya and Zurbarán, while the **Museo de Prehistoria y Arqueología** displays local finds, including Neolithic axe heads, Roman coins, pottery, and figurines.

On the Península de la Magdalena stands the **Palacio de la Magdalena**, built for Alfonso XIII in 1912. The upscale seaside resort of **El Sardinero**, to the north, has a long beach, chic cafés, and a majestic white casino.

🏛 **Museo de Bellas Artes**
Calle Rubio 6. **Tel** *942-20 31 20.*
◯ *Mon–Sat.* 📷
🏛 **Museo de Prehistoria y Arqueología**
Calle Casimiro Saenz 4. **Tel** *942-20 71 09.* ◯ *Tue–Sun.* ♿ 📷

19th-century Neo-Romanesque basilica in Covadonga, Picos de Europa

Frank Gehry's ultramodern Museo Guggenheim building in Bilbao

Bilbao ⓮

Vizcaya. 🏛 360,000. ✈ 🚢 🚉
🚌 🛈 Pl Ensanche 11 (944-79 57
60). 🎉 Fiesta (third week Aug).

Bilbao (Bilbo) is the center of Basque industry and Spain's leading commercial port, yet it has many cultural attractions worth visiting. In the city's medieval quarter – the *Casco Viejo* – the **Museo Arqueológico, Etnográfico e Histórico Vasco** displays Basque art and folk artifacts, while in the newer town, the **Museo de Bellas Artes** is one of Spain's best art museums.

The jewel in Bilbao's cultural crown, however, is the **Museo Guggenheim Bilbao**, which has a superb collection of Modern and contemporary art. It is just one of the city's many pieces of modern architecture, which also include the striking **Palacio de la Música y Congresos Euskalduna**.

🏛 **Museo Guggenheim**
Avenida Abandoibarra. **Tel** 944-35
90 80. ◯ 10am–8pm. ◯ Sep–Jun:
Mon; public hols. 🎫 🅿 ⬛ ♿
www.guggenheim-bilbao.es

San Sebastián ⓯

Guipúzcoa. 🏛 180,000. 🚉 🚌 🛈
Reina Regente 3 (943-48 11 66). 🎉
International Film Festival (late-Sep).

Popular with the aristocracy, San Sebastián (Donostia) became a fashionable seaside resort in the late 19th century.

At the heart of the old town are the handsome Plaza de la Constitución and the church of **Santa María del Coro**, with its Baroque portal. Behind the old town, Monte Urgull is worth climbing for the superb views from its summit. At the foot of the hill, the **Museo de San Telmo** holds exhibits ranging from Basque funerary columns to works by El Greco.

A short bus ride from the Calle Oquendo takes you to **Chillida-Leku**, a display of works by renowned Basque sculptor, Eduardo Chillida.

Between the city's two main beaches – the Playa de la Concha and the Playa de Ondarreta – is the **Palacio Miramar** (1889), built for Queen María Cristina.

🏛 **Museo de San Telmo**
Plaza Zuloaga. **Tel** 943-48 15 80.
◯ Tue–Sun. ♿

Mural by Josep Maria Sert in the Museo de San Telmo, San Sebastián

Bulls scattering the runners during Sanfermines in Pamplona

Pamplona ⓰

Navarra. 🏛 200,000. ✈ 🚉 🚌
🛈 Calle Eslava 1 (848-420 420).
🎉 Sanfermines (Jul 6–14).

Supposedly founded by the Roman general, Pompey, Pamplona is most famous for the fiesta of Los Sanfermines, with its daredevil bull running.

West of the city's mainly Gothic **cathedral** lies the old Jewish quarter, with the Neo-Classic **Palacio del Gobierno de Navarra** and the medieval **Iglesia de San Saturnino**.

The **Museo de Navarra** is a museum of regional history, archaeology, and art.

Southeast of the center is Felipe II's massive **citadel**, erected in the 16th century.

🏛 **Museo de Navarra**
Calle Santo Domingo. **Tel** 848-42
64 92. ◯ Tue–Sun. 🎫 free Sat
pm, Sun. ♿ 📷 by appointment.

BASQUE CULTURE

Possibly Europe's oldest race, the Basques are thought to be descended from Cro-Magnon people, who lived in the Pyrenees 40,000 years ago. Long isolated in their mountain villages, the Basques preserved their unique language (Euskera), myths, and art for millennia, almost untouched by other influences. Many families still live in the stone *caseríos*, or farmhouses, built by their forebears. The *fueros*, or ancient Basque laws, were suppressed under General Franco, but since 1975 the Basque region (Euskadi) has had its own parliament. Nevertheless, there is still a strong separatist movement seeking to sever links with the government in Madrid.

The Ikurriña, the flag of the Basque region

Catalonia

A nation-within-a-nation, Catalonia has its own semi-autonomous regional government, and its own language. Spoken by more than eight million people, Catalan has supplanted Castilian Spanish as the first language of the region, and is used on road signs and in place names everywhere. Barcelona is the region's capital, rivaling Madrid in economic and cultural importance. Catalonia offers a variety of attractions. The flower-filled valleys of the Pyrenees offer a paradise for naturalists and walkers, while inland are medieval towns, Roman ruins, and spectacular monasteries, such as Montserrat.

Parc Nacional d'Aigüestortes ⑰

Lleida. 🚆 *La Pobla de Segur.*
🚌 *El Pont de Suert, La Pobla de Segur.* 🛈 *Barruera (973-69 61 89).*

The pristine mountain scenery of Catalonia's only national park is among the most spectacular in the Pyrenees. The main village in the area is the mountain settlement of Espot, on the park's eastern edge. Dotted around the park are waterfalls and more than a hundred lakes and tarns.

The most beautiful scenery is around Sant Maurici lake, from where several walks lead north to the towering peaks of Agulles d'Amitges. The park is home to an impressive variety of wildlife: chamois, beavers, otters, and golden eagles have all found a habitat here.

Barcelona ⑱

See pp306–15.

Monestir de Montserrat ⑲

See pp316–7.

Poblet ⑳

Off N240, 10 km (6 miles) from Montblanc. *Tel* 977-87 00 89.
🚆 *to L'Espluga de Francolí, then taxi.*
🚌 ○ *9:30am–1pm, 3:30–5:30pm daily.* ● *Jan 1, Dec 25 & 26.* 📷

Santa Maria de Poblet was the first and most important of three medieval monasteries, known as the "Cistercian triangle." In 1835, during the

The superb high altar reredos at Santa Maria de Poblet

Carlist upheavals, the abbey sustained serious damage. Restoration began in 1930, and monks returned a decade later.

Poblet is enclosed by fortified walls that have hardly changed since the Middle Ages. Its evocative, vaulted cloisters were built in the 12th and 13th centuries. Beautiful, carved scrollwork decorates the capitals. Behind the stone altar, an impressive alabaster reredos, carved by Damià Forment in 1527, fills the apse. Other highlights include the

Royal Tombs, where many Spanish monarchs are buried. Begun in 1359, they were reconstructed by Marès in 1950.

Tarragona ㉑

Tarragona. 🏛 *125,000.* ✈ 🚆 🚌
🛈 *Carrer Major 39 (977-25 07 95).*

Now a major industrial port, Tarragona preserves many remnants of its Roman past, when it was the capital of the Roman province, Tarraconensis.

Among the extensive ruins are the **Anfiteatro Romano** (Roman Amphitheater) and the Praetorium, a Roman tower that was later converted into a medieval palace. Also known as the Castell de Pilato (after Pontius Pilate), the tower houses the **Museu de la Romanitat**, which contains Roman and medieval finds and gives access to the cavernous passageways of the 1st-century AD Roman circus. In the adjacent building is the **Museu Nacional Arqueològic**, which holds the most important collection of Roman artifacts in Catalonia, including some beautiful frescoes. An archaeological walk follows part of the Roman city wall.

Tarragona's 12th-century **cathedral** was built on the site of a Roman temple and an Arab mosque, and exhibits a harmonious blend of styles.

🏛 **Museu Nacional Arqueològic de Tarragona**
Plaça del Rei 5. *Tel* 977-23 62 09.
○ *Jun–Sep: Tue–Sat, am Sun; Oct–May: 10am–1:30pm, 4–7pm Tue–Sat, am Sun.* 📷 ♿

View across the Roman amphitheater at Tarragona to the sea

Barcelona ⑱

Barcelona, one of the Mediterranean's busiest ports, is more than the capital of Catalonia. In culture, commerce, and sport, it rivals not only Madrid, but also many of Europe's greatest cities. The success of the 1992 Olympic Games, staged in the Parc de Montjuïc, confirmed this to the world. Although there are many historical monuments in the Old Town, the city is best known for the scores of superb buildings left behind by the artistic explosion of Modernisme in the decades around 1900. Today, Barcelona still sizzles with creativity; its bars and public parks speak more of bold contemporary design than of tradition.

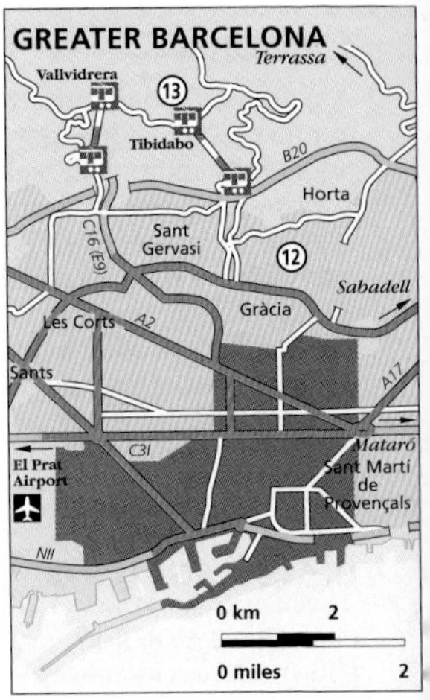

GREATER BARCELONA

SIGHTS AT A GLANCE

Barcelona Cathedral ①
Basílica de Santa
 Maria del Mar ④
Fundació Joan Miró ⑩
Montjuïc ⑨
Museu Nacional d'Art
 de Catalunya ⑪
Museu Picasso ⑤
Palau Reial & Museu
 d'Historia de la Ciutat ②
Quadrat d'Or ⑧
La Rambla ③
Sagrada Família
 pp312–13 ⑦
Vila Olímpica ⑥

Greater Barcelona
(see inset map)
Parc Güell ⑫
Tibidabo ⑬

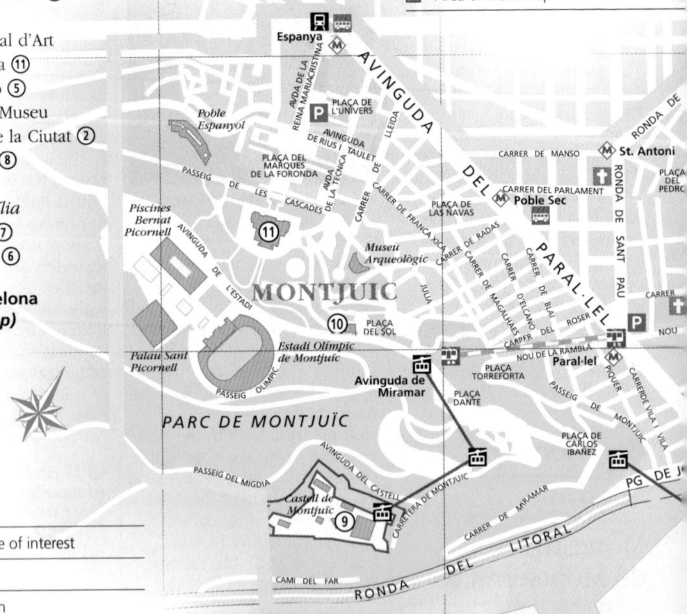

KEY

Area of main map

KEY

■	Sight / Place of interest
✈	Airport
🚆	Train station
Ⓜ	Metro station
🚌	Main bus stop
🚊	Tram stop
🚠	Cable car station
🚟	Funicular station
P	Parking
ℹ	Tourist information
✝	Church
---	Pedestrian street

Pedestrian swing bridge in Port Vell, at the end of La Rambla

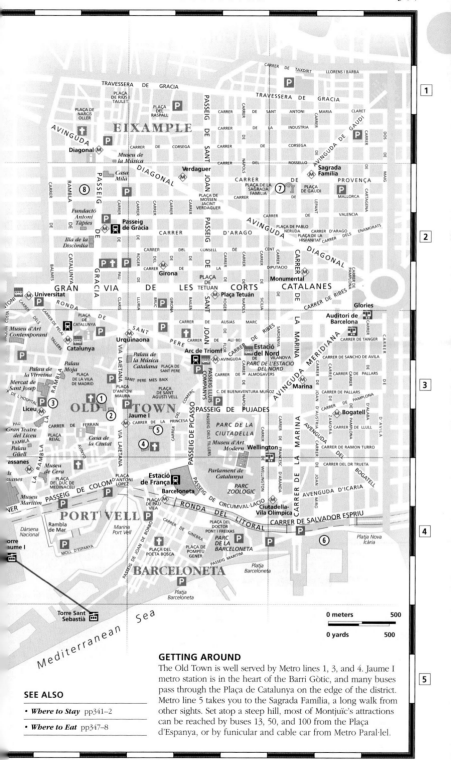

0 meters 500

0 yards 500

GETTING AROUND

The Old Town is well served by Metro lines 1, 3, and 4. Jaume I metro station is in the heart of the Barri Gòtic, and many buses pass through the Plaça de Catalunya on the edge of the district. Metro line 5 takes you to the Sagrada Família, a long walk from other sights. Set atop a steep hill, most of Montjuïc's attractions can be reached by buses 13, 50, and 100 from the Plaça d'Espanya, or by funicular and cable car from Metro Paral·lel.

SEE ALSO

• **Where to Stay** pp341–2

• **Where to Eat** pp347–8

D E F

Street-by-Street: Barri Gòtic

The Barri Gòtic (Gothic Quarter) is the true heart of Barcelona. This site was chosen by the Romans in the reign of Augustus (27 BC–AD 14) to found a new *colonia* (town), and has been the location of the city's administrative buildings ever since. The Roman forum was on the Plaça de Sant Jaume, where the medieval Palau de la Generalitat, Catalonia's parliament, and the Casa de la Ciutat, the town hall, now stand. Nearby are the Gothic cathedral and royal palace, where Columbus was received by the Catholic Monarchs on his return from the New World in 1492.

The Casa de l'Ardiaca (Archdeacon's House), a Gothic-Renaissance building on the Roman city wall, now houses Barcelona's historical archives.

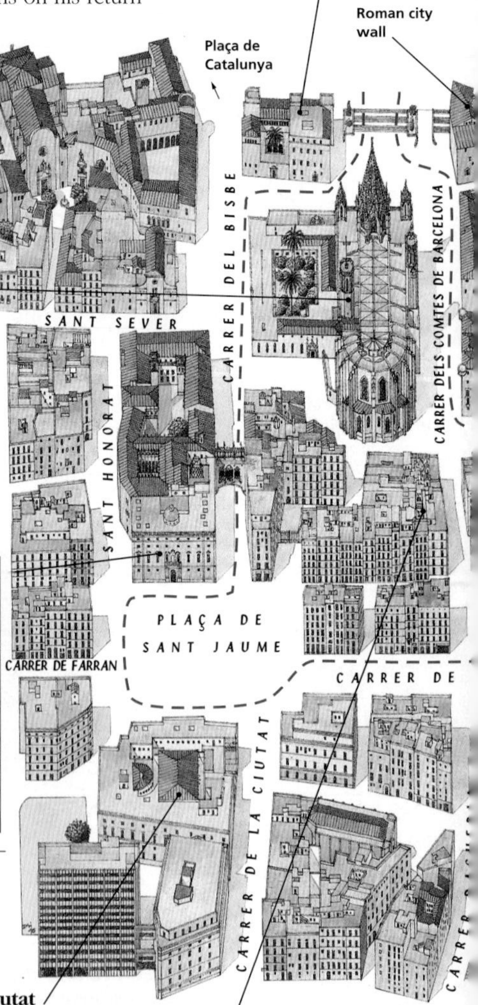

Roman city wall

Plaça de Catalunya

★ Cathedral
The façade and spire are 19th-century additions to the original building. The cathedral's treasures include medieval Catalan paintings.

Palau de la Generalitat
The superb Gothic features of the Catalan Parliament include the chapel and a stone staircase rising to an arcaded gallery.

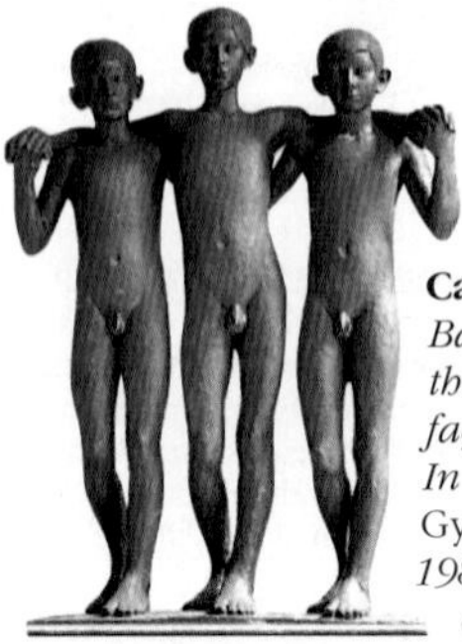

La Rambla ←

Casa de la Ciutat
Barcelona's town hall was built in the 14th and 15th centuries. The façade is a Neoclassical addition. In the entrance hall stands Three Gypsy Boys *by Joan Rebull (1899–1981), a 1976 copy of a sculpture he originally created in 1946.*

The Centre Excursionista de Catalunya, housed in a medieval mansion, displays Roman columns from the Temple of Augustus, whose site is marked by a millstone in the street outside.

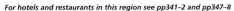

Museu Frederic Marès

This medieval doorway is from an extensive display of Spanish sculpture – the mainstay of this museum's extraordinarily eclectic and high-quality collections.

Capella Reial de Santa Àgata

Plaça del Rei

Palau del Lloctinent

★ Palau Reial & Museu d'Història de la Ciutat
The 14th-century Capella Reial de Santa Àgata, with its 1466 altarpiece, is one of the best-preserved sections of the palace.

Jaume I

Museu d'Història de la Ciutat

Housed in a 14th-century mansion are the most extensive subterranean Roman ruins in the world. Visitors can see the streets of Roman Barcelona, as well as an exhibition focusing on Barcelona's rapid development in the 13th and 14th centuries.

KEY

– – – Suggested route

0 meters   100
0 yards   100

STAR SIGHTS

★ Cathedral

★ Palau Reial

Barcelona Cathedral ①

Plaça de la Seu. **Tel** *93-315 15 54.*
Ⓜ *Jaume I.* 🚌 *17, 19, 45.*
⬤ *8am–7:30pm daily.* 📷 🚻

Begun in 1298 under Jaime II, on the foundations of a site dating back to Visigothic times, this compact Gothic cathedral was not finished until the late 19th century. The interior has beautiful Gothic cloisters and carved 15th-century choir stalls with painted coats of arms. Beneath the main altar, the crypt houses the sarcophagus of St. Eulalia, martyred in the 4th century AD. The nave has 28 side chapels, and a vaulted ceiling that rises to 26 m (85 ft).

The wide Catalan Gothic nave of Barcelona Cathedral

Palau Reial & Museu d'Història de la Ciutat ②

Plaça del Rei. **Tel** *93-315 11 11.*
Ⓜ *Jaume I.* ⬤ *Tue–Sat (only pm Oct–May), am Sun.* ⬤ *Jan 1, Good Fri, Jun 25, Dec 25–26.* 📷 🎫 *by appt.*

The Royal Palace, founded in the 13th century, was the residence of the count-kings of Barcelona. The complex includes the Gothic Saló del Tinell, with arches spanning 17 m (56 ft) and, on the right, the Capella de Santa Àgata, with a painted wood ceiling by Jaume Huguet. The main attraction of the museum lies underground. Entire streets and squares of old Barcino are accessible via walkways suspended over the ruins.

Las Ramblas ③

Ⓜ *Drassanes, Liceu, Catalunya.*

Busy around the clock, this is one of the most famous streets in Spain. A stroll down its tree-shaded, central walkway to the seafront, taking in the mansions, shops, and cafés, makes a perfect introduction to Barcelona life.

The name (Les Rambles in Catalan) comes from the Arabic *ramla*, meaning the dried-up bed of a seasonal river. Barcelona's 13th-century city wall followed the left bank of one such river. During the 16th century, convents, monasteries, and a university were built on the opposite bank. Later demolished, they have left their legacy in the names of the five sections of the street. Today Las Ramblas is thronged by street vendors, tarot readers, musicians, and mime artists.

Among its many famous buildings is the **Palau Güell**, a Neo-Gothic mansion that established the international reputation of Catalan architect Antoni Gaudí for outstanding,

The Gothic interior of the Basílica de Santa Maria del Mar

original architecture. Built in 1889, this fascinating work of art is located on a narrow street just off Las Ramblas. Nearby, the **Gran Teatre del Liceu**, the city's fine opera house, has been restored twice after fires iˆn 1861 and 1994. Further along is the huge **Mercat de Sant Josep**, a colorful food market popularly known as "La Boqueria."

On the opposite side of Las Ramblas, midway between the Drassanes and Liceu metro stations, the **Plaça Reial** is Barcelona's liveliest square and dates from the 1850s. Also worth visiting, the **Museu de Cera** (wax-work museum) is housed in an atmospheric 19th-century building, and holds around 300 exhibits.

🏛 **Palau Güell**
Carrer Nou de la Rambla 3–5.
Tel *93-317 39 74.* Ⓜ *Drassanes, Liceu.* ⃝ *Mar–Sep: 10am–8pm Mon–Sat; Oct–Feb: 10am–5pm Mon–Sat.* 📷 📹

Basílica de Santa Maria del Mar ④

Plaza Sta Maria 1. ***Tel*** *93-310 23 90.* Ⓜ *Jaume I.* ⃝ *9am–1:30pm, 4:30–8pm daily (from 10am Sun).*

This beautiful building, the city's favorite church, has superb acoustics for concerts. It is also the only surviving example of an entirely Catalan Gothic-style church.

The church took just 55 years to build. The speed of its construction – unrivaled in the Middle Ages – gave it a unity of style both inside and out. The west front has a 15th-century rose window of the Coronation of the Virgin. More stained glass, dating from the 15th to the 18th centuries, lights the wide nave and high aisles.

The choir and furnishings were destroyed during the Spanish Civil War (1936–9), which only serves to enhance the sense of space and simplicity.

Monument to Columbus at the southern end of the tree-lined Ramblas

For hotels and restaurants in this region see pp341–2 and pp347–8

Museu Picasso ⑤

Carrer Montcada 15–23. **Tel** *93-256 30 00.* Ⓜ *Jaume I.* ◷ *10am–7pm Tue–Sat, 10am–2:30pm Sun.* ◯ *Jan 1, May 1, Jun 24, Dec 25–26.* 🖼 ♿ **www**.museupicasso.bcn.es

One of Barcelona's most popular attractions, the Picasso Museum is housed in five adjoining palaces on the Carrer Montcada. It was founded in 1963, displaying works donated by Jaime Sabartes, a great friend of Picasso. Later, Picasso himself donated paintings, including some graphic works left in his will. Several ceramic pieces were given to the museum by his widow, Jacqueline.

The strength of the 3,000-piece collection is Picasso's early drawings and paintings, such as *The First Communion* (1896), produced when he was still an adolescent. The most famous work on show is the series *Las Meninas*, based on Velázquez's 1656 masterpiece *(see p290)*.

Yachts in the marina at the Port Olímpic, overlooked by skyscrapers

Vila Olímpica ⑥

Ⓜ *Ciutadella-Vila Olímpica.*

The most dramatic rebuilding for the 1992 Olympics was the demolition of the old industrial waterfront and the laying out of 4 km (2 miles) of promenade and pristine sandy

The rippled façade of Gaudí's Casa Milà "La Pedrera" in the Quadrat d'Or

beaches. Suddenly Barcelona seemed like a seaside resort, with a new estate of 2,000 apartments and parks called Nova Icària. The area is still popularly known as the Vila Olímpica because the buildings once housed Olympic athletes.

On the seafront there are twin 44-floor towers – Spain's tallest skyscrapers. They stand beside the Port Olímpic, also built for the Olympics. Two levels of restaurants, shops, and nightclubs around the marina attract business people at lunchtimes and pleasure seekers at weekends.

Sagrada Família ⑦

See pp312–3.

Quadrat d'Or ⑧

Ⓜ *Diagonal, Passeig de Gracia.*

Called the "Golden Square" because it contains so many of the city's best Modernista buildings, the Quadrat d'Or is made up of around a hundred city blocks centering on the Passeig de Gràcia. The wealthy bourgeoisie, who favored this area of the Eixample, embraced the new artistic and architectural style, both

for their homes and offices. Many interiors are open to the public, revealing a feast of stained glass, ceramics, and ironwork.

The most remarkable single block is the **Illa de la Discòrdia**, where four of Barcelona's most famous Modernista houses – all built between 1900 and 1910 – vie for attention. Nearby, the late 19th-century **Fundació Tàpies**, by Domènech i Montaner, houses paintings, sculptures, and graphics, and is topped by Tàpies' wire sculpture, *Cloud and Chair*.

Gaudí's famous **Casa Milà "La Pedrera"** has a wave-like façade and a roofscape of chimneys and vents resembling abstract sculptures. The Palau Baró de Quadras, designed by Puig i Cadalfalch in 1904, is now home to the Casa Asia, which holds occasional exhibitions dedicated to Asian art and culture.

Carving of a coiled beast on the doorway of the Casa Asia, Quadrat d'Or

Sagrada Família ⑦

Europe's most unconventional church, the Temple
Expiatori de la Sagrada Família is an emblem of a
city that likes to think of itself as individualistic. Full of
symbolism inspired by nature and striving for originality, it
is the greatest work of Catalan architect Antoni Gaudí
(1852–1926). In 1883, a year after work began on a Neo-
Gothic church on the site, he was given the task of
completing it. Gaudí changed everything, extemporizing
as he went along. It became his life's work and he lived
like a recluse on the site for 14 years. He is buried in the
crypt. By the time of his death only one tower on the
Nativity façade had been completed, but several more
have since been finished to his original plans. After the
Civil War, work resumed and continues today, financed
by public subscription.

Bell Towers
*Eight of the 12 spires, one
for each apostle, have
been built. Each is topped
by Venetian mosaics.*

THE FINISHED CHURCH

Gaudí's initial ambitions have been
scaled down over the years, but the
design for the building's completion
remains impressive. Still to come
is the central tower,
which is to be encir-
cled by four large tow-
ers representing the
Evangelists. Four
towers on the Glory
(south) façade will
match the existing four
on the Passion (west)
and Nativity (east)
façades. An
ambulatory – like an
inside-out cloister –
will run round the out-
side of the building.

**Tower
with
elevator**

The apse was the first
part of the church
Gaudí completed.
Stairs lead down
from here to the
crypt below.

The altar canopy,
designed by Gaudí, is
still waiting for the altar.

★ Passion Façade
*This bleak façade was completed
from 1986 to 2000 by artist Josep
Maria Subirachs. A controversial
work, its sculpted figures are
angular and often sinister.*

**Entrance to
Crypt Museum**

Main entrance

Spiral Staircases

Steep stone steps allow access to the towers and upper galleries. Majestic views reward those who climb them or take the elevator.

Tower with elevator

VISITORS' CHECKLIST

Calle Mallorca 401. **Tel** 93-207 30 31. M Sagrada Familia. 19, 33, 34, 43, 44, 50, 51, 54. 9am–8pm (Nov–Feb: to 6pm; Mar & Oct: to 7pm). Jan 1 & 6, Dec 25 & 26 (pm). Apr–Sep: 9am, 10:30am, 11:45am, 1pm, 8:15pm. ground floor. **www**.sagradafamilia.org

★ Nativity Façade

The most complete part of Gaudí's church has doorways representing Faith, Hope, and Charity. Scenes of the Nativity and Christ's childhood contain imagery, such as doves, which symbolize the congregation.

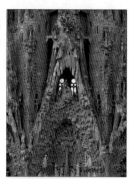

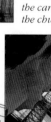

★ Crypt

The crypt, where Gaudí is buried and services are currently held, was begun by the original architect, Francesc de Paula Villar i Lozano, in 1882. A small museum traces the careers of both architects and the church's complicated history.

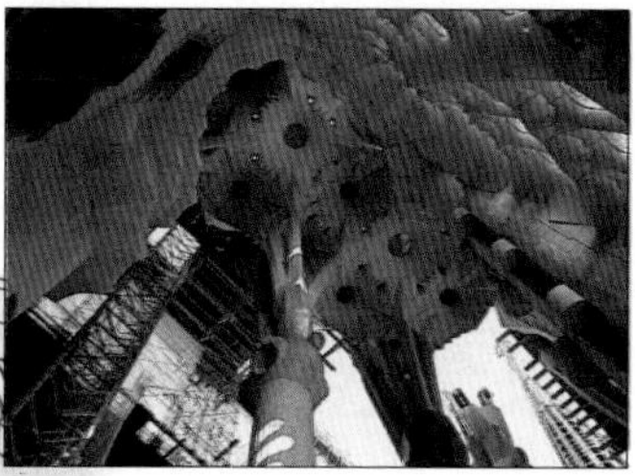

Nave

In the nave, which is still under construction, a forest of fluted pillars will support four galleries above the side aisles, while skylights let in natural light.

STAR FEATURES

★ Passion Façade

★ Nativity Façade

★ Crypt

Pretty whitewashed houses in Poble Espanyol, Montjuïc

Montjuïc ⑨

Ⓜ Espanya, Poble Sec, Paral·lel.
🚌 13, 50 from Plaça Espanya.

The hill of Montjuic, rising to 213 m (699 ft) above the commercial port on the south side of the city, is Barcelona's biggest recreation area. Its museums, art galleries, funfair, and nightclubs make it popular night and day.
The hill is also a spectacular vantage point from which to view the city.

There was probably a Celt-iberian settlement here before the Romans built a temple to Jupiter on their Mons Jovis, which may have given Montjuïc its name. Another theory suggests that a Jewish cemetery on the hill inspired the name Mount of the Jews. Many buildings were erected in 1929, when an International Exhibition was held here, and later for the 1992 Olympics.

On Montjuïc's western edge is the popular **Poble Espanyol** – a "village" of cobbled streets and squares, created in 1929 to showcase different Spanish architectural styles. Also of interest, the **Museu Arqueo-lògic** holds important finds from prehistoric cultures in Catalonia and the Balearic Islands. In the same complex, the **Museu Etnològic** houses artifacts from Oceania, Africa, Asia, and Latin America.

The summit of Montjuïc is occupied by the huge 18th-century **Castell de Montjuïc**, built for the Bourbon family. The castle is now a military museum with an extensive display of ancient weaponry.

♣ **Castell de Montjuïc**
Parc de Montjuïc. **Tel** 93-329 86 13.
Ⓜ Paral·lel, then funicular & cable car. **Museum** ◯ Tue–Sun. ● Jan 1, Good Fri, May 1, Dec 25–26.

🏛 **Museu Arqueològic**
Passeig Santa Madrona 39. **Tel** 93-424 65 77. Ⓜ Espanya, Poble Sec. ◯ Tue–Sat, am Sun & public hols. ● Jan 1, Dec 25–26.
📷 ♿ www.mac.es

Fundació Joan Miró ⑩

Parc de Montjuïc. **Tel** 93-443 94 70.
www.bcn.fjmiro.es Ⓜ Espanya or Paral·lel, then bus 50 or 55.
◯ Tue–Sat, am Sun & public hols.
● Jan 1, Dec 25 & 26. 📷 ♿

Housed in a boldly modern building designed in 1975 by Josep Lluís Sert, this collection of paintings, sculptures, and tapestries by Catalan artist Joan Miró (1893– 1983) is lit by natural light.

An admirer of primitive Catalan art and Gaudí's Modernism, Miró developed a Surrealistic style, with vivid colors and fantastical forms that suggested dreamlike situations. Miró himself donated the works displayed here. Some of the best pieces at the museum include his *Barcelona Series* (1939–44), a set of 50 black-and-white lithographs. Temporary exhibitions of other artists' work are also held here.

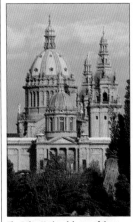

The Palau Nacional, home of the Museu Nacional d'Art de Catalunya

Museu Nacional d'Art de Catalunya ⑪

Palau Nacional, Parc de Montjuïc.
Tel 93-622 03 76. Ⓜ Espanya.
◯ Tue–Sat, am Sun & public hols.
● Jan 1, May 1, Dec 25–26. 📷 📷
call 93-622 03 75 in advance. ♿

Originally built for the 1929 International Exhibition, since 1934 the austere Palau Nacional (National Palace) has been used to house the city's most important art collection.

The museum contains one of the greatest displays of Romanesque art in the world, its centerpiece being a series of magnificent 12th-century frescoes. These have been peeled from Catalan Pyrenean churches (to save them from the ravages of pollution and time) and pasted on to replicas of the original vaulted ceilings

A section of the 18th-century castle on the summit of Montjuïc

and apses they adorned. The most remarkable are the wall paintings from the churches of Santa Maria de Taüll and Sant Climent de Taüll in Vall de Boí.

The museum's superb Gothic collection covers the whole of Spain, but is particularly good on Catalonia. Several outstanding works by El Greco, Velázquez, and Zurbarán are on display in the Renaissance and Baroque section.

Parc Güell ⑫

Carrer d'Olot. **Tel** *93-413 24 00.* M *Lesseps.* ⬚ *daily.* 🎫 & **Casa-Museu Gaudí** *Tel 93-219 38 11.* ⬚ *daily.* ● *Dec 25 & 26 (am), Jan 1 & 6.* 📷

Designated a World Heritage Site by UNESCO, the Parc Güell is Gaudí's most colorful creation. He was commissioned in the 1890s by Count Eusebi Güell to design a garden city on 20 hectares (50 acres) of family estate. Little of Gaudí's grand plan for decorative buildings among landscaped gardens became reality. What we see today was completed between 1910 and 1914.

Most atmospheric is the Room of a Hundred Columns, a cavernous covered hall of 84 crooked pillars, which is brightened by glass and ceramic mosaics. Above it, reached by a flight of steps flanked by ceramic animals, is the Gran Plaça Circular, an

Mosaic-encrusted chimney by Gaudí at the entrance of the Parc Güell

open space with a snaking balcony of colored mosaics, said to have the longest bench in the world. It was executed by Josep Jujol, one of Gaudí's chief collaborators.

The two mosaic-decorated pavilions at the entrance are by Gaudí, but the **Casa-Museu Gaudí**, a gingerbread-style house where he lived from 1906–26, was built by Francesc Berenguer. The drawings and furniture inside are all by Gaudí.

Tibidabo ⑬

Plaça del Tibidabo 3–4. **Tel** *93-211 79 42.* M *Avda Tibidabo, then Tramvia Blau & funicular, or TibiBus from Plaça Catalunya.* **Funfair** ⬚ *call to check.* ● *Oct–Apr: Mon–Fri.* & **Temple del Sagrat Cor** *Tel 93-417 56 86.* ⬚ *daily.* **www**.tibidabo.es

The heights of Tibidabo are reached by Barcelona's last surviving tram, the Tramvia Blau, and a funicular railway.

An ornate merry-go-round at the Parc d'Atraccions, Tibidabo

The name, inspired by Tibidabo's views of the city, comes from the Latin *tibi dabo* (I shall give you) – a reference to the Temptation of Christ, who was taken up a mountain by Satan and offered the world spread at his feet.

The hugely popular funfair at **Parc d'Atraccions** first opened in 1908. The rides were completely renovated in the 1980s. While the old ones retain their charm, the newer ones provide the latest in vertiginous experiences. Their hilltop location at 517 m (1,696 ft) adds to the thrill. Also in the park is the **Museu d'Automates**, which displays automated toys, jukeboxes, and gaming machines.

Tibidabo is crowned by the **Temple Expiatori del Sagrat Cor** (Church of the Sacred Heart), built with religious zeal but little taste by Enric Sagnier between 1902 and 1911. Inside one of its towers, an elevator takes you up to an enormous statue of Christ.

Monestir de Montserrat ⑲

A Benedictine monk

Its highest peak rising to 1,236 m (4,055 ft), the "Serrated Mountain" *(mont serrat)* is a magnificent setting for Catalonia's holiest place, the Monastery of Montserrat, which is surrounded by chapels and hermits' caves. The earliest record of a chapel on this site is from the 9th century. The monastery was founded in the 11th century. In 1811, when the French attacked Catalonia in the War of Independence, the monastery was destroyed and the monks killed. Rebuilt and repopulated in 1844, it was a beacon of Catalan culture during the Franco years. Today Benedictine monks live here. Visitors can hear the famous male choir, the Escolania, singing the *Salve Regina i Virolai* (the Montserrat hymn) at 1pm and 7pm every day, except in July and August, and from December 26 to January 8.

Gothic cloister

Funicular to the holy site of Santa Cova

Plaça de Santa Maria
The focal points of the square are two wings of the Gothic cloister built in 1477. The modern monastery façade is by Françesc Folguera.

The Museum holds 19th- and 20th-century Catalan paintings and many archaeological exhibits from West Asia.

The Way of the Cross
This path passes 14 statues representing the Stations of the Cross. It begins near the Plaça de l'Abat Oliba.

View of Montserrat
The complex includes cafés and a hotel. A second funicular railway takes visitors to nature trails above the monastery.

STAR FEATURES

★ Basilica Façade

★ Black Virgin

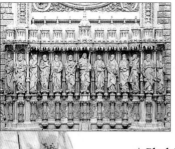

★ **Basilica Façade**
Agapit and Venanci Vallmitjana sculpted Christ and the apostles on the basilica's Neo-Renaissance façade. It was built in 1900 to replace the Renaissance façade of the original church, consecrated in 1592.

★ **Black Virgin**
La Moreneta looks down from behind the altar, protected behind glass. Her wooden orb protrudes for pilgrims to touch.

VISITORS' CHECKLIST

Montserrat (Barcelona province).
Tel 93-877 77 77. 🚉 to Aeri de Montserrat (from Barcelona via Monistrol), then cable car. 🚌 from Barcelona. **Basilica** ◯ 7:30am–7:30pm daily (Jul–Sep: to 8:30pm). 🕇 from 9am Mon–Fri, from 7:30am Sat, from 8am Sun & religious hols. 🖼 **Museum** ◯ 10am–6pm Mon–Fri, 9:30am–6:30pm Sat, Sun & public hols. 🖼 🎥 🚻 **www**.abadiamontserrat.net

Basilica Interior
The sanctuary in the domed basilica is adorned by a richly enameled altar and paintings by Catalan artists.

The rack railway, opened in 2003, follows the course of a historic rail line built in 1880.

Terminal for cable car from Aeri de Montserrat train station

THE VIRGIN OF MONTSERRAT

The small wooden statue of La Moreneta ("the dark one") is the soul of Montserrat. It is said to have been made by St. Luke and brought here by St. Peter in AD 50. Centuries later, the statue is believed to have been hidden from the Moors in the nearby Santa Cova (Holy Cave). Carbon dating suggests, however, that the statue was carved around the 12th century. In 1881 Montserrat's Black Virgin became patroness of Catalonia.

The Black Virgin of Montserrat

Inner Courtyard
On one side of the courtyard is the baptistry (1902), with sculptures by Charles Collet. Pilgrims may approach the Virgin through a door to the right.

Eastern Spain and the Balearic Islands

Eastern Spain covers an extraordinary range of climates and landscapes, from the snowbound peaks of the Pyrenees in Aragón to the beaches of the Costa Blanca. The region has many historical sights, including the striking Mudéjar churches of Zaragoza and the great cathedral of Valencia. The coastal resorts of Eastern Spain are a popular destination, as are the Balearic Islands. Mallorca is the most culturally rich of the islands, while Menorca is dotted with prehistoric sites. Ibiza is chiefly known for its exuberant nightlife, but Formentera remains largely unspoiled. A dialect of the Catalan language, brought by 13th-century settlers, is still widely spoken on the islands.

Cupolas of the Basílica de Nuestra Señora del Pilar in Zaragoza

Zaragoza ②

Zaragoza. 🏠 700,000. ✈ 🚉 🚌
ℹ Plaza del Pilar (902-20 12 12).
🗓 Wed, Sun.

The Roman settlement of Caesaraugusta gave Zaragoza its name. Located on the fertile banks of the Río Ebro, it grew to become Spain's fifth largest city, and the capital of Aragón.

Badly damaged during the early 19th-century War of Independence, the old center nevertheless retains several fine monuments. Overlooking the vast Plaza del Pilar is the **Basílica de Nuestra Señora del Pilar**. With its 11 brightly tiled cupolas, it is one of the city's most impressive sights.

Also on the square are the Gothic-Plateresque **Lonja** (commodities exchange), the **Palacio Episcopal**, and Zaragoza's cathedral, **La Seo**, which displays a great mix of styles. Part of the exterior is faced with typical Mudéjar brick and ceramic decoration, while inside are a fine Gothic reredos and splendid Flemish tapestries. Nearby is the flamboyant Mudéjar bell tower of the **Iglesia de la Magdalena**, and remains of the Roman forum.

Parts of the Roman walls can be seen on the opposite side of the Plaza del Pilar near the **Mercado de Lanuza**, a market with sinuous ironwork in Art Nouveau style. The **Museo Camón Aznar** houses the eclectic collection of an art historian, whose special interest was the locally-born artist Goya.

The **Alfajería**, a beautiful 11th-century Moorish palace with gardens and a mosque, lies on the main road to Bilbao.

🏛 **Museo Camón Aznar**
Calle Espoz y Mina 23. **Tel** 976-39 73 28. ⬜ Tue–Sun. 📷 by appt. ♿

Valencia ㉓

Valencia. 🏠 764,000. ✈ 8 km (5 miles) SW. 🚉 🚆 🚌 ℹ Plaza de la Reina 19 (963-15 39 31). 🗓 Las Fallas (Mar 15–19).

Valencia, Spain's third largest city, is famous for its ceramics, and for the spectacular fiesta of Las Fallas, marked by the erection and burning of elaborate papier-mâché monuments (fallas).

Among the city's finest buildings are **La Lonja**, an exquisite Late Gothic hall built between 1482 and 1498, and the **cathedral** (1262) on Plaza de la Reina. Other monuments worth visiting include the Gothic **Palau de la Generalitat**, with its splendidly decorated first-floor chambers, and the 17th-century **Basílica de la Virgen de los Desamparados**.

Beyond the city center is the **Torres de Serranos** gateway, erected in 1391.

Valencia has a number of fine museums. The **Museo de Bellas Artes** holds 2,000 paintings and statues dating from antiquity to the 19th century, including six paintings by Goya, while the **Museo Domingo Fletcher** has a unique collection of local Stone Age engravings. Valencia's metro system takes tourists to the extensive beaches of El Cabañal and La Malvarrosa, east of the city.

🏛 **La Lonja**
Plaza del Mercado s/n. **Tel** 96-352 54 78 (ext. 4153). ⬜ Tue–Sun. 📷

Effigy burning in Valencia during the annual fiesta of Las Fallas

The mountain village of Castell de Guadalest, Costa Blanca

🏛 Palau de la Generalitat
Plaza des Manises. **Tel** 96-386 61 00 or 96-386 34 61. ☐ by prior appointment only.

🏛 Museo de Bellas Artes
Museo San Pio V, Calle San Pio V 9. **Tel** 96-387 03 00. ☐ Tue –Sun. ● Jan 1, Good Friday, Dec 25. 🎫 ♿

Costa Blanca ㉔

🛬 🚢 🚉 🚌 Alicante. **ℹ** Calle Portugal 17, Alicante (96-592 98 02). **www**.comunidadvalenciana.com

The Costa Blanca occupies a prime stretch of Spain's Mediterranean coastline. The main city, **Alicante** (Alacant), has an 18th-century Baroque town hall and a 16th-century castle, the Castillo de Santa Bárbara. The nearest beach to the city center is the popular Postiguet; slightly farther afield are the vast beaches of La Albufereta and Sant Joan.

The massive, rocky outcrop of the **Penyal d'Ifach** towers over Calp harbor, and is one of the Costa Blanca's most dramatic sights. Its summit offers spectacular views. A short drive inland, **Castell de Guadalest** is a pretty mountain village with castle ruins and a distinctive belfry perched precariously on top of a rock.

Also worth visiting are the whitewashed hilltop town of **Altea, Denia**, which has good snorkeling, and the cliffs and coves around **Xabia**. South of Alicante, **Guardamar del Segura** has a quiet beach bordered by aromatic pine woods, while **Torrevieja** is a highly-developed resort with sweeping, sandy shores.

Mallorca and the Balearic Islands ㉕

🛬 🚢 🚌 Palma, Mallorca; Maó, Menorca. **ℹ** Plaça Reina 2, Palma, Mallorca (971-71 22 16).

The largest of the Balearic islands, Mallorca has a varied landscape and a rich cultural heritage. A massive Gothic cathedral is poised high on the sea wall of **Palma**, its capital. Completed in 1587 and known locally as Sa Seu, the cathedral is one of Spain's most breathtaking buildings. The interior was remodeled by Antoni Gaudí and a highlight is the Baldachino, his bizarre wrought-iron canopy above the altar.

Also worth visiting in Palma are the Basílica de Sant Francesc, the Moorish Palau de l'Almudaina, and the Fundació Pilar i Joan Miró – a stunning modern building housing Miró's studio and a collection of the artist's work.

Around the island, **Andratx** is a chic and affluent town with yachts moored along its harbor, while **Pollença** is a popular tourist resort which has remained relatively unspoiled. The 18th-century

family home, **La Granja**, and **Alfàbia**, which exudes a Moorish atmosphere, are aristocratic estates open to the public. The **Monasteri de Lluc**, in the remote mountain village of the same name, incorporates a guesthouse, a museum, and a church.

Menorca

Menorca's capital, **Maó**, has one of the finest harbors in the Mediterranean, an 18th-century Carmelite church, and a museum, the Collecció Hernández Mora, housing Menorcan art and antiques. The town of **Ciutadella** boasts an impressive main square and a delightful Árt Nouveau market. Menorca's many Bronze Age villages – to which there is usually free access – are mostly the work of the "talaiotic" people, who lived from 2000–1000 BC.

Ibiza and Formentera

A popular package-tour destination, Ibiza has some of the wildest nightclubs in Europe. An hour's boat ride from Ibiza harbor are the tranquil shores of Formentera. The capital, **Sant Francesc**, has a pretty 18th-century church and a folk museum.

View across the marina at Palma, Mallorca to the spectacular cathedral

Southern Spain

One large region – Andalusia – extends across the south of Spain. It was here that the Moors lingered longest and left their greatest monuments in the cities of Granada, Córdoba, Málaga, and Seville. The eight southern provinces span a wide range of landscapes, with deserts in the east, sandy beaches along the Costa del Sol, and sherry-producing vineyards around Jerez. From flamingoes in the wetland Doñana National Park to flamenco – the uniquely Andalusian art form – the region has something to interest every visitor.

Antonio Palamino's cupola in the Monasterio de la Cartuja, Granada

Granada ㉖

Granada. 🕍 241,000. ✈ 12 km (7 miles) SW. 🚉 🚌 ℹ Corral del Carbón, Calle Mariana Pineda (958-24 71 28). 🎭 Corpus Christi (May–Jun). **www**.turismodegranada.org

The ancient city of Granada, founded by the Iberians, was for 250 years the capital of a Moorish kingdom. The Nasrid dynasty, who ruled from 1238 until 1492 when Granada fell to the Catholic Monarchs, left some outstanding examples of Moorish architecture here. The greatest legacy of their rule is the spectacular palace complex of the Alhambra (see pp322–3). Under the Nasrids the city enjoyed a golden age, acquiring an international reputation as a major cultural center. Later, under Christian rule, the city became a focus for the Renaissance.

Granada's 16th-century Gothic **cathedral** has a Renaissance façade and a Baroque west front. Nearby, the **Capilla Real** (Royal Chapel), built between 1505

and 1507, houses Carrara marble figures of the Catholic Monarchs, whose bodies lie in the crypt. Equally impressive are the **Casa de los Tiros**, a fortress-like palace built in Mudéjar style, and the **Monasterio de la Cartuja**, both dating from the 16th century. Founded by a Christian warrior, the latter has a dazzling cupola by Antonio Palomino.

Relics of the Moorish era in the old town include the **Corral del Carbón**, a former storehouse and inn for merchants, and the **Palacio de la Madraza**. Originally an Arab university, the palace has a splendid Moorish hall with a finely decorated *mihrab* (prayer niche). Renovated in 2006, it holds temporary art exhibitions.

Granada's Moorish ancestry is most evident in the hillside Albaicín district, which faces the Alhambra. Along its cobbled alleys stand *cármenes* – villas with Moorish decor and gardens – and **El Bañuelo**, the 11th-century brick-vaulted

Arab baths. The churches here were mostly built on the sites of mosques. The most beautiful of these, the **Iglesia de Santa Ana**, has an elegant Plateresque portal. The **Real Chancillería**, or Royal Chancery (1530), boasts a beautiful Renaissance façade.

Also worth visiting in the Albaicín district is the **Museo Arqueológico**, with Iberian, Phoenician, and Roman finds.

From one end of the district, a road leads up to **Sacromonte**. Granada's gypsies once lived in the caves lining this hillside. Their legacy lives on in the flamenco shows performed here in the evenings.

From the northern side of the Alhambra, a footpath leads to the **Generalife** (see pp322–3), the country estate of the Nasrid kings. The gardens, begun in the 13th century, originally contained orchards and pastures. Today, their lush greenery, pools, and graceful water fountains provide a magical setting for the many events staged each year between mid-June and early July on the occasion of the city's international music and dance festival.

🏛 **Casa de los Tiros**
Calle Pavaneras. **Tel** 958-22 10 72. ⏱ Tue–Sun. ● main public hols.

🏛 **Palacio de la Madraza**
Calle Oficios 14. **Tel** 958-24 34 84. ⏱ 8am–10pm Mon–Fri.

🏛 **Museo Arqueológico**
Carrera del Darro 43. **Tel** 958-22 56 40. ⏱ Tue pm, 9am–8pm Wed–Sat, Sun am. ● main public hols.

Entrance to the Moorish *mihrab* in the Palacio de la Madraza, Granada

The main façade of Málaga's unusual cathedral, consecrated in 1588

Málaga ㉗

Málaga. 650,000. 🛬 🚢 🚆 🚌 Pasaje de Chinitas 4 (95-221 34 45).

Málaga, the second largest city in Andalusia, was a thriving port under Phoenician, Roman, and Moorish rule. It also flourished during the 19th century, when sweet Málaga wine was one of Europe's most popular drinks.

At the heart of the old town is the **cathedral**, begun in 1528 by Diego de Siloé. The half-built second tower, abandoned in 1765 when funds ran out, gave the cathedral its nickname: La Manquita ("the one-armed one").

The **Casa Natal de Picasso**, where the painter spent his early years, is now the headquarters of the international Picasso Foundation. Málaga's old Museo de Bellas Artes has recently been renovated and transformed into a new museum dedicated to the painter.

The city's vast fortress – the **Alcazaba** – was built between the 8th and 11th centuries. Its major attractions are the display of Phoenician, Roman, and Moorish artifacts, as well as a recently restored Roman theater. The ruined **Castillo de Gibralfaro**, a 14th-century Moorish castle, lies behind the Alcazaba.

🏛 Alcazaba
Calle Alcazabilla. **Tel** 95-221 60 05.
◻ 9:30am–7:30pm Tue–Sun.

Costa del Sol ㉘

🛬 🚢 🚆 🚌 Málaga. 🛈 Pasaje de Chinitas 4, Málaga (95-221 34 45).

With its year-round sunshine and varied coastline, the Costa del Sol attracts crowds of vacationers every year and also has half a million foreign residents.

Its most stylish resort is **Marbella**, frequented by royalty and film stars, who spend their summers here in the smart villas or luxury hotels overlooking the area's 28 beaches. Puerto Banús is its ostentatious marina. In winter the major attraction is golf: 30 of Europe's finest golf courses lie just inland.

Among the highlights of Marbella's old town is the Museo de Grabado Contemporáneo, which displays some of Picasso's least-known work, the peaceful Iglesia de Nuestra Señora de la Encarnación, and the town hall, with its exquisite, panelled Mudéjar ceiling.

Sotogrande, to the west of Marbella, is an exclusive resort of luxury villas. The marina is fronted by good seafood restaurants. In spite of tourism, **Estepona** preserves its Spanish character, with pretty tree-filled squares and inexpensive tapas bars.

To the east are the package-holiday resorts of **Fuengirola** and **Torremolinos**. Once the brash haunt of young northern European tourists, they are now more family-oriented.

Player on a green at one of Marbella's high-profile golf courses

MOORISH SPAIN

Typical Moorish *alcazaba*, dating from the 10th century

In the 8th century, the Iberian Peninsula came almost entirely under Moorish rule. The Muslim settlers called Spain "Al Andalus." A powerful caliphate was established in Córdoba, which became the center of one of the most brilliant civilizations of early medieval Europe. The Moors erected *alcazabas* (castles built into city ramparts) and palaces surrounded by patios, pools, and gardens, making lavish use of arches, stucco work, glazed wall tiles *(azulejos)*, and ornamental calligraphy. They also introduced new crops to Spain, such as oranges and rice. By the 11th century the caliphate had collapsed into 30 *taifas* (splinter states) and the northern Christian kingdoms were reconquering parts of Moorish Spain. In 1492 the Catholic Monarchs took Granada, its last stronghold. Though many Muslims were expelled from Spain following the Reconquest, some were employed to build new churches and palaces for the Christian rulers. Known as Mudéjares (the name literally means "those permitted to stay"), these craftsmen developed a hybrid Christian-Islamic style that survived into the 18th century.

Granada: the Alhambra

A magical use of space, light, water, and decoration characterizes this most sensual piece of architecture. It was built under Ismail I, Yusuf I, and Muhammad V, caliphs when the Nasrid dynasty (1238–1492) ruled Granada. Seeking to belie an image of waning power, they created their idea of paradise on earth. Modest materials were used (plaster, timber, and tiles), but they were superbly worked. Although the Alhambra suffered decay and pillage, including an attempt by Napoleon's troops to blow it up, it has recently been restored and its delicate craftsmanship still dazzles the eye.

Sala de la Barca

★ Salón de Embajadores
The ceiling of this sumptuous throne room, built between 1334 and 1354, represents the seven heavens of the Muslim cosmos.

★ Patio de Arrayanes
This pool, set amid myrtle hedges and graceful arcades, reflects light into the surrounding halls.

Patio de Machuca

Entrance

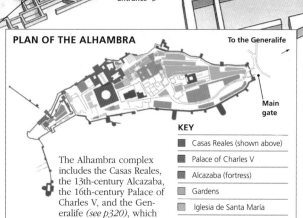

PLAN OF THE ALHAMBRA

To the Generalife

Main gate

KEY

■	Casas Reales (shown above)
▨	Palace of Charles V
▨	Alcazaba (fortress)
▨	Gardens
▨	Iglesia de Santa María
■	Other buildings

The Alhambra complex includes the Casas Reales, the 13th-century Alcazaba, the 16th-century Palace of Charles V, and the Generalife *(see p320)*, which is located just off the map.

Patio del Mexuar
This council chamber, completed in 1365, was where the reigning sultan listened to the petitions of his subjects and held meetings with his ministers.

Palacio del Partal

A pavilion with an arched portico and a tower is all that remains of this palace, the oldest building in the Alhambra.

VISITORS' CHECKLIST

For the Alhambra and Generalife. **Tel** *902-22 44 60.* **Group reservations Tel** *902-22 09 12 or 0034-915 37 91 78 (from abroad).* 🚌 *2.* ⏰ *8:30am–8pm daily (Nov–Feb: to 6pm).* **Night visits:** *Mar–Oct: 10–11:30pm daily; Nov–Feb: 8–9:30pm Fri & Sat.* 🎫 ▶ **www.**alhambra-patronato.es

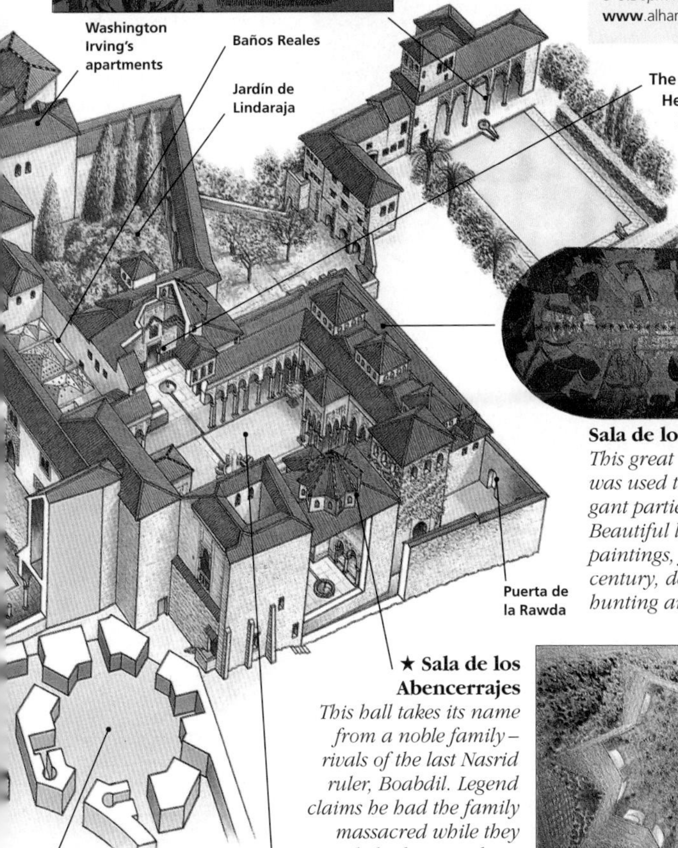

Washington Irving's apartments

Baños Reales

Jardín de Lindaraja

The Sala de las Dos Hermanas, with its honeycomb dome, is regarded as a splendid example of Spanish-Islamic architecture.

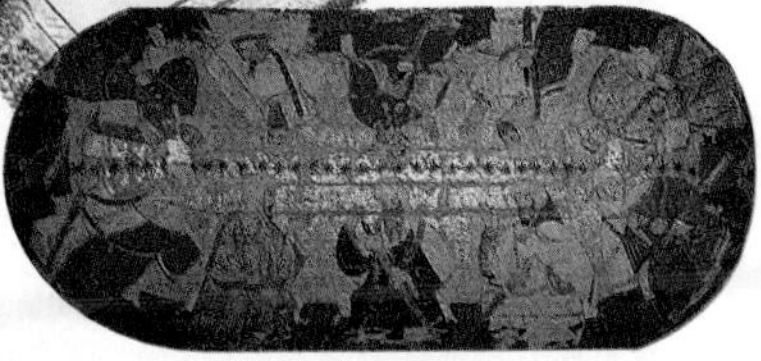

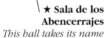

Sala de los Reyes

This great banqueting hall was used to hold extravagant parties and feasts. Beautiful leather ceiling paintings, from the 14th century, depict tales of hunting and chivalry.

Puerta de la Rawda

★ Sala de los Abencerrajes

This hall takes its name from a noble family – rivals of the last Nasrid ruler, Boabdil. Legend claims he had the family massacred while they attended a banquet here. The geometrical ceiling was inspired by Pythagoras' theorem.

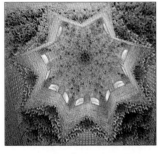

The Palace of Charles V (1526) houses a collection of Spanish-Islamic art, whose highlight is the Alhambra vase.

★ Patio de los Leones

Built by Muhammad V, this patio is lined with arcades supported by 124 slender marble columns. At its center, a fountain rests on 12 stocky marble lions.

STAR FEATURES

★ Salón de Embajadores

★ Patio de Arrayanes

★ Sala de los Abencerrajes

★ Patio de los Leones

The Puente Nuevo, spanning the deep Tajo gorge at Ronda

Ronda ㉙

Málaga. 🏘 *35,000.* 🚉 🚌
ℹ *Plaza de España 9 (95-287 12 72).*

Ronda sits on a massive, rocky outcrop, straddling a precipitous limestone cleft. Because of its impregnable position, it was one of the last Moorish bastions, finally falling to the Christians in 1485.

On the south side perches a classic *pueblo blanco* – a white town – so-called because the houses are whitewashed in the Moorish tradition.

Among Ronda's historic buildings is the **Palacio Mondragón**, adorned with original Moorish mosaics. The façade of the 18th-century **Palacio del Marqués de Salvatierra** is decorated with images of South American Indians. From the **Casa del Rey Moro**, built on the site of a Moorish palace, 365 steps lead down to the river.

Across the **Puente Nuevo** or 'New Bridge,' which spans the deep Tajo gorge, is the modern town, and the site of one of Spain's oldest bullrings.

Inaugurated in 1785, the **Plaza de Toros** and its bull-fighting museum, the **Museo Taurino**, attract aficionados from all over the country.

🏟 Plaza de Toros & Museo Taurino
Calle Virgen de la Paz. *Tel* 952-87 41 32. ⬤ *daily.* 🌐 ♿

Córdoba ㉚

Córdoba. 🏘 *330,000.* 🚉 🚌
ℹ *Palacio de Congresos, Calle Torrijos 10 (957-47 12 35).*

With its glorious mosque and pretty Moorish patios, Córdoba is northern Andalusia's star attraction. Its name may derive from Kartuba, Phoenician for "rich and precious city." In the 10th century the city enjoyed a golden age as the western capital of the Islamic empire.

Córdoba's most impressive Moorish monument is the mighty Mezquita *(see pp326–7)*. To the west of its towering walls, the **Alcázar de los Reyes Cristianos**, in the old Jewish

quarter, is a stunning 14th-century palace-fortress built by Alfonso XI. The Catholic Monarchs stayed here during their campaign to wrest Granada from Moorish rule.

The small Mudéjar-style **synagogue** (c.1315) has decorative plasterwork with Hebrew script. Nearby, the **Museo Taurino**, a bullfighting museum, contains a replica of the tomb of Manolete, a famous matador, and the hide of the bull that killed him.

A Roman bridge, spanning the Río Guadalquivir, links the old town to the 14th-century **Torre de la Calahorra**. This defensive tower houses a small museum depicting life in 10th-century Córdoba.

In the newer part of the city, the **Museo Arqueológico** displays Roman and Moorish artifacts. The **Museo de Bellas Artes** contains sculptures by local artist Mateo Inurria (1867–1924) and paintings by Murillo and Zurbarán. Other notable buildings are the beautiful 17th-century **Palacio de Viana**, filled with works of art, and the handsome arcades of the **Plaza de la Corredera**.

♜ Alcázar de los Reyes Cristianos
Calle Caballerizas Reales s/n.
Tel 957-42 01 51. ⬤ *10am–2pm & 5:30–7:30pm Mon–Sat, 9:30am–2:30pm Sun & public hols.* ⬛ *Jan 1, Dec 25.* 🌐

Seville ㉛

See pp328–31.

Water gardens at the Alcázar de los Reyes Cristianos, Córdoba

Marshes and sand dunes of the Parque Nacional de Doñana

Parque Nacional de Doñana ❷

Huelva & Sevilla. *La Rocina (959-44 23 40)* or *El Acebuche (959-44 87 11)*. **Park interior** ○ summer: Mon–Sat; winter: Tue–Sun. **Tel** 959-43 04 32 for reservations. www.turismodedonana.com

Doñana National Park is ranked among Europe's greatest wetlands, comprising more than 185,000 acres of marshes and sand dunes. The area, officially protected since 1969, was once a ducal hunting ground *(coto)*.

A road runs through part of the park, with information points located along it. There are also several self-guided walks on the park outskirts, but the interior can be visited on official guided day tours only.

Doñana is home to wild cattle, fallow and red deer, and the lynx – one of Europe's rarest mammals. The greater flamingo and the rare imperial eagle can also be seen.

Jerez de la Frontera ❸

Cádiz. 🏛 250,000. ✈ 🚆 🚌 ℹ Alameda Cristina 7 (956-32 47 47).

Jerez is the capital of sherry production and many *bodegas* (cellars) can be visited. Among the well-known names are **González Byass** and **Pedro Domecq**.

The city is also famous for its **Real Escuela Andaluza de Arte Ecuestre**, a school

of equestrian skills. Public dressage displays are held on Thursdays. On the Plaza de San Juan, the 18th-century **Palacio de Penmartín** houses the Centro Andaluz de Flamenco, with exhibitions on this music and dance tradition. The 11th-century **Alcázar** encompasses a well-preserved mosque, now a church.

Just to the north is the **cathedral**. Its most famous treasure, *The Sleeping Girl* by Zurbarán.

Golden chalice from the treasury of Cádiz cathedral

🍷 **Sherry Bodegas**
González Byass, Calle Manuel María González 12, Jerez. **Tel** 956-35 70 00. **Pedro Domecq**, Calle San Ildefonso 3, Jerez. **Tel** 956-15 15 00. ○ call for tour times.

Cádiz ❸

Cádiz. 🏛 160,000. 🚆 🚌 ℹ Plaza de San Juan de Dios 11 (956-24 10 01) or Calle Nueva 6 (956-25 86 46).

Surrounded almost entirely by water, Cádiz lays claim to being Europe's oldest city. After the Catholic reconquest, the city prospered on wealth brought from the New World.

Modern Cádiz is a busy port, with a pleasant water-front, while the old town has narrow alleys and lively markets. The Baroque and Neoclassical **cathedral**, with its dome of golden yellow tiles, is one of Spain's largest. The **Museo de Cádiz** has one of the largest art collections in Andalusia, and arch-aeological exhibits chart the history of the city .

The 18th-century **Oratorio de San Felipe Neri** has been a shrine to liberalism since 1812 when a provisional government assembled in the church to try to establish Spain's first con-stitutional monarchy. The **Torre Tavira**, an 18th-century watchtower, offers spectacular views of the city.

🏛 **Museo de Cádiz**
Plaza de Mina. **Tel** 956-21 22 81. ○ Tue–Sun. ● public hols. ♿

TAPAS

The light snacks known as tapas – and sometimes as *pinchos* – originated in Andalusia in the 19th century as an accompaniment to sherry. The name derives from a bartender's practice of covering a glass with a saucer or *tapa* (cover) to keep out flies. The custom progressed to a chunk of cheese, or a few olives, placed on a platter to serve with a drink. Today tapas range from cold snacks to elaborately prepared hot dishes, generally eaten standing at the bar rather than sitting at a table. Almost every village in Spain has a tapas bar. In the larger towns it is customary to move from bar to bar, sampling the specialties of each.

Olives

Jamón serrano (salt-cured ham)

Patatas bravas (potatoes in spicy tomato sauce)

Córdoba: the Mezquita

Córdoba's great mosque, dating back 12 centuries, embodied the power of Islam on the Iberian Peninsula. Abd al Rahman I built the original mosque between 785 and 787. The building evolved over the centuries, blending many architectural forms. In the 10th century al Hakam II made some of the most lavish additions, including the elaborate *mihrab* (prayer niche) and the *maqsura* (caliph's enclosure). During the 16th century a cathedral was built in the heart of the mosque, part of which was destroyed.

Patio de los Naranjos
Orange trees grow in the courtyard where the faithful washed before prayer.

Torre del Alminar
This bell tower, 93 m (305 ft) high, is built on the site of the original minaret. Steep steps lead to the top for a fine view of the city.

The Puerta del Perdón is a Mudéjar-style entrance gate, built during Christian rule in 1377. Penitents were pardoned here.

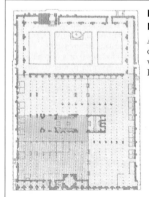

EXPANSION OF THE MEZQUITA

Abd al Rahman I built the original mosque. Extensions were added by Abd al Rahman II, al Hakam II, and al Mansur.

The Puerta de San Esteban is set in a section of wall from an earlier Visigothic church.

KEY TO ADDITIONS

- ☐ Original mosque (785–787)
- ☐ Added by Abd al Rahman II (848)
- ☐ Added by al Hakam II (c.961)
- ☐ Added by al Mansur (c.987)
- ☐ Patio de los Naranjos

STAR FEATURES

- ★ Arches and Pillars
- ★ Mihrab
- ★ Capilla de Villaviciosa

Cathedral

Part of the mosque was destroyed to accommodate the cathedral, begun in 1523. Featuring an Italianate dome, it was designed chiefly by members of the Hernán Ruiz family.

VISITORS' CHECKLIST

Calle Torrijos 10. **Tel** 957-47 05 12. ◯ 10am–7pm Mon–Sat, 9–10:15am, 2–7pm Sun (winter: closes 1–2 hours earlier). 9:30am Mon–Sat; 11am, noon & 1pm Sun and public hols.

The cathedral choir has Churrigueresque – excessive Baroque-style – stalls carved by Pedro Duque Cornejo in 1758.

Capilla Mayor

Capilla Real

★ Arches and Pillars

More than 850 columns of granite, jasper, and marble support the roof, creating a dazzling visual effect. Many were taken from Roman and Visigothic buildings.

★ Mihrab

This prayer niche, richly ornamented, held a gilded copy of the Koran. The worn flagstones indicate where pilgrims circled it seven times on their knees.

★ Capilla de Villaviciosa

The first Christian chapel was built in the mosque in 1371 by Mudéjar crafts-men (see p321). Its multi-lobed arches are stunning.

Street-by-Street: Seville ③

The maze of narrow streets that makes up the Barrio de Santa Cruz represents Seville at its most romantic and compact. This is a good place to begin an exploration of the city, since many of the best-known sights are located here. As well as the expected souvenir shops, tapas bars, and strolling guitarists, there are plenty of picturesque alleys, hidden plazas, and flower-decked patios to reward the casual wanderer. Once a Jewish ghetto, its restored buildings, with characteristic window grilles, are now a harmonious mix of upscale residences and tourist accommodations. Good restaurants and bars make the area well worth an evening visit.

Plaza Virgen de los Reyes
This delightful square, which is often lined with horse-drawn carriages, has an early 20th-century fountain by José Lafita.

Palacio Arzobispal, the 18th-century Archbishop's Palace, is still used by Seville's clergy.

Bus station

★ Cathedral and La Giralda
This huge Gothic cathedral and its Moorish bell tower are Seville's most popular sights (see p330).

Convento de la Encarnación (1591)

Archivo de Indias
Built in the 16th century as a merchants' exchange, the Archive of the Indies now houses documents and maps relating to the Spanish colonization of the Americas.

Plaza del Triunfo
The square was built to celebrate the city's survival of the great earthquake of 1755. In the center is a modern statue of the Virgin Mary.

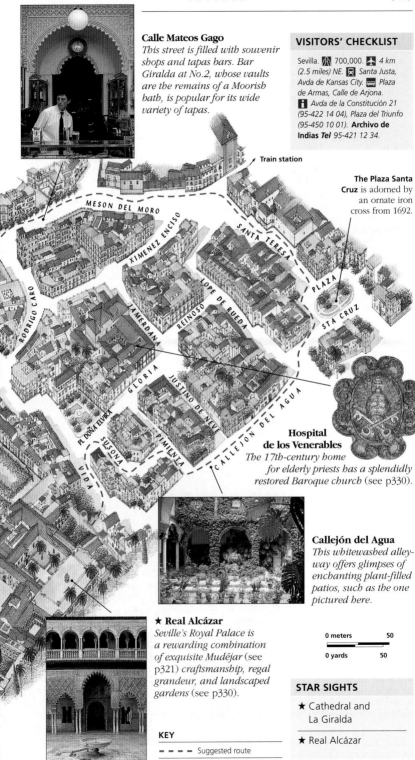

Calle Mateos Gago
This street is filled with souvenir shops and tapas bars. Bar Giralda at No.2, whose vaults are the remains of a Moorish bath, is popular for its wide variety of tapas.

VISITORS' CHECKLIST

Sevilla. 🏛 700,000. ✈ 4 km (2.5 miles) NE. 🚉 Santa Justa, Avda de Kansas City. 🚌 Plaza de Armas, Calle de Arjona. ℹ Avda de la Constitución 21 (95-422 14 04), Plaza del Triunfo (95-450 10 01). **Archivo de Indias Tel** 95-421 12 34.

Train station

The Plaza Santa Cruz is adorned by an ornate iron cross from 1692.

MESON DEL MORO

XIMENEZ ENCISO

SANTA TERESA

RODRIGO CARO

JAMERDANA

LOPE DE RUEDA

REINOSO

PLAZA

STA CRUZ

GLORIA

JUSTINO DE NEVE

PL. DOÑA ELVIRA

SUSONA

PIMIENTA

CALLEJON DEL AGUA

VIDA

Hospital de los Venerables
The 17th-century home for elderly priests has a splendidly restored Baroque church (see p330).

Callejón del Agua
This whitewashed alley-way offers glimpses of enchanting plant-filled patios, such as the one pictured here.

★ **Real Alcázar**
Seville's Royal Palace is a rewarding combination of exquisite Mudéjar (see p321) craftsmanship, regal grandeur, and landscaped gardens (see p330).

0 meters 50
0 yards 50

STAR SIGHTS

★ Cathedral and La Giralda

★ Real Alcázar

KEY

- - - Suggested route

The mighty Giralda bell tower rising above the Gothic cathedral

🔒 Cathedral and La Giralda

Avenida de la Constitución. **Tel** 954-21 49 71. ◯ 11am–5pm daily (Jul–Aug: 9:30am–3:30pm; Sun: pm only). 📷 ⛔ except Giralda tower.

Seville's cathedral occupies the site of a great mosque, built by the Almohads in the late 12th century. La Giralda, its huge bell tower, and the beautiful Patio de los Naranjos, which is filled with orange trees, are a legacy of this Moorish structure. Work on the Christian cathedral began in 1401. The bronze spheres on the original Moorish minaret were replaced by Christian symbols, though the Giralda did not assume its present appearance until 1568. Today it is crowned by a bronze sculpture portraying Faith. This weathervane (*giraldillo*) has given the tower its name. Visitors can climb La Giralda for superb views of the city.

The cathedral houses many fine works of art, including the stunning high altar reredos with its 44 gilded reliefs, carved by Spanish and Flemish sculptors in 1482–1564.

🏛 Real Alcázar

Patio de Banderas. **Tel** 95-450 23 23. ◯ Apr–Sep: Tue–Sun & pub hols; Oct–Mar: Tue–Sat, am Sun & pub hols. 📷 **www**.patronato-alcazarsevilla.es

In 1364 Pedro I of Castile ordered the construction of a royal residence within the palaces that had been built in the 12th century by the Moors.

Craftsmen from Granada and Toledo created a stunning complex of Mudéjar patios and halls, the Palacio Pedro I, now at the heart of Seville's Real Alcázar. Successive monarchs added their own distinguishing marks: Isabel I dispatched navigators to explore the New World from her Casa de Contratación, while Carlos I (the Holy Roman Emperor Charles V) had grandiose, richly decorated apartments built.

A star feature of the palace is the Salón de Embajadores (Ambassadors' Hall), with its dazzling dome of carved and gilded, interlaced wood. The hall overlooks the Patio de las Doncellas (Patio of the Maidens), which boasts some exquisite plasterwork and has been restored to its function as a "floating garden", as it was during Pedro I's reign.

Laid out with terraces, fountains, and pavilions, the tranquil gardens of the Real Alcázar provide a delightful refuge from the heat and bustle of the center of Seville.

🏛 Hospital de los Venerables

Plaza de los Venerables 8. **Tel** 95-456 26 96. ◯ 10am–2pm, 4–8pm daily. ⬤ Jan 1, Good Friday, Dec 25. 📷 📷 ⛔

This late 17th-century home for elderly priests has recently been restored as a cultural center, its upper floors, cellar, and infirmary serving as exhibition galleries. The Hospital church is a showcase of Baroque splendors, with frescoes by both Juan de Valdés Leal and his son Lucas Valdés. There are also fine sculptures by Pedro Roldán.

🏛 Torre del Oro

Paseo de Cristóbal Colón. **Tel** 95-422 24 19. ◯ 10am–2pm Tue–Fri, 11am–2pm Sat & Sun. ⬤ Aug. 📷 except Tue.

The Moors built Seville's Torre del Oro (Tower of Gold) as a defensive lookout in 1220. Its turret was not added until 1760. The gold in the tower's name may refer to the gilded *azulejos* (ceramic tiles) that once clad its walls, or to treasures from

Fresco by Juan de Valdés Leal in the Hospital de los Venerables

For hotels and restaurants in this region see pp340–45 and pp346–51

Arcaded arena of the Plaza de Toros de la Maestranza, begun in 1761

the Americas unloaded here. It now houses the **Museo Marítimo**, which exhibits maritime maps and antiques.

🏟 Plaza de Toros de la Maestranza

Paseo de Cristóbal Colón 12. *Tel 95-422 45 77.* ◯ *daily.* ● *for bullfights.* 🈺 🎫

Built between 1761 and 1881, Seville's famous bullring seats up to 14,000 spectators.

Visitors who take a guided tour of this enormous building are shown many interesting features, including a chapel where the matadors pray for success, and the stables where the horses of the *picadores* (lance-carrying horsemen) are kept. There is also a small museum.

Between Easter Sunday and October, *corridas* (bullfights) take place every Sunday evening. Tickets can be bought from the *taquilla* (ticket office) at the bullring.

🏛 Museo de Bellas Artes

Plaza del Museo 9. *Tel 95-478 64 82.* ◯ *Wed–Sat, am Sun, pm Tue.* 🈺 ♿

The magnificently restored Convento de la Merced Calzada houses one of Spain's best art museums. Delightful tree-filled patios, colorful *azulejos*, and a church with a beautiful Baroque painted ceiling make this a wonderful setting for the fine works of art on display here.

The museum's collection of Spanish art and sculpture – which covers all periods from the medieval to the modern – focuses on the work of the Seville School artists. Among the star attractions are masterpieces by Murillo, Juan de Valdés Leal, and Zurbarán.

🌿 Parque María Luisa

In 1893 Princess María Luisa donated part of the grounds of the Palacio San Telmo to the city for this park. Its most extravagant feature is the semicircular Plaza de España, designed by Aníbal González for the 1929 Ibero-American Exposition. At the center of the park, the Pabellón Mudéjar houses the **Museo de Artes y Costumbres Populares**, with displays of traditional Andalusian folk arts. Nearby, located in the grand Neo-Renaissance Pabellón de Bellas Artes, is the provincial **Museo Arqueológico** (Archaeological Museum).

⛪ Monasterio de Santa María de las Cuevas

Calle Americo Vespucio 2, Isla de la Cartuja. *Tel 95-503 70 70.* ◯ *Tue–Sat, am Sun.* 🈺 🎫 *by prior appointment only.* ♿

This 15th-century Carthusian monastery was inhabited by monks until 1836. Columbus lay buried in the crypt of its church between 1507 and 1542.

FLAMENCO

More than just a dance, flamenco is an artistic expression of the joys and sorrows of life. A uniquely Andalusian art, its origins are hard to trace. Gypsies may have been the main creators of the art, mixing their own Indian-influenced culture with existing Moorish and Andalusian folklore, and with Jewish and Christian music. Gypsies were already living in Andalusia by the early Middle Ages, but only in the 18th century did flamenco begin to develop into its present form. There are many styles of *cante* (song) from different parts of Andalusia, but no strict choreography – dancers *(bailaores)* improvise from basic movements, following the rhythm of the guitar and their feelings.

Flamenco dancer *(bailaora)*

The monastery stands at the heart of the Isla de Cartuja, the site of Expo '92, and also houses the **Museo de Arte Contemporáneo**, with its collection of Spanish and international art. The **Isla Mágica** theme park is also nearby.

Seville's dazzling Plaza de España in the Parque María Luisa

Practical Information

Spain's tourist information service is efficient and extensive, with offices in most towns providing advice on lodgings, restaurants, and local events. In August, many businesses close and roads are busy. It is worth finding out whether local fiestas will coincide with your visit, as while these are enjoyable, they may also cause closures. Public telephones are widely available, but international call charges are high. When changing money, credit cards often offer the best exchange rate and can be used in cash dispensers. The Spanish lunch hour extends from 2pm to 5pm.

WHEN TO VISIT

August is Spain's busiest vacation month. Spanish holidaymakers and millions of foreign tourists flock to the coast. Easter is a good time to visit: temperatures are more bearable, especially in the south, the countryside is in full bloom, and the country's most important fiestas take place. In the Sierra Nevada and the Pyrenees the ski season is from mid-December until May.

TOURIST INFORMATION

All major cities and towns have a tourist information office (oficina de turismo), which will provide town plans, lists of hotels and restaurants, and details of local activities. There is a **Spanish National Tourist Office** in several large cities worldwide.

OPENING HOURS

Most monuments and museums in Spain close on Mondays. On other days they are generally open from 10am to 2pm, and, in some cases, reopen from 5pm to 8pm. Most charge for entry. Some churches may only be opened for services.

In smaller towns, churches, castles, and other sights are often kept locked. The key, available on request, will be lodged in a neighboring house, in the town hall, or perhaps with the local bar owners.

VISA REQUIREMENTS AND CUSTOMS

Citizens of the EU, Switzerland, Iceland, and Norway do not require a visa for entry to Spain. A list of entry requirements – available from Spanish embassies – specifies other countries, including Canada and New Zealand, whose nationals do not need a visa for visits of less than 90 days. US and Australian citizens must have a valid visa to travel.

Non-EU residents can reclaim IVA (sales tax) on some single items. You pay the full price and ask the sales assistant for a formulario (tax exemption form). On leaving Spain, you must ask customs to stamp your formulario (this must be within six months of the purchase). You receive the refund by mail or on your credit card account.

PERSONAL SECURITY

Violent crime is rare in Spain. Petty theft is the main problem in the cities, especially Barcelona, where visitors should be extra vigilant. Men may make complimentary remarks (piropos) to women in the street. This is customary and not intended to be intimidating.

POLICE

There are essentially three types of police force in Spain. The Guardia Civil (National Guard) mainly police rural areas and impose fines for traffic offenses. The Policía Nacional operate in larger towns. They are replaced by a regional force, the Ertzaintza, in the Basque country, and by the Mossos d'Esquadra in Catalonia. The Policía Local, also called Policía Municipal or Guardia Urbana, operate independently in each town and have a branch for city traffic control.

All three services will direct you to the relevant authority in the event of an incident requiring police help.

EMERGENCY SERVICES

Only the Policía Nacional operates a nationwide emergency phone number (see Directory). Telephone

---

THE CLIMATE OF SPAIN

Spain's large landmass, with its mountain ranges and the influences of the Atlantic and Mediterranean, accounts for a varied climate. The eastern and southern coasts and islands have mild winters, but winter temperatures in the interior often fall below freezing. Summers everywhere are hot, except in upland areas. Northern Spain is wettest year round.

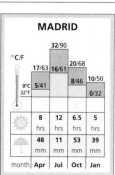

MADRID			
°C/F		32/90	
	17/63 16/61	20/68	
0°C 5/41		8/46	10/50
32°F			0/32
8 hrs	12 hrs	6.5 hrs	5 hrs
48 mm	11 mm	53 mm	39 mm
month Apr	Jul	Oct	Jan

SEVILLE			
		35/95	
°C/F	21/70	18/64 25/77	
	10/50	13/55	16/61
0°C 32°F			5/41
6 hrs	8 hrs	4.5 hrs	2 hrs
50 mm	58 mm	55 mm	55 mm
month Apr	Jul	Oct	Jan

directories list local emergency numbers under *Servicios de Urgencia*. For emergency medical treatment call the Cruz Roja (Red Cross), look under *Ambulancias* in the phone book, or go to a hospital emergency room *(Urgencias)*.

HEALTH ISSUES

Spanish pharmacists have wide responsibilities. They can advise and, in certain cases, prescribe without consulting a doctor. In a non-emergency, a *farmacéutico* is a good person to see first. It is usually easy to find one who speaks English.

The pharmacy *(farmacia)* sign is a green or red illuminated cross. Those open at night are listed in the windows of all the local pharmacies.

FACILITIES FOR THE DISABLED

Spain's national association for the disabled, the Confederación Coordinadora Estatal de Minusválidos Físicos de España (**COCEMFE**), has a tour company, Servi-COCEMFE, which publishes

guides to facilities in Spain and will help plan a vacation to individual requirements. A Spanish travel agency, **Viajes 2000**, specializes in vacations for disabled people.

LANGUAGE AND ETIQUETTE

The Spanish commonly greet and say goodbye to strangers at bus stops and in stores and other public places. People shake hands when introduced and whenever they meet. In Catalonia and the Basque country, regional languages are as much in use as the national tongue, Castilian Spanish.

BANKING AND CURRENCY

The Spanish unit of currency is the euro *(see p15)*, which replaced the peseta on January 1, 2002.

Generally, banks are open from 8am to 2pm Monday to Friday. Some branches, especially those in the larger towns and cities, open until 1pm on Saturdays, except in August. Most have a foreign exchange desk with the sign *Cambio* or *Extranjero*. Take some form of ID when

changing money. Bureaux de change charge higher rates of commission but are open longer hours and are commonly found in the main tourist destinations.

COMMUNICATIONS

As well as public telephone booths *(cabinas)*, there are nearly always pay phones in bars. Most take coins, but some take tokens. Phone-cards can be bought at newsstands and *estancos* (tobacconists). At public telephone offices, which are called *locutorios*, you can make a call and pay for it afterwards. Telefónica run the official ones, which are less expensive than private offices.

The Spanish postal service, Correos, is rather slow: a national or international delivery may take more than a week. Send important mail by *urgente* (express) or *certificado* (registered) mail. The main Correos offices open from 8am to 9pm from Monday to Friday and from 9am to 7pm on Saturday. Conveniently, you will find that stamps for letters and postcards can also be bought from an *estanco*.

DIRECTORY

SPANISH NATIONAL TOURIST OFFICES ABROAD

Australia
Level 24,
St Martin's Tower,
31 Market Street,
Sydney, NSW 2000.
Tel 292 61 24 33.

United Kingdom
79 New Cavendish Street,
London W1W 6XB.
Tel 020-7486 8077.
www.tourspain.co.uk

United States
35th Floor,
666 Fifth Avenue,
New York,
NY 10103.
Tel 212-265 8822.
www.okspain.org

TOURIST OFFICES IN SPAIN

Barcelona
Palau Robert,
Passeig de Gràcia 107,
08008 Barcelona.
Tel 93-238 40 00.

Madrid
Calle Duque de Medinaceli
2, 28014 Madrid.
Tel 91-429 49 51.

Seville
Avenida de la
Constitución 21b,
41004 Seville.
Tel 95-422 14 04.

EMBASSIES

Australia
Plaza del Descubridor
Diego de Ordás 3,
28003 Madrid.
Tel 91-441 60 25.

Canada
Calle de Núñez
de Balboa 35, Madrid.
Tel 91-423 32 50.

UK
Calle de Fernando El Santo
16, 28010 Madrid.
Tel 91-319 02 00.
Consulate:
Paseo Recoletos 7–9,
28004 Madrid.
Tel 91-524 97 00.

US
Calle Serrano 75,
28006 Madrid.
Tel 91-587 22 00.

EMERGENCY NUMBERS

Emergency: all services
Tel 112 (most large cities).

Police
Tel 091 (nationwide).

Ambulance
(Red Cross, Cruz Roja)
Tel 112 or 91-522 22 22
(This Madrid number is now the national number for the Red Cross.)
For other cities' emergency services, consult the local phone directory.

Fire Brigade (Bomberos)
Tel 080 (in most large cities).

FACILITIES FOR THE DISABLED

COCEMFE
Calle de Luis Cabrera 63,
28002 Madrid.
Tel 91-744 36 00.

Viajes 2000
Paseo de la Castellana
228–230, 28046 Madrid .
Tel 91-323 10 29.

Travel Information

Spain has an increasingly efficient transportation system. All the major cities and islands have airports, and flights from around the globe arrive at those of Madrid and Barcelona. Both the road and rail networks were greatly improved during the 1980s and in the run-up to the Barcelona Olympics in 1992. Intercity rail services are reliable, but buses are a faster and more frequent option between smaller towns. In much of rural Spain, however, public transportation is limited and a car is the most practical solution for getting around. Ferries connect mainland Spain with the Balearic Islands and ports in the UK.

FLYING TO SPAIN

Of the several US airlines serving Spain, **American Airlines** flies to Madrid, while **Delta Air Lines** flies to both Madrid and Barcelona. **Iberia**, the Spanish national airline, has direct flights to Madrid from New York, Miami, and Los Angeles, as well as flights to many destinations in Spain from Toronto and Montreal.

Iberia also offers scheduled flights daily to Madrid and Barcelona from all Western European capitals (except Dublin, which has four flights a week). **British Airways** has scheduled flights to Madrid and Barcelona and several other cities daily from London Heathrow or Gatwick; also Madrid from Manchester.

From Australasia the best connections are via Athens, Bangkok, and London.

CHARTERS AND PACKAGE DEALS

Charter flights from the UK serve airports such as Alicante, Málaga, and Girona. These can be inexpensive, but are less reliable and often fly at unsociable hours. Make sure your agent is ABTA bonded before making a reservation. Special deals are often offered in the winter and may include a number of nights at a hotel. Low-cost airline **easyJet** serves Madrid, Barcelona, Mallorca, and Málaga from London Luton and Liverpool, while **Bmibaby** and **Ryanair** fly from London Stansted and other UK regional airports to mainland and island Spain.

DOMESTIC FLIGHTS

Most of Spain's domestic flights have traditionally been operated by **Iberia**. In recent years, however, this monopoly has been broken to encourage competition. The two main alternative Spanish carriers are **Air Europa** and **Spanair**.

The most frequent shuttle service is the Puente Aéreo, run between Barcelona and Madrid by Iberia. Flights leave every 15 minutes at peak business times. A ticket machine allows passengers to buy tickets up to 15 minutes before departure. The journey usually takes 50 minutes.

Air Europa and Spanair services between Madrid and the regional capitals are not as frequent as the Puente Aéreo, but their prices are usually slightly lower. Flights to provincial cities usually operate in the morning and evening. Air services to and within the Balearic Islands are run by **Binter**, which is affiliated to Iberia Airlines.

GETTING AROUND MADRID AND BARCELONA

The metro is the quickest and least expensive way to travel around Madrid. It is open from 6am to 1:30am and consists of 11 color-coded lines, plus the Ópera-Príncipe Pío link and a service to the airport. Day buses run from 6am until midnight; night buses continue operating until 6am and leave from the Plaza de Cibeles. A *Metrobus* ticket, valid for ten trips on the buses and metro, can be bought at any metro station, as well as from newsstands and *estancos* (tobacconists). Sightseeing bus tours are run by **Madrid Vision** and **Juliá Tours**.

Barcelona's metro system generally runs from 5am to 11pm; on Fridays and Saturdays it stays open until 2am. There are various types of travelcard available, valid for bus, metro, and the FGC (*Ferrocarrils de la Generalitat de Catalunya*) suburban train network. The city buses in Barcelona are usually colored white and red. The *Nitbus* (night bus) runs from around 10pm to 5am; the *TombBus* covers the main shopping streets; and the *Aerobus* provides an excellent service between the Plaça de Catalunya and the airport.

Sightseeing tours in Barcelona are operated by Bus Turístic from April through to February on two routes from the Plaça de Catalunya.

RAIL TRAVEL

Spain offers many options for users of the state railroad **RENFE**. The two high-speed services are the intercity TALGO trains and the AVE service between Madrid and Seville via Córdoba. Tickets for these are the most expensive and may be bought at train stations from the *taquilla* (ticket office) or obtained from travel agents. On certain days, so-called *días azules*, or blue days, there is a 10 percent discount on usual rail fares.

The *largo recorrido* (long-distance trains) and *regionales y cercanías* (regional and local) services are frequent, inexpensive, but slower. Tickets for local travel may be purchased from machines at the station.

In Madrid the major stations for long-distance trains are Atocha, Chamartín, and Norte. Barcelona's two principal train stations are Sants and Francia.

Regional rail companies operate in three areas of Spain. Catalonia and Valencia each has its own *Ferrocarrils de la Generalitat*, known respectively as the **FGC** and the **FGV**. The Basque country has the **ET** (*Eusko Trenbideale*).

Iberrail holidays offer rail-plus-hotel deals for traveling between Spanish cities. Two services similar to the Orient Express are also operated by Iberrail. The El Andalus Expres tours Andalusia, stopping at Seville, Córdoba, Granada, Jerez, and Ronda. The Transcantábrico, run by **FEVE** *(Ferrocarriles de Vía Estrecha)* leaves San Sebastián to travel the length of Spain's north coast, ending its journey in Santiago de Compostela. Passengers travel in style in 14 restored period carriages dating from between 1900–30.

LONG-DISTANCE BUSES

Spain has no national long-distance bus company. The largest private company, **Alsa**, offers a variety of bus tours and sightseeing trips throughout Spain.

Other companies operate in particular regions. Tickets and information for long-distance travel are available at main bus stations and from travel agents.

TRAVELING BY ROAD

Spain's fastest roads are its *autopistas*. They are normally dual carriageways subject to *peajes* (tolls). *Autovías* are similar but have no tolls. Smaller roads are less well kept but are a more relaxed way to see rural Spain.

As well as the international car rental companies, a few Spanish companies, such as **Atesa**, operate nationwide. You can probably negotiate the best deal with an international company from home. There are also fly-drive package deals, which include car rental. *Gasolina* (gas) is priced by the liter.

Spanish law requires drivers to carry at all times valid insurance and registration documents, a driver's license, and ID, usually in the form of a passport.

FERRY SERVICES

Two car ferry routes link the Spanish mainland with the UK. **Brittany Ferries** sails between Plymouth in the UK and Santander in Cantabria; **P&O European Ferries** sails from Portsmouth to Bilbao. The crossings take over 24 hours. Advance reservations are essential in the summer.

Trasmediterránea runs car ferry services from Barcelona and Valencia on the Spanish mainland to the Balearic Islands. The crossing takes about eight hours. The same company also operates frequent inter-island services.

DIRECTORY

IBERIA AND AFFILIATES

International and domestic flights
Tel 902-400 500 (Spain).
Tel 0845-601 2854 (UK).
Tel 800-772 4642 (US).
www.iberia.com

OTHER AIRLINES

Air Europa
Tel 902-401 501 (Spain).
www.aireuropa.com

American Airlines
Tel 902-115 570 (Spain).
Tel 800-633 3711 (US).
www.aa.com

Bmibaby
www.bmibaby.com

British Airways
Tel 902-111 333 (Spain).
Tel 08708-509 850 (UK).
Tel 800-247 92 97 (US).
www.britishairways.com

Delta Air Lines
Tel 91-749 66 30 (Spain).
Tel 800-241 41 41 (US).
www.delta.com

easyJet
www.easyJet.com

Ryanair
www.ryanair.com

Spanair
Tel 902-13 14 15 (Spain).
www.spanair.com

MADRID TOURS

Juliá Tours
Gran Via 68, Madrid.
Tel 93-402 69 00.
www.juliatours.com

RAIL TRAVEL

ET
Tel 902-54 32 10.
www.euskotren.es

FEVE
Tel 985-29 76 56.
www.feve.es

FGC
Tel 93-205 15 15.
www.fgc.catalunya.net

FGV
Tel 96-526 27 31.
www.fgv.es

Iberrail
Tel 91-571 66 96.
www.iberrail.es

RENFE
Tel 902-24 02 02.
www.renfe.es

BUS COMPANIES

Alsa
Tel 90-242 22 42 (Spain).
www.alsa.es

Eurolines
Tel 90-240 50 40 (Spain).
Tel 08705-14 32 19 (UK).
www.eurolines.es
www.eurolines.com

BUS STATIONS

Madrid
Estación Sur
(for whole of Spain).
Tel 91-468 42 00.
Intercambiador des Autobuses
(for northern Spain).
Tel 91-745 63 00.
Terminal Auto Res
(for Valencia, Extremadura, Andalusia).
Tel 90-202 09 99.

Barcelona
Estació del Nord.
Tel 90-226 06 06.

Seville
Estación Plaza de Armas.
Tel 95-490 80 40.

CAR RENTAL

Atesa
Tel 902-10 01 01 (Spain).
www.atesa.com

Avis
Tel 90-213 55 31 (Spain).
Tel 0870-60 60 100 (UK).
www.avis.com

Europcar
Tel 902-10 50 30 (Spain).
Tel 08457-222 525 (UK).
www.europcar.com

Hertz
Tel 901-10 10 01 (Spain).
Tel 0870-844 8844 (UK).
www.hertz.es
www.hertz.co.uk

FERRY SERVICES

Brittany Ferries
Tel 942-36 06 11 (Spain).
Tel 0870-536 0360 (UK).
www.brittany-ferries.com

P&O European Ferries
Tel 90-202 0461 (Spain).
Tel 0870-520 2020 (UK).
www.poferries.com

Trasmediterránea
Tel 93-295 91 34 (Barcelona).
Tel 971-70 73 45 (Palma de Mallorca).
Tel 96-316 48 55 (Valencia).
Tel 0870-499 1305 (UK).
www. trasmediterranea.es

Shopping

Shopping in Spain is a pleasurable activity, particularly if you approach it in a leisurely way, punctuating it with frequent breaks for coffee. In small, family-run shops especially, people will go out of their way to fulfill your smallest request. Markets sell the freshest of produce and quality wines can be found at almost any grocer. Leatherwork is still highly regarded among Spain's many traditional crafts. Spanish design has come to the forefront in both fashion and decor.

OPENING HOURS

Shops usually open at 10am, close at 2pm, and reopen from 5pm to 8pm. Bakeries generally open early, at around 8am. Supermarkets and department stores stay open over lunchtime.

Rural markets are held in the morning only. In some regions Sunday trading is just limited to the bakeries, *pastelerías* (pastry shops), and newspaper kiosks, but in many tourist resorts stores open on Sunday.

LARGER STORES

The *hipermercados* (superstores) are sited outside towns and can often be found by following signs to the *centro comercial*. The best known are Carrefour, Alcampo, and Hipercor.

Spain's leading department store is **El Corte Inglés**. It has branches in all cities and in the larger regional towns.

Major seasonal sales are advertised by the word *Rebajas* displayed in store windows.

CLOTHING STORES

The larger cities naturally offer the widest selection of clothing stores, but Spanish designer labels can be found even in the smaller towns.

The Calle de Serrano and Calle de José Ortega y Gasset are the main streets for fashionwear in Madrid, while the work of young designers is mostly located in the Chueca district. **Adolfo Domínguez** is the doyen of Madrid's minimalist look. The adventurous will appreciate the designs of **Agatha Ruiz de la Prada**.

In Barcelona, international fashion labels and clothes by young designers can be found in and around the Passeig de Gràcia, including **Armand Basi**, vendors of quality leisure and sportswear.

Victorio & Lucchino in Seville sells clothes with a distinctly Andalusian style.

LEATHER GOODS

Leather accessories and shoes are a popular purchase and there is a wide range in terms of quality and price. It is the practice in mid-range stores for customers to choose from the selection in the window and give the sales assistant the code number indicated and the *talla* (size) required. If you want an all-leather shoe, look for *cuero*, the hide label mark. **Calçats Sole** in Barcelona is well known for its classic hand-made shoes and boots.

Leather clothes and bags of all kinds are usually of good quality and well designed. The prestigious **Loewe** handbags are sold in retail outlets in Madrid and other major Spanish cities. Madrid's **Piamonte** also offers stylish bags at affordable prices.

SPECIALTY STORES

Specialty stores are often run by generations of the same family. *Panaderías* (also called *hornos*) are bakeries selling bread and *bollos* (sweet buns). Cakes and pastries are sold in *pastelerías*.

Fresh meat can be bought in a *carnicería*, but a *charcutería* will have the best selection of cold, cooked meats, and also sells a wide selection of cheeses.

Pescaderías sell fish and shellfish, although the best fish is often to be found on the local market stands.

For fruit and vegetables, a *frutería* or *verdulería* will have better produce, because they stock only what is in season.

Hardware stores are called *ferreterías*. *Librerías* are in fact bookshops, not libraries, and *papelerías* are stationers. Anything you buy as a *regalo* (gift) will be gift-wrapped on request. When you buy flowers from a *floristería*, the assistant will expect to arrange them.

MARKETS

Every large town has a daily market *(mercado)*, open from 9am to 2pm, and from 5pm to 8pm. Small towns have one or more market days a week.

Markets usually have the best fresh produce, but they sell all types of food, including *frutos secos* (dried fruits) and seasonal produce, such as mushrooms, soft fruit, and game. There are also usually other types of goods on sale, such as flowers, hardware, and clothes.

Flea markets *(rastros)* are held everywhere in Spain, but the largest – known as **El Rastro** – is in Madrid, and is held on Sundays and public holidays. Prices on the clothes, records, antiques, and other items sold here can be bargained down. Madrid also has a coin, stamp, and postcard market held on Sundays in the Plaza Mayor.

The **Encants Vells**, the flea market in Barcelona, is held on Mondays, Wednesdays, Fridays, and Saturdays. The food market, **La Boqueria**, is open daily on La Rambla.

FOOD AND DRINK

Spanish regional specialties are often better value when bought where they are made. Each region produces its own type of sausage. In Burgos, for example, *morcilla* (blood sausage) is made, while a fiery red *chorizo* comes from Guijuelo, Extremadura. Andalusia is renowned for olives and olive oil, and Galicia for its cheeses.

Among the preserves and sweets of Spain, Seville marmalade is famous. The delicious almond-based nougat, called *turrón*, can be purchased from food stores around the country.

Wine can be bought by the liter at a *bodega* (local wine shop). It can also be purchased directly from vineyards (also called *bodegas*), but you may need an appointment to visit.

Spain's most famous vine-growing regions are La Rioja and Navarra, Penedés, home of *cava* (sparkling wine), Valdepeñas, Ribera del Duero, and Jerez, the sherry region.

TRADITIONAL CRAFTS

Authentic items such as guitars, fans, castanets, and flamenco shoes are sold in major cities. Madrid's **Moda y Ole** has a good selection of hand-painted fans. **Guitarrería F. Manzanero** sells handmade guitars. Some traditional crafts originated with the Moors, such as Toledo's filigree metalwork and the *azulejos* (ceramic tiles) of Andalusia. **Cántaro**, near the Plaza de España in Madrid, **La Caixa de Fang** in Barcelona, and **Azulejos Santa Isabel** in Seville all sell ceramics.

Catalan-style espadrilles are another popular buy. **La Manual Alpargatera** in Barcelona makes them by hand on the premises and sells them in a wide range of colors.

Lace from the villages of the Sierra de Gata in Extremadura and Galicia's Costa da Morte is prized. Spanish linen and silk shawls can be purchased from **Borca**, off the Puerta del Sol in Madrid. In Barcelona, **L'Arca de l'Avia** sells antique silk and lace. One of the most celebrated traditional hat makers in Spain is the **Sombrerería Herederos de J. Russi** in Córdoba.

HOUSEHOLD AND KITCHEN GOODS

Department stores have a good selection of household goods, but the *ferreterías* (small hardware shops) often have the more authentic selection. Traditional pottery, such as red clay *cazuelas* (dishes) that can be used in the oven and on the hob are inexpensive. Paella pans have always been made of iron or enamel, but now come in stainless steel or with non-stick finishes. Table linen is often a bargain on market stands. Spanish lighting design is widely admired and sold in *lampisterías*. Traditional wrought-iron goods, such as candlesticks and door hardware, are always popular.

DIRECTORY

DEPARTMENT STORES

El Corte Inglés
Calle de Preciados 1–3,
Madrid.
Tel 93-306 38 00.
www.elcorteingles.es
Plaça Catalunya 14,
Barcelona.
Tel 93-306 38 00.
Plaza Duque de la Victoria 10, Seville.
Tel 95-459 70 00.

CLOTHING STORES

Adolfo Domínguez
Calle de Serrano 18,
Madrid.
Tel 91-577 82 80.
Passeig de Gràcia 89,
Barcelona.
Tel 93-215 13 39.

Armand Basi
Passeig de Gràcia 49,
Barcelona.
Tel 93-215 14 21.
www.armandbasi.com

Agatha Ruiz de la Prada
Calle de Serrano 27,
Madrid.
Tel 91-781 10 74.

Victorio & Lucchino
Calle de las Sierpes 87,
Seville.
Tel 95-422 79 51.

LEATHER GOODS

Calçats Sole
Carrer Ample 7,
Barcelona.
Tel 93-301 69 84

Loewe
Calle de Serrano 34,
Madrid.
Tel 91-426 35 88.
Plaza Nueva 12,
Seville.
Tel 95-422 52 53.

Piamonte
Calle del Marqués de Monasterio 5,
Madrid.
Tel 91-575 55 20.

MARKETS

La Boqueria
Las Ramblas 100,
Barcelona.

Encants Vells
Plaça de les Glòries Catalanes,
Barcelona.

El Rastro
Calle de la Ribera de Curtidores,
Madrid.

TRADITIONAL CRAFTS

L'Arca de l'Avia
Carrer dels Banys Nous 20, Barcelona.
Tel 93-302 15 98.

Azulejos Santa Isabel
Calle Alfarería 12,
Triana, Seville.
Tel 95-434 46 08.

Borca
Calle del Marqués Viudo de Pontejos 2,
Madrid.
Tel 91-532 61 53.

La Caixa de Fang
Calle Freneria 1,
Barcelona.
Tel 93-315 17 04.

Cántaro
Calle de la Flor Baja 8,
Madrid.
Tel 91-547 95 14.

Guitarrería F. Manzanero
Calle de Santa Ana 12,
Madrid.
Tel 91-366 00 47.

La Manual Alpargatera
Calle d'Avinyó 7,
Barcelona.
Tel 93-301 01 72.

Moda y Ole
Plaza Mayor 12,
Madrid.
Tel 91-365 42 89.

Sombrerería Herederos de J. Russi
Cde Cardenas 1,
Córdoba.
Tel 957-47 79 53.

Entertainment

The Spanish take particular pride in their cultural heritage. As well as the traditional art form of flamenco dance and the three-act drama of the bullfight (*corrida*), the theaters and opera houses of Spanish cities provide one of the best ways of sharing the experience of Spain. Many activities begin well after midnight and taking full advantage of the afternoon siesta is a good way to prepare for the evening ahead. Spain's mountain ranges, woodlands, and extensive coast offer great potential for scenic tours and sports vacations as alternatives to lounging on the beach.

ENTERTAINMENT LISTINGS

For Spanish speakers, the most complete guide to what's going on in Madrid and Barcelona can be found in the weekly *Guía del Ocio* (published on Fridays in Madrid, and Thursdays in Barcelona). Daily newspapers such as *El País*, *El Mundo*, and *ABC* have weekly entertainment supplements. The free monthly English-language publication, *In Madrid*, can be found in bookshops and Irish bars.

SEASONS AND TICKETS

The main concert and theater season in Spain runs from September to June.
In Madrid, the easiest way to acquire tickets for the theater, concerts, and opera is by telephone. **Casa Madrid** and **Tel-Entrada** accept credit card payment and do not charge for the service. The **TEYCI** agency sells tickets for most events, but charges up to 20 percent commission. Another agency that holds tickets for a variety of events is **El Corte Inglés**.
In Barcelona, theater tickets can be bought from branches of the Caixa de Catalunya or La Caixa savings banks. Tickets for special events are sold at tourist offices.
In other parts of Spain, your hotel or local tourist office will provide details of events and where to purchase tickets.
Tickets for bullfights, generally held between mid-March and mid-October, are sold at the reservations office (*taquilla*) of the bullring.

OPERA AND ZARZUELA

A visit to the Spanish capital would not be complete without spending a night at the *zarzuela*, Madrid's own variety of comic opera. The best productions are those staged at the **Teatro de la Zarzuela**. Other venues include the **Teatro Albéniz** and the recently reopened **Teatro Príncipe – Palacio de las Variedades**. Several other theaters offer *zarzuela* productions in the summer.
The best place to see national and international opera, including Madrid's own opera company, is the **Teatro Real de Madrid**. The Teatro Calderón also hosts excellent classical and modern opera productions. Barcelona's opera house, the **Gran Teatre del Liceu**, is now fully operational following a fire in 1994.

THEATER

Madrid's most prestigious theaters are the **Teatro de la Comedia** and the **Teatro María Guerrero**. The former stages classic works by Spanish playwrights, while the latter hosts foreign productions and modern Spanish drama. The **Teatro Muñoz Seca** and **Teatro Reina Victoria** put on comedy productions. Madrid's autumn festival of classical and modern drama (Festival de Otoño) takes place between mid-September and mid-November.
In Barcelona, the new **Teatre Nacional de Catalunya** is a fine show-case for Catalan drama.

CLASSICAL MUSIC

In Madrid, the two concert halls of the **Auditorio Nacional de Música** host international classical music performances. The Orquesta Nacional de España plays here regularly. The newly-renovated **Teatro Real de Madrid** also hosts important classical music concerts.
Barcelona's Modernista **Palau de la Música Catalana** is one of the world's most beautiful concert halls, with world-renowned acoustics.

BULLFIGHTING

Bullfighting continues to be a popular spectacle throughout the country, but it is not for the squeamish. The **Plaza de Toros de Las Ventas** in Madrid is the most famous bullring in the world. It holds *corridas* every Sunday during the bullfighting season. During the May Fiestas de San Isidro fights are held every day. Some of Spain's most important fights are held at the **Maestranza** bullring in Seville during the Feria de Abril (a spring fair held during the fortnight after Easter). Most towns in Andalusia have their own bullrings: Ronda, Córdoba, and Granada are among the best-known venues.

FLAMENCO

A spontaneous musical art form, flamenco has its roots in the gypsy culture of Andalusia. However, many of the best exponents are now based in the capital.
In Madrid, **Casa Patas** is still the best place to catch the raw power of genuine flamenco guitar and *cante* singing. Both music and dance can be enjoyed at **Café de Chinitas**.
Flamenco is performed late at night with most venues offering dinner and a show. In Andalusia, visitors can enjoy top-quality performances in the *tablaos* (flamenco bars) of the Barrio de Santa Cruz, in Seville, and listen to soul-stirring songs in the bars of another of the city's districts,

Triana. One of the best-known flamenco venues in Granada is in the gypsy caves of Sacromonte *(see p320).*

SPECIAL INTEREST VACATIONS

All tourist offices in Spain can provide details of special interest vacations. Cookery, wine, and painting courses, as well as history and archaeology tours, are popular. Nature lovers and hikers head for Spain's many national parks.

Information about Spanish language courses is provided by **Canning House** in London and the **Instituto Cervantes**.

OUTDOOR ACTIVITIES

For information on horse riding and pony trekking in most regions, contact the **Real Federación Hípica Española** or local Spanish tourist offices.

Picturesque minor roads in many parts of Spain are excellent for cycle-touring. Walking tours are also popular. The **Federación Española de Montaña y Escalada** can provide information about climbing and many other mountain sports.

Spain's most popular resorts for downhill skiing are the Vall d'Aran in Catalonia and the Sierra Nevada, near Granada.

As well as white-water rafting and canoeing, a wide variety of water sports is possible in Spain. Jet skis and windsurfing equipment are available to rent in many coastal resorts. Information about sailing can be obtained from the **Real Federación Española de Vela**.

Spain has an abundance of top-quality golf courses. The **Real Federación Española de Golf** will give locations and more detailed information. In most tourist areas there are tennis courts for rental by the hour. Travel agents arrange tennis holidays for enthusiasts. More information is available from the **Real Federación Española de Tenis**.

DIRECTORY

TICKETS

Casa Madrid
Tel 902-48 84 88
(Madrid).

El Corte Inglés
Tel 902-40 02 22
(Madrid).
www.elcorteingles.es

Tel-Entrada
Tel 902-10 12 12 (Madrid).
www.tel-entrada.com

TEYCI
Calle de Goya 7, Madrid.
Tel 91-576 45 32.
www.softguides.com

OPERA AND ZARZUELA

Gran Teatre del Liceu
Rambla de los Capuchinos 63, Barcelona.
Tel 93-485 99 00.

Teatro Albéniz
Calle de la Paz 11, Madrid.
Tel 91-531 83 11.

Teatro Príncipe – Palacio de las Variedades
Calle de las Tres Cruces 8, Madrid.
Tel 91-521 83 81.

Teatro Real de Madrid
Plaza de Oriente, Madrid.
Tel 91-516 06 06.

Teatro de la Zarzuela
Calle de Jovellanos 4, Madrid.
Tel 91-524 54 00.

THEATER

Teatre Nacional de Catalunya
Plaça de les Arts 1, Barcelona.
Tel 93-306 57 00.

Teatro de la Comedia
Calle del Príncipe 14, Madrid.
Tel 91-521 49 31.

Teatro María Guerrero
Calle de Tamayo y Baus 4, Madrid.
Tel 91-310 15 00.

Teatro Muñoz Seca
Plaza del Carmen 1, Madrid.
Tel 91-523 21 28.

Teatro Reina Victoria
Carrera de San Jerónimo 24, Madrid.
Tel 91-369 22 88.

CLASSICAL MUSIC

Auditorio Nacional de Música
Calle del Príncipe de Vergara 146, Madrid.
Tel 91-337 01 34.

Palau de la Música Catalana
Carrer de Sant Francesc de Paula 2, Barcelona.
Tel 90-244 28 82.

BULLFIGHTING

Plaza de Toros de la Maestranza
Paseo de Cristóbal Cólon 1, Seville.
Tel 95-422 45 77.

Plaza de Toros de las Ventas
Calle de Alcalá 237, Madrid.
Tel 91-356 22 00.

FLAMENCO

Café de Chinitas
Calle de Torija 7, Madrid.
Tel 91-547 15 02.

Casa Patas
Calle de Cañizares 10, Madrid.
Tel 91-369 04 96.

SPECIAL INTEREST VACATIONS

Canning House
2 Belgrave Square, London SW1X 8PJ.
Tel 020-7235 2303.

Instituto Cervantes (Spain)
Calle Libreros 23, 28801 Alcalá de Henares, Madrid.
Tel 91-885 61 00.

Instituto Cervantes (UK)
102 Eaton Square, London SW1W 9AN.
Tel 020-7235 0353.

OUTDOOR ACTIVITIES

Federación Española de Montaña y Escalada
Calle Floridablanca 84, 08015 Barcelona.
Tel 93-426 42 67.
www.fedme.es

Real Federación Hípica Española
Plaza del Marqués de Salamanca 2, 28006 Madrid.
Tel 91-577 77 25.

Real Federación Española de Golf
Calle Capitán Haya 5–9, 28002 Madrid.
Tel 91-555 26 82.
www.golfspain federacion.com

Real Federación Española de Tenis
Avenida Diagonal 618 2°B, 08021 Barcelona.
Tel 93-200 53 55.

Real Federación Española de Vela
Calle Luis Salazar 9, 28002 Madrid.
Tel 91-519 50 08.
www.rfev.es

Where to Stay in Spain

Visitors to Spain have a wide variety of accommodations to choose from, at a range of prices. At the top of the scale are elegant suites in converted medieval castles or royal palaces – many of these are paradors, luxurious state-run hotels. Then there are stylish beach hotels and villas or family-run guesthouses for the budget traveler.

MADRID

OLD MADRID Hostal Madrid
€

Map C4

C/ Esparteros 6–2°, 28012 **Tel** *915-22 00 60* **Fax** *915-32 35 10* **Rooms** *15*

One of the best budget options in Madrid, this hotel is set in the heart of the old city. Offers both rooms and apartments decorated in a mixture of traditional and modern styles, with amenities such as Wi-Fi. The staff is friendly, and the city's sights, restaurants, bars, and nightlife are right on the doorstep. **www.hostal-madrid.info**

OLD MADRID Hotel Plaza Mayor
€€

Map D5

C/ Atocha 2, 28012 **Tel** *913-60 06 06* **Fax** *913-60 06 10* **Rooms** *34*

Just around the corner of Madrid's central square, this popular hotel fills up fast, so book well in advance. Rooms vary in size and decor, but are spotless and brightly painted. The attic suite is more expensive, but offers fine views from its private terrace. Also has a reading room. Free wireless internet in cafeteria. **www.h-plazamayor.com**

OLD MADRID Carlos V
€€€

Map C4

C/ Maestro Victoria 5, 28013 **Tel** *915-31 41 00* **Fax** *915-31 37 61* **Rooms** *67*

A city-center hotel in a pedestrian street beside the Puerta del Sol. This family-run hotel has interconnecting bedrooms as well as family rooms. Some of the rooms also have balconies and sun terraces. A generous buffet breakfast is served in the café bar, and the staff are friendly and helpful. **www.hotelcarlosv.com**

OLD MADRID Tryp Rex
€€€

Map B3

Gran Via 43, 28013 **Tel** *915-47 48 00* **Fax** *915-47 12 38* **Rooms** *145*

This expansive hotel, renovated in 2004, is situated in an old building between the Plaza del Callao and the Plaza de España, close to a large public car park. It has spacious public rooms and well-equipped bedrooms, each with its own safe. Offers good value for money considering the central location and reasonable amenities. **www.solmelia.com**

OLD MADRID Casa de Madrid
€€€€€

Map B4

C/ Arrieta 2, 28013 **Tel** *915-59 57 91* **Fax** *915-40 11 00* **Rooms** *7*

Housed in an 18th-century palace, this stylish little hotel is ideal for a romantic getaway. The seven rooms – two of which are suites – are exquisitely decorated with antiques. The breakfast includes freshly squeezed juice and home-made marmalade. Highly recommended. **www.casademadrid.com**

BOURBON MADRID Hostal Gonzalo
€

Map D4

C/ Cervantes 34, 28014 **Tel** *914-29 27 14* **Fax** *914-20 20 07* **Rooms** *15*

A family-run hostal, which often fills up well in advance. Provides good facilities, immaculate bedrooms, and excellent value for money. The multi-lingual owners are hospitable and offer helpful information regarding nearby attractions and entertainments. Several restaurants can be found within walking distance. **www.hostalgonzalo.com**

BOURBON MADRID Mora
€€

Map D4

Paseo del Prado 32, 28014 **Tel** *914-20 15 69* **Fax** *914-20 05 64* **Rooms** *62*

A 1930s hotel with an attractive entrance and a lobby with an original glass skylight. The recently renovated rooms are modern, functional, and brightly furnished. Located near the Prado, the hotel offers very good value for money. Families can request an extra bed in the room for a small surcharge. **www.hotelmora.com**

BOURBON MADRID Hotel Liabeny
€€€

Map C4

C/ Salud 3, 28013 **Tel** *915-31 90 00* **Fax** *915-32 74 21* **Rooms** *220*

An elegant, modern hotel, located just a short walk from the main sights, yet away from the hubbub of the city center. The extensively renovated hotel features traditionally decorated rooms and suites with every modern amenity, a good restaurant, and excellent service. The private parking and disabled access is a plus. **www.liabeny.es**

BOURBON MADRID Villa Real
€€€€

Map D4

Plaza de las Cortes 10, 28014 **Tel** *914-20 37 67* **Fax** *914-20 25 47* **Rooms** *115*

Close to the Prado and the Retiro gardens, this stylish hotel is based in an opulent, early 19th-century building. One of Madrid's smartest hotels, the spacious rooms and suites are decorated in a tasteful mixture of traditional and contemporary styles, and scattered with ancient Roman art. Some suites even have a jacuzzi. **www.derbyhotels.es**

Key to Symbols *see back cover flap*

BOURBON MADRID Ritz
Plaza de la Lealtad 5, 28014 **Tel** *917-01 67 67* **Fax** *917-01 67 76* **Rooms** *167*   **Map** *D4*

Inaugurated in 1910 as a hotel for aristocrats, the Ritz is still one of Spain's most elegant hotels. Close to the Prado, the hotel has an ornate, circular foyer, and a terraced garden, and serves tea and brunch along with live music. Rooms are luxurious and offer every imaginable comfort. **www.ritz.es**

FARTHER AFIELD NH Alcalá
C/ de Alcalá 66, 28009 **Tel** *914-35 10 60* **Fax** *914-35 11 05* **Rooms** *146*   **Map** *E3*

A large, chain hotel close to the lovely Retiro gardens. Features spacious, well-equipped rooms with amenities that include Wi-Fi and internet access. This reasonably priced hotel also has a café, a bar, and private car park. It is within walking distance to the up-market shopping district in Salamanca, and three museums. **www.nh-hotels.com**

FARTHER AFIELD Santo Mauro
C/ Zurbano 36, 28010 **Tel** *913-19 69 00* **Fax** *913-08 54 77* **Rooms** *51*

This palace, built in 1894 on one of Madrid's most elegant streets, is surrounded by beautiful wooded gardens. The rooms and suites are stylishly decorated, and the two fine restaurants offer romantic outdoor dining in summer. Also houses a swimming pool in the vaulted cellars. **www.ac-hotels.com**

BARCELONA

EIXAMPLE Hostal Palacios
Rambla Catalunya 27, 08007 **Tel** *933-01 3079* **Fax** *933-01 3792* **Rooms** *11*   **Map** *D3*

This friendly hostal is housed in a magnificent Modernista building. Many of the original fittings, including the huge carved doors and colorful tiles, have been retained, and are stylishly complemented by modern fabrics and contemporary bathrooms. Guests can use the piano in the comfortable lounge. **www.hostalpalacios.com**

EIXAMPLE Actual
Carrer Rosselló 238, 08008 **Tel** *935-52 05 50* **Fax** *935-52 05 55* **Rooms** *29*   **Map** *F2*

This modern hotel is fashionably decorated in sleek minimalist style. It has a superb location on the same block as Gaudí's La Pedrera, and the upmarket boutiques of the Passeig de Gràcia are on the doorstep. Like many hotels in this area, it is geared toward business travelers, which means good weekend deals. **www.hotelactual.com**

EIXAMPLE Condes de Barcelona
Passeig de Gràcia 73–75, 08008 **Tel** *934-45 00 00* **Fax** *934-45 32 32* **Rooms** *235*   **Map** *D2*

This hotel is located in two handsomely renovated Modernista palaces, with marble lobbies and creamy façades. The rooms in both locations are cool and contemporary, and some have jacuzzis. Choose a room with a terrace to admire Gaudí's "La Pedrera" building directly across the street. **www.condesdebarcelona.com**

EIXAMPLE Palace
Gran Via de les Corts Catalanes 668, 08010 **Tel** *935-10 11 30* **Fax** *933-18 01 48* **Rooms** *125*   **Map** *E2*

"Palace" has recently been refurbished and is the most elegant of Barcelona's grand hotels. The large luxurious bedrooms are decorated in classical style and boast huge marble bathrooms. Contains a health club and a beauty parlor. Famous guests have included the Spanish royal family and Frank Sinatra. **www.hotelpalacebarcelona.com**

OLD TOWN Fontanella
Via Laietana 71–2°, 08003 **Tel** *933-17 59 43* **Fax** *933-17 59 43* **Rooms** *11*   **Map** *D3*

Fontanella is a simple, family-run hostal where the owners do their best to make visitors feel at home. There is a wonderful antique lift, which creaks up to a knick-knack filled lobby. The basic rooms are made cozy and welcoming with flowery prints and lots of goodies in the bathrooms. **www.hostalfontanella.com**

OLD TOWN Peninsular
Carrer de Sant Pau 34, 08001 **Tel** *933-02 31 38* **Fax** *934-12 36 99* **Rooms** *59*   **Map** *D3*

Rooms are truly basic, but of good value in this former Carmelite convent. Just off La Rambla behind the Liceu opera house, this hotel's charms lie in its luminous, plant-filled inner courtyard and friendly staff. Breakfast is served in an old-fashioned dining room with a high ceiling, but there is no restaurant. **www.hpeninsular.com**

OLD TOWN Jardí
Plaça Sant Josep Oriol 1, 08002 **Tel** *933-01 59 00* **Fax** *933-42 57 33* **Rooms** *42*   **Map** *D3*

A popular hostal overlooking a pretty leafy square in the heart of the Barri Gòtic quarter. Some bedrooms have been renovated and have good views of the square and the handsome Gothic church of Santa María del Pi; others are cheaper but not as atmospheric. Because of its location, this is the best place for nightowls.

OLD TOWN Jazz Hotel
Carrer Pelai 3, 08001 **Tel** *935-52 96 96* **Fax** *935-52 96 97* **Rooms** *108*   **Map** *D3*

A glassy ultra-modern hotel, close to the Plaça de Catalunya, Jazz offers better facilities than its three-star rating would suggest. There is a rooftop pool with sun deck, and the rooms (all soundproofed) are stylishly decorated with contemporary furniture and fabrics. **www.hoteljazzbarcelona.com**

Map References *see maps of Madrid pp282–3 and Barcelona pp306–7*

OLD TOWN Montecarlo

La Rambla 124, 08002 **Tel** *934-12 04 04* **Fax** *933-18 73 23* **Rooms** *76*   **Map** *D3*

This beautiful hotel right on La Rambla in the center of Barcelona occupies a former 19th-century palace. The lobby is a gorgeous whirl of gilt and marble, while the rooms are smart and modern. Staff are particularly helpful here, and there are fantastic deals available on the website. **www.montecarlobcn.com**

OLD TOWN Colón

Avda de la Catedral 7, 08002 **Tel** *933-01 14 04* **Fax** *933-17 29 15* **Rooms** *145*   **Map** *D3*

A classic in Barcelona, this traditional, rather formal hotel has a fabulous location opposite the Gothic cathedral. The best rooms have terraces overlooking the square, where guests can watch the Sardana, the traditional Catalan folk dance, performed in the Plaça de Catedral on Sunday mornings. **www.hotelcolon.es**

OLD TOWN Arts

Carrer de Marina 19–21, 08005 **Tel** *932-21 10 00* **Fax** *932-21 10 70* **Rooms** *455*   **Map** *F4*

Set in a soaring tower overlooking the Port Olímpic, Arts is one of the most luxurious and glamorous hotels in Europe. Huge rooms boast spectacular views along with every imaginable modern convenience. There are stunning suites on the upper floors for those with very deep pockets. **www.hotelartsbarcelona.com**

NORTHERN SPAIN

BAIONA, RIAS BAIXAS Parador de Baiona

Castillo Monterreal, 36300 (Pontevedra) **Tel** *986-35 50 00* **Fax** *986-35 50 76* **Rooms** *122*

This parador, built in an old Galician *pazo* (manor house) style, is located within the walls of Monterreal castle. The restaurant serves seafood accompanied by the local Ribeiro wine. Some rooms have four-poster beds and offer sea views, while others look out on to the gardens. **www.parador.es**

BILBAO (BILBO) Mirohotel

Alameda Mazarredo 77, 48009 (Vicaya) **Tel** *946-61 18 80* **Fax** *944-25 51 82* **Rooms** *50*

This glass-fronted boutique hotel designed by Antonio Miró is located between the Guggenheim and Fine Arts Museums. Facilities include a library, a gym, and a spa. The bar, which hosts jazz or other live music some evenings, acts as a meeting point for art lovers. **www.mirohotelbilbao.com**

CANGAS DE ONIS Parador de Cangas de Onis

Villanueva (km 2 from Cangas), 33550 (Asturias) **Tel** *985-84 94 02* **Fax** *985-84 95 20* **Rooms** *64*

A restored 12th-century Benedictine monastery with magnificent cloisters, located on the bank of the Río Sellar just outside the town of Cangas de Onis. The rooms are spacious and comfortable, and the restaurant serves regional dishes. Includes facilities such as meeting rooms. **www.parador.es**

OVIEDO Hotel de la Reconquista

C/ Gil de Jaz 16, 33004 (Asturias) **Tel** *985-24 11 00* **Fax** *985-24 11 66* **Rooms** *142*

A luxury hotel in a magnificent 18th-century building, originally an orphanage, with a massive stone coat of arms above the main entrance. Its name commemorates the Reconquest of Spain which was launched from Asturias. The public rooms are arranged around several courtyards. **www.hoteldelareconquista.com**

PAMPLONA (IRUNA) Ciudad de Pamplona

Iturrama 21, 31007 (Navarra) **Tel** *948-26 60 11* **Fax** *948-17 36 26* **Rooms** *117*

An ultra-modern luxury hotel, decorated in warm tones and scattered with avant-garde furniture. It has four sitting rooms and ample facilities for business people. The hotel is at some distance from the old part of Pamplona, in one of the streets behind the Ciudadela fortress. The restaurant serves classic Navarran dishes. **www.ac-hotels.com**

PONTEVEDRA Parador de Pontevedra

Rua del Barón 19, 36002 **Tel** *986-85 58 00* **Fax** *986-85 21 95* **Rooms** *45*

A parador in a 16–18th-century Renaissance palace, which was once a school, granary, masonic lodge, and an aristocratic residence. The decor incorporates antiques, gilt mirrors, chandeliers, and tapestries. Some rooms are in a new wing. The restaurant specializes in seafood of the Rías Baixas. **www.parador.es**

SAN SEBASTIAN (DONOSTIA) María Cristina

C/ Oquendo 1, 20004 (Guipúzcoa) **Tel** *943-43 76 00* **Fax** *943-43 76 76* **Rooms** *136*

Built in 1912 and named after Queen Maria Cristina, this is a landmark of the city and one of the most historic hotels in Spain. It was designed by the architect of the London and Paris Ritz hotels and is decorated in belle époque style. It is also the venue of the San Sebastián film festival. **www.mariacristina.es**

SANTANDER Las Brisas

La Braña 14, El Sardinero, 39005 (Cantabria) **Tel** *942-27 50 11* **Fax** *942-28 11 73* **Rooms** *13*

A recently-refurbished homely hotel in a 19th-century white turret-shaped villa, close to the popular Sardinero beach. Each room is different with floral fabrics predominating. Breakfast, included in the price, can be served on a seaside terrace. The hotel also has five self-catering apartments. Closed 22 Dec–15 Jan. **www.hotellasbrisas.net**

SANTIAGO DE COMPOSTELA Parador Hostal Dos Reis Catolicos   🖼️🍴📋♿   €€€€€
Praza do Obradoiro 1, 15705 (A Coruña) **Tel** *981-58 22 00* **Fax** *981-56 30 94* **Rooms** *137*

Built under the Catholic monarchs as a hospice for poor pilgrims, this luxurious 16th-century parador, on the same square as Santiago de Compostela's famous cathedral, is one of the world's grandest hotels. It is built around four arcaded courtyards with fountains. The public rooms have regal touches such as hanging tapestries. **www.parador.es**

CATALONIA & EASTERN SPAIN

ALICANTE (ALACANT) Sidi San Juan   🖼️🍴🏊🏋️📺📋♿   €€€€€
La Doblada 8, Playa San Juan, 03540 (Alicante) **Tel** *965-16 13 00* **Fax** *965-16 33 46* **Rooms** *176*

A gleaming, modern luxury hotel overlooking the lively and popular San Juan beach on the outskirts of the city center. Surrounded by beautiful gardens, the hotel hosts a spa, health center, and various sports facilities, as well as a play area and paddling pool for kids. **www.hotelessidi.es**

DENIA Rosa   🖼️🍴🏊📋♿   €
C/ Congre 3, Las Marinas, 03700 (Alicante) **Tel** *965-78 15 73* **Fax** *966-42 47 74* **Rooms** *40*

A modern, white villa with a perfect location close to the beach. It was built and is run by a hospitable Parisian expat who has several repeat customers. Comfortable rooms have sun-trapping, Florentine-style balconies. Guests can also opt for one of the garden bungalows. The family-friendly pool has a section for toddlers. **www.hotelrosadenia.com**

FIGUERES Hotel Durán   🖼️🍴📋   €€
Carrer de Lasauca 5, 17600 (Girona) **Tel** *972-50 12 50* **Fax** *972-50 26 09* **Rooms** *60*

Established in 1855, this ochre-and-pink hotel is set above one of the finest restaurants in the region. It is still owned by the same family, who are warm and friendly. Rooms are attractively, if simply, furnished, and many have pretty wrought-iron balconies overlooking the street below. **www.hotelduran.com**

TARRAGONA Imperial Tarraco   🖼️🍴🏊📋   €€
Passeig Les Palmeres s/n, 43004 (Tarragona) **Tel** *977-23 30 40* **Fax** *977-21 65 66* **Rooms** *170*

The plushest option in Tarragona, this large, modern hotel has a panoramic location right on the balcón del Mediterrani (the balcony of the Mediterranean). Many of the spacious, elegant rooms and suites have large terraces. The hotel is conveniently close to the historic center of the city. **www.husa.es**

VALENCIA Meliá Inglés   🖼️🍴📋♿   €€€
C/ Marqués de Dos Aguas 6, 46002 (Valencia) **Tel** *963-51 64 26* **Fax** *963-94 02 51* **Rooms** *63*

This convenient and stylish city-center hotel is in the old palace of the Dukes of Cardona, next to the National Ceramics Museum. The rooms and suites overlook the street, and are equipped with amenities such as internet access, a TV, a minibar, and a safe. The restaurant serves regional specialties. **www.meliaingles.solmelia.com**

XABIA (JAVEA) Parador de Jávea   🖼️🏊📺📋   €€€€
Avda Mediterráneo 233, 03730 (Alicante) **Tel** *965-79 02 00* **Fax** *965-79 03 08* **Rooms** *70*

A large, modern parador surrounded by lush Mediterranean gardens right on the beach. The rooms are bright and spacious and almost all have balconies overlooking the sea. Offers a wide range of sports facilities, including horse riding, diving, sailing, and golf. The restaurant serves regional cuisine. Lunch or dinner included. **www.parador.es**

ZARAGOZA Palafox   🖼️🍴🏊🏋️📺📋♿   €€€€
Casa Jimenez s/n, 50004 **Tel** *976-23 77 00* **Fax** *976-23 47 05* **Rooms** *179*

The Spanish architect Pascua Ortega went to town on his design for this luxurious hotel. The grand entrance is flanked by full-scale representations of the old gates to the city. The rooms, on the other hand, are tasteful and minimalist. In terms of location and facilities this is one of the best places in the city. **www.palafoxhoteles.com**

CENTRAL SPAIN

AVILA Parador de Ávila   🖼️🍴📋   €€€
C/ Marqués Canales de Chozas 2, 05001 **Tel** *920-21 13 40* **Fax** *920-22 61 66* **Rooms** *61*

Ideal for history lovers, this hotel is set in a 16th-century palace, next to the walls that surround Ávila's old town. Refurbished with stone and adobe, the hotel is furnished with many antiques. It also boasts a covered interior patio and a garden replete with archaeological remains. **www.parador.es**

BURGOS Landa Palace   🖼️🍴🏊📺📋♿   €€€€€
Ctra AI (E-5) de Madrid a Irún km 235, 09001 **Tel** *947-25 77 77* **Fax** *947-26 46 76* **Rooms** *39*

Considered one of the best hotels in the region, this family-run establishment offers guests a taste of luxurious living with large, elegant, and comfortable rooms equipped with DVD players and other creature comforts. Some rooms have jacuzzis. The highlight, however, is the magnificent swimming pool covered by Gothic arches. **www.landapalace.es**

Key to Symbols *see back cover flap*

LEON Parador de San Marcos

Plaza de San Marcos 7, 24001 **Tel** *987-23 73 00* **Fax** *987-23 34 58* **Rooms** *226*

The dramatic Renaissance façade of this former San Marcos monastery gives way to an interior full of stone work and wooden masterpieces by medieval maestros. The rooms are comfortable and luxurious. A stay at this museum-like hotel is an experience in itself. **www.parador.es**

SALAMANCA AC Palacio de San Esteban

Arroyo de Santo Domingo 3, 37001 **Tel** *923-26 22 96* **Fax** *923-26 88 72* **Rooms** *51*

The AC hotel chain took over this old convent in 2002 and converted it into one of the city's finest hotels. The original character of the building has been kept alive within the context of a modern hotel. The vaulted ceilings and stone walls breathe history, while the comfortable rooms do not lack any amenities. **www.ac-hotels.com**

SAN LORENZO DE EL ESCORIAL El Botánico

C/ Timoteo Padrós 16, 28200 **Tel** *918-90 78 79* **Fax** *918-90 81 58* **Rooms** *20*

An appealing hotel, housed in a handsome, whitewashed country mansion. A stone's throw from the vast El Escorial monastery, it is surrounded by beautiful gardens and is situated opposite the golf course. The bedrooms are decorated with modern furnishings, and offer great views. Breakfast included. **www.valdesimonte.com**

SEGOVIA Parador de Segovia

Ctra de Valadolid s/n, 40003 **Tel** *921-44 37 37* **Fax** *921-43 73 62* **Rooms** *113*

This country house is just a short distance from the aqueduct and offers magnificent views of Segovia. The abstract art in the large lobby forms a nice contrast to the sober lines of the classical interior. The restaurant is one of the best places to sample the city's favorite dish, *cochinillo* (suckling pig). **www.parador.es**

TOLEDO Pintor El Greco

C/ Alamillos del Tránsito 13, 45002 (Toledo) **Tel** *925-28 51 91* **Fax** *925-21 58 19* **Rooms** *33*

A 17th-century bakery in Toledo's former Jewish quarter has been discreetly extended behind the original façade and patio. Wrought iron, traditional ceramics, and lots of flowering plants add character to the hotel. The bedrooms are modern, yet in keeping with the historic surroundings. **www.hotel-pintorelgreco.com**

SOUTHERN SPAIN

ARCOS DE LA FRONTERA Parador de Arcos de Frontera

Plaza del Cabildo s/n, 11630 (Cádiz) **Tel** *956-70 05 00* **Fax** *956-70 11 16* **Rooms** *24*

Formerly a magistrate's house, this mansion perched on a cliff above the old city is now a smart parador. A huge terrace offers great views of ancient spires and rooftops below, and the rooms are set around a series of beautifully tiled patios with wells and fountains. Rooms are plush and comfortable and some have jacuzzis. **www.parador.es**

CORDOBA Casa de los Azulejos

C/ Fernando Colón 5, 14002 (Córdoba) **Tel** *957-47 00 00* **Fax** *957-47 54 96* **Rooms** *8*

The "House of the Tiles" is an enchanting 17th-century mansion set around a typical patio with exquisite local tiles, pretty wrought iron, and lush greenery. The pretty rooms are cool and modern, with extras such as internet. A terrific restaurant offers a fusion of Andalusian and South American cuisine. **www.casadelosazulejos.com**

GRANADA Posada Pilar del Toro

C/ Elvira 25, 18010 (Granada) **Tel** *958-22 73 33* **Fax** *958-21 62 18* **Rooms** *15*

Rustic charm and a historic ambiance are combined with modern comforts in this welcoming hotel which is located close to Albaícin, Plaza Nueva, and the cathedral. There is an attractive central courtyard where guests can relax. **www.posadapilardeltoro.com**

GRANADA Parador de Granada

C/ Real de la Alhambra, 18009 (Granada) **Tel** *958-22 14 40* **Fax** *958-22 22 64* **Rooms** *36*

This elegant parador in the jasmine-scented gardens of the Alhambra was once a convent, and the cloister has been transformed into a tree-filled oasis filled with flowers. From the elegant bedrooms, you can hear the fountains of the Generalife and enjoy blissful views of the city and the ancient palace. Book well in advance. **www.parador.es**

MALAGA Don Curro

C/ Sancha de Lara 7, 29015 (Málaga) **Tel** *952-22 72 00* **Fax** *952-21 59 46* **Rooms** *118*

The exterior may not be attractive, but this hotel's interior is charming and comfortable, with a welcoming ambiance. Rooms are tastefully furnished with dark wood and marble, and they offer some thoughtful extras, including a valet parking service. Houses a simple bar-restaurant and is popular with business travelers. **www.hoteldoncurro.com**

MARBELLA El Fuerte

Av El Fuerte, 29600 (Málaga) **Tel** *952-92 00 00* **Fax** *952-82 44 11* **Rooms** *263*

El Fuerte was the first purpose-built hotel in Marbella and is still one of the best. It is unmissable – a big pink building surrounded by tropical gardens. Some rooms have mountain views but the best look out to sea. Next to the beachfront, it has a heated, glassed-in pool, an outdoor pool, and a health and beauty center. **www.fuertehoteles.com**

RONDA Parador de Ronda €€€

Plaza España, 29400 (Málaga) **Tel** *952-87 75 00* **Fax** *952-87 81 88* **Rooms** *78*

Edging up to Ronda's famous cliff, yet close to the town center, this modern, purpose-built parador has stunning views over the gorge, especially from the top-floor suites. The bedrooms are full of light and stylishly decorated. The parador is surrounded by huge gardens with an outdoor pool right on the cliff edge. **www.parador.es**

SEVILLE La Casa del Maestro €€€

C/ Almudena 5, 41002 **Tel** *954-50 00 07* **Fax** *954-50 00 06* **Rooms** *11*

Once the home of celebrated flamenco guitarist Niño Ricardo, this charming yellow-and-ochre painted town house is built around a patio bursting with plants and flowers. Rooms are on the small side, but full of thoughtful touches such as a jug of iced water and chocolates placed by the bed. Has a lovely roof terrace. **www.lacasadelmaestro.com**

SEVILLE Vincci la Rabida €€€

C/ Castelar 24, 41001 **Tel** *954-50 12 80* **Fax** *954-21 66 00* **Rooms** *81*

Located in El Arenal district, close to shops, restaurants, and a bullring, this 18th-century palace was restored and opened as a four-star hotel in 2003. The guest rooms combine warm, earthy tones with dark furnishings and wrought-iron beds. Some rooms have views of the central courtyard. **www.vinccihoteles.com**

SEVILLE Casa Numero Siete €€€€

C/ Virgenes 7, 41004 **Tel** *954-22 15 81* **Fax** *954-21 45 27* **Rooms** *7*

One of the loveliest and most romantic hotels in Seville. This elegant guesthouse occupies a mansion and features just a handful of rooms. The decor includes a range of antiques and family heirlooms. Also has an opulent sitting room with a bar. The breakfasts here are delicious. **www.casanumero7.com**

TORREMOLINOS Hotel Miami €

C/ Aladino 14, 29620 (Málaga) **Tel** *952-38 52 55* **Fax** *952-38 52 55* **Rooms** *26*

The Miami offers welcome respite from the Costa del Sol's modern growth. It has whitewashed walls, tiles, iron grilles, balconies, and potted plants. Rooms are simple, and vary in terms of size and amenities, but they are all comfortable and the staff are friendly and helpful. The pool is an added bonus. **www.residencia-miami.com**

THE BALEARIC ISLANDS

FORMENTERA, ES PUJOLS Sa Volta €€€

C/ Miramar 94, 07871 (Formentera) **Tel** *971-32 81 25* **Fax** *971-32 82 28* **Rooms** *25*

A family-run hostal in a modern block close to the beach in one of Formentera's main resorts. The standard rooms are simple, but comfortable. It is worth splashing out on one of the three semi-suites, which have plush modern decor, including canopied beds and spacious private terraces. Charming staff. Open Mar–Dec. **www.savolta.com**

IBIZA, IBIZA TOWN Hostal La Marina €€

C/ Barcelona 7, 07800 (Formentera) **Tel** *971-31 01 72* **Fax** *971-31 48 94* **Rooms** *25*

A classic on the seafront, Hostal La Marina is located in a modernized 19th-century building, which retains some charming original details. Rooms are brightly painted in Mediterranean colors and the best have lovely sea views. In high season, it is a little overpriced, but a good deal otherwise. **www.hostal-lamarina.com**

MALLORCA, PALMA DE MALLORCA Born €€

C/ Sant Jaume 3, 07012 (Mallorca) **Tel** *971-71 29 42* **Fax** *971-71 86 18* **Rooms** *30*

The Marquis of Ferrandell's town mansion, built in the 16th century and restored in the 18th, makes a splendid little hotel. The simple but comfortable bedrooms are set around a typical Mallorcan courtyard with palms and a grand staircase. A few have tiny balconies overlooking the courtyard. One of the best budget options. **www.hotelborn.com**

MALLORCA, PORT DE POLLENCA Formentor €€€€€

Playa de Formentor, 07470 (Mallorca) **Tel** *971-89 91 01* **Fax** *971-86 51 55* **Rooms** *127*

Writers, opera singers, film stars, and the Dalai Lama have signed the visitors' book of this luxury hotel on the island's northwest tip. No longer quite the celebrity haunt that it was, it still remains an elegant retreat. The rooms are traditionally decorated. Superb sports facilities available and the beach is on the doorstep. **www.hotelformentor.net**

MENORCA, CIUTADELLA Patricia €€€

Paseo San Nicolás 90–92, 07760 (Menorca) **Tel** *971-38 55 11* **Fax** *978-48 11 20* **Rooms** *44*

A modern, cream-colored chain hotel with white bay windows overlooking the harbor. Rooms are spacious and blandly furnished. Geared toward business travelers, it has conference facilities and a business center. The convenient location and efficient staff make it a good bet for tourists. Offers weekend discounts. **www.hesperia-patricia.com**

MENORCA, MAO Port Mahón €€

C/ Fort de l'Eau 13, 07701 (Menorca) **Tel** *971-36 26 00* **Fax** *971-35 10 50* **Rooms** *82*

Housed in an attractive red and white colonial-style building, this hotel – probably the most luxurious in the city – overlooks Maó harbor. Its grounds include wide terraces and a curving swimming pool surrounded by lawns. The best rooms, comfortably furnished in chain-hotel style, have private terraces. **www.sethotels.com**

Where to Eat in Spain

The quickest and best-value places to eat in Spain are bars that serve tapas, small appetizers traditionally eaten standing at the bar (*see p325*). Family-run *posadas* or *mesones* serve reasonably priced, sit-down meals. Spain also has many top-quality restaurants, notably in the Basque Country, Galicia, Madrid, and Barcelona.

PRICE CATEGORIES
Price categories are for a three-course meal for one, including a half-bottle of house wine, tax and service:

€ Under 25 euros
€€ 25–35 euros
€€€ 35–45 euros
€€€€ Over 45 euros

MADRID

OLD MADRID Casa Patas
Tapas   €
C/ Cañizares 10, 28012 **Tel** *913-69 04 96*   **Map** *C4*

Casa Patas is primarily known for its flamenco shows in the evenings, which are among the best in the city. It is also an original place to eat in the heart of Old Madrid, with a well-stocked tapas bar and an unbeatable fixed-price lunch menu. Wheelchair-users must call in advance for assistance. There is an admission charge. Closed Sun.

OLD MADRID El Estragón
€
Plaza de la Paja 10, 28005 **Tel** *913-65 89 82*   **Map** *B4*

El Estragón is located in a pretty spot, overlooking one of Madrid's loveliest and most fashionable squares. *Madrileño* cuisine is decidedly meaty, but this long-standing vegetarian restaurant provides a welcome break for veggies. The menu features a variety of delectable vegetable- and soy-based dishes. Note that there are two sittings for dinner.

OLD MADRID Delic
Tapas   €€
Plaza de la Paja s/n, 28005 **Tel** *913-64 54 50*   **Map** *B4*

Stylish Delic is a popular café-bar, doubling as a hip local drinking hole. It serves everything from delicious breakfasts, to light snacks and more substantial cuisine with an exotic touch. With a perfect location on the trendy Plaza de la Paja, the terrace is a good place to watch a smart crowd of locals hang out on hot summer nights.

OLD MADRID Taberna Bilbao
Tapas   €€
C/ Costanilla de San Andrés 8, 28005 **Tel** *913-65 61 25*   **Map** *B4*

A hugely popular Basque tavern, Taberna Bilbao serves home-made specialties such as *bacalao* (cod) cooked in a range of styles. The *chipirones* (baby squid), prepared in their own ink, are excellent. Try the house *txakoli*, a light, tart, and very refreshing Basque wine. Reservations are highly recommended. Closed Mon lunch.

OLD MADRID Botín
€€€
C/ de Cuchilleros 17, 28011 **Tel** *913-66 42 17*   **Map** *B4*

Dating back to 1725, Botín is reputedly the oldest restaurant in the world. With its brick-lined vaults and heavy wooden beams, it has changed little since. Even the original wood-burning oven is still used to cook the traditional roast lamb and suckling pig. There is a reasonable fixed-price lunch menu. Book well in advance.

OLD MADRID Casa Lucio
Tapas   €€€€
C/ Cava Baja 35, 28005 **Tel** *913-65 32 52*   **Map** *B4*

Casa Lucio is a historic tavern serving Castillian specialties. The *huevos estrellados* (fried eggs with potatoes) are so exquisite that they have even made it into a celebrated Spanish poem. The typical *Madrileño* tripe and rice pudding are equally renowned. The wine list has some fine wines from around Spain. Closed Sat lunch & Aug.

BOURBON MADRID Café Gijón
Tapas   €
Paseo Recoletos 21, 28007 **Tel** *915-21 54 25*   **Map** *D3*

A legendary café, established in 1888 and still decorated with original Art Nouveau style furnishings, Café Gijón is perfect for breakfast, a fixed-price lunch, or afternoon tea with cakes. Specialties include hake with cider and seafood *paella*. There is an elegant terrace, frequented by the well-heeled.

BOURBON MADRID Casa Labra
Tapas   €
C/ Tetuán 12, 28013 **Tel** *915-32 14 05*   **Map** *C4*

Founded in 1860, Casa Labra is one of Madrid's most atmospheric tapas bars. It is tucked away on a small street close to the Puerta del Sol, and retains its gleaming wood panels and pretty tiles. In the same family since 1947, the restaurant is renowned for its *bacalao* (cod). Closed Jan 1.

BOURBON MADRID El Amparo
€€€€
Callejón de Puigcerdá 8, 28001 **Tel** *914-31 64 56*   **Map** *E2*

Enjoy new Basque cuisine in what many consider to be Madrid's nicest setting, with a skylight that lets you gaze up at the stars. The dining rooms are spread out over three levels, and the cuisine is assured and highly creative, such as tuna mousse with lobster and parsley oil. Closed Sat lunch, Sun & Easter.

Key to Symbols *see back cover flap*

BOURBON MADRID Teatriz   *Tapas* 🏢📋   €€€€

C/ Hermosilla 15, 28001 **Tel** *915-77 53 79*   **Map** *E3*

Formerly a theater, Teatriz was completely transformed by French designer Philippe Starck in 1989 and now houses a chic restaurant and a stylish tapas bar. In the restaurant, you can dine on fresh Mediterranean cuisine with Italian influences, while the tapas bar offers gourmet tapas. Prices reflect the glamorous setting.

BOURBON MADRID Viridiana   📋🍷   €€€€

C/ Juan de Mena 14, 28014 **Tel** *915-23 44 78*   **Map** *E4*

Innovative Spanish cuisine, complemented by an encyclopedic wine list, is offered in this restaurant decorated with stills from Luís Buñuel's film, Viridiana. The creative menu changes frequently, and features elaborate creations prepared with the best seasonal produce. The wine list was recently voted one of the best in the world. Closed Sun.

BARCELONA

EIXAMPLE Alkimia   🏢📋🍷   €€€€

C/ Indústria 79, 08025 **Tel** *932-07 61 15*   **Map** *F2*

One of the rising stars of Barcelona's gastronomic scene, this small designer restaurant revitalizes traditional Catalan dishes with new techniques and foreign flavors. Signature dishes include creamy rice with crayfish and nyora peppers, sticky, slow roasted bull tail and mandarin essence with *horchata* (tiger nut) foam. Closed Sat lunch & Sun.

EIXAMPLE Casa Calvet   🏢📋🍷   €€€€

C/ Casp 48, 08010 **Tel** *934-12 40 12*   **Map** *D2*

A beautiful restaurant that was originally designed by Gaudí as a private home and offices for a wealthy textile merchant. The cozy seating booths, formal table settings, and old-school service set the ambiance. Try the lamb meatballs with creamy risotto and pine nut tart with foamed *crema catalana*. Closed Sun.

OLD TOWN Bar Pinotxo   *Tapas* 🍷   €

C/ Mercat de la Boqueria (La Rambla 89), 08002 **Tel** *933-17 17 31*   **Map** *E4*

The most famous of all the bars in the Boqueria. Steel buckets hold chilled bottles of cava (Catalan champagne-style wine), and fresh ingredients from neighboring market stalls are cooked and served hot on the spot. Try the squid cooked in diverse styles and the fresh oysters. The bar is closed on Sundays and in the evenings after 6pm.

OLD TOWN Elisabets   *Tapas* 🍷📋   €

C/ Elisabets 2, 08001 **Tel** *933-17 58 26*   **Map** *D3*

A local institution, this homely bustling restaurant specializes in traditional Catalan cuisine. It is a favorite for diners in search of hearty, home-cooked mid-day meals and Friday night tapas. Dishes include rabbit stew, chicken cooked in beer, and a variety of *bocadillos* (sandwiches). Closed Sun (the bar is open) & three weeks in Aug.

OLD TOWN El Salón   📋🍷   €€

C/ Hostal d'en Sol 6–8, 08002 **Tel** *933-15 21 59*   **Map** *D3*

The Baroque-style interior gives this establishment the feel of an 18th-century boudoir. The menu changes constantly but promises sumptuous ingredients and inventive dishes, often featuring French and Catalan specialties. Closed Sun & Sat lunch.

OLD TOWN Euskal Etxea   *Tapas* 🏢📋🍷   €€

C/ Placeta Montcada 1–3, 08003 **Tel** *933-10 21 85*   **Map** *E3*

Home to the Basque Cultural Institute, the Euskal Etxea is one of the best places in town for Basque *pintxos* (small rounds of bread with myriad toppings). Other specialties include fish and meat stews, roasted meat, and fresh seafood dishes. It also serves exceptionally good à la carte meals. Closed Sun & Mon lunch.

OLD TOWN 7 Portes   🏢📋🍷   €€€

Passeig Isabel II 14, 08003 **Tel** *933-19 30 33*   **Map** *E3*

A long-standing Barcelona institution since 1836, with a who's who of past guests, including Winston Churchill and Che Guevara. It is famed for its classic marble tiles and wood-paneled dining room, and most of all for *paella*, which comes in 10 different varieties. They serve a different *paella* every day of the week.

OLD TOWN Taxidermista   🏢📋🍷   €€€

Plaça Reial 8, 08002 **Tel** *934-12 45 36*   **Map** *D3*

Soft color schemes and high ceilings give this trendy restaurant an edge over the touristy competition on the bustling Plaça Reial. Inventive market cooking offers a wide range of dishes from around the Mediterranean Rim, including *baba ghanoush* (Lebanese eggplant purée), sardine tarts, and duck confit. Closed Mon.

OLD TOWN Cal Pep   📋🍷   €€€€

Plaça de les Olles 8, 08003 **Tel** *933-10 79 61*   **Map** *E3*

Arguably the best bar in town for fresh fish and seafood, right off the boats. Cal Pep has an excellent selection of tapas as well. The long, narrow, standing bar means it gets crowded at peak times. Arrive early for one of five tables out back. Closed Sun, Mon lunch, & Aug.

Map References *see maps of Madrid pp282–3 and Barcelona pp306–7*

OLD TOWN Hofmann 🖩🍴🍷 €€€€

C/ Argenteria 74–78, 08003 **Tel** *933-19 58 89* **Map** *E3*

The recent recipient of a Michelin star, this restaurant-cum-cookery school produces high-quality cuisine in a sophisticated locale with attentive service. Daily specials are always a good bet. Do not miss the desserts as they are highly elaborate and artistic. Closed Sat & Sun, Easter, & Aug.

NORTHERN SPAIN

BAIONA, RIAS BAIXAS Moscón ♿🚇🖩🍷 €€

C/ Alférez Barreiro 2, 36300 (Pontevedra) **Tel** *986-35 50 08*

This restaurant in Baiona serves mainly Galician cuisine with fish stews predominating on the menu. These include a tasty fish *caldeirada* (casserole) spiced with paprika. There is also seafood from the estuary; all complemented by a good selection of Galician wines. The harbor view makes for a pleasant dining experience. Outside tables in summer.

BILBAO (BILBO) Zortziko 🖩🍴🍷 €€€€

C/ Alameda Mazarredo 17, 48001 (Vizcaya) **Tel** *944-23 97 43*

Contemporary haute cuisine served in a beautiful building, not far from the Guggenheim Museum. The menu is seasonal with creative Basque touches. Among the specialties are *pintada a baja temperatura* (guinea fowl cooked at a low temperature), *foie gras*, turbot and a delicious tiramisu. Closed Sun, Mon, & 20 Aug–15 Sep.

CANGAS DE ONIS El Molín de la Pedrera *Tapas* ♿🚇🖩 €

C/ Río Güeña 2, 33550 (Asturias) **Tel** *985-84 91 09*

A stylish *sidrería* (cider house), decorated with traditional objects and implements which give it a rustic air. It serves original combinations such as *crujiente de cabrales con avellanas* (Cabrales cheese from the Picos de Europa with hazelnuts) and more traditional dishes such as *bonito* fish and *frixuelos* (crêpes). Closed Wed except in summer & Jan.

OVIEDO Casa Fermín ♿🖩🍷 €€€

C/ San Francisco 8, 33003 (Asturias) **Tel** *985-21 64 52*

The cozy Casa Fermín is one of Oviedo's most classic restaurants offering a combination of traditional and modern, seasonal cuisine. Try the green beans with goats' cheese or the *salmonetes* (red mullet) with black rice. For dessert, try copa de *tiramisú con frambuesa* (tiramisu with raspberries). Closed Sun.

PAMPLONA (IRUNA) Europa 🖩🍷 €€€€

C/ Espoz y Mina 11, 31002 (Navarra) **Tel** *948-22 18 00*

Located in the Hotel Europa, in the old part of the city near the cathedral, is one of Pamplona's best places to eat. It offers a range of traditional Navarrese dishes such as *menestra de verduras* (vegetable stew), *sopa de castañas* (chestnut soup), and *chateaubriand de lomo de ciervo con mango a la parrilla* (grilled deer with mango). Closed Sun.

PONTEVEDRA, RIAS BAIXAS Alameda de Doña Antonia 🖩🍷 €€€

C/ Soportales de la Herrería 4–1°, 36002 **Tel** *986-84 72 74*

Regional cuisine in a refined and beautiful setting overlooking the lovely Plaza de la Herrería. Monkfish salad, marinated sea bass salad, oven-cooked lamb with honey, and *mero al vapor* (grouper) with vegetables and olive oil are favorites. Closed Sun & Mon evening (except December and August), two weeks in Sep and May.

SAN SEBASTIAN (DONOSTIA) Arzak ♿🖩🍴🍷 €€€€

Av Alcalde José Elósegui 273, 20015 (Guipúzcoa) **Tel** *943-27 84 65*

Celebrity chef Juan Mari Arzak has earned a reputation beyond Spain for his perfectly presented, creative dishes. His daughter Elena works here as well. They even run a "laboratory" where a team of cooks experiment. Closed Sun evenings Mon, & Tue (Jan–Jun); Sun evenings & Mon (Jul–Dec); two weeks in Jun & Nov.

SANTANDER El Nuevo Molino ♿🚇🖩🍷 €€€€

Ctra N611 Santander Torrelavega km 13, Barrio Monseñor 18, Puente Arce, 39478 (Cantabria) **Tel** *942-57 50 55*

Sited in Puente Arce, this ancient mill belongs to El Serbal in Santander. It offers creative cooking with dishes such as cod salad with mushrooms and *pil pil* (a creamy parsley sauce) and monkfish ravioli filled with king prawn and cream. There is a divine ice cream with sultanas and brandy over toffee cream. Closed Sun evenings & Tue.

SANTIAGO DE COMPOSTELA Toñi Vicente ♿🖩🍷 €€€€

C/ Rosalia de Castro 24, 15706 (A Coruña) **Tel** *981-59 41 00*

Worshippers of Galician haute cuisine flock faithfully to Toñi Vicente's culinary temple. Among her creations are the marinated sea bass salad, the duck liver sautéed with apple, the red tuna fish in pickle, and the carpaccio of venison with truffle oil, salad, and parmesan. Closed Sun & some weeks during the year (call ahead).

VILAGARCIA DE AROUSA, RIAS BAIXAS Casa Bóveda ♿🚇🖩 €€€

C/ La Marina 2, Carril, 36610 (Pontevedra) **Tel** *986-51 12 04*

It is better to book in advance to eat in this busy restaurant situated on Carril harbor, a short way from Vilagarcía de Arousa. It specializes in fish and shellfish from the Rias Baixas and also prepares excellent *guisos* (stews) and rice dishes. Closed Sun evenings & Mon (except Aug) and 20 Dec–20 Jan.

Key to Price Guide *see p346* **Map References** *see map of Barcelona pp306–7*

CATALONIA & EASTERN SPAIN

ALICANTE (ALACANT) Nou Manolín
Tapas 🅰️📶📋🍷 €€€€
C/ Villegas 3, 03001 (Alicante) **Tel** 965-20 03 68

An Alicantino favorite, this attractive restaurant is tucked away in the old quarter in the former home of local author Gabriel Miró. There is an excellent tapas bar downstairs, while upstairs you can dine in an elegant brick-lined salon on classic Valencian seafood, rice dishes, accompanied by an extensive wine list.

ALTEA, COSTA BLANCA Racó de Toni
Tapas 🅰️📋🍷 €€
C/ de la Mar 127, 03590 (Alicante) **Tel** 965-84 17 63

An old-fashioned charmer, this cozy, traditional *mesón* serves good regional specialties including excellent rice dishes and locally caught fish. Specialties include rice with salt cod and vegetables, and peppers stuffed with anchovies. There's a good-value *menú del día*, or you can join the lively crowd of locals in the tapas bar. Closed 20–30 Nov.

TARRAGONA El Merlot
📶📋🍷 €€€
C/ Cavallers 6, 43003 (Tarragona) **Tel** 977-22 06 52

Situated in the old part of town, this restaurant serves classic Mediterranean dishes. House specials include game in season, fresh fish, and home-made desserts. Specialties include flower salad with vinaigrette of seeds and apples tartar with *foie gras*, and anise ice cream. Also good wines. Closed Sun & Mon lunch, 1–15 Feb, & Christmas.

VALENCIA Corretgeria 33
🅰️📶📋🍷 €€€
C/ Corretgeria 33, 46001 (Valencia) **Tel** 963-92 41 61

A stylish little restaurant painted in bright colors, Corretgeria 33 serves a good-value menú del día for lunch. There is an elaborate menu of creative versions of local dishes in the evenings. The handful of tables, out on the pavement terrace, are great people-watching spots. Closed Mon, Sat lunch, Sun evenings, 15 days in Nov.

ZARAGOZA Don Pascual
🅰️📶📋🍷 €€€
C/ Residencial Paraíso 48, 50008 **Tel** 976-21 87 14

Inside this romantic, intimate space, creative cooking wows the regulars. The promise of using only the freshest market ingredients is reflected in the dishes. The king prawns in curry and the steak tartar are very popular choices. Closed Sun (except May & Dec), Easter, & 1–15 Aug.

CENTRAL SPAIN

AVILA El Almacén
🅰️📶📋🍷 €€€
Crta Salamanca 6, 05002 **Tel** 920-25 44 55

This restaurant, located in an old warehouse, is generally regarded as one of the best in all of Castilla, and is particularly noted for its wine cellar. It offers creative cooking with prime-quality local produce, all cooked to perfection. There are views of Ávila's famous wall from the dining room. Closed Sun evenings, Mon, & Sep.

BURGOS Mesón del Cid
📋 €€€
Plaza Santa María 8, 09003 **Tel** 947-20 87 15

In a 15th-century edifice located in front of the cathedral, this rustic place is named after Spain's most notorious conqueror. A favorite among locals, it is celebrated for its home-style cooking. The menu features traditional fare such as roast lamb, garlic soup, and cod cooked with garlic. There is an excellent house wine. Closed Sun evenings.

LEON Vivaldi
📋🍷 €€€€
Platerias 4, 24003 **Tel** 987-26 07 60

In the historic Húmedo district, Vivaldi is one of the better-known restaurants in León. Original creations include fresh pasta with fungi and *foie gras*, sautéed vegetables with octopus, and chickpeas with garlic prawns. There is a bar for pre-dinner drinks. Closed Sun evenings and Mon (except in Jul & Aug).

SALAMANCA El Río de la Plata
Tapas 📋🍷 €€€
Plaza del Peso 1, 37001 **Tel** 923-21 90 05

Located in the heart of the old town, this traditional restaurant, run by the locally celebrated Andrés brothers, serves slow-cooked lamb, pork and veal stews, and suckling pig. Lighter eaters may wish to stick to the excellent selection of tapas. Among the tasty desserts is apple baked in a secret sauce! Closed Mon, 8–20 Jan, & 15–20 days in Jul.

SAN LORENZO DE EL ESCORIAL Taberna La Cueva
Tapas 📶🍷 €
C/ San Antón 4, 28200 **Tel** 918-90 15 16

Juan de Villanueva, architect of the Prado, designed this 18th-century inn whose specialties include the *heuvos a la cueva* (fried eggs and ham served in a nest of straw potatoes). A cool stone house, it is cozy in winter and cool in summer, when you can also tuck into tapas out on the terrace. A good range of local wines. Closed Mon.

Key to Symbols see back cover flap

SEGOVIA Mesón de Cándido
Tapas 🅰️🔲🈯️📶 €€€

Azoguejo 5, 40001 **Tel** *921-42 59 11*

One of the region's better-known restaurants, Mesón de Candido is located in a 15th-century home, close to the Roman aqueduct. The restaurant is famed for its roast suckling pig (so tender they carve it for you with the side of a plate) and hearty Castillian soups. A favorite among locals, it is always busy, so reservations are recommended.

TOLEDO Hostal del Cardenal
🈯️🔲 €€

Paseo de Recadero 24, 45004 (Toledo) **Tel** *925-22 08 62*

Once the summer residence of Cardinal Lorenzana, this 18th-century palace retains its beautiful Arabic-style gardens, enclosed by the city walls. It serves suckling pig, traditionally roasted in a brick oven, along with game (particularly pheasant) in season. Desserts always feature the famous Toledo *mazapán* (marzipan).

SOUTHERN SPAIN

CADIZ El Faro
Tapas 🅰️🔲📶 €€€

C/ San Félix 15, 11011 (Cádiz) **Tel** *956-21 10 68*

El Faro restaurant has a warm atmosphere in the old fishermen's barrio of Cádiz. The menu, a wonderful blend of modern and traditional, changes daily but always features local seafood, such as the *tortillitas de camarones* (fritters of tiny shrimps), or the rice dishes flavored with shellfish from the bay. There is a popular tapas bar too.

CORDOBA Casa Pepe de la Judería
Tapas 🅰️🔲🈯️ €€€

C/ Romero 1, 14003 (Córdoba) **Tel** *957-20 07 44*

This has been one of Córdoba's most appealing restaurants since it opened in 1928. Dine on a lovely Córdoban patio blazing with flowers, or sit in the dining rooms festooned with photos of notable customers. Try the *flamenquin* (fried rolls of veal and ham), or the unusual cherry gazpacho flavored with mint. Closed 24–31 Dec.

ESTEPONA La Alborada
🅰️🈯️🔲 €€

Puerto Deportivo de Estepona, 29680 (Málaga) **Tel** *952-80 20 47*

This quayside eatery serves excellent *paella* and other rice dishes, such as *arroz a la banda* (a kind of fish risotto). It also serves delicious *pescaito frito* (white bait) and has tasty home-made desserts such as the *pudin de almendras* (creamy almond pudding). There are lovely views of the yacht-filled harbor from the terrace. Closed Wed.

FUENGIROLA Portofino
🅰️🈯️🔲📶 €€

Edificio Perla 1, Paseo Marítimo 29, 29640 (Málaga) **Tel** *952-47 06 43*

This seafront restaurant is popular for its friendly service and good international food, such as the fish brochette or delicious pastas with rich sauces. It also prepares traditional Andalusian dishes, all served in generous portions. The terrace has views over the glossy, yacht-filled port. Closed Mon & Jul.

GRANADA Mirador de Morayma
🈯️🎵🔲 €€

C/ Pianista Garcia Carrillo 2, 18010 (Granada) **Tel** *958-22 82 90*

Situated in the Albaícin with views of the Alhambra, this charming patio-restaurant specializes in typical dishes of Granada, such as *remojón* (a salad of oranges and codfish) and lamb sautéed with garlic. The wine list includes organic wines produced on the restaurant's own estate. Flamenco on Tuesdays, call to confirm times. Closed Sun pm.

GRANADA Carmen de San Miguel
🅰️🈯️🔲 €€€€

Plaza Torres Bermejas 3, 18009 (Granada) **Tel** *958-22 67 23*

The Andalusian specialties at this pretty restaurant with Moorish-style decor include the seabass with aubergine (eggplant) and the *foie gras* pastry with mango chutney. Everything is fresh and prepared with imagination by a talented young chef. There are wonderful views of the whitewashed maze of the Albaícin from the terrace. Closed Sun.

JEREZ DE LA FRONTERA La Mesa Redonda
🔲 €€

C/ Manuel de la Quintana 3, 11402 (Cádiz) **Tel** *956-34 00 69*

A charming, family-run restaurant, which remains a favorite with locals for the quality and excellence of its cuisine. The creative menu changes with the seasons offering seafood, meat dishes, and game. Try the *mojama* (cured tuna) as a starter, and do not miss the spectacular beef *salteado* (sautéed with black sausage). Closed Sun, 15 Jul–16 Aug.

MALAGA Mesón Astorga
Tapas 🅰️🈯️🔲 €€

C/ Gerona 11, 29006 (Málaga) **Tel** *952-34 25 63*

Using Málaga's superb local produce with flair, makes this classically decorated and typically Andalusian restaurant popular. Try the fried aubergine (eggplant) drizzled with molasses or the salad of fresh tuna with sherry vinegar dressing. At the lively tapas bar, you can join the locals tucking into generous *raciones*. Closed Sun.

MARBELLA Santiago
Tapas 🅰️🈯️🔲📶 €€€€

C/ Paseo Marítimo 5, 29600 (Málaga) **Tel** *952-77 00 78*

This is probably the best place for seafood on the Costa del Sol. On any day, there might be 40 or 50 fish and shellfish dishes, all very fresh. Famous for more than 50 years, it's essential to book your table well in advance. Tapas are served at the bar, but there is a huge variety (more than 500) on offer at the adjoining Tabernita de Santiago.

Key to Price Guide *see p346* **Key to Symbols** *see back cover flap*

RONDA Del Escudero
Paseo de Blás Infante 1, 29400 (Málaga) **Tel** *952-87 13 67*

With an incomparable garden setting near Ronda's famous bullring, this elegant restaurant offers spectacular views over the valley to go with its traditional Andalusian cuisine. Go for the good-value fixed-price lunch menu which you can enjoy on the panoramic garden terrace. Closed Sun evenings.

SEVILLE El Cabildo
Plaza del Cabildo, 41001 (Seville) **Tel** *954-22 79 70*

Part of the ancient Arabic walls have been conserved in this classic and delightfully old-fashioned restaurant. All the traditional Andalusian favorites are on the menu, excellently cooked with fresh local ingredients. Try a platter of fresh fried fish, Sevillian *revueltos* (scrambled eggs with different fillings) accompanied by sturdy local wine.

SEVILLE La Isla
C/ Arfe 25, 41001 **Tel** *954-21 26 31*

This attractive, centrally located restaurant features superb seafood specialties from Galicia, including turbot, bream, and delicacies such as *percebes* (sea barnacles). Some Andalusian dishes, such as a meaty beef stew, also feature. There is a small tapas bar where you can enjoy fabulous prawns, oysters, and a wide range of local hams.

SEVILLE Corral del Agua
Callejón del Agua 6, 41004 **Tel** *954-22 48 41*

Dine on the cool patio of the Reales Alcázares gardens, with plants trailing romantically around wrought-iron grilles and a marble fountain burbling quietly. Antique furniture and paintings adorn the dining room, and the menu emphasizes seasonal specialties, traditionally prepared. Closed Sun.

TORREMOLINOS Frutos
Av de la Riviera 80, 29620 (Málaga) **Tel** *952-38 14 50*

The grande dame of Costa del Sol restaurants, serving superb meat and fish. There is a terrace, and two glassy dining areas where you can enjoy suckling pig, followed by *arroz con leche* (rice pudding). The remarkable wine cellar in the basement can be visited. An informal tapas bar at the entrance serves lighter meals. Closed Sun evenings.

THE BALEARIC ISLANDS

FORMENTERA, ES PUJOLS Sa Palmera
Playa Es Pujols, C/Aguadulce 15–31, 07871 (Formentera) **Tel** *971-32 83 56*

Freshly caught seafood is served at this classic seafront restaurant, which specializes in traditionally prepared regional cuisine. Try the mixed fish *paella* or the *zarzuela de mariscos* (shellfish casserole), although you will also find a few meat dishes on the menu. You can eat out on the breezy terrace and enjoy great sea views. Closed Nov–Apr.

IBIZA, IBIZA TOWN La Masía d'en Sort
Ctra San Miguel km 1, 07814 (Ibiza) **Tel** *971-31 02 28*

A sturdy Ibizan *masia* (farmhouse) set in orange groves is home to this elegant restaurant, with stylish dining rooms which double as art galleries. The food is no less artistic, and features reinventions of classic Balearic cuisine prepared with fresh local ingredients. Try the refreshing langoustine salad. Closed Mon (except in Jul & Aug); Nov–Mar.

MALLORCA, PALMA DE MALLORCA Porto Pí
C/ Garita 25, 07015 (Mallorca) **Tel** *971-40 00 87*

This elegant old house, surrounded by gardens, is an ideal spot to savor creative Mediterranean and international cuisine using first-class ingredients. Try the sea bream cooked in wine or the duck with lime and curry spices. They also offer a range of elaborate dishes using *foie gras*. Delicious desserts. Closed Sat lunch & Sun.

MALLORCA, PORT DE POLLENCA Stay
C/ Muelle Nuevo s/n, 07470 (Mallorca) **Tel** *971-86 40 13*

With tables right on the bay, this popular local restaurant serves tasty regional cuisine with emphasis on fish and seafood. Try the *salsa de eneldo* (fillets of white fish grilled with vegetables and served with a dill sauce). They also have a cheap and cheerful snack bar (for sandwiches and burgers), good for families coming off the beaches.

MENORCA, CIUTADELLA Café Balear
C/ Pla de Sant Joan 15, 07760 (Menorca) **Tel** *971-38 00 05*

A legendary restaurant right on the port, Café Balear specializes in fish and seafood including *caldera de langosta* (lobster casserole) and *fritada de gambas* (fried prawns). The fish arrives on the restaurant's own boat, and is prepared with the minimum of fuss to better appreciate its freshness. Reservations essential. Closed Sun.

MENORCA, MAO Jágaro
Moll de Levant 334, 07701 (Menorca) **Tel** *971-36 23 90*

A classic restaurant right on the harbor, with a cozy dining room filled with knick knacks and a popular breezy terrace. It serves fine Mediterranean seafood dishes, including the Menorcan specialty *caldereta de langosta* (lobster stew). There are over 100 wines on their wine list. Closed Mon, Feb, & Sun evenings in winter.

PORTUGAL

Most visitors to Portugal head for the sandy coves, pretty fishing villages, and manicured golf courses of the Algarve. But beyond the south coast resorts lies the least explored corner of Western Europe: a country of rugged landscapes, ancient cities with proud traditions, and quiet rural backwaters.

Portugal appears to have no obvious geographical claim to nationhood, yet the country has existed within borders virtually unchanged for nearly 800 years, making it one of the oldest nation states in Europe. Its ten million people are proudly independent from, and distrustful of, neighboring Spain.

For a small country, the regions of Portugal are immensely varied. The rural Minho and Trás-os-Montes in the north are the most traditional – some might say backward. Over the last few decades many inhabitants of these neglected regions have been forced to emigrate in search of work. At the same time, the Algarve, with its beautiful sandy beaches and warm Mediterranean climate, has become a vacation playground for North Europeans as well as the Portuguese themselves. Lisbon, the capital, at the mouth of the Tagus, is a cosmopolitan metropolis with a rich cultural life. Oporto is a serious rival, especially in terms of commerce and industry, and is the center for the production and export of Portugal's most famous product – port wine, grown on steeply terraced vineyards hewn out of mountainsides in the wild upper reaches of the Douro valley.

HISTORY

The Romans, who arrived in 216 BC, called the whole peninsula Hispania, but the region between the Douro and Tagus rivers was named Lusitania after the Celtiberian tribe that lived there. After the collapse of the Roman Empire in the 5th century, Hispania was overrun first by Germanic tribes, then by Moors from North Africa in 711.

Reconquest by the Christian kingdoms of the north began in earnest in the 11th century. In the process Portucale, a small county of the kingdom of León and Castile, was declared an independent kingdom by its ruler, Afonso Henriques, in 1139. With the aid of English crusaders, he succeeded in recapturing Lisbon in 1147.

Fishing boats on the beach at the popular Algarve resort of Albufeira

◁ Nave of the Manueline church of Santa Maria in the Jerónimos monastery, Belém, Lisbon

The kingdom expanded south to the Algarve, and Portuguese sailors began to explore the African coast and the Atlantic. Portugal's golden age reached its zenith in the reign of Manuel I, with Vasco da Gama's voyage to India in 1498 and the discovery of Brazil in 1500. The era also produced the one uniquely Portuguese style of architecture: the Manueline. Trade with the East brought incredible wealth, but military defeat in Morocco meant that the prosperity was short-lived. Spain invaded in 1580 and ruled Portugal for the next 60 years.

After Portugal regained independence, its fortunes were restored by gold from Brazil. In the late 18th century, the chief minister, the Marquês de Pombal, began to modernize the country. However, Napoleon's invasion in 1807 and the

Manuel I (reigned 1495–1521), who made vast profits from Portugal's spice trade

loss of Brazil in 1825 left Portugal impoverished and divided. Absolutists and Constitutionalists struggled for power, until, in 1910, a republican revolution overthrew the monarchy.

The weakness of the economy led to a military coup in 1926 and a long period of dictatorship. António Salazar, who held power from 1928 to 1968, rid the country of its debts, but poverty was widespread and all opposition banned. The country was a virtual recluse in the world community, the prime concern of foreign policy being the defense of its African and Asian colonies. The bloodless Carnation Revolution ended the dictatorship in 1974, and full democracy was restored in 1976. Since its entry into the European Community in 1986, Portugal has enjoyed rapid economic growth and assumed the self-confident attitude of a modern Western European state.

KEY DATES IN PORTUGUESE HISTORY

139 BC Romans subdue the Lusitani

415 AD Visigoths invade Iberian Peninsula

711 Muslim army conquers Visigothic kingdom

1139 Afonso Henriques declares himself king

1147 Afonso Henriques takes Lisbon

1249 Conquest of Algarve complete

1385 João I defeats Castilians at Aljubarrota

1418 Prince Henry the Navigator made governor of Algarve; sponsors expeditions to Africa

1498 Vasco da Gama reaches India

1578 King Sebastião killed on ill-fated expedition to Morocco

1580 Philip II of Spain becomes king of Portugal

1640 Restoration; Duke of Bragança crowned João IV; start of war of independence

1668 Spain recognizes Portugal's independence

1755 Lisbon earthquake

1807 French invade; royal family flees to Brazil

1910 Revolution; Manuel II abdicates and flees to England; republic proclaimed

1932 António Salazar becomes prime minister

1974 Carnation Revolution

2000 Portugal joins European single currency

2005 Socialists win first outright majority in parliament since democracy began in 1974

LANGUAGE AND CULTURE

The family is the hub of Portuguese daily life and Catholicism remains a powerful force in rural communities. But the country has come a long way since the repression and self-censorship of the Salazar era. Urban Portugal, in particular, presents a fairly emancipated and eagerly consumerist face to the world.

The national psyche encapsulates this dualism in its struggle between a forward-looking, realistic approach to life and the dreamy, inward-looking side that finds expression in the Portuguese notion of *saudade*, a melancholy yearning for something lost or unattainable.

The Portuguese language is a source of national pride, and visitors should not assume that it is interchangeable with Spanish. Portuguese people are also often eager to speak English. Pride, too, is taken in *fado*, the native musical tradition that expresses *saudade*.

Exploring Portugal

Portugal is a small country and there are fast road
and train links between the country's three great cities,
Lisbon, Coimbra, and Oporto. Many of the most
famous sights, such as the royal palaces at Sintra and
the monastery of Alcobaça, make a good day's outing
from Lisbon. In the south, the great attractions are the
sandy beaches of the Algarve. With the completion of
the Lisbon-Algarve motorway, arriving from the north
is quite easy, but most visitors fly direct to Faro airport
and once there, traveling between the various resorts
is no problem.

Sintra, dominated by the conical
chimneys of the old royal palace

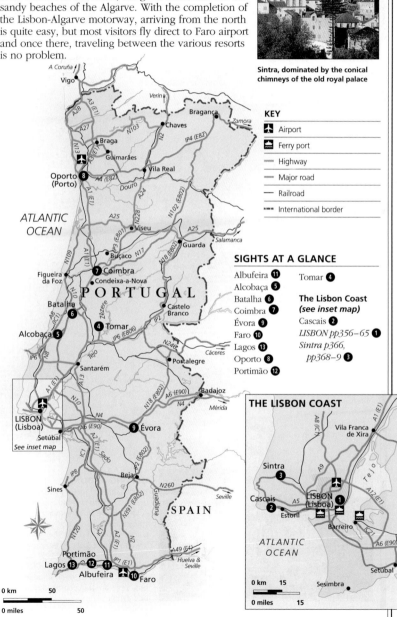

KEY

✈ Airport

⛴ Ferry port

━ Highway

━ Major road

━ Railroad

┅ International border

SIGHTS AT A GLANCE

Albufeira ⑪
Alcobaça ⑤
Batalha ⑥
Coimbra ⑦
Évora ⑨
Faro ⑩
Lagos ⑬
Oporto ⑧
Portimão ⑫

Tomar ④

The Lisbon Coast
(see inset map)
Cascais ②
LISBON pp356–65 ①
Sintra p366,
*   pp368–9* ③

THE LISBON COAST

ATLANTIC
OCEAN

0 km   50

0 miles   50

0 km   15

0 miles   15

Lisbon ❶

The capital of Portugal occupies a hilly site on the estuary of the Tagus. Over the centuries, the city expanded along the coast to Belém, the starting point for the voyages of discovery in the 15th century, and even to the other side of the river, known as the Outra Banda. It has now spread far inland, making the population of Greater Lisbon nearly two million. The historic center (the Baixa) is a small, low-lying area, pinned between the heights of the Alfama to the east and the Bairro Alto to the west. The city underwent a great cleanup for the Expo '98 exhibition, especially in the old docks and industrial areas along the waterfront.

Portugal's coat of arms in the treasury of the Sé (cathedral)

SIGHTS AT A GLANCE

Alfama ④
Bairro Alto ⑨
Baixa ⑧
Castelo de São Jorge ⑤
Museu Nacional de Arte
 Antiga ⑪
Praça do Comércio ⑦
São Vicente de Fora ③
Sé ⑥

Greater Lisbon
(see inset map)
Museu Calouste
 Gulbenkian ⑩
Museu Nacional do
 Azulejo ②
Oceanário de
 Lisboa ①

Belém *(see inset map)*
Monument to the
 Discoveries ⑬
*Mosteiro dos Jerónimos
 pp364–5* ⑭
Museu da Marinha ⑮
Museu Nacional dos
 Coches ⑫
Torre de Belém ⑯

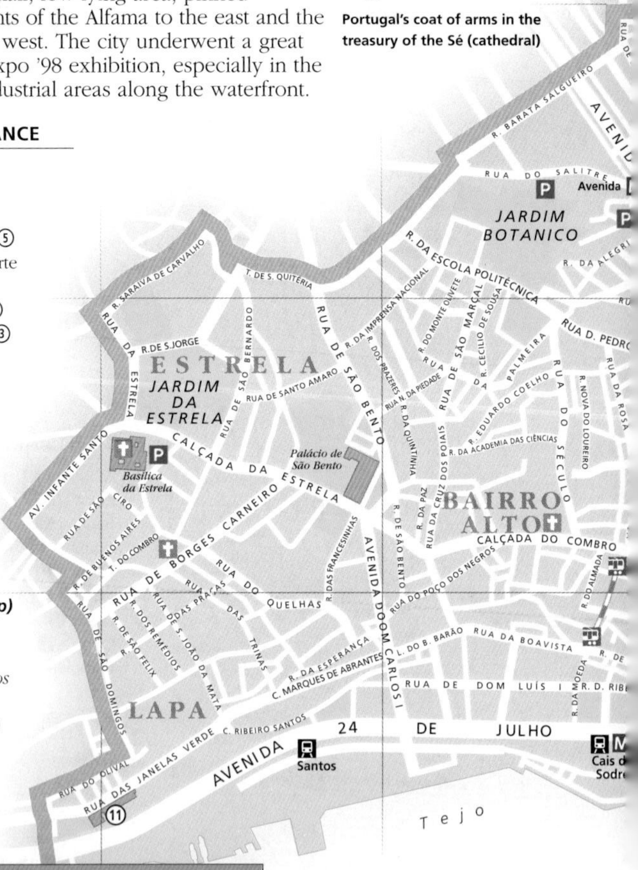

Mosteiro dos Jerónimos overlooking Praça do Império

GETTING AROUND

Lisbon's limited metro system links the north of the city with sights in the center around Rossio square. Buses cover the whole city and are the most common form of public transportation. Take the Santa Justa lift to reach the Bairro Alto district and the 28 tram to climb the steep hill up to the Alfama. Belém is served by tram, train, and bus. Taxis are inexpensive, but a taxi ride can be alarming, as can any experience of driving in Lisbon.

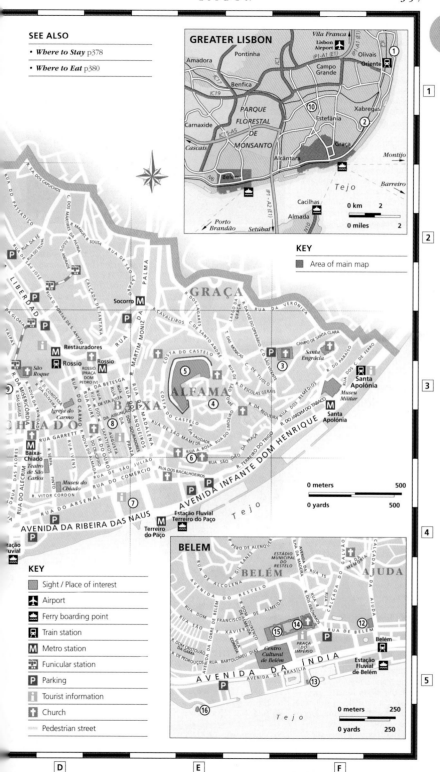

SEE ALSO
• *Where to Stay* p378
• *Where to Eat* p380

GREATER LISBON

Vila Franca
Lisbon Airport
Olivais
Oriente
Amadora
Pontinha
Campo Grande
Benfica
Xabregas
PARQUE FLORESTAL DE MONSONTO
Estefânia
Carnaxide
Graça
Cascais
Alcântara
Montijo
Belém
Tejo
Barreiro
Cacilhas
Almada
Porto Brandão
Setúbal

0 km   2
0 miles   2

KEY
Area of main map

Socorro
GRAÇA
Restauradores
Rossio
Santa Engrácia
São Roque
Santa Apolónia
Igreja do Carmo
ALFAMA
Museu Militar
Santa Apolónia
CHIADO
BAIXA
Baixa-Chiado
Teatro de São Carlos
Museu do Chiado
AVENIDA INFANTE DOM HENRIQUE

0 meters   500
0 yards   500

AVENIDA DA RIBEIRA DAS NAUS
Estação Fluvial Terreiro do Paço
Terreiro do Paço
Tejo

KEY
Sight / Place of interest
Airport
Ferry boarding point
Train station
Metro station
Funicular station
Parking
Tourist information
Church
Pedestrian street

BELÉM
ESTÁDIO MUNICIPAL DO RESTELO
BELÉM
AJUDA
Centro Cultural de Belém
PRAÇA DO IMPÉRIO
Belém
Estação Fluvial de Belém
AVENIDA DA ÍNDIA
Tejo

0 meters   250
0 yards   250

Oceanário de Lisboa ①

Esplanada dom Carlos I, Parque das Nações. **Tel** *21-891 70 02.* **M** *Oriente.* 🚌 *5, 10, 19, 21, 28, 44, 750, 768, 208 (night).* 🚈 *Gare do Oriente.* ⬜ *daily.* ⬤ *Dec 25.* 🗗 ♿

This huge oceanarium, on the banks of the Tagus, is the second largest in the world. It was designed for Expo '98 by the American architect, Peter Chermayeff, to illustrate the environmental theme of "The Oceans: A Heritage for the Future."

The central feature is a gigantic aquarium, the "Open Tank," with enough water to fill four Olympic swimming pools. Representing the open ocean, this contains fauna of the high seas, from sea bream to sharks. Around the main tank four smaller aquariums reconstruct the ecosystems of the Atlantic, Antarctic, Pacific, and Indian oceans.

Museu Nacional do Azulejo ②

Rua da Madre de Deus 4. **Tel** *21-810 03 40.* 🚌 *60, 727, 751.* ⬜ *Tue pm–Sun.* ⬤ *Jan 1, Easter, May 1, Dec 25.* 🖳 🍴 🗗 www.mnazulejo-ipmuseus.pt

The idea of decorative tiles was a legacy of the Moors. From the 16th century onward, Portugal started producing its own painted ceramic tiles *(azulejos)*. The blue-and-white tiles of the Baroque era are considered by many to be the finest.

The National Tile Museum is housed in the Convento da Madre de Deus, founded by Dona Leonor (widow of João II) in 1509. The interior of the church has striking Baroque decoration, added by João V.

An important surviving feature of the original convent is the Manueline cloister. Along with the larger Renaissance cloister, it provides a stunning setting for the museum. Decorative panels, individual tiles, and photographs trace tile-making from its introduction, through Spanish influence and

Statue of woman praying beside tomb of Carlos I in São Vicente de Fora

the development of Portugal's own styles, to today. Panels from churches, monasteries, and other sites around Portugal have been reassembled here. Highlights include a blue-and-white, 18th-century panorama showing Lisbon before the earthquake, and the colorful 17th-century carpet tiles (so-called because they imitated the patterns of Moorish rugs).

Detail from 16th-century altarpiece in the Museu Nacional do Azulejo

São Vicente de Fora ③

Largo de São Vicente. **Tel** *21-882 44 00.* 🚈 *28.* 🚌 *12, 34.* ⬜ *Tue–Sun.* ⬤ *public hols.* 🗗 *to cloisters.*

St. Vincent was proclaimed Lisbon's patron saint in 1173, when his relics were brought

to a church on this site. The present church was completed in 1627. The Italianate façade has statues of Saints Vincent, Augustine, and Sebastian over the entrance. Inside, one's eye is immediately drawn to the striking Baroque altar canopy.

Behind the church is the old refectory, transformed into the Bragança Pantheon in 1885. The tombs of almost every Bragança king and queen are here, from João IV, who died in 1656, to Manuel II, last king of Portugal. Only Maria I and Pedro IV are not buried here. A stone mourner kneels at the tomb of Carlos I and his son Luís Felipe, assassinated in Praça do Comércio (*see p360*) in 1908.

Alfama ④

🚌 *12, 37, 107, 701, 746.* 🚈 *12, 28.*

A fascinating quarter at any time of day, the Alfama comes to life in the late afternoon and early evening, when the small restaurants and bars start to fill and music, often *fado*, can be heard in the alleyways. It is hard to believe that this, the oldest part of Lisbon, was once the most desirable quarter of the city. In the Middle Ages wealthy residents started to move away, fearing earthquakes, leaving the quarter to fishermen and paupers. Ironically, the Alfama was spared by the earthquake of 1755. Today, the area is a warren of narrow streets and small, picturesque houses clinging to the hillside below the Castelo de São Jorge.

The least strenuous way to see this area is to start at the castle at the top and work your way down. Attractions on the way include the **Museo de Artes Decorativas** (Museum of Decorative Arts), which has its own workshops, and the sweeping views from the terrace of the **Miradouro de Santa Luzia**. You could also visit, on a Tuesday or Saturday, the colorful **Feira da Ladra** (Thieves' Market) in Campo de Santa Clara to the east of the castle or the early morning fish market in Rua de São Pedro.

Castelo de São Jorge ⑤

Porta de S. Jorge, Rua do Chão da Feira. *Tel* 21-880 06 20. 🚌 37. 🚋 28. ⭕ daily. 🎟

Following the recapture of Lisbon from the Moors in 1147, King Afonso Henriques transformed their citadel – which crowned Lisbon's eastern hill – into the residence of the Portuguese kings. In 1511 Manuel I built a more lavish palace beside the river (*see p360*). In the centuries that followed the Castelo de São Jorge was used variously as a theater, a prison, and an arms depot. After the 1755 earthquake, the ramparts lay in ruins until 1938 when the castle was completely rebuilt. It was restored again, along with parts of the Santa Cruz district, in 2006.

The castle gardens and narrow streets of the old Santa Cruz district, which lies within the walls, are a pleasant place for a stroll, and the views are the finest in Lisbon. Visitors can climb the towers, one of which has a camera obscura, walk along the reconstructed ramparts, or stand on the shaded observation terrace.

The Sé, Lisbon's austere 12th-century cathedral

Sé ⑥

Largo da Sé. *Tel* 21-886 67 52. 🚌 37. 🚋 12, 28. ⭕ daily. **Cloister & treasury** ⭕ daily. 🎟

In 1150, Afonso Henriques built a cathedral for the first bishop of Lisbon (Gilbert of Hastings) on the site of the Moorish mosque. Sé denotes the seat of a bishop.

Though much renovated over the centuries, the Sé has kept its solid Romanesque façade. The Capela de Santo Ildefonso, one of nine Gothic chapels in the ambulatory behind the altar, contains two fine 14th-century tombs and in the Franciscan chapel by the entrance stands the font where St. Antony of Padua was baptized in 1195. In the Gothic cloister behind the Sé, excavations have unearthed Roman and other remains.

The treasury, located in one of the towers, has a splendid collection of exhibits, including the relics of St. Vincent. Legend has it that his remains were watched over by two ravens on their journey to Lisbon in 1173, hence the raven on the city's coat of arms.

View of the Castelo de São Jorge across the Baixa, Lisbon's lower town

Praça do Comércio, a grand entrance to the city of Lisbon

Praça do Comércio ⑦

🚌 2, 40, 714, 746, & many others.
🚋 15, 18.

More commonly known as *Terreiro do Paço* (Palace Square), this was the site of the royal palace for 400 years. Manuel I transferred the royal residence here, from the Castelo de São Jorge, in 1511. The first palace, together with its library and 70,000 books, was destroyed in the 1755 earthquake. Its replacement was built around three sides of the square. After the 1910 revolution it became government administrative offices.

The south side looks across the Tagus and was once the finest gateway to Lisbon – used by royalty and ambassadors – with marble steps up from the river. In the center of the square is an equestrian statue of José I (1775) by Machado de Castro, leading Portuguese sculptor of the 18th century.

The impressive triumphal arch on the north side, decorated with statues of historical figures, leads into Rua Augusta and the Baixa.

On February 1, 1908, King Carlos and his son, Luís Felipe, were assassinated in the square. In 1974 it witnessed the first uprising of the Armed Forces Movement, which overthrew the Caetano regime in a bloodless coup that became known as the Carnation Revolution.

Baixa ⑧

🚌 2, 9, 36, 40, 44, 714, 746, & many others. 🚋 15, 18. Ⓜ Rossio, Restauradores, Terreiro do Paço.

Following the 1755 earthquake, the Marquês de Pombal created an entirely new city center, one of Europe's first examples of town planning. Using a grid layout of streets, the Praça do Comércio was linked with the busy central square of Rossio. The streets were flanked by splendid Neoclassical buildings.

The Baixa (lower town) is still the commercial hub of the city, housing banks, offices, and stores. The streets are crowded by day, especially the central Rua Augusta, but less so after dark.

By the Restauradores metro station is the **Palácio Foz**, an 18th-century palace. Tourists are naturally drawn to Rossio, an elegant square and social focal point with cafés and *pastelarias*. The **National Theater** stands on the north side. Just to the east of Rossio is the less attractive Praça da Figueira, the city's main marketplace in Pombal's time. Rua das Portas de Santo Antão, north of the two squares, is a lively pedestrian street full of restaurants.

Bairro Alto ⑨

🚌 6, 9, 22, 714, 720, 727, 732, 738, & many others. 🚋 28 (also Elevador da Glória & Elevador da Santa Justa). Ⓜ Baixa-Chiado.

The hilltop Bairro Alto quarter, dating from the 16th century, is one of Lisbon's most picturesque districts. Its narrow, cobbled streets house a traditional, close-knit community, with small workshops and family-run *tascas* (cheap restaurants). This predominantly residential area has become fashionable at night for its bars, night clubs, and *fado* houses (see p377).

Rossio Square and the Neoclassical National Theater in the Baixa

For hotels and restaurants in this region see p378 and p380

The first tremor of the devastating earthquake was felt at 9:30am on November 1. It was followed by a second, far more violent, shock a few minutes later, which reduced over half the city to rubble. A third shock was followed by fires which quickly spread. An hour later huge waves came rolling in from the Tagus, flooding the lower part of the city. Most of Portugal suffered damage, but Lisbon was the worst affected: an estimated 15,000 people died in the city. Sebastião José de Carvalho e Melo, chief minister to King José I, later Marquês de Pombal, restored order and began a progressive town-planning scheme. His cool efficiency gained him almost total political control.

Marquês de Pombal

The Elevador de Santa Justa, which links the Baixa to the Carmo district

Very different in character is the neighboring, elegant, commercial district known as the Chiado, where affluent Lisboetas shop. On the main street, Rua Garrett, the Café Brasileira – once frequented by writers and intellectuals – remains popular. The Chiado was devastated by fire in 1988, but has been painstakingly renovated.

The best way to reach the Bairro Alto from the Baixa is via the Carmo district and the **Elevador de Santa Justa**, a Neo-Gothic elevator dating from 1901–2. Tourist attractions include the richly decorated **São Roque** church, the ruined **Igreja do Carmo**, the largest church in Lisbon, and the **Museu do Chiado**, which houses art from 1850–1950.

Museu Calouste Gulbenkian ⑩

Avenida de Berna 45. **Tel** 21-782 34 02. **M** Praça de Espanha, São Sebastião. ⚏ 16, 31,56, 726, 746. 🚊 24. ◯ Tue–Sun (Tue: pm only). ⬤ Mon & public hols. ▨ (free Sun). ⬤ ⬤ ⬤ www.museu.gulbenkian.pt

Thanks to wealthy Armenian oil magnate, Calouste Gulbenkian, Portugal owns one of the finest personal art collections assembled during the 20th century. Gulbenkian moved to Portugal in World War II, because of the country's neutral status. This museum was inaugurated in 1969, as part of the charitable institution bequeathed to the nation. The building was devised to create the best layout for the founder's varied collection: the exhibits span over 4,000 years, from ancient Egypt and China, through an extensive collection of Islamic ceramics and carpets, to Art Nouveau. Gulbenkian was a friend of René Lalique, the great glassware and jewelry maker and one room is filled with his work.

Highlights of the European art collection include Van der Weyden's *St. Catherine* and Rembrandt's

Portrait of an Old Man. Other major artists exhibited include Ghirlandaio, Rubens, Guardi, Gainsborough, Turner, Manet, and Renoir. The collection also includes sculpture, jewelry, textiles, manuscripts, porcelain, and a variety of decorative arts.

Museu Nacional de Arte Antiga ⑪

Rua das Janelas Verdes. **Tel** 21-391 28 00. ⚏ 40, 49, 60, 727, 751. 🚊 15, 18. ◯ Tue–Sun (Tue: pm only). ⬤ public hols. ▨ ⬤ ⬤ ⬤ www.mnarteantiga-ipmuseus.pt

The national art collection, housed in a 17th-century palace, was inaugurated in 1770. In 1940 a modern annex (including the main façade) was added. This was built on the site of a monastery, largely destroyed in the 1755 earthquake. Its only surviving feature, the chapel, has been integrated into the museum.

The ground floor houses 14th–19th-century European paintings, decorative arts, and furniture. Artists exhibited include Piero della Francesca, Hans Holbein the Elder, Raphael, Lucas Cranach the Elder, Hieronymus Bosch, and Albrecht Dürer. Oriental and African art, Chinese ceramics, and the gold, silver, and jewelry collection are on the second floor. The top floor houses Portuguese works.

The pride of the Portuguese collection is the *Adoration of St. Vincent* (c.1467–70), attributed to Nuno Gonçalves. It is an altarpiece painted on six panels, featuring portraits of a wide range of contemporary figures, from beggars and sailors to bishops and princes, including Henry the Navigator and the future João II, all paying homage to the saint. Another fascinating aspect of the Age of Exploration is recorded in the 16th-century Japanese screens, which show Portuguese traders arriving in Japan.

Statue of the founder at Gulbenkian Museum

Belém

At the mouth of the Tagus, where the Portuguese mariners set sail on their voyages of discovery, Manuel I commissioned two grand monuments in the exuberant Manueline style of architecture: the Mosteiro dos Jerónimos and the Torre de Belém. Today Belém is a spacious, relatively green suburb with museums and gardens, including the vast Praça do Império, a formal square with a central fountain in front of the monastery. The area enjoys an attractive riverside setting with cafés and a promenade; on sunny days it has a distinct seaside feel. In Rua de Belém is the Antiga Confeitaria de Belém, a 19th-century café that sells the local specialty: *pastéis de Belém*, rich flaky-pastry custard tarts.

chaises used by young members of the royal family. There is also a 19th-century Lisbon cab, painted black and green, the colors of taxis right up to the 1990s. The 18th-century Eyeglass Chaise has a black leather hood pierced with sinister eyelike windows. It dates from the era of Pombal (*see p361*), when lavish decoration was discouraged.

Baroque coach in the Museu Nacional dos Coches

Museu Nacional dos Coches ⑫

Praça Afonso de Albuquerque. *Tel* 21-361 08 50. 🚌 28, 714, 727, 729, 751. 🚋 15. 🚉 Belém. ◯ Tue–Sun. ● Jan 1, Easter, May 1, Dec 25. 🎫 (free 10am–2pm Sun). ♿ www.museudoscoches-ipmuseus.pt

The National Coach Museum was established in 1905 by King Carlos's wife, Dona Amélia, whose pink riding cloak can be seen on display. It occupies the former riding school of the Palace of Belém. The rest of the elegant pink palace is now the residence of the president of Portugal.

The coaches on display span three centuries and range from

the practical to the preposterous. The main gallery, in Louis XVI style with a splendid painted ceiling, is the setting for two rows of coaches created for Portuguese royalty. The oldest is the comparatively plain 16th-century red leather and wood coach of Philip II of Spain. The coaches become increasingly sumptuous, interiors lined with red velvet and gold, exteriors carved with allegorical figures. The most extravagant of all are three Baroque coaches made in Rome for the Portuguese ambassador to the Vatican in the early 18th century.

The neighboring gallery has more royal carriages, including pony-drawn

Monument to the Discoveries ⑬

Padrão dos Descobrimentos, Avenida de Brasília. *Tel* 21-303 19 50. 🚌 28, 727, 729, 751. 🚋 15. ◯ Tue–Sun. ● public hols. 🎫 for elevator. www.egeac.pt

Standing prominently on the Belém waterfront, the Padrão dos Descobrimentos was built in 1960 to mark the 500th anniversary of the death of Henry the Navigator (*see p354*). The 52-m (170-ft) high monument resembles a caravel – the small, lateen-rigged ship used by Portuguese sailors to explore the coast of

EASTERN FACE OF THE MONUMENT TO THE DISCOVERIES

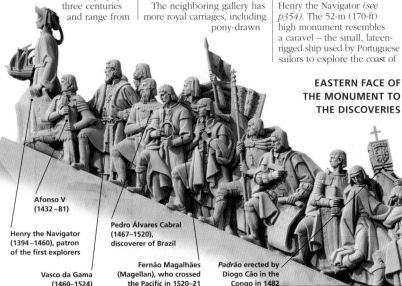

Afonso V (1432–81)

Henry the Navigator (1394–1460), patron of the first explorers

Pedro Álvares Cabral (1467–1520), discoverer of Brazil

Vasco da Gama (1460–1524)

Fernão Magalhães (Magellan), who crossed the Pacific in 1520–21

Padrão erected by **Diogo Cão in the Congo in 1482**

For hotels and restaurants in this region see p378 and p380

Africa – with Portugal's coat of arms on the sides. Henry the Navigator stands at the prow with a caravel in hand. In two sloping lines either side of the monument are heroes linked with the Discoveries.

In front of the monument is a huge mariner's compass cut into the paving. The central map, dotted with galleons and mermaids, shows the routes of the discoverers in the 15th and 16th centuries. Inside the monument, an elevator whisks you to the sixth floor where steps lead to the top for a splendid panorama.

Mosteiro dos Jerónimos ⑭

See pp364–5.

Museu de Marinha ⑮

Praça do Império. *Tel* 21-362 00 19.
🚌 28, 727, 729, 751. 🚊 15.
⬤ *Tue–Sun.* ⬤ *public hols.* 🎫 ♿
www.museu.marinha.pt

The Maritime Museum was inaugurated in 1962 in the west wing of the Jerónimos monastery. A hall devoted to the Discoveries illustrates the rapid progress in ship design from the mid-15th century. Small replicas show the transition from the bark to the lateen-rigged caravel, through the faster square-rigged caravel, to the Portuguese *nau* or great ship. There is also a display of astrolabes and navigational instruments, and replicas of 16th-century maps. The pillars carved with the Cross of the Order of Christ are replicas of various kinds of *padrão*, a stone marker set up to denote sovereignty over the new lands discovered.

Beyond the Hall of Discoveries are models of modern Portuguese ships and the Royal Quarters, housing the exquisitely furnished wood-paneled cabin of King Carlos and Queen Amélia from the royal yacht *Amélia*, built in Scotland in 1900. The modern pavilion opposite houses original royal barges and a display of seaplanes.

The Torre de Belém, a landmark for sailors returning to Lisbon

Torre de Belém ⑯

Avenida da India. *Tel* 21-362 00 34.
🚌 28, 727, 729, 751. 🚊 15. 🚂
Belém ⬤ *Tue–Sun.* ⬤ *Jan 1, Easter, May 1, Dec 25.* 🎫 *(free 10am–2pm Sun).* ♿ *ground floor only.*
www.mosteirojeronimos.pt

Commissioned by Manuel I, the tower was built as a fortress in the middle of the Tagus in 1515–21. Before nearby land was reclaimed in the 19th century, the tower stood much further from the shore than it does today. As the starting point for the navigators who set out to discover the trade routes to the east, this Manueline gem became a symbol of Portugal's great era of expansion. On the terrace,

Royal coat of arms on the Torre de Belém

facing the sea, stands a statue of Our Lady of Safe Home-coming, watching over the lives of Portugal's sailors.

The beauty of the tower lies in the exterior decoration: Manueline ropework carved in stone, openwork balconies, and Moorish-style watchtowers. The distinctive battlements are in the shape of shields, decorated with the squared cross of the Order of Christ, the emblem that also adorned the sails of Portuguese ships. The space below the terrace, which served as a store-room and a prison, is very austere, but the private quarters in the tower are worth visiting for the elegant arcaded Renaissance loggia and the wonderful panorama.

VASCO DA GAMA (C.1460–1524)

In 1498 Vasco da Gama sailed around the Cape of Good Hope and opened the sea route to India. Although the Hindu ruler of Calicut, who received him wearing diamond and ruby rings, was not impressed by his humble offerings of cloth and wash basins, da Gama returned to Portugal with a valuable cargo of spices. In 1502 he sailed again to India, establishing Portuguese trade routes in the Indian Ocean. João III nominated him Viceroy of India in 1524, but he died of a fever soon after.

Portrait of Vasco da Gama, painted in India

Mosteiro dos Jerónimos ⑭

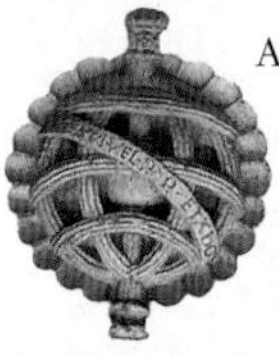

A monument to the wealth of Portugal's Age of Discovery, the monastery is the culmination of the Manueline style of architecture. Commissioned by Manuel I around 1501, soon after Vasco da Gama's return from his historic voyage, it was funded largely by "pepper money," taxes on spices, precious stones, and gold. Various masterbuilders worked on the building, the most notable being Diogo Boitac, replaced by João de Castilho in 1517. The monastery was entrusted to the Order of St. Jerome (Hieronymites) until 1834, when all religious orders were disbanded.

Armillary sphere in the cloister

Tomb of Vasco da Gama
The 19th-century tomb of the explorer (see p361) is carved with ropes, armillary spheres, and other seafaring symbols.

Refectory
The walls of the refectory are tiled with 18th-century azulejos. The panel at the northern end depicts the Feeding of the Five Thousand.

The fountain is in the shape of a lion, the heraldic animal of St. Jerome.

The modern wing, built in 1850 in Neo-Manueline style, houses the National Museum of Archaeology and part of the Maritime Museum *(see p361).*

Entrance to church and cloister

Gallery

View of the Monastery
The façade of the monastery church is dominated by the magnificent South Portal. This makes dramatic use of the Manueline style of architecture, essentially a Portuguese variant of Late Gothic.

The West Portal was designed by the French sculptor Nicolau Chanterène. One of the niches holds a sculpture of the kneeling figure of King Manuel I.

STAR FEATURES

★ South Portal

★ Cloister

★ Cloister

João de Castilho's pure Manueline creation was completed in 1544. Delicate tracery and richly carved images decorate the arches and balustrades.

VISITORS' CHECKLIST

Praça do Império. *Tel* 21-362 00 34. 28, 727, 729, 751. 15. 10am–6pm (6:30pm May–Sep) Tue–Sun (last adm: 1 hr before closing). public hols. (free am Sun). cloister.

Nave

The spectacular vaulting in the church of Santa Maria is held aloft by slender octagonal pillars. These rise like palm trees to the roof creating a feeling of space and harmony.

The chapter house holds the tomb of Alexandre Herculano (1810–77), historian and first mayor of Belém.

The chancel was commissioned in 1572 by Dona Catarina, wife of João III.

The tombs of Manuel I, his wife Dona Maria, João III and Catarina are supported by elephants.

★ South Portal

The strict geometrical architecture of the portal is almost obscured by the exuberant decoration. João de Castilho unites religious themes, such as this image of St. Jerome, with the secular, exalting the kings of Portugal.

Tomb of King Sebastião
The tomb of the "longed for" Dom Sebastião stands empty. The young king never returned from battle in 1578 (see p354).

Beach at Estoril, east of Cascais

Cascais ➋

🏛 33,000. 🚉 🚌 ℹ️ *Rua Visconde da Luz 14 (21-486 82 04).* 🛍 *first and third Sundays in month.*

A harbor since prehistoric times, Cascais became a fashionable resort in the 1870s, when Luís I's summer palace was sited here. Today it is a bustling cosmopolitan resort, with many upscale shops in the pedestrian streets of the old town and a new marina complex. Fishing is still an important activity, and the day's catch is auctioned near the harbor in the afternoon.

Environs
Along the coast, 3 km (2 miles) to the east, the resort of **Estoril** has been home to exiled European royalty. It has retained its sense of place with grand villas and hotels lining the coast.

Guincho, 10 km (6 miles) west of Cascais, has a magnificent sandy beach. Its Atlantic breakers make it popular with surfers. Further north is **Cabo da Roca**, the most westerly point of mainland Europe.

Sintra ➌

🏛 25,000. 🚉 🚌 ℹ️ *Praça da República 23 (21-923 39 19).* 🛍 *2nd and 4th Sun of month in São Pedro.* 🎵 *Festival de Música (Jun–Jul).*

Sintra's setting among wooded ravines and fresh water springs made it a favorite summer retreat for the kings of Portugal, who built the fabulous **Palácio Nacional de Sintra** (*see pp368–9*) here.

Designated a UNESCO World Heritage Site in 1995, the town draws thousands of visitors, yet there are many tranquil walks in the surrounding hills.

Present-day Sintra is a maze of winding roads, and exploring the town on foot involves much walking and climbing; for a more leisurely tour, take a horse and carriage ride. The **Miradouro da Vigia** in São Pedro offers impressive views, as does the cozy **Casa de Sapa** café, where you can sample *queijadas*, cheese tarts spiced with cinnamon.

High above the town is the **Castelo dos Mouros**, an 8th-century Moorish castle. On a nearby hilltop stands the **Palácio da Pena**, built in the 19th century for Ferdinand, King Consort of Maria II, in a bizarre medley of architectural styles. A magnificent park surrounds the fairytale castle.

Palácio da Pena in Sintra, the hilltop retreat of the last kings of Portugal

⚓ **Castelo dos Mouros**
Estrada da Pena, 5 km (3 miles) S. **Tel** *21-923 73 00.* 🚌 *(in summer) or taxi from Sintra.* 🕙 *daily.* ⚫ *Jan 1, Dec 25.*

🏰 **Palácio da Pena**
Estrada da Pena, 5 km (3 miles) S. **Tel** *21-910 53 40.* 🚌 *(in summer) or taxi from Sintra.* 🕙 *Tue–Sun.* ⚫ *Jan 1, Easter, May 1, Jun 29, Dec 25.* 🖱 *www.ippar.pt*

Tomar ➍

🏛 43,000. 🚉 🚌 ℹ️ *Avenida Dr. Cândido Madureira (24-932 24 27).* 🛍 *Fri.* 🎵 *Festa dos Tabuleiros (Jul, every 4 years).*

Founded in 1157 by Gualdim Pais, the first Grand Master of the Order of the Templars in Portugal, Tomar is dominated by the castle containing the **Convento de Cristo**. It was begun in 1162, built on land given to the Templars for services in battle, and preserves many traces of its founders and the inheritors of their mantle, the Order of Christ. The nucleus of the castle is the 12th-century Charola, the Templars' octagonal oratory. In 1356, Tomar became the headquarters of the Order of Christ.

Manueline window at Tomar's monastery

Cloisters were built in the time of Henry the Navigator, but it was in the reigns of Manuel I (1495–1521) and his successor, João III (1521–57), that the greatest changes were made, with the addition of the Manueline church and Renaissance cloisters. The church window (c.1510), commissioned by Manuel I, is probably the best-known single example of the Manueline style of architecture.

Other fascinating features include the Terrace of Wax, where honeycombs were left to dry, and the "bread" cloister, where loaves were handed out to the poor.

The town of Tomar is the site of the curious Festa dos Tabuleiros, in which young girls carry towering structures made of 30 loaves of bread on their heads. They parade through the main square, Praça da República. The square's focal point is the 15th-century Gothic church of **São João Baptista**. Tomar is also home to one of Portugal's oldest synagogues, now the **Museu Luso-Hebraico de Abraham Zacuto**, a Jewish museum.

🏛 **Convento de Cristo**
Tel 24-931 34 81. ⭕ *daily.*
⬤ *Jan 1, Easter, May 1, Dec 25.* 📷

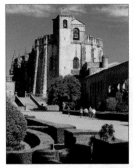

The Convento de Cristo, Tomar

Alcobaça ❺

Praça 25 de Abril, Alcobaça.
Tel 262-50 51 20. 🚌 *from Lisbon or Coimbra.* ⭕ *daily.* ⬤ *Jan 1, Easter, May 1, Dec 25.* 📷

The Mosteiro de Santa Maria de Alcobaça is Portugal's largest church and a UNESCO World Heritage site. Founded in 1153, the abbey is closely linked to the arrival of the Cistercian order in Portugal in 1138 as well as to the birth of the nation. In March 1147, Afonso Henriques conquered the Moorish stronghold of Santarém. To commemorate the victory, he gave land and money to build a church to the Cistercians. Completed in 1223, the church is a beautiful building of austere simplicity. Portugal's rulers continued to endow the monastery, notably King Dinis (1279–1325), who added the main cloister, known as the Cloister of Silence. In the Sala dos Reis, 18th-century tiles depict the founding of the abbey, and statues of Portuguese kings adorn the walls.

Among those buried here are the tragic lovers King Pedro (1357–67) and his murdered mistress, Inês de Castro (d.1355), whose tombs face each other across the transept of the abbey church. Inês' death was ordered by Pedro's father, Afonso IV (1325–57). After Afonso's death, Pedro had two of Inês' murderers killed brutally. He then had her body exhumed and reburied.

One of Alcobaça's most popular features is the vast kitchen. Here whole oxen could be roasted on a spit inside the fireplace and a specially diverted stream provided a constant water supply.

Batalha ❻

Mosteiro de Santa Maria da Vitória, Batalha. *Tel 244-76 54 97.* 🚌 *from Lisbon, Leiria, Porto de Mós, & Fátima.* ⭕ *daily.* ⬤ *Jan 1, Easter, May 1, Dec 25.* 📷 *(free 9am–2pm Sun).*

The Dominican Abbey of Santa Maria da Vitória at Batalha is a masterpiece of Portuguese Gothic architecture and a UNESCO World Heritage site.

Manueline portal leading to the Unfinished Chapels at Batalha

The pale limestone monastery was built to celebrate João I's historic victory at Aljubarrota in 1385. Today, the abbey still has military significance: two unknown soldiers from World War I lie in the chapter house. João I, his English wife, Philippa of Lancaster, and their son, Henry the Navigator, are also buried here, in the Founder's Chapel.

The abbey was begun in 1388 and work continued for the next two centuries. King Duarte, João's son, began an octagonal mausoleum for the royal house of Avis. The project was taken up again but then abandoned by Manuel I. It is now known as the Unfinished Chapels. Much of the decoration of the abbey is in the Manueline style.

The magnificent Gothic tomb of Pedro I in the transept of the monastery church at Alcobaça

Palácio Nacional de Sintra ❶

At the heart of the old town of Sintra (Sintra Vila), a pair of strange conical chimneys rises high above the Royal Palace. The main part of the palace, including the central block with its plain Gothic façade and the large kitchens beneath the chimneys, was built by João I in the late 14th century, on a site once occupied by the Moorish rulers. The Paço Real, as it is also known, became the favorite summer retreat for the court and continued as a residence for Portuguese royalty until the 1880s. Additions to the building by the wealthy Manuel I, in the early 16th century, echo the Moorish style. Gradual rebuilding of the palace has resulted in a fascinating amalgamation of various different styles.

Swan panel, Sala dos Cisnes

★ Sala das Pegas
It is said that King João I had the ceiling panels painted as a rebuke to the court women for indulging in idle gossip like chattering magpies (pegas).

The Torre da Meca has dovecotes below the cornice decorated with armillary spheres and nautical rope.

The Sala das Galés (galleons) houses temporary exhibitions.

★ Sala dos Brasões
The domed ceiling of this majestic room is decorated with stags holding the coats of arms (brasões) of 72 noble Portuguese families. The lower walls are lined with 18th-century Delft-like tiled panels.

Jardim da Preta, a walled garden

Sala de Dom Sebastião, the audience chamber

AZULEJOS – PAINTED CERAMIC TILES

Spanish-made, Moorish-style tiles from the palace chapel (1510)

The Palácio Nacional de Sintra contains *azulejos* from the 16th–18th centuries, many painted with Moorish-influenced designs. In the early 16th century, tiles were produced by compartmental techniques, using raised and depressed areas to prevent the tin-glaze colors from running. The maiolica technique appeared in the mid-16th century. This allowed artists to paint directly onto prepared flat tiles using several colors, as these did not run in the firing process.
By the 18th century, no other European country was producing as many decorative tiles as Portugal, and there are many examples of 18th-century blue-and-white *azulejos* in the palace at Sintra, notably in the Sala dos Brasões.

★ Sala dos Cisnes

The magnificent ceiling of the former banqueting hall, painted in the 17th century, is divided into octagonal panels decorated with swans (cisnes).

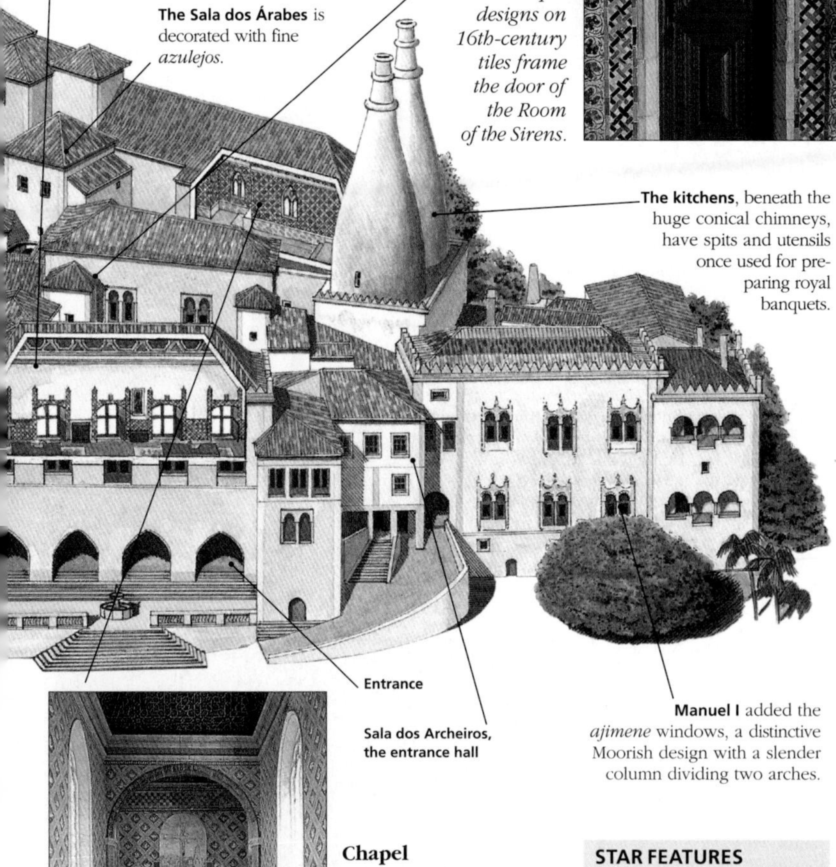

The Sala dos Árabes is decorated with fine *azulejos*.

VISITORS' CHECKLIST

Largo Rainha Dona Amélia. **Tel** 21-910 68 40. ☐ *10am–5:30pm Thu–Tue (last adm: 30 mins before closing).* ⬤ *Jan 1, Easter, May 1, Jun 29, Dec 25.* 🎫 🖼 *(free 10am–2pm Sun).* **www**.ippar.pt

Sala das Sereias
Intricate Arabesque designs on 16th-century tiles frame the door of the Room of the Sirens.

The kitchens, beneath the huge conical chimneys, have spits and utensils once used for preparing royal banquets.

Manuel I added the *ajimene* windows, a distinctive Moorish design with a slender column dividing two arches.

Entrance

Sala dos Archeiros, the entrance hall

Chapel
Symmetrical Moorish patterns decorate the original 15th-century chestnut and oak ceiling and the mosaic floor of the private chapel.

STAR FEATURES

★ Sala dos Brasões

★ Sala dos Cisnes

★ Sala das Pegas

18th-century library of Coimbra University

Coimbra ⑦

🚶 144,000. 🚉 🚌 🛈 *Largo Dom Dinis (239-83 25 91); Largo da Portajem (239-48 81 20).* 🎫 *Mon–Fri.* 🎭 *Queima das Fitas (early May).*

Afonso Henriques chose Coimbra as his capital in 1139, an honor it retained until 1256. Today, the city on the Mondego is famous as the home of Portugal's oldest university. Most sights are within walking distance of each other, so Coimbra is best explored on foot, despite the steep hill on which it is built.

Coimbra's two cathedrals, the **Sé Velha** ("old") and **Sé Nova** ("new"), lie in the shadow of the hilltop University. The Sé Velha, begun in 1064, is seen as the finest Romanesque building in Portugal. The Sé Nova was founded in 1598 by the Jesuits.

The **University**, a short walk away, was founded in 1290 by King Dinis. Originally its location alternated between Lisbon and Coimbra, but it was finally installed in Coimbra's royal palace in 1537. Its oldest buildings are grouped around the Pátio das Escolas. The **belltower** (1733), symbol of the university, can be seen from all over the city. The **Library** was a gift of João V (1706–50). Its rooms, of gilt and exotic wood, are lined with 300,000 books. Nearby is the similarly ornate **Capela de**

São Miguel. Each May, at the end of the academic year, the Queima das Fitas takes place, at which students hold a ceremonial burning of their faculty ribbons, a tradition that dates back 700 years.

Another fascinating site is the **Museu Nacional Machado de Castro**, which holds some of Portugal's finest sculpture set among the elegant 16th-century loggias and courtyards of the former bishops' palace. However, this site has been undergoing restoration.

After visiting this area (the "upper town"), head to the "lower town." Largo da Portagem is a useful starting point, and river trips depart from nearby. In the Praça do Comércio, alongside coffee shops and bars, is the restored 12th-century church of **São Tiago**. North of this is **Santa Cruz**, founded in 1131, where Portugal's first two kings are buried.

In the southeast of the city is the **Jardim Botânico**. The gardens, which are Portugal's largest, were created in 1772 and house 1,200 plant species.

On the opposite bank of the Mondego are the two convents of **Santa Clara**; these have ties with Santa Isabel, the widow of King Dinis

(1279–1325), and Inês de Castro, stabbed to death here in 1355 *(see p367)*. Nearby is a fun place for those with children: the **Portugal dos Pequenitos** theme park.

🏛 **University**
Paço das Escolas. **Tel** 239-85 98 00. 🕐 *daily.* ● *Dec 25.* 🎫 ♿ *Library only.* **www.uc.pt**

🏛 **Museu Nacional Machado de Castro**
Largo Dr. José Rodrigues. **Tel** 239-82 37 27. ● *for refurbishment.* 🎫

🎡 **Portugal dos Pequenitos**
Santa Clara. **Tel** 239-80 11 70. 🕐 *daily.* ● *Dec 25.* 🎫 ♿

Environs
Buçaco National Forest, 16 km (10 miles) north of Coimbra, was once the retreat of Carmelite monks. Part ancient woodland and part arboretum, it is dotted with chapels and fountains. It also houses the splendid Palace Hotel Bussaco, built in Neo-Manueline style as a royal hunting lodge in 1907. Buçaco was also the site of a crucial battle (1810) in the Peninsular War.

The Roman town of **Conímbriga** lay south of modern Coimbra. Portugal's largest Roman site, it has some opulent villas with fine floor mosaics, and an excellent museum.

Student in May celebrations

🏛 **Conímbriga**
2 km (1 mile) S of Condeixa-a-Nova. 🚌 *from Coimbra.* **Site** 🕐 *daily.* ● *Dec 25.* **Museum Tel** 239-94 11 77. 🕐 *Tue–Sun.* 🎫 ♿ *museum only.*

The Palace Hotel Bussaco *(see p381)* in its enchanting woodland setting

The river Douro and old city of Oporto, with the Ponte de Dom Luís I and modern metro line in the foreground

Oporto ⑧

🏛 245,000. ✈ 10 km (6 miles) N.
🚉 🚌 🛈 Rua Clube dos Fenianos
25 (22-339 34 72); Rua Infante Dom
Henrique 63 (22-200 97 70); Praça
Dom João I 43 (22-205 75 14).
🎎 São João do Porto (Jun 23–24).

Ever since the Romans built a fort here, at the mouth of the Douro, Oporto (Porto in Portuguese) has prospered from commerce. Today it is Portugal's second city and a thriving industrial center.

The commercial center of the city and the Baixa ("lower") district attract fashionable shoppers. Also in the Baixa is the colorful Bolhão market. Most of the tourist sights, however, are to be found in the older riverside quarters.

High above the river, on Penaventosa Hill, stands Oporto's cathedral, or **Sé,** originally a fortress church. A noteworthy 13th-century feature is the rose window, while the upper level of the beautiful 14th-century cloister affords splendid views.

Nearby are the Renaissance church of **Santa Clara,** and **São Bento Station,** completed in 1916, decorated with spectacular azulejo panels.

Below the Sé is the hillside **Barredo** quarter, seemingly unchanged since medieval days. This leads down to the riverside quarter, the **Ribeira,** its houses decorated with tiled or pastel-painted façades. The district is being restored, attracting restaurants and clubs.

Sights close to the river include the **Palácio da Bolsa,** the city's stock exchange,

built in 1842. Its highlight is the Arabian Room decorated in the style of the Alhambra. Close by is the 14th-century **São Francisco** church. Its interior is richly covered in carved and gilded wood.

In the Cordoaria district, west of the Sé, stands the 18th-century **Igreja dos Clérigos.** The church tower, at 75 m (246 ft), offers superb views.

Situated in the lovely Serralves park, the **Fundação de Serralves** is dedicated to contemporary art. It presents temporary exhibitions in the Art Deco Casa de Serralves, and its art collection, from the 1960s to the present, in the Modernist Museu de Arte Contemporânea, designed by Alvaro Siza Vieira.

The oldest of the five bridges spanning the Douro are the Dona Maria Pia rail bridge (1877), designed by Gustave Eiffel, and the two-tiered Ponte de Dom Luís I (1886), by one of Eiffel's assistants.

Across the river is the town of **Vila Nova de Gaia,** the center of port production, housing the lodges (armazéns) of over 50 companies. Many offer guided tours.

🏛 **Fundação Serralves**
Rua Dom João de Castro 210.
Tel 80-820 05 43. ⏰ 10am–7pm
Tue–Wed Fri–Sun, 10am–10pm
Thu. ⏰ Jan 1, Dec 25. 🎫 (free
10am–2pm Sun). ♿ 📷 📷
www.serralves.pt

THE STORY OF PORT

Port comes only from a demarcated region of the upper Douro valley. Its "discovery" dates from the 17th century, when British merchants added brandy to Douro wine to stop it turning sour in transit. Over the years, methods of maturing and blending were refined and continue today in the port lodges of Vila Nova de Gaia. Much of the trade is still in British control.

A classic after-dinner drink, port is rich and usually full-bodied. The tawnies are lighter in color than ruby or vintage, but can be more complex. All ports are blended from several wines, selected from scores of samples. White port, unlike the other styles, is drunk chilled as an aperitif.

Tiled panel of a barco rabelo on the Douro

Traditionally the wine was shipped down the Douro from the wine-growing estates (quintas) to the port lodges on narrow sailing barges called barcos rabelos. Some of these can still be seen moored along the quay at Vila Nova de Gaia.

Southern Portugal

Southern Portugal encompasses the Alentejo and the Algarve, which are separated by ranges of hills. The Alentejo, nearly one-third of Portugal, stretches south from the Tagus. It is typified by vast rolling plains of olive trees, cork oaks, or wheat, as well as whitewashed villages, castles, and a sense of space and tranquility. The Algarve is very different from the rest of Portugal in climate, culture, and scenery. Its stunning coastline and year-round mild weather make it a popular vacation resort.

Renaissance fountain in Évora's main square, Praça do Giraldo

Carved figures of the Apostles on the portal of the Sé, Évora

Évora ❾

🏛 55,000. 🚉 🚌 🛈 Praça do Giraldo (266-73 00 30). 🍴 Sat & 2nd Tue of month. 🎭 Festa de São João (Jun).

Rising dramatically out of the Alentejo plain, the enchanting city of Évora is set in Roman, medieval, and 17th-century walls. In 1986, UNESCO declared it a World Heritage Site.

The fortresslike cathedral, the **Sé**, on the Largo do Marquês de Marialva, was begun in 1186. The portal is flanked by a pair of unmatched towers. Inside, a glittering treasury houses sacred art. Beside it stands a 16th-century palace that houses the newly renovated **Museu de Évora**, which has exhibits on the history of the city from Roman columns to modern sculpture. Opposite the museum is a **Roman temple** – erected in the 2nd or 3rd century AD – believed to have been dedicated to Diana.

Walk from the Sé past the craft shops of Rua 5 de Outubro to reach Praça do Giraldo, the main square, with its Moorish arcades and central fountain (1571). In 1573 the square was the site of an Inquisitional burning.

Just outside the city's Roman walls stands the **University**, founded by the Jesuits in 1559. It was closed in 1759 by the Marquês de Pombal (*see p361*). The building, with its graceful cloister and notable *azulejos*, forms part of the present-day university and the 18th-century Baroque chapel is used for graduation ceremonies.

Évora has over 20 churches and monasteries, including the 15th-century **São Francisco**. The church's gruesome 17th-century **Capela dos Ossos** was created from the bones of 5,000 monks.

Northwest of the city stands the remaining 5 miles (9 km) of Évora's aqueduct, **Aqueduto da Água de Prata**, (1531–37), which was damaged in the 17th century, during the Restoration War with Spain.

🏛 Museu de Évora
Largo do Conde de Vila Flor. **Tel** 266-70 80 95. ☐ Tue–Sun. ● some public hols. 🎟

🏛 University
Largo dos Colegiais. **Tel** 266-74 08 75. ☐ Mon–Sat. ● public hols. 🎟 Sat pm.

Faro ❿

🏛 55,000. ✈ 🚉 🚌 🛈 Av. 5 de Outubro 18 (289-80 04 00). 🍴 daily. 🎭 Dia da Cidade (Sep 7).

Faro has been the capital of the Algarve since 1756. It was damaged by the 1755 earthquake and, although some parts of the ancient city walls remain, most of the buildings date from the 18th or 19th centuries.

The old city is easy to explore on foot. At its heart is the Largo da Sé, lined with orange trees and flanked by the 18th-century bishops' palace, the **Paço Episcopal**, which is still in use today.

The **Sé** itself is a mixture of Baroque and Renaissance styles and has a fine 18th-century organ. Next to the Sé is the **Museu Arqueológico**, which contains local Roman, medieval, and Manueline archeological finds from all over the region. On the other side of the Old City wall is the impressive 18th-century church of **São Francisco**.

Orange trees in front of the Bishops' Palace in the old city of Faro

The lively center of modern Faro, along the Rua de Santo António, is stylish and pedestrianized, full of shops, bars, and restaurants. A little to the north is Faro's parish church, the Baroque and Italianate **São Pedro**. In the nearby Largo do Carmo is the impressive **Igreja do Carmo**. Its magnificent façade and richly decorated interior are in sharp contrast to its somber **Capela dos Ossos** (Chapel of Bones), built in 1816.

At the far northeast corner of the town is the **Cemitério dos Judeus**. The Jewish cemetery served from 1838 until 1932; there is no Jewish community in Faro today.

🏛 **Museu Arqueológico**
Largo Dom Afonso III. *Tel 289-89 74 00.* 🔲 *Mon–Sat.* ⬤ *public hols.* 📷

Ocher sandstone rocks sheltering the Praia de Dona Ana beach, Lagos

Yachts and power boats at the Vilamoura marina, near Albufeira

Albufeira ⓫

👥 *31,000.* 🚃 🚌 🛈 *Rua 5 de Outubro (289-58 52 79).* 🗓 *1st & 3rd Tue of month.*

This charming fishing port has become the tourist capital of the Algarve. The Romans built a castle here and under the Arabs the town prospered from trade with North Africa. The oldest part of the town, around Rua da Igreja Velha, retains some original Moorish arches.

Environs
From **Praia de São Rafael**, 1 mile (2 km) west of Albufeira, to **Praia da Oura** due east, the area is punctuated by small sandy coves set between eroded ocher rocks.

East of Albufeira, **Vilamoura** is set to become Europe's largest leisure complex. It has a large marina with lively cafés, shops, and restaurants.

Portimão ⓬

👥 *40,000.* 🚃 🚌 🛈 *Avenida Zeca Afonso (282-47 07 17).* 🗓 *first Mon of month.*

The Romans were attracted to Portimão by its natural harbor. It is still a flourishing fishing port and one of the largest towns in the Algarve.

The town center, around the pedestrianized Rua Vasco da Gama, dates mainly from the 18th century, since it was rebuilt after the 1755 earthquake. The 14th-century origins of the church of Nossa Senhora da Conceição are revealed in its portico. The interior contains 17th- and 18th-century *azulejo* panels.

Environs
Just 3 km (2 miles) south of Portimão is **Praia da Rocha**, a series of fabulous sandy coves. At its east end is the 16th-century castle, Fortaleza de Santa Catarina, with a superb view of the beach and cliffs – and a swathe of high-rise hotels. Inland from Portimão is the town of **Silves**, once the Moorish capital, Xelb. It has an impressive castle and picturesque groves of orange and lemon trees.

Lagos ⓭

👥 *16,000.* 🚃 🚌 🛈 *Sítio de São João (282-76 30 31).* 🗓 *first Sat of month.*

Lagos is set on one of the Algarve's largest bays; it was the region's capital from 1576–1756. The town suffered badly in the 1755 earthquake, so as a result most of the buildings date from the late 18th and 19th centuries.

In the 15th century Lagos became an important naval center, unfortunately also becoming the site of the first slave market in Europe.

Lagos's parish church is the 16th-century **Santa Maria**. The 18th-century **Santo António** is worth a visit for its Baroque *azulejos* and carving. The statue of St. Antony, kept in the church, accompanied the local regiment during the Peninsular War (1807–11).

Environs
The promontory, **Ponta da Piedade**, shelters the bay of Lagos and should not be missed. **Praia de Dona Ana** beach is 25 minutes' walk from the town center, but **Praia do Camilo** may be less crowded. **Meia Praia**, east of Lagos, stretches for 4 km (2 miles).

Lying 10 km (6 miles) north is the peaceful **Barragem de Bravura** reservoir. Another popular excursion is southwest to **Sagres** and the rocky headland of **Cabo de São Vicente**.

Practical & Travel Information

The Portuguese are a hospitable people and in Lisbon, Oporto and the Algarve the choice of hotels, restaurants and entertainment is vast, and English is widely spoken. Elsewhere, visitors will usually find help easily available, with locals keen to show off their region.

Travel and communication networks in Portugal have improved greatly in recent years. For national travel there are efficient rail and bus services. Cities have buses and trams, and Lisbon has a metro as well.

TOURIST INFORMATION

The country is divided into tourist regions, separate from its administrative districts. All cities and large towns have a *Posto de Turismo* (tourist office), where you can obtain information about the region, lists of hotels, and details of regional events. Visitors can also consult Portuguese tourist offices abroad.

Most state museums open from 10am to 5pm and are usually closed on Mondays. Many museums and sights also close for lunch for one, or even two hours.

In Lisbon, the convenient Lisboa Card entitles visitors to free public transportation and free or reduced entry to museums. It can be bought at the airport, the city's tourist offices, and some hotels, travel agents, and major sights. It is valid for up to three days.

VISA REQUIREMENTS

There are currently no visa requirements for American, Canadian, Australian, and New Zealand nationals for stays up to 90 days. It is worth checking with the nearest Portuguese

embassy or consulate as this may change. Citizens of the EU need only a valid passport to enter Portugal.

PERSONAL SECURITY

Violent crime is rare, but sensible precautions should be taken after dark, especially in Lisbon, Oporto, and the Algarve. To report a crime, contact the nearest police station. Ask for an interpreter if necessary. Theft of documents, such as a passport, should also be reported to your consulate or embassy. Remember that many travel insurance companies insist on policy holders reporting thefts within 24 hours to substantiate any subsequent claim.

EMERGENCY SERVICES

The number to call in an emergency is 112. Ask for either *polícia* (the police), *ambulância* (an ambulance), or *bombeiros* (the fire brigade). For emergency medical treatment you should go to the emergency room (*serviço de urgência*) of the nearest main hospital.

HEALTH ISSUES

For non-emergency medical treatment, details of how to contact an English-speaking doctor can be found in English-language newspapers, such as *The Resident*.

Pharmacies (*farmácias*) can dispense a range of drugs that would require a prescription in many other countries. They open from 9am to 1pm and 3 to 7pm (not Sat) and carry a sign with a green illuminated cross. No vaccinations are needed for Portugal, although a typhoid shot and polio booster are recommended.

FACILITIES FOR THE DISABLED

These are limited, although the situation is improving. Wheelchairs and adapted restrooms are available at airports and major stations, and ramps, reserved parking, and elevators are becoming more common. Lisbon has a special taxi service, but you have to book well in advance.

LANGUAGE AND ETIQUETTE

Written Portuguese looks similar to Spanish, but its pronunciation is very different. The Portuguese do not take kindly to being spoken to in Spanish, so it is useful to learn a few basic phrases before you go. It is polite to address strangers as *senhor* or *senhora* and, when introduced to someone, to shake their hand.

Although dress is generally relaxed, especially in the more tourist-oriented areas, when visiting religious buildings arms and knees should be kept covered.

BANKING AND CURRENCY

The Euro replaced the traditional Portuguese currency, the escudo, on January 1, 2002 (*see p15*).

Money can be changed at most banks, hotels, and bureaux de change (*câmbio*). Banks tend to offer a good rate of exchange. Traveler's checks can often be expensive to cash in Portugal

THE CLIMATE OF PORTUGAL

In the south, especially along the sheltered coast of the Algarve, winters are very mild, but July and August can be extremely hot. Between April and October, the north is pleasantly warm, though rain is not unusual. Winters in the north can be very cold, especially in the mountainous inland regions. The best times to visit are spring and fall.

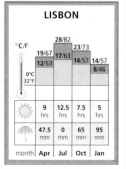

LISBON

°C/F	Apr	Jul	Oct	Jan
	19/67	28/82	23/73	14/57
	12/53	17/63	14/57	8/46
☀ hrs	9	12.5	7.5	5
☂ mm	47.5	0	65	95
month	Apr	Jul	Oct	Jan

although they are a safe way of carrying money. Most major credit cards can be used to make withdrawals from ATMs.

COMMUNICATIONS

The postal service is known as *Correios*. First-class mail *(correio azul)* and overseas letters are posted in blue mailboxes; second-class mail *(normal)* is posted in red mailboxes. Public payphones take either coins or cards (including credit cards). You can also make calls from post offices.

FLYING TO PORTUGAL

The only direct flight from New York (Newark) to Lisbon is operated by **TAP Air Portugal**. Once in Lisbon, passengers can change for Faro or Oporto. Internal flights are operated by **Portugália** and **SATA**.

Many airlines operate flights from the US to European hubs, such as London, Paris, or Madrid, where passengers can change for Lisbon.

There are no direct flights to Portugal from Australia or New Zealand; visitors from these countries should fly via London or Madrid. Regular flights go from many European cities direct to Lisbon, Faro, and Oporto in Portugal.

RAIL TRAVEL

Direct trains to Portugal go from Paris and Madrid. Once in Portugal, you can reach many places by rail, but services vary enormously. The high-speed Alfa service from Lisbon to Oporto via Coimbra is good, but local trains can be slow and infrequent. Fares are cheap compared to other parts of Europe and tourist tickets, valid for 7, 14, or 21 days, are available. It is always best to book in advance.

Lisbon can be confusing for visitors as there are five main stations. **Santa Apolónia** and **Oriente** (on the same line) serve international routes and the north; for the Algarve and the Alentejo, you must take a ferry to Barreiro on the south bank of the Tagus. Trains from Rossio go to Sintra and a few destinations on the coast; trains from Cais do Sodré serve Estoril and Cascais.

LONG-DISTANCE BUSES

Some long-distance bus services – Lisbon to Évora for example – are quicker and more comfortable than going by train. There are no central bus stations because companies are private and operate separately, but tourist offices and travel agencies have information on routes.

TRAVELING BY CAR

Portugal's highway network is expanding, but many older roads are in need of repair and minor roads can be treacherous. Driving can be a hair-raising experience – the country has one of the highest accident rates in Europe and traffic jams are a problem in and near cities. Beware of reckless drivers and do not drive in the rush hour if you can possibly avoid it.

If renting a car, check its condition and insurance very carefully. Always carry your passport, car insurance, license, and rental contract with you (or you may incur a fine).

Traffic drives on the right hand side and Continental European regulations apply. Seat belts must be worn. Speed limits are 50 kph (31 mph) in towns, 90 kph (55 mph) on other roads, and 120 kph (74 mph) on highways. Tolls are payable on highways and some bridges. Do not use the *Via Verde* (green lane) at tolls; this is for the use of drivers who have paid automatically. If you are involved in a car accident on a highway or a main road, use one of the orange SOS telephones to call for help.

Gas stations can be scarce in remote areas, so always fill up your car before leaving a town.

DIRECTORY

TOURIST OFFICES

Lisbon
Lisboa Welcome Center, Rue do Arsenal 15.
Tel 21-031 27 00.

Oporto
Rua Clube dos Fenianos 25. *Tel* 22-339 34 72.
www.portoturismo.pt

UK
11 Belgrave Square, London SWX 8PP.
Tel 020-7201 6666.

US
590 Fifth Ave, 3rd floor, New York, NY 10036.
Tel 212-354 44 03.
www.portugal.org

EMBASSIES

Australia
Av. de Liberdade 196–200, 2° (Edifício Victoria), 1269-121 Lisbon.
Tel 21-310 15 00.

Canada
Av. de Liberdade 196–200, 3° (Edifício Victoria), 1269-121 Lisbon.
Tel 21-316 46 00.

Ireland
Rua da Imprensa à Estrela 1, 4°, 1250-684 Lisbon.
Tel 21-392 94 40.

UK
Rua de São Bernardo 33, 1249-082 Lisbon.
Tel 21-392 40 00.

US
Avenida das Forças Armadas, 1600-081 Lisbon.
Tel 21-727 33 00.

EMERGENCIES

Ambulance, Police, and Fire services
Tel 112.

AIRLINES

Portugália
Tel 21-842 55 00.

SATA
Tel 707-22 72 82.

TAP Air Portugal
Tel 70-720 57 00 (Portugal).
Tel 0845-601 0932 (UK).
Tel 800-221 73 70 (US).
www.tap-airportugal.us

TRAIN INFORMATION

Tel 80-820 82 08.
www.cp.pt

CAR RENTAL

Auto Jardim, Faro
Tel 289-81 84 91.

Budget, Oporto
Tel 22-607 69 70.
www.budgetrentacar.com

Sixt, Lisbon
Tel 21-781 61 01.
www.e-sixt.com

Europcar, Faro
Tel 289-82 37 78 or 707-200 399 (toll-free).

Hertz, Lisbon
Tel 21-381 24 30.
www.hertz.com

Shopping & Entertainment

Traditional arts and crafts flourish in Portugal. A wide range of interesting pottery can be found in all parts of the country, while in the north embroidery, lace, and gold filigree jewelry from the Minho region make unusual presents. Many visitors come to Portugal for the sporting facilities, principally the golf courses of the Algarve. Water sports, both in the Algarve and on the wilder west coast, are another great attraction. Tourists are usually encouraged to sample *fado*, Lisbon's native folk music, and there are also classical cultural events to be enjoyed in the big cities and at annual festivals.

WHERE TO SHOP

Although it is not difficult to find shops that seem a little behind the times when compared with other European countries, modern shopping malls are now a common feature of most cities. In Lisbon, the **Amoreiras** shopping center led the way, with 370 shops, underground parking, cinemas, and restaurants. **Cascaishopping**, between Sintra and Estoril, is similar in style. Opening times for shopping centers are usually from 10am until 11pm daily (including Sunday). Ordinary stores open at 9 or 10am and close at 7pm, though smaller stores and those in quieter areas usually close for lunch between 1 and 3pm.

RECLAIMING TAX

Value Added Tax (IVA) can be reclaimed by non-EU residents who stay for less than 180 days. Ask for an *Isenção de IVA* form or invoice in triplicate, describing the goods, quantity, value, and buyer's identity (best done where you see the "Tax Free for Tourists" signs). Present the forms at customs on departure.

WHAT TO BUY

Portugal is not expensive when compared with the rest of Europe, and prices are very reasonable for traditional crafts, especially away from the big cities and tourist centers. The Portuguese are well known for their delicate embroidery and fine lace. Some of the finest examples come from towns in the Minho such as Viana do Castelo, also famous for its brightly printed shawls. Embroidered bedspreads are made in Castelo Branco in the Beira Baixa, and colorful carpets are sold in the Alentejo.

Filigree jewelry (*filigrana*) from the Minho is typically worn at local festivals. Gold and silver threads are worked into intricate brooches, earrings, and pendants.

Woven baskets, produced throughout the country, make delightful souvenirs. Cork from the Alentejo is used to make articles such as mats and ice buckets.

CERAMICS

In most cities you can buy as well as commission ceramic tiles and panels. Portugal has a long-standing tradition in ceramics, both for decorative purposes and for home use. Styles range from elegant Vista Alegre porcelain to simple glazed brown earthenware, plain or painted with simple patterns. Antique *azulejos* are highly sought after and very expensive, but you can buy reproductions of well-known historic designs at places such as Lisbon's Museu Nacional do Azulejo (*see p358*).

MARKETS

A social and commercial occasion, the street market is integral to Portuguese life. It is usually held in the town's main square. Most markets sell a wide range of goods, from food to household items and clothes, but you will also see sites devoted to antiques, pottery, lace, rugs, clothes, and local crafts. Most markets are held in the morning only, but in tourist areas they may go on until late afternoon.

FOOD AND DRINK

Some visitors may want to buy regional produce such as Serra cheese from the Serra da Estrela mountains. However, more are likely to bring back a bottle as a souvenir – most probably of port. It is not especially cheap, but you will never have the opportunity to sample so many styles and vintages as you will on a tour of the port lodges of Vila Nova de Gaia (*see p371*). Of table wines you might enjoy the young, slightly sparkling *vinho verde* from Douro in the north, an aged red Dão, or one of the new southern wines from the Alentejo.

ENTERTAINMENT LISTINGS AND TICKETS

Tickets for almost all events in Lisbon can be reserved by visiting or phoning the Agência de Bilhetes para Espectáculos **(ABEP)**. Pay in cash when you collect them from the kiosk. Cinemas and theaters will not take phone or credit card reservations.

Previews of forthcoming events and listings of bars and clubs appear in several magazines in Lisbon. English-language publications include the monthly *Follow Me Lisbon*, which is available free from tourist offices.

CLASSICAL MUSIC, OPERA, AND DANCE

Lisbon's top cultural centers are the **Fundação Calouste Gulbenkian** and the vast **Centro Cultural de Belém**. These host national and international events including ballet, opera, and concerts. The Portuguese national opera house is the **Teatro Nacional de São Carlos**.

Classical music festivals are also held in many areas. One of the best is the annual summer festival which takes place in Sintra (*see p366*).

THEATER AND CINEMA

In Lisbon theater-lovers can enjoy performances of Portuguese and foreign-language plays at the **Teatro Nacional Dona Maria II**.

Cult movies and international arthouse films can be seen at the **Cinemateca Portuguesa**, which has a comprehensive monthly film calendar.

In Portugal movies are almost always shown in the original language version with Portuguese subtitles.

FADO

Fado is an expression of longing and sorrow. Literally meaning "fate," the term may be applied to an individual song as well as the genre itself. The dominant emotion is *saudade* – a longing for what has been lost or has never been attained. It is sung as often by women as men, accompanied by the *guitarra* (a flat-backed instrument shaped like a mandolin, with paired strings) and the *viola* (acoustic Spanish guitar).

The traditional way to enjoy *fado* is with a meal at a *fado* house. It can be an expensive night out, so make sure you like *fado* before you go. The best establishments are run by the *fadistas* themselves, for example the **Parreirinha de Alfama**, which is now run by the legendary performer, Argentina Santos.

OUTDOOR ACTIVITIES

Although a small country, Portugal offers a great variety of terrain, with sports and activities to match. Water sports are extremely popular along its 500 miles of coast. The best beach for surfing is the world-famous Guincho, near Cascais (*see p366*). However, the ocean breakers there are only suitable for experienced surfers. In fact, all along the Atlantic coast conditions can be dangerous for swimming and water sports, hence the appeal of the sheltered bays of the Algarve. These are well-equipped for all kinds of activities. Windsurfing boards and small sailboats can be rented at most resorts and lessons are easily arranged. The marinas at Lagos and the giant vacation complex of Vilamoura are the most important yachting centers.

Many parts of Portugal's rugged interior are excellent for hiking, cycling, and horseback riding.

GOLF AND TENNIS

Most of Portugal's best golf courses are concentrated in the Algarve, which has gained a reputation as one of Europe's prime destinations for golfing vacations. The mild climate ensures that a game can be enjoyed all year round and many courses have been designed by top professionals. Some of the best courses insist that players show a reasonable degree of proficiency, while others welcome golfers of any ability and provide excellent coaching. Serious golfers might consider booking a specialist golf vacation. For information on golfing activities and vacations, contact the **Federação Portuguesa de Golfe**.

Tennis courts are found virtually all over Portugal, especially alongside tourist facilities. Some of the larger Algarve resorts offer tennis coaching vacations. Based in London, **Jonathon Markson Tennis** organizes special vacation packages at resorts in Portugal for tennis enthusiasts.

BULLFIGHTING

Portuguese bullfighting differs from the Spanish version in many ways. The bull is not killed in the ring and the star of the show is the horseman (*cavaleiro*). An added attraction is the *pega*, in which a team of men, the *forcados*, attempts to topple the bull and immobilize it with their bare hands.

The traditional center for bullfighting is the Ribatejo, but Lisbon has a splendid Neo-Moorish arena at Campo Pequeno, which is currently closed for renovation.

DIRECTORY

SHOPPING MALLS

Amoreiras
Avenida Eng. Duarte Pacheco.
Tel 21-381 02 00.

Cascaishopping
Estrada Nacional 9,
Alcabideche - Estoril.
Tel 21-012 16 28.

ENTERTAINMENT TICKETS

ABEP
Praça dos Restauradores,
Lisbon.
Tel 21-347 58 24.

CLASSICAL MUSIC, OPERA, & DANCE

Centro Cultural de Belém
Praça do Império, Belém,
Lisbon.
Tel 21-361 24 00.

Fundação Calouste Gulbenkian
Avenida de Berna 45,
Lisbon.
Tel 21-782 30 00 (tickets).

Teatro Nacional de São Carlos
Rua Serpa Pinto 9,
Lisbon.
Tel 21-325 30 00.

THEATER

Cinemateca Portuguesa
Rua Barata Salgueiro 39,
Lisbon.
Tel 21-359 62 62.

Teatro Nacional Dona Maria II
Praça Dom Pedro IV,
Lisbon.
Tel 21-325 08 00.

FADO

Parreirinha de Alfama
Beco do Espírito Santo 1,
Lisbon.
Tel 21-886 82 09.

GOLF AND TENNIS

Federação Portuguesa de Golfe
Ave das Túlipas,
Edifício Miraflores,
17º, 1495-161 Algés.
Tel 21-412 37 80.

Jonathon Markson Tennis
Springside House,
84 North End Road,
London
W14 9ES,
UK.
Tel 020-7603 2422.

Where to Stay in Portugal

Hotels in Portugal vary enormously in quality, price, and facilities – from huge resort villages in the Algarve to the simple *pensão*, or guesthouse. In Lisbon and the Algarve, there are hotels to suite every budget. Many hotels have great character, especially the *pousadas*, or state-run inns, which are often housed in converted historic buildings.

PRICE CATEGORIES
Price categories are for a standard double room per night, including breakfast:

€ Under 60 euros
€€ 60–90 euros
€€€ 90–140 euros
€€€€ 140–200 euros
€€€€€ Over 200 euros

LISBON

AVENIDA Lisboa Plaza
Map C2

Travessa do Salitre 7, 1269-066 **Tel** *21-321 82 18* **Fax** *21-347 16 30* **Rooms** *112*

Built in 1953, and situated off Praça da Alegria and Av. da Liberdade, this boutique hotel possesses an air of informal good taste and understated charm. The decor is by the Portuguese interior designer Graça Viterbo, and her characteristic color-coordinated fabrics and furnishings are carried through the entire property. **www.heritage.pt**

AVENIDA Tivoli Lisboa
Map D2

Avenida da Liberdade 185, 1269-050 **Tel** *21-319 89 00* **Fax** *21-319 89 50* **Rooms** *329*

One of Lisbon's most emblematic hotels, the Tivoli holds court over Avenida da Liberdade and is renowned for its high levels of service and personal attention. The 329 rooms are fully insulated and sound proofed, and the rooftop Terrace Grill is a gourmet hotspot. The property regularly hosts VIP conferences. **www.tivolihotels.com**

BAIXA Duas Nações
Map D3

Rua da Vitória 41, 1100-618 **Tel** *21-346 07 10* **Fax** *21-347 02 06* **Rooms** *54*

The "Two Nations" is a rather grand building straddling the corner of Rua Augusta and Rua da Vitória, both pedestrianized. The property is fashioned as a traditional Lisbon boarding house with rooms that are well appointed and have private bathroom facilities. Those overlooking Rua Augusta can be noisy at times. **www.duasnacoes.com**

CASTELO Ninho das Águias
Map E3

Costa do Castelo 74, 1100-179 **Tel** *21-885 40 70* **Rooms** *16*

Easily identified by its rooftop turret, the unusual "Eagle's Nest" *pensão* perches under the castle walls. A huge stuffed eagle greets visitors at reception. The bright and sometimes breezy rooms are very popular so it's wise to book ahead. The terraced flower garden offers peace and solitude. No breakfast.

CHIADO Lisboa Regency Chiado
Map D4

Rua Nova do Almada 114, 1200-290 **Tel** *21-325 61 00* **Fax** *21-325 61 61* **Rooms** *40*

Japanese silk-screen prints adorn the lobby of this prestigious boutique hotel in Lisbon's most fashionable district. It was designed by Portuguese architect Álvaro Siza Vieira who has cleverly blended Oriental and colonial Portuguese influences with a modern and stylish functionality. Some rooms offer outstanding views.

LAPA York House
Map B4

Rua das Janelas Verdes 32, 1200-691 **Tel** *21-396 24 35* **Fax** *21-397 27 93* **Rooms** *32*

Behind the rose-pink walls of this enchanting 17th-century *pensão* are luxurious rooms with wooden or terracotta floors, and elegant antique furniture. There is a charming, plant-filled courtyard and the atmosphere is one of peace and serenity. Wholly inviting. **www.yorkhouselisboa.com**

MARQUES DE POMBAL Jorge V

Rua Mouzinho da Silveira 3, 1250-165 **Tel** *21-356 25 25* **Fax** *21-315 03 19* **Rooms** *49*

Considering the central location, this pleasant, comfortable hotel offers good value for money. Roughly half the rooms have balconies, so request one when checking in. There are also six suites. The downstairs bar is a good place to mingle with fellow guests, and there are internet facilities in the lobby. **www.hoteljorgev.com**

MARQUES DE POMBAL Ritz Four Seasons

Rua Rodrigo da Fonseca 88, 1099-039 **Tel** *21-381 14 00* **Fax** *21-383 17 83* **Rooms** *282*

Hospitality at the legendary Ritz combines luxury and elegance in a grand style. The hotel is a prominent landmark and a stunning locale from which to experience the city. A major draw is the spa. Designed in marble and rich oak, the facility offers a wealth of treatments and therapies. **www.fourseasons.com**

ROSSIO Metrópole
Map D3

Praça Dom PedroIV 30, 1100-200 **Tel** *21-321 90 30* **Fax** *21-346 91 66* **Rooms** *36*

Inaugurated in 1917, this hotel was a favorite haunt of spies and double agents during World War II. The individually styled and elegant rooms are partly furnished with original pieces from the 1920s, and the whole building exudes a distinctly retro atmosphere. The balcony views across Rossio are picture-postcard. **www.almeidahotels.com**

Key to Symbols *see back cover flap* **Map References** *see map of Lisbon pp356–7*

REST OF PORTUGAL

ALBUFERA Falésia
Praia da Falésia, 8299-911 Tel 289-50 12 37 Fax 289-50 12 70 Rooms 172

Located near Falésia beach surrounded by umbrella pine, this smart hotel has brightly furnished and airy rooms that enjoy either pool or garden views. A huge, marble floor atrium decorated with hanging plants is a central featrue. A piano bar provides nightly entertainment, and reception can arrange various outdoor activities. **www.falesia.com**

CASCAIS Albatroz
Rua Frederico Arouca 100, 21-275 03 53 Tel 214 847 380 Fax 21-484 48 27 Rooms 59

Built in the 19th century as a retreat for the Portuguese royal family, the Albatroz sits perched on the rocks directly overlooking the ocean. Notable for its traditional style of luxury and exceptional design, the service is first class and discreet. The hotel has its own outdoor salt-water swimming pool. **www.albatrozhotels.com**

COIMBRA Astória
Avenida Emidio Navarro 21, 3000-150 Tel 239-85 30 20 Fax 239-82 20 57 Rooms 62

One of Coimbra's best-known hotels, the Astória has preserved its Art Deco heritage and 1920s ambiance while modernizing its extensive facilities. Stylish rooms offer fine views across the River Mondego, especially those in the turret façade. The first-class restaurant, L'Amphitryon, features the original orchestra gallery. **www.almeidahotels.com**

COIMBRA Quinta das Lágrimas
Rua António Augusto Gonçalves, 3041-901 Tel 239-80 23 80 Fax 239-44 16 95 Rooms 54

The renowned Quinta das Lágrimas offers three accommodation options: the palace, the garden, and spa guest rooms. The beautiful 18th-century manor house, forever associated with lovers Pedro andInês, is complemented by a modern hotel wing with guest rooms and a luxury spa. The restaurant is Michelin starred. **www.lagrimashotels.com**

EVORA Pousada dos Lóios
Largo Conde Vila Flor, 7000-804 Tel 266-73 00 70 Fax 266-70 72 48 Rooms 32

Originally a 15th-century monastery, the decorative public spaces in this elegant *pousada* contrast with the simple but characterful rooms that were converted from the monks' cells. An intricately embroidered carpet hangs from the wall skirting the marble staircase. The delightful swimming pool is sunk into an inner courtyard. **www.pousadas.pt**

FARO Alnacir
Estrada Senhor da Saúde 24, 8000-500 Tel 289-80 36 78 Fax 289-80 35 48 Rooms 53

A tidy, modern hotel located on a quiet street close to the center of the Algarve's regional capital. Pleasantly decorated throughout, two of the double rooms have a panoramic terrace overlooking the Ria Formosa Natural Park. Breakfast is served in a light, airy dining room. A laundry service is available. **www.alnacir.netfirms.com**

LAGOS Hotel Tivoli Lagos
Rua António Crisógono Santos, 8600-678 Tel 282-79 00 79 Fax 282-79 03 45 Rooms 324

Built to exude the charm and character of a small village, this pleasant complex has five restaurants, a health club, and swimming pool surrounded by trim gardens. The hotel operates its own beach club and barbeques are organized for hotel guests during the summer. A free shuttle service is also provided. **www.tivolihotels.com**

OPORTO Malaposta
Rua da Conceição 80, 4050-214 Tel 22-200 62 78 Fax 22-200 62 95 Rooms 37

Tucked away on a quiet side street, the attractive and modern Malaposta is a friendly, good-value hotel and benefits from its city-center location. Within walking distance are some of Oporto's best-known historical monuments. Guests can use the nearby car park, free from 8pm-8am, and on weekends and bank holidays. **www.hotelmalaposta.com**

OPORTO Pestana Porto
Praça da Ribeira 1, 4050-513 Tel 22-340 23 00 Fax 22-340 24 00 Rooms 48

One of the most desirable hotels in the city, this charming boutique property is located on the Praça da Ribeira, in a block of carefully restored riverfront buildings. The rooms are contemporary in style and fashionable in taste and offer gracious living and fabulous views. The romantic setting makes advance booking advisable. **www.pestana.com**

PORTIMAO Bela Vista
Avenida Tomas Cabreira, Praia da Rocha, 8500-802 Tel 282-45 04 80 Fax 282-41 53 69 Rooms 21

This delightful hotel is housed in one of the few surviving examples of early 19th-century manor houses that once lined this stretch of coast. The interior maintains much of the original decoration, including in some rooms and public spaces, dazzling *azulejo* tiles, and ceilings fashioned out of Brazilian wood. **www.hotelbelavista.net**

SINTRA Tivoli Palácio de Seteais
Avenida Barbosa do Bocage 10, 2710-517 Tel 21-923 32 00 Fax 21-923 42 77 Rooms 30

One of the most cherished and romantic hotels in the country, this splendid property is a magnificent example of 18th-century architecture, with rooms that dazzle in the classical style of the era. Rare period furniture graces the public areas and guests are free to wander the beautifully landscaped topiary gardens. **www.tivolihotels.com**

Where to Eat in Portugal

Many restaurants in Lisbon and the Algarve serve international cuisine, but the Portuguese like to stick to their culinary traditions, so salted cod (*bacalhau*) and unusual combinations such as pork and clams are often on the menu. Marvelous fish dishes are available all along the coast, but choices for vegetarians are limited.

PRICE CATEGORIES
Price categories are for a three-course meal for one, including a half-bottle of house wine, tax and service:

€ Under 20 euros
€€ 20–25 euros
€€€ 25–30 euros
€€€€ 30–35 euros
€€€€€ Over 35 euros

LISBON

ALFAMA Lautasco   €
Beco do Azinhal 7a (off Rua de São Pedro), 1100-067 **Tel** *21-886 01 73*   **Map** *E3*

Rustically decorated with wooden paneling and wagon-wheel chandeliers, Lautasco specializes in typical Portuguese cuisine that can be enjoyed on the outside terrace. Decorative streamers and colorful spotlights enhance an already atmospheric setting and the restaurant is extremely popular in summer. Reservations recommended. Closed Sun.

BAIRRO ALTO Buenos Aires   €
Calçada Escadinhas do Duque 31b, 1200-155 **Tel** *21-342 07 39*   **Map** *D3*

The generous cuts of Argentine beef served with potatoes and a crispy green salad are the obvious choice at this decorative eatery that draws a young, attractive crowd. Cozy and intimate, the walls are festooned with colorful cards and posters. The menu features some truly memorable chocolate desserts. Reservations recommended. Closed Sun.

BAIRRO ALTO Casonostra   €
Travessa do Poço da Cidade 60, 1200-334 **Tel** *21-342 59 31*   **Map** *D3*

A favorite haunt of Lisbon's artistic and intellectual set, this Italian restaurant is renowned for its creative six-page menu. Popular choices include *penne all'arrabbiata* (pasta with bacon smothered in spicy tomato and garlic sauce). The wine list has been carefully chosen to complemenet each dish. Closed Mon & Sun lunch.

BAIRRO ALTO Pap'Açorda   €€€€€
Rua da Atalaia 57, 1200-037 **Tel** *21-346 48 11*   **Map** *D3*

One of Lisbon's great gastronomic landmarks, this establishment was one of the first to modernize Portuguese food and remains one of the most successful restaurants in the city. Both locals and tourists come here for the delicious *açorda de mariscos* (bread stew and seafood). Comprehensive wine list. Reservations essential. Closed Sun & Mon.

BAIXA Terreiro do Paco   €€€€€
Lisbon Welcome Centre, Praça do Comércio, 1100-148 **Tel** *21-031 28 50*   **Map** *D4*

Tucked under a colonnaded building overlooking Praça do Comércio, this is a wonderful example of how 18th-century elegance can be enriched by 21st-century style. There are two restaurants – downstairs for light dishes, upstairs for an à la carte menu paying homage to Portugal's great culinary traditions. Excellent wine list. Closed Sun eve & Sat lunch.

BELEM Ja Sei   €€€€
Avenida Brasilia 202, 1400-038 **Tel** *21-301 59 69*

This restaurant sits right at the edge of a small lake that's situated in front of the Monument to the Discoveries, with the river beyond. At night the monument is illuminated and the view from a waterside table is quite remarkable. So is the food, with a seafood-based menu that includes grilled catch of the day. Closed Sun eve and Mon.

LAPA Sua Excelência   €€€
Rua do Conde 34, 1200-637 **Tel** *21-390 36 14*   **Map** *B4*

At "His Excellency", in Lisbon's diplomatic quarter, the proprietor can recite the menu in five languages. The food is classic Portuguese, with the *cogumelos salteados em manteiga com natas e vinho da Madeira* (fried mushrooms in a butter, cream and Madeira wine sauce) just one example of the chef's creativity. Booking advised. Closed Sat & Sun lunch.

RESTAURADORES Casa do Alentejo   €
Rua das Portas de Santo Antão 58, 1150-268 **Tel** *21-340 51 40*   **Map** *D3*

Visitors to this extraordinary 19th-century house are in for a surprise. Behind the unremarkable façade is a beautiful Moorish-style courtyard decorated with tiles inlaid with intricate Arabic calligraphy. Art exhibitions regularly take place here, as do choral recitals. The food is standard regional fare, but the exuberant surroundings more than compensate.

RESTAURADORES Gambrinus   €€€€€
Rua das Portas de Santo Antão 23, 1150-264 **Tel** *21-342 14 66*   **Map** *D3*

One of the best seafood restaurants in the country, Gambrinus is exclusive and expensive.It is not only shellfish that attracts visitors, the menu lists Iranian Beluga caviar and truffle *foie gras*, among the starters. Fresh fish is the mainstay, however, with a carefully selected choice available. The extensive wine list includes an array of vintage ports.

Key to Symbols *see back cover flap*   **Map References** *see map of Lisbon pp356–7*

REST OF PORTUGAL

ALBUFEIRA Evaristo
Praia do Evaristo, 8200-903 **Tel** *289-59 16 66*

This contemporary beachfront restaurant enjoys fabulous views over Praia do Evaristo, west of Albufeira. The fish and seafood is first class and the menu features *lagosta na grelha* (broiled lobster), *lulas grelhadas em olho* (grilled squid with garlic) and an array of fresh fish. Meat choices include entrecote steak and fried chicken. Closed Mon; Jan.

BATALHA Mestre Afonso Domingues
Largo Mestre Afonso Domingues, 2440-102 **Tel** *244-76 52 60*

This centrally located restaurant, found in the *pousada* named after the architect of the nearby Santa Maria da Vitória monastery, serves such regional delights as fried pork with turnip tops and bream fillet with spinach. The terrace offers a superb view of the 14th-century monument and the whole experience is infused with a palatable sense of history.

CASCAIS O Pescador
Rua das Flores 10b, 2750-348 **Tel** *21-483 20 54*

This well-established seafood restaurant has lured Mick Jagger and Julio Iglesias, among many other famous personalities. It is decorated with quirky maritime artifacts. An ocean of choice leaps from the menu, with lobster soup, rose shrimp cocktail, spidercrab platter, swordfish steak, and codfish *cataplana*. Closed Sun.

COIMBRA Arcadas da Capela
Quinta das Lágrimas, Rua António Augusto Gonçalves, 3041-901 **Tel** *239-80 23 80*

A luxury gourmet restaurant, dining here is a Michelin-starred treat. Executive chef Albano Lourenço changes the menu four times a year. One dish is themed around Portugal's enduring love story – that of the doomed, 14th-century affair between Pedro and Inês de Castro. The kitchen celebrates the couple's lives with a Pedro & Inês 4-course dinner.

EVORA Fialho
Travessa das Mascarenhas 16, 7000-557 **Tel** *266-70 30 79*

Arguably the best restaurant in the Alentejo, and highly regarded throughout Portugal, Fialho has collected many awards for its inventive cuisine, such as *atum grelhado e amêijoas na cataplana* (grilled tuna and cockle *cataplana*) and *medalhões de porco preto* (medallions of black pork). Reservations essential. Closed Mon; 1–24 Sep.

FARO Mesa dos Mouros
Largo Sé 10, 8000-138 **Tel** *289-87 88 73*

The "Moor's Table" lies in the shadow of Faro's historic 13th-century cathedral on a corner of a large square lined with fragrant orange trees. The *javoli com molho frutos* (wild boar with rice, sultanas and mango sauce) is a specialty. Service is friendly and relaxed, and the outdoor terrace is a wonderful option in warm weather. Closed Sat lunch; Sun.

LAGOS No Pátio
Rua Lançarote de Freitas 46, 8600-605 **Tel** *282-76 37 77*

The creative, British-run kitchen serves international-themed cuisine exemplified by dishes like seared salmon with asparagus risotto, white wine and watercress cream. Good wine selection from Portuguese, Australian, and US labels. There is a charming rear patio for secluded dining. Open for lunch Sun, & dinner Thu–Sat (Tue–Sat from Apr–Oct).

OPORTO Restaurante Kool
Casa da Música, Avenida da Boavista, 4100-111 **Tel** *226-09 28 76*

On the 7th floor of the city's Casa da Musica building, this stark, angular restaurant is named after Dutch architect Rem Koolhaas. The menu is haute cuisine at accessible prices. Choices include poached eggs with warm Brie cheese, Savoy cabbage and bacon, and grilled lamb cutlets with country parsley sauce with baby potatoes. Closed Mon, Sun evening.

OPORTO Dom Tonho
Cais da Ribeira, 4050-509 **Tel** *22-200 43 07*

Located in a refurbished 17th-century warehouse on the historic *ribeira* (quayside) in the shadow of the Dom Luís bridge, the menu here restpects the culinary traditions of northern Portugal. Dishes like *arroz de pato à moda antiga* (duck rice-traditional style) are served in a contemporary space under soft spotlight. Good wine list. Closed Sun & Wed lunch.

PORTIMAO Simsa
Rua São Gonçalo 7, 8500-164 **Tel** *282-42 30 57*

The Dutch andIndonesian owners are not afraid to experiment here. This is one of the few places where you can order *avestruz com molho de ervas* (ostrich in herb sauce). They also offer specialties like *pato com molho de morangos* (duck in strawberry sauce), but the signature *bife holandês* (beef steak) is a firm favorite. Closed Sun & Mon.

SINTRA Tulhas
Rua Gil Vicente 4-6, 2710-568 **Tel** *21-923 23 78*

The mysterious hole near the entrance is the last vestige of a series of medieval granaries that once stood here (the Portuguese word for granary is Tulhas). Small and down-to-earth, the homemade food is wholesome and great value. The veal steak in Madeira wine is particularly flavorsome, but leave room for the cheesecake. Closed Wed.

ITALY AND GREECE

ITALY AND GREECE
AT A GLANCE 384–385

ITALY 386–467

GREECE 468–517

Italy and Greece at a Glance

The appeal of Italy and Greece is both cultural and
hedonistic. As the cradles of Europe's two great
Classical civilizations, both countries are famous for
their ancient temples and monuments, concentrated
principally in the cities of Rome and Athens. Located
in the southern half of Europe, Italy and Greece share
a sunny Mediterranean climate and a correspondingly
laid-back way of life. Away from the main cultural
sights, the peaceful countryside, beautiful
beaches, and warm
seas guarantee
a relaxed vacation.

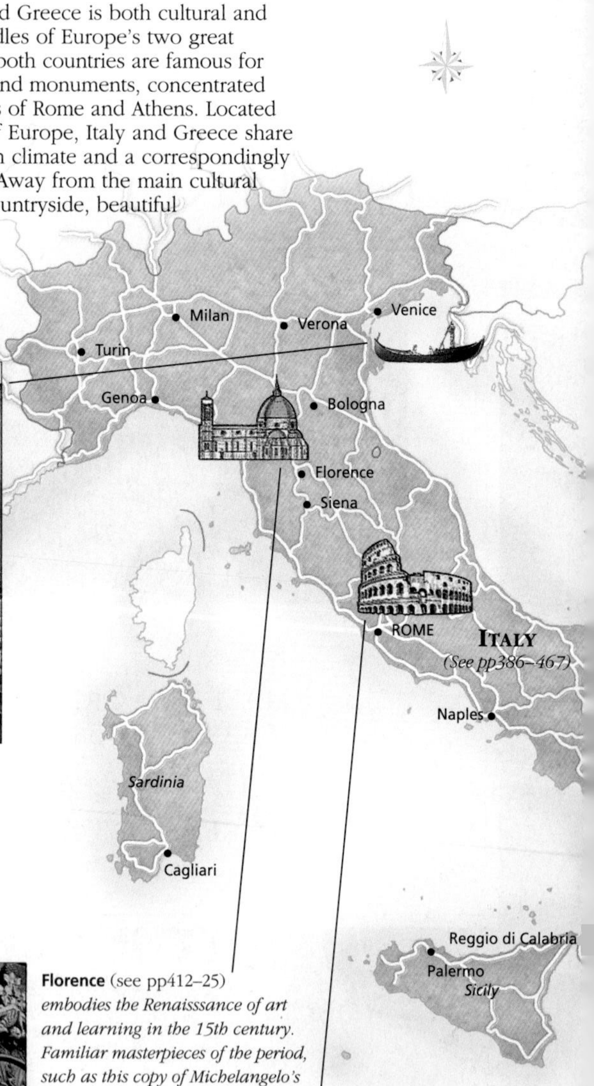

ITALY
(See pp386–467)

Milan

Turin

Verona

Venice

Genoa

Bologna

Florence

Siena

ROME

Naples

Sardinia

Cagliari

Reggio di Calabria

Palermo
Sicily

Venice (see pp432–41) *is a
city quite unlike any other:
a fabulous treasure house
of art and architecture,
built on a series of islands,
where there are no cars
and the streets are canals.*

Florence (see pp412–25)
*embodies the Renaissance of art
and learning in the 15th century.
Familiar masterpieces of the period,
such as this copy of Michelangelo's
David, adorn the streets.*

Rome (see pp392–
405) *owes its grandest
monuments to the era
of papal rule. The vast
colonnaded square
in front of St. Peter's
and the Vatican was
created by Bernini in
the 17th century.*

◁ Fishermen unloading their catch on the island of Mýkonos in the Cyclades, Greece

LOCATOR MAP

The Peloponnese (see pp490–93), *a large peninsula, connected to the rest of the Greek mainland by the Corinth isthmus, abounds in ancient and medieval ruins. The heavily fortified sea port of Monemvasía, in the southeastern corner, has many well-preserved Byzantine and Venetian buildings.*

Athens (see pp474–81) *is renowned for its unrivaled collection of Classical antiquities. The world-famous Acropolis is dominated by the 2,500-year-old Parthenon, built as an expression of the glory of ancient Greece.*

Brindisi

Corfu

● Thessaloníki

● Neápoli

● Metéora

GREECE
(See pp468–517)

Ancient Olympia ●   ● Náfplio

● **ATHENS**

● Monemvasía

0 km   100

0 miles   100

Rhodes Town ●

Rhodes

● Irákleio

Crete

Crete (see pp500–501), *the largest and most southerly of the Greek islands, boasts clear blue seas and fine sandy beaches. Inland there are ancient Minoan palaces and dramatic mountainous landscapes.*

ITALY

I *taly has drawn people in search of culture and romance for centuries. Few countries can compete with its Classical origins, its art, architecture, musical, and literary traditions, its scenery, or its food and wine. Since World War II Italy has climbed into the top ten world economies, yet at its heart it retains many of the customs, traditions, and regional allegiances of its agricultural heritage.*

Italy has no single cultural identity. Between the snowy peaks of the Alps and the rugged shores of Sicily lies a whole series of regions, each with its own distinctive dialect, architecture, and cuisine. There is also a larger regional division. People speak of two Italies: the rich industrial north and the poorer agricultural south, known as *Il Mezzogiorno* (Land of the Midday Sun).

The north is directly responsible for Italy's place among the world's top industrial nations, a success achieved by names such as Fiat, Pirelli, Olivetti, Zanussi, Alessi, and Armani. The south, in contrast, has high unemployment, many areas in the grip of organized crime, and regions that rank among the most depressed in Europe.

History and geography have both contributed to the division. The north is closer both in location and spirit to Germany and France while the south has suffered a succession of invasions from foreign powers: Carthaginians and Greeks in ancient times, Saracens and Normans in the Middle Ages and until the middle of the last century, the Bourbons from Spain held sway.

HISTORY

Italy is a young country: it did not exist as a unified nation state until 1861. The idea of Italy as a geographic entity goes back to the time of the Etruscans, but prior to the 19th century, the only time the peninsula was united was under the Romans, who by the 2nd century BC had subdued the other Italian tribes and the Greek colonies around the coast. Rome became the capital of a huge empire, introducing its language, laws, and calendar to most of Europe before falling to Germanic invaders in the 5th century AD.

A timeless view and way of life: peaceful old age amid the hills of Tuscany

◁ Piazza Navona, a Baroque fantasy created in papal Rome in the 17th century

The ostentatious Victor Emmanuel Monument in Rome, built to commemorate the completion of the unification of Italy in 1870

Another important legacy of the Roman Empire was Christianity, with the pope as head of the Catholic church throughout western Europe. The medieval papacy summoned the Franks to drive out the Lombards from Italy and, in AD 800, crowned the Frankish king Charlemagne Holy Roman Emperor. Unfortunately, for five centuries popes and emperors fought to decide which of them should be in charge of their nebulous empire.

KEY DATES IN ITALIAN HISTORY

c.800 BC First Greek colonists reach Italy

c.700 BC Rise of the Etruscans

509 BC Foundation of Roman Republic

202 BC Victory over Carthaginians makes Rome dominant power in the Mediterranean

27 BC Augustus establishes Roman Empire

AD 476 Collapse of Western Roman Empire

564 Lombards invade northern Italy

878 Saracens gain control of Sicily

1061 Start of Norman conquest of Sicily

11th–13th century Constant struggles between rival supporters of popes and emperors

1321 Dante writes *The Divine Comedy*

15th century Medici rule Florence; Renaissance

1527 Sack of Rome by Emperor's troops puts end to political ambitions of the papacy

1713 Much of the north passes to Austria

1735 Bourbon dynasty become rulers of Naples and Sicily (Kingdom of the Two Sicilies)

1860 Garibaldi and the Thousand capture Kingdom of the Two Sicilies

1861 Unification of most of Italy under House of Savoy, rulers of Piedmont and Sardinia

1870 Rome becomes capital of modern Italy

1922 Fascists come to power under Mussolini

1946 Foundation of modern Italian republic

2002 Italy joins European single currency

2005 Pope John Paul II dies

2006 Italy wins World Cup in Germany

Meanwhile, a succession of foreign invaders – Normans, Angevins, and Aragonese – conquered Sicily and the south. The north, in contrast, saw a growth of independent city states, the most powerful being Venice, fabulously wealthy from trade with the East. Northern Italy became the most prosperous and cultured region in western Europe and it was the artists and scholars of 15th-century Florence who inspired the Renaissance. Small, fragmented states, however, could not compete with great powers. In the 16th century Italy's petty kingdoms fell prey to a foreign invader, this time to Spain. The north subsequently came under the control of Austria, while the papacy ruled a small region in the center.

One small kingdom that remained independent was Piedmont and in the 19th century it was Piedmont that became the focus for a movement towards a united Italy, a goal that was achieved in 1870, thanks largely to the heroic military exploits of Garibaldi. In the 1920s, the Fascists seized power and, in 1946, the monarchy was abandoned for today's republic.

Governments in the postwar era have consistently been short-lived coalitions, dominated by the Christian Democrats. Investigations in Milan in 1992 revealed an organized network of corruption which exposed a huge number of politicians and businessmen. Silvio Berlusconi, Prime Minister from 2001–2006, was succeeded by Romano Prodi.

TRADITION AND PROGRESS
Variations between Italy's regions have much to do with the mountainous landscape and inaccessible valleys. Throughout the country, ancient techniques of husbandry endure and many livelihoods are linked to the land and the seasons. Main crops include wheat, olives, and grapes. Although some of the north's postwar economic prosperity can be attributed to industry (especially car production in Turin),

much of it has grown from the expansion of family-owned artisan businesses exporting handmade goods abroad. The clothes chain, Benetton, is a typical example of Italian design flair capturing a large slice of the global market.

LANGUAGE AND CULTURE

A tradition of literary Italian was established back in the 14th century by the poets Dante and Petrarch, who wrote in a cultured Florentine dialect. Yet, even today, with national television and radio stations, Italy's regional dialects show an astonishing resilience and northerners have great difficulty understanding a Neapolitan or Sicilian.

The arts in Italy have enjoyed a long and glorious history and Italians are very proud of this. Given the fact that Italy has some 100,000 monuments of major historical significance, it is not surprising that there is a shortage of funds to keep them in good repair. However, with tourism accounting for 3 percent of Italy's GDP, efforts are being made to put as many great buildings and art collections on show as possible.

The performing arts are also underfunded, yet there are spectacular cultural festivals. In the land of Verdi and Rossini, opera is naturally well supported, with almost every town of any size having its own opera house. Cinema is another art form that flourishes, keeping alive the tradition of great directors of the second half of the 20th century, such as Federico Fellini, Vittorio de Sica, and Luchino Visconti.

Children on their way to take First Communion in the Basilica di Monte Berico in Vicenza

MODERN LIFE

The number of practising Catholics in Italy has been in decline for years. In spite of this, Italian society is still highly traditional, and Italians can be very formal. Italian chic decrees that whatever clothes you wear should give the impression of wealth. If people wear similar outfits, it is because Italians are conformists in fashion as in many other aspects of daily life.

The emphasis on conformity and a commitment to the family remain key factors in Italian society despite the country's low, and falling, birth rate. Grandparents, children and grandchildren still live in family units, although this is becoming less common. All children are pampered but the most cherished ones are, usually, male. Attitudes to women in the workplace have changed, particularly in the cities. However, the idea that men should help with housework is still a fairly foreign notion to the older generation.

Food and football are the great constants; Italians live for both. Much time is spent on preparing food and eating. The Italian diet, particularly in the south, is among the healthiest in the world. Football is a national passion and inspires massive public interest.

Despite the political upheaval and corruption scandals of the 1990s, Italy appears little changed to foreign visitors, maintaining its regional identities and traditional values. The cost of living has soared, however, since the introduction of the Euro in 2002, leading to increased poverty for some.

Alessi kettle, an icon of modern Italian design

The Italian football team, World Cup winners in 2006

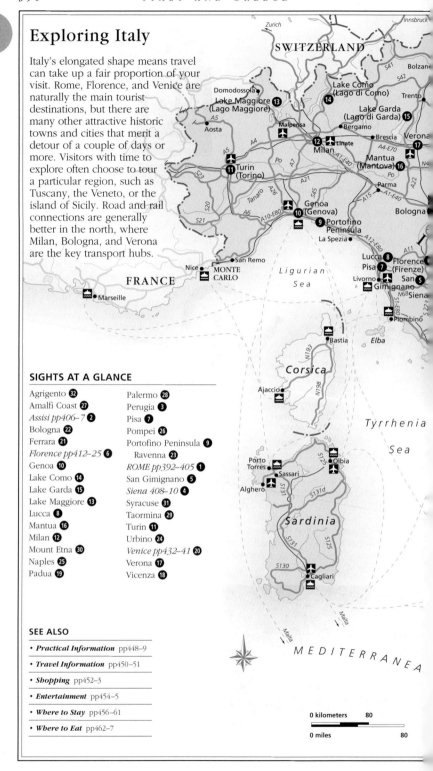

Exploring Italy

Italy's elongated shape means travel can take up a fair proportion of your visit. Rome, Florence, and Venice are naturally the main tourist destinations, but there are many other attractive historic towns and cities that merit a detour of a couple of days or more. Visitors with time to explore often choose to tour a particular region, such as Tuscany, the Veneto, or the island of Sicily. Road and rail connections are generally better in the north, where Milan, Bologna, and Verona are the key transport hubs.

SIGHTS AT A GLANCE

Agrigento **32**
Amalfi Coast **27**
Assisi pp406–7 **2**
Bologna **22**
Ferrara **21**
Florence pp412–25 **6**
Genoa **10**
Lake Como **14**
Lake Garda **15**
Lake Maggiore **13**
Lucca **8**
Mantua **16**
Milan **12**
Mount Etna **30**
Naples **25**
Padua **19**

Palermo **28**
Perugia **3**
Pisa **7**
Pompei **26**
Portofino Peninsula **9**
Ravenna **23**
ROME pp392–405 **1**
San Gimignano **5**
Siena 408–10 **4**
Syracuse **31**
Taormina **29**
Turin **11**
Urbino **24**
Venice pp432–41 **20**
Verona **17**
Vicenza **18**

SEE ALSO

- *Practical Information* pp448–9
- *Travel Information* pp450–51
- *Shopping* pp452–3
- *Entertainment* pp454–5
- *Where to Stay* pp456–61
- *Where to Eat* pp462–7

0 kilometers 80

0 miles 80

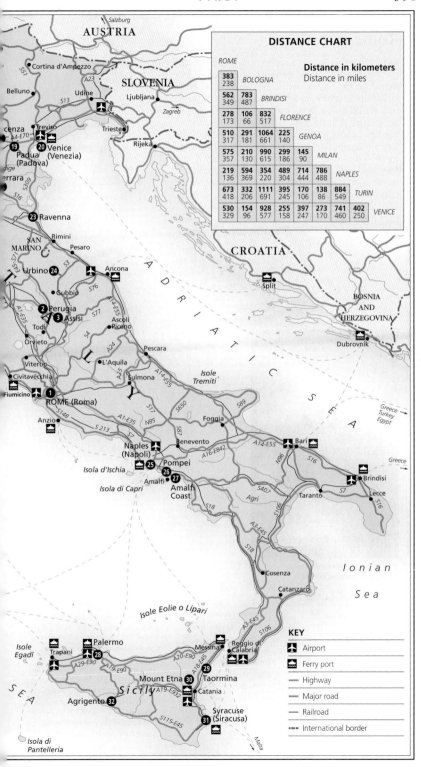

DISTANCE CHART

Distance in kilometers
Distance in miles

ROME								
383								
238	*BOLOGNA*							
562	**783**							
349	487	*BRINDISI*						
278	**106**	**832**						
173	66	517	*FLORENCE*					
510	**291**	**1064**	**225**					
317	181	661	140	*GENOA*				
575	**210**	**990**	**299**	**145**				
357	130	615	186	90	*MILAN*			
219	**594**	**354**	**489**	**714**	**786**			
136	369	220	304	444	488	*NAPLES*		
673	**332**	**1111**	**395**	**170**	**138**	**884**		
418	206	691	245	106	86	549	*TURIN*	
530	**154**	**928**	**255**	**397**	**273**	**741**	**402**	
329	96	577	158	247	170	460	250	*VENICE*

KEY

✈	Airport
⛴	Ferry port
—	Highway
—	Major road
—	Railroad
▪▪▪	International border

Rome ●

From its early days as a settlement of shepherds on the Palatine hill, Rome grew to rule a vast empire stretching beyond western Europe. Later, after the fall of the Roman empire, Rome became the center of the Christian world. The legacy of this history can be seen all over the city. The Pope, head of the Roman Catholic Church, still resides in the Vatican City, an independent enclave at the heart of Rome. In 1870 Rome became the capital of a newly unified Italy, and now has over 2.8 million inhabitants. In summer, many of the grand Baroque piazzas and narrow medieval streets are crammed with attractive sidewalk bars and restaurants.

View of the Roman Forum with the Colosseum rising behind

SIGHTS AT A GLANCE

Capitoline Museums ⑩
Castel Sant'Angelo ③
Colosseum ⑭
Gesù ⑨
Museo e Galleria
  Borghese ⑲
Palatine ⑬
Palazzo Doria Pamphilj ⑧
Pantheon ⑦
Piazza Navona ⑥
Roman Forum ⑫

St. Peter's pp394–5 ①
Santa Maria Maggiore ⑮
Santa Maria del Popolo ⑱
Santa Maria in
  Trastevere ⑤
Spanish Steps ⑰
Trajan's Markets ⑪
Trevi Fountain ⑯
Vatican Museums pp396–8 ②
Villa Farnesina ④
Villa Giulia ⑳

GETTING AROUND

Rome has a subway system known as *la metropolitana* (metro for short). Line A crosses the city from northwest to southeast, Line B from southwest to northeast. The two lines meet at Stazione Termini, the city's central station, which is also the starting point for many bus routes. These cover most parts of the city. Official taxis are white or yellow. Driving is not advisable in Rome – walking is the easiest way to negotiate the city's narrow streets.

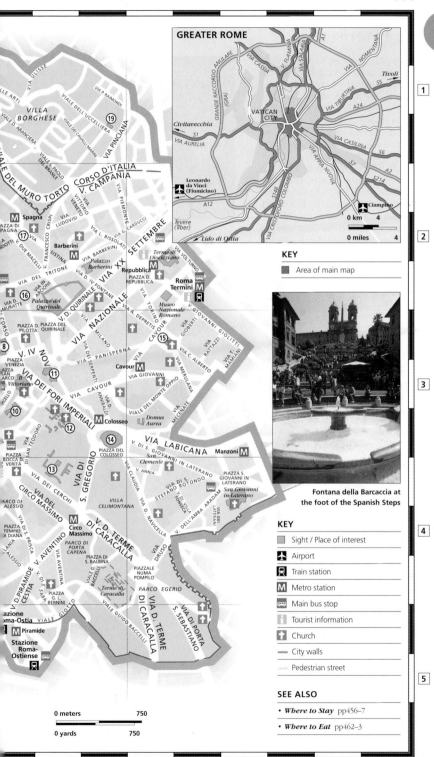

GREATER ROME

VILLA BORGHESE

Tivoli

Civitavecchia

VATICAN CITY

Leonardo
da Vinci
(Fiumicino)

Tevere
(Tiber)

Lido di Ostia

Ciampino

0 km 4

0 miles 4

KEY

Area of main map

Fontana della Barcaccia at
the foot of the Spanish Steps

KEY

Sight / Place of interest

✈ Airport

🚆 Train station

Ⓜ Metro station

Main bus stop

ℹ Tourist information

✝ Church

City walls

Pedestrian street

SEE ALSO

• *Where to Stay* pp456–7

• *Where to Eat* pp462–3

0 meters 750

0 yards 750

D E F

St. Peter's ①

Catholicism's most sacred shrine, the vast, marble-encrusted basilica draws pilgrims and tourists from all over the world. A shrine was erected on the site of St. Peter's tomb in the 2nd century and the first basilica, commissioned by Constantine, was completed around AD 349. By the 15th century it was falling down and in 1506 Pope Julius II laid the first stone of a new church. The present basilica, 187 m (615 ft) long, took more than a century to build and all the great architects of the Roman Renaissance and Baroque had a hand in its design. The dominant tone of the interior is set by Bernini, creator of the *baldacchino* below Michelangelo's magnificent dome.

★ Dome
The 137-m (448-ft) dome, designed by Michelangelo, was not completed until 1590, long after his death.

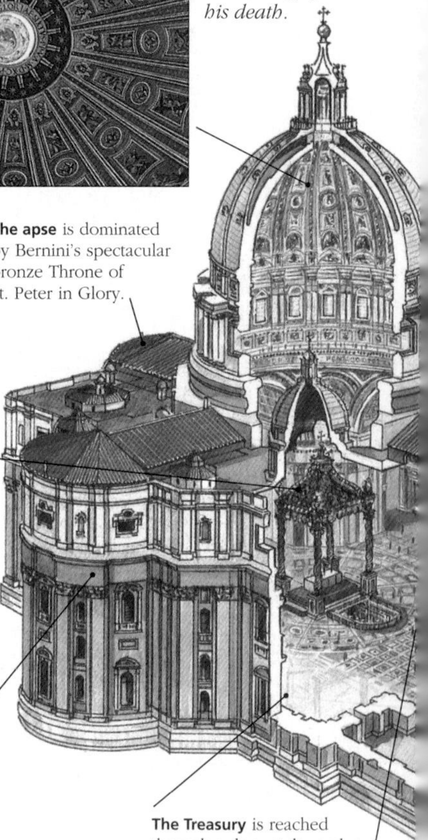

The apse is dominated by Bernini's spectacular bronze Throne of St. Peter in Glory.

Baldacchino
Commissioned by Urban VIII in 1624, Bernini's extravagant Baroque canopy stands above the Papal Altar, a plain slab of marble, at which only the pope may say mass. The altar is sited directly above the tomb of St. Peter in the Grottoes below.

Monument to Pope Alexander VII
Bernini's last work in St. Peter's was finished in 1678 and shows the pope surrounded by the allegorical figures of Truth, Justice, Charity, and Prudence.

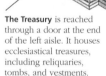

The Treasury is reached through a door at the end of the left aisle. It houses ecclesiastical treasures, including reliquaries, tombs, and vestments.

The Grottoes
A fragment of this 13th-century mosaic by Giotto, salvaged from the old basilica, is now in the Grottoes, where many popes are buried.

STAR FEATURES

★ Statue of St. Peter

★ Michelangelo's Pietà

★ Dome

For hotels and restaurants in this region see pp456–7 and pp462–3

★ **Statue of St. Peter**
This 13th-century bronze is thought to be by Arnolfo di Cambio. The foot of the statue has worn thin from the kisses of millions of pilgrims over the centuries.

Two minor cupolas by Vignola (1507–73)

★ **Michelangelo's Pietà**
Protected by glass since an attack in 1972, the Pietà stands in the first side chapel on the right. It was created in 1499 when Michelangelo was only 25.

VISITORS' CHECKLIST

Piazza San Pietro. **Tel** 06-69 88 16 62. Ⓜ Ottaviano S. Pietro. 🚌 23, 40, 49, 64, 81, 492. **Basilica** ◯ 7am–7pm (Oct–Mar: 6pm) daily. 🚻 **Treasury** ◯ 9am–6:15pm (Oct–Mar: 5:45pm) daily. 🚫 **Grottoes** ◯ 8am–5:45pm daily. **Dome** ◯ 8am–5:45pm daily (steep climb). 🚫 Strict dress code inside church. **www**.vatican.va

The façade (1614) is by Carlo Maderno, who lengthened the basilica to create its Latin-cross floorplan.

From this window, the pope blesses the faithful gathered in the piazza below.

Filarete Door
This bronze door, decorated with reliefs by Filarete (1439–45), was one of the doors of the old St. Peter's.

Entrance for stairs to dome

The nave floor has markings that show the lengths of other churches compared with St. Peter's.

Main entrance

Piazza San Pietro
The piazza in front of St. Peter's is enclosed by a vast pincer-shaped colonnade by Bernini. It is topped by statues of saints.

Vatican Museums ②

Four centuries of papal patronage and connoisseurship have resulted in one of the world's great collections of Classical and Renaissance art. The Vatican houses many of the great archaeological finds of central Italy, including the *Laocoön* group and the *Apollo del Belvedere*. The museums are housed in palaces originally built for wealthy Renaissance popes such as Innocent VIII, Sixtus IV, and Julius II. Parts of these were decorated with wonderful frescoes by the finest painters of the age – most notably the Borgia Apartment, the Raphael Rooms and the Sistine Chapel *(see p398).*

Gallery of the Candelabra
Once an open loggia, this gallery of Greek and Roman sculpture has a fine view of the Vatican Gardens.

Room of the Biga (a two-horse chariot)

Gallery of Tapestries

Gallery of Maps
The gallery is an important record of 16th-century cartography and history. This painting shows the Turkish siege of Malta in 1565.

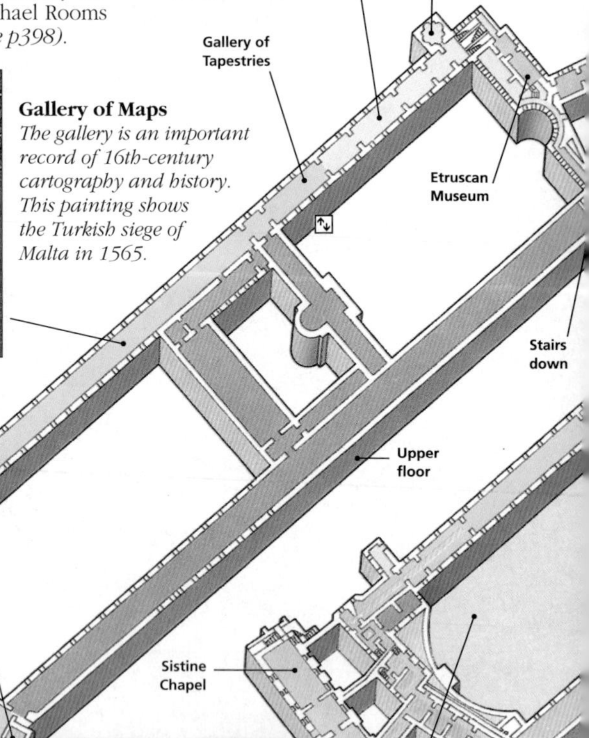

Etruscan Museum

The Raphael Loggia
contains Raphael frescoes, but special permission is needed to visit it.

Stairs down

Upper floor

Sistine Chapel

Raphael Rooms
This detail from the Expulsion of Heliodorus from the Temple *contains a portrait of Julius II. It is one of a series of frescoes painted by Raphael for the pope's private apartments (see p398).*

The Cortile del Belvedere
was laid out by Bramante in 1503.

The Borgia Apartment, frescoed by Pinturicchio in a highly decorative style in the 1490s, also houses a collection of modern religious art.

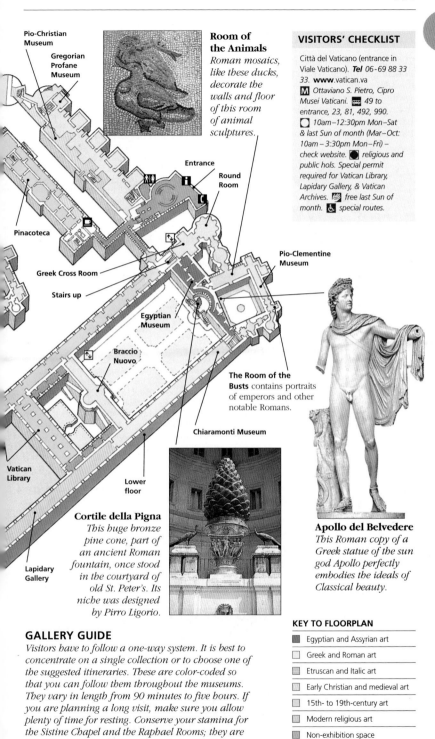

Pio-Christian Museum

Gregorian Profane Museum

Room of the Animals

Roman mosaics, like these ducks, decorate the walls and floor of this room of animal sculptures.

Entrance

Round Room

Pinacoteca

Greek Cross Room

Stairs up

Pio-Clementine Museum

Egyptian Museum

Braccio Nuovo

The Room of the Busts contains portraits of emperors and other notable Romans.

Chiaramonti Museum

Vatican Library

Lower floor

Cortile della Pigna

This huge bronze pine cone, part of an ancient Roman fountain, once stood in the courtyard of old St. Peter's. Its niche was designed by Pirro Ligorio.

Lapidary Gallery

Apollo del Belvedere

This Roman copy of a Greek statue of the sun god Apollo perfectly embodies the ideals of Classical beauty.

VISITORS' CHECKLIST

Città del Vaticano (entrance in Viale Vaticano). **Tel** 06-69 88 33 33. **www**.vatican.va

Ⓜ Ottaviano S. Pietro, Cipro Musei Vaticani. 🚌 49 to entrance, 23, 81, 492, 990. ⬤ 10am–12:30pm Mon–Sat & last Sun of month (Mar–Oct: 10am–3:30pm Mon–Fri) – check website. ⬤ religious and public hols. Special permit required for Vatican Library, Lapidary Gallery, & Vatican Archives. 📷 free last Sun of month. ♿ special routes.

KEY TO FLOORPLAN

- ⬛ Egyptian and Assyrian art
- ⬜ Greek and Roman art
- ⬜ Etruscan and Italic art
- ⬜ Early Christian and medieval art
- ⬜ 15th- to 19th-century art
- ⬜ Modern religious art
- ⬜ Non-exhibition space
- ⬜ Open by special permit only

GALLERY GUIDE

Visitors have to follow a one-way system. It is best to concentrate on a single collection or to choose one of the suggested itineraries. These are color-coded so that you can follow them throughout the museums. They vary in length from 90 minutes to five hours. If you are planning a long visit, make sure you allow plenty of time for resting. Conserve your stamina for the Sistine Chapel and the Raphael Rooms; they are 20–30 minutes' walk from the entrance, without allowing for any viewing time along the way.

Exploring the Vatican's Collections

The Vatican's greatest treasures are its Greek and Roman antiquities, which have been on display since the 18th century. The 19th century saw the addition of exciting discoveries from Etruscan tombs and excavations in Egypt. Then there are works by many of Italy's greatest Renaissance artists housed in the Pinacoteca (art gallery) and decorating the walls of chapels and papal apartments.

The *Laocoön*, a Roman copy of a Greek original, excavated in Rome in 1506

ANCIENT ART

The Egyptian collection contains finds from 19th- and 20th-century excavations, as well as items brought to Rome in Imperial times. There are also Roman imitations of Egyptian art. Genuine Egyptian works include the tomb of Iri, guardian of the Pyramid of Cheops (22nd century BC).

Prize Greek and Roman art in the Pio-Clementine Museum includes Roman copies of the 4th-century BC Greek statues *Apoxyomenos* and the *Apollo del Belvedere,* and a splendid *Laocoön* from the 1st century AD.

The Chiaramonti Museum is lined with ancient busts, and its extension, the Braccio Nuovo, has a 1st-century BC statue of Emperor Augustus.

The Etruscan Museum houses a superb collection, including the bronze throne, bed, and funeral cart, found in the 650 BC Regolini-Galassi tomb in Cerveteri.

In the Vatican Library is the *Aldobrandini Wedding*, a beautiful Roman fresco from the 1st century AD.

CHRISTIAN ART

The Pio-Christian Museum has Early Christian art, such as inscriptions and sculpture from catacombs and basilicas. The first two rooms of the Pinacoteca house medieval art, including Giotto's *Stefaneschi Triptych* (c.1300), which decorated the main altar of the old St. Peter's. Other rooms in the Pinacoteca contain Renaissance works. 15th-century highlights are a *Pietà* by Giovanni Bellini and Leonardo da Vinci's unfinished *St. Jerome.* Exceptional 16th-century pieces include an altarpiece by Titian, a *Deposition* by Caravaggio, *St. Helen* by Paolo Veronese, and a whole room devoted to Raphael.

THE SISTINE CHAPEL

The Sistine Chapel takes its name from Pope Sixtus IV: it was built in 1473 at his request. The walls were frescoed by some of the finest artists of the age, including Signorelli, Botticelli, Roselli, Ghirlandaio, and Perugino (who is credited with having overseen the project). There are 12 frescoes on the side walls, painted between 1481 and 1483. Their subjects are parallel episodes in the lives of Moses and Christ.

In 1508–12, at the request of Pope Julius II, Michelangelo created what has become his most famous work, the chapel ceiling. The main panels chart the *Creation of the World* and *Fall of Man.* They are surrounded by subjects from the Old and New Testaments.

In 1534–41 Michelangelo completed the chapel walls, painting *The Last Judgment* on the altar wall. It depicts the souls of the dead rising up to face the wrath of God and the damned being hurled down to hell. The artist's own tormented attitude to his faith is seen in his self-portrait, painted on the skin held by the martyr, St. Bartholomew.

RAPHAEL ROOMS

Pope Julius II chose Raphael (1483–1520) to redecorate four rooms *(stanze)* of his apartments. The frescoes in the Room of the Segnatura (1508–11) include the famous *School of Athens,* which centers on a debate between Plato and Aristotle. Raphael depicted Leonardo da Vinci and Michelangelo as philosophers. The decoration of the Room of Heliodorus (1512–4) incorporates a famous portrait of Julius II, whereas the Room of the Fire in the Borgo (1514–7) was painted during the reign of Pope Leo X, Julius II's successor. All the frescoes here exalt the new pope or his earlier namesakes.

The Hall of Constantine (1517–25) was largely the work of Raphael's pupils.

Original Sin, from Michelangelo's fresco on the Sistine Chapel ceiling

View across the Tiber to Castel Sant'Angelo, crowned by the figure of the angel that gave it its name

Castel Sant'Angelo ③

Lungotevere Castello. **Tel** 06-681 91 11. 🚌 23, 34, 280. ⬜ Tue–Sun. ⬤ pub hols. 📷 ♿ **www**.galleria borghese.it/castello/it

This massive cylindrical fortress takes its name from the vision of the Archangel Michael, experienced by Pope Gregory the Great in the 6th century, as he led a procession across the bridge, fervently praying for the end of the plague.

The castle began life in AD 139 as the Emperor Hadrian's mausoleum. Since then it has been a bridgehead in the Emperor Aurelian's city wall, a medieval citadel and prison, and a place of safety for popes during times of war or political unrest.

Visitors are given a glimpse into all aspects of the castle's history – from its dank prison cells to the lavish apartments of Renaissance popes.

Villa Farnesina ④

Via della Lungara 230. **Tel** 06-68 02 72 68. 🚌 23, 280. ⬜ Mon–Sat. 📷

The fabulously wealthy Sienese banker, Agostino Chigi, commissioned this villa in 1508 from his fellow Sienese, Baldassare Peruzzi. Chigi's main home was across the Tiber – the villa was just for extravagant banquets. Chigi also used it for sojourns

with the courtesan Imperia, who allegedly inspired one of the *Three Graces* painted by Raphael in the Loggia of Cupid and Psyche.

The simple, harmonious design of the Farnesina, with a central block and projecting wings, made it one of the first true villas of the Renaissance. Peruzzi decorated some of the interiors himself, such as the Sala della Prospettiva upstairs, in which illusionistic frescoes create the impression of looking out over Rome through a marble colonnade.

The painted vault of the main hall, the Sala di Galatea, shows the position of the stars at the time of Chigi's birth. After his death the banking business collapsed, and in 1577 the villa was sold off to the Farnese family.

Trompe l'oeil view in the Sala della Prospettiva, Villa Farnesina

Santa Maria in Trastevere ⑤

Piazza Santa Maria in Trastevere. **Tel** 06-581 48 02. 🚌 H, 23, 280. ⬜ daily. ♿

Trastevere, the area "across the Tiber," is one of the city's most attractive quarters: a maze of narrow, cobbled alleys. Once home to the city's poor, it has witnessed a proliferation of fashionable clubs, restaurants, and boutiques.

At the heart of Trastevere, overlooking an attractive traffic-free square stands the Basilica of Santa Maria – probably the first official place of Christian worship in Rome. It was founded by Pope Callixtus I in the 3rd century, when Christianity was still a minority cult. According to legend, it was built on the site where a fountain of oil had sprung up miraculously on the day that Christ was born.

The basilica became the focus of devotion to the Madonna. Mary and Christ are among the figures depicted in the façade mosaics (c.12th century). In the apse is a stylized 12th-century mosaic *Coronation of the Virgin*, and below it, a series of realistic mosaic scenes from the life of Mary by the 13th-century artist Pietro Cavallini. The oldest image of the Virgin is a 7th-century icon, which depicts her as a Byzantine empress flanked by a guard of angels.

Piazza Navona ⑥

🚌 *40, 46, 62, 64, 81, 87, 116, 492, 628.*

Rome's most spectacular Baroque piazza follows the shape of a 1st-century AD stadium, built by Domitian and used for athletic contests *(agones)*, chariot races, and other sports. The foundations of the surrounding buildings come from the ruined stadium, traces of which are visible below the church of Sant' Agnese in Agone. The church, created by the architects Girolamo and Carlo Rainaldi and Francesco Borromini, is dedicated to the virgin martyr, St. Agnes. When she was stripped naked to force her to renounce her faith, her hair grew miraculously long, concealing her body.

The piazza began to take on its present appearance in the 17th century, when Pope Innocent X commissioned a new church, palace, and fountain. The fountain, the Fontana dei Quattro Fiumi, is Bernini's most magnificent,

The Pantheon, a place of worship since the 2nd century AD

with statues of four gods personifying the world's greatest known rivers at the time – the Nile, the Plate, the Ganges, and the Danube – sitting on rocks below an obelisk. Bernini also sculpted the muscle-bound Moor in the Fontana del Moro, though the present statue is a copy.

Pantheon ⑦

Piazza della Rotonda. **Tel** *06-68 30 02 30.* 🚌 *116 & many others.* ⬜ *daily.* ⬤ *Jan 1, May 1, Dec 25.* ♿

The Pantheon, the Roman "temple of all the gods," is the most extraordinary and best preserved ancient building in Rome. The first temple on the site is thought to have been a conventional rectangular affair erected by Agrippa between 27 and 25 BC. The present structure was built, and possibly designed, by Emperor Hadrian in AD 118.

The temple is fronted by a massive pedimented portico, screening what appears to be a cylinder fused to a shallow dome. Only from the inside can the true scale and beauty of the temple be appreciated: a vast hemispherical dome equal in radius to the height of the cylinder gives perfectly harmonious proportions to the building. A circular opening in the center of the coffered dome, the *oculus*, lets in the only light.

In the 7th century, Christians claimed that they were being plagued by demons as they passed by, and permission was given to turn the Pantheon into a church. Today it is lined with tombs, ranging from the restrained monument to Raphael to the huge marble and porphyry sarcophagi holding the bodies of Italian monarchs.

Palazzo Doria Pamphilj ⑧

Piazza del Collegio Romano 2. **Tel** *06-679 73 23.* 🚌 *64, 70, 81, 85, 117, 119, 492.* ⬜ *Fri – Wed.* ⬤ *Jan 1, Easter Sun, May 1, Aug 15, Dec 25.* 📷 www.doriapamphilj.it ♿

Palazzo Doria Pamphilj is a vast stone edifice, whose oldest parts date from 1435. It was owned by the della Rovere family and then by the Aldobrandini family, before the Pamphilj family took possession of it in 1647. The Pamphilj added a new wing, a splendid chapel, and a theater.

Personification of the Ganges, Fontana dei Quattro Fiumi, Piazza Navona

For hotels and restaurants in this region see pp456–7 and pp462–3

The family art collection has over 400 paintings dating from the 15th to the 18th century, including a portrait of Pope Innocent X by Velázquez and works by Caravaggio, Titian, Guercino, and Claude Lorrain. The opulent rooms of the private apartments retain many of their original furnishings, including Brussels and Gobelins tapestries, Murano chandeliers, and a gilded crib.

In the first half of the 18th century, Gabriele Valvassori created the gallery above the courtyard and a new façade along the Corso, using the highly decorative style of the period, known as the *barocchetto*, which now dominates the building.

Triumph of Faith over Heresy by Pierre Legros in the Gesù

Gesù ⑨

Piazza del Gesù. *Tel* 06-69 70 01. H, 46, 62, 64, 70, 81, 87, 186, 492, 628 & other routes. daily.

The Gesù, built between 1568 and 1584, was Rome's first Jesuit church. The Jesuit order was founded in Rome in 1537 by a Basque soldier, Ignatius Loyola, who became a Christian after he was wounded in battle. The order was intellectual, austere, and heavily engaged in teaching and missionary activities.

The much-imitated design of the Gesù typifies Counter Reformation architecture: a large nave with side pulpits for preaching to crowds, and a main altar as the centerpiece for the mass. The illusionistic decoration that covers the nave ceiling and the dome was

added by Il Baciccia in the 17th century. The painting in the nave depicts the *Triumph of the Name of Jesus* and its message is clear: faithful, Catholic worshippers will be joyfully uplifted to heaven while Protestants and heretics are flung into the fires of hell. The message is reiterated in the Cappella di Sant'Ignazio, a rich display of lapis lazuli, serpentine, silver, and gold. The Baroque marble by Legros, *Triumph of Faith over Idolatry*, shows a female "Religion" trampling on the head of the serpent "Idolatry."

Capitoline Museums ⑩

Musei Capitolini, Piazza del Campidoglio. *Tel* 06-67 10 24 75. 40, 63, 64, 70, 75 & many others. Tue–Sun. Jan 1, May 1, Dec 25. www.museicapitolini.org

When Emperor Charles V announced he was to visit Rome in 1536, Pope Paul III asked Michelangelo to give the Capitol, formerly the citadel of Ancient Rome, a facelift. He redesigned the piazza, renovated the façades of its palaces and built a new staircase, the Cordonata. This gently rising ramp is now crowned with the massive Classical statues of Castor and Pollux.

The Capitoline Museums – the Palazzo Nuovo and the Palazzo dei Conservatori – stand on opposite sides of the impressive Piazza del Campidoglio. In the center of the piazza is an equestrian statue of Marcus Aurelius (it is a copy; the original bronze is in the Palazzo Nuovo).

The façade of the Palazzo Nuovo was designed by Michelangelo, but the work was finished in 1655 by the brothers Carlo and Girolamo Rainaldi.

The Palazzo dei Conservatori had been the seat of the city's magistrates during the late

Statue of Marcus Aurelius in the center of Piazza del Campidoglio

Middle Ages. Its frescoed halls are still used occasionally for political meetings and the ground floor houses the municipal registry office. The current building was begun in 1536, built by Giacomo della Porta, who also carried out Michelangelo's other designs for Piazza del Campidoglio.

A collection of Classical statues has been kept on the Capitoline Hill since the Renaissance. When the Palazzo Nuovo was completed, some of the statues were transferred there. In 1734 Pope Clement XII decreed that the building be turned into the world's first public museum.

The museum is still devoted chiefly to sculpture. Most of its finest works, such as *The Dying Galatian*, are Roman copies of Greek masterpieces. There are also two collections of busts, assembled in the 18th century, of the philosophers and poets of ancient Greece and the rulers of ancient Rome.

Although much of the museum is given over to sculpture, it also houses a collection of porcelain, and its art galleries contain various works by Veronese, Titian, Caravaggio, Rubens, van Dyck, and Tintoretto.

The two museums have recently been restored, and a new subterranean passage now links them.

Esquiline Venus, Capitoline Museums

Ancient Rome

Traces of ancient Rome are visible all over the city, occasionally a whole building, often just a column from a temple or an arch of an aqueduct recycled in a later construction. The major archaeological sites are to be found along Via dei Fori Imperiali, which runs from Piazza Venezia to the Colosseum. On the north side lie Trajan's Markets and the forums of various emperors; on the south side are the Roman Forum and the Palatine Hill. Many museums hold extensive collections of antiquities excavated in the city.

Romans fortifying a town in a detail from Trajan's Column

Trajan's Markets ⑪

Via IV Novembre. **Tel** 06-679 00 48.
🚌 64, 70, 170, 640 & many others.
🕐 Tue–Sun. ⬤ public hols. 🖼

Originally considered among the wonders of the Classical world, Trajan's Markets now show only a hint of their former splendor.

Emperor Trajan and his architect, Apollodorus of Damascus, built this visionary complex of 150 shops and offices in the early 2nd century AD. The Markets sold everything from Middle Eastern silks and spices to fresh fish, fruit, and flowers. It was also the place where the corn dole was administered: a free ration for Roman men.

Shops opened early and closed about noon. Almost all the shopping was done by men and the traders were almost exclusively male.

The **Forum of Trajan** (AD 107–13) was built in front of the market complex. It was a vast colonnaded open space with a huge basilica, and included two libraries.

Dominating the ruins today is **Trajan's Column**. Spiralling up its 30 m (98 ft) high stem its minutely detailed scenes showing episodes from Trajan's successful campaigns in Dacia (present-day Romania).

Roman Forum ⑫

Entrances: Largo Romolo e Remo, Via del Foro Romano, and near the Arch of Titus on Via Sacra. **Tel** 06-39 96 77 00. Ⓜ Colosseo. 🚌 75, 81, 85, 87, 117, 175, 186, 810, 850. 🕐 daily. ⬤ Jan 1, May 1, Dec 25. 🖼

The Forum was the center of political, commercial, and judicial life in ancient Rome. As Rome's population grew, however, this ancient Forum became too small, so Julius Caesar built a new one (46 BC). This move was emulated by successive emperors. The newer forums are known as the "Imperial Fora."

The ruins of the Roman Forum date from many eras and the layout is confusing. It is a good idea to view them from the vantage point of the

Capitoline Hill, before walking around. From there you can make out the Via Sacra, the route of religious and triumphal processions.

The best preserved monuments are two triumphal arches. The **Arch of Titus** commemorates the crushing of the Jewish Revolt by Titus in AD 70. The later **Arch of Septimius Severus** (AD 203) records the emperor's victories over the Parthians.

Most of the other ruins are temples or basilicas. The latter were huge public buildings, which served as law courts and places of business. At the western end of the forum are the scant remains of the **Basilica Julia**, named after Julius Caesar, and the earlier **Basilica Aemilia**. Close to the latter stands the reconstructed **Curia**, where the Roman Senate once met.

The eastern end of the Forum is dominated by the shell of the **Basilica of Constantine and Maxentius** (4th century AD). The adjacent **Temple of Romulus** is now part of a church. Cross the Via Sacra from here to see the partly reconstructed **Temple of Vesta** and the **House of the Vestal Virgins**.

Further east past the Arch of Titus are the extensive ruins of the **Temple of Venus and Rome**, built in AD 121 by Hadrian. Attached to the ruined temple is the church of **Santa Francesca Romana** – patron saint of motorists. On March 9, drivers bring their cars here to have them blessed.

Central garden of the House of the Vestal Virgins in the Roman Forum

Ruins of oval fountain in the Domus
Flavia on the Palatine

Palatine ⑬

Entrances: Via di San Gregorio and
near the Arch of Titus on Via Sacra.
Tel 06-39 96 77 00. Ⓜ Colosseo. 🚍
75, 85, 87, 117, 175 & many others.
🚋 3. ☐ daily. ● public hols. 🎫
(includes entry to the Colosseum). 🎫

The Palatine, the hill where
the Roman aristocracy lived
and emperors built their
palaces, is the most pleasant
and relaxing of the city's
ancient sites. Shaded by pines
and carpeted with wild flowers
in the spring, it is dominated
by the imposing ruins of the
Domus Augustana and the
Domus Flavia, two parts of
Domitian's huge palace (1st
century AD).

Other remains here include
the **House of Augustus** and
the **House of Livia**, where the
Emperor Augustus lived with
his wife Livia; and the
Cryptoporticus, a long underground gallery built by Nero.

The **Huts of Romulus**, not
far from the House of
Augustus, are Iron Age huts
(10th century BC), which
provide archaeological support
for the area's legendary links
with the founding of Rome.
According to legend Romulus
and Remus grew up on this
hill in the 8th century BC.

After admiring the ancient
sights, visit the **Farnese
Gardens**, created in the
mid-16th century by Cardinal
Alessandro Farnese, with
tree-lined avenues, rose
gardens, and glorious views.

Colosseum ⑭

Piazza del Colosseo. **Tel** 06-3996 77
00. Ⓜ Colosseo. 🚍 75, 81, 85, 87,
117, 175, 673, 810. 🚋 3. ☐ daily.
● Jan 1, May 1, Dec 25. 🎫 (includes
entry to the Palatine). 🎫 🚻 limited.

Rome's great amphitheater,
commissioned by the
Emperor Vespasian in AD 72,
was built on the marshy site
of a lake in the grounds of
Nero's palace.

It is likely that the arena
took its name, not from its
own size, but from that of an
enormous statue, the Colossus
of Nero, that stood nearby.

The Colosseum was the site
of deadly gladiatorial combats
and wild animal fights, staged
free of charge by the emperor
and wealthy citizens. It was
built to a very practical design,
its 80 entrances allowing easy
access for 55,000 spectators.
Excavations in the 19th century
exposed a network of rooms
under the arena, from which
animals could be released.

The four tiers of the outside
walls were built in differing
styles. The lower three are
arched: the bottom with Doric
columns, the next with Ionic,
and the third with Corinthian.
The top level supported a
huge awning, used to shade
spectators from the sun.

Beside the Colosseum stands
the **Arch of Constantine**,
commemorating Constantine's
victory in AD 312 over his
co-emperor Maxentius. Most
of the medallions, reliefs, and
statues were scavenged from
earlier monuments. Inside the
arch are reliefs showing one
of Trajan's victories.

The Colosseum, a majestic sight despite centuries of damage and neglect

Santa Maria Maggiore ⑮

Piazza di Santa Maria Maggiore.
Tel 06-48 31 95. M *Termini,
Cavour.* 🚌 *16, 70, 71, 714.* 🚋 *14.*
◻ *daily.* 📷

Of all the great Roman
basilicas, Santa Maria has the
most successful blend of
different architectural styles.
Its colonnaded triple nave is
part of the original 5th-century
building; the marble floor and
Romanesque bell tower, with
its blue ceramic roundels, are
medieval; the Renaissance saw
a new coffered ceiling; and
the Baroque gave the church
twin domes and its imposing
front and rear façades.

Santa Maria is most famous
for its mosaics. Those in the
nave and on the triumphal
arch date from the 5th century.
Medieval mosaics include a
13th-century enthroned Christ
in the loggia and Jacopo
Torriti's *Coronation of the
Virgin* (1295) in the apse.

The gilded ceiling was a gift
of Alexander VI, the Borgia
pope. The gold used is said
to be the first brought back
from America by Columbus.

The Spanish Steps, with the church of Trinità dei Monti above

Trevi Fountain ⑯

Piazza di Trevi. 🚌 *52, 53, 61, 62, 63,
71, 80, 95, 116, 119 & many others.*

Most visitors gathering around
the coin-filled fountain
assume that it has always
been there, but by the
standards of the Eternal City,
the Trevi is a fairly recent
creation. Nicola Salvi's

theatrical design for Rome's
largest and most famous
fountain was completed only
in 1762. The central figure is
Neptune, flanked by two
Tritons. One Triton struggles
to master a very unruly "sea-
horse," the other leads a far
more docile animal. These
symbolize the two contrasting
moods of the sea.

The site was originally the
terminal of the Aqua Virgo
aqueduct (19 BC). A relief
shows the legendary virgin,
after whom the aqueduct was
named, pointing to the spring
from which the water flows.

Spanish Steps ⑰

Scalinata della Trinità dei Monti,
Piazza di Spagna. M *Spagna.*
🚌 *116, 117.*

The steps, which link the
church of Trinità dei Monti
with Piazza di Spagna below,
were completed in 1726.
They combine straight
sections, curves, and terraces
to create one of the city's
most dramatic and distinctive
landmarks. To the right as
you look at the steps from the
square is the **Keats-Shelley
Memorial House**, a small
museum in the house where
the poet John Keats died of
consumption in 1821.

In the 19th century the
steps were a meeting place
for artists' models; today they
are filled with people sitting,
writing postcards, taking
photos, flirting, busking, or
just watching the passers-by.
Eating here is not allowed.

The steps overlook Via
Condotti and the surrounding
streets. In the 18th century
this area was full of hotels for
foreigners doing the Grand
Tour. It now contains the
smartest shops in Rome.

The Trevi Fountain, the most famous of Rome's Baroque landmarks

For hotels and restaurants in this region see pp456–7 and pp462–3

Santa Maria del Popolo ⑱

Piazza del Popolo 12. **Tel** 06-361 08 36. **M** Flaminio. 95, 117, 119, 490, 495, 926. ◯ daily.

Santa Maria del Popolo was commissioned by Sixtus IV in 1472. After his death in 1484, the pope's family chapel, the Della Rovere Chapel (first on the right), was frescoed by Pinturicchio.

In 1503 Sixtus IV's nephew Giuliano became Pope Julius II and had Bramante build a new apse. Pinturicchio was called in again to paint its vaults with Sibyls and Apostles framed by freakish beasts.

In 1513 Raphael created the Chigi Chapel (second on the left) – a Renaissance fusion of the sacred and profane – for the banker Agostino Chigi. Bernini later added the statues of Daniel and Habakkuk. In the Cerasi Chapel, left of the altar, are two Caravaggios: *The Crucifixion of St Peter* and *The Conversion of St Paul.*

The Chigi Chapel in Santa Maria del Popolo, designed by Raphael

Museo e Galleria Borghese ⑲

Piazzale Scipione Borghese 5. **Tel** 06-328 10 (reservations). 52, 53, 116, 910. 3, 19. ◯ Tue–Sun (reservations obligatory). ● pub hols. www.galleriaborghese.it

The Villa Borghese and its park were designed in 1605 for Cardinal Scipione Borghese, nephew of Pope

Detail from Bernini's *Rape of Proserpine* in the Museo Borghese

Paul V. The park was the first of its kind in Rome. It was laid out with 400 pine trees, sculpture by Bernini, and dramatic water features.

The villa was used for entertaining and displaying the cardinal's impressive collection of paintings and sculpture. Unfortunately, between 1801 and 1809 Prince Camillo Borghese, husband to Napoleon's sister Pauline, sold many of these to his brother-in-law, and swapped 200 of Scipione's Classical statues for an estate in Piedmont. The statues are still in the Louvre. However, some Classical treasures remain, including fragments of a 3rd-century AD mosaic of gladiators fighting wild animals.

The highlights of the remaining collection are the sculptures by the young Bernini. *Apollo and Daphne* (1624), shows the nymph Daphne being transformed into a laurel tree to escape being abducted by Apollo. Other striking works are *The Rape of Proserpine* and a *David*, whose face is said to be a self-portrait of Bernini.

The most notorious work is a sculpture by Canova of Pauline Borghese as *Venus Victrix* (1805), in which the semi-naked Pauline reclines on a chaise longue.

The Galleria Borghese, on the upper floor, houses some fine Renaissance and Baroque paintings. These include Raphael's *Deposition*, along with works by Pinturicchio, Correggio, Caravaggio, Rubens, and Titian.

Within the Villa Borghese park are other museums and galleries, foreign academies, a zoo, schools of archaeology, an artificial lake, and an array of fountains and follies.

Villa Giulia ⑳

Piazzale di Villa Giulia 9. **Tel** 06-322 65 71. 52, 926, 88, 95, 490, 495. 3, 19. ◯ Tue–Sun. ● Jan 1, May 1, Dec 25. audio. ♿

Villa Giulia was built as a country retreat for Pope Julius III. Today it houses a world-famous collection of Etruscan and other pre-Roman remains. There are fascinating pieces of jewelry, bronzes, mirrors, and a marvelous terra-cotta sarcophagus of a husband and wife from Cerveteri.

The delightful villa was the work of architects Vasari and Vignola, and the sculptor Ammannati. Michelangelo also contributed. At the center of the garden is a *nympheum* – a sunken courtyard decorated with mosaics, statues, and fountains, built in imitation of ancient Roman models.

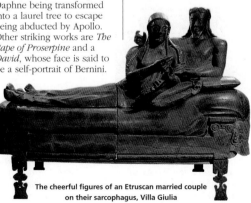

The cheerful figures of an Etruscan married couple on their sarcophagus, Villa Giulia

Assisi: Basilica di San Francesco

The burial place of St. Francis, this basilica was begun in 1228, two years after the saint's death. Over the next century its Upper and Lower Churches were decorated by the foremost artists of their day, among them Cimabue, Simone Martini, Pietro Lorenzetti, and Giotto, whose frescoes of the *Life of St. Francis* are some of the most renowned in Italy. Many of the basilica's frescoes were badly damaged in the earthquake that hit Assisi in 1997, but all have been restored. The basilica, which dominates Assisi, is one of the great Christian shrines and receives vast numbers of pilgrims throughout the year.

★ Frescoes by Giotto
The Ecstasy of St. Francis is one of 28 panels that make up Giotto's cycle on the Life of St. Francis (c.1290–95).

St. Francis
Cimabue's simple painting (c.1280) captures the humility of the revered saint, who stood for poverty, chastity, and obedience.

Faded paintings by Roman artists line the walls above Giotto's *Life of St. Francis.*

The choir (1501) features a 13th-century stone papal throne.

The vaulting of the Lower Church is covered almost entirely in frescoes.

Steps to the Treasury

The crypt contains the tomb of St. Francis.

A Renaissance portico shelters the original Gothic portal of the Lower Church.

★ Frescoes by Lorenzetti
The bold composition of Pietro Lorenzetti's fresco, entitled The Deposition (1323), is based around the truncated Cross, focusing attention on the twisted figure of Christ.

★ Cappella di San Martino
The frescoes in this chapel on the life of St. Martin (1315) are by the Sienese painter Simone Martini. This panel shows the death of the Saint. Martini was also responsible for the fine stained glass in the chapel.

The Upper Church has soaring Gothic vaulting painted with a starry sky, symbolizing the heavenly glory of St. Francis. Its style influenced that of many later Franciscan churches.

The rose window is framed by the carved symbols of the four Evangelists.

Entrance to Upper Church

The façade and its rose window are early examples of Italian Gothic.

STAR FEATURES

★ Frescoes by Giotto

★ Frescoes by Lorenzetti

★ Cappella di San Martino

The ancient Tempio di Minerva in the Piazza del Comune, Assisi

Assisi ❷

🏠 25,000. 🚉 🚌 ℹ️ Piazza del Comune (075-81 25 34). 🗓 Sat.
www.assisi.umbria2000.it

This beautiful medieval town, with its geranium-hung streets, lovely views, and fountain-splashed piazzas, is heir to the legacy of St. Francis (c.1181–1226), who is buried in the **Basilica di San Francesco**.

Piazza del Comune, Assisi's main square, is dominated by the columns of the **Tempio di Minerva**, a Roman temple-front from the Augustan age. The Palazzo Comunale, opposite, houses an art gallery the **Pinacoteca Comunale**.

The town has many other interesting churches. On Corso Mazzini is the **Basilica di Santa Chiara**. Here, St. Clare – Francis's companion and the founder of the Poor Clares (an order of nuns) – is buried. The **Duomo** has a superb Romanesque façade. **San Pietro** is a simple, well-restored Romanesque church, while the nearby **Oratorio dei Pellegrini**, a 15th-century pilgrims' hospice, contains well-preserved frescoes by Matteo da Gualdo.

Perugia ❸

🏠 160,000. 🚉 🚌 ℹ️ Corso Vanucci 19 (075-572 33 27). 🗓 Tue, Sat.

Perugia's old center hinges around Corso Vannucci, named after the local painter Pietro Vannucci (Perugino). It is dominated by Umbria's finest building and former town hall, the monumental **Palazzo dei Priori**. Among its richly decorated rooms is the Sala dei Notari or Lawyers' Hall (c.1295), vividly frescoed with scenes from the Old Testament. Superlative frescoes (1498–1500) by Perugino cover the walls of the Collegio del Cambio, Perugia's medieval money exchange. The **Galleria Nazionale dell'Umbria** on the third floor displays a fine collection of paintings.

The Cappella del Santo Anello in Perugia's 15th-century **Duomo** houses the Virgin's agate "wedding ring," said to change color according to the character of its wearer. The Renaissance *Madonna delle Grazie* by Gian Nicola di Paolo hangs in the nave.

On Piazza San Francesco the **Oratorio di San Bernardino** (1457–61), has a colorful façade by Agostino di Duccio. Beyond the old city walls, the 10th-century **San Pietro** is Perugia's most extravagantly decorated church. **San Domenico** (1305–1632), on Piazza Giordano Bruno, is Umbria's largest church. It houses the tomb of Pope Benedict XI (c.1304) and the **Museo Archeologico Nazionale dell'Umbria**, a collection of prehistoric, Etruscan, and Roman artifacts.

Palazzo dei Priori, Perugia's imposing medieval town hall

Street-by-Street: Siena ●

Unicorn contrada

Siena's principal sights cluster in the maze of narrow streets and alleys around the fan-shaped Piazza del Campo. One of Europe's greatest medieval squares, the piazza sits at the heart of the city's 17 *contrade*, the historic districts whose ancient rivalries are still acted out in the twice-yearly Palio *(see p410)*. Loyalty to the *contrada* of one's birth is fierce, and as you wander the streets you will see the parishes' animal symbols repeated on flags, plaques, and carvings.

The Duomo dominating Siena's skyline

Bus station ↑

Train station

Via della Galluzza leads to the house of St. Catherine, Siena's patron saint *(see p410)*.

The Baptistry has fine frescoes and a font with reliefs by Donatello, Jacopo della Quercia, and Ghiberti.

VIA D. GALLUZZA

PIAZZA INDIPENDENZA

VIA DI DIACCETO

VIA DI FONTEBRANDA

VIA DI CITTÀ

VIA DEI PELLEGRINI

VIA FRANCIOSA

PIAZZA SAN GIOVANNI

VIC. D. CAMPANE

★ Duomo

Striped black and white marble pillars, surmounted by a carved frieze of the popes, support the Duomo's vaulted ceiling, painted blue with gold stars to resemble the night sky (see p410).

Each tier of the Duomo's bell tower has one more window than the floor below.

Cafés and shops fill the streets around Piazza del Duomo.

VIA DEL FUSARI

VIA DEL POGGIO

VIA DI CITTÀ

PIAZZA DEL DUOMO

VIA DEL CAPITANO

KEY

   Suggested route

0 meters		300
0 yards		300

Museo dell'Opera del Duomo

The museum (see p410) houses weathered sculptures from the cathedral, including this battered she-wolf suckling Romulus and Remus.

For hotels and restaurants in this region see pp456–61 and pp462–7

Loggia della Mercanzia
*This graceful arcade (1417)
was used by Siena's medieval
merchants and money dealers.*

**Tourist
information**

Palazzo Piccolomini,
built in 1460, now
holds the Sienese state
archives. Many of the
original painted
wooden bindings
are on display.

VIA BANCHI DI SOTTO

VIA RINALDINA

VIA DI PANTANETO

VIA DEL PORRIONE

VIA DI SALICOTTO

PIAZZA
DEL
CAMPO

PIAZZA
DEL
MERCATO

VIA DUPRÈ

★ Palazzo Pubblico
*The graceful Gothic town
hall was completed in
1342. At 102 m (330 ft),
the bell tower, the Torre
del Mangia, is the second
highest medieval tower
ever built in Italy.*

Fonte Gaia
*The reliefs on the fountain
are 19th-century copies of
the 15th-century originals
by Jacopo della Quercia.*

STAR SIGHTS

★ Duomo

★ Palazzo Pubblico

🏛 Palazzo Pubblico
Piazza del Campo 1. *Tel 0577-22 62
30.* **Museo Civico & Torre del
Mangia** 🕐 daily. 🌑 Dec 25. 🎟
Although the Palazzo Pubblico
(1297–1342) continues in its
ancient role as Siena's town
hall, the **Museo Civico** is also
housed here. Many of the
medieval rooms, some decorated with paintings of the
Sienese School, are open to
the public. They include the
main council chamber, or Sala
del Mappamondo, named
after a map of the world
painted here by Ambrogio
Lorenzetti in the early 14th
century. One wall is covered
by Simone Martini's fresco
Maestà (1315), which depicts
the Virgin in Majesty. The Sala
della Pace houses the famous
*Allegory of Good and Bad
Government*, a pair of frescoes
by Lorenzetti finished in 1338.
In the palace courtyard is
the magnificent **Torre del
Mangia** bell tower, which
offers superb views of the city.

🏛 Piazza del Campo
Italy's loveliest piazza
occupies the site of the old
Roman forum, and for much
of Siena's early history was
the city's principal marketplace. The Council of Nine,
Siena's ruling body, gave the
order for work to start on the
piazza in 1293. The red brick
paving was finished in 1349.
It is divided into nine sections,
representing not only the
authority of the council, but
also the protective folds of
the Madonna's cloak. The
piazza has been the focus of
city life ever since, a setting
for executions, bullfights, and
the drama of the Palio. Cafés,
restaurants, and fine medieval
palazzi now line the square,
which is dominated by the
Palazzo Pubblico and the
Torre del Mangia.

**Piazza del Campo, viewed from the
top of the Torre del Mangia**

Exploring Siena

Once a capital to rival Florence, Siena is still unspoiled and endowed with the grandeur of the age in which it was at its peak (1260–1348). The magnificent Duomo is one of Italy's greatest cathedrals. The best place to begin an exploration of the historic city center is Piazza del Campo and the surrounding maze of medieval streets. Siena's hilly position means that walks through the city are rewarded with countless sudden views of the surrounding countryside.

Massacre of the Innocents, a detail from the Duomo's marble floor

Richly decorated façade of Siena's Duomo

🏛 Duomo
Piazza del Duomo. **Tel** 0577-28 30 48. 🕐 daily. 🌑 Nov–May: 1:30–5:30pm.
Museo dell'Opera del Duomo *Tel* 0577-28 30 48. 🕐 mid-Mar–Oct: 9am–7pm daily; Nov–mid-Mar: 10am–5pm daily. 🌑 Jan 1, Dec 25. 🖼

Siena's cathedral (1136–1382) is a spectacular example of Pisan-influenced Romanesque-Gothic architecture. Had the 14th-century plan to create a new nave come to fruition, it would have become the largest church in Christendom, but the idea was abandoned when the Black Death of 1348 virtually halved the city's population. Among the Duomo's treasures are sculptural masterpieces by Nicola Pisano, Donatello, and Michelangelo, a fine inlaid marble floor, and a magnificent fresco cycle by Pinturicchio.

In the side aisle of the unfinished nave, which has been roofed over, is the **Museo dell'Opera del Duomo**. The museum is devoted mainly to sculpture removed from the exterior of the Duomo, including a tondo (circular relief) of a Madonna and Child, probably by Donatello. The highlight is Duccio's huge altarpiece, *Maestà* (1308–11), which depicts the *Madonna and Child* on one side, and *Scenes from the Life of Christ* on the other.

🏛 Pinacoteca Nazionale
Via San Pietro 29. **Tel** 0577-28 11 61. 🕐 daily. 🌑 Mon pm, Jan 1, Dec 25. 🖼 🖼

Housed in the Palazzo Buonsignori, this gallery contains an unsurpassed collection of paintings by artists of the Sienese School. Highlights include Duccio's *Madonna dei Franceschi* (1285) and Simone Martini's *The Blessed Agostino Novello and Four of his Miracles* (c.1330).

🏛 San Domenico
Piazza San Domenico. 🕐 daily.

The preserved head of the city's patroness, St. Catherine of Siena (1347–80), can be seen in a gilded tabernacle on the altar of a chapel dedicated to her in this huge, barn-like Gothic church. The chapel itself was built in 1460 and is dominated by Sodoma's frescoes (1526), which show Catherine in states of religious fervor. The church has the only portrait of St. Catherine considered authentic, painted by her friend Andrea Vanni.

St. Catherine's house, the **Casa di Santa Caterina**, is also a popular shrine for visitors to Siena.

🏛 Fortezza Medicea
Viale Maccari. **Fortezza** 🕐 daily. **Enoteca Italica** *Tel* 0577-28 88 11. 🕐 noon–8pm Mon, noon–1am Tue–Sat. 🖼

This huge red-brick fortress was built by Cosimo I in 1560, following Siena's defeat by Florence in the 1554–5 war. After an 18-month siege, during which more than 8,000 Sienese died, the town's banking and wool industries were suppressed by the Florentines.

The fortress now houses the **Enoteca Italica**, where you can taste and buy Italian wines.

THE PALIO

The Palio is Tuscany's most celebrated festival and it occurs in the Campo each year on July 2 and August 16. This bareback horse race was first recorded in 1283, but it may have had its origins in Roman military training. The jockeys represent Siena's 17 *contrade* (districts) and the horses are chosen by the drawing of lots. Preceded by days of colorful pageantry and heavy betting, the races themselves last only 90 seconds each, the winner being rewarded with a silk *palio* (banner).

Drummer taking part in the Palio's noisy pre-race pageant

The skyline of San Gimignano, bristling with medieval towers

the 17th centuries. Major 15th-century works include Masaccio's *St. Paul*, Gentile da Fabriano's radiant *Madonna of Humility*, and Donatello's reliquary bust of *San Rossore*.

🏛 Museo Nazionale di San Matteo
Piazza San Matteo 1. *Tel 050-54 18 65.* 🕙 Tue–Sun. 🖼

San Gimignano ❺

Siena. 🏘 *7,000.* 🚌 🚏 ℹ️ *Piazza del Duomo 1 (0577-94 00 08).* 🗓 *Thu.* 🎉 *San Gimignano (Jan 31).*

The thirteen towers that dominate San Gimignano's skyline were built by rival noble families in the 12th and 13th centuries, when the town's position on the main pilgrim route to Rome brought it great prosperity. The plague of 1348, and later the diversion of the pilgrim route, led to its economic decline and its miraculous preservation.

Full of good restaurants and shops, the town is also home to many fine works of art. The **Museo Civico** holds works by Pinturicchio, Benozzo Gozzoli, and Filippino Lippi, while the church of **Sant'Agostino** has a Baroque interior by Vanvitelli (c.1740) and a fresco cycle on *The Life of St. Augustine* by Benozzo Gozzoli (1465).

Florence ❻

See pp412–25.

Pisa ❼

🏘 *90,000.* ✈ *Galileo Galilei, 5 km (3 miles) S.* 🚉 🚌 ℹ️ *Piazza Duomo (050-56 04 64).* 🗓 *Wed & Sat.* **www**.pisa.turismo.it

In the Middle Ages, Pisa's navy dominated the western Mediterranean. Trade with Spain and North Africa brought vast wealth, reflected in the city's splendid buildings. The **Duomo**, begun in 1064, is a magnificent example of Pisan-Romanesque architecture, its four-tiered façade an

intricate medley of creamy colonnades and blind arcades. Inside, highlights include a pulpit (1302–11) by Giovanni Pisano and a mosaic of *Christ in Majesty* by Cimabue (1302).

Begun in 1173 on sandy silt subsoil, the famous **Leaning Tower** (Torre Pendente) was completed in 1350. The tower has attracted many visitors over the centuries, including Galileo, who came here to conduct experiments on falling objects. Recent engineering work has reduced the tower's tilt to approximately 4.12 m (13.5 ft).

The graceful **Baptistry** was begun in 1152 and finished a century later by Nicola and Giovanni Pisano.

The **Museo Nazionale di San Matteo** holds Pisan and Florentine art from the 12th to

Lucca ❽

🏘 *85,000.* 🚉 🚌 ℹ️ *Piazza Santa Maria 35 (0583-91 99 31).* 🗓 *Wed, Sat, 3rd Sun of month (antiques).*

The city of Lucca is still enclosed within its 17th-century walls, and visitors can stroll along the ramparts, which were converted into a public park in the early 19th century. Within the walls, narrow lanes wind among dark medieval buildings, opening suddenly to reveal stunning churches and piazzas, including the vast Piazza del Anfiteatro, which traces the outline of the old Roman amphitheater. The finest of the churches are all Romanesque: **San Martino**, the 11th-century cathedral, **San Michele in Foro**, built on the sight of the old Roman forum, and **San Frediano**.

The Baptistry in front of Pisa's Duomo, with the Leaning Tower behind

Florence ⑥

Florence is a monument to the Renaissance, the artistic and cultural reawakening of the 15th century. The buildings of Brunelleschi and the paintings and sculptures of artists such as Botticelli and Michelangelo turned the city into one of the world's greatest artistic capitals. During this time Florence was at the cultural and intellectual heart of Europe, its cosmopolitan atmosphere and wealthy patrons, such as the Medici, providing the impetus for a period of unparalleled artistic growth. The legacy of the Renaissance draws many visitors to the city today, with its numerous museums, galleries, churches, and monuments the major attractions. Florence's best sights are encompassed within such a compact area that the city seems to reveal its treasures at every step.

SIGHTS AT A GLANCE

Bargello ⑥
Boboli Gardens ⑭
Duomo pp416–17 ①
Galleria dell'Accademia ④
Museo di Storia
   della Scienza ⑩
Palazzo Pitti ⑬
Palazzo Vecchio ⑨
Piazza della Signoria ⑧
Ponte Vecchio ⑫
San Lorenzo ②
San Marco ⑤
Santa Croce ⑦
Santa Maria Novella ③
Uffizi pp422–4 ⑪

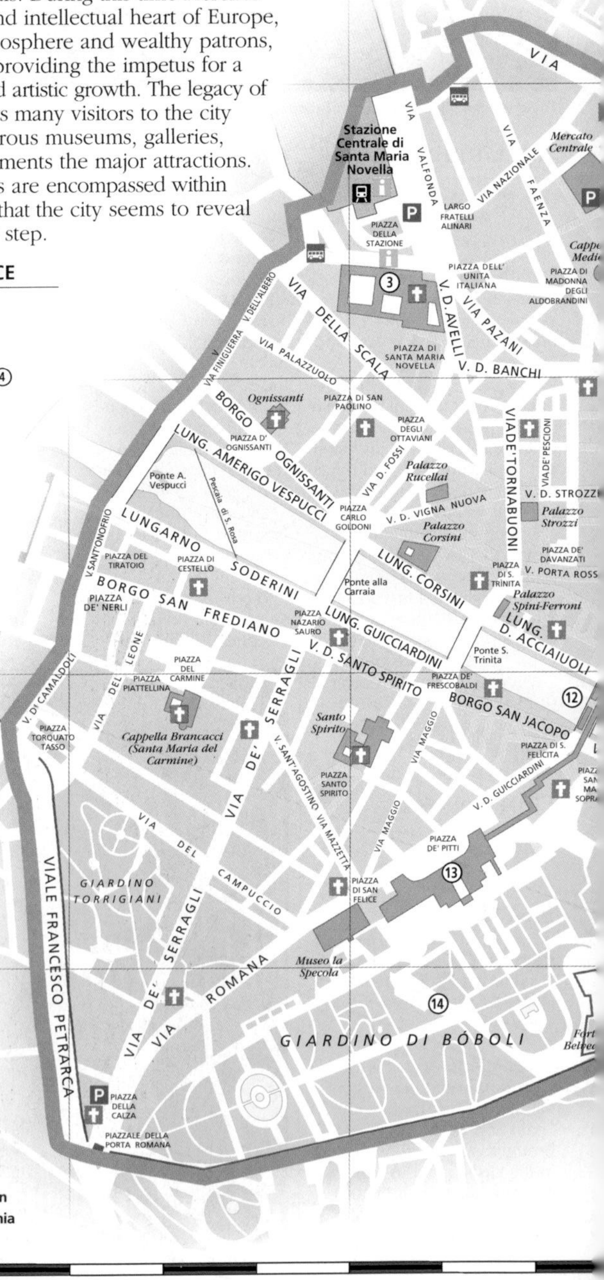

Michelangelo's *David* in
the Galleria dell'Accademia

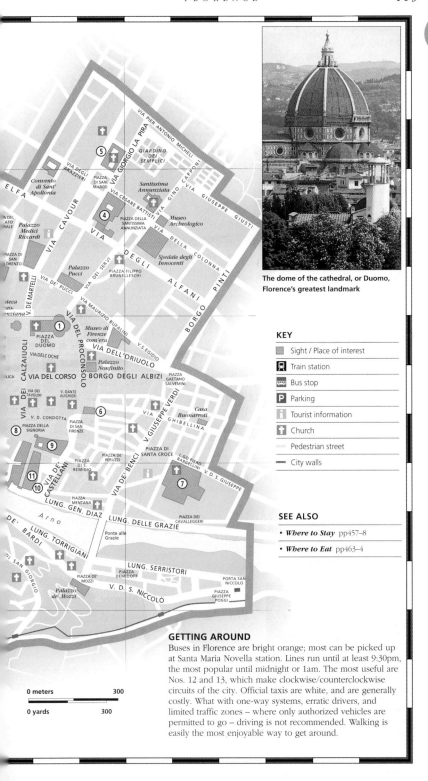

The dome of the cathedral, or Duomo, Florence's greatest landmark

KEY

Sight / Place of interest

Train station

Bus stop

Parking

Tourist information

Church

Pedestrian street

City walls

SEE ALSO

- *Where to Stay* pp457–8

- *Where to Eat* pp463–4

GETTING AROUND

Buses in Florence are bright orange; most can be picked up at Santa Maria Novella station. Lines run until at least 9:30pm, the most popular until midnight or 1am. The most useful are Nos. 12 and 13, which make clockwise/counterclockwise circuits of the city. Official taxis are white, and are generally costly. What with one-way systems, erratic drivers, and limited traffic zones – where only authorized vehicles are permitted to go – driving is not recommended. Walking is easily the most enjoyable way to get around.

0 meters   300

0 yards   300

Duomo ①

See pp416–17.

San Lorenzo ②

Piazza di San Lorenzo. 🚌 *many routes.*
Basilica *Tel* 055-21 66 34. ◯ *Mon–
Sat.* ● *religious hols.* 🖼 **Biblioteca**
Tel 055-21 44 43. ◯ *am Mon–Sat.*
Tel public hols. **Cappelle Medicee**
Piazza di Madonna degli Aldobrandini.
Tel 055-29 48 83. ◯ *daily (am only
public hols).* ● *alternate Mon & Sun
of month, Jan 1, May 1 & Dec 25.* ⓺

San Lorenzo was the parish
church of the Medici family,
who lavished their wealth on
its adornment. Rebuilt in
Renaissance Classical style in
1419, the outer façade was
never completed.

The inner façade of the
Basilica was designed by
Michelangelo. Cosimo il
Vecchio, founder of the Medici
dynasty, is buried under a
stone slab before the High
Altar. The bronze pulpits in the
nave are Donatello's last
works. Opposite is Bronzino's
vast fresco of the human form
in various poses (1659).

The **Biblioteca Mediceo-
Laurenzia**, which housed the
family's manuscripts, has an
elaborate sandstone staircase,
desks, and ceilings designed
by Michelangelo in 1524.

The **Cappelle Medicee**
incorporate three sacristies
which epitomize different
periods of art. Donatello's
decoration of the Old
Sacristy contrasts
with the design
of the New
Sacristy

Detail from Donatello pulpit, San Lorenzo

Façade of Santa Maria Novella, redesigned by Alberti in 1456–70

by Michelangelo. The latter's
funerary figures (1520–34)
around its walls are among
his greatest works. The
Chapel of the Princes (1604),
is opulently decorated with
inlaid semiprecious stones
and bright frescoes. Six Grand
Dukes of the Medici family
are buried here.

Santa Maria Novella ③

Piazza di Santa Maria Novella. 🚌 *A,
11, 12, 36, 37.* ⓺ **Church** *Tel* 055-
21 92 57. ◯ *daily (pm only Fri–Sun &
religious hols).* 🖼 **Museum** *Tel* 055-
28 21 87. ◯ *9am–2pm Sat–Thu.* ●
Jan 1, Easter Sun, May 1. 🖼 ⓺

The Gothic church of Santa
Maria Novella, built by the
Dominicans between 1279 and
1357, contains some of the
most important works of art in
Florence. The interior displays
a number of superb
frescoes, including
Masaccio's *Trinity*
(c.1428), which is
renowned as a master-
piece of perspective
and portraiture. The
close spacing of the
nave piers at the east
end accentuates the
illusion of length. The
Tornabuoni Chapel
contains Ghirlandaio's
famous fresco cycle,
*The Life of John the
Baptist* (1485). In the
Filippo Strozzi Chapel,
Lippi's dramatic frescoes

show St. John raising Drusiana
from the dead and St. Philip
slaying a dragon. Boccaccio
set the beginning of *The
Decameron* in this chapel.
The Strozzi Tomb (1493) is
by Florentine sculptor
Benedetto da Maiano.

The 14th-century frescoes
in the Strozzi Chapel are by
two brothers (Nardo di Cione
and Andrea Orcagna) and
were inspired by Dante's
Divine Comedy.

Beside the church is a
walled cemetery with grave
niches. The cloisters on the
other side of the church form
a museum. The Green
Cloister's name derives from
the green tinge to Uccello's
Noah and the Flood frescoes,
damaged by the 1966 floods.
The adjoining Spanish
Chapel contains frescoes
on the theme of salvation
and damnation.

Galleria dell'Accademia ④

Via Ricasoli 60. 🚌 *many routes.*
Tel 055-29 48 83. ◯ *Tue–Sun
(until midnight Jun–Sep).* ● *Mon &
public hols.* 🖼 ⓺

The Academy of Fine Arts in
Florence, founded in 1563,
was the first school in Europe
set up to teach drawing,
painting, and sculpture.

Since 1873, many of Michelangelo's most important works
have been in the Accademia.
Perhaps the most famous of

all dominates the collection: Michelangelo's *David* (1504). This colossal nude depicts the biblical hero who killed the giant Goliath; it established Michelangelo, then aged 29, as the foremost sculptor of his time. The statue was moved here from the Palazzo Vecchio in 1873 to protect it from the elements.

Michelangelo's other masterpieces include a statue of St. Matthew finished in 1508, and the *Quattro Prigioni* (four prisoners), sculpted between 1521 and 1523. The muscular figures struggling to free themselves from the stone are among the most dramatic of his works.

The gallery contains an important collection of paintings by 15th- and 16th-century Florentine artists, and many major works including the *Madonna del Mare* attributed to Botticelli (1445–1510), Pacino di Bonaguida's *Tree of Life* (1310), and *Venus and Cupid* by Jacopo Pontormo (1494–1556). Also on display is an elaborately painted wooden chest, the *Cassone Adimari* (c.1440) by Lo Scheggia. It was originally used as part of a bride's trousseau, and is covered with details of Florentine daily life, clothing, and architecture.

The Salone della Toscana (Tuscany Room) exhibits more modest 19th-century sculpture and paintings by members of the Accademia.

Fra Angelico's *Annunciation*, in the monastery of San Marco

San Marco ⑤

Piazza di San Marco. 🚌 many routes. 🚻 partial. **Church Tel** *055-28 76 28.* ◯ *daily (pm only Sun and religious hols).* **Museum Tel** *055-29 48 83.* ◯ *daily.* ⬤ *Jan 1, May 1, Dec 25, 2nd & 4th Mon and 1st, 3rd, & 5th Sun each month.* 🎫 🚻

The church of San Marco, and the monastery built around it, date from the 13th century. Following the transfer of the site to the Dominicans of Fiesole by Pope Eugene IV in 1436, Cosimo il Vecchio paid a considerable sum for its reconstruction, overseen by his favorite architect, Michelozzo. The single-naved church holds valuable works of art, and the funerary chapel of St. Antony is considered Giambologna's main work of architecture.

To the right of the church, the oldest part of the monastery is now a museum. It contains a remarkable series of devotional frescoes by Fra Angelico. The former Pilgrims' Hospice houses *The Deposition* (1435–40), a poignant scene of the dead Christ; his *Crucifixion* (1441–2) can be seen in the Chapter House.

There are over 40 cells adorned with frescoes by Fra Angelico. *The Annunciation* (c.1445) demonstrates his mastery of perspective. Relics of the fiery orator Savonarola (1452–98), dragged from here and executed in Piazza della Signoria, are also on display.

The monastery houses Europe's first public library, designed by Michelozzo in a light and airy colonnaded hall. Valuable manuscripts and bibles are held here.

A scene from Lo Scheggia's *Cassone Adimari* in the Galleria dell'Accademia

Duomo ①

Set in the heart of Florence, Santa Maria del
Fiore – the Duomo, or cathedral, of
Florence – dominates the city with its
enormous dome. Its sheer size was typical of
Florentine determination to lead in all things,
and to this day, no other building stands
taller in the city. The Baptistry, with its
celebrated doors, is one of Florence's oldest
buildings, dating perhaps from the 4th century.
In his capacity as city architect, Giotto
designed the Campanile in 1334; it was
completed in 1359, 22 years after his death.

★ Campanile
*At 85 m (276 ft),
the Campanile is
6 m (20 ft) shorter
than the dome. It
is clad in white ,
green and pink
Tuscan marble. The
first-floor reliefs are
by Andrea Pisano.*

Gothic windows

**The Neo-Gothic
marble façade** echoes
the style of Giotto's
campanile, but was
only added in
1871–87.

★ Baptistry
*Colorful 13th-century mosaics
illustrating* The Last Judgment *decorate
the ceiling above the large octagonal
font where many famous Florentines,
including Dante, were baptized.*

The Baptistry doors
demonstrate the
artistic ideas that
led to the
Renaissance.

Main
entrance

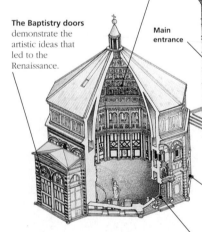

The east doors
known as the "Gate
of Paradise" (1424–52)
were made by Ghiberti.
The originals are in the
Duomo museum.

STAR FEATURES

★ Dome

★ Baptistry

★ Campanile

South Door Panels
*This scene from the south
doors of the Baptistry,
completed by the sculptor
Andrea Pisano in 1336,
depicts* The Baptism of
St. John the Baptist.

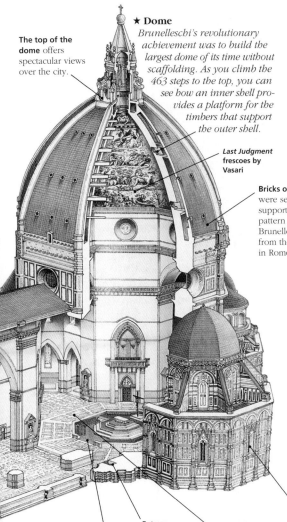

★ Dome
Brunelleschi's revolutionary achievement was to build the largest dome of its time without scaffolding. As you climb the 463 steps to the top, you can see how an inner shell provides a platform for the timbers that support the outer shell.

The top of the dome offers spectacular views over the city.

Last Judgment frescoes by Vasari

Bricks of varying size were set in a self-supporting herringbone pattern – a technique Brunelleschi copied from the Pantheon in Rome.

VISITORS' CHECKLIST

Piazza del Duomo. *Tel* 055-230 28 85. 🚌 1, 6, 14, 17, 23. ⬜ Mon – Sat, Sun pm. 🔴 religious hols. ♿ ⬜ **Crypt** ⬜ Mon–Sat. 📷 **Dome** ⬜ Mon–Sat. 📷 **Campanile** ⬜ daily. 📷 **Baptistry** ⬜ pm Mon–Sat; Sun am. All buildings 🔴 Jan 1 & religious hols. 📷 **www.**duomofirenze.it

Chapels at the East End
The three apses each house five chapels and are crowned by a miniature copy of the dome. The 15th-century stained glass is by Lorenzo Ghiberti and other artists.

The octagonal marble sanctuary around the High Altar was decorated by Baccio Bandinelli.

Entrance to steps to the dome

Marble Pavement
As you climb up to the dome, you can see that the 16th-century marble pavement, designed in part by Baccio d'Agnelo, is laid out as a maze.

Steps to Santa Reparata
The crypt contains the remains of the church of Santa Reparata, built in the 4th century, and demolished in 1296 to make way for a cathedral which would more fittingly represent Florence and rival those of Siena and Pisa.

Bargello ⑥

Via del Proconsolo 4. *Tel 055-29 48 83.* 🚌 *A, 14.* ⏰ *8:30am–1:50pm daily.* ● *1st, 3rd & 5th Sun and 2nd & 4th Mon of each month, Jan 1, May 1, Dec 25.* 📷 ♿

Florence's second-ranking museum after the Uffizi, the Bargello houses Italy's finest collection of Renaissance sculpture and some superb Mannerist bronzes. Begun in 1255, the fortress-like building was initially the town hall but later home to the chief of police (the *Bargello*). The renovated building opened as one of Italy's first national museums in 1865.

The key exhibits range over three floors, beginning with the Michelangelo Room. Here visitors can admire *Bacchus* (1497), the sculptor's first large free-standing work, a delicate circular relief depicting the *Madonna and Child* (1503–5), and *Brutus* (1539–40), his only known portrait bust. Among other sculptors' works in the same room is *Mercury* (1564), Giambologna's famous bronze. Across the courtyard, two more rooms contain exterior sculptures removed from sites around the city and an external

Donatello's statue of *David* in the Bargello

staircase leads to a first-floor collection of bronze birds by Giambologna. To the right, the Salone del Consiglio Generale contains the cream of the museum's Early Renaissance sculpture, including Donatello's heroic *St George* (1416) and his androgynous *David* (c.1430), famous as the first free-standing nude by a Western artist since antiquity.

Beyond the Salone, the Bargello's emphasis shifts to the applied arts, with room after room devoted to rugs, ceramics, silverware, and

Gaddi's night scene fresco in the Baroncelli Chapel, Santa Croce

other *objets d'art*. The Salone del Camino on the second floor holds the finest collection of small bronzes in Italy. Benvenuto Cellini (1500–71) is among the artists featured.

Santa Croce ⑦

Piazza di Santa Croce. *Tel 055-246 61 05.* 🚌 *C, 23.* ⏰ *daily (Sun: pm only).* 📷 ♿

The Gothic church of Santa Croce (1294) contains the tombs and monuments of many famous Florentines, among them Galileo, Michelangelo, and Machiavelli, as well as radiant early 14th-century frescoes by Giotto and his gifted pupil, Taddeo Gaddi. In 1842 the Neo-Gothic campanile of Santa Croce was added, and the façade in 1863.

In the Basilica, Rossellino's effigy (1447) of Leonardo Bruni, the great Humanist depicted in serene old age, is a triumph of realistic portraiture. Close by it is the 15th-century *Annunciation* by Donatello. The remainder of the monastic buildings scattered around the cloister form a museum of religious painting and sculpture.

The museum houses Cimabue's *Crucifixion*, a 13th-century masterpiece damaged in the flood of 1966, and Gaddi's magnificent *Last Supper* (c.1355–60).

Of the church's many chapels, the most famous is the Bardi Chapel, decorated by Giotto with frescoes of the life of St. Francis (1315–23). The Peruzzi Chapel houses further Giotto frescoes. Gaddi's 1338 fresco in the Baroncelli Chapel of an angel appearing to sleeping shepherds is notable as the first true night scene in Western art.

In the cloister alongside the church is Brunelleschi's Cappella de' Pazzi (Pazzi Chapel), a masterpiece of Renaissance architecture. The delicate gray stonework of the domed chapel is set off by white plaster, which is inset with terra-cotta roundels of the Evangelists by Luca della Robbia.

Piazza della Signoria ⑧

🚌 *A, B.*

Piazza della Signoria has been at the heart of Florence's political and social life for centuries. Citizens were once summoned to public meetings here, and the square's statues

Statue of Cosimo I in Piazza della Signoria

celebrate events in the city's history. That of Grand Duke Cosimo I (1595) by Giambologna commemorates the man who subjugated all Tuscany, while Ammannati's *Neptune Fountain* honors Tuscan naval victories. Michelangelo's original *David* stood here until 1873, when it was replaced by a copy. Donatello's original statue of the heraldic lion of Florence, known as the *Marzocco*, is now in the Bargello.

Other notable statues include Cellini's bronze *Perseus*, and *The Rape of the Sabine Women* by Giambologna, carved from a single block of marble.

Painting of Penelope in Eleonora's rooms in the Palazzo Vecchio

The Putto fountain in Vasari's courtyard, at the Palazzo Vecchio

Palazzo Vecchio ⑨

Piazza della Signoria. **Tel** 055-276 84 65. ▥ A, B. ◯ daily (Thu & Sun, am only). ◉ Jan 1, Easter, May 1, Aug 15, Dec 25. ▨ ⓐ

Palazzo Vecchio, completed in 1322, has retained its external medieval appearance, and its imposing bell tower dominates the square. The "Old Palace" still fulfils its original role as Florence's town hall. Much of the interior was remodeled for Duke Cosimo I in the mid-16th century by Vasari, whose work includes several frescoes that laud the Duke's achievements.

The palazzo is entered via a courtyard, in which stands Verrochio's *Putto* fountain. A staircase leads to the Salone dei Cinquecento, which is graced by Michelangelo's

Victory statue (1525), and to the tiny Studiolo decorated by 30 of Florence's leading Mannerist painters.

Eleonora of Toledo, wife of Cosimo I, had a suite of rooms in the palace, decorated with scenes of virtuous women. Highlights of the palace include the paintings by Il Bronzino in the Cappella di Eleonora and the loggia, which has wonderful views over the city. The Sala dei Gigli (Room of Lilies), contains frescoes of Roman heroes and Donatello's *Judith and Holofernes*.

A new Children's Museum is open at weekends to families, and several formerly secret passages and private rooms can now be visited.

Museo di Storia della Scienza ⑩

Piazza de' Giudici 1. **Tel** 055-26 53 11. ◯ summer: 9:30am–5pm Mon–Sat (to 1pm Tue & Sat); winter: 9:30am–5pm Mon & Wed–Sat (to 1pm Tue). ◉ public hols. ▨

This lively museum devotes numerous rooms on two floors to different scientific themes, illustrating each with fine displays and beautifully made early scientific instruments. It is also something of a shrine to the Pisa-born scientist, Galileo Galilei (1564–1642), and features two of his telescopes as well as large-scale reconstructions of his experiments into motion, weight, velocity, and

acceleration. These are sometimes demonstrated by the attendants. Other exhibits come from the Accademia del Cimento (Academy for Experimentation), founded in memory of Galileo by Grand Duke Ferdinand II in 1657.

Some of the finest exhibits include early maps, antique microscopes, astrolabes, and barometers. Of equal interest are the huge 16th- and 17th-century globes illustrating the motion of the planets and stars. Be sure to see Lopo Homem's 16th-century map of the world, showing the newly charted coasts of the Americas, and the nautical instruments invented by Sir Robert Dudley, an Elizabethan marine engineer employed by the Medicis.

The second-floor rooms display fine old clocks, calculators, and a horrifying collection of 19th-century surgical instruments, weights and measures, and graphic anatomical models.

Armillary sphere, Museo di Storia della Scienza

The Florentine Renaissance

Fifteenth-century Italy saw a flowering of the arts and scholarship unmatched in Europe since Ancient Greek and Roman times. It was in wealthy Florence that this artistic and intellectual activity, later dubbed the Renaissance, was at its most intense. The patronage of the rich banking dynasty, the Medici, rulers of Florence from 1434, was lavished on the city, especially under Lorenzo the Magnificent (1469–92), and the city aspired to become the new Rome. Architects turned to Classical models for inspiration, while the art world, with a new understanding of perspective and anatomy, produced a series of painters and sculptors that included such giants as Donatello, Botticelli, Leonardo da Vinci, and Michelangelo.

ITALY IN 1492

- Republic of Florence
- Papal States
- Aragonese possessions

THE PROCESSION OF THE MAGI

Benozzo Gozzoli's fresco (1459) in the Palazzo Medici-Riccardi, Florence, depicts members of the Medici family and other contemporary notables. It contains references to the church council held in Florence in 1439, which, it was hoped, would effect a reconciliation between the Church of Rome and the Eastern Church.

Giuliano was the younger son of Piero de' Medici.

Piero de' Medici, Lorenzo's father, was given the nickname "the Gouty."

Self-portrait of the artist

Pope Leo X
There were two Medici popes: Giovanni, who reigned as Leo X (1513–21), and Giulio, who took his place as Clement VII (1521–34). Corruption in the church under Leo inspired Luther and the growth of Protestantism.

TIMELINE

1420 Martin V re-establishes papacy in Rome

Cosimo de' Medici

1434 Cosimo de' Medici comes to power in Florence

1435 Publication of *On Painting* by Alberti, which contains the first system for the use of linear perspective

1425

1436 Brunelleschi completes dome of Florence cathedral

1450

1452 Birth of Leonardo da Vinci

1453 Fall of Constantinople

1464 Death of Cosimo il Vecchio

1469 Lorenzo the Magnificent becomes ruler of Florence

Michelangelo's Sculpture

The Quattro Prigioni *(see p415), unfinished works intended for the tomb of Pope Julius II, illustrate Michelangelo's ideal of liberating "the figure imprisoned in the marble."*

Filippo Brunelleschi

In order to realize his design for the dome of Florence's cathedral, Brunelleschi devised engineering techniques decades ahead of their time.

RENAISSANCE ARCHITECTURE

In place of the spectacular Gothic style, Renaissance architects favored the rational, orderly, human scale of Greek and Roman buildings. The various stories of a palazzo were designed according to Classical proportions and there was a widespread revival in the use of Roman arches and the Doric, Ionic, and Corinthian orders of columns.

Palazzo Strozzi
(1489–1536) is a typical Florentine building of the period. Rusticated stonework gives an impression of great strength. Decorative detail is largely on the upper stories above the fortress-like ground floor.

Lorenzo de' Medici (the Magnificent) is depicted as one of the three kings traveling to Bethlehem.

The Medici emblem of seven balls appears on the trappings of Lorenzo's horse.

The Spedale degli Innocenti, *an orphanage, was one of Brunelleschi's first buildings in Florence. Slender Corinthian columns support a delicate arcade.*

Humanism

Carpaccio's painting St. Augustine in his Study *(1502) is thought to show Cardinal Bessarion (c.1395–1472), one of the scholars who revived interest in Classical philosophy, especially Plato.*

	1498 Savonarola executed; Machiavelli secretary to ruling Council in Florence	**1513** Giovanni de' Medici crowned Pope Leo X	**1532** Machiavelli's book *The Prince* is published, five years after his death

1530 Medici restored as rulers of Florence

1475 — **1500** — **1525**

1475 Birth of Michelangelo

1483 Birth of Raphael

1494 Italy invaded by Charles VIII of France. Florence declared republic under leadership of the religious fanatic Savonarola

1512 Michelangelo completes Sistine Chapel ceiling

Niccolò Machiavelli

Uffizi ⑪

The Uffizi was built in 1560–80 as a suite of offices *(uffici)* for Duke Cosimo I's new Tuscan administration. The architect, Vasari, used iron reinforcement to create an almost continuous wall of glass on the upper story. From 1581 Cosimo's heirs, beginning with Francesco I, used this well-lit space to display the Medici family art treasures, thus creating what is now the oldest art gallery in the world.

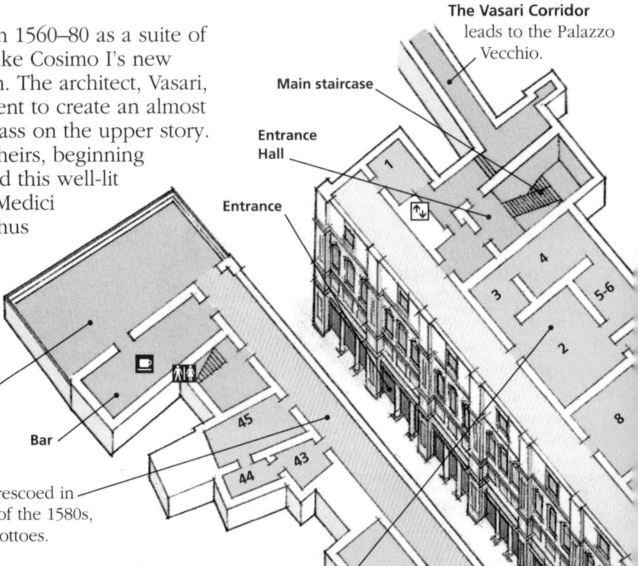

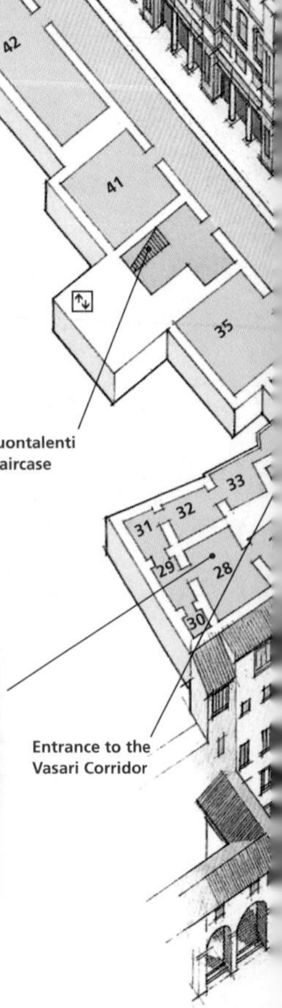

The Vasari Corridor leads to the Palazzo Vecchio.

Main staircase

Entrance Hall

Entrance

The café terrace merits a visit for its unusual views of Piazza della Signoria *(see pp418–19).*

Bar

Corridor ceilings are frescoed in the "grotesque" style of the 1580s, inspired by Roman grottoes.

GALLERY GUIDE

The Uffizi art collection is housed on the top floor. Ancient Greek and Roman sculptures are displayed in the corridor running round the inner side of the building. The paintings are hung in a series of rooms off the main corridor, in chronological order, to reveal the development of Florentine art from Gothic to High Renaissance and beyond. Most of the best-known paintings are grouped in rooms 7–18. To avoid the long queues, book your visiting time in advance.

The Ognissanti Madonna
Giotto's grasp of spatial depth in this altarpiece (1310) was a milestone in the mastery of perspective.

Buontalenti staircase

Entrance to the Vasari Corridor

STAR PAINTINGS

- ★ The Duke and Duchess of Urbino by Piero della Francesca
- ★ The Birth of Venus by Botticelli
- ★ The Holy Family by Michelangelo
- ★ The Venus of Urbino by Titian

★ The Venus of Urbino *(1538)*
Titian's sensuous nude was condemned for portraying the goddess in such an immodest pose.

VISITORS' CHECKLIST

Piazzale degli Uffizi 6.
*Tel 055-238 86 51
(to reserve time of visit call
055-29 48 83).* B, 23.
8:15am–6:50pm Tue–Sun
*(last adm: 45 mins before
closing).* Jan 1, May 1, Dec
25. *(partial)*
Vasari Corridor *Tel 055-2654
321 for guided tours.*
www.uffizi.firenze.it

★ **The Duke and Duchess of Urbino** *(1460)*
*Piero della Francesca's panels are among the first
true Renaissance portraits. He even recorded the
Duke's hooked nose – broken by a sword blow.*

The Tribune,
decorated in
red and gold,
contains the
works that
the Medici
valued most.

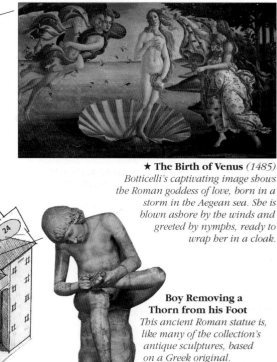

★ **The Birth of Venus** *(1485)*
*Botticelli's captivating image shows
the Roman goddess of love, born in a
storm in the Aegean sea. She is
blown ashore by the winds and
greeted by nymphs, ready to
wrap her in a cloak.*

**Boy Removing a
Thorn from his Foot**
*This ancient Roman statue is,
like many of the collection's
antique sculptures, based
on a Greek original.*

**Vasari's Classical
Arno façade**

KEY

- East Corridor
- West Corridor
- Arno Corridor
- Gallery Rooms 1–45
- Non-exhibition space

★ **The Holy Family** *(1507)*
*Michelangelo's painting, the
first to break with the
convention of showing
Christ on the Virgin's lap,
inspired subsequent Mannerist
artists through its expressive
handling of color and posture.*

Exploring the Uffizi's Collection

The Uffizi houses some of the greatest art of the Renaissance. Accumulated over the centuries by the Medici, the collection was first housed in the Uffizi in 1581, and eventually bequeathed to the people of Florence by Anna Maria Lodovica, the last of the Medici (1667–1743). Roman statues collected by the Medici are on display in the Arno Corridor, but the pride of the gallery is its matchless collection of paintings.

Madonna of the Long Neck by Parmigianino (c.1534)

GOTHIC ART

Following the collection of statues and antiquities in room 1, the gallery's next six rooms are devoted to Tuscan art from the 12th to the 14th centuries, notably works by Cimabue, Duccio, and Giotto, the three greatest artists of this period. Giotto (1266–1337) introduced a degree of naturalism new to Tuscan art. This is apparent in the range of emotions expressed by the angels and saints in his *Ognissanti Madonna* (1310). There are also fine works by Ambrogio and Pietro Lorenzetti, and Simone Martini of the Sienese School.

EARLY RENAISSANCE

A better understanding of geometry and perspective allowed Renaissance artists to create an illusion of space and depth in their works. No artist was more obsessed with perspective than Paolo Uccello

(1397–1475), whose *Battle of San Romano* is displayed in room 7. Portraits include two panels by Piero della Francesca (1410–92), depicting the Duke and Duchess of Urbino, while Fra Filippo Lippi's *Madonna and Child with Angels* (1455–66) is a work of great warmth and humanity.

For most visitors, however, the famous Botticellis in rooms 10–14 are the highlight of the gallery. In *The Birth of Venus*, Botticelli replaces the Virgin with the Classical goddess of love, while in *Primavera* (1480), he breaks with Christian religious painting to depict the pagan rite of spring.

HIGH RENAISSANCE AND MANNERISM

Room 15 contains works attributed to the young Leonardo da Vinci. The evolution of his masterly style can be traced in *The Annunciation* (1472–5) and his unfinished *Adoration of the Magi* (1481). The octagonal Tribune (room 18) displays some of the best-loved pieces of the Medici collection, including the 1st century BC *Medici Venus*, considered the most erotic of ancient statues. There are also paintings of family members, including Bronzino's fine portrait of Eleonora of Toledo, Cosimo I's wife (1545).

Rooms 19 to 23 illustrate the spread of Renaissance ideas and techniques beyond Florence to other parts of Italy and beyond. The Umbrian artist Perugino (1446–1523)

and northern European painters such as Dürer (1471–1528) are well represented.

Michelangelo's *Holy Family* (1507), in Room 25, is striking for its vibrant colors and the curious twisted pose of the Virgin. This painting had great influence on the next generation of Tuscan painters, notably Bronzino (1503–72), Pontormo (1494–1556), and Parmigianino (1503–40), whose *Madonna of the Long Neck* with its contorted anatomy and unusual colors is a classic example of what came to be known as Mannerism.

Sublime examples of High Renaissance art located nearby include Raphael's *Madonna of the Goldfinch* and Titian's notorious *Venus of Urbino* (1538), considered by many to be the most beautiful nude ever painted.

LATER PAINTINGS

Rooms 41–45 of the Uffizi hold paintings acquired by the Medici in the 17th and 18th centuries. These include works by Rubens (1577–1640) and van Dyck (1599–1641) and three paintings by Caravaggio – *Bacchus* (c.1589), *The Sacrifice of Isaac* (c.1590), and *Medusa* (1596–8). Room 44 is dedicated to northern European painting, and features *Portrait of an Old Man* (1665) by Rembrandt.

Madonna of the Golfinch (1506) by Raphael

Ponte Vecchio ⑫

🚌 *many routes.*

The Ponte Vecchio, the oldest surviving bridge in the city, was designed by Taddeo Gaddi, and built in 1345. The three-arched bridge rests on two stout piers with boat-shaped cutwaters. Its picturesque shops were originally occcupied by black-smiths, butchers, and tanners (who used the river as a convenient garbage dump). They were evicted in 1593 by Duke Ferdinando I and replaced by jewelers and goldsmiths who were able to pay higher rents. A bust of the most famous of Florence's goldsmiths, Benvenuto Cellini (1500–71), is located in the middle of the bridge.

The elevated Vasari Corridor runs along the eastern side of the bridge, above the shops. It was designed in 1565 to allow the Medici to move from the Palazzo Vecchio to Palazzo Pitti via the Uffizi, without having to mix with the public. The Mannelli family refused to demolish their tower to make way for the corridor, and it stands there defiantly to this day. The corridor passes around it, supported on brackets.

The "Old Bridge," at its most attractive when viewed at sunset, was the only one to escape destruction during World War II. Visitors today come to admire the views and to browse among the antiques and specialized jewelry shops.

The massive Renaissance Palazzo Pitti, home to several museums

Palazzo Pitti ⑬

Piazza Pitti. 🚌 D, 11, 36, 37. **Tel** *055-29 48 83.* ⏲ *8:15am–6:50pm Tue–Sun.* ⬤ *public hols.* 📷 ♿

Palazzo Pitti was originally built for the banker Luca Pitti, but his attempt to outrival the Medici backfired when costs of the building, begun in 1457, bankrupted his heirs. The Medici moved in and subsequent rulers of the city lived here. Today the richly decorated rooms exhibit many treasures from the Medici collections.

The Palatine Gallery contains numerous works of art and ceiling frescoes glorifying the Medici. Raphael's *Madonna dalla Seggiola* (c.1515) and Titian's *Portrait of a Gentleman* (1540) are among the exhibits.

On the first floor of the south wing, the royal apartments – Appartamenti Reali – are opulently decorated with ornate gold and white stuccoed ceilings. The rooms are hung with portraits of the Medici family and decorated with beautiful frescoes and Gobelins tapestries.

Other collections at the Palazzo include the Galleria d'Arte Moderna, with mainly 19th-century works of art, the Galleria del Costume, opened in 1983, which reflects changing taste in courtly fashions, and the Museo degli Argenti which displays the family's lavish tastes in silverware and furniture.

L'Isolotto with Giambologna's *Oceanus Fountain***, Boboli Gardens**

Boboli Gardens ⑭

Piazza de' Pitti. 🚌 D, 11, 36, 37. ⏲ *daily.* ⬤ *1st & last Mon of month, Jan 1, May 1, Dec 25.* 📷 ♿

Laid out behind the Palazzo Pitti, the Boboli Gardens are an excellent example of highly stylized Renaissance gardening. Formal box hedges lead to peaceful groves of holly and cypress trees, inter-spersed with Classical statues.

Highlights include the stone amphitheater where early opera performances were staged and L'Isolotto (Little Island), with its statues of dancing peasants around a moated garden. The Grotta Grande is a Mannerist folly, which houses several statues including *Venus Bathing* (1565) by Giambologna and Vincenzo de' Rossi's *Paris with Helen of Troy* (1560).

View of the Ponte Vecchio and the Arno at sunset

For hotels and restaurants in this region see pp457–8 and pp463–4

Portofino Peninsula ❾

🛏️ 🚌 ℹ️ *Via Roma 35, Portofino (0185-26 90 24).*
www.apttigullio-liguria.it

Portofino is the most exclusive harbor and resort town in Italy, crammed with the yachts of the wealthy. Cars are not allowed in the village but boats run regularly between here and the resort of **Santa Margherita Ligure**. Boats also run to the **Abbazia di San Fruttuoso**, an 11th-century abbey situated on the other side of the peninsula.

Further west along the coast is **Punta Chiappa**, a rocky promontory famous for the changing colors of the sea. Other attractive resorts along the Ligurian coast include the fishing village of **Camogli**, **Rapallo** and its patrician villas, and romantic **Portovenere**.

Genoa ❿

🏛️ *660,000.* ✈️ *Cristoforo Colombo 6 km (4 miles) W.* 🛏️ 🚂 🚌 ℹ️ *Aeroporto C. Colombo (010-601 52 47); Stazione Principe (010-246 26 33).* 🎭 *Mon, Wed, & Thu.* 🎟️ *International Ballet Festival (Jul); Fiera Nautica (Oct).*

The most important commercial port in Italy, Genoa (Genova in Italian) also possesses palaces, paintings,

Gothic façade of San Lorenzo, Genoa

and sculptures dotted around the city, which are among the finest in northwestern Italy.

The austere-looking **Palazzo Reale**, one-time residence of the Kings of Savoy, has a highly ornate Rococo interior, a collection of paintings including works by Parodi and van Dyck, and an attractive garden. Opposite the palace is the old **University** (1634), built on four levels and designed by the architect Bartolomeo Bianco.

Palazzo Bianco, on the **Via Garibaldi**, contains the city's prime collection of paintings, including works by Lippi, van Dyck, and Rubens. Across the

street, **Palazzo Rosso** houses works by Dürer and Caravaggio, and 17th-century frescoes by local artists.

Once the seat of the doges of Genoa and now an arts and cultural center, the **Palazzo Ducale** is located between **San Lorenzo** cathedral with its attached museum, and **Il Gesù**, a Baroque church.

All that remains of the Gothic church of **Sant' Agostino**, bombed in World War II, is the bell tower, which is decorated with colored tiles. Two surviving cloisters of its surrounding monastery have been turned into the **Museo di Sant' Agostino**, which contains the city's collection of sculptural and architectural fragments.

🏛️ **Palazzo Reale**
Via Balbi 10. **Tel** 010-271 010 236.
⏰ *Tue–Sun (Tue & Wed pm only).*
🚫 *Jan 1, Apr 25, May 1, Dec 25.*

🏛️ **Palazzo Bianco**
Via Garibaldi 1. **Tel** 010-557 2193.
⏰ *Tue–Sun.* 🔗 **Palazzo Rosso**
Tel 010-247 63 51. ⏰ *Tue–Sun.* 🔗

🏛️ **Museo di Sant' Agostino**
Piazza Sarzano 35. **Tel** 010-251 12 63. ⏰ *Tue–Sun.* 🚫 *public hols.*
🔗 ♿

Portofino's famous harbor, showing the large yachts moored here

The Dome of San Lorenzo in Turin

Turin ⓫

🏙 940,000. ✈ Caselle 15 km
(9 miles) N. 🚌 🚆 🛈 Stazione
Porta Nuova (011-53 51 81). 🚢 Sat.
🎭 Festa di San Giovanni (Jun 24).

Home of the Fiat car company, the famous Shroud, and the Juventus football team, Turin (Torino to the Italians) is also a town of grace and charm, with superb Baroque architecture.

Many of Turin's monuments were erected by the House of Savoy (rulers of Piedmont and Sardinia) from their capital here, before Italian unification in 1861 made the head of the House of Savoy King of Italy.

The **Museo Egizio** – one of the world's great collections of Egyptian artifacts – was amassed by Bernardo Drovetti, Napoleon's Consul General in Egypt. Wall and tomb paintings, papyri, sculptures, and a reconstruction of the 15th-century BC **Rock Temple of Ellessya** are among its marvels.

The **Galleria Sabauda**, in the same building, was the House of Savoy's main painting collection, and houses a stunning array of works by Italian, French, Flemish, and Dutch masters.

Other notable buildings in the city include **San Lorenzo**, the former Royal Chapel designed by Guarino Guarini (1624–83), which boasts an extraordinary geometric dome. Inside the **Palazzo Reale**, seat of the Savoys, the **Armeria Reale** holds one of the largest arms collections in the world.

The **Duomo** (1497–8), Turin's cathedral dedicated to St. John the Baptist, is the only example of Renaissance architecture in the city. Inside, the **Cappella della Sacra Sindone**, also designed by Guarini, houses the famous Turin Shroud.

Inside the **Palazzo Madama**, the recently renovated **Museo Civico d'Arte Antica** contains a variety of Classical and antique treasures.

🏛 **Museo Egizio**
Via Accademia delle Scienze 6. *Tel* 011-561 77 76. �”Tue–Sun. ● Jan 1, May 1, Dec 25. 🏷 🔌 🛈

🏛 **Palazzo Reale**
Piazzetta Reale. *Tel* 011-436 14 55. �”Tue–Sun. ● Jan 1, May 1, Dec 25. 🏷 🔌 🔌 🔲 🛈

🏛 **Armeria Reale**
Piazza Castello 191. *Tel* 011-54 38 89. �” 1:30–7:30pm Tue & Thu, 8:30am–2pm Wed & Fri, 10:30am–7:30pm Sat & Sun. ● Jan 1, Aug 15, Dec 25. 🏷

The imposing façade of the Baroque Basilica di Superga

Environs

In the countryside near Turin, two superb monuments to the House of Savoy are worth visiting. About 9 km (5 miles) southwest of Turin, **Stupinigi** is a magnificent hunting lodge, sumptuously decorated with frescoes and paintings. It has a vast collection of 17th- and 18th-century furniture.

The Baroque **Basilica di Superga**, on a hill to the east of Turin, offers good views of the city. Its mausoleum commemorates kings of Sardinia and other royals.

🏛 **Stupinigi**
Piazza Principe Amedeo 7.
Tel 011-358 12 20. 🚌 63 to Piazza Caio Mario, then 41. �” Tue–Sun. ● Jan 1, Dec 25. 🏷 🔌
www.mauriziano.it

🔓 **Basilica di Superga**
Strada Basilica di Superga 73. *Tel* 011-898 00 83. 🚊 Sassi, then 79 bus. �” daily. **Tombs** 🏷

THE TURIN SHROUD

The most famous – and most dubious – holy relic of them all is kept in Turin's Duomo. The shroud, said to be the sheet in which the body of Christ was wrapped after the Crucifixion, bears the imprint of a man with a side wound, and bruises, possibly from a crown of thorns.

The shroud's early history is unclear, but the House of Savoy was in possession of it around 1450, and displayed it in Guarini's chapel in the Duomo from 1694. The "original" shroud sits in a silver casket inside an iron box within a marble coffer. This has been placed inside an urn on the chapel altar. A replica shroud is on view. Tests done in 1988 claiming the shroud to be only a 12th-century relic have recently been discredited. The shroud may be 1,300–3,000 years old, pending further tests.

The supposed face of Christ imprinted on the Turin Shroud

The giant Gothic Duomo in central Milan, crowned with spires

Milan ⓬

🏛 1,350,000. ✈ Malpensa 55 km (34 miles) NW; Linate 8 km (5 miles) E. 🚉 🚌 🛈 Via Marconi 1 (02-72 52 43 01). 🛍 daily, major market Sat. 🎉 Sant'Ambrogio (Dec 7). www.milanoinfotourist.com

Center of fashion and business, Milan (Milano in Italian) also has a wealth of impressive sights reflecting its long and checkered history.

An important trading center since it was founded by the Romans in 222 BC, Milan's central position made it a favored location for the empire's rulers. It was here that Emperor Constantine declared that Christianity was officially recognized, following his own conversion (known as the Edict of Milan, AD 313).

By the Middle Ages Milan was one of many cities in Lombardy which opposed the power of the Holy Roman Emperor. A period of local dynastic rule followed the fall of the region to the Visconti family in 1277. They were succeeded by the Sforzas during the Renaissance.

These dynasties became great patrons of the arts, with the result that Milan has acquired a host of artistic treasures. Today this chic, bustling, and prosperous metropolis also offers opportunities for designer shopping and gastronomic pleasures.

Situated at the very heart of Milan, the giant **Duomo** is one of the largest Gothic churches in the world. The roof is extraordinary with 135 spires and innumerable statues and gargoyles. Inside, there are remarkable stained-glass windows, bas-reliefs, and a medieval treasury. More religious artifacts can be seen in the **Museo del Duomo**, located in the Palazzo Reale.

An ornate shopping arcade completed in 1878, the **Galleria Vittorio Emanuele II** links the Piazza del Duomo with the Piazza della Scala. It boasts a superb metal and glass roof crowned with a central dome, has mosaic floors, and houses stylish shops and restaurants.

The Neo-Classical **Teatro alla Scala** opened in 1778 and is among the most prestigious opera houses in the world. Closed until 2005 for renovation, its stage is one of the largest in Europe. The adjoining **Museo Teatrale** displays past sets and costumes and offers a glimpse of the auditorium.

The **Castello Sforzesco**, a symbol of Milan, was initially the palace of the Visconti family. Francesco Sforza, who became lord of Milan in 1450, embellished it, turning it into a magnificent Renaissance residence. The building has a forbidding exterior, a delightful interior, and contains an impressive collection of furniture, antiquities, and paintings. Michelangelo's unfinished sculpture, known as the *Rondanini Pietà*, can also be seen here.

Milan's finest art collection is held in the imposing 17th-century Palazzo di Brera. Major works of Italian Renaissance and Baroque painters including *The Marriage of the Virgin* by Raphael, and Mantegna's

The glass dome of the Galleria Vittorio Emanuele II in Milan

Dead Christ, hang in the 38 rooms of the **Pinacoteca di Brera**. Works by some of Italy's 20th-century artists are also on display.

The beautiful 15th-century Renaissance convent of **Santa Maria delle Grazie**, in the southwest of the city, is a must-see because it contains one of the key images of western civilization: the *Last Supper* (or *Cenacolo*) of Leonardo da Vinci. The large wall painting has deteriorated badly but remains an iconic work of great subtlety.

Sant'Ambrogio is a mainly 10th-century Romanesque basilica dedicated to the patron saint of Milan whose tomb lies in the crypt. The 4th-century church of **San Lorenzo** holds an important collection of Roman and early Christian remains.

⌂ Duomo
Piazza del Duomo. 🖼 for roof. ♿
Museo del Duomo Tel 02-86 03 58 02. ◯ Tue–Sun. ● public hols. 🖼

♦ Castello Sforzesco
Piazza Castello.
Tel 02-88 46 37 00. ◯ Tue–Sun. ● public hols. ♿

🏛 Pinacoteca di Brera
Via Brera 28. **Tel** 02-72 26 31.
◯ Tue–Sun. ● Jan 1, May 1, Dec 25. 🖼 ♿ ▯

⌂ Santa Maria delle Grazie
Piazza Santa Maria delle Grazie 2.
Cenacolo Tel 02-89 42 11 46.
◯ Tue –Sun (booking compulsory).
● public hols. 🖼 ♿

Lake Maggiore ⑬

🚂 to Stresa and Laveno. 🚌
🚢 Navigazione Lago Maggiore (032-33 03 92). 🛈 Piazza Marconi 16, Stresa (0323-301 50).

Lake Maggiore is a long expanse of water that nestles right against the mountains and stretches away into Alpine Switzerland. In the center lie the exquisite Borromean islands named after the chief patron of the lake, St. Carlo Borromeo, of whom there is a giant statue in **Arona**.

Further up the western coast of the lake is **Stresa**, the chief resort and main jumping-off point for visits to the islands. From here **Monte**

Statue of Carlo Borromeo, patron saint of Lake Maggiore, in Arona

Mottarone, a snow-capped peak offering spectacular panoramic views, can be reached by cable car.

Lake Como ⑭

🚂 to Como and Lecco. 🚌 🚢 Navigazione Lago di Como (024-67 61 01). 🛈 Piazza Cavour 17, Como (031-269 712).

Set in an idyllic landscape, Como has long attracted visitors who come to walk in the hills or to go boating. The long, narrow lake, also

known as Lario, is shaped like an upside-down Y, and offers fine views of the Alps.

In the heart of the town of **Como** lies the elegant Piazza Cavour. The beautiful 14th-century **Duomo** nearby has 15th- and 16th-century reliefs and paintings, and fine tombs.

Bellagio, at the junction of the "Y," has spectacular views, and is one of the most popular spots on Lake Como.

In the lakeside town of **Tremezzo**, the 18th-century **Villa Carlotta** is adorned with sculptures and celebrated for its terraced gardens.

Lake Garda ⑮

🚂 to Desenzano and Orta San Giulio. 🚌 🚢 Navigazione Lago di Garda (800-55 18 01). 🛈 Viale Marconi 2, Sirmione (030-91 61 14).

Garda, the largest of the northern lakes, borders the three regions of Trentino, Lombardy, and Veneto.

Hydrofoils and catamarans ply the lake, offering stops at **Sirmione**, site of a medieval castle, **Gardone** with the curiosity-filled **Villa il Vittoriale**, and **Salò** where Mussolini established a short-lived Republic in 1943.

Lake Como, one of the most attractive summer resorts of northern Italy

The Arena, Verona's Roman amphitheater – the setting for spectacular summer opera performances

Mantua ⑯

🏛 55,000. 🚏 🚌 🛈 Piazza Andrea Mantegna 6 (0376-43 24 32). 🛐 Thu.

A striking if stern-looking city of fine squares and aristocratic architecture, Mantua (Mantova in Italian) is bordered on three sides by lakes. It was the birthplace of the poet Virgil and playground for three centuries of the Gonzaga dukes. Mantua was also the setting for Verdi's opera *Rigoletto*, and is mentioned in Shakespeare's *Romeo and Juliet*. These theatrical connections are celebrated in local street-names and monuments and are reinforced by the presence in the town of the 18th-century **Teatro Scientifico Bibiena**, a masterpiece of late Baroque theater architecture.

Mantua is focused on three attractive main squares. Piazza Sordello is the site of the **Palazzo Ducale**, the vast former home of the Gonzaga family which also incorporates

a 14th-century fortress and a basilica. The frescoes by Mantegna in the **Camera degli Sposi** (1465–74), are a highlight. They portray the Gonzaga family and court, and the room is completed by a light-hearted *trompe l'oeil* ceiling. The nearby **Duomo** has an 18th-century façade and fine interior stuccoes by Giulio Romano (c.1492–1546).

Piazza dell'Erbe is dominated by the Basilica di Sant' Andrea (15th century), designed largely by the early Renaissance architect and theorist, Alberti.

Across town is the early 16th-century Palazzo del Tè, designed as the Gonzaga family's summer retreat. This extraordinary palace is decorated with frescoes by Giulio Romano and has rooms lavishly painted with horses and signs of the zodiac.

🏛 **Palazzo Ducale**
Piazza Sordello. *Tel 0376-22 48 32.* 🕙 Tue–Sun. ● Jan 1, May 1, Dec 25. 🖼 **Camera degli Sposi** *Tel 041-241 18 97.* 🕙 mid-Sep–mid-Dec: Tue–Sun.

Verona ⑰

🏛 261,000. ✈ Villafranca 14 km (9 miles) SW. 🚏 🚌 🛈 Via degli Alpini 9 (045-806 86 80). 🛐 daily. 🎭 Estate Teatrale Veronese (Jun–Aug); Opera Festival (Jun–Sep).

Verona, a large and prosperous city of the Veneto region, boasts magnificent Roman ruins, second only to those of Rome itself, as well as some important medieval monuments.

The Arena, Verona's Roman amphitheater completed in AD 30, is the third largest in the world. Bullfights, fairs, and opera productions are staged here. Other Roman sites include the Roman Theater, and artifacts from Roman times can be seen in the Museo Archeologico.

The tragic story of Romeo and Juliet, first set here by Luigi da Porto in the 1520s and immortalized by Shakespeare, has inspired local monuments such as Romeo's House and the so-called Tomb of Juliet. Verona's focal point is Piazza Erbe, scene of colorful markets for 2,000 years.

The ornate tombs of members of the Scaglieri family, who ruled the city for 127 years from 1263, are situated beside the entrance to the church of Santa Maria Antica. Another legacy of the family is Castelvecchio, an impressive castle built by Cangrande II between 1355 and 1375. There is a fine art gallery in the castle, which has a collection of 15th-century late Renaissance Madonnas.

The 13th-century façade of the Palazzo Ducale in Mantua

For hotels and restaurants in this region see pp456–61 and pp462–7

Built in 1125–35 to house the shrine of Verona's patron saint, **San Zeno Maggiore** is the most ornate Romanesque church in northern Italy, famous for its unusual medieval bronze door panels.

The **Duomo** also dates from the 12th century and displays Titian's *Assumption*. Other notable medieval churches in Verona are **San Fermo Maggiore** with many interior frescoes including the *Annunciation* by Pisanello (1377–1455), and **Sant' Anastasia**, which houses 15th-century frescoes and holy water stoups supported by figures of beggars known locally as *i gobbi*.

⚑ Arena
Piazza Brà. **Tel** 045-800 32 04.
◯ daily. ◉ Jan 1, Dec 25–26. ☒

♟ Castelvecchio
Corso Castelvecchio 2. **Tel** 045-806 26 11. ◯ daily. ☒ ◻ ☒ (audio).

Vicenza ⑱

☒ 116,000. ☒ ☒ ℹ Piazza Matteotti 12 (0444-32 08 54). ☒ Tue & Thu. ☒ Concert season (May–Jun).

Vicenza is celebrated for its splendid, varied architecture. Known as the city of Andrea Palladio (1508–80), stone-mason turned architect, it offers a unique opportunity to study the evolution of his distinctive style.

Piazza dei Signori at the heart of Vicenza is dominated by the Palazzo della Ragione, known also as the **Basilica**. Palladio's first public

The illusionistic stage set of the Teatro Olimpico in Vicenza

commission, it has a roof like an upturned boat, and a balus-trade bristling with statues. Beside it stands the 12th-century **Torre di Piazza**.

The **Loggia del Capitaniato**, to the northwest, was built by Palladio in 1571. Its upper rooms contain the city's council chamber.

Europe's oldest surviving indoor theater, the **Teatro Olimpico** was begun by Palladio in 1579 and completed by his pupil, Vincenzo Scamozzi. It was Scamozzi who created the permanent stage, built largely of wood and plaster and painted to look like marble. It represents Thebes, a Greek city, and uses perspective to create an illusion of depth.

Palladio was also responsible for the design of **Palazzo Chiericati** which houses the **Museo Civico**, but the epitome of his work can be seen in the villa known as **La Rotonda**, located in the countryside to the south of Vicenza.

Memorial to Andrea Palladio in Vicenza

⛪ Piazza dei Signori
Basilica **Tel** 0444-32 36 81.
◯ Tue–Sun. ☒

⛪ Teatro Olimpico
Piazza Matteotti. **Tel** 0444-22 28 00. ◯ Tue–Sun. ◉ 1 Jan, 25 Dec.
☒ ♿

⛪ La Rotonda
Via Rotonda 25. **Tel** 0444-32 17 93.
Villa ◯ Mar–Nov: Wed. ☒
Garden ◯ Tue–Thu. ☒

The Basilica di Sant'Antonio in Padua, with its Byzantine domes

Padua ⑲

☒ 220,000. ☒ ☒ ℹ Piazzale della Stazione (049-875 20 77).
☒ Mon–Sat at Piazza delle Erbe.
☒ Cultural Festival (Jun–Sep).

Padua is an old university town with an illustrious academic history. The city (Padova in Italian) has two major attractions – the **Basilica di Sant' Antonio**, one of the most popular sites of pilgrimage in Italy, and the **Cappella degli Scrovegni**, a beautifully decorated chapel. The exotic Basilica was built from 1232 to house the remains of the great Franciscan preacher, St. Antony of Padua.

The chapel (1303) features a series of frescoes depicting the life of Christ, painted by Giotto. The **Museo Civico Eremitani** on the same site has a rich coin collection and an art gallery.

Other attractions include the **Duomo** and **Baptistry**, which contains one of Italy's most complete medieval fresco cycles (painted by Giusto de'Menabuoi in 1378), and the **Palazzo della Ragione**, built in 1218 to serve as Padua's law court and council chamber.

⛪ Cappella degli Scrovegni
Piazza Eremitani. **Tel** 049-201 00 20. ◯ daily (advance booking necessary). ◉ public hols. ☒ ♿

Venice ⑳

Created on a series of mud banks in a lagoon, with
canals in place of roads, Venice can truly claim to be
unique. Originally a province of the Byzantine
Empire, by the 12th century Venice was an
independent city-state and, through its control
of the spice and silk trade from the East, the
richest trading nation in Europe. The banks
of its canals are lined with magnificent
palaces dating from this period up until
the 18th century. By then Venice's
power and influence were waning.
It finally lost its independence
in 1797, since when this
astonishing city has remained
more or less frozen in time.

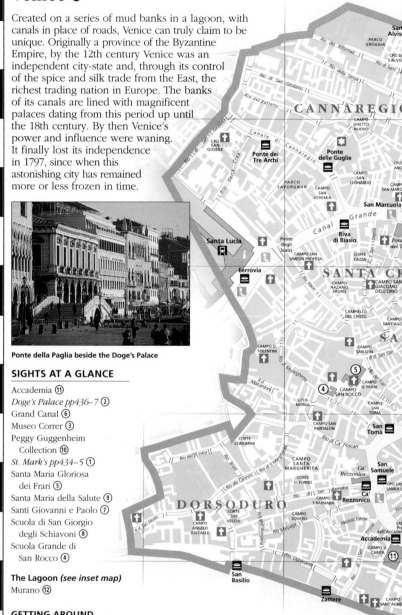

Ponte della Paglia beside the Doge's Palace

SIGHTS AT A GLANCE

Accademia ⑪
Doge's Palace pp436–7 ②
Grand Canal ⑥
Museo Correr ③
Peggy Guggenheim
   Collection ⑩
St. Mark's pp434–5 ①
Santa Maria Gloriosa
   dei Frari ⑤
Santa Maria della Salute ⑨
Santi Giovanni e Paolo ⑦
Scuola di San Giorgio
   degli Schiavoni ⑧
Scuola Grande di
   San Rocco ④

The Lagoon *(see inset map)*
Murano ⑫

GETTING AROUND

On land, the only way to get around Venice is by foot, and
strolling through the city's narrow streets is one its greatest
pleasures. By water, the *vaporetto (see p450)* water bus
plies the canals of the city and links it to the various lagoon
islands. More exotic craft include gondolas, which are very
expensive, and the more reasonable *traghetti* (gondola
ferries). The speediest means of travel is water taxi.

SEE ALSO

• *Where to Stay* p458

• *Where to Eat* p464

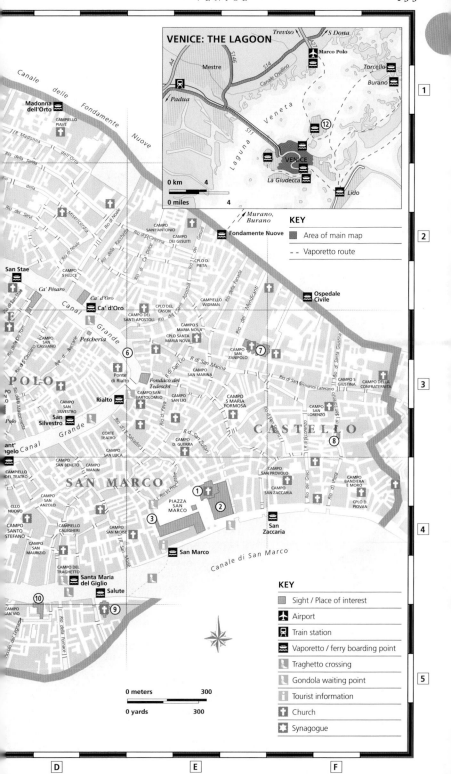

VENICE: THE LAGOON

Treviso

S Dona

Marco Polo

Mestre

Canale Oxillino

Torcello

Padua

Burano

Veneta

12

Laguna

VENICE

La Giudecca

Lido

0 km   4

0 miles   4

Murano, Burano

KEY

Area of main map

-- Vaporetto route

Canale delle Fondamente Nuove

Madonna dell'Orto

CAMPIELLO PIAVE

R Madonna dell'Orto

Rio della Sensa

Rio della Misericordia

Rio dei Servi

San Stae

Ca' Pésaro

CAMPO S FELICE

Ca' d'Oro

Ca' d'Oro

Canal

Grande

CPLO DEL CASON

Pescheria

CAMPO DEI SANTI APOSTOLI

Fondamente Nuove

CAMPO SANT'ANTONIO

CAMPO DEI GESUITI

CPLO D. PIETA

CAMPIELLO WIDMAN

Ospedale Civile

CAMPO S MARIA NOVA

CPLO SANTA MARIA NOVA

CAMPO S ZANIPOLO

7

POLO

6

Ponte di Rialto

Fondaco dei Tedeschi

CAMPO SAN BARTOLOMEO

Rialto

CAMPO SAN SILVESTRO

San Silvestro

Grande

CORTE TEATRO

CAMPO SAN LUCA

CAMPO D. GUERRA

CAMPO SAN MARINA

CAMPO SAN LIO

CAMPO S MARIA FORMOSA

R di San Lio

R di San Zulian

CASTELLO

CAMPO S GIOVANNI LATERANO

CAMPO S LORENZO

8

CAMPO S GIUSTINA

CAMPO DELLA CONFRATERNITA

Sant' angelo Canal

CAMPIELLO DEL TEATRO

CAMPO SAN BENETO

CAMPO MANIN

CAMPO SAN ANZOLO

CLLO NUOVO

CAMPO SANTO STEFANO

CAMPO SAN MAURIZIO

CAMPIELLO CALEGHERI

CAMPO SAN MOISE

CAMPO DEL TRAGHETTO

Santa Maria del Giglio

Salute

10

9

CAMPO SAN VIO

SAN MARCO

1

PIAZZA SAN MARCO

2

3

San Marco

CAMPO SAN PROVOLO

CAMPO SAN ZACCARIA

CAMPO BANDIERA E MORO

CPLO D. PIOVAN

San Zaccaria

Canale di San Marco

0 meters   300

0 yards   300

KEY

Sight / Place of interest

Airport

Train station

Vaporetto / ferry boarding point

Traghetto crossing

Gondola waiting point

Tourist information

Church

Synagogue

D

E

F

1

2

3

4

5

St. Mark's ①

The basilica blends architectural and decorative styles from East and West to create one of Europe's greatest buildings. Built on a Greek-cross plan and crowned with five huge domes, it is the third church to stand on this site. The first, built to enshrine the body of St. Mark in the 9th century, was destroyed by fire. The second was pulled down in the 11th century to make way for a truly spectacular edifice, reflecting the growing power of the Republic and its links with Byzantium. The dark interior is clad in wonderful mosaics, gleaming with gold. Many treasures – statues, icons, and the famous horses – were brought to St. Mark's after the 4th Crusade had plundered Constantinople in 1204.

★ Pentecost Mosaic
The interior of the dome above the nave is decorated with a 12th-century mosaic of the Holy Spirit descending on the Apostles in tongues of fire.

St. Mark flanked by Angels
The statues crowning the central arch were added in the early 15th century.

The atrium, or narthex, contains many fine mosaics, notably those of the Genesis Cupola showing the Creation.

The central arch features 13th-century carvings of the Labours of the Months.

★ Horses of St. Mark
The four horses are replicas of the gilded bronze originals, kept in the Museo Marciano, reached from the atrium.

Main entrance

★ Façade Mosaics
These are either heavily restored or replacements of the originals. This 17th-century work shows the body of St. Mark being smuggled out of Alexandria.

The Ascension Dome features a magnificent 13th-century mosaic of Christ surrounded by angels, the 12 Apostles, and the Virgin Mary.

VISITORS' CHECKLIST

Piazza San Marco. **Tel** 041-522 52 05. 🚤 San Marco. ⬭ Apr–Oct: 9:45am–5:30pm Mon–Sat, 2–4pm Sun; Nov–Mar: 9:45am–4:30pm Mon–Sat, 2–4pm Sun. ✠ sightseeing limited during services. 📷 📹 📷 ♿ Strict dress code applies in the church.

★ Pala d'Oro

The greatest treasure of St. Mark's is kept behind the high altar. The magnificent altarpiece, created originally in the 10th century, is made up of 250 gold panels, adorned with enamels and precious stones.

The altar canopy, or baldacchino, has alabaster columns carved with New Testament scenes.

St. Mark's body, thought to have been lost in the fire of 976, reappeared when the new church was consecrated in 1094. The remains are housed below the altar.

★ Treasury

This contains many treasures looted from Constantinople by the Venetians in 1204. This 11th-century silver-gilt reliquary is in the shape of a domed basilica.

Allegorical mosaics decorate the floor of the south transept.

Baptistry

The Tetrarchs

This porphyry sculptural group (4th-century Egyptian) may represent Diocletian, Maximian, Constantius, and Valerian – the four joint rulers of the Roman Empire c. AD 300, known as the tetrarchs.

STAR FEATURES

★ Mosaics

★ Horses of St. Mark

★ Pala d'Oro

★ Treasury

Doge's Palace ②

The official residence of the Venetian ruler (doge) was founded in the 9th century. The present palace owes its external appearance to the building work of the 14th and early 15th centuries. To create their airy Gothic masterpiece, the Venetians broke with tradition by perching the bulk of the palace (built of pink Veronese marble) on top of an apparent fretwork of loggias and arcades (built of white Istrian stone). A tour of the palace leads through a succession of richly decorated chambers and halls, ending with the Bridge of Sighs and the prisons.

Mars by
Sansovino

In the Sala del Collegio the doge would receive ambassadors. The ceiling is decorated with 11 paintings by Veronese.

The Sala del Senato was the home of the senate, which had some 200 members.

Anticollegio

Arco Foscari

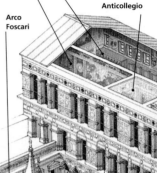

★ **Porta della Carta**
This 15th-century Gothic gate was the principal entrance to the palace. From it, a vaulted passageway leads to the Arco Foscari and the internal courtyard.

Exit

STAR FEATURES

★ Giants' Staircase
★ Porta della Carta
★ Sala del Maggior Consiglio

The balcony on the west façade was added in 1536 to mirror the early 15th-century balcony looking onto the quay.

★ **Giants' Staircase**
Statues by Sansovino of Neptune and Mars at the top of this late 15th-century staircase symbolize Venice's power at sea and on land. Doges were crowned with the glittering zogia or ducal cap on the landing.

Torture Chamber
Suspects under interrogation were hung on the walls of this room by cords tied around their wrists.

VISITORS' CHECKLIST

Piazzetta. **Tel** 041-271 59 11.
San Marco. Apr–Oct: 9am–7pm daily; Nov–Mar: 9am–5pm daily (last adm 1hr 30 mins before closing). Jan 1, Dec 25. (audio). limited.

The Sala del Consiglio dei Dieci was once the meeting place of the powerful Council of Ten.

Bridge of Sighs
The bridge was built in 1600 to link the palace with the state prisons. It reputedly acquired its name from the sighs of prisoners being led across it to face trial.

Sala della Bussola (Compass Room)

Drunkenness of Noah
This early 15th-century sculpture, symbolic of the frailty of man, is set on the corner of the palace.

Ponte della Paglia

Main entrance

★ Sala del Maggior Consiglio
This vast chamber was the meeting hall of Venice's Great Council. By the 16th century this had over 2,000 members. The entire end wall is taken up by Tintoretto's Paradise (1588–92).

Carpaccio's *Portrait of a Young Man in a Red Hat*, Museo Correr

Museo Correr ③

Procuratie Nuove. Entrance in Ala Napoleonica. *Tel* 041-240 52 11. San Marco. daily. Jan 1, Dec 25.

Teodoro Correr bequeathed his extensive collection of works of art to Venice in 1830, thus forming the core of the city's fine civic museum.

Its first rooms form a suitably Neoclassical backdrop for early statues by Antonio Canova (1757–1822). The rest of the floor covers the history of the Venetian Republic, with maps, coins, armor, and a host of doge-related exhibits.

The second floor contains the picture gallery. Works are hung chronologically, enabling one to trace the evolution of Venetian painting. The most famous are by Carpaccio: *Portrait of a Young Man in a Red Hat* (c.1490), and *Two Venetian Ladies* (c.1507). The Museo del Risorgimento on the same floor looks at the history of Venice until unification with Italy in 1866.

Scuola Grande di San Rocco ④

Campo San Rocco. *Tel* 041-523 48 64. San Tomà. daily. Jan 1, Easter, Dec 25. (audio).

Founded in honor of San Rocco (St. Roch), a saint who dedicated his life to helping the sick, the Scuola started out as a charitable

confraternity. Construction began in 1515. The work was financed by donations from Venetians keen to invoke San Rocco's protection, and the Scuola quickly became one of the wealthiest in Venice. In 1564 its members decided to commission Tintoretto to decorate its walls and ceilings. His earliest paintings, the first of over 50 works he eventually created for the Scuola, fill the small Sala dell'Albergo off the Upper Hall. His later paintings are in the Ground Floor Hall, just inside the entrance.

The ground floor cycle was executed in 1583–7, when Tintoretto was in his sixties, and consists of eight episodes from the life of Mary. They are remarkable for the tranquil serenity of paintings such as *The Flight into Egypt* and *St. Mary of Egypt*.

Scarpagnino's great staircase (1544–6), leads to the Upper Hall, which was decorated by Tintoretto in 1575–81. The ceiling is painted with scenes from the Old Testament. The three large square paintings in the center show episodes from the Book of Exodus, all alluding to the charitable aims of the Scuola in alleviating thirst, sickness, and hunger. The vast wall paintings feature episodes from the New Testament, linking with the ceiling paintings. Two of the most striking are *The Temptation of Christ*, which shows a handsome young Satan offering Christ two loaves of bread, and *The Adoration of the Shepherds*.

The carvings below the paintings were added in the 17th century by sculptor Francesco Pianta. They include (near the altar) a caricature of Tintoretto with his palette and brushes.

The Sala dell'Albergo contains perhaps the most breathtaking of all Tintoretto's masterpieces – the *Crucifixion* (1565). Henry James once remarked of this painting: "no single picture contains more of human life; there is everything in it, including the most exquisite beauty."

Santa Maria Gloriosa dei Frari ⑤

Campo dei Frari. *Tel* 041-275 04 62. San Tomà. Mon–Sat & Sun pm. Jan 1, Jan 6, Easter, Dec 25. unless attending mass.

More commonly known as the Frari (a corruption of Frati, meaning brothers), this vast Gothic church dwarfs the eastern area of San Polo. Its 83-m (272-ft) campanile is the tallest in the city after that of San Marco. The first church on the site was built by the Franciscans in 1250–1338, but was replaced by a larger building completed in the mid-15th century. The airy interior is striking for its sheer size and for the quality of its works of art, including masterpieces by Titian and Giovanni Bellini, a statue by Donatello, and several grandiose tombs.

The sacristy altarpiece *The Madonna and Child* (1488)

Detail from Tintoretto's *Flight into Egypt*, Scuola Grande di San Rocco

by Bellini, with its sublime use of color, is one of Venice's most beautiful Renaissance paintings. The main altarpiece is *The Assumption of the Virgin*, a spectacular, glowing work by Titian (1518), which draws the eye through the Renaissance rood screen to the altar. Between the altar and the screen is the Monks' Choir (1468), its three-tiered stalls lavishly carved with saints and Venetian city scenes.

The Tomb of Canova, a marble, pyramid-shaped tomb, was built after Canova's death in 1822 by his pupils. It is similar to a design Canova himself had planned for a memorial for Titian. The Titian monument in the shape of a triumphal arch that stands opposite was built by two of Canova's pupils in 1853.

View across the Grand Canal to the Pescheria (fishmarket)

High altar of the Frari church with Titian's *Assumption of the Virgin*

Grand Canal ⑥

🚤 *1 from Ferrovia and many others.*

The best way to view the Grand Canal as it winds through the heart of the city is from a *vaporetto*, or water bus. Several lines travel the length of the canal. The palaces lining the waterway were built over a span of five centuries and present a panoramic survey of the city's history, almost all bearing the name of some once-great Venetian family.

Nearly 4 km (2.5 miles) long, the canal varies in width from 30 to 70 m (100 to 230 ft) and is spanned by three bridges, the Scalzi, the Rialto, and the Accademia. After passing the Rialto, the canal doubles back on itself along a stretch known as La Volta (the bend). It then widens out and the views become more spectacular approaching San Marco. Façades may have faded and foundations rotted, yet the canal remains, in the words of the French ambassador in 1495, "the most beautiful street in the world."

Santi Giovanni e Paolo ⑦

Campo Santi Giovanni e Paolo (also signposted San Zanipolo). *Tel 041-523 59 13.* 🚤 *Fondamente Nuove or Ospedale Civile.* ⬜ *daily.* 🔵 *Sun am for mass.* ♿ 🚻

Known colloquially as San Zanipolo, Santi Giovanni e Paolo vies with the Frari as the city's greatest Gothic church. Built by the Dominicans in the 14th century, it is striking for its vast scale and architectural austerity. Known as the Pantheon of Venice, it houses monuments to no fewer than 25 doges. Among these are several fine works of art, executed by the Lombardi family and other leading sculptors. Pietro Lombardo created the magnificent tombs of the doges Nicolò Marcello (died 1474) and Pietro Mocenigo (died 1476). His masterpiece, the Tomb of Andrea Vendramin (died 1478), takes the form of a Roman triumphal arch.

The main doorway, which is decorated with Byzantine reliefs and carvings, is one of Venice's earliest Renaissance architectural works. On the right as you enter the church is a polyptych by Giovanni Bellini (c.1465) showing St. Vincent Ferrer, a Spanish cleric, flanked by St. Sebastian and St. Christopher.

THE GONDOLAS OF VENICE

The gondola has been a part of Venice since the 11th century. With its slim hull and flat underside, the craft is perfectly adapted to negotiating narrow, shallow canals. There is a slight leftward curve to the prow, which counteracts the force of the oar, preventing the gondola from going around in circles.

In 1562 it was decreed that all gondolas should be black to stop people making an ostentatious show of their wealth. For special occasions they were decorated with flowers. Today, gondola rides are expensive and usually taken by tourists.

Gondolas moored in a Venice canal

Scuola di San Giorgio degli Schiavoni ⑧

Calle Furlani. **Tel** *041-522 88 28.*
🚣 *San Zaccaria.* ⬭ *Tue–Sun (Sun: am only).* ⬤ *Jan 1, May 1, Dec 25 and other religious hols.* 📷

Within this small Scuola, established in 1451 and rebuilt in 1551, are some of the finest paintings of Vittore Carpaccio (c.1460–1525). Commissioned by the Schiavoni, or Dalmatian Slav trading community in Venice, Carpaccio's exquisite frieze (1502–08) shows scenes from the lives of three saints: St. George, St. Tryphon, and St. Jerome. Each episode of the narrative cycle is remarkable for its vivid coloring and minutely observed detail of Venetian life. *St. George Slaying the Dragon* and *The Vision of St. Jerome* are outstanding.

Santa Maria della Salute ⑨

Campo della Salute. **Tel** *041-274 39 11.* 🚣 *Salute.* ⬭ *daily.* 📷 *to sacristy.*

The great Baroque church of Santa Maria della Salute, standing at the entrance of the Grand Canal, is an imposing

The single-story palazzo housing the Peggy Guggenheim Collection

architectural landmark of Venice. Construction of the church, begun in 1630 by Baldassare Longhena, was not completed until 1687, five years after his death.

The comparatively sober interior of Santa Maria della Salute consists of a large octagonal space below the cupola and six chapels radiating from the ambulatory. The sculptural group around the grandiose high altar is by Giusto Le Corte and represents the Virgin and Child protecting the city of Venice from the plague.

In the sacristy to the left of the altar, Titian's early altarpiece *St. Mark Enthroned with St. Cosmas, St. Damian, St. Roch and St. Sebastian* (1511–12) and his dramatic ceiling paintings of *David and Goliath*, *Cain and Abel*, and *The Sacrifice of Isaac* (1540–9) are considered the finest paintings in the church. *The Wedding at Cana* (1551) on the wall opposite the entrance, is a major work by Jacopo Tintoretto.

The church was named *Salute*, which means both "health" and "salvation," in thanksgiving for the deliverance of the city from the plague epidemic of 1630. Each November, in a moving ceremony of remembrance, worshipers light candles and approach the church across a bridge of boats which spans the mouth of the Grand Canal.

Peggy Guggenheim Collection ⑩

Palazzo Venier dei Leoni. **Tel** *041-240 54 11.* 🚣 *Accademia.* ⬭ *Wed–Mon.* ⬤ *Dec 25.* 📷 📷 *(audio).* 🔲 🔲
www.guggenheim-venice.it

Intended as a four-story palace, the 18th-century Palazzo Venier dei Leoni in fact never rose beyond the ground floor – hence its nickname "The Unfinished Palace." In 1949 the building was bought by Peggy Guggenheim (1898–1979), an American collector, dealer, and patron of the arts. One of the most visited sights of Venice, the palace is the best place in the city to see modern art. The light-filled rooms and modern canvases are in striking contrast to the majority of the art on display in Venice.

Her collection consists of 200 fine paintings and sculptures, representing the 20th century's most influential modern art movements. The dining room has notable Cubist works of art, including *The Poet* by Pablo Picasso, and an entire room is devoted to Jackson Pollock, who was "discovered" by Guggenheim. There are also works by Braque, Chagall, Dalí, Klee, Mondrian, and Magritte, whose Surreal *Empire of Light* (1953–4) shows a night scene of a darkened house with bright daylight above.

The sculpture collection, which includes Constantin Brancusi's elegant *Bird in Space* (c.1923), is laid out in the house and the garden.

Perhaps the most provocative piece, on the canal terrace, is Marino Marini's *Angelo della Città* (1948). It shows a man sitting on a horse, erect in all respects.

The Baroque church of Santa Maria della Salute, viewed from the other side of the Grand Canal

Accademia ⑪

Campo della Carità. *Tel* 041-522 22 47. 🚤 *Accademia.* ⬜ *daily (Mon: am only).* 🌑 *Jan 1, May 1, Dec 25.* 🎫 🎧 *(audio).* 📱 **www**.galleriaaccademia.org

Spanning five centuries, the matchless collection of paintings in the Accademia provides a complete spectrum of the Venetian school, from the Byzantine period through the Renaissance to the Baroque and later.

Housed in three former religious buildings, the basis of the collection was the Accademia di Belle Arti, founded in 1750 by the painter Giovanni Battista Piazzetta. In 1807 Napoleon moved the academy to its present premises, greatly enlarging the collection with artworks from churches and monasteries he suppressed.

The paintings are housed on one floor divided into 24 rooms, more or less in date order. A highlight of the Byzantine and Gothic section is Paolo Veneziano's *Coronation of the Virgin* (1325), which contrasts with the delicate naturalism of Giambono's painting of the same name (1448).

The Bellini family played a dominant role in the early Venetian Renaissance, and outstanding examples of their work include Giovanni Bellini's *Madonna and Child between St. John the Baptist and a Saint* (c.1504), and other paintings of his Madonna collection in rooms 4 and 5. One of Bellini's students, Giorgione, painted the famous,

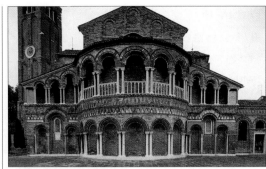

The colonnaded apse of Murano's Basilica dei Santi Maria e Donato

atmospheric *Tempest* (c.1507). Among Renaissance works on display are Veronese's *Feast in the House of Levi* (1573), and *The Miracle of the Slave* (1548) which made the reputation of Jacopo Tintoretto.

The long gallery of Baroque, genre, and landscape paintings alongside Palladio's inner courtyard (1561) features works by Giambattista Tiepolo, the greatest Venetian painter of the 18th century, and a view of Venice (1763) by Canaletto.

Rooms 20 and 21 contain two cycles of paintings portraying Venetian settings: *The Stories of the Cross*, and *Scenes from the Legend of St. Ursula*, painted by Carpaccio (1490s).

Murano ⑫

🚤 *LN, 41 and 42 from Fondamente Nuove; DM from Ferrovia and Piazzale Roma.*

Like the city of Venice, Murano consists of a cluster of small islands, connected by bridges. In the 15th and 16th

centuries Murano was the principal glass-producing center in Europe and today most tourists visit to tour the furnaces and buy traditionally designed glass from the manufacturers' showrooms.

The **Museo Vetrario** in the Palazzo Giustinian houses a fine collection of antique pieces. The prize exhibit is the dark blue wedding cup (1470–80) with enamel work by Angelo Barovier.

The architectural highlight of the island is the 12th-century **Basilica dei Santi Maria e Donato** with its lovely colonnaded apse. Of particular note are the Gothic ship's-keel roof, the mosaic Madonna in the apse, and the beautiful medieval mosaic floor, which dates from 1140.

🏛 **Museo Vetrario**
Palazzo Giustinian. *Tel* 041-73 95 86. ⬜ *Thu–Tue.* 🌑 *Jan 1, May 1, Dec 25.* 🎫 📱

⛪ **Basilica dei Santi Maria e Donato**
Fondamenta Giustinian. *Tel* 041-73 90 56. ⬜ *daily (Sun: pm only).*

Veronese's painting of Christ's Last Supper, retitled *The Feast in the House of Levi* (1573), in the Accademia

Ferrara 21

140,000. Castello Estense, Largo Castello (0532-20 93 70). Mon & Fri.

The D'este Dynasty has left an indelible mark on Ferrara, one of the Emilia-Romagna region's greatest walled towns. The noble family took control of the town under Nicolò II in the late 13th century, holding power until 1598. **Castello Estense**, the family's formidable dynastic seat, with its moats, towers, and battlements, looms over the town center.

Bronze statues of Nicolò III and Borso d'Este, one of Nicolò's reputed 27 children, adorn the medieval **Palazzo del Comune**. The d'Este summer retreat was the **Palazzo Schifanoia**. Begun in 1385, it is famous for its Salone dei Mesi, whose walls are covered with murals by Cosmè Tura and other Ferrarese painters.

Ferrara's **cathedral** has an excellent museum, which contains marble reliefs of the *Labours of the Months* (late 12th century), two painted organ shutters (1469) of *St. George* and the *Annunciation* by Tura, and the *Madonna of the Pomegranate* (1408) by Sienese sculptor Jacopo della Quercia (c.1374–1438).

Castello Estense
Largo Castello. ***Tel*** *0532-29 92 33.*
Tue–Sun. Dec 25.

Palazzo Schifanoia
Via Scandiana 23. ***Tel*** *0532-641 78.*
Tue–Sun. public hols.

The medieval Castello Estense and surrounding moat in Ferrara

Flagged medieval street with shady, arcaded buildings, typical of central Bologna

Bologna 22

385,000. Marconi 9 km (5 miles) NW. Piazza Maggiore 6 (051-23 96 60). Fri & Sat. Bologna Music Festival (Mar–Jun).

Capital of Emilia-Romagna and one of Italy's most prosperous cities, Bologna has a rich cultural heritage, ranging from medieval palaces and churches to leaning towers.

Celebrated in the Middle Ages for its university – believed to be the oldest in Europe – Bologna came under papal rule in 1506 and a large part of the city was given over to monasteries and convents. After the arrival of Napoleon's occupying force in 1797, the university was moved from its Catholic cradle in the **Archiginnasio** to a science building where Marconi later studied. After unification the old city walls were demolished and an era of prosperity was ushered in.

The two central squares of the city, the Piazza Maggiore and the Piazza del Nettuno, are bordered to the south by the churches of **San Petronio** and **San Domenico**. The former ranks among the greatest of Italy's brick-built medieval buildings. Founded in 1390, its construction was halted halfway due to financial constraints, and the planned central row of columns became the eastern flank. Twenty-two chapels open off the nave of the Gothic interior, many with fine works of art.

San Domenico is the most important of Italy's many Dominican churches, housing, as it does, the tomb of St. Dominic himself. A magnificent composite work, the tomb features statues and reliefs by Nicola Pisano, while the figures of angels and saints are early works by Michelangelo.

The **Torri degli Asinelli e Garisenda** are among the few surviving towers of the 200 that once formed the skyline of Bologna. Both were begun in the 12th century. The Garisenda tower (closed to the public) leans some 3 m (10 ft), while the Asinelli tower has a 500-step ascent and offers fine views.

The Romanesque-Gothic church of **San Giacomo Maggiore**, begun in 1267 but altered substantially since, is visited mainly for the superb Bentivoglio family chapel, decorated with frescoes by Lorenzo Costa (1460–1535). The Bentivoglio tomb is among the last works of Jacopo della Quercia.

Bologna's main art gallery, the **Pinacoteca Nazionale**, stands on the edge of the university district. Its two highlights are Perugino's *Madonna in Glory* (c.1491) and Raphael's famous *Ecstasy of St. Cecilia*, painted around 1515.

The cuisine of Bologna is reputed to be Italy's finest. To try the famous Bolognese meat sauce you should order *spaghetti al ragù*.

Torri degli Asinelli e Garisenda
Piazza di Porta Ravegnana. *Tue–Sun. May 1, Aug 16.*

Pinacoteca Nazionale
Via delle Belle Arti 56. ***Tel*** *051-420 94 11. Tue–Sun. Jan 1, May 1, Aug 15, Dec 25.*
www.pinacotecabologna.it

For hotels and restaurants in this region see pp456–61 and pp462–7

Ravenna ㉓

🏠 140,000. 🚉 🚌 ℹ️ *Via Salara 8–12 (0544-354 04).* 🚢 *Wed & Sat.*

Ravenna rose to power in the 1st century BC when Emperor Augustus built a port and naval base nearby, but gained further prominence after becoming the administrative capital of the Byzantine Empire in AD 402.

Most people visit the city for its superb early Christian mosaics. Spanning the years of Roman and Byzantine rule, they can be seen in many of Ravenna's 5th- and 6th-century buildings. In the church of **San Vitale**, apse mosaics (526–547) show the saint being handed a martyr's crown. Another mosaic depicts Emperor Justinian, who ruled from 527 to 565, and members of his court. Next door, the tiny **Mausoleo di Galla Placidia** is adorned with a mosaic of *The Good*

Apse of San Vitale, Ravenna, showing 6th-century mosaics

Shepherd. Galla Placidia ran the Western Empire for 20 years after the death of her husband, the Visigothic King Altauf. The 6th-century church of **Sant'Apollinare Nuovo** is dominated by two rows of mosaics which depict processions of martyrs and virgins bearing gifts.

Travelers in Ravenna can also visit **Dante's Tomb** – the great writer died here in 1321 – and the **Museo Nazionale**, which houses icons, paintings, and archaeological displays. The best place to relax and take a break from sightseeing is among the lovely ensemble of medieval buildings in the Piazza del Popolo.

🔒 **San Vitale & Mausoleo di Galla Placidia**
Via Fiandrini. **Tel** *0544-54 16 88.* ⬜ *daily.* ● *Jan 1, Dec 25.* 🎦 ♿

🔒 **Sant'Apollinare Nuovo**
Via di Roma. **Tel** *0544-54 16 88.* ⬜ *daily.* ● *Jan 1, Dec 25.* 🎦 ♿

BYZANTINE ITALY

By the 5th century AD the Roman Empire was split into two. Rome and the Western Empire could not stem the tide of Germanic invaders as they migrated southwards and Italy fell to the Goths. In the years after 535 AD, however, the Eastern Empire reconquered most of Italy. Its stronghold, Ravenna, became the richest, most powerful Italian city. Most of the peninsula was subsequently lost to the Lombards who invaded in 564, but Ravenna, protected by marshes and lagoons, was able to hold out until 752 when the Lombard King Aistulf finally recaptured the city.

Byzantine Emperor Justinian

Urbino ㉔

🏠 16,000. 🚌 ℹ️ *Piazza Rinascimento 1 (0722-26 13).* 🚢 *Sat.*

Urbino traces its origins to the Umbrians, centuries before Christ, and became a Roman municipality in the 3rd century BC. The city's zenith, however, came in the 15th century under the rule of the philosopher-warrior Federico da Montefeltro, who commissioned the building of the **Palazzo Ducale** in 1444. This beautiful Renaissance palace has an extensive library, hanging gardens, and numerous fine paintings. Two great 15th-century works, *The Flagellation* by Piero della Francesca, and *Ideal City* attributed to Luciano Laurana, are notable for their use of perspective.

Of special interest in the Neoclassical **Duomo**, built in 1789, is the painting of the *Last Supper* by Federico Barocci (c.1535–1612). The **Museo Diocesano** contains a collection of ceramics, glass, and religious artifacts.

The **Casa Natale di Raffaello**, home of Urbino's famous son, the painter Raphael (1483–1520), is also open to visitors.

🏛️ **Palazzo Ducale**
Piazza Duca Federico 13. **Tel** *0722-32 26 25.* ⬜ *8:30am–7:15pm Tue–Sun, 8:30am–2pm Mon.* ● *Jan 1, Dec 25.* 🎦 📷

🏛️ **Casa Natale di Raffaello**
Via di Raffaello 57. **Tel** *0722-32 01 05.* ⬜ *Mon–Sat, Sun am.* ● *Jan 1, Dec 25.* 🎦

The Palazzo Ducale, rising above the rooftops of Urbino

View across the Bay of Naples to the slopes of Mount Vesuvius

Naples ㉕

🏃 1,100,000. ✈ Capodichino 4 km (2.5 miles) NW. 🚢 🚌 🚃 ℹ Piazza del Gesù Nuovo (081-552 33 28). 🗓 daily. 🎉 Maggio dei Monumenti (May), San Gennaro (Sep 19).

The chaotic yet spectacular city of Naples (Napoli) sprawls around the edge of a beautiful bay in the shadow of Mount Vesuvius.

Originally a Greek city named Neapolis, founded in 600 BC, Naples became an "allied city" of Rome two centuries later. It has since had many foreign rulers. The French House of Anjou controled Naples between 1266 and 1421, when power passed to Alfonso V of Aragón. A colony of Spain by 1503, in 1707 Naples was ceded to Austria, and in 1734 Charles III of Bourbon took over. In 1860, Naples became part of the

Tomb of King Ladislas of Naples in San Giovanni a Carbonara

new kingdom of Italy. The centuries of occupation have left Naples with a rich store of ancient ruins, churches, and palaces, many of which can be seen in the compact center of the old city. The **Museo Archeologico Nazionale** holds treasures from Pompeii and Herculaneum, including a bust of Seneca, fine glassware, frescoes, mosaics, and the fabulous Farnese Classical sculptures. Nearby, the church of **San Giovanni a Carbonara** houses some glorious medieval works of art, such as the tomb of King Ladislas of Naples (1386–1414). The French Gothic **Duomo** holds the relics of San Gennaro, martyred in 305 AD. Next to it is one of Italy's finest Renaissance gateways, the **Porta Capuana**, completed in 1490.

Also worth visiting, the **Monte della Misericordia**, a 17th-century octagonal church, houses Caravaggio's huge *Seven Acts of Mercy* (1607).

Central Naples is particularly rich in 14th- and 15th-century churches. **San Domenico Maggiore** contains some fine Renaissance sculpture while **Santa Chiara** houses the tombs of the Angevin monarchs and a museum whose exhibits include the

ruins of a Roman bathhouse. Southeast Naples is home to the city's castles and the royal palace of **Castel Nuovo**, built for Charles of Anjou in 1279–82. Another star sight, the **Palazzo Reale** was designed for the viceroy Ruiz de Castro, and has a superb library, richly adorned royal apartments, and a court theater. Begun in 1600, the palace was not completed until 1843.

The Palazzo Reale di Capodimonte, once a hunting lodge, now houses the **Museo di Capodimonte**, with its magnificent collection of Italian paintings, including works by Titian, Botticelli, and Raphael. This part of Naples is also known for its "Spanish Quarter," or **Quartieri Spagnoli**, a neighborhood of narrow, cobbled alleys often used to represent the archetypal Neapolitan street scene.

Farnese Hercules, Museo Archeologico Nazionale

Environs
A trip by funicular railway up **Vomero** hill brings you to the **Certosa di San Martino**. This 14th-century charterhouse has been lavishly redecorated over the centuries. The Church and the Prior's Residence are particularly impressive. Just behind the Certosa lies the **Castel Sant Elmo**, which offers fine views.

Boat excursions can be taken along the Posillipo coast, and to the islands of **Capri, Ischia**, and **Procida**. Inland, **Caserta** has its own **Palazzo Reale**, which boasts over 1,000 sumptuously decorated rooms. The town of **Santa Maria Capua Vetere** has a Roman amphitheater and a Mithraeum.

🏛 **Museo Archeologico Nazionale**
Piazza Museo Nazionale 19. **Tel** 081-29 28 23. **M** Piazza Cavour. 🔴 Wed–Mon. 🔴 May 1, Dec 25. 🖼

🏛 **Museo di Capodimonte**
Parco di Capodimonte. **Tel** 081-749 91 11. 🔴 Tue–Sun. 🖼 ♿

A breathtaking view of the steep village of Positano on the Amalfi Coast

Pompeii ㉖

Piazza Esedra 5. **Tel** *081-861 07 44.*
🚆 🚌 ◯ *daily.* ◐ *Jan 1, Easter Mon,*
May 1, Aug 15, Dec 25. 🌐 ♿ 🎫

Ancient Pompeii, destroyed in
AD 79 by an eruption of
Vesuvius, lay buried under
rock and ash until the 18th
century. When excavations
began in 1748, a city frozen
in time was revealed. Many
buildings survived, some
complete with paintings and
sculptures. The villa of the
wealthy patrician Casii is
known as House of the Faun
after its bronze statuette. The
House of the Vettii, named
after its owners, contains rich
wall decorations.

The original layout of the
city can be clearly seen. The
Forum was the center of
public life, with administrative
and religious institutions
grouped around it. Theaters,
the marketplace, temples,
stores, and even brothels can
be visited. Around 2,000
people died at Pompeii and
casts of numerous recumbent
figures have been made.

Much of our knowledge of
the daily lives of the ancient
Romans has been derived
from the excavations at
Pompeii and nearby
Herculaneum. The baths were
divided into separate sections
for men and women, but the

citizens of Pompeii were not
prudish – graphic frescoes
reveal the services offered by
male and female prostitutes in
the *lupanares*, or brothels.

Many works of art, domestic
items, and other artifacts were
preserved by the mud and
ash are on permanent display
in the Museo Archeologico
Nazionale in Naples.

Amalfi Coast ㉗

🚉 🚌 *Amalfi.* 🛈 *Corso Roma*
19–21, Amalfi (089-87 11 07).

The most enchanting and
most visited route in
Campania is that skirting the
southern flank of Sorrento's
peninsula: the Amalfi Coast
(Costiera Amalfitana). Among

the popular pleasures here
are dining on locally caught
grilled fish and sipping icy
Lacrima Christi from Vesuvian
vineyards, interspersed with
beach-hopping.

From **Sorrento**, a well-
developed holiday resort, the
road winds down to **Positano**,
a village clambering down a
vertiginous slope to the sea.
Further on, **Praiano** is another
fashionable resort.

Amalfi – the coast's largest
town – was a maritime power
before it was subdued in 1131
by King Roger of Naples. Its
most illustrious citizens were
buried in the 13th-century
Chiostro del Paradiso, flanking
the 9th-century Duomo.
Above Amalfi, **Ravello** offers
peace and quiet and superb
views of the coast.

Sacrarium of the Lares, shrine of Pompeii's guardian deities

Sicily

Located at a crossroads in the Mediterranean, Sicily was a magnet for colonists and invaders from half the ancient civilized world. As Greek, Arab, and Norman conquerors came and went, they left behind a rich and varied cultural heritage. This has evolved into a colorful mixture of language, customs, and cuisine, and is reflected in the diverse art and architecture of the island. Sicily has magnificent beaches, remote hilltowns, flower-covered mountain ranges, and an active volcano whose lava flows over the centuries have created a fertile land of walnut trees, citrus groves, and vineyards.

Front façade of the Norman Duomo (cathedral) in Palermo

Palermo 28

🏛 700,000. ✈ Punta Raisi 32 km (20 miles) W. 🚌 🚉 🚌 ⓘ Piazza Castelnuovo 35 (091-605 81 11) and railway station. 🛍 Mon–Sat. 🎉 U Festinu for Santa Rosalia (Jul 10–15).

Capital of Sicily and situated along the bay at the foot of Monte Pellegrino, Palermo was originally called Panormos, or "port" by the Phoenicians. A prosperous Roman town, Palermo's golden age came later, while under Arab domination. The Baroque period (17th–18th centuries) has also left a lasting mark on the city's civic and religious buildings.

Palermo suffered heavy bombardment by the Allies in World War II, but, despite chaotic rebuilding, the city remains an exotic mix of the oriental and the European, and an exciting place to explore.

The old Arab quarter can be found in North Palermo, typified by the medieval, casbah-style market of **Vucciria**. On Piazza Marina, the focal point of North Palermo, the 15th-century

Palazzo Abatellis houses the **Galleria Regionale di Sicilia**, which has a fine collection of sculptures, medieval crucifixes, frescoes, and paintings.

On the Piazza della Vittoria in South Palermo, the **Palazzo Reale** – a focus of power since Byzantine rule – is now home to Sicily's regional government. Its splendid **Cappella Palatina** is adorned with mosaics. The **Duomo**, founded in 1184, has a Catalan Gothic portico (1430), a cupola in Baroque style, and slender turrets with lancet windows.

🏛 Galleria Regionale di Sicilia

Via Alloro 4. **Tel** 091-623 00 11. ◯ am daily, pm Tue–Thu. 📷

🏛 Palazzo Reale

Piazza Indipendenza. **Tel** 091-705 11 11. ◯ daily. **Cappella Palatina** ◯ daily. ● Easter, Apr 25, May 1, Dec 26. 📷

Environs

A few miles inland from Palermo, the cathedral at **Monreale**, founded in 1172, is one of the great sights of Norman Sicily. The interior glitters with mosaics and the cloisters, with their Saracenic-style arches, represent Norman artistry at its peak.

R Monreale

Piazza Vittorio Emanuele. 🚌 🖼 **Cloister Tel** 091-640 44 13. ◯ daily (am only Sun & hols). 📷 for treasury & terrace.

Taormina 29

Messina. 🏛 10,000. 🚉 🚌 ⓘ Palazzo Corvaja, Piazza Santa Caterina (0942 232 43). 🛍 Wed.

Sicily's most popular tourist resort, Taormina is a delight to visit, with sandy beaches and numerous restaurants.

The most illustrious relic of the past is the 3rd-century BC **Theater**, begun by the Greeks, and rebuilt by the Romans. Among other Classical ruins are the **Odeon** (a musical theater) and the **Naumachia** (a man-made lake for mock battles).

The 14th-century **Palazzo Corvaja** and the 13th-century **Duomo**, renovated in 1636, are also worth visiting.

Taormina's Greek theater with Mount Etna in the background

Fishing boats moored in the picturesque harbor of Syracuse

Mount Etna 30

Catania. 🚉 to Linguaglossa or Randazzo; Circumetnea (095-374 842). 🚌 to Nicolosi. 🚶 Via G Garibaldi 63, Nicolosi (095-91 15 05).

One of the world's largest active volcanoes, Mount Etna was thought by the Romans to have been the forge of Vulcan, the god of fire. To view it in comfort, take the Circumetnea railway, which runs around the base from Catania to Riposto.

Now a protected area, about 58 sq km (22 sq miles) in size, Etna offers numerous opportunities for excursions. One of the most popular is from Zafferana to the Valle del Bove. Hikes can also be taken up to the large craters at the summit.

Syracuse 31

🏛 118,000. 🛥 🚉 🚌 🚶 Via Maestranza (0931-464 255). 🛥 Wed.

The most important and powerful Greek city from 400 to 211 BC when it fell to the Romans, Syracuse (Siracusa in Italian) was also regarded as the most beautiful.

The peninsula of Ortigia is the hub of the old city. A highlight is the 18th-century **Duomo**. Its Baroque façade masks the **Temple of Athena** (5th century BC), which has been absorbed into it. Nearby is the **Palazzo Beneventano del Bosco** (1778–88) where

Admiral Nelson once stayed. At Ortigia's farthest point is the **Castello Maniace**, built by Frederick II around 1239, and the **Galleria Regionale di Palazzo Bellomo**, where Caravaggio's *Burial of St. Lucy* (1608) may be seen.

One of the most important examples of ancient theater architecture, the 5th-century BC **Greek Theater** has a 67-tier auditorium or *cavea*. The great Greek playwrights staged their works here.

At Tyche, north of Syracuse, the **Museo Archeologico Regionale Paolo Orsi** houses an important collection of artifacts excavated from local digs, which date from the Paleolithic to the Byzantine era.

🏛 Galleria Regionale di Palazzo Bellomo
Palazzo Bellomo, Via Capodieci 16. **Tel** 0931-696 17. 🔲 Tue–Sat, Sun am.

🏛 Museo Archeologico Regionale Paolo Orsi
Viale Teocrito 66. **Tel** 0931-46 40 22. 🔲 Mon–Sat, Sun am.

Agrigento 32

🏛 57,000. 🛥 🚉 🚌 🚶 Via Empedocle 73 (0922-203 91). 🛥 Fri.

Modern Agrigento occupies the site of Akragas, an important city of the ancient Greeks. Following the Roman conquest of 210 BC, Agrigento was renamed and successively occupied by Byzantines, Arabs, and Normans. The historic medieval core of the

city focuses on the Via Atenea. The 13th-century abbey complex of **Santo Spirito** houses stuccoes by Giacomo Serpotta (1695).

Environs
South of Agrigento, the **Valley of Temples** is the principal sacred site of ancient Akragas. The mainly 5th- and 6th-century ruins rank among the most impressive complexes of ancient Greek buildings outside Greece. **Museo Regionale Archeologico** houses outstanding artifacts from the temples and the city.

🏛 Museo Regionale Archeologico
Contrada San Nicola, Viale Panoramica. **Tel** 0922-40 15 65. 🔲 for restoration. 📷

The Temple of Concord (c.430 BC) in the Valley of Temples, Agrigento

Practical Information

Italy's charm and allure help to mask an idiosyncratic public sector in which delays and long lines are common. Be prepared to wait in offices and banks, and to persevere when seeking information. However, communications – other than the post office – are good, and banking and exchange facilities are widely available. Italy is generally safe for visitors and there is a visible police presence should a crisis arise. Personal belongings should nevertheless be watched at all times. Many shops and offices close at lunch for the siesta, reopening in the late afternoon. Pharmacies are a useful first stop for health advice.

WHEN TO VISIT

Italy's towns and historic sites are extremely popular attractions and it is worth considering this when planning your trip. Rome, Florence, and Venice are all crowded from spring to October and it is advisable to reserve a hotel well in advance. In August the cities are generally slightly less busy, and the seaside resorts fill up. June and September can be as hot as midsummer, but the beaches are less crowded. The skiing season runs from December to March.

TOURIST INFORMATION

The national tourist board, **ENIT**, has branches in capital cities worldwide and offers general information on Italy. Locally, there are two types of tourist office: an EPT *(Ente Provinciale di Turismo)* has information on its town and surrounding province, whereas an **APT** *(Azienda di Promozione Turistica)* deals exclusively with an individual town. Both can help with practical issues such as hotel reservations and local tour guides. They also provide free maps and guide-books in several languages.

OPENING HOURS

Italian museums are gradually conforming to new regulations, particularly in the north, opening daily from 9am to 7pm, except for two or more Mondays each month. In summer, many museums stay open longer at weekends. In winter, opening times are more limited. It is advisable to check beforehand. Archaeological sites usually open from 9am to an hour before sunset, Tuesday to Sunday. Churches are open from about 7am to 12:30pm and 4 to 7pm, but they often prefer not to admit tourists during services.

Visits to some of the more popular tourist sights, such as Leonardo da Vinci's painting of *The Last Supper* in Milan, must be organized in advance.

VISA REQUIREMENTS

Citizens of the European Union (EU), US, Canada, Australia, and New Zealand do not require a visa for stays of up to three months. Most European Union visitors need only a valid identity document to enter Italy, but visitors from the UK, Ireland, Sweden, and Denmark need a passport.

PERSONAL SECURITY

Although petty crime in the cities is frequent, violent crime in Italy is rare. However, it is common for people to raise their voices aggressively during an argument. Usually, remaining calm and being polite will help to defuse the situation. Unofficial tour guides, taxi drivers, or strangers who try to advise you on accommodations may expect money in return.

Women traveling alone in Italy are likely to meet with a lot of attention, although this is often more of an irritation than a danger. Staff at hotels and restaurants generally treat their single female customers with extra care and attention.

POLICE

There are several different police forces in Italy and each one fulfills a particular role. The state police, *la polizia*, deals with most crimes. The *carabinieri* deal with a variety of offences, and also conduct random security checks. The *vigili urbani*, the municipal traffic police, issue fines for traffic and parking offences. If

---

THE CLIMATE OF ITALY

The Italian peninsula has a varied climate falling into three distinct geographical regions. Cold Alpine winters and warm, increasingly wet summers characterize the northern regions. In the extensive Po Valley, arid summers contrast with freezing, damp winters. The rest of Italy has long, and often very hot, summers and mild, sunny winters.

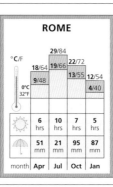

ROME			
°C/F			
	29/84		
	18/64 19/66	22/72	
9/48		13/55	12/54
0°C 32°F			4/40
6 hrs	10 hrs	7 hrs	5 hrs
51 mm	21 mm	95 mm	87 mm
month Apr	Jul	Oct	Jan

VENICE			
°C/F			
	28/82		
	17/63 18/64 18/64		
7/44		9/48	7/44
0°C 32°F			0/32
7 hrs	9 hrs	4 hrs	2 hrs
112 mm	108 mm	134 mm	90 mm
month Apr	Jul	Oct	Jan

you have anything stolen, you should go to the nearest police station and file a report *(denuncia)*.

EMERGENCY SERVICES

In case of emergencies while on vacation the appropriate numbers to call are listed in the directory below.

HEALTH ISSUES

No inoculations are needed for Italy, but it is advisable to carry mosquito repellent in the summer months. If emergency medical treatment becomes necessary, you should go to the *Pronto Soccorso* (emergency room) of the nearest hospital.

Various medical products, including homeopathic medicines, are available in any pharmacy *(farmacia)*, but a prescription is often required. Thanks to a night rota *(servizio notturno)* – listed in the local pages of daily newspapers and on pharmacy doors – there is always a pharmacy open in all cities and most towns.

LANGUAGE AND ETIQUETTE

People in Italy are very dress-conscious and unusual or risqué clothes get noticed. Strict dress codes are enforced in many places of worship, where your torso, knees, and upper arms should be covered.

Forms of address are still governed by traditional social formalities. *Ciao* should only be used as a greeting for familiar friends, otherwise *piacere* (pleased to meet you), *buon giorno* (good day), or *buona sera* (good evening) are polite greetings. Say *arrivederci* on parting. Kissing on the cheeks is common among friends, but shake hands with strangers.

A tip of around 5 percent is sufficient in restaurants when the service charge (usually 15 percent) is not included. In tourist areas, however, the service and cover charge are often added to your bill and are non-negotiable. Taxi drivers and hotel porters expect a reasonable tip if they have been helpful.

FACILITIES FOR THE DISABLED

Public awareness of the needs of the disabled is low, but improving. **CO.IN.Sociale** (Consorzio Cooperative Integrale) provides information on facilities for the disabled.

BANKING AND CURRENCY

Italy's currency was the lira (plural lire). However, on January 1, 2002 it was replaced by the euro *(see p15)*.

Banks open between 8:30am and 1:30pm Monday to Friday. Most also open from 2:15 to 3pm or 2:30 to 3:30pm. Electronic exchange

machines, with multilingual instructions, are located at all major airports, train stations, and banks. Bureaux de change can be found in main towns, and are usually open all day, and into the evening in resorts. However, they quite often tend to have less favorable exchange rates and charge a higher commission than banks.

COMMUNICATIONS

Post offices open from 8:25am to 1:50pm weekdays, and from 8:25am to noon on Saturday. Main post offices are open from 8:25am to 7pm non-stop. The red mailboxes (blue in the Vatican City) usually have two slots labeled *per la città* (for the city only) and *tutte le altre destinazioni* (for all other destinations). Italian post is renowned for its unreliability, and letters can take from four days to two weeks to arrive. For a faster service, send mail *prioritaria*.

Public telephones are increasingly card-operated. A telephone card *(carta* or *scheda telefonica)* can be purchased from bars, newspaper kiosks, post offices, and tobacconists *(tabacchi)*. Remember to break off the corner of the card before attempting to make a call. Alternatively, main towns have telephone offices *(Telefoni)* where you are assigned a booth and pay after calls are completed. No premium is charged.

DIRECTORY

TOURIST OFFICES

APT Florence
Via Manzoni 16.
Tel 055-23 320.

APT Milan
Via Marconi 1.
Tel 02-72 52 43 01.

APT Rome
Via Parigi 5.
Tel 06-488 991.

APT Venice
Castello 5050.
Tel 041-529 87 11.

ENIT Rome
Via Marghera 2.
Tel 06-497 11.

ENIT UK
1 Princes St, London, W1.
Tel 020-7408 1254
www.italiantourist
board.co.uk

ENIT US
630 Fifth Ave, New York,
NY 10111.
Tel 212-245 4822. 56.514
www.italian tourism.com

EMBASSIES

Australia
Via A. Bosio 5, Rome
Tel 06-85 27 21. **www**.
italy.embassy.gov.au

Canada
Via Zara 30, Rome.
Tel 06-854 44 29 11.
www.rome.qc.ca

UK
Via XX Settembre 80A,
Rome. *Tel* 06-42 20 00
01. **www**.britain.it

US
Via Veneto 119A, Rome.
Tel 06-467 41.
www.usembassy.it

EMERGENCY NUMBERS

General Emergency
Tel 113.

Medical Emergency
Tel 118.

Police (Carabinieri)
Tel 112.

FACILITIES FOR THE DISABLED

CO.IN.Sociale
Via Enrico Giglioli 54A,
Rome.
Tel 06-232 675 82.

Travel Information

Italy has transportation systems of varying efficiency, from the modern road, bus, and rail networks of the north to the slower and more antiquated systems of the south. Numerous airlines operate flights to the country's major airports. Highways are good, but busy at weekends and peak periods, and delays are common at Alpine passes. Train travel is inexpensive and services generally frequent, although they can be overcrowded during local holidays. The major Italian cities have a number of transportation options and that most suited to the tourist varies from place to place: the bus is more practical in Rome and the metro in Milan.

FLYING TO ITALY

If you are flying from the United States, **United Airlines** operates direct scheduled flights to Rome and Milan from New York. **Delta** has flights from New York to Rome and from Boston to Milan. **Air Canada** flies from Montreal and Toronto, and **Qantas** flies from Sydney and Melbourne to Hong Kong, and from there to Rome.

Alitalia has regular services between Rome and Milan and New York, Los Angeles, Boston, Miami, Chicago, and Atlanta. It may, however, be more convenient and less expensive for long-haul passengers to take a budget flight to London, Frankfurt, Paris, or Amsterdam before continuing their journey to Italy from there. **Eurofly** also has direct flights from New York to Rome and Milan.

Low-cost airlines **easyJet** and **Ryanair** offer flights from London Stansted and Gatwick to as many as 15 Italian airports according to season.

Rome's Leonardo da Vinci (Fiumicino) and Milan's Malpensa are the key airports for long-haul flights into Italy. Milan's Linate airport handles European flights.

CHARTERS AND PACKAGE DEALS

Package holidays to Italy are usually less costly than traveling independently, unless you are on a tight budget and are prepared to make use of youth hostels and campsites. Rome, Florence, and Venice are often offered as separate or linked package deals, and many operators have packages to Tuscany and Umbria, the Lakes, the Riviera, Naples, Sicily, and the Amalfi Coast. Several firms organize fly-drive packages. In winter, ski packages to many Alpine resorts are available. Specialty walking, gastronomy, and art tours are increasingly common.

DOMESTIC FLIGHTS

Alitalia runs regular services between many Italian cities. Long-haul passengers can transfer to domestic flights in Rome and Milan.

As internal flights are expensive, and busy at peak periods, trains are a good alternative. Flights to airports in the north can be disrupted by fog in the winter.

TRAVELING IN CITIES

Milan and Rome both have a metro system known as *la metropolitana* (*metro* for short). Rome's network amounts to just two lines – A and B – which converge at Stazione Termini, the city's central train station. Several stations are useful for key sights but the system is designed for commuters and carriages are usually stiflingly hot in summer.

Milan has three principal lines – MM1 (the red line), MM2 (green), and MM3 (yellow) – that give easy access to the city's main sights.

Cars are a liability in all city centers and some, such as Florence, have a large limited-traffic zone. Walking is in many cases the easiest way to negotiate the narrow streets of historic town centers. Trams still run in some cities such as Milan and Rome. Taxis must be met at official taxi stands or reserved by telephone; in theory, you cannot hail a taxi in the street.

Most Italian cities and towns have a bus system which is inexpensive, comprehensive, and as efficient as traffic will allow. Bus stops are known as *fermate*, and buses (*autobus*) usually run from about 6am to midnight. Train stations are invariably linked to the city centers by shuttle buses. Tickets (*biglietti*) must usually be bought before boarding the bus, and are available from kiosks, bars, and *tabacchi* (tobacconists). Buses are boarded via the front and rear doors and exited via the central doors. Tickets are validated by being punched in machines on board.

GETTING AROUND VENICE

The water buses (*vaporetti*) are an entertaining form of public transportation in Venice, although most journeys within the city can easily be covered on foot. The main route for the water buses is the Grand Canal. They also link the city to the islands in the lagoon. Tickets can be purchased from kiosks at each stop, and the main routes run every 10 to 20 minutes until early evening. For general inquiries, contact the **ACTV Information Office**.

Gondolas are a luxury form of transportation. Before boarding, agree on a price with the gondolier. *Traghetti* (gondola ferries), on the other hand, are an inexpensive, convenient way of crossing the Grand Canal.

For those with sufficient funds, the most practical means of traveling around Venice is by water taxi. These motorboats run from 16 water taxi ranks and can reach the airport in 20 minutes. Extra charges are made for luggage, waiting, night service, and calling out a taxi.

RAIL TRAVEL

The bulk of Italy's rail network is an integrated state-run system operated by the **Ferrovie dello Stato** (FS). Train journeys into Italy from other parts of Europe wind through the Alps and are an exciting way to travel to the country. High-speed trains, which operate on main lines to the coast or between cities, almost always require pre-booking of seats. Intercity (IC) trains and Eurocity (EC) trains only stop at main stations and require the payment of a first- or second-class supplement (*supplemento*). *Espresso* and *Diretto* trains make more stops and require no supplement.

The most useful pass for visitors is the Trenitalia Pass, which gives unlimited travel for 4–10 consecutive or non-consecutive days over a two-month period, with special rates for those under 26. This pass can be purchased at most mainline stations and various agencies outside Italy. It is available only to non-residents.

Before traveling, all tickets need to be validated in one of the machines on the platform.

TRAVELING BY BUS

Long-distance buses (*pullman* or *corriere*) operate between towns and can be less expensive and more frequent than the trains. Tickets can be purchased on board, and services usually depart from a town's train station or main square. Buses in some areas may be run by several companies (*see Directory below*).

TRAVELING BY ROAD

A car is invaluable for touring the Italian countryside. Drivers should take into account high gas (*benzina*) prices, the difficulty of parking in towns, and the Italians' often erratic approach to driving. Italy has a good network of highways, but most have tollbooths, often leading to congestion. Care should be taken at night when many traffic lights switch to flashing amber. Car theft is rife in Italy and valuables should not be left unattended.

Car rental (*autonoleggio*) is expensive in Italy, and should be organized beforehand through fly-drive deals or prebooked with firms that have branches in Italy. Local firms may be less expensive than the international firms. Most airports have rental offices on site (*see Directory below*). Visitors from outside the EU need an international license, but in practice not all rental firms insist on this.

FERRY SERVICES

Italy's large number of off-shore islands means that it has a well-developed network of ferries. Boats of various kinds also operate on the Italian Lakes.

Ferries depart for Sicily from Naples and Reggio di Calabria. They also run from the mainland and from Sicily to surrounding islands and archipelagoes, for example from Naples to Capri and Ischia. Boats for Sardinia leave from Civitavecchia near Rome, Livorno, and Genoa. There are car ferry services from Brindisi to Corfu and Patras in Greece. In summer, these ferries can get very crowded, so make sure you reserve well in advance.

DIRECTORY

AIRLINES

Air Canada
Tel 888-247 2262
(Canada).
www.aircanada.com

Alitalia (Italy)
Tel 06-22 22.
www.alitalia.it

Alitalia (UK)
Tel 0870-544 8259.
www.alitalia.co.uk

Alitalia (US)
Tel 800-223 5730.
www.
alitaliausa.com

British Airways
Tel 199-71 22 66
(Italy).
Tel 0870-850 9850
(UK).
www.ba.com

Delta
Tel 800-221 1212
(US).
www.delta.com

easyJet
www.easyjet.com

Eurofly (Italy)
Tel 199-509 960.
www.eurofly.it

Qantas
Tel 848-35 00 10
(Italy).
Tel 612-13 13 13
(Australia).
www.qantas.com

Ryanair
www.ryanair.com

United Airlines
Tel 02-69 63 37 07
(Italy).
Tel 800-622 1015
(US).
www.united.com

GETTING AROUND VENICE

ACTV Information Office
Piazzale Roma, Venice.
Tel 041-24 24.
www.actv.it

Consorzio Motoscafi Rialto (Water Taxis)
Tel 041-522 23 03.

RAIL TRAVEL

Ferrovie dello Stato
Toll-free number;
information and inquiries.
Tel 89-20 21.
www.trenitalia.com

BUS COMPANIES

Cotral
Rome: **Tel** 800-150 008.

Lazzi
Rome: **Tel** 06-884 0840.
Florence and national:
Tel 055-215 155.

Sita
Florence: **Tel** 800-373 760.
National & international:
Tel 800-001 311.

CAR RENTAL

Avis
Tel 199-10 01 33
(Rome).
www.avis.com

Europcar
Tel 800-01 44 10
(Rome).
www.europcar.co.it

Hertz
Tel 199-11 22 11
(Rome airport).
www.hertz.it

Maggiore
Tel 06-854 86 98
(Rome).
www.maggiore.it

Sixt
Tel 06-474 0014 (Rome).

Shopping

Italy is known for its quality designer goods, ranging from chic clothing and sleek cars to stylish household items. There is a strong tradition of craftsmanship, often from family-run businesses, and there are numerous markets selling regional specialties. Apart from the town markets, it is not a country for bargains, but the joys of window-shopping will offer plenty of compensation.

OPENING HOURS

Opening times for shops are usually 9:30am–1pm and 3:30 or 5–8pm. Stores are traditionally closed on Monday mornings, but shopkeepers are increasingly working more flexible hours.

DEPARTMENT STORES

Department stores are often open without a lunchbreak *(orario continuato)* from 9am until 8pm Monday to Saturday. **La Rinascente** stores are good for ready-to-wear clothes, haberdashery, and perfumes.

DESIGNER FASHION

Italy is famous worldwide for its fashion industry. Milan, its designer capital, is stormed each year by Italians and foreigners alike in search of the latest catwalk novelty. **Giò Moretti**, in Via della Spiga, features articles by the top names, as well as pieces by up-and-coming designers.

Retail outlets of famous designers can be found in most Italian city centers. In Venice, **Armani** and others have stylish shops just off the Piazza San Marco. Rome's most famous designer is **Valentino**. His and other top fashion names dominate Rome's Via Condotti, Via de' Tornabuoni in Florence, and the Chiaia district of Naples.

CLOTHING STORES

Less expensive clothes are available in high-street stores, where the styles tend to be more conventional and classical. Sales, called *saldi*, are held during summer and winter. Secondhand shops may seem expensive, but the quality of the clothes is good.

JEWELRY

Glitzy gold jewelry is very popular in Italy and every *gioielleria* (jewelry shop) will offer a wide selection of items. Elegant, classic jewelry can be purchased at **Cusi** in Milan, while Venice's smartest jewelers are **Missiaglia** and **Nardi** in Piazza San Marco. **Bulgari**, known for its beautiful jewelry and watches, has a number of retail outlets, as does **Buccellati**, famous for its delicately engraved designs inspired by the Italian Renaissance. For reasonably priced jewelry try **Gioie** in Rome. Naples has several jewelers' and goldsmiths' shops where traditional engraving and cameo work can still be seen. Unusual and original items can often be found in artisan shops *(oreficeria)*.

ACCESSORIES

Stylish Italian leather shoes and handbags have an international market, and are a popular purchase of visitors to all parts of the country. **Ferragamo**, the well-known Italian designer, has stores in most Italian cities, offering elegant, classic shoes. Mandarina Duck bags and luggage are available at **Gatti Francesco** and **Ottica Nuova di Malizia Michela** as well as many other stores. **Borsalino** is the place for top-quality classic hats.

One-off pieces by local designers can also be found by the intrepid shopper. In Naples, **Marinella** has a store selling her famous ties worn by many celebrities.

HOUSEHOLD ITEMS

Household stores in cities and towns throughout the country sell the well-designed utensils for which Italy is famous.

Stainless steel and copper kitchenware is a favorite buy with visitors.

REGIONAL CRAFTS

Traditional crafts are still practised in Italy and range from delicate lacework and glassware in the Veneto to leatherwork, jewelry, and marbled paper in Florence. Elaborate Tuscan pottery, hand-painted dishes from around Amalfi, and De Simone's stylized designer plates from Sicily are among many ceramic styles available.

Among the best craft workshops in Rome is **Arte e Mestieri**, which specializes in original, hand-made wood and terra-cotta items. Naples' **Il Cantuccio della Ceramica** is the place to go for ceramics.

In Venice, the best place to buy local blue- and claret-colored glass is the island of Murano. Here, **Barovier e Toso** produce original designs. Some of the most expensive glass in Venice can be bought from **Venini**. Carnival masks, available from **Tragicomica**, and traditional Burano lace are also popular buys.

The Etruscan art of working alabaster is best seen in Volterra. Hand-made perfumes and toiletries, and hand-painted majolica are favorite purchases in Tuscany. Sicily is well known for its ceramics, and for traditional rod puppets. The latter, now rare, can still be found in antique shops.

GOURMET FOODS

Many of Italy's regional food specialties are world-famous: Parma ham, Chianti wine, olive oil, and grappa. Regional sweets, including the Sienese *panforte* and Sicilian marzipan, are also well-known, as are cheeses such as Gorgonzola from Lombardy and Parmesan from Emilia-Romagna. Tuscan delicacies include bottled *antipasti* and sunflower honey. The Veneto region produces the famous *panettone* cake and *amaretto* biscuits. *Vesuvio* chocolate with rum from Naples is also delicious.

To make the most of Italian food, try to buy what is in season. Mushrooms and grapes are best in the fall, whereas spring is the season for asparagus, strawberries, and artichokes. In winter, cauliflower and broccoli are at their best, as are lemons from Amalfi and Sicilian blood oranges. Summer is the time for plums, pears, and cherries, as well as zucchini, eggplant, tomatoes, and melon.

FOOD STORES

Specialty stores are the most interesting way to shop for food in Italy. A *fornaio* has the best bread and a *macellaio* has the finest meat (go to a *norceria* for pork products). Vegetables are freshest from market stands or the *frutti-vendolo*. You can buy cakes at the *pasticceria*, milk at the *latteria*, and pasta, ham, and cheese at the well-stocked *alimentari* and delicatessens.

To buy wine, head for the *enoteca*, *vineria*, or *vinaio*, where you can sometimes taste the products first. Italy is a major wine producer and stores stock a wide range of labels, from the prized Barolo and Barbaresco vintages to the inexpensive but palatable local *vino da tavola*.

MARKETS

All Italian towns have at least one market a week. Large towns have small, daily markets in addition to a weekly flea market, usually held on a Sunday. Traders set up at 5am and start to clear away at about 1:30pm. Bargaining is not usual when buying food, but it is worth asking for a discount *(sconto)* for clothes and other items.

Larger markets have stands piled high with secondhand clothes, and many markets sell fake Rayban sunglasses, Lacoste T-shirts, and Levi's jeans. Popular gifts from Italy include the characteristic brown espresso and cappuccino cups sold in all markets.

Specialty markets can be found in many cities. Milan's antique market, the Mercatone dell'Antiquariato, is held on the last Sunday of the month, and the Via Sannio and Porta Portese markets of Rome are a mecca for secondhand clothes. The fish market by the Grand Canal in Venice is an interesting place to visit.

DIRECTORY

DEPARTMENT STORES

La Rinascente
Via del Corso, Rome.
Tel 06-679 76 91.

Piazza Fiume, Rome.
Tel 06-884 12 31.

Piazza della Repubblica 1, Florence.
Tel 055-21 91 13.

Piazza Duomo, Milan.
Tel 02-885 21.

DESIGNER FASHION

Armani
Via Condotti 77, Rome.
Tel 06-699 14 60.

Via de Tornabuoni 48r, Florence.
Tel 055-265 81 21.

Via Montenapoleone 2, Milan. **Tel** 02-76 39 00 68.

Piazza Martiri 61, Naples.
Tel 081-40 63 63.

San Marco 989, Venice.
Tel 041-523 78 08.

Giò Moretti
Via della Spiga 4, Milan.
Tel 02-76 00 73 27.

Valentino
Via Bocca di Leone 16, Rome.
Tel 06-678 75 85.

Via dei Tosinghi 52r, Florence.
Tel 055-29 31 42.

JEWELRY

Buccellati
Via Condotti 31, Rome.
Tel 06-679 03 29.

Via della Vigna Nuova 73, Florence.
Tel 055-239 65 79.

Via Monte Napoleone 23, Milan.
Tel 02-79 50 59.

Bulgari
Via Condotti 10, Rome.
Tel 06-679 38 76.

Via della Spiga 6, Milan.
Tel 02-77 70 01.

Cusi
Via Monte Napoleone 21a, Milan.
Tel 02-76 02 19 77.

Gioie
Via di Grotta Rossa 126, Rome.
Tel 06-33 26 03 51.

Missiaglia
Procuratie Vecchie, San Marco 125, Venice.
Tel 041-522 44 64.

Nardi
Procuratie Nuove, Piazza San Marco 69, Venice.
Tel 041-522 57 33.

ACCESSORIES

Borsalino
Piazza del Popolo 20, Rome.
Tel 06-32 60 92 56.

Galleria Vittorio Emanuele II, Milan.
Tel 02-804 337.

Ferragamo
Via Condotti 73–74, Rome.
Tel 06-679 71 01.

Via de' Tornabuoni 16r, Florence.
Tel 055-29 21 23.

Via Borgospesso 2, Milan.
Tel 02-76 00 66 60.

Gatti Francesco
Via di Propaganda 19, Rome.
Tel 06-679 39 58.

Marinella
Riviera di Chiaia 287, Naples.
Tel 081-764 32 65.

Ottica Nuova di Malizia Michela
Via P. Rossi 38, Milan.
Tel 02-648 03 10.

REGIONAL CRAFTS

Studio Arti e Mestieri
Via dei Baullari 146, Rome.
Tel 06-687 24 67.

Barovier e Toso
Fondamenta Vetrai 28, Murano.
Tel 041-73 90 49.

Il Cantuccio della Ceramica
Via Benedetto Croce 38, Naples.
Tel 081-552 58 57.

Tragicomica
Calle dei Nomboli, San Polo 2800, Venice.
Tel 041-72 11 02.

Venini
Piazzetta dei Leoncini, San Marco 314, Venice.
Tel 041-522 40 45.

Entertainment

With world-class sporting and a host of cultural events, Italy has something to offer everyone. The cities boast a varied and lively nightlife, while its Riviera resorts, hill villages, and classical sites are ideal for the avid sightseer or walker. Skiing in the Alps, water sports of all kinds on the coast, and pony trekking in the countryside, are tourist favorites. The open-air theater and music performances in summer are world-famous. Or simply join the Italians in their traditional evening stroll, the *passeggiata*, followed by a drink at a bar or café in a picturesque piazza.

ENTERTAINMENT LISTINGS

Information about what's on in Rome can be found in *Trovaroma*, the weekly Thursday supplement to the *La Repubblica* newspaper. There is also a weekly listings publication, *Roma C'è*, which has a section in English.

In Florence, the monthly magazines *Firenze Spettacolo* and *Florence Today* have restaurant and café guides, as well as details of concerts, exhibitions, and sporting events. *Milano Mese* is a free brochure listing concerts and other cultural events held in and around the city.

Un Ospite di Venezia (A Guest in Venice), produced by the Hotels' Association, comes out fortnightly in summer and monthly in winter and is free.

If you can read Italian, regional newspapers are also a good source of information about current events. Local tourist offices display posters advertising forthcoming events.

TICKETS

Making advance reservations for concerts is not the custom in Italy, where decisions are often made on the spur of the moment. To guarantee a seat you will have to visit the box office in person, as reservations are not usually taken over the telephone. You may also have to pay an advance booking supplement, or *prevendita,* which is generally about 10 percent of the price of the seat.

Tickets for popular music concerts are normally sold through record and music shops, whose names are displayed on the publicity material distributed.

Whereas tickets for classical concerts are sold on the spot for same-day performances, opera tickets are purchased months in advance. Prices vary significantly according to the artists scheduled to perform and the type of venue.

ENTERTAINMENT VENUES

Rome's city churches and the new **Parco della Musica** are favorite venues for classical music lovers. Venice also makes good use of its most magnificent churches as concert halls. **La Pietà** was Vivaldi's own church and is still used for classical music performances. In Milan, by contrast, the **San Siro** football stadium is often used as a concert venue along with the 5,000-capacity Palalido and the even larger **Mazdapalace**.

OPEN-AIR VENUES

During the summer months, Italy's historic buildings and classical ruins become dramatic settings for open-air events. Concerts are held in the grounds of Rome's 16th-century Villa Giulia *(see p405)* while Greek and Roman plays are staged in the restored theater of **Ostia Antica**, southwest of Rome.

In Venice the gardens of the Baroque palace, **Ca'Rezzonico**, and the ornate, enclosed courtyard of the Doge's Palace *(see pp436–7)* are used as outdoor concert venues. The 1st-century Teatro Romano *(see pp430–31)* in Verona also stages open-air concerts.

OPERA

Opera is one of the great cultural delights of Italy, whether experienced in the magnificent opera houses of **La Scala** in Milan or Venice's **La Fenice Viva!**, or in a spectacular open-air venue like Verona's superb **Arena**. The opera house of Naples, **San Carlo**, also boasts world-class performers. The **Teatro dell'Opera** in Rome has a late winter season and an open-air summer festival.

The opera season at the Verona Arena runs from the first week in July until the beginning of September, and every year features a lavish production of Verdi's *Aida*.

CLUBS AND DISCOS

Cities and resorts in Italy are packed with trendy discos, and upscale night-clubs. **Gilda**, with its two elegant restaurants and large dancefloor, is a favorite with Rome's jet set. A younger crowd frequents **Alien**. In the summer months the nightlife shifts to the Roman seaside resort of Fregene.

Currently drawing in the fashion crowd of Milan is the **Hollywood** club. Also popular with celebrities is the **Iron**. The **Martini Scala** is a well-known late-night club in Venice and there are a number of discos at Mestre on the mainland.

ITALIAN FESTIVALS

The distinctive regionalism which has survived in modern Italy is marked by the diverse local festivals celebrated each year. For example, on April 25 Venetians commemorate St. Mark with a gondola race and on June 24 Florence relives its past with a procession of people in 16th-century costumes. The Sienese celebrate the Palio – a bareback horse race dating from 1283 – on July 2 and August 16 each year. Traditional dress is worn in the processions and pre-race pageants. Other *festas* celebrate the harvesting of local produce: the wine festivals held in September and October in Chianti, Tuscany, and the Castelli Romani south of Rome, are popular with visitors.

Many events have an international flavor, such as the film festivals held in Venice (Aug–Sep), Taormina, (Jul–Aug), and Rome (Oct). From May to June Florence hosts an arts festival and Syracuse celebrates Greek drama. Ravello, near Naples, hosts an international festival of music each May.

Masked Venetians spill onto the streets during Carnival in February, and on summer evenings throughout Italy tourists can join in street dancing at local *festas*.

SPECIAL INTEREST VACATIONS

In recent years, culinary holidays run by English-speaking experts in Italian cooking have become very popular. **Tasting Places**, for example, organizes wine tours and week-long courses in Italian cuisine. The course locations include the Veneto, Sicily, Tuscany, and Umbria.

The **Società Dante Alighieri** provides courses in the Italian language, literature, history of art, and culture. There are both full- and part-time courses available, for every level of ability.

The **Gruppo Archeologico Romano** runs two-week digs in various regions. There are summer and winter trips for both adults and children.

For those with an interest in more energetic activities, the **Federazione Arrampicata Sportiva Italiana** has a list of mountain-climbing schools that organize climbs for people of all abilities. Ski holidays are best arranged with agents offering package deals. Trekking excursions can be organized with **Club Alpino Italiano (CAI)**. Nature walks and bird-watching trips are run by the **Italian Birds Protection League (LIPU)**. Cyclists will find miles of flat and scenic cycling routes in the Po Delta.

WATER SPORTS

Most lakeside towns and many seaside resorts in Italy rent out sailboats, canoes, and windsurfing equipment. Lessons and courses in a variety of water sports are organized by clubs, which usually require membership.

The **Federazione Italiana Attività Subacquee** runs underwater diving courses. Most travel agents have a selection of sailing vacations.

Swimming pools are expensive in Italy and you often have to pay a membership fee and a monthly tariff. Water parks are popular and provide pools, slides, wave machines, and games.

DIRECTORY

ENTERTAINMENT VENUES

Ca'Rezzonico
Fondamenta Rezzonico 3136, Venice.
Tel 041-241 01 00.

La Pietà
Riva degli Schiavoni, Venice.
Tel 041-523 10 96.

Mazdapalace
Via San Elia 33, Milan.
Tel 02-33 40 05 51.

Ostia Antica
Viale dei Romagnoli 717, Rome.
Tel 06-56 35 80 99.

Parco della Musica
Viale de Coubertin, Rome.
Tel 06-80 24 11.

San Siro
Via Piccolomini 5, Milan.
Tel 02-48 71 37 13.

OPERA

La Fenice Viva!
Cassa di Risparmio, Campo San Luca, Venice.
Tel 041-24 24.

Teatro alla Scala
Piazza alla Scala, Milan.
Tel 02-720 03 744.

Teatro dell'Opera
Piazza Beniamino Gigli 1, Rome.
Tel 06-48 16 01.

Teatro San Carlo
Via San Carlo 98/f, Naples.
Tel 081-797 23 31.

Verona Arena
Box Office
ENTE Arena, Piazza Brà 28, 37121 Verona.
Tel 045-800 51 51.

Ticket Agent
Vertours, Galleria Pelliciai 13, 37121 Verona.
Tel 045-59 49 88.

CLUBS AND DISCOS

Alien
Via Velletri 13–19, Rome.
Tel 06-841 22 12.

Gilda
Via Mario de' Fiori 97, Rome.
Tel 06-67 84 83 88.

Hollywood
Corso Como 15, Milan.
3 1111 02-655 55 74.

Iron
Corso di Porta Ticinese 60, Via Vetere, Milan.
Tel 02-89 40 07 09.

Martini Scala
San Marco 1980, Venice.
Tel 041-522 41 21.

SPECIAL INTEREST VACATIONS

Club Alpino Italiano
Via Galvani 10, 00153 Rome.
Tel 06-57 28 71 43.

Federazione Arrampicata Sportiva Italiana
Via del Terrapieno 27, Bologna.
Tel 051-601 48 90.
www.federclimb.it

Gruppo Archeologico Romano
Via Baldi degli Ubaldi 168, Rome. *Tel 06-638 52 56.*

Italian Birds Protection League
Via Trento 49, 43100 Parma.
Tel 0521-27 30 43.
www.lipu.it

Società Dante Alighieri
Piazza Firenze 27, 00186 Rome.
Tel 06-687 36 94.
www.soc.dante-al.it

Tasting Places
PO Box 38174, London W10 52P, England.
Tel 0208-964 5333.
www.tastingplaces.com

WATER SPORTS

Federazione Italiana Attività Subacquee
Via Vittoria Colonna 27, 00193 Rome.
Tel 06-322 56 87.

Where to Stay in Italy

Accommodations in Italy range from the family-run *pensione* to the Renaissance palazzo, and prices vary accordingly. Top hotels in Venice and Florence are very expensive. Italian lodgings tend to have fewer facilities, but you can find excellent value in all price ranges. Book early, especially if you want a room with a view.

PRICE CATEGORIES
Price categories are for a standard double room per night, including tax and service charges but not breakfast.
€ Under 85 euros
€€ 85–150 euros
€€€ 150–250 euros
€€€€ 250–350 euros
€€€€€ Over 350 euros

ROME

AVENTINE Sant'Anselmo
€€€ Map D4
Piazza di Sant'Anselmo 2, 00153 **Tel** 06-570 057 **Fax** 06-578 36 04 **Rooms** 45

This pretty villa is on a peaceful square halfway up the Aventine hill. The entrance hall is stenciled with flowers; there are chandeliers and corridors with floors of inlaid marble. The lounge looks onto the hotel's garden. Many of the rooms have terraces. The staff provide a warm service. **www.aventinohotels.com**

CAMPO DE' FIORI Teatro di Pompeo
€€€ Map C3
Largo del Pallaro 8, 00186 **Tel** 06-687 28 12 **Fax** 06-68 80 55 31 **Rooms** 12

A lovely little hotel built on the remains of the ancient theater of the same name, where Julius Caesar is said to have met his destiny. Rooms are large and comfortable with wooden beams and dark wooden furniture. Breakfast is served in the basement under a Roman vault. **www.hotelteatrodipompeo.it**

FORUM Lancelot
€€€ Map E4
Via Capo d'Africa 47, 00184 **Tel** 06-70 45 06 15 **Fax** 06-70 45 06 40 **Rooms** 60

A popular place to stay near the Colosseum with very friendly, helpful staff. Rooms are spacious and charming. Some have private terraces with views, and two are specially adapted for guests with disabilities. A half-board option is available and a hearty breakfast is served in the patio garden. **www.lancelothotel.com**

PANTHEON Grand Hotel de la Minerve
€€€€€ Map C3
Piazza della Minerva 69, 00186 **Tel** 06-69 52 01 **Fax** 06-679 41 65 **Rooms** 135

Favoured by Italy's first Grand Tourists, with generations following ever since, the charismatic Minerve is a fusion of Old World elegance and contemporary styling. Marble and chandeliers abound, as do wonderful frescoes, tastefully blended with cutting-edge design. Excellent rooftop bar and restaurant. **www.grandhoteldelaminerve.com**

PIAZZA DI SPAGNA Panda
€€ Map C2
Via della Croce 35, 00187 **Tel** 06-678 01 79 **Fax** 06-69 94 21 51 **Rooms** 28

Panda is an appealing little hotel with a faithful clientele, offering unpretentious, cheap accommodations in one of Rome's most expensive areas. Clean rooms with or without bathrooms, but all with air conditioning, telephone, and internet access. A couple of the rooms feature original 19th-century frescoes. **www.hotelpanda.it**

PIAZZA DI SPAGNA Hassler
€€€€€ Map D2
Piazza Trinità dei Monti 6, 00187 **Tel** 06-69 93 40 **Fax** 06-678 99 91 **Rooms** 98

At the top of the Spanish Steps, this is the glitterati's choice and the grande dame of Rome's hotels. Service is impeccable and the public spaces are luxurious with marble, chandeliers, and wood paneling. Bedrooms and suites are plush, styled individually and most have views. Legendary roof restaurant. **www.hotelhasslerroma.com**

PIAZZA NAVONA Raphael
€€€€ Map C3
Largo Febo 2, 00186 **Tel** 06-68 28 31 **Fax** 06-687 89 93 **Rooms** 59

A lovely burnt sienna palazzo, strewn with ivy and fairy lights just off the piazza, Raphael is romantic and stylish. There are breathtaking views from its roof terrace, where meals are served in summer. Rooms are well appointed, if fairly small. The lobby is filled with art, including a Picasso porcelain collection. **www.raphaelhotelrome.com**

TERMINI Hotel Columbia
€€€ Map C3
Via del Viminale 15, 00184 **Tel** 06-488 35 09 **Fax** 06-474 02 09 **Rooms** 45

A quiet gem of a hotel in one of Rome's busiest neighbourhoods. Dark wood and light colored fabrics give the rooms (some with balconies) an airy, Mediterranean feel. The extensive buffet breakfast can be enjoyed on the pretty roof terrace. **www.hotelcolumbia.com**

TRASTEVERE San Francesco
€€€ Map C4
Via Jacopa de' Settesoli 7, 00153 **Tel** 06-58 30 00 51 **Fax** 06-58 33 34 13 **Rooms** 24

A lovely little hotel, away from the crowds, with the perfect roof terrace. Very stylish, modern rooms in a converted Franciscan convent. Professional and friendly staff. A tiny shuttle bus on the adjacent square takes you to the heart of Trastevere and a tram takes you across the river to the centre. **www.hotelsanfrancesco.net**

Key to Symbols *see back cover flap*

VATICAN Hilton Cavalieri

Via Cadlolo 101, 00136 **Tel** *06-35 09 20 31* **Fax** *06-35 09 22 41* **Rooms** *370*　　　　　　　**Map** *B2*

Although a 15-minute drive from the centre of Rome, Hilton Cavalieri is one of the city's top hotels, with the finest restaurant, La Pergola. Set in large, lush gardens, it has a huge pool and a sumptuous spa. Rooms are beautifully decorated and some have spectacular views over Rome. Extras are expensive. **www.cavalierihilton.it**

VIA VENETO Westin Excelsior

Via Veneto 125, 00187 **Tel** *06-470 81* **Fax** *06-482 62 05* **Rooms** *317*　　　　　　　**Map** *D2*

Exotically sculpted balconies with caryatid figures announce the presence of this extravagant hotel on Via Veneto. Inside are boutiques, a wonderful new spa with pool, excellent panoramic restaurants and bar, and even a children's club. The rooms are classically sumptuous throughout. **excelsior.hotelinroma.com**

VILLA BORGHESE Villa Mangili

Via G Mangili 31, 00197 **Tel** *06-321 71 30* **Fax** *06-322 43 13* **Rooms** *12*　　　　　　　**Map** *D1*

In a pleasant, quiet part of Parioli, Villa Mangili is close to the Villa Borghese park near the new auditorium and the Villa Giulia. Although small, it has spacious and beautifully decorated rooms with wooden parquet floors. Breakfast is served in a lovely garden. The hotel exhibits and sells the works of new artists. **www.hotelvillamangili.it**

FLORENCE

CITY CENTER Hermitage

Vicolo Marzio 1, 50122 **Tel** *055-28 72 16* **Fax** *055-21 22 08* **Rooms** *28*　　　　　　　**Map** *D4*

This hotel is on four floors of a medieval tower: the reception and common areas are on the fifth floor; the roof-garden on the sixth offers a panoramic view of the Vasari Corridor, the Ponte Vecchio, the Arno and beyond. Rooms facing the Duomo are quieter. **www.hermitagehotel.com**

CITY CENTER Loggiato dei Serviti

Via dei Servi 49 (Piazza Santissima Annunziata 3), 50122 **Tel** *055-28 95 92* **Fax** *055-28 95 95* **Rooms** *39* **Map** *D3*

Built in the 16th-century by the Padri Serviti order to house traveling prelates. A mirror-image of Brunelleschi's Spedale degli Innocenti across the square. All the rooms are different. Rooms overlook either the piazza or the garden of the Accademia delle Belle Arti. Advanced booking essential. **www.loggiatodeiservitihotel.it**

CITY CENTER Palazzo Niccolini al Duomo

Via dei Servi 2, 50122 **Tel** *055-28 24 12?* **Fax** *055-29 09 79* **Rooms** *10*　　　　　　　**Map** *D4*

In a prime location directly facing the Duomo, this 16th-century palazzo is run by descendants of the original owners. Reception and rooms are on the second floor. Public rooms have paintings and antiques. Rooms have marble bathrooms. The living room of the suite has a unique view of Brunelleschi's dome. **www.niccolinidomepalace.com**

CITY CENTER Porta Rossa

Via Porta Rossa 19, 50123 **Tel** *055-28 75 51* **Fax** *055-28 21 79* **Rooms** *78*　　　　　　　**Map** *D2*

Located between the Ponte Vecchio and Piazza Santa Trinità. While the current building dates from 1500, documents confirm that a house stood here as early as 1386. The vaulted entrance hall is decorated in the Italian Art Nouveau style known as Liberty. All rooms are large and furnished with antiques. **www.hotelportarossa.it**

CITY CENTER Grand Hotel Minerva

Piazza Santa Maria Novella 16, 50123 **Tel** *055-272 30* **Fax** *055-26 82 81* **Rooms** *102*　　　　　　　**Map** *C2*

The only hotel in Florence to have a rooftop swimming pool. Watching the sunset from here or from the adjacent bar, is a totally memorable experience. Recently refurbished from top-to-toe, this hotel has welcomed a long line of famous guests, including Henry James. Family suites have two bathrooms. **www.grandhotelminerva.com**

CITY CENTER Excelsior

Piazza Ognissanti 3, 50123 **Tel** *055-271 51* **Fax** *055-21 02 78* **Rooms** *171*　　　　　　　**Map** *B3*

The Excelsior excels. Marble floor and columns, grand staircases, stained-glass windows, statues, and period paintings. The rooms are equally opulent, and the service impeccable. The restaurant Il Cestello serves Tuscan and international cuisine; the ground-floor terrace provides splendid views. **www.westin.com/excelsiorflorence**

CITY CENTER Savoy

Piazza della Repubblica 7, 50123 **Tel** *055-273 51/28 33 13* **Fax** *055-273 58 88* **Rooms** *102*　　　　　　　**Map** *B2*

Architecturally magnificent, lavish interiors, elegantly appointed rooms with 14 suites (two of which have a *hammam*). The sixth-floor gym has spectacular views of the Duomo and Giotto's *campanile*. The L'Incontro bar on the piazza is a rendezvous point for the Florentines. **www.hotelsavoy.it**

SOUTH OF THE ARNO Silla

Via dè Renai 5, 50126 **Tel** *055-234 28 88* **Fax** *055-234 14 37* **Rooms** *35*　　　　　　　**Map** *E4*

Located in a 16th-century building, this family-run hotel on the Oltrarno side of the river is reached through an elegant courtyard. A grand staircase leads to the entrance of this hotel (also lift). Breakfast is served on the terrace in the summer, overlooking the river and the city. **www.hotelsilla.it**

Map References *see maps of Rome pp392–3 and Florence pp412–3*

VENICE

CANNAREGIO Continental
€€€

Lista di Spagna 166, 30121 **Tel** *041-71 51 22* **Fax** *041-524 24 32* **Rooms** *93*   **Map** *C2*

This sizeable modern hotel caters mainly to large groups. It boasts a restaurant with panoramic views next to the Grand Canal. Many rooms have views of the canals, while others overlook a shady square. The hotel's location is especially handy for one of the city's main tourist shopping districts. **www.hotelcontinentalvenice.com**

CASTELLO Paganelli
€€€

Riva degli Schiavoni 4687, 30122 **Tel** *041-522 43 24* **Fax** *041-523 92 67* **Rooms** *22*   **Map** *F4*

This hotel has an excellent location on the San Marco waterfront, close to ferry services, with wonderful views from the front rooms, which are furnished in an old style but are cosy all the same. The accommodations in the annexe (*dipendenza*) are quieter but less attractive. Babysitting can be arranged. **www.hotelpaganelli.com**

CASTELLO Londra Palace
€€€€

Riva degli Schiavoni 4171, 30122 **Tel** *041-520 05 33* **Fax** *041-522 50 32* **Rooms** *53*   **Map** *F4*

Elegance, excellent service, and spacious rooms characterize this top hotel. Located close to the monument to King Vittorio Emanuele on the broad bustling Riva a short stroll from the Piazza, it has splendid views over the water. It was here that Tchaikovsky composed his Fourth Symphony. **www.hotellondra.it**

DORSODURO Ca' Pisani
€€€

Rio Terrà Foscarini 979a, 30123 **Tel** *041-240 14 11* **Fax** *041-277 10 61* **Rooms** *29*   **Map** *C5*

This converted 15th-century palace is very handily located for the Accademia galleries and the Peggy Guggenheim Collection. The atmosphere is compounded by stunning modern design, a roof terrace, and a relaxing steam bath. **www.capisanihotel.it**

LIDO DI VENEZIA Hotel des Bains
€€€

Lungomare Marconi 17, 30126 **Tel** *041-526 59 21* **Fax** *041-526 01 13* **Rooms** *192*

Wonderful Art Deco ambience, cool arcades with plush armchairs, and top-level service. The superb rooms have everything. Across the road from the beach, the Des Bains is open for guests from mid-Mar to Nov. Thomas Mann set his famous novel *Death in Venice* here. **www.westin.com**

LIDO DI VENEZIA Villa Mabapa
€€€

Riviera San Nicolò 16, 30126 **Tel** *041-526 05 90* **Fax** *041-526 94 41* **Rooms** *73*

This 1930s villa, originally built as a private residence, has been converted into a comfortable guesthouse. An attractive shady garden welcomes guests back from sightseeing expeditions. Close to the *vaporetto* landing stages, it stands on a promenade overlooking the lagoon. **www.villamabapa.com**

RIALTO Rialto
€€€€

Riva di Ferro 5149, 30124 **Tel** *041-520 91 66* **Fax** *041-523 89 58* **Rooms** *79*   **Map** *D3*

This rambling establishment has good family rooms, excellent facilities and a canalside restaurant in the summer months. The marvelous position at the foot of the Rialto bridge ensures spectacular views from many of its rooms and the *vaporetto* is very convenient. **www.rialtohotel.com**

SAN MARCO Flora
€€€

Via XXII Marzo 2283a, 30124 **Tel** *041-520 58 44* **Fax** *041-522 82 17* **Rooms** *43*   **Map** *D4*

This tiny hotel is squeezed in a narrow alley just off a major fashion shopping street, close to Piazza San Marco and the *vaporetto* landing stages. The rooms are a little cramped, but well equipped. A small but pleasant garden can be enjoyed when the weather is fine. It is advisable to reserve in advance. **www.hotelflora.it**

SAN MARCO Gritti Palace
€€€€

Santa Maria del Giglio 2467, 30124 **Tel** *041-79 46 11* **Fax** *041-520 09 42* **Rooms** *91*   **Map** *D4*

Ernest Hemingway described this as "the best hotel in a city of great hotels". Deluxe standards are combined with a superb setting on the magnificent Grand Canal for this sumptuous 15th-century palace. Service is meticulous and a meal at the waterside restaurant highly recommended. **www.luxurycollection.com/grittipalace**

SAN MARCO Europa & Regina
€€€€

Calle Larga XXII Marzo 2159, 30124 **Tel** *041-520 04 77* **Fax** *041-523 15 33* **Rooms** *185*   **Map** *D4*

This splendid establishment was the home of 18th-century artist Tiepolo. In an inspiring position on the Grand Canal, close to Piazza San Marco, it has beautifully decorated spacious rooms and sumptuous public areas. The excellent alfresco waterside restaurant is recommended. **www.westin.com**

SANTA CROCE Al Sole
€€

Fondamenta Minotto 136, 30135 **Tel** *041-244 03 28* **Fax** *041-72 22 87* **Rooms** *60*   **Map** *C4*

Book well in advance to stay in this lovely 14th-century palace, with its marble-floored reception area and photogenic façade. Its courtyard is a blaze of scented blooms in summer. Handy for Piazzale Roma for buses and *vaporetti*. The inviting rooms have views over the canal or private garden. **www.alsolehotels.com**

Key to Price Guide *see p456* **Map References** *see map of Venice pp432–3*

NORTHERN ITALY

GENOA Torre Cambiaso

🍴🏊⛱🅿 €€

Via Scarpanto 49, 16157 **Tel** *010-698 06 36* **Fax** *010-697 30 22* **Rooms** *45*

A unique noble villa with romantic tower, orchards, formal gardens and a tree-lined avenue leading up to the entrance. Rooms with swathes of fabric and period furniture are located in the villa or elegantly restored stables. Guests can enjoy the hotel's heated outdoor pool and the restaurant's Ligurian cuisine. **www.antichedimore.com**

LAKE COMO Hotel du Lac

🛗🍴📋🅿 €€

Via del Prestino 4, 23829 **Tel** *0341-83 02 38* **Fax** *0341-83 10 81* **Rooms** *17*

A peaceful hotel at the water's edge with enchanting views from the lake-facing rooms. Enjoy the terrace restaurant, looking out over the water. Charming features include marble columns, wrought-iron balustrades and floral names for every room. Tranquil and relaxing. Closed mid-Nov–end-Feb. **www.albergodulac.com**

LAKE GARDA Locanda San Vigilio

🍴🏊📋🅿 €€€€

San Vigilio, 37016 **Tel** *045-725 66 88* **Fax** *045-627 81 82* **Rooms** *7*

One of the loveliest, most exclusive hotels on Lake Garda, exuding Old World charm. Set in tranquil grounds with a small church dedicated to Saint Vigilio. Comfort and service live up to all expectations and there is a private beach and free mooring for waterborne guests. Closed Dec–Feb. **www.punta-sanvigilio.it**

LAKE MAGGIORE Giardino

🛗🍴📋 €€

Corso Repubblica 1, 28041 **Tel** *0322-459 94* **Fax** *0322-24 94 01* **Rooms** *56*

The Giardino Hotel is in the centre of town and faces the lake. It is comfortable but sparsely decorated, with a light airy feel. In addition to a garden and large terrace with views across Lake Maggiore, it has a landing stage for boats. **www.giardinoarona.com**

MANTUA Rechigi

🛗🍴🅿 €€€

Via Pier Fortunato Calvi 30, 46100 **Tel** *0376-32 07 81* **Fax** *0376-22 02 91* **Rooms** *56*

A bright contemporary hotel in the historic center of Mantua with a spacious, modern entrance hall, gleaming in white marble. Innovative art is displayed at intervals on the ground floor and the hotel boasts a lovely little indoor garden. Close to the great monuments and restaurants of the town. **www.rechigi.com**

MILAN Antica Locanda Leonardo

🛗📋🅿 €€€

Corso Magenta 78, 20123 **Tel** *02-46 33 17* **Fax** *02-48 01 90 12* **Rooms** *20*

A chic family-run guesthouse with bar and dining room, and a wonderful terraced garden at the back. This 19th-century palazzo has antiques mixed with more contemporary decor, and is close to Leonardo da Vinci's Last Supper. Wi-Fi internet connection in every room. Closed 3 weeks Aug. **www.anticalocandaleonardo.com**

MILAN Park Hyatt Milano

🛗🍴🏊🎮📋 €€€€€

Via Tommaso Grossi 1, 20121 **Tel** *02-88 21 12 34* **Fax** *02-88 21 12 35* **Rooms** *117*

Housed in an old bank, this relaxed hotel is an elegant modern addition to Milan's more traditional hotels. You can't get more central: from the front doors you step into the beautiful domed Galleria, Milan's central walkway of shops alongside the Duomo cathedral. Excellent restaurant, facilities, and service. **www.milan.park.hyatt.com**

PADUA Plaza

🍴🎮📋🅿 €€

Corso Milano 40, 35139 **Tel** *049-65 68 22* **Fax** *049-66 11 17* **Rooms** *139*

An established and efficiently run hotel with a deservedly good reputation. Though its 1970s exterior appears somewhat unattractive, inside it offers up-to-date technology and modern comforts. It provides a full range of services and a thoroughly warm welcome. **www.plazapadova.it**

PORTOFINO Splendido

🛗🍴🏊🎮🅿 €€€€€

Salita Baratta 16, 16034 **Tel** *0185-26 78 01* **Fax** *0185-26 78 06* **Rooms** *64*

Positioned on a series of terraces and housed in a former monastery overlooking Italy's luxurious fishing village resort of Portofino, this is a truly magnificent place to stay. Service is impeccable and the views from all rooms are unforgettable. Closed mid-Nov–end-Mar. **www.hotelsplendido.com**

TURIN Turin Palace

🛗🍴🏊📋🅿 €€€

Via P. Sacchi 8, 10128 **Tel** *011-562 55 11* **Fax** *011-561 21 87* **Rooms** *122*

Impeccable service and traditional luxury can be expected in this palazzo dating back to 1872. The refined tranquil atmosphere also includes modern facilities. The Vigna Reale restaurant serves regional dishes and an old-style cuisine. Central for shopping, museums, and sightseeing. **www.turinpalace.thi.it**

VERONA Giulietta e Romeo

🛗🏊📋🅿 €€

Vicolo Tre Marchetti 3, 37121 **Tel** *045-800 35 54* **Fax** *045-801 08 62* **Rooms** *31*

This prettily named hotel is situated in a quiet street just behind the Arena, which is just a few minutes' walk away. The city's main attractions are also nearby. The refurbished bedrooms are bright and comfortable with modern furnishings. Breakfast is served in the bar. The hotel also offers free bike hire. **www.giuliettaeromeo.com**

Key to Symbols *see back cover flap*

VERONA Due Torri Hotel Baglioni　　　　🔲⏸️💈📺🅿️　　€€€
Piazza Sant'Anastasia 4, 37121 **Tel** *045-59 50 44* **Fax** *045-800 41 30* **Rooms** *90*

Standing alongside a beautiful church in the heart of medieval Verona, this sumptuous 14th-century building is one of Italy's most eccentric hotels. Each bedroom is decorated and furnished in the style of a different era. The public areas are equally opulent in this unique hotel. **www.baglionihotels.com**

VICENZA Campo Marzio　　　　🔲⏸️📋🅿️　　€€
Via Roma 21, 36100 **Tel** *0444-54 57 00* **Fax** *0444-02 04 95* **Rooms** *35*

A stylish boutique hotel with good facilities, just a short stroll from the city center and the principal Palladian sites. The bedrooms are large and beautifully furnished – each room with its own individual decor and Wi-Fi connection. It is situated in a peaceful location. **www.hotelcampomarzio.com**

CENTRAL ITALY

ASSISI Hotel Umbra　　　　🔲⏸️📋　　€€
Via degli Archi 6 (Piazza del Comune), 06081 **Tel** *075-81 22 40* **Fax** *075-81 36 53* **Rooms** *25*

Tucked away on a small street, not far from the town hall, this is a very popular little hotel and restaurant with a courtyard garden offering alfresco dining in summer. Quiet and family run, it has tiled floors and antiques throughout. Bedrooms are airy and elegantly decorated. **www.hotelumbra.it**

BOLOGNA De Commercianti　　　　🔲📋🅿️　　€€€
Via De'Pignattari 11, 40124 **Tel** *051-745 75 11* **Fax** *051-745 75 22* **Rooms** *36*

In the heart of the city, just off Piazza Maggiore, this historic building dates from the 12th century. Delightful bedrooms and suites, some with wooden beams or frescoes, others with a private terrace overlooking the church of San Petronio. Prices surge during the trade fairs. Bicycles and internet access available. **www.bolognarthotels.it**

FERRARA Duchessa Isabella　　　　🔲⏸️📋🅿️　　€€€€
Via Palestro 70, 44100 **Tel** *0532-20 21 21* **Fax** *0532-20 26 38* **Rooms** *27*

A Relais & Chateaux hotel in a delightful 16th-century palazzo. Bedrooms are named after flowers, with plasma-screen televisions and lovely bathrooms. The hotel offers its horse and carriage for glamorous rides around Ferrara. Bicycles for hire; fitness center nearby. Relaxing grounds and excellent restaurant. **www.duchessaisabella.it**

LUCCA Piccolo Hotel Puccini　　　　€
Via di Poggio 9, 55100 **Tel** *0583-554 21* **Fax** *0583-534 87* **Rooms** *14*

A small, friendly hotel in an attractive stone building in the very heart of Lucca, just over the road from the house in which Giacomo Puccini was born (now a museum) and the busy central square of San Michele. The rooms are small but well priced for the location. Courtesy car to airport and train station. **www.hotelpuccini.com**

PERUGIA Albergo Brufani Palace　　　　🔲⏸️💈📺📋🅿️　　€€€€€
Piazza Italia 12, 06100 **Tel** *075-573 25 41* **Fax** *075-572 02 10* **Rooms** *94*

A four-storey luxury hotel on a hill in central Perugia with lovely views over the valleys below. High, frescoed ceilings, parquet floors, stone fireplaces, chandeliers and antiques abound; bedrooms are particularly sumptuous. The swimming pool has a glass floor above Etruscan ruins. Fine restaurant. **www.brufanipalace.com**

PISA Royal Victoria Hotel　　　　🔲📋🅿️　　€€
Lungarno Pacinotti 12, 56126 **Tel** *050-94 01 11* **Fax** *050-94 01 80* **Rooms** *48*

The Royal Victoria occupies a 10th-century tower built to house the Winemaker's Guild. It became Pisa's first hotel in 1837, combining several medieval tower houses in the process. Run by the welcoming Piegaja family, the rooms are charming in their size and decor. Bike rental and private garage. **www.royalvictoria.it**

RAVENNA Albergo Cappello　　　　🔲⏸️💈📋🅿️　　€€
Via IV Novembre 41, 48100 **Tel** *0544-21 98 13* **Fax** *0544-21 98 14* **Rooms** *7*

Extremely central, on a pedestrianized street, this small boutique hotel is Ravenna's prettiest, though bedrooms are fairly small. Each bedroom has been individually styled and furnished with antiques. Renowned restaurant and wine bar. Non-smoking rooms/disabled access. **www.albergocappello.it**

SIENA Pensione Palazzo Ravizza　　　　⏸️📋　　€€€
Pian dei Mantellini 34, 53100 **Tel** *0577-28 04 62* **Fax** *0577-22 15 97* **Rooms** *30*

A *pensione* in a quiet, Renaissance palace in the historical center of Siena. Rooms come with original terracotta floors, frescoed ceilings, carved wooden doorways, and antique furnishings. Suites have their own lounge areas. Gourmet evening restaurant and a garden terrace overlooking the Tuscan hills. **www.palazzoravizza.it**

URBINO Hotel Bonconte　　　　🔲🚻📋　　€€
Via delle Mura 28, 61029 **Tel** *0722-24 63* **Fax** *0722-47 82* **Rooms** *23*

A short walk away from the centro storico, just within the city walls, this hotel has lovely views of the countryside around Urbino. This elegant old villa below the town is filled with antiques and set in a garden oasis, where breakfast is served in summer (not included in room rate). Good restaurant. **www.viphotels.it**

Key to Price Guide *see p456* **Key to Symbols** *see back cover flap*

NAPLES AND THE SOUTH

AMALFI Hotel Santa Caterina
SS Amalfitana 9, 84011 **Tel** *089-87 10 12* **Fax** *089-87 13 51* **Rooms** *70*

Run by the same family since 1880, this luxury hotel is one of the Amalfi Coast's finest. High over Amalfi, perched on a promontory tumbling down to the sea, it has extensive gardens and terraces. Rooms and suites are lavish, all with antiques, *majolica* floor tiles and balconies or terraces. Spa and excellent restaurant. **www.hotelsantacaterina.it**

CAPRI Hotel La Minerva
Via Occhio Marina, 80073 **Tel** *081-837 03 74* **Fax** *081-837 52 21* **Rooms** *19*

A pretty five-story hotel with flower-filled terraces, in a quiet, picturesque spot not far from the center of Capri town. *Majolica* tile floors, antiques, and sea views. Superior rooms have a terrace, deluxe rooms have whirlpool bathtubs and sea-facing terraces, while standard rooms are much cheaper. **www.laminervacapri.com**

NAPLES Hotel Chiaja de Charme
Via Chiaia 216, 81021 **Tel** *081-41 55 55* **Fax** *081-42 23 44* **Rooms** *14*

A lovely intimate hotel with reception on the first floor of a noble palazzo on the pedestrian street of Via Chiaia, two minutes' walk from Piazza Plebescito. All the rooms are soundproofed and individually furnished with antiques. Some of the bathrooms have whirlpool bathtubs. Charming, professional staff. **www.hotelchiaia.it**

NAPLES Hotel Vesuvio
Via Partenope 45, 81021 **Tel** *081-764 00 44* **Fax** *081-764 44 83* **Rooms** *143*

In Santa Lucia, the Vesuvio is unarguably Naples' most luxurious hotel, with a spectacular penthouse. All bedrooms and suites are extremely comfortable, furnished with antiques and have a terrace or balcony with sea or street views. Spa and gym, terrace restaurant, babysitting room, and a hotel boat. **www.vesuvio.it**

POSITANO Palazzo Murat
Via dei Mulini 23, 84017 **Tel** *089-87 51 77* **Fax** *089-81 14 19* **Rooms** *30*

The genteel Palazzo Murat was once the summer residence of Napoleon's brother-in-law Murat. Set in an enchanting courtyard with an excellent restaurant, the bedrooms are in the old 18th-century wing – and are complete with stucco, wooden beams, and frescoes – or in the elegant modern annex. **www.palazzomurat.it**

SICILY

AGRIGENTO Hotel Colleverde
Valle dei Templi, 92100 **Tel** *0922-295 55* **Fax** *0922-290 12* **Rooms** *48*

A modern hotel with a fine view of the Valley of the Temples from its landscaped gardens. The bedrooms are comfortable and nicely furnished: deluxe rooms have wonderful views. Close to Agrigento's center and train station. The restaurant has a terrace. Two rooms have disabled facilities. **www.colleverde-hotel.it**

CATANIA Hotel Katane Palace
Via Finocchiaro April 110, 95129 **Tel** *095-747 07 02* **Fax** *095-747 01 72* **Rooms** *58*

In a central position, convenient for the port, railway station and visiting the old quarter. Bedrooms are spacious, elegantly furnished and soundproofed; the en suite bathrooms are very smart. Cuciniere, the hotel's restaurant, is critically renowned and an annual series of music concerts is held here. **www.katanepalace.com**

PALERMO Massimo Plaza Hotel
Via Maqueda 437, 90133 **Tel** *091-32 56 57* **Fax** *091-32 57 11* **Rooms** *15*

In an extremely central position, opposite the Teatro Massimo, this lovingly restored palazzo has stylish decor and an air of calm. Bedrooms are large and fresh, with soundproofing – some have prime views over the elegant square. There is a welcoming bar and lounge area, and service is excellent. **www.massimoplazahotel.com**

PALERMO Grand Hotel Villa Igiea
Salita Belmonte 43, 90142 **Tel** *091-631 21 11* **Fax** *091-54 76 54* **Rooms** *110*

A romantic Hilton hotel outside Palermo, with jasmine-scented gardens overlooking the sea. Built in 1908 by Ernesto Basile, a key proponent of the Italian Art Nouveau style, there are exquisite frescoes in the public areas and original furniture. Elegant bedrooms with garden views or private sea-facing terraces. **www.hilton.co.uk**

TAORMINA Villa Belvedere
Via Bagnoli Croce 79, 98039 **Tel** *0942-237 91* **Fax** *0942-62 58 30* **Rooms** *47*

A pretty, yellow Liberty style villa in a garden of orange and lemon trees surrounding a pool facing the sea. Five minutes from both the old quarter and the funicular down to the beach. Its public rooms are cool and welcoming and the bedrooms are generally airy and light, most with a balcony or terrace. **www.villabelvedere.it**

Where to Eat in Italy

Each region has its own distinctive cuisine, using local, seasonal ingredients, although national favorites, such as classic pasta dishes, pizzas, and desserts are produced all over the country. Among the countless delights of Italian food, look out for Sicilian fish, game and steaks in Tuscany, and the rich cuisine of Emilia-Romagna.

PRICE CATEGORIES
Price categories are for a three-course meal for one, including half a bottle of house wine, tax, and service.
€ Under 25 euros
€€ 25–35 euros
€€€ 35–45 euros
€€€€ 45–55 euros
€€€€€ Over 55 euros

ROME

CAMPO DE' FIORI Al Pompiere
€€

Via S. M. del Calderari 38, 00186 **Tel** *06-686 83 77*   **Map** *C3*

On the first floor of Palazzo Cenci, in the Ghetto, Al Pompiere has an attractive dining room with frescoes and wooden beams. The Roman-Jewish menu features *carciofi alla giudia* (fried artichokes), pasta with *la pajata* (calf intestines), and beef stew. Desserts include *crema fritta* (deep-fried custard).

CAMPO DE' FIORI Camponeschi
€€€€€

Piazza Farnese 50, 00186 **Tel** *06-687 49 27*   **Map** *C3*

One of Rome's finest restaurants, Camponeschi offers wonderful views of the Piazza Farnese. Its cuisine, a fusion of Italian, Mediterranean and French, is extremely refined. Superb fish and meat dishes. Its *cantina* contains over 400 wines, including its own prestigious label from the family vineyard. Open in evenings only.

CAMPO DE' FIORI Piperno
€€€€€

Via Monte de' Cenci 9, 00186 **Tel** *06-68 80 66 29*   **Map** *C3*

A restaurant has been here since the mid-1800s, though the original Piperno has long gone. His name still carries great kudos, though as one of the finest in Roman-Jewish cooking. The pasta is handmade every day; the fish arrives daily. The house wine is a delicious Frascati. Don't miss the *carciofi alla giudia* (fried artichokes). Book ahead.

PANTHEON Da Gino
€€

Vicolo Rosini 4, 00186 **Tel** *06-687 34 34*   **Map** *C2*

Da Gino is a friendly restaurant packed to the gills with politicans and journalists. The frescoed, old-fashioned interior opens on to a charming *pergola* in good weather. Classic Roman dishes include *spaghetti alla carbonara*, *abbacchio alla cacciatora* (a lamb dish), *seppie con piselli* (cuttlefish with peas), and rabbit.

PANTHEON El Toulà
€€€€€

Via della Lupa 29B, 00186 **Tel** *06-687 34 98*   **Map** *C2*

Justly renowned as one of Rome's most exclusive and luxurious restaurants, El Toulà serves Mediterranean cuisine, but is strongly inspired by the Veneto region. The elegant vaulted dining room and excellent service are perfect for a special lunch or dinner. The risotto, pasta, fish, and meat dishes change with the seasons.

PIAZZA DI SPAGNA Margutta Vegetariana
€€

Via Margutta 118, 00187 **Tel** *06-32 65 05 77*   **Map** *C2*

A colorful, plant-filled dining room with modern art in profusion and a jazz soundtrack, this is Rome's first and finest vegetarian eatery. Opened 20 years ago, it offers a hearty buffet lunch and an excellent value Sunday brunch. The adjacent restaurant prepares vegetarian meals with creative flair at much higher prices.

PIAZZA NAVONA Il Primoli
€€

Via dei Soldati 22, 00186 **Tel** *06-68 13 51 12*   **Map** *C2*

On the ground floor of the Museo Napoleonico in Palazzo Primoli, the elegant Primoli has modern decor, blown-up fin-de-siècle images on the walls, and candlelit tables. Typical fare is air-dried beef with courgette flowers and *robiola* cheese, pasta with ricotta and asparagus tips, fish tempura, and chocolate soufflé. Great value.

QUIRINAL Al Presidente
€€€€

Via in Arcione 95, 00187 **Tel** *06-679 73 42*   **Map** *D3*

One of the city's best restaurants, with wonderful, modern Roman cuisine, elegant decor and fine wine – ideal for intimate chats. Only a short walk from the Trevi Fountain, it also has a great outdoor terrace. Ingredients are expertly researched, with the menu changing accordingly. Three taster menus are available at dinner.

TRASTEVERE Ripa 12
€€€

Via di San Francesco a Ripa 1, 00153 **Tel** *06-580 9093*   **Map** *C4*

In Southern Trastevere, far from the tourist trail, Ripa 12 serves excellent Calabrian cuisine, with the focus firmly on fish. Marinated sea bass *carpaccio* (wafer-thin slices) is the house starter, followed by fresh fish of the day or a platter of fried seafood. Very much a locals' favorite.

Key to Symbols *see back cover flap*

VATICANO Dal Toscano
🚻♿📷🍴   €€€

Via Germanico 58, 00192 **Tel** *06-39 72 57 17*   **Map** *B2*

A popular and ever-reliable restaurant, Dal Toscano has outside tables in summer and a wood-paneled dining room. Expect exquisitely cooked meat dishes and excellent red wines. *Pappardelle sulla lepre* (pasta in a hare sauce), polenta and porcini mushrooms or *bistecca alla Fiorentina* (steak on the bone) on the menu.

VIA VENETO Papà Baccus
🍴   €€€€€

Via Toscana 36, 00184 **Tel** *06-42 74 28 08*   **Map** *D2*

One of the best addresses in the city for bona fide Tuscan cuisine. From the classic ribollita (a soup of beans, vegetables, and bread) to the various cuts of Chianina beef, every option here is a good one. The simply seared fillet steak reigns supreme, though the baked *rombo* (turbot) and *baccalà* (salt cod) should also satisfy the fish eater.

VILLA BORGHESE Baby
♿🚻👔🍴   €€€€€

Via Ulisse Aldrovandi 15, 00197 **Tel** *06-321 61 26*   **Map** *D1*

A relative newcomer to Rome's restaurant scene, Baby is run by the renowned husband-and-wife team behind Don Alfonso (one of Italy's finest restaurants) on the Amalfi Coast. Outstanding Neapolitan-inspired cuisine is served in a delightful dining room and terrace at one of Rome's top hotels, the Hotel Aldrovandi Palace.

FLORENCE

CITY CENTER Coquinaros
🍴   €€

Via delle Oche 15r, 50122 **Tel** *055-230 21 53*   **Map** *D3*

A convenient, cosy little place, just behind the Duomo, where you can eat at almost any time of the day or evening. There are some delicious pasta dishes (try the ravioli with pecorino and pears). You can also order a salad, a plate of cheese or cured meats or a toasted open sandwich. There are good wines by the glass and bottle too.

CITY CENTER Frescobaldi Wine Bar
🍴   €€

Via dei Magazzini 2/4r, 50122 **Tel** *055-28 47 24*   **Map** *B4*

This wine bar and restaurant is owned by one of Tuscany's foremost wine producers. Lunch is a casual affair, while dinner is a little more formal, with white tablecloths and gleaming crystal. Creative, elegant food is accompanied by some fine in-house wines; if you just want a snack and a glass, pop into Frescobaldino next door.

CITY CENTER Il Santo Bevitore
♿🚻🍴   €€

Via Santo Spirito 64/66r, 50125 **Tel** *055-21 12 64*   **Map** *D4*

Housed in an ex-stable, this relaxed restaurant/wine bar features delicately flavored innovative dishes. The menu changes seasonally, but there is always a selection of soups and home-made pastas, fish and grilled meat. Or you can choose from a selction of well-sourced cheese and cured meats. The wine list is interesting too.

CITY CENTER Ristorante Ricchi
♿🚻🍴   €€

Piazza Santo Spirito 8r, 50125 **Tel** *055-21 58 64*   **Map** *B4*

With elegant, modern decor and a lovely terrace, this small fish restaurant is situated on one of Florence's most beautiful squares. Oriental influences are evident in dishes such as pasta with shrimps and mint, swordfish with Sichuan pepper, and salt cod in a spice crust. There's a limited choice for carnivores too.

CITY CENTER I Latini
♿🍴   €€€

Via dei Palchetti 6r, 50123 **Tel** *055-21 09 16*   **Map** *C3*

There is always a crowd of both foreigners and locals clamoring for a table outside this large, noisy *trattoria* where huge hams hang from the ceiling. The food is traditional and the portions are enormous. Try the succulent grilled and roasted meats; *bistecca alla fiorentina* (broiled T-bone steak) is an experience.

CITY CENTER Targa
♿🚻👔🍴   €€€

Lungarno C Colombo 7, 50136 (east of city centre) **Tel** *055-67 73 77*

Background jazz and a warm wood-and-glass interior, softened by lots of greenery, make for a relaxed setting in this bistro on the Arno. The food is understated and based on seasonal local traditions; crêpes with artichokes and *taleggio* (cheese), rack of lamb with asparagus and broad beans. Fantastic wine list.

CITY CENTER San Jacopo
♿🚻🍴   €€€

Borgo San Jacopo 62r, 50125 **Tel** *055-28 16 61*   **Map** *C4*

One of the city's newer restaurants, San Jacopo enjoys a fabulous setting on the south bank of the Arno. Book ahead and ask for one of the coveted tables on the tiny terrace. The chic and breezy atmosphere suits the unpretentious but beautifully served food very well. Fish fans should try the *brodetto* (fish soup), an Adriatic specialty.

CITY CENTER Enoteca Pinchiorri
♿🚻👔🍴   €€€€€

Via Ghibellina 87, 50122 **Tel** *055-24 27 57*   **Map** *E4*

Pinchiorri is frequently described as Italy's finest restaurant and it has one of Europe's best-stocked cellars, boasting over 80,000 bottles. On the ground floor of a 15th-century palazzo, the ambience is very special too, but the food (ultra-refined Tuscan/French) and the fussy service will not please all.

Map References see maps of Rome pp392–3 and Florence pp412–3

VENICE

BURANO Da Romano
�&ℝ⌨🖹 €€€€
Via Galuppi 221, 30012 **Tel** *041-73 00 30*

It is advisable to book ahead to avoid disappointment since this is the leading restaurant on the island of Burano. A wide range of fish is served in traditional Venetian fashion, under the watchful eye of a descendant of the original 19th-century owner. Closed Sun dinner, Tue; mid-Dec–Jan.

CANNAREGIO Vini Da Gigio
🖹 €€€€
Fondamenta San Felice 3628A, 30121 **Tel** *041-528 51 40* **Map** *E2*

Elegant atmosphere and refined dishes that use seasonal produce. Risotto with prawns or grilled cuttlefish often feature on the menu, or delicious duck and local artichokes. There is also a vast wine list. Advance booking is advisable. Closed Mon, Tue; mid-Jan–5 Feb, 3 wks Aug.

CASTELLO La Corte Sconta
🖹🖹 €€€€€
Calle del Pestrin 3886, 30122 **Tel** *041-522 70 24* **Map** *D4*

Tricky to find, but worth the effort, this simple, laid-back eatery rates among the city's best restaurants. The fresh fish and home-made pasta are superb, and desserts such as *pincia* (a traditional Venetian cake) round off the meal. Closed Sun, Mon; 7 Jan–7 Feb, mid-Jul–mid-Aug.

DORSODURO La Rivista
�&ℝ⌨🖹 €€€
Rio Terrà Foscarini 979/A, 30123 **Tel** *041-240 14 25* **Map** *C4*

A modern, welcoming establishment close to the Accademia, La Rivista also does light salads and cold platters for lunch. Imaginative meat, pasta and vegetable dishes are also on offer, as are divine desserts such as wild-berry cream. The creative menu changes on a monthly basis. Closed Mon.

GIUDECCA Cipriani
�&ℝ🎵🖹 €€€€€
Giudecca 10, 30122 **Tel** *041-520 77 44*

A courtesy launch ferries guests from the San Marco waterfront to this exclusive island hotel/restaurant for a unique meal. The food and service are impeccable and the views stunning. Children under 8 are not admitted and there is a dress code. Closed Nov–March.

SAN MARCO Da Raffaelle
🖹🖹 €€€€€
Ponte delle Ostreghe 2347, 30124 **Tel** *041-523 23 17* **Map** *D4*

This well-established bustling restaurant offers a vast range of regional dishes in an especially romantic setting. Dishes worth trying include *granseola* (spider crab) as an antipasto, and risotto with scampi and turbot as a main course. Closed Thu; Dec–late Jan.

SAN MARCO Harry's Bar
🖹 €€€€€
Calle Vallaresso 1323, 30124 **Tel** *041-528 57 77* **Map** *D4*

Known the world over as Ernest Hemingway's favorite watering hole in Venice, Harry's Bar is a hallowed institution as well as a cosy café. Coffee and toasted sandwiches can be ordered, or a Bellini cocktail. The renowned food on the menu includes *carpaccio* (raw marinated beef), a dish invented by the owner.

SAN POLO Da Fiore
🖹🖹 €€€€€
Calle del Scaleter 2202, 30125 **Tel** *041-72 13 08* **Map** *C3*

An exclusive establishment hidden behind Campo San Polo, Da Fiore is probably the city's best restaurant. Seasonal produce is the rule. Gourmet diners appreciate the sea bass with balsamic vinegar, tuna with rosemary, and *molecche* (soft-shelled crabs). Leave room for a delicate fruit sorbet. Closed Sun, Mon; 3 wks Aug, Christmas–mid–Jan.

NORTHERN ITALY

GENOA Da Genio
€€
Salita San Leonardo 61r, 16128 **Tel** *010-58 84 63*

One of Genoa's best-loved *trattorias*, with a loyal clientele, situated in the old quarter. The menu includes well-prepared fish dishes, such as fresh swordfish stuffed with anchovies and capers, but the famous starter is the traditional Ligurian dish *trenette al pesto* (pasta with pesto sauce). Closed Sun; 3 wks Aug.

LAKE COMO Albergo Ristorante Silvio
ℝ €€€
Via Carcano 12, 22021 **Tel** *031-95 03 22*

Silvio and Cristian Ponzini, the owner and his son, are the professional fishermen providing an abundant catch of fine freshwater fish for their restaurant. Visitors can even arrange a fishing trip with them, or stay at the self-catering apartments. The views over Lake Como are enchanting, especially from the vine-clad terrace. Closed Jan–Feb.

Key to Price Guide *see p462* **Map References** *see map of Venice pp432–3*

LAKE GARDA Capriccio 🔢📋 €€€€€
Piazza S. Bernardo 6, 25080 **Tel** *0365-55 11 24*

This refined establishment with views of Lake Garda offers high-quality cuisine such as sea bass, scallops on fennel cream with a grapefruit sauce, or medallions of *ricciola* (greater amberjack fish) and prawns in fennel sauce. Closed Tue; Jan–Feb.

MANTUA Il Cigno Trattoria dei Martini 📋 €€€€€
Piazza Carlo d'Arco 1, 46100 **Tel** *0376-32 71 01*

Il Cigno Trattoria dei Martini is a forerunner of the new Mantuan cuisine that simplified traditional heavy dishes and reduced prices. Its signature dish, *cappone in agrodolce* (sweet-and-sour capon) still survives. The fine Mantuan fare is complemented by a good wine list. Closed Mon, Tue; first wk Jan, Aug.

MILAN La Trattoria Milanese 📋 €€€
Via Santa Marta 11, 20123 **Tel** *02-86 45 19 91*

This trattoria is a Milan institution. With modest decor and sober professional staff, it has served genuine Milanese food near the Stock Exchange for generations. Classics include *ossobuco* (veal shank), great saffron risotto and *carpione* (cold mini-cutlets in onion and vinegar dressing). Closed Tue, mid-Jul–1 Sep, Christmas–10 Jan.

MILAN Da Giacomo 📋 €€€€€
Via B Cellini, corner Via Sottocorno 6, 20129 **Tel** *02-76 02 33 13*

A peaceful and stylish family-run establishment, and an insider address for the well-heeled and fashionable Milanese. The dining room is decorated with Art Deco lamps and photos of famous faces. House specialties are fish such as swordfish steak alla Giacomo. The wine list offers a wide choice of quality vintages. Closed Aug, 2wks Christmas.

PADUA San Pietro 📋 €€
Via San Pietro 95, 35100 **Tel** *049-876 03 30*

The perfect place for regional dishes cooked with fresh, local ingredients. This traditional Paduan restaurant offers attentive, though not always friendly, service in an informal atmosphere. Many dishes come from the Lombardy region of Italy. Closed Sun; summer Sat and Sun; Jul.

PORTOFINO Da Puny 📋🔢 €€€€€
Piazza Martiri dell'Olivetta 5, 16034 **Tel** *0185-26 90 37*

One of the best restaurants lining the tiny harbor square. The proprietor is a gregarious character, happy to recount anecdotes and flatter his guests. Fresh fish, pasta in *pesto corto* (the rich basil, cheese and pine nut sauce lifted with a dash of tomato) and house antipasti are excellent. Closed Thu; mid-Dec–mid-Feb.

TURIN Porto di Savona 🔢📋 €€
Piazza Vittorio Veneto 2, 10100 **Tel** *011-817 35 00*

This restaurant is housed in an 18th-century building near the River Po. It offers regional dishes such as gnocchi with gorgonzola cheese, local pasta varieties *tajarin* and *agnolotti*, asparagus risotto, *vitello tonnato* (thin slices of veal in tuna and caper sauce), and other specials using Barolo wine. Closed Jan.

VERONA Il Desco 📋 €€€€€
Via Dietro San Sebastiano 5–7, 37121 **Tel** *045-59 53 58*

One of Italy's finest restaurants, set in a 16th-century palazzo, Il Desco truly deserves its two Michelin stars. It is both romantic and understated. Dishes include pumpkin and Amarone wine risotto and the famous aubergine (eggplant) ravioli. A gourmet menu offers a staggering seven courses. Closed Sun, Mon; 2 wks Christmas, 2 wks Jun.

VICENZA Taverna Aeolia ♿🔢📋 €€
Piazza Conte da Schio 1, Costozza di Longare, 36023 **Tel** *0444-55 50 36*

This restaurant is housed in an elegant villa with a beautiful frescoed ceiling. The menu specializes in creative meat dishes, with kangaroo, bison, and frog all available. Vegetarians can enjoy the lemon risotto, and a children's menu is also available. Closed Tue; 1–15 Nov.

CENTRAL ITALY

ASSISI Medioevo 🎵 €€
Via Arco dei Priori 4B, 06081 **Tel** *075-81 30 68*

An elegant restaurant set under the medieval stone vaults of an ancient palazzo in the centre of Assisi. Try the home-made pastas (featuring black truffles in season). Meat, such as *agnello al tartufo* (lamb with truffles), is cooked to traditional recipes and they work wonders with steak. Great home-made desserts.

BOLOGNA Antica Trattoria Spiga 📋 €€
Via Broccaindosso 21a, 40125? **Tel** *051-23 00 63*

Family-run, old-fashioned trattoria popular with the locals for its authentic and immaculately prepared traditional cuisine. Among the specialties: lasagne, *tagliatelle al ragù*, *pasta e fagioli* (pasta and bean soup), and stuffed pasta smothered in walnuts and gorgonzola cheese.

Key to Symbols *see back cover flap*

BOLOGNA Pappagallo   🅰🗐   €€€€
Piazza Mercanzia 3c, 40125 **Tel** *051-23 28 07*

Since 1919, princes, artists, and actors have left signed photos to line the walls of this elegant restaurant housed in a 14th-century palazzo practically underneath Bologna's twin towers. The cuisine is traditional Bolognese, including tortellini (in broth or meat ragout), lasagne, and veal.

FERRARA La Sgarbata   🅰🗐   €€
Via Sgarbata 84, 44046 **Tel** *0532-71 21 10*

This countryside *trattoria* on the outskirts of the city serves up tasty local dishes such as *cappellacci di zucca alla ferrarese* (Ferrara's signature pumpkin-stuffed pasta), as well as specialty fish dishes based on the catch of the day. Locals often make plans to meet here just for the tasty pizzas. Occasional live music in summer.

LUCCA Buca di Sant'Antonio   🅰🗐   €€
Via della Cervia 3, 55100 **Tel** *0583-558 81*

This duly restored 19th-century tavern, with an excellent location, serves classic local fare with the occasional innovative touch. The stuffed rabbit en croute with mushrooms is excellent. In winter, several dishes feature locally grown chestnuts. Try *buccellato*, the tasty local pudding. Interesting wines.

PERUGIA Giò Arte e Vini   🅰🗐   €€
Via Ruggero d'Andreotto 19, 06124 **Tel** *075-573 11 00*

This modern hotel and restaurant on the outskirts of town is famous for its spectacular selection of wines (some 1,200 choices), modern art on the walls, and well-chosen regional dishes prepared with special touches. The pumpkin ravioli and the *treccia di agnello* (lamb) are particularly good.

PISA Ristorante V. Beni   🅰🗐🗐   €€€€
Piazza Gambacorti Chiara 22, 56125 **Tel** *050-25 067*

In a building dating back to the 14th century, this restaurant is situated a 15-minute walk from the Leaning Tower of Pisa, meaning that it is relatively off the tourist trail. Even so, it is enormously popular with the locals, and it is best to book in advance. Fish-based dishes are a specialty. Closed Sun.

RAVENNA Ca de Ven   €€
Via C. Ricci 24, 48100 **Tel** *0544-301 63*

They say Dante lived in a boarding house on this site, now occupied by a 16th-century palazzo next to the poet's tomb. Its brick vaulted cellars are lined with wine bottles and host one of Ravenna's best *trattoria*. The speciality is *piadine*, the local flatbread, topped with meat, cheeses, or vegetables.

SAM GIMGNANO Dorandò   🅰🗐   €€€
Vicolo dell'Oro 2, 53037 **Tel** *0577-94 18 62*

This restaurant is small and very select, so booking is advised. Impressive wine list, and dishes to go with it. The pasta with pigeon sauce on a bed of creamed mushrooms is delicious. There are various fish specialities, including angler fish in a nutty crust served with leeks. Take your time to enjoy it all.

SIENA Osteria Le Logge   🗐🗐   €€€
Via del Porrione 33, 53100 **Tel** *0577-480 13*

Siena's prettiest, and often full, restaurant has a dark wood and marble interior. The tables are laid with crisp linen cloths and decorated with plants. Home-produced oils and Montalcino wines accompny dishes that wander slightly from mainstream Tuscan cooking. The stuffed guinea fowl is delicious.

URBINO Vecchia Urbino   🅰🗐   €€€
Via dei Vasari 3–5, 61029 **Tel** *0722-44 47*

An elegantly rustic restaurant in a 16th-century structure serving simply prepared traditional dishes, including *vincigrassi* (the local lasagne of chicken, ham, and veal), *raviolone al tartufo* (a giant pasta parcel stuffed with ricotta and dressed in black truffles), rabbit, and polenta with mushrooms.

NAPLES AND THE SOUTH

AMALFI La Marinella   🅰🗐   €€
Via Lungomare dei Cavalieri di San Giovanni di Gerusalemme 1, 84011 **Tel** *089-87 10 43*

A lively, friendly restaurant overlooking the Amalfi Coast just two meters from the sea. Much fish is served, as well as traditional local specialties such as *scialatelli ai frutti di mare* (home-made pasta with seafood and crustaceans). Open for lunch only, except in high season.

CAPRI La Savardina da Eduardo   🗐   €€
Via Lo Capo 8, 80073 **Tel** *081-837 63 00*

This is one of the most traditional restaurants on Capri, with an outdoor pergola, orange trees, sea views, and tasty regional specialties such as *ravioli alla caprese* (cheese ravioli in a tomato and mozzarella sauce), *linguini all'Eduardo* (noodles with anchovies and capers), and stewed rabbit.

Key to Price Guide *see p462* **Key to Symbols** *see back cover flap*

NAPLES Amici Miei

Via Monte di Dio 78, 80123 **Tel** *081-764 60 63*

A classic menu, though it concentrates mainly on meat dishes (a rarity in fish-oriented Naples). Excellent pasta with vegetables and pulses and main courses, especially the char-grilled meats and the *braciola di maiale al ragù* (pork chop smothered in sauce with pine nuts). Cosy atmosphere and an excellent wine list.

NAPLES Da Ettore

Via Santa Lucia 56, 80123 **Tel** *081-76 404 98*

Unpretentious neighborhood *trattoria* and pizzeria serving typical Neapolitan cuisine. Good pizzas and excellent seafood pasta with mussels or clams. Also sample the *parmigiana di melanzane* (a baked casserole of aubergines/eggplant, mozzarella and tomatoes). Excellent buffalo mozzarella antipasto.

NAPLES La Cantinella

Via N. Sauro 23/Lungomare di Santa Lucia, 80132 **Tel** *081-764 86 84*

One of Naples's most famous restaurants, this place has a distinctly colonial feel. Diners are attracted by the sea views, the impeccable service, and a reputation for carefully and successfully prepared regional and international cuisine based around seafood and traditional dishes.

POMPEII Il Principe

Piazza B. Longo 8, 80045 **Tel** *081-850 55 66*

This airy, refined, and elegant restaurant with a seasonally changing menu is close to the excavations. The cuisine is based on fish, including fish-filled ravioli, and turbot with vegetables. Dishes may be inspired by 17th-century Neapolitan recipes, ancient Roman spices, or desserts pictured in Pompeii frescoes.

POSITANO La Sponda

Via Colombo 30, 84017 **Tel** *089-87 50 66*

A sumptuous restaurant in one of Italy's most elegant hotels, where guests are treated like wealthy family friends. A tempting range of modern and traditional dishes based on fresh fish and seasonal ingredients is on offer. Try *gragnano paccheri* (large pasta tubes with anchovies, roasted peppers, and basil).

SICILY

AGRIGENTO Trattoria il Pescatore

Lungomare Falcone e Borsellino 20, Località Lido di San Leone, 92100 **Tel** *0922-41 43 42*

The chef chooses the fish daily and uses it, sometimes raw, in simple but delicious dishes – often just roasting or grilling it, and drizzling on some olive oil and lemon juice. The pasta specialties are spaghetti served with a lobster sauce or tossed with chunks of swordfish, aubergines, and fresh basil.

PALERMO Trattoria Sympaty

Via Piano Gallo 18, Località Mondello, 90151 **Tel** *091-45 44 70*

The dining room has good views over the bay of Mondello – Palermo's most popular beach resort – and the menu is, appropriately, almost exclusively fish-based. Try the *fettuccini all'aragosta* (noodles with lobster), spaghetti alle sarde (with sardines), ricci (sea urchins), octopus or squid.

PALERMO La Scuderia

Viale del Fante 9, 90146 **Tel** *091-52 03 23*

This elegant restaurant set in the Parco della Favorita, on the north edge of Palermo, sticks to traditional Sicilian cuisine, carefully and deliciously prepared. Do not miss the *merluzzetti alla ghiotta* (whiting stewed with capers, potatoes, saffron and cherry tomatoes).

SYRACUSE Jonico 'a Rutta 'e Ciauli

Riviera Dionisio il Grande 194, 96100 **Tel** *0931-655 40*

This refined restaurant has a dining room with walls covered in Sicilian ceramics and agricultural artifacts, plus seating on a terrace just above the waves. Regional cuisine on a menu written mostly in Sicilian dialect; try the *cernia alla mattalotta* (grouper in white wine, onions, olives, capers and tomatoes).

TAORMINA Al Duomo

Vico degli Ebrei 11, 98039 **Tel** *0942-62 56 56*

A typical Sicilian restaurant with an outdoor terrace. Dishes make good use of Sicily's twin fish specialities: tuna and swordfish. But the chef's signature dish is *pasta ca 'nocca* (home-made macaroni with fresh anchovies, bread crumbs and wild fennel), followed by grilled *agnello* (lamb).

TAORMINA La Giara

Vicolo La Floresta 1, 98039 **Tel** *0942-233 60*

A pretty restaurant of columns and arches with beautiful views over the bay from tables out on the terrace. Try the lobster cocktail, the *petto d'oca affumicato* (smoked duck breast), ravioli with aubergine (eggplant), and *pesce alla eoliana* (baked grouper with potatoes, tomatoes and capers). It also has a piano bar/club. Closed lunch.

GREECE

Greece is one of the most visited countries in Europe, yet remains one of the least known. Although most visitors will be familiar with the images of Ancient Greece, the modern Greek state dates only from 1830. Situated at a geographical crossroads, Greece combines cultural elements of the Balkans, the Middle East, and the Mediterranean.

For a small country, Greece possesses marked regional differences. Nearly three-quarters of the land is mountainous, uninhabited, or uncultivated. On the mainland, fertile agricultural land supports tobacco farming in the northeast, with orchard fruits and vegetables grown farther south. A third of the population lives in the capital, Athens, the cultural, financial, and political center, where ancient and modern stand side by side. Of the myriad islands, only about a hundred are today inhabited.

For centuries a large number of Greeks have lived abroad. Currently there are over half as many Greeks outside the country as in, although recent years have seen reverse immigration, with expatriates returning home, especially to the islands.

Rural and urban life in contemporary Greece has been transformed since the start of the 20th century, despite foreign occupation and civil war. Until the 1960s, the country remained underdeveloped, with many rural areas lacking basic amenities. Since then, a number of improvements, including the growth of tourism, the country's largest hard-currency earner, have helped Greece develop into a relatively wealthy, modern state.

HISTORY

Early Greek history is marked by a series of internal struggles, from the Mycenaean and Minoan cultures of the Bronze Age to the competing city-states of the 1st millennium BC. In spite of warfare, the 4th and 5th centuries BC were the high point of ancient Greek civilization, a golden age of exceptional creativity in philosophy and the arts.

In 338 BC the Greeks were conquered by Philip II of Macedonia at Chaironeia, and Greece soon became absorbed into Alexander the Great's vast empire. With the defeat of

Whitewashed stone windmills, a common feature of the Cyclades and the Dodecanese islands

◁ The awe-inspiring rock "towers" of Metéora in central Greece, first settled by hermits in the 10th century

the Macedonians by the Romans in 168 BC, Greece was made a province of Rome. As part of the Eastern Empire, it was ruled from Constantinople and became a powerful element within the Orthodox Christian, Byzantine world.

Following the Ottomans' momentous capture of Constantinople in 1453, the Greek mainland was ruled by the Turks for the next 350 years. Crete and the Ionian islands were seized for long periods by the Venetians. Eventually the Greeks rebelled and, in 1821, the Greek War of Independence began. In 1832 the Great Powers that dominated Europe established a protectorate over Greece, marking the end of Ottoman rule. During the 19th century the Greeks expanded their national territory, reasserting Greek sovereignty over many of the islands.

Almost a century of significant territorial gains came to a disastrous end in 1922, when millions of Greeks were expelled from Smyrna in Turkish Anatolia, bringing to a close thousands of years of Greek presence in Asia

19th-century lithograph celebrating the Greek War of Independence

Minor. The ensuing years were a time of hardship and instability. The Metaxás dictatorship was followed by Italian, German, and Bulgarian occupation during World War II, and then a bitter civil war. The present boundaries of the Greek state date from 1948, when the Dodecanese were finally returned by the Italians. Today, Greece is a stable democracy and has been a member of the European Union since 1981.

RELIGION, LANGUAGE, AND CULTURE

During Venetian and Ottoman domination, the Greek Orthodox church succeeded in preserving the Greek language and identity. Today, the Orthodox church is still a powerful force. Great importance is placed on baptisms and church weddings, although civil marriages are valid in law. Sunday mass is very popular with women, for whom church is a meeting place for socializing, just as the *kafeneía* (cafés) are for men.

The Greek language was for a long time a field of conflict between *katharévousa*, an artificial form devised around the time of independence, and the slowly evolved everyday speech, or *dimotikí*. Today's prevalence of *dimotikí* was perhaps a foregone conclusion in an oral culture. The art of storytelling is as prized now as it was in Homer's time, with conversation

KEY DATES IN GREEK HISTORY

3000–1200 BC Bronze Age; Cycladic, Minoan, and Mycenaean cultures flourish

800 Emergence of city-states

5th century Classical period; high point of Athenian culture under Perikles

431–404 Peloponnesian Wars; defeat of the Athenians by the city-state of Sparta

338 Greek army conquered by Philip II of Macedonia

333 Alexander the Great declares himself king of Asia; Greece absorbed into his vast empire

168 Greece becomes province of Rome

AD 49–54 St. Paul preaches Christianity in Greece

395 Greece becomes part of the new Eastern Roman Empire, ruled from Constantinople

1453 Constantinople falls to the Ottoman Turks

1821 Start of the Greek War of Independence

1832 Great Powers establish protectorate over Greece, and appoint Otto of Bavaria king

1922 Greeks fail to capture Smyrna from Turks

1946–9 Civil war leaves thousands dead or homeless

1981 Admission to the European Union

2002 Euro becomes legal currency

2004 Greece hosts Olympic Games and wins the football European Cup

pursued for its own sake in *kafeneía* and at dinner tables. Singers, writers, and poet-lyricists have all kept *dimotikí* alive until the present day.

DEVELOPMENT AND DIPLOMACY

Compared to its Balkan neighbors, Greece is a wealthy country, but it remains one of the poorer members of the European Union. It still bears the hallmarks of a developing economy, with agriculture and the service sector accounting for two-thirds of the GNP. Nevertheless, with a nominally capitalist orientation, it has overcome its resemblance to pre-1989 Eastern Europe. Loss-making state enterprises have been sold off, and inflation and interest rates have fallen. However, unemployment remains high. Tourism has compensated for the decline in other industries, such as world shipping.

The fact that the Greek state is less than 200 years old, combined with recent periods of political instability, means that there is little faith in government institutions. Life operates on networks of personal friendships and official contacts. In the political sphere, the years following World War II were largely shaped by the influence of two men: Andréas Papandréou of the Pan-hellenic Socialist Movement (PASOK) and Conservative Konstantínos Karamanlís, who between them held office for the most part of the 1980s and 90s.

Typical scene at a Greek taverna, a popular place for friends and family to socialize

The conservative New Democracy Party led by Costas Karamanlís (nephew of Konstantínos) took over from PASOK after a convincing election win in 2004.

The late Andréas Papandréou, three times Greek premier

HOME LIFE

The family is still the basic Greek social unit. Traditionally, one family would farm its own land independently, and today family-run businesses are common in urban settings. Family life and social life are usually one and the same, and tend to revolve around eating out. Arranged marriages and dowries, though officially banned, persist. Most single young adults live with their parents and outside the largest cities, few unmarried couples dare to cohabit. Despite the renowned Greek love of children, Greece has one of the lowest birth rates in Europe. Recently, the status of urban Greek women has greatly improved. They are now better represented in medicine and law, and many women run their own firms. However, in the country macho attitudes still exist, women often sacrificing a career to look after the house and children. New imported attitudes have crept in, especially in the cities, but generally the Greek traditional way of life remains resolutely strong.

Fishermen mending their nets on one of the Greek islands

Exploring Greece

From beaches to ancient archaeological sites, Greece boasts a wide range of attractions. The nation's greatest ancient monuments are located in the capital, Athens, but relics of the Mycenaean, Minoan, Classical, and Byzantine civilizations can be found all over. The Greek islands attract thousands of tourists, many of whom come simply to enjoy the sun and sand and the relaxed pace of life. Ferries link the different island groups to the mainland, and "island-hopping" is a popular way to explore the many archipelagos.

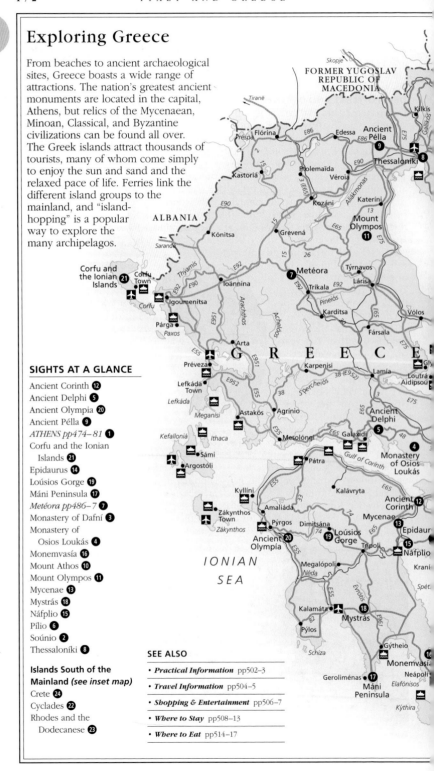

SIGHTS AT A GLANCE

Ancient Corinth **12**
Ancient Delphi **5**
Ancient Olympia **20**
Ancient Péla **9**
ATHENS pp474–81 **1**
Corfu and the Ionian
    Islands **21**
Epidaurus **14**
Loúsios Gorge **19**
Máni Peninsula **17**
Metéora pp486–7 **7**
Monastery of Dafní **3**
Monastery of
    Osios Loukás **4**
Monemvasía **16**
Mount Athos **10**
Mount Olympos **11**
Mycenae **13**
Mystrás **18**
Náfplio **15**
Pílio **6**
Soúnio **2**
Thessaloníki **8**

Islands South of the
Mainland *(see inset map)*

Crete **24**
Cyclades **22**
Rhodes and the
    Dodecanese **23**

SEE ALSO

• *Practical Information* pp502–3

• *Travel Information* pp504–5

• *Shopping & Entertainment* pp506–7

• *Where to Stay* pp508–13

• *Where to Eat* pp514–17

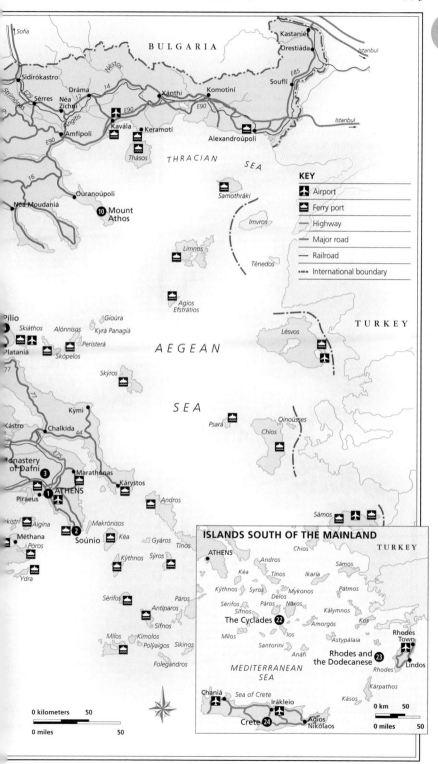

Sofia

BULGARIA

Kastaniés
Orestiáda
Istanbul

Sidirókastro
Néstos
Dráma
14
Xánthi
Komotiní
Souflí
E85
E79
Sérres
Néa
Zíchni
12
E90
E90
Istanbul
Amfípoli
Kavála
Keramotí
Alexandroúpoli
E90
Thásos
16
THRACIAN
SEA
Ouranoúpoli
Samothráki
Néa Moudaniá
10 Mount
Athos
Ímvros
KEY

✈ Airport
🚢 Ferry port
— Highway
— Major road
— Railroad
·–·– International boundary

Límnos
Ténedos
TURKEY

Agios
Efstrátios
Pílio
Gioúra
Skiáthos
Alónnisos
Kyrá Panagiá
Lésvos
Plataniá
Peristerá
Skópelos
77
Skýros
AEGEAN
Kými
SEA
Kástro
Chalkída
44
Psará
Qinoússes
Monastery
of Dafní
Marathónas
Chíos
ATHENS
Kárystos
Piraeus
Andros
Sámos
Aígina
Makrónisos
Méthana
Soúnio
Kéa
Póros
Gyáros
Tínos
Kýthnos
Sýros
Ýdra
Sérifos
Páros
Antíparos
Sífnos
Mílos
Kímolos
Polýaigos
Síkinos
Folégandros

ISLANDS SOUTH OF THE MAINLAND

TURKEY

ATHENS
Andros
Chíos
Kéa
Tínos
Ikaría
Sámos
Kýthnos
Sýros
Mýkonos
Pátmos
Delos
Sérifos
Páros
Náxos
Kálymnos
Sífnos
The Cyclades 22
Amorgós
Kos
Mílos
Íos
Astypálaia
Rhodes
Town
Santorini
Anáfi
Rhodes and 23
the Dodecanese
Rhodes
Lindos

Kárpathos

MEDITERRANEAN
SEA
Kásos

Chaniá
Sea of Crete
Irákleio
Crete 24
Agios
Nikólaos

0 kilometers   50

0 miles   50

0 km   50

0 miles   50

Athens ●

Athens has been inhabited for 7,000 years. The city's greatest glory was during the Classical period (4th and 5th centuries BC) of ancient Greece, from which so many buildings and artifacts survive. The city is dominated by the world-famous Acropolis and its theaters and temples, including the Parthenon, erected by Perikles as part of his grand building plan in the mid-5th century BC. Within the Byzantine Empire and under Ottoman rule, Athens played only a minor role. It returned to prominence in 1834, when King Otto made it capital of Greece. When the king's architects planned the new, European-style city, they included many splendid Neoclassical public buildings, which today provide elegant homes for some of Athens' best museums and galleries.

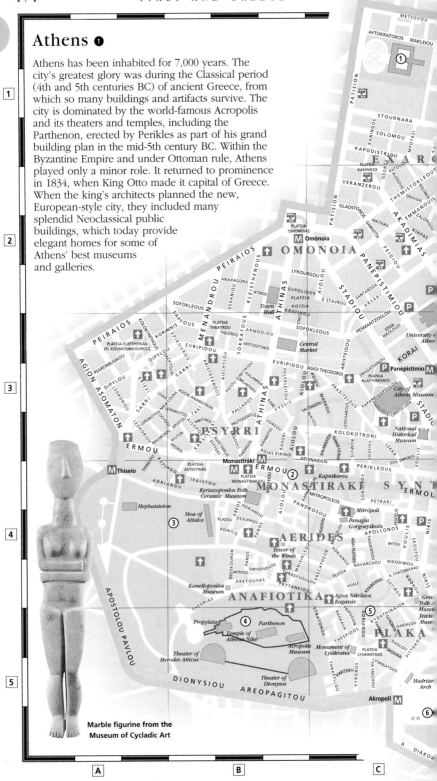

Marble figurine from the
Museum of Cycladic Art

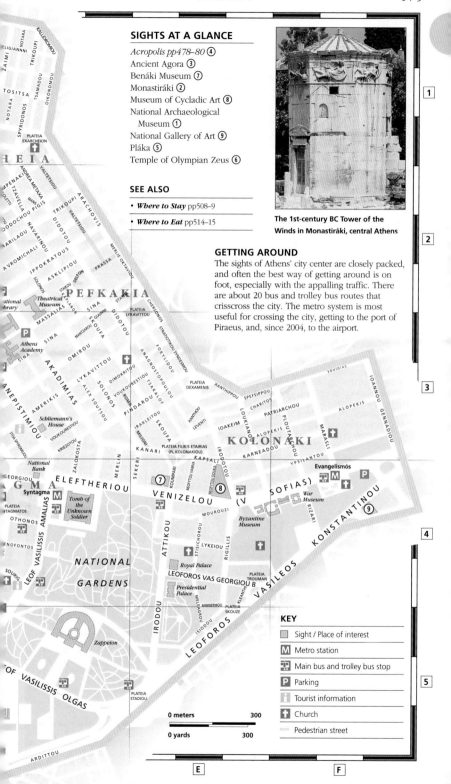

SIGHTS AT A GLANCE

Acropolis pp478–80 ④
Ancient Agora ③
Benáki Museum ⑦
Monastiráki ②
Museum of Cycladic Art ⑧
National Archaeological
    Museum ①
National Gallery of Art ⑨
Pláka ⑤
Temple of Olympian Zeus ⑥

SEE ALSO

• **Where to Stay** pp508–9

• **Where to Eat** pp514–15

The 1st-century BC Tower of the
Winds in Monastiráki, central Athens

GETTING AROUND

The sights of Athens' city center are closely packed,
and often the best way of getting around is on
foot, especially with the appalling traffic. There
are about 20 bus and trolley bus routes that
crisscross the city. The metro system is most
useful for crossing the city, getting to the port of
Piraeus, and, since 2004, to the airport.

KEY

▪	Sight / Place of interest
Ⓜ	Metro station
🚌	Main bus and trolley bus stop
🅿	Parking
ⓘ	Tourist information
✚	Church
⋯	Pedestrian street

0 meters   300

0 yards   300

Neoclassical entrance to the National Archaeological Museum

National Archaeological Museum ①

Patissíon 44, Exárcheia. **Tel** 210-821 7717. Ⓜ Omónoia. ☐ summer: 8am–7pm daily; winter 1–7:30pm Mon, 8:30am–3pm Tue–Sun. 📷 📹 ⓰ www.culture.gr

When it was opened in 1891, this museum brought together antiquities that had previously been stored in different places all over the city. New wings were added in 1939, but during World War II the museum's priceless exhibits were dispersed and buried underground to protect them from possible damage. The museum reopened in 1946, but it has taken another 50 or so years of renovation and reorganization to finally do justice to its formidable collection. With the combination of such unique exhibits as the Mycenaean gold, and an unrivaled assembly of sculpture, pottery, and jewelry, it can definitely be claimed as one of the finest museums in the world. It is a good idea to plan ahead and be selective when visiting the museum and not attempt to cover everything in one visit.

The museum's exhibits can be divided into seven main collections: Neolithic and Cycladic, Mycenaean, Geometric and Archaic sculpture, Classical sculpture, Roman and Hellenistic sculpture, the pottery collections, and the Thíra frescoes. There are also other smaller collections that are well worth seeing. These include the stunning Eléni Stathátou jewelry collection and the recently opened Egyptian rooms.

High points of the museum include the unique finds from the grave circle at Mycenae (see p490), in particular the gold Mask of Agamemnon. Also not to be missed are the Archaic *kouroi* statues and the unrivaled collection of Classical and Hellenistic statues. Two of the most important and finest of the bronzes are the *Horse with the Little Jockey* and *Poseidon*. One of the world's largest collections of ancient ceramics can also be found here, comprising a vast array of elegant red- and black-figure vases from the 6th and 5th centuries BC and some Geometric funerary vases that date back as far as 1000 BC.

Monastiráki ②

Ⓜ Monastiráki. **Market** ☐ daily.

This lively and atmospheric area, which is named after the little monastery in Plateía Monastirakíou, is synonymous with Athens' famous flea market. Located next to the ancient Agora, it is bounded by Sari in the west and Aiólou in the east. The streets of Pandrósou, Ifaístou, and Areos leading off Plateía Monastirakíou are full of shops, selling a range of goods from expensive antiques, leather, and silver to tourist trinkets.

The heart of the flea market is in Plateía Avyssinías, west of Plateía Monastirakíou, where every morning junk dealers arrive with pieces of furniture and various odds and ends. During the week the shops and stalls are filled with antiques, second-hand books, rugs, leatherware, taverna chairs, army surplus gear, and tools.

On Sunday mornings, when the shops are closed, the market itself still flourishes along Adrianoú and in Plateía Agíou Filíppou. There are always numerous bargains to be had. Items particularly worth investing in include some of the brightly colored woven and embroidered cloths and an abundance of good silver jewelry.

Shoppers browsing in Athens' lively Monastiráki market

For hotels and restaurants in this region see pp508–9 and pp514–15

View across the Agora, showing the reconstructed Stoa of Attalos on the right

Ancient Agora ③

Main entrance at Adrianoú,
Monastiráki. **Tel** *210-321 0185.*
Ⓜ *Thiseío, Monastiráki.* **Museum
and site** ◯ *daily.* ● *main public
hols.* 🔌 🚻 *limited.*

The American School of
Archaeology commenced
excavations of the Ancient
Agora in the 1930s, and since
then a complex array of
public buildings and temples
has been revealed. The
democratically governed
Agora was the political and
religious heart of ancient
Athens. Also the center of
commercial and daily life, it
abounded with schools and
elegant stoas, or roofed
arcades, filled with shops.
The state prison was here, as
was the city's mint. Even the
remains of an olive oil mill
have been found.
   The main building standing
today is the impressive two-
story Stoa of Attalos. This was
rebuilt in the 1950s on the
original foundations and
using ancient building
materials. Founded by King
Attalos of Pergamon (ruled
159–138 BC), it dominated
the eastern quarter of the
Agora until it was destroyed
in AD 267. It is used today as
a museum, exhibiting the
finds from the Agora. These
include a *klepsydra* (a water
clock that was used for timing
plaintiffs' speeches), bronze
ballots, and items from
everyday life such as some
terra-cotta toys and leather
sandals. The best-preserved
ruins on the site are the

Odeion of Agrippa, a covered
theater, and the Hephaisteion,
a temple to Hephaistos, also
known as the Theseion.

Acropolis ④

See pp478–80.

Pláka ⑤

Ⓜ *Monastiráki, Acropolis.* 🚌 *1, 2,
4, 5, and many others.*

The area of Plaka is the
historic heart of Athens. Even
though only a few buildings
date back farther than the
Ottoman period, it remains
the oldest continually
inhabited area in the city.
One probable explanation of
its name comes from the
word used by Albanian
soldiers in the service of the
Turks who settled here in the
16th century – *pliaka* (old)
was how they used to
describe the area. Despite the

constant swarm of tourists
and Athenians, who come to
eat in old-fashioned tavernas
or browse in the antique and
icon shops, Pláka still retains
the atmosphere of a traditional neighborhood. The
Lysikrates Monument in
Plateía Lysikrátous is one of a
number of monuments that
were built to commemorate
the victors at the annual
choral and dramatic festival
at the Theater of Dionysos.
Taking its name from the
sponsor of the winning team,
it is the only such monument
still intact in Athens.
   Many churches are worth a
visit: the 11th-century **Agios
Nikólaos Ragavás** has ancient
columns built into the walls.
   The **Tower of the Winds**, in
the far west of Pláka, lies in
the grounds of the Roman
Agora. It was built by a Syrian
astronomer in the 2nd century
BC as a weather vane and
water clock. The name comes
from external friezes depicting
the eight mythological winds.

The Byzantine church of Agios Nikólaos Ragavás in Pláka

Acropolis ④

In the mid-5th century BC, Perikles persuaded the Athenians to begin a grand program of new building work. The resulting transformation has come to embody the political and cultural achievements of ancient Greece. Three contrasting temples were built on the Acropolis, together with a monumental gateway. The Theater of Dionysos and the Theater of Herodes Atticus were added later, in the 4th century BC and the 2nd century AD respectively.

LOCATOR MAP

★ Porch of the Caryatids
These statues of women were used in place of columns on the south porch of the Erechtheion. The originals, four of which can be seen in the Acropolis Museum, have been replaced by casts.

An olive tree now grows where Athena first planted her tree in a competition against Poseidon.

The Propylaia was built in 437–432 BC to form a new entrance to the Acropolis.

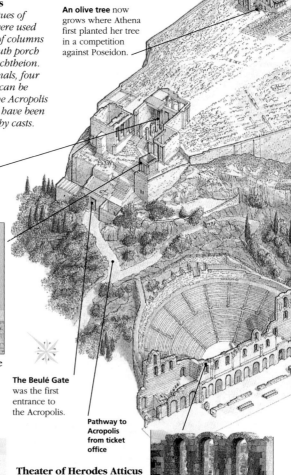

★ Temple of Athena Nike
This temple to Athena of Victory is on the west side of the Propylaia. It was built in 426–421 BC.

The Beulé Gate was the first entrance to the Acropolis.

Pathway to Acropolis from ticket office

Theater of Herodes Atticus
Also known as the Odeion of Herodes Atticus, this superb theater was originally built in AD 161. It was restored in 1955 and is used today for outdoor concerts.

STAR SIGHTS

★ Parthenon

★ Porch of the Caryatids

★ Temple of Athena Nike

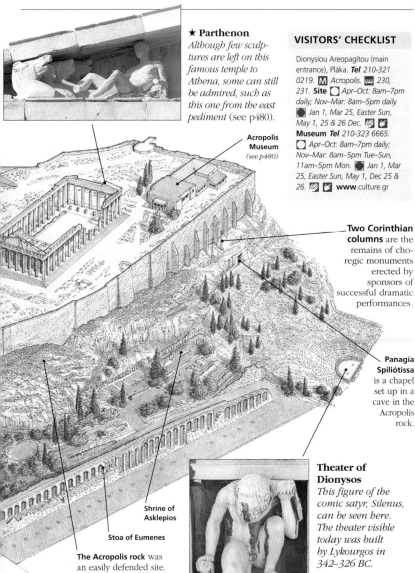

★ Parthenon
Although few sculptures are left on this famous temple to Athena, some can still be admired, such as this one from the east pediment (see p480).

Acropolis Museum
(see p480)

VISITORS' CHECKLIST

Dionysíou Areopagítou (main entrance), Pláka. *Tel 210-321 0219.* M *Acropolis.* 🚌 *230, 231.* **Site** 🕐 *Apr–Oct: 8am–7pm daily; Nov–Mar: 8am–5pm daily.* ⬤ *Jan 1, Mar 25, Easter Sun, May 1, 25 & 26 Dec.* 🎫 🗲 **Museum** *Tel 210-323 6665.* 🕐 *Apr–Oct: 8am–7pm daily; Nov–Mar: 8am–5pm Tue–Sun, 11am–5pm Mon.* ⬤ *Jan 1, Mar 25, Easter Sun, May 1, Dec 25 & 26.* 🎫 🗲 www.culture.gr

Two Corinthian columns are the remains of choregic monuments erected by sponsors of successful dramatic performances.

Panagía Spiliótissa is a chapel set up in a cave in the Acropolis rock.

Shrine of Asklepios

Stoa of Eumenes

The Acropolis rock was an easily defended site. It has been in use for nearly 5,000 years.

Theater of Dionysos
This figure of the comic satyr, Silenus, can be seen here. The theater visible today was built by Lykourgos in 342–326 BC.

THE ELGIN MARBLES

These famous sculptures, also called the Parthenon Marbles, are held in the British Museum in London. They were acquired from the occupying Turkish authorities by Lord Elgin in 1801–3. He sold them to the British nation for £35,000 in 1816. There is great controversy surrounding the Marbles. While some argue that they are more carefully preserved in the British Museum, the Greek government does not accept the legality of the sale and believes they belong in Athens.

The newly arrived Elgin Marbles at the British Museum, in a painting by A. Archer

Exploring the Acropolis

Once you are through the Propylaia, the grand entrance to the site, the Parthenon exerts an overwhelming fascination. The other fine temples on "the Rock" include the Erechtheion and the Temple of Athena Nike. Since 1975, access to all the temple precincts has been banned. However, it is a miracle that anything remains at all. The ravages of war, the removal of treasures, and pollution have all taken their irrevocable toll on the Acropolis.

View of the Parthenon from the southwest at sunrise

∩ The Parthenon
One of the world's most famous monuments, the Parthenon was commissioned by Perikles as part of his rebuilding plan. Work began in 447 BC, when the sculptor Pheidias was entrusted with supervising the building of a new Doric temple to Athena, the patron goddess of the city. Built on the site of earlier Archaic temples, it was designed primarily to house the *Parthenos*, Pheidias's impressive cult statue of Athena.

Taking just nine years to complete, the temple was dedicated to the goddess in the course of the Great Panathenaia festival of 438 BC. Designed and constructed in Pentelic marble by the architects Kallikrates and Iktinos, the Parthenon replaces straight lines with slight curves. It is thought that this complex architectural style was used to create an illusion of perfection *(see pp482–3)*.

For the pediments and the friezes that ran all the way around the temple, an army of sculptors and painters was employed. Agorakritos and Alkamenes, both pupils of Pheidias, are two of the sculptors who worked on the frieze, which depicted the people and horses in the Panathenaic procession.

Despite much damage and alterations made to adapt it to various uses, which have included a church, a mosque, and even an arsenal, the Parthenon remains a majestic sight today.

🏛 Acropolis Museum
Opened in 1878, this museum houses a collection devoted solely to finds from the Acropolis. Among the treasures are some beautiful statues dating from the 5th century BC and segments of the Parthenon frieze. The museum is transferring to a new building, which is opening in stages from 2007.

The collection includes 6th-century BC works such as the *Moschophoros* or Calf-bearer (c.570 BC), along with fragments of pedimental statues of mythological scenes. Further rooms contain a pediment from the old Temple of Athena and a collection of

kórai (550–500 BC), votive statues of maidens offered to the goddess Athena.

Treasures from later periods include fragments from the Erechtheion frieze and a well-preserved *metope* from the the Parthenon showing the battle between the Lapiths and centaurs. The collection ends with the four remaining caryatids from the Erechtheion, carefully kept in a temperature-controlled environment.

Around the Acropolis
The area around the Acropolis was the center of public life in Athens. In addition to the Agora in the north *(see p477)*, there were two theaters on the southern slope, the Theater of Herodes Atticus and the Theater of Dionysos. Political life was largely centered on the Areopagos and the Pynx Hills to the west of the Acropolis: the *Ekklesia* (citizens' assembly) met on the latter, while the former was the seat of the Supreme Judicial Court. Filopáppos Hill, the highest summit in the south of Athens, has always played an important defensive role in the city's history – an important fort was built here overlooking the strategic Piraeus road in 294 BC. On the tree-clad Hill of the Nymphs, the 19th-century Danish-built Asteroskopeíon (Observatory) occupies the site of an old sanctuary dedicated to nymphs associated with childbirth.

The Asteroskopeíon (Observatory) on the Hill of the Nymphs

Temple of Olympian Zeus ⑥

Corner of Amalías & Vasilíssis Olgas, Pláka. *Tel 210-922 6330.* 🚇 *2, 4, 11.* ⬜ *daily.* ⬛ *main public hols.* 🔲 🚻 *limited.*

This vast temple is the largest in Greece, exceeding even the Parthenon in size. The tyrant Peisistratos allegedly initiated the building of the temple in the 6th century BC to gain public favor. It was not completed until 650 years later.

In AD 132 the Roman Emperor Hadrian dedicated the temple to Zeus Olympios and set up a statue of the god inside, a copy of the original by Pheidias at Olympia *(see p493).* Next to it he placed a huge statue of himself. Both statues have since been lost.

Only 15 of the original 104 columns remain, but enough to give a sense of the once enormous size of this temple – approximately 96 m (315 ft) long and 40 m (130 ft) wide. Roman-style Corinthian capitals were added to the original, Doric columns in 174 BC.

The temple lies next to Hadrian's Arch, which was built in AD 131 and marked the boundary between the ancient city and the new Athens of Hadrian.

Benáki Museum ⑦

Corner of Koumpári & Vasilíssis Sofías, Kolonáki. *Tel 210-367 1000.* 🚇 *3, 7, 8, 13.* ⬜ *Mon & Wed–Sun.* ⬛ *public hols.* 🔲 *except Thu.* 🚻 *limited.* **www**.benaki.gr

This museum contains a superb collection of Greek art and crafts, jewelry, regional costumes, and political memorabilia from the Neolithic era to the 20th century. It was founded by Antónios Benákis (1873–1954), who was interested in Greek, Persian, Egyptian, and Ottoman art from an early age and started collecting while living in Alexandria. On moving to Athens in 1926, he donated his collection to the Greek state. The family home, an elegant 19th-century

The remains of the Temple of Olympian Zeus

Neoclassical mansion, was used as a museum and opened to the public in 1931.

A major part of the Benáki collection consists of gold jewelry dating from as far back as 3000 BC. Also on display are icons, liturgical silverware, Egyptian artifacts, and Greek embroideries.

Museum of Cycladic Art ⑧

Neofýtou Doúka 4 (new wing at Irodótou 1), Kolonáki. *Tel 210-722 8321.* 🚇 *3, 7, 8, 13.* ⬜ *Mon–Sat.* ⬛ *main public hols.* 🔲 🚻 **www**.cycladic.gr

A magnificent selection of ancient Greek art, including the world's most important collection of Cycladic figurines, is on view at this modern museum.

The displays start on the first floor, with the Cycladic collection. Dating back to the 3rd millennium BC, the Cycladic figurines were found mostly in graves, although their exact usage remains a mystery. Ancient Greek art is exhibited on the second floor and the Charles Polítis collection of Classical and Prehistoric art on the fourth floor. The third floor displays some excellent ancient Cypriot art. A new wing, which opened in the adjoining Stathátos Mansion in 1992, contains the Greek Art Collection of the Athens Academy.

National Gallery of Art ⑨

Vasiléos Konstantínou 50, Ilísia. *Tel 210-723 5937.* 🚇 *3, 13.* ⬜ *9am–3pm Mon, Wed–Sat, 10am–2pm Sun.* ⬛ *main public hols.* 🔲 🚻

This modern building holds a permanent collection of European and Greek art. European exhibits include various works by van Dyck, Cézanne, Dürer, Rembrandt, Picasso, and Caravaggio. The majority of the collection, however, is made up of Greek art from the 18th to 20th centuries, and includes paintings of the Greek War of Independence, seascapes, and some excellent portraits.

Modern sculpture outside the National Gallery of Art

Temple Architecture

Temples were the most important public buildings in ancient Greece, largely because religion was a central part of everyday life. Often placed in prominent positions, temples were also statements about political and divine power. The earliest temples, in the 8th century BC, were built of wood and sun-dried bricks. Many of their features were copied in marble buildings from the 6th century BC onward.

The Parthenon on the Acropolis in Athens

TEMPLE CONSTRUCTION

This drawing is of an idealized Doric temple, showing how it was both built and used.

The cult statue was of the god or goddess to whom the temple was dedicated.

The cella, or inner sanctum, housed the cult statue.

The pediment, triangular in shape, often held sculpture.

Fluting on the columns was carved *in situ*, guided by that on the top and bottom drums.

The column drums were initially carved with bosses for lifting them into place.

A ramp led up to the temple entrance.

The stepped platform was built on a stone foundation.

THE ILLUSION OF PERFECTION

Every aspect of the Parthenon was built on a 9:4 ratio to make the temple completely symmetrical. The sculptors also used visual trickery to counteract the laws of perspective. The illustration *(right)* is exaggerated to show the techniques they employed.

The base of the temple is higher in the middle than at the edges.

Entasis (a bulge in the middle) makes each column look straight.

Each column leans slightly inward.

THE DEVELOPMENT OF TEMPLE ARCHITECTURE

Greek temple architecture is divided into three styles, which evolved chronologically, and are most easily distinguished by the column capitals.

The gable ends of the roof were surmounted by statues, known as *akroteria*, in this case of a Nike or "Winged Victory". Almost no upper portions of Greek temples survive.

The roof was supported on wooden beams and covered in rows of terra-cotta tiles, each ending in an upright antefix.

Doric *temples were surrounded by sturdy columns with plain capitals and no bases. As the earliest style of stone buildings, they recall wooden prototypes.*

Triangular pediment filled with sculpture

Guttae imitated the pegs for fastening the wooden roof beams.

Triglyphs resembled the ends of cross beams.

Metopes could contain sculpture.

Doric capital

Stone blocks were smoothly fitted together and held by metal clamps and dowels: no mortar was used in the temple's construction.

The ground plan was derived from the megaron of the Mycenaean house: a rectangular hall with a front porch that was supported by columns.

Ionic *temples differed from Doric in their tendency to have more columns, of a different form. The capital has a pair of volutes, like rams' horns, front and back.*

Akroteria, at the roof corners, could look Persian in style.

The frieze was a continuous band of decoration.

The Ionic architrave was subdivided into projecting bands.

The Ionic frieze took the place of Doric *triglyphs* and *metopes.*

Ionic capital

Caryatids, *or figures of women, were used instead of columns in the Erechtheion at Athens' Acropolis. In Athens' Agora (see p477), tritons (half-fish, half-human creatures) were used.*

Corinthian *temples in Greece were built under the Romans and only in Athens. They feature columns with slender shafts and elaborate capitals decorated with acanthus leaves.*

The pediment was decorated with a variety of moldings.

Akroterion in the shape of a griffin

The cella entrance was at the east end.

The entablature was everything above the capitals.

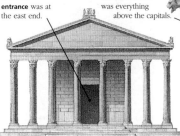

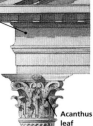

Acanthus leaf capital

Central Greece

Beyond the endless urban sprawl of Athens, the vast expanse of central Greece has a little of everything for the visitor, from sandy beaches and fishing ports, to one of the country's most important archaeological sites, Ancient Delphi. Not to be missed is the Byzantine splendor of the monasteries of Dafní and Osios Loúkas, while the extraordinary mountain-top monasteries of Metéora are another of the region's principal attractions. The beautiful wooded mountain slopes of the Pílio offer some of the best scenery on the mainland.

The Temple of Poseidon on the cape at Soúnio

Soúnio ❷

9 km (5.5 miles) S of Lávrio, Attica. **Tel** 22920-39363. 🚌 to Lávrio. ◯ daily. 🐾

The temple of Poseidon, situated at the top of sheer cliffs tumbling into the Aegean Sea at Soúnio (Cape Sounion), was ideally located as a place to worship the powerful god of the sea. Its brilliant white marble columns have been a landmark for ancient and modern mariners alike.

The present temple, built in 444 BC, stands on the site of older ruins. An Ionic frieze, made from 13 slabs of Parian marble, is located on the east side of the temple's main approach path. It is very eroded, but is known to have depicted scenes from mythological battles, as well as the adventures of the hero Theseus, said in some legends to be the son of Poseidon.

Local marble from the quarries at Agriléza was used for the temple's 34 slender Doric columns, of which 15 survive today. In 1810 the British Romantic poet, Lord

Byron, carved his name on one of the columns, setting an unfortunate precedent of vandalism at the temple.

Monastery of Dafní ❸

10 km (6 miles) NW of Athens, Attica. **Tel** 210-581 1558. 🚌 ◯ for restoration (phone for details). 🐾 ♿ limited.

Founded in the 5th century AD, the Monastery of Dafní is named after the laurels (dáfnes) that once grew here.

The 5th-century Byzantine Monastery of Dafní near Athens

It was built with the remains of an ancient sanctuary of Apollo, which had occupied the site until it was destroyed in AD 395. In the early 13th century, Otto de la Roche, the first Frankish Duke of Athens, bequeathed it to Cistercian monks in Burgundy. Greek Orthodox monks took the site in the 16th century, erecting the elegant cloisters just south of the church. The monastery is presently closed for restoration, due to an earthquake which hit in the year 2000.

Among the monastery's principal attractions are the beautiful gold-leaf Byzantine mosaics in the *katholikón* (main church). Byzantine church architecture was concerned almost exclusively with decoration. Mosaics and frescoes portraying the whole body of the Church, from Christ downward, had a dual purpose: they gave inspiration to worshipers and represented windows to the spiritual world. The most impressive mosaics at Dafní are the Esonarthex Mosaics, which include the *Last Supper,* the *Washing of the Feet,* and the *Betrayal of Judas.* Equally magnificent, the *Christ Pantokrátor* is a mosaic of Christ in judgement that fills the church's huge dome.

Monastery of Osios Loúkas ❹

8 km (5 miles) E of Dístomo, Stereá Elláda. **Tel** 22670-22797. 🚌 ◯ daily. 🐾

Dedicated to a local hermit and healer, Osios Loúkas ("Holy Luke"), who lived in the 10th century, this splendid monastery was one of medieval Greece's most important buildings architecturally. It was built around AD 1011 by the Emperor Romanós, who extended an earlier church dating from 944. The octagonal style of the main church, the *katholikón*, became a hallmark of late Byzantine church design, while the mosaics inside lifted Byzantine art into its final great period.

Among the most impressive features of the monastery are the 10th-century crypt, which

Detail from an 11th-century mosaic in the Monastery of Osios Loúkas

is from the original church and contains the sarcophagus of Holy Luke, and a mosaic entitled *Washing of the Apostles' Feet*. This 11th-century work, based on a style dating back to the 6th century, is the finest of a number of mosaics found in the narthex, the western entrance hall. The monastery's main dome is decorated with an imposing mural of Christ, painted in the 16th century to replace fallen mosaics.

Ancient Delphi ❺

Mount Parnassus, Stereá Elláda.
Tel *22650-82312.* 🚌 ⬜ *daily.*
⬤ *main public hols.* 📷 ♿

In ancient times Delphi was believed to be the center of the earth. The site was renowned as a dwelling place of Apollo, and from the late 8th century BC people came here to worship and seek advice from the god. With the political rise of Delphi in the 6th century BC, and the establishment of the Pythian Games – a cultural, religious, and athletic festival – the site entered a golden age that lasted until the arrival of the Romans in 191 BC. The Delphic Oracle was abolished in AD 393 after Christianity was introduced as the state religion.

The Sanctuary of Apollo, also known as the Sacred Precinct, forms the heart of the complex, and one of its most impressive sights is the **Temple of Apollo**. A temple has stood on this spot since the 6th century BC, but the

remains visible today date from the 4th century BC. Leading from the sanctuary entrance to the Temple of Apollo is the **Sacred Way**, once lined with some 3,000 statues and treasuries. Also worth seeing is the well-preserved **Stadium**. The present structure dates from Roman times, and most of the seating is still intact.

The Marmaria Precinct, or marble quarry, is where the **Sanctuary of Athena Pronaia** is found. Here, the most remarkable monument is the *tholos*, which dates from the 4th century BC. The purpose of this circular structure, originally surrounded by 20 columns, remains a mystery.

The museum at Ancient Delphi houses an impressive collection of sculptures and architectural remains.

Pílio ❻

Thessaly. 🚌 *Vólos.* 🚉 ℹ️ *Plateía Riga Feraíou, Vólos (24210-23500).*

The Pílio Peninsula is one of the most beautiful areas of the mainland. The mountain air is sweet with the scent of herbs, which in ancient times were renowned for their healing properties. The area became populated in the 13th century by Greeks retreating

Traditional-style guesthouses in the Pílio village of Vyzítsa

from the Ottomans. After centuries of protecting its culture, the Pílio is known for its strong local cuisine.

The main town on the peninsula is **Vólos**, which has an excellent Archaeological Museum. From here you can make a tour of the many traditional hillside villages and fishing ports. Worth visiting are **Miliés**, with its Folk Museum and fresco-adorned church, and picturesque **Vyzítsa**. **Argalastí** has a busy market, though its tavernas and cafés retain a peaceful atmosphere. For fine sandy beaches and excellent seafood, visit the popular coastal resorts of **Plataniá** or **Agios Ioánnis**.

The *tholos* beside the Sanctuary of Athena Pronaia at Ancient Delphi

Metéora ❼

The extraordinary sandstone towers of Metéora (or "suspended rocks") were formed by the action of the sea that covered the plain of Thessaly around 30 million years ago. The huge columns of rock were first used as a religious retreat in AD 985, when a hermit named Barnabas occupied a cave here. In the mid-14th century Neílos, the Prior of Stagai convent, built a small church. A few years later, in 1382, the monk Athanásios, from Mount Athos, founded the huge monastery of Megálo Metéoro on one of the many pinnacles. A further 23 monasteries were built, though most had fallen into ruin by the 19th century. In the 1920s stairs were cut in the rock faces to make the remaining six monasteries more accessible, and today a religious revival has seen the return of a number of monks and nuns.

Monastic cells

Outer walls

LOCATION OF MONASTERIES OF METEORA

Rousánou

Moní Rousánou, perched precariously on the very tip of a narrow spire of rock, is the most spectacularly located of all the monasteries. Its church of the Metamórfosis (1545) is renowned for its harrowing frescoes, painted in 1560 by the iconographers of the Cretan school.

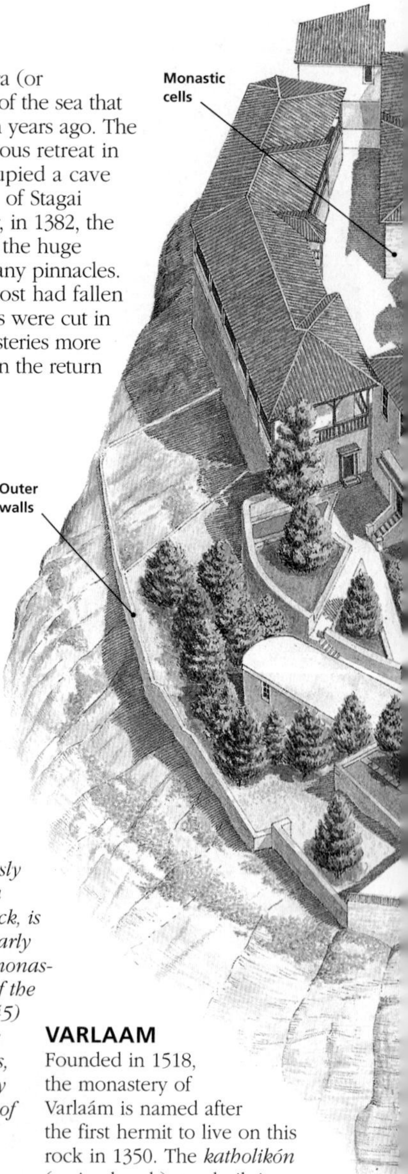

VARLAAM

Founded in 1518, the monastery of Varlaám is named after the first hermit to live on this rock in 1350. The *katholikón* (main church) was built in 1542 and contains frescoes by the Theban iconographer Frágkos Katelános.

Megálo Metéoro

Also known as the Great Meteoron, this was the first and, at 623 m (2,045 ft), highest monastery to be founded. By the entrance is a cave in which Athanásios first lived. His body is buried in the main church.

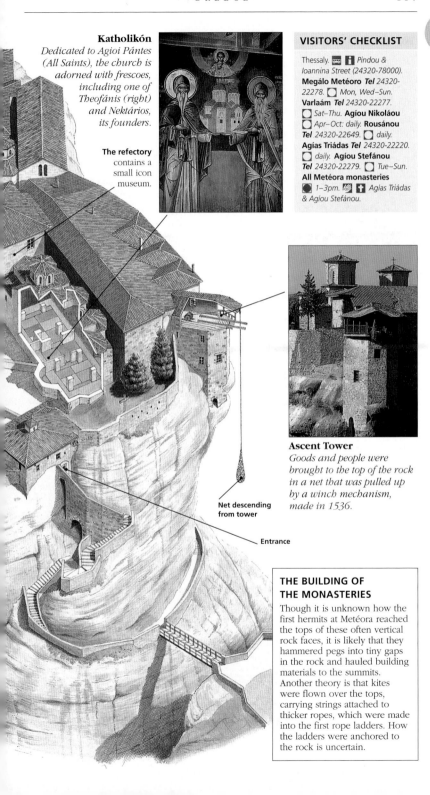

Katholikón
Dedicated to Agioi Pántes (All Saints), the church is adorned with frescoes, including one of Theofánis (right) and Nektários, its founders.

The refectory contains a small icon museum.

VISITORS' CHECKLIST

Thessaly. Pindou & Ioannina Street (24320-78000).
Megálo Metéoro *Tel* 24320-22278. Mon, Wed–Sun.
Varlaám *Tel* 24320-22277. Sat–Thu. **Agíou Nikoláou** Apr–Oct: daily. **Rousánou** *Tel* 24320-22649. daily.
Agías Triádas *Tel* 24320-22220. daily. **Agíou Stefánou** *Tel* 24320-22279. Tue–Sun.
All Metéora monasteries 1–3pm. Agías Triádas & Agíou Stefánou.

Ascent Tower
Goods and people were brought to the top of the rock in a net that was pulled up by a winch mechanism, made in 1536.

Net descending from tower

Entrance

THE BUILDING OF THE MONASTERIES
Though it is unknown how the first hermits at Metéora reached the tops of these often vertical rock faces, it is likely that they hammered pegs into tiny gaps in the rock and hauled building materials to the summits. Another theory is that kites were flown over the tops, carrying strings attached to thicker ropes, which were made into the first rope ladders. How the ladders were anchored to the rock is uncertain.

Northern Greece

Northern Greece offers an appealing combination of comparatively unexplored natural beauty and a rich cultural heritage. The stunning scenery of places like Mount Olympos holds special appeal to walking enthusiasts, while of historical interest in the region are several ancient archaeological sites, including Pélla, the birthplace of Alexander the Great. Many of northern Greece's finest examples of Byzantine architecture and art are to be found on the Athos Peninsula and in the bustling city of Thessaloníki.

The 15th-century White Tower on the waterfront in Thessaloníki

Thessaloníki ❽

🏠 1,000,000. ✈ 25 km (15 miles) SE. 🚢 🚃 🚍 ℹ 136 Tsimiski (2310-221100).

Thessaloniki, also known as Salonica, is Greece's second city, and was founded by King Kassandros in 315 BC. The capital of the Roman province of Macedonia Prima from 146 BC, it later became part of the Byzantine Empire. In 1430 it was captured by the Turks, who held it until 1912. Today Thessaloníki is a bustling cosmopolitan city and a major religious center.

On the *paralía*, the city's attractive waterfront, stands one of Thessaloníki's most famous sights, the **White Tower**. Built in 1430, this is one of three towers that were added to the city walls by the Turks. Today it houses special exhibitions, though it may be closed for restoration.

The **Arch of Galerius** was built in AD 303 by the Emperor Galerius to celebrate victory over the Persians, and is the principal architectural legacy of Roman rule. Standing north of the arch is the **Rotónda**, believed to have been constructed as a mausoleum for Galerius. Now closed, it has been used in the past as both a church and a mosque.

Thessaloníki has a number of museums, including the **Museum of Byzantine Culture** and the **Museum of the Macedonian Struggle**, which focuses on the centuries of Turkish domination. The star attractions at the city's newly refurbished **Archaeological Museum** are the Roman floor mosaics, and the splendid Dervéni Krater, a 4th-century BC bronze wine-mixing bowl. You should also make time to see the museum's stunning collection of Macedonian gold.

Visitors should not miss the city's rich array of UNESCO-listed Byzantine churches, which include the 5th-century **Agios Dimítrios** – the largest church in Greece. Dating from the mid-8th century, **Agía Sofía** is an important building, both for its mosaics and for its role in influencing future architectural development, while the 14th-century **Agios Nikólaos Orfanós** contains the best-preserved collection of late Byzantine frescoes in the city.

🏛 **Archaeological Museum**
Manóli Andrónikou & Leof Stratoú.
Tel 2310-830538. 🚃 3. ◯ daily (Mon: pm only). ◉ main public hols.
🅿 ♿

Ancient Pélla ❾

38 km (24 miles) NW of Thessaloníki. **Tel** 23820-33094. 🚃 ◯ daily (winter: Tue–Sun). ◉ main public hols. 🅿 ♿

This small site was once the flourishing capital of Macedonia. The court was moved here from Aigai (near modern Vergína) in 410 BC

THE MACEDONIAN ROYAL FAMILY

The gold burial casket found at Vergína is emblazoned with the Macedonian Sun, the symbol of the king. Philip II was from a long line of Macedonian kings that began in about 640 BC with Perdiccas I. Philip was the first ruler to unite the whole of Greece as it existed at that time. Much of Greece's pride in the symbol lies in the fact that Alexander the Great used it throughout his empire. He was just 20 when his father was assassinated in 336 BC. He inherited his father's already large empire and also his ambition to conquer the Persians. In 334 BC Alexander crossed the Dardanelles with 40,000 men and defeated the Persians in three different battles, advancing as far as the Indus Valley before he died at the age of 33. With his death the Macedonian empire divided.

Gold burial casket from the Royal Tombs at Vergina

Russian Orthodox monastery, Agíou Panteleímonos, on Mount Athos

by King Archelaos, who ruled from 413 to 399 BC. It is here that Alexander the Great was born in 356 BC, and was later tutored by the philosopher Aristotle. Some sense of the existence of a city can be gained from a plan of the site, which shows where the main street and stores were located. The palace, believed to have been north of the main site, is still being excavated.

At the site, and in the museum, are some of the best-preserved pebble mosaics in Greece. Dating from about 300 BC, the mosaics depict vivid hunting scenes. One of the most famous is of Dionysos riding a panther; it is housed in the now-covered, 4th-century BC House of the Lion Hunt. Originally comprising 12 rooms around three open courtyards, this building was constructed at the end of the 4th century BC.

Mount Athos ⓾

Athos Peninsula. 🚢 *Dáfni (boat trips from Ouranoúpoli & Thessaloniki for the west coast, or from Ierissós for the east coast).* 🚌 *to Karyés.* 🎫 *donation.*

Also known as the Holy Mountain, Mount Athos is the highest point on the Athos Peninsula – an autonomous republic, ruled by the 1,700 monks who live in its 20 monasteries. Only adult males may visit the peninsula, but it is possible to see many of the monasteries from a boat trip along the coast. They include some fine

examples of Byzantine architecture and provide a fascinating insight into Orthodox monastic life.

For the monks who live here, the day begins at 3 or 4am with morning services and prayers. They eat two meals a day, which consist mainly of food they grow themselves. There are 159 fasting days in the year. Between meals the monks spend their time working, resting, and praying.

Ouranoúpoli is the main town on Athos and where the boat trips for the peninsula's west coast start. Among the monasteries that can be viewed are the 10th-century **Docheiaríou, Agíou Panteleímonos**, an 11th-century Russian Orthodox monastery, and **Moní Agíou Pávlou**. On the east coast, **Megístis Lávras** was the first monastery to be founded on Athos, while 10th-century **Moní Vatopedíou**, farther north, is one of the largest and best-preserved buildings.

Adult males wishing to visit any of the monasteries must obtain a letter of recommendation from the Greek consul in their country. The Ministry of Foreign Affairs in Athens, or Ministry of Macedonia and Thrace in Thessaloníki, will then issue a permit allowing a stay of up to four nights. Accommodations are free, though donations are expected.

Mount Olympos ⓫

17 km (10 miles) W of Litóchoro. 🚌 *Litóchoro.* 🚶 *EOS: Evángelou Karavákou 20, Litóchoro (23520-82444).*

The name Mount Olympos refers to a whole range of mountains, 20 km (12 miles) across. The highest peak in the range is Mýtikas, at 2,917 m (9,570 ft). The entire area constitutes the Olympos National Park, an area of outstanding natural beauty that attracts naturalists and walkers alike. The park's rich flora and fauna include 1,700 plant species, in addition to chamois, boars, and roe deer. From **Litóchoro**, which has several hotels and tavernas, walkers can follow a series of trails.

A short distance from Litóchoro is **Ancient Díon**, considered a holy city by the ancient Macedonians. The flat plains were used as a military camp by King Philip II of Macedon in the 4th century BC. The ruins visible today – which include mosaics, baths, and a theater – date mainly from the Roman era. A museum shows finds from the site.

The peaks of the Mount Olympos range rising above Litóchoro

The Peloponnese

One of the primary strongholds and battlefields of the 1821–31 Revolution, the Peloponnese is the kernel from which the modern Greek state grew. The region boasts a wealth of ancient and medieval ruins, from Bronze Age Mycenae to the Byzantine town of Mystrás. As popular as its vast array of historical sites is the Peloponnese's spectacularly varied landscape. The breathtaking scenery of places like the Loúsios Gorge attracts walkers and naturalists in their thousands.

The ruins of Acrocorinth, south of Ancient Corinth

Ancient Corinth ⑫

7 km (4 miles) SW of modern Corinth. *Tel* 27410-31207. 🚌 ⏰ *daily.* 🔴 *main public hols.* 🎫 ♿ *limited.*

A settlement since Neolithic times, Ancient Corinth was razed in 146 BC by the Romans, who rebuilt it a century later. Attaining a population of 750,000 under the patronage of the Roman emperors, the town gained a reputation for licentious living, which St. Paul attacked when he came here in AD 52. Excavations have revealed the vast extent of the ancient city, which was destroyed by earthquakes in Byzantine times. The ruins constitute the largest Roman township in Greece.

Among the most impressive remains are the **Lechaion Way**, the marble-paved road that linked the nearby port of Lechaion with the city, and the **Temple of Apollo**, with its striking Doric columns. The temple was one of the few buildings preserved by the Romans when they rebuilt the city in 44 BC. Of the **Temple of Octavia**, once dedicated to the sister of Emperor Augustus, three ornate Corinthian columns, overarched by a restored architrave, are all that remain. The **Odeion** is one of several buildings endowed to the city by Herodes Atticus, the wealthy Athenian and friend of the Emperor Hadrian.

Close to the Odeion, the **Museum** houses a collection of exhibits representing all periods of the town's history. The Roman gallery is particularly rich, containing some spectacular 2nd-century AD mosaics lifted from the floors of nearby villas.

Just 4 km (2 miles) south of Ancient Corinth is the bastion of **Acrocorinth**, to which there is access between 8:30am and 3pm each day. Held and refortified by every occupying power in Greece from Roman times onward, it was one of the country's most important fortresses in medieval times. The ruins show evidence of Byzantine, Turkish, Frankish, and Venetian occupation. The summit of Acrocorinth affords one of the most sweeping views in the whole of Greece.

RECONSTRUCTION OF ANCIENT CORINTH (C.AD 100)

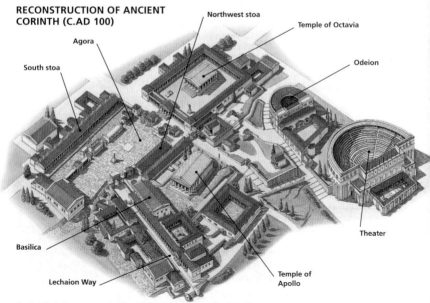

Northwest stoa

Temple of Octavia

Agora

Odeion

South stoa

Basilica

Theater

Lechaion Way

Temple of Apollo

For hotels and restaurants in this region see pp510–13 and pp514–17

Interior of the tomb known as the Treasury of Atreus, at Mycenae

Mycenae ⑬

2 km (1 mile) N of Mykínes. *Tel* 27510-76803. 🚌 to Mykínes. ⬜ daily. ⬤ main public hols. 🈺 ♿ Treasury of Atreus and museum only.

Discovered in 1874, the fortified palace complex of Mycenae is an early example of sophisticated citadel architecture. The Mycenaeans were a Bronze Age culture that existed between 1700 and 1100 BC. Only the ruling class inhabited the palace, with artisans and merchants living outside the city walls. The citadel was abandoned in 1100 BC after much disruption in the region.

The tombs at Mycenae are one of the most famous attractions of the site. The city's nobles were entombed in shaft graves, such as those at **Grave Circle A**, or, later, in *tholos* ("beehive") tombs, so-called because of their shape. The *tholos* tombs, found outside the palace walls, were buried under an earth mound, the only entrance being via a *dromos*, or open-air corridor. The 14th-century BC **Treasury of Atreus** is the most outstanding of the *tholos* tombs. Here a Mycenaean king was buried with his weapons and enough food and drink for his journey to the underworld. The so-called **Tomb of Klytemnestra** is equally well preserved.

Also of interest at the site are the remains of the **Royal Palace**, the **Secret Stairway**, which leads down to a cistern deep beneath the citadel, and the 13th-century BC **Lion Gate**, the grand entrance to Mycenae.

Epidaurus ⑭

30 km (19 miles) E of Náfplio. *Tel* 27530-22009. 🚌 ⬜ daily ⬤ main public hols. 🈺 ♿ limited. 🈸

Active from the 6th century BC until at least the 2nd century AD, the Sanctuary of Epidaurus was an extensive therapeutic and religious center, dedicated to the healing god Asklepios. The site is most renowned for its magnificent **Theater**, whose *cavea* (cavity) is 114 m (374 ft) across and surrounds a 20-m (66-ft) diameter *orchestra* (stage). Designed in the late 4th century BC, the theater is well known for near-perfect acoustics, and has the only circular *orchestra* to have survived from antiquity. Today, it is the venue for an annual summer festival of ancient drama.

Most of the **Asklepieion**, or Sanctuary of Asklepios, is currently being re-excavated. Accessible remains include the *propylaia*, or monumental gateway, a late Classical stadium, and the *tholos* – a circular building, thought to have been used either as a pit for sacred serpents, or as the setting for religious rites. Of Asklepios's temple, to the east of the *tholos*, only the foundations have survived.

Náfplio ⑮

🏃 12,000. 🚗 🚌 ⓘ *Ikosispémptis Martíou 24 (27520-24444).*

One of the most elegant towns in mainland Greece, Náfplio emerged in the 13th century and later endured many sieges during the struggles between the Turks and the Venetians for the ports of the Peloponnese. From 1829 to 1834, it was the first capital of liberated Greece.

A number of fortifications today testify to the town's checkered history. The island fortress of **Boúrtzi** is a legacy of the second Venetian occupation (1686–1715). **Akronafplía**, also known as Its Kale ("Inner Castle" in Turkish), was the site of the Byzantine and early medieval town, while the huge Venetian citadel of **Palamídi** was built between 1711 and 1714.

The Plateía Syntágmatos, the hub of public life, looks much as it did three centuries ago, when two mosques were built by the victorious Ottomans. These are now the cathedral, **Agios Geórgios**, and the **Catholic church**.

The town has two museums of note: the award-winning **Folk Art Museum**, and the **Archaeological Museum**, which houses mainly local pre-Mycenaean artifacts.

Located 4 km (2 miles) outside Náfplio, the 12th-century convent of **Agía Moní** is worth visiting.

🏛 **Archaeological Museum**
Plateía Syntágmatos. *Tel* 27520-27502. ⬜ 8:30am–3pm Tue–Sun. ⬤ main public hols.

The fortified isle of Boúrtzi, north of Náfplio harbor

The cliff-top church of Agía Sofía, Monemvasía upper town

Monemvasía ⓰

🏛 *800*. 🚌 🚢 ℹ *27320-61210.*

This fortified town is built on two levels on a rock rising 350 m (1,150 ft) above the sea. A town of 50,000 in its 15th-century halcyon days, Monemvasía was for centuries a semi-autonomous city-state, which prospered thanks to its strategic position astride the sea lanes from Italy to the Black Sea. After a long and protracted siege, the town was finally surrendered by the Turks in 1821 during the War of Independence.

In the restored lower town, enclosed by the formidable 16th-century walls, are a number of mosques and churches. They include the 18th-century **Panagía Myrtidióssa** and the 13th-century cathedral, **Christós Elkómenos**, with its Venetian belfry. Also found in the lower town is **Giánnis Rítsos's House**, where this prominent 20th-century Greek poet and communist was born.

The upper town, which lies largely in ruins, has been uninhabited since 1911. It was first fortified in the 6th century, and is the oldest part of Monemvasía. Here, the most impressive sight is the still-intact, cliff-top church of **Agía Sofía**, founded by Emperor Andronikos II (1282–1328) and modeled on the Monastery of Dafní (*see p484*). Visitors can also see the remains of a 13th-century fortress.

Máni Peninsula ⓱

🚌 *Gýtheio.* 🚍 *Kalamáta (Outer Máni), Areópoli (Inner Máni).* ℹ *Vasiléos Georgiou 20, Gýtheio (27330-24484).*

The harsh and remote Máni Peninsula is divided into two areas, Outer Máni and Inner Máni, separated by a ravine at Oítylo. The area is most famous for its history of internal feuding, which led to the building of many fine tower houses. From the 15th century, rival clansmen, fighting over the inadequate land, used the towers to shoot at their opponents. After years of bloodshed, the clans finally united, instigating the Greek Independence uprising in 1821.

The main places of interest in more fertile Outer Máni are **Oítylo**, with its elegant 19th-century mansions, and **Kardamýli**, the lair of the Troupákis family, one of the most important Maniot clans. In the environs of Kardamýli are the stunning **Vyrós Gorge**, and **Stoúpa**, popular for its two sandy bays. **Mount Taÿgetos** is one of the area's beauty spots, and can offer several days of wilderness trekking to experienced, well-equipped mountaineers.

In Inner Máni, bustling **Gýtheio** is one of the most attractive coastal towns in the southern Peloponnese. Its 18th-century fortress houses the Museum of the Máni. **Areópoli**, "the city of Ares" (god of war), was where the Maniot uprising against the Turks was proclaimed by Pétros Mavromichális. Nearby

Fishing boats moored in Gýtheio harbor in Inner Máni

is the 17th-century Ottoman **Kelefá Castle**. Visitors to Inner Máni should also see the **Pýrgos Diroú** cave system, and the many Byzantine churches scattered along the west coast. Built between the 10th and 14th centuries, the finest churches include **Taxiarchón**, at Charoúda, **Agios Theódoros**, at Vámvaka, and, near Ano Mpoulárioi village, **Agios Panteleímon** contains 10th-century frescoes. Overlooking the sea and Cape Taínaro, **Vátheia** is one of the most dramatically located of the villages in the Máni. It is worth visiting just to see its collection of tower houses.

Ruins of the Despots' Palace in the Byzantine town of Mystrás

Mystrás ⓲

5 km (3 miles) W of Spárti. **Tel** *27310-83377.* 🚍 *to Néos Mystrás.* 🕐 *daily.* ⬤ *main public hols.* 🅿

Majestic Mystras occupies a panoramic site on a spur of the severe Taÿgetos range. Founded by the Franks in 1249, the town soon passed to the Byzantines, under whom it attained a population of 20,000 and, after 1348, became the seat of the Despots of Morea. The despotate acted semi-independently and, by the 15th century, Mystrás had become the last major Byzantine cultural center, attracting scholars and artists from Italy, Constantinople, and Serbia. One result was the uniquely cosmopolitan decoration of Mystrás's churches, whose pastel-colored frescoes, crowded with detail, reflect Italian Renaissance influence.

Now in ruins, Mystrás consists of an upper and lower town, with a wealth of churches, monasteries, palaces, and houses lining its narrow, winding streets. Among the churches and monasteries worth visiting are **Mitrópoli** – the oldest church in Mystrás, dating from 1291 – **Moní Perivléptou**, and **Moní Pantánassas**. The **Vrontóchion**, a 13th-century monastic complex, was the cultural heart of medieval Mystrás. Visitors can also explore the ruins of the **Despots' Palace**, and the **Kástro**, an impressive fortification that crowns the summit of the upper town, and affords magnificent views of the entire site.

Loúsios Gorge ⑲

🚌 Dimitsána. **All monasteries** ⏰ dawn to dusk daily. **Moní Aimyalón** ⏰ 2–5pm.

Although merely a tributary of the Alfeiós River, the Loúsios stream boasts one of the most impressive canyons in Greece. Scarcely 5 km (3 miles) long, the Loúsios Gorge is nearly 300 m (985 ft) deep at its narrowest section.

Moní Agíou Ioánnou Prodrómou in the Loúsios Gorge

Remains of the Palaestra, or training center, at Ancient Olympia

A number of hiking trails connect the area's highlights, which include several churches and monasteries clinging to the steep cliffs of the gorge. Of these, the most impressive are **Moní Aimyalón**, founded in 1605 and containing some magnificent frescoes, the 17th-century **Néa Moní Filosófou**, and the 10th-century **Moní Agíou Ioánnou Prodrómou**, wedged into the canyon's east flank. Occupying a sunken excavation on the stream's west bank is the Asklepieion, or therapeutic center, of **Ancient Gortys**. On this site lie the foundations of a 4th-century BC temple to Asklepios, the god of healing.

Overlooking the gorge, the beautiful hillside towns of **Dimitsána** and **Stemnítsa** make a good base from which to explore the area.

🏛 **Ancient Gortys** ⏰ daily. ⚫ main public hols.

Ancient Olympia ⑳

Tel 26240-22742. 🚗 🚌 ⏰ daily (winter: Tue–Sun). ⚫ main public hols, May–mid-Oct: Mon am. 🎫

The sanctuary of Olympia enjoyed over 1,000 years of renown as a religious and athletics center. Though it flourished in Mycenaean times, its historic importance dates to the coming of the Dorians, at the beginning of the first millennium BC. They brought the worship of Zeus, after whose abode on Mount Olympos the site was named. Olympia reached its zenith in the 5th century BC, but by the end of the reign of Roman Emperor Hadrian (AD 117–38), it had begun to have less religious and political significance. The first Olympian Games, the forerunner of the Olympic Games, took place here in 776 BC, but were banned in AD 393 by Emperor Theodosius I, who took a dim view of the pagan festival.

The most important ruins include the 5th-century BC Doric **Temple of Zeus**, of which only column bases and tumbled sections remain, and the partly reconstructed **Palaestra**, which was a training center for athletes. In **Pheidias's Workshop**, a huge statue of Zeus was sculpted in the 5th century BC.

Also not to be missed is the **Archaeological Museum**, one of the richest museums in Greece, with exhibits from prehistory, through to the Classical period and the Roman era. The central hall houses the pediment and metope sculpture from the Temple of Zeus. There is also a small museum dedicated to the Olympic Games.

🏛 **Archaeological Museum** **Tel** 26240-22742. ⏰ daily. ⚫ main public hols, May–mid-Oct. 🎫 📷 ♿

Corfu and the Ionian Islands ⑳

The Ionian Islands are the greenest and most fertile of all the island groups. Lying off the west coast of mainland Greece, they have been greatly influenced by Western Europe. Periods of rule by the Venetians, French, and British have left their mark on many of the islands, especially in the mixed architecture of places like Corfu town. The Ionians first became a holiday destination during the Roman era, and today their beaches remain one of their most popular attractions.

LOCATOR MAP

The elegant parade of cafés known as the Liston in Corfu town

Corfu

🏙 100,000. ✈ 3 km (1.5 miles) S of Corfu town. ⛴ Xenofóntos Stratigoú, Corfu town. ▦ ℹ Rizospaston Vouleuton (26610-37520).

Corfu offers the diverse attractions of secluded coves, bustling resorts, and traditional hill villages. Between 229 BC and AD 337 it was part of the Roman empire. It remained under Byzantine rule until the 14th century, when the Venetians took control. French and British occupation followed, before unification with Greece in 1864. Though the island is most popular for its beaches, inland there are many places where you can still observe the traditional lifestyle of the Corfiot people.

Corfu Town

The checkered history of the island is reflected in Corfu town's varied architecture. With its grand French-style colonnades, elegant Italianate buildings, and famous cricket pitch, the town is a delightful blend of European influences.

The **Palace of St. Michael and St. George** was built by the British between 1819 and 1824 to serve as the residence of a high commissioner. Used for a short time by the Greek royal family after the British left the island, the palace is now home to the **Museum of Asiatic Art**.

The palace overlooks the Esplanade, or Spianáda, a mixture of park and town square, and the site of the cricket ground. Once a Venetian firing range, the cricket pitch was developed by the British, and local teams play here regularly. Nearby, the Enosis Monument commemorates the 1864 union of the Ionian Islands with the rest of Greece. The **Liston**, a parade of cafés that was built in 1807 as a copy of the Rue de Rivoli in Paris, lines one side of the square.

Another of the town's most famous sights, the distinctive red-domed belfry of **Agios Spyrídon** is the tallest belfry on Corfu. The church was built in 1589 and dedicated to the island's patron saint.

Also worth seeing are the **Town Hall** – a grand Venetian building located in the Plateía Dimarcheíou – the **Byzantine Museum**, and the fascinating **Archaeological Museum**. The latter's centerpiece is a stunning Gorgon frieze.

On the town's eastern side stands the 16th-century Venetian-built **Old Fortress**, which affords magnificent views of the town and along the island's east coast. The **New Fortress** was built shortly after the old one to strengthen the town's defenses.

🏛 **Palace of St. Michael and St. George**
Plateía Spianáda. *Tel* 26610-30443. ◷ Tue–Sun. ● main public hols.

Northern Corfu

Northern Corfu, in particular the northeast coast, is a busy vacation destination, which boasts a whole host of popular resorts and beaches.

The multiple picturesque bays of Palaiokastrítsa in northern Corfu

For hotels and restaurants in this region see pp510–13 and pp514–17

Mount Aínos and the **Mount Aínos National Park**, in the south, and the haunting, subterranean **Melissaní Cave-Lake** are sights not to be missed. **Fiskárdo**, with its 18th-century Venetian houses clustered by the harbor, is Kefalloniá's prettiest village. From here ferry services are available to the islands of **Ithaca** and **Lefkáda**.

Vacation apartments at Fiskárdo on the island of Kefalloniá

Set around a fishing harbor, **Kassiópi** has retained its character in spite of the influx of tourists. Nearby are the ruins of a 13th-century castle, and the church of Kassiopítissa, which occupies the site of a former temple of Jupiter.

The bustling vacation center of **Sidári** is famous for its sandy beaches and unusual rock formations, while picturesque **Palaiokastrítsa** has safe swimming and water sports, as well as boat trips to nearby grottoes. Vacationers wanting a diversion from the busy resort atmosphere can visit the 17th-century monastery, **Moní Theotókou**.

Mount Pantokrátor, a short drive north of Corfu town, is popular with walkers and naturalists. The highest point on Corfu, it offers fine views of the whole island.

Southern Corfu

More varied than the north, southern Corfu offers other attractions apart from beaches. Tranquil hillside villages, such as **Vátos** and **Pélekas**, contrast with noisy resorts like **Benítses**, offering a more traditional image of Greece.

Among the more peaceful spots in the south is the **Korisíon Lagoon**, a 5-km (3-mile) stretch of water, separated from the sea by some of the most beautiful dunes and beaches on Corfu. The area provides a habitat for many species of birds and wild flowers.

A popular day trip from any of Corfu's resorts is to the **Achílleion Palace**, built between 1890 and 1891 as a personal retreat for the Empress Elizabeth of Austria (1837–98). After a tour of the palace and its gardens, visit the Vasilákis Tastery opposite, and sample this local distiller's products.

🏛 **Achílleion Palace**
19 km (12 miles) SW of Corfu town.
🚌 **Tel** 26610-56210. ◯ daily.

Kefalloniá

🏠 31,000. ✈ 9 km (6 miles) S of Argostóli. ⛴ Argostóli. 🚌 Ioánnou Metaxá, Argostóli. ℹ Waterfront, Argostóli (26710-22248).

The largest island in the Ionians, Kefalloniá has a range of attractions, from busy beach resorts to areas of outstanding natural beauty.

The capital, **Argostóli**, is a busy town located by a bay. Of interest are the Historical and Folk Museum and the Archaeological Museum.

Around the island the liveliest places are **Lássi** and the south-coast resorts, but elsewhere there are quiet villages and stunning scenery.

Zákynthos

🏠 30,000. ✈ 4 km (2.5 miles) S of Zákynthos town. ⛴ Zákynthos town, Agios Nikólaos. 🚌 Zákynthos town. ℹ Tzouláti 2, Zákynthos town (26950-48073).

Zákynthos is an attractive and green island, with good beaches and beautiful scenery to be enjoyed.

Zákynthos town is the point of arrival on the island. Here, the impressive church of Agios Dionýsios, and the Byzantine Museum, which houses a breathtaking array of frescoes, both deserve a visit.

The growth of tourism on Zákynthos has been heavily concentrated in **Laganás** and its 14-km (9-mile) sweep of soft sand. The town's hectic nightlife continues until dawn. Alternatively, visitors can head to the island's north coast for the beach resorts of **Tsiliví** and **Alykés**, the latter being especially good for windsurfing. At the northern-most tip of the island are the unusual and spectacular **Blue Caves**. The caves can be visited by boat from the resort of **Agios Nikólaos**.

The Blue Caves of Zákynthos at the northern tip of the island

Cyclades ㉒

The most visited island group, the Cyclades are
everyone's Greek island ideal, with their whitewashed,
cliff-top villages, blue-domed churches, and stunning
beaches. The islands vary greatly, from the quiet and
traditional to the more nightlife-oriented. The cradle of
the Cycladic civilization (3000–1000 BC), they also offer
a rich ancient history. Important archaeological sites,
such as those on Delos and Santoríni, provide a
fascinating insight into the past.

LOCATOR MAP

Working 16th-century windmill, part of the
Folk Museum in Mýkonos town

Mýkonos

🏛 4,500. ✈ 3 km (1.5 miles) SE of
Mýkonos town. 🚢 Mýkonos town.
🚌 Polykandrióti, Mýkonos town (for
north of island); on road to Ornós,
Mýkonos town (for south of island).
🛈 Harborfront, Mýkonos town
(22890-22482).

Sandy beaches and dynamic
nightlife combine to make
Mýkonos one of the most
popular islands in the
Cyclades. Visited by
intellectuals in the early days
of tourism, today it thrives on
its reputation as the glitziest
island in Greece. In addition
to offering sun, sea, and sand,
the island is a good base from
which to visit the ancient
archaeological site on Delos.

Mýkonos Town

The supreme example of a
Cycladic town, Mýkonos town
(or Chóra) is a tangle of
dazzling white alleys and
cube-shaped houses. It has a
bustling port, from where taxi
boats for the island of **Delos**
leave. To the south, the

**Archaeological
Museum** has a fine
collection of exhibits,
including finds from
the excavations of the
ruins on Delos.
  In the Kástro, the
oldest part of town, is
the excellent **Folk
Museum**. The 16th-
century Vonís Windmill,
still in working order, is
part of the museum.
Nearby, the most
famous church on the
island is **Panagía Para-
portianí**, which dates
back to 1425. From
Kástro, the lanes run
down into picturesque
Venetía, or Little
Venice, the artists'
quarter. Also worth visiting
are the **Maritime Museum
of the Aegean** and the
Municipal Art Gallery.

🏛 **Archaeological Museum**
Harborfront. **Tel** 22890-22325.
⏰ Tue–Sun. ● main public hols. 🏷

Around the Island

Mýkonos is popular primarily
for its beaches and one of the
best is stylish **Platýs Gialós**,
3.5 km (2 miles) south of
Mýkonos town. There are
also several nudist beaches,

including quiet **Parága** and
the more lively **Paradise,
Super Paradise,** and **Eliá**.
  Inland, the traditional
village of **Ano Merá** remains
largely unspoiled by tourism.
The main attraction here is
the 16th-century monastery
Panagía i Tourlianí.

🏛 **Delos**
2.5 km (1 mile) SW of Mýkonos
town. **Tel** 22890-22259. 🚢
8–10am daily from Mýkonos town
returning 12–2pm. ⏰ Tue–Sun. ●
main public hols. 🏷 📷
The tiny, uninhabited island
of Delos is one of the most
important archaeological sites
in Greece. The legendary
birthplace of Artemis and
Apollo, from 1000 BC it was
home to the annual Delian
Festival, held in honor of
the god Apollo. By 700 BC
it had become a major
religious center and place
of pilgrimage. In addition to
some impressive 2nd-century
BC mosaics and temple ruins,
the most important remains
on Delos are the magnificent
7th-century BC **Lion Terrace**,
the **Theater**, built in 300 BC
to hold 5,500 people, and the
Theater Quarter.

Lions carved from Naxian marble along the Lion Terrace on Delos

Whitewashed buildings lining the cliff top in Firá, Santoríni

Santoríni

👥 *12,500.* ✈ *5 km (3 miles) SE of Firá.* ⛴ *Skála Firón.* 🚌 *50 m (160 ft) S of main square, Firá.* ℹ *Firá (22860-22220).*

Colonized by the Minoans in 3000 BC, this volcanic island erupted in 1450 BC, forming Santoríni's distinct crescent shape. A popular tourist destination, it is a stunning island, as famous for its ancient archaeological sites as for its white-washed villages, volcanic cliffs, and black sand beaches.

Firá
Founded in the late 18th century, Firá was destroyed by an earthquake in 1956 and rebuilt along terraces in the volcanic cliffs. Packed with hotels, bars, and restaurants, its streets enjoy magnificent views out to sea. The tiny port of Skála Firón, 270 m (890 ft) below, is connected to the town by cable car or by mule up 580 steps.

Among Firá's most interesting sights are the **Archaeological Museum**, with finds from Ancient Thíra and Minoan Akrotíri, and the 18th-century church of **Agíos Minás**. The pretty ocher chapel of **Agios Stylianós** is also worth a visit on the way to the Frangika, or Frankish quarter, with its maze of arcaded streets.

🏛 **Archaeological Museum**
Opposite cable car station. **Tel** 22860-22217. ⏺ *Tue–Sun.* ⬛ *main public hols.* ♿

Around the Island
Within easy reach of Firá, on the headland of Mésa Vounó, the ruins of the Dorian town of **Ancient Thíra** are not to be missed. Most of the ruins date from the Ptolemies, who built temples to the Egyptian gods in the 4th and 3rd centuries BC. There are also Hellenistic and Roman remains. Below the site are the popular beaches of **Períssa** and **Kamári**.

Another of the Cyclades' most inspiring archaeological sites, the Minoan settlement of **Akrotíri** was unearthed in 1967, still wonderfully preserved after some 3,500 years of burial under volcanic ash. Some of the frescoes discovered here are now on display in the National Archaeological Museum in Athens *(see p476)*.

A donkey ride in Firá, Santoríni

🏛 **Ancient Thira**
11 km (7 miles) SW of Firá. **Tel** 22860-23217. 🚌 *to Kamári.* ⏺ *Tue–Sun.* ⬛ *main public hols.*

Náxos

👥 *20,000.* ✈ *2 km (1 mile) S of Náxos town.* ⛴ 🚌 *Harborfront, Náxos town.* ℹ *Harborfront, Náxos town (22850-25201).*

The largest of the Cyclades, Náxos was a major center of the Cycladic civilization. The Venetians, who arrived in the 13th century, built many fortifications that still stand on the island today. History and superb beaches make Náxos an ideal vacation destination.

Náxos Town
Overlooking Náxos town's bustling harbor is the huge, marble, 6th-century BC Portára gateway, built as the entrance to the unfinished Temple of Apollo. To the south, **Agios Geórgios** is the main tourist center, with a wealth of hotels, apartments, and restaurants. The old town divides into the Kástro – the 13th-century Venetian fortifications – and the medieval Bourg. The fine 18th-century Orthodox cathedral, the **Mitrópoli Zoödóchou Pigís**, stands in the Bourg, which also has a busy market area. In the Kástro, the **Archaeological Museum**, in the Palace of Sanoúdo, has one of the best collections of Cycladic marble figurines in the Greek islands.

🏛 **Archaeological Museum**
Palace of Sanoúdo. **Tel** 22850-22725. ⏺ *Tue–Sun.* ⬛ *main public hols.* ♿

Around the Island
South of Náxos town are many fine beaches, including **Agía Anna** and **Kastráki** – both good for water sports – and tranquil **Pláka**.

Inland the Tragaía Valley is a walkers' paradise. It is dotted with picturesque villages, such as **Chalkí**, with its Byzantine and Venetian architecture, and **Filóti**, which sits on the slopes of 1,000-m (3,300-ft) Mount Zas.

The Portára gateway that overlooks Náxos town's harbor

Rhodes and the Dodecanese ㉓

The Dodecanese offer a wide range of landscapes and activities. Their hot climate and fine beaches attract many visitors, but the islands also boast lush, fertile valleys and wooded mountains. The Dodecanese have been subject to several invasions, with periods of occupation by the medieval Knights of St. John, the Ottomans, and the Italians. This checkered history is still apparent in the islands' impressively varied architecture and wealth of historical sites.

LOCATOR MAP

The Palace of the Grand Masters in Rhodes town

Rhodes

🏛 100,000. ✈ 25 km (15 miles) SW of Rhodes town. ⛴ Commercial harbor, Rhodes town. 🚌 Mandráki, Rhodes town. ℹ Archiepiskopou Makariou 1, Rhodes town (22410-44330).

An important center from the 5th to 3rd centuries BC, Rhodes was later part of both the Roman and Byzantine empires before being conquered by the Knights of St. John, the order founded in the 11th century to tend Christian pilgrims in Jerusalem. They occupied the island from 1306 to 1522, and their medieval walled city still dominates Rhodes town. Ottoman and Italian rulers followed, leaving their own traces of occupation. Rhodes' rich and varied history, sandy beaches, and lively nightlife attract tens of thousands of tourists each year.

Rhodes Old Town
The town of Rhodes has been inhabited for over 2,400 years. A city was first built here in 408 BC, and when the Knights of St. John arrived in

1306 they built their citadel over these ancient remains. Surrounded by moats and 3 km (2 miles) of walls, the Knights' medieval citadel forms the center of the Old Town, which is divided into the Collachium and the Bourg. The Collachium was the Knights' quarter, while the Bourg was home to the rest of the population.

Dominating the Old Town is the 14th-century **Palace of the Grand Masters**, the seat of 19 Grand Masters of the Knights during two centuries of occupation. The palace houses several priceless mosaics from sites in Kos, as well as two permanent exhibitions about ancient and medieval Rhodes.

The medieval **Street of the Knights** is lined by the Inns of the Tongues of the Order of St. John. The Inns – there was one for each of the seven Tongues, or nationalities, into which the Order was

divided – were used as meeting places for the Knights. Begun in the 14th century in Gothic style, they were restored by the Italians in the early 20th century.

The **Archaeological Museum** and the **Byzantine Museum**, both located in the Collachium, contain many fine exhibits from different periods in Rhodes' history.

In the Bourg area, the **Mosque of Suleiman the Magnificent** was built to commemorate the Sultan's victory over the Knights in 1522. The **Library of Ahmet Havuz**, which houses the chronicle of the Turks' siege of Rhodes, and the **Hammam**, the public baths, provide further reminders of the town's Turkish past.

🏛 Palace of the Grand Masters
Ippotón. **Tel** 22410-75674/31048.
🕐 Tue–Sun. 🌑 main public hols.
🎫 ♿ limited.

Rhodes New Town
Beyond the original citadel walls, the new town of Rhodes is made up of a number of areas. These include **Néa Agora**, with its Moorish domes and lively market, and **Mandráki harbor** in the eastern half of town. Close to the harbor are the mock Venetian Gothic **Government House** – a legacy of the Italian occupation of the 1920s – and the **Mosque of Murad Reis**, with its graceful minaret. The west side of town is a busy tourist center, with lively streets and a packed beach.

The minaret of the Mosque of Murad Reis

For hotels and restaurants in this region see pp510–13 and pp514–17

The acropolis overlooking Líndos town on Rhodes

Western Rhodes

A short distance southwest of Rhodes town, set on the beautiful green and wooded hillsides of Filérimos, is **Moní Filerímou**. A place of worship for 2,000 years, this monastery has layers of history and tradition, from Phoenician to Byzantine, Orthodox, and Catholic.

A few kilometers farther southwest, **Ancient Kámeiros** is one of the best-preserved Classical Greek cities. Its remains include a 3rd-century BC Doric temple.

Also worth visiting are the wine-making village of **Emponas**, and **Petaloúdes**, or Butterfly Valley. Popular with walkers, this valley teems with Jersey tiger moths from June to September.

⌂ Ancient Kámeiros
36 km (22 miles) SW of Rhodes town.
⌂ *Tue–Sun.* ● *main public hols.* 🈯
🈯 *to lower sections only*

Eastern Rhodes

Halfway along Rhodes' sheltered east coast, **Líndos** is one of the island's most popular resorts. A magnet for tourists seeking sun, sea, and sand, it is also famous for its cliff-top acropolis overlooking the bay. This temple site, crowned by the 4th-century BC Temple of Lindian Athena, was one of the most sacred spots in the ancient world.

Located in the Valley of Aíthona, between Líndos and Rhodes town, **Archángelos** is famous for its pottery, hand-woven rugs and leather boots. Above the town are the ruins

of the Crusader Castle, built in 1467 by the Knights of St. John as a defense against the Turks.

⌂ Acropolis at Líndos
1 km (0.5 miles) E of Líndos village.
***Tel** 22440-31258.* ⌂ *Jul–Sep: daily; Oct–Jun: Tue–Sun.* ● *main public hols.* 🈯

Kos

🈯 *27,000.* ✈ *27 km (16 miles) W of Kos town.* ⛴ ➡ *Aktí Koudouriótou, Kos town.* 🛈 *Vasiléos Georgíou 1, Kos town (22420-28724).*

Mainly flat and fertile, Kos is known as the "Floating Garden." It has a wealth of archaeological sites, Hellenistic and Roman ruins, and Byzantine and Venetian castles, many of which can be found in **Kos town**. Here, the 16th-century Castle of the Knights, the Ancient Agora, and the Roman remains should not be missed.

Most visitors to Kos come for the sandy beaches. The best of these are easily reached from the resort of **Kamári** on the island's southwest coast. **Kardámaina** is Kos's biggest and noisiest resort, while the northwest bays, such as **Tigkáki**, are ideal for water sports. In spite of tourist development, inland you can still see remnants of Kos's traditional lifestyle.

Kos is a good base from which to explore the more northerly islands of the Dodecanese, including **Pátmos**, home to the 11th-century Monastery of St. John.

Kárpathos

🈯 *5,000.* ✈ *17 km (11 miles) S of Kárpathos town.* ➡ *corner of 28 Oktovríou & Dimokratías, Kárpathos town.* ⛴ *Kárpathos town, Diáfani.* 🛈 *Kárpathos town (22450-22222).*

Despite a recent increase in tourism, wild and rugged Kárpathos remains largely unspoiled. Its capital, **Kárpathos town**, is a busy center, with hotels, cafés, and restaurants around its bay. Nearby is the main resort of **Amoopí**, with its sweep of sandy shore. In addition to some magnificent beaches on the west coast, including **Lefkós** and **Apélla,** the island has places of archaeological and historical interest. **Vroukoúnda** is the site of a 6th-century BC city, while in the village of **Olympos** traditional Greek life and customs can still be observed.

Windmills in the traditional village of Olympos on Kárpathos

Crete ㉔

Rugged mountains, sparkling seas, and ancient history combine with the Cretans' relaxed nature to make this island an idyllic vacation destination. The center of the Minoan civilization over 3,000 years ago, Crete has also been occupied by Romans, Byzantines, Venetians, and Turks. Historic towns such as Irákleio, Chaniá, and Réthymno, and the famous Minoan palaces at Knossos and Phaestos, give a fascinating insight into some of the most important periods in Cretan history.

LOCATOR MAP

Irákleio's boat-lined harbor, dominated by the vast Venetian fortress

Irákleio

🏘 116,000. ✈ 5 km (3 miles) E.
🚢 🚌 🚍 ℹ Xanthoudídou 1 (2810-246299).

A busy, sprawling town of concrete buildings, Irákleio nevertheless has much of interest to the visitor. Four centuries of Venetian rule have left a rich architectural legacy, evident in the imposing 16th-century **fortress** overlooking the harbor, and the elegantly-restored 17th-century **Loggia**, a former meeting place for the island's nobility. Among Irákleio's many churches, **Agios Márkos**, built by the Venetians in 1239, and 16th-century **Agios Títos** deserve a visit. Also not to be missed are the Archaeological Museum *(see below)* and the **Historical Museum**, which traces the history of Crete from early Christian times. The heart of the town is the Plateía Eleftheríou Venizélou, a bustling pedestrianized zone of cafés and shops.

Those interested in the beaches should head to the package-tour resorts of **Mália** and **Chersónisos**, just a short drive east of the town.

🏛 Irákleio Archaeological Museum

Corner of Xanthoudídou & Mpofór, Plateía Eleftherías.
Tel 2810-280370.
⬤ for restoration until 2009.

This impressive museum displays Minoan artifacts from all over Crete. Its most magnificent exhibits include the famous Minoan frescoes from Knossos, and the Phaestos Disk, which was discovered at the site of the palace of Phaestos in 1903. Inscribed with pictorial symbols, the disk's meaning and origin remain a mystery. Among the museum's many other treasures are the Snake Goddesses, two figurines dating from around 1600 BC.

♠ Palace of Knossos

5 km (3 miles) S of Irákleio.
Tel 2810-231 940. 🚌 ⬤ daily.
⬤ main public hols.
The capital of Minoan Crete, Knossos was the largest and most sophisticated of the Minoan palaces on the island. Built around 1900 BC, the first palace of Knossos was destroyed by an earthquake in about 1700 BC and was soon completely rebuilt. The ruins visible today are almost entirely from this second palace. They were restored by Sir Arthur Evans in the early 20th century; although the subject of academic controversy, his reconstructions give one of the best impressions of life in Minoan Crete to be found anywhere on the island.

Highlights of a tour of the site – the focal point of which is the vast Central Court – include the replica of the Priest-King Fresco, the Giant Pithoi, one of over 100 *pithoi* (storage jars) unearthed at Knossos, the Throne Room, believed to have served as a shrine, and the Royal Apartments. The original frescoes from the palace are now housed in Irákleio's Archaeological Museum.

The South Propylon (entrance) of the Palace of Knossos

Phaestos

65 km (40 miles) SW of Irákleio.
Tel 28920-42315. ▦ ◯ *daily.*
⬤ *main public hols.* ▨

Phaestos was one of the
most important Minoan
palaces on Crete. In 1900
Italian-led excavations
unearthed two palaces.
Remains of the first palace,
constructed around 1900 BC
and destroyed by an
earthquake in 1700 BC, are
still visible. Most of the
present ruins, however, are of
the second palace. Phaestos
was finally destroyed in the
2nd century BC by the
ancient city-state of Górtys.

The most impressive
remains are the Grand
Staircase, which was the main
entrance to the palace, and
the Central Court.

A few kilometers northeast
of Phaestos, the archaeological
remains of ancient **Górtys**
date from about 1000 BC to
the late 7th century AD.

Agios Nikólaos

🏛 10,000. 🚌 ▦ ﹗ *Koundoúrou
21 (28410-22357).* 🛒 *Wed.*

The main transport hub for
the east of the island,
delightful Agios Nikólaos is
a thriving vacation center
with an attractive harbor and
fine beaches, as well as an
interesting **Folk Museum** and
an **Archaeological Museum**.

A few kilometers north is
the well-established resort of
Eloúnda, boasting attractive
sandy coves and a good
range of accommodations.

Chaniá

🏛 50,000. ✈ 16 km (10 miles) E.
🚢 ▦ ﹗ *Kriári 40 (28210-92943).*

One of Crete's most
appealing cities, Chánia
was ruled by the Venetians
from 1204 to 1669, and is
dotted with elegant houses,
churches, and fortifications
dating from this period. Many
of these can be found in the
Venetian quarter around the
harbor, and in the picturesque

Splántzia district. The
Mosque of the Janissaries,
on one side of the harbor,
dates back to the arrival of
the Turks in 1645, and is the
oldest Ottoman building on
Crete. The lively covered
market, with its many shops
and fresh produce stalls, is an
area worth exploring. Nearby
the **Archaeological Museum**
is housed in the Venetian
church of San Francesco.

A short walk west of Chaniá
is the relatively undisturbed
beach of **Agioi Apóstoloi**.

Samariá Gorge

44 km (27 miles) S of Chaniá. ▦ *to
Xylóskalo.* 🚢 *Agía Rouméli to Sfakiá
or Palaiochóra (via Soúgia); last boat
back leaves at 5pm.* ◯ *May–mid-
Oct: 6am–4pm daily; Apr 10–30 &
Oct 16–31: if weather permits.*

Crete's most spectacular
scenery lies along the
Samariá Gorge, the longest
ravine in Europe. When it
became a national park, the
inhabitants of the village of
Samariá moved elsewhere,
leaving behind the ruined
buildings and chapels seen
here today. Starting from the
Xylóskalo (Wooden Stairs), an
18-km (11-mile) trail leads to
the seaside village of Agía
Rouméli. A truly impressive
sight along the route is the
Sideróportes, or Iron Gates,
where the path squeezes
between two towering walls
of rock, only 3 m (9 ft) apart.
Upon reaching Agía Rouméli
walkers can take a boat to
Sfakiá, Soúgia, or Palaiochóra
to join the road and buses
back to Chaniá.

The narrow defile known as the
Iron Gates in the Samariá Gorge

Réthymno

🏛 24,000. 🚌 ▦ ﹗ *Eleftheríou
Venizélou (28310-29148).* 🍷 *Wine
Festival (mid-Jul).*

Despite tourism and modern
development, Réthymno has
retained much of its charm.
The old quarter is rich in
well-preserved Venetian and
Ottoman architecture,
including the elegant 16th-
century Venetian **Lótzia**
(Loggia) and the **Nerantzés
Mosque**, converted from a
church by the Turks in 1675.
The huge **Fortétsa** was built
by the Venetians in the 16th
century to defend the port
against both pirates and the
Turks. Below it is a pretty
harbor, lined with cafés and
restaurants. Also worth
visiting in the town is the
Archaeological Museum.

East of Réthymno there are
several resorts, while to the
west lies a 20-km (12-mile)
stretch of uncrowded beach.

Tavernas and bars along Réthymno's waterfront

Practical Information

Tourism is one of Greece's most important industries, and as a consequence, visitors to the country are well catered for: transportation networks are relatively efficient, there are banks and exchange facilities in all the major resorts, and telecommunications have improved dramatically in recent years. The country's hot climate, together with the easy-going outlook of its people, are conducive to a relaxed vacation, and it is usually best to adopt the philosophy *sigá, sigá* (slowly, slowly). In summer, almost everything closes for a few hours after lunch, reopening later in the day when the air cools and Greece comes to life again.

WHEN TO VISIT

Tourist season in Greece – late June to early September – is the hottest and most expensive time to visit, as well as being very crowded. December to March are the coldest and wettest months, with reduced public transportation facilities, and many hotels and restaurants closed for the winter. Spring is a good time to visit; there are fewer tourists, and the weather and the countryside are at their best.

TOURIST INFORMATION

Tourist information is available in many towns and villages throughout Greece, from government-run **EOT** offices (Ellinikós Organismós Tourismoú), municipally run tourist offices, the local tourist police, or privately owned travel agencies. However, visitors should be aware that not all of the information published by the EOT is reliable or up-to-date.

OPENING HOURS

Opening hours tend to be vague in Greece, varying from day to day, season to season, and place to place. To avoid disappointment, visitors are advised to confirm the opening times of sites covered in this chapter once they arrive in the country.

All post offices and banks, and most stores, offices, state-run museums, and archaeological sites close on public holidays. Some facilities may also be closed on local festival days.

The main public holidays in Greece are as follows: January 1, March 25, Good Friday, Easter Sunday, May 1, December 25 and 26.

VISA REQUIREMENTS AND CUSTOMS

Visitors from EU countries, the US, Canada, Australia, and New Zealand need only a valid passport for entry to Greece (no visa is required), and can stay for up to 90 days.

The unauthorized export of antiquities and archaeological artifacts from Greece is treated as a serious offence, incurring hefty fines or even a prison sentence.

Prescription drugs brought into the country should be accompanied by a prescription note for the purposes of the customs authorities.

PERSONAL SECURITY

The crime rate in Greece is very low compared with other European countries, but it is worth taking a few sensible precautions, such as keeping all personal possessions secure. If you have anything stolen, you should contact either the police or the tourist police.

Foreign women traveling alone in Greece are usually treated with respect, especially if they are dressed modestly. However, hitchhiking alone is not advisable.

POLICE

Greece's police are split into three forces: the regular police, the port police, and the tourist police. The tourist police provide advice to vacationers in addition to carrying out normal police duties. Should you suffer a theft, lose your passport, or have cause to complain about shops, restaurants, tour guides, or taxi drivers, you should contact them first. Every tourist police office claims to have at least one English speaker. Their offices also offer maps, brochures, and useful advice on finding accommodations in Greece.

EMERGENCY SERVICES

In the unlikely event of an emergency while on vacation, the appropriate numbers to call are listed in the Directory opposite.

HEALTH ISSUES

No inoculations are required for visitors to Greece, though tetanus and typhoid boosters may be recommended by your doctor.

THE CLIMATE OF GREECE

On the mainland, summers are very hot, while spring and autumn generally bring milder but wetter weather. In winter, rainfall is at its greatest everywhere. Mountainous regions usually get heavy snow, but around Athens, temperatures rarely drop below freezing. Throughout the islands, the tendency is for long, dry summers and mild but rainy winters.

ATHENS

°C/F	Apr	Jul	Oct	Jan
		31/88		
		22/72	22/72	
	18/64		15/59	
	11/52			12/54
0°C 32°F				6/43
☀	8 hrs	12 hrs	7 hrs	4 hrs
☔	23 mm	6 mm	51 mm	62 mm
month	Apr	Jul	Oct	Jan

Tap water in Greece is generally safe to drink, but in remote communities it is a good precaution to check with the locals.

Jellyfish, sea urchins, and weaver fish are potential hazards on beach holidays.

PHARMACIES

Greek pharmacies, *farmakeía*, are open from 8:30am to 2pm Monday to Friday, but are usually closed in the afternoon and all day on Saturdays. In larger towns there is often a rota system to maintain a service from 7:30am to 2pm and from 5:30 to 10pm. Details are posted in pharmacy windows, in both Greek and English.

FACILITIES FOR THE DISABLED

There are few facilities in Greece for assisting the disabled,.so careful, advance planning is essential.

ETIQUETTE

Though formal attire is rarely needed, modest clothing (trousers for men and skirts for women) should be worn when visiting churches and monasteries.

In restaurants, the service charge is always included in the check, but tips are still appreciated – the custom is to leave between 10 and 15 percent. Public restroom attendants should also be tipped. Taxi drivers, hotel porters, and chambermaids do not expect a tip, but are not averse to them either.

PHOTOGRAPHY

Taking photographs inside churches and monasteries is officially forbidden in Greece. Inside museums, photography is usually permitted, although flashes and tripods are often not. Wherever you go, it is best to gain permission before using a camera, as rules vary.

BANKING AND CURRENCY

The Greek unit of currency was the drachma, but since January 2002 it has been replaced by the euro *(see p15)*.

Greek banks open from 8am to 2pm Monday to Thursday, and 8am to 1:30pm on Friday. In major cities and resorts, at least one bank usually opens its exchange desk for a few hours on weekday evenings and on Saturday mornings in summer.

Exchange facilities are also available at post offices, travel agents, hotels, tourist offices, and car rental agencies. Take your passport with you when cashing traveler's checks. Cash point machines (ATMs) operate 24 hours a day.

COMMUNICATIONS

Public telephones can be found in many locales, including hotel lobbies, street kiosks, or local offices of the **OTE** (Organismós Tilepikoinonión Elládos – the Greek national telephone company). OTE offices are open daily from 7am to 10pm or midnight in larger towns, or until around 3pm in smaller communities. Long-distance calls are very expensive in Greece. They are best made in a telephone booth using a phonecard – available at any street kiosk.

Greek post offices *(tachydromeía)* are generally open from 7:30am to 2pm Monday to Friday; some main branches close as late as 8pm and occasionally open for a few hours at weekends. All post offices are closed on public holidays. Those displaying an "Exchange" sign will change money in addition to offering the usual services.

DIRECTORY

TOURIST INFORMATION

Greek National Tourist Board
www.gnto.gr

EOT in Greece:
Tsoha 7,
10564 Athens.
Tel 210-870 7000.

In Australia:
51–57 Pitt St,
Sydney, NSW 2000.
Tel 2-9241 1663.

In Canada:
1500 Don Mills Road
Suite 102, Toronto,
Ontario M3B 3K4.
Tel 416-968-2220.

In the UK:
4 Conduit St,
London W15 2DJ.
Tel 020-7495 9300.

In the US:
Olympic Tower, 645 Fifth
Ave, New York, NY 10022.
Tel 212-421-5777.

EMBASSIES

Australia
Thon Building, Kiasias &
Alexandras, Ambelopiki,
11521 Athens.
Tel 210-870 4000.

Canada
Gennadíou 4,
11521 Athens.
Tel 210-727 3400.

New Zealand
Kifissías 268, 11528
Athens. *Tel 210-687 4700.*

Ireland
Vassiléos Konstantínou 7,
10674 Athens.
Tel 210-723 2405.

UK
Ploutárchou 1,
10675 Athens.
Tel 210-727 2600.

US
Vasilíssis Sofías 91,
10160 Athens.
Tel 210-721 2951

EMERGENCY NUMBERS (NATIONWIDE)

Police
Tel 100.

Ambulance
Tel 166.

Fire
Tel 199.

Road assistance
Tel 104.

Coastguard patrol
Tel 108.

EMERGENCY NUMBERS (ATHENS)

Tourist police
Tel 171.

Doctors
Tel 1016 (2pm–7am).

Pharmacies
For information on
24-hour pharmacies:
Tel 1434.

Travel Information

During the tourist season (late June–early September), there are countless international flights bringing millions of vacationers to the shores of Greece, especially from the colder parts of northern Europe and North America. Traveling within Greece is easy enough. While many of the larger islands can be reached from the mainland by plane, there are ferry routes to even the remotest destinations. Greece's extensive bus network serves virtually everywhere, from the largest city to the tiniest community. Renting a car or motorcycle is another popular way of exploring the country.

FLYING TO GREECE

There are around 20 international airports in Greece that can be reached directly from Europe. Only Crete, Rhodes, and Corfu among the islands, and Athens and Thessaloníki on the mainland, handle both charter and scheduled flights. The other international airports can only be reached directly by charter flights.

Direct scheduled flights from London to Athens and Thessaloníki are operated by **Olympic Airlines** (the Greek national airline), British Airways, and easyJet (Athens only). From outside Europe, all scheduled flights to Greece arrive in Athens, and only a few airlines offer direct flights. Olympic and Delta Air Lines operate direct flights daily from New York.

Flights from Australasia to Athens are run by Qantas, Singapore Airlines, Thai Airways, and KLM.

Athens' new international airport, Eléfthérios Venizélos, opened in 2001 and is located 27 km (17 miles) north-east of the center. There are two 24-hour bus services from the city to the airport: the E95 from the Plateía Syntágmatos takes approximately 1 hour; the E96 departs from Piraeus and takes 1 hour and 20 minutes. Metro line 3 now runs from Syntagma to the airport.

CHARTERS AND PACKAGE DEALS

Charter flights to Greece are nearly all from within Europe, and mostly operate between May and October.

Tickets are sold by travel agencies either as part of an all-inclusive package tour or as a flight-only deal.

DOMESTIC FLIGHTS

Most internal flights in Greece and the Greek Islands are operated by **Olympic Airlines**. Olympic Airlines operates direct flights from Athens and Thessaloníki to many of the islands. In addition, there are a number of inter-island services available throughout the year. Private companies, such as **Aegean Airlines**, also provide services between Athens and some of the major mainland and island destinations. Fares for domestic flights are at least double the equivalent bus journey or deck-class ferry trip.

GETTING AROUND ATHENS

Athens has a network of buses, trolley buses, and trams, in addition to a metro system. Buses are inexpensive, but can be very slow, as well as crowded. Tickets for buses and trams must be purchased in advance from a *períptero* (street kiosk), a transport booth, or certain other designated places. A brown, red, and white logo, with the words *eisitíria edó*, indicates where you can buy them. Each ticket is valid for one journey only, regardless of the distance traveled.

Since most of the major sights in the city center are within walking distance of one another, you can avoid using public transportation.

RAIL TRAVEL

Greece's rail network is operated by the state-owned **OSE** (Organismós Sidirodrómon Elládos). Limited to the mainland, it is fairly skeletal by European standards. First- and second-class tickets are less expensive than the equivalent bus journey, but services tend to be slower. Though more costly, tickets for intercity express trains are worth it for the time they save. A Greek Rail Pass allows the user three or five days of unlimited rail travel in one month on first- and second-class services, anywhere in Greece.

TRAVELING BY BUS

International buses connect Greece with eastern Europe, though during the tourist season fares are more expensive than charter flights.

Within Greece, the long-distance bus network is extensive, with buses stopping at least once a day at even the remotest destinations, and frequent express services on all the major routes.

From Athens there are regular departures to all the larger mainland towns, apart from those in Thrace, which are served by buses from Thessaloníki. Athens' Terminal A serves Epirus, Macedonia, the Peloponnese, and the Ionian islands of Corfu, Kefalloniá, Lefkáda, and Zákynthos. Terminal B serves most destinations in central Greece, including Delphi.

TRAVELING BY CAR

On the mainland there are express highways between Athens, Thessaloníki, Vólos, and Pátra. These roads are very fast, but tolls are charged for their use. There has been much upgrading of the roads on the islands, but they are still often poorly surfaced, particularly in more remote areas.

Car rental agencies are found in every tourist resort and major town. International companies such as **Budget, Avis, Hertz,** and **Europcar** tend to be more expensive than their local counterparts. The car rental agency should have an agreement with an emergency recovery company, such as Express, Hellas, or the InterAmerican Towing Company, in the event of a vehicle breakdown. Mopeds and motorcycles are also available for rent in many tourist resorts.

Greece has one of the highest road traffic accident rates in Europe; visitors are advised to take extra care when driving around.

FERRY SERVICES

There are regular, year-round ferry crossings from Italy, Israel, and Turkey to the Greek mainland and islands.

Piraeus, the port of Athens, is Greece's busiest port, with ferry routes to international destinations, as well as to scores of locations on the mainland and islands. A number of companies run the ferry services, each with their own ticket agency on the dockside. All fares except first class are set by the Ministry of Transport, so a journey should cost you the same, regardless of which shipping company you choose.

Ferry tickets can be purchased from the shipping line office on the dockside, or any authorized travel agency. Advance reservations are essential in peak season, which runs from June to August. In off season, services may be reduced or suspended altogether. Check local sources – such as the Greek tourist office or a travel agency – for the latest information before you travel. The port police, who have an office at Piraeus, are also a good source of reliable, up-to-date information.

In addition to the large ferries, there are smaller vessels that make inter-island crossings in summer.

HYDROFOILS AND CATAMARANS

The main operators of hydrofoil and catamaran services between the mainland and the islands are **Dodecanese Hydrofoils** and **Flying Dolphin** (run by Minoan Lines). However, all hydrofoils, regardless of which company they are operated by, are known locally as "Flying Dolphins." They are twice as fast as ferries, but twice as expensive. Most vessels function only in the summer months and are often cancelled in bad weather.

DIRECTORY

OLYMPIC AIRLINES

www.olympic-airlines.gr

Athens
Syngroú 96,
11741 Athens.
Tel 210-926 9111.

Thessaloníki
Kountouriótou 3,
Thessaloníki.
Tel 2310-368 311.

UK
11 Conduit Street,
London W1R OLP.
Tel 020-7399 1500 or 0870-606 0460.

US
Satellite Airlines Terminal,
125 Park Ave, New York,
NY 10017.
Tel 718-269 2200.

DOMESTIC AIRLINES

Aegean Airlines
Viltanoti 31,
14561 Athens.
Tel 80-11 12 00 00.
www.aegeanair.com

TRAVEL AGENCIES IN GREECE

National Travel Information.
Tel 1440 (boat, train, coach times).

American Express Travel Services
Messogion Ave 318,
15341 Athens.
Tel 210-659 0700.

Oxygen Travel
Eslin 4,
Athens.
Tel 210-641 0881.
www.oxygentravel.gr

Superfast Ferries
Amalias 30,
10563 Athens.
Tel 210-891 9130.
www.superfast.com

RAIL TRAVEL

OSE (Information & Reservations)
Sína 6, Athens.
Tel 1110.
www.ose.gr

Rail Europe
Tel 08708-371 371 (UK).
www.raileurope.co.uk

Train Stations in Athens

Laríssis station (for northern Greece)
Tel 210-823 1514.

Peloponnísou station
(for Peloponnese)
Tel 210-513 1601.

BUSES

Bus Terminals in Athens
Terminal A:
Kifisoú 100
Tel 210-513 2834.

Terminal B:
Liosíon 260
Tel 210-832 9585.

CAR RENTAL AGENCIES

Avis
Leofóros Amalías 48,
10558 Athens.
Tel 210-322 4951.
www.avis.com

Budget
Syngroú 8,
11742 Athens.
Tel 210-921 4771.
www.budget.com

Europcar
Syngroú 43,
11742 Athens.
Tel 210-924 8810.
www.europcar.com

Hertz
Syngroú 12,
11742 Athens.
Tel 210-922 0102.
www.hertz.gr

PIRAEUS PORT

Tel 210-422 6000 (port police).
Tel 1440 (ferry timetable).

HYDROFOIL AND CATAMARAN SERVICES

Dodecanese Hydrofoils
Mandráki Harbor,
Rhodes.
Tel 224-107 8052.

Flying Dolphin
Goúnari 2,
Piraeus.
Tel 210-419 9200.

Shopping & Entertainment

The choice of places to shop in Greece ranges from colorful, bustling street markets, found in almost every town and village, through traditional arts and crafts shops, to the designer fashion boutiques of Athens. Entertainment is as varied; visitors can try an open-air concert in the atmospheric setting of an ancient theater, or enjoy some late-night dining in a local taverna before heading for a bar or disco. With its dry, sunny climate and clear, warm seas, Greece offers countless opportunities for outdoor activities, from snorkeling to windsurfing, sailing, and hiking.

WHAT TO BUY

Traditional handicrafts, though often expensive, are the most genuinely Greek souvenirs. In Athens, Monastiráki and Pláka are the best places to purchase such items. There are also many unusual shops offering unique services, such as that of self-styled poet, **Stávros Melissinós**, who makes a wide variety of sturdy sandals and leather items. An excellent selection of goods, including tapestries and rugs, is available at **Ikpa Ipoteknia**, while at the fascinating **Center of Hellenic Tradition** you can buy, among other things, finely crafted ceramics.

Some of the country's best ceramics can be found in the markets and shops of Athens' northern suburb Maroúsi, and on the island of Crete.

Brightly colored embroidery and wall-hangings are produced in many Greek villages. Colorful *flokáti* rugs, which are handwoven from sheep or goat's wool, are made mainly in the Píndos mountains, but can also be found in other parts of the mainland and on the islands.

Sold throughout Greece, leather goods are particularly noted on Crete, where the town of Chaniá hosts a huge leather market.

Well-crafted copies of ancient and Byzantine Greek art can be found in museum shops in many of the major cities. In Pláka in Athens, **Orféas** offers good quality marble and pottery copies of Classical Greek works, in addition to glittering Byzantine icons.

For jewelry, Athens is the best place to shop. Exclusive names include **Vourákis** and **Anagnostópoulos**, on Voukourestíou. The **Ilías Lalaoúnis Jewelry Museum** has over 3,000 designs, inspired by Classical and other archaeological sources.

MARKETS

Most towns in Greece have a weekly street market (*laïkí agorá*), where fresh produce is sold alongside shoes, fabrics, and sundry household items. In Athens, the one on Xenokrátous in centrally located Kolonáki takes place every Friday. The busy Central Market is excellent for food, while the famous Sunday-morning flea market in Monastiráki should not be missed.

FOOD AND DRINK

Culinary delights to look for in Greece include honey, olives, olive oil, pistachios, and cheeses, such as the salty feta. Also worth trying are ouzo (an anise-flavored liquor), retsina (wine flavored with pine resin), and the fire-water *tsípouro*.

ENTERTAINMENT LISTINGS AND TICKETS

For detailed information on entertainment in Athens, try the weekly *Athinorama*, (in Greek only), or the English-language *Athens News*.

Most theaters and music clubs in the capital sell tickets at the door on the day of the performance. However, tickets for the summer Athens

Festival and for concerts at the Mousikís Mégaron Concert Hall should be purchased in advance; there is a central ticket office, open daily from 10am to 4pm, located near the Plateía Syntágmatos.

Elsewhere, your nearest tourist office should be able to provide information on what is happening locally.

ENTERTAINMENT VENUES

The main entertainment venues in Athens host a wide variety of events. As well as excellent productions of 19th-century Greek and European plays, the **National Theater** puts on opera, ballet, and contemporary dance. The **Mousikís Mégaron Concert Hall** is a first-class classical concert venue, while the Olýmpia Theater is home to the **Lyrikí Skiní** (National Opera). At the **Dóra Strátou Dance Theater** there is traditional regional Greek dancing nightly between May and September.

OPEN-AIR CINEMAS AND THEATERS

Found in towns and cities all over Greece, the outdoor cinema is extremely popular with Greeks and an experience not to be missed by anyone visiting the country in summer. Most movies are in English with Greek subtitles.

Open-air performances of Classical and modern drama, held at famous ancient archaeological sites, are an equally popular form of entertainment. The **Herodes Atticus Theater** hosts plays, as well as opera, ballet, and classical music concerts, during the annual Athens Festival (mid-June to mid-September). The theater at **Epidaurus** in the Peloponnese is another well-known venue.

TRADITIONAL GREEK MUSIC

To hear traditional Greek music in Athens head for **Diogénis Studio** or **Rex**. At **Taksími** and **Rempétiki Istoría** you can hear genuine *bouzouki* (Greek mandolin)

music. In smaller towns and resorts around the country, the local taverna is often a good place to see traditional musicians perform while you dine.

SPECIAL INTEREST VACATIONS

Companies offering special interest vacations include **Filoxenía** and **Ramblers Holidays**, which organize archaeological tours, and **Andante Travels**. Filoxenía also runs courses on creative writing, drawing, and painting in Greece.

For specialist wildlife tours contact **Naturetrek, Limosa Holidays**, or the **Hellenic Ornithological Society**.

OUTDOOR ACTIVITIES

With miles of coastline, and crystal clear seas, Greece is the perfect place to pursue water sports. Windsurfing, water-skiing, jet-skiing, and parasailing are all available in the larger resorts. Snorkeling and scuba diving are also popular, although the latter is restricted. A list of places where it is permissible to dive with oxygen equipment can be obtained from the EOT (Greek Tourist Office) *(see p502).*

For information on sailing vacations and chartering yachts, contact the **Hellenic Yachting Federation**. Cruises on luxury liners can be booked through **Swan Hellenic Cruises**, while inexpensive minicruises and boat trips are best arranged at a local travel agent on the spot.

Those wishing to simply relax on the beach should look for one with a Blue Flag; this indicates that the water is regularly tested for purity, and that the beach meets over a dozen other environmental criteria for both cleanliness and safety.

Inland the range of leisure opportunities is very varied, ranging from kayaking, white-water rafting, and canoeing, to hiking. **Trekking Hellas** organizes vacations based on these and other activities.

DIRECTORY

ART AND CRAFTS

Center of Hellenic Tradition
Mitropóleos 59 (Arcade) –
Pandrósou 36,
Monastiráki, Athens.
Tel 210-321 3023.

Ikpa Ipoteknia
Filenninon 14,
Syntagma, Athens.
Tel 210-321 8272.

Stávros Melissinós
Ag.Theklas 2,
Psyrri, Athens.
Tel 210-321 9247.

MUSEUM COPIES

Orféas
Pandrósou 28, Pláka,
Athens.
Tel 210-324 5034.

JEWELRY

Anagnostópoulos
Voukourestíou 6,
Kolonáki,
Athens.
Tel 210-360 4426.

Ilías Lalaoúnis Jewelry Museum
Karyatidon 4a,
Pláka, Athens.
Tel 210-922 1044.

Vourákis
Voukourestíou 8, Kolonáki,
Athens.
Tel 210-331 1089.

THEATERS

Dóra Strátou Dance Theater
Filopáppou Hill,
Filopáppou, Athens.
Tel 210-324 6188.

National Theater
Agíou Konstantínou 22,
Omónoia, Athens.
Tel 210-522 0585.

CLASSICAL MUSIC AND OPERA

Lyrikí Skiní, Olympia Theater
Akadimías 59,
Omónoia, Athens.
Tel 210-361 2461.

Mousikís Mégaron Concert Hall
V Sofías & Kókkali,
Stégi Patrídos, Athens.
Tel 210-728 2333.

OPEN-AIR THEATERS

Herodes Atticus Theater
Dionysíou Areopagítou,
Acropolis, Athens.
Tel 210-323 9132.

TRADITIONAL GREEK MUSIC

Diogénis Studio
Leof A Syngroú 259,
N. Smyrni, Athens.
Tel 210-942 5754.

Rempétiki Istoría
Ippokrátous 181,
Neápoli, Athens.
Tel 210-642 4937.

Rex
Panepistimíou 48,
Omonoia, Athens.
Tel 210-381 4591.

Taksími
C Trikoúpi & Isávron 29,
Neápoli, Athens.
Tel 210-363 9919.

SPECIAL INTEREST VACATIONS

Andante Travels
The Old Barn,
Old Road, Alderbury,
Salisbury SP5 3AR, England.
Tel 01722-713 800.
www.andante
travels.co.uk

Filoxenía
Castle Howard, York,
YO60 7JU, England.
Tel 01653-617 755.
www.filoxenia.co.uk

Hellenic Ornithological Society
Vasileos Irakleion 24,
10682 Athens.
Tel 210-822 7937.

Limosa Holidays
Suffield House,
Northrepps, Norfolk NR27
0LZ, England.
Tel 01263-578 143.
www.limosaholidays.co.uk

Naturetrek
Cheriton Mill, Cheriton,
Alresford, Hants
SO24 0NG,
England.
Tel 01962-733 051.
www.naturetrek.co.uk

Ramblers Holidays
Box 43, Welwyn Garden
City, Herts AL8 6PQ,
England.
Tel 01707-331 133.
www.ramblers
holidays.co.uk

OUTDOOR ACTIVITIES

Hellenic Yachting Federation
Akti Possidónas 51,
Moschato, Athens,
Greece.
Tel 210-940 3111.

Swan Hellenic Cruises
Richmond Hse,
Perminus Terrace,
Southampton,
SO14 3PN, England.
Tel 0845-355 5111.
www.swanhellenic.com

Trekking Hellas
Filellinou 7, 10557 Athens.
Tel 210-331 0323.
www.trekking.gr

Where to Stay in Greece

In a country so heavily dependent on tourism, accommodations are always easily found, and are very inexpensive compared with those in most other European destinations. Visitors to Greece can choose to stay in a range of surroundings, from modern luxury chain hotels to restored historic buildings.

PRICE CATEGORIES
The following price ranges are for a standard double room with tax per night during the high season. Breakfast is not included, unless specified:
€ Under 50 euros
€€ 50–90 euros
€€€ 90–130 euros
€€€€ 130–200 euros
€€€€€ Over 200 euros

ATHENS

EXARCHEIA Exarchion   🔲♿   €
Themistokléous 55, 106 83 **Tel** *210-38 01256* **Fax** *210-38 03296* **Rooms** *58*   **Map** *D1*

The dated rooms of this 1960s high-rise, with their linoleum floors and dark furniture, are ready for a facelift, but they do have fridges, air conditioning and TVs; given the price and the location in the heart of the district's nightlife scene, you can't complain. The mezzanine breakfast room is cheerful enough. **www.exarchion.gr**

EXARCHEIA Best Western Museum   🔲🔲📶♿   €€€
Mpoumpoulínas 16, 106 82 **Tel** *210-38 05611* **Fax** *210-38 00507* **Rooms** *90*   **Map** *C1*

Renovated recently, this hotel takes its name from the National Archaeological Museum at the front, and is popular with academic visitors. The rooms are up to the standards of the Best Western chain without being especially distinctive. There are also triples and quads for families. **www.bestwestern.gr**

ILISIA Hilton   🔲🔲🔲📶♿   €€€€€
Vassilísis Sofías 46, 115 28 **Tel** *210-72 81000* **Fax** *210-72 81111* **Rooms** *306*   **Map** *F3*

For years the only five-star hotel in the city center, the Hilton's pre-Olympics overhaul has vaulted back into the top rank, with the rooms retaining their large balconies. The hotel's three restaurants and huge outdoor pool (open to the public for a fee) are still major meeting points. **www.athens.hilton.com**

KOLONAKI St. George Lycabettus   🔲🔲🔲📶♿   €€€€
Kleoménous 2, 106 75 **Tel** *210-72 90711* **Fax** *210-72 90439* **Rooms** *157*   **Map** *E3*

Situated just off Platía Dexamenís halfway up Lykavittós Hill, the St. George offers a rooftop pool, two well-regarded restaurants, and a bar that's a popular local hangout. The rooms are a mix of retro and modern minimalist; try to get a south-facing one with a view over the city. **www.sglycabettus.gr**

KOUKAKI Marble House   🔲   €
Alley off Anastasíou Zínni 35, 11741 **Tel** *210-92 28294* **Fax** *210-92 34058* **Rooms** *16*   **Map** *B5*

The helpful Nikoloulias family's pension has an enviable location on a quiet cul-de-sac. The simple but tidy rooms upstairs, most with bath and balcony, are complete with pine furniture and white tiles. There are two slightly larger ground floor studios. Very popular in season, so book well in advance. **www.marblehouse.gr**

MAKRYGIANNI Herodion   🔲🔲   €€€
Rovértou Gkálli 4, 117 42 **Tel** *210-92 36832* **Fax** *210-92 11650* **Rooms** *90*   **Map** *B5*

The Herodion has lovely common areas: the café-restaurant with patio seating shaded by wild pistachios, and the roof garden with two Jacuzzi tubs and the Acropolis a stone's throw away. Functional but fair-sized rooms, some with disabled-friendly baths and Acropolis views, have coco-fiber mattresses. **www.herodion.gr**

MAKRYGIANNI Divani Palace Acropolis   🔲🔲🔲📶   €€€€
Parthenónos 19–25, 117 42 **Tel** *210-92 80100* **Fax** *210-92 14993* **Rooms** *250*   **Map** *B5*

This popular business and conference hotel has vast common facilities, though the underground restaurant is gloomily lit. Equally subterranean are exhibited sections of the Themistoklean Long Walls, discovered when the hotel was built. Rooms are a good size; there's also a small pool area and summer rooftop garden. **www.divanis.gr**

MONASTIRAKI Cecil   🔲   €€
Athinás 39, 105 54 **Tel** *210-32 17079* **Fax** *210-32 19606* **Rooms** *40*   **Map** *B3*

One of the oldest buildings in central Athens, dating from the 1850s, has been restored as a good-value character hotel with soundproofed, tastefully decorated, en suite rooms. Breakfast (charged separately) is abundant, featuring homemade jams, plus there's a roof terrace. **www.cecil.gr**

OMONOIA Art Athens Hotel   🔲🔲   €€
Márnis 27/Aristotélous 16, 104 32 **Tel** *210-52 40501* **Fax** *210-52 43384* **Rooms** *30*   **Map** *B1*

Boutique hotels are now ten a penny in Athens, but this one – occupying a converted Neo-Classical mansion – is one of the best. Light cream tones characterize the wood-floored rooms, accented by colorful original artwork. Everything is hi-tech, from lighting to voice mail to individual thermostats. Service is excellent. **www.arthotelathens.gr**

Key to Symbols *see back cover flap*

OMONOIA The Alassia

🍴🛏️🅿️♿   €€€

Sokrátou 50, 104 31 **Tel** *210-52 74000* **Fax** *210-52 74029* **Rooms** *82*   **Map** *B2*

A designer hotel, deploying lots of polished metal, futuristic furniture, recessed lighting and marble surfaces in the common areas, and understated, soundproofed (if slightly small) guest rooms with internet access. The location doesn't get much more central, but this is the least interesting corner of Omónoia. **www.thealassia.com.gr**

OMONOIA Delphi Art Hotel

🍴🛏️   €€€€

Agíou Konstantínou 27, 104 37 **Tel** *210-52 44004* **Fax** *210-52 39564* **Rooms** *40*   **Map** *B2*

Formerly a six-story 1930s apartment block next to the National Theatre, this has been converted into a stylish hotel with all mod cons (including internet access), without sacrificing original features such as bay windows and French doors opening onto balconies with wrought-iron railings. Common areas include three bar-cafés. **www.delphiarthotel.com**

PLAKA Phaedra

📄🛏️   €

Chairefontos 16, corner of Adrianoú, 105 58 **Tel** *210-32 38461* **Fax** *210-32 27795* **Rooms** *21*   **Map** *C5*

Located at the intersection of two pedestrian lanes, the Phaedra had a thorough makeover before the Olympics and offers the best budget value in the area. Although not all tiled-floor rooms are en suite, each has an allocated bathroom and TV, while some have balconies. Pleasant ground floor breakfast room.

PLAKA Central

🍴🛏️🅿️   €€€

Apóllonos 21, 105 57 **Tel** *210-32 34357* **Fax** *210-32 25244* **Rooms** *84*   **Map** *C4*

Italian designer furniture, marble-clad bathrooms, and wooden flooring set the tone for this revamped hotel, with warm-toned soft furnishings in the comfortable, soundproofed rooms, some of which interconnect. There are four conference rooms, and a rooftop bar with a small spa and view of the Acropolis. **www.centralhotel.gr**

PLAKA Plaka

🍴🛏️   €€€€

Kapnikaréa 7, corner of Mitropóleos, 105 66 **Tel** *210-32 22096* **Fax** *210-32 22412* **Rooms** *67*   **Map** *C4*

A sister hotel to the Hermes, the Plaka anticipated by some years the Olympic Games renovation frenzy, and has worn well. From the leather sofas in the lobby to the striking color schemes in the wood-floored rooms, the place is sleek and tasteful. Many nearby hotels boast of roof gardens; the Plaka's is one of the best. **www.plakahotel.gr**

PLAKA Electra Palace

🍴🏊🛏️🅿️   €€€€€

Navárchou Nikodhímou 18–20, 105 57 **Tel** *210-33 70000* **Fax** *210-32 41875* **Rooms** *131*   **Map** *C4*

The only de luxe hotel in Pláka attracts attention with its Neo-Classical façade. The interior lives up to this promise, with plush rooms, antique and mock-antique decor, a wellness centre, plus plans for a rooftop pool. Rooms facing the garden are quieter. It's worth paying extra for a suite. **www.electrahotels.gr**

PSYRRI Fresh

🍴🏊🛏️   €€€€

Sofokléous 26 & Kleisthénous, 105 52 **Tel** *210-52 48511* **Fax** *210-52 48517* **Rooms** *133*   **Map** *B3*

The closest design hotel to the town centre, Fresh combines minimalist chic with shockingly vibrant colors, right down to the balcony partitions. Rooms are small but cleverly designed – you can control the blinds from your bed to reveal views of the interior rock gardens. Stylish rooftop pool and bar. Wi-Fi access. **www.freshhotel.gr**

STATHMOS LARISSIS Oscar

🍴🏊🛏️🅿️   €€€

Filadélfias 25, 104 39 **Tel** *210-88 34315* **Fax** *210-82 16368* **Rooms** *124*

The Oscar's main advantage is its position opposite the main Athens train station – ideal for late-night arrivals or early-morning departures to/from the airport or the north mainland. The common facilities, including a rooftop pool, are more than you would expect for this price, though rooms are a little dull. **www.oscar.gr**

SYNTAGMA Metropolis

📄🛏️🅿️   €€

Mitropóleos 46, 105 63 **Tel** *210-32 17469* **Fax** *210-32 17871* **Rooms** *25*   **Map** *C4*

This small, five-story hotel enjoys views over its namesake, the Mitrópoli (Cathedral), and on to the Acropolis from the upper rooms. Rooms are basic, with vinyl floors and balconies, though the staff are friendly and the price is reasonable. There are no common areas, and breakfast is not provided. **www.hotelmetropolis.gr**

SYNTAGMA Athens Cypria

🛏️   €€€

Diomeias 5, 105 57 **Tel** *210-32 38034* **Fax** *210-32 48792* **Rooms** *71*   **Map** *C4*

The exterior of this hotel just off pedestrianized Ermoú is deceptively bland. Inside, earth-toned rooms with small balconies are matched by the color scheme and stone dressing in the lobby. A disadvantage is the complete lack of common areas, other than a small café-bar with tables on the pavement. **www.athenscypria.com**

SYNTAGMA Grande Bretagne

🍴🏊🛏️♿   €€€€€

Vassíleos Georgíou 1, Plateía Syntágmatos, 105 63 **Tel** *210-33 30000* **Fax** *210-32 28034* **Rooms** *321*   **Map** *D4*

Originally built in 1842 for King Otto, the Grande Bretagne has always been Athens' most exclusive hotel. Its restaurants and bars stand out in their own right: Alexander's Bar has an 18th-century tapestry of Alexander the Great, and the brasserie and rooftop restaurant are justifiably busy. **www.grandebretagne.gr**

SYNTAGMA King George II

🍴🏊🛏️♿   €€€€€

Vassíleos Georgíou 3, Plateía Syntágmatos, 105 64 **Tel** *210-32 22210* **Fax** *210-32 50504* **Rooms** *102*   **Map** *D4*

The 1936-founded King George is more intimate and personal than other luxury hotels in the immediate vicinity, but boasts similar antique Belle Époque decor, a small pool in the fitness center, and a rooftop restaurant. Rooms are a good size, all unique, with handmade furniture in Second Empire style, and all mod cons. **www.grecotel.gr**

Map References *see map of Athens pp474–5*

REST OF MAINLAND GREECE

ÁGIOS IOANNIS Sofoklis
Seafront, north end, 370 12 **Tel** *24260-31230* **Fax** *24260-31021* **Rooms** *20*

This professionally run hotel tries a bit harder than the competition at this beach resort. There is a century-old stone-walled ground floor lounge, oblique or direct sea views from most rooms, a tasteful breakfast terrace, and an attractive pool. Unusually for this area, it's open all year. **www.sofokleshotel.pelionet.gr**

ANCIENT CORINTH Shadow
On access road to village, 200 07 **Tel/Fax** *27410-31481* **Rooms** *12*

A small, friendly pension, well-placed for the ruins at Ancient Corinth and Acrocorinth, and far preferable to staying in noisy Kórinthos. The back rooms have good views out to the west. Excellent breakfasts are served in the downstairs area, which also houses a collection of rocks, crystals, and natural history items. All rooms have fridges.

AREOPOLI Xenonas Lontas
Off Plateía Taxiarchón, 23062 **Tel** *27330-51360* **Fax** *27330-51012* **Rooms** *4*

This tower-mansion has been sympathetically converted into a small, sophisticated inn by Iakovos, painter and chef, and Han Jakob. The colorful textiles and wall tones are in the best of taste. Local honey and Iakovos' marmalade is served at breakfast.

DELFOI Pan
Pávlou ké Fredherikís 53, 330 54 **Tel** *22650-82294* **Fax** *22650-83244* **Rooms** *15*

Most rooms here have fine views of the gulf. The best and newest rooms sleep four and are in the attic. Immediately across the street is a slightly pricier annex, with larger rooms and bathrooms, including bathtubs, but without the views of the older building.

DIMITSANA Xenonas Kazakou
Near the top of the village, 220 07 **Tel** *27950-31660* **Fax** *27950-31660* **Rooms** *5*

Externally austere, this tastefully restored, stone and wood mansion is discreetly comfortable inside – with central heating for the chilly mountain winters. It is very quiet, apart from the Sunday church-bells. A rich traditional breakfast, including *loukomádes*, is served in the vaulted cellar. **www.xensonaskazakou.gr**

GYTHEIO Githio
Vassiléos Pávlou 33, 232 00 **Tel** *27330-23452* **Fax** *27330-23523* **Rooms** *7*

This fine Neo-Classical building from 1864 was formerly a gentleman's club; it's now a stylishly refurbished hotel above an ice cream parlor, overlooking the seafront and harbor. Elegant, high-ceilinged rooms sleep two or three; two four-bed apartments have kitchen facilities. Breakfast served in an area carved out of the natural rock. **www.gythionhotel.gr**

KALAMPAKA Alsos House
Kanári 5, 422 00 **Tel** *24320-24097* **Fax** *24320-79191* **Rooms** *6*

Remodelled in 2004, this small inn at the heart of Kalampáka's oldest quarter offers a mix of doubles, triples and a 4-bed family suite, all with balconies and sharing a well-equipped communal kitchen. The multilingual proprietor is a mine of information on the surrounding area. **www.kalampaka.com/alsoshous**

KARDAMYLI Cardamili Beach
Northern end of Ritsia beach, 240 22 **Tel** *27210-73180* **Fax** *27210-73184* **Rooms** *29*

Situated in a large orchard on the beachfront, and a short distance from the village, the hotel has rooms in the main building and a number of garden bungalows; some of the latter have kitchen facilities. All rooms have a fridge and views of the sea or mountains. Taverna and swimming pool on site. Open Apr–Oct.

LITOCHORO Villa Drosos
Archeláou 20, Ágios Geórgios district, 602 00 **Tel** *23520-84561* **Fax** *23520-84563* **Rooms** *13*

The Villa Drosos may not have the unimpeded mountain views of the central-square hotels, but it does offer excellent standards in its small but balconied rooms, the best of which overlook the swimming pool and a small wood. The breakfast room has a fireplace, and the restaurant serves good grills. Open all year. **grigoris@kat.forthnet.gr**

MONEMVASIA Malvasia
Inside the Kástro, 230 70 **Tel** *27320-61160* **Fax** *27320-61722* **Rooms** *34*

Named after the malmsey wine historically grown in the area and spread over three sites in the old city, Malvasia offers sympathetically restored rooms, each different, with traditional, low-key furnishings and antique furniture, some with wooden floors, fireplaces and kitchenette facilities. Most rooms have terraces or sea views. Competitively priced.

MYKINES Belle Helene
Tsoúnta 15, 212 00 **Tel** *27510-76225* **Fax** *27510-76179* **Rooms** *5*

This historical building (built in 1862) is where Heinrich Schliemann stayed for some of his excavations in the 1870s – his bed is still in use. Later visitors included Agatha Christie and Virginia Woolf. The ambience is still almost Victorian and bathrooms are not en suite, but the restaurant and hospitality are excellent.

Key to Price Guide *see p508* **Key to Symbols** *see back cover flap*

NAFPLIO Byron

Plátonos 2, 211 00 **Tel** *27520-22351* **Fax** *27520-26338* **Rooms** *18*

An elegant hotel with antique furniture, in a tastefully restored mansion above Ágios Spyrídon church. Rooms are modestly decorated in a simple but charming style, with wooden floors and rugs. Some rooms have a view or balcony. Breakfast can be taken on the patio. Internet facilities are available. **www.byronhotel.gr**

NAFPLIO King Othon 1 & 2

Farmakopoúlou 4/Spiliádou 5, 211 00 **Tel** *27520-27585* **Fax** *27520-27595* **Rooms** *20*

This restored mansion, originally the Ionian Bank and retaining its spectacular curving wooden staircase, is near the old town center. Rooms vary, some having balconies, but bathrooms are small. Breakfast is served in a flowery courtyard. Othon 2, nearby, has slightly larger rooms and suites. **www.kingothon.gr**

NAFPLIO Grande Bretagne

Plateía Filellínon, 211 00 **Tel** *27520-96200* **Fax** *27520-96209* **Rooms** *20*

This three-storey Neo-Classical building on the seafront has been transformed into an elegant hotel. All rooms feature dark hardwood furniture, high ceilings and marble-trimmed bathrooms; a few lucky ones have balconies. The restaurant here serves international cuisine. **www.grandebretagne.com.gr**

NEOS MYSTRAS Byzantion

Village center, 231 00 **Tel** *27310-83309* **Fax** *27310-20019* **Rooms** *22*

Ideally situated for exploration of the nearby Mystras site or walking in the foothills of Taygetos, the Byzantion offers quiet, spacious rooms with castle views and a pleasant pool-garden. The hotel has a bar and café, and tavernas are a few minutes stroll away. Popular with groups, so book early. **www.byzantionhotel.gr**

OLYMPIA Pelops

Varelás 2, 270 65 **Tel** *26240-22543* **Fax** *26240-22213* **Rooms** *18*

Stylishly refurbished in 2004 by friendly Greek-Australian owners Theodore and Susanna, the well-equipped rooms all have balconies, and wireless internet access is available. The hotel, where the Olympics Committee stays, is within easy walking distance of the archaeological sites. Cooking and art courses are offered. Open Mar–Oct. **www.hotelpelops.gr**

THESSALONIKI Tourist

Mitropóleos 21, 546 24 **Tel** *2310-270501* **Fax** *2310-226865* **Rooms** *37*

One of the few surviving interwar buildings in this area, the Tourist features parquet-floored lounges, a breakfast room accessed by a period lift, and irregularly shaped rooms with en suite. It's been featured in many publications on the city and has a staunchly loyal word-of-mouth clientele, so reservations are mandatory. **www.touristhotel.gr**

THESSALONIKI Le Palace

Tsimiskí 12, 546 24 **Tel** *2310-257400* **Fax** *2310-256589* **Rooms** *54*

The city's first boutique hotel is located in a 1926 Art Deco building, transformed from 1998–2002. The large, double-glazed rooms have contemporary bathrooms, while the common areas preserve some interwar touches. There's a mezzanine lounge and restaurant, which serves an outstanding buffet breakfast, and a café. **www.lepalace.gr**

THESSALONIKI Electra Palace

Plateía Aristotélous 9, 546 24 **Tel** *2310-232221* **Fax** *2310-294001* **Rooms** *131*

This landmark semicircular building recently underwent a refurbishment; common areas are palatially fitted with walnut and marble trim as well as chandeliers, while the wood-trimmed rooms – with every conceivable gadget – have ochre and red decor. Rooftop pool, fitness center, English-themed bar, and two restaurants. **www.electrahotels.gr**

CORFU AND THE IONIAN ISLANDS

CORFU Akrotiri Beach

T Desylla 155, Palaiokastrítsa, 49100 **Tel** *26630-41237* **Fax** *26630-41277* **Rooms** *127*

Largest and best of the hotels around popular Palaiokastrítsa. The hotel offers a plethora of facilities including 2 pools, restaurant, 3 bars, live entertainment, and watersports including scuba diving nearby. Comfortable, well-equipped rooms with balconies and some of Corfu's best views. Closed Oct–Apr. **www.akrotiri-beach.com**

CORFU Bella Venezia

N. Zambeli 4, Corfu Town, 49100 **Tel** *26610-46500* **Fax** *26610-20707* **Rooms** *32*

Close to the center of Corfu town, this dignified Neo-Classical mansion has been restored and converted into a pleasant boutique hotel. High-ceilinged rooms are comfortable and tasteful without being extravagant. Hospitable, friendly staff. Public areas and some rooms are wheelchair-accessible. **www.bellaveneziahotel.com**

CORFU Corfu Palace

Dimoktratias 2, Corfu Town, 49100 **Tel** *26610-39485* **Fax** *26610-31749* **Rooms** *115*

The "grande dame" of Corfu hotels, built in 1954 and still the best place to stay in Corfu town. The marble bathrooms, cheerfully decorated rooms and suites, and grand public areas lend a touch of class. The rooms at the front have fine sea views. Large pool with shaded terrace. **www.corfupalace.com**

KEFALLONIA Linardos

Asos, 28085 **Tel** *26740-51563* **Fax** *26740-51563* **Rooms** *12*

Located in the center of the pretty village of Asos, Linardos offers rooms with fine views across the bay to the ruins of the Venetian castle. A choice of doubles, triples, twins and family rooms, each with a well-equipped mini-kitchen. Hire a motor boat at the harbor to explore the nearby coast. Closed Oct–May. **www.linardosapartments.gr**

KEFALLONIA Emelisse Art Hotel

Eblisi, Fiskárdo, 28084 **Tel** *26740-41200* **Fax** *26740-41026* **Rooms** *65*

Fourteen traditional-style stone houses with stylish rooms boasting four-poster beds and private terraces. Facilities include a poolside bar and restaurant, breakfast terrace, tennis court, gym and billiards. Mountain bikes are also available for guests to use. Good views over bay area. Closed Oct–Apr. **www.arthotel.gr**

ZAKYNTHOS Leedas Village

Lithákia, Agios Sóstis, 29092 **Tel** *26950-51305* **Fax** *26950-53491* **Rooms** *20*

Self-catering apartments for 2–9 people in 5 attractive stone villas, all with terraces. Apartments are plain and cool, with terracotta paved floors and fully equipped kitchens. The villas are set in pretty, flower-filled gardens and are a short walk from the beach. Children's playground. Closed Nov–Apr. **www.leedas-village.com**

THE CYCLADES

MYKONOS Cavo Tagoo

Thesi Tagkou, Mýkonos, 84600 **Tel** *22890-23692* **Fax** *22890-24923* **Rooms** *72*

Located on a hillside about 2 km (1 mile) from the center of Mýkonos Town, Cavo Tagoo stands in splendid isolation away from the bustle of the island capital, but within a short drive of its shops, restaurants and nightlife. Built in village style, with white walls and blue woodwork. Shady eucalyptus trees and fine views. Closed Nov–Mar. **www.cavotagoo.gr**

MYKONOS Princess of Mýkonos

Agios Stéfanos, 84600 **Tel** *22890-24713* **Fax** *22890-23031* **Rooms** *38*

Situated on one of the island's most exclusive beaches, 4 km (2.5 miles) from Mýkonos town, this hotel is chic and stylish. Its small size allows for personal, attentive service and, like most Mýkonos hotels, it is designed in much-Cycladic style. The pool is on the small side, but the beach is nearby. Closed Nov–Mar. **www.princessofmykonos.gr**

NAXOS Kavos

Agios Prokopios, 84300 **Tel** *22850-23355* **Fax** *22850-26031* **Rooms** *19*

Located on one of the best beaches in the Aegean, Kavos offers a collection of excellent value studios, apartments, and suites with self catering facilities. Rooms are in simple white cottages, surrounded by greenery, and each has painted furniture and galleried bed spaces. Closed Nov–Mar. **www.kavos-naxos.com**

SANTORINI Keti

Thíra, 84700 **Tel** *22860-22324* **Fax** *22860-22380* **Rooms** *7*

Just off the steep steps that lead from Thira Town to the harbor below, Hotel Keti shares the same stunning crater view as the much more costly boutique hotels elsewhere on the island. The whitewashed rooms have arched ceilings, marble floors and are simply furnished and decorated. Closed Oct–Apr. **www.hotelketi.gr**

SANTORINI Katikies

Oía, Santoríni, 84700 **Tel** *22860-71401* **Fax** *22860-71129* **Rooms** *22*

Stunning views from the horizon pool make this the best hotel on Santoríni. The elegantly-appointed, traditional cave-rooms are whitewashed, each has a private terrace, some terraces also have whirlpools. Fine restaurant and attentive service. Closed Nov–Apr. **www.slh.com**

RHODES AND THE DODECANESE

KOS Afendoulis

Evripidou 1, Kos Town, 85300 **Tel** *22420-25321* **Fax** *22420-25797* **Rooms** *23*

A small, family hotel in the center of Kos town with friendly, English-speaking management and comfortable, simple rooms. Fairly quiet (by Kos Town standards) and a short walk from the good town beach. Breakfast and drinks are served in a lovely garden filled with jasmine and bougainvillea. Closed Nov–Apr.

KOS Porto Bello Beach

Kardámaina, 85302 **Tel** *22420-91217* **Fax** *22420-91168* **Rooms** *340*

Billed as an 'ultra all-inclusive' resort, the luxury Porto Bello is located on a 5 km (3 miles) long beach, 2 km (1 mile) from Kardámaina. Rate includes buffet breakfast, lunch and dinner, snacks, drinks, non-motorised water sports, a wide range of land sports, and live entertainment. Closed Nov–Apr.

Key to Price Guide *see p508* **Key to Symbols** *see back cover flap*

KOS Grecotel Kos Royal Park
Agios Geórgios, Marmári, 85300 **Tel** *22420-41488* **Fax** *22420-41373* **Rooms** *236*

This well-appointed and well-located luxury resort on sandy Marmári beach, offers all-inclusive packages as well as standard rates. Facilities and activities include pools for adults and children, windsurfing, pedaloes, canoes, beach sports, and live entertainment. Bicycle rental and horse riding are available nearby. Closed Nov–Apr. **www.grecotel.gr**

RHODES Apollo
Omirou 82, 85100 **Tel** *22410-32003* **Rooms** *6*

This restored old house has bright, breezy rooms with four-poster beds – spend a bit extra for the more expensive top-floor rooms at the front which have wonderful Old Town views. Set in a quieter part of the Old Town with a pretty inner courtyard. Short walk to sights and shopping. Closed Nov–Apr. **www.apollo-touristhouse.com**

RHODES San Nikolis Hotel
Ipodamou, Rhodes Old Town, 85100 **Tel** *22410-34561* **Fax** *22410-32034* **Rooms** *18*

Nestling under the walls of the Old Town is this charming, small hotel housed in an old Rhodian townhouse with stone walls covered with ivy and bougainvillea. Rooms are very comfortable, with antique furnishings, and some with balconies. Excellent views from the rooftop terrace. Closed Nov–Apr. **www.s-nikolis.gr**

RHODES Rodos Palace
Leofóros Triádon, ixia, 85100 **Tel** *22410-25222* **Fax** *22410-25350* **Rooms** *470*

Built in the 1960s and completely renovated in 2001, the Rodos Palace is the island's flagship luxury hotel. Rooms and suites surround a central 20-storey tower with world-class views from the upper floor rooms. Choice of bars and restaurants, indoor and outdoor pools, excellent leisure and business facilities. **www.rodos-palace.gr**

CRETE

AGIOS NIKOLAOS St Nicolas Bay
Agios Nikólaos, 72100 **Tel** *28410-25041* **Fax** *28410-24556* **Rooms** *108*

Magnificent complex of bungalows and luxury suites – some with private pool – on an enviable seaside site just outside Agios Nikólaos. Landscaped gardens full of citrus and olive trees surround the buildings and the hotel has its own virtually private beach. Watersports and choice of 8 restaurants and bars. Closed Nov–Mar. **www.stnicolasbay.com**

CHANIA Amfora
Parodos Theotokopoulou 20, 73131 **Tel** *28210-93224* **Fax** *28210-93226* **Rooms** *21*

This 13th-century Venetian mansion has tastefully appointed rooms and a charming roof terrace overlooking Chaniá's picturesque harbor. Situated in the heart of Chaniá's old quarter, on a mostly traffic free street just a few steps from the waterfront with its numerous restaurants, shops and bars.

CHANIA Villa Andromeda
Venizelou 150, 73133 **Tel** *28210-28300* **Fax** *28210-28303* **Rooms** *8*

Oozing period dignity, this 19th-century building was once the German consulate. There are eight plainly-furnished suites. The grand sitting rooms, by contrast, glow with yellow stucco. Large pool and terrace outside. Located 2 km (1 mile) from the harbor front. Closed Nov–Mar. **www.villandromeda.gr**

ELOUNTA Eloúnda Beach Hotel
Eloúnta, 72053 **Tel** *28410-63000* **Fax** *28410-41373* **Rooms** *258*

The "grande dame" of Greek resorts, the Eloúnda Beach offers luxurious villas – some with private pools – scattered around a picturesque headland and a private beach. Excellent water sports, fine dining, very attentive service. Closed Nov–Mar. **www.eloundabeach.gr**

IRAKLEIO Lato Hotel
Epimenidou 15, 71202 **Tel** *28102-28103* **Fax** *28103-34955* **Rooms** *58*

Formerly comfortable but undistinguished, the Lato – in the center of the old town – has been reborn as Irákleio's first boutique hotel. Its rooms are stylish with balconies, terraces or glassed-in mini-conservatories, satellite TV and, internet access. There is also a roof garden, mini-gym, and sauna. **www.lato.gr**

IRAKLEIO Sofitel Capsis Palace Hotel and Capsis Beach Hotel
Agía Pelagía, 71000 **Tel** *28108-11112* **Fax** *28018-11314* **Rooms** *420*

This huge, self-contained luxury complex stands on its own promontory and combines two hotels and a conference center. The complex offers a full range of watersports and other facilities and activities, including its own zoo. Rooms range from standard doubles to large suites with private pool, butler and maid service. Private beach. **www.capsis.gr**

RETHYMNO Palazzo Vecchio
Iroon Polytechniou/Melissinou, 74100 **Tel** *28310-35351* **Fax** *28310-25479* **Rooms** *23*

New meets old in this 15th-century townhouse which has been converted into a stylishly grand modern hotel with in-room facilities including satellite TV, mini-kitchen and full-sized bathrooms (a rarity in most historic hotels in Réthymno). Pleasant courtyard bar with fountain, attentive service, central location. Closed Nov–Mar. **www.palazzovecchio.gr**

Where to Eat in Greece

Eating out is an important part of Greek social life, enjoyed by rich and poor, old and young alike. As a result, the country boasts a vast array of eating places. With a host of stylish restaurants serving international fare, friendly tavernas offering traditional, local cooking, and lively cafés and bars, Greece caters for all tastes.

PRICE CATEGORIES
The following price ranges are for a three-course meal for one, including a half bottle of house wine, tax and service:
€ Under 15 euros
€€ 15–25 euros
€€€ 25–35 euros
€€€€ 35–45 euros
€€€€€ Over 45 euros

ATHENS

EXARCHEIA Mparmpa Giannis   €
Emmanouíl Mpenáki 94, 106 81 **Tel** *210-38 24138*   **Map** *C2*

A favorite that hasn't changed much in decades, this place dishes up consistently good *mageireftá* (baked dishes) and a handful of grills. On any given day there might be *giouvarláki* (rice & meat balls in *avgolémono*), stewed okra or baked *pérka* fish. The tables in pedestrianised Dervenión fill first in summer. Closed Sun dinner; Aug.

GAZI Mamacas   €€€
Persefónis 41, 104 35 **Tel** *210-34 64984*

The original new wave taverna that kick-started the gentrification of Gázi, Mamacas is still steaming along after its 1998 opening. The fare is wholesome, updated Greek like Cretan *dákos* salad (rusks, tomato, cheese, oregano) and cuttlefish with greens. The decor is trendy and the clientele equally so. After midnight DJ sounds predominate.

KOLONAKI Ouzadiko   €€€
Karneádou 25–29, 106 76 **Tel** *210-72 95484*   **Map** *E3*

This *ouzerí* claims to offer more varieties of *ouzo* and *tsípouro* (wine spirit) to wash down *lakérda* (white fleshed marinated bonito), *hortópitta* and *revythokeftédes* (chickpea croquettes) than anywhere else in town. Always crowded and convivial, it's a popular hangout for politicians and journalists. Closed Sun–Mon; Aug.

KOLONAKI Orizontes Lykavittou   €€€€€
Lykavittós Hill, 106 75 **Tel** *210-72 27065*   **Map** *E3*

The views are sky-high and so are the prices (for dishes like sea bass in sauce with tagliatelle) at this spot near the summit of the hill, accessible only by the funicular or a long hike up through the pines. Seating is either in a conservatory or on a terrace.

MONASTIRAKI Thanassis   €
Mitropóleos 69, 105 55 **Tel** *210-32 44705*   **Map** *B4*

Perennial candidate for best purveyor of *souvláki* and *yíros* in town, Thanassis is always packed with Athenians queuing for a take-out or waiting for a table (you can't book ahead). It's frenetic and there's pressure to give up your seat quickly, but for a quick bite you can't beat it. The side dish of peppers is delicious.

MONASTIRAKI Café Avissynia   €€€
Kynéttou 7, off Plateía Avissynías, 105 55 **Tel** *210-32 17047*   **Map** *B4*

Tables indoors and out are always packed at weekend lunchtimes and Friday evenings when entertainment is provided by an accordionist and singer. The food – Macedonian staples, mussel *pilaf*, baked feta – is rich and the clientele verging on the bohemian. Closed Sun dinner, Mon; summer.

OMONOIA Ideal   €€
Panepistimíou 46, 106 78 **Tel** *210-33 03000*   **Map** *C2*

A city center institution since 1922, serving international cuisine (*schnitzel* and chops) along with more exciting, more Hellenic dishes of the day such as milk-fed veal with aubergine (eggplant) and stuffed courgettes (zucchini). Locals love both the consistent food quality and the Art Nouveau interior. Closed Sun.

PLAKA O Platanos   €
Diogénous 4, 105 57 **Tel** *210-32 20666*   **Map** *C4*

Taking its name from the *plátanos* (plane) tree outside, this 1932-founded taverna emphasises meat-based stews and *laderá* (cooked vegetable dishes) in its repertoire. Their exceptionally good barrelled *retsina* has been profiled in Niko Manesi's *The Greek Wine Guide*. Closed Sun.

PLAKA Eden   €€
Lysiou 12, 105 56 **Tel** *210-32 48858*   **Map** *B4*

Installed on the ground floor of a Neo-Classical dwelling, the city's only exclusively vegetarian restaurant offers a menu where beans, lentils, spinach, mushrooms, and soya-based products predominate, although there are good desserts and herbal teas as well. Portions are on the small side. Closed Tue.

Key to Symbols *see back cover flap* **Map References** *see map of Athens pp474–5*

PSYRRI Zeideron

Taki 10–12, 105 52 **Tel** *210-32 15368* **Map** *B3*

Psyrri has firmly established itself as Athens' favorite nighttime playground and Zeideron is a fine place to kick off the evening. Diners feast on modern taverna fare in an old stone building with a light and airy upper-level glass extension. There are also several highly coveted tables outside on the street.

THISEIO Pil Poul

Apostólou Pávlou 51corner Poulopoúlou, 118 51 **Tel** *210-34 23665* **Map** *A4*

Diners sit in tastefully decorated rooms at this former Neo-Classical mansion, with roof-terrace seating in summer. The menu offers French and Mediterranean-tinged creative cooking like fillet with truffles or grouper baked in champagne sauce, served by uniformed waiters. Open dinner; closed Mon.

REST OF MAINLAND GREECE

ANCIENT CORINTH Archontikó

Paralía Lechaíou, 200 06 **Tel** *27410-27968*

Overlooking the coastal road, about 3.5 km (2 miles) west of town, near the Lechaion archaeological site, this taverna offers well-prepared meat dishes and *mezédes*. Specialties include *kokkinistó Archontiko*, a wine-based meat stew with mushrooms, and cockerel *kokkinistó* with pasta. Popular with locals, so book ahead. Open lunch (weekends only).

GYTHEIO Saga

Odós Tzanetáki, opposite Marathonísi, 232 00 **Tel** *27330-23220*

From ground floor premises under the eponymous French-Greek-owned pension, this restaurant spreads tables across the narrow pavement and along the sea wall opposite. Excellent for fresh fish, with a wide choice in the chiller cabinet – including several types of sea bream – plus fish soup, shrimp *saganáki* (fried cheese), and charcoal-grilled octopus.

KALAMPAKA Hoútos

Town center, close to City Hall, 422 00 **Tel** *24320-24754*

Locals know all about this grillhouse, with its superb and reasonable lamb kebab, chops, *biftéki* (rissoles) and *kokorétsi* (offal roulade) made from local lamb and pork. At peak seasons it is wise to book ahead, as the premises are relatively small. Dine on the terrace in summer.

LITOCHORO Gastrodromeío en Olympo

Kentrikí Plateía, 602 00 **Tel** *23520-21300*

Most tavernas in Litóchoro, used to a stream of visitors heading quickly through town en route to the mountain, don't make a special effort; Gastrodromeío does, with good renditions of suckling pig and rabbit stew, plus a decent wine list – at a price.

MONEMVASIA Skorpiós

South coast road, Géfyra district, 230 70 **Tel** *27320-62090*

South of the bridge linking the mainland with the rock of Monemvasiá is Skorpios, with seating outside and unimpeded views towards the rock. Good *mezédes* like *tzatzíki* and *tyrokafteri* (spicy cheese dip) and simple small fish like marinated *gávros* and *atherina* are served. Good wine.

NAFPLIO Ta Fanária

Staïkopoúlou 13 corner Soútsou, 211 00 **Tel** *27520-27141*

This long-running restaurant offers outdoor seating under climbing vines; indoor seating is limited and for winter only. Ta Fanária is best for lunch when *maghireftá* (baked dishes) such as *moussakás* and *soutzoukákia* (minced lamb and tomato dish) emerge fresh from the oven. There's good bulk *retsina* from Mégara to wash it all down.

OLYMPIA Kladaíos

2 km (1 mile) NW of village, 270 65 **Tel** *26240-23322*

On the west bank of the eponymous river, beyond the rail station, this small, unpretentious, rural taverna offers delicious food in relaxed surroundings. Lamb is one of the mainstays. Popular with both visitors to the site and locals. Excellent rosé house wine. Closed Nov–Mar.

THESSALONIKI Kamares

Plateía Agíou Georgíou 11 **Tel** *23102-19686*

Located close to the Roman-Byzantine *Rotónda*, this neighbourhood favorite offers the usual range of salads, attractively priced seafood and a few meat grills, accompanied by white wine from Límnos. In summer Kamares has seating beside the little park.

THESSALONIKI Ta Nisiá

Proxénou Koromilá 13, 546 23 **Tel** *23210-22447*

Open since 1981, this upscale restaurant purveys a balanced mix of fish, shellfish and meat recipes. Typical platters include *kakaviá* (fish soup), stewed octopus, roast pork in wine sauce and creative desserts. The wine list is unusually comprehensive. Pleasant interior, with island colors and decor. Closed Sun; Aug.

CORFU AND THE IONIAN ISLANDS

CORFU Rouvas 📋 €

St. Desillas 13, Corfu Town **Tel** *26610-31182*

One of the most affordable traditional eating places in Corfu Town, with a well-established reputation for some of the best Greek, Corfiot and international dishes. Located in the center of town, near the main produce market, so the ingredients are usually very fresh. Closed dinner; Sun.

CORFU Rex 🍴📋 €€

Kapodistriou 66, Corfu Town **Tel** *26610-39649*

Housed in a mid-19th-century building, one block behind the arcades and cafés of the Spianádha, the Rex is a Corfu institution – a truly traditional Greek restaurant serving genuine Corfiot food. Specialities include swordfish *bourthéto* (a spicy fish stew with tomatoes, peppers and potatoes). Good, attentive service.

KEFALLONIA Patsouras 🍴 €

Ioannou Metaxas 40, Argostóli **Tel** *26710-22779*

Surprisingly cheap taverna in the center of Kefalloniá's island capital. Patsouras is family-run, and its menu includes all the traditional taverna favorites plus Kefallonian island specialties such as *kreatópita* (meat pie) and *krasáto* (pork in wine sauce). Enjoy lunch or dinner in a pleasant garden setting.

KEFALLONIA Tassia 🍴📋🎵 €€€€

Limáni Fiskardou **Tel** *26740-41205*

This internationally-acclaimed restaurant sits right on the harbor and features a good wine list which emphasizes some of Kefalloniá's own vintages, recognised as among the best in Greece. The menu includes fine seafood, simply but well-prepared, as well as pasta dishes, salads, appetizers, and desserts. Closed Oct–Apr.

ZAKYNTHOS Zakanthi 🍴 €€

Kalamáki **Tel** *26950-43586*

This lively restaurant and bar is a good place to spend the evening whether you are looking for a light snack with drinks or something more substantial. The menu is eclectic, with a reasonable selection of Greek favorites along with pasta, pizza, burgers and other international dishes. Closed lunch; Oct–May.

THE CYCLADES

MYKONOS Sea Satin Market Caprice 🍴 €€€€

Mýloi, Mýkonos Town **Tel** *22890-24676*

This lively fish restaurant and traditional grill is located by the sea with open-air tables below the village's famous windmills and with views of Little Venice. The restaurant is a delight for seafood lovers and carnivores alike, this is one of the few places you can get a really good steak. Closed lunch; Nov–Apr.

MYKONOS Katrine's 🍴📋🎵🍷 €€€€€

Matogiannia **Tel** *22890-22169*

Katrine's enjoys a long-standing reputation for fine French and Greek cuisine and has an outstanding list of Greek and imported wines. A very good choice of Greek appetizers and more sophisticated main dishes, attentive service and a dressed-up clientele. Booking is advisable. Closed May–Sep: lunch; Nov–Mar.

NAXOS Manolis 🍴🍴 €

Bourgos, Náxos Town **Tel** *22850-25168*

This garden taverna, in the heart of the old town, serves traditional Greek cuisine in very pleasant surroundings. Dishes on offer include *melitzánes* (fried aubergines), *skordaliá* (potato and garlic purée) and other well-known favorites at prices to suit even smaller budgets. Closed lunch; Nov–Mar.

SANTORINI Iliovasilema 🍴🍴 €€

Ammoudi, Oía **Tel** *22860-71614*

A delightfully simple quayside restaurant where the fish comes straight off the boat and onto the grill. The menu here mainly depends on the catch of the day which can be enjoyed at rickety wooden tables beside a tiny pebbly beach. Extremely good value. Closed Nov–Apr.

SANTORINI 1800 🍴📋🍷 €€€€€

Main street, Oía **Tel** *22860-71485*

Book ahead for an evening at Oía's swankiest restaurant where the sophisticated menu blends Greek and European influences. There is an extensive wine list with a good sampling of Santorini's more interesting labels and vintages. Not too formal, but not ideal for children. Closed lunch; Oct–Apr.

Key to Price Guide *see p514* **Key to Symbols** *see back cover flap*

THE DODECANESE

KARPATHOS Anoisis

Diafáni **Tel** *22450-51226*

A classic summer taverna serving old-fashioned island cooking such as oven-cooked meat and vegetable dishes, salads and meat grills – lamb, pork chops and chicken. Occasionally served are fish, stuffed peppers, and kid in red sauce with roast potatoes. Nice location by the harbor at Diafáni. Closed Oct–Jul.

KOS O Makis

Mastichári **Tel** *22420-59061*

One of the best little fish tavernas on the island, O Makis is located next to an attractive little fishing harbor from which comes most of the seafood that it serves. Expect sea-fresh *tsipoura* and *fagri* as well as prawns, squid, octopus and – for special occasions, and worth ordering a couple of days in advance – langouste. Closed lunch.

KOS Plátanos

Plateía Platanou **Tel** *22420-28991*

Located on the square beside the Castle of Knights, this café-restaurant overlooks the ancient agora. More peaceful than Kos Town's parade of harbor-side restaurants, it serves light meals, snacks and drinks, and is reasonably priced compared with many eating places in town. Closed Nov–May.

RHODES Meltemi

Akti Koundourioti

Newly-renovated, unpretentious family-run restaurant right on the beach. The simple menu has a good choice of hot and cold appetizers, grills, and fish dishes – a basket of fresh hot bread is served with every meal. Its terrace with sea views makes it an ideal spot for lunch. Closed Nov–Mar.

RHODES Alexis

Sokratous 18, Old Town **Tel** *22410-29347*

This wonderful restaurant in the heart of the picturesque Old Town has been specializing in seafood since it opened in 1957. A host of celebrity guests have come to enjoy the perfectly-grilled fresh fish, good wines and professional but friendly service. Choice of tables on two floors and sunny terrace. Better for dinner than lunch. Closed Nov–Mar.

CRETE

AGIOS NIKOLAOS Itanos

Plateía Venizélou **Tel** *28410-25340*

Popular taverna in a lane just off Agios Nikólaos's main square. The menu includes spit-roasted chicken, lamb and goat, oven-baked dishes, and an assortment of stuffed and stewed vegetables. Good value and a decent choice of local wines. Seats inside or out. Closed Nov–Mar.

CHANIA To Pigadi tou Tourkou (The Well of the Turk)

1–3 Kallinikou Sarpaki, Splantzia, 73100 **Tel** *28210-54547*

This cosy restaurant is housed in the arched stone cellar of an ancient Chaniá mansion, with candle-lit tables and Cretan and Levantine background music. The menu is more imaginative than most – try the aubergine meatballs, or the spicy stuffed squid – and uses local produce. Closed lunch; Wed; mid-Nov–Feb.

IRAKLEIO O Kyriákos

Leofóros Dimokratías 53 **Tel** *28102-22464*

You will be beckoned into the kitchen of this old-fashioned restaurant to choose your meal from bubbling pots or glass cases filled with fish, vegetables and cuts of meat. O Kyriakós is an Irákleio institution, unpretentious and catering to a loyal local following. Wine from the barrel.

IRAKLEIO Loukoulos

Korai 5 **Tel** *28102-24435*

A mainly Italian menu in up-market surroundings – with white linen tablecloths, candles in the evening, and a dining room decorated with antique prints and paintings. With its excellent food, Loukoulos has been regarded for years as one of the best restaurants in Irákleio.

RETHYMNO Avlí

22 Xanthoudidou, 74100 **Tel** *28310-26213*

This charming restaurant offers dining in vaulted rooms or in the courtyard of an old mansion. The menu consists mainly of grilled and roast meat and there is an extensive wine list featuring some of the best Greek wines. Attentive service and spotless interior.

GERMANY, AUSTRIA, AND SWITZERLAND

GERMANY, AUSTRIA, AND
SWITZERLAND AT A GLANCE 520–521

GERMANY 522–585

AUSTRIA 586–611

SWITZERLAND 612–633

Germany, Austria, and Switzerland at a Glance

Europe's three main German-speaking countries occupy a broad swathe of Europe stretching from the Alps to the North Sea and the Baltic. Germany has many great cities, the former capitals of the small states that made up Germany under the Holy Roman Empire. It also has beautiful countryside, rivers, and forests. Austria's main attractions are the former imperial capital Vienna, the river Danube, and its mountains. More than half of Switzerland, which also has important French- and Italian-speaking regions, is mountainous, dominated by its permanently snow-capped Alpine peaks.

Lübeck

Hamburg

Bremen

Hanover

Münster

GERMANY
(See pp520–585)

Düsseldorf

Cologne

Kassel

Bonn

Frankfurt
am Main

Trier

Mainz

Würzburg

Stuttgart

Freiburg
im Breisgau

Basel

Zürich

BERN

SWITZERLAND
(See pp612–633)

Geneva

The Rhine Valley (see pp558–9) *attracts hordes of visitors in summer, drawn by the beautiful scenery, medieval and mock-medieval castles, and Germany's finest white wines. You can either tour by car or take a river cruise from cities such as Mainz and Koblenz.*

The Swiss Alps (see pp619–24) *are a popular destination all year round: in winter for the skiing and other winter sports, in summer for the excellent walking or simply for the crisp, clean air and unrivaled scenery.*

Salzburg (see pp602–3) *trades on the legacy of Mozart, its most famous son, and stages one of the world's great music festivals. It also boasts a rich architectural heritage from the prince-archbishops who ruled the city from 1278 to 1816.*

◁ **Swiss lakeland scene, Interlaken**

LOCATOR MAP

Rostock

BERLIN

Magdeburg

Leipzig

Dresden

Berlin (see pp528–41), *since 1990 once more the capital of a united Germany, combines relics of its imperial past, such as the Berliner Dom, with modern landmarks such as the towering Fernsehturm.*

Munich (see pp546–54) *is the cultural capital of southern Germany. It owes many of its great buildings and art collections to the kings of Bavaria. The city is also remarkable for its 18th-century churches, such as the astonishingly ornate Asamkirche.*

uremberg

Munich

Linz

VIENNA

Salzburg

AUSTRIA
(See pp586–611)

Innsbruck

Graz

0 kilometers   100

0 miles   100

Vienna (see pp590–99) *was largely the the creation of the 18th- and 19th- century Habsburg emperors. More modern land- marks include the ferris wheel in the Prater funfair, immortalized in* The Third Man, *the 1949 film starring Orson Welles.*

GERMANY

By reputation the Germans are a hard-working, efficient, competitive people and this is borne out by their recent economic success. However, Germany's turbulent, divided past and the centuries when it was a patchwork of many tiny states mean that there are profound regional differences, apparent in a wealth of fascinating historical sights and colorful local traditions.

Thanks initially to American aid, industry and commerce boomed in West Germany following World War II. This so-called *Wirtschaftswunder* (economic miracle) made West Germany a dominant member of the European Economic Community (now the European Union). Demand for labor led to reliance on migrant workers or *Gastarbeiter* (guest workers). As a result, over 7 million immigrants now live in Germany, the largest number coming from Turkey, but many too from Italy, Greece, and increasingly the former Yugoslavia. In the manufacturing city of Stuttgart one inhabitant in three is an immigrant.

Despite its many industrial cities and a population of over 80 million, Germany is large enough to also possess a great variety of attractive rural landscapes. For many the Rhine epitomizes Germany, especially the romantic stretch between Mainz and Cologne. However, the country has much more to offer in the way of scenery, especially its forests, heaths, and mountains. In the far south the Alps are the major attraction, especially around Lake Constance (the Bodensee), the large lake that borders Austria and Switzerland.

HISTORY

Germanic tribes became established in the region sometime during the 1st millennium BC. They clashed with the Romans, defeating them in AD 9 at the Teutoburger forest. Thereafter the Romans fixed their frontier along the Rhine and the Danube. Although relations were often hostile, the Goths and other Germanic tribes traded and made alliances with Rome, and as the Roman Empire collapsed, these peoples carved out kingdoms of their own.

The dome of Berlin's Reichstag – home to the Bundestag (Federal Parliament)

◁ Neuschwanstein, King Ludwig II's theatrical castle in the Bavarian Alps

The people who eventually inherited the largest kingdom were the Franks, who conquered France and in the early 9th century, under Charlemagne, subdued most of the German tribes, including the Saxons, Swabians, and Bavarians. The pope gave his blessing to Charlemagne's overlordship, thus creating the Holy Roman Empire.

After Charlemagne, the German kingdom became separated from the rest of the empire. The next strong German ruler was the Saxon Otto I, who increased his power further after his defeat of the Magyars in 955.

Frederick II (the Great), King of Prussia (1740–86)

The Middle Ages saw the development of a complicated feudal system with hundreds of dukedoms, counties, and ecclesiastical estates owing allegiance to the German emperor, as well as free "imperial cities." In the 11th and 12th centuries popes and emperors joined in a fierce struggle over who should grant lands,

appoint bishops, and collect revenues. Each would try to bribe the Electors *(Kurfürsten)* – princes and bishops who chose the emperor. The role of the Electors was clarified in the Golden Bull issued by Emperor Charles IV in 1356, but by the 16th century the position had become the more or less hereditary right of the Austrian Habsburgs.

The power of the church created many problems and it was no surprise that the Reformation began in Germany in 1517 with Martin Luther's *95 Theses* pointing out the abuses of the clergy. In the ensuing wars of religion, princes saw a chance to increase their lands at the expense of the Church. The Peace of Augsburg in 1555 established the principle *cuius regio eius religio* – each state followed the religion of its ruler. In the 17th century religious differences were again a major factor in the Thirty Years' War. Other countries, such as France and Sweden, joined the conflict, which laid waste most of Germany.

In the 17th and 18th centuries Germany remained a patchwork of small states, theoretically still part of the Habsburg Empire. However, Prussia gradually became a power to rival the Habsburgs. During the Enlightenment and Romantic periods German literature found its voice, especially in the dramas of Goethe and Schiller, and Napoleon's invasion of Germany sparked ideas of nationalism. In the mid-19th century it was Prussia that assumed the leadership of Germany through the skilful politics of Otto von Bismarck, the Prussian chancellor. After the Prussians had defeated the Austrians in 1866 and the French in 1870, the Second German Reich was declared with the Prussian King as Kaiser Wilhelm I.

Wilhelm's grandson Wilhelm II had great ambitions for the new empire and rivalry with Britain, France, and Russia plunged Europe into World War I. The humiliation of defeat and the terms of the Treaty of Versailles (1919) left

KEY DATES IN GERMAN HISTORY

5th century AD Germanic peoples overrun large parts of Roman Empire

c.750 Mission of St. Boniface to Germany

843 Charlemagne's empire divided; Louis the German rules lands east of the Rhine

962 Otto I crowned emperor

1077 Pope Gregory VII and Emperor Heinrich IV clash over investiture of bishops

1155 Frederick Barbarossa crowned Emperor

13th century North German Hanseatic League starts to dominate trade in Baltic region

1356 Golden Bull establishes role of Electors

1517 Martin Luther attaches his *95 Theses to* the door of a church in Wittenberg

1555 Peace of Augsburg ends religious wars

1618–48 Germany ravaged by Thirty Years' War

1740–86 Reign of Frederick the Great

1806 Napoleon abolishes Holy Roman Empire

1871 German Empire proclaimed

1914–18 World War I

1933 End of Weimar Republic; Hitler comes to power

1939–45 World War II: after Germany's defeat country divided into West and East

1990 Reunification of Germany

2002 Germany joins single European currency

Germany in economic chaos. The Weimar Republic struggled on until 1933 when Hitler seized power. His nationalist policies appealed to a demoralized people, but his territorial ambitions led the country into World War II and a second defeat.

Despite the atrocities committed by the Nazis, the Germans were soon forgiven by both America and Russia as they divided the country in such a way that it became the theater for the Cold War between East and West. The Berlin Wall erected in 1961 to stop East Germans fleeing to the West became the symbol of an era. Its fall in 1989 was the start of the process of reunification.

Modern Germany, the Bundesrepublik, is a federal country, with each *Land* (state) electing its own parliament. Regional differences due to Germany's checkered history are still much in evidence, the Catholic south being much more conservative than the north. Differences between the former West Germany and the old DDR (East Germany) are also very visible. The East suffers from high unemployment and its people tend to be suspicious of the motives of the West Germans, despite all the money poured into the region to equalize living standards.

CULTURE AND THE ARTS

Germany is rich in legends and sagas, such as the tale of Siegfried told in the epic poem the *Nibelungenlied*, written down around 1200. It has been reworked many times, notably in Richard Wagner's great *Ring* opera cycle.

Celebrating the fall of the Berlin Wall in 1989

Of all the arts it is to classical music that Germany has made the greatest contribution, Johann Sebastian Bach from the Baroque period and Ludwig van Beethoven from the Classical period being perhaps the two most influential figures. In the 19th century poems by Goethe, Schiller, and others were set to music by composers Robert Schumann, Johannes Brahms, and Hugo Wolf.

Germany has also produced many of the world's most influential philosophers: from Immanuel Kant (1724–1804), father of modern philosophy, to Karl Marx (1818–83), founder of the 20th century's most potent political ideology.

MODERN LIFE

The German economy tends to be dominated by long-established giants such as Siemens in the electrical and electronic sectors, Volkswagen and BMW in cars, and BASF in chemicals. Despite the continuing success of German industry and banking, and the people's reputation for hard work, the Germans actually enjoy longer annual holidays and spend more money on foreign travel than any other European nation. When at home they are enthusiastic participants in many sports, and have enjoyed great success in recent years at football, motor racing, and tennis. They also enjoy gregarious public merrymaking, for example at *Fasching* (carnival) and the Oktoberfest, Munich's annual beer festival.

Munich's Olympic Stadium, created for the 1972 Olympic Games

Exploring Germany

Visitors in search of classical German landscapes flock
to the Black Forest, the Rhine Valley, and the Bavarian
Alps. The attractive German countryside is easily accessed
thanks to the best road network in Europe. Of the cities,
the most popular destinations are the capital Berlin, a
vibrant metropolis in a state of transition since
reunification in 1990, and Munich, the historic
former capital of the Kingdom of Bavaria. East
Germany, now open for tourism, has many
attractions to draw visitors – particularly the
city of Dresden, rebuilt after World War II.

SIGHTS AT A GLANCE

Bamberg ❻
Bayreuth ❺
BERLIN pp528–41 ❶
Black Forest ❶❺
Bonn ❷❹
Bremen ❷❽
Cologne pp562–3 ❷❺
Dresden ❷
Frankfurt am Main ❷❸
Freiburg im Breisgau ❶❹
Hamburg ❷❾
Hanover ❷❼
Heidelberg ❶❼
Koblenz ❷❷
Lake Constance ❶❸
Leipzig ❸
Lübeck ❸⓿
Mainz ❷⓿
Mosel Valley ❶❾
Munich pp546–53 ❶⓿
Münster ❷❻
Neuschwanstein ❶❷
Nuremberg ❾
Passau ❶❶
Rhine Valley ❷❶
Rothenburg ob
   der Tauber ❽
Stuttgart ❶❻
Trier ❶❽
Weimar ❹
Würzburg ❼

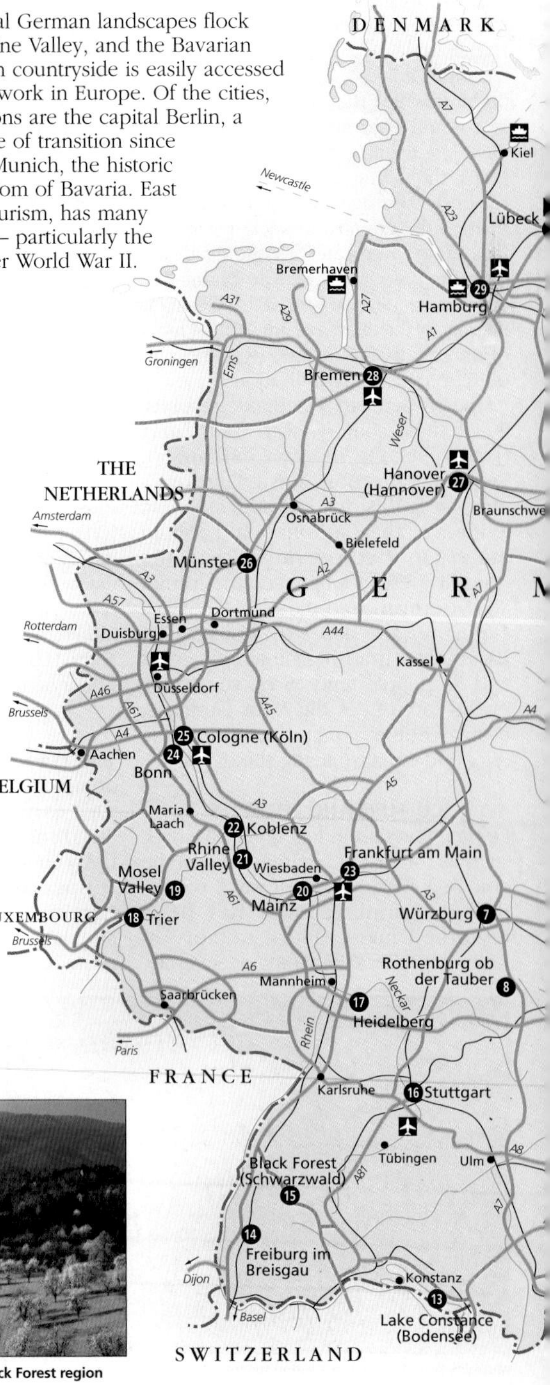

Thickly wooded landscape of the Black Forest region

DENMARK

Newcastle

Kiel

Lübeck

Bremerhaven

Hamburg ❷❾

Bremen ❷❽

Groningen

THE
NETHERLANDS

Amsterdam

Hanover
(Hannover) ❷❼

Osnabrück

Braunschwe

Bielefeld

Münster ❷❻

G   E   R

Rotterdam

Essen   Dortmund

Duisburg

Kassel

A44

Düsseldorf

Brussels

Cologne (Köln) ❷❺

Aachen   Bonn ❷❹

BELGIUM

Maria
Laach

Koblenz ❷❷

Frankfurt am Main ❷❸

Rhine
Valley ❷❶   Wiesbaden

LUXEMBOURG

Mosel
Valley ❶❾

Mainz ❷⓿

Würzburg ❼

Brussels

Trier ❶❽

Rothenburg ob
der Tauber ❽

Saarbrücken

Mannheim

Heidelberg ❶❼

Paris

Rhein

FRANCE

Karlsruhe

Stuttgart ❶❻

Tübingen   Ulm

Black Forest
(Schwarzwald) ❶❺

Dijon

Freiburg im
Breisgau ❶❹

Konstanz

Basel

Lake Constance ❶❸
(Bodensee)

SWITZERLAND

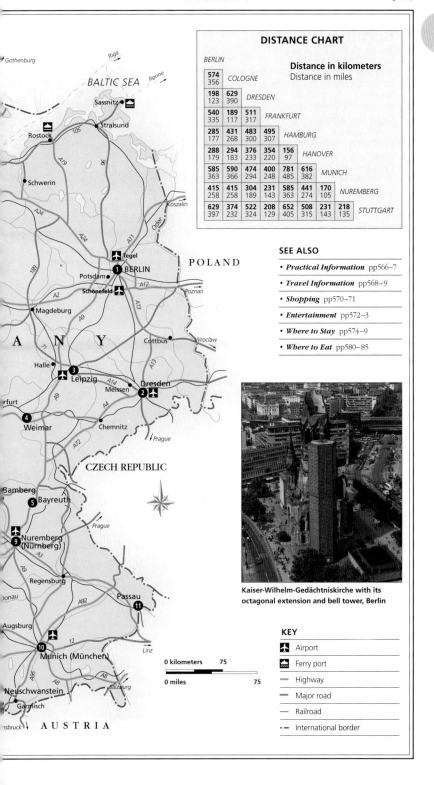

DISTANCE CHART

Distance in kilometers
Distance in miles

BERLIN								
574 356	COLOGNE							
198 123	**629** 390	DRESDEN						
540 335	**189** 117	**511** 317	FRANKFURT					
285 177	**431** 268	**483** 300	**495** 307	HAMBURG				
288 179	**294** 183	**376** 233	**354** 220	**156** 97	HANOVER			
585 363	**590** 366	**474** 294	**400** 248	**781** 485	**616** 382	MUNICH		
415 258	**415** 258	**304** 189	**231** 143	**585** 363	**441** 274	**170** 105	NUREMBERG	
629 397	**374** 232	**522** 324	**208** 129	**652** 405	**508** 315	**231** 143	**218** 135	STUTTGART

SEE ALSO

- *Practical Information* pp566–7
- *Travel Information* pp568–9
- *Shopping* pp570–71
- *Entertainment* pp572–3
- *Where to Stay* pp574–9
- *Where to Eat* pp580–85

Kaiser-Wilhelm-Gedächtniskirche with its octagonal extension and bell tower, Berlin

KEY

- ✈ Airport
- ⛴ Ferry port
- — Highway
- = = Major road
- — Railroad
- · – International border

Berlin ●

Since becoming the capital of the Federal Republic of Germany following reunification in 1990, Berlin has become an ever popular destination for visitors. The historic heart of the city is located around the wide avenue Unter den Linden and on Museum Island, which takes its name from the fine museums built there in the 19th and early 20th centuries. South of Unter den Linden is Checkpoint Charlie, a legacy of Berlin's status as a divided city during the Cold War. To the west are the green open spaces of Tiergarten and Kurfürstendamm, the center of the former West Berlin. Farther afield, the splendid palaces of Potsdam, now almost a suburb of Berlin, are not to be missed.

The grand approach to the 18th-century Rococo Schloss Sanssouci in Potsdam

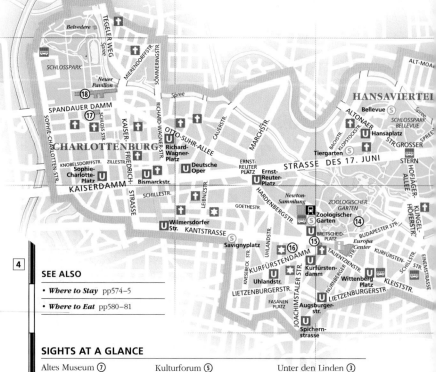

SEE ALSO

- **Where to Stay** pp574–5
- **Where to Eat** pp580–81

SIGHTS AT A GLANCE

Altes Museum ⑦
Berliner Dom pp534–5 ⑨
Brandenburg Gate ①
Centrum Judaicum &
  Neue Synagoge ⑩
Fernsehturm ⑪
Kaiser-Wilhelm-
  Gedächtniskirche ⑮
Kreuzberg ⑬

Kulturforum ⑤
Kurfürstendamm ⑯
Nikolaiviertel ⑫
Pergamonmuseum ⑧
Potsdamer Platz ④
Reichstag ②
Sammlung Berggruen ⑰
Schloss Charlottenburg ⑱
Tiergarten ⑥

Unter den Linden ③
Zoologischer Garten ⑭

Greater Berlin
(see inset map)
Dahlem ⑳
Grunewald ⑲
Potsdam and Park
  Sanssouci ㉑

GETTING AROUND

Berlin's U- and S-Bahn trains are the quickest way of getting around the city. They also serve outlying areas, such as Grunewald, Dahlem, and Potsdam. Buses are reliable, but slow, especially during rush hour, owing to congestion. Trams are another option in the east of the city, and accept the same tickets as the buses and S-Bahn lines.

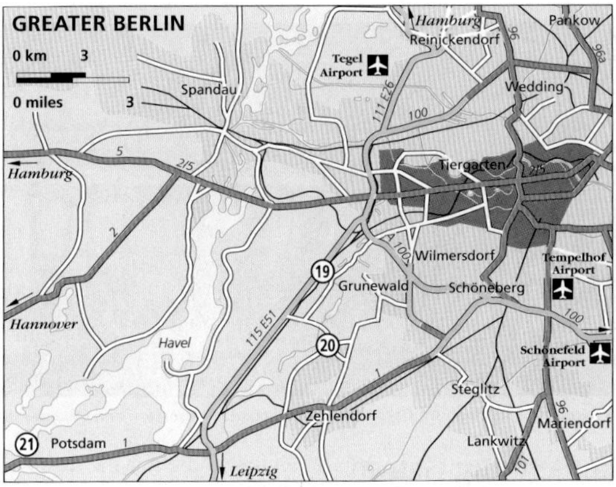

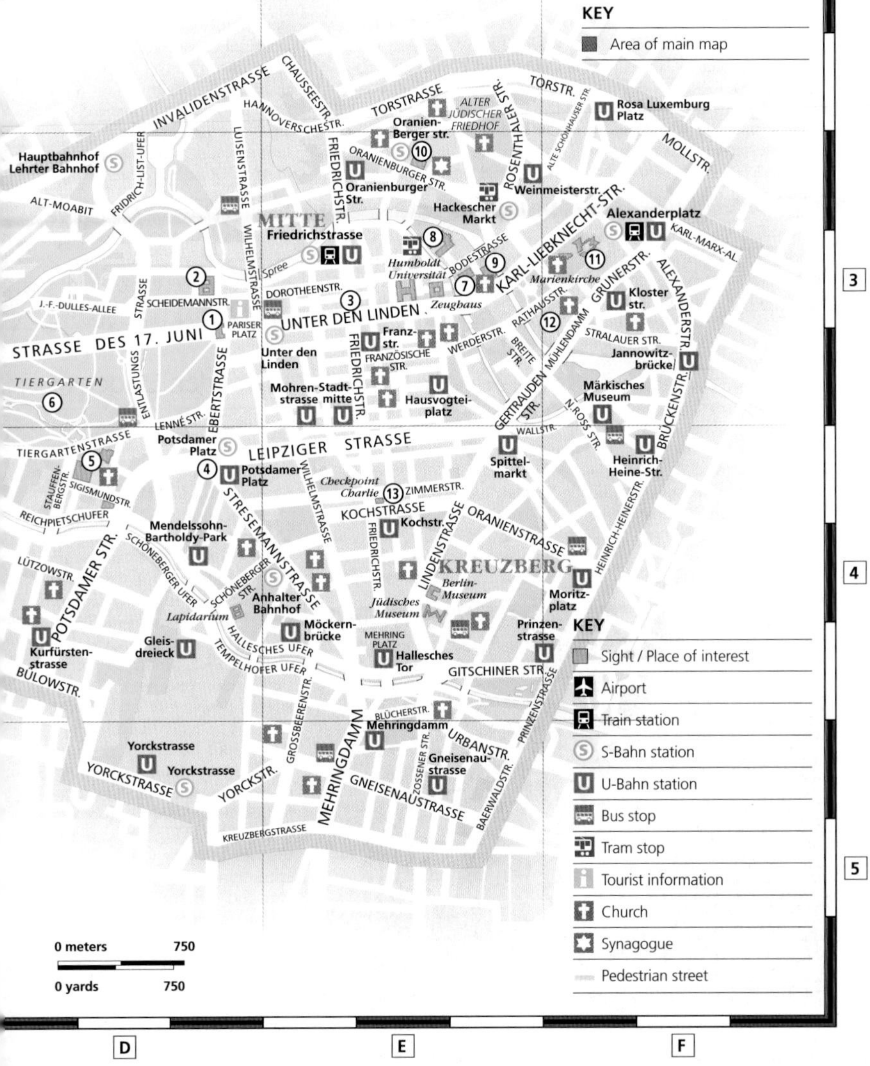

GREATER BERLIN

0 km 3
0 miles 3

Hamburg — Reinickendorf — Pankow
Tegel Airport
Spandau — Wedding
Hamburg
Tiergarten
Hannover
Havel — Grunewald — Wilmersdorf — Schöneberg — Tempelhof Airport
Leipzig — Potsdam — Zehlendorf — Steglitz — Mariendorf — Lankwitz — Schönefeld Airport

KEY

■ Area of main map

Main map labels:

Hauptbahnhof Lehrter Bahnhof
ALT-MOABIT
J.-F.-DULLES-ALLEE
STRASSE DES 17. JUNI
TIERGARTEN
INVALIDENSTRASSE
CHAUSSEESTR.
HANNOVERSCHESTR.
LUISENSTRASSE
FRIEDRICHSTR.
WILHELMSTRASSE
TORSTRASSE
ALTER JÜDISCHER FRIEDHOF
Oranien-Berger str.
ORANIENBURGER STR.
Oranienburger Str.
Hackescher Markt
Weinmeisterstr.
TORSTR.
ROSENTHALER STR.
ALTE SCHÖNHAUSER STR.
Rosa Luxemburg Platz
MOLLSTR.
MITTE
Friedrichstrasse
Spree
Humboldt Universität
Zeughaus
KARL-LIEBKNECHT-STR.
Alexanderplatz
KARL-MARX-AL.
Marienkirche
ALEXANDERSTR.
Kloster str.
GRUNERSTR.
DOROTHEENSTR.
UNTER DEN LINDEN
Franz-str.
FRANZÖSISCHE STR.
WERDERSTR.
BODESTRASSE
RATHAUSSTR.
BREITE STR.
Jannowitz-brücke
STRALAUER STR.
Märkisches Museum
Unter den Linden
Mohren-Strasse mitte
FRIEDRICHSTR.
Hausvogteiplatz
GERTRAUDEN
MÜHLENDAMM
WALLSTR.
Spittelmarkt
Heinrich-Heine-Str.
BRÜCKENSTR.
HEINRICH-HEINER-STR.
SCHEIDEMANNSTR.
PARISER PLATZ
EBERTSTRASSE
ENTLASTUNGS
LENNÉ-STR.
Potsdamer Platz
LEIPZIGER STRASSE
Potsdamer Platz
STRESEMANNSTRASSE
WILHELMSTRASSE
Checkpoint Charlie
ZIMMERSTR.
KOCHSTRASSE
Kochstr.
LINDENSTRASSE
ORANIENSTRASSE
KREUZBERG
Moritzplatz
TIERGARTENSTRASSE
STAUFFENBERGER STR.
SIGISMUNDSTR.
REICHPIETSCHUFER
POTSDAMER STR.
Mendelssohn-Bartholdy-Park
SCHÖNEBERGER UFER
SCHÖNEBERGER STR.
Berlin-Museum
Jüdisches Museum
Prinzen-strasse
LÜTZOWSTR.
Anhalter Bahnhof
Lapidarium
Möckern-brücke
MEHRING PLATZ
Hallesches Tor
GITSCHINER STR.
Kurfürstenstrasse
BÜLOWSTR.
Gleisdreieck
HALLESCHES UFER
TEMPELHOFER UFER
BLÜCHERSTR.
Mehringdamm
URBANSTR.
PRINZENSTRASSE
Yorckstrasse
YORCKSTRASSE
Yorckstrasse
YORCKSTR.
GROSSBEERENSTR.
MEHRINGDAMM
ZOSSENER STR.
Gneisenaustrasse
GNEISENAUSTRASSE
BAERWALDSTR.
KREUZBERGSTRASSE

KEY

□ Sight / Place of interest
✈ Airport
▣ Train station
Ⓢ S-Bahn station
Ⓤ U-Bahn station
▦ Bus stop
▥ Tram stop
ⓘ Tourist information
✝ Church
✡ Synagogue
▨ Pedestrian street

0 meters 750
0 yards 750

The imposing Brandenburg Gate at Pariser Platz, at the western end of Unter den Linden

Brandenburg Gate ①

Pariser Platz. Ⓢ *Unter den Linden.*
🚌 *100.*

The Brandenburg Gate is the quintessential symbol of Berlin. This magnificent Neo-classical structure was designed by Carl Gotthard Langhans and modeled on the Propylaia of the Acropolis in Athens *(see p478)*. It was erected between 1788 and 1791, although the sculptural decorations were not completed until 1795. Pavilions frame its simple Doric colonnade, and bas-reliefs on the entablature above the columns depict scenes from Greek myth. The structure is crowned by the famous sculpture of a *quadriga* – a chariot drawn by four horses – designed by Johann Gottfried Schadow.

The Brandenburg Gate has witnessed many important historical events. Military parades and demonstrating workers have marched under its arches, and it was the site of celebrations marking the birth of the Deutsches Reich in 1871. It was here, too, that the Soviet flag was raised in 1945.

Restored between 1956 and 1958, for the next 30 years the gate stood watch over the divided city, until the fall of the Berlin Wall in 1989. It was renovated once again in 2002.

Reichstag ②

Platz der Republik. Ⓢ *Unter den Linden.* 🚌 *100, 248, 257.*
***Tel** 030-2273 2152.* **Dome & Assembly Hall** ☐ *daily.* ⬤ *Dec 24, Dec 31.* 🖼

Built to house the German Parliament, the Reichstag was intended as a symbol of national unity and to showcase the aspirations of the new German Empire, declared in 1871. Constructed between 1884 and 1894, the Neo-Renaissance building by Paul Wallot captured the prevailing spirit of German optimism. On the night of February 27, 1933, a fire destroyed the main hall. Rebuilding work undertaken between 1957 and 1972 removed the dome and most of the ornamentation on the façades. On December 2, 1990, the Reichstag was the first meeting place of a newly-elected Bundestag following German reunification.

The latest rebuilding project, completed in 1999 to a design by Sir Norman Foster, transformed the Reichstag into a modern meeting hall crowned by an elliptical glass dome.

Unter den Linden ③

🚇 *Unter den Linden.* 🚌 *100, 157, 348.*

One of the most famous streets in Berlin, Unter den Linden was once the route to the royal hunting grounds that were transformed into the Tiergarten. In the 17th century it was planted with lime trees, to which it owes its name.

In the 18th century, Unter den Linden became the main street of the westward-growing city. It gradually filled with prestigious buildings, such as the Baroque **Zeughaus**, home of the Deutsches Historisches Museum, and the **Humboldt Universität** (1753). Next door, the **Neue Wache** (1816–1818) commemorates the victims of war and dictatorship.

Since reunification, Unter den Linden has acquired several cafés and restaurants, as well as many smart new shops. The street is also the venue for many outdoor events.

The Reichstag, crowned by a dome designed by Sir Norman Foster

For hotels and restaurants in this region see pp574–5 and pp580–81

Potsdamer Platz ④

U Ⓢ *Potsdamer Platz.*

Before the onset of World War II, Potsdamer Platz was one of the busiest and most densely built-up areas of Berlin. Most of the area's landmarks ceased to exist after the bombing of 1945, and the destruction was completed when the burned-out ruins were finally pulled down to build the Berlin Wall.

Since the mid-1990s a new financial and business district has sprung up on this empty wasteland, which once divided East and West Berlin. The huge new complex comprises not only office buildings, but also a concert hall, a multi-screen cinema, and the Arkaden shopping mall. The first finished structure was the Daimler-Benz-Areal office block, designed by Renzo Piano and Christoph Kohlbecker. To the north lies the impressive Sony-Center complex, by Helmut Jahn.

Kulturforum ⑤

U Ⓢ *Potsdamer Platz.* **Tel** *030-266 3666.* **Kunstgewerbemuseum** ⬜ *Tue–Sun.* ⬤ *first Tue after Easter, Whitsun, Oct 1, Dec 24, 25 & 31.* 📷 ♿ **Gemäldegalerie** ⬜ *Tue–Sun.* ⬤ *first Tue after Easter, Whitsun, May 1, Dec 24, 25 & 31.* 📷 ♿ **Neue Nationalgalerie** ⬜ *Tue–Sun.* 📷 ♿

The idea of creating a new cultural center in West Berlin was first mooted in 1956. The first building to go up was the

Silver and ivory tankard from the Kunstgewerbemuseum

Philharmonie (Berlin Philharmonic concert hall), built to an innovative design by Hans Scharoun in 1961. Most of the other plans for the Kulturforum were realized between 1961 and 1987. With many museums and galleries, the area attracts millions of visitors every year.

The **Kunstgewerbemuseum** (Museum of Arts and Crafts) holds a rich collection of decorative art and crafts dating from the early Middle Ages to the modern day. Goldwork is very well represented, and the museum takes great pride in its late Gothic and Renaissance silver.

The **Gemäldegalerie** fine art collection is in a modern building designed by Heinz Hilmer and Christopher Sattler. Works by German Renaissance artists, including Albrecht Dürer and Hans Holbein, dominate the exhibition space, but there are also pieces by van Dyck, Rembrandt, Raphael, Velázquez, and Caravaggio.

Housed in a striking building with a flat steel roof over a glass hall, the **Neue Nationalgalerie** contains mainly 20th-century art, but begins with artists of the late 19th century, such as Edvard Munch and Ferdinand Hodler. Paintings from the *Die Brücke* movement include pieces by Ernst Ludwig Kirchner and Karl Schmidt-Rottluff. Also on display are works by Picasso, Léger, Dalí, Magritte, and Max Ernst.

A tranquil stretch of water in Berlin's 19th-century Tiergarten

Tiergarten ⑥

Ⓢ *Tiergarten, Bellevue.* 🚌 *100, 187, 200, 341.*

The Tiergarten is the largest park in Berlin. Situated at the geographical center of the city, it occupies a 210-ha (520-acre) area. Once the Elector's hunting reserve, the forest was transformed into a landscaped park by Peter Joseph Lenné in the 1830s. A triumphal avenue was built at the end of the 19th century, lined with statues of the nation's rulers and statesmen.

World War II inflicted huge damage on the Tiergarten, including the destruction of the triumphal avenue, many of whose surviving monuments can now be seen in the Lapidarium in Kreuzberg. Replanting has restored the Tiergarten, and many of its avenues are now lined with statues of national celebrities, including Goethe and Wagner.

The Philharmonie, with the later addition of the Kammermusiksaal (1984–7) in front, at Kulturforum

Mosaic from Hadrian's Villa (2nd century AD), at the Altes Museum

Altes Museum ⑦

Am Lustgarten. *Tel* 030-266 3660.
Ⓢ Hackescher Markt. 🚌 100, 157,
348. ☐ daily. 📷

The Altes Museum, designed by Karl Friedrich Schinkel, is undoubtedly one of the world's most beautiful Neo-classical structures, with an impressive 87-m (285-ft) high portico supported by Ionic columns. The stately rotunda is decorated with sculptures and ringed by a colonnade.

Officially opened in 1830, this was one of the first purpose-built museums in Europe, designed to house the royal collection of paintings and antiquities. Following World War II, the building was used to display temporary exhibitions. Since 1998 the Altes Museum has housed a portion of the Antikensammlung, a magnifi-cent collection of Greek and Roman antiquities. Among the

highlights of the collection are a colorful floor mosaic from Hadrian's Villa near Tivoli, and Perikles' Head, a Roman copy of the sculpture by Kresilas that stood at the entrance to the Acropolis in Athens.

Pergamon-museum ⑧

Bodestrasse 1–3 (entrance from Am Kupfergraben). *Tel* 030-266 3666.
Ⓢ Hackescher Markt, Friedrich-strasse. 🚌 100, 147, 257, 348.
☐ daily. ● Jan 1, first Tue after Easter and Pentecost, Dec 24, 25 & 31. 📷 ♿ 📷 (no flash).

Built between 1912 and 1930 to a design by Alfred Messel and Ludwig Hoffmann, the Pergamonmuseum is one of Berlin's major attractions. Its three large independent col-lections, the result of exten-sive archaeological excavations, form one of Europe's most famous archives of antiquities.

The highlight of Berlin's collection of Greek and Roman antiquities (Antikensammlung) is the huge Pergamon Altar from the acropolis of ancient Pergamon in Asia Minor. This magnificently restored altar, which gives the museum its name, is thought to have been commissioned by King Eumenes in 160 BC. Roman architecture is represented by the market gate from the Roman city of Miletus, which dates from the 2nd century BC.

Major excavations begun in the 1820s form the basis of a royal collection at the Museum of Near Eastern Antiquities (Vorderasiatisches Museum). One striking exhibit is the splendid Ishtar Gate, built during the reign of Nebuchadnezzar II (604–562 BC) in ancient Babylon. Also on display are pieces from the neighboring regions of Persia, Syria, and Pales-tine, including a basalt sculpture of a bird from Tel Halaf and a glazed wall relief of a spear-bearer from Artaxerxes II's palace in Susa, capital of the Persian Empire.

Persian relief, Pergamon-museum

The history of the Museum of Islamic Art (Museum für Islamische Kunst) begins in 1904 when Wilhelm von Bode donated his extensive collection of carpets. He also brought to Berlin a 45-m (150-ft) long section of the façade of a Jordanian desert palace, dating from the Oma-yyad period (AD 661–750). Another fascinating exhibit is a beautiful 13th-century *mihrab* (Islamic prayer niche). Made in the Iranian town of Kashan, the *mihrab* is covered in lustrous metallic glazed tiles. The collection's many carpets come from as far afield as Iran, Asia Minor, Egypt, and the Caucasus.

Berliner Dom ⑨

See pp534–5.

Relief carving of Athena from the Pergamon Altar, Pergamonmuseum

For hotels and restaurants in this region see pp574–5 and pp580–81

The splendidly reconstructed gilded domes of the Neue Synagoge

Centrum Judaicum & Neue Synagoge ⑩

Oranienburger Strasse 28 & 30. *Tel 030-8802 8316 (Centrum Judaicum).* Ⓢ *Oranienburger Strasse.* 🚋 *1, 13.* 🚌 *157.* ⃝ *Sun–Thu, am Fri.* ● *Jewish festivals.*

Occupying the former premises of the Jewish community council, the Centrum Judaicum contains an extensive library, archives, and a research center all devoted to the history and cultural heritage of Berlin's Jews. Next door, the restored rooms of the Neue Synagoge are used as a museum, exhibiting material relating to the local Jewish community.

The building of the New Synagogue was started in 1859 and completed in 1866. The narrow façade is flanked by a pair of towers and crowned with a dome containing a round vestibule. Now in use again for services, the synagogue's main hall has space for 3,000 worshipers.

This fascinating structure was Berlin's largest synagogue. However, on November 9, 1938, it was partially destroyed during the infamous "*Kristallnacht*" ("Night of the Broken Glass"), when thousands of synagogues, cemeteries, and Jewish homes and shops all over Germany were looted and burned. The building was damaged further by Allied bombing in 1943, and was finally demolished in 1958. Reconstruction began in 1988 and was completed in 1995.

Fernsehturm ⑪

Panoramastrasse. Ⓤ Ⓢ *Alexanderplatz.* 🚌 *100, 157.* ⃝ *daily.*

Known as the *Telespargel,* or toothpick, by the locals, this 368-m (1,206-ft) high television mast soars above the massive Alexanderplatz. It is the third tallest structure in Europe – after Moscow's Ostankino Tower and Riga Radio and TV Tower.

The concrete shaft contains elevators that carry passengers to the viewing platform. Situated inside a steel-clad giant sphere, this platform is 203 m (666 ft) above the ground. Visitors can also enjoy the revolving café, from where it is possible to get a bird's-eye view of the whole city while sipping a cup of coffee. Visibility can reach up to 40 km (25 miles).

Nikolaiviertel ⑫

Ⓤ *Alexanderplatz, Klosterstrasse.* Ⓢ *Alexanderplatz.* 🚌 *100, 143, 148, 200, 348.*

This small area on the bank of the Spree, known as the Nikolaiviertel (St. Nicholas Quarter), is a favorite strolling ground for both Berliners and tourists. Some of Berlin's oldest houses stood here until they were destroyed in World War II. The redevelopment of the area, carried out between

Berlin's massive Fernsehturm, towering over the city

1979 and 1987, proved to be an interesting, if somewhat controversial, attempt at recreating a medieval village.

Today the area consists mostly of newly built replicas of historic buildings. The narrow streets are filled with small shops, cafés, bars, and restaurants, among them the popular Zum Nussbaum, a historical inn that was once located on Fischer Island. Dating from 1507, the original building was destroyed, and subsequently reconstructed at the junction of Am Nussbaum and Propststrasse.

Riverside buildings of the Nikolaiviertel

Berliner Dom ⑨

Royal crest of Friedrich III

This Protestant cathedral was built by Johann Boumann between 1747 and 1750 on the site of a Dominican church. It incorporated the crypt of the Hohenzollern dynasty, which ruled the city for nearly 500 years, and is one of the largest of its kind in Europe. The present Neo-Baroque structure is the work of Julius Raschdorff and dates from 1894–1905. The central copper dome reaches 98 m (322 ft), with an inner cupola which is 70 m (230 ft) high. Following severe damage sustained in World War II, the building has been restored in a simplified form, including the dismantling of the Hohenzollern memorial chapel, which originally adjoined the northern wall.

Figures of the Apostles

Philipp der Grossmütige
At the base of the arcade stand statues of church reformers and princes who supported the Reformation. The statue of Philip the Magnanimous, Landgrave of Hesse (1509–67) is the work of Walter Schott.

★ **Church Interior**
The impressive, richly-decorated interior was designed by Julius Raschdorff at the turn of the 20th century.

Sauer's Organ
The organ, the work of Wilhelm Sauer, has an exquisitely carved case. The instrument contains some 7,200 pipes.

Main entrance

★ **Hohenzollern Sarcophagi**
The imperial Hohenzollern family crypt, hidden beneath the floor of the cathedral, contains 100 richly decorated sarcophagi, including that of Prince Friedrich Ludwig.

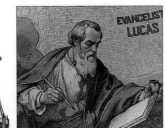

The Four Evangelists
Mosaics depicting the Four Evangelists decorate the ceilings of the smaller niches in the cathedral. They were designed by Woldemar Friedrich.

VISITORS' CHECKLIST

Am Lustgarten. *Tel* 030-20 26 91 19. Ⓢ Hackescher Markt. 🚌 100, 157, 200, 348. ⏰ 9am–8pm Mon–Sat, noon–8pm Sun (Oct–Mar: until 7pm). ♿ ✝ 10am & 6pm Sun.

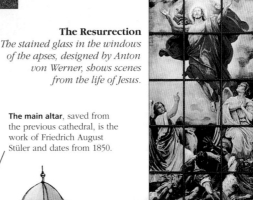

The Resurrection
The stained glass in the windows of the apses, designed by Anton von Werner, shows scenes from the life of Jesus.

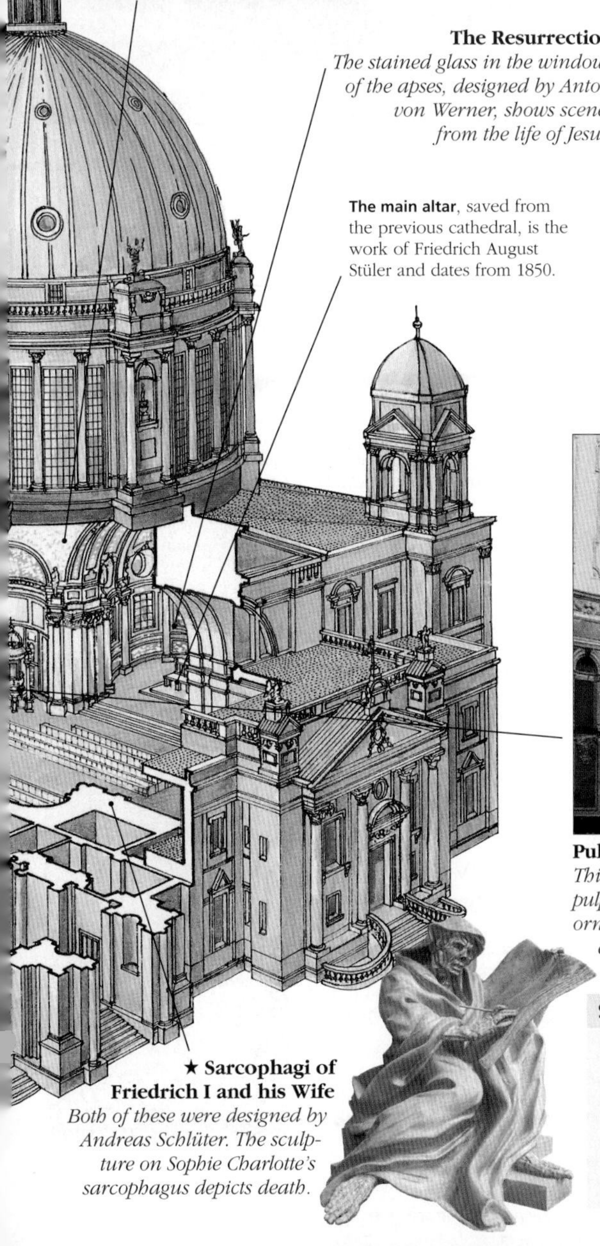

The main altar, saved from the previous cathedral, is the work of Friedrich August Stüler and dates from 1850.

Pulpit
This elaborate Neo-Baroque pulpit is part of the cathedral's ornate decor dating from the early 20th century.

★ Sarcophagi of Friedrich I and his Wife
Both of these were designed by Andreas Schlüter. The sculpture on Sophie Charlotte's sarcophagus depicts death.

STAR FEATURES

★ Hohenzollern Sarcophagi

★ Church Interior

★ Sarcophagi of Friedrich I and his Wife

Kreuzberg ⑬

Checkpoint Charlie Friedrichstrasse 43–45. **Tel** 030-253 7250. U Kochstrasse. 🚌 129. ◯ 9am–10pm daily. 🎫 **Jüdisches Museum** Lindenstrasse 14. U Hallesches Tor, Kochstrasse. 🚌 240. **Tel** 030-2599 3300. ◯ 10am–10pm Mon, 10am–8pm Tue–Sun.

Kreuzberg is an area of contrasts, with luxury apartments next to dilapidated buildings. The district's attractions are its wealth of restaurants and Turkish bazaars, as well as a wide selection of theaters, cinemas, and galleries.

Checkpoint Charlie was once the notorious border crossing between the Soviet and American sectors, and witness to a number of dramatic events during the Cold War. The museum close by, Haus am Checkpoint Charlie, houses exhibits connected with the ingenious attempts by East Germans to escape to the West.

The imaginative architecture of the **Jüdisches Museum**, dedicated to Jewish history and art, conveys something of the tragic history of the millions of Jews who lost their lives in the Holocaust. The zigzag layout recalls a torn Star of David, while the interior arrangement is dominated by a long empty area, which symbolizes the void left in Europe by the exile and murder of countless thousands of Jews.

Berlin Wall sculpture at entrance to Haus am Checkpoint Charlie

Zoologischer Garten, home to over 1,400 animal species

Zoologischer Garten ⑭

Hardenbergplatz 8 or Budapester Strasse 34. **Tel** 030-254 010. U ⓢ Zoologischer Garten. 🚌 100, 109, 145, 146 & many others. ◯ daily. 🎫

The Zoological Garden forms part of the Tiergarten and dates from 1844, making it the oldest zoo in Germany. It offers a number of attractions, including the monkey house, which contains a family of gorillas, and a specially darkened pavilion for observing nocturnal animals. The hippopotamus pool has a glazed wall that enables visitors to watch these enormous creatures moving through the water. The aquarium, one of the largest in Europe, contains sharks, piranhas, and unusual animals from coral reefs. There is also a huge terrarium with an overgrown jungle that is home to a group of crocodiles.

Kaiser-Wilhelm-Gedächtniskirche ⑮

Breitscheidplatz. **Tel** 030-218 5023. U Zoologischer Garten, Kurfürstenstrasse. ⓢ Zoologischer Garten. 🚌 100, 200, X-9. **Gedenkhalle** ◯ Mon–Sat. 🎫

The damaged roof of this former church has become one of the best-known symbols of postwar Berlin. The vast Neo-Romanesque building was consecrated in 1895, but was destroyed by bombs in 1943. After World War II the ruins were removed, leaving only the massive front tower, at the base of which the Gedenkhalle (Memorial Hall) is situated. This hall documents the history of the church and contains some of the original ceiling mosaics, marble reliefs, and liturgical objects. The latter include the Coventry Crucifix, a modest cross fashioned from nails found in the ashes of Coventry Cathedral, England, which was destroyed in the bombing raids of the 1940s.

In 1963, Egon Eiermann designed a new octagonal church in blue glass. His hexagonal bell tower stands on the site of the former nave of the destroyed church.

New and old bell towers of the Kaiser-Wilhelm-Gedächtniskirche

A bustling outdoor café on the Kurfürstendamm

Kurfürstendamm ⑯

Ⓤ *Kurfürstendamm.* 🚌 *109, 119, 129, 219.*

This wide avenue was established in the 1880s on the site of a former track that led to the Grunewald forest *(see p538)*. It quickly acquired many imposing buildings and grand hotels. In the 20 years between World Wars I and II, the Ku'damm, as it is popularly called, was renowned for its cafés, visited by famous film directors, writers, and painters.

After World War II, new buildings replaced the damaged houses, but this did not change the character of the street. Elegant shops and pretty cafés still attract a chic crowd. Not far from here is the city's newest photography museum, the **Newton-Sammlung**.

Sammlung Berggruen ⑰

Schlossstrasse 1. *Tel 030-326 9580.* Ⓤ *Richard-Wagner-Platz, Sophie-Charlotte-Platz.* Ⓢ *Westend.* 🚌 *109, 145, 309.* ◻ *10am–6pm Tue–Sun.* 📷 ♿

Heinz Berggruen assembled this tasteful collection of art dating from the late 19th and first half of the 20th centuries. The museum is well-known for its impressive array of paintings, drawings, and gouaches by Pablo Picasso. There is also a display of more than 20 works by Paul Klee and paintings by Van Gogh, Braque, and Cézanne. The exhibition is supplemented by some excellent sculptures.

Schloss Charlottenburg ⑱

Spandauer Damm. *Tel 030-3209 1440.* Ⓤ *Richard-Wagner-Platz, Sophie-Charlotte-Platz.* Ⓢ *Westend.* 🚌 *109, 110, 145, X-26.* ◻ *Tue–Sun.* 📷 *compulsory on ground floor.* 🎫

The palace in Charlottenburg was intended as a summer residence for Sophie Charlotte, Elector Friedrich III's wife. Construction began in 1695 to a design by Johann Arnold Nering. Between 1701 and 1713 the palace was enlarged, and a Baroque cupola and an orangery were added. Subsequent extensions were undertaken by Frederick the Great (King Friedrich II), who added the Neuer Flügel (New Wing) between 1740 and 1746.

Restored to its former elegance after World War II, the palace's richly decorated interior is unequalled in Berlin. In the central section of the palace, the mirrored gallery of the Porzellankabinett has walls lined with fine Japanese and Chinese porcelain.

The Neuer Flügel, the new wing of the palace, used to house the popular Galerie der Romantik. The former private apartment of Friedrik the Great, it now has displays of the king's exquisite furniture. The Neuer Flügel and the upper floor can be visited independently.

The Neoclassical pavilion that houses the **Museum für Vor- und Frühgeschichte**, a museum of pre- and early history, was added to the orangery wing in 1787–91.

The park surrounding the palace is one of the most picturesque places in Berlin. Among the many fine monuments dotted around the grounds are the charming Neoclassical **Neuer Pavillion** (New Pavilion), whose interior is furnished in period style, and the **Belvedere** (1788), housing a large collection of porcelain.

Central tower and 18th-century cupola of Schloss Charlottenburg

Restaurant in the Forsthaus Paulsborn in the Grunewald

Grunewald ⑲

Ⓢ Grunewald. 🚌 115. **Jagdschloss Grunewald**. *Tel* 030-813 3597. ⬤ *for renovation until 2009.*

Just a short S-Bahn ride from central Berlin lie the vast forests of the Grunewald, bordering some of the city's most elegant suburbs. Once the haunt of politicians, wealthy industrialists, and renowned artists, some of the villas here now serve as the headquarters of Berlin's academic institutes.

On the shore of the picturesque Grunewaldsee is the **Jagdschloss Grunewald**, one of the oldest civic buildings in Berlin. Built by Elector Joachim II in 1542, it was rebuilt in the Baroque style around 1700. Inside the small palace is Berlin's only surviving Renaissance hall, which houses canvases by Rubens and van Dyck among others. Opposite the Jagdschloss, the **Jagdzeugmagazin** (Hunting Museum) holds displays of historic hunting equipment. Just 4 km (2 miles) away is the Wald-museum, the only museum devoted to forest life in the Berlin area.

To the southwest of the Grunewaldsee is **Forsthaus Paulsborn**. This rather pictur-esque hunting lodge, which nowadays houses a very good restaurant, was constructed in 1905.

Dahlem ⑳

Ⓤ *Dahlem Dorf.* 🚌 *110, 183, X-11, X-83.* **Museumszentrum** *Tel* 030-83010. ⬤ *Tue– Sun.*

First mentioned in 1275, by the 19th century Dahlem had grown from a small village into an affluent, tranquil city suburb. At the beginning of the 20th century, a number of museums, designed by Bruno Paul, were built. They were extended considerably in the 1960s, when the **Museums-zentrum** was created to rival East Berlin's Museum Island (*see pp532– 4*).

Highlights from this cluster of museums include bronzes from Benin in West Africa and gold Inca jewelry from South America at the Ethnologisches Museum (Museum of Ethnography). The other collections range from the Museum für Indische Kunst (Museum of Indian Art) and the Museum für Ostasiatische Kunst (Museum of Far Eastern Art), to the Nordamerica Ausstellung (Exhibition of Native North American Cultures).

Not far from the Museums-zentrum, the **Museum Europäischer Kulturen** specializes in European folk art and culture. Among the exhibits you can expect to see are earthenware items, cos-tumes, jewelry, toys, and tools.

Domäne Dahlem is a rare oasis of country life in the Berlin suburbs. Part of the Stadtmuseum Berlin (Museum of the City of Berlin), the Baroque manor house (c.1680) boasts splendid period interiors, while the 19th-century farm buildings hold a collection of agricultural tools.

The elegant Functionalist building occupied by the **Brücke-Museum** was built by Werner Düttmann in 1966–7. The museum houses a collection of German Expressionist paintings by members of the artistic group known as *Die Brücke*.

The combined museum and working farm of Domäne Dahlem

Potsdam and Park Sanssouci ㉑

An independent city close to Berlin, Potsdam has almost 150,000 inhabitants and is the capital of Brandenburg. The first documented reference to the town dates from AD 993; it was later granted municipal rights in 1317. The town blossomed in the 1600s, during the era of the Great Elector, and then again in the 18th century, when the splendid summer palace, Schloss Sanssouci, was built for Frederick the Great. Potsdam suffered badly in World War II, particularly on April 14 and 15, 1945, when the Allies bombed the town's center.

VISITORS' CHECKLIST

Brandenburg. 🚶 150,000.
🚆 from Bahnhof Zoo, Berlin
to Potsdam-Stadt. Ⓢ 🚌 🚊
🛈 Brandenburger Strasse 3
(0331-27 55 80).
www.potsdam.de

A Russian-style wooden house in the charming Alexandrowka district

Exploring Potsdam

Despite its wartime losses, today Potsdam is one of Germany's most attractive towns. Tourists flock to see the magnificent royal estate, Park Sanssouci (*see pp540–41*), to stroll in the Neuer Garten, which boasts its own grand palaces, and to see the pretty Alexandrowka district and the historic Dutch quarter.

🏛 Marmorpalais

Am Ufer des Heiligen Sees (Neuer Garten). **Tel** 0331-969 4246.
🚌 692, 695. ◯ Apr–Oct 31:
Tue–Sun; Nov 1–Mar: Sat & Sun.
The Marmorpalais (Marble Palace) is located on the edge of the lake in the Neuer Garten, a park northeast of Potsdam's center. Completed in 1791, the grand Neoclassical building owes its name to the Silesian marble that decorates its façade. The rooms in the main part of the palace contain Neoclassical furnishings from the late 18th century, including Wedgwood porcelain and furniture from the workshops of Roentgen. The concert hall in the right wing, whose interior dates from the 1840s, is particularly impressive.

🏛 Schloss Cecilienhof

Am Neuen Garten. **Tel** 0331-969 4244. 🚌 692, 695. ◯ Apr–Oct: Tue–Sun; Nov–Mar: Tue–Sun.
Schloss Cecilienhof was built for the Hohenzollern family between 1914 and 1917. In July 1945 the palace played an important role in history, when it served as the venue for the Potsdam Conference – an event that played a major part in establishing the political balance of power in Europe following the end of World War II.

🏛 Alexandrowka

Russische Kolonie Allee/ Puschkinallee.
🚌 604, 609, 638, 639. 🚊 92, 95.
A trip to Alexandrowka, in the northeast of the city, takes the visitor into the world of Pushkin's fairy tales. Wooden log cabins, set in their own gardens, form a charming residential estate. The houses were built in 1826 for singers in a Russian choir established to entertain military troops. Peter Joseph Lenné was responsible for the overall appearance of the estate, named after the Tsarina, the Prussian Princess Charlotte.

🏛 Holländisches Viertel

Friedrich-Ebertstrasse/ Kurfürsten-strasse/ Hebbelstrasse/ Gutenberg-strasse. 🚌 138, 601, 602, 603, 604 & many others.
The Dutch Quarter attracts crowds of tourists, with numerous stores, galleries, cafés, and beer cellars, especially along Mittelstrasse. The area was built up in the first half of the 18th century, when Dutch workers, invited by Friedrich Wilhelm I, began to settle in Potsdam. Today, you can still see the pretty red-brick, gabled houses that were built for them.

🏛 Filmpark Babelsberg

Grossbeerenstrasse. **Tel** 0331-721 2750. ◯ Apr–Oct: daily.
This amazing film park was laid out on the site of the film studios where Germany's first movies were made in 1912. From 1917, the studios belonged to Universum-Film-AG, which produced some of the most renowned movies of the silent era, such as Fritz Lang's futuristic *Metropolis* (1927) and films starring Marlene Dietrich and Greta Garbo. Later, Nazi propaganda films were also made here. The studio is still in operation today, but part of the complex is open to the public. Visitors can see old film sets, exciting special effects demonstrations, and stuntmen in action.

Original film prop on display at the Filmpark Babelsberg

Park Sanssouci

The enormous Park Sanssouci, covering an area of 287 hectares (709 acres), is among the most beautiful palace complexes in Europe. The first building to be constructed, Frederick the Great's Schloss Sanssouci, was built on the site of an orchard in 1745–7. Its name – *sans souci* is French for "without a care" – gives an indication of the building's flamboyant character. Over the years, the park has been enriched by other palaces and pavilions. Today, the park is made up of small gardens dating from different eras, all maintained in their original style.

Communs (1766–9)
This house for the palace staff has an unusually elegant character, and is situated next to a pretty courtyard.

★ Neues Palais
The monumental New Palace, constructed in 1763–1769, is crowned by a massive dome. Bas-reliefs on the triangular tympanum depict figures from Greek mythology.

| 0 meters | 200 |
| 0 yards | 200 |

Schloss Charlottenhof
The most interesting interior of this Neoclassical palace is the Humboldt Room, also called the Tent Room due to its resemblance to a marquee.

STAR SIGHTS

★ Schloss Sanssouci

★ Neues Palais

The Römische Bäder
(Roman Baths) date from 1829 and include a mock-Renaissance villa and a suite of Roman-style rooms.

The Lustgarten
(pleasure garden) has a symmetrical layout lined with rose beds.

The Chinesisches Teehaus
(Chinese Teahouse) features an exhibition of exquisite Oriental porcelain.

Schopenhauerstrasse/Zur
Historischen Mühle. 🚌 *612,
614, 695.* **Chinesisches Teehaus**
Ökonomieweg (Rehgarten). *Tel
0331-969 4202.* 🚌 *606.* 🚃
94, 96. 🕐 *May–Oct: Tue–Sun.*
Communs Am Neuen Palais. 🚌
606, 695. **Römische Bäder**
Lenné-Strasse (Park Charlottenhof). *Tel 0331-969 4202.* 🚌
606. 🚃 *94, 96.* 🕐 *May–Oct:
Tue–Sun.*

Orangerie
*This Neo-Renaissance palace,
the largest in the park, was
built in the mid-19th
century to house
foreign royalty
and guests.*

**Neue
Kammern**

**Bildergalerie
(art gallery)**

🏛 Neues Palais
Am Neuen Palais. *Tel 0331-969 4202.*
🚌 *606, 695.* 🕐 *Sat–Thu.* 🖼
This imposing Baroque palace
was begun at the request of
Frederick the Great in 1763.
Decorated with hundreds of
sculptures, the vast two-story
building contains more than
200 richly adorned rooms.
Especially unusual is the
Grottensaal (Grotto Salon),
where man-made stalactites
hang from the ceiling.

🏛 Schloss Sanssouci
Zur Historischen Mühle.
Tel 0331-969 4202. 🚌 *695.*
🚃 *94, 96.* 🕐 *Tue–Sun.* 🖼
Schloss Sanssouci is an enchanting Rococo palace, built in
1745–7. The original sketches
for the building were made
by Frederick the Great.
Inside, the walls of the
Konzertzimmer (Concert Hall)
are lined with paintings by
Antoine Pesne. The greatest
treasures are the paintings
of *fêtes galantes* by Antoine
Watteau (1684–1721), a favorite
artist of Frederick the Great.

🏛 Orangerie
Maulbeerallee (Nordischer Garten).
Tel 0331-969 4202. 🚌 *695.*
🕐 *May–Oct: Tue–Sun.*
The highlight of this guest
house is the Raphael Hall,
which is decorated with copies
of works by the great Italian
Renaissance artist. The view
from the observation terrace
extends over Potsdam.

🏛 Schloss Charlottenhof
Geschwister-Scholl-Strasse. *Tel 0331-
969 4202.* 🚌 *606.* 🚃 *94, 96.*
🕐 *May–Oct: Tue–Sun.*
This small Neoclassical palace
was designed by Friedrich
Schinkel and Ludwig

**The elegant Baroque exterior
of the Neue Kammern**

Persius in 1829, in the style of
a Roman villa. The rear of the
palace has a portico that
opens out onto the garden
terrace. Some of the wall
paintings, produced by
Schinkel, are still in place.

🏛 Neue Kammern
Zur Historischen Mühle (Lustgarten).
Tel 0331-969 4202. 🚌 *612, 614,
695.* 🕐 *Apr: Sat–Sun; May–Oct:
Tue–Sun.* 🖼
Originally built as an orangery
for Schloss Sanssouci in 1747,
the Neue Kammern (New
Chambers) was remodeled
as guest accommodations in
1777. The most impressive
of the building's four elegant
Rococo halls is the Ovidsaal,
with its rich reliefs and
marble floors.

🏛 Bildergalerie
Zur Historischen Mühle.
Tel 0331-969 4202. 🚌 *695.*
🕐 *May–Oct: Tue–Sun.* 🖼
Constructed between 1755
and 1764 to a design by
J.G. Buring, the Bildergalerie
holds an exhibition of paintings
once owned by Frederick
the Great. Highlights include
Caravaggio's *Doubting
Thomas* (1597), and Guido
Reni's *Cleopatra's Death* (1626),
as well as a number of works
by Rubens and van Dyck.

★ Schloss Sanssouci
*The oldest building in
the complex, this palace
contains the imposing
Marmorsaal (Marble
Hall), decorated with
pairs of columns made
from Carrara marble.
Frederick the Great
wanted the room to be
based on the Pantheon
in Rome (see p400).*

Eastern Germany

Closed to the West for over 40 years of Communist rule, Eastern Germany is now fast rebuilding its reputation as an attractive tourist destination. The powerful duchy of Saxony, whose rulers were also Electors and, in the early 18th century, kings of Poland, has left behind a rich cultural heritage for visitors to explore. After Berlin, the area's main attractions are Dresden, the ancient capital of Saxony, the old university town of Leipzig, and the important cultural center of Weimar in Thuringia.

Dresden ②

Saxony. ⛰ 480,000. ✈ 15 km (9 miles) N. ▣ ▦ ▤ ⓘ Prager Strasse 10–11 (0351- 49 19 20). www.dresden.de

One of Germany's most beautiful cities, Dresden blossomed during the 18th century, when it became a cultural center and acquired many magnificent buildings. Almost all of these, however, were completely destroyed during World War II, when Allied air forces mounted vast carpet-bombing raids on the city.

Today, meticulous restoration work is in progress to return the city to its former glory.

The most celebrated building in Dresden is the **Frauenkirche**. The landmark Church of Our Lady (1726–43) was left in ruins during the communist era to serve as a reminder of World War II damage but reconstruction began after reunification. The church was finally reconsecrated in 2005, and now serves as a symbol of reconciliation between former warring nations.

The **Zwinger** is an imposing Baroque building constructed in

Vermeer's *Girl Reading a Letter*, **Gemäldegalerie Alte Meister**

1709–32 with a spacious courtyard surrounded on all sides by galleries housing several museums, including the **Gemäldegalerie Alte Meister**. This contains one of Europe's finest art collections, with works by Antoine Watteau, Rembrandt, van Eyck, Velázquez, Vermeer, Raphael, Titian, and Albrecht Dürer.

The 19th-century **Sächsische Staatsoper** (Saxon State Opera) has been the venue for many world premieres, including *The Flying Dutchman* and *Tannhäuser* by Wagner, as well as works by Richard Strauss.

Dresden's **Residenzschloss** was built in stages from the late 15th to the 17th centuries. The palace now houses some of the most beautiful art collections in Eastern Germany. The Verkehrsmuseum has been a museum of transportation since 1956. The Residenzschloss also houses the famous **Grünes Gewölbe**, a vast royal treasury.

Once part of the town's fortifications, the **Brühlsche Terrasse** was subsequently transformed into magnificent

The Baroque Wallpavilion, part of the Zwinger building in Dresden

REBUILT FROM THE ASHES

Once known as the "Florence of the north," Dresden was one of the most beautiful cities in Europe. Then, on the night of February 13, 1945, 800 British aircraft launched the first of five massive firebomb raids on the city made by Allied air forces. The raids completely destroyed the greater part of the city, killing over 35,000 people, many of whom were refugees. The rebuilding of Dresden began soon after the war, when it was decided to restore the Zwinger and other historic buildings, and create a new city of modern developments on the levelled land around the old city center. Much of Dresden has now been reconstructed, though some reminders of the city's destruction remain.

The center of Dresden after Allied carpet-bombing

gardens by Heinrich von Brühl. Offering splendid views over the Elbe river, it is known as "the balcony of Europe." The **Albertinum** houses several magnificent collections, including the **Gemäldegalerie Neue Meister**, which holds paintings from the 19th and 20th centuries. These include landscapes by Caspar David Friedrich, canvases by the Nazarene group of painters, and works by Degas, van Gogh, Manet, and Monet.

On the banks of the Elbe stands **Schloss Pillnitz**, the charming summer residence of Augustus the Strong. The main attraction is the park, laid out in English and Chinese styles.

🏛 **Gemäldegalerie Alte Meister**
Theaterplatz 1. **Tel** 0351-4914 2000. ◻ Tue–Sun. 📷

Environs
Meissen, 19 km (12 miles) northwest of Dresden, is famous for its porcelain manufacture. The **Albrechtsburg** is a vast fortified hilltop complex with a cathedral and a palace once used by the Electors. Europe's first porcelain factory was set up in the palace in 1710 but moved to premises in Talstrasse in 1865. Documents relating to the history of the factory and examples of its products are on display in the palace rooms.

⛪ **Albrechtsburg**
Domplatz 1. **Tel** 03521-470 70. ◻ daily. ● Jan 10–31. 📷

Leipzig ❸

Saxony. 👥 493,000. 🚆 🚌 ✈
🛈 Richard-Wagner-Strasse 1 (0341-710 42 60).

Leipzig is not only one of Germany's leading commercial towns, but also a center of culture and learning. Most of the interesting sights can be found in the old town, including Europe's biggest train station, the **Hauptbahnhof**.

Lovers of Johann Sebastian Bach's music can visit the **Thomaskirche** (1482–96), where he was choirmaster

The lofty Neoclassical interior of the Nikolaikirche, Leipzig

from 1723. It now contains his tomb. The **Bacharchive und Bachmuseum** houses items relating to the composer.

The 16th-century **Nikolaikirche** (Church of St. Nicholas) was redecorated in Neoclassical style in 1784–97. The grand Renaissance **Altes Rathaus** (Old Town Hall), built in only nine months in 1556, is now the municipal museum. The **Museum der Bildenden Künste** has an excellent collection of German masters, including works by Caspar David Friedrich and Lucas Cranach the Elder, as well as van Eyck, Rubens, and Rodin.

Currently under renovation, the **Grassimuseum** complex houses three collections: a museum of ethnography, a museum of decorative arts, and a large collection of musical instruments.

🏛 **Museum der Bildenden Künste**
Katharinenstr 10. **Tel** 0341-216 9914. ◻ Tue–Sun (Wed: noon–8pm).

Weimar ❹

Thuringia. 🏛 62,000. 🚆 🚌
🛈 Markt 10 (03643-7450).
www.weimar.de

Weimar rose to prominence due to the enlightened sponsorship of its rulers, particularly Duke Carl Augustus and his wife Anna Amalia in the 18th century. Former residents include Goethe, Schiller, and Nietzsche, as well as the designers of the Bauhaus School, founded here in 1919.

Weimar is relatively small, and most of its museums are in the town center. To the north stands the **Neues Museum**, which holds a large collection of modern art. The nearby **Stadtmuseum** (currently closed for renovation) is devoted to Weimar's history, while the **Goethe-Museum** displays items associated with the famous writer.

The Neoclassical **Deutsches Nationaltheater**, built in 1906–7, was the venue for the world premiere of Wagner's *Lohengrin*. In 1919 the National Congress sat here to pass the new constitution for the Weimar Republic.

The vast ducal castle, **Weimar Schloss**, has original interiors and fine paintings by Peter Paul Rubens. Also known as the Grünes Schloss (Green Castle), the **Herzogin-Anna-Amalia Bibliothek** was converted into the duchess' library in 1761–6. It has a splendid Rococo interior.

Set in attractive Belvedere Park, the ducal summer residence of **Schloss Belvedere** (1761–6) has fine collections of Rococo decorative art and vintage vehicles.

⛪ **Weimar Schloss**
Burgplatz 4. **Tel** 03643-54 59 60. ◻ Tue–Sun. 📷

Weimar Schloss in Burgplatz, with its tall Renaissance tower

Bavaria

Bavaria is the largest state in the Federal Republic of Germany. Ruled by the Wittelsbach dynasty from 1180, the duchy of Bavaria was elevated to the status of a kingdom in 1806. In addition to historic cities, fairy-tale castles, and exquisite Baroque and Renaissance palaces, the region has more than its fair share of glorious Alpine scenery, beer halls, and colorful festivals.

The auditorium of Bayreuth's Markgräfliches Opernhaus

Bayreuth ❺

🏠 75,000. 🔲 🚹 Luitpoldplatz 9 (0921-885 88). 🎭 Richard-Wagner-Festspiele (Jul–Aug).

Music lovers associate this city with the German composer Richard Wagner (1813–83), who took up residence here in 1872. The **Villa Wahnfried** was built for Wagner by Carl Wölfel and today houses a museum dedicated to the famous musician. Nearby, the **Franz-Liszt-Museum** occupies the house where the Hungarian composer died in 1886.

Other sights of interest in Bayreuth include the **Markgräfliches Opernhaus**, the lavish Baroque opera house, which dates from the mid-18th century, and the **Neues Schloss**. Built for Margravine Wilhelmine in the 18th century, the palace retains its splendid Baroque and Rococo interiors, and its English-style gardens.

Bamberg ❻

🏠 71,000. 🔲 🚹 Geyerswörth-strasse 3 (0951-297 62 00).

Bamberg's most interesting historical monuments are clustered around Domplatz, including the magnificent **Cathedral of St. Peter and St. George**. Begun around 1211, the cathedral combines the late Romanesque and early French-Gothic styles. The eastern choir contains the famous equestrian statue of the "Bamberg Rider" (1225–30), whose identity remains a mystery to this day.

The west side of Domplatz is flanked by the **Alte Hofhaltung**, the former bishop's residence. Built in the 15th and 16th centuries, it houses a museum of local history. The more recent Baroque **Bishop's Palace** (1763) stands behind the cathedral.

Also on Domplatz is the **Neue Residenz** (1695–1704), with its richly decorated apartments. Inside, the Staatsgalerie has a collection of old German masters.

On the east side of the town, the **Altes Rathaus** was originally Gothic in style, but was remodeled in 1744–56 by Jakob Michael Küchel.

Bamberger Reiter (Bamberg Rider) in the city's cathedral

🏛 **Neue Residenz**
Domplatz 8. **Tel** 0951-519 390.
⭘ daily. 🖼

Würzburg ❼

🏠 130,000. 🔲 🚹 Marktplatz, Am Falkenhaus (0931-37 23 35).

Located on the bank of the Main river, Würzburg is an important cultural and commercial center, and home of the excellent Franconian wine.

The city's most impressive landmark is the **Residenz**, where Würzburg's prince-bishops lived from 1744. A highlight of this lavish Baroque palace is the huge Treppenhaus (staircase), by Balthasar Neumann (1687–1753). Above it is a glorious ceiling fresco by the Venetian artist, Giovanni Battista Tiepolo.

Before the Residenz was built, the city's prince-bishops resided in the fortress known as the **Festung Marienberg**, which has stood on a hill overlooking the river since 1210. The Mainfränkisches Museum, housed inside the fortress, illustrates the history of the town and holds a number of works by the renowned German sculptor Tilman Riemen-schneider (1460–1531).

Würzburg's cathedral, the **Dom St. Kilian**, dates from 1045 and is one of Germany's largest Romanesque churches. North of it is the 11th-century basilica **Neumünster**. Its imposing Baroque dome and sandstone façade are 18th-century additions. Dating from the 13th century, the picturesque **Rathaus** (Town Hall) has a late-Renaissance tower, added in 1660.

🏛 **Residenz**
Residenzplatz 2. **Tel** 0931-35 51 70. ⭘ daily. 🖼

♠ **Festung Marienberg**
🎨 Apr–Oct: 11am, 2pm, 3pm Tue–Fri; 10am, 11am, 1pm, 2pm, 3pm, 4pm Sat–Sun. 🖼 **Mainfränkisches Museum Tel** 0931-205 940. ⭘ Tue–Sun. 🖼

Neumann's stunning Treppenhaus (staircase) at Würzburg's Residenz

Rothenburg ob der Tauber ❽

🏘 *12,000.* 🚉 ℹ️ *Marktplatz 2 (09861-40 48 00).*

Encircled by ramparts, Rothenburg is a perfectly preserved medieval town in a picturesque setting on the banks of the Tauber river.

At the heart of the town is Marktplatz, whose focal point is the **Rathaus** (Town Hall), combining Renaissance and Gothic styles. Off the main square, **St. Jakobs Kirche** (1373–1464) and the **Franziskanerkirche** both contain many historical treasures.

Two museums of note are the **Reichsstadtmuseum**, devoted to the town's history, and the **Mittelalterliches Museum**, which contains a large collection of medieval instruments of torture.

Through the Burgtor, a gateway in the city walls, you arrive at the **Burggarten** – pretty gardens giving views over the town and river.

Rothenburg's Rathaus (Town Hall), begun in the 14th century

massive 15th and 16th-century ramparts. A short walk away is the **Germanisches Nationalmuseum**. Founded in 1853, the museum houses a superb collection of antiquities from the German-speaking world, including masterworks by Tilman Riemenschneider, Lucas Cranach the Elder (1472–1553), and Albrecht Dürer (1471–1528).

Overlooking the bustling Lorenzer Platz, the Gothic **St. Lorenz-Kirche** is one of the city's most important churches. Begun in 1270, it boasts some glorious stained-glass windows.

As you cross over the Pegnitz to the north side of town, look out for the **Heilig-Geist-Spital** (Hospital of the Holy Spirit), which dates from 1332 and spans the river.

A major landmark north of the river is the **Frauenkirche**, commissioned by the Holy Roman Emperor Charles IV in the mid-14th century. Also of importance is the **Albrecht-Dürer-Haus**, where the

celebrated Renaissance painter lived in 1509–28. Copies of a wide selection of his works are on display here.

A climb up Burgstrasse brings you to the **Kaiserburg**, the imperial castle complex. The oldest surviving part is a pentagonal tower, the **Fünfeckturm**, which dates from 1040. At its foot is the Kaiserstallung (Imperial Stables), now a youth hostel.

At the Christkindlmarkt, the lively Christmas fair held during Advent in the Hauptmarkt, you can warm yourself with a glass of hot red wine spiced with cloves and buy locally made crafts.

🏛 **Germanisches Nationalmuseum**
Kornmarkt. *Tel 0911-13 310.* 🕐 *Tue–Sun.* 🈚

🏛 **Albrecht-Dürer-Haus**
Albrecht–Dürer-Strasse 39. *Tel 0911-231 25 68.* 🕐 *Tue–Sun.* 🈚 🈲

Nuremberg ❾

🏘 *490,000.* ✈️ 🚉 ℹ️ *Königstrasse 93 (0911-233 60).*

The largest town in Bavaria after Munich, Nuremberg (Nürnberg) flourished in the 15th and 16th centuries, when many prominent artists, craftsmen, and intellectuals worked here, making it a leading European cultural center. The city is divided in two by the Pegnitz river. In the southern half, the mighty **Frauentor** is one of several gateways in the

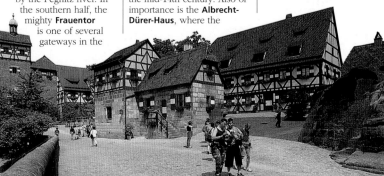
The half-timbered buildings of Nuremberg's Kaiserburg at the top of Burgstrasse

Munich ⑩

Founded in 1158, Munich became the capital of Bavaria in the 16th century. The town rapidly overshadowed once powerful neighbors, such as Augsburg and Nuremberg, to become southern Germany's main metropolis. The period of greatest growth was in the 19th century, when the city was developed along Neoclassical lines. Many of the grand buildings around Königsplatz and along Ludwigstrasse date from this time. As well as historic monuments, Munich has first-class museums and excellent shopping. It also hosts the world-famous annual beer festival, the Oktoberfest.

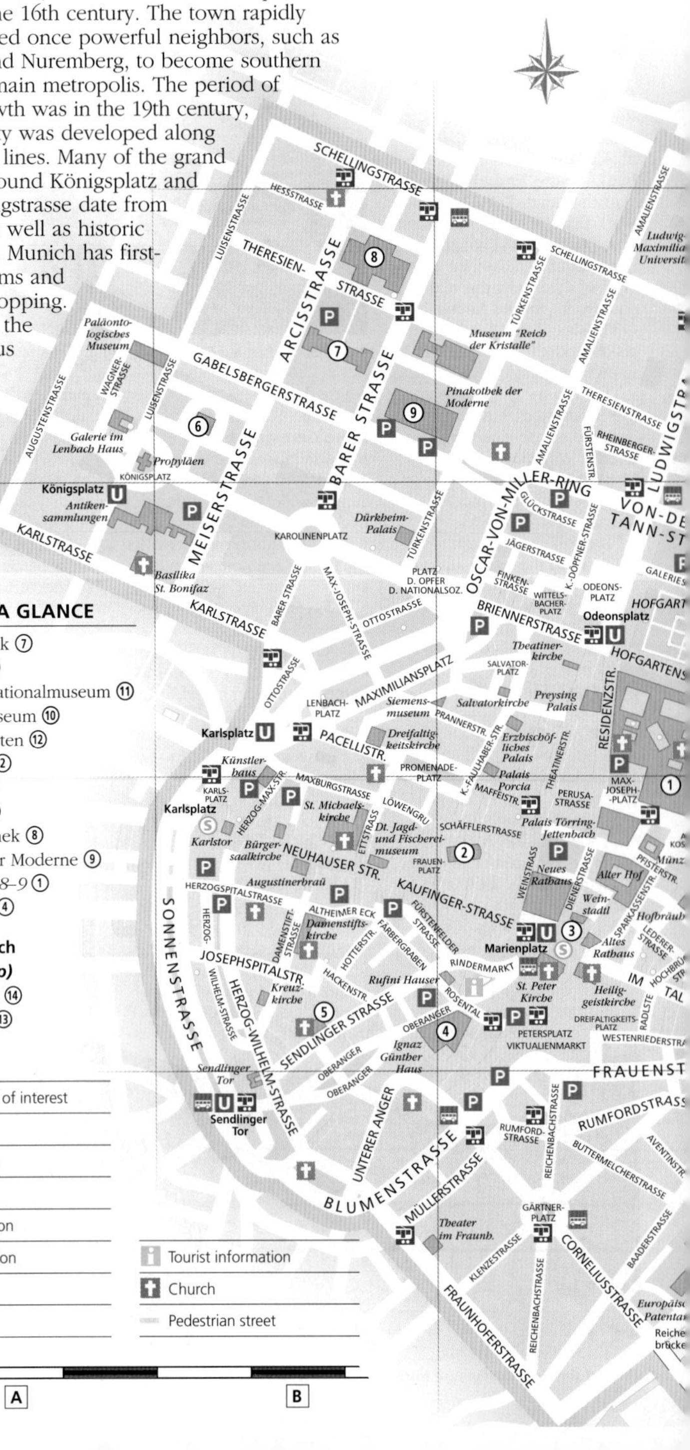

SIGHTS AT A GLANCE

Alte Pinakothek ⑦
Asamkirche ⑤
Bayerisches Nationalmuseum ⑪
Deutsches Museum ⑩
Englischer Garten ⑫
Frauenkirche ②
Glyptothek ⑥
Marienplatz ③
Neue Pinakothek ⑧
Pinakothek der Moderne ⑨
Residenz pp548–9 ①
Stadtmuseum ④

**Greater Munich
(see inset map)**
Nymphenburg ⑭
Olympiapark ⑬

KEY

- ▪ Sight / Place of interest
- ✈ Airport
- 🚉 Train station
- 🚋 Tram stop
- Ⓢ S-Bahn station
- Ⓤ U-Bahn station
- 🚌 Bus stop
- 🅿 Parking
- ℹ Tourist information
- ✝ Church
- — Pedestrian street

A   B

GETTING AROUND

Most of the main sights of interest can be reached by Munich's efficient U- and S-Bahn train networks, including sights located farther afield, such as Olympia-park and Nymphenburg. Buses and trams also serve many of the main tourist spots. There is a large pedestrianized zone at the heart of the city making walking a pleasant alternative to public transportation.

GREATER MUNICH

Nuremberg
Freimann
Munich Airport

Moosach

Ober-menzing

Gern

⑬

Schwabing

Bogenhausen

Nymphen-burg ⑭

Neuhsn.

Hauptbahnhof

Laim

Haid-hausen

Berg am Laim

Landsberg

Giesing

Salzburg

0 km 3

0 miles 3

1

2

KEY

■ Area of main map

PROF.-HUBER-PLATZ

VETERINÄRSTR.

versität

Ludwigskirche

KAULBACHSTRASSE

ENGLISCHER GARTEN

Bayerische Staatsbibliothek

KÖNIGINSTRASSE

SCHÖNFELDSTRASSE

⑫

HAHNEN-STRASSE

LERCHENFELDSTRASSE

ROSEN-BUSCHSTR.

Haus der Kunst

PRINZREGENTENSTRASSE

Prähistorische Staatssamm-lung

OETTINGENSTRASSE

REITMORSTRASSE

AM GRIES

Neue Staats-kanzlei

STRAUSS-RING

SEITZSTRASSE

PILOTYSTR.

BRUDERSTRASSE

UNSÖLDSTRASSE

WAGMÜLLER-STRASSE

ALEXANDRASTR.

⑪

Schackgalerie

REITMORSTR.

Luitpoldbr.

3

Marstall

SCHARNAGL-RING

SEITZSTRASSE

ST. LIEBIGSTRASSE

Anna-kirche

ST.-ANNA-PLATZ

ST.-ANNA-STRASSE

R.-KOCH-STR.

TATTENBACH-STRASSE

LIEBIGSTRASSE

STERNSTRASSE

WIDENMAYERSTRASSE

Isar

MARSTALLSTR.

Anna Klosterkirche

U Lehel

BÜRKLEINSTRASSE

Regierung von Oberbayern

THIERSCH-TRIFTSTR.-STRASSE

GEWÜRZMÜHL-STRASSE

SEE ALSO

• **Where to Stay** pp575–6

• **Where to Eat** p582

MAXIMILIANSTRASSE

Kammer-spiele

HILDEGARDSTRASSE

HERRNSTRASSE

MARIENSTR.

TH. WIMMER-RING

KNÖBELSTRASSE

ADELGUNDEN-STRASSE

Völkerkunde-museum

Maximiliansbr.

PRATER-INSEL

4

MANNHARDT-STRASSE

THIERSCHSTRASSE

Mariannenbr.

PRATERINSEL

Isartor-PLATZ

Isartor

THIERSCHSTR.

Kabelsteg

ISARTOR-PLATZ

ZWEIBRÜCKENSTR.

STEINSDORFSTRASSE

WEINSTEG

Weur

AUF DER INSEL

MORASSTRASSE

ERHARDTSTRASSE

Ludwigsbr.

MUSEUMS-INSEL

Bosch-br.

⑩

Zenneckbr.

0 meters 400

0 yards 400

St. Mary's column and the Neo-Gothic Neues Rathaus towering over Marienplatz

5

E

F

Residenz ①

The origins of Munich's grand Residenz – the former residence of Bavarian kings – go back to the 14th century, when a castle was built here for the Wittelsbach dynasty. In the following centuries the fortress was replaced by a palace complex, which in turn was gradually modified and extended. Major work in the 17th century included the construction of two chapels, the Reiche Kapelle and the Hofkapelle. The Königsbau, containing the superb Nibelungensäle, was added by Leo von Klenze in the first half of the 19th century. Since 1920 the palace has been open to the public as a museum, displaying a wealth of magnificent treasures. In addition to the collections of the Residenzmuseum and the Schatzkammer (Treasury), there is an interesting museum of Egyptian art, the Staatliches Museum Ägyptischer Kunst.

Hofkapelle
This imposing chapel, which dates from the early 17th century, was modeled on nearby St. Michael's Church.

The Staatliches Museum Ägyptischer Kunst (Museum of Egyptian Art) is housed in this wing of the Residenz.

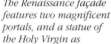

Patrona Boiariae
The Renaissance façade features two magnificent portals, and a statue of the Holy Virgin as Patroness of Bavaria (Patrona Boiariae).

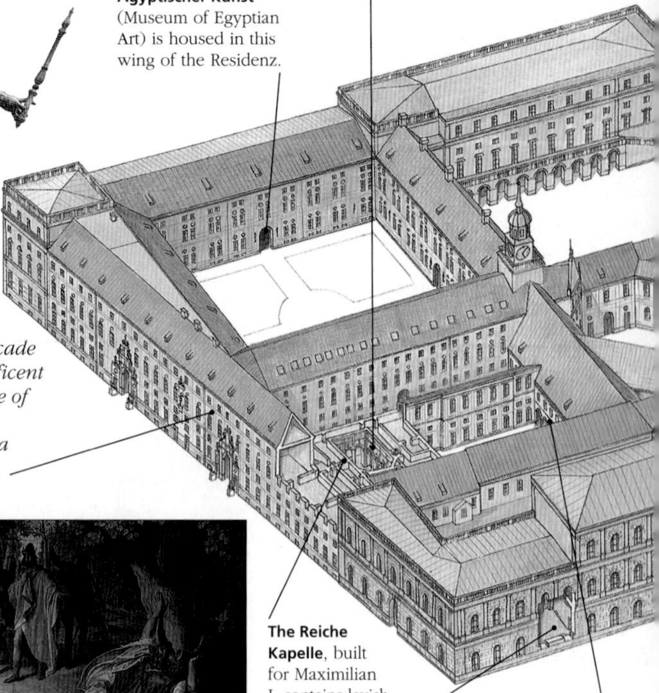

The Reiche Kapelle, built for Maximilian I, contains lavish furnishings.

Grottenhof (Grotto Court)

★ **Nibelungensäle**
The Nibelungensäle (Halls of the Nibelungs), a series of five rooms in the Königsbau, take their name from the wall paintings depicting scenes from the great German epic, the Nibelungenlied.

STAR FEATURES

★ Nibelungensäle

★ Schatzkammer

★ Antiquarium

For hotels and restaurants in this region see pp575–6 and p582

★ **Antiquarium**
This magnificent vaulted chamber, with its stunning frescoes, was begun in the second half of the 16th century to house the royal collection of antiquities.

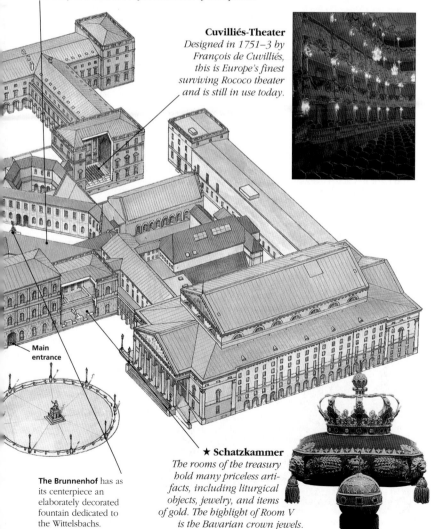

Cuvilliés-Theater
Designed in 1751–3 by François de Cuvilliés, this is Europe's finest surviving Rococo theater and is still in use today.

Main entrance

The Brunnenhof has as its centerpiece an elaborately decorated fountain dedicated to the Wittelsbachs.

★ **Schatzkammer**
The rooms of the treasury hold many priceless arti-facts, including liturgical objects, jewelry, and items of gold. The highlight of Room V is the Bavarian crown jewels.

Frauenkirche ②

Frauenplatz 1. **U** or **S** *Karlsplatz, Marienplatz.* 🚋 19. **Tower** ◯ *Apr–Oct: Mon–Sat.*

The site of the Frauenkirche was originally occupied by a small chapel dedicated to the Virgin Mary, built in the 13th century. Some 200 years later, a new, much larger church was built here by the architects Jörg von Halspach and Lukas Rottaler. The new Frauenkirche (or Dom) was completed in 1488, although the distinctive copper onion domes were not added to its towers until 1525. The church is one of southern Germany's largest Gothic structures. Over 100 m (330 ft) long and 40 m (130 ft) wide, it can accommodate a congregation of about 2,000 people. The vast triple-naved hall has no transept. There are long rows of side chapels and a gallery surrounding the choir. For a good view of central Munich, you can take an elevator to the top of one of the towers.

Partly demolished in 1944–5, the church was rebuilt after World War II. Church treasures that escaped destruction include a painting of the Virgin by Jan Polack (c.1500), the altar of St. Andrew in the Chapel of St. Sebastian, and the huge monumental tomb of Ludwig IV the Bavarian, the first member of the house of Wittelsbach to be elected Holy Roman Emperor (c.1283–1347). The monument was the work of Hans Krumpper (1619–22).

Altes Rathaus and the Talbruktor on Marienplatz

Marienplatz ③

U or **S** *Marienplatz.* **Spielzeugmuseum** *Tel 089-29 40 01.* ◯ *daily.* www.toymuseum.de

In medieval times Marienplatz was Munich's salt- and corn-market. In the center stands a column with a statue of the Virgin Mary dating from 1623. The square is dominated by the Neo-Gothic **Neues Rathaus** (New Town Hall), built in 1867–1909. Its walls are adorned with statues of Bavarian rulers, mythological figures, saints, and monstrous gargoyles. At 11am and 5pm the center of attention is the clocktower. The bells ring out a carillon, while figures of knights fight a tournament and a crowd dances. The dance is the "Coopers' Dance," first performed in 1517 to raise citizens' morale during a plague epidemic.

At the eastern end of the square stands the **Altes Rathaus** (Old Town Hall). Originally built in the late 15th century, it has been rebuilt many times since. The high tower, above the old city gate beside the town hall, was rebuilt in 1975 to a design based on pictures dating from 1493. Since 1983 the tower has been the home of the city's **Spielzeugmuseum** (toy museum).

Stadtmuseum ④

St. Jakobsplatz 1. *Tel 089-23 32 23 70.* **U** or **S** *Marienplatz.* **U** *Sendlinger Tor.* ◯ *Tue–Sun.*

The collection of the city museum has been housed since 1880 in the former arsenal, built in 1491–3 by Lukas Rottaler. It is filled with exhibits illustrating daily life in Munich throughout the ages. One of the museum's greatest treasures is the "Dancing Moors" by Erasmus Grasser (1480), which used to decorate the ballroom of the Altes Rathaus. Originally there were 18 highly expressive limewood carvings of dancing figures surrounding the figure of a woman, but only ten survive.

The Waffenhalle on the ground floor has a fine collection of arms and armor. There are also fascinating displays of furniture, paintings, prints, posters, photographs, brewing equipment, dolls, and musical instruments. The vast doll collection includes paper dolls from India and China, as well as automata and puppets. The museum stages regular temporary exhibitions and there is also a film museum and a cinema with nightly screenings.

Asamkirche ⑤

Sendlinger Strasse 32. **U** *Sendlinger Tor.* 🚋 16, 17, 18, 27. 🚌 52, 152. ◯ *daily.*

This extraordinary Rococo church is dedicated to St. John Nepomuk, but is known as the Asamkirche after the brothers Cosmas Damian and

The distinctive onion domes of the Frauenkirche rising above the city

For hotels and restaurants in this region see pp575–6 and p582

Egid Quirin Asam, who built it as a private family church. Completed in 1746, the tiny church is a riot of decoration with a dynamically shaped single nave, where no surface is left unembellished. The eye is drawn to the altar, and its sculptural group of the Holy Trinity. The house next door to the church was the residence of Egid Quirin Asam, who was a stuccoist and sculptor. From one of the windows of his house he could see the altar.

The richly decorated altar of the Rococo Asamkirche

Glyptothek ⑥

Königsplatz 3. **Tel** 089-28 61 00. **U** Königsplatz. ◯ Tue–Sun. 📷
Staatliche Antikensammlung
Königsplatz 1. **Tel** 089-59 98 88 30. ◯ Tue–Sun. 📷

On the northern side of Königsplatz stands the Glyptothek, a collection of Greek and Roman sculpture, notably statues from the Temple of Aphaia on the Greek island of Aegina. The museum's imposing façade, with the portico of an Ionic temple at the center, is part of a kind of Neoclassical forum created in the first half of the 19th century to house the archaeological finds acquired by King Ludwig I of Bavaria. On the opposite side of the square, the **Staatliche Antikensammlung** houses smaller treasures, in particular a vast array of Greek vases.

Alte Pinakothek ⑦

Barer Strasse 27. **Tel** 089-23 80 52 16. **U** Königsplatz. 🚊 27. 🚌 53. ◯ Tue–Sun. 📷 ♿

This magnificent gallery is filled with masterpieces of European art from the Middle Ages to the mid-18th century. Many of the Wittelsbach rulers of Bavaria were great collectors, the first being Wilhelm IV the Steadfast, who ruled from 1508 to 1550. The Alte Pinakothek (Old Picture Gallery) was built for Ludwig I by Leo von Klenze in 1826–36 in the form of a Florentine Renaissance palazzo. The ground floor is devoted to the works of German and Flemish Old Masters from the 16th and 17th centuries. On the first floor are works by Dutch, Flemish, French, German, Italian, and Spanish artists.

Of the German works, pride of place goes to Albrecht Dürer's famous *Self-Portrait* (1500) and two panels of an altarpiece showing *Four Apostles*. Among the other German artists represented are Lucas Cranach the Elder and Grünewald. Early Flemish

Four Apostles (1526) by Albrecht Dürer, in the Alte Pinakothek

masterpieces include *St. Luke Painting the Madonna* by Rogier van der Weyden, and works by Hans Memling and Pieter Brueghel the Elder.

Of later artists, the one with most works on display is the prolific Rubens. There are also interesting works by El Greco, Rembrandt, Raphael, Titian, and Tintoretto.

Neue Pinakothek ⑧

Barer Strasse 29. **Tel** 089-23 80 51 95. **U** Theresienstrasse. 🚊 2. 🚌 27. ◯ Wed–Mon. 📷

Bavaria's collection of late 18th- and 19th-century European painting and sculpture occupies a purpose-built gallery completed in 1981. German painting of every artistic movement of the 19th century, including Romanticism, the "Nazarenes", German and Austrian Biedermeier, and Impressionism is well represented. There are also works by French Realists, Impressionists, and Symbolists purchased when the gallery's director was the art historian Hugo von Tschudi.

The open space between the Neue and Alte Pinakothek has been turned into a sculpture park.

Neoclassical façade of the Glyptothek, which houses a collection of Greek and Roman sculpture

Pinakothek der Moderne ⑨

Barer Strasse 40. *Tel* 089-23 80 53 60. **U** *Königsplatz.* 🚋 27. 🚌 53. ⭘ *10am–6pm Tue–Sun (to 8pm Thu).* 🎦 *except Sun.* ♿ ▣
www.pinakothek-der-moderne.de

Designed by the German architect Stephan Braunfels, this new museum brings together the worlds of art, design, graphics, and architecture under one roof. The collections of four previously separate museums, including the Staatliche Graphische Sammlung, the design collection of Die Neue Sammlung, and the models, drawings, and objects of the Architekturmuseum, are now housed here. As well as the individual permanent displays, there are also temporary and mixed exhibitions.

Deutsches Museum ⑩

Museuminsel 1. *Tel* 089-217 91. Ⓢ *Isartor.* 🚋 18. 🚌 52, 56. ⭘ *daily.* 🎦 www.deutsches-museum.de

Reputed to be the largest science and technology museum in the world, the Deutsches Museum is also the most popular museum in Germany. Founded in 1904, the vast collection features more than 18,000 exhibits across a wide range of subject areas, from agriculture to telecommunications.

In the basement and on the ground floor are some of the museum's largest exhibits. The aeronautics section holds an aeroplane that belonged to the Wright brothers and a 1936

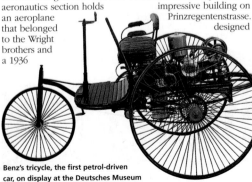

Benz's tricycle, the first petrol-driven car, on display at the Deutsches Museum

Neapolitan crib in the Bayerisches Nationalmuseum

Messerschmitt ME 109. A hall charting the history of seafaring houses a 14th-century cog, a trading ship used by the Hanseatic League, and a 19th-century fishing vessel.

The museums's superb collection of automobiles and other exhibits related to land travel is now largely on display in the Deutsches Museum Verkehrszentrum at Theresienhöhe 14a, in the west of the city.

Temporary exhibitions are regularly held at the museum, which also has an excellent library archive and a range of multimedia facilities.

Bayerisches Nationalmuseum ⑪

Prinzregentenstrasse 3. *Tel* 089 211 24 01. 🚋 17. 🚌 100. ⭘ *Tue –Sun.*

Founded in 1855 by King Maximilian II, the Bavarian National Museum holds a superb collection of fine and applied arts and historical artifacts. Since 1900 the museum has occupied an impressive building on Prinzregentenstrasse. designed

by Gabriel von Seidl. The ground floor contains works from the Romanesque, Gothic, Renaissance, Baroque, and Neoclassical periods. Star exhibits are German sculptor Conrat Meit's *Judith* (1515) and a beautiful sculpture of the Madonna by Tilman Riemenschneider (c.1460 --1531). The first-floor collections include German porcelain, clocks, glassware, ivory carvings, textiles, and items of gold.

In the basement rooms, the Christmas nativity scenes by Bavarian and Italian artists are especially worth seeing.

Englischer Garten ⑫

U *Giselastrasse.* 🚌 54.

The idea of creating a park in the heart of the city open to all Munich's citizens came from the American-born Count von Rumford, who lived in Bavaria from 1784. In 1789, taking advantage of his position as Bavaria's Minister of War, he persuaded Elector Karl Theodor to put his plans into action. Opened in 1808, the Karl-Theodor-Park is today simply known as the Englischer Garten (English Garden). The park covers an area of 3.7 sq km (914 acres), and has become a popular place for walking, jogging, or simply relaxing.

Several interesting buildings dotted about the gardens include the Monopteros, a Neoclassical temple (1837) by Leo von Klenze, and the Chinese Tower (1789–90), similar to the pagoda in

London's Kew Gardens *(see p63)*. In the delightful Japanese Teahouse, demonstrations on the art of tea brewing are held. Within the Englischer Garten are three beer gardens, where locals and tourists alike come to drink and listen to live music. Visitors can also take out rowing boats on the park's lake, the Kleinhesseloher See.

The late 18th-century Chinese Tower in the Englischer Garten

Olympiapark ⑬

Tel 089-30 67 24 14. **U** *Olympia-zentrum.* 🚊 *20, 25, 27.* **Pavilion** ◯ *Apr–Oct: daily; Nov–Mar: Mon–Fri.*

Built for the 1972 Olympic Games, the Olympiapark is visible from almost anywhere in Munich, identifiable by the 290-m (950-ft) high television tower, the Olympiaturm. The site has three main facilities: the Olympic stadium, which seats over 60,000 spectators, the Olympic Hall, and the Swimming Hall. All three are covered by a vast transparent canopy, stretched between several tall masts to form an irregular-shaped pavilion. Also within the complex are an indoor skating rink, a cycle racing track, and tennis courts.

As well as sporting occasions, the Olympiapark hosts many popular cultural events, such as fireworks displays and open-air rock and pop concerts during the summer months.

Schloss Nymphenburg ⑭

Tel 089-17 90 80. **U** *Rotkreuzplatz.* ◯ *daily.* 🎟 **Botanischer Garten** ◯ *daily.* 🎟

Located northwest of the city center, the stunning Schloss Nymphenburg grew up around an Italianate villa, built in 1663–4 for Electress Henrietta-Adelaide. The Electress dedicated the palace, which became the summer residence of the Wittelsbachs, to the pastoral pleasures of the goddess Flora and her nymphs, hence the name. Several additions were made in the following century, including the construction of four pavilions, connected to the original villa by arcaded passageways.

The palace's interior boasts some magnificent examples of the Rococo style. One of the most impressive rooms is the **Festsaal** – a sumptuous ballroom, designed by father and son, Johann Baptiste and Franz Zimmermann. Equally impressive is the **Schön-heitengalerie** (Gallery of Beauties). Hanging here are 38 portraits of beautiful women – favorites of King Ludwig I. The palace also houses a small natural history and science museum. The old stables are now home to the **Marstallmuseum**, a collection of wonderfully ornate carriages that once belonged to Bavarian rulers.

Interior of the Amalienburg, in the grounds of Schloss Nymphenburg

The approach to the palace is dominated by a broad canal, bordered by immac-ulately presented gardens. On the edge of the gardens is the Porcelain Factory, established in 1741, and one of the oldest factories of its type in Europe.

Behind the palace stretches the **Schlosspark**, an English-style country park dotted with lakes and various royal lodges. The most notable of these is François de Cuvilliés's **Amalienburg**, a hunting lodge with a lavish Rococo interior. Its highlight is the splendid Spiegelsaal (Hall of Mirrors). Joseph Effner, the principal architect of the palace's extensions, was also responsible for designing the **Pagodenburg**, used for entertaining, and the Baroque bathing house, the **Badenburg**. Also in the park is the **Magdalenenklause**, built as a hermitage for Maximilian Emmanuel, but not completed until after the Elector's death in 1725.

North of the palace, the **Botanischer Garten** (Botanical Garden) holds many rare and exotic species.

Façade of the splendid Schloss Nymphenburg, begun in the 17th century

The Beers of Germany

Although Germany produces many fine wines, it is for its beer that the country has won worldwide renown. Nowhere is the business of brewing and beer drinking taken so seriously as in Munich. Bavarians are probably the world's greatest consumers of beer, with an annual average intake of 240 liters per head. However, this figure is possibly inflated by the vast

Logo of the Paulaner brewery in Munich

quantities downed at the annual Oktoberfest, during which some 7 million lovers of beer converge on Munich for 16 days of revelry lasting from late September to early October. When traveling in Germany, make a point of trying the specialties of the local brewery, in a *Bierkeller* (beer cellar) or *Bierstube* (pub) in winter, and in summer in a *Biergarten* (beer garden).

The tankard *known as a* Mass *(measure) holds one liter, although German beer is always served with a considerable head on it. Waitresses at the Oktoberfest have no difficulty carrying eight or nine of these at once.*

Munich's Oktoberfest *attracts so many visitors, a great tented village, with stalls, a funfair, and loud music, is set up on Theresienwiese, just to the west of the city center. This open space was where the marriage of King Ludwig was celebrated in 1810.*

Paulaner Pilsener   **Löwenbräu Pilsener**

PILSENER

The most widely drunk beer in Germany is Pils (short for Pilsener), a light lager-style beer produced by bottom-fermentation. This method was perfected in Pilsen (Plzeň in the Czech Republic) in the 19th century. Fermentation occurs at low temperatures, so takes longer than with other beers. The essential ingredients are barley, hops, and crystal-clear water. Two of the main breweries producing this kind of beer in Munich are Löwenbräu and Paulaner.

OTHER GERMAN BEERS

Germany produces many varieties of beer, some of which are brewed only at certain times of year. Of these seasonal beers, it is worth trying spring beers such as the strong *Maibock*. Other interesting beers include dark styles – known as *Dunkelbier* or *Schwarzbier* – and *Weizenbier*, a beer made from wheat rather than barley. The Berlin version of the latter, *Berliner Weisse* (white beer), is served with fruit juice. Many local breweries have their own specialties. Bamberg is famous for its *Rauchbier*, which has a light smokiness. In the lower Rhine valley, *Altbier* is still produced; this is a top-fermented beer, prepared by traditional methods.

Berliner Weisse (wheat beer)   **Dunkel-bier**   **Oktoberfest beer**

St. Stephans Dom, Passau's imposing Baroque cathedral

Passau ⑪

🏛 50,000. 🚉 🚌 ℹ Rathaus-
platz 3 (0851-95 59 80).

Passau lies on a peninsula
between the Danube and the
Inn, near the Austrian border.
In 739 the Irish monk St.
Boniface founded a major
bishopric here. After two
destructive fires
in 1662 and 1680,
the town was
rebuilt by Italian
architects, who
left many fine
Baroque build-
ings, including
the cathedral, **St.
Stephans Dom**.
However, the
town retains a
medieval feel in
its narrow alleys
and archways. The Gothic
town hall dates from the 14th
and 15th centuries. Opposite it
is the **Passauer Glasmuseum**,
which has a fine collection of
Bohemian, Austrian, and
Bavarian glass. High above the
Inn stands a pretty Baroque
pilgrimage church, the
Wallfahrtskirche Mariahilf.

Neuschwanstein ⑫

🚌 to Schwangau. **Tel** 08362-93 98
80. ⭕ Oct–Mar: 10am–4pm daily;
Apr–Sep: 9am–6pm daily. 📷 📹
♿ (limited access).

Set amid magnificent
mountain scenery on the
shores of the Alpsee, this
fairy-tale castle was built in

1869–86 for the eccentric
Bavarian King Ludwig II, to a
design by the theater designer
Christian Jank. Its pinnacled
turrets have provided the
inspiration for countless
models, book illustrations,
and film sets.

The walls of the vestibule
and other rooms in the castle
are lavishly covered with paintings depicting
scenes from
German myths
and legends. The
gilded interior of
the throne room
is reminiscent
of a Byzantine
basilica, while the
dining room has
intricately carved
panels and fabu-
lous pictures and
furniture. The
pale grey granite castle, which
draws on a variety of historical
styles, is a 20-minute walk
from the village of Schwangau.

In the village itself is
another castle, **Schloss
Hohenschwangau**, built in
1832 by Maximilian, heir to
the throne of Bavaria, over
the ruins of a medieval castle.
A tour of the Neo-Gothic
castle gives a fascinating
insight into the history of the
Wittelsbach family, rulers of
Bavaria from 1180 to 1918.
There are also some fine
19th-century furnishings and
the castle's terraced gardens
afford magnificent views.

**Gilded apse of the throne
room, Neuschwanstein**

⛪ **Schloss Hohenschwangau**
Tel 08362-819 80. ⭕ daily.
⬤ Dec 24. 📷 📹

Lake Constance ⑬

🚉 Konstanz. 🚌 ℹ Bahnhofsplatz
13, Konstanz (07531-13 30 30).

Lake Constance (in German,
the Bodensee) lies on the
borders of Germany, Austria,
and Switzerland. The area
surrounding the lake is one of
the most attractive in Germany,
in terms of both natural beauty
and cultural heritage. The best
time to visit is summer, when
local fishermen stage colorful
festivals and there are plenty
of opportunities for water
sports and cruises on the lake.

Konstanz (Constance) is the
largest town in the region,
and its main attraction is the
magnificent 11th-century
Romanesque cathedral. The
town is in two parts: the old
town (Altstadt) is a German
enclave in Switzerland on the
southern shore, while the
newer part stands on a
peninsula between the two
main arms of the lake.

The many romantic old
towns and beautiful islands
of Lake Constance attract
hordes of visitors every
summer. The exquisite little
town of **Meersburg** opposite
Konstanz is a very popular
destination. So too is **Mainau**,
the "Island of Flowers." The
most beautiful gardens on the
island are in the park of the
Baroque palace, built in
1739–46. At the northeastern
(Bavarian) end of the lake,
the medieval island town of
Lindau is the major draw.

Lake Constance, with the Swiss Alps
rising above the southern shore

For hotels and restaurants in this region see pp574–9 and pp580–85

Baden-Württemberg

Baden-Württemberg, which includes territories of the former Grand Duchy of Baden, is one of Germany's most popular tourist destinations. Its magnificent castles, luxurious resorts, and the beautiful recreation areas of the Black Forest guarantee a memorable vacation, while the region's long and turbulent history has given it a rich cultural and religious diversity. Germany's oldest university, Heidelberg, is also located in the region.

Rembrandt's *St. Paul in Prison* (1627), Staatsgalerie, Stuttgart

The Kaufhaus, Freiburg's historic merchants' meeting hall

Freiburg im Breisgau ⑭

🏠 *197,000.* 🚉 🚌 🛈 *Rotteckring 14 (0761-388 18 80).* 🎭 *Fasnet (end of carnival), Weintage (Jun).*

Freiburg is a natural gateway to the Black Forest. The counts von Zähringen first established the town in 1120, and since 1805 it has been part of Baden. From the Middle Ages, fast-flowing canals, or *bächle*, have run through the town, providing water to help extinguish the once frequent fires.

The **cathedral** was built in the 13th century in Gothic style. Münsterplatz, the picturesque cathedral square, is lined with houses from various architectural periods.

Completed in 1520, with ground-floor arcades and richly adorned gables, the **Kaufhaus** was used by merchants for meetings and conferences.

Black Forest ⑮

🚉 *to Freiburg.* 🚌 *to all towns.* 🛈 *Wehratalstrasse 19, Todtmoos (07674-906 00).* **www**.todtmoos.de

Densely planted with tall firs and spruces, the Black Forest (Schwarzwald) is one of Germany's most picturesque

regions. The area is famous for *Schwarzwälder Kirschtorte* (Black Forest gateau) and *Kirschwasser* (schnaps), as well as for its therapeutic spring waters.

Todtnau is a popular sports center and a base for hikers. Nearby, Hangloch-Wasserfall is one of the most magnificent waterfalls in the region.

The heart of the resort of **Todtmoos** is the Baroque pilgrimage church, which dates from the 17th–18th centuries. Popular dog-sled races are held annually in the town.

In the health resort of **St. Blasien** stands a Benedictine Abbey, founded in the 9th century. Its church (1783) is an excellent example of early Neoclassical style.

The main attraction of **Furtwangen** is its clock museum (Uhrenmuseum), which houses a collection of more than 4,000 chronometers.

In the open-air museum near the small town of **Gutach** visitors can see the Black Forest's oldest house – the 16th-century Vogtsbauernhof.

Stuttgart ⑯

🏠 *586,000.* ✈ 🚉 🚌
🛈 *Königstrasse 1A (0711-222 820).*

Stuttgart grew from humble beginnings as a stud farm to become the ducal and royal capital of Württemberg. It is now one of the largest and most important towns of the Federal Republic. Beautifully situated among picturesque hills, the town is a major industrial and cultural center, with a world-famous ballet company, chamber orchestra, and splendid art collections.

When Württemberg castle burned down in 1311, the family seat was moved to Stuttgart. The ducal residence, the **Altes Schloss**, was given its present square layout in 1553–78. The palace now houses the Württembergisches Landesmuseum, which holds vast collections of decorative art and jewelry.

The Vogtsbauernhof in Gutach, the oldest house in the Black Forest

On the east side of Stuttgart's main square is a huge palace complex, the **Neues Schloss**, built in 1746–1807. The palace gardens have maintained much of their original charm, with neat avenues and impressive sculptures.

The **Staatsgalerie** grew from a fine art museum containing King Wilhelm I of Württemberg's private collection. Among the Old Masters on display are Rembrandt and Bellini, while modern artists include Monet, Picasso, and Modigliani.

A building exhibition held in 1927 left behind a complete housing estate, the **Weissenhofsiedlung**, which contains houses by Mies van der Rohe, Le Corbusier, Peter Behrens, and Hans Scharoun. Another must for all lovers of modern architecture, the **Liederhalle** congress center is a successful synthesis of tradition and modernism.

The **Linden Museum** is one of Germany's finest ethnology museums, containing exhibits from all over the world. Figures from the Indonesian theater of shadows and a 6th–8th-century mask from Peru are among the eclectic items on display.

To the east of the center is the famous **Mercedes-Benz-Museum**. Its splendid collection illustrates the development of the automobile with over 70 historic vehicles, all in immaculate condition. Stuttgart's other famous car manufacturer has created the **Porsche-Museum**, which includes around 50 examples of these high-speed, expensive vehicles.

Once an independent health resort, **Bad Cannstatt** is now a district of Stuttgart. Set in a beautiful park, it has a late-Gothic church, a Neoclassical town hall, and a *kursaal* (spa-house). One of its main attractions is the Neoclassical Schloss Rosenstein (1824–9).

🏛 **Staatsgalerie**
Konrad-Adenauer-Strasse 30–32.
Tel 0711-470 400. ◻ *Tue–Sun.*
🎫 (free Wed).

🏛 **Mercedes-Benz-Museum**
Mercedesstrasse 137. *Tel* 0711-172 25 78. ◻ *Tue–Sun.*

Classic cars on display in the Mercedes-Benz-Museum, Stuttgart

Heidelberg ⓱

🏘 *139,000.* 🚉 🚌
ℹ *Hauptbahnhof (06221-194 33).*

Situated on the banks of the Neckar river, Heidelberg is one of Germany's most beautiful towns. For centuries it was a center of political power, with a lively and influential cultural life. In 1386, Germany's first university was established here by the Elector Ruprecht I. The construction of the town's palace began during his reign, continuing until the mid-17th century. However,

French incursions in the late 17th century totally destroyed medieval Heidelberg. The town was subsequently rebuilt in the 18th-century in Baroque style.

Towering over the town, the **Heidelberger Schloss** is a vast residential complex that was built and repeatedly extended between the 13th and 17th centuries. Originally a supremely well-fortified Gothic castle, it is now mostly in ruins.

The **Universitätsbibliothek** (University Library), erected in 1901–5, has one of the largest book collections in Germany, with over two million volumes.

The French Count Charles de Graimberg built up an extensive collection of fine drawings, paintings, arms, and other curios. His collection forms the core of the **Kurpfälzisches Museum**, which also has a fascinating archaeology section.

The Baroque domes of the **Heiliggeistkirche** are city landmarks. Former canons of the college were university scholars, and the church aisle features extensive galleries of books.

🏛 **Kurpfälzisches Museum**
Hauptstrasse 97. *Tel* 06221-583 40 20. ◻ *Tue–Sun (Wed: 10am–9pm).* 🎫

Heidelberger Schloss rising above Heidelberg's Alte Brücke (Old Bridge)

The Rhine and Mosel Valleys

The Rhine and Mosel Valleys offer a series of fairy-tale landscapes – spectacular gorges, rocky crags topped by romantic castles, and picturesque villages surrounded by vineyards producing excellent white wines. After flowing into Germany from France, the Mosel meanders between steep-sided banks to join the Rhine at Koblenz. South of Koblenz lies one of the most stunning stretches of the Rhine, which is also the birthplace of German myths such as the Lorelei and the *Nibelungenlied*, the great medieval epic poem of vengeance and honor.

The colorful portal of Trier's Kurfürstliches Schloss

Trier ⑱

Rhineland-Palatinate. 🏛 99,000.
🚊 🚌 🛈 An der Porta Nigra
(0651-97 80 80). **www**.trier.de

Germany's oldest town, Trier was founded by the Emperor Augustus in 16 BC. Its monumental Roman gateway, the **Porta Nigra**, was built in the 3rd century AD. Among the city's other Roman relics are the **Aula Palatina**, a vast, austere building that served as the throne hall of Roman emperors and also as a church, the **Basilika und Kurfürstliches Schloss**. The basilica was built for Emperor Constantine around AD 305. In the 16th century part of it was incorporated into a Renaissance castle, later transformed into a Baroque palace for the archbishop-electors of Trier. The 4th-century **Kaiserthermen** (Imperial Baths) are also in the same building. A superb collection of Roman artifacts is held in the **Rheinisches Landesmuseum** close by.

🏛 **Rheinisches Landesmuseum**
Weimarer Allee 1. **Tel** 0651-977 40.
◯ daily. ● Mon (Nov–Apr). 🎫

Mosel Valley ⑲

🛈 Am Gestade 6, Bernkastel-Kues
(06531-4023). 🚢 Hans Michels
(06531-8222); Gebrüder Kolb,
Briedern (02673-1515).

On the stretch of the Mosel between Trier and Koblenz, romantic castles tower above extensive vineyards. Between May and October river trips are available all along the river – either short daytrips or longer cruises. However, progress can be slow because of the number of locks. A tour by car or bus is an attractive alternative. Two of the most popular excursions are from Trier to Bernkastel-Kues and from Koblenz to Cochem. Wine-tasting and eating play a big part in visitors' enjoyment of the region. Of the many castles that line the river be sure to visit **Burg Eltz** – the core of which has survived more or less intact since it was built in the 12th century – a short walk from the town of Wierschem.

⛫ **Burg Eltz**
🚌 to Wierschem. ◯ Apr – Oct: daily. 🎫

Mainz ⑳

Rhineland-Palatinate. 🏛 190,000.
🚊 🚌 🛈 Im Brückenturm am
Rathaus (06131-28 62 10).

Mainz enjoyed power and influence under the Holy Roman Empire, as the city's Archbishop was one of the Electors. The **Kaiserdom**, the Romanesque cathedral, dates back to the 11th century. Like others from this period it has a choir at each end – one for the emperor and one for the clergy. The nave is

Burg Eltz, the most authentic and evocative castle in the Mosel Valley

The apse and towers at the east end of the Kaiserdom, Mainz

filled with the splendid tombs of the archbishops, ranging in date from the 13th to the 19th century. The **St. Gotthard-Kapelle** beside the cathedral was the private chapel of the archbishops. It has a fine 12th-century arcaded loggia.

Other attractions include the well-preserved old half-timbered houses of the **Kirschgarten** area and the Baroque **Kurfürstliches Schloss**, now a museum of Roman and other relics.

Mainz is also famous for the development in the 1440s by Johannes Gutenberg of printing with movable metal type. The **Gutenberg Museum** has a recreation of his studio and a copy of his famous 42-line Bible.

🏛 Gutenberg Museum
Liebfrauenplatz 5. *Tel* 06131-12 26 40. ◻ Tue–Sun. ● public hols.

Rhine Valley ㉑

🛈 Bahnhofplatz 17, Koblenz (0261-313 04). 🚢 K-D Linie, Rheinwerft, Koblenz (0261-310 30).

Cruises on the Rhine are available along much of its length, but the most scenic and popular stretch is the Rhine Gorge between Mainz and Bonn. The gorge starts at Bingen, where the Nahe joins the Rhine on its 1,320-km (825-mile) journey from Switzerland to the North Sea. Popular sights along the route include **Bacharach**, a pretty

town on the left bank, and the striking white-walled island castle of **Pfalzgrafenstein**, which levied tolls on passing ships until the mid-19th century. Past the town of Kaub on the right bank is the rock of the **Lorelei**, a legendary siren who lured sailors to their deaths with her song and her beauty. A modern statue marks the spot. Across the river is the town of **St. Goar**, dominated by the ruined Burg Rheinfels, blown up by French troops in 1797. **Burg Katz** offers one of the best-known views of the Rhine valley. At **Boppard** the attractions include the 13th-century Church of St. Severus and more spectacular views of the Rhine. Just south of Koblenz stands **Schloss Stolzenfels**, created in the early 19th century for King Friedrich Wilhelm IV. There are no bridges on this stretch of the river, but if you are exploring by car, there are ferries at various points along the route. However, the best way to enjoy the Rhine's magnificent scenery is by boat.

Koblenz ㉒

Rhineland-Palatinate. 🏠 109,300. 🚌 🚉 🛈 Bahnhofplatz 17 (0261-313 04), Jesuitenplatz (0261-13 09 20).

Koblenz stands at the confluence of the Mosel and Rhine rivers. On the **Deutsches Eck**, the spur of land between the

two rivers, stands a huge equestrian statue of Emperor Wilhelm I.

Florinsmarkt takes its name from the Romanesque-Gothic **Church of St. Florin**, which dates from the 12th century. Nestling among the square's historic buildings is the **Mittelrheinisches Museum**, with medieval art and archaeological collections.

The present appearance of the **Alte Burg**, with its fine Renaissance façade, dates from the 17th century, but a fortress has stood on this site since the early Middle Ages.

Other sights of interest are the **Liebfrauenkirche**, which has a beautiful Gothic choir, the **Kurfürstliches Schloss** (the Electors' palace), and **Festung Ehrenbreitstein**, where the archbishops of Trier resided from 1648–1786.

Detail on tomb of Heinrich II, Maria Laach

Environs

Northwest of Koblenz, the Benedictine abbey of **Maria Laach** is a masterpiece of Romanesque architecture. It was begun in 1093 on the orders of Count Palatine Heinrich II, who lies buried here. The Paradise courtyard, meant to symbolize the Garden of Eden, resembles the Alhambra in Granada (*see pp322–3*).

🏰 Maria Laach
Off A61, 25 km (16 miles) NW of Koblenz. *Tel* 02652-590. 🚌 *from Andernach or Niedermendig*. ◻ *daily.*

Burg Katz above the town of St. Goarhausen in the Rhine Gorge

Frankfurt's skyscraper district, nicknamed "Mainhattan"

Frankfurt am Main ㉓

Hesse. 660,000. 🚉 Hauptbahnhof (069-21 23 88 00).

Frankfurt am Main is one of the main economic and cultural centers of Europe. The headquarters of many major banks and newspaper publishers are based here, and the city's International Book Fair is the world's largest event of its kind.

Since 1878, the **Städelsches Kunstinstitut** has occupied a Neo-Renaissance building on Schaumainkai, the picturesque "museum embankment." The ground floor houses a collection of Dutch and German prints and drawings, the first floor is devoted to 19th- and 20th-century art, and the second floor displays works by Old Masters such as Botticelli, van Eyck, Vermeer, and Rembrandt.

Another interesting museum in the Schaumainkai complex is the **Deutsches Architektur-museum**, which concentrates mainly on developments in 20th-century architecture.

Nearby is the **Deutsches Filmmuseum**, which holds documents and objects relating to the art of filmmaking and the development of film technology. The museum has its own cinema, which shows old and often long-forgotten films.

The great German poet, novelist, and dramatist Johann Wolfgang von Goethe was born at the **Goethehaus** in 1749. The house was totally destroyed in World War II, but later lovingly restored, its interior reconstructed in typical 18th-century style. The desk at which Goethe wrote his early works, such as *The Sorrows of Young Werther* (1774), remains.

Located in the center of the old town, the **Römer** is a collection of 15th- to 18th-century houses, including the Altes Rathaus (Old Town Hall), rebuilt after World War II. Opposite is a group of half-timbered houses, known as the **Ostzeile**.

On the banks of the Main stands **St. Leonhardkirche**, a fine example of Gothic and Romanesque architecture.

Portrait of a Woman (c.1480) by Botticelli, Städelsches Kunstinstitut

Built in stages in the 13th and 15th centuries, the church contains many treasures, including a copy of Leonardo da Vinci's *Last Supper* by Hans Holbein the Elder, from 1501.

The **Historisches Museum** has an interesting display of items relating to Frankfurt's history, including a fascinating model of the medieval town, a collection of local prehistoric finds, and several decorative fragments from buildings destroyed during World War II.

The twin-naved **Alte Nikolaikirche**, or Church of St. Nicholas, is popular with visitors for its fine statues of St. Nicholas and the 40-bell carillon, which plays German folk songs twice a day.

The **Kaiserdom**, an imperial cathedral, was built between the 13th and 15th centuries. It has several priceless masterpieces of Gothic artwork, including the 15th-century Maria-Schlaf-Altar.

The collection at the **Museum für Moderne Kunst** (Museum of Modern Art) represents all the major artistic trends from the 1960s until the present day, with works by Roy Lichtenstein and Andy Warhol.

The **Liebieghaus**, a museum of sculpture, has works ranging from antiquity through to Mannerism and Rococo. There are some superb examples of ancient Egyptian and Far Eastern art, as well as splendid works from the Middle Ages and the Renaissance.

🏛 **Städelsches Kunstinstitut**
Schaumainkai 63. **Tel** 069-605 09 80. ◻ Tue–Sun. 🖼 🗙

🏛 **Museum für Moderne Kunst**
Domstrasse 10. **Tel** 069-21 23 04 47. ◻ Tue–Sun. 🖼

Environs
Hanau, 30 km (19 miles) east of Frankfurt, is the birthplace of the brothers Wilhelm and Jakob Grimm. There is an exhibition devoted to their lives and work at the local historical museum.

The Ostzeile on the Römerberg, one of the symbols of Frankfurt

The Baroque Elector's palace, housing Bonn University

Bonn ㉔

North Rhine-Westphalia. 🏛
310,000. ✈ 🚉 🚌 🚹
Windeckstrasse 1 (0228-77 50 00).

There has been a crossing over the Rhine at Bonn since pre-Roman times, but the settlement first rose to prominence under the Archbishops of Cologne in the 13th century. Bonn was the capital of the Federal Republic of Germany between 1949 and 1991.

The central market square is surrounded by a mixture of modern and Baroque architecture, including the late-Baroque **Rathaus** (Town Hall), built in 1737–8. Just north of the market square stands the 18th-century Baroque house where Beethoven was born. The **Beethovenhaus** is now a museum housing an impressive collection of memorabilia.

Bonn has many fine museums. The **Rheinisches Landesmuseum** has a vast collection of archaeological exhibits dating back to Roman times, as well as medieval and modern art. A Neanderthal skull is also exhibited here. The **Kunstmuseum Bonn**, a museum of modern art, has a superb display of Expressionist paintings.

Cologne ㉕

North Rhine-Westphalia. 🏛
1,005,000. ✈ 🚉 🚌 🚹 *Unter Fettenhennen 19 (0221-22 13 04 00).*

Originally founded by the Romans, Cologne (Köln) is one of the oldest settlements in Germany. Present-day Cologne is an important ecclesiastical and cultural center, boasting 12 Romanesque churches and the famous cathedral *(see pp562–3),* as well as several excellent museums, historic buildings, and superb galleries.

The **Wallraf-Richartz-Museum** contains 14th- to 19th-century paintings organized by the schools of art they represent. Featured artists include Rubens, Dürer, Munch, and Max Liebermann.

Housing archaeological finds from Cologne and the Rhine Valley, the modern **Römisch-Germanisches Museum** displays Roman weapons, tools, and decorative objects, as well as the superb Dionysus mosaic from around 250 BC.

The **Museum Ludwig** boasts one of Europe's best collections of modern art. German Expressionists, Surrealists, and American Pop Artists are all represented.

The Romans built a sports arena on the site now occupied by the 12th-century **Groß St. Martin**. Remains of the baths have been uncovered underneath the crypt.

Cologne's **Rathaus** (Town Hall) is an irregular-shaped building, the result of successive modifications after 1330. Under a glass pyramid at the front are the remains of 12th-century Jewish baths.

Highlights of the late-Gothic **Church of St. Peter**, built in 1515–39, are its stained-glass windows and the magnificent *Crucifixion of St. Peter* (c.1637) by Peter Paul Rubens.

The southern chamber of the **Church of St. Ursula** is lined with many shrines. According to legend, they hold the remains of St. Ursula and 11,000 virgins, reputedly killed by the Huns.

🏛 **Wallraf-Richartz-Museum**
Martinstrasse 39. *Tel 0221-22 12 11 19.* 🕐 *Tue–Sun.* 🔲

Skyline of Cologne, dominated by the spires of the Rathaus, Gross St. Martin, and the cathedral

Cologne Cathedral

The history of Germany's greatest Gothic cathedral is long and complicated. The foundation stone was laid on August 15, 1248, the chancel was consecrated in 1322, and building work continued until about 1520. The cathedral then stood unfinished until the 19th century, when the original Gothic designs were rediscovered. It was finally completed in 1842–80. Precious works of art include the fabulous Shrine of the Three Kings, the Altar of the Magi, and an early-Gothic carving of the Virgin Mary (c.1290) known as the Mailänder (Milanese) Madonna.

Mailänder Madonna

The north tower, at 157.38 m (516 ft), is slightly higher than the south tower.

Elaborately decorated pinnacles top the supporting pillars.

Cathedral Interior
The chancel, the ambulatory, and the chapels retain a large number of Gothic, mainly early 14th-century, stained-glass windows.

Main entrance

The Petrusportal is the only entrance built in the Middle Ages. Of the figures flanking the doorway, five were original Gothic statues, but these have been replaced by copies.

Buttresses support the entire bulk of the cathedral.

Englebert Reliquary (c.1630)
The treasury in the cloister on the north side of the cathedral is famous for its large collection of gold objects, vestments, and the beautifully decorated liturgical books.

For hotels and restaurants in this region see pp574–9 and pp580–85

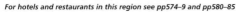

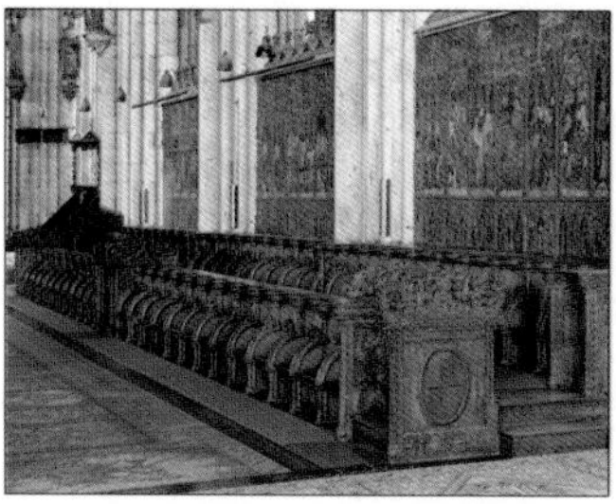

★ Choir
The massive oak stalls were built in 1308–11. They are backed by beautiful painted wooden panels.

VISITORS' CHECKLIST

Kölner Dom. *6am–7:30pm daily.* **Domforum (Visitors' Center)** ***Tel*** *0221-92 58 47 30.* **Treasury** Domkloster 4. ***Tel*** *0221-92 58 47 30.* *10am–6pm daily.* **Tower** *May–Sep: 9am–6pm; Oct–Apr 10am–4pm.*

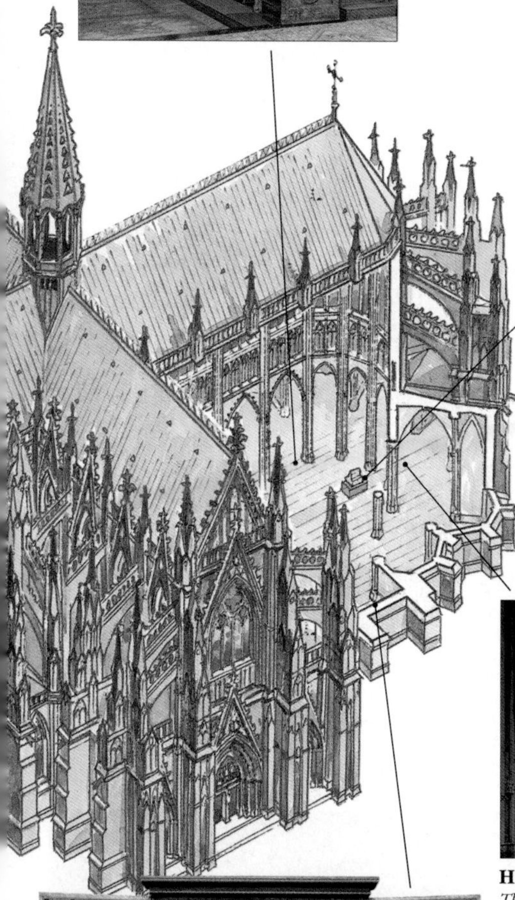

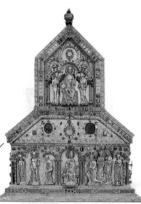

★ Shrine of the Three Kings
This huge Romanesque reliquary was made by Nikolaus von Verdun in 1181–1220, to hold the relics of the Three Kings. These were brought to Cologne from Italy in 1164 by Emperor Friedrich I Barbarossa.

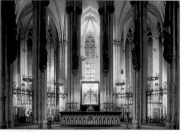

High Altar
The Gothic altar dates back to the consecration of the chancel. The frieze depicts the Coronation of the Virgin Mary, flanked by the twelve Apostles.

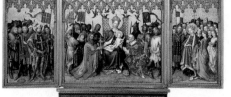

★ Altar of the Magi
This magnificent altarpiece (c.1442) by Stephan Lochner depicts The Adoration of the Magi. *When the panels are closed, it shows* The Annunciation.

STAR FEATURES

- ★ Choir
- ★ Shrine of the Three Kings
- ★ Altar of the Magi

Northern Germany

Three federal states – Lower Saxony and the city-states of Hamburg and Bremen – occupy a huge swathe of northern Germany. Lower Saxony's capital, Hanover, has splendid architecture and fine museums. Hamburg and Bremen were wealthy Hanseatic trading towns, and today their ports still play an important role in city life. The region's other main attractions are the well-preserved medieval towns of Münster, in North Rhine-Westphalia, and Lübeck in Schleswig-Holstein.

The beautifully restored façade of Münster's Gothic Rathaus

Münster ㉖

🏯 280,000. 🛬 🚊 🛈 *Heinrich-Brüning-Strasse 9 (0251-492 27 10).*

Münster's main sights of interest are located in the Altstadt, the historic heart of the city. The imposing Gothic **Rathaus** (Town Hall), carefully restored following damage during World War II, dates from the late 12th century. In 1648 the Treaty of Westphalia was signed here, ending the Thirty Years' War.

Münster's great cathedral, the **Dom St. Paulus**, on Domplatz, was built in 1225–65. Its best-known treasure is the astronomical clock (1540). Also on the square is the **Westfälisches Landesmuseum**, which specializes in Gothic art. Nearby, the **Lambertikirche** (1375–1450) is a fine example of the hall-churches typical of Westphalia.

West of the center stands the **Residenzschloss**. Built in 1767–87, the splendid Baroque palace, now the headquarters of Münster's university, overlooks pleasant gardens.

Hanover ㉗

🏯 522,000. 🚊 🛈 *Ernst-August-Platz 8 (0511-12 34 51 11).*
🎪 *Schützenfest (Jun–Jul).*

Hanover (Hannover) is the capital of Lower Saxony, and for more than a century, from 1714 to 1837, shared a succession of rulers with Britain. Heavily bombed during World War II, the city has been largely rebuilt.

Among the city's finest landmarks are the grand **Opernhaus** (Opera House), built in Neoclassical style in 1845–57, and, on Tramm-platz, the **Neues Rathaus** (Town Hall), which dates from 1901–13 and combines Neo-Gothic and Secessionist detail. The latter's massive central dome offers fine views of the city.

On Marktplatz, in the old town, are many restored, 15th-century, half-timbered houses, as well as the **Markt-kirche St. Georg und St. Jacobus** with its 14th-century nave and fine Gothic altar.

One of Europe's best museums of modern art, the **Sprengel-Museum** holds works by Munch, Chagall, Picasso, and Christo. Also worth visiting is the **Niedersächsisches Landesmuseum**, whose picture gallery has German medieval and Renaissance paintings, Dutch and Flemish works by Rubens, Rembrandt, and van Dyck, and 19th- and 20th-century German art.

West of the city center, the **Herrenhauser Gärten** are among the most beautiful Baroque gardens in Germany.

🏛 **Sprengel-Museum**
Kurt-Schwitters-Platz. **Tel** 0511-16 84 62 10. 🕐 Tue–Sun. 🈴
🏛 **Niedersächsisches Landesmuseum**
Willy-Brandt-Allee 5.
Tel 0511-980 7686. 🕐 Tue–Sun.

Bremen ㉘

🏯 556,000. 🚉 🚊 🛈 *Im Bahnhof (0421-308 000).*

A member of the Hanseatic League from 1358, in the Middle Ages Bremen was a thriving seaport, trading in grain, wine, and salt. Today, the independent city-state still prospers from its port, Germany's second-largest.

Bremen's **Rathaus** (Town Hall), on Marktplatz, was built in 1405–10 and boasts a fine Renaissance façade, added to the original Gothic structure 200 years later. Opposite is the 11th-century Romanesque

Hanover's medieval quarter, with the Church of St. George and St. Jacobus

For hotels and restaurants in this region see pp574–9 and pp580–85

Attractive gabled houses and the statue of Roland in Bremen's Marktplatz

Dom, which contains some fine bas-reliefs. In Marktplatz itself stand a tall statue of Charlemagne's knight Roland (1404) and a sculpture of the *Musicians of Bremen* (1953), recalling the Grimm fairy tale.

Two museums of note are the **Kunsthalle**, with European art dating from the Middle Ages to the 20th century, and the **Focke Museum**, a museum of local history and decorative arts.

Musicians of Bremen sculpture

🏛 **Rathaus**
Marktplatz. ⬚ *for guided tours only (11am, noon, 3pm, 4pm daily)*
book at 🛈 📷 ✓

🏛 **Kunsthalle**
Am Wall 207. **Tel** *0421-32 90 80.*
⬚ *Tue–Sun.* 📷

Hamburg ㉙

🏚 *1,700,000.* ✈ 🚢 🚊 🛈
uptbahnhof, Kirchenallee (040-30 05 12 00).

For many years Hamburg, Germany's second largest city, was a leading member of the Hanseatic League and an independent trading town. In 1945 it became a city-state of the Federal Republic.

Hamburg sustained considerable damage during World War II, and little of the old town remains. The ruined tower of the Neo-Gothic **Nikolai-kirche** serves as a

monument to the tragic consequences of war. Nearby, the **Jakobikirche** (1340) has been rebuilt in its original style. Inside is a massive 17th-century Baroque organ by Arp Schnitger. Another fine church is the Baroque **Michaeliskirche**, whose 132-m (433-ft) tower gives splendid views of the city.

Hamburg's Neo-Renaissance town hall, on the Rathausmarkt, is the fifth in the city's history. Just north of it is a large recreational lake, the Binnenalster. Also nearby, the prestigious **Kunst-halle** traces the history of European art from medieval times to the 20th century. The section devoted to the 19th-century German Romantics is especially good.

The best-known example of the city's collection of Expressionist buildings is Fritz Höger's **Chilehaus** (1922–4) in Kontorhausviertel.

Hamburg is the second largest port in Europe after Rotterdam, and a tour is

Triptych adorning the main altar in Hamburg's Jakobikirche

highly recommended. There are two museum ships moored here: the freighter *Cap San Diego* and the sailing boat *Rickmer Rickmers* (1896).

🏛 **Kunsthalle**
Glockengießerwall. **Tel** *040-428 13 12 00.* ⬚ *Tue–Sun.*

🚢 **Port**
Ⓤ *Baumwall or St-Pauli-Landungs-brücken.* **Cap San Diego Tel** *040-36 42 09.* ⬚ *daily.* **Rickmer Rickmers Tel** *040-319 59 59.* ⬚ *daily.*

Lübeck's 15th-century Holstentor, on the western edge of the town

Lübeck ㉚

🏚 *215,000.* 🚉 🛈 *Holstentor-Platz 1 (0451-409 1950).*

The most important town in the Baltic basin at the end of the Middle Ages, Lübeck is known for its wealth of superb medieval architecture.

The city's 13th-century **Marienkirche** (St. Mary's Church), boasts the highest vaulted brick nave in the world. A short walk away, the turreted **Rathaus** (Town Hall) dates from 1226 and is a fine example of Lübeck's distinctive Gothic brick architecture. The Gothic **Dom** (Cathedral) was begun in 1173. Nearby, the **St.-Annen-Museum** has historical artifacts dating from the 13th to the 18th centuries. Another famous monument is the **Holstentor** (1466–78), the western gateway to the city.

The **Buddenbrook-Haus** is a museum devoted to the great writers Thomas and Heinrich Mann, whose family lived here in 1841–91.

🏛 **Buddenbrook-Haus**
Heinrich-und-Thomas-Mann-Zentrum, Mengstrasse 4. **Tel** *0451-122 4192.*
⬚ *daily.* ⬤ *Dec 24, 25 & 31.* 📷

Practical Information

Germany is renowned as a safe, clean, and efficient country to visit. Travelers will find that every town has a helpful tourist information center offering advice on restaurants, attractions, and activities. Larger cities also have Internet web sites which give up-to-the-minute information. Hotels are plentiful but may be busy during the festivals and fairs which occur throughout the year in different parts of the country.

WHEN TO VISIT

The climate in Germany is pleasantly temperate. Cities and historic monuments are best visited in spring or early fall, particularly in the south of the country where it can be very warm. July and August are ideal months for a restful holiday by the sea, in the lake districts or in the mountains. In Bavaria during the second half of September and early October the Oktoberfest takes place. This is an annual beer-drinking event which is open to all visitors. In December everybody is preoccupied with Christmas shopping, while during winter, skiing is a popular pursuit in the Black Forest, the Alps, and the Harz Mountains. The roads are busiest during the school holidays, dates of which vary from state to state, and during the "long weekends" at Easter, Whitsun, and other national public holidays.

VISA REQUIREMENTS AND CUSTOMS

Citizens of countries that are members of the EU, as well as citizens from the US, Canada, Australia, and New Zealand, do not need a visa to visit Germany, so long as their stay does not exceed three months. Visitors from South Africa must have a visa. Visitors from EU countries do not require a passport to enter Germany, as long as they have a national ID card.

Drugs, animals, animal products, such as cured meats, and exotic plants under special protection are totally prohibited from importation into Germany. Regulations also restrict the importation of cigarettes and wine.

PERSONAL SECURITY

As in other countries, visitors are far safer in small towns and villages than in big cities, where extra care must be taken against street theft – particularly when traveling on public transport during the rush hour. Pickpockets tend to frequent popular tourist sights and any events where large groups of people gather. It is worth using a money belt to conceal your money and documents. Also keep cameras and audio equipment out of sight. Better still, leave valuable items in the hotel safe.

POLICE

German police uniforms and signs are mostly green. Look out for motorized police units, the *Verkehrspolizei*, which are concerned with safety on the streets, roads, and highways, and are distinguished by their white caps. Uniformed police officers patroling city streets have a green cap. Certain town police have navy-blue uniforms and their job is to catch motorists for parking offences for which they can impose an on-the-spot fine. Remember that you should carry ID such as a passport, driving license or student card with you at all times.

PHARMACIES

Look out for the stylized letter "A" *(Apotheke)* which indicates a pharmacy. They are usually open from 8am to 6pm; in small towns they close between 1 and 3pm. In larger towns there is always a rota and this is displayed in the window of each pharmacy with a note of addresses. Information on rota pharmacies may also be obtained from tourist offices.

ACCIDENTS AND EMERGENCIES

If you have an accident or a serious breakdown on the motorway, it is best to use one of the special telephones that are situated at regular intervals along the hard shoulder. Throughout the country a special emergency

THE CLIMATE OF GERMANY

Germany lies in a temperate climatic zone. In the north, with marine influences predominating, summers tend to be quite cool and winters mild, with relatively high rainfall. In the eastern part of the country, however, the climate is more continental and this produces harsher winters and hotter summers. Germany's highest rainfall and lowest temperatures are recorded in the Alps.

BERLIN

°C/F		23/73	
	13/56	12/54	14/57
0°C 32°F	3/37		3/37
			1/34
			-5/23

	6 hrs	8 hrs	4 hrs	2 hrs
	24 mm	60 mm	41 mm	31 mm
month	Apr	Jul	Oct	Jan

MUNICH

°C/F		23/73	
	14/57	11/53	13/56
0°C 32°F	3/37		3/37
			2/36
			-5/23

	5 hrs	8 hrs	5 hrs	2 hrs
	56 mm	99 mm	48 mm	46 mm
month	Apr	Jul	Oct	Jan

number, 110, is answered by an operator who will inform the appropriate emergency services. This number is free on all telephones, including mobiles. If you lose your passport, you should go to your consulate.

TOURIST INFORMATION

A well-developed network of tourist information centers exists in Germany. These are usually run by the city or regional tourist authorities, *Verkehrsamt*. They provide advice on accommodations, addresses, and opening hours of monuments, museums, tours, and excursions, as well as brochures covering the most important tourist attractions. They may also be able to find and book you a hotel room.

OPENING HOURS

The opening hours of stores, offices, and most other businesses depend to a great extent on the size of the town. In larger cities, office hours are usually from 9am until 6pm, and larger shops are open

from 9am to 8pm weekdays, and until 6pm on Saturday. Banks operate shorter hours: 9am–3:30pm Monday–Friday, with a lunchbreak between noon and 1pm. They usually stay open later one evening a week until 6pm. Some new shopping malls are open on Sundays. In smaller towns, not much tends to open before 10am, and many businesses close from 1–2pm for lunch, on Saturday afternoons, Sundays and public holidays

DISABLED TRAVELERS

There are ramps or lifts for people confined to wheelchairs at large museums and major historical sites. Banks are also accessible by wheelchair and there are lifts at railroad stations and larger underground stations. Some public transport is adapted to take wheelchairs. Most higher grade hotels have suitably equipped bedrooms. Public restroom facilities in parking lots, train stations, and airports usually have suitable cubicles. For information contact **Bundesverband Selbsthilfe Körperbehinderter (BSK)**.

COMMUNICATIONS

Mail and telephone services in Germany are very efficient. Mailboxes are bright yellow and call booths can be found everywhere. The oldest types are coin-operated, but others take telephone cards which can be bought at mail offices. Many public phone booths have a number so they can receive incoming calls. Call booths with the word *"National"* can only be used to ring numbers with German dialling codes, but overseas calls can be made from other phones. You can book a call at mail offices at the window marked *"Ferngespräche."* Calls are cheaper in the evening from 6–9pm and at weekends.

BANKING AND CURRENCY

The Deutschmark was the German currency until 2002 when the euro, common currency of the European Union, was introduced into general circulation. Foreign currency can be changed at banks, most hotels, or bureau de change (*Wechselstube*).

DIRECTORY

TOURIST INFORMATION

German National Tourist Office
Tel 069-97 46 40.
www.germany-tourism.de

Berlin
Am Karlsbad 11, 10785 Berlin.
Tel 030-25 00 25.
www.btm.de

Frankfurt am Main
Hauptbahnhof Empfangshalle,
60329 Frankfurt am Main.
Tel 069-21 23 88 00.
www.frankfurt-tourismus.de

Munich
Marienplatz, Rathaus,
80331 Munich.
Tel 089-233 0300.
www.munich-tourist.de

Stuttgart
Königstrasse 1a,
70173 Stuttgart.
Tel 0711-222 80.
www.stuttgart-tourist.de

EMBASSIES

Australia
Wallstrasse 76–79,
10179 Berlin.
Tel 030-880 08 80.
Fax 030-88 08 83 10.
www.australian-embassy.de

Canada
Leipziger Platz 17,
10117 Berlin.
Tel 030-20 31 20.
Fax 030-20 31 25 90.
www.kanada-info.de

New Zealand
Friedrichstrasse 60,
10117 Berlin.
Tel 030-20 62 10.
Fax 030-20 62 11 14.
@ nzemb@t-online.de

South Africa
Tiergartenstrasse 17–18,
12683 Berlin.
Tel 030-22 07 30.
Fax 030-22 07 31 90.
www.suedafrika.org

UNITED KINGDOM

Embassy
Wilhelmstrasse 70,
10117 Berlin.
Tel 030-20 45 70.
Fax 030-20 45 75 74.
www.britischebotschaft.de

Consulate
Harvestehuder Weg 8a,
20148 Hamburg.
Tel 040-448 03 20.
Fax 040-410 72 59.

United States

Embassy
Neustädtische Kirchstrasse 4–5,
10117 Berlin.
Tel 030-83050.
Fax 030-238 62 90.
www.usembassy.de

Consulate
Königinstrasse 5,
80539 Munich.
Tel 089-288 80.
Fax 089-280 99 98.

EMERGENCY NUMBERS

Police and Fire services
Tel 110.

Ambulance
Tel 19222.

DISABLED TRAVELERS

Mobility International
North America
Tel 541-343 1284.

Bundesverband Selbsthilfe Körperbehinderter (BSK)
Postfach 20,
74238 Krautheim.
Tel 06294-42810.
www.bsk-ev.de

Travel Information

Traveling to and around Germany is fast and easy. In every large city there is an airport, and most of these offer international connections. The whole of Germany is linked by a dense network of highways, while the main roads are of a high standard and well signposted. Train travel throughout the country is comfortable and reliable; for longer journeys it is worth taking advantage of the fast connections offered by InterCityExpress (ICE). Buses are also comfortable and efficient and can be essential in rural areas that cannot be reached by train. Large cities have tram, bus, and sometimes subway services.

ARRIVING BY AIR

Germany's most important airports are Berlin, Frankfurt am Main, Munich and Düsseldorf. You can get connecting flights from these to other cities such as Hamburg and Stuttgart. The country's national airline is **Lufthansa**, which flies between Germany and most of the world's major destinations. From the UK, flights are operated by **BA** and **BMI. Ryanair, Air Berlin**, and **easyJet** all offer cheaper alternatives as well.

There are frequent flights from the US to Germany, mainly to Berlin and Frankfurt, which is Germany's largest airport and one of the busiest in Europe. Direct flights are available from many major US cities.

Although Canada does not have many direct flights to Germany, **Air Canada** operates a regular flight from Toronto to Frankfurt and its subsidiary Canadian Airlines flies from Vancouver to Frankfurt.

DOMESTIC FLIGHTS

In addition to Lufthansa, there are a number of smaller airlines in Germany including the **dba**, which may offer cheaper fares than Lufthansa on internal routes, as well as providing air links with small airports, such as Augsburg, Dortmund, and Erfurt.

BORDER CROSSINGS

There are many crossings into Germany and provided that you carry the necessary documents and your car does not look disreputable, you should experience a minimum of delay and formalities at the border. There are limits on the amount of duty-free items that can be brought in by non-EU citizens *(see p13)*.

TRAVELING BY CAR

The fastest and most comfortable way to travel around the country is by road. Germany's excellent network of toll-free highway routes guarantees fast journeys over long distances, while a well-maintained system of good smaller roads means that many interesting places throughout the country are within easy reach. On smaller roads and in remote areas, filling stations may be few and far between.

The German *Autobahn* (highway) network is extensive. An *Autobahn* is indicated by the letter "A" followed by a number – some also have an "E" and a number, denoting that the road crosses the German border. They are all toll-free and have regularly spaced filling stations, as well as parking lots with restrooms, restaurants, and motels. A *Bundesstrasse* (main road) has the letter "B" and a number.

In the event of an accident on an *Autobahn*, or if sudden traffic congestion means you have to brake hard, drivers should turn on their flashing emergency lights to warn drivers behind of the danger. Along the hard shoulder there are yellow poles with emergency buttons, which can be used to call for help if you have a breakdown or an accident. The two automobile associations **Allgemeiner Deutscher Automobil Club (ADAC)** and **Automobilclub von Deutschland (AvD)** offer roadside assistance.

RULES OF THE ROAD

In Germany, the same road traffic regulations apply as in most European countries. The car must carry a plate indicating country of origin, and be equipped with a red warning triangle for use in case of breakdown.

The wearing of seatbelts is compulsory and children under 12 must sit in the back, with babies and toddlers secured in child-seats.

Driving after drinking a small amount of alcohol is allowed, but if you have an accident, the consequences will be more severe if a breathalyzer shows alcohol in your blood.

In built-up areas the speed limit is 50 km/h (31 mph); beyond this it is 100 km/h (62 mph), and on highways there is no limit, of which many drivers take full advantage. When traveling with a caravan or camping trailer outside built-up areas, drivers should not exceed 70 km/h (44 mph), and on highways 100 km/h (62 mph). Road traffic police are strict about imposing fines for speeding. Drivers can also be fined for driving too close to the vehicle in front and for parking in prohibited areas.

PARKING IN TOWNS

Finding a place to park is not easy: it is often best to use a multi-level parking lot, which is indicated by *"Parkhaus"*; a sign with the word *"Frei"* indicates that spaces are available. It is never worth leaving your car in a prohibited area. If you do risk it, a traffic warden may find your car, immediately impose a fine and arrange for the car to be towed away. Retrieving your car is then expensive and difficult.

Cars left in a parking zone must either display a parking ticket or be at a meter.

TRAVELING BY TRAIN

Traveling around Germany by train is not the cheapest form of transport, but it is undoubtedly one of the most efficient. Trains operated by **Deutsche Bahn**, the German rail company, are renowned for their punctuality, safety, and cleanliness. The fastest are InterCityExpress (ICE) trains; these are aerodynamically designed, painted white, with air-conditioning in the coaches and airline-style seats. Unfortunately, there is not much room for luggage. These trains can travel at more than 200 km/h (125 mph), which means that a journey from Hamburg to Munich takes just under six hours. ICE trains operate on just a few routes linking the largest cities. The InterCity (IC) trains, which stop only at certain stations, are cheaper but still offer an express service. For short distances, it is best to take the Regional Express (RE) trains. The S-Bahn (short for *Schnellbahn*) is a fast commuter rail network which operates in some of the major German cities.

TRAIN FARES

Train fares in Germany are quite expensive and there is a compulsory surcharge (*Zuschlag*) for express train travel. It is not usually necessary to reserve seats, but in the high season this is a good idea and it does not cost a lot. If you are staying for some time and want to use trains frequently, one way to travel more cheaply is to buy a *BahnCard*. After an initial hefty outlay, this gives you a 50 percent discount on rail tickets for a whole year.

CITY TRANSPORT

Several major cities in Germany, including Berlin, Hamburg, Munich, and Nuremberg, have a network of fast connections by subway (*U-Bahn*). U-Bahn stations are indicated by square signs with a white "U" on a dark blue background, while S-Bahn stations have round signs with a white "S" on a green background. The U-Bahn offers very frequent services – at peak hours trains normally run every 3–5 minutes – and stations are only a short distance from each other. The S-Bahn trains are less frequent and the stations are farther apart.

In some cities (especially in eastern Germany) trams are the most common method of travel; in some cities they also have underground sections. Trams are ideal urban transport because they do not get stuck in traffic jams. You can use the same tickets as on buses and the S-Bahn. When they are above ground, remember that trams have right of way.

Various types of ticket can be bought from machines located by the entrance to stations. Children under six travel free while those under 14 get a reduced rate.

TRAVELING BY BUS

There is a good network of inter-city bus services in Germany, though journeys are generally no cheaper than traveling by train. Most towns have a *Zentraler Omnibus Bahnhof* (ZOB) close to the train station. Most bus services originate here and you can also get timetables and buy your tickets here.

CYCLING TOURS

Cycling is a slow but environmentally friendly means of getting around. It also enables you to combine sightseeing with physical exercise. It is easy to rent bikes in some tourist areas, particularly at main train stations from April to October. Bikes can be taken on trains, on the U-Bahn, and the S-Bahn. For cycling routes, you will find that many newsstands, bookstores, and tourist offices have excellent maps.

DIRECTORY

AIRLINES

Air Berlin
www.airberlin.com

Air Canada
Tel 069-27 11 51 11.
www.aircanada.ca

American Airlines
US: Tel 800-433 7300.
Frankfurt: Tel 1803-242324. www.AA.com

BMI
www.flybmi.com

British Airways
UK: Tel 0845-773 3377.
Frankfurt: Tel 01805-26 65 22. www.
britishairways.com

Delta Air Lines
US: Tel 800-221 12 12.
Berlin: Tel 0180-333 78 80.
www.delta.com

dba
Tel 01805-35 93 22.
www.flydba.com

easyJet
www.easyjet.com

Lufthansa
US: Tel 800-645 3880.
Berlin: Tel 01805-83 84 26.
www.lufthansa.com

Qantas
Australia: Tel 612-131313.
Frankfurt: Tel 01805-25 06 20. www.qantas.com

Ryanair
www.ryanair.com

United Airlines
US: Tel 800-241 6522.
Frankfurt: Tel 069-50 07 03 87. www.
unitedairlines.de

AIRPORT INFORMATION

Berlin Schönefeld
Tel 0180-500 01 86.

Frankfurt am Main
Tel 0180-53 72 46 36.

Munich
Tel 089-97 52 13 13.

CAR RENTAL

Avis
Tel 06171-68 18 00.
www.avis.com

Hertz
Tel 0180-533 35 35.
www.hertz.com

Sixt Rent-a-Car
Tel 0180-525 25 25.
www.e-sixt.com

EMERGENCY SERVICES

ADAC
Tel 01802-222 222.

AvD
Tel 069-660 60.

TRAIN TRAVEL

Deutsche Bahn
National Rail Inquiries
Tel 11861. www.bahn.de

Shopping

Stores in Germany are generally of high quality but many products are not cheap. In Berlin almost anything can be bought, so long as you know where to look; outside Berlin, you'll discover that in many areas of the country the tradition of producing handicrafts and various types of folk art continues. A visit to a local market could give you the chance to buy a regional specialty to take home as a souvenir. The vast shopping malls that are springing up in every large city offer a wide choice of stores and top-quality brands.

MARKETS

A weekly market, known as a *Wochenmarkt*, is held in many towns throughout Germany. In smaller towns, stalls are set up in the market square, while in larger towns and cities markets may be held in specially designated squares in different neighborhoods. At these markets, you can buy fresh fruit and vegetables, cheeses, and many everyday items. Specialist fairs are often held at weekends – for example *Blumenmärkte*, where flowers are sold, or *Kunstmärkte*, where artists and craftsmen display their work for sale.

Every large town also has its *Flohmarkt* (fleamarket) where, among the masses of junk, pieces of amusing kitsch and genuine antiques can sometimes be found. In Berlin the **Antik-und Trödelmarkt** is worth a visit.

In Munich there is a famous market specializing in crafts, antiques, and hardware called **Auer Dult**. This is held during the last weeks of April, July, and October.

REGIONAL SPECIALTIES

Almost every state in Germany produces its own regional specialty and although you might not be able to take certain fresh foods back home, you could try them while you are visiting. For example, Lübeck is known for marzipan, while Nuremberg is synonymous with gingerbread. The Spreewald region is known for its pickled cucumbers, while you'll find the cherry jam produced in the Black Forest region is excellent. In Friesland

and Schleswig in the north, marinated herrings and excellent cheeses are worth trying. The hams of Westphalia have a well-deserved reputation, as do sausages from Braunschweig (Brunswick).

GIFTS AND SOUVENIRS

Just about every region of Germany has something special to offer. You could buy a beer stein from a beer hall, or a cuckoo clock from the Black Forest, for instance. If you are keen on dressing up, traditional clothes such as lederhosen and dirndl skirts can be found in Bavaria. For children, handmade puppets and marionettes are good gifts, while in Nuremberg there is a wide selection of toys. Don't forget that German optical items such as cameras, binoculars, and lenses are top quality and may be cheaper than at home.

ALCOHOLIC DRINKS

Renowned German beers are best drunk straight from the barrel, but it is also worth looking out for the bottled beers that are rarely seen outside Germany.

There are a number of fine German wines, especially those from vineyards in the Mosel and Rhine valleys. Excellent wines are also produced in Bavaria and Baden-Württemberg.

Various types of spirits, as well as herbal and root-flavored liqueurs and bitters, are produced on a large scale. If you visit a monastery you may be able to buy a bottle of a herbal infusion or a liqueur that is made to a centuries-old recipe.

SHOPPING IN BERLIN

Although German cities all boast shopping malls and every town has a shopping district popular with local residents, Berlin stands out with its choice and quality of shops. If it is luxury you want, you must head for the large stores on the Kurfürstendamm, Friedrichstrasse, and Potsdamer Platz, where all the major fashion houses and perfume makers have their stores. Alternatively, if you want to explore the smaller boutiques of lesser-known designers, make your way to Berlin's Hackescher Markt in the Mitte district, or to Prenzlauer Berg.

Kaufhaus des Westens, better known as **KaDeWe** in Wittenbergplatz, is the biggest and the best department store in Berlin. Only products of the highest quality are sold in these luxurious halls, where virtually everything you need is on sale – from unusual perfumes and elegant underwear to *haute couture*, all sold in a system of stores-within-stores. The food hall on the sixth floor is legendary for its restaurant overlooking Tauentzienstrasse.

Galeries Lafayette on Friedrichstrasse is nothing less than a slice of Paris placed in the heart of Berlin. Its perfumes, household items, and clothing attract an enormous clientele, many of whom also visit the food counter, which offers a wide range of French specialties. An extraordinary glass cone rises through the middle of the store, reflecting the interiors of the stores.

Another very popular store is **Wertheim** on the Kurfürstendamm. Although its range of goods is not as broad as that at Galeries Lafayette, there is still an enormous choice and its top-floor restaurant offers excellent views over the city.

New shopping malls are being opened all the time, usually situated conveniently close to S-Bahn stations. *Passagen* (arcades) are massive three-level structures, resembling huge arcaded passageways, which contain an enormous number of stores, ranging from supermarkets and pharmacies to bars, fashion outlets, and bookstores. Like most of the stores in Berlin, they stay open until 8pm during the week and are open on Sundays.

One of the newest shopping malls is the **Potsdamer Platz Arkaden**. Built in October 1998 this is now very popular both as a shopping mall and a meeting place for Berliners and visitors.

The **Gesundbrunnen-Center** is the biggest shopping arcade in Berlin, and has countless stalls and tables offering every kind of bargain. A large number of bars also makes this a popular place to meet friends for a beer or a coffee.

SHOPPING IN OTHER CITIES

Most shoppers in Munich make a beeline for the pedestrian precinct in the old town center between Karlsplatz and Marienplatz. Here you will find many big department stores such as **Ludwig Beck am Rathauseck** and chain stores where you can buy fashion and shoes as well as jewelry, souvenirs, and music.

For haute couture in Munich, the big-name stores are concentrated in these streets: Maximilianstrasse, Theatinerstrasse, Residenzstrasse, and Briennerstrasse.

The place to shop for food in Munich is the colorful **Viktualienmarkt** near Marienplatz. This has been the city's main food market for over 200 years.

The largest and most interesting shopping area in Frankfurt is the Zeil, while in Hamburg it is the Alsterhaus. Hamburg also prides itself on its many fine shopping arcades, several of which are covered and heated, making them ideal for window shopping.

CERAMICS AND GLASS

Porcelain made by Meissen is among the most sought-after in the world but it is expensive. Meissen porcelain can be found in the town itself at the **Staatliche Porzellan-Manufaktur** *(see p543)* or in several shops situated along the popular Kurfürstendamm in Berlin. Munich's **Porzellan Manufaktur Nymphenburg**, which has a factory and a shop in the grounds of Schloss Nymphenburg *(see*

p553), produces china of similarly exquisite quality. Berlin's **KPM** (Königliche Porzellan-Manufaktur), which has been in operation for over 250 years, also makes excellent porcelain.

German glassware is renowned. Old glassworks in Saxony and Bavaria still make glassware by traditional techniques: for example, beautifully cut and polished crystal tableware and ruby-colored glassware.

Some porcelain and glassware factories operate retail outlets with showrooms. Visitors can arrange to have purchases sent to their home.

BOOKSTORES

When you need a book in English or an American newspaper, **Buchexpress** is the place to go in Berlin. In Munich, look for the **Words'Worth** and **Geobuch** for good maps and guides. In Frankfurt try the **British Bookshop**.

The **Bücherbogen** chain offers a huge choice of books and has several outlets in Berlin and elsewhere; the one under the S-Bahn bridge near Savignyplatz in Berlin has the largest stock.

DIRECTORY

MARKETS

Antik-und Trödelmarkt
Ostbahnhof, Erich-Steinfurth-Strasse, Berlin.
⬭ *10am–5pm Sun.*

Auer Dult
Mariahilfplatz, Munich.
⬭ *last weeks of Apr, Jul & Oct.*

SHOPPING IN BERLIN

Galeries Lafayette
Französische Strasse 23, Berlin.
Tel 030-20 94 80.

Gesundbrunnen-Center
Badstrasse 4, Berlin.
Tel 030-493 00 00.

KaDeWe
Tauentzienstrasse 21–24, Berlin. *Tel 030-212 10.*

Potsdamer Platz Arkaden
Alte Potsdamer Strasse 7, Berlin. *Tel 030-255 92 70.*

Wertheim
Kurfürstendamm 231, Berlin.
Tel 030-88 00 33 00.

SHOPPING IN OTHER CITIES

Ludwig Beck am Rathauseck
Am Marienplatz 11, Munich.
Tel 089-23 69 10.

Viktualienmarkt
Peterplatz–Frauenstrasse, Munich. ⬭ *Mon–Sat.*

CERAMICS AND GLASS

KPM
Wegelystrasse 1, Berlin.
Tel 030-39 00 90.

Porzellan Manufaktur Nymphenburg
Schloss Nymphenburg, Nördliches Schloßrondell 8, Munich.
Tel 089-179 19 70.
Odeonsplatz 1, Munich.
Tel 089-28 24 28.

Staatliche Porzellan-Manufaktur
Talstrasse 9, Meissen.
Showroom ⬭ *9am–6pm (Nov–Apr: to 5pm).*
Tel 03521-4680.

BOOKSTORES

British Bookshop
Börsenstrasse 17, Frankfurt am Main.
Tel 069-28 04 92.

Bücherbogen
Savignyplatz, Berlin.
Tel 030-31 86 95 11.

Buchexpress
Unter den Eichen 57, Berlin.
Tel 030-831 40 04.

Geobuch
Rosental 6, Munich.
Tel 089-26 50 30.

Words'Worth
Schellingstrasse 3 & 21, Munich.
Tel 089-280 9141.

Entertainment

With so much on offer in Germany, it is possible to indulge just about any taste, whether you are looking for avant-garde theater and performance art, atmospheric clubs, or prestigious music festivals. Outside Berlin the larger cosmopolitan cities, such as Munich and Frankfurt, also offer a wide range of entertainment, from classical drama to eclectic nightclubs, from grand opera to discos.

ENTERTAINMENT LISTINGS

Tourist information centers offer basic information in every city and town, but the most comprehensive guides are in the local press and listings magazines. In Berlin there are *Tip* and *Zitty*, which are published every other Wednesday. The daily *Berliner Morgenpost* publishes its supplement *bm Live* on Fridays, while *Ticket* comes out on Wednesdays, together with *Tagesspiegel*.

Useful listing magazines in Munich are *In München* and *Münchener Stadtmagazin*. There is also a monthly review in English called *Munich Found*, available from the Tourist Office. You can get a monthly jazz magazine called *Münchener Jazz-Zeitung* in music shops and at jazz cafés and clubs.

In Frankfurt a magazine detailing events called *Prinz* is on sale from news kiosks. There are also free publications such as *Fritz*, while the *Frankfurter Woche* is available from the tourist office for a small sum.

BOOKING TICKETS

Theater and concert tickets can usually be booked up to two weeks in advance, and you can buy directly at the box office or by telephone. Reserved tickets must be picked up and paid for at least half an hour before the performance. For many performances in Berlin you can also pre-book tickets at **Ticket Online**.

One Berlin agency that specializes in last-minute ticket purchase is **Hekticket Theaterkassen** on Hardenbergerstrasse, where

you can get tickets on the day, even up to as little as an hour before a show. These tickets are usually sold at a 50 percent discount.

Students, senior citizens, and the disabled are entitled to a 50 percent discount on tickets, for which they must present proof of their status.

THEATER

As you would expect in the land of Goethe and Schiller, theatrical traditions are very strong in Germany. Almost every large town has a good local theater. Berlin's most famous theater is the magnificent **Berliner Ensemble**, which was once managed by Bertold Brecht. The **Deutsches Theater** offers an ambitious program, while the **Volksbühne** stages works by young playwrights. Munich has many theaters, with most of the productions in German. A venerable venue is the **Cuvilliéstheater** in the Residenz (*see pp548–9*), while the **Deutsches Theater** offers some foreign plays. The **Kammerspiele** is dedicated to contemporary works.

Frankfurt has a theater that offers productions in English, aptly called the **English Theatre**. You will find a range of old and new plays put on at the city's main theater, the **Schauspiel Frankfurt**.

CLASSICAL MUSIC AND DANCE

Berlin has one of the finest orchestras in the world — the Berlin Philharmonic Orchestra, whose home, the **Philharmonie**, is also one of the world's most beautiful concert halls. The city boasts three opera houses: the **Staatsoper Unter den Linden**

and the **Komische Oper** are in the eastern part of city, while the **Deutsche Oper Berlin** is in the west. The three opera houses have ballet programs built into their repertoires and these are performed largely by resident dance companies.

Munich has two opera houses and several distinguished resident orchestras. A visit to the **Bayerische Staatsoper** is a must if you appreciate grand opera and ballet. The **Gasteig** is a modern complex offering a range of classical concerts, large and small. Munich's **Prinzregententheater** is the main venue for ballet and other musical performances.

Frankfurt has a wide choice of musical events. At the **Alte Oper**, there are three halls for orchestral and vocal performances, while the **Jahrhunderthalle** also offers classical recitals and concerts.

JAZZ, ROCK, AND POP

Berlin is always a popular destination for world-famous musicians, whose concerts are often held in the **Waldbühne**. Numerous music clubs offer daily opportunities to hear good music. Favorite venues are **Quasimodo** in the western part of the city center, **Schlot** in Prenzlauer Berg and **Junction Bar** in Kreuzberg. Good traditional jazz can be heard at Berlin's annual Jazzfest in the first week of November. At the same time experimental modern works are performed at the Total Music Meeting.

In Munich in the late evening you could drop into a small, hip club like **Atomic Café** or go to hear blues, rock, or jazz at **Feierwerk**. Dixieland jazz is played at the **Alabamahalle** and traditional jazz at **Jazzclub Unterfahrt**. There are often free rock concerts in Munich in summer at the Theatron in Olympiapark. Frankfurt has an enthusiastic jazz scene which is centered around *Jazzgasse* (Jazz Alley) or Kleine Bockenheimer Strasse. Here you will find the city's top jazz venue, **Jazzkeller**, in a cellar. If you like to listen to different kinds of live music such as African, Asian, and salsa, try **Brotfabrik**, which also has a café.

Discos in Munich and Frankfurt mainly cater, naturally enough, for a young crowd and play music of all kinds: from chart hits, funk, and techno to heavy metal. Some have a dress policy.

FESTIVALS AND FAIRS

Germans love festivals and fairs and this country probably has more than most other European countries. The most famous is the *Oktoberfest* in Munich *(see p554)*, which is a huge event that celebrates beer with two weeks of drinking, from the last week in September. Not to be outdone, wine-drinkers can enjoy a wine festival *(Weinfest)* in August in the Rhine-Mosel area and in October in the Rhineland.

Germany has produced many of the world's foremost musicians, so classical music festivals are popular and take place in many German towns. To give a few examples, there is a Bach Festival in May in Leipzig *(see p543)*, while Bonn *(see p561)* is the venue for the International Beethoven Festival from late September. Beginning in late July, Bayreuth *(see p540)* hosts the annual *Opernfest* of Richard Wagner's *Ring Cycle*. However, be aware that you cannot just turn up for a performance here – you will have to book tickets at least a year in advance or else get them with a package holiday.

December brings a rush of fairs. Many towns and cities, including Berlin and Munich, stage a Christmas market *(Christkindlmarkt)*, but the one in Nuremberg is considered to be the most impressive.

OUTDOOR ACTIVITIES

Germany is the ideal destination for a range of outdoor activities, including hiking, cycling, fishing, and sailing. It also has a number of winter-sports resorts with first-class ski slopes, the best being in the Bavarian Alps, which lie only an hour's drive from Munich.

There is a tradition of great horsemanship in Germany. Keen riders will find excellent facilities in many areas, as well as the chance to attend international competitions.

Tennis is the second most popular sport (after soccer) and there are several annual professional tournaments. You can play on the many public courts, or find a hotel with its own facilities. Golfers with the appropriate handicap can play on most golf courses simply by paying a green fee.

DIRECTORY

BOOKING TICKETS

Ticket Online
Tel 01805-4470.
www.ticketonline.de

Hekticket Theaterkassen
Hardenbergstrasse 29d, Berlin.
Tel 030-23 09 93 33.

THEATER

Berliner Ensemble
Bertold-Brecht-Platz 1, Berlin.
Tel 030-28 40 80.

Cuvilliéstheater
Residenzstrasse 1, Munich.
Tel 089-21 85 19 40.

Deutsches Theater
Schumannstrasse 13a, Berlin.
Tel 030-28 44 12 25.

Deutsches Theater
Schwanthalerstrasse 13, Munich.
Tel 089-55 23 44 44.

English Theatre
Kaiserstrasse 34, Frankfurt.
Tel 069-24 23 16 20.

Kammerspiele
Maximillianstrasse 28, Munich.
Tel 089-233 966 00.

Schauspiel Frankfurt
Neue Mainter Strasse 17, Frankfurt.
Tel 069-13 40 400.

Volksbühne
Rosa-Luxemburg-Platz, Berlin.
Tel 030-247 7694.

CLASSICAL MUSIC AND DANCE

Alte Oper
Opernplatz, Frankfurt.
Tel 069-134 04 00

Bayerische Staatsoper
Max-Joseph-Platz 1, Munich.
Tel 089-21 85 19 20.

Deutsche Oper
Bismarckstrasse 35, Berlin.
Tel 030-343 84 01.

Gasteig
Rosenheimer Strasse 5, Munich.
Tel 089-480 980.

Jahrhunderthalle
Pffafenwiese, Frankfurt.
Tel 069-360 12 36.

Komische Oper
Behrenstrasse 55–57, Berlin.
Tel 030-47 99 74 00.

Philharmonie
Herbert-von-Karajan-Strasse 1, Berlin.
Tel 030-25 48 89 99.

Prinzregenten-theater
Prinzregentenplatz 12, Munich.
Tel 089-21 85 19 20.

Staatsoper
Unter den Linden 7, Berlin.
Tel 030-20 35 45 55.

JAZZ, ROCK, AND POP

Alabamahalle
Domagkstrasse 33, Munich.
Tel 089-368 14 50.

Atomic Café
Neuturmstrasse 5, Munich.
Tel 089-228 30 52.

Brotfabrik
Bachmannstrasse 2–4, Frankfurt.
Tel 069-789 55 13.

Feierwerk
Hansastrasse 39, Munich.
Tel 089-72 48 80.

Jazzclub Unterfahrt
Einsteinstrasse 42, Munich.
Tel 089-448 2794.

Jazzkeller
Kleine Bockenheimer Strasse 18a, Frankfurt.
Tel 069-28 85 37.

Junction Bar
Gneisenaustrasse 18, Berlin.
Tel 030-694 66 02.

Quasimodo
Kantstrasse 12a, Berlin.
Tel 030-312 80 86.

Schlot
Chausseestrasse 18, Berlin.
Tel 030-448 21 60.

Waldbühne
Am Glockenturm, Berlin.
Tel 030-23 09 93 33.

Where to Stay in Germany

Most German cities have several deluxe and international chain hotels offering a high level of comfort. Finding less expensive accommodations can be difficult, unless you stay outside the center. Away from the cities, high prices generally apply to hotels in historic or peaceful locations; a room in a pension or private home is usually cheaper.

PRICE CATEGORIES
Price categories are for a standard double room for one night in peak season, including tax, service charges, and breakfast:
€ Under 75 euros
€€ 75–125 euros
€€€ 125–175 euros
€€€€ 175–225 euros
€€€€€ Over 225 euros

BERLIN

EAST OF CENTER Alexander Plaza Berlin
€€€

Rosenstraße 1, 10178 **Tel** *030-240 010* **Fax** *030-240 017 77* **Rooms** *92*   **Map** *F3*

This top-quality hotel, opened in 1997, is located near the S-Bahn station Hackescher Markt. Rooms in the late 19th-century building, an intriguing mixture of stucco ceilings, glass and steel, are large, comfortable, and full of light, with soundproofed windows. There is a nice lobby bar and café. **www.alexander-plaza.de**

EAST OF CENTER Art'otel Berlin Mitte
€€€

Wallstraße 70–73, 10179 **Tel** *030-240 620* **Fax** *030-240 622 22* **Rooms** *109*   **Map** *F3*

Overlooking the Spree river, this upmarket hotel is well priced and one of the most popular establishments in Mitte. Inside, it is modern with simple and elegant furniture. In summer there is a café on a riverboat tied to the riverbank. The hotel is popular with young, culture-oriented guests. **www.artotel.de**

EAST OF CENTER Derag Residenz Hotel Henriette
€€€€

Neue Rossstraße 13, 10179 **Tel** *030-246 009 00* **Fax** *030-246 009 40* **Rooms** *54*   **Map** *F3/4*

The small and intimate Henriette is the nicest – and the most unknown – of the many Derag hotels in town. Although built recently, it exudes an incredibly elegant, historic flair, with oak furniture, precious carpets and beds. The hotel provides excellent service. **www.deraghotels.de**

EAST OF CENTER Hotel Gendarm
€€€€

Charlottenstraße 61, 10117 **Tel** *030-206 06 60* **Fax** *030-206 066 66* **Rooms** *27*   **Map** *E4*

The Gendarm's reputation as one of the best and most popular smaller hotels in Berlin is more than justified. An excellent service, a great location off Gendarmenmarkt and traditional, elegantly furnished rooms make this a serious competitor of the big five-star hotels nearby. **www.hotel-gendarm-berlin.de**

EAST OF CENTER Hotel de Rome
€€€€€

Behrenstraße 37, 10117 **Tel** *030-460 60 90* **Fax** *030-460 60 92 000* **Rooms** *146*   **Map** *E3*

Hidden behind the classicist façade of a former 19th-century bank, this is a new shining star among the city's first-class hotels. The interior design is very modern, with subdued colors complementing the historic setting. The service is impeccable and the fairly large rooms offer wonderful views of Opernplatz. **www.hotelderome.com**

EAST OF CENTER Sofitel am Gendarmenmarkt
€€€€€

Charlottenstraße 50–52, 10117 **Tel** *030-203 750* **Fax** *030-203 751 00* **Rooms** *92*   **Map** *E4*

This luxury hotel offers well-furnished rooms and excellent service. It is conveniently located near the Gendarmenmarkt, not far from Unter den Linden and sights such as the Brandenburg Gate and the Reichstag. The Aigner restaurant downstairs specializes in good Austrian food. **www.sofitel.com**

WEST OF CENTER Ellington Hotel
€€

Nürnberger Straße 50–55, 10789 **Tel** *030-683 150* **Fax** *030-683 55 555* **Rooms** *285*   **Map** *C4*

An oasis of modern design behind the stunning façade of a 1920s Bauhaus-style office building, the Ellington is an affordable stylish alternative to other central hotels. The bright colors, perfect service, and great location more than make up for the small rooms, with many thoughtful touches ensuring a comfortable stay. **www.ellingtonhotel.de**

WEST OF CENTER Arte Luise Kunsthotel
€€€

Luisenstraße 19, 10117 **Tel** *030-284 480* **Fax** *030-284 484 48* **Rooms** *50*   **Map** *E3*

An authentic Berlin artist's hotel, the Künstlerheim (literally "home for artists") welcomes the artsy crowd into individually designed rooms, created by various German artists, in an early 19th-century house. It is steps away from the Scheunenviertel and offers great service. **www.arte-luise.com**

WEST OF CENTER Hotel Brandenburger Hof
€€€€

Eislebener Straße 14, 10789 **Tel** *030-214 050* **Fax** *030-214 051 00* **Rooms** *72*   **Map** *B4*

An intimate family atmosphere, impeccable service and quiet luxurious rooms make this one of the most desirable top-notch hotels in Berlin. The enchanting building has been restored and rooms feature Bauhaus furniture. The Michelin-awarded restaurant, Die Quadriga is a must. **www.brandenburger-hof.com**

Key to Symbols *see back cover flap*

WEST OF CENTER Hotel Concorde Berlin

Augsburger Straße 41, 10789 **Tel** *030-800 999 0* **Fax** *030-800 999 99* **Rooms** *311* **Map** *C4*

Offering sophisticated charm, this modern hotel is decorated in minimalist style, with a lot of glass, warm lights, and wooden paneling. The large comfortable rooms, impeccable service and French restaurant, Faubourg, all contribute to its appeal, as do the views of bustling street life on Kurfürstendamm. **www.hotelconcordeberlin.com**

FARTHER AFIELD Hotel-Pension Kastanienhof

Kastanienallee 65, 10119 **Tel** *030-44 30 50* **Fax** *030-443 051 11* **Rooms** *35*

The Kastanienhof is a budget *Pension* hidden in a fully restored, typical Berlin tenement house. Its location is perfect for exploring the clubbing scene in Prenzlauer Berg. The rooms are surprisingly nice and come equipped with a hairdryer, mini bar and safe. **www.hotel-kastanienhof-berlin.de**

FARTHER AFIELD Honigmond

Tieckstraße 11, 10115 **Tel** *030-284 45 50* **Fax** *030-284 455 11* **Rooms** *60*

The Honigmond is great for exploring the Mitte and Prenzlauer Berg arts scenes. Originally a traditional 19th-century tenement house with a courtyard, it has individuallly designed rooms, some of which feature four-poster beds and parquet floors, while other rooms entice you with their summerhouse feel. **www.honigmond.de**

EASTERN GERMANY

DRESDEN Romantik Hotel Pattis

Merbitzer Straße 53, 1157 **Tel** *0351-42 55 0* **Fax** *0351-42 55 25 5* **Rooms** *46*

This is very much a family-run hotel (pictures, birth dates, and other family information are given on the website) and offers a rather effective mix of business-class standards and personal touches that will make you feel both important and relaxed at the same time. **www.pattis.de**

DRESDEN Steigenberger Hotel de Saxe

Neumarkt 9, 1067 **Tel** *0351-43 86 0* **Fax** *0351-43 86 88 8* **Rooms** *185*

Even the simple rooms are vast and elegant and offer internet, satellite television, safes, and the usual list of comforts and conveniences. There is a definite sense of sparkle and fresh opulence in the dining areas. This is a very refined establishment. **www.desaxe-dresden.steigenberger.de**

LEIPZIG Alt-Connewitz Hotel-Restaurant

Meusdorfer Straße 47a, 4277 **Tel** *0341-30 13 77 0* **Fax** *0341-30 13 80 0* **Rooms** *33*

A simple and straightforward hotel with very reasonable prices. The comfortable guest rooms have a fresh, clean decor and include internet access and TV. They also have a good restaurant with a fine selection of wines. **www.alt-connewitz.de**

LEIPZIG Hotel Fürstenhof

Tröndlinring 8, 4105 **Tel** *0341-14 00* **Fax** *0341-14 03 70 0* **Rooms** *92*

A hotel with a bright and confident classiness. Its rooms are colorfully decorated and furnished, and tall slim windows offer plenty of light and a feeling of space. All rooms have a mini bar and satellite television, but the ones that overlook the courtyard are worth requesting. A bold and luxurious hotel. **www.luxurycollection.com/fuerstenhof**

WEIMAR Hotel Elephant

Markt 19, 99423 **Tel** *03643-80 20* **Fax** *03643-80 26 10* **Rooms** *99*

Despite the hotel's name, the style here is very refined and stately. Everything is squared-off, neat, respectable, and comfortable. All rooms also have original artworks, and the hotel has a tradition of being a meeting place for artists, poets, and intellectuals. **www.luxurycollection.com/elephant**

MUNICH

CENTRAL MUNICH Gästehaus Englischer Garten

Liebergesellstraße 8, 80802 **Tel** *089-3839410* **Fax** *089-38394-133* **Rooms** *25*

A cosy little guesthouse with pleasant, if small rooms. The hotel is quiet and family run. Longer-stay apartments are also available, offering more space and a balcony. Once a watermill, the now listed building has a lovely garden where you can sit out and enjoy breakfast. **www.hotelenglischergarten.de**

CENTRAL MUNICH Cosmopolitan Hotel

Hohenzollernstraße 5, 80801 **Tel** *089-383810* **Fax** *089-38381-111* **Rooms** *71* **Map** *2 C1*

A contemporary hotel in a quieter side street in the fashionable Schwabing district. There is a modern design feel throughout and rooms have Ligne Roset furniture. Enjoy breakfast on the outdoor terrace in warmer weather. It is located just a short walk from the English Garden. **www.geisel-privathotels.de**

Map References *see maps of Berlin pp528–9 and Munich pp546–7*

CENTRAL MUNICH Insel Mühle
Von-Kahr-Straße 87, 80999 **Tel** *089-810 10* **Fax** *089-812 05 71* **Rooms** *38*

This hotel has a dreamy romantic setting in an old mill with beautiful gardens by a small river. The style is simple, rustic and comfortable. There is also an excellent restaurant, beer garden, wine cellar, and bar. Choose tables in shady spots, under trees, or simply relax and wander around the grounds. **www.insel-muehle.com**

CENTRAL MUNICH Novotel Muenchen City
Hochstraße 11, 81669 **Tel** *089-661 070* **Fax** *089-66 10 79 99* **Rooms** *307*

A very contemporary four-star hotel with simple, sleek, bright decor. The welcoming breakfast room has large floral photographs. There is also a spacious pool and relaxation room plus fitness area. Its central location means that you can walk to Marienplatz, the Gasteig cultural center or museums. **www.novotel.com**

CENTRAL MUNICH Bayerischer Hof
Promenadeplatz 2–6, 80333 **Tel** *089-212 00* **Fax** *089-212 09 06* **Rooms** *395* **Map** *2 A3*

A large luxurious hotel in a prominent central location near the best shops, museums, opera house, theaters and restaurants. Elegant rooms with swathes of fabrics mixing plaids and florals in a country-house style. It also has a spa, three restaurants, including the Garden Restaurant, and a great bar. **www.bayerischerhof.de**

CENTRAL MUNICH Kempinski Hotel Vier Jahreszeiten
Maximilianstraße 17, 80539 **Tel** *089-212 50* **Fax** *089-21 25 20 00* **Rooms** *308* **Map** *2 C4*

The top address in Munich (built for King Maximilian II in 1858) nestled among the designer stores on Maximilianstraße. Excellent service, gastronomy, and bars. A stunning entrance hall in rich gold and reds sets the tone. The pool and wellness floor was completely revamped in 2006. **www.kempinski-vierjahreszeiten.de**

SOUTHERN GERMANY

BAMBERG Alt Ringlein
Dominikanerstraße 9, 96049 **Tel** *0951-953 20* **Fax** *0951-953 25 00* **Rooms** *33*

A pleasant and comfortable hotel in Bamberg's center. Enjoy the choice of Franconian meals in its restaurant of the same name and try one of several local beers, including their own home-brewed one. In the wing dating back to 1296 they have Franconian styled rooms. Make sure you spend time in the nice beer garden. **www.alt-ringlein.com**

BAMBERG Welcome Hotel Residenzschloss
Untere Sandstraße 32, 96049 **Tel** *0951-609 10* **Fax** *0951-609 17 01* **Rooms** *184*

This hotel has classic rooms in a listed building on the banks of the river Regnitz. Now a spa and conference hotel, it began life as a hospital back in 1789. Guests can choose between two restaurants, and there is also a piano bar and small chapel, which sometimes holds classical concerts. **www.residenzschloss.com**

FREIBURG IM BREISGAU Zum Roten Bären
Oberlinden 12, 79098 **Tel** *0761-387 870* **Rooms** *25*

Situated in a building that dates back to the 12th century, just minutes from the center of Freiburg, this hotel also has a lovely traditional *Stube*, a tavern-style restaurant serving regional seasonal food. The guest rooms are comfortable and there is also a peaceful courtyard. **www.roter-baeren.de**

HEIDELBERG Holländer Hof
Neckarstaden 66, 69117 **Tel** *06221-605 00* **Rooms** *39*

An old house in the center of town with a pretty façade and classic, elegant rooms, this hotel is within easy reach of the famous castle and not far from the shops, restaurants, churches, and pedestrianized area of Heidelberg. It is also close to where boat rides are run up and down the Neckar. **www.hollaender-hof.de**

HEIDELBERG Europäischer Hof Hotel Europa
Friedrich-Ebert-Anlage 1, 69117 **Tel** *06221-515 0* **Rooms** *118*

The best in the area this hotel has luxurious suites, high quality rooms, courteous and helpful staff, à la carte dinners in the Kurfürstenstube, a terrace overlooking a garden, a shopping arcade, and the Panorama spa and fitness club. There is everything you could possibly want to make it a memorable stay. **www.europaeischerhof.com**

LINDAU Bayerischer Hof
Seepromenade, 88131 **Tel** *08382-9150* **Fax** *08382-915 591* **Rooms** *97*

A luxurious Neo-Classical building dating back to 1854, located on the harbor front which has spacious rooms and suites, good service and excellent fitness, pool, sauna, and wellbeing facilities. Enjoy the international cuisine in the restaurant of the same name and unforgettable lake views from the bar. **www.bayerischerhof-lindau.de**

NUREMBERG Burghotel
Lammgaße 3, 90403 **Tel** *0911-238 890* **Fax** *0911-2388 9100* **Rooms** *58*

Charming simple rooms filled with light offer some great views over the roofs of the old town. Burghotel has traces of ancient castle life, such as armour and coats-of-arms. There is also a lounge with an open fire, rustic bar, sun terrace, and sauna. **www.altstadthotels-nuernberg.de**

NUREMBERG Romantik Hotel am Josephplatz 🖼️🏃🛏️📧 €€
*Josephsplatz 30–32, 90403 **Tel** 0911-214 470 **Fax** 0911-21 44 72 00 **Rooms** 36*

A romantic hotel dating back to 1675 located within walking distance of Nuremburg's old center. There are small apartments which would suit a family. Enjoy the good breakfast buffet, roof terrace, sauna, solarium, fitness room, and winter garden. There are also several restaurants close by. **www.romantikhotels.com/Nuernberg**

NUREMBERG Maritim Hotel Nürnberg 🖼️🍴♨️🏃🛏️📧 €€€€
*Frauentorgraben 11, 90443 **Tel** 0911-236 30 **Fax** 0911-236 38 23 **Rooms** 316*

The Maritim has a slightly corporate feel (it is run by a large German chain), but has an excellent central location opposite the ancient city wall. There are good swimming and wellbeing facilities plus a choice of restaurants – Stube for international cuisine, the Blauer Salon café or the piano bar. **www.maritim.de**

PASSAU Passauer Wolf 🖼️ €€€
*Rindermarkt 6–8, 94032 **Tel** 0851-931 510 **Fax** 0851-931 5150 **Rooms** 41*

This hotel is located in the old town of Passau, next to the pedestrian precinct and on the banks of the Danube. The St. Stephan cathedral and several museums and unique sights are within walking distance. Choose between rooms with a view over the river, the old town or the courtyard. **www.hotel-passauer-wolf.de**

ROTHENBURG OB DER TAUBER Prinzhotel 🖼️🍴 €€
*An der Hofstett 3, 91541 **Tel** 09861-9750 **Fax** 09861-97575 **Rooms** 52*

Within the old town walls, this historic hotel is in a very quiet location surrounded by the town's medieval history. All the sights are within walking distance. The hotel's restaurant serves Franconian-Italian cuisine. Parking is available in front of the hotel. **www.prinzhotel.rothenburg.de**

STUTTGART Hansa Hotel 🖼️🍴🏃 €€
*Silberburgstraße 114–116, 70176 **Tel** 0711-656 7800 **Fax** 0711-617 349 **Rooms** 80*

This is located near the pedestrianized area, so it is a good central base for exploring the Swabian capital of Stuttgart. It is also close to shops, restaurants, the station, and museums. There is internet access, bike hire, a restaurant, Petrarca, offering Mediterranean specials, and a beer garden. **www.hansa-stuttgart.de**

STUTTGART Kronen Hotel 🖼️📧 €€€
*Kronenstraße 48, 70174 **Tel** 0711-225 10 **Rooms** 80*

Located in a quiet spot, but still with easy access to the railway station, this hotel has a nice garden with terrace. Enjoy the great breakfast buffet in the modern breakfast room, looking out onto a palmed terrace. Guests can also take drinks at the little lobby bar or use the hotel sauna. **www.kronenhotel-stuttgart.de**

WÜRZBURG/ HOCHBERG Minotel Zum Lamm 🖼️🍴🏃 €€
*Hauptstraße 76, 97204 **Tel** 0931-304 5630 **Fax** 0931-408 973 **Rooms** 37*

The hotel lies in Höchberg, outside the Baroque center of Würzburg and offers guests a typical Franconian hospitality and great gourmet food. It also boasts a lovely courtyard and garden. Guests are spoiled with great food and wine, and it is popular with cyclists, motorcyclists, and hikers touring the area. **www.lamm-hoechberg.de**

WESTERN GERMANY

BONN Schlosshotel Kommende Ramersdorf 🖼️🍴 €€
*Oberkasslerstraße 10, 53227 **Tel** 0228-440 734 **Fax** 0228-444 400 **Rooms** 18*

Situated in a fairytale castle, the rooms and hallways here are filled with antiques and works of art that help set it apart from other hotels. There is a medieval feel to the hotel, and each room is individual. The restaurant is also worth a visit. **www.schlosshotel-kommende-ramersdorf.de**

BONN Kaiser Karl 🖼️🍴 €€€
*Vorgebirgsstraße 56, 53119 **Tel** 0228-985 570 **Fax** 0228-985 5777 **Rooms** 42*

Exquisitely decorated rooms and a keen eye for detail make this hotel a welcome oasis of leisure and pleasure. All rooms cater to those with allergies. Many famous guests have passed through the doors, and more than a few have tinkled the keys of the piano in the old-fashioned and dignified bar. **www.kaiser-karl-hotel-bonn.de**

BONN Dorint Sofitel Venusberg 🖼️🍴🏃🛏️📧 €€€€€
*An der Casselsruhe 1, 53127 **Tel** 0228-2880 **Fax** 0228-288 288 **Rooms** 85*

This hotel sits on the banks of the Rhine and has colorful and decadent rooms that overlook the surrounding forest. There are a number of sporting facilities in the area, such as golf and tennis, and there is a jogging track inside the hotel for fitness fans. **www.accorhotels.com**

COLOGNE Hotel Kosmos 🖼️🍴♨️🏃🛏️📧 €€
*Waldecker Straße 11–15, 51065 **Tel** 0221-67090 **Fax** 0221-6709321 **Rooms** 161*

Set in an otherwise dull area this hotel is an oasis of comfort and hospitality. The air-conditioned rooms are spacious and well equipped. The hotel is still family run and great care has gone into retaining its charm. They have a large pool and good fitness facilities. It attracts mostly business guests for trade fairs. **www.kosmos-hotel-koeln.de**

Key to Symbols *see back cover flap*

COLOGNE Hyatt Regency
Kennedy-Ufer 2a, 50679 **Tel** *0221-828 12 34* **Fax** *0221-828 1370* **Rooms** *306*

One of the best hotels in Germany, this Hyatt has a prime location perfect both for crossing the bridge into the Old Town and visiting the trade fairs. All tastes are catered for and the view over the Rhine and the Old Town is unparalleled. **www.cologne.regency.hyatt.de**

COLOGNE Hotel im Wasserturm
Kaygasse 2, 50676 **Tel** *0221-200 80* **Fax** *0221-200 88 88* **Rooms** *88*

Integrated into a historic water tower in the heart of Cologne, this top class hotel is one of the most distinctive in the city. The building's shape has spawned oddly shaped rooms, some with two levels. On the 11th floor is an opulent restaurant, La Vision, that has been awarded a Michelin star. **www.hotel-im-wasserturm.de**

COLOGNE Jolly Hotel MediaPark
Im MediaPark 8b, 50670 **Tel** *0221-271 50* **Fax** *0221-271 59 99* **Rooms** *217*

Part of an Italian chain of hotels, this one displays the subtle and refined styling that serves them well. There are luxurious and comfortable rooms and facilities, situated in the MediaPark, next to the tall tower. There are excellent fitness and wellness facilities, and guests receive discounts at the nearby Holmes gym. **www.jollyhotels.de**

FRANKFURT AM MAIN Hotel Borger
Triebstraße 51, 60388 **Tel** *06109-309 00* **Fax** *06109-309 030* **Rooms** *36*

A family-styled hotel with a comfortable atmosphere and a convenient location, the rooms here offer the basic amenities, and the hotel is the perfect base for exploring the city and surrounding areas. The villa has been in the family for over a hundred years and was renovated late in the 20th century. **www.hotel-borger.de**

FRANKFURT AM MAIN Frankfurt Hotel Savoy
Wiesenhüttenstraße 42, 60329 **Tel** *069-273 960* **Fax** *069-273 967 95* **Rooms** *144*

This hotel has a classy attitude. Situated in a convenient location for trade fairs and with good access to the airport, guests will find the hotel itself a charming place to explore. There is a swimming pool on the top floor, which offers a rare and beautiful skyline view of Frankfurt am Main. **www.savoyhotel.de**

FRANKFURT AM MAIN Hessischer Hof
Friedrich Ebert Anlage 40, 60325 **Tel** *069-754 00* **Fax** *069-754 029 24* **Rooms** *117*

An exquisitely styled hotel with a sense of class. The rooms are styled either in a modern manner or with more of an antique feel about them, with some of the suites furnished with pieces from the Prince of Hesse. The restaurant and bar compliment each other well. **www.hessischer-hof.de**

FRANKFURT AM MAIN Steigenberger Frankfurter Hof
Am Kaiserplatz, 60311 **Tel** *069-215 02* **Fax** *069-215 09 00* **Rooms** *321*

A very large and comprehensive hotel where everything you desire is catered for and is done in style. The rooms are impeccable and the restaurants are among the best in the city. It is situated less than a kilometer away from the main station and has very helpful and friendly staff. **www.frankfurter-hof.steigenberger.de**

KOBLENZ Top Hotel Krämer Garni
Kardinal-Krementz-Straße 12, 56073 **Tel** *0261-406 200* **Fax** *0261-413 40* **Rooms** *25*

A comfortable and new hotel, with a touch of the traditional German style. The rooms have a modern feel about them, and fresh flowers are a colorful touch which contrast well with the somewhat minimalist decor. The service is friendly and enhances the personal atmosphere of the hotel. **www.tophotel-k.de**

KOBLENZ Mercure
Julius-Wegeler-Straße 6, 56068 **Tel** *0261-136 0* **Fax** *0261-1361199* **Rooms** *169*

There is a home-like feeling to the colorful and comfortable rooms, which also offer nice views. The hotel has an elegant restaurant and a stylish lounge bar. There is also a good view from the higher floors of the hotel looking over Koblenz and the surrounding district. **www.mercure.com**

MAINZ Favorite Parkhotel
Karl-Weiser-Straße 1, 55131 **Tel** *06131-801 50* **Fax** *06131-801 54 20* **Rooms** *122*

There is a pleasant surprise around every door here. Apart from the ultra-comfortable rooms and suites, there is a greenhouse with different varieties of palms, a gourmet restaurant, and a beer garden that is a favorite meeting place for locals as well as guests. **www.favorite-mainz.de**

MAINZ Novotel Mainz
Augustusstraße 6, 55131 **Tel** *06131-954 0* **Fax** *06131-954 100* **Rooms** *217*

The bright and well-equipped rooms are very comfortable, and there is a spacious and relaxing pool area. Their restaurant offers elegant dining and a must-see wine bar, Kasematten, which is situated in a 17th-century vaulted cellar, providing a distinctive atmosphere for wine tastings. **www.novotel.com**

TRIER Römischer Kaiser
Porta-Nigra-Platz 6, 54292 **Tel** *0651-977 0100* **Fax** *0651-977 019 99* **Rooms** *43*

This hotel is housed in part of a historic building in the illustrious Porta Nigra Square. First mentioned in 1885, the hotel was refurbished in 1994, and now offers a decadent retreat in the heart of Trier. The rooms are tastefully furnished and spacious. It has a highly recommended restaurant of the same name. **www.hotels-trier.de**

Key to Price Guide *see p574* **Key to Symbols** *see back cover flap*

NORTHERN GERMANY

BREMEN Park Hotel

Im Bürgerpark, 28209 **Tel** *0421-340 80* **Fax** *0421-340 86 02* **Rooms** *177*

Opulent and expansive, the Park Hotel brings to life all your dreams of luxury and comfort. The grounds are well sculpted and spectacular, as are the rooms which are guaranteed to make you feel relaxed. There are several restaurants, bars, and bistros, so take your pick. **www.park-hotel-bremen.de**

BREMEN Landhaus Radler Garni

Kastanienweg 17, 27404 **Tel** *04281-988 20* **Fax** *04281-988 210* **Rooms** *16*

A family-owned and managed hotel, this place is a little distant from the center of Bremen, but offers a peaceful atmosphere that is appreciated by families. There is a playground for children and the surrounding area is perfect for cycling and exploring on foot. Nestled in the rear is a well-maintained little garden. **www.landhaus-radler.de**

HAMBURG Le Royal Meridien

An Der Auster 52–56, 20099 **Tel** *040-210 00* **Fax** *040-210 011 11* **Rooms** *284*

Situated on the banks of Alster lake this modern, luxury hotel offers some of the best views Hamburg has to offer. Rooms are sparsely furnished but offer all the amenities of a first-class hotel. The Meridien spa and fitness club is considered to be one of the best designed in Germany. **www.leroyalmeridien-hamburg.com**

HAMBURG Side Hotel Hamburg

Drehbahn 49, 20354 **Tel** *040-309 990* **Fax** *040-309 993 99* **Rooms** *178*

This five-star dream of a hotel is a comfortable and centrally located alternative to the more classic top hotels in the downtown area. The architecture and interior design is cutting edge; rooms are decorated in soft, shiny beige and white colors. For a little extra you can book an Executive room with a kitchenette. **www.side-hamburg.de**

HAMBURG Park Hyatt

Bugenhagenstrasse 8, 20095 **Tel** *040-332 12 34* **Fax** *040-333 212 35* **Rooms** *252*

The Park Hyatt is located in the heart of historic Hamburg and off Mönckebergstrasse – the city's main shopping pedestrian zone. Rooms are modern and feature large-screen TVs and moveable bathroom doors. The breakfast buffet offers a huge range of international and German dishes. **www.hamburg.park.hyatt.com**

HANNOVER Best Western Parkhotel Kronsberg

Gut Kronsberg 1, 30539 **Tel** *0511-874 00* **Fax** *0511-867 112* **Rooms** *200*

Conveniently located opposite the fairground, the hotel has become a favorite with business guests. With lots of light and space, the lobby is crowned with a glass dome. There is a mixture of room styles which are all comfortable and spacious. The restaurants and bistros offer character and good food. **www.kronsberg.bestwestern.de**

HANNOVER Hotel Kaiserhof

Ernst-August-Platz 4, 30159 **Tel** *0511-368 30* **Fax** *0511-368 31 14* **Rooms** *78*

Housed in a historic building constructed in 1915, this hotel has been well preserved. There is a subtle French style to the tastefully detailed rooms. It is located opposite the main train station and close to the city center. The restaurant is highly acclaimed, and serves trout that they raise themselves in a courtyard fountain. **www.centralhotel.de**

HANNOVER Novotel Hannover

Podbielskistraße 21–23, 30163 **Tel** *0511-390 40* **Fax** *0511-390 41 00* **Rooms** *206*

Housed in an old biscuit factory, this hotel has luxurious amenities and guest rooms, with a playground for children, as well as a babysitting service if required. It also has extensive conference facilities, indeed one conference room still retains some old machinery from the factory days. **www.novotel.de**

LÜBECK Kaiserhof

Kronsforder Allee 11–13, 23560 **Tel** *0451-703 301* **Fax** *0451-795 083* **Rooms** *58*

Sitting in the middle of the "island", you could not ask for a better location. Close to historic attractions and museums, some guest rooms here have a balcony. Their restaurant focuses on fish and there is an elegant banquet hall which is often used for weddings and other functions. **www.kaiserhof-luebeck.de**

LÜBECK Radisson SAS Senator Hotel

Willy-Brandt-Allee 6, 23554 **Tel** *0451-14 20* **Fax** *0451-142 22 22* **Rooms** *224*

Overlooking the river and close to the center, the rooms here are very comfortable and bright. There are many facilities to keep children occupied and when accompanied by parents they eat in the restaurant for free. Along with the restaurant, there is a cocktail bar, a café, and a tavern with adjoining beer garden. **www.senatorhotel.de**

MÜNSTER Schloss Wilkinghege

Steinfurter Straße 374, 48159 **Tel** *0251-144 270* **Fax** *0251-212 898* **Rooms** *35*

A successful blend of modern comfort and historic charm, the top suite here has been furnished with antiques, and the bathroom adorned with Philippe Starck fixtures. The restaurant serves refined cuisine with a subtle French flair. Next door there is a golf course and tennis courts. **www.schloss-wilkinghege.de**

Where to Eat in Germany

German cuisine does not enjoy the same reputation as that of some European countries. Nevertheless you can eat very well here with many restaurants specializing in appetizing, if somewhat heavy, regional dishes. In the past few years, some fine restaurants have opened seving excellent international cuisine.

PRICE CATEGORIES
The following price ranges are for a three-course meal for one, including a half-bottle of house wine, tax, and service:
€ Under 30 euros
€€ 30–45 euros
€€€ 45–60 euros
€€€€ 60–90 euros
€€€€€ Over 90 euros

BERLIN

EAST OF CENTER Historische Weinstuben
€€
Poststraße 23, 10178 **Tel** *030-242 41 07*
Map *5 E2*

This popular wine bar is housed in one of the most decorative buildings of the Nicolaiviertel. Traditional dishes from Berlin, such as *Kohl* or *Rinderrouladen* (rolled and roasted stuffed beef), can be accompanied by a drink from a small but exquisite wine list of 50 mostly German vintages.

EAST OF CENTER Zum Nussbaum
€€€
Am Nussbaum 3, 10178 **Tel** *030-242 30 95*
Map *5 E2*

Situated in an alley in the Nicolaiviertel, this is a reconstruction of a 16th-century country inn, serving traditional Berlin cuisine, with tender pork knuckle, rollmops or *Berliner Boulette*, a spicy hamburger pattie without a bun. In summer, dine in its garden and enjoy the various brands of local beer.

EAST OF CENTER Lutter & Wegner
€€€€
Charlottenstraße 56, 10117 **Tel** *030-202 954 17*
Map *4 C3*

The first restaurant to start the revitalization of the gourmet scene in the historic center of Eastern Berlin. Formerly know as a fine German champagne brand, it now serves delicious German–Austrian food. The huge *Wiener Schnitzel* with potato salad, best served lukewarm, is a delight as are the duck and goose specialties in winter.

EAST OF CENTER Vau
€€€€€
Jägerstraße 54–55, 10117 **Tel** *030-202 97 30*
Map *4 B2*

This restaurant stands out with its elegant and unpretentious interior. The excellent and imaginative Austrian- and French-based dishes are created by Berlin's star chef, Kolja Kleeberg. The service is welcoming and there is a selection of good wines. The small courtyard is used during lunch. Closed Sun.

WEST OF CENTER Nolle
€€
Georgenstraße 203, 10117 **Tel** *030-208 26 55*
Map *4 C1*

The Nolle is a pleasantly decorated, 1920s-style Berlin restaurant tucked way under the S-Bahn tracks. The lush greenery around the place, the elegantly appointed tables, and candlelight make a perfect setting for its international and German dishes. The *Schnitzel* selection is impressive.

WEST OF CENTER Francucci's
€€€
Kurfürstendamm 90, 10711 **Tel** *030-327 647 95*
Map *4 B1*

One of Berlin's best-kept secrets and a favorite among locals is this upscale neighborhood restaurant offering hearty but supreme Tuscan country cooking. Specialties include the homemade pasta dishes and meat recipes as well as Berlin classics such as their signature pizza, served by the slice.

WEST OF CENTER Ganymed
€€€
Schiffbauerdamm 5, 10117 **Tel** *030-285 852 42*
Map *4 B1*

A good-quality brasserie restaurant in charming surroundings with a small garden and views of the Spree river. The chef favors fish dishes, including Berlin fish specialties, but also offers traditional French fare such as steak tartare, fresh scallops sautéed in white wine, and a good cheese selection.

WEST OF CENTER Desbrosses
€€€€
Potsdamer Platz 3, 10785 **Tel** *030-337 776 400*
Map *4 A3*

Desbrosses has the most authentic French brasserie interior in all of Berlin. Dark wood-paneled walls, comfortable, plush leather bistro chairs, an open show kitchen and recordings of Piaf, all make for a real French experience. A must here is the seafood platter.

WEST OF CENTER Hugo's
€€€€€
Budapester Straße 2, 10787 **Tel** *030-260 212 63*
Map *2 C4*

This newly opened restaurant, in the Inter-Continental Hotel, is one of the best in Berlin. Unusual French and international dishes are prepared with a German influence. The fish and seafood dishes are proof of the chef's real mastery. An attraction is the restaurant's rooftop location with great views. Reservations necessary. Closed Sun.

Key to Symbols *see back cover flap*

POTSDAM Restaurant Juliette �? ⚡ €€€€€

Jägerstraße 39, 14467 **Tel** *0331-270 17 91*

A French restaurant with all the romantic trimmings you would expect – candles, white tablecloths and a lit fireplace. French food traditionalists beware, the decorated and imaginative chef serves up both traditional and experimental cuisine. Try the ever-popular *crème brûlée* for dessert. There are vegetarian options on the menu.

FARTHER AFIELD Mutter 🍽🚻⚡ €€€€€

Hohenstaufenstraße 4, 10781 **Tel** *030-216 49 90*

True to its name, Mutter (German for "mother") serves generous portions to its patrons. A fixture of the bustling Winterfeldplatz nightlife scene, it offers cool Caribbean drinks and an eclectic mix of some traditional German, Italian and Asian dishes, with an emphasis on sushi and Thai food.

FARTHER AFIELD Remise im Schloss Klein-Glienicke ?⚡ €€€€€

Königstraße 36, 14109 **Tel** *030-805 40 00*

This is the ideal place for an elegant meal on the outskirts of Berlin. Now run by Franz Raneberger, one of Berlin's most prominent chefs, the restaurant offers excellent German cuisine, with perch, crayfish, and game, all prepared with a dose of imagination. The restaurant is also a good choice for lunch. Closed Mon–Tue.

EASTERN GERMANY

DRESDEN Sophienkeller 🍽🚻🚗⚡ €€

Taschenberg 3, 0-1067 **Tel** *0351-49 72 60*

One of the most popular and lively restaurants in Dresden. It is one of three eateries located in the Taschenbergpalais. Come here for the re-created rustic atmosphere of an 18th-century beer cellar. They have authentic regional cuisine on the menu. The staff wear period costumes. Ask to sit at the indoor carousel table.

DRESDEN Intermezzo 🚻🚗?⚡ €€€

Taschenberg 3, 0-1067 **Tel** *0351-49 12 0*

This restaurant is in the Kempinski Taschenbergpalais and serves unconventional dishes with a touch of the Mediterranean. Try one of the delicious salads or soups for lunch. Desserts are also worth noting as is the extensive wine list. The dining area of the hotel also includes an American-style bar, café, and other dining options.

DRESDEN Das Caroussel 🚻🚗?⚡ €€€€€

Rähnitzgasse 19, 0-1097 **Tel** *0351-800 30*

The hotel and restaurant are based within a recently restored Baroque palace in the historic city center, dating from the 18th century. Famed in the region as one of the best restaurants in Saxony, dine on Mediterranean cuisine while sipping one of the first-class wines. Truly spectacular.

LEIPZIG Kaiser Maximilian 🚗?⚡ €€€

Neumarkt 9, 4109 **Tel** *0341-355 33 333*

A bright restaurant, pleasantly decorated and with small recesses for the tables, the menu here is largely influenced by Italian dishes, but several regions of the world are also represented, and changes every other week, ensuring that the best in-season produce is used for the head chef's fabulous new creations.

LEIPZIG Medici 🚻🚗?⚡ €€€€€

Nikolaikirchhof 5, 4109 **Tel** *0341-211 38 78*

A hip, up-market restaurant located in the center of the city. The menu focuses on the Mediterranean with fresh, high quality ingredients, specially vegetables and fish. Take your pick of lighter or heavier meals. The wine list is certainly better than average. Open daily at noon and closed between 3pm and 6pm.

MEISSEN Mercure Grandhotel Meissen 🚗⚡ €€

Hafenstr. 27–31, 1662 **Tel** *03521-722 50*

This classy hotel-restaurant, based in a large Art Nouveau villa on the bank of the Elbe, serves regional and international food. Look for a wide selection of fish dishes on the menu. Their wine list is superb. Guests can also dine in the café, which has a terrace, or in the intimate hotel bar.

WEIMAR Brasserie Central 🚗?⚡ €€

Rollplatz 8a, 99423 **Tel** *03643-85 27 74*

Typical French provincial cuisine with some international influences, mostly German and Italian. Sweet or savory crêpes are made to order. The menu changes constantly, so check with the staff for current offerings. They have a vast wine list, so it is a great place to try a new wine or enjoy an old favorite.

WEIMAR Anna Amalia 🚻🚗?⚡ €€€€€

Markt 19, 99423 **Tel** *03643-80 20*

This restaurant has a venerable tradition, with famous customers such as Richard Wagner and Thomas Mann, and remains popular to this day. You will enjoy some of the finest Italian cooking in all of Thuringia, with an ever-evolving menu. The interior is decorated in Art Deco style. Service is first class.

Map References *see map of Berlin pp528–9*

MUNICH

Zum Franziskaner   €€
Residenzstraße 9, Perusastraße 5, 80331 **Tel** *089-2318120*   **Map** *2 B4*

Rich in tradition and one of the best places to head for typical Bavarian specials. Their home-made white sausage, *Weißwurst*, is famous in Munich. Also, try the Bavarian meatloaf with mustard, fillet of ox, plus a variety of salads and vegetarian dishes. Being the brewery's restaurant, you must try the Franziskaner beer, originally brewed by monks.

Dallmayr   €€€
Dienerstraße 14–15, 80331 **Tel** *089-2135100*   **Map** *2 B4*

Dallmayr is a Munich institution, famous for its coffee house and café. The elegant restaurant offers delicious treats such as courgette (zucchini) flowers with lobster on a bed of ratatouille in curry sauce, plus a selection of superb wines. Very popular with locals and tourists for its high level of service, patisserie, and cuisine.

Ederer   €€€€€
Kardinal-Faulhaber-Straße 10, 80333 **Tel** *089-24231310*   **Map** *2 B3*

A first-floor restaurant within the Fünf Höfe building opposite a large bank. Excellent fish and seafood is available, such as terrine of sardines and sweet peppers or pea soup and gambas, all fresh from the market. Also, over 500 great wines from their cellar. Diners can enjoy the courtyard terrace in summer.

Käfer Schänke   €€€€€
Prinzregentenstraße 73, 81675 **Tel** *089-4168247*

Michael Käfer's renowned gourmet restaurant attracts a mix of politicians and artsy and business types. Open all day from 11am for lunch and dinner whenever you want. There are cosy, intimate dining rooms in contemporary chic mixed with traditional Bavaria – hunting room, opera room, and a lounge with an open fire.

Tantris   €€€€€
Johann-Fichte Straße 7, 80805 **Tel** *089-3619590*

A classic establishment and a Munich institution for over 30 years. Designed in a 1970s style it offers gourmet menus, a high standard of luxury and also has two Michelin stars, a garden, and a terrace. Booking is essential. Try the specials, aubergine (eggplant) and sardine terrine with pesto or salmon with leek purée and brown butter.

BAVARIA

BAMBERG St Nepomuk   €€
Obere Mühlbrücke 9, 96049 **Tel** *0951-98420*

Dine in a traditional restaurant which has been a staple in the community for centuries. Good selection of game and fish dishes as well as accompanying local wines and beers. The cuisine is generally international. Part of a former mill, it has a charming atmosphere and great views across the river and the town.

BAYREUTH Schlossgaststätte Eremitage   €€€
Eremitage 6, 95448 **Tel** *0921-799970*

An incredibly beautiful setting in the castle where there is also a terrace for alfresco summer dining, an orangerie for the afternoon or aperitifs and a café. Excellent cuisine, service, and international wines. Highly recommended is the fine perch, or steak in balsamic and shallot sauce with rocket roast potatoes. The desserts are also exquisite.

BAYREUTH Jagdschloss Thiergarten   €€€€
Oberthiergärtner Straße 36, 95448 **Tel** *09209-9840*

This romantic setting is popular for special occasions as well as romantic dinners. The castle provides a cosy tavern, with a hunting lodge feel, serving traditional game dishes, or the more formal, elegant Schloss restaurant serving nouvelle cuisine. Try the tuna *carpaccio*, fish, duck, lobster or lamb.

FREIBURG Enoteca   €€€€
Gerberau 21, 79098 **Tel** *0761-3899130*

With 20 years of experience, Enoteca is one of Freiburg's leading restaurants. It offers a high level of light but classic Italian cuisine, where the emphasis is on simplicity and wonderful fresh produce. There are several menus to choose from, a simple choice, the fish menu, daily menu or à la carte. The dining room is stylish and understated.

HEIDELBERG Schlossweinstube Schönmehls   €€€€
Im Schlosshof, 69117 **Tel** *06221-97970*

In the magnificent old Heidelberg castle, this stylish and spacious restaurant offers modern cuisine of international and regional dishes. Good choices are fish, duck or game. For a special treat book a candlelit dinner for two. There is also a lovely terrace to dine outdoors on warm evenings. There are fish and vegetarian menus.

Key to Price Guide *see p580* **Key to Symbols** *see back cover flap*

HEIDELBERG Simplicissimus

Ingrimstraße 16, 69117 **Tel** *06221-183336*

Owing to the busy central location in Heidelberg's old town, booking is recommended. Tourists and locals flock here for the simple but outstanding cuisine, combining regional fresh produce, French flavors and good wines. Sit in the intimate dining room or in the flower-filled courtyard. Wine-tasting events take place every first Friday of the month.

NUREMBERG Sebald

Weinmarkt 14, 90403 **Tel** *0911-381303*

A smart contemporary restaurant in the center of the old town. The chef combines his global experience to serve appetizing dishes with a German and Italian predominance, from *vitello tonnato* (chilled veal in a tuna sauce) to clear oxtail soup, scallops, and *Wiener Schnitzel*. The cuisine does not disappoint. It is very popular, so be sure to book.

NUREMBERG Essigbrätlein

Weinmarkt 3, 90403 **Tel** *0911-225131*

Just a stroll away from the main market square, this small intimate restaurant only has 20 tables so booking ahead is essential. Tightly packed, cosy and familiar, there is excellent food, staff, and wines. You can choose from the daily changing menu or let the head waiter and sommelier advise you. Delicious fish dishes plus exquisite desserts.

PASSAU Christophorus Stüberl

Pfaffengasse 7, 94032 **Tel** *0851-7568090*

For hearty home cooking head to the old-fashioned Christophorus Stüberl in a narrow old street in the heart of Passau. In addition to traditional regional cuisine they offer international dishes such as steaks and fish. It is nestled in a cobbled street between the cathedral and the Danube. The owners also sell fine Italian gourmet products.

PASSAU Heilig-Geist-Stift Stiftskeller

Heilig-Geist-Gasse 4, 94032 **Tel** *0851-2607*

Dark wood panelling throughout with a historical feel and old tiled stoves. Dinner is served in the hunting room or bishop's room, where coats of arms, hunting trophies and old prints adorn the walls. This rustic restaurant and wine bar specialize in Bavarian food. Try the locally caught freshwater fish. Closed Wednesday.

ROTHENBURG OB DER TAUBER Gerberhaus Cafe

Spitalgasse 25, 91541 **Tel** *09861-94900*

Try a local Franconian specialty such as *Nürnberger Bratwürstl mit Sauerkraut* (Nuremberg sausages with Sauerkraut) in the lovely beer garden of the Hotel Gerberhaus, below the city wall. The popular café offers great pastries and cappuccino. Other light meals are served accompanied by local wine from the Tauber valley.

STUTTGART Hotel Traube

Brabandtgasse 2, 70599 **Tel** *0711-458920*

Steeped in history, the Traube is a half-timbered, small hotel in Plieningen, a village just outside Stuttgart. From its antique furniture to old doors, cobblestones, and gabled roof, it exudes a romantic charm. The wood-panelled dining room is cosy indoors and the summer terrace is a pretty alternative. Good Swabian game and fish.

STUTTGART Schlossgastronomie Solitude

Solitude 2, 70197 **Tel** *0711-692025*

An impressive sprawling Rococo castle from 1775 is the setting for this restaurant. The elegant restaurant offers dinners only. The chef concentrates on French cuisine with light dishes using fresh local produce, but also serves regional specials and international cooking. It has a lovely garden terrace. Closed Sun–Mon.

STUTTGART Cube

Kleiner Schlossplatz 1, 70173 **Tel** *0711-2804441*

A gastronomic delight within Stuttgart's modern art museum. The vast glass cube houses this excellent restaurant for cultured dining on the fourth floor. Minimal, stylish, and cosmopolitan, the Pacific Rim cuisine in the evenings offers fusion dishes such as honey-and-soya-glazed duck breast on chilli-vanilla cabbage.

WÜRZBURG Schloss Steinburg

Auf dem Steinberg, 97080 **Tel** *0931-97020*

The romantic Steinburg castle provides the attractive setting for this hotel and restaurant. It boasts fabulous views over the town from the garden terrace in fine weather. Steeped in history the castle was first mentioned in 1236. Enjoy German gourmet specialties with excellent service. Perhaps book a romantic candlelit dinner for two.

WESTERN GERMANY

BONN Zur Lindenwirtin Aennchen

Aennchenplatz 2, 53173 **Tel** *0228-312051*

The interior is very ornate and the stylish setting creates an intimate and romantic atmosphere. The kitchen produces international dishes with a leaning towards France. Their carefully chosen wine list encompasses great wines from nine different countries. The service is impeccable and polite.

Map References *see map of Munich pp546–7*

BONN-BAD GODESBERG Halbedel's Gasthaus   €€€€€
Rheinallee 47, 53173 **Tel** *0228-354253*

A stone's throw from the Rhine in an exclusive part of town in a nondescript villa. The chef concocts fantastic and interesting international cuisine and is constantly inventing new dishes. They cater to the serious wine lover, too, with more than 700 different wines. The service is first rate.

COLOGNE Restaurant Pöttgen   €
Landmannstraße 19, 50825 **Tel** *0221-555246*

This traditional and cheerful restaurant has been in the Pöttgen family for four generations and is still going strong. The history of the restaurant and family can be seen in the charming decor. The food is always very tasty and is fantastic value. The chef has kept some dishes from the menus of his ancestors.

COLOGNE Fischers   €€€
Hohenstaufenring 53, 50674 **Tel** *0221-3108470*

This restaurant centers around wine. The cellar is vastly stocked and they operate a wine club as well. The dining area is spacious and simple, which suits the earthy cuisine that focuses on fresh produce. They also have a wine bar and terrace, which is very pleasant in the evenings.

COLOGNE Börsen-Restaurant Maître   €€€€€
Unter Sachsenhausen 10–26, 50667 **Tel** *0221-133021*

A very elegant and romantic restaurant in the shadow of the Cologne Dom cathedral. The kitchen produces high quality French cuisine in a stunning location. The stylish yet comfortable dining area is an ideal place for a romantic evening, and it is a good idea to book ahead because it can fill up quickly.

FRANKFURT AM MAIN Zum Schwarzen Stern   €€€
Römerberg 6, 60311 **Tel** *069-291279*

A restaurant serving traditional fare as well as international dishes. There is a specific menu section called "Grandmother's recipes" which caters to the taste for regional cuisine. It is located next to the cathedral in a very old building and there are references to it dating back to 1453.

FRANKFURT AM MAIN Tigerpalast   €€€€€
Heiligkreuzgasse 16–20, 60313 **Tel** *069-92002225*

This rare find combines Michelin-starred dining with a variety show. Light Mediterranean dishes are served with flair and passion. The walls are adorned with show posters from all over the world. It is common for guests to combine dining in the restaurant with watching the show.

KOBLENZ Da Vinci   €€
Firmungstraße 32b, 56068 **Tel** *0261-9215444*

An Italian restaurant with a sophisticated atmosphere and superb cuisine. There are often functions held here, such as wine tastings and fashion shows. The walls are covered with paintings and there is often soft music playing. The fresh ingredients and traditional Italian dishes have made this new restaurant popular amongst the locals.

KOBLENZ Loup de mer   €€€
Neustadt 12, 88250 **Tel** *0261-16138*

This could possibly be the best seafood restaurant in Koblenz. The dishes are imaginative and comprehensive and not restricted to fish. The menu also contains tasty dishes for vegetarians and non-fish eaters. Their *loup de mer* dish, after which the restaurant is named, is divine. There is a great dining area outside on their terrace.

MAINZ Der Halbe Mond   €€€€
In der Witz 12, 55252 **Tel** *06134-23913*

A tiny restaurant offering some very special creations. Because there are only five tables it is a good idea to make reservations first. The dishes have a refined flavor and a French influence. The night is not complete without sampling their white and dark chocolate mousse with caramelized hazelnuts.

MARIA LAACH Seespiegel-Seehotel Maria Laach   €€€€
Orsteil Maria Laach, 56653 **Tel** *02652-584512*

This unique and well-respected restaurant is located in a hotel close to a 900-year-old monastery, which provides the kitchen with fresh produce. Seafood has a starring role on the menu, although their lamb fillet salad is tempting and seductive. The chef is sympathetic to vegetarians and provides them with fantastic fare.

TRIER Römischer Kaiser-Taverne   €€
Porta-Nigra-Platz 6, 54292 **Tel** *0651-97700*

This restaurant is inside the Römischer Kaiser hotel, which is located at the edge of a scenic square in Trier. The specials are often interesting and tasty, especially the game dishes. There is an extensive wine list that has a number of international wines as well as a good selection of German wines. It is best to book on weekends.

TRIER Pfeffermühle   €€€€
Zurlaubener Ufer 76, 54292 **Tel** *0651-26133*

This restaurant overlooks the Mosel river and has a great view that can be enjoyed from their terrace in the warmer months. The building dates back to the 19th century and provides an intimate location to enjoy their international cuisine. The terrace is a little more sociable, as there are more tables outside.

Key to Price Guide *see p580* **Key to Symbols** *see back cover flap*

NORTHERN GERMANY

BREMEN L'Orchidée
Am Markt, 28195 **Tel** *0421-3059888*

L'Orchidée is housed in the oldest operating wine cellar in Germany, established over 600 years ago. There is a wine bar which offers over 600 different wines. The restaurant serves great international food in a truly magnificent dining area, complete with wood-panelled walls, chandeliers, and wall paintings.

BREMEN Meierei
Im Bürgerpark, 28209 **Tel** *0421-3408619*

This restaurant first opened in 1881. There is a Mediterranean flavor running through the menu, however, one should not overlook their fabulous rabbit *ragout*. The inside is inviting with a warm fireplace in the dining area which is dominated by earth tones. There is a large wine selection, specially the Italian wines.

HAMBURG Au Quai
Grosse Elbstraße 145, 22767 **Tel** *040-38037730*

Housed in a refurbished cold storage depot, the conversion has resulted in a fantastic place to try the best of Hamburg's seafood. Operated by a brother and sister, the kitchen reflects their heritage with great Mediterranean dishes and a subtle French influence that works well with the delicate fish-dominated menu.

HAMBURG Fischereihafen-Restaurant
Grosse Elbstraße 143, 22767 **Tel** *040-381816*

This is the place to go for fresh, delicious seafood (though other dishes are offered). The large menu is changed often to suit the seasons. The terrace overlooks the water and has one of the best views of the harbor. The list of famous guests is longer than the extensive wine list and reflects the great food and outstanding service.

HAMBURG Jacobs Restaurant
Elbchaussee 401–403, 22609 **Tel** *040-822550*

This restaurant, situated in the beautiful Hotel Louis C. Jacob, is among the best in the city. The cuisine is international with a definite French infusion. There is also a wine cellar that keeps connoisseurs happily occupied for hours, with the help of the master sommelier. There is an adjacent wine bar and a terrace.

HANNOVER Die Insel
Rudolf-von-Bennigsen-Ufer 81, 30519 **Tel** *0511-831214*

There is a picturesque view of nearby Lake Masch from the dining area. This restaurant attracts customers from the music industry to politics. The cuisine is hard to pin down, with some great regional dishes as well as some great oriental creations. The food is matched by the equally impressive wine selection.

HANNOVER Gallo Nero
Gross-Buchholzer Kirchweg 72b, 30655 **Tel** *0511-5463434*

The "Black Rooster" offers top-quality Northern Italian cuisine, ranging from basic flavors and produce to more refined sauces and spices. The interior of the restaurant resembles a Tuscan art gallery, which gives a very intimate and unique atmosphere to enjoy their unpretentious food. They have a large selection of Italian wines.

HANNOVER Le Chalet
Isernhagener Straße 21, 30161 **Tel** *0511-319588*

An intimate dining experience in an elegant part of town. The French cuisine has won popularity amongst patrons with their rich sauces and exquisite salads. The staff blend into the background until they are needed, at which time they seem to materialize out of thin air. This is particularly helpful when selecting wines, as they are experts.

LÜBECK Historischer Weinkeller
Koberg 6–8, 23552 **Tel** *0451-76234*

This unique restaurant is located in an 800-year-old wine cellar under a historic hospital. There is a medieval tone to the restaurant, which has retained the ambience of its heritage while at the same time creating a light and friendly atmosphere. Their game dishes have won the hearts of locals and tourists.

LÜBECK Wullenwever
Beckergrube 71, 23552 **Tel** *0451-704333*

A very elegant restaurant that offers a number of unique rooms and dining areas, the chef is liberal with his creations, happily giving out recipes to interested patrons. The set menus have been artfully chosen to give a perfect balance of tastes, and there are wine suggestions for each dish. It has become rather well-known, so book ahead.

MÜNSTER Landhaus Eggert
Zur Haskenau 81, 48157 **Tel** *0251-328040*

The hotel and restaurant are family owned and run, and there is a personal approach to the service. The chef produces fantastic and varied menus, exploring international cuisine while also showcasing the region's best dishes. The setting is a peaceful country area and the hotel was once a farm.

AUSTRIA

*A*ustria has existed as a country for less than 100 years but, despite inauspicious beginnings, has thrived thanks to its position at the heart of Europe. Visitors are attracted by the glories of its Imperial Habsburg past, especially in the capital, Vienna. Austria also has a strong musical tradition and great natural beauty, especially in the Alps and the valley of the Danube.

Present-day Austria emerged in 1919, when the lands of its former empire were granted independence, as a curiously shaped, landlocked country. It is bordered by Switzerland and Germany to the west and north. Along the rest of its border lie the former lands of the old Habsburg Empire, the Czech Republic, Slovakia, Hungary, Slovenia, and the South Tyrol. The regions of the west, the Vorarlberg and the Tyrol, are mountainous, dominated by the eastern Alps. This is where you will find the most familiar images of Austria: well-appointed skiing resorts, snow-capped peaks, and beautiful valleys cloaked in forest.

The Alps are not the traditional heart of Austria – this lies in the regions of Upper and Lower Austria in the northeast, where the Danube (Donau) flows eastwards across the country for 360 km (225 miles). Vienna stands at a point just beyond where the great river emerges from the mountains to flow into the Hungarian plain. The east of the country is more populous, with more agriculture and industry.

HISTORY

In the 1st millennium BC, settlements in the region of present-day Austria prospered from mining iron and salt. One settlement, Hallstatt, has given its name to an important Iron Age culture that spread across Europe. It was iron that first drew the Romans to occupy the region, where they established the provinces of Rhaetia, Noricum, and Pannonia, making the Danube the frontier of their empire. When the Romans withdrew, the region was settled by Germanic tribes, such as the Alemanni and the Bavarians, and Slavs, but it was the German-speaking peoples who prevailed.

Ruined castle of Aggstein overlooking the Danube in the Wachau region

◁ **The magnificent staircase at the entrance to the Vienna State Opera House**

The geographical kernel of Austria (Österreich) was the Ostmark (eastern march or border county) established by Charlemagne in the 9th century to protect the frontier of his empire. In the 10th century, the Babenbergs acquired the county, which was elevated to a dukedom in 1156. Their dynasty died out in the 13th century and their lands were fought over until they came under the control of Rudolf of Habsburg, who was elected Holy Roman Emperor in 1273 .

The Central, one of the grandest of Vienna's coffee houses

Over the next three centuries the Habsburg domains grew, occasionally by conquest, but usually by means of marriages and inheritances. In time it became a matter of course that they were elected as Holy Roman Emperors.

From the 15th century, Turkish invasions threatened the Habsburg lands. In 1683 the Turks laid siege to Vienna, but they were dispersed by a relieving army. This marked the start of many successful campaigns in the Balkans. In the 18th century Austria was a major power, although the rise of Prussia and Napoleon's occupation of Vienna in 1809 dented Habsburg pride.

The Austrian empire was considerably weakened in the 19th century by the growth of nationalist movements, but Vienna enjoyed its heyday as a great cosmopolitan European capital.

After World War I, the defeated Austrian Empire was dismembered and countries such as Czechoslovakia and Hungary gained their independence. There followed bitter struggles between Right and Left for control of the new Austrian republic. The country was annexed by Germany in 1938 and then, following Hitler's defeat in 1945, came under Allied control until 1955, when it

Exploring Austria

Austria's main attractions are the alpine resorts in the west of the country around Innsbruck and the capital, Vienna, in the east. In between there are many other sights worth seeking out: ancient monasteries and castles, well-preserved medieval cities, such as Salzburg and Graz, the picturesque lakes of the Salzkammergut region, and the scenic stretch of the Danube known as the Wachau. Road and rail communications along the main axis of the country between Vienna, Linz, Salzburg, and Innsbruck are very good.

SIGHTS AT A GLANCE

Eisenstadt ❷
Graz ❸
Hallstatt ❻
Innsbruck ❽
Linz ❺
Melk and the Wachau ❹
Salzburg ❼
VIENNA pp590–99 ❶

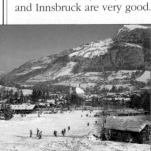
Skiing at the fashionable resort of
Kitzbühel in the Austrian Alps

0 kilometers 50

0 miles 50

became a sovereign state once more. As a keen member of the European Union, Austria has flourished economically, but the old political divisions have arisen in a new form. The ultra-conservative nationalist party, the FPÖ (then led by Jörg Haider), were part of government coalitions from 2000 – resulting in international outrage – until the Social Democratic party (SPO) took over in 2006.

LANGUAGE AND CULTURE

Austria is linguistically homogenous, with 98 percent of the population speaking German. There are, however, considerable differences in dialect between the various regions.

Culturally, Austria is synonymous with music, the long list of great Austrian composers containing names such as Mozart, Haydn, Schubert, and Mahler, not forgetting the Strausses, father and son, and their famous waltzes. Vienna's intellectual and artistic life enjoyed an extraordinary flowering in the late 19th and early 20th century with the Secession movement in painting, architecture, and design. It was also the period of Sigmund Freud's investigations, which

KEY DATES IN AUSTRIAN HISTORY

c.800 BC Rise of Hallstatt culture
15 BC Noricum occupied by Romans
AD 976–1246 Babenberg dynasty rules Eastern March of the Holy Roman Empire
1276 Rudolf of Habsburg ruler of Austria
1519 Charles V is elected Holy Roman Emperor
1618–48 Thirty Years' War
1683 Siege of Vienna
1740–80 Reign of Maria Theresa
1805 Napoleon defeats Austrians at Austerlitz
1815 Congress of Vienna
1848 Revolutions throughout Habsburg Empire
1918 Defeat in World War I brings Habsburg rule to an end – Austria declared republic
1938 Anschluss – Austria absorbed by Germany
1945–55 Vienna occupied by Allies
1994 Austria joins EU
2004 Elfriede Jelinek receives Nobel Prize for Literature
2006 After FPÖ party splits in 2005, Social Democrats defeat conservatives in elections

laid the foundations of modern psychology. Alongside all this intellectual excitement, older Austrian values survived. One still cherished today is the idea of *Gemütlichkeit*, coziness, embodied in family life, coffee and cakes, and old-fashioned courtesy.

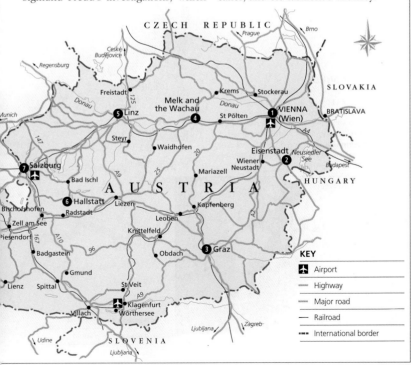

KEY

🛫 Airport
— Highway
— Major road
— Railroad
▪▪▪ International border

Vienna ❶

Greater Vienna has a population of 1.5 million, but the Austrian capital is a compact city with many of the important sights, especially those that date from the Habsburg era, clustered around the Hofburg, the former imperial court. In the mid-19th century the city's old defenses were pulled down and a wide circular boulevard, the Ringstrasse, was built linking new political and cultural institutions, such as Vienna's great art gallery, the Kunsthistorisches Museum. Completed in the 1880s, the Ringstrasse still defines the Innere Stadt or heart of the city. The Danube (Donau) river flows through the east of the city, where it has been canalized to prevent flooding.

SIGHTS AT A GLANCE

Albertina ⑫
Applied Arts Museum ⑨
Burgtheater ②
Freud Museum ⑧
Hofburg pp592–4 ①
Karlskirche ⑪
Kunsthistorisches Museum ⑥
MuseumsQuartier Wien ⑦
Naturhistorisches Museum ⑤
Secession Building ⑩
Staatsoper ④
Stephansdom ③

Greater Vienna *(see inset map)*

Belvedere ⑭
Prater ⑬
Schönbrunn Palace
  and Gardens ⑮

GETTING AROUND

The center of the city is easily explored on foot. Trams 1 and 2 take you round the Ringstrasse past many of the important sights. To see these in old-world style, but at great expense, hire a horse-drawn *Fiaker*. The suburbs are served by the U-bahn (subway) and S-bahn services, although the latter is of more use to locals.

Lipizzaner stallion at the Winter Riding School in the Hofburg

SEE ALSO

- *Where to Stay* pp608–9
- *Where to Eat* pp610–11

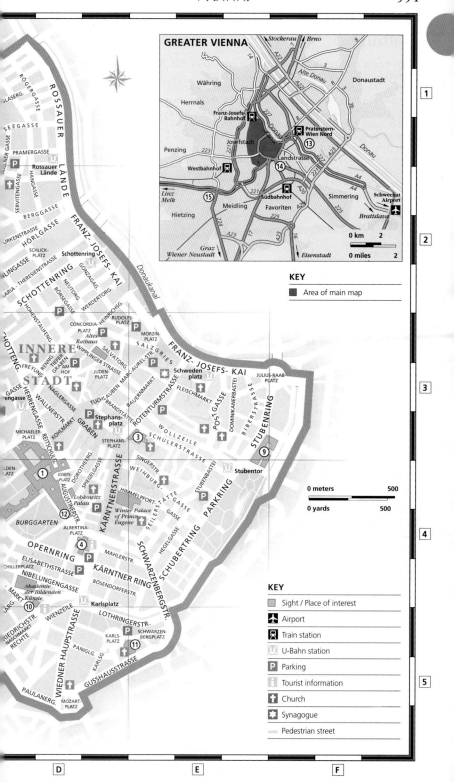

GREATER VIENNA

Stockerau   Brno

Währing

Herrnals

Franz-Josefs-Bahnhof

Josefstadt

Penzing

Westbahnhof

Linz
Melk

Hietzing

Graz
Wiener Neustadt

Alte Donau

Donaustadt

Praterstern-
Wien Nord **13**

Landstrasse **14**

15

Meidling

Südbahnhof

Favoriten

Simmering

Schwechat
Airport

Bratislava

Eisenstadt

0 km   2

0 miles   2

KEY

▨ Area of main map

ROSSAUER LÄNDE

ROGERGASSE

SEEGASSE

PRAMERGASSE

Rossauer
Lände

BERGGASSE

HÖRLGASSE

SCHLICK-
PLATZ

Schottenring

SCHOTTENRING

GONZAGAG.

WERDERTORG.

RUDOLFS-
PLATZ

CONCORDIA
PLATZ

Altes
Rathaus

MORZIN-
PLATZ

SALZGRIES

MARC-AUREL-STR.

Schweden
platz

FLEISCHMARKT

INNERE
STADT

FREYUNG

AM HOF

JUDEN-
PLATZ

BAUERNMARKT

ROTENTURMSTRASSE

POSTGASSE

DOMINIKANERBASTEI

FRANZ-
JOSEFS-
KAI

JULIUS-RAAB-
PLATZ

BIBERSTRASSE

STUBENRING

Stephans-
platz

KOHLMARKT

GRABEN

NAGLERGASSE

WOLLZEILE

SCHULERSTRASSE

STEPHANS-
PLATZ

3

SINGERSTR.

WEIHBURG.

STUBENBASTEI

9

Stubentor

MICHAELER-
PLATZ

JOSEFS-
PLATZ

DOROTHERG.

SPIEGELG.

HIMMELPFORT.

SEILERS-TÄTTE

HEGELGASSE

PARKRING

BURGGARTEN

AUGUSTINERSTR.

Lobkowitz
Palais

Winter Palace
of Prince
Eugene

ALBERTINA-
PLATZ

12

4

MAHLERSTR.

SCHWARZENBERGSTR.

SCHUBERTRING

OPERNRING

ELISABETHSTRASSE

KÄRNTNER RING

BÖSENDORFERSTR.

NIBELUNGENGASSE

Akademie
der Bildenden
Künste

WIENZEILE

Karlsplatz

LOTHRINGERSTR.

10

SCHWARZEN-
BERGPLATZ

KARLS
PLATZ

11

WIEDNER HAUPTSTRASSE

PANIGLG.

KARLSG.

GUSSHAUSSTRASSE

PAULANERG.

MOZART-
PLATZ

0 meters   500

0 yards   500

KEY

▨ Sight / Place of interest

✈ Airport

🚉 Train station

Ⓤ U-Bahn station

🅿 Parking

ℹ Tourist information

✝ Church

✡ Synagogue

— Pedestrian street

Hofburg ①

What began as a small fortress in 1275 grew over the centuries into a vast palace, the Hofburg. It was the seat of Austrian power for over six centuries, and successive rulers were all anxious to leave their mark. The various buildings range in style from Gothic to late 19th-century Neo-Renaissance. The complex was still expanding up until a few years before the Habsburgs fell from power in 1918. The presence of the imperial court had a profound effect on the surrounding area, with noble families competing to site their palaces as close as possible to the Hofburg.

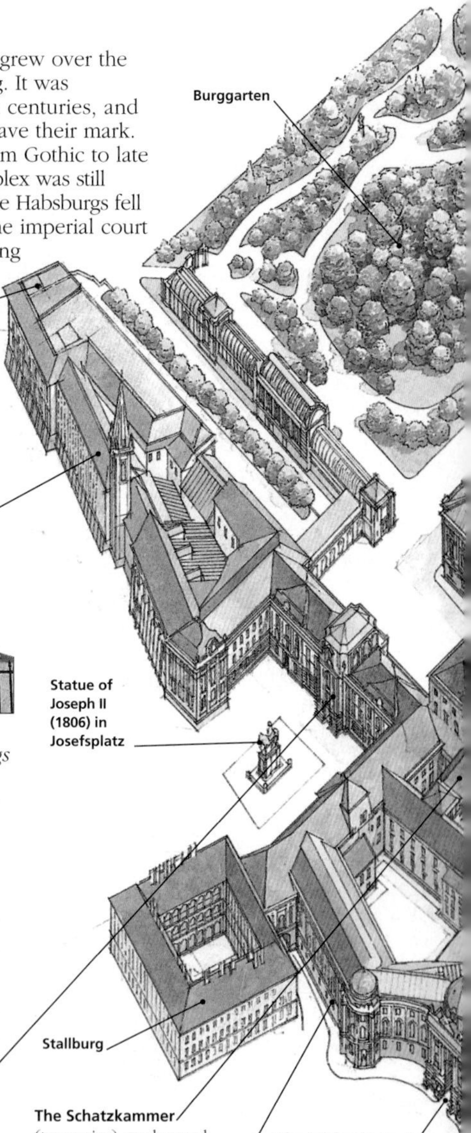

Burggarten

The Albertina, recently renovated, houses a collection of Old Master drawings and prints.

★ Augustinerkirche
The former parish church of the Habsburgs houses the spectacular late 18th-century tomb of Maria Christina, Maria Theresa's favorite daughter, by Antonio Canova.

Statue of Joseph II (1806) in Josefsplatz

Prunksaal
The showpiece of the Austrian National Library (1722–35) is the grand, wood-paneled Prunksaal, or Hall of Honor.

Stallburg

The Schatzkammer (treasuries) are housed in the Alte Burg, the core of the old palace.

The Michaelertor is the gate through which visitors reach the older parts of the palace.

★ Winter Riding School
The white Lipizzaner horses are stabled in the Stallburg opposite the Riding School itself, where they are trained and give performances.

STAR FEATURES

★ State Apartments

★ Winter Riding School

★ Augustinerkirche

Mozart Memorial (1896)
Viktor Tilgner's statue of
the composer stands just
inside the Ringstrasse
entrance.

VISITORS' CHECKLIST

Michaelerplatz 1, A-1010.
Ⓤ Stephansplatz, Herrengasse,
Volkstheater. 🚌 2A, 3A. 🚋 D,
J, 1. For details of individual
museums, see p594.

The Burgtor or outer
gate was built to a
design by Peter Nobile
in 1821–4.

Neue Burg
A monument to
the great general,
Eugene of Savoy
(1663–1736), stands
in front of the newest
wing of the palace,
completed in 1913.

Volksgarten

Heldenplatz

Schweizertor
This 16th-century
gateway leads to the
Schweizerhof, the oldest part
of the Hofburg, originally a
stronghold with four towers.

The Burgkapelle,
the Hofburg's
chapel, is where the
famous Vienna
Boys' Choir sings.

★ State Apartments
The table in the state
banqueting hall is laid
as it used to be in the latter
part of the reign of Franz
Joseph I (1848–1916).

Exploring the Hofburg Complex

The vast Hofburg complex contains the former imperial apartments and treasuries (Schatzkammer) of the Habsburgs, several museums, a chapel, a church, the Austrian National Library, the Winter Riding School, and the President of Austria's offices. The entrance to the imperial apartments and the treasuries is through the Michaelertor on Michaelerplatz.

10th-century crown of the Holy Roman Empire, Schatzkammer

Portrait of the Empress Elisabeth by Winterhalter (1865)

Neue Burg
Heldenplatz. **Tel** 01-5252 4484.
🕐 Wed–Mon. 🌐
The massive curved Neue Burg on Heldenplatz was added to the Hofburg in 1881–1913. Archaeological finds from Ephesus are on display in the **Ephesos Museum**, while pianos that belonged to Beethoven, Schubert, and Haydn are housed in the musical instrument museum – the **Sammlung alter Musikinstrumente**. The weapons collection in the **Hofjagd und Rüstkammer** is one of the finest in Europe. There is also an excellent ethnological collection – the **Völkerkundemuseum**, as well as collections from the Kunsthistorisches Museum (see p596).

Augusti nerkirche
Augustinerstrasse 3. **Tel** 01-533 7099. 🕐 daily.
The church has one of the best-preserved 14th-century Gothic interiors in Vienna. In the Loreto Chapel are a series of silver urns that contain the hearts of the Habsburg family. The church is also celebrated for its music, with masses by Schubert or Haydn performed here on Sundays.

State Apartments
Michaelerkuppel-Feststiege.
Tel 01-533 7570. 🕐 9am–5pm daily. 🌐 🎫 Sat & Sun.
The State Apartments (Kaiserappartements) in the Reichkanzleitrakt (1726–30) and the Amalienburg (1575) include the rooms occupied by Franz Joseph from 1857 to 1916, Empress Elisabeth's apartments from 1854 to 1898, and the rooms where Czar Alexander I lived during the Congress of Vienna in 1815.

Winter Riding School
Tel 01-533 9031. 🕐 for performances.
🌑 public hols. 🌐 👟 some areas.
The Spanish Riding School is believed to have been founded in 1572 to cultivate the classic skills of *haute école* horsemanship. By breeding and training horses from Spain, the Habsburgs formed the Spanische Reitschule. Today, 80-minute shows take place in the building known as the Winter Riding School, built in 1729–35 to a design by Josef Emanuel Fischer von Erlach.

Schatzkammer
Schweizerhof. **Tel** 01-525 240.
🕐 10am–6pm Wed–Mon. 🌑 Jan 1, May 1, Nov 1, Dec 25. 🌐 👟
Sacred and secular treasures amassed during centuries of Habsburg rule are displayed

in 21 rooms, known as the Schatzkammer or Treasury. They include relics of the Holy Roman Empire, the crown jewels, and liturgical objects of the imperial court. Visitors can also admire the dazzling gold, silver, and porcelain once used at state banquets.

Burgkapelle
Schweizerhof. **Tel** 01-533 9927. 🕐 11am–3pm Mon–Thu, 11am–1pm Fri. 🌑 Nov 1, Dec 8, Jan 1, Jul, Aug. 🌐
Vienna Boys' Choir Jan–Jun & Sep–Dec: 9:15am Sun (book by phone). 🌐
From the Schweizerhof, steps lead up to the Burgkapelle, originally constructed in 1296. The interior has Gothic statues in canopied niches. On Sundays, visitors can hear the Wiener Sängerknaben, the Vienna Boys' Choir (see p607).

Burggarten and Volksgarten
Burgring/Opernring/Dr-Karl-Renner-Ring. 🕐 daily.
Some of the space left around the Hofburg after Napoleon had razed part of the city walls was transformed by the Habsburgs into gardens. The Volksgarten opened to the public in 1820, but the Burggarten remained the palace's private garden until 1918.

Ornamental pond in the Volksgarten, with Burgtheater in the background

Burgtheater ②

Dr.-Karl-Lueger-Ring 2, A-1014.
Tel 01-5144 42613. **U** Schottentor.
🚋 1, 2, D. 🅾 for performances.
⬤ Good Fri, Dec 24; Jul & Aug
(except for guided tours). 📷 ♿
📷 afternoons (call 01-5144 44140).

The Burgtheater is the most
prestigious stage in the
German-speaking world. The
original theater, built in Maria
Theresa's reign, was replaced
in 1888 by today's Italian
Renaissance-style building by
Karl von Hasenauer and
Gottfried Semper. It closed for
refurbishment in 1897 after the
discovery that several seats had
no view of the stage. At the
end of World War II a bomb
devastated the building, leaving
only the side wings containing
the Grand Staircases intact. The
restoration was so successful
that today it is hard to tell the
new parts from the old.

**Detail from the Wiener Neustädter
Altar in the Stephansdom**

Stephansdom ③

Stephansplatz 3, A-1010. **Tel** 01-
51552 3526. **U** Stephansplatz.
🚋 1A. 🅾 daily. ♿

The Stephansdom, with its
magnificent glazed-tile roof, is
the heart and soul of Vienna.
It is no mere coincidence that
the urns containing the
entrails of some of the
Habsburgs lie in a vault
beneath its main altar.

A church has stood on the
site for over 800 years, but
all that remains of the original
13th-century Romanesque
church are the Giants'
Doorway and Heathen

Auditorium of the Staatsoper, the Vienna State Opera House

Towers. The Gothic nave, the
choir, and the side chapels are
the result of rebuilding in the
14th and 15th centuries, while
some of the outbuildings,
such as the Lower Vestry, are
Baroque additions.

The lofty vaulted interior
contains an impressive
collection of works of art.
Masterpieces of Gothic sculpture include the fabulously
intricate pulpit, several of the
figures of saints adorning
the piers, and the canopies
over many of the side altars.
To the left of the High Altar
is the 15th-century winged
Wiener Neustädter Altar
bearing the painted images
of 72 saints. The altar panels
open out to reveal delicate
sculpture groups. The most
spectacular Renaissance work
is the tomb of Friedrich III,
while the High Altar adds a
flamboyant Baroque note.

Staatsoper ④

Opernring 2, A-1010. **Tel** 01-51444-
2606. **U** Karlsplatz. 🚋 1, 2, D, J.
🅾 for performances. 📷 ♿ 📷 by
arrangement (call 51444-2613).
www.wiener-staatsoper.at

Vienna's opera
house, the Staatsoper,
was the first of the
grand Ringstrasse
buildings to be
completed; it
opened on May 25,
1869 to the strains
of Mozart's Don
Giovanni. Built in Neo-
Renaissance style, it
initially failed to impress
the Viennese.
Yet when it was

hit by a bomb in 1945
and largely destroyed, the
event was seen as a symbolic
blow to the city. With a
brand new auditorium and
stage, the Opera House
reopened in November 1955
with a performance of
Beethoven's Fidelio.

Naturhistorisches Museum ⑤

Burgring 7, A-1014. **Tel** 01-521 770.
U Volkstheater. 🚌 2A, 48A.
🚋 2, D, J, 46, 49. 🅾 9am–6:30pm
Thu– Mon (to 9pm Wed). ⬤ Jan 1,
May 1, Nov 1, Dec 25. 📷 ♿
www.nhm-wien.ac.at

Almost the mirror image of
the Kunsthistorisches
Museum, the Natural History
Museum was designed by
the same architects, and
opened in 1889. Its collections include archaeological,
anthropological, mineralogical,
zoological, and geological
displays. There are casts of
dinosaur skeletons, the
world's largest display of
skulls illustrating the history
of man, one of Europe's
most comprehensive
collections of gems,
prehistoric sculpture,
Bronze Age items,
and extinct birds
and mammals. In
the archaeological
section look out
for the celebrated
Venus of Willendorf,
a 25,000-year-old
Palaeolithic fertility
figurine, and finds from
the early Iron Age
settlement at
Hallstatt (see p602).

**Venus of Willendorf,
Naturhistorisches Museum**

Hunters in the Snow by Peter Brueghel the Elder (1565)

Kunsthistorisches Museum ⑥

Maria-Theresien-Platz. **Tel** 01-525 24-0. **U** Babenberger Strasse, Volks-theater. 🚌 2A, 57A. ⬜ 10am–6pm Tue–Sun; picture gallery also 6–9pm Thu. ⬤ Jan 1, May 1, Nov 1, Dec 25. 🎦 🔊 📷 🎬 www.khm.at

The Museum of the History of Art attracts more than one and a half million visitors each year. Its collections are based largely on those built up over a number of centuries by the Habsburgs.

The picture gallery occupies the whole of the first floor. The collection focuses on Old Masters from the 15th to the 18th centuries. Because of the links between the Habsburgs and the Netherlands, Flemish painting is especially well represented. About half the surviving works of Peter Brueghel the Elder (c.1525–69) are held by the museum, including *The Tower of Babel* and most of the cycle of *The Seasons*.

The Dutch paintings range from genre scenes of great domestic charm to magnificent landscapes. All the Rembrandts on show are portraits, including the famous *Large Self-Portrait* of the artist in a plain smock (1652). The only Vermeer is the enigmatic allegorical painting, *The Artist's Studio* (1665). The

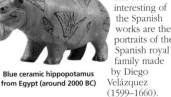

Blue ceramic hippopotamus from Egypt (around 2000 BC)

Italian galleries have a strong collection of 16th-century Venetian paintings, with a comprehensive range of Titians and great works by Giovanni Bellini and Tintoretto. Also on show are the bizarre vegetable portrait heads, representing the four seasons, made for Emperor Rudolf II by Giuseppe Arcimboldo (1527–93).

The German section is rich in 16th-century paintings. There are several works by Dürer, including his *Madonna with the Pear* (1512). The most interesting of the Spanish works are the portraits of the Spanish royal family made by Diego Velázquez (1599–1660).

On the ground floor are the Greek, Roman, Egyptian, and Near Eastern collections, with new rooms devoted specifically to Greek and Roman antiquities. Among the Egyptian and Near Eastern antiquities is an entire 5th-Dynasty tomb chapel from Giza (c.2400 BC) and a splendid bust of King Tuthmosis III (c.1460 BC).

The sculpture and decorative arts collection contains some fine, late Gothic religious statues by artists such as Tilman Riemenschneider (c.1460–1531). There is also a collection of curiosities bought or commissioned by various Habsburg monarchs, such as automata and scientific instruments.

MuseumsQuartier Wien ⑦

Museumsplatz 1. **Tel** 523-5881/1723. **U** MuseumsQuartier, Volkstheater. 🚌 2a to the MuseumsQuartier, 48a to Volkstheater. 🚊 49 to Volkstheater. **Visitor Centre** ⬜ 10am–7pm daily. 🎦 🎬 🔊 🍴 📷 www.mqw.at

This museum complex is one of the largest cultural centers in the world, housed in what was once the imperial stables and carriage houses. Here you will find art museums, venues for film, theater, architecture, dance, new media, and a children's creativity center. The visitor center is a good starting point.

Among the attractions is the **Leopold Museum** which focuses on Austrian art, including many works by Egon Schiele and Gustav Klimt. The **Museum of Modern Art Ludwig Foundation Vienna** shows contemporary and modern art from around the world. **ZOOM Kinder-museum** offers a lively introduction to the world of the museum for children. **Architekturzentrum** is dedicated to 20th- and 21st-century architecture.

Freud Museum ⑧

Berggasse 19. **Tel** 01-319 1596. **U** Schottentor. ⬜ 9am–5pm daily. 🎦

No. 19 Berggasse is very like any other 19th-century apartment in Vienna, yet it is now one of the city's most famous addresses. The father of psychoanalysis, Sigmund Freud, received patients here from 1891 to 1938. The flat housed Freud's family as well as his practice. Memorabilia

Beautifully restored patients' waiting room in the Freud Museum

on display include letters and books, furnishings, photographs, and various antiquities. Even his hat and cane are on show. Although it was abandoned when the Nazis forced Freud to leave, the apartment still preserves an intimate domestic atmosphere.

Applied Arts Museum ⑨

Stubenring 5. **Tel** 01-711 360.
Ⓤ Stubentor, Landstrasse. 🚌 74A.
🚊 1, 2. ◯ 10am–midnight Tue,
10am–6pm Wed–Sun. ⬤ Jan 1, May
1, Nov 1, Dec 25. 🈂 ♿ 🍴 🛗 ⬛

The MAK (Museum für angewandte Kunst) was founded in 1864 as a museum for art and industry. Over the years, it also acquired objects representing new artistic movements. The museum has a fine collection of furniture, including some classical works of the German cabinet-maker David Roentgen, textiles, glass, Islamic and East Asian art, and fine Renaissance jewelry. There is also a whole room full of Biedermeier furniture. The most important Austrian artistic movement was the Secession, formed by artists who seceded from the Vienna academy in 1897. Their style, also known as Jugend-stil, is represented through the many and varied productions of the Wiener Werkstätte (Viennese Work-shops), a cooperative arts and crafts studio, founded in 1903.

Brass vase (1903) by Kolo Moser

Secession Building ⑩

Friedrichstrasse 12. **Tel** 01-587 5307.
Ⓤ Karlsplatz. ◯ 10am–6pm Tue–Sun. 🈂 ♿

Joseph Maria Olbrich designed the unusual Secession Building in *Jugendstil* style as a

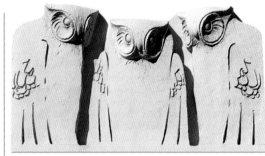

Group of stone owls decorating the Secession Building

showcase for the Secession movement's artists in 1898. The almost windowless building is a squat cube with four towers. The filigree globe of entwined laurel leaves on the roof gave rise to the building's nickname: "The Golden Cabbage."

Inside, Gustav Klimt's famous *Beethoven Frieze*, designed in 1902, covers three walls and stretches 34 m (110 ft) from end to end.

Karlskirche ⑪

Karlsplatz. **Tel** 01-504 6187.
Ⓤ Karlsplatz. 🚌 4A. ◯ daily. 🈂

During Vienna's plague epidemic of 1713, Karl VI vowed that, as soon as the city was delivered, he would build a church dedicated to St. Charles Borromeo (1538–84),

Karlskirche, with column showing scenes from the life of St. Charles Borromeo

a patron saint of the plague. Johann Bernhard Fischer von Erlach's eclectic Baroque masterpiece borrows from the architecture of ancient Greece and Rome. The interior was embellished with carvings and altarpieces by leading artists of the day.

Johann Michael Rottmayr's huge fresco in the cupola (1725–30) depicts St. Charles in heaven interceding for deliverance from the plague.

Albertina ⑫

Albertinaplatz 1. **Tel** 01-534 830.
Ⓤ Karlsplatz, Stephansplatz. ◯
10am–6pm daily (to 9pm Wed). 🈂
♿ 🛗 🍴 www.albertina.at

Hidden away in a corner of the Hofburg is the Albertina, a palace named after Duke Albert of Sachsen-Teschen, Maria Theresa's son-in-law. Its collection includes one million prints, 65,000 water-colors and drawings, and over 70,000 photographs. The gems of the collection are by Dürer, with Michelangelo and Rubens also well represented. Picasso heads a fine 20th-century section. These are dis-played through a series of high-profile temporary exhibitions in three halls.

The palace was recently restored to its former glory and now, for the first time in over 200 years, it is possible to visit the Hapsburg State Rooms, a fine example of Neo-classical architecture and interior decoration.

Vienna: Farther Afield

For a city of 1.6 million inhabitants, Vienna is surprisingly compact. Nonetheless, some of the most interesting sights are away from the city center. At Belvedere, the palace and gardens of Prince Eugene impress with their scale and grandeur. Farther away at Schönbrunn sprawls the immense palace and gardens so loved by Empress Maria Theresa. There are also many parks and gardens around the city, the largest and most interesting of which is the Prater. A former hunting ground of the Habsburgs, it is now open to the public for numerous leisure activities.

The colorful Volksprater Funfair, Prater

Prater ⑬

Prater. **U** *Praterstern.* 🚌 *74A.*
Park ◯ *daily.* **Ferris Wheel** ◯
daily. 📧 **www**.wiener-prater.at

Originally an imperial hunting ground, this huge area of woods and meadows between the Danube and the Danube Canal was opened to the public by Joseph II in 1766. The central avenue, or Hauptallee, stretches for 5 km (3 miles) through the center of the Prater, and was for a long time the preserve of the nobility and their footmen. During the 19th century the northern end of the Prater became a massive funfair,

dominated by a giant ferris wheel, one of Vienna's most famous landmarks. There is also a planetarium, an exhibition center, and a trotting stadium nearby.

The southern side of the Prater contains extensive woodland – interlaced with cycle paths, a municipal golf course, and the Freudenau Racetrack, where flat racing meetings are held from April to November.

Belvedere ⑭

Upper Belvedere Prinz-Eugen-Strasse 27. **Tel** 01-795 570. 🚌 13A. ⑤ Süd-bahnhof. 🚊 0, 18, D, 71. ◯ 10am–6pm Tue–Sun (Good Fri, Dec 24 & 31: 10am–3pm). ● Jan 1, May 1, Nov 1, Dec 25. 📷 ♿ 📧 **Lower Belvedere** Rennweg 6a. **Tel** 01-795 570. 🚊 71, D. ◯ as above. ● as above. 📷 ♿ 📧 **Gardens** ◯ daily. ♿

The Belvedere was built by Johann Lukas von Hildebrandt as the summer residence of Prince Eugene of Savoy, the brilliant military

commander whose strategies helped vanquish the Turks in 1683. Situated on a gently sloping hill, the Belvedere consists of two palaces linked by a formal garden laid out in the French style by Dominique Girard. The huge garden is sited on three levels, linked by two elaborate cascading waterfalls. Different areas of the garden are meant to convey a complicated series of Classical allusions: the lower part of the garden represents the domain of the Four Elements, the center is Parnassus, and the upper section is Olympus.

Standing at the highest point of the garden, the Upper Belvedere has a more elaborate façade than the Lower Belvedere, with lavish stone ornamentation, statues, and balustrades. The domed copper roofs of the end pavilions were designed to resemble Turkish tents – an allusion to Prince Eugene's many victories over the Turks. In fact, the

Sphinx from Upper Belvedere garden

whole palace was intended to be a symbolic reflection of the prince's power and glory, and was appropriate to the grand festive occasions for which it was originally used. The many impressive interiors include the Sala Terrena, with four Herculean figures supporting the ceiling, and a grand, sweeping staircase, the ornately decorated chapel, and the opulent Marble Hall.

Imposing Baroque façade of Prince Eugene's Upper Belvedere palace

For hotels and restaurants in this region see pp608–9 and pp610–11

The Sala Terrena, the grand entrance hall of the Upper Belvedere

The building also houses the collections of 19th- and 20th-century paintings belonging to the Austrian Gallery. Many of the works are by Austrian painters, including an excellent collection by Gustav Klimt. There are also works by Ferdinand Georg Waldmüller and Van Gogh.

The Lower Belvedere was used by Prince Eugene for day-to-day living, and the building itself is less elaborate than the Upper Belvedere. Many of the rooms are just as grand, however, for example the ornate, golden Hall of Mirrors. Part of the palace now houses the Museum of Austrian Baroque Art, which displays works of art by the artists and sculptors who shaped the city during Vienna's Golden Age (c.1683–1780). There are paintings by J. M. Rottmayr, Martino Altomonte, Daniel Gran, and Paul Troger among others, and sculptures by Franz Xavier Messerschmidt and Georg Raphael Donner.

Next door to the Lower Belvedere is the handsome Orangery, originally used to shelter tender garden plants in winter. The Museum of Austrian Medieval Art is housed here, and the gallery contains masterpieces of Gothic and early Renaissance painting and sculpture. Notable among the sculptures is the 12th-century Romanesque Stammerberg Crucifix, one of the oldest surviving examples of Tyrolean woodcarving. The seven painted panels by Rueland Frueauf the Elder (1490–94) show the Passion taking place in an Austrian setting.

Schönbrunn Palace and Gardens ⑮

Schönbrunner Schloss Strasse 147, Schönbrunn. **Tel** *01-811 13239.* Ⓤ *Schönbrunn.* 🚌 *10A.* 🚊 *10, 58.* ◐ *daily.* 🎟️ *(gardens free).* ♿ 🏪 ⓘ 🚾

This magnificent former summer residence of the imperial family takes its name from a "beautiful spring" that was found nearby. An earlier hunting lodge was destroyed by the Turks, so Leopold I asked Johann Bernhard Fischer von Erlach to design a grand Baroque residence here in 1695. The project was finally completed by Nikolaus Pacassi in the mid-18th century, under Empress Maria Theresa.

The strict symmetry of the architecture is complemented by the extensive formal gardens, with their neat lawns and careful planting. An array of fountains and statues is framed by trees and alleyways. The gardens also contain a huge tropical Palm House with an interesting collection of exotic plants, a small zoo, a butterfly house, an orangery, and the Gloriette – a large Neoclassical arcade which crowns the hill behind the palace. Inside the palace, the Rococo decorative schemes were devised by Nikolaus Pacassi. In the state rooms, the dominant features are white paneling, often adorned with gilded ornamental framework. The rooms vary from the extremely sumptuous – such as the Millionen-Zimmer, paneled with fig-wood inlaid with Persian miniatures – to the quite plain apartments of Franz Joseph and Empress Elisabeth. The Memorial Room contains the portrait and effigy of the Duke of Reichstadt, the son of Napoleon and Princess Maria Louisa, daughter of Austrian Emperor Franz I. A virtual prisoner in the palace after Napoleon's fall from power, the duke died here in 1832 aged 21. Alongside the palace is a museum of imperial coaches and sleighs.

The beautiful Schönbrunn Palace, as seen from the gardens

The historic center of Graz, overlooked by the thickly-wooded Schlossberg

Eisenstadt ❷

🏃 14,000. 🚪 🚅 🛈 *Schloss Esterházy (02682-67390).*

The principal attraction of Eisenstadt is the grand residence of the Esterházy princes, the Hungarian aristocrats who claimed to be descendants of Attila. **Schloss Esterházy** was built for Prince Paul Esterházy in 1663–73. In the Haydnsaal, a huge hall of state decorated with 18th-century frescoes, the famous composer Joseph Haydn (1732–1809) conducted the family orchestra. Haydn lived on Haydngasse, and his house is now a museum. He is buried in the **Bergkirche**, west of the palace.

Until World War II, Eisenstadt had a large Jewish community, and there is a **Jewish Museum** near the palace.

Schloss Esterházy, a mix of Baroque and Neoclassical styles

🏰 **Schloss Esterházy**
Esterházyplatz. *Tel 02682-719 3000.* ⬤ *Apr–mid-Nov: daily; mid-Nov–Mar: Mon–Fri.* 🎦

Graz ❸

🏃 254,000. ✈ 9 km (6 miles) S. 🚉 🚅 🛈 *Herrengasse 16 (0316-807 50).*

Almost entirely surrounded by mountains, Graz is Austria's second largest city. During the Middle Ages its importance rivaled that of Vienna. In the late 14th century, the Habsburg Duke Leopold III chose Graz as his base, and in the following century the town played a vital strategic role in the war against the invading Turks.

The city is dominated by the Schlossberg, the huge hill on which the town's medieval defenses were built. During the Napoleonic Wars Graz was occupied by French troops, who blew up most of the fortifications in 1809. Among the ruins visible today are a 28-m (92-ft) high clock tower, the **Uhrturm**, dating from 1561, and the **Glockenturm** (bell tower), from 1588. The former houses the **Schlossbergmuseum**, with exhibits illustrating the history of Graz. From the summit of the hill there are splendid views over the city and the Mur valley.

At the foot of the Schlossberg lies the Old Town, a UNESCO World Heritage site. The medieval **Burg** (fortress)

was built in several stages and completed in 1500. To the south are the late-Gothic **Cathedral of St. Ägydius**, with its striking Baroque interior, and the **Mausoleum of Ferdinand II**, designed by the Italian Pietro de Pomis in the late 17th century.

Graz's **Landesmuseum Joanneum** includes the Alte Galerie (Old Gallery) at Schloss Eggenberg, and a natural science department. Also of interest are the **Landeszeughaus**, with its impressive array of over 30,000 weapons and pieces of armor, and the **Neue Galerie**.

🏛 **Landesmuseum Joanneum**
Raubergasse 10 (Natural Science). *Tel 0316-8017 9660.* ⬤ *Tue–Sun.* 🎦
🏛 **Neue Galerie**
Herberstein Palace, Sackstrasse 16. *0316-829 155.* ⬤ *Tue–Sun.* 🎦

Environs
A few kilometers west of the city, **Schloss Eggenberg** was built by Johann Ulrich von Eggenberg in 1625–35. Open daily, the Baroque palace houses the Alte Galerie, a collection of 19th- and 20th-century art, as well as a collection of local prehistoric finds, coins, antiquities, and gemstones. Its rich collection of paintings includes works by Lucas Cranach the Elder (1472–1553) and Peter Brueghel the Younger (1564–1638). There are displays of stuffed animals in the Jagd-museum (Hunting Museum).

Melk and the Wachau ❹

Melk. Babenbergerstr., Melk (02752-5230 7410).
Benedictine abbey May–Sep: 9am–6pm daily; Apr & Oct: 9am–5pm daily; winter: guided tours only (11am and 2pm daily).

Melk lies at the western end of one of the loveliest stretches of the River Danube, the Wachau, which extends some 40 km (25 miles) downstream to Krems.

Dotted with Renaissance houses and old towers, **Melk** itself is most famous for its Baroque Benedictine abbey, a treasure trove of paintings, sculptures, and decorative art. One of its most impressive rooms is the Marble Hall, with beautiful ceiling paintings depicting mythological scenes.

A boat trip is the best way to enjoy the Wachau, though for the energetic there are cycle paths along the banks of the river. Landmarks to look for traveling downstream include the picturesque castle of **Schönbühel** and the ruined medieval fortress at **Aggstein**. Though not visible from the river, nearby **Willendorf** is the site of famous prehistoric finds.

At the eastern end of the Wachau are the well-preserved medieval towns of **Dürnstein** and **Krems**. The latter's tiny hillside streets offer fine views across the Danube to the Baroque **Göttweig Abbey**.

The opulent interior of the 17th-century Church of St. Ignatius in Linz

Linz ❺

186,000. 10 km (6 miles) SW. Hauptplatz 1 (070-7070 1777).

Austria's third city, Linz has been inhabited since Roman times, when it was a port called Lentia. In the early 16th century it developed into an important trading center. Although, today, Linz is a busy industrial city, the Old Town contains many historic buildings and monuments.

The Hauptplatz, one of the largest medieval squares in Europe, is bordered by splendid Baroque façades.

Among the finest buildings is the **Town Hall**, home to the Museum Linz Genesis, which tells the history of the city. The 20-m (66-ft) high marble Dreifaltigkeitssäule (Trinity Column) was completed in 1723.

In the southeast corner of the square is the **Church of St. Ignatius**. Also known as the Alter Dom, it was built in the 17th century in Baroque style and boasts a wonderfully ornate pulpit and altarpiece. Nearby, the **Landhaus** is well worth seeing for its three beautiful Renaissance courtyards and loggia.

The streets west of the Hauptplatz lead up to Linz's hilltop **castle**, built for Friedrich V (Holy Roman Emperor Friedrich III) in the 15th century. The castle houses the Schlossmuseum, with paintings, sculptures, and historical artifacts.

On the other side of the river, the **Ars Electronica Center** is a superb new museum that allows visitors to experiment with the latest technological innovations. Hidden away in the Lentia 2000 shopping mall is the **Lentos Kunstmuseum**, containing a fine collection of 19th- and 20th-century Austrian art, including works by Egon Schiele (1890–1918) and Gustav Klimt (1862–1918).

For splendid views of Linz, take a ride on the Pöstling-bergbahn train, which climbs to the top of Pöstlingberg Hill.

River cruises along the Danube west to Passau, in Germany, and east to Vienna depart from the quay at the Nibelungenbrücke. On-board entertainment includes themed events, such as a "Bavarian afternoon" or an "Italian night".

Ⅲ Ars Electronica Center
Hauptstrasse 2. *Tel* 0732-727 22.
Wed–Sun. www.aec.at
Ⅲ Lentos Kunstmuseum
Ernst-Koref-Promenade 11.
Tel 070-7070 3614. Wed–Mon.
www.lentos.at

Melk's massive Benedictine abbey on the banks of the Danube

Hallstatt, an attractive lakeside village in the Salzkammergut

Hallstatt

1,000. Seestrasse 169 (06134-8208).

This pretty village on the bank of the Hallstätter See lies in the Salzkammergut, a stunning region of lakes and mountains. The area takes its name from the rich deposits of salt *(salz)* that have been mined here since the 1st millennium BC. From Hallstatt, it is possible to visit a working mine, the **Salzbergwerk**, by taking the cable car from the southern end of the village up to the mine entrance on the Salzberg mountain. The **Rudolfsturm**, the tower that stands close to the station at the top, was completed in 1284 to defend the mine workings.

Hallstatt's **Prähistorisches Museum** contains Celtic Iron Age artifacts discovered near the mines. Today, the name Hallstatt is used to refer to the Celtic culture that flourished from the 9th to the 5th centuries BC.

Behind the **Pfarrkirche**, the town's late-Gothic parish church, the **Beinhaus** (Charnel House) has been used to store human remains since 1600.

Salzbergwerk Hallstatt
Tel 06132-200 2400. end Apr–Oct: daily.

Prähistorisches Museum
Tel 06134-828 015. Apr–Oct: daily; Nov–Mar: Wed–Sun.

Environs

The mountains and the crystal clear waters of the Hallstätter See offer many opportunities for swimming, water sports, scuba diving, hiking, and cycling. There are also boat trips on the lake.

At the southern end of the Hallstätter See, about 2 km (1 mile) from Hallstatt, are the **Dachstein limestone caves**, open daily from May to mid-October. A cable car from south of Obertraun climbs to the entrance of the caves, giving superb views of the lake and surrounding mountains.

Salzburg ❼

150,000. 3 km (2 miles) W. Mozartplatz 5 (0662-8898 7330). Salzburger Festspiele (late Jul–Aug). **www**.salzburg.info

Salzburg first rose to prominence in about AD 700, when a church and a monastery were established here. Until 1816, when it became part of the Habsburg empire, the independent city-state of Salzburg was ruled by a succession of prince-archbishops. Best known as the birthplace of Wolfgang Amadeus Mozart, today the city has a thriving musical tradition. Each summer large numbers of tourists arrive for the Salzburger Festspiele, a festival of opera, classical music concerts, and theater.

Salzburg's medieval fortress, the **Festung Hohensalzburg**, looms over the city from its hilltop position. The castle dates from the 11th century, but the state apartments are an early 16th-century addition.

The **Residenz**, where Salzburg's prince-archbishops lived and held court, owes its early Baroque appearance to Archbishop Wolf Dietrich von Raiteneau, who resided here from 1587. The palace contains the Residenzgalerie, a collection of European art of the 16th to 19th centuries.

WOLFGANG AMADEUS MOZART

Wolfgang Amadeus Mozart (1756–91)

Salzburg's most famous son, Wolfgang Amadeus Mozart, was born in 1756, the son of Leopold, a member of the Prince-Archbishop's chamber orchestra. He learnt to play the harpsichord at the age of 3, and by the age of 5 had already written his first compositions. From 1763 Mozart traveled widely, performing for the aristocracy across Europe. His mastery of all the musical genres of the day swiftly earned him renown at home and abroad. During his short life, his prodigious output included 56 symphonies, over 20 concertos, and 15 operas, among them *The Marriage of Figaro* and *Don Giovanni*. Mozart's aspirations to lead the kind of lifestyle enjoyed by his patrons, however, led him into financial difficulties. In his final years, the musician was continually debt-ridden and prone to depression. He died in 1791 and was buried in a mass grave.

For hotels and restaurants in this region see pp608–9 and pp610–11

Among the city's fine religious buildings are **St. Peter's Abbey** and **Benedictine monastery**, dating from c.AD 700, and the **Cathedral** (Dom), begun in 1614 to a design by Santino Solari. The **Franziskanerkirche** boasts a magnificent Baroque altarpiece (1709) by Johann Bernhard Fischer von Erlach.

Notable museums include the **Museum Carolino Augusteum**, with its historical and fine arts collections, and the **Haus der Natur**, a museum of natural history. The **Mozarts Geburtshaus** is Mozart's birthplace, while the **Mozart Wohnhaus** features audio-visual displays telling the story of his life.

On the right bank of the Salzach, **Schloss Mirabell** was built by Archbishop Wolf Dietrich for his Jewish mistress, Salome Alt. The palace gardens house the **Barock-Museum** (Baroque Museum), with its collection of 17th- and 18th-century works of art.

⛪ Festung Hohensalzburg
Mönchsberg 34. **Tel** 0662-8424 3011. ⬜ daily. 🖼 🚻

🏛 Residenz
Residenzplatz 1. **Tel** 0662-8042 2690. ⬜ daily. (Residenzgalerie Tue–Sun ● Feb–mid-Mar & 1st 2 weeks Nov.) 🖼 🚻

🏛 Museum Carolino Augusteum
Museumplatz 1. **Tel** 0662-6208 08200. ⬜ daily. 🖼

🏛 Barockmuseum
Tel 0662-877 432. ⬜ Tue–Sun. 🖼

Innsbruck's Annasäule, crowned by a statue of the Virgin Mary

Innsbruck ❽

🏨 124,000. ✈ 4 km (2.5 miles) W. 🚉 🚌 ℹ Burggraben 3 (0512-59850). www.innsbruck-tourismus.com

Capital of the Tyrol region, Innsbruck grew up at the crossroads of the old trade routes between Germany and Italy, Vienna, and Switzerland.

One of the city's finest pieces of architecture is the **Goldenes Dachl** (Golden Roof), commissioned by Emperor Maximilian I, who chose Innsbruck as his imperial capital at the end of the 15th century. Made of gilded copper tiles, the roof was constructed in the 1490s to cover a balcony used by members of the court to observe events in the square below. Beneath the balcony is the **Museum Maximilianeum**, which focuses on the life of the Habsburg emperor, who ruled from 1493 to 1519.

Innsbruck's **Hofburg** (Imperial Palace) dates from the 15th century, but was rebuilt in Rococo style in the 18th century by Empress Maria Theresa (ruled 1740–80).

Built in 1555–65, the **Hofkirche** contains the impressive mausoleum of Maximilian I, which features 28 bronze statues. The high-light of the **Domkirche St. Jakob** (1717–22) is Lucas Cranach the Elder's painting of the *Madonna and Child*, which adorns the high altar.

Innsbruck's many museums include the **Tiroler Landes-museum Ferdinandeum**, which has European art from the 15th to the 20th centuries, and the **Tiroler Volkskunst-museum**, with exhibitions of local folk art and crafts.

🏛 Museum Maximilianeum
Herzog-Friedrichstrasse 15. **Tel** 0512-581 111. ⬜ daily. ● Oct–Apr: Mon. 🖼

🏛 Hofburg
Rennweg 1. **Tel** 0512-587 186. ⬜ daily. ● Aug 15. 🖼

🏛 Tiroler Landesmuseum Ferdinandeum
Museumstrasse 15. **Tel** 0512-59489. ⬜ daily. ● Oct–May: Mon. 🖼

🏛 Tiroler Volkskunst-museum
Universitätsstrasse 2. **Tel** 0512-584 302. ⬜ daily. 🖼

Salzburg's magnificent Baroque cathedral, dominating the skyline of the Old Town

Practical & Travel Information

Austria is well-equipped for tourism in both winter and summer. The extensive winter-sports facilities mean that even in the mountainous west of the country, communications are good and most roads are kept open all year. Public transport, especially the train services between the main cities, is reliable, and banking and exchange facilities are widely available. The country is generally safe for visitors except for a few unsavory bits of Vienna. Hospitals are of a high standard and, for lesser ailments, pharmacists are highly respected.

TOURIST INFORMATION

Austria has a wide network of local and regional tourist offices and the **Austrian National Tourist Office** has branches in many countries abroad. In the busier skiing resorts in winter, local offices often stay open as late as 9pm. In Vienna, **Wiener Tourismusverband** is a very helpful organization, especially with regard to forthcoming events and booking accommodations.

VISA REQUIREMENTS

Citizens of the US, Canada, Australia, and New Zealand need just a passport to visit Austria. No visa is required for stays of up to three months. Most European Union (EU) visitors need only a valid identity card to enter the country.

PERSONAL SECURITY

Although crime in the cities is rare, there are a few parts of Vienna that are best avoided at night, especially around the Karlsplatz station. Fights and pickpocketing are quite common at the Prater funfair at night.

In case of emergencies while on vacation, the appropriate services to call are listed in the Directory opposite.

HEALTH ISSUES

It is best to take out full health insurance which also covers flights home for medical reasons. This is true even for visitors from EU countries such as Great Britain. There is a reciprocal arrangement with Austria whereby emergency hospital treatment is free upon presentation of a British passport, but obtaining free treatment can involve rather a lot of bureaucracy.

In the case of a medical emergency, call an ambulance *(Rettungsdienst)* or the local **Doctor on Call**. For minor ailments or injuries, visit an *Apotheke* (pharmacy). All pharmacies display a distinctive red "A" sign. When closed, they give the address of the nearest open pharmacy.

FACILITIES FOR THE DISABLED

Public awareness of the needs of the disabled is growing in Austria. Wiener Tourismusverband has a good online information service with details of the ease of wheelchair access at tourist sights, hotels, and public restrooms.

ETIQUETTE

Austrians on the whole are a conservative people and formal in their modes of address. Waiters are summoned with a deferential "Herr Ober," and greetings in the street are accompanied by the use of titles, such as "Herr Doktor," and much handshaking.

BANKING AND CURRENCY

The unit of currency in Austria was, until 2002, the Austrian Schilling. On January 1, 2002, it was replaced by the euro *(see p15)*.

Banks are usually the best places to change money. Most are open Monday to Friday from 8am to 12:30pm and from 1:30pm to 3pm (5:30pm on Thursdays). Some banks, generally those at main train stations and at airports, stay open longer and do not close for lunch. Though major credit cards are accepted at most large stores, hotels, and restaurants, they are not used as frequently as, for instance, in the UK or France, so it is a good idea to carry some cash with you.

COMMUNICATIONS

The Austrian telecommunications network is run by Telekom Austria. Calls are among the most expensive in Europe. Public phones are coin- or card-operated, and you can buy phonecards from post offices and newsagents. Lower-rate calling times from Vienna are from 6pm to 8am Monday to Friday, and all day on Saturday and Sunday. Numbers starting in 05- can be dialled from anywhere in Austria at a local call rate. The postal service is reliable, verging on the pedantic, and

THE CLIMATE OF AUSTRIA

Altitude obviously plays an important role in the climate of Austria, the Alpine part of the country experiencing lower temperatures and receiving more rain and snow than Vienna and the east. Snow cover in the Alps lasts from November to May. Daytime temperatures in summer can be high, but the evenings are cool. There is a risk of thunderstorms from June to August.

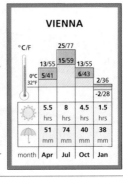

VIENNA			
°C/F	25/77		
	13/55 15/59 13/55		
0°C 5/41		6/43	2/36
32°F			-2/28
5.5 hrs	8 hrs	4.5 hrs	1.5 hrs
51 mm	74 mm	40 mm	38 mm
month Apr	Jul	Oct	Jan

posting a letter can take some time. Each letter is carefully weighed and every size and shape coded separately.

Most post offices are open between 8am and noon and 2pm and 6pm from Monday to Friday. You can also buy stamps at newsagents.

FLYING TO AUSTRIA

If you fly from the United States, there are direct flights with **Delta Air Lines** from New York and Orlando to Vienna's Schwechat airport. **Austrian Airlines** flies from New York, Washington, and Chicago and **Lauda Air** has flights from Miami. The only direct flights from Australia are run by Lauda Air, which operates charter services from Sydney and Melbourne.

Connections to all of the major European cities are good. There are several flights a day from London's Gatwick and Heathrow airports. British Airways is the main British airline with regular flights to Vienna, and the main Austrian carrier is Austrian Airlines. Ryanair also offers regular services at low prices.

You can get APEX tickets if you book two weeks in advance, and charters are available at very competitive prices. Weekend package deals, including the price of

two nights at a good Viennese hotel, can be excellent value, sometimes costing less than the economy-class ticket price.

RAIL TRAVEL

Austria's rail network is run by the state-owned Österreichische Bundesbahnen (ÖBB). Like London and Paris, Vienna has several mainline stations, three of which serve international connections. Generally, the Westbahnhof handles trains from the west, with good, frequent services to Innsbruck and Salzburg. Southern and eastern areas are served by the Südbahnhof, and trains from the north arrive at Franz-Josefs-Bahnhof.

The city of Vienna has two local train services: the U-Bahn (subway) and the Schnellbahn (a fast commuter service). The Westbahnhof has interchanges with the U3 and U6 subway lines, the Schnellbahn, and several tram and bus routes. The Südbahnhof is linked to the Schnellbahn and tram and bus lines, while Franz-Josefs-Bahnhof is served by the Schnellbahn and the cross-city D tram, which goes directly to the Ringstrasse.

The travel agency (*Veerkehrsverein*) at Westbahnhof, open from 8am to 9pm daily, provides rail information and also helps

with hotel bookings. In Vienna there is a telephone number for obtaining railway information in English (*see below*).

TRAVELING BY BUS

Austria's long-distance buses serve those parts of the country that are not reached by train. Bus and train timetables are well integrated. In most towns, buses leave from the train station or the post office.

TRAVELING BY CAR

Even in winter, Austrian road conditions are good and autobahns (highways) link all the major cities. There are also convenient routes into Austria from neighboring countries, such as those from Munich to Salzburg and Innsbruck. Highways are subject to a toll, which is paid by buying a windshield sticker valid for a certain period of time, ranging from a week to two months to a year. Stickers can be bought at the border or at post offices, gas stations, and tobacconists throughout the country. Tolls are also payable on certain mountain roads and tunnels. All drivers in Austria must carry their driver's license, car registration documents, and insurance documents.

DIRECTORY

TOURIST OFFICES

Austrian National Tourist Office
www.austria.info

In Australia:
36 Carrington Street,
1st floor, Sydney,
NSW 2000.
Tel 02-9299 3621.

In Canada:
2 Bloor Street West,
400 Toronto,
Ontario M4W 3E2.
Tel 416-967 3381.

In the UK:
9–11 Richmond Bldgs,
London W1D 3HF.
Tel 207-318 1651.

In the US:
PO Box 1142,
New York,
NY 10018-114.
Tel 212-944 6885.

Wiener Tourismusverband
Corner of Albertinaplatz/
Tegethoffstrasse/
Meysedergasse, Vienna.
Tel 01-24555.
www.wien.info

EMBASSIES

Australia
Mattiellistrasse 2–4,
A-1010 Vienna.
Tel 01-506740.

Canada
Laurenzerberg 2,
A-1010 Vienna.
Tel 01-5313 83000.

UK
Jaurèsgasse 12,
A-1030 Vienna.
Tel 01-716130.

US
Boltzmanngasse 16,
A-1090 Vienna.
Tel 01-31339.

EMERGENCY NUMBERS

Ambulance
Tel 144.

Doctor on Call
Tel 141.

Fire
Tel 122.

Police
Tel 133.

AIRLINES

Austrian Airlines
Tel 05-1789 (Austria).
Tel 020-7434 7350 (UK).
Tel 800-843 0002 (US).
www.aua.com

Delta Air Lines
Tel 01-79567 023 (Vienna).
Tel 800-221 1212 (US).
www.delta.com

Lauda Air
Tel 0820-320 321 (Vienna).
Tel 800-588 8399 (US).

Ryanair
Tel 0871-246 0000 (UK).
www.ryanair.com

RAIL INFORMATION

Tel 05-1717.
www.oebb.at

Shopping and Entertainment

Shopping in Austria can be expensive, but it is a good place to buy certain high-quality traditional goods, such as Loden coats, porcelain, and glass. Famous for its coffee shops, Christmas markets, world-class opera, and orchestras, Vienna is the center of entertainment in Austria, although some important music festivals are held across the country. Outside the city, such rural pleasures as skiing and hiking are available in the west of the country, in the Tyrol, Salzburger Land, and Salzkammergut regions.

OPENING HOURS

Stores usually open at 8:30 or 9am and close at 6 or 7pm. Smaller ones may close for an hour at lunch. In the past all stores closed at noon on Saturday, a routine that some still follow, though most now stay open until 5pm. Shops are still closed on Sundays and public holidays, but you can buy items such as groceries, flowers, books, camera film, and newspapers at major train stations.

FOOD AND DRINK

Austria is justly famous for its cakes and pastries, and in Vienna and large towns a good *Café-Konditorei* (cake shop and café) will mail cakes back home for you. Buy a prettily-packaged *Sachertorte*, the world-famous Viennese chocolate cake. In November and December try the buttery Advent *Stollen*, stuffed with fruit and nuts and dusted with icing sugar, available from the **Meinl am Graben** delicatessen or any good baker. Specialist chocolate shops, such as **Altmann & Kühne**, are also worth a visit, both for the unusual packaging and the chocolates themselves.

Sweet *Eiswein* (so-called because the grapes are left on the vines until the first frosts) is an unusual and delicious white dessert wine. **Zum Schwarzen Kameel** in Vienna also sells the rarer red variety.

LUXURY GOODS

Desirable Austrian goods include clothes made of *Loden*, a felt-like woollen fabric, custom-made sheets, and high-quality down pillows and duvets. Petit point embroidery, which adorns handbags, powder compacts, and similar articles, is a Viennese specialty. A wide range is available at **Petit Point** and **Maria Stransky**.

Trachten (Austrian costume) shops are fun, selling a wide selection of hats, children's dresses, jackets, and blouses.

Glassware – including superb chandeliers – and Augarten porcelain come in highly original designs, but are very expensive. **Rasper & Söhne** is a good glass and porcelain shop for such items. The **Schloss Augarten** porcelain factory is open to visitors.

BOOKING TICKETS

You can buy tickets direct from the appropriate box office or reserve them by phone. Agencies are reliable; try the **Reisebüro Mondial**. Vienna's four state theaters, the Burgtheater, Akademietheater, Opera House, and Volksoper have a central booking office, the **Bundestheaterkassen**. In most cases tickets go on sale one month before the performance. Written applications for tickets must reach the Österreichische Bundestheater Verband (address as Bundestheaterkassen) at least three weeks in advance for opera tickets, and 10 days ahead for the theaters. Standing-room tickets (over 500 at the Opera House) are sold at the evening box office one hour before the start of the performance.

THEATER

Viennese theater enjoys a high reputation and the Burgtheater *(see p594)* is the most prestigious venue.

Classic and modern plays are performed here and at the associated Akademietheater.

The **Volkstheater** offers more modern plays as well as the occasional classic and some operetta performances.

The historic **Theater an der Wien** and the large **Raimund Theater** are part of the Vereinigte Bühnen Wien, the city's own theaters. Both specialize in lavish musicals. The Wiener Festwochen is held in May and June, and includes productions by guest companies, which are staged at these two theaters as part of the festival programme.

Vienna has a wide range of fringe theater from one-man shows to *Kabarett* – satirical shows not cabarets – but fairly fluent German is needed to appreciate them.

OPERA AND OPERETTA

The opera season runs from September to June. At the Staatsoper in Vienna, operas are normally performed in the original language. At the **Wiener Volksoper**, where the repertoire includes light opera by Mozart and Puccini and operettas by Strauss and Lehár, they are sung in German. The same singers often appear at the two venues. The New Year's Eve performance at the Opera House is always Johan Strauss the Younger's *Die Fledermaus*, and famous guests sometimes make surprise appearances during the second act.

A wonderful smaller opera house is the **Wiener Kammeroper**. Here you can expect anything from Rossini and classic operetta to rock versions of familiar operas and opera parodies. From mid-July until mid-August the Wiener Kammeroper also plays at the **Soirée bei Prinz Orlofsky** festival at the Schönbrunner Schlosstheater.

CLASSICAL MUSIC

The principal venues for classical music concerts are the **Musikverein** (including the restored Brahms-Saal) and the concert halls of the **Konzerthaus**. Performances are also held in many other halls and historic palaces around Vienna.

The New Year's Concert is televised live from the Grosser Musikvereinsaal in the Musikverein every year. You can apply for tickets by writing direct to the **Wiener Philharmoniker**. Applications must be received on January 2 (not before, not after) for the next year's concert. You can order from abroad by telegram.

The city supports two great orchestras, the Wiener Philharmoniker and the Wiener Symphoniker. There are also a number of chamber music ensembles and church music is often of concert quality. The world-famous Vienna Boys' Choir can be heard during mass at the Burgkapelle in the Hofburg complex *(see p594)* every Sunday and religious holiday at 9:15am except from July to about mid-September (the box office is open the Friday before). You can also hear them at the Konzerthaus every Friday at 3:30pm in May, June, September, and October. Tickets are available from hotel porters and from Reisebüro Mondial.

MUSIC FESTIVALS

Seasonal events in Vienna include the Vienna Festival in May and June, and the Klangbogen Wien in July and August, which includes opera performances held at the Theater an der Wien.

Inaugurated in 1920, the **Salzburg Festival** of opera, drama, and music claims to be the largest of its kind in the world. It is held annually in late July and August, attracting the world's finest conductors, soloists, and opera and theater companies. The spectacular venues include the Felsenreitschule, the riding school of the prince-archbishops of Salzburg. There is always a strong emphasis on Mozart, the city's most famous son, but the festival has also won acclaim for its contemporary music and innovative productions of classic and modern drama.

Another smaller festival is the **Haydn Festspiele**, held at the magnificent Schloss Esterházy in Eisenstadt *(see p600)*. The festival itself is in September, but Haydn concerts are given in the palace throughout the summer.

COFFEE HOUSES AND HEURIGE

The Viennese coffee house is a throwback to a more leisured age, serving coffee in a bewildering range of styles and allowing patrons to sit and read newspapers at their leisure. The *Heuriger* is a uniquely Austrian establishment. Its literal meaning is "this year's," and it refers both to the youngest available local wine and to venues that sell it. The most famous are in villages to the north and west of Vienna, such as Heiligenstadt and Grinzing. A sign reading *Eigenbau* means that the wine is from the owner's vineyards.

WINTER SPORTS

Austria's facilities for winter sports are second only to Switzerland's. Ski resorts vary from fashionable Kitzbühel and St. Anton to small family resorts with less demanding slopes. Package tours are available from many countries around the world. Information on 800 resorts can be found on the **Austria Tourism** website, along with snow reports and other useful information.

DIRECTORY

FOOD AND DRINK

Altmann & Kühne
Graben 30, Vienna.
Tel 01-533 0927.

Meinl am Graben
Graben 19, Vienna.
Tel 01-532 3334.

Zum Schwarzen Kameel
Bognergasse 5, Vienna.
Tel 01-533 8125.

LUXURY GOODS

Maria Stransky
Hofburg Passage 2, Vienna.
Tel 01-533 6098.

Petit Point
Kärntner Strasse 16, Vienna.
Tel 01-512 4886.

Rasper & Söhne
Am Graben 15, Vienna.
Tel 01-534 33.

Schloss Augarten
Obere Augartenstrasse 1, Vienna.
Tel 01-211 24123.

BOOKING TICKETS

Bundestheaterkassen
Opernring 2, Vienna.
Tel 01-514 440.

Reisebüro Mondial
Operngasse 206, Vienna.
Tel 01-5880 4150.

THEATER

Raimund Theater
Wallgasse 18, Vienna.
Tel 01-599 770.

Theater an der Wien
Linke Wienzeile 6, Vienna.
Tel 01-58885.

Volkstheater
Neustiftgasse 1, Vienna.
Tel 01-521 110.

OPERA AND OPERETTA

Soirée bei Prinz Orlofsky
Schönbrunner Schlosstheater, Schönbrunn.
Tel 01-71155 6100.

Wiener Kammeroper
Fleischmarkt 24, Vienna.
Tel 01-512 010077.

Wiener Volksoper
Währinger Strasse 78, Vienna.
Tel 01-514 4430.

CLASSICAL MUSIC

Konzerthaus
Lothringerstrasse 20, Vienna.
Tel 01-242 002.

Musikverein
Bösendorferstrasse 12, Vienna.
Tel 01-505 8190.

Wiener Philharmoniker
Bösendorferstrasse 12, Vienna.
Tel 01-505 8190.

MUSIC FESTIVALS

Haydn Festspiele
Schloss Esterházy, A-7000 Eisenstadt.
Tel 02682-618 66.

Salzburg Festival
Hofstallgasse 1, Postfach 140, A-5100 Salzburg.
Tel 0662-804 5579.

WINTER SPORTS

Austria Tourism
www.austria.info

Where to Stay in Austria

Accommodations in Austria range from large, well-equipped, five-star hotels to simple pensions, and generally you can expect a high standard of comfort and cleanliness everywhere. Room rates in Vienna are disproportionately high compared to other costs. Save money by staying in a hotel outside the Ringstrasse.

PRICE CATEGORIES
Price categories for a standard double room per night, including tax, service and breakfast:

€ Under 90 euros
€€ 90–140 euros
€€€ 140–180 euros
€€€€ 180–260 euros
€€€€€ Over 260 euros

VIENNA

CENTRAL VIENNA Neuer Markt
€

*Seilergasse 9, 1010 **Tel** 01-512 23 16 **Fax** 01-513 9105 **Rooms** 37* **Map** D4

A pension has existed on this site since the 1920s, and the Neuer Markt continues the tradition in true Viennese style. Plenty of dusty-rose colored furnishings. Friendly, personal service. For those staying longer than seven nights, a pick-up service upon arrival at the airport or train stations is provided free of charge. **www.hotelpension.at**

CENTRAL VIENNA Arenberg
€€

*Stubenring 2, 1010 **Tel** 01-512 52 91 **Fax** 01-513 93 56 **Rooms** 22* **Map** E3, F3

Located directly on the Ringstrasse, the Arenberg is a stylishly elegant establishment. The bedrooms reflect traditional decor and provide comfort and charm as well as sound-proofed windows. The bathrooms are modern and gleaming. Several good value weekend stay packages are available. **www.arenberg.at**

CENTRAL VIENNA Aviano
€€

*Marco d'Avianogasse 1, 1010 **Tel** 01-512 83 30 **Fax** 01-512 83 30 6 **Rooms** 17* **Map** D4

Located only one minute from the Opera House, this four-star pension offers a friendly, welcoming atmosphere with very personalized service. The staff can help organize site-seeing tours and tickets to concerts. Cheerful, well-decorated rooms. Good value for money. **www.pertschy.com**

CENTRAL VIENNA Pension Christina
€€

*Hafnersteig 7, 1010 **Tel** 01-533 29 61 **Fax** 01-533 29 61 11 **Rooms** 33* **Map** E3

Located on a quiet, cobbled side street just a few minutes from St. Stephen's Cathedral, this small unassuming pension is decorated in Art Deco style. The comfortable rooms feature a TV, mini-bar and shower. The friendly staff can help arrange entertainment and tour tickets. **www.pertschy.com**

CENTRAL VIENNA Mailberger Hof
€€€

*Annagasse 7, 1010 **Tel** 01-512 06 41 **Fax** 01-512 06 41 10 **Rooms** 40* **Map** E4

Two Gothic houses have merged to create a Baroque palace, this building is owned by the Knights of Malta and is under landmark protection. You can dine in the striking vaulted restaurant. A wide, stone staircase leads to the spacious, tastefully furnished bedrooms. **www.mailbergerhof.at**

CENTRAL VIENNA Wandl
€€€

*Peterplatz 9, 1010 **Tel** 01-534 55 0 **Fax** 01-534 55 77 **Rooms** 138* **Map** D3

Located close to the Peterskirche, this charming, old-fashioned hotel has been in the same family for generations. Fine stuccoed features are in some of the bedrooms as well as in the covered courtyard that serves as a breakfast room. Other rooms are simpler, but large, and feature parquet floors. **www.hotel-wandl.com**

CENTRAL VIENNA Astoria
€€€€

*Kärntner Strasse 32–34, 1015 **Tel** 01-515 77 **Fax** 01-515 77 58 2 **Rooms** 118* **Map** D4

A hotel since 1912, it features a paneled Jugendstil foyer leading to a grand dining room on the first floor. Some of the splendid bedrooms feature their own brass letter boxes. The spacious rooms are traditionally furnished, often with period decor. Ideally located near the Opera House. **www.austria-trend.at**

CENTRAL VIENNA Kaiserin Elisabeth
€€€€

*Weihburggasse 3, 1010 **Tel** 01-512 26 0 **Fax** 01-515 26 7 **Rooms** 63* **Map** E4

This elegant hotel, named after the indomitable Habsburg empress, is located just off the Stephansplatz. In the 1800s, it played host to many famous musicians such as Wagner and Liszt. The *fin-de-siècle*-style bedrooms are smart, and Persian rugs lie on parquet floors in the public rooms. Pets are permitted. **www.kaiserinelisabeth.at**

CENTRAL VIENNA Palais Coburg Hotel Residenz
€€€€€

*Coburgbastei 4, 1010 **Tel** 01-518 18 0 **Fax** 01-512 22 47 66 **Rooms** 35* **Map** E4

This 19th-century former Saxe-Coburg-Gotha palace was renovated in 2003 for $100 million, and is now a luxury Relais & Chateaux hotel. There are 35 elegant suites, from traditional to contemporary, plus a unique rooftop spa and two fine restaurants. The wine cellar is stocked with one of Europe's finest collections. **www.palaiscoburg.at**

Map References *see map of Vienna pp590–91*

REST OF AUSTRIA

GRAZ Hotel Zum Dom

Bürgergasse 14, Graz, 8010 **Tel** *0316-82 48 00* **Fax** *0316-82 48 00 8* **Rooms** *29*

A unique boutique hotel incorporating modern luxuries within the structure of the handsome historic building. Well located in the picturesque old city and close to shopping, restaurants and bars. Its 29 rooms and suites have striking pieces of art, decadent baths and a real sense of style. **www.domhotel.co.at**

GRAZ Erzherzog Johann

Sackstraße 3–5, 8010 **Tel** *0316-81 16 16* **Fax** *0316-81 15 15* **Rooms** *62*

Elegant old-world hotel which was an inn since the 16th century, and a grand *palais* during the 18th century. The beautifully crafted interior iron work dates from this period. Rooms and grand suites are furnished with lovely antiques and parquet floors. There is an elegant winter garden restaurant and Viennese-style café. **www.erzherzog-johann.com**

HALLSTATT Seehotel Grüner Baum

Marktplatz 104, 4830 **Tel** *06134-82 63* **Fax** *06134-82 63 44* **Rooms** *20*

The lakeside hotel dates to at least 1700, its splendid façade dominating the quaint Hallstatt marketplace. An inviting terrace looks directly on to the lake. An impressive guest list includes Empress Elisabeth (Sissy) of Austria and Agatha Christie. Rooms are charmingly furnished with a mixture of contemporary and antique pieces. **www.gruenerbaum.cc**

INNSBRUCK Goldener Adler

Herzog-Friedrich-Straße 6, 6020 **Tel** *0512-57 11 11* **Fax** *0512-58 44 09* **Rooms** *34*

Located in the heart of the old town, this is one of the first inns in Europe, built in 1390. The rooms are named after former guests, which have included emperors, kings and Mozart himself. Several restaurants serve fine Tyrolean cuisine. The Goethe Stube is a fine place to drink in living history. **www.goldeneradler.com**

INNSBRUCK Parkhotel Leipzigerhof

Defreggerstraße 13, 6020 **Tel** *0512-34 35 25* **Fax** *0512-39 43 57* **Rooms** *55*

A fully modernised, family-owned, four-star hotel in the centre of Innsbruck. Bright en-suite bathrooms, elegant traditional restaurant, plus recreation centre with sauna and solarium. Rooms are equipped with high-speed Internet. **www.bestwestern.com**

INNSBRUCK Schlosshotel Igls

A-6080 Igls **Tel** *05123-77 21 7* **Fax** *05123-77 21 71 98* **Rooms** *18*

At this luxurious and discreet mountain castle every guest is treated royally. The elegant Blue Saloon serves as breakfast room, and the mahogany-paneled restaurant offers fine seasonally influenced menus. Each of the bedrooms is uniquely furnished. Combined indoor-outdoor pool, sauna, steam-bath, solarium and massage. **www.schlosshotel-igls.com**

LINZ Arcotel Nike

Untere Donaulände 9, 4020 **Tel** *0732-76 26 0* **Fax** *0732-76 26 2* **Rooms** *176*

The River Danube makes an idyllic backdrop for this modern, efficiently appointed hotel. A five-minute walk from the old centre, its rooms are furnished in a clean, modern style. A restaurant and café as well as wellness centre with hammam, indoor pool, sauna and steam bath are in house. Bright conference rooms. **www.arcotel.at**

LINZ Austria Trend Hotel Schillerpark

Rainerstraße 2–4, 4020 **Tel** *0732-69 50 0* **Fax** *0732-69 50 9* **Rooms** *111*

This rectangular glass and steel designed building offers functional modern rooms and suites with en-suite bathrooms, air-conditioning, TV, Pay-TV, minibar and safe. All single rooms feature double beds. Rooms located on the executive floor are more luxuriously equipped. There is a restaurant and several cafés and bars. **www.austria-trend.at**

SALZBURG Bergland

Rupertgasse 15, 5020 **Tel** *0662-87 23 18 0* **Fax** *0662-87 23 18 8* **Rooms** *18*

Located in a quiet street just 10 minutes walk to the centre, this is a small family-run hotel. Bathrooms are large and stylish, and downstairs a music room with piano and small English library make a cosy spot. Bicycles are available to hire. Rooms are non-smoking and have satellite TV. **www.berglandhotel.at**

SALZBURG NH Salzburg City

Franz-Josef-Straße 26, 5020 **Tel** *0662-88 20 41* **Fax** *0662-87 42 40* **Rooms** *140*

This sleek, stylishly designed hotel serves both business and holiday travelers looking to be near the historical centre and Mirabell Gardens. The hotel offers access to wireless Internet and concierge services. There is an underground garage as well as public parking. The train station is 2 km (1 mile) away. **www.nh-hotels.com**

SALZBURG Hotel Sacher Salzburg

Schwarzstraße 5–7, 5020 **Tel** *0662-88 97 7* **Fax** *0662-88 97 71 4* **Rooms** *118*

Residing here in five-star splendor comes with unlimited access to Sachertorte, the chocolate cake Austria is famous for. The completely renovated turn-of-the-century hotel offers state-of-the-art luxury paired with grand tradition. Rich red interiors, bright marble bathrooms and splendid views of the Salzach River and the Old Town. **www.sacher.com**

Key to Symbols *see back cover flap*

Where to Eat in Austria

Austria has a range of restaurants to suit most tastes and budgets. In the capital, the most luxurious establishments are found in or near the Stephansdom Quarter. Some, including those in the big hotels, offer international menus. There are also many ethnic restaurants. In smaller towns, most venues prepare local specialties

PRICE CATEGORIES
Price categories for a three-course meal for one, without drinks, including tax and service:

€ Under 20 euros
€€ 20–35 euros
€€€ 35–45 euros
€€€€ 45–55 euros
€€€€€ Over 55 euros

VIENNA

CENTRAL VIENNA Glacis Beisl
🔲 V   €

Museumsquartier, Zugang Breitegasse 4, 1070 **Tel** *01-526 56 60*   **Map** *C4*

This is a moderately priced restaurant in the museum district that has a huge aquarium at the entrance. A popular restaurant with tourists, it offers carefully chosen dishes of meats, dumplings, pasta, and fish. Shady summer garden for fine weather as well as an enclosed winter garden. Menu in English. Open daily until 2am.

CENTRAL VIENNA Ofenloch
🔲🔲🔲   €€

Kurrentgasse 8, 1010 **Tel** *01-533 88 44*   **Map** *D3*

Classic Viennese dishes are served in this historic restaurant with a traditional *Wirtshaus* (tavern) interior. The dishes are prepared using only the very best local products, which are largely organically grown. Weather permitting, diners can eat outside on one of Vienna's oldest streets. Closed Sun.

CENTRAL VIENNA Zu den 3 Hacken
🔲 V   €€

Singerstrasse 28, 1010 **Tel** *01-512 58 95*   **Map** *E4*

Said to be the oldest tavern in Vienna, Zu den 3 Hacken is made up of four old-fashioned wood paneled stube dining rooms, one dedicated to the composer Schubert (a regular guest in his day). Small tasting room in the wine cellar. This is classic Viennese cooking in a friendly ambience.

CENTRAL VIENNA Drei Husaren
🔲 V 🔲   €€€

Weihburggasse 4, 1010 **Tel** *01-512 10 92*   **Map** *E4*

Touted as Vienna's oldest luxury restaurant, Drei Husaren offers fine Viennese cuisine in an environment fit for a Habsburg. Meat, fish, and other fare is prepared and served elegantly. For dessert, try the Drei Husaren Torte. Men must wear a jacket and tie. Reservations are recommended.

CENTRAL VIENNA Plachutta
🔲   €€€

Wollzeile 38, 1010 **Tel** *01-512 15 77*   **Map** *E3*

This is the flagship restaurant of the Plachutta chain and the unrivalled headquarters of Austria's famous *Taflspitz* dish of boiled beef. The Plachutta restaurants are dedicated to keeping Viennese traditional cooking alive, using classic ingredients and methods. Open daily until midnight.

CENTRAL VIENNA Wrenkh
🔲 V   €€€

Bauernmarkt 10, 1010 **Tel** *01-533 15 26*   **Map** *E3*

Famous for years as Vienna's premier strictly vegetarian restaurant, Wrenkh's now serves chicken and fish as well, though tofu still figures prominently on the menu. Its unique "happy cuisine" philosophy tries to take the seriousness out of *haute cuisine*, and is demonstrated in cooking workshops open to the public. Menus in English. Closed Sun.

CENTRAL VIENNA Do & Co
🔲 V 🔲   €€€€

Stephansplatz 12, 1010 **Tel** *01-533 39 69*   **Map** *D3*

Part of a catering empire as well as a Viennese institution, Do & Co is on the 7th floor of the Haas-Haus building and has a striking view of the Stephansdom. Excellent international and regional dishes are served, and the specialities include kebabs. Reservations are required.

CENTRAL VIENNA Meinl am Graben
🔲🔲 V 🔲   €€€€€

Graben 19, 1010 **Tel** *01-532 33 34 6000*   **Map** *D3*

Meinl is the biggest name in Austria for food. The downstairs wine bar always has 30 open wine varieties to taste. The café with attached garden offers unlimited blends of coffee beans. And naturally the restaurant is one of the best in the country, and is applauded for its creativity and superb presentation.

FARTHER AFIELD Steman
🔲🔲   €€

Otto/Bauer Gasse 7, 1060 **Tel** *01-597 85 09*

This is a comfortable and homely guest house, retaining many period features. Diners eat family-style at long tables in a dining room of paneled wood and old oil paintings. The Viennese dishes produced have won favorable comment in the local press. Closed Sat & Sun.

Map References *see map of Vienna pp590–91*

REST OF AUSTRIA

GRAZ Wintergarten €€
Sackstrasse 3–5, 8010 **Tel** *0316-81 16 16*

This spacious and spectacular atrium restaurant is built into the old courtyard of the majestic palace hotel, Erzherzog Johann. The glass-roofed dining area is overflowing with vegetation. Classic Austrian cuisine is enlivened by Italian influences. An ideal setting for afternoon coffee and cakes. Tables are limited, so reservations advised. Closed Mon–Tue.

GRAZ Iohan €€€
Landhausgasse 1, 8010 **Tel** *0316-82 13 12*

One of the busiest and most popular eating spots in Graz, especially for the young and hip. One reason is the stunning architecture of the ancient Landhaus building. Squat stone columns support vaulted ceilings under which acres of white tablecloths are spread. There is also a courtyard terrace for summer dining. Eclectic cuisine. Closed Sun–Mon.

HALLSTATT Gasthof Zauner-Seewirt €€
Marktplatz 51, 4830 **Tel** *06134-82 46*

Don't be surprised if the food is a bit salty here as this town boasts the world's oldest salt mine. The trademark *Salzfürstenplatte* includes both savory boar and fish. The Seewirt dates back a century, and fish has always been the main item on the menu. An all-wooden interior, and very attentive service.

LINZ Der Neue Vogelkäfig €€
Holzstraße 8, 4020 **Tel** *0732-77 01 93*

"The Birdcage" is an upmarket and culinarily ambitious restaurant, offering a range of French, Italian, and classic Austrian cuisine in an elegant dining room. Tables are well spread out to give privacy. The well stocked wine cellar, claims the largest collection of magnums in Austria. Large garden. Reservations essential. Closed Sat–Mon.

LINZ Chizuru €€€
Johann-Konrad-Vogel-Straße 11, 4020 **Tel** *0732-77 27 79*

An authentic Japanese restaurant in Linz with a real sushi bar, where diners sit close up to the chef slicing and dicing. The interior is somewhat spartan in decor and limited in space; however, in summer there is garden seating for an additional 60 guests. Reservations are advised, as Chizuru is very popular with local residents. Closed Sun.

INNSBRUCK Kapeller €€
Philippine-Welser-Straße 96, 6020 **Tel** *0512-34 31 06*

The Kappeller is a tastefully appointed historic guest house in the centre of Innsbruck. The Dorfstube offers intimacy and Tyrolean traditional dishes. Most attractive is the small dining terrace, partly covered in glass, in an interior courtyard with views of the old town. Closed Sun.

INNSBRUCK Goldener Adler €€€
Altstadt, 6020 **Tel** *0512-57 11 11*

The restaurant of the Best Western Hotel Goldener Adler is one of the oldest inns in Europe, dating from 1390. Mozart is said to have eaten here. There are five dining areas, including one intimate and cosy stube rooms. Outdoor dining on the pavement outside the hotel. Open daily until midnight, but kitchen closes at 10:30pm.

SALZBURG Die Gersberg Alm €€
Gersberg 37, 5020 **Tel** *0662-64 12 57*

Just outside Salzburg in an extensive park on a hill, Die Gersberg Alm offers organic beef, fresh fish and a wide range of mouth-watering pastries. The wine list features mostly Austrian vintages and many local schnapps. One of the most enticing garden areas in which to eat in the Salzburg region. Open daily until midnight.

SALZBURG Stieglbräu €€
Rainerstrasse 14, 5020 **Tel** *0662-87 76 94*

Stieglbräu is a restaurant, beer garden, and bar in a Best Western hotel within walking distance of the train station and most tourist attractions in downtown Salzburg. The menu features typical international dishes and standard Austrian specialties. The bar is a popular meeting place. There is also a beer garden, which becomes lively in summer.

SALZBURG Alt Salzburg €€€€
Bürgerspitalgasse 2, 5020 **Tel** *0662-84 14 76*

In the historical centre of Salzburg, this is a popular and lively restaurant with a high reputation for good food at a reasonable price. Three dining areas, including one carved out of solid rock at the rear. The menu concentrates on standard Austrian and Salzburg favorites. No menus in English, but waiters are happy to translate. Closed Sun.

SALZBURG Hotel Sacher Salzburg €€€€
Schwarzstrasse 5–7, 5020 **Tel** *0662-88 997*

The Hotel Sacher is no place to contemplate starting a diet. Home of the famous chocolate cake of the same name, the hotel emphasizes that nothing you eat elsewhere can compare. The recipe remains a 175-year-old secret. Among three restaurants, one a grill and one for local specialties, is the opulent gourmet room, the Zirbelzimmer.

Key to Symbols *see back cover flap*

SWITZERLAND

T*he stereotypical images of Switzerland – cozy wooden chalets, alpine meadows, and chic skiing resorts – are easy to find. But there are many other sides to this small, diverse country that are equally accessible, from picturesque medieval towns to world-class art and fine gastronomy. Switzerland's rural retreats offer wonderful opportunities for relaxing and recharging.*

Switzerland lies at the very heart of Europe, landlocked between the Alps and the Jura mountains. It is bordered to the west by France, to the north by Germany, to the east by Austria and Liechtenstein, and to the south by Italy.

Mountains make up 30 percent of Switzerland's 41,285 sq km (15,949 sq miles). The St. Gotthard Massif is the source of many lakes and two major rivers, the Rhine and the Rhône. Central Switzerland has the highest concentration of picturesque Alpine peaks, although the loftiest Alps are those of the Valais in the southwest. The valleys of Graubünden in the east provide the setting for many winter resorts. In the west, the cities lining the northern shore of Lake Geneva make up the bulk of French Switzerland, while a series of high passes provides overland access from German-speaking Switzerland to the Ticino, the Italian-speaking part of the country, and to Italy.

With almost a quarter of its area comprising high Alps, lakes, and barren rock, and with no seaboard and few natural resources other than water power, the country has managed to preserve a proud and united spirit of independence.

HISTORY

Switzerland's unique geography has presented both opportunities and disadvantages. Its story has been of a gradual coming together, not without bloodshed, of a population of diverse races, religions, and languages, making what is today viewed as a haven of peace and reason.

The Jura mountains provide the earliest evidence of Switzerland's habitation, which dates to over 50,000 years ago. By the start of the Christian era, Celtic peoples were living in western Switzerland and Germanic tribes in the north and east. Many of

The snow-capped Jungfrau, one of the Alps' most famous peaks

◁ The colorful façade of a typical Swiss chalet, Interlaken

these communities were under the control of the expanding Roman Empire, whose influence spread after 58 BC.

The Germanic tribes to the north eventually broke through Roman defenses; by the 5th century AD the era of Roman rule had ended. During the so-called "Dark Ages," the Burgundian tribe controlled the west, the Alemanni the center and east. In the 5th century, both tribes came under the control of the Franks, and later the Holy Roman Empire. The 13th century saw the rise of powerful local families such as the Habsburgs and the Zähringen, who established feudal rule over the area.

In 1291 three forest cantons around Lake Lucerne – Uri, Schwyz, and Unterwalden – came together to swear an Oath of Allegiance, thus forming an independent Swiss state. Over the coming centuries, more cantons came to join the Confederation. These

Huldrych Zwingli (1484–1531), leader of the Swiss Reformation

included lands south of the Alps known as the Ticino, and those to the west, where Charles of Burgundy was defeated by the Swiss in 1477. Switzerland was famous at this period for producing skilled mercenaries, who were paid handsomely to fight battles well beyond Swiss frontiers.

Protestantism took root in Switzerland in the 16th century, spread by the teachings of Zwingli and Calvin. Swiss cities embraced the new doctrines, whereas rural cantons remained mostly Catholic. Tensions between the two communities erupted into violence from time to time, and apart from a brief period at the turn of the 19th century when Napoleon established the Helvetic Republic, these issues were not resolved until the adoption of a federal constitution in 1848.

With stability came development – railways were built, agriculture diversified, resorts developed. A tradition

Exploring Switzerland

Switzerland is a small country – only 350 km (220 miles) by 220 km (140 miles) at its greatest extent. The Alps run across the southern part of the country, and in the northwest, the Jura mountains stretch along the French border. Mediterranean influences can be felt and seen in mild winters and palm-lined esplanades south of the Alps. Traveling by car is the most flexible mode of transportation, but the reliable rail network makes sightseeing by train easy and surprisingly affordable.

SIGHTS AT A GLANCE

Basel ❹
Bern ❺
Chur ❿
Geneva ❶
Interlaken and the Jungfrau ❻
Lake Geneva ❷
Lucerne ❽
Neuchâtel ❸
Swiss National Park ⓫
Ticino ⓬
Zermatt ❼
Zürich ❾

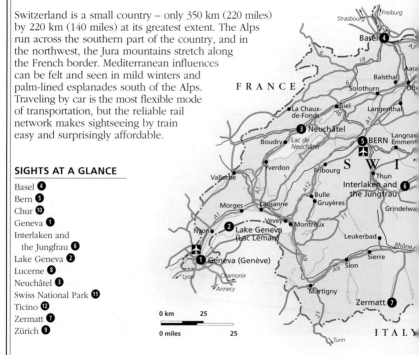

of humanitarianism began in the mid-19th century with the founding of the International Red Cross. In the 20th century Switzerland remained neutral during the two world wars, and concentrated on furthering its economic development, notably in the sectors of finance and pharmaceuticals.

LANGUAGE AND CULTURE

Switzerland is a quadrilingual nation. German, French, Italian, and Romansch (the language of a few valleys in the canton of Graubünden) are spoken in different parts of the country, though German is the language of the majority.

For many centuries Swiss culture had a predominantly rural tradition, and wine festivals are still a feature of village life. Great pride is taken in traditional crafts and regional specialties, such as the famous Emmental cheese. Swiss chocolate is also renowned for its high quality. Switzerland is now an outward-looking country, keen to export its expertise in finance and watchmaking worldwide.

KEY DATES IN SWISS HISTORY

58 BC–AD 400 Roman occupation

AD 400–1100 Germanic peoples – the Allemani and Burgundians – inhabit the area

12th century Holy Roman Empire extends feudal law over much of present-day Switzerland

1220 Gotthard Pass opened

1291 Oath of Allegiance marks beginning of the Swiss Confederation

1351 Zürich joins the Confederation

1477 Charles the Bold of Burgundy defeated by Swiss troops at Battle of Nancy

16th century Reformation; Protestantism takes firm hold in Swiss cities

1798 Napoleon creates the Helvetic Republic

1815 Power of cantons re-established

1830–48 Federal constitution drawn up

1864 International Red Cross set up

1914–18 & 1939–45 Switzerland remains neutral during two world wars

1946 UN offices established in Geneva

1998 Global settlement sum agreed by Swiss banks by way of reparations for Holocaust claims

2002 Switzerland declared member of the UN

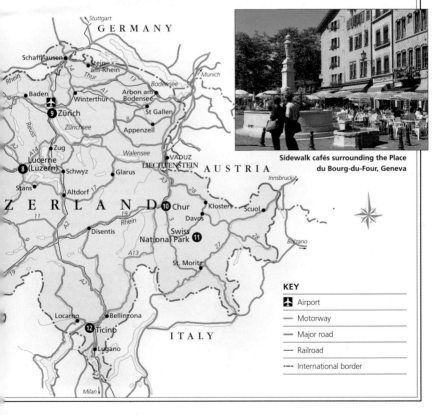

Sidewalk cafés surrounding the Place du Bourg-du-Four, Geneva

KEY

✈ Airport

— Motorway

--- Major road

— Railroad

- - - International border

Narrow, winding street in Geneva's historic old town

Geneva ❶

Geneva. 🏛 *416,000.* ✈ 🚉 🚌
ℹ *Rue du Mont-Blanc 18 (022-909 7000).* 🎭 *Fêtes de Genève (early Aug).* **www**.geneva-tourism.ch

Geneva is an ancient settlement with origins that go back to Roman times. The **old town**, situated on a craggy hill up above the western end of Lake Geneva, is the most attractive part of the city, with narrow, cobbled lanes and streets, fountain-filled squares, and an array of galleries, shops, and cafés.

In the heart of the old town stands the **Cathédrale St-Pierre**. Although the building dates from the 12th century it was much altered in the 16th century – the plain façade and interiors are in keeping with its Reformist heritage. A splendid 14th-century townhouse close by, the **Maison Tavel**, gives a good insight into life in the developing city of Geneva through the centuries. In Rue Jean-Calvin the **Barbier-Müller Museum** displays artifacts and objects from traditional societies in Africa and the Asia-Pacific region. There is a mesmerizing array of beautiful carvings, jewelry, and textiles.

Geneva's grandest museum, however, is the **Musée d'Art et d'Histoire**, at the eastern end of the old town. The stately early 19th-century edifice houses a diverse array of Swiss and European art and artifacts, from prehistory to the modern age. It also has a sizeable collection of Egyptian antiquities.

At the foot of the old town Geneva's main shopping street – the Rue de Rive – runs parallel to the lake shore. The quays either side of the lake are pleasant places to stroll, with the Jardin Anglais and the **Jet d'Eau** (one of the world's largest fountains) on the Left Bank, and the Quai du Mont-Blanc on the right. It is from the latter that the ferries and paddle-steamers operate pleasure cruises and regular services to towns along the lake. Farther along the Right Bank are the city's **botanic gardens**, and if you take the road bordering them you will come to the international quarter of the city. Here the **Palais des Nations** – European head-quarters of the UN – runs frequent guided tours through the day. Opposite, the **International Red Cross and Red Crescent Museum** offers a moving testimony to the need for such an organization.

Jet d'Eau fountain, Geneva harbor

🏛 **Musée d'Art et d'Histoire**
Rue Charles-Galland 2. **Tel** *022-418 2600.* ⏰ *Tue–Sun.* ♿ 📷 *for temporary exhibitions.*
http://mah.ville-ge.ch

🏛 **Palais des Nations**
Avenue de la Paix 14. **Tel** *022-917 4896.* ⏰ *daily.* 📷 *obligatory.* ⬤ *Nov–Mar: Sat & Sun.* 🎫 ♿
www.unog.ch

Lake Geneva ❷

Vaud. 🚉 🚌 🚢 ℹ *Avenue d' Ouchy 60, Lausanne (021-613 2626).* 🎭 *Nyon Paléo Music Festival (Jul).* **www**.region-du-leman.ch

The region skirting Lake Geneva offers a string of interesting settlements in a landscape replete with rolling hills, pretty stone-built villages, vine-clad slopes, and palm-fringed esplanades.

Coppet, 15 km (10 miles) north of Geneva, is a quaint medieval village. The 17th-century Château de Coppet was the home of Madame de Staël, whose literary soirées and opposition to Napoleon enhanced the popularity of the château in the 18th century.

Farther along the lake, **Nyon** is a charming lakeside town dating from Roman times, a heritage displayed at the excellent Roman Museum. With its fortress-like château and network of lanes, Nyon commands a fine hilltop view over the lake.

Lausanne, 60 km (38 miles) east of Geneva, is a bustling city with a fine old town, a beautiful Gothic cathedral, and excellent shopping. The city is also home to the international Olympic movement – at the lakeside district of Ouchy, the Musée Olympique (www.museum.olympic.org) is a must for all sports enthusiasts.

Wine château and vineyards near the town of Nyon

The resort of **Montreux** at the eastern end of the lake has a palm-lined promenade and a busy marina. As well as Belle Epoque hotels and health resorts, the town boasts one of Switzerland's top attractions – the **Château de Chillon**. This former bastion of the dukes of Savoy has all the accoutrements of a medieval castle – damp dungeons, weaponry, and huge banqueting halls.

About 25 km (15 miles) north of Montreux, the wonderfully preserved medieval hilltop town of **Gruyères** is also a major tourist attraction. The walled town is divided by a cobbled main street flanked by tempting restaurants. You can see the famous cheese being made in the traditional way in Moléson-sur-Gruyères.

♣ **Château de Chillon**
1820 Veytaux, Montreux. **Tel** 021-966 8910. ◯ daily. ● Dec 25, Jan 1. ▨ **www**.chillon.ch

Pit Stop **(1984), sculpture in the Museum Jean Tinguely, Basel**

Neuchâtel ❸

Neuchâtel. ▨ *32,000.* 🚆 🚌
ℹ *Hôtel des Postes (032- 889 6890).*
🍷 *Wine Festival (late Sep).*
www.neuchatel-tourisme.ch

Neuchâtel, an old religious center and university town, lies at the eastern end of Lake Neuchâtel at the base of the Jura mountains. It is a little off the beaten track, but has an extensive and attractive old town overlooked by the partly Romanesque **Collegiate Church**. Just below the church, the **Tour des Prisons** offers a stunning view of the lake and city. The market square – Place des Halles – is bounded by elegant 17th-century buildings, including the turreted **Maison des Halles**, now a restaurant. The area around Neuchâtel is known for its wines, including Perdrix Blanche.

Environs
20 km (12 miles) northwest of Neuchâtel lies **La Chaux-de-Fonds**, the largest of Switzerland's watchmaking towns. Located 992 m (3,255 ft) above sea level, it does not have the feel of a typical Swiss town. Its rigid grid pattern was

adopted when the town was rebuilt after a devastating fire in the 18th century. Le Corbusier and Louis Chevrolet are famous sons, though there is little evidence of the former in the town's architecture. The **Musée International d'Horlogerie** has a wonderful collection devoted to the watch industry, and is well worth a visit.

🏛 **Musée International d'Horlogerie**
Rue des Musées 29. **Tel** 032-967 6861. ◯ Tue–Sun. ● public hols. ▨ **www**.mih.ch

Enameled watch (c.1665) in the Musée International d'Horlogerie

Basel ❹

Basel. ▨ *188,000.* ✈ 🚆 🚌
ℹ *Basel Tourismus, Steinenberg 14 (061-268 6868).* 🎪 *Fair (Oct–Nov).*
www.baseltourismus.ch

Basel sits in the northernmost corner of Switzerland, straddling the Rhine at the farthest point that the river is navigable to sea-going vessels. It is a large commercial city,

and a world center for the chemical and pharmaceutical industries. This specialization is a legacy of its liberal past, when the city offered a home to Huguenots fleeing persecution. Their traditional silk-weaving skills eventually led to the development of synthetic dyes, and to pharmaceutical processes.

The **old town** remains the heart of the city and is a maze of fine streets and squares, including Marktplatz with its daily fruit and vegetable market. The striking red painted **Rathaus** (city hall) stands here, on the southern bank of the Rhine.

The twin sandstone towers of the Gothic **cathedral** are major landmarks. This imposing 12th-century building stands in a grand square – site of the famous autumn fair that has been an annual event since the 15th century.

Basel has a modern side too, with a vibrant cultural scene and a number of interesting museums, most notably the **Kunstmuseum**, which includes an impressive range of 20th-century artists such as Picasso, and the **Beyeler Foundation**, in Baselstrasse, a collection of around 200 paintings by modern masters.

Switzerland's most famous artist, Jean Tinguely (1925–91), has a museum devoted to his outlandish mechanical sculptures – **Museum Tinguely**.

🏛 **Kunstmuseum**
St. Alban-Graben 16. **Tel** 061-206 6262. ◯ Tue–Sun. ▨ 🗓 ♿

🏛 **Museum Tinguely**
Paul Sacher Imlage 1. **Tel** 061-681 9320. ◯ Wed–Sun. ▨ ♿

The tall spire of Bern Cathedral rising above the city skyline

Bern ⑤

Bern. 🏛 *300,000.* 🚉 🚌 🚋
🛈 *Central Railway Station (031-328 1212).* 🎭 *Ziebelemaerit (Nov).*
www.berninfo.com

Bern is the capital of Switzerland and its most attractive city – it has the best-preserved medieval town center in the country. It is located on raised land in a bend of the Aare River. From the city's terraces there are spectacular views over the river and across to the peaks of the distant Alps.

The city was founded at the end of the 12th century by the Duke of Zähringen and allegedly named after the first animal – a bear – killed in the forests which previously covered the area. The bear has been the city's emblem ever since. Most of the center of Bern, with its many fine stone Renaissance houses and covered arcades, dates from the 16th and 17th centuries.

Since 1848 Bern has been the capital of the Confederation. The massive **Bundeshaus** (Parliament House) is the home of the Swiss Parliament, and the building is open to visitors when parliament is not in session. It is situated at the end of the city's main market squares – Bärenplatz and Bundesplatz. These linked squares are also the site of the annual onion market which takes place on the fourth Monday in November, when the local onion harvest is traditionally celebrated.

The grotesque **Kindlifresser or Ogre Fountain**

The attractive **old town** at the heart of Bern is a UNESCO World Heritage site, famous for its arcaded streets, which offer comprehensive protection in the event of bad weather. The main streets – Kramgasse, Spitalgasse, Marktgasse, and Gerechtigkeitsgasse – are all lined with tempting shops, galleries, and cafés.

The city's famous **clocktower** stands where Kramgasse meets Marktgasse. The clock dates from 1530, and on the hour a series of figures – including bears, a jester, and a rooster – plays out its performance. The old town is filled with magnificent fountains, each of which depicts a famous historical or legendary figure. A wander around the city center will reveal the likenesses of Moses, the Duke of Zähringen, and the gruesome child-eating ogre, the Kindlifresser.

The **cathedral** on Münstergasse was built in the 15th century and is a beautiful example of late Gothic architecture. The building's most magnificent element is

the main portal – a masterpiece of carved and painted stone, which depicts the Last Judgment. The tall spire was only added in the late 19th century. To the right of the cathedral is a delightful small park overlooking the Aare flowing far below. This makes a good picnic spot in summer.

The **Bärengraben**, or bear pits, are to be found at the eastern end of the old town, over the Nydeggbrücke bridge. These date from the mid-1800s and today only a handful of bears are kept here. The city's **Historical Museum** – located just south of the old town over the river across Kirchenfeldbrücke – provides a great introduction to the city's history. Among the notable exhibits are wonderful Flemish tapestries. There is also the brand-new **Paul Klee Centre**, on Monument in Fruchtland, which contains around 4,000 works by the renowned Expressionist artist, who lived in Bern for 33 years.

🏛 **Historical Museum**
Helvetiaplatz 5. **Tel** *031-350 7711.*
⏰ *Tue–Sun.* 🎫 ♿ 📷
www.bhm.ch

Environs

To the southeast of Bern is the **Emmental Valley**. This verdant agricultural region, with its lush grazing, is famous for the cheese of the same name. A drive around the region can make an ideal half-day countryside tour. Take in some of the delightful towns and villages – Burgdorf, Affoltern, or Langnau im Emmental – and the gentle rolling hills dotted with covered wooden bridges and distinctive gabled wooden farm-houses of the area.

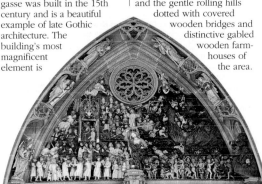

The Last Judgment, in the tympanum of Bern Cathedral's main portal

Interlaken cruise ship moored by the banks of the Thunersee

Interlaken and the Jungfrau ❻

Bern. 🏠 *15,000.* 🚆 🚌 ℹ️
Höheweg 37 (033-826 5300).
www.interlaken.ch

Interlaken, as its name suggests, lies between two lakes – the Thunersee and the Brienzersee – in the foothills of the Alps. To the south is the classic landscape of the Jungfrau mountains – one of the first regions of Switzerland to be opened up to tourism in the middle of the 19th century. Tourism is virtually the only industry in town, which caters for skiers in winter and sightseers by the busload in summer. A **funicular**, built in 1906, takes visitors up to the summit of the Heimwehfluh (669 m/ 2,195 ft), a wonderful vantage point above Interlaken. From here you can walk along woodland paths, visit an open-air model railway, or take the bob-run all the way down to the base station in Interlaken. There is also a restaurant and a children's play area.

Environs
One of the Alps' most famous peaks, the 4,158-m (13,642-ft) **Jungfrau** lies 20 km (12 miles) to the south of Interlaken. The almost equally high **Mönch** and **Eiger** mountains are neighbors and the stretch between Interlaken and the mountains is full of pretty alpine valleys and villages. From **Wengen** and **Grindel-**

wald you can take a train up to Kleine Scheidegg, and another to Jungfraujoch, a viewpoint high on the Jungfrau. Another popular viewpoint is the **Schilthorn** peak at the head of the Lauterbrunnen valley. This can be reached via **Mürren** and **Gimmelwald**, by cable car on the last stretch. The region is perfect skiing and hiking territory, with walking trails to suit all ability levels.

A few kilometers east of Brienz, the main town on Brienzersee, lies the Swiss Open Air Museum (known as the **Ballenberg**). Original buildings from all over the country have been brought to this living museum. A special bus runs from Brienz train station to the Ballenberg.

🏛️ **Ballenberg**
Tel *033-952 1030.* ⏰ *Apr–Oct: daily.* 📷 ♿ 🎞️ **www**.ballenberg.ch

Zermatt ❼

Valais. 🏠 *6,000.* 🚆
ℹ️ *Bahnhofplatz (027-966 8100).*
www.zermatt.ch

The chalet-filled resort of Zermatt sits directly below the **Matterhorn**, a peak of 4,478 m (14,688 ft), which has been a mountain-climbers' mecca for the best part of two centuries. In addition to mountaineering, Zermatt offers top-quality skiing and hiking. Skiing is possible all year round at this, the highest of Swiss resorts, and there are miles of well-marked trails accessible to all walkers.

The most scenic way to arrive in Zermatt is via the Glacier Express from St. Moritz, but you can also take the less expensive train from Täsch 5 km (3 miles) down the valley. The only other alternative is a minibus service, as Zermatt is car free. If driving, leave your car in Täsch.

Hinterdorf is the most historic part of town. The parish church and cemetery contain some poignant reminders of the dangers of the high mountains. The displays at **Atlantis**, an alpine museum near the church, reflect the importance of the region's mountaineering tradition.

Gornergrat is probably the best viewing point for the Matterhorn, and can be reached by taking a cog-wheel railroad. You can carry on by cable car to the **Stockhorn** peak for more mountain views.

Cog-wheel mountain railroad, with the Matterhorn peak rising behind

The Alps

The Alps are one of the oldest mountain ranges in the world, formed 65 million years ago when the Eurasian and African tectonic plates collided. They dominate Switzerland's landscape, covering more than half its surface area, and have shaped its history and economy. Switzerland is home to many well-known, distinctive peaks – such as the Matterhorn, Jungfrau, and Eiger – which were early tourist attractions in the 18th and 19th centuries. Trade and pilgrimage routes have crossed the Alps since Roman times but it is only in the last century that this wild and beautiful landscape has become truly accessible, with the development of long road and rail tunnels, mountain railroads, and cable cars.

Peak of the Matterhorn and the Gornergrat mountain railroad

Lake Lucerne surrounded by peaks and alpine meadows

ALPINE FLORA

Deciduous trees are common on the lower slopes of the Alps, but these gradually give way to coniferous spruce and pine. Between the tree line and the snow line lie lush alpine meadows famous for their wildflowers.

The Alpine aster *is one of many beautiful, brief-flowering, alpine plants found throughout the higher slopes and pastures. It blooms from July to August.*

Androsace alpina, *or rock jasmine, grows in mats which cling to alpine rockfaces. The shoots produce pinky-white flowers between July and August.*

Edelweiss *is the country's most famous flower, a symbol of purity and everlasting love. Increasingly rare, it is now a protected species.*

ALPINE WILDLIFE

Several national parks amid the Alps ensure the preservation of the unique native fauna. Although some animals have disappeared, a few species have adapted well to the higher altitudes, such as the marmot, chamois, ibex, mountain hare, and alpine chough.

Marmots *are difficult to spot but quite easy to hear, and live in burrows high on the valley slopes. Found throughout the Alps, these mammals are particularly abundant in Graubünden and Ticino.*

Chamois *are goat-like antelopes which can be seen adeptly scaling the highest mountain ridges. In the past they were hunted for their hide, which makes a very soft leather, but strict hunting controls are now imposed.*

The alpine chough, *a crow-like bird with a yellow bill, glossy blue-black plumage, and gregarious disposition, spends the summer above the tree line. They descend to the valleys and villages in winter, where they accept food from tourists.*

THE ALPS IN SUMMER

Long before skiing became popular, foreign visitors were coming to Switzerland's alpine areas for quiet, relaxing holidays full of fabulous vistas and fresh air. In general, alpine resorts are quieter in summer than during the ski season, but there are good outdoor activities provided in most areas. Some resorts, such as Verbier and Gstaad, host summer music festivals of some note. Most cable cars and mountain railroads operate throughout the summer, transporting hikers and sightseers.

Hikers and mountain bikers *are very well-catered for in summer, as Switzerland has thousands of kilometers of designated footpaths. Trails are well-marked and maintained, with regular refreshment stops en route.*

Désalpe, *a traditional Swiss festival, celebrates the return of herds of cows from the high mountain pastures at the end of summer. In alpine valleys and the Jura, lines of groomed and festooned cattle are herded down the country roads, stopping off at village cattle troughs and fountains for refreshment, on their way back to the lowland farms.*

THE ALPS IN WINTER

Switzerland has ski resorts to suit most tastes and budgets, from the chic, five-star hotels of St. Moritz, where celebrity spotting is almost as popular as skiing, to family-oriented resorts with facilities and slopes for all abilities such as Grindelwald. Some are predominantly modern – Verbier has grown from the unvisited hamlet of 50 years ago into one of the biggest ski resorts in Switzerland. Others, such as Zermatt – with its historic town center, alpine museum, and slow pace of life – are more traditional.

Davos *is the largest resort in Switzerland, attracting visitors from all over the world. The twin towns of Davos Dorf and Davos Platz offer a wide choice of activities off piste, with an indoor sports center and many bars, nightclubs, and restaurants.*

EDWARD WHYMPER

An illustrator by profession, the mountaineeer Edward Whymper (1840–1911) was one of a long line of British climbers who came to the Swiss Alps in the 19th century to scale hitherto unconquered peaks. In 1865, he reached the peak of the Matterhorn at 4,478 m (14,688 ft), together with two Swiss guides. Today, the Matterhorn remains one of the key challenges on the international mountaineering list.

Winter snow *is what draws most visitors to the Alps, whether for traditional skiing or trendy snowboarding. More bizarre sports include horseboarding (like water-skiing with a horse) and "zorbing" (tumbling down the slopes strapped to the inside of a balloon).*

Breathtaking Lake Lucerne and its surrounding mountain peaks

Lucerne ⑧

Lucerne. 🏙 60,000. 🚇 🚌
🛈 Zentralstrasse 5 (041-227 1717).
🎫 Lucerne Festival Sommer (mid-Aug–mid-Sep). **www**.luzern.org

The city of Lucerne makes a good base for touring most of central Switzerland. The surrounding countryside is possibly the most stereo-typically Swiss – crystal-clear lakes ringed with snow-capped mountains, hemmed with lush pastures in summer, and criss-crossed with cog-wheel rail-roads. This is also the heartland of the Swiss Confederation – the three forest cantons of Uri, Schwyz, and Unterwalden, which swore the original Oath of Allegiance in 1291 (see p614), border the shores of Lake Lucerne. Today the region remains the most conservative part of Switzerland.

The town's historic center stands on the north bank of the Reuss river, which flows out of Lake Lucerne at its westernmost corner. Stretches of the ancient city wall and its watchtowers can be clearly seen bounding a ridge that marks the northern edge of the old town. The cobbled streets and shady squares are bustling both day and night.

The **Kapellbrücke** is the city's most famous symbol. Spanning the river at the lake end, this covered wooden bridge was built in 1333, and formed part of the city's original boundary. Much of the bridge, including its decorative paintings, had to be renovated following a destructive fire in 1993. Also nearby is the **Rosengart Collection**, with over 200 works by various classic Modernist artists such as Klee, Picasso, and Cézanne.

Next to the town hall on Furrengasse lies the **Picasso Museum**, which focuses on the later works of the artist. Photographs of Picasso, taken during the last 20 years of his life by British photographer David Douglas Duncan, further illuminate the artist's character.

🏛 Picasso Museum
Furrengasse 21. **Tel** 041-410 3533.
◯ daily. 📷 ♿ w www.
kulturluzern.ch/picasso-museum

Environs

Less than 2 km (1 mile) southeast of the town center stands the **Richard Wagner Museum**, where the composer lived and worked from 1866 to 1872. There are letters, manuscripts, and photographs relating to Wagner's life, and a fine collection of 17th-, 18th-, and 19th-century instruments.

About 28 km (17 miles) east of Lucerne, **Schwyz** is the capital of one of the original three forest cantons, and has given the country its name. The charter detailing the 1291 Oath of Allegiance which marks the beginning of the Swiss Confederation is housed in the town's Bundesbriefmuseum. More interesting is the **Ital Reding Hofstatt**, a fine 17th-century mansion on the northwest side of town, built on the proceeds of one of Switzerland's first exports – mercenaries. The fighting skills of the men of Schwyz were highly prized by warring European rulers until well into the 18th century.

Pilatus and **Rigi** mountains tower over the area and both are easily accessible. Mount Rigi has the distinction of being the first mountain in Europe to have a rail line constructed to the summit. This starts at Vitznau on the lake shore. Mount Pilatus to the south is higher and gives unrivaled views of the Alps. Its peak can be reached either by cable car from Kriens or cog-wheel railroad from Alpnachstad.

🏛 Richard Wagner Museum
Wagnerweg 27. **Tel** 041-360 2370.
◯ mid-Mar–Nov: Tue–Sun. 📷 ♿

The 17th-century mansion of Ital Reding Hofstatt in Schwyz

Zürich **❾**

Zürich. 364,000.
10 km (6 miles) N.
Hauptbahnhof (044-215 4000).
www.zuerich.com

The dominant position of Zürich in the nation's economy has long been felt – in medieval times the guilds ruled the city and, boosted by the Reformation, Zürich and its inhabitants developed a talent for hard work and accumulating wealth. The stock exchange, which is the world's fourth largest, opened in 1877, and today Swiss bankers control the purse strings of many international companies and organizations.

Despite this tradition, the city also knows how to enjoy itself, and the medieval town center, which stretches either side of the Limmat river, is a

Grossmünster and Fraumünster in Zürich, separated by the Limmat river

Lively flea market at a lakeside park in Zürich's old town

hive of cafés, bars, and hip boutiques. On the east bank the warren of streets and alleys lies close to the university, adding to the café culture of this district. Also on the east bank, the extremely austere **Grossmünster** dominates the city. This was the church from which Ulrich Zwingli launched the Reformation on the receptive burghers of Zürich in 1520. Along Limmat Quai you can see the town hall (*rathaus*) built out on supports over the river, opposite one of Zürich's grand guildhalls.

On the other side of the river there are a number of interesting sights. **Lindenhof**, a small hill, overlooks the city and was the site chosen by the Romans to build a customs post and thus found the city. **Fraumünster** and **St. Peter's** churches are nearby; the latter, with its Romanesque cloisters and stained-glass windows created by Marc Chagall, is well worth a visit.

Augustinergasse, which leads down from St. Peter's, is a delightful street with traces of medieval storefronts. It is a world away from Zürich's main shopping street, which it meets; Bahnhofstrasse is one of the world's most famous shopping areas – a wide, tree-lined avenue with trams running along its length. There are plenty of high-priced emporia, especially towards the southern lake end, but interesting and reasonably priced shops and department stores can be found here or in the streets nearby. At No. 70, **Orell Füssli** is Switzerland's largest English-language bookshop, and nearby on Löwenplatz you will find hard-to-resist outlets of the celebrated **Confiserie Sprüngli**.

Just behind the main train station at the top of Bahnhofstrasse, housed in a suitably Schloss-like building, the **Swiss National Museum** contains a comprehensive collection of art and artifacts detailing the history and cultural diversity of the country.

🏛 Swiss National Museum
Museumstrasse 2.
Tel 044-218 6511. ☐ Tue–Sun.
🌐 ♿ www.musee-suisse.ch

Environs
Winterthur, 25 km (15 miles) northwest of Zürich, is an interesting and little visited Swiss town. Its history as an industrial center in the 19th century has left a legacy of old factory and mill architecture. It also boasts excellent museums; the best of these are the eclectic Oskar Reinhart Collection am Römerholz and the Fotomuseum.

The nucleus of medieval **Stein-am-Rhein**, 40 km (25 miles) northeast of Zürich, is unchanged since the 16th century. Rathausplatz and Understadt, at its heart, are lined with buildings covered in colorful frescoes, oriel windows, and window boxes.

Oriel window and frescoed façade of the Gasthaus zur Sonne, Stein-am-Rhein

Chur ⓾

Graubünden. 🏛 35,000. 🚉
ℹ️ Bahnhofplat 3 (081-252 1818).
www.churtourismus.ch

Chur, the capital of Switzerland's largest canton Graubünden, is a quiet, ancient town with origins that go back 2,000 years. It is located on the upper reaches of the Rhine, on an ancient route between northern Europe and Italy. It has long been a religious center – the bishop of Chur controls dioceses as far away as Zürich – as well as a commercial center, and is famous throughout the country for the Passugger mineral water which is bottled just outside the town.

The pedestrianized historic town center is a maze of cobbled streets and small squares, including Arcas Square with its sunny, café-filled corners in summer. At the southern tip of the old town the late-Romanesque **cathedral**, set in a square, overlooks the rest of town. The highlight of the cathedral is its intricately carved and gilded 15th-century altarpiece, depicting Christ stumbling under the weight of the cross and scenes from the life of St. Catherine. Unfortunately, lighting levels are so low inside the building that its full glory is hard to discern. Next

Elaborate 15th-century gilded altarpiece in Chur Cathedral

to the cathedral stands the **Bishop's Palace** (not open to the public) and at the bottom of the small flight of steps leading up to the cathedral square is the **Rätisches Museum**, which focuses on the history and culture of the canton of Graubünden.

🏛 **Rätisches Museum**
Hofstrasse 1. **Tel** 081-257 2889.
🕐 Tue–Sun. 🖥 **www**.rm.gr.ch

Environs
To the east of Chur there are a number of world-class ski resorts. The two best-known, with very different characters, are **Klosters** (www.klosters.ch) and **Davos** (www.davos.ch). The former, famous as the

favorite ski destination of British royalty, is a small traditional resort filled with charming chalets. Davos, on the other hand, is a big, brash town with plenty in the way of diversions away from the slopes. It has grown from a mountain health resort in the 19th century to a major winter-sports venue – apart from skiing, there are opportunities for snowboarding, tobogganing, and paragliding.

Swiss National Park ⓫

Graubünden. 🚉 Zernez, Scuol, S-Chanf. ℹ️ National Park House, Zernez (081-856 1378). 🕐 May–Oct: daily. 🖥 **www**.nationalpark.ch

Switzerland has many small nature reserves but only one national park. By international standards it is small, covering only 172 sq km (66 sq miles), but it is an area where conservation measures have been strictly enforced for the best part of a century, and people always take second place to the natural environment.

The Ofenpass road, linking Switzerland with Austria, cuts through the center of the park and affords good views of one of the park's valleys. Otherwise the best way to see the park is to take some of the 80 km (50 miles) of marked trails – walkers are not allowed to deviate off the paths.

The landscape is one of wooded lower slopes and jagged scree-covered ridges, including the park's highest peak at 3,173 m (10,407 ft) – Piz Pisoc. Among the abundant wildlife you may see are chamois, ibex, marmots, and the glorious bearded vultures, which are very rare in Europe and were reintroduced into the park in 1991. From June to August, with the retreat of the snows at higher altitudes, a carpet of beautiful alpine flowers, including edelweiss and Swiss androsace, appears. Plans to enlarge the park, since its small size is compromising the range of creatures that can be conserved and reintroduced, have recently been shelved.

The lively winter-sports resort of Davos, in the mountains east of Chur

For hotels and restaurants in this region see pp630–31 and pp632–3

Hilltop sanctuary of Madonna del Sasso, Ticino, with its lakeside views

Ticino ⑫

🛬 Agno. 🚆 Bellinzona, Locarno,
Lugano. 🛈 Palazzo Civico, Bellinzona (091-825 2131); Riva Albertolli
5, Lugano (091-913 3232). 🎬
Locarno International Film Festival
(early Aug). www.ticino-tourism.ch

The Ticino, Switzerland's
most southerly canton, feels
much more Italian than Swiss
with its mild climate and
Italian cuisine and language.
It lies south of the Alps,
bordering the Italian lakes
(see p429), and is traversed by
routes up the Alpine passes of
St. Gotthard and San Berna-
dino. The three main towns
of Bellinzona, Locarno, and
Lugano all make attractive
bases for exploring the area,
with plenty of attractions, cafés
and restaurants. Beyond, the
valleys of the Ticino offer great
sightseeing opportunities.

Bellinzona is the capital of
the canton. Lying on the main
north–south route between
the Alps and Italy, it provides
the first hint of Italian life

with elegant piazzas, hilltop
fortresses, and fine Renaissance
churches. The three castles of
Castelgrande, in the town,
Montebello, in the middle, and
Sasso Corbaro, on top of the
hill, feature on UNESCO's list of
protected monuments.
Castelgrande, with its imposing
battlements, was the stronghold of the Visconti family in
medieval times. Bellinzona is
also appealing on Saturdays,
when the streets are filled
with tempting market stalls.

Locarno is located at the
northern end of Lake
Maggiore. The suitably named
Piazza Grande is the heart of
town, which for two weeks

in August becomes a giant
open-air cinema during the
International Film Festival.
The festival aims to keep alive
experimentation, discovery,
eclecticism, and passion for
auteur cinema. Moviegoers
of all ages and nationalities
gather in the square to watch
a movie on one of the world's
biggest screens.

Winding lanes filled with
restaurants and boutiques
radiate off the piazza. Above
the town, easily accessible by a
funicular railroad, the sanctuary
of **Madonna del Sasso** is a
major tourist and pilgrimage
site. There has been a church
here since 1480 when a vision
of the Virgin Mary appeared
to a local monk. The Baroque
church is filled with marvelous
frescoes and commands a
fantastic view over the lake.

Probably the most charming
of the three main centers of
the region is **Lugano**, with its
palm-lined lakeside location
and attractive historic center
of elegant piazzas. The arcaded
streets are full of interesting old
shops selling local produce.

Away from the main centers
there are plenty of quaint
villages along the Maggiore
and Lugano lakes, such as
Ascona and **Gandria**. These
are now filled with waterside
restaurants and arts and crafts
shops. The valleys to the
north offer great hiking and
beautiful, peaceful scenery.
Val Verzasca, north of Locarno,
is one such valley, with the
photogenic stone hamlet of
Corippo clinging to the steep
sides, and the pretty villages
of **Brione** and **Sonogno**
towards the head of the valley.

⛪ **Castelgrande**
Monte San Michele, Bellinzona.
Tel 091-825 8145. ◯ daily. 🎬
🛈 **Madonna del Sasso**
Locarno. **Tel** 091-743 6265. ◯ daily.

Crowd gathered for Locarno's annual International Film Festival

Practical & Travel Information

Thanks to the famous Swiss efficiency, traveling around Switzerland is generally a pleasant and hassle-free experience. The country prides itself on its excellent transportation systems, with an extensive national rail network and frequent tram and bus services in the big cities. There are abundant tourist information offices and banking and communication facilities are of a high standard. Switzerland has four national languages – German, French, Italian, and Romansh – but the use of English is widespread, especially in tourist destinations.

TOURIST INFORMATION

Up-to-date information on many of Switzerland's towns and cities can be obtained from brochures and internet sites. Most large cities have at least one centrally located tourist information office (*Verkehrsverein, Tourismus,* or *Office du Tourisme*), offering a wide range of information and facilities. Even the smallest towns and resorts have tourist offices, but the opening hours of those in ski resorts may be limited in summer. Most embassies are located in Bern, but many countries also have a consulate in Geneva.

OPENING HOURS

The 24-hour society has yet to reach Switzerland and while large stores in cities may have late-night opening (usually on a Thursday), most shops, museums, and offices close at 5 or 6pm. Many museums are closed on Mondays and village restaurants often close on one or two days a week.

VISA REQUIREMENTS

Visitors to Switzerland must have a valid passport to enter the country. A visa is not required for visitors from the UK, Ireland, the United States, Canada, Australia, and New Zealand for stays of up to 90 days. EU citizens should remember that Switzerland is not a member of the European Union, so there is no "express" blue channel at customs.

SAFETY AND EMERGENCIES

Switzerland is one of the world's safest countries but you should still take all the usual precautions. Since Switzerland has no public health system, travel and health insurance are essential, especially considering the medical costs associated with skiing accidents. Hospitals have 24-hour emergency cover and in cities and towns there is always a pharmacy open. All pharmacies should post details of a 24-hour roster in their window.

Emergency services, including **helicopter rescue**, are very efficient, and there is also an **avalanche bulletin** hotline. If skiing or hiking at altitude, remember that dehydration or sunburn can cause problems.

BANKING AND CURRENCY

The unit of currency in Switzerland is the Swiss franc (CHF). Banking hours are generally 8:30am–4:30pm Monday to Friday, with some branches in tourist resorts also opening on Saturdays. Outside the big cities some banks may close for lunch between noon and 2pm. Money can be changed at banks or at bureaux de change. The latter can be found in hundreds of locations across the country, including at major train stations. Credit cards are widely accepted in Switzerland.

COMMUNICATIONS

Even the smallest villages in Switzerland have a post office, and the bright yellow mail boxes are easy to spot. Post offices usually open from 7:30am to noon and 1:30 to 6:30pm Monday to Friday, and from 8 to 11am on Saturday. However, times can vary from region to region, and smaller post offices often have more restricted hours. Public telephones are plentiful, and take both phonecards – available from post offices and newsagents – and credit cards. Internet facilities are found at airports and train stations, among other places.

The principal newspapers with nationwide circulation are the *Neue Zürcher Zeitung* from Zürich and *Le Temps* from Geneva. Most British newspapers are available in major centers from lunchtime.

FLYING TO SWITZERLAND

Switzerland has international airports at Zürich, Geneva, Basel, Bern, and Lugano. Among the major airlines that fly to Switzerland are Swiss International Airlines (Swiss), Qantas, American Airlines, and British Airways. Low-cost

THE CLIMATE OF SWITZERLAND

Generally summers are sunny with temperatures frequently reaching 25° C (77° F), though thunderstorms can be a feature of summer evenings. Winters are cold with plenty of snow, but many places get a lot of winter sunshine, especially the ski resorts of the Valais. South of the Alps, in the Ticino, the climate is milder and much more Mediterranean in character.

BERN			
°C/F	23/73		
	12/54 13/55 13/55		
0°C 32°F 3/37		6/43	2/36
			-2/38
6 hrs	8 hrs	4 hrs	2 hrs
70 mm	85 mm	65 mm	75 mm
month Apr	Jul	Oct	Jan

airline easyJet *(see p17)* flies from London Gatwick, London Luton, and other European cities to Zürich and Geneva.

Because of the many business travelers who fly to Switzerland on a weekly basis, Monday and Friday flights can be hard to obtain, especially during the skiing season.

TRAVELING BY TRAIN

Switzerland is at the heart of Europe and rail links to major European cities are fast and efficient. The journey time from Zürich to Paris is six hours; from Geneva to Paris it is three and a half hours.

Switzerland's rail network is operated by the state-owned **Swiss Federal Railways** and private companies. It reaches all major cities and towns and even the smallest villages in the mountains. There is an integrated ticketing and fare system. When traveling to a major city, ask for a ticket that covers your destination's transportation network too – this usually costs only a small amount more. Swiss Passes allow unlimited travel on trains, lake ferries, and many mountain railroads. They are available for 4-, 8-, 15- or 22-day periods, or for a month (www.swisstravelsystem.com).

Switzerland has a number of spectacular train routes. The best-known are those that pass through the Alps, such as the Glacier Express between St. Moritz and Zermatt. These services are included in the Swiss Passes and are reasonably priced. Local tourist offices and Swiss Federal Railways can provide details.

TRAVELING BY CAR

The most direct route by car from Great Britain to Switzerland is via the Channel Tunnel and French freeways to western Switzerland. Drivers must carry a driver's license and a valid vehicle registration document. If you want to make use of Switzerland's excellent freeway network you will need to purchase a freeway sticker *(vignette)*, available at border crossings, tourist offices, and gas stations.

Renting a car in Switzerland is expensive. Most of the international rental firms have offices at airports and in major towns. Many allow you to leave the car at a destination in France, Germany, or Italy.

As in the rest of continental Europe, the Swiss drive on the right. Since most freight is moved by rail in Switzerland, the majority of country routes,

main roads, and freeways are free of congestion. Driving around major cities, however, can be more difficult. Road signs are generally clear, with main roads in blue and freeways in green. Historic sights are usually signposted in brown. Speed limits are strictly enforced – 120 km/h (75 mph) on freeways, 80 km/h (50 mph) on main roads, and 50 km/h (30 mph) in built-up areas. Many mountain passes are closed from November to June. A sign at the foot of the pass will indicate whether the road is open or closed.

GETTING AROUND CITIES AND TOWNS

Buses and trams are found in the major cities and they provide frequent and reliable services. Tickets can be purchased from machines at bus and tram stops. Taxis are generally very expensive. Some cities such as Bern offer bicycle rental facilities, as do most of the major train stations. Many small villages that are not served by trains are on a "post bus" route, which usually originates at the train station of the nearest main town. Buses are timed to coincide with the arrival and departure of trains.

DIRECTORY

TOURIST INFORMATION

UK
Switzerland Tourism,
30 Bedford Street,
London WC2E 9ED.
Tel 00800-100 200 30
(international toll free).

US & Canada
Swiss Center, 608 Fifth
Ave, New York, NY 10020.
Tel 00800-100 200 30
(international toll free).

Switzerland & all other countries
P.O. Box 695, 8027 Zürich.
Tel 00800-100 200 30
(international toll free).
www.
myswitzerland.com

EMBASSIES

Australia
Chemin des Fins 2,
Case Postale 172,
Geneva 1211.
Tel 02-2799 9100.

Canada
Kirchenfeldstrasse 88,
3005 Bern.
Tel 031-357 3200.

Ireland
Kirchenfeldstrasse 68,
3005 Bern.
Tel 031-352 1442.

UK
Thunstrasse 50, 3000
Bern. **Tel** 031-359 7700.

US
Jubiläumstrasse 93, 3001
Bern. **Tel** 031-357 7011.

EMERGENCY NUMBERS

Ambulance
Tel 144.

Avalanche Bulletin
Tel 187.

Fire
Tel 118.

Helicopter Rescue
Tel 1414 / 1415.

Police
Tel 117.

Weather Forecast
Tel 162.

SWISS INTERNATIONAL AIRLINES

Australia
Tel 1-800 883 199.

Ireland
Tel 01-890 200 515.

New Zealand
Tel 09-977 2238.

Switzerland
Tel 0848-852 000.
Tel 0820-040 506 (24 hrs).

UK
Tel 0845-601 0956.
www.swiss.com

US & Canada
Tel 1-877 359 7947.

TRAVELING BY TRAIN

Swiss Federal Railways
Hochschulstrasse 6, 3000
Bern. **Tel** 0900-300 300.
www.sbb.ch

Shopping & Entertainment

There are plenty of high-quality Swiss-made products to take away from your trip, including, of course, watches and chocolate. Porcelain, lace, wine, and cheese are also popular purchases. Apart from major events, such as the Montreux Jazz Festival, there is entertainment on a smaller scale throughout the country. Classical and jazz concerts abound in the large cities, which also have cinemas, opera halls, and dance venues. Most regions hold a number of seasonal local events, from wine festivals to antiques and bric-à-brac fairs. Switzerland's greatest attractions, however, are its landscape and outdoor sports. The mountains welcome skiers in winter and climbers, hikers, and cyclists in summer, with all levels of ability catered for.

WHERE TO SHOP

In the large cities the old town areas usually have the most rewarding shopping – often you'll find narrow streets crammed with interesting, if often expensive, specialist stores and galleries. Bern's old town, with its arcaded streets, offers varied and sheltered shopping whatever the weather. The major department stores, such as Globus, offer a fairly standard international shopping experience, but in nationwide chains such as Coop and Migros (both supermarkets) you can pick up some interesting and reasonably priced items, especially when it comes to food and wine.

WHAT TO BUY

After you have stocked up with Swiss chocolate, other items you might consider taking away with you as souvenirs and gifts are linen and lace. Switzerland has a long tradition of textile-working in the northeast of the country and the quality is generally very good.

Swiss army knives are popular and incredibly useful. Victorinox is the make to look out for. Swiss porcelain and pottery can also be a good buy. Many of the designs favor strong colors and rural motifs.

Basketry and carved wooden items (such as toys) make ideal gifts, and these can sometimes be found on market stalls. A wide range of watches and jewelry is available, particularly at the top end of the market. Watches are one of Switzerland's most important exports, so the quality of Swiss watchmaking is very high.

Other places where you might find suitable gifts include any branch of **Schweizer Heimatwerk**, which is a national chain of Swiss handicraft stores. They have outlets in many large towns and cities, as well as at the airports if you leave your present-buying late.

Major museums, cheese showrooms and similar locations will often have a small store. In the major tourist destinations, such as Gruyères, there is no shortage of shops selling cheap tourist souvenirs, but you will also find knowledgeable retailers offering high-quality genuine Swiss-made items.

MARKETS

Outdoor produce and craft markets are common in Switzerland. Most towns and cities have a market on one or two mornings a week, and almost always on a Saturday morning. These are great places to try out local wines and cheeses, as well as simply to savor the lively atmosphere.

FOOD AND DRINK

Very little Swiss wine is exported, so it makes an unusual gift. Some of the Valais wines, such as *Fendant* (white) and *Dôle* (red), are the best.

Among more transportable food items are dried meats from the German parts of Switzerland, such as *Bündner-fleisch*, alpine cheeses such as Gruyère, and spicy *Leckerli* biscuits from Lucerne or Basel. Even packets of ready-made *rösti* mixture from supermarkets can make a fun gift.

ENTERTAINMENT LISTINGS AND TICKETS

A great variety of small town- and village-based concerts, festivals, and events takes place in Switzerland throughout the year. Local tourist offices can supply details of what's happening during your visit, while the Swiss Tourist Board offices abroad can provide comprehensive listings of all major sporting and cultural events taking place in Switzerland over the coming year.

Most major cities have a variety of venues dedicated to the arts, whether it be classical music, theater, cabaret, or jazz. Information about events can be found on the websites of the local tourist offices (for example, www.zuerich.com/events), on www.my switzerland.com or via the ticket office **Ticketcorner**. Tickets for most events in Zürich are available from **Billettzentrale BIZZ**.

ENTERTAINMENT VENUES

Many venues in Switzerland are not dedicated to a specific type of entertainment. The **Reitschule** in Bern is used for live music, theater, film, and dance, while the **Théâtre de l'Usine** in Geneva hosts concerts, theater, film, and cabaret.

The Zürich Tonhalle Orchestra is based at the **Opernhaus**, a popular venue for opera and ballet. Zürich's nightlife is centered on the Niederdorfstrasse, where the **Casa Bar** and the **Widder Bar** are popular venues to hear live jazz performances.

Cinemas in Switzerland usually show films in their original language, often with subtitles in French, German, Italian, or English. Zürich has more than 40 cinemas, almost all of which have regular showings of English-language films.

FESTIVALS AND PUBLIC HOLIDAYS

Across Switzerland, public holidays and religious events are celebrated in different ways. Lent and Easter are marked by masked parades, lantern processions, music concerts, and tree- and fountain-dressing in many parts of the country. Swiss National Day (August 1) commemorates the swearing of the Oath of Allegiance between the original forest cantons. Bonfires are lit and huge firework displays put on all over the country. Even the smallest village has a party with wine, food, and music.

Switzerland has many other annual festivals and themed events. Geneva's famous International Motor Show is held every year in the spring. The **Montreux International Jazz Festival** takes place in July, as does the **Paléo Music Festival**, a week-long open-air concert of world music at the town of Nyon on Lake Geneva. August brings the **Locarno International Film Festival** and Lucerne's International Music Festival.

Other annual festivals include the huge autumn fair in Basel, harvest festivals in the country's wine-growing regions, and the summer-long Combats de Reines, a form of cow fighting popular in the Valais. The animals are pitted against each other to determine which cow will lead the herds to the summer pastures – the animals themselves are rarely hurt.

WINTER SPORTS

Skiing and snowboarding are just a couple of the many activities that Switzerland has to offer. Despite the country's reputation for high costs, it is possible to ski inexpensively. There is a wide range of options, from small, traditional villages to large modern resorts packed with lots of additional facilities such as swimming pools and ice-skating rinks. Advice on the range and suitability of different resorts can be sought from Switzerland Tourism (see p626) or the **Ski Club of Great Britain**, which provides information, advice, and holiday and tuition packages. Cross-country skiing is very popular – some of the best places to try this are the villages of the Jura and the Lower Engadine Valley.

SUMMER SPORTS

In the summer, mountaineering and hiking take over from skiing as the most popular draw, though skiing all year round is an option at one or two high-altitude resorts, such as Zermatt. There are thousands of kilometers of marked hiking trails all over the country, including some long-distance ancient trade and pilgrimage routes, such as the Grand St-Bernard trail. Yellow markers indicate standard hiking trails. Higher, rougher trails have red and white markers and the very high-altitude trails are marked in blue. These should only be attempted with an experienced guide. Mountain biking is also catered for, with trails clearly indicated. Maps and information are available from the **Swiss Alpine Club** or the **Swiss Hiking Federation**.

OTHER OUTDOOR ACTIVITIES

Sailing and swimming are possible during summer at the country's clean lakes. River rafting is also a popular activity, especially along the Rhine. If slightly gentler sports – such as hot-air ballooning or horseback riding – are more your thing, tourist offices will be able to provide suggestions.

DIRECTORY

HANDICRAFTS

Schweizer Heimatwerk
www.heimatwerk.ch
Schneidergasse 2, Basel.
Tel 061-261 9178.
Airport, Geneva.
Tel 022-788 3300.
Bahnhofstrasse 2, Zürich.
Tel 044-221 0837.
Rudolf-Brun-Brücke, Zürich.
Tel 044-217 8317.

ENTERTAINMENT TICKETS

Billettzentrale BIZZ
Bahnhofstrasse 9, Zürich.
Tel 044-221 2283.
www.bizz-online.ch

Ticketcorner
Tel 0900-800 800.
www.ticketcorner.com

ENTERTAINMENT VENUES

Casa Bar
Münstergasse 30, Zürich.
Tel 044-261 2002.

Opernhaus
Falkenstrasse 1, Zürich.
Tel 044-268 6400.
Fax 044-268 6401.
www.opernhaus.ch

Reitschule
Neubrückstrasse 8, Bern.
Tel 031-306 6969.
Fax 031-306 6967.
www.reitschule.ch

Théâtre de l'Usine
4 Place des Volontaires, Geneva.
Tel 022-328 0818.
Fax 022-781 4138.
www.usine.ch/theatre

Widder Bar
Widdergasse 6, Zürich.
Tel 044-224 2526.
www.widderhotel.ch

FESTIVALS

Locarno International Film Festival
www.pardo.ch

Montreux International Jazz Festival
www.
montreuxjazz.com

Paléo Music Festival
www.paleo.ch

OUTDOOR ACTIVITIES

Ski Club of Great Britain
57–63 Church Road, London SW19.
Tel 0845-458 0780.
www.skiclub.co.uk

Swiss Alpine Club
Monbijoustrasse 61, Bern.
Tel 031-370 1818.
www.sac-cas.ch

Swiss Hiking Federation
Im Hirshalm 49, Reihen.
Tel 031-370 1020.
www.swisshiking.ch

Where to Stay in Switzerland

Switzerland has always been a highly popular European tourist destination and its hoteliers are famous for their courteous enthusiasm and attention to detail. It is all too easy to think of Switzerland only as mountains and wooden chalets, but there are many smart town hotels, too, as well as spectacular lakeside accommodations.

PRICE CATEGORIES
Price categories for a standard double room with bathroom or shower, including tax and service:

Ⓕ Under 150 CHF
ⒻⒻ 150–250 CHF
ⒻⒻⒻ 250–350 CHF
ⒻⒻⒻⒻ 350–500 CHF
ⒻⒻⒻⒻⒻ Over 500 CHF

LAKE GENEVA

GENEVA Hôtel de la Cloche   Ⓕ

6 Rue de la Cloche, 1201 **Tel** *022-732 94 81* **Fax** *022-738 16 12* **Rooms** *8*

A very popular bijou hotel in a quiet neighborhood in the center of Geneva, just behind the Quai du Mont Blanc, with the unique appeal of a 19th-century family home. Elegant stone exterior. Small but perfect rooms with parquet flooring, fireplace, and balconies with wrought-iron railings. Reserve well in advance. **www.geneva-hotel.ch/cloche**

GENEVA L'Auberge d'Hermance   ⒻⒻ

12 Rue du Midi, Hermance, 1248 **Tel** *022-751 13 68* **Fax** *022-751 16 31* **Rooms** *6*

Intimate, elegant, and an escape from downtown Geneva. Tucked away in the picturesque hamlet of Hermance, the Auberge has just six romantic rooms, three of which are suites. Rooms feature original paintings, hand-painted furniture, open beams, stone walls, and gorgeously tiled bathrooms. Exceptional restaurant. **www.hotel-hermance.ch**

GENEVA Hôtel Beau-Rivage   ⒻⒻⒻⒻⒻ

13 Quai du Mont-Blanc, 1201 **Tel** *022-716 66 66* **Fax** *022-716 60 60* **Rooms** *93*

Geneva's oldest family-run hotel, poised on the edge of the lake, close to all major attractions with views of the famous *jet d'eau*. An architectural gem, with crystal chandeliers, soaring four-story interior atrium with bubbling fountain, marble walls, and Grecian columns. Exceptional concierge services and opulent rooms. Four apartments. **www.beau-rivage.ch**

GRUYERES Hostellerie des Chevaliers   ⒻⒻ

Route de la Cité, 1663 **Tel** *026-921 19 33* **Fax** *026-921 25 52* **Rooms** *34*

The hotel looks like a rambling old farmhouse, painted white and set by itself in the verdant pastures of the Gruyères countryside. Tranquil and evocative location, cyclists particularly welcome. Rooms range from the simply furnished to those with antiques and lavish colorful old fabrics covering beds and walls alike. **www.gruyeres-hotels.ch**

LAUSANNE Elite   ⒻⒻ

1 Avenue Sainte-Luce, 1003 **Tel** *021-320 23 61* **Fax** *021-320 39 63* **Rooms** *33*

Elite is a large townhouse of pink stone with white shutters and red-striped awnings, with a large leafy garden, in the heart of downtown Lausanne between the cathedral and train station. Top rooms have views of the lake; all are non-smoking, and some have spacious wrought-iron balconies. Urban address with relaxed country ambiance. **www.elite-lausanne.ch**

LAUSANNE Lausanne Palace & Spa   ⒻⒻⒻⒻⒻ

7–9 Rue du Grand-Chêne, 1002 **Tel** *021-331 31 31* **Fax** *021-323 25 71* **Rooms** *154*

The epitome of the grand old Belle Époque hotel, evoking the heyday of the Swiss Riviera, with one of the most elaborately equipped spa centers in Switzerland. City center location. Rooms range in size from 30 sq m (322 sq ft) to the 95 sq m (1,020 sq ft) Presidential Suites. Black marble bathrooms. Indoor pool. **www.lausanne-palace.ch**

WESTERN SWITZERLAND

BASEL Teufelhof   ⒻⒻⒻ

Leonhardsgraben 47–49, 4051 **Tel** *061-261 10 10* **Fax** *061-261 10 04* **Rooms** *33*

Very special art and entertainment themed twin hotels. The Art Hotel has 8 exceptional rooms and a suite. Each room is a work of art. One room features a huge painted Bible. The Gallery Hotel's 24 rooms and suites are each given over to a specific artist to display his design sense. Superb restaurant, in-house theater. **www.teufelhof.com**

BERN Belle Époque   ⒻⒻⒻ

Gerechtigkeitsgasse 18, 3011 **Tel** *031-311 43 36* **Fax** *031-311 39 36* **Rooms** *17*

An oasis of art and individual design in the Old Town, this hotel lives up to its name. Each guest room is unique not only in size and ambiance, but furnished with Art Nouveau or Belle Époque antiques and paintings. One room even contains original works by the Swiss painter Ferdinand Hodler. **www.belle-epoque.ch**

Key to Symbols *see back cover flap*

GRINDELWALD Parkhotel Schoenegg

Dorfstrasse, 3818 **Tel** *033-854 18 18* **Fax** *033-854 18 18* **Rooms** *49*

Run by the same family for four generations, the Parkhotel Schoenegg is a quiet luxury hotel with top spa facilities, private garden, and cosy reading room with wood-burning stove. There is an indoor swimming pool, a whirlpool with floor to ceiling views of the Eiger and a Finnish log sauna. Well equipped rooms. **www.parkhotelschoenegg.ch**

INTERLAKEN Victoria-Jungfrau

Höhenweg 41, 3800 **Tel** *033-828 28 28* **Fax** *033-828 28 80* **Rooms** *212*

This is one of the most majestic and impressive grand old hotels in the palace style to be found anywhere in Europe. Convenient for lake excursions, the hotel also has extensive, state-of-the-art spa, and fitness and beauty facilities. The public rooms are opulent, bedrooms generously sized and elegantly appointed. **www.victoria-jungfrau.ch**

ZERMATT Riffelalp

Riffelalp, 3920 **Tel** *027-966 05 55* **Fax** *027-966 05 50* **Rooms** *72*

Arguably the most desirable hotel in Zermatt. Tranquillity is assured, the only way up to the hotel being by train. The hotel complex dates back to 1884, but since total reconstruction in 2000 with a new spa, indoor swimming pool, and bowling alley, the hotel's rooms are among the most luxurious in the Alps. **www.riffelalp.com**

ZURICH AND LUCERNE

LUCERNE Jailhotel Löwengraben

Löwengraben 18, 6004 **Tel** *041-410 78 30* **Fax** *041-410 78 32* **Rooms** *56*

This former prison was converted in 1998, and now offers "Unplugged" rooms that resemble cells but with more comfort, modernized "Most Wanted" rooms with showers and toilet, and attractive suites (the best is the former visitors' room). The "Warden's" room has a safe, and the library suite is filled with books. **www.loewengraben.com**

LUCERNE Art Deco Hotel Montana

Adligenswilerstrasse 22, 6002 **Tel** *041-419 00 00* **Fax** *041-419 00 01* **Rooms** *62*

This historic hotel overlooks Lake Lucerne. Each room is a unique Art Deco experience, with furniture, paint colors, and tiles chosen to complement the theme, which extends to the bathrooms. A funicular delivers guests from the lakeside right into the hotel lobby. Two towers with suites. **www.hotel-montana.ch**

ZURICH Lady's First

Mainaustrasse 24, 8008 **Tel** *044-380 80 10* **Fax** *044-380 80 20* **Rooms** *28*

Owned and operated by a team of five women, this unusual fashion hotel is aimed toward women. Although the "modern man" is welcomed, he is not permitted on the upper floors, which house a spa, recreation rooms, and terrace. The hotel occupies an elegant 19th-century townhouse with exceptional decor. Rose garden. **www.ladysfirst.ch**

ZURICH Widder

Rennweg 7, 8001 **Tel** *044-224 25 26* **Fax** *044-224 24 24* **Rooms** *49*

Unusual, wildly popular luxury hotel spread out over eight former historic townhouses in the Augustiner Quarter. Very high reputation for service. No two rooms are remotely alike. Some have old hand-carved oak furnishings and four-poster beds, others have hanging steel staircases and hip leather furniture. Latest high-tech gadgets. **www.widderhotel.ch**

GRAUBUNDEN AND TICINO

DAVOS Schatzalp

Bobbahnstrasse 23, 7270 **Tel** *081-415 51 51* **Fax** *081-415 52 52* **Rooms** *92*

Featured in Thomas Mann's *The Magic Mountain*, the Art Nouveau Schatzalp is spectacularly situated 300 m (1,000 ft) above Davos on a sunny terrace at the tree line. The only access is by private funicular. The hotel's Alpinum Schatzalp is a beautiful botanical garden with 3,000 species of alpine plants. **www.schatzalp.ch**

KLOSTERS Wynegg

Landstrasse 205, 7250 **Tel** *081-422 13 40* **Fax** *081-422 41 31* **Rooms** *20*

A charming old wooden chalet painted blue, with wooden ceilings decorated with frescoes, the hotel is famous for its food, and for being the favorite haunt of Prince Charles. Aside from royals, the clientele is almost entirely repeat customers of long standing. Rooms are cozy and comfortable rather than chic. The decor verges on kitsch.

LOCARNO Belvedere

Via ai Monti della Trinita 44, 6600 **Tel** *091-751 03 63* **Fax** *091-751 52 39* **Rooms** *81*

This luxury hotel in a former 16th-century palazzo lies on a sunny hill overlooking Locarno and Lake Maggiore. The public rooms have marble and frescoed ceilings. Large garden for dining, games, or sunbathing and an outdoor pool. Four restaurants, including an outdoor grotto. Spa with indoor pool, gym, sauna, and solarium. **www.belvedere-locarno.ch**

Where to Eat in Switzerland

There is no "national dish" in Switzerland, since menus vary from region to region. In French Switzerland, fondue is a local specialty, while in German Swiss restaurants *rösti* (hash brown potatoes) are a favorite. Pizzerias are most numerous in the Italian-speaking Ticino region. For a landlocked country, seafood is surprisingly popular.

PRICE CATEGORIES
Price categories for a three-course meal for one person, including tax and service but without wine:

Ⓕ Under 30 CHF
ⒻⒻ 30–60 CHF
ⒻⒻⒻ 60–90 CHF
ⒻⒻⒻⒻ 90–120 CHF
ⒻⒻⒻⒻⒻ Over 120 CHF

LAKE GENEVA

GENEVA Bistrot du Bœuf Rouge
ⒻⒻ
Rue Alfred-Vincent 17, 1201 **Tel** *022-732 75 37*

A gastronomic restaurant at the top of its game masquerading as a small family bistro. The cooking is heavily influenced by the Lyon region of France,with savory and substantial sauces. Many Swiss wines are on the list, as are impeccable vintages from France: Louis Latour for burgundies and choice northern Rhône wines. Closed Sat and Sun.

GENEVA Café de Paris
ⒻⒻ
Rue du Mont-Blanc 26, 1201 **Tel** *022-732 84 50*

A short stroll from the lake, the Café de Paris is a venerable Geneva institution, famous for being written up as having only one item on the menu: entrecôte steak with chips, green salad, and the eponymous still secret butter sauce first developed in 1930. Short list of a dozen Swiss and French wines.

GENEVA L'Entrecôte Couronnée
ⒻⒻⒻ
5 rue des Pâquis, 1201 **Tel** *022-732 84 45*

Small, intimate bistro in downtown Geneva popular with the locals. The wine list emphasizes wines from canton Geneva and the restaurant has been awarded a certificate for its use of local meats and produce. Genuinely charming interior with retro style wooden floors and period tables. Try the steak with butter sauce. Closed Sun.

GENEVA Du Parc des Eaux-Vives
ⒻⒻⒻⒻⒻ
82 Quai Gustave Ador, 1211 **Tel** *022-849 75 75*

This historic château houses both a brasserie and a superbly elegant fine dining room in the grounds of a leafy park of the same name near Lake Geneva. Said to have the most beautiful summer dining terrace in Geneva. Classic French cuisine with great Simmental beef and Paulliac lamb. Two Michelin stars. Closed Sun and Mon.

LAUSANNE (OUCHY) La Croix d'Ouchy
ⒻⒻ
Avenue d'Ouchy 43, 1006 **Tel** *021-616 22 33*

A highly regarded gourmet restaurant on the outskirts of Lausanne by the lake. The menu offers French and Italian cuisine with good vegetarian choices. Service can be slow, but the risottos are sublime and the *escalopines au miel et citron* (escalope with honey and lemon) is also superb, as is the black truffle ravioli. Sunny terrace.

MONTREUX Palais Oriental
ⒻⒻⒻ
6 Quai Ernest-Ansermet, 1820 **Tel** *021-963 12 71*

A Montreux landmark, the Palais Oriental is entertaining and exotic, with its ornate Islamic carpets (for sale) and metal work. It is a good spot to take afternoon tea. The meals are somewhat pricey, but there is an authentic range of Iranian, Moroccan, Lebanese, and Egyptian cuisine. The restaurant is right on the shores of Lake Geneva.

WESTERN SWITZERLAND

BASEL Goldenen Sternen
ⒻⒻⒻ
St. Alban-Rheinweg 70, 4052 **Tel** *061-272 16 66*

The oldest restaurant in Basel (and one of the oldest in Europe), dating from the 15th century, with old-fashioned decor and standards of service. Tables are laid with starched white linen and sterling silver. A loyal clientele of locals. Wide range of Swiss German specialties as well as international fare like grilled meats. The wine list is impressive.

BERN Kornhauskeller
ⒻⒻⒻ
Kornhausplatz 18, 3000 **Tel** *031-327 72 72*

A treat for the eyes as much as for the palate, the cellar dining room of the Kornhaus features dramatic, soaring vaulted arches painted with frescoes. In the past the Kornhaus fulfilled many functions, including a grain storage facility. Restored to its glory, the cellar is now immensely popular with tourists. The menu is Mediterranean.

Key to Symbols *see back cover flap*

INTERLAKEN Schuh

Höheweg 56, 3800 **Tel** *033-822 94 41*

An Interlaken institution since the beginning of the 19th century, the "Grand Restaurant Schuh" to give its full title, is deservedly renowned for its chocolates, many of which are unique concoctions. But the dining room menu ventures into the Orient, with Japanese and Thai dishes, as well as Swiss-German terrain with veal *schnitzel*, Zürich style.

ZERMATT Zum See

Zum See, 3920 **Tel** *027-967 20 45*

One of the most highly regarded mountain restaurants in the Alps, with an ever changing menu. In summer, mountain berries and vegetables from the garden right outside the old chalet add a wonderful freshness to the menu. In autumn there is game. In winter the rustic hut is filled to the rafters with skiers in the know.

ZURICH AND LUCERNE

LUCERNE Movie

Metzgerrainle 9, 6400 **Tel** *041-410 36 31*

A popular riverside restaurant with a cinema theme. The menus come on metal film-reel canisters and the dishes are named after classic movies. Generous portions of American burgers with french fries and a good selection of beers. Mexican food is also on the menu, with tasty tacos. Reservations recommended. Young and hip crowd.

LUCERNE Old Swiss House

Löwenplatz 4, 6002 **Tel** *041-410 61 71*

This landmark half-timbered house in the city center near the Lion Monument has fabulous decor, with oil paintings and a wooden interior. The innovative cuisine is impeccably presented, deserving its 15 Gault Millau points. The *Wienerschnitzel* simply cannot be missed. Wine cellar with 30,000 bottles includes Château Mouton Rothschild from 1911 onwards.

ZURICH Haus zum Rüden

Limmatquai 42, 8001 **Tel** *044-261 95 66*

The "House of the Hounds", as the name translates, has a Gothic dining hall with an 11 m (36 ft) high curved wooden ceiling, and dark wood wainscoting. The architecture is stunning, but the menu is even more compelling. French cuisine dominates the menu, with special attention to game, vegetables, and mushrooms as they come into season.

ZURICH Kronenhalle

Rämistrasse 4, 8001 **Tel** *044-262 99 00*

An unmissable Zürich institution, as compelling for its interior as for its cooking. The dark-panelled walls contain original artwork from Picasso, Matisse, and Braque. The restaurant is always filled with locals, as well as tourists. Swiss German dishes vie with French classics on the menu, and portions are generous. The chocolate mousse is famous.

GRAUBUNDEN AND TICINO

BELLINZONA Ristorante Castelgrande

Salita al Castello, 6500 **Tel** *091-826 23 53*

An outstanding restaurant with two dining options, both located in the imposing stone fortress Castlegrande. The Grotto is a relaxed dining area with a cavern-like feel where local specialties like risotto and gnocchi are served. There is also game when in season, including wild boar. The gourmet dining room, by contrast, is sleek and modern. Closed Mon.

KLOSTERS Rustico

Landstrasse 194, 7250 **Tel** *081-410 22 88*

A rare treat, real Asian cooking with a chef from Hong Kong in the middle of Graubünden. Japanese, Chinese, Vietnamese, and Malaysian influences. Sushi and sashimi of course but also delicacies such as roe deer satay. Local Graubünden dishes are not ignored, either, and there is a good wine list. In summer Asian cooking courses are offered.

LOCARNO La Cittadella Trattoria

Via Cittadella 18, 6600 **Tel** *091-751 58 85*

This restaurant occupies two floors in a rose-colored stone building in the heart of the Old Town in a quiet pedestrian zone. Downstairs the trattoria has a wood-burning oven, and seafood is the theme. Upstairs in a more elegant dining room, fish and shellfish are more elaborately prepared. Closed Mon.

LUGANO Al Portone

Viale Cassarate 3, 6900 **Tel** *091-923 55 11*

A gourmet restaurant near the business district of Lugano with superb presentation. Refined and inventive Mediterranean cuisine is served in an exclusive atmosphere. The wine cellar has the best Ticino wines and a fine choice of other wines from all over the globe. The specialties include risotto and homemade pastas.

SCANDINAVIA

SCANDINAVIA AT A GLANCE 636–637

SWEDEN 638–655

NORWAY 656–671

DENMARK 672–687

FINLAND 688–701

SIDE TRIP TO ST. PETERSBURG 696–697

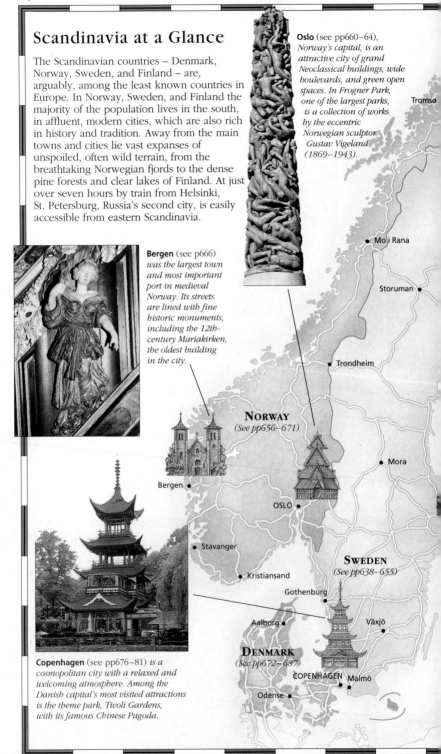

Scandinavia at a Glance

The Scandinavian countries – Denmark, Norway, Sweden, and Finland – are, arguably, among the least known countries in Europe. In Norway, Sweden, and Finland the majority of the population lives in the south, in affluent, modern cities, which are also rich in history and tradition. Away from the main towns and cities lie vast expanses of unspoiled, often wild terrain, from the breathtaking Norwegian fjords to the dense pine forests and clear lakes of Finland. At just over seven hours by train from Helsinki, St. Petersburg, Russia's second city, is easily accessible from eastern Scandinavia.

Oslo (see pp660–64), *Norway's capital, is an attractive city of grand Neoclassical buildings, wide boulevards, and green open spaces. In Frogner Park, one of the largest parks, is a collection of works by the eccentric Norwegian sculptor Gustav Vigeland (1869–1943).*

Bergen (see p666) *was the largest town and most important port in medieval Norway. Its streets are lined with fine historic monuments, including the 12th-century Mariakirken, the oldest building in the city.*

Copenhagen (see pp676–81) *is a cosmopolitan city with a relaxed and welcoming atmosphere. Among the Danish capital's most visited attractions is the theme park, Tivoli Gardens, with its famous Chinese Pagoda.*

Tromsø

Mo i Rana

Storuman

Trondheim

NORWAY
(See pp656–671)

Mora

Bergen

OSLO

Stavanger

SWEDEN
(See pp638–655)

Kristiansand

Gothenburg

Aalborg

Växjö

DENMARK
(See pp672–687)

COPENHAGEN   Malmö

Odense

◁ Pulpit Rock, giving spectacular views of the Lysefjord near Stavanger in Norway

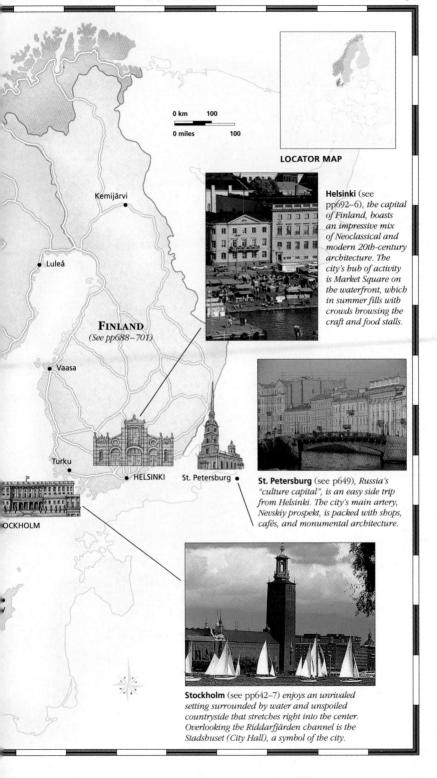

LOCATOR MAP

0 km 100
0 miles 100

Kemijärvi

Luleå

FINLAND
(See pp688–701)

Vaasa

Turku

HELSINKI · St. Petersburg ·

OCKHOLM

Helsinki (see pp692–6), *the capital of Finland, boasts an impressive mix of Neoclassical and modern 20th-century architecture. The city's hub of activity is Market Square on the waterfront, which in summer fills with crowds browsing the craft and food stalls.*

St. Petersburg (see p649), *Russia's "culture capital", is an easy side trip from Helsinki. The city's main artery, Nevskiy prospekt, is packed with shops, cafés, and monumental architecture.*

Stockholm (see pp642–7) *enjoys an unrivaled setting surrounded by water and unspoiled countryside that stretches right into the center. Overlooking the Riddarfjärden channel is the Stadshuset (City Hall), a symbol of the city.*

SWEDEN

The Swedes are justly proud of the natural beauty of their country. From the snow-capped mountains of the north, through rolling countryside dotted with forests and lakes, to the tiny islands of the Baltic archipelagos around Stockholm, the country is a mecca for outdoor enthusiasts. Like its people, Sweden's cities are modern and dynamic, but also rich in tradition.

Sweden is Europe's fifth-largest country, with an area about the size of California. Roughly 1,600 km (1,000 miles) lie between its southernmost and northernmost points. About 15 percent of its area lies north of the Arctic Circle, where, for a few days each summer, the sun never sets, and never rises for a similar period in winter. The Swedish climate is not severe, thanks to the warming influence of the Gulf Stream.

Only 7 percent of Sweden's area is cultivated farmland; more than half the country is covered by timberlands, consisting mainly of coniferous forests. Mountains, fells, and wetlands occupy nearly a quarter of the country. Sweden has about 100,000 lakes, which include Vänern, the third-largest body of fresh water in Europe. Norrland, the northern three-fifths of the country, is rich in natural resources, including timber, ore deposits, and rivers, whose waterfalls contribute to the national energy supply. It is here that the Sami (formerly known as the Lapps) earn their traditional livelihood herding reindeer.

HISTORY

Although the Swedish Vikings were seafaring warriors like their Danish and Norwegian cousins, they were primarily known as Sweden's first traders, opening up routes along the Russian rivers to the east as far as the Black Sea. Ruthlessly exploiting the Slav population of the area, they dealt mainly in slaves and furs. The Viking reign ended with the successful Christianization of Sweden at the end of the 11th century.

The German traders of the Hanseatic League arrived in Sweden some time during the 13th century, and dominated Swedish life for the next hundred years. In 1397, the Germans were forced out by the Union of Kalmar, which brought

Dancers in traditional folk costume in the village of Sundborn, Dalarna province

◁ View across the Strömmen in Stockholm to the dome of Katarina Kyrka on Södermalm

Scandinavia under Danish rule. This state of affairs continued until Gustav Vasa, resenting Denmark's influence, succeeded in ousting the Danes in 1523, becoming king of an independent Sweden.

The 17th and early 18th centuries were dominated by two military giants, Gustav II Adolf and Karl XII, whose conquests made Sweden for the first time more powerful than Denmark. In the 18th century, the Swedes contributed to Europe's Age of Enlightenment with advances in science and major developments in the arts, especially under the patronage of Gustav III. He opened the magnificent Royal Opera House in 1782, and was responsible for the construction of the Royal Dramatic Theater in 1788.

Karl XII of Sweden (1697–1718), the "warrior king"

By 1809, Sweden's military power had waned to such an extent that the country was forced to surrender Finland to Russia. A new constitution transferred power from the king to Parliament, marking the beginning of Sweden's democratic monarchy. In the early 19th century, Sweden was also a poor country, suffering from stagnation in agriculture and trade. In the course of the century nearly one million Swedes migrated, mostly to America. Their departure was a sobering lesson to those that remained, inspiring the philosophy of cradle-to-grave care that was put into practice in 20th-century Sweden's welfare state.

In a single century, Sweden grew from a poor rural economy to a leading industrial nation.

The 1990s saw many significant changes take place. Engineering expanded rapidly, particularly in the field of telecommunications, led by the Ericsson company. Sweden joined the EU, and the church severed its role with the state after more than 400 years. In the year 2000, Malmö in Sweden and the Danish capital of Copenhagen were connected by the completion of the Öresund Bridge, symbolic of the long-standing friendship that has replaced the animosity between these once warring nations.

KEY DATES IN SWEDISH HISTORY

AD 800–1060 Era of the Swedish Vikings

13th century Hanseatic League of German merchants at height of its power in Sweden

1397 Kalmar Union links the Nordic countries

1523 Gustav Vasa becomes king of an independent Sweden

1611–32 Reign of Gustav II Adolf, "the Lion of the North," whose campaigns turn Sweden into a great European power

1718 Death of Karl XII, Sweden's last great military king, at siege of Fredriksten in Norway

1721 Sweden cedes Baltic provinces to Russia

1772 Gustav III crowned and mounts coup d'état giving the monarchy absolute power

1809 Sweden loses Finland to Russia

1814 Sweden gains Norway from Denmark

1869 Emigration to North America increases due to crop failure

1905 Parliament dissolves union with Norway

1939 Sweden declares neutrality in World War II

1995 Sweden joins European Union

2000 Öresund Bridge opens, finally connecting Sweden and Denmark

2001 EU presidency held by Sweden

2003 Single European currency rejected

LANGUAGE AND CULTURE

Swedish belongs to the northern group of Germanic languages, along with Norwegian, Danish, Icelandic, and Faeroese. Various dialects are spoken, most notably in Skåne, southern Sweden, where the accent is almost Danish.

A nation of nature lovers, the Swedes are apt to retreat to their country cottages in all seasons. Deeply traditional, they love their rituals, from maypole dances at midsummer to the St. Lucia procession in December. Beneath their reserve the Swedes are a friendly people, their warmth readily unleashed with a *skål* (toast) and a round of schnapps.

Swedes are open-minded, trend-hungry, and tech-friendly. Stockholm offers the latest in design and architecture, and Sweden has become increasingly multicultural. While this new Sweden doesn't always blend easily with the old, most Swedes recognize that the country is richer for its diversity.

Exploring Sweden

The natural starting point for exploring Sweden is the capital Stockholm, built on a cluster of Baltic Sea islands. From here, visitors can explore the castles of Lake Mälaren or head north to Uppsala, a thriving university town. On the way south to Malmö or west to Gothenburg lies the Glass Kingdom, where some of the world's best-known glassmakers ply their trade. Travel throughout Sweden can be conducted quite easily by high-speed trains or by car, though the long distances involved make travel quite expensive.

SWEDEN

0 km 250
0 miles 250

NORWAY   SWEDEN   FINLAND

See main map   Helsinki

Oslo   STOCKHOLM   ESTONIA

Gothenburg   LATVIA

DENMARK   LITHUANIA
Copenhagen

SIGHTS AT A GLANCE

Dalarna ④
Gothenburg ⑥
Gotland and Visby ⑤
Lake Mälaren ②
Malmö ⑧
STOCKHOLM pp642–7 ①
Uppsala ③
Växjö ⑦

Gulf of Bothnia

Gävle

④ Dalarna

Borlänge

Grisslehamn

Uppsala ③

Kapellskär

Lake Mälaren ②

STOCKHOLM

Nynäshamn

Oxelösund

Norrköping

Örebro

Karlstad

Vänern

Vättern

Skagerrak

Strömstad

Sandefjord

OSLO

NORWAY

S W E D E N

Newcastle, Harwich

Gothenburg (Göteborg) ⑥

Jönköping

Borås

Västervik

Visby ⑤

Gotland

Oskarshamn

⑦ Växjö

Öland

Halmstad

Kalmar

Helsingør · Helsingborg

COPENHAGEN   Kristianstad

Karlskrona

Malmö ⑧   Simrishamn

Trelleborg   Ystad   Allinge

Rønne

Bornholm (Denmark)

Rostock

0 kilometers   100
0 miles   100

KEY

✈ Airport

⚓ Ferry port

— Highway

-- Major road

— Railroad

···· International border

The Göteborgsutkiken building, overlooking Gothenburg Harbor

Stockholm ❶

Stockholm was founded around 1250 on a small island in the narrow Strömmen channel between the Baltic Sea and Lake Mälaren. Today, the Swedish capital stretches across 14 islands. As well as a stunning waterside location, Stockholm boasts a rich cultural heritage. Its 750-year history has produced a wealth of beautiful buildings, such as the Royal Palace and Drottningholm – symbols of Sweden's era as a great power in the 17th and early 18th centuries. Many other impressive treasures from the past can be discovered in the city's fine museums.

The Stadshuset, Stockholm's City Hall, on the island of Kungsholmen

GETTING AROUND

Most of the main sights are served by Tunnel-bana (underground train), and there are also numerous bus routes. Bus 47 goes to the Vasamuseet, the Nordiska Museet, and Skansen, which you cannot reach by Tunnelbana. Small ferries travel between the city center and Djurgården, while archipelago boats take visitors on day trips to some of the thousands of islands in the Stockholm archipelago.

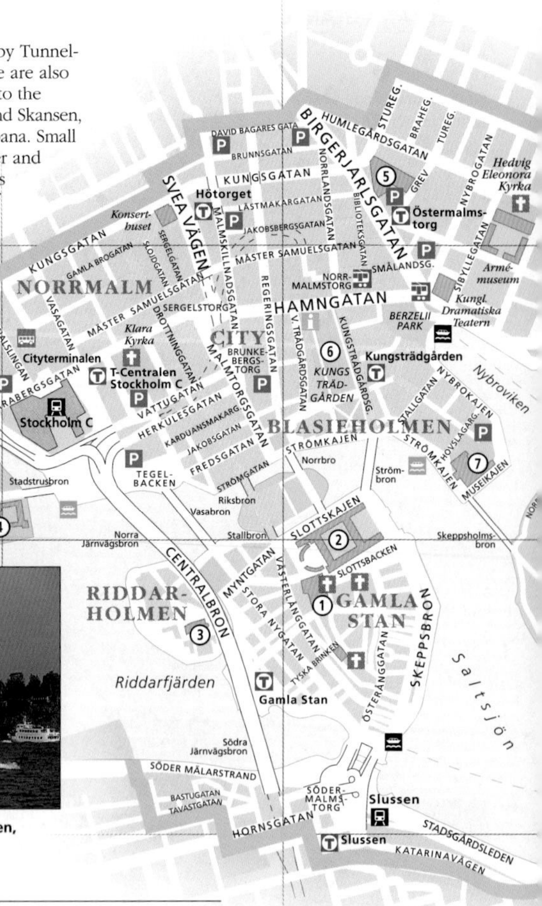

Archipelago boats moored at Strömkajen, outside the Nationalmuseum

SIGHTS AT A GLANCE

Historiska Museet ⑫
Kungsträdgården ⑥
Moderna Museet ⑧
Nationalmuseum ⑦
Nordiska Museet ⑪
Riddarholmskyrkan ③
Royal Palace ②
Skansen ⑩

Stadshuset ④
Storkyrkan ①
Stureplan & Sturegallerian ⑤
Vasamuseet ⑨

Greater Stockholm
(see inset map)
Drottningholm ⑬

SEE ALSO

• *Where to Stay* p654

• *Where to Eat* p655

GREATER STOCKHOLM

Uppsala
Sundbyberg
Lidingö
Solna
Bromma Airport
Ängby
Alvik
Tappström
⑬
Lovön
Hägersten
Bredäng
Norrköping, Södertälje

0 km 2
0 miles 2

KEY

■ Area of main map

ÖSTERMALM
⑫
NARVAVÄGEN
INNEGATAN
GUMSHORNSG.
STORGATAN
GREVGATAN
GREV MAGNIGATAN
TORSTENSSONSG.
BANERGATAN
ULRIKAGATAN
STORGATAN
STORGATAN
STRANDVÄGEN
NOBEL-PARKEN
STRANDVÄGEN P
Ladugårdslandsviken Djurgårdsbron
GALÄR-PARKEN
⑪
⑨
DJUR-GÅRDEN
DJURGÅRDSVÄGEN
P
⑧
SKEPPS HOLMEN
SVENSKSUNDSVÄGEN
LÅNGA RADEN
FALKENBERG
⑩
Kastellholms-bron
KASTELL-HOLMEN

0 meters 400
0 yards 400

KEY

■	Sights / Place of interest	Ⓣ	Tunnelbana station
✈	Airport	🚊	Tram stop
⛴	Long-distance ferry	P	Parking
🚢	Djurgården ferry	ℹ	Tourist information
🚢	Archipelago boat	✝	Church
🚉	Train station	⚊	Pedestrian street
🚌	Bus station		

D   E

Storkyrkan ①

Trångsund 1. **Tel** 08-723 30 16.
Ⓣ *Gamla Stan.* 🚌 *2, 3, 43, 53, 55, 71, 76.* ☐ *daily.* 📷 *May–Aug.* 📷 *in English: Jul–mid-Aug: 1pm.* ♿ 📷

Stockholm's 700-year-old cathedral, known as the Storkyrkan, or, literally, "big church," is of great national religious importance. From here the Swedish reformer Olaus Petri (1493–1552) spread his Lutheran message around the kingdom. The cathedral is also used for royal ceremonies.

A small church was built on this site in the 13th century, probably by the city's founder Birger Jarl. In 1306 it was replaced by a much bigger basilica, St. Nicholas.

The 15th-century Gothic interior was revealed in 1908 during restoration work. The late Baroque period provided the cathedral's so-called "royal chairs," the pews nearest the chancel, which were designed by Nicodemus Tessin the Younger (1654–1728) to be used by royal guests on special occasions. The 66-m (216-ft) high tower was added in 1743.

The cathedral houses some priceless artifacts, such as Bernt Notke's late-Gothic sculpture of *St. George and the Dragon* (1489), celebrating Sten Sture the Elder's 1471 victory over the Danes. Other prized treasures are the silver altar (1650s) and the *Parhelion Painting*, which depicts a light phenomenon observed over Stockholm in 1535. Recent research has proved the painting is not the original, but a copy from the 1630s.

The Italian Baroque-style façade of Stockholm's Storkyrkan

The grand façade of Stockholm's Kungliga Slottet (Royal Palace)

Royal Palace ②

Kungliga Slottet. **Tel** *08-402 61 30.*
Ⓣ *Gamla Stan.* 🚌 *2, 3, 43, 53, 55,
71, 76.* ⬜ *mid-May–mid-Sep:
daily; mid-Sep–mid-May: noon–
3pm Tue–Sun (except Royal Chapel
& Museum of Antiquities).*
⬛ *during official functions of the
Court.* 🖼 🎫 ♿
www.royalcourt.se

Completed in the mid-13th
century, the Tre Kronor
(Three Crowns) fortress was
turned into a royal residence
by the Vasa kings during the
following century. In 1697 it
was destroyed by fire. In its
place the architect Nicodemus
Tessin the Younger (1654–
1728) created a new palace
with an Italianate exterior and
a French interior that also
shows Swedish influences.

Though the palace is no
longer the king's
residence, the **State
Apartments** are still
used for official
functions. Banquets for
visiting heads of state
are often held in the
magnificent Karl XI's
Gallery, which is
modeled on the Hall
of Mirrors at Versailles
outside Paris *(see
pp168–9),* and is
a fine example of
Swedish Late Baroque.
Look out for the
exquisite ivory and
silver saltcellar,
designed by Flemish
painter Rubens. The
two-story Hall of State,
designed by Tessin
and Carl Hårleman,
combines Rococo
and Classical
elements, and contains

one of the palace's most
valuable treasures, the
splendid silver coronation
throne of Queen Kristina
(reigned 1633–54).

Below the Hall of State is
the **Treasury**, where the State
regalia are kept, including King
Erik XIV's crown, scepter, and
orb. Other priceless artifacts,
such as two crystal crowns
belonging to the present
monarchs, King Carl XVI
Gustaf and Queen Silvia, are
on view in the **Royal Chapel**.
Within the palace are two
museums. **Gustav III's
Museum of Antiquities**
opened in 1794 in memory
of the murdered king, and
contains artifacts collected
during his journey to Italy in
1783–4. The **Tre Kronor
Museum** illustrates the palace's
1,000-year history, and has
relics rescued from the

Tre Kronor (Three Crowns) symbol atop the
106-m (348-ft) tower of the Stadshuset

burning palace in 1697. A
very popular tourist event, the
daily changing of the guard,
takes place at midday in the
palace's Outer Courtyard.

Riddarholms-
kyrkan ③

Birger Jarls Torg. **Tel** *08-402 61 30.*
Ⓣ *Gamla Stan.* 🚌 *3, 53.* ⬜ *mid-
May–Sep: 10am–4pm daily.* 🖼 🎫
(call ahead for tours in English). ♿

Built on the site of the
late 13th-century Greyfriars
abbey, founded by Magnus
Ladulås, this majestic
brick church is best known
for its ornate burial vaults.
Dating back to the 16th
century, the vaults hold the
remains of all the Swedish
monarchs, from Gustav II
Adolf in the 17th century,
with two exceptions: Queen
Kristina, buried at St. Peter's
in Rome in 1689, and Gustav
VI Adolf, who was interred at
Haga, on the city outskirts, in
1973. Especially moving are
the graves of royal children,
including the many small tin
coffins that surround the
tombs of Gustav II Adolf and
his queen, Maria Eleonora.

Stadshuset ④

Hantverkargatan 1. **Tel** *08-508 290
58.* Ⓣ *Centralen.* 🚌 *3, 62.* ⬜ *for
guided tours.* ⬛ *Jan 1, Easter,
Dec 24–26 & 31, and during special
activities.* 🖼 🎫 *obligatory.* ♿
www.stockholm.se/cityhall

Probably Sweden's biggest
architectural project of the
20th century, the Stadshuset
(City Hall) was completed in

1923 and has become a symbol of Stockholm. It was designed by Ragnar Östberg (1866–1945) and displays influences of both the Nordic Gothic and Northern Italian schools. Many leading Swedish artists contributed to the rich interior design, including Einar Forseth (1892–1988), who created the stunning Byzantine-inspired gold-leaf wall mosaics in the Golden Room.

The building contains the Council Chamber and 250 offices for administrative staff. As well as a work place for the city's councillors, the Stadshuset also provides a venue for special events, such as the annual Nobel Prize ceremony, which takes place in the lavish Blue Hall.

Kungsträdgården, known as Stockholm's "open-air living room"

Kungsträdgården ⑥

ⓣ Kungsträdgården. 🚌 2, 47, 55, 62, 65, 69, 71, 76. **Kungliga Operan Tel** 08-791 44 00. 📷 Sep–May: 1pm Sat. ♿

The city's oldest park, the Kungsträdgården (King's Garden) takes its name from when it was a royal kitchen garden in the 15th century. During the summer open-air theater, dancing, concerts, and food festivals take place here. In winter the skating rink is a popular attraction. At the center of the park is a bronze fountain (1866) by J.P. Molin, who also designed the statue of Karl XII (1868) at the park's southern end. Overlooking this part of the park is the city's royal opera house, the **Kungliga Operan** (1898), whose ornate interior includes the Gold Foyer, with ceiling paintings by Carl Larsson.

In the 16th century, the kitchen garden was transformed into a Renaissance garden. The 17th-century summer house built for Queen Kristina still stands on the park's western flank.

Nationalmuseum ⑦

Södra Blasieholmshamnen. **Tel** 08-519 543 00. ⓣ Kungsträdgården. 🚌 2, 55, 62, 65, 71, 76. ◻ Tue–Sun. ● some public hols. 📷 🎥 ♿ ◻ 🏠 www.nationalmuseum.se

The location of the National-museum, on the Strömmen channel, inspired the 19th-century German architect August Stüler to design a building in the Venetian and Florentine Renaissance styles. Completed in 1866, the museum houses some 500,000 paintings, sculptures, prints, and drawings from the 15th to the early 20th centuries. The focus of the painting and sculpture section is Swedish 18th- to early 20th-century art, but the 17th-century Dutch and Flemish, and 18th-century French schools are also well represented. Highlights include Rembrandt's *The Conspiracy of the Batavians under Claudius Civilis* (1661–62) and *The Lady with the Veil* (1769) by Swedish portrait painter Alexander Roslin. There is also a decorative arts department, which contains 30,000 works spanning the last five centuries. Among the wide range of exhibits on show is Scandinavia's largest display of porcelain, glass, silver-ware, and furniture. Another exhibit, Design 1900–2000, tracks the history of design to the present day.

The opulent interior of Stockholm's Nationalmuseum

Stureplan, a popular meeting place for Stockholmers

Stureplan and Sturegallerian ⑤

ⓣ Östermalmstorg. 🚌 1, 2, 55, 56, 91. **Sturegallerian** Stureplan 4. **Tel** 08-611 46 06. ◻ daily (Sun: pm only). **Sturebadet Tel** 08-545 015 00. ◻ daily.

After a fire at the Sturebadet swimming pool in 1985, the Stureplan district was revamped and restored to its late 19th-century glory.

Part of the renovation of the area included building a stylish shopping mall, the Sture-gallerian, which boasts some 50 retail outlets. The Sturebadet public baths, within the mall, have been rebuilt according to their original late 19th-century Art Nouveau design.

The Moderna Museet's airy interior, designed by Catalan Rafael Moneo

Moderna Museet ⑧

Skeppsholmen. **Tel** 08-519 552 00. ⑦ Centralen. 🚃 65. ⬚ Tue–Sun. ● Jan 1, Mar 28, May 16, Jun 25, Dec 24, 25 & 31. 🚻 🛇 🔲 🎦 **www**.modernamuseet.se

The light and spacious building that the Moderna Museet has occupied since 1998 provides a perfect setting for the museum's world-class collection of modern art, photography, and film.

Following a recent period of renovation, during which the museum moved to another location and put on a variety of exhibitions and events, it is now back in its own building.

All the works on display date from between 1900 and the present day. Two of the star exhibits are *The Child's Brain* (1914) by Italian artist Giorgio de Chirico, widely considered a precursor to the

Surrealists, and *Monogram* (1955–59) by the American Robert Rauschenberg. Among the collection of Swedish works is Nils Dardel's Expressionistic painting, *The Dying Dandy* (1918).

Vasamuseet ⑨

Galärvarvsvägen, Djurgården. **Tel** 08-519 548 00. 🚃 44, 47. 🚋 7. ⛴ Djurgårdsfärja. ⬚ daily. ● Jan 1, Dec 23–25 & 31. 🚻 🛇 🔲 🔳 ❑ **Museifartygen Tel** 519 548 91. ⬚ Jun 10–Aug: pm daily. 🚻 🎦 **www**.vasamuseet.se

The centerpiece of the city's most popular museum is the massive royal warship, *Vasa*, which capsized in Stockholm harbor on its maiden voyage in 1628. Rediscovered in 1956, the vessel has been painstakingly restored to 95 percent of its original appearance.

The warship is decorated with around 700 sculpted figures and carved ornaments, designed as a type of war propaganda. King Gustav II Adolf, who commissioned *Vasa*, was known as the Lion of the North, so a springing lion was the obvious choice for the figurehead on the ship's prow. It is 4 m (13 ft) long and weighs 450 kg (990 lb).

Although visitors cannot board the ship, full-scale models of *Vasa's* upper gun deck and the Admiral's cabin provide a glimpse of what life

on board was like. There is also a fascinating display of items retrieved in the salvage operation, including medical equipment, an officer's backgammon set, and a chest still neatly packed with clothing and other personal belongings.

Moored in the dock alongside the museum are two other historic vessels, collectively referred to as the **Museifartygen**. The lightship *Finngrundet* was built in 1903 and worked for 60 years before becoming a museum. *Sankt Erik* was commissioned in 1915 and was Sweden's first sea-going icebreaker.

Midsummer celebrations at the open-air museum, Skansen

Skansen ⑩

Djurgårdsslätten 49–51. **Tel** 08-442 80 00. 🚃 44, 47. 🚋 7. ⛴ Djurgårdsfärja. ⬚ daily. ● Dec 24. 🚻 🎦 Jun–Aug (call in advance). 🛗 ❑ **www**.skansen.se

The world's first open-air museum opened in 1891 to show an increasingly industrialized society how people once lived. Around 150 buildings were assembled from all over Scandinavia, to portray the life of peasants and landed gentry, as well as Lapp *(Same)* culture.

In the Town Quarter are 19th-century town-houses, where glassblowers and other craftsmen demonstrate their skills. Two of Skansen's oldest "exhibits" are a 650-year-old wooden farmhouse from Dalarna, and a 14th-century storehouse from Norway.

Nordic flora and fauna can be seen, with elks, bears, and wolves in natural habitat enclosures and marine animals in an aquarium. Traditional festivals and concerts are held here throughout the year.

The restored 17th-century royal warship, *Vasa*, at the Vasamuseet

For hotels and restaurants in this region see p654 and p655

Nordiska Museet ⑪

Djurgårdsvägen 6–16. **Tel** *08-519
546 00.* 🚌 *44, 47.* 🚃 *7.* ⛴ *Djur-
gårds-färja.* ○ *late Jun–Aug: daily;
Sep–mid-Jun: Tue–Sun.*
⬤ *midsummer hol, Dec 24, 25, 31;
Jan 1.* 📷 🚫 ♿ 🎧 🏪
www.nordiskamuseet.se

Housed in a Renaissance-
style building, the Nordiska
Museet's collection was
started by Artur Hazelius
(1833–1901), founder of the
Skansen open-air museum,
with the intention of
reminding future generations
of the old Nordic farming
culture. Today, the museum
has over 1.5 million exhibits
portraying everyday life in
Sweden from the 1520s to the
present day. Items on display
range from priceless jewelry,
to furniture, dolls' houses,
and replicas of period rooms,
such as the splendid 17th-
century state bedchamber
from Ulvsunda Castle. Highlights include the monumental
gilded oak statue of King
Gustav Vasa (1924), and
16 paintings by the Swedish
author and dramatist August
Strindberg (1849–1912).

**Carl Milles' huge statue of King
Gustav Vasa in the Nordiska Museet**

Historiska Museet ⑫

Narvavägen 13–17. **Tel** *08-519 556
00.* Ⓣ *Karlaplan, Östermalmstorg.*
🚌 *44, 56.* ○ *daily.* ⬤ *some public
hols.* 📷 ♿ 🎧 **www**.historiska.se

Sweden's Museum of National
Antiquities was opened in
1943. It originally made its

The magnificent Drottningholm palace, on the island of Lovön

name with relics from the
Viking era, as well as its
outstanding collections from
the Middle Ages. The latter
include one of the museum's
star exhibits – a richly gilded
wooden Madonna figure,
from Sweden's early medieval
period. In the prehistoric
collection is the Alunda
Elk, a ceremonial stone
axe, discovered in 1920
at Alunda and thought
to have been made
around 2000 BC.

Since the early
1990s the museum's
priceless collection
of gold and silver,
dating from the
Bronze Age to the
Middle Ages, has
been on show in
the Guld-rummet
(Gold Room). Look
out for the stunning Elisabeth
Reliquary, an 11th-century
goblet, with a silver cover
made in 1230 to enclose the
skull of St. Elisabeth.

**Madonna figure in the
Historiska Museet**

Drottningholm ⑬

10 km (6 miles) W of Stockholm.
Tel *08-402 62 80.* Ⓣ *Brommaplan,
then bus 177, 178.* 🚢 *May–Sep
from Stadshusbron.* ○ *May–Sep:
daily; Oct–Apr: Sat & Sun. (Chinese
Pavilion: May–Sep only; Theater
Museum: May–Sep only.)* ⬤ *Dec
22–Jan 5.* 📷 **www**.royalcourt.se

With its sumptuous palace,
theater, park, and Chinese
pavilion, the whole of the
Drottningholm estate has
been included in UNESCO's
World Heritage list. Contemporary Italian and French

architecture inspired Nicodemus Tessin the Elder
(1615–81) in his design of the
royal palace. Begun in the
1660s on the orders of King
Karl X Gustav's widow, Queen
Hedvig Eleonora, the building
was completed by Tessin the
Younger. Today, the present
royal family still uses parts of
the palace as a private
residence. The most lavish
rooms open to the public
include Queen Lovisa
Ulrika's library, designed
by Jean Eric Rehn
(1717–93), and
Queen Hedvig
Eleonora's state
bedroom, decorated
in Baroque style.

The Baroque and
Rococo gardens and
lush parkland
surrounding the
palace are dotted with
monuments and splendid
buildings. The blue and gold
Chinese Pavilion (Kina Slott)
was built for Queen Lovisa
Ulrika in the latter half of the
18th century, and contains
many interesting artifacts from
China and Japan. The designer
of the Chinese Pavilion, Carl
Fredrik Adelcrantz, was also
responsible for the Drottningholm Court Theater
(Slottsteatern), which dates
from 1766. This simple
wooden building is the world's
oldest theater still preserved
in its original form. The
scenery, with its wooden
hand driven machinery, is still
in working order. In summer
the theater hosts opera and
ballet. There is also a
museum, which focuses on
18th-century theater.

The Renaissance Gripsholms Slott, on the shore of Lake Mälaren

🏛 **Birkamuseet**
Tel 08-560 514 45. ⬜ May 1–
Sep 26: daily. 📷 📶

🎪 **Gripsholms Slott**
Tel 0159-101 94. ⬜ mid-May–mid-
Sep: daily; mid-Sep–mid-May: Sat &
Sun. ● Dec 18–Jan 2. 📶 📷 🚽

Uppsala ❸

🏯 190,000. 🚶 🚊 🚌
ℹ️ Fyris Torg 8 (018-727 48 00).
www.uppland.nu

One of Sweden's oldest settlements, Uppsala, on the banks of the Fyrisån river, is also a lively university town. On the last day of April, crowds of students wearing white caps parade through the town for the traditional spring season celebrations.

Dominating the town's attractive medieval center is the **Domkyrkan**, Scandinavia's largest Gothic cathedral. Its chapel contains the relics of Sweden's patron saint, Saint Erik. The onion-domed **Gustavianum**, opposite the cathedral, dates from the 1620s and houses the Uppsala University Museum. The museum's exhibits include a 17th-century anatomical theater and Egyptian, Classical, and Nordic antiquities. Just a short walk away stands the **Carolina Rediviva**, the impressive university library.

Uppsala Slott, the town's hilltop fortress, was built in the 16th century by King Gustav Vasa, although it was later destroyed by fire. Now restored, it also houses the Uppsala Art Museum.

Lake Mälaren ❷

Birka 🚢 May–Sep daily from Stadshusbron, Stockholm. **Mariefred** 🚢 in summer from Stadshusbron, Stockholm. 🚂 from Centralstationen, Stockholm to Läggesta, then bus or steam train.

To the west of Stockholm lies Lake Mälaren, a vast stretch of water, whose pretty shores and islands offer several day excursions from the city.

Sweden's first town, **Birka**, was founded on the island of Björkö in the 8th century, although archaeological finds indicate that trading activity took place here at least 1,500 years ago. In the 9th and 10th centuries Birka grew into a busy Viking center. The **Birkamuseet** has displays of local archaeological finds and provides a fascinating insight into the daily lives of the town's early inhabitants. There are also guided tours of ongoing excavations.

The most striking feature of the pretty town of **Mariefred** is the majestic **Gripsholms Slott**, built for King Gustav Vasa in 1537, and later modified under Gustav III in the 18th century. The palace is known for its well-preserved interiors, and also houses the National Portrait Gallery, with over 4,000 paintings spanning some 500 years.

Mariefred itself has a lovely 17th-century church and an 18th-century timber Rådhus (law courts' building), as well as several specialist stores, galleries, and antique shops. In summer, one of the most enjoyable ways to travel there from Stockholm is aboard the *Mariefred*, a historic, coal-fired steamboat. The trip takes around three and a half hours and allows passengers to enjoy the spectacular scenery along the route.

Aerial view of Uppsala, with its massive Gothic cathedral, the Domkyrkan

A short bus ride north of the town center, Gamla Uppsala is the site of the Kungshögarna, royal burial mounds believed to date from the 6th century. The **Historiskt Centrum** acquaints visitors with the history, legends, and lore surrounding the burial mounds and contains displays of local archaeological finds.

ffi Gustavianum
Akademigatan 3. *Tel* 018-471 75 71. ◯ *Tue–Sun.* 🎥 ✗ 📷 ♿
🌐 www.gustavianum.uu.se

⚓ Uppsala Slott
Slottet, entrance E. *Tel* 018-727 24 82. ◯ *Wed–Sun.* 🎥 📷 *Jun–Aug.*
♿ 🅿

ffi Historiskt Centrum
Disavägen. *Tel* 018-23 93 00.
◯ *May–Sep: daily; at other times: call for information.* 🎥 ♿ 📷

Dalarna ❹

🗺 *Falun, Mora.* 🚌 *Falun, Mora.*
ℹ *Trotzgatan 10–12 (023-640 04); Stationsväg 3, Mora (0250-59 23 10).*

With its proud tradition of music, dance, and handicrafts, Dalarna is Sweden's folklore district. The charming rural landscape, dotted with red, wooden cottages, attracts many tourists seeking a quiet country retreat in the summer. In winter, the area's mountain resorts, Sälen and Idre, are packed with skiers.

The main sights of interest are located around Lake Siljan. **Mora**, the largest of the lakeside towns, was home to one of Sweden's best-known artists, Anders Zorn (1860–1920). Open daily, the Zorn Museum, at No. 36 Vasagatan, holds paintings by the artist, and you can also visit his former home and studio.

Dalarna is famous for its midsummer festivals. In **Leksand** and **Rättvik** you may see traditionally dressed locals dancing and playing musical instruments or rowing on the lake in wooden longboats during the towns' colorful celebrations.

Around 15 km (9 miles) from the provincial capital and largely industrial town of

The Norderport, one of the gateways in Visby's medieval city walls

Falun is **Sundborn**, where Swedish painter Carl Larsson (1853–1919) and his wife, Karin, a textile artist, lived in the early 20th century. Their work still has a big influence on contemporary Swedish design. The couple's lakeside house is open to the public.

Gotland and Visby ❺

🏛 *60,000.* ✈ 🚢 *to Visby.*
ℹ *Hamngatan 4, Visby (0498-20 17 00).* **www**.gotland.info

The island of Gotland, Sweden's most popular holiday destination, boasts a stunning coastline, a rich cultural heritage, and a superb climate, enjoying more hours of sunshine than anywhere else in the country.

In the Viking Age, Gotland, the largest island in the Baltic Sea, was a major trading post and later its capital, Visby, became a prosperous Hanseatic port. Surrounded by one of the best-preserved city walls in the world, Visby is like a living museum, with pretty step-gabled houses and a web of narrow cobbled streets and small squares. The original Hanseatic harbor is now a park, but the **Burmeisterska Huset** (Burmeister's House), dating

Female musician at a midsummer festival in Dalarna

from 1645, is a fine surviving example of the architecture of the Post-Hanseatic period. Strandgatan contains some of Visby's most attractive historic buildings, the former homes of wealthy merchants. In the same street is the excellent historical museum, **Gotlands Fornsal**, which holds a collection of artifacts spanning 8,000 years. The **Domkyrkan** (Cathedral of St. Maria) below Kyrkberget is the only medieval church still intact and in use in Visby.

Away from Visby, the rest of Gotland is dotted with many unspoilt farmhouses, old medieval churches, and secluded beaches. Among the most impressive sights are the subterranean limestone caves of **Lummelundagrottorna**, 13 km (8 miles) north of the city, and, off the northeastern tip of the island, **Fårö**. This island, known for its severe beauty, can be reached by a daily, half-hourly ferry from Fårösund. Besides old fishing hamlets such as Helgumannen, visitors can enjoy the long stretch of white sandy beach and the swimming at Sudersands. Look out for Fårö's spectacular *raukar*. These are huge limestone rock formations, rising out of the sea on the west side of the island.

ffi Gotlands Fornsal
Strandgatan 14. *Tel* 0498-29 27 00.
◯ *May–mid-Sep: daily; mid-Sep–Apr: pm Tue–Sun.* 🎥 📷 *in summer.* ♿

Poseidon fountain, at the end of Kungsportsavenyn in Gothenburg

Gothenburg ❻

🏙 478,000. ✈ 25 km (16 miles) E.
🚉 🚌 ⛴ ℹ Kungsportsplatsen 2
(031-612 500).
www.gothenburg.com

Gothenburg (Göteborg), Sweden's second largest city, has a distinctive character, with beautiful architecture, pleasant café-lined boulevards, a bustling harbor, and a dynamic cultural life.

Scandinavia's largest seaport is dominated by the **Göteborgsutkiken**, a huge lookout tower providing stunning panoramic views of the city and its surroundings. A short walk west along the quayside are the daring, industrial-style **Göteborgsoperan** (Opera House), built in 1994, and the **Maritiman**, reputedly the world's largest floating ship museum. Moored in the dock are a dozen different types of vessel, all open to the public. They include a light ship, a destroyer, and a submarine.

The pulse of the city is Kungsportsavenyn, simply known as Avenyn, or "The Avenue." This 900-m (2952-ft) long boulevard is lined with restaurants, pubs, and cafés, and is a favorite haunt of street musicians and hawkers. On a side street off Avenyn, **Röhsska Museet** is Sweden's only museum devoted to arts, crafts, and industrial design. At the southern end of the avenue is Götaplatsen, whose focal point is the famous Poseidon fountain by the Swedish sculptor Carl Milles. The square is flanked by the fine **Konstmuseet** (Art Museum), which specializes in 19th- and 20th-century Scandinavian art.

Southeast of Götaplatsen is **Lisebergs Nöjespark**, the largest amusement park in Sweden.

🏛 **Maritiman**
Packhuskajen 8. **Tel** 031-10 59 50.
◻ Mar–Nov: daily; Dec–Feb:
advance bookings only. 🎫 ▢ ▢

🏛 **Röhsska Museet**
Vasagatan 37–39. **Tel** 031-61 38
50. ◻ pm Tue–Sun. 🎫 ▢ ▢
▢ www.designmuseum.se

🏛 **Konstmuseet**
Götaplatsen. **Tel** 031-61 29 80.
◻ Tue–Sun. 🎫 ▢ 🎫 ▢ ▢ ▢

Växjö ❼

🏙 56,000. 🚉 🚌 ℹ Västra
Esplanaden 7 (0470-414 10).
www.turism.vaxjo.se

Located right at the heart of Småland, Växjö is an ideal base from which to explore the Glasriket, or "Kingdom of Glass," Sweden's world-famous region of glassworks. The town's main attraction is the **Smålands Museum**, which tells the story of 400 years of glassmaking, and provides a good introduction to a visit to any one of the many glassworks scattered throughout the surrounding forests.

The best-known glassworks are at **Orrefors** and **Kosta**, within 90 km (56 miles) of Växjö, but other factories worth visiting include **Åfors** and **Strömbergshyttan**. Most of the factories have excellent glassblowing demonstrations, and all have a shop where you can choose from a wide selection of products. In the past, Småland's glassworks were more than just a place of work. Locals used to meet here in the evenings to bake herrings and potatoes in the furnace, while music was provided by a fiddler. Today the Orrefors and Kosta glassworks arrange similar forms of entertainment, known as *hyttsill* evenings.

Visitors to Växjö should not miss the **Utvandrarnas Hus** (House of Emigrants). This interesting museum recounts the story of the one million Swedes who, in the face of famine in the late 19th and early 20th centuries, left Småland for a better life in America.

Swedish glassware from Småland

🏛 **Smålands Museum**
Södra Järnvägsgatan 2. **Tel** 0470-
7042 00. ◻ Jun–Aug: daily; Sep–
May: Tue–Sun. 🎫 ▢ 🎫 ▢ ▢

🏛 **Kosta Glassworks**
Kosta, on route 28. **Tel** 0478-
34529. ◻ daily. ● some public
hols. 🎫 ▢

🏛 **Utvandrarnas Hus**
Vilhelm Mobergsgatan 4. **Tel** 0470-
201 20. ◻ daily. 🎫

Malmö

🏊 265,000. 🛬 🚢 🚆 🚌 ℹ️
Central Station (040-34 1200).

Malmö is the capital of the province of Skåne in southwestern Sweden. In the 16th century, it was a major fishing port, competing with Copenhagen as Scandinavia's most influential city. Today the city is well-known for its busy harbor, as well as for its rich architectural heritage.

The imposing 16th-century Malmöhus was built by the Danish king Christian III, when Skåne formed part of Denmark. It contains the **Malmömuseer** (Malmö Museums), which include the Art Museum, the Museum of Natural History, the City Museum, the Science & Technology and Maritime Museum, and the Kommendants Hus (Commander's House).

The Dutch Renaissance style is evident in Malmö's impressive **Rådhuset** (Town Hall), which dates from 1546 and dominates the city's main square, Stortorget. Northeast of here is the 14th-century **St. Petri's Kyrka**, built in the Baltic Gothic style. The church's most beautiful features include the altarpiece (1611), Scandinavia's largest, and a

Mälmo's main square, overlooked by the Renaissance Rådhuset

wonderfully ornate pulpit. Amid the city's maze of café-lined pedestrianized streets is Lilla Torg (Little Square), with its cobblestones and charmingly restored houses. The square has a lively atmosphere and draws crowds of tourists and locals alike, especially in fine weather. At the northwest corner of the square, the bustling Saluhallen is a covered market, with many restaurants, cafés, and specialist food stores.

Heading east from Lilla Torg brings you to the **Rooseum**.

This excellent museum of modern art was founded in 1988 by the Swedish art collector and financier Fredrik Roos. Retrospectives of leading international contemporary artists are held here regularly.

🏛 **Malmömuseer**
Malmöhus, Malmöhusvägen. **Tel** *040-34 44 37.* ⏰ *pm daily.* ⏺
Dec 24, 25, 31, Jan 1. 📷 ♿ ♿
www.malmo.se/museer

🏛 **Rooseum**
Gasverksgatan 22. **Tel** *040-12 17 16.* ⏰ *pm Wed–Sun.* ⏺ *some public hols.* 📷 ♿

THE ORESUND LINK

Despite a legacy of mutual warfare and rivalry, in May 2000 the close ties between Denmark and Sweden were strengthened with the inauguration of the Öresund Link. A 16-km (10-mile) long combined suspension bridge and tunnel now connects the Danish capital, Copenhagen, with the Swedish provincial capital Malmö on either side of the channel of water known as the Öresund. The bridge is the strongest cable stay bridge in the world, designed to carry the combined weight of a motorway and a dual-track railway, while the tunnel is the world's largest immersed tunnel in terms of volume. The project has been hailed as a renaissance for southern Sweden, which now seems poised to become a prospering center of trade, science, industry, and culture at the heart of the cross-border Danish-Swedish Öresund region.

The newly constructed Öresund Link, spanning the Öresund channel

Practical & Travel Information

With Sweden growing rapidly as an important tourist destination, standards in the travel industry have improved greatly. Foreign visitors will enjoy a comfortable stay in Sweden, not least because most people speak English. Sweden's infrastructure is constantly being improved – there are many new highways and the rail system has recently been upgraded for high-speed trains. There is also a direct link to Denmark via the new Öresund Bridge. In Stockholm, public transportation on buses, subway trains, ferries, and local trains is efficient, and covers the entire city and surrounding region.

TOURIST INFORMATION

Tourist information offices are located throughout Sweden, and are run by the **Swedish Travel & Tourism Council**. Stockholm's official tourist information organization is the **Stockholm Visitors Board**. Most hotels in the capital, as well as many department stores and museums, stock the free monthly listings brochure *What's On Stockholm*.

Most museums and other sights in Sweden are open between 10 or 11am and 5 or 6pm all year round, and often have longer opening hours in the summer. They are usually closed on Monday.

VISA REQUIREMENTS

Passports are not required for visitors from most EU countries, but visitors from the US, Canada, the UK, Ireland, Australia, and New Zealand still need a valid passport. Citizens of almost all countries can enter Sweden without a visa.

PERSONAL SECURITY

Violent crime against tourists is rare in Sweden, although pickpockets are known to frequent the busier pedestrian shopping streets in the main cities. Sweden has a well-developed network of emergency services, which are efficient and reliable. Swedish police are extremely helpful and most speak good English.

HEALTH ISSUES

No special vaccinations are necessary to visit Sweden. Hygiene standards are among the highest in the world, and the tap water is safe to drink. For prescription and non-prescription medicines visit a pharmacy *(apotek)*, open during normal store hours. A 24-hour *apotek* service is also available in major cities.

CURRENCY AND BANKING

The Swedish unit of currency is the krona, abbreviated to SEK or kr. Banking hours are generally 10am–3pm Monday to Friday, though some banks stay open until 6pm at least one day a week. Traveler's checks can be changed at all banks. Bureaux de change are located throughout the main cities and airports, and normally provide a better exchange rate than banks.

All the well-known credit cards are widely accepted in Sweden. Withdrawals can be made from cash machines using all internationally accepted credit cards.

COMMUNICATIONS

Public telephone kiosks are owned by the state-run Telia company, and are usually operated by card only. Phonecards can be bought at tobacconists and newspaper kiosks, though normal credit cards or international telephone cards work just as well.

Post offices are open from 10am to 6pm on weekdays and from 10am to 1pm on Saturdays. Many of the post offices have recently been closed and postal services moved to gas stations and stores instead. Stamps can be purchased at these locations as well as at post offices, Pressbyrån kiosks, and tourist information offices.

FLYING TO SWEDEN

Most major European cities have direct flights to Stockholm. Many of the world's leading airlines serve Arlanda Airport, located about 40 km (25 miles) north of the city center. International flights also serve Gothenburg and Malmö. Services from the UK are operated by **Finnair**, **SAS** (Scandinavian Airlines), British Airways, and low-cost airline **Ryanair**. Direct flights from North America are available from SAS and Finnair, and from the US airline American.

TRAVELING BY FERRY

Ferries to Gothenburg from Fredrikshavn in Denmark (2–3 hours), and from Kiel in Germany (20–22 hours), are operated by **Stena Line**.

THE CLIMATE OF SWEDEN

Sweden's summers are usually fairly cool, although sometimes there can be heatwaves for several weeks at a time. Winter temperatures often fall below freezing, but it is rarely severely cold, except in the far north. The snow may lie until well after March in the north, but in the rest of the country some recent winters have been virtually free of snow.

STOCKHOLM

	Apr	Jul	Oct	Jan
°C/F high		23/73		
	10/50	14/57	12/54	
	2/36		7/44	0/32
0°C 32°F				-4/25
sun (hrs)	6 hrs	8 hrs	3.5 hrs	1.5 hrs
rain (mm)	21 mm	65 mm	48 mm	27 mm

Large passenger and car ferries sail to Stockholm from Finland; both **Viking Line** and **Silja Line** operate daily services from Helsinki (with a crossing time of about 15 hours) and Turku (with a crossing time of about 11 hours).

DFDS Seaways has a year-round service twice a week from Newcastle in Great Britain to Gothenburg via Kristiansand (with a crossing time of about 24 hours).

Within Sweden, ferries to Visby in Gotland leave from Nynäshamn, about 75 km (47 miles) south of Stockholm. There are two crossings daily by catamaran (2 hours 50 mins) and one or two crossings daily by regular ferry (5 hours). Both services are run by **Destination Gotland**.

RAIL TRAVEL

Rail travel to Sweden from mainland Europe is fast and comfortable. Journey times have been cut considerably with the opening of the Öresund Bridge; traveling from Copenhagen to Malmö now takes only 40 minutes.

Within Sweden, the state-owned rail company Statens Järnvägar (SJ) operates many of the long-distance trains. Some routes are run by private companies – Tågkompaniet runs trains from Stockholm to Narvik, Umeå, and Luleå in the far north of Sweden.

In recent years domestic air travel in Sweden has faced strong competition from the new X 2000 high-speed trains. The journey time by train from Malmö to Stockholm is about 5 hours, and from Gothenburg to the capital takes about 3 hours.

TRAVELING BY CAR

Visitors driving from Denmark can use the spectacular Öresund toll bridge between Copenhagen and Malmö. On the Swedish side, the bridge connects with the E4, a 550-km (340-mile) highway to Stockholm.

Fines for speeding are high, and even if the limit is only slightly exceeded, you can lose your license. The maximum permitted blood alcohol level is so low that drinking is effectively banned for drivers. When driving in the Swedish countryside, be particularly cautious, as elk and deer may appear unexpectedly in the middle of the road.

TRAVELING IN STOCKHOLM

Virtually all of Stockholm's sights and attractions can be reached by subway train or bus. Tunnelbana, the underground rail system, has 100 stations on three main routes. Travelcards are available for one-day, three-day, and monthly periods, and are also valid on bus and ferry services.

Traveling by bus is a pleasant and economical way to see the city. The best routes for sight-seeing are 3, 4, 46, 47, 62, and 69, which cover the central area and stop near many sights.

Stockholm's waterways play an important role in urban life, and boats and ferries provide a delightful way of getting to know the city and its environs. **Strömma Kanalbolaget** runs various hour-long excursions during the summer months, and also organizes longer tours of the archipelago and Lake Mälaren throughout the year.

A worthwhile purchase for any visitor to the capital is the Stockholm Card, which allow free travel on Tunnelbana trains, local buses, and local trains, free parking at official city parking areas, and free admission to more than 70 museums and attractions.

DIRECTORY

TOURIST OFFICES

Stockholm Visitors Board
Drottninggatan 33, Stockholm.
Tel 08-50 82 85 00.
www. stockholmtown. com

Swedish Travel & Tourism Council
Kungsgatan 36, Stockholm.
Tel 08-789 10 00.
www.visitsweden.com

In the UK:
5 Upper Montague Street, London W1H 2AG.
Tel 0800-3080 3080.

In the US:
655 Third Ave, 18th Floor, New York, NY 10017.
Tel 212-885 9700.
Fax 212-885 9764.

EMBASSIES

Australia
11th floor, Sergels Torg 12, Stockholm. **Tel** 08-613 29 00. **www**.sweden. embassy.gov.au

Canada
Tegelbacken 4, Stockholm.
Tel 08-453 30 00.
www.canadaemb.se

Ireland
Östermalmsgatan 97, Stockholm.
Tel 08-661 80 05.

UK
Skarpögatan 6-8, Stockholm.
Tel 08-671 30 00.
www.britishembassy.se

US
Dag Hammarskjölds Väg 31, Stockholm.
Tel 08-783 53 00.
www.usemb.se

EMERGENCY NUMBERS

Ambulance, Police and Fire
Tel 112.

AIRLINES

Finnair
Tel 0771-55 00 10
(toll-free in Sweden).
Tel 0870-241 4411 (UK).
Tel 800-950 5000 (US).
www.finnair.com

Malmö Aviation
Tel 0771-78 11 00.
www.malmoaviation.se

Ryanair
www.ryanair.com

SAS
Tel 0770-727 727
(toll-free in Sweden).
Tel 0870-6072 7727 (UK).
Tel 800-221 2350 (US).
www.scandinavian.net

FERRY SERVICES

Destination Gotland
Tel 0771-22 33 00.
www.destination gotland.com

DFDS Seaways
Tel 042-26 60 00.
www.dfdsseaways.com

Silja Line
Tel 08-22 21 40.
www.silja.com

Stena Line
Tel 031-704 00 00.
www.stenaline.se

Viking Line
Tel 08-452 40 00.
www.vikingline.se

TRAVELING IN STOCKHOLM

Strömma Kanalbolaget
Tel 08-587 140 00.
www.strommakanal-bolaget.com

Where to Stay in Sweden

Sweden's hotels are not usually built on the same grandiose scale as their counterparts in southern Europe, but they offer a high level of comfort and service and often have magnificent views or locations. Major hotels in the larger cities can be fairly expensive, but rooms are often available at reduced rates for weekend breaks.

PRICE CATEGORIES
The following price ranges are for a standard double room with taxes per night during the high season. Breakfast is not included, unless specified:

Ⓚ Under 700 SEK
ⓀⓀ 700–1,500 SEK
ⓀⓀⓀ 1,500–2,100 SEK
ⓀⓀⓀⓀ Over 2,100 SEK

STOCKHOLM

CENTRAL STOCKHOLM Hotel Riddargatan   🅿   ⓀⓀⓀ
Riddargatan 14, 114 35 **Tel** *08-55 57 30 00* **Fax** *08-55 57 30 11* **Rooms** *58*   **Map** *C3/D3*

Refurbished in 2002 but having retained its 1930s Art Deco styling, this hotel has a good location in Stockholm's "golden triangle", just behind the Royal Dramatic Theatre. Close to restaurants, bars, and nightlife – sometimes visiting world-famous jazz musicians stay and perform here. **www.profilhotels.se**

CENTRAL STOCKHOLM Hotel Rival   🅱🅿🍴   ⓀⓀⓀⓀ
Mariatorget 3 **Tel** *08-545 789 00* **Fax** *08-545 789 24* **Rooms** *99*   **Map** *B5*

This trendy boutique hotel comes equipped with its own cinema and has a great location in the heart of Stockholm. Built in the 1930s, the owner, Benny Andersson (of Abba fame) has recaptured the glamour of the era in the hotel's design. Each of the 99 guest rooms are individually designed. **www.rival.se**

CENTRAL STOCKHOLM Radisson SAS Royal Viking Hotel   🍴🅿🍴   ⓀⓀⓀⓀ
Vasagatan 1, 101 24 **Tel** *08-50 65 40 00* **Fax** *08-50 65 40 01* **Rooms** *459*   **Map** *B3*

One of Stockholm's best-known hotels, the Royal Viking offers two bars, one in the ground floor atrium and the exciting Sky Bar on the top floor, as well as the excellent Stockholm Fisk Restaurant. This hotel maintains high standards suited to both business and leisure travellers. **www.radissonsas.com**

SOUTHERN STOCKHOLM Tre Små Rum Hotel   Ⓚ
Högbergsgatan 81, 118 54 **Tel** *08-641 23 71* **Fax** *08-642 88 08* **Rooms** *7*   **Map** *C5*

This inexpensive but cosy modern hotel was started by a traveler hoping to offer an economical and friendly hotel option with a central location. All the rooms are non-smoking, and none en suite. Healthy breakfasts are created to guests' individual order. Early booking is essential. Bicycles are available for hire. **www.tresmarum.se**

WESTERN STOCKHOLM Långholmen Hotel   🅿🍴   ⓀⓀⓀ
Kronohäketet, Långholmen, 102 72 **Tel** *08-720 85 00* **Fax** *08-720 85 75* **Rooms** *102*

A converted prison, the Långholmen offers accommodation in modernised "cells" in the city center. There is a restaurant in the warden's residence and also a pub, wine cellar, prison museum, and even a private bathing beach. Youth hostel available from mid-June to mid-August. **www.langholmen.com**

REST OF SWEDEN

GOTHENBURG Eggers Hotell & Restaurang   🅱🍴   ⓀⓀⓀ
Drottningtorget, 401 25 **Tel** *031-333 44 40* **Fax** *031-333 44 49* **Rooms** *69*

A listed building and Sweden's third oldest hotel. Built on historic ground in the center of Gothenburg, this classic hotel offers a mix of early 20th-century charm and modern conveniences. No one room is the same as another, all are tastefully furnished to reflect the historical character of the building. **www.hoteleggers.se**

MALMÖ Hotel Mäster Johan   🍴🅱🅿🍴   ⓀⓀⓀⓀ
Mäster Johansgatan 13, 211 21 **Tel** *040-664 64 00* **Fax** *040-664 64 01* **Rooms** *69*

The first class Hotel Mäster Johan is a modern building in the culturally protected part of Malmö known as Gamla Väster. The interior design theme is based on natural materials such as stone, glass, and wood. All rooms have plush bathrooms, Bang & Olufsen TVs, and luxury Swedish-made beds. A real modern classic. **www.masterjohan.se**

UPPSALA First Hotel Linné   🍴   ⓀⓀ
Skolgatan 45, 750 02 **Tel** *018-10 20 00* **Fax** *018-13 75 97* **Rooms** *116*

Well managed hotel at the edge of the impressive Linnaeus Botanical Garden. Interior design is inspired by the garden, which most rooms overlook. Less expensive doubles can be a bit cramped. The Alex Vinbar & Kök serves an international menu and the wine bar offers some 200 wines by the glass. **www.firsthotels.com/Linne**

Key to Symbols *see back cover flap*

Where to Eat in Sweden

Good Swedish restaurants tend to be small and informal. Food can be very expensive, with lunch often the best value. Some restaurants serve *smörgåsbord*, where you can eat as much as you like at a fixed price. Many menus feature *husmanskost* – traditional dishes of Swedish "home cooking" – such as Swedish meatballs.

PRICE CATEGORIES
Average price for a three-course meal for one, including half a bottle of house wine, tax, and service:

Ⓚ Under 400 SEK
ⓀⓀ 400–550 SEK
ⓀⓀⓀ 550–700 SEK
ⓀⓀⓀⓀ Over 700 SEK

STOCKHOLM

CENTRAL STOCKHOLM Bakfickan
ⓀⓀ
Kungliga Operan, Karl XII's Torg, Stockholm, 111 86 **Tel** *08-676 58 09*　　**Map** *C3*

A real little gem for its many regular customers, including artists from the nearby opera house, Bakfickan is ideal for those looking for a quick bite to eat. The bar menu consists of Swedish "home-cooked" specials, along with a selection of open sandwiches. More complex meals are also available. Closed Sundays.

CENTRAL STOCKHOLM Nalen
ⓀⓀⓀ
Regeringsgatan 74, Stockholm, 111 39 **Tel** *08-50 52 92 01*　　**Map** *C3*

Formerly the Grand National, this eatery now has the same name as the jazz club around the corner. The food is traditional Swedish using the best local ingredients such as reindeer, bleak roe and cloudberries. Since Mathias Nordin became the new head chef, it can be difficult to get a table, so book ahead. Closed Sundays.

CENTRAL STOCKHOLM Operakällaren
ⓀⓀⓀⓀ
Operahuset, Karl XII's Torg, Stockholm, 111 86 **Tel** *08-676 58 01*　　**Map** *C3*

The capital's classic temple of gastronomy. The chefs are young and creative, the dining room with its lavish 19th-century ceiling paintings and the Jugendstil bar are attractions in themselves. Café Opera has lower prices and a famous afternoon cake buffet. One Michelin star.

SOUTHERN STOCKHOLM Pontus by the Sea
ⓀⓀ
Tullhus 2, Skeppsbron, Stockholm, 111 30 **Tel** *08-20 20 95*　　**Map** *C4*

Owned by one of Stockholm's star chefs Pontus Frithiof, this restaurant offers a reasonably priced, accessible menu including a large seafood platter and cold meat platter. The food is excellent. In summer diners can sit outside and watch the ships come into port. Closed Sundays.

EASTERN STOCKHOLM Teatergrillen
Ⓚ
Nybrogatan 3, Stockholm, 114 34 **Tel** *08-54 50 65*　　**Map** *C2*

One of Stockholm's oldest restaurants, Teatergrillen is beautifully old fashioned; for example, diners can order desserts from a silver trolley brought to the table, making a refreshing change from the many modern restaurants now in the city. A favorite among celebrities and media workers. Closed Sundays.

REST OF SWEDEN

GOTHENBURG 28+
ⓀⓀⓀⓀ
Götabergsgatan 28, 411 34 **Tel** *031-20 21 61*

Regarded by many as the best restaurant in Gothenburg, 28+ offers a luxurious menu created by Swedish master chef Ulf Johansson. The restaurant itself is located in a cellar, and the tiled floor and antique furniture can feel a little cold, but the food is the star here. Sample the pan-seared zander fillet with king crab and ravioli.

MALMÖ Salt & Brygga
ⓀⓀⓀ
Sundspromenaden 7, 211 18 **Tel** *040-611 59 40*

The row of award plaques outside the front door of this seaside restaurant pay testament to its food and service. A strong environmental philosophy runs through the entire business, with ingredients sourced locally and organic foods used whenever possible. A healthy and happy place to eat.

UPPSALA Wermlandskällaren
ⓀⓀⓀⓀ
Nedre Slottsgatan 2, 753 09 **Tel** *018-13 22 00*

Both set menus and à la carte meals have a modern Swedish-French twist. Inspiration drawn from the forest, sea, and meadows are the hallmarks of this traditional restaurant set in the cellars of a 13th-century building. Regarded as one of Uppsala's must-visit restaurants, it has exceptionally good standards of service.

Map References *see map of Stockholm pp642–3*

NORWAY

N orway's great attraction is the grandeur of its scenery. The landscape is one of dramatic contrasts: great mountain ranges, sheer river valleys, mighty glaciers, deep green forests, and the spectacular fjords that indent the western coast. In the far north, above the Arctic Circle, visitors can marvel at the Northern Lights and the long summer nights of the Land of the Midnight Sun.

The fjords that make the coastline of Norway one of the most jagged in the world were carved by glaciers during the last Ice Age. As the glaciers began to recede about 12,000 years ago, the sea level rose and seawater flooded back to fill the deep, eroded valleys. Norway's extraordinary geography has had a great influence on its people and development. In the past, scarcity of agricultural land led to economic dependence on the sea. In contrast, Norway today has abundant hydro-electric power as well as rich oil and gas deposits on its continental shelf.

The first settlers arrived 10,000 years ago as the Scandinavian icesheets retreated. They were hunters of reindeer, deer, bears, and fish. By the Bronze Age (1500–500 BC) rock carvings show that these early Norwegians had learnt to ski. Other inhabitants of the region were the Sami (formerly known as the Lapps), with origins in the northern regions of Russia, Finland, Sweden, and Norway, where they haved lived for thousands of years by fishing and herding reindeer. Some still follow the nomadic life of their forefathers but the majority now live and work in much the same way as Norwegians.

HISTORY

It is for the Viking Age (c.800–1050) that Norway is best known. As a result of overpopulation and clan warfare, the Norwegian Vikings traveled to find new lands. They mostly sailed west, their longships reaching the British Isles, Iceland, Greenland, and even America. The raiders soon became settlers and those who remained at home benefited both from the spoils of war and the fact that farmland was no longer in such short supply. The country was united by Harald the Fairhaired in the 9th century. This

The harbor at Bergen, the main center for tours of Norway's fjords

◁ Borgund stave church, one of the best-preserved of Norway's distinctive medieval churches

The Norwegian explorer, Roald Amundsen, checking his position after reaching the South Pole in 1911

great age of expansion, however, effectively ended in 1066, when King Harald Hardråde was defeated at the battle of Stamford Bridge in England.

The 11th and 12th centuries were marked by dynastic conflicts and the rising influence of the church. I n 1217 Haakon IV came to power, ushering in a "Golden Age," when Norway flourished under strong centralized government. In 1262 both Iceland and Greenland came under Norwegian rule. However, in the following century, after suffering terrible losses in the Black Death, Norway was reduced to being the least important of the Scandinavian countries. From 1380 to 1905 it was under the rule first of Denmark and then of Sweden.

The 19th century saw the growth of a national identity and a blossoming of Norwegian culture. Most of Norway's most famous individuals were born in this century, among them the composer Edvard Grieg, dramatist Henrik Ibsen, Expressionist painter Edvard Munch, and polar explorer Roald Amundsen.

Following independence from Sweden in 1905, the government set about industrializing the country, expanding the merchant fleet, and establishing healthcare and education as the cornerstones of a welfare state.

Norway pursued a policy of neutrality in World War I and World War II. The price was high in World War I, since German submarines attacked shipping indiscriminately and Norway lost half its chartered tonnage. In World War II Germany occupied the country, but encountered a massive resistance movement. Norway's part in the war helped it gain in status and it became one of the founding members of the UN in 1945 and entered NATO in 1949.

The biggest issue of the postwar years has been whether or not to join the EU. Twice Norway has refused, but the economy thrives regardless, thanks in large part to revenues from North Sea oil.

KEY DATES IN NORWEGIAN HISTORY

AD 800–1050 Viking Age

866 Vikings control most of England

900 Norway united under hereditary rule

1030 Christianity established

1217–63 Reign of Haakon IV

1380–1814 Norway in union with Denmark

1397 Kalmar Union unites crowns of Denmark, Sweden, and Norway

1660 Modern boundaries of Norway established, through peace of Copenhagen

1814 Union with Sweden, but Norwegian parliament, the Storting, has extensive powers

1887 Norwegian Labour party is founded

1905 Norway established as a separate kingdom

1940–45 German occupation of Norway during World War II

1969 Discovery of oil and gas in North Sea

1972 Following a referendum Norway declines membership of the EU

1994 Second referendum on membership of the EU; majority again votes "no"

LANGUAGE AND CULTURE

There are two official Norwegian languages: *Bokmål* (book language), a modernization of old Dano-Norwegian used in the days of Danish rule, and *Nynorsk*, based on rural dialects, which was codified in the 19th century as part of the resurgence of nationalism. Despite the government's efforts to preserve the use of *Nynorsk*, it is in decline. As in other parts of Scandinavia, you don't need to speak Norwegian to get by, since most people speak English.

Perhaps because independence was so long in coming, most Norwegians are great patriots. National Independence Day (May 17) is celebrated the length and breadth of the country, with festive gatherings even at remote farms. Norwegians also have a great attachment to outdoor pursuits – fishing, hiking, walking, and skiing – and many families have a *hytte* (cottage or cabin) in the mountains or on the coast.

Exploring Norway

Norway is so long and narrow that, if Oslo remained fixed and the rest were turned upside down, it would stretch all the way to Rome. There are two main areas of attraction: Oslo, a lively, open city, particularly in summer, and Bergen and the fjords in the west. Elsewhere, up to 95 percent of the country is forested or uncultivated. Transportation (which comprises trains, buses, and coastal ferries) is reliable, though services can be cut back severely in the winter months, especially in the north.

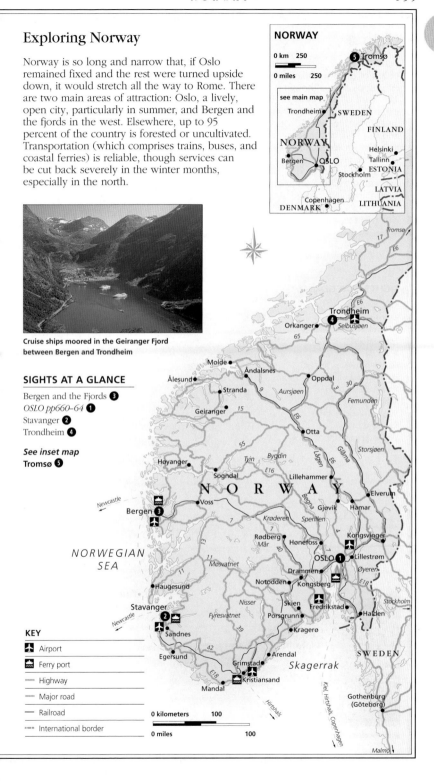

Cruise ships moored in the Geiranger Fjord between Bergen and Trondheim

SIGHTS AT A GLANCE

Bergen and the Fjords ❸
OSLO pp660–64 ❶
Stavanger ❷
Trondheim ❹

See inset map
Tromsø ❺

KEY

✈	Airport
⛴	Ferry port
—	Highway
—	Major road
—	Railroad
•••	International border

NORWAY

0 km 250
0 miles 250

see main map

Tromsø ❺

Trondheim   SWEDEN

FINLAND

NORWAY   Helsinki

Bergen   OSLO   Tallinn   ESTONIA
Stockholm
LATVIA
Copenhagen   LITHUANIA
DENMARK

Map labels:

Tromsø
17
E6

Trondheim
Orkanger   ❹ Selbusjøen
65

Molde
Ålesund   Åndalsnes   Oppdal
Stranda   Aursjøen   30
Geiranger   15   Femunden
E6
Otta
55   Bygdin   Storsjøen
Høyanger   Tyin   Lågen   E6
E16
Sogndal   Lillehammer
N O R W A Y   Elverum
Voss   Begna   Gjøvik   Hamar
Bergen ❸   Kröderen   Sperillen
7
Rødberg   Hønefoss   Kongsvinger
Mår   40
Møsvatnet   OSLO ❶   Lillestrøm
NORWEGIAN   Drammen   Øyeren
SEA   Notodden   Kongsberg   E18
Haugesund   Nisser   Skien   Fredrikstad   Stockholm
Stavanger   Fyresvatnet   Porsgrunn   Halden
❷   39   Kragerø
Sandnes   SWEDEN
42   Arendal
Egersund   Grimstad   Skagerrak
E18
Mandal   Kristiansand   Gothenburg (Göteborg)
Newcastle
Kiel, Hirtshals, Copenhagen
Hirtshals
Malmö

0 kilometers   100
0 miles   100

Oslo ❶

Founded around 1048 by Harald Hardråde, Oslo is the
oldest of the Scandinavian capital cities and occupies an
enormous area, although it has only 500,000 inhabitants.
The heart of the city is largely made up of late 19th- and
early 20th-century Neoclassical buildings, wide avenues,
and landscaped parks. Once the poor cousin to Stockholm
and Copenhagen in terms of nightlife and cultural
activities, in recent years Oslo has undergone a rebirth,
and there are now more restaurants and entertainment
venues than ever before. Most of the city's sights
are within walking distance of each other. The
Nordmarka area of forests to the north of the
center gives a glimpse of the beautiful
Norwegian countryside.

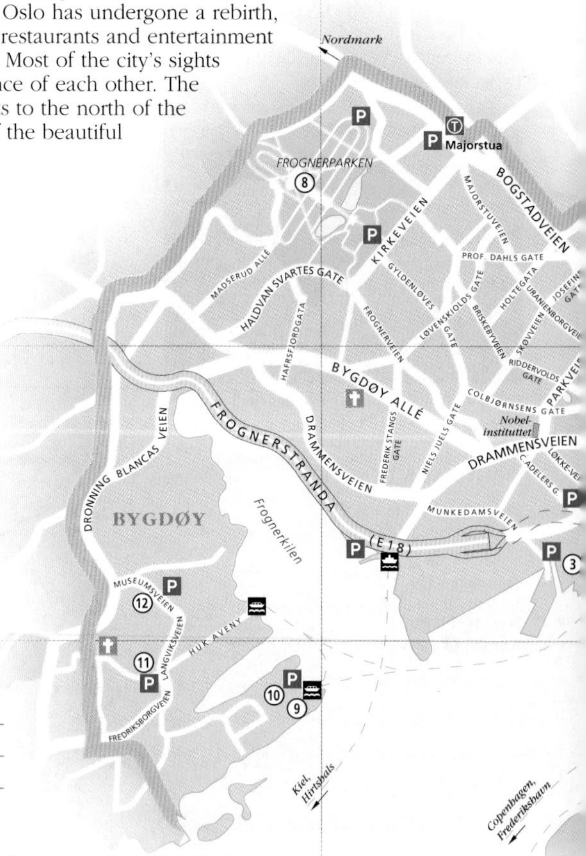

SIGHTS AT A GLANCE

Aker Brygge ③
Akershus Slott and
    Hjemmefrontmuseet ①
Frammuseet ⑨
Kongelige Slottet ④
Kon-Tiki Museum ⑩
Munch-museet ⑦
Nasjonalgalleriet ⑥
Nationaltheatret ⑤
Norsk Folkemuseum ⑫
Rådhus ②
Vigelandsparken ⑧
Vikingsskipshuset ⑪

SEE ALSO

• *Where to Stay* p670

• *Where to Eat* p671

Boats moored along the quayside, in front of the Akershus Slott

GETTING AROUND

Oslo has around 60 bus and tram
routes. Buses are faster than trams,
and most set out from the terminal
a few hundred meters northwest of
Oslo Sentralstasjon, the main train
station. Route 30 goes to the
museums on the Bygdøy Peninsula.
From late April to September you
can also reach the peninsula by
ferry from the boarding point by
the Rådhus. The Tunnelbanen is
most useful for reaching the city
suburbs, including Nordmarka.

Busy shopping street in Oslo's city center

KEY

▨ Sight / Place of interest		🚌 Bus station	
✈ Airport		P Parking	
⬇ Long-distance ferry		ℹ Tourist information	
⬇ Local ferry		✝ Church	
🚆 Train station		Pedestrian street	
Ⓣ T-bane station			

0 meters 750

0 yards 750

Akershus Slott and Hjemmefront-museet ①

Festningsplassen. 🚃 10, 12.
Akershus Slott Ⓣ Stortinget.
Tel 23 09 39 17. ⬤ May 2–Sep 15:
daily. ⬤ Sun am, public hols.
▨ 🖥 **Hjemmefrontmuseet**
Tel 23 09 32 80. ⬤ daily.
⬤ public hols. ▨ 🏛

Located on a knoll over-
looking the Oslofjorden, the
Akershus Slott (Akershus
Castle) is the city's most
notable memorial to medieval
times. Built around 1300, the
castle was besieged several
times before King Christian
IV of Denmark transformed
it into a lavish Renaissance
residence in the 1620s. He also
built a new fortress around the
castle. Known as the Akershus
Festning, it is still in use today.
Little remains of the castle's
former glory, most of the
rooms being relatively bare,
although the tapestries in the
Romerike Hall are impressive.
You can also visit the
royal chapel and the royal
mausoleum, where members
of the present Norwegian
dynasty lie buried.

The most somber period
in the Akershus Slott's history
was during World War II,
when the occupying Nazis
tortured and shot members
of the Norwegian resistance
here. Pictorial displays at the
Hjemmefrontmuseet
(Resistance Museum), located
by the gates of the castle,
provide a moving account
of the war in Norway, from
occupation through resistance
to liberation.

**Akershus Slott, Oslo's finest
surviving medieval monument**

Rådhus ②

Rådhuset i Oslo, Fridtjof Nansens Plass.
Tel 23 46 16 00. ⓣ Nationaltheatret,
Stortinget. ▦ 30, 31, 32, 45, 81, 83.
▦ 10, 12, 13, 15, 19. ◯ daily. ◉
public hols. ▨ (May–Sep). ⅋ ▯
www.oslokommune.no

Inaugurated in 1950 to
commemorate Oslo's 900th
year, the brown brick Rådhus
(City Hall) is the city's most
conspicuous landmark. The
building was a subject of con-
tention when it opened, with
many commenting that it
seemed un-Norwegian, but in
time the Rådhus has become a
popular symbol of civic pride.
Providing a complete contrast
to the exterior, the colorful
murals, sculptures, and frescoes
inside the building
celebrate Norwegian
artistic and intellectual
achievements, as
well as those in
exploration.
  The Rådhus is
famous as the place
where the Nobel
Peace Prize is
presented. This award
owes its inception,
ironically enough, to
a Swedish chemist,
Alfred Nobel, who
invented dynamite in
1867 and a smokeless
gunpowder in 1889.
He left his fortune in
trust for the endow-
ment of five Nobel prizes –
for physics, chemistry,
medicine, literature, and
peace. All the other prizes
are awarded at the Stadshuset
in Stockholm (see p644). Past
recipients of the prize have
included the Red Cross,
Martin Luther King, and
Mother Teresa.

**Viking warrior
detail from Rådhus
main doors**

Aker Brygge ③

Aker Brygge. ⓣ Nationaltheatret.
▦ 21. ▦ 10, 12.

This old shipyard is now a
glass-and-chrome leisure
complex, centered around an
open sculpture court, which
includes shops, restaurants,
bars, cinemas, and a theater.
It is one of the most popular
places in the city to go for a

beer and a meal, especially
during the long Scandinavian
summer evenings, when you
can sit outside and enjoy the
scenery of the Oslo Fjord.

Kongelige Slottet ④

Drammensveien 1. **Tel** 22 04 87 00.
ⓣ Nationaltheatret. ▦ 30, 31, 32,
34, 45, 81, 83. ▦ 11, 13, 17, 18,
19. ◯ end Jun–mid-Aug: 6am–9pm
daily. ▨ ▣ compulsory. ⅋ ▯

The Neoclassical Royal Palace
is a monument to openness,
standing as it does in the
freely accessible Palace
gardens (Slottsparken). Without gates or walls, the gardens
symbolize Norway's "open"
monarchy. The palace itself
was built in 1825–48 at
the request of King
Karl Johan. An
equestrian statue of
the king stands in
front of the building.
Every day at 1:30pm
the ceremony of the
changing of the
guard takes place.
Once a year during
Norway's National
Day on May 17, the
palace becomes the
focal point of cele-
brations when the
royal family stands
on the balcony to
greet the processions
of school children.

Oslo's Nationaltheatret, overlooking
its attractive, busy piazza

Nationaltheatret ⑤

Johanne Dybwads Plass 1. **Tel** 22 00
14 00. ⓣ Nationaltheatret. ▦ 30,
31, 32, 34, 45, 81, 83. ▦ 11, 13,
17, 18, 19. ◯ Aug–mid-Jun: daily.
▣ (call in advance). ▯▮ ▯

Built in 1899, Norway's
National Theater is Neo-
classical in style, and flanked
by imposing statues of the
nation's two greatest 19th-
century playwrights – Henrik
Johan Ibsen and Bjørnstjerne
Bjørnson, who is little known
outside Scandinavia these days,
but was a prolific writer of
plays and poetry during the
19th century. The theater has
four stages, and a varied
program, with all perfor-
mances given in Norwegian.
Visitors can make special
arrangements to have a
guided tour of the interior.

HENRIK JOHAN IBSEN (1828–1906)

Born in the southern town of Skien, the young Ibsen was
brought up in poverty, after his timber merchant father
suffered bankruptcy in 1836. Managing to escape, he lived first
in Kristiania and then Bergen, where he began writing and
producing his first dramas. In 1864 he left for
Germany and Italy, where he spent the
next 27 years. His most famous plays
include Peer Gynt (1867), A Doll's
House (1879), and Hedda Gabler
(1890). Regarded as one of the
founders of modern drama, Ibsen's
legacy to the European stage was
his introduction of themes such as
the alienation of the individual
from a morally bankrupt society,
loss of religious faith, and women's
desire to free themselves of their
roles as wives and mothers – a clear
departure from the unchallenging theater
of the time. After returning to
Norway, he died in 1906.

**Playwright Henrik
Johan Ibsen**

Simple, red brick façade of the Nasjonalgalleriet

Nasjonalgalleriet ⑥

Universitetsgaten 13. **Tel** 22 20 04 04. ⓣ Nationaltheatret. 🚌 30, 31, 32, 45, 81, 83. 🚊 13, 15, 19. ⬜ Tue–Sun. ● public hols. 🅿 ♿ **www**.nasjonalmuseet.no

Norway's biggest collection of art is housed in this grand 19th-century building. It includes an impressive collection of works by the country's most famous painter, Edvard Munch, from the 1880s to 1916. The main part of the collection is housed on the second floor. There is a strong international collection including Impressionist paintings by Manet, Monet,

Young Woman on the Shore (1896) by Edvard Munch, at the Munch-museet

and Degas, Post-Impressionist works by Gauguin and Cézanne, and early 20th-century paintings by Picasso and Braque. The museum also holds an important collection of Norwegian art. Among the paintings on display are some spectacular fjord and country scenes from the 19th-century National Romantic period by leading Norwegian landscape painters, notably Johan Christian Dahl. There are also works by Realist artists such as Harriet Becker, Christian Krohg, and Erik Werenskiold, as well as sculptures by Gustav Vigeland. The Munch room contains such important works as *The Sick Child* (1885) and *The Scream* (1893), the swirling forms and colours of which were to greatly inspire the growing Expressionist movement.

Munch-museet ⑦

Tøyengata 53. **Tel** 23 49 35 00. ⓣ Tøyen. 🚌 20, 60. ⬜ Jun–Aug: daily; Sep–May: Tue–Sun. ● Jan 1, May 1, May 12, Dec 24–25. ♿ 📷 🅿 🍴 **www**.munch.museum.no

One of Scandinavia's leading artists, Edvard Munch (1863–1944) left an amazing 1,100 paintings, 4,500 drawings, and 18,000 graphic works to the city of Oslo when he died. Most of these are housed at the Munch-museet, which opened in 1963.

Munch led a troubled life, plagued by melancholy and depression due, in part, to the untimely deaths of his favorite sister and younger brother. He nevertheless remained a highly prolific artist whose intensely psychological work remains one of the great corner-stones of early Expressionist art. Since the Munch-

museet is a fairly small museum, only a fraction of his work can be shown at any one time, which prevents it from being overwhelming and means that displays are frequently changed. The core of the collection is the series of outstanding paintings from the 1890s, although other periods of his life are well represented. Munch was also a prolific graphic artist, and the print room reveals his talents using etching, lithographic, and woodcut techniques. The basement houses a permanent display of Munch's life and times, and there is also a comprehensive library.

View back towards the city across Vigelandsparken sculpture park

Vigelandsparken ⑧

Kirkeveien. **Tel** 23 49 37 00. ⓣ Majorstuen. 🚌 20, 45. 🚊 12, 15. ⬜ daily. 🍴 ⬛

Vigelandsparken lies within the larger green expanse of Frognerparken. The park takes its name from the larger-than-life sculptures of Gustav Vigeland (1869–1943), which form extraordinary tableaux of fighting, play, and love. Work on display includes a series of 58 bronzes of men, women, and infants, flanking the footbridge over the river and leading up to his most famous creation, a 17-m (56-ft) granite obelisk of no fewer than 121 intertwined figures depicting the cycle of life. One of Oslo's most visited attractions, the park is a massive artistic creation that took Vigeland 40 years to complete. Some other examples of his work can be seen at Vigelandsmuseet near the park or at the Nasjonalgalleriet.

The Bygdøy Peninsula

No trip to Oslo is complete without a visit to the Bygdøy Peninsula, which lies off the western edge of the city. The area offers beaches, walking, numerous historic sites, and fascinating museums. These include a folk museum showing traditional ways of life, the Vikingsskipshuset, which traces Norway's maritime history, and others celebrating the famous Norwegian explorers Roald Amundsen and Thor Heyerdahl.

Frammuseet ⑨

Bygdøynesveien 36. **Tel** *23 28 29 50.*
🚌 *30.* 🚢 ☐ *daily.* ● *public hols.*
🌐 *www.fram.museum.no*

Designed in 1892 by Scottish-Norwegian shipbuilder Colin Archer, the *Fram* is best known as the ship that carried Norwegian explorer Roald Amundsen on his epic journey to the South Pole in 1911. The *Fram* was an ideal vessel for this undertaking. Its sides are perfectly smooth, making it impossible for ice to get a grip on the hull. Visitors can ease themselves between the remarkable array of beams in the ship's hull and marvel at the assortment of equipment – ranging from a piano to surgical instruments – that the crew managed to take with them. A series of fascinating displays around the ship relate the history of Arctic exploration.

Kon-Tiki Museum ⑩

Bygdøynesveien 36. **Tel** *23 08 67 67.*
🚌 *30.* 🚢 ☐ *daily.* ● *public hols.*
♿ 🌐 *www.kon-tiki.no*

On display at the superb Kon-Tiki Museum are the unbelievably fragile-looking vessels used by Thor Heyerdahl to make his legendary journeys across the Pacific and Atlantic Oceans. The aim of his voyages was to prove that transoceanic contact was possible between ancient civilisations. The balsawood *Kon-Tiki* raft carried Heyerdahl and a crew from Peru to Polynesia in 1947, confirming his theory that the first Poly-nesian settlers could have sailed from pre-Inca Peru. In 1970 he sailed a papyrus boat, *Ra II*, from Morocco to the

Thor Heyerdahl's vessel, *Ra II*, at the Kon-Tiki Museum

Caribbean to prove that the ancient peoples of Africa or Europe might have had contact with South America. These, and other eventful sagas, are outlined in the exhibition.

Vikingskipshuset ⑪

Huk Aveny 35. **Tel** *22 43 83 79.* 🚌 *30.*
🚢 ☐ *daily.* ● *public hols.* 🌐 ♿
www.khm.uio.no/info/vskip_huset

Norway is best known for its Viking explorers, and this museum contains three beautifully preserved 9th-

century longships. All three were unearthed from burial mounds in Norway, and funeral goods from each of the vessels are on display, including ceremonial sleighs, chests, and tapestries. Viewing platforms allow visitors to study the magnificent 22 m by 5 m (72 ft by 16 ft) Oseberg ship and the slightly larger Gokstad boat, both of which were discovered on the western side of the Oslofjord. Fragmented sections of a smaller boat, the Tune, remain much as they were when they were found on the eastern side of the fjord in 1867.

Norsk Folkemuseum ⑫

Museumsveien 10. **Tel** *22 12 37 00.*
🚌 *30.* 🚢 ☐ *daily.* ● *Jan 1,*
May 17, Dec 24, 25 & 31. 🌐 ♿
www.norskfolkemuseum.no

Established in 1894, this excellent attraction is devoted largely to Norwegian rural life, and visitors should set aside half a day to view the many (over 150) restored buildings. These include barns, storehouses, and a splendid stave church (c.1200) with typical steep, shingle-covered roofs and dramatic dragon finials. The indoor collections consist of displays of folk art, toys, folk dress, the playwright Ibsen's study, and a pharmacy museum. On Sundays in the summer there are displays of folk dancing, and guides demonstrate skills such as weaving tapestries or baking traditional flatbread.

A reassembled grass-roofed house at the Norsk Folkemuseum

For hotels and restaurants in this region see p670 and p671

The Vikings

From the 8th to the 11th century the Vikings, or Northmen, sailed from their overpopulated fjords in Scandinavia and made their way across Europe, plundering, looking for trade, and offering mercenary service. The Swedes (or Varangians) established themselves throughout the Baltic and controlled the overland route to the Black Sea, while the Danes invaded parts of England, Portugal, and France. The Norwegians, however, were unparalleled in their success, and their adventures became the stuff of Viking legend. After overrunning the Orkneys,

Gold and silver box brooch

the Shetlands, the Hebrides, and parts of Ireland, the Norwegians established colonies in the Faroes, Iceland, and Greenland. They even sailed to the coast of North America. The Vikings were undoubtedly the most feared Europeans of their day, and their impact on history was immense. Fear of the Viking raid unified many otherwise disparate tribes and kingdoms, and many new political states were created by the Vikings themselves. Despite profiting from the spoils of war, it was their success as settlers and traders that was the Vikings' greatest achievement.

Burial "ships" made of stone for warriors from poorer families, near Aalborg in Denmark

Viking religion *was dominated by the supreme gods Odin (god of war), Thor (thunder), and Frey (fertility). Valhalla was their equivalent of heaven. Warriors were buried with whatever it was thought the afterlife required, and the rich were entombed in ships, often with their servants. Most had converted to Christianity by the late 10th century, but Sweden remained pagan well into the 11th century.*

Frey, god of fertility

The longship *was the main vessel of the Viking raid. Longer, slimmer, and faster than the usual Viking ship, it had a large rectangular sail and between 24 and 50 oars. The sail was used in open sea and navigation was achieved by taking bearings from the stars.*

The prow, curled into a "shepherd's crook," formed a high defensive barrier.

The keel was characteristically shallow to allow for flat beach landings.

The beautifully restored Oseberg ship, unearthed in 1904, on display at the Vikingsskipshuset in Oslo

Weapons and armor *were the backbone of Viking culture, so the blacksmith's art was always in demand. Bronze and iron swords were endlessly produced, many of which followed their bearers to the grave. Arrows, axes, shields, helmets, and coats of mail were standard military gear, examples of which survive in pristine condition today.*

Gold armlet

Jewelry design *often showed Arab and eastern European influence, which illustrates the extent of the Viking trading network. Gold and silver were a sign of wealth and prestige, although many ornaments were made of bronze, pewter, colored glass, jet, and amber.*

Picture stones *were memorial blocks that celebrated the glory of dead relatives. They were carved with pictures and runic writing.*

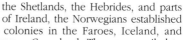

Viking helmet with noseguard

Picture stone from Gotland

View of the waterfront at Stavanger's attractive marina

Stavanger ❷

🏛 110,000. 🛬 🚢 🚉 🚌
ℹ️ Rosenkildetorget 1 (51 85 92 00).
🎭 Maijazz (May); Glamat Food Festival (Jul).

Stavanger is best known today as Norway's major oil town, with North Sea oil having provided its prosperity since the 1970s. Earlier in its history, in the mid-19th century, the town grew rich on herring exports.

Small enough to be seen on foot, much of the center of Stavanger is modern. One exception is the cathedral, the **Stavanger Domkirke**, which dates back to the 12th century but has been restored several times since. Later 17th-century additions include a flamboyant pulpit and a number of huge, richly carved memorial tablets hanging in the aisles.

Stavanger's main attraction is Gamle Stavanger (Old Stavanger), west of the harbor. Visitors can wander down the narrow cobblestone streets of this old city quarter, amid the whitepainted wooden houses, and imagine life here in the 19th century. An interesting museum in the town is the **Hermetikkmuseet** (Canning Museum) at No. 88 Øvre Strandgate, which tells the story of Stavanger's fisheries. Overlooking the harbor, the **Norsk Oljemuseum** (Norwegian Petroleum Museum) gives an insight into North Sea oil exploration.

Bergen and the Fjords ❸

🏛 235,000. 🛬 🚢 🚉 🚌 ℹ️
Vågsallmenningen 1 (55 55 20 00). 🎭
Bergen International Festival (May–Jun).

Surrounded by no fewer than seven mountains, Norway's most westerly port offers the visitor plenty to do and see, although it rains relentlessly here. Founded in the 12th century, Bergen is one of Norway's prettiest cities, with a medieval quarter dating back to the days when the port was an important center of European trade for the allpowerful German Hanseatic League. Many of the surviving Hanseatic buildings are found on the **Bryggen** (quay), where brightly-painted old wooden warehouses – now museums, shops, and restaurants – make up an attractive harborside.

Close by the harbor is the busy Fisketorvet (Fish Market) where fresh fish, produce, and local crafts can be found. Also nearby are the 11th-century **Mariakirken** (St. Mary's Church) and the **Hanseatiske Museum** – an excellently preserved late Hansa house from the 18th century.

Around Lille Lungegårdsvann, the city's central lake, are a number of interesting art galleries. Finally, no visitor to Bergen should miss the chance to take a trip up Mount Ulriken for a panoramic view of the area. A cable car takes you from the edge of the city to the summit.

Elaborate Baroque pulpit in the Mariakirken, Bergen

Environs

Just outside the city is **Troldhaugen**, an enchanting villa filled with paintings, prints, and other memorabilia, where Norway's most famous composer Edvard Grieg (1843–1907) spent the later years of his life and composed much of his work. A short way beyond is **Fantoft Stavkirke**, a traditional, ancient wooden church, originally built in Sognefjord, but moved here.

Bergen also makes a good base for viewing the western fjord scenery, which extends from south of Bergen to distant Kristiansund in the north. Boat trips leave from Bergen throughout the summer (a few run yearround), visiting local fjords. One of the closest is **Osterfjord**, but **Hardangerfjord**, with its majestic waterfalls, is perhaps the most spectacular. To the north,

The stunning scenery of the Sognefjord, north of Bergen

For hotels and restaurants in this region see p670 and p671

Sognefjord, at 206 km (128 miles) long and 1,308 m (4,291 ft) deep, is the deepest and longest fjord in the world.

� Troldhaugen
Troldhaugveien 65, Paradis.
Tel 55 92 29 92. ◯ *Apr–Nov: daily; mid-Jan–Mar: Mon–Fri.* 🈸 ⛧
🖼 🖳 🏠 www.troldhaugen.com

Trondheim ❹

🏯 *152,000.* ✈ 🚢 🚉 🚌
🛈 *Munkegaten 19 (73 80 76 60).*
🎭 *St. Olav Festival (Jul).*
www.trondheim.com

Called Nidaros (which means the mouth of the River Nid) until the 16th century, Trondheim has benefited from having a good harbor and being situated in a wide and fertile valley. Founded in AD 997, the city was for many centuries the political and religious capital of Norway, with the earliest Parliament (or *Ting*) being held here. This period saw the construction of Trondheim's most beautiful building – and one of Norway's architectural highlights – the **Nidaros Cathedral**, begun around 1077. Until the Reformation in the 16th century, the cathedral attracted pilgrims from all over Scandinavia. Notable features of this colossal building include the Gothic-style great arched nave and a magnificent stained-glass rose window above the entrance – the work of Gabriel Kjelland

Detail from the façade of Nidaros Cathedral, Trondheim

in 1930. Since 1988, the cathedral has been home to the Norwegian Crown jewels and the modest but beautiful regalia of the King, Queen, and Crown Prince, which are on display in a side chapel.

Another reminder of Trondheim's medieval past is provided by the wharves alongside the harbor and the narrow streets that wind between brightly painted warehouses. Although the buildings you see today only date back to the 18th century, the layout of the area is much as it was in earlier times when fishing and timber were the main source of the town's wealth.

Other attractions of the city include Scandinavia's largest wooden building, the **Stiftsgården**, built between 1774 and 1778 as a private home. Today it serves as the king's official residence in Trondheim. The **Nordenfjeldske Kunstindustrimuseum** (Decorative Arts Museum) houses an extensive collection of furniture, tapestries, ceramics, silver, and glassware from the 16th to the 20th century, including a fine collection of Art Nouveau pieces, plus contemporary arts, crafts, and design.

🏛 Nordenfjeldske Kunstindustrimuseum
Munkegaten 5. *Tel* 73 80 89 50.
◯ *Jun–Aug: daily; Sep–May: Tue–Sun.* ● *some public hols.* 🈸
🖼 🖿 ⛧

Tromsø ❺

🏯 *61,000.* ✈ 🚢 🚌
🛈 *Storgaten 61–63 (77 61 00 00).*
🎭 *Northern Lights Festival (Jan).*

Situated inside the Arctic circle, Tromsø, the so-called capital of North Norway, is a lively university town. There are not many specific sights and attractions in the town itself, but its fine mountain and fjord setting makes it well worth a visit. The most spectacular time to stay is in

Tromsø's modern concrete and glass Arctic Cathedral

the summer, during the period of the "midnight sun." Due to the high latitude, the sun remains above the horizon from May 21 to July 21, and the sky often glows red throughout the night. Tromsø is also a good place to view the Northern Lights.

Since Tromsø is a compact town, it is possible to stroll through the center, which sits upon a small hilly island reached by a bridge, in around 15 minutes. The major sight here is the striking white **Ishavskatedralen** (Arctic Cathedral). The cathedral is intended to represent the type of tent used by the Sami, the region's indigenous semi-nomadic people. Tromsø's **Polarmuseet** (Polar Museum) documents the history of the local economy – seal trapping played a big part until the 1950s – and polar expeditions, in particular the voyages undertaken by Norwegian explorer Roald Amundsen. Tromsø is a famous starting point for Arctic expeditions, and Amundsen made his last expedition from here to the Arctic ice cap, where he died in 1928. Visitors should not miss the opportunity to take the cable car (Fjellheisen) up the mountain behind the city to get a real sense of the setting of this polar town.

🏛 Polarmuseet
Søndre Tollbugata 11. *Tel* 77 68 43 73. ◯ *daily.* ● *public hols.*
🈸 🏠

Practical & Travel Information

Norway has a reputation as an expensive destination, but the cost of traveling around the country is fairly reasonable. Norway's public transportation system is comprehensive and reliable, although visitors should expect a reduced service during winter. Once within the Arctic Circle, there is a period around midsummer during which the sun never sets (the "midnight sun"). Conversely, there is a "polar night" around midwinter, during which the sun never rises at all. These effects occur for longer periods the farther north you travel.

TOURIST INFORMATION

Norway has around 350 local tourist offices, as well as almost 20 regional offices. Visitors to the capital can use **Oslo Promotion Tourist Information** in the center of town. For brochures and more general information on all parts of the country, contact the **Norwegian Tourist Board** before you leave home.

As well as providing information on hiking routes and guided mountain tours, **Den Norske Turistforening** (Norwegian Mountain Touring Association) sells maps and hiking gear, and maintains more than 300 mountain huts throughout the country.

OPENING HOURS

Many attractions are open all year round, although a few have seasonal opening hours. Stores are generally open from 9am to 5pm Monday to Friday, and from 9am to 1 or 3pm on Saturday. Many stores stay open until 7 or 8pm on Thursdays.

VISA REQUIREMENTS

Citizens of the EU, the US, Canada, Australia, and New Zealand do not require a visa for stays of less than three months. Citizens of most EU countries can use a national identity card instead of a passport for entry to Norway.

SAFETY AND EMERGENCIES

Norway is a safe country, and crime against tourists is relatively rare. Standards of healthcare are excellent. Hotels and tourist offices have lists of local doctors, or you can look in the telephone directory under doctors *(leger)*. You will have to pay a fee for a doctor's appointment and for prescriptions, but EU citizens with an E111 form will be reimbursed for part of the cost of any treatment.

BANKING AND CURRENCY

The Norwegian unit of currency is the Norwegian krone, abbreviated to NOK. Cash and traveler's checks can be changed at banks and post offices for a small commission. Outside banking hours, you can change money at hotels, some campsites, and (in Oslo) exchange booths, although exchange rates are less favorable. Major credit and charge cards are accepted in most places.

Banks are open from 8:15am to 4pm Monday to Wednesday and Friday, and 8:15am to 5pm on Thursday. Between June and August, they close 30 minutes earlier.

COMMUNICATIONS

Telecommunications and postal services in Norway are very efficient and reliable. Coin-operated phone booths are gradually being phased out in favor of those that will only take phonecards (Telekort). These cards can be purchased in news kiosks.

E-mail can be collected at the country's growing number of Internet cafés (all major cities have at least a couple) or at most public libraries.

Thanks to state subsidies and loans there is a large number of newspapers in Norway. Most British and some American newspapers are sold in large towns from Narvesen newsstands.

TAX-FREE SHOPPING

Visitors to Norway can benefit from the nation's decision not to join the EU by taking advantage of the tax-free shopping scheme. This means that if you purchase goods over a certain value from any one of the 3,000 outlets that participate in the scheme you can have the VAT refunded. You will receive a tax-free voucher, which you must present upon your departure from the country. The goods must be unused for you to receive the refund.

ARRIVING BY AIR

Most international flights arrive at Oslo's new airport, **Gardermoen**, 60 km (37 miles) north of the city, although some carriers also

THE CLIMATE OF NORWAY

The climate of Norway experiences intense seasonal changes. The short summer (roughly mid-June to mid-August) can be quite hot, though rain is regular and temperatures in the far north can plunge during the summer nights. Winter is long and dark, and the north is subject to sub-zero temperatures which can persist for months at a time.

OSLO

	Apr	Jul	Oct	Jan
°C/F high	9/48	21/70	9/48	0/32
°C/F mid		12/54		
°C/F low	1/34		3/37	-6/21
sun (hrs)	5 hrs	7 hrs	3 hrs	2 hrs
rain (mm)	48 mm	79 mm	99 mm	58 mm

0°C 32°F

fly to Stavanger, Bergen, Tromsø, and Kristiansand. From Britain, daily direct flights are operated by British Airways, **SAS** (Scandinavian Airline System), **Norwegian**, and Ryanair. SAS offers direct flights from other major European cities, such as Stockholm, Berlin, and Amsterdam.

Flying to Norway from North America may involve changing planes, although SAS offers a direct service from New York to Oslo.

Domestic flights can be useful if you are short on time – especially if you wish to visit the far north – and are operated by a variety of carriers, including SAS.

TRAVELING BY SEA

Ferries from Germany, Denmark, and Sweden make daily crossings to Norway. It is also possible to travel directly from Newcastle in the UK, but the journey can take as long as 27 hours. Routes are operated by **Fjord Line** and **DFDS Seaways**.

Once in Norway, you are never very far from the sea and local ferries are an invaluable means of transportation across the fjords.

Hurtigruten, the Norwegian Coastal Express service, sails from Bergen to Kirkenes, far above the Arctic Circle, putting in at 35 ports en route. It is a superb way to see Norway's dramatic coastline. Call ferry companies **OVDS** or **TFDS** to make a reservation.

RAIL TRAVEL

Many rail services link Norway with the rest of Scandinavia and mainland Europe. The major point of entry to Scandinavia from mainland Europe is Copenhagen, where trains cross the new Øresund Bridge before heading to Oslo. Within Norway, the **Norges Statsbaner** (Norwegian State Railroad) operates a more extensive network in the south than in the north, but there are routes to all the major towns.

A Norway rail pass allows unlimited travel on all trains in Norway for a specified number of days in a given period. The pass is available from rail ticket agents in Norway and abroad.

Oslo's Tunnelbanen (T-bane) consists of eight metro lines, which converge in the city center. The system runs from around 6am to 12:30am.

BUSES AND TAXIS

Buses cover the length and breadth of Norway, and are useful for getting to places the train network does not reach. Bus journeys are also reasonably priced. Most long-distance buses are operated by the national company, **NOR-WAY Bussekspress**.

Taxis are extremely expensive in the cities and towns, but in Oslo the excellent public transportation network generally means that you can avoid having to use taxis at all.

TRAVELING BY CAR

Car rental is fairly costly, although Norway's main roads are fast and extremely well maintained. All of the major international car rental companies are represented. EU driver's licenses are honored in Norway, but visitors from other countries will need an international driver's license. Road regulations are strictly enforced, particularly those relating to drunken driving.

Due to poor visibility and bad weather, many minor roads in Norway close during the dark winter months.

DIRECTORY

TOURIST INFORMATION

Den Norske Turistforening
Tel 22 82 28 00.
www. turistforeningen.no

Oslo Turistinformasjon
Rådhuset, Fridtjof Nansens Plass 5, 0160 Oslo.
Tel 81 53 05 55.
www.visitoslo.com

Norwegian Tourist Board
www.visitnorway.com
In Norway:
Innovasjon Norge,
Akersgate 13, Postboks
440 Sentrum, 0104 Oslo.
Tel 22 00 25 00.

In the UK:
5th Floor, Charles House,
5 Regent Street,
London SW1Y 4LR.
Tel 020-7839 2650.

In the US:
655 Third Avenue,
Suite 1810, New York 1.
Tel 212-885 9700.

EMBASSIES

Australian Consulate
Jernbane Torget 2, Oslo.
Tel 22 47 91 70.

Canada
Wergelandsveien 7, Oslo.
Tel 22 99 53 00.

UK
Thomas Heftyes Gate 8,
Oslo. *Tel 23 13 27 00.*

US
Drammensveien 18, Oslo.
Tel 22 44 85 50.

EMERGENCIES

Ambulance
Tel 113.

Fire
Tel 110.

Police
Tel 112.

AIR TRAVEL

Gardermoen Airport
Tel 815-502 50.

Norwegian
www.norwegian.no

SAS
Tel 815-20 400 (Norway).
Tel 0845-60 727 727 (UK).
Tel 800-221 2350 (US).
www.scandinavian.net

FERRY SERVICES

DFDS Seaways
Tel 22 41 90 90 (Norway).
Tel 08702 520 524 (UK).
www.dfds.co.uk

Fjord Line
Tel 55 54 87 00 (Norway).
Tel 0191-296 1313 (UK).
www.fjordline.co.uk

OVDS/TFDS
Tel 76 96 76 93 (OVDS).
Tel 77 64 82 00 (TFDS).

RAIL TRAVEL

Norges Statsbaner
Tel 81 50 08 88.

BUSES

NOR-WAY Bussekspress
Schweigaardsgata 8–10
(Visitor Centre), Oslo.
Tel 815-444 44.
www.nor-way.no

Where to Stay in Norway

Accommodations in Norway are not as expensive as might be expected for Scandinavia; almost all hotels offer weekend and summer discounts, which can reduce the cost considerably. Hotel breakfasts are huge, all-you-can-eat buffet affairs, and are normally included in the price. Guests can expect attentive service and spotless rooms.

PRICE CATEGORIES
Price categories for a standard double room (not per person) per night, including tax, service, and breakfast:

Ⓚ Under 1,000 NOK
ⓀⓀ 1,000–1,400 NOK
ⓀⓀⓀ 1,400–1,800 NOK
ⓀⓀⓀⓀ Over 1,800 NOK

OSLO

CENTRAL OSLO WEST Thon Hotel Gyldenløve
Bogstadveien 20, 0355 Oslo **Tel** *23-33 23 00* **Fax** *23-33 23 03* **Rooms** *164*   **Map** *C2*

The Gyldenløve is superbly located in Oslo's west quarter, on one of the city's best shopping avenues. It has recently undergone a major refurbishment program and now has a modern, stylish, Scandinavian feel. There is a reasonable menu at the hotel's Portofino Café and Wine Bar. **www.thonhotels.com/gyldenlove**

CENTRAL OSLO WEST Hotel Bristol
Kristian IV's gate 7, 0164 Oslo **Tel** *22-82 60 00* **Fax** *22-82 60 01* **Rooms** *251*   **Map** *D3*

The classy Bristol has been one of Oslo's top hotels since the 1920s and is a regular choice for visiting celebrities. Dripping in traditional elegance, the hotel's Library Bar and Wintergarden is a popular meeting point, and the Bristol Grill offers both international and Norwegian dishes. A luxurious stay is guaranteed. **www.bristol.no**

CENTRAL OSLO EAST Rica Oslo Hotel
Nr.1 Europarådets Plass, 0154 Oslo **Tel** *23-10 42 00* **Fax** *23-10 42 10* **Rooms** *175*

Leather furniture and marble floors decorate this hotel's lobby, while art and sculpture from prominent Norwegian artists further adds to the artistic atmosphere. Rooms are individually decorated with paintings. Buffet meals and an à la carte menu are served at the Bjorgvigen Mat & Vinhus restaurant. **www.rica-hotels.com**

CENTRAL OSLO EAST Grand Hotel
Karl Johans Gate 31, 0159 Oslo **Tel** *23-21 20 00* **Fax** *23-21 21 00* **Rooms** *290*   **Map** *D3*

The Grand Hotel first opened its doors in 1874. Built in Louis XVI revival style, it is now a deluxe hotel with a hint of Nordic Art Nouveau. It has been extended and modernized over the years, and today is a superb mix of tradition and modern comfort. The hotel has a great choice of bars and restaurants. **www.grand.no**

WEST OSLO Clarion Collection Hotel Gabelhus
Gabelsgate 16, 0272 Oslo **Tel** *23-27 65 00* **Fax** *23-27 65 60* **Rooms** *114*   **Map** *C3*

The ivy-covered Gabelshus is located in an exclusive residential area with beautiful townhouses, embassies, high-class restaurants and cafés all within walking distance. Thoroughly renovated in 2004, it is now a stylish and charming boutique hotel that combines modern Scandinavian design with traditional architectural features. **www.gabelshus.no**

REST OF NORWAY

BERGEN Clarion Hotel Admiral
C. Sundtsgate 9, 5004 Bergen **Tel** *55-23 64 00* **Fax** *55-23 64 64* **Rooms** *210*

Known as "the hotel with the sea on three sides," the top-class Clarion has stunning views of the wharf, the fish market and Mt. Fløien. Built at the turn of the century as a boat warehouse, it was turned into a waterside hotel in 1987. All 210 rooms have large windows, and 40 have harbor views. **www.admiral.no**

STAVANGER Radisson SAS Atlantic Hotel
Olav V's Gate 3, 4002 Stavanger **Tel** *51-76 10 00* **Fax** *51-76 10 01* **Rooms** *350*

Overlooking Lake Breiavatnet and next to the historic Old Stavanger area, this modern top-class hotel has 350 air-conditioned rooms spread over 13 floors. The hotel's Restaurant Ajax has a bright dining room serving breakfast, while the Antique Restaurant is a more formal eatery serving à la carte international cuisine. **www.radissonsas.com**

TRONDHEIM Britannia Hotel
Dronningensgate 5, 7011 Trondheim **Tel** *73-80 08 00* **Fax** *73-80 08 01* **Rooms** *247*

The Britannia, which opened in 1897, was Trondheim's first luxury hotel and has been synonymous with the highest standards of service, comfort, and cuisine ever since. Behind the elegant façade and stylish interior is a modern hotel offering the latest facilities, with four restaurants as well as a piano and cocktail bar. **www.britannia.no**

Key to Symbols *see back cover flap*

Where to Eat in Norway

Eating out, and food in general, is often expensive in Norway, especially when the price of alcohol is added to the bill. Lunchtimes are usually simple affairs, consisting of *smørbrød* (open sandwiches) and light pastries. A three-course evening meal in a Norwegian restaurant will often involve soup as a starter and fruits for dessert.

PRICE CATEGORIES
Price categories for a three-course meal for one person, including half a bottle of house wine, tax and service:

Ⓚ Under 400 NOK
ⓀⓀ 400–500 NOK
ⓀⓀⓀ 500–700 NOK
ⓀⓀⓀⓀ Over 700 NOK

OSLO

CENTRAL OSLO WEST Lofoten Fiskerestaurant 🦐🍴Ⓥ ⓀⓀⓀ
Stranden 75, 0250 Oslo **Tel** *22-83 08 08* **Map** *C3*

This fish and seafood restaurant located next to Oslo's quay is elegantly decorated in a maritime theme and offers some of the best views of the Oslo fjord. It serves high-quality dishes with a seasonal twist such as scallop, king crab, and calamari, accompanied by a herb salad, smoked bell-pepper aioli, and croutons.

CENTRAL OSLO WEST Theatercafeen Ⓥ ⓀⓀⓀ
Stortingsgata 24–26, 0161 Oslo **Tel** *22-82 40 50* **Map** *D3*

Theatercafeen has a lively atmosphere and attracts guests from all walks of life, ranging from the rich and famous to tourists. On *The New York Times*' Top Ten list of the world's most famous cafés, there's live piano and violin music in the evenings and during the day on Saturdays. The menu is international and reservations are recommended.

CENTRAL OSLO EAST Kaffistova 🧍Ⓥ Ⓚ
Rosenkrantz' Gate 8, 0159 Oslo **Tel** *23-21 42 10* **Map** *D3*

Part of the Hotel Bondeheimen and located a stone's throw from Karl Johans Gate, the Kaffistova offers a buffet with a comprehensive choice of traditional Norwegian dishes. A popular place for Norwegian specialties such as *raspeballer* (potato dumplings), *boknafisk* (dried and salted cod) and *rømmegrøt* (sour cream porridge).

CENTRAL OSLO EAST Det Gamle Raadhus Restaurant 🍴Ⓥ ⓀⓀⓀ
Nedre Slottsgate 1, 0157 Oslo **Tel** *22-42 01 07* **Map** *D3*

Steeped in tradition, this popular restaurant close to Akershus Festning is housed in one of Oslo's oldest buildings (which was the first City Hall) dating from 1641. Today it is well known for its fish and game dishes. Their *lutefisk* platter, served just before Christmas, is one of the house specialties. There's outdoor service in the summer.

CENTRAL OSLO EAST Statholdergaarden Ⓥ ⓀⓀⓀⓀ
Rådhusgaten 11, 0151 Oslo **Tel** *22-41 88 00* **Map** *D3*

Statholdergaarden is a Norwegian gourmet restaurant where culinary world champion Bent Stiansen is in charge of the kitchen. He creates a new six-course menu every day based on the freshest ingredients inspired by European food traditions. Statholderens Krostue is the more informal restaurant in the cellar serving open sandwiches at lunchtime.

REST OF NORWAY

BERGEN Fløien Folkerestaurant 🧍🍴Ⓥ ⓀⓀⓀ
Fløifjellet 2, 5014 Bergen **Tel** *55-32 18 75*

At the top of the famous Funicular in Bergen, high above sea level, you will find Fløien Folkerestaurant. Opened in 1925, it has been completely restored and, with its distinctive architecture, prominent location and breathtaking views, is a tourist attraction in itself. On the large outdoor terrace you can gaze over Bergen while enjoying your meal.

STAVANGER Straen Fiskerestaurant ⓀⓀⓀⓀ
Nedre Strandgate 15, 4005 Stavanger **Tel** *51-84 37 00*

Amusingly touted as being "world famous throughout Norway", this really is one of the best seafood restaurants in Stavanger. The old-fashioned interior is straight out of the 1950s and the windows open out to give fantastic views of the harbor. There is a nightclub upstairs and another restaurant downstairs that's served by the same kitchen.

TRONDHEIM Havfruen Fiskerestaurant ⓀⓀⓀ
Kjøpmannsgata 7, 7013 Trondheim **Tel** *73-87 40 70*

One of the foremost fish restaurants in Trondheim, Havfruen offers a distinctive atmosphere in an 18th-century wharf warehouse. The menu ranges from *bouillabaisse* to fish varieties from the Norwegian coastal waters, as well as meat dishes. Instead of a standard à la carte concept there's an eight-course menu that changes each month.

Map References *see map of Oslo pp660–1*

DENMARK

enmark is a peaceful and pleasant place. Its landscape is largely green, flat, and rural – with a host of half-timbered villages reminiscent of a Hans Christian Andersen fairy tale. It is an easy country to visit – not only do the majority of Danes speak English, but they are friendly and extremely hospitable. Above all, the pace of life is not as frenetic as in some European mainland countries.

Denmark consists of no fewer than 405 islands and the Jutland peninsula, which extends north from Germany. Located as it is between Scandinavia proper and mainland Europe, Denmark not surprisingly shares characteristics with both. It has the least dramatic countryside of the Scandinavian countries, yet there are also a number of important Viking sites dotted throughout the land. Zealand, the largest island, is the focal point for Denmark's 5.3 million inhabitants, a quarter of whom live in Copenhagen. Funen is a much more tranquil island, its sandy beaches popular with Danish youth. The Jutland peninsula has Denmark's most varied scenery, with marshland and desolate moors alternating with agricultural land.

HISTORY

Although nomadic hunters inhabited Jutland some 25,000 years ago, the first mention of the Danes as a distinct people is in the chronicles of Bishop Gregor of Tours from 590. Their strategic position in the north made them a central power in the Viking expansion that followed. Constant struggles for control of the North Sea with England and western Europe, for the Skagerrak – the straits between Denmark and Norway – with Norway and Sweden, and for the Baltic Sea with Germany, Poland, and Russia, ensued. But thanks to their fast ships and fearless warriors, by 1033 the Danes controlled much of England and Normandy, as well as most trading routes in the Baltic.

The next three hundred years were characterized by Denmark's attempts to maintain its power in the Baltic with the help of the German Hanseatic League. During the reign of Valdemar IV (1340–1375), Sweden, Norway, Iceland, Greenland, and the Faroe Isles came under Danish rule.

Ice skating in the Tivoli Gardens, Copenhagen

◁ Frederiksborg Slot, a grand Renaissance palace northwest of Copenhagen

Valdemar's daughter Margrethe presided over this first Scandinavian federation, known as the Kalmar Union.

The next period of Danish prosperity occurred in the 16th century, when Denmark profited from the Sound dues, a levy charged to ships traversing the Øresund, the narrow channel between Denmark and Sweden. Christian IV (reigned 1588–1648), the "builder king," instigated a huge program of construction that provided Denmark with a number of architectural masterpieces, such as the Rosenborg Palace in Copenhagen (see p681).

Christian IV of Denmark (1588–1648)

By the 18th century, Denmark had discovered lucrative trading opportunities in the Far East, and consolidated its position in the Baltic. However, an alliance with the French in the Napoleonic Wars (1803–15) led to the bombardment of Copenhagen by Britain's Admiral Nelson, and King Frederik VI was forced to hand over Norway to Sweden in 1814.

The remainder of the 19th century witnessed the rise of the social democrats and the trade unions. The year 1901 saw the beginnings of parliamentary democracy and a number of social reforms, including income tax on a sliding scale and free schooling.

Denmark was neutral during both world wars, but during World War II the country was occupied by the Nazis, a move that heralded the development of a huge resistance movement. Social reforms continued after the war, and in the 1960s laws were passed allowing abortion on demand and the abolition of all forms of censorship. In 1972, Denmark became the first Scandinavian country to join the European Community, and has developed a reputation for addressing environmental issues and supporting the economies of developing nations.

As the 21st century begins, Danish citizens have a high standard of living and state-funded education and health systems, although this has been achieved through high tax bills. Nevertheless, Denmark remains less expensive than either Norway or Sweden.

KEY DATES IN DANISH HISTORY

AD 590 First written account of the Danes in the chronicle of Bishop Gregor of Tours

960 Denmark becomes officially Christian with the baptism of King Harald "Bluetooth"

1033 Danes control much of England and Normandy and dominate trade in the Baltic

1282 Erik V forced to grant nobles a charter limiting his powers – first Danish constitution

1397 Queen Margrethe I unites Scandinavia under the Danish throne in the Kalmar Union

1814 Norway transferred from the Danish to the Swedish crown

1849 Under Frederik VII, Denmark becomes a constitutional monarchy

1890s Social reforms lay the foundations of the present welfare state

1914–18 Denmark neutral in World War I

1940–45 Despite declaring its neutrality, Denmark invaded and occupied by the Nazis

1945 Becomes a charter member of the United Nations and signs the North Atlantic Treaty

1972 Denmark joins the EC (now the EU)

2000 Danes reject euro as their currency

2002 EU presidency held by Denmark

LANGUAGE AND CULTURE

A North Germanic language, Danish is similar to Norwegian and Swedish, but there are some significant differences in word meaning ("frokost" for example, means "lunch" in Danish, but "breakfast" in Norwegian) and pronunciation. English and German are widely spoken, so visitors should have few problems in making themselves understood.

For such a small country Denmark has produced a number of world-famous writers and philosophers, including Hans Christian Andersen (see p683) and the 19th-century philosopher Søren Kierkegaard, who is claimed to have laid the foundations of modern existentialism. However, it is best known for its 20th-century design and craftsmanship, which have given the country an international reputation. The works of companies such as Georg Jensen silversmiths and Royal Copenhagen porcelain, and the furniture of architect Arne Jacobsen, enjoy a worldwide reputation.

Exploring Denmark

Copenhagen is Denmark's main attraction, a small
yet lively capital with a considerable number of
sights concentrated in the center. Outside the
capital, the pace of life is slow, and the flat
countryside is punctuated by half-timbered
villages and the occasional manor house. Roads
are of a high standard, and the trains and buses
extremely punctual and efficient. Denmark's lack
of hills makes it an excellent place for cycling.

**Tranquil park at Odense, the principal
town of the fertile island of Funen**

SIGHTS AT A GLANCE

Aalborg **7**
Århus **6**
COPENHAGEN pp676–81 **1**
Frederiksborg Slot **3**
Helsingør **2**
Legoland **8**
Odense **5**
Roskilde **4**

KEY

✈	Airport
⛴	Ferry port
—	Highway
—	Major road
—	Railroad
-∙-∙-	International border

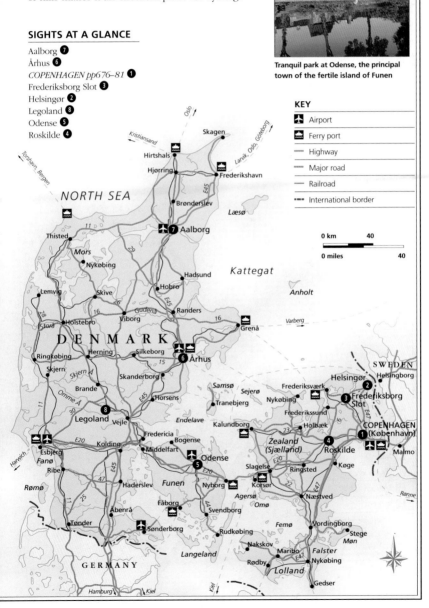

0 km   40
0 miles   40

Copenhagen ●

Copenhagen is Denmark's largest city, with a
population of around 1.4 million. Founded in 1167
by Bishop Absalon, who built a fortress on
the island of Slotsholmen, the town grew quickly,
prospering from trade in the Baltic. In 1461 it was
declared the capital of Denmark. During the reign
of Christian IV (1588–1648), the city was endowed
with many fine Renaissance buildings, some of
which still stand today, including the splendid
Rosenborg Slot and the Børsen. As a change from
sightseeing, visitors can head for the lively,
cosmopolitan shopping area of Strøget, Europe's
longest pedestrian street, or simply relax in one of
the many restaurants and cafés of bustling Nyhavn,
with its charming, gabled townhouses.

**Cannon in the grounds of the city's
16th-century fortress, the Kastellet**

SIGHTS AT A GLANCE

Amalienborg ⑨
Børsen ⑥
Christiania ⑭
Christiansborg Palace ⑤
Kastellet and
 Frihedsmuseet ⑪
Little Mermaid ⑩
National Museum ④
Ny Carlsberg Glyptotek ②
Nyhavn ⑧
Rådhuset ③
Rosenborg Slot ⑬
Statens Museum for Kunst ⑫
Strøget ⑦
Tivoli Gardens ①

SEE ALSO

- **Where to Stay** p686
- **Where to Eat** p687

KEY

▨	Sight / Place of interest
⛴	Ferry boarding point
🚉	Train station
🚌	Bus station
Ⓜ	Metro station
Ⓟ	Parking
ℹ	Tourist information
✝	Church
✡	Synagogue
—	Pedestrian street

A   B   C

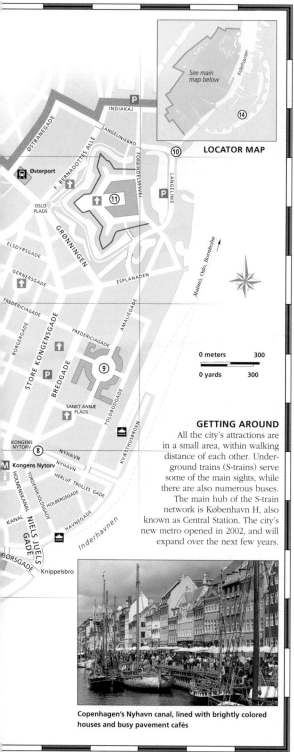

LOCATOR MAP

GETTING AROUND

All the city's attractions are in a small area, within walking distance of each other. Underground trains (S-trains) serve some of the main sights, while there are also numerous buses.

The main hub of the S-train network is København H, also known as Central Station. The city's new metro opened in 2002, and will expand over the next few years.

Copenhagen's Nyhavn canal, lined with brightly colored houses and busy pavement cafés

The Nimb building, with its domes and minarets, at Tivoli Gardens

Tivoli Gardens ①

Vesterbrogade 3. **Tel** 33 15 10 01. 🚉 København H. 🚌 1A, 2A, 10, 15, 30, 33, 40, 47, 66, 67, 68, 2505. ◯ mid-Apr–Sep, mid Oct (Halloween), & mid-Nov–late Dec: daily.

One of Copenhagen's most famous tourist attractions, the Tivoli Gardens opened in 1843. This highly popular entertainment park combines all the fun of fairground rides with fountains and fireworks, concerts and ballets, top-quality restaurants and fast-food outlets. Based on the 18th-century ornamental gardens popular in Europe at the time, Tivoli features Chinese-style pagodas and Moorish pavilions, as well as modern additions, such as the Hanging Gardens and the Bubble Fountain.

Among the many fairground rides are a traditional roller coaster, a ferris wheel, and a "freefall" tower, as well as rides designed for children. There are also amusement arcades and shooting galleries.

The gardens are at their most enthralling after dusk, when thousands of tiny lights illuminate the park. At night, open-air theaters host all forms of entertainment, from jugglers to jazz bands and performances of Italian *Commedia dell'Arte*. On Wednesdays and Saturdays there is a spectacular fireworks display just before midnight.

A good time to visit Tivoli is between late November and Christmas. At this time, the gardens are transformed into a bustling Christmas fair, where you can sample traditional Danish seasonal fare, buy many specialty Christmas gifts, and ice-skate on Tivoli Lake.

The richly decorated Neoclassical façade of Ny Carlsberg Glyptotek art gallery

Ny Carlsberg Glyptotek ②

Dantes Plads 7. **Tel** 33 41 81 41. 🚇 København H. 🚌 1A, 2A, 15, 33, 65E. 🕐 Tue–Sun. 🌑 Jan 1, Jun 5, Dec 24, 25. 🎟 except Sun. &
🏠 www.glyptoteket.dk

Copenhagen's most elegant art gallery was opened in 1897 by Carl Jacobsen, son of the founder of the Carlsberg Brewery, to give more people the chance to see classical art. Housed in a magnificent Neoclassical building, the Glyptotek is best-known for its exquisite antiquities, in particular a collection of Etruscan art and what is claimed to be Europe's finest collection of Roman portraits.

The main building's collections are completed with Egyptian, Greek, Roman, and French sculpture and works from the "Golden Age" of Danish painting (1800–1850). A modern wing, designed by acclaimed Danish architect Henning Larsen, contains Impressionist paintings by Monet, Sisley, Pissarro, and works by David and Bonnard.

Rådhuset ③

Rådhuspladsen. **Tel** 33 66 25 83. 🚇 København H. 🚌 10, 12, 14, 26, 29, 33 & many others. 🌑 Sun, public hols. 🎟 in English with 🎧 3pm Mon–Fri, 10am & 11am Sat. &
🏠 www.kk.dk

At the edge of the Indre By (city center), in the middle of a wide open square, is the Baroque-style Rådhuset or City Hall, built in the early 1900s. A statue of Copenhagen's 11th-century founder, Bishop Absalon, sits above the entrance. A 300-step staircase leads to the top of the bell tower for a view of the city. The tower also houses the first World Clock. This super-accurate timepiece, with a 570,000-year calendar, was designed by Jens Olsen and took 27 years to complete. The clock was started in 1955.

The modern, central atrium of Denmark's National Museum

National Museum ④

Ny Vestergade 10. **Tel** 33 13 44 11. 🚇 København H. 🚌 1A, 2A, 6A, 12, 15, 26, 29, 33. 🕐 10am–5pm Tue–Sun. 🌑 Dec 24–25 & 31. & 🎧 🍴 www.natmus.dk

Like so many of Denmark's museums, the National Museum contains beautifully presented exhibits. The extensive ethnographic and antiquities collections detail Danish history from prehistoric to modern times, and include some fascinating exhibits of Viking life.

Many of the items on display come from the Danish isles, such as items of jewelry, bones, and even several bodies found preserved in peat bogs, as well as imposing rune stones with inscriptions dating from around AD 1000. There is also a children's museum and a host of educational activities, all housed in the restored 18th-century royal residence. Close by, and part of the museum, is a Danish home with authentic interiors from the 1890s, complete with decorated panels and carvings, a profusion of paintings, and elaborately carved furniture.

Christiansborg Palace ⑤

Slotsholmen. **Tel** 33 92 64 92. 🚌 1A, 2A, 15, 26, 29, 6505. 🕐 May–Sep: daily; Oct–Apr: Tue–Thu, Sat, Sun. 🎟 🎧 🏠 www.slotte.dk **Teater-museet:** Christiansborg Ridebane 18. **Tel** 33 11 51 76. 🕐 Wed, Sat, Sun. 🌑 Dec 23–Jan 1. 🎟 **Thorvaldsen's Museum:** Bertil Thorvaldsens Plads 2. **Tel** 33 32 15 32. 🕐 Tue–Sun. 🎟 🎧

Situated on the island of Slotsholmen, the **Christians-borg Palace** has been the seat of the Danish Parliament since 1918, and also houses the Royal Reception Rooms, the Queen's Library, the Supreme Court, and the Prime Minister's Office. Built on the site of a fortress constructed in 1167 by Copenhagen's founder, Bishop Absalon, the palace has twice burnt down and been rebuilt, then altered and extended. Much of this work was carried out during the 18th century under Christian VI, whose elaborate visions were realized both in the architecture and in the lavish interiors. The current palace dates mostly from the early 20th century, and it is possible to visit the Royal Reception Rooms, the Harness Room, the Stables and Coach House, and some ruins from the original fortress.

Above the riding stables is the Royal Court Theater, built by Christian VI in 1767. Now a museum, much of it has been restored to its original 18th-century appearance. Exhibits illustrate the history of Danish theater up to the present day. The auditorium, with its plush, red furnishings and small, gold side boxes, houses a wealth of memorabilia – including costumes, old theater programs, wigs, and even old make-up boxes and a reconstructed dressing room. The whole theater is dominated, however, by the grand royal box, built for King Frederik VII in 1852. Situated at the back of the auditorium, it seems almost to upstage the stage itself. Unusually, the king's wife, the former ballet dancer Louise Rasmussen, had a private box to the right of the royal box, where she sat if she was alone.

Along the north side of the palace, the **Thorvaldsen's Museum** houses the work of the country's most celebrated sculptor, Bertel Thorvaldsen (1770–1844). After completing his education in Denmark, Thorvaldsen lived for nearly 40 years in Rome, where he gained a worldwide reputation. As well as his own impressive Neoclassical sculptures, the museum houses his collection of antiquities and 19th-century Danish art. There is also a detailed account of his life.

The Børsen, Copenhagen's beautiful old stock exchange

Børsen ⑥

Børsgade. 🚌 2A, 19, 66.
🚫 to public.

Built in 1619–40 by King Christian IV, Denmark's old stock exchange is an architectural masterpiece. The building combines tiny windows, steep roofs, and decorative gables, and is topped by a spire representing four intertwined dragon's tails. Originally a marketplace, it became a commodities and stock exchange in the 19th century. Today the building is used only for special occasions, since the main stock exchange has long since moved to the Strøget. It is not open to the public.

Strøget ⑦

Frederiksberggade to Østergade. 🚇
København H, Nørreport. 🚌 1A, 2A, 5A, 6A, 10, 12, 14, 15 & many others.

Running between Rådhuspladsen (town hall square) and Kongens Nytorv (marketplace), Strøget (pronounced "Stroyet") is the world's longest pedestrian street. Located at the center of a large traffic-free zone in the heart of the city, Strøget consists of five streets – Frederiksberggade, Nygade, Vimmelskaftet, Amagertorv, and Østergade. The area is home to several exclusive stores, including top international designers Hermes, Gucci, and Chanel. Other stores sell the best in Danish porcelain, modern design, glass, and furnishings – all areas in which Denmark has a world-class reputation.

The best selection can be found in the Royal Copenhagen shopping mall, facing Amagertorv, which includes Royal Copenhagen, Georg Jensen, and Illums Bolighus. There are also many bustling cafés and restaurants, street performers, and musicians, making it a lively place for walking or for relaxing with a coffee. The area is extremely popular with locals and visitors, particularly on a Saturday, but it is still possible to enjoy the atmosphere and admire the many surviving 18th-century buildings.

The impressive Christiansborg Palace, once a seat of royalty and now home to the Danish Parliament

Nyhavn ⑧

Kongens Nytorv. 🚌 1A, 15, 19, 26, 29, 3505. 🚢 901, 902.

A narrow canal flanked by a wide promenade, Nyhavn (New Harbor) was originally built 300 years ago to attract trade. It leads up to the Kongens Nytorv (New Royal Market). For much of its history the district was far from inviting, being mainly frequented by sailors, but after the 1970s the area was transformed. The harbor is lined either side with brightly painted town houses, a number of which date from the 18th century. Author Hans Christian Andersen lived in three of them (numbers 18, 20, and 67). Shops, restaurants, and bars have replaced all but one or two of the tattoo parlors that used to be here.

The attractive buildings, as well as the dozens of old wooden sailing ships moored on the water, make Nyhavn a lively and picturesque place to spend an hour or two enjoying a meal or a beer. It is also a good starting point for seeing the city, as some pleasure-boat tours of Copenhagen's canals leave from here.

Nyhavn, Copenhagen's picturesque and popular harborside promenade

Changing of Queen Margrethe's guard, Amalienborg

Amalienborg ⑨

Amaliegade. **Tel** 33 92 64 51. 🚇 Østerport. 🚌 1A, 15, 19, 26, 29, 650S, 901, 902. ◯ May–Oct: daily. 🏛 for museum. 🎫 call in advance. 🛡 **Changing of the guard:** noon daily. **www**.slotte.dk

The Amalienborg (Amalia's Castle) consists of four identical Rococo buildings arranged symmetrically around a large cobbled square with an imposing equestrian statue of Frederik V in the middle. The buildings have housed the Danish royal family since 1784; two of them still serve as royal residences. Changing of the guard takes place every day at noon outside the palace of the present queen, Margrethe II. The palace directly opposite is now a museum and is home to part of the Royal Collection, the bulk of which is housed at the Rosenborg Slot. Some of the official and private rooms have been opened to the public, the latest of which to be shown is the study of Frederik IX. However the highlights are undoubtedly the study of King Christian IX (1818–1906) and the drawing room of his wife, Queen Louise, which are filled with family presents, photographs, and the occasional Fabergé treasure.

There are two attractive, but completely contrasting views from the square. On the harborside is Amaliehaven (Amalia's Garden), with lush greenery and a fountain; in the opposite direction lies the Marmorkirken, a white marble church officially known as Frederikskirken, which has one of Europe's largest domes, inspired by St. Peter's in Rome. Its construction was begun in 1749 with expensive Norwegian marble, but was not completed until 150 years later (with less expensive Danish limestone) owing to the huge costs incurred. Inside, the church is decorated with many frescoes and statues.

Little Mermaid ⑩

Langelinie. 🚇 Østerport. 🚌 1A, 15, 19, then a short walk. 🚢 901, 902.

The subject of many Danish postcards, the Little Mermaid (Den Lille Havfrue) has become the emblem of Copenhagen and is much visited by tourists. Sitting on a stone by the promenade at Langelinie, and looking out over the Øresund, she is difficult to spot from the road and smaller than her pictures would have you believe. Sculpted by Edvard Erichsen and first unveiled in 1913, this bronze statue was inspired by the Hans Christian Andersen character, who left the sea after falling in love with a prince. The mermaid has suffered over the years at the hands of mischievous pranksters, even losing her head and an arm. Happily, she is currently in possession of all her "parts."

Copenhagen's famous Little Mermaid

Kastellet and Frihedsmuseet ⑪

Churchillparken. **Tel** *33 13 77 14.*
🚇 *Østerport.* 🚌 *1A, 15, 19, 26.*
🚢 *901, 902.* **Kastellet** ◯ *daily.*
Frihedsmuseet ◯ *Tue–Sun.*
📷 ♿

The grassy grounds of this fortress, built by Christian IV in the 16th century (and added to by his successors), are good for strolling around or sitting quietly by the moat. Currently occupied by the Danish army, its buildings are closed to the public, but near the south entrance is the Danish Resistance Movement Museum (Frihedsmuseet). This charts the German occupation of Denmark in World War II and the growth of the organization that saved more than 7,000 Jews from the Nazis by hiding them in "safe houses" and helping them escape to neutral Sweden.

Statens Museum for Kunst ⑫

Sølvgade 48–50. **Tel** *33 74 84 94.*
🚇 *Nørreport, Østerport.* 🚌 *6A, 14, 184, 185.* ◯ *Tue–Sun.* 📷 ♿ 🖥

The extensive Statens Museum for Kunst (State Art Museum) holds Danish and European art from the 14th century to the present day. Among its many paintings and sculptures are works by Titian, Rubens, Rembrandt, El Greco, Picasso, and Matisse. Danish artists are particularly well represented in the new modern art wing. There is also a vast collection of prints and drawings.

The enchanting Rosenborg Slot, set within magnificent parkland

Rosenborg Slot ⑬

Østervoldgade 4A. **Tel** *33 15 32 86.*
🚇 *Nørreport.* 🚌 *6A, 26, 3505.* ◯
May–Oct: daily; Nov–Apr: Tue–Sun.
⚫ *Jan 1, end Dec.* 📷 📷 🖥 📷
www.rosenborgcastle.dk

Originally built by Christian IV as a summer residence in 1606–7, the Rosenborg Slot was inspired by the Renaissance architecture of the Netherlands. The "builder king" continued to add to it over the next 30 years until the castle looked much as it does today – a playful version of a fortress. The interiors are particularly well preserved and its sumptuous chambers, halls, and ballrooms are full of objects including amber chandeliers, life-size silver lions, tapestries, thrones, portraits, and gilded chairs.

Two of the 24 rooms open to the public are stacked from floor to ceiling with porcelain and glass. The Porcelain Cabinet includes examples from the famous *Flora Danica* dinner service made for 100 guests, created by the Royal Copenhagen Porcelain factory between 1790 and 1803. The colorful Glass Cabinet houses nearly 1,000 examples of old Venetian glass as well as glass from the Netherlands, Bohemia, England, and most of the German glassworks.

Christiania ⑭

Bådsmandsstræde 43. **Tel** *32 95 65 07.* 🚇 *Christianshavn.* 🚌 *66, 2A, 19, 47, 350S.* ◯ *daily.* 📷 *for prebooked groups only.*
www.christiania.org

Originally set up in 1971, this "free town" is an enclave of an alternative lifestyle: colorful, anarchic, community-based, self-governing, and with an active drug scene. With around 1,000 permanent inhabitants, it has also become Denmark's third largest tourist attraction. Shops, galleries, workshops, cafes, bakeries, and music venues cater for the 500,000 visitors a year.

Modern art wing of the Statens Museum for Kunst

Helsingør ❷

Zealand. 🏃 61,300. ⊠ 🚃 ⛴
🛈 *Havnepladsen 3 (49 21 13 33).*
www.visithelsingor.dk

Helsingør, or Elsinore, lies
at the narrowest point of the
Øresund, the waterway
dividing Denmark and Sweden.
Its attractive medieval quarter
has many well-preserved merchants' and ferrymen's houses.

The town is dominated by
the **Kronborg Slot** (Kronborg
Castle), which stands on a spit
of land overlooking the sea.
Famous as the setting of
Hamlet, the fortress actually
dates from the 1500s, much
later than Shakespeare's
character would have lived.
Highlights include the 62-m
(210-ft) banqueting hall. A
statue of the Viking chief
Holger Danske slumbers in
the castle cellars – according
to legend he will awaken to
defend Denmark if needed.

The spires and turrets of the Kronborg Slot, Helsingør

⚓ **Kronborg Slot**
Kronborg. *Tel 42 21 30 78.* 🚃 340,
347, 801, 802, 803. ⬜ *May–Sep:*
daily; Oct–Apr: Tue–Sun. 📷 🎦 🍴

Frederiksborg Slot ❸

Hillerød, Zealand. *Tel 42 26 04 39.*
🚊 *to Hillerød, then bus 701 or 702.*
⬜ *daily.* 📷 ♿ 🖥 🛍
www.frederiksborgslot.dk

One of Scandinavia's most
magnificent royal castles,
the Frederiksborg Slot is built
across three small islands

surrounded by an artificial
lake. Created as a residence
for Frederik II (1559–88), the
castle was rebuilt in the Dutch
Renaissance style by his son,
Christian IV (1588–1648).

The vaulted black marble
chapel, where monarchs were
once crowned, sits directly
below the Great Hall, with its
fine tapestries, paintings, and
reliefs. The castle also houses
the National History Museum.

Roskilde ❹

Zealand. 🏃 52,000. 🚊 🚃
🛈 *Gullandstræde 15 (46 31 65 65).*
www.visitroskilde.com

The settlement of Roskilde
first came to prominence in
AD 980, when a Viking king,
Harald Bluetooth, built
Zealand's first Christian
church here. Once the center
of Danish Catholicism, the
town declined after the
Reformation. Today Roskilde
is a quiet town, although it
also hosts northern Europe's
largest annual music festival.

View from the outer courtyard of the Frederiksborg Slot

For hotels and restaurants in this region see p686 and p687

The **Roskilde Domkirke** stands
on the site of Harald
Bluetooth's original church.
Begun by Bishop Absalon in
1170, the building is now a
mix of architectural styles.
The cathedral also functions
as Denmark's royal mausoleum
– some 39 Danish kings and
queens are buried here.

Overlooking Roskilde Fjord
is the **Vikingeskibsmuseet**. This
Viking ship museum contains
five reconstructed Viking
ships, first built around AD
1000, excavated from the
bottom of the fjord in 1962. In
the waterside workshops
Viking ship replicas are built
using authentic period tools
and traditional techniques.

🏛 **Vikingeskibsmuseet**
Strandengen. *Tel 46 30 02 00.* ⬜
daily. ⬛ *Dec 24–25 & 31.* 📷 🎦 *in*
summer. ♿ *call in advance.* 🖥 🛍

Odense ❺

Funen. 🏃 182,000. 🚊 🚃
🛈 *Rådhus, Vestergade (66 12 75*
20). **www**.visitodense.com

Looking like a storybook
village, Odense is never-
theless Denmark's third-largest
urban center. It lies at the
heart of an area dubbed the
"Garden of Denmark" for the
variety of fruits and vegetables
produced here. The town is
most famous as the birthplace
of Hans Christian Andersen.

Odense is easily explored on
foot. The old town contains
some fine museums, including
three art museums, one of
which is dedicated to photography. Odense's showpiece is
the **Hans Christian Andersen Hus,**
where the storyteller's life is
detailed through drawings,

photographs, letters, and personal belongings. A library contains his works in more than 90 languages. The **H.C. Andersens Barndomshjem** (H.C. Andersen's Childhood Home) shows where the writer lived with his parents in a room measuring barely 2 m (6 ft) by 1.5 m (5 ft).

Ⅲ Hans Christian Andersen Hus
Munkemollestræde 3–5. **Tel** 65 51 46 01. ◯ mid-Jun–Aug: daily; Sep–mid-Jun: Tue–Sun. 🎫 ✆ by prior arrangement only. **www**.odmus.dk

Half-timbered buildings at Den Gamle By outdoor museum, Århus

Århus ❻

Jutland. 🏙 300,000. ✈ 44 km (27 miles) NE. 🚆 🚌 🛈 Rådhus, Park Allé (89 40 67 00). **www**.visitaarhus.com

Denmark's second city and Jutland's main urban center, Århus is small enough to see within a few hours. The city is something of a showcase for innovative 20th-century architecture.

Århus divides clearly into two parts. The old town is a cluster of medieval streets with several fine churches. **Den Gamle By**, the city's open-air museum, consists of 60 or so half-timbered houses and a watermill, transported from locations all over Jutland and carefully reconstructed.

In the modern part of the city, the controversial **Rådhus** (City Hall) was built by Arne Jakobsen and Erik Møller in 1941. Its coating of pale Norwegian marble still provokes differing opinions to this day.

Ⅲ Den Gamle By
Viborgvej. **Tel** 86 12 31 88. ◯ daily. ◯ Jan 1, Dec 24–25 & 31. 🎫 🚻 🛈

Aalborg ❼

Jutland. 🏙 160,000. 🚆 🚌 🛈 📮 🛈 Østerågade 8 (99 30 60 90). **www**.visitaalborg.com

The port of Aalborg spreads across both sides of the Limfjord, which slices through the tip of the Jutland peninsula. Aalborg is the leading producer of the spirit aquavit, the fiery Danish national drink.

The well-preserved old town has several sights of interest, including the suitably dark and atmospheric dungeons of the town castle, the **Aalborghus Slot** (1539). The **Budolfi Domkirke**, a 16th-century Gothic cathedral, houses a collection of portraits depicting Aalborg merchants from the town's prosperous past.

The **Nordjyllands Kunstmuseum** (North Jutland Art Museum) houses a collection of Danish modern art, as well as works by foreign artists such as Max Ernst and Chagall.

On the edge of Aalborg is the important historical site of **Lindholm Høje**. Set on a hilltop overlooking the city, it contains more than 650 marked graves from the Iron Age and Viking Age (see p665). A museum depicting the history of the site stands nearby.

♫ Lindholm Høje
Vendilavej. **Tel** 99 31 74 40. ◯ daily. **Museum** ◯ Easter–mid-Oct: daily; in winter: Tue & Sun. 🎫 🚻 ✆ 🛈 🛈

Legoland transportation – the colorful Lego train and monorail

Legoland ❽

Billund, Jutland. **Tel** 75 33 13 33. ✈ 🚌 to Vejle, then bus. ◯ Mar 19–Oct: daily. 🎫 🚻 🛈

The Legoland Billund theme park celebrates the tiny plastic blocks that have become a household name worldwide. The park opened in 1968, and more than 45 million Lego bricks were used in its construction.

Aimed primarily at 3–13 year olds, Legoland is divided into different zones. As well as Lego sculptures of animals, buildings, and landscapes, there are many rides and stage shows. Highlights include Miniland, a collection of miniature Lego towns that represent places around the world, and a driving track where children can take a safety test in a Lego car.

HANS CHRISTIAN ANDERSEN

Denmark's most internationally famous writer, Hans Christian Andersen (1805–75) was born in Odense, the son of a poor cobbler. Andersen was admitted to the University of Copenhagen in 1832, and the following year made his debut as an author with his first novel. Several plays and other novels followed but he remains best known for his children's fairy tales, published between 1835 and 1872. Andersen used everyday language, thus breaking with the literary tradition of the time. Some of his tales, such as "The Little Mermaid" (see p680), are deeply pessimistic and unhappy. A strong autobiographical element runs through these sadder tales; throughout his life Andersen saw himself as an outsider and he also suffered deeply in his closest relationships.

Statue of Hans Christian Andersen, Copenhagen

Practical & Travel Information

Visitors are always treated with courtesy and hospitality in Denmark; the Danes are one of the most tolerant nations in the world, and the Danish concept of *hygge* (coziness) makes the country a very comfortable place to stay. Denmark's travel facilities are plentiful, reliable, and easy to use. There is an extensive rail network and city public transportation services function efficiently. The capital, Copenhagen, is a compact city, which makes getting around by public transport quite straightforward. Since most Danes speak fluent English, you should have no problems with communication.

TOURIST INFORMATION

General and location-specific information on all parts of Denmark can be obtained from the **Danish Tourist Board**, which has offices in many countries worldwide, including the US and the UK. Visitors to the capital can obtain brochures, maps, and other useful information at the **Wonderful Copenhagen** office.

OPENING HOURS

Many tourist attractions close on Mondays, and a few have seasonal opening hours. Stores are open 10am to 5:30pm Monday to Thursday, 10am to 7 or 8pm on Friday, and 9am to 2pm on Saturday. Office hours are generally 9am to 4pm Monday to Friday.

VISA REQUIREMENTS

Visitors who are not citizens of a Scandinavian country require a valid passport to enter Denmark. Citizens of the EU may use a national identity card in lieu of their passport. No visa is required for visitors from the US, Canada, the UK, Ireland, Australia, or New Zealand.

SAFETY AND EMERGENCIES

Denmark is a peaceful country and street crime is rare, although travelers are advised to take out comprehensive travel insurance. Danish tourist offices and health offices have lists of doctors and local hospitals. For prescriptions (obtainable at a pharmacy or *apotek*) or a doctor's consultation, you will have to pay the full cost on the spot, but EU citizens can obtain a refund by taking their passport and European Health Insurance Card (EHIC) to a local health office.

BANKING AND CURRENCY

The Danish unit of currency is the krone (DKr), which is divided into 100 øre.

Danish banks usually open from 9:30am to 4pm Monday to Wednesday and Friday, and from 9:30am to 6pm on Thursday. For the most favorable exchange rates, change money and traveler's checks at a bank. Outside bank opening hours there are exchange booths at post offices, and most airports, main train stations, and ferry terminals. Major credit and charge cards are accepted in most places, and local currency can be obtained with credit or debit cards from cashpoint machines (ATMs).

COMMUNICATIONS

Public phone booths are plentiful and generally very reliable. Phone cards are becoming common in the larger cities and can be purchased from all post offices and kiosks.

Most post offices open from 10am to 6pm Monday to Friday, and 10am to 1pm on Saturday, although smaller branches may have restricted opening times. Visitors can have letters sent *poste restante* to anywhere in Denmark (some places will even hold mail ahead of your arrival). Cyber cafés are springing up in many of the larger cities.

English-language newspapers are usually available the day after publication at train stations and many of the larger newsagents.

FLYING TO DENMARK

Most international flights arrive at Copenhagen's **Kastrup Airport**, 8 km (5 miles) from the city center. British Airways, British Midland, Go, Ryanair, and **SAS** (Scandinavian Airline System) operate direct flights from Britain. SAS also offers direct flights from New York; most flights from North America, however, require a stopover. **Sterling** is the largest Danish domestic airline.

TRAVELING BY SEA

If you are considering traveling to Denmark by sea, **DFDS Seaways** operates a ferry service between Harwich in England and Esbjerg, on Denmark's west

---

THE CLIMATE OF DENMARK

The climate of Denmark is the least extreme of the Scandinavian countries, but the country's close proximity to the sea means that the weather can change very quickly. The summer months are generally sunny; temperatures in July can top 26° C (78° F). Winters are cold and rainy, although not severe, and there may be snow from December to February.

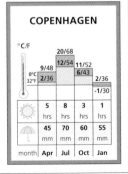

COPENHAGEN

°C/F	Apr	Jul	Oct	Jan
	9/48	20/68 12/54	11/52	
0°C 32°F	2/36		6/43	2/36 -1/30
	5 hrs	8 hrs	3 hrs	1 hrs
	45 mm	70 mm	60 mm	55 mm
month	Apr	Jul	Oct	Jan

coast, three or four times a week. The crossing takes around 20 hours. Special midweek offers are often available, which can cut the cost of travel considerably.

Norway and Sweden are also well connected to Denmark by sea. Ferries from Oslo call at Copenhagen, Hirtshals, and Frederikshavn, and journeys to Helsingør from Helsingborg in Sweden take just 15 minutes.

Ferries also link all the Danish islands and range in size from the car- and bus-carrying catamarans and ferries of **Mols-Linien**, which travel between Zealand and Jutland, to tiny vessels serving small settlements off the mainland and major islands.

RAIL TRAVEL

Like the rest of the public transportation system in Denmark, the trains are clean and reliable, and are by far the best way to get around. **Danish State Railways** – Danske Statsbaner (DSB) – operates an efficient network that covers most parts of the country, with the exception of Funen and northeast Jutland.

In Copenhagen a local train service, the **S-tog**, provides transportation between the city center and the surrounding areas, including Helsingør.

TRAVELING BY CAR

Car rental in Denmark is expensive. To rent a vehicle you must be at least 20 years of age, and hold an international driver's license.

Driving in central Copenhagen is not advisable due to the traffic and lack of parking.

The Danish authorities conduct random breath tests, and penalties for driving under the influence of alcohol are severe. The **Forenede Danske Motorejere (FDM)**, offers a breakdown service to Automobile Association (AA) members.

BUSES, TAXIS, AND BICYCLES

Buses are cheaper than trains, but on the whole not as comfortable. However, they are useful for traveling to remote areas not covered by the train network. Copenhagen's **HUR Kunde-center** has a bus information hotline.

Most taxi drivers speak English, but cabs are often expensive, especially at night and all day at weekends.

Cycling is an excellent way to enjoy Denmark's mostly flat landscape, since traffic is light on the country roads and most towns have cycle tracks. Bikes can be rented at most youth hostels, tourist offices, and bike stores, and at some train stations. In Copenhagen, **Kobenhavns Cykelbørs** is a reliable bike rental store. Contact the **Dansk Cyklist Forbund** (Danish Cycling Association) for more information.

SIGHTSEEING IN COPENHAGEN

If you plan to do a lot of sightseeing in Copenhagen, it is worth investing in a Copenhagen Card (valid for one, two, or three days). The card gives unlimited use of public transportation in the metropolitan area (including North Zealand), free or discounted admission to many museums, as well as price reductions with certain car rental companies and on ferry crossings to Sweden.

DIRECTORY

TOURIST OFFICES

Danish Tourist Board
www.visitdenmark.com

In Denmark:
Vesterbrogade 4a,
Copenhagen V.
Tel 70 22 24 42.

In the UK:
55 Sloane Street,
London SW1X 9SY.
Tel 020-7259 5959.
Fax 020-7259 5955.

In the US:
655 Third Avenue,
Suite 1810, New York.
Tel 212-885 9700.
Fax 212-885 9726.

Wonderful Copenhagen
Gammel Kongevej 1,
Copenhagen V.
Tel 70 22 24 42.
www.woco.dk

EMBASSIES

Australia
Dampførgevej 26,
Copenhagen Ø. *Tel 70 26 36 76*. **www**.denmark.
embassy.gov.au

Canada
Kristen Bernikows Gade 1,
Copenhagen K.
Tel 33 48 32 00.
www.dfait-maeci.gc.ca

Ireland
Østbanegade 21,
Copenhagen Ø.
Tel 35 42 32 33.

UK
Kastelsvej 36–40,
Copenhagen Ø.
Tel 35 44 52 00.
www.britishembassy.dk

US
Dag Hammarskjölds Allé
24, Copenhagen Ø.
Tel 33 41 71 00.
www.usembassy.dk

EMERGENCY NUMBERS

Ambulance, Fire and Police
Tel 112.

AIR TRAVEL

Kastrup Airport
Tel 32 31 32 31.
www.cph.dk

SAS
Tel 70 10 20 00 (Denmark).
Tel 0870-60 727 727 (UK).
Tel 800-221 2350 (US).
www.sas.dk

Sterling
Tel 70 10 84 84 (Denmark).
Tel 0870-78 78 038 (UK).
www.sterling.dk

FERRY SERVICES

DFDS Seaways
Tel 33 42 30 80 (Denmark).
Tel 08702-520 524 (UK).
www.dfdseaways.com

Mols-Linien
Tel 70 10 14 18 (Denmark).

RAIL TRAVEL

Danish State Railways
Tel 70 13 14 15.
www.dsb.dk

S-tog Information
Tel 33 14 17 01.

ROAD TRAVEL

HUR Kunde-center (bus information)
Tel 36 13 14 15.
trafikinfo.hur.dk

Dansk Cyklist Forbund
Tel 33 32 31 21.
www.dcf.dk

Forenede Danske Motorejere (FDM)
Tel 45 27 07 07.

Kobenhavns Cykelbørs
Gothersgade 157,
Copenhagen K.
Tel 33 14 07 17.
www.cykelboersen.dk

Where to Stay in Denmark

Although Denmark is less expensive to visit than either Sweden or Norway, a large chunk of a traveler's budget will still be spent on accommodations. However, most hotels offer discount rates for summer or weekend stays. As many Danish hotels are found in very old buildings, rooms can vary enormously, but are always clean.

PRICE CATEGORIES
Price categories are for a standard double room with bath or shower per night in high season including breakfast, tax, and service.
Ⓚ Under 600 DKr
ⓀⓀ 600–1,000 DKr
ⓀⓀⓀ 1,000–1,500 DKr
ⓀⓀⓀⓀ 1,500–2,000 DKr
ⓀⓀⓀⓀⓀ Over 2,000 DKr

COPENHAGEN

CENTRAL COPENHAGEN Danhostel Copenhagen City   Ⓚ
H.C. Andersens Boulevard 50, 1553 **Tel** *33-18 83 32* **Fax** *33-29 80 59* **Rooms** *192*   **Map** *B4/C5*

Do not be deceived by the anonymous high-rise exterior: the interior furnishings and sleekly-styled rooms would put most mid-level hotels to shame. Many of the rooms have superb views over the city. Facilities include an internet café, comfortable TV lounge, laundry, and large kitchen. **www.danhostel.dk/copenhagencity**

CENTRAL COPENHAGEN Hotel Fox   ⓀⓀ
Jarmers Plads 3, 1551 **Tel** *33-95 77 55* **Fax** *33-14 30 33* **Rooms** *61*   **Map** *B4*

Easily one of the most unusual hotels in the city, the Fox was fashioned by a group of graphic designers, street artists and illustrators. Their off-the-wall creations range from the ultra-minimalist (floor-to-ceiling white formica) to the fantastical (walls covered in outlandish murals). Friendly reception and a great restaurant to boot. **www.hotelfox.dk**

CENTRAL COPENHAGEN Ibsens   ⓀⓀⓀ
Vendersgade 23, 1363 **Tel** *33-13 19 13* **Fax** *33-13 19 16* **Rooms** *118*

Set within a classic French-style apartment building, this modern boutique hotel has individually-styled rooms, ranging from modern Scandinavian to classical English, though all are modestly decorated. The hotel is hidden away in a narrow café-lined street close to Nansensgade – great for a night out. **www.ibsenshotel.dk**

CENTRAL COPENHAGEN Radisson SAS Royal Hotel   ⓀⓀⓀⓀⓀ
Hammerichsgade 1, 1611 **Tel** *33-42 60 00* **Fax** *33-42 63 00* **Rooms** *260*   **Map** *B4*

This is *the* designer hotel. The entire place, inside and out, was designed in 1960 by Arne Jacobsen, including Swan and Egg chairs, a spiral staircase, and anodized doorknobs. The comfortable rooms have recently been renovated bringing them up-to-date; all have internet access. **www.royal.copenhagen.radissonsas.com**

CENTRAL COPENHAGEN Hotel d'Angleterre   ⓀⓀⓀⓀⓀⓀ
Kongens Nytorv 34, 1022 **Tel** *33-12 00 95* **Fax** *33-12 11 18* **Rooms** *123*   **Map** *D4*

One of the most respected hotels in Copenhagen, the Angleterre has been in business for more than 250 years and remains the choice for visiting dignitaries. The rooms are very large, classic in decor, and filled with every amenity you could want. The queen's official residence is just around the corner. **www.remmen.dk/dangleterre**

REST OF DENMARK

ODENSE Hotel Ansgar   ⓀⓀ
Østre Stationsvej 32, 5000 **Tel** *66-11 96 93* **Fax** *66-11 96 75* **Rooms** *74*

The rooms here have just been renovated and now boast plenty of classical charm thanks to their Italian-style chairs and window sashes. Catering to business and leisure travelers alike, the Ansgar has recently opened a bar and restaurant, which offers a very good lunchtime buffet. **www.hotel-ansgar.dk**

AALBORG Helnan Phønix Hotel   ⓀⓀ
Vesterbro 77, 9000 **Tel** *98-12 00 11* **Fax** *98-10 10 20* **Rooms** *210*

A major feature of the town, this historic hotel was built in 1783 as a palace to Brigadier William Von Halling and converted into a hotel just over 100 years later. Located in the heart of Aalborg, the hotel provides classic hospitality in an elegant setting. **www.helnan.dk**

ÅRHUS Best Western Hotel Ritz   ⓀⓀⓀ
Banegårdspladsen 12, 8000 **Tel** *86-13 44 44* **Fax** *86-13 45 87* **Rooms** *67*

Built in 1932 near to the town's Musikhuset (concert hall), theatres and restaurants, Best Western's Ritz has been redecorated and carefully refurbished in keeping with the original architecture. The hotel restaurant is one of the best in town. Access to the internet is available in the lobby. **www.hotelritz.dk**

Key to Symbols *see back cover flap*

Where to Eat in Denmark

An evening meal can be expensive in Denmark, especially in the capital. Visitors are advised to have a hearty meal at lunchtime, when a few helpings of *smørrebrød* (Danish open sandwiches piled with meat, fish, cheese, and vegetables) will reduce the need for a large dinner – without reducing the size of your wallet.

PRICE CATEGORIES
The following price categories are for a three-course meal for one without alcohol or tip, but including tax:
Ⓚ Under 150 DKr
ⓀⓀ 150–200 DKr
ⓀⓀⓀ 200–300 DKr
ⓀⓀⓀⓀ 300–350 DKr
ⓀⓀⓀⓀⓀ Over 350 DKr

COPENHAGEN

CENTRAL COPENHAGEN Slotskælderen   🅰🛉   Ⓚ
Fortunstræde 4, 1065 **Tel** *33-11 15 37*   **Map** *C4*

Excellent, well-known lunch-only spot right by the Strøget that specializes is *smørrebrød*. Select what you want from behind the glass counters and they bring it to your table. Slotskælderen also serve good *frikadeller* (meatballs) and *sild* (herring). Popular with the parliamentarians who hold sessions nearby.

CENTRAL COPENHAGEN Restaurant Cap Horn   🆅   ⓀⓀ
Nyhavn 21 3tv, 1051 **Tel** *33-12 85 04*   **Map** *D4*

Weathered walls, original wood floors, and an open fireplace are the setting for the Cap Horn's classic Danish menu, which focuses on regularly changing seafood and organic dishes. The organic theme extends to the beer, wine, and coffee. Service is fast and courteous and they occasionally have live jazz sessions.

CENTRAL COPENHAGEN Det Lille Apotek   🅰🛉🆅   ⓀⓀⓀ
Store Kannikestrade 15, 1169 **Tel** *33-12 56 06*   **Map** *C4*

The interior of Det Lille Apotek is decorated in deep, dark woods and gilded lamps. The menu features classic Danish dishes incluning roast pork, prawn cocktail with tournedos, and a wide variety of pickled *sild* (herring). Their specialty is *apotekaregrytan*, a tasty stew of pork tenderloin in a paprika cream sauce with mushrooms and pineapple.

CENTRAL COPENHAGEN Thorvaldsens Hus   🅰🛉🆅   ⓀⓀⓀⓀ
Gammel Strand 34, 1202 **Tel** *33-32 04 00*   **Map** *C4*

This modern restaurant is perfect for a fairly-priced gourmet meal after visiting the nearby Thorvaldsens Museum. Try the ten-course "Taste the Thorvaldsens Hus" menu, which features a little bit of everything good in the kitchen. Otherwise, excellent *smørrebrød* and simple Danish dishes are served on the courtyard terrace overlooking the canal.

CENTRAL COPENHAGEN Noma   🆃🆅   ⓀⓀⓀⓀⓀ
Strandgade 93, 1401 **Tel** *32-96 32 97*

One of the city's several Michelin-starred restaurants, the Noma draws upon Greenland, Iceland, and the Faroe Islands for its inspiration. Though there are only a handful of dishes on the menu, they are all prepared with immaculate attention to detail. A meal to remember.

REST OF DENMARK

AALBORG Duus Vinkælder   🖻🛉   Ⓚ
Østerågade 9, 9000 **Tel** *98-12 50 56*

Located in the cellar of the famous Jens Bang's Stenhus, this is a convivial restaurant and bar serving light lunches only. They are known for their delicious *frikadeller*, and in summer serve a wide variety of Danish *smørrebrød*. This place is full of character and makes a good stopping-off point while sightseeing.

ÅRHUS Navigator   🅰🛉   ⓀⓀⓀⓀ
Marselisborg Havnevej 46D, 8000 **Tel** *86-20 20 58*

A lively restaurant, decked out in cobalt blue and creamy white, serving well-cooked Danish-French staples in tune with the seasons. When the weather permits, there is an outdoor grill and salad bar. Dinner and dance evenings are on every Saturday. It is necessary to book in advance.

ODENSE Den Gamle Kro   🅰🛉🆅   ⓀⓀⓀ
Overgade 23, 5000 **Tel** *66-12 14 33*

Set in a wonderful old building dating from 1683, this atmospheric restaurant is decorated with memorabilia from the past. Some of the more unexpected Danish dishes on the menu include fried mullet with shellfish ragout, and strawberries soaked in champagne. There are several dining rooms to choose from and a great wine cellar.

Map References *see map of Copenhagen pp676–7*

FINLAND

inland is perhaps the least known of the Nordic countries. Historically, geographically, and economically, the country straddles East and West, trading and maintaining links with both Western Europe and the former states of the Soviet Union. The Finnish have a strong sense of national identity, and are rightly proud of their beautiful unspoiled landscape of forest, lakes, coast, and islands.

About a third of Finland (*Suomi* in Finnish) is covered by native pine, spruce, and birch forests. Most of the rest is covered by water – an estimated 188,000 lakes, numerous rivers, and extensive areas of marshland. Finland's coastline is extremely indented and dotted with thousands of islands, most of which can be found in the archipelagos of the southwest. The land is generally flat, apart from mountainous areas in Lapland. About one third of the territory lies within the Arctic Circle, where the landscape is strikingly beautiful, if sometimes bleak.

Most of Finland's towns and cities are found in the southern coastal region, where they vie for space with extensive stretches of farmland. The lake district, at the heart of Finland, is not so populous, but industrialization of the area has been steadily increasing since the mid-20th century. Northern Finland is still fairly undeveloped, with small pockets of Finns inhabiting the south, while the Sami (the nomadic people of Lapland) are spread over the far north.

Although by nature modest and not very practised at marketing themselves, the Finns have achieved much economic success, excelling in the fields of technology and design. Nokia, the mobile phone giant, is Finland's best-known success story in global terms, although many people are unaware of the company's Finnish origins.

HISTORY

Little is known of early Finnish history, although it is believed that the ancestors of the Sami first arrived in Finland about 9,000 years ago. Another group, whose language evolved into modern Finnish, arrived some 3,000 years later. In the

A busy main street in central Helsinki

◁ Peaceful summer cottage in Finland's extensive Lakelands region

1st millennium BC the arrival of more groups, including the ancestors of the present-day Finns, forced the Sami to withdraw northwards to Lapland.

Even before the beginning of the Viking age (8th–11th century AD), Swedes had settled on the southwest coast of Finland, and in 1216 Finland became part of Sweden. Under Swedish sovereignty, the Finnish tribes gradually developed a sense of unity, which would later form the basis for a proud national identity.

From the 13th to the 18th centuries, Finland was a battleground for power struggles between Sweden and Russia. In 1809 Sweden ceded Finland to Russia, and the territory became an autonomous Grand Duchy of Russia. Helsinki was decreed the Finnish capital in 1812, and by the 1830s the transformation of this rocky fishing harbor into a major Baltic trading city was well underway.

When Czar Nicholas II unwisely removed Finland's autonomous status, a determination to achieve independence took root. This independence was finally won in 1917, aided by the maneuverings of General Carl Gustaf Emil Mannerheim (1867–1951). Mannerheim ousted the Russian soldiers still garrisoned in Finland and thus averted the immediate danger

Statue of General Mannerheim, architect of independence

that the fledging USSR might extend its Communist regime into the country. Finland's declaration of independence was finally recognized by the Soviet government on December 31, 1917.

Between the two world wars, Finland was dominated by a controversy over language. The Finns fought for the supremacy of their native tongue, and the use of Swedish declined sharply.

Despite its independent status, tensions between Finland and the Soviet Union remained throughout the early 20th century. Years of fear culminated in the 1939–40 Winter War against an invading Soviet army, swiftly followed by the "War of Continuation" (1941–44), in which Finland aided German troops against the Soviet Union. Deep suspicion of the Soviet Union continued for decades, but following the demise of the USSR in 1991, Finland reached a new agreement with Russia which pledged to end disputes between them peacefully.

In recent years, Finland has carved for itself a peace-brokering reputation, and has expanded economically through membership of the European Union and the efforts of its entrepreneurs.

LANGUAGE AND CULTURE

What began as a tentative linguistic and cultural exploration of Finnishness in the 19th century has evolved into a confident, outward-looking sense of nationhood. At the heart of Finnishness lies the notion of *sisu*, a kind of courage against the odds, but it also embraces everything in which the Finns take pride, such as the freedom to harvest berries and mushrooms in the forests.

Outdoor pursuits have an important place in the national psyche, especially cross-country skiing, swimming, boating, and cycling. Finland is also successful in some competitive sports, such as long-distance running and rally driving.

In the arts, the music of composer Jean Sibelius remains Finland's best known cultural export. Finnish architects and designers, in particular Alvar Aalto (1898–1976), are renowned worldwide.

KEY DATES IN FINNISH HISTORY

1155 First Swedish crusade to Finland
1216 Finland becomes a duchy of Sweden
1550 New market town of Helsinki established
1714 & 1721 Russia and Finland are at war
1748 Island fortress of Suomenlinna under construction to defend Finland against Russians
1809 Finland is separated from Sweden and becomes an autonomous Grand Duchy of Russia
1812 Helsinki becomes capital of Grand Duchy
1917 Declaration of independence
1939–44 Russia and Finland at war
1995 Finland joins the European Union
2000 Helsinki is European City of Culture and celebrates its 450th anniversary
2002 Finnish mark replaced by Euro
2006 Finland assumes EU presidency

Exploring Finland

After many years in the tourism wilderness, Finns are working hard to put their country on the map of world travel destinations. Wonderful natural amenities, a manageable and attractive capital city, and excellent public transportation make Finland an easy country to promote. Trains are the most convenient way to get around the country, although long-distance buses are often faster on east–west journeys. Destinations in the populous south are all easy to reach, but in the far north traveling takes more time and planning.

SIGHTS AT A GLANCE

HELSINKI pp692–6 **①**
Savonlinna **③**
Turku **②**
Side Trip to St. Petersburg
pp696–7 **④**

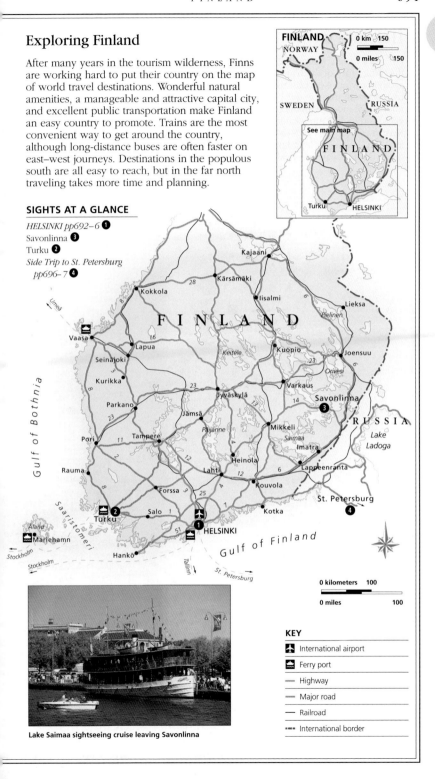

Lake Saimaa sightseeing cruise leaving Savonlinna

KEY

- ✈ International airport
- ⚓ Ferry port
- — Highway
- — Major road
- — Railroad
- ▪▪▪ International border

Helsinki ❶

Finland's capital since 1812, Helsinki is called the "White City of the North," a reference to the gleaming white Neoclassical buildings commissioned by its Russian rulers in the 19th century. It also boasts impressive modern architecture, from the copper, glass, and rock Temppeliaukio Church to the futuristic Kiasma center. The city is at its best in summer, when long days and clear light lift the mood of Finns, and the parks and waterfront cafés fill with lively crowds.

KEY

	Sight / Place of interest
	Long-distance ferry
	Local ferry
	Train station
M	Metro station
	Bus station
P	Parking
	Tourist information
	Church
	Synagogue
	Pedestrian street

SIGHTS AT A GLANCE

Finlandia Hall ⑥
Helsinki Cathedral ④
Kiasma, Museum of
    Contemporary Art ⑤
Market Square ①
National Museum ⑦
Senate Square ③
Temppeliaukio Church ⑧
Uspenski Cathedral ②

Greater Helsinki

Suomenlinna Island Fortress ⑨

GETTING AROUND

The center of Helsinki is easily explored on foot. The city's efficient transportation network consists of buses, trams, and a metro system, although the latter is of limited use to tourists. Virtually all bus and tram routes converge on the streets around Helsinki Central Station. Suomenlinna Island Fortress can be reached by ferry only, from Market Square.

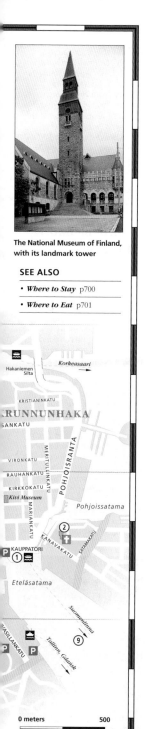

The National Museum of Finland, with its landmark tower

SEE ALSO

- **Where to Stay** p700
- **Where to Eat** p701

[Map of Helsinki with labels: Korkeasaari, Hakaniemen Silta, KRISTIANINKATU, KRUUNUNHAKA, SANKATU, VIRONKATU, RAUHANKATU, KIRKKOKATU, Kivi Museum, MERITULLINKATU, POHJOISRANTA, Pohjoissatama, KAUPPATORI, Eteläsatama, KANAVAKATU, SATAMAKATU, MARIANKATU, Suomenlinna, VASILLANKATU, Tullinn Graani]

0 meters   500
0 yards   500

D

Stall holder moored alongside the quay at Helsinki's Market Square

Market Square ①

Head of South Harbor. 🚋 13, 16.
🚊 1, 1A, 2, 3B, 3T, 4. 🕐 6.30am–
6pm Mon–Fri, 6:30am–4pm Sat,
9am–4pm Sun. ◐ Sun in winter.

In summer, a short season that must sustain a nation through a long winter, the people of Helsinki sun themselves in the cobbled Market Square (Kauppatori).

Finnish craftsmen sell handmade wares alongside fish, fruit, and vegetable stalls. Farmers will often travel for many miles by small wooden boat to sell fresh produce grown on their small holdings just like their forefathers did.

Among the fine buildings lining the square are the blue-painted **City Hall**, by Carl Ludwig Engel (1778–1840), and the 19th-century red- and yellow-brick **Old Market Hall**, containing several gourmet and specialist food shops.

Leading westward from Market Square is **Esplanadi** park, a favorite gathering place for Finns, who can be seen strolling down its wide boulevards. At the eastern end of the park is a bronze statue of a nude, *Havis Amanda* (1905) by Ville Vallgren, now a symbol of the city.

Uspenski Cathedral ②

Kanavakatu 1. **Tel** 09-634 267. 🚊
2, 4. ◯ May–Sep: daily; Oct–Apr:
Tue–Sun. 🚻 ask for assistance.

With its dark red-brick exterior, this Russian Orthodox cathedral is a colorful landmark in the ubiquitous white of the historic city center. Its green copper roof and gold "onion" domes make it highly visible on Helsinki's skyline.

Designed in the Byzantine-Russian architectural tradition by A.M. Gornostayev of St. Petersburg, the cathedral was built in 1868. Uspenski is the biggest Russian Orthodox church in Scandinavia, and its spacious interior is resplendent in gold, silver, red, and blue. The terrace gives magnificent views over the heart of Helsinki, and the immediate area has been improved by converting old warehouses into shops and restaurants. The sheer exuberance of the building forms a sharp contrast to the Lutheran austerity of Helsinki Cathedral.

The red-brick exterior and "onion" domes of Uspenski Cathedral

Senate Square ③

🚊 1, 1A, 2, 3B, 3T, 4, 7A, 7B. 🚋 16.

Senate Square (Senaatintori) is the masterpiece of Carl Ludwig Engel (1778–1840). It was built by Finland's Russian rulers in the early 1800s, and a statue of Czar Alexander II of Russia stands in the center.

The pleasing proportions of the square are best viewed from the top of the steps to Helsinki Cathedral. From here, the **Senate Building** lies to the left and the **University of Helsinki** to the right. Adjacent to the square is **Sederholm House** (1757), the oldest stone building in Helsinki.

The steep south-facing steps leading to the Neoclassical Helsinki Cathedral

Helsinki Cathedral ④

Unioninkatu 29, Senaatintori.
Tel 09-709 2455. 🚇 1, 1A, 2, 3B,
3T, 4, 7A, 7B. 🚌 16. ⬜ daily
(Sun: pm only). ♿ call in advance.
Crypt ⬜ Jun–Aug: daily.

The five green cupolas of the
gleaming white Lutheran
Cathedral are a landmark on
Helsinki's skyline. Designed
by C.L. Engel, the Neoclassical
building sits at the top of a
steep flight of steps.

White Corinthian columns
decorate the splendid exterior,
while the inside is rather
spartan. There are, however,
statues of the 16th-century
Protestant reformers Martin
Luther, Philipp Melanchthon,
the great humanist scholar,
and Mikael Agricola,
translator of the Bible into
Finnish. Beneath the cathedral
is a crypt, now used for
concerts and exhibitions.

Kiasma, Museum of Contemporary Art ⑤

Mannerheiminaukio 2. **Tel** 09-173
36501. 🚌 🚇 3T & many routes.
⬜ 10am–8:30pm Wed–Sun, 9am–
5pm Tue. ● public hols. 🎫 📷 ♿
🖥 📱 www.kiasma.fi

This glass and metal-paneled
building, designed by
American architect Steven
Holl, was completed in 1998
at a cost of over 227 million
Finnish markka. With its fluid
lines and white interior, the
museum is built in a curve to
maximize natural light in the
exhibition spaces.

Intended as an exhibition
space for post-1960 art,
Kiasma hosts mixed media

shows, art installations,
contemporary drama, and art
workshops. There is also a
children's technological center.

**The glass entrance to Kiasma,
Museum of Contemporary Art**

Finlandia Hall ⑥

Mannerheimintie 13E. **Tel** 09-40241.
🚇 4, 7A, 7B, 10. 🚌 40. 🎫
📷 by arrangement. ♿
www.finlandia.talo.fi

Located in the tranquil setting
of Hesperia Park, striking
Finlandia Hall is one of
architect Alvar Aalto's best
known works. Despite the
hall's poor acoustics, it is a
leading international concert
venue, hosting regular
performances by the
Helsinki Philharmonic.

National Museum ⑦

Mannerheimintie 34. **Tel** 09-405 09
544. 🚌 40. 🚇 4, 10 & many routes.
⬜ 11am–8pm Tue–Wed,
11am–6pm Thu–Sun. ● public hols.
🎫 ♿ 📷 🖥 📱 www.nba.fi

Dating from the start of the
20th century, the National
Museum is one of Helsinki's

most notable examples of
Finnish National-Romantic
architecture. The museum
illustrates the history of
Finland, from prehistory to
the present day through a
variety of artifacts. One of the
highlights is the throne of
Czar Alexander I from 1809.

The striking wall painting
by Akseli Gallen-Kallela
(1865–1931) in the entrance
hall depicts scenes from
Finland's national epic, a
poem known as the *Kalevala*.

Temppeliaukio Church ⑧

Lutherinkatu 3. **Tel** 09-494 698.
🚇 3B, 3T. 🚌 14, 14B, 18, 24, 39,
39A. ⬜ daily. ♿

Built into a granite outcrop
with walls of stone, this
circular "Church in the Rock" is
an astonishing piece of modern
architecture. Consecrated in
1969, it is the work of architects Timo and Tuomo
Suomalainen. The ceiling is
an enormous, domed, copper
disk, separated from the
rough-surfaced rock walls by
a ribbed ring of glass, which
allows light to filter in from
outside. The austere interior is
relatively free of iconography
and religious symbolism.

As well as being a major
visitor attraction – some half a
million people come to admire
the church each year – this
popular Lutheran place of
worship is also used for organ
concerts and choral music.

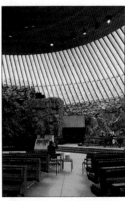

**Interior of Temppeliaukio Church,
with its copper and glass dome**

Suomenlinna Island Fortress ⑨

🚢 from Market Square to residential area of island. **Tel** 09-684 1880. 🗹 by appointment. 🕭 limited. 🍴 🛈

Constructed by the Swedes between 1748 and 1772, this island fortress is the biggest in Scandinavia, and is now a UNESCO World Heritage Site. Designed to defend the Finnish coast, Suomenlinna offered security to Helsinki's burghers and merchants, enabling the city to flourish. The fortress contains about 200 buildings, most of which date from the 18th century. Until the early 19th century, the fortress had more residents than Helsinki.

900 people still live on the islands which receive around 700,000 visitors a year who come to enjoy the cobbled castle courtyards and marinas. There are many eateries, galleries, and museums, including a doll and toy museum.

Turku ②

🏘 175,000. ✈ 🚇 🚌 🚢 🚢 🛈 Aurakatu 4 (02-262 7444). 🗹 Medieval Market (late Jun–Jul), Music Festival (Aug). **www**.turkutouring.fi

Turku (Åbo in Swedish), a bustling port with a modern city center, was Finland's principal city during the sovereignty of Sweden, and remains the center of Finland's second language, Swedish.

Completed in 1300, **Turku Cathedral** is the principal place of worship for the Evangelical-Lutheran Church of Finland. The museum holds many ecclesiastical treasures.

Work on **Turku Castle** began in the late 13th century, but reached its prime in the mid-1500s with the addition of further rooms. The history of Turku and the castle are presented in the **Historical Museum of Turku**.

A double museum comprising **Aboa Vetus** and **Ars Nova** focus on life in medieval Turku and 20th-century Finnish and international art respectively.

Suomenlinna Island Fortress, the largest sea fortress in Scandinavia

Other attractions include the west bank of the River Aura and the indoor market. Archipelago steamship cruises are also available.

⚓ Turku Castle
Linnankatu 80. **Tel** 02-262 0300. ◯ Mid-Apr–mid-Sep: daily; mid-Sep–mid-Apr: Tue–Sun. ● public hols. 🗹 in summer. 🖬 🍴 🛈

🏛 Aboa Vetus and Ars Nova
Itäinen Rantakatu 4–7. **Tel** 02-250 0552. ◯ Apr–mid-Sep: daily; mid-Sep–Mar: Tue–Sun. ● public hols. 🖬 🗹 in summer. 🕭

Environs
Just west of Turku lies **Naantali**, a popular seaside resort with cruises available from the harbor. **Moominworld**, a childrens' theme park based on Tove Jansson's creations is also here.

Moominworld
Naantali. 🚌 11, 110, 111 from Turku. **Tel** 02-511 1111. ◯ Jun 11–Aug 21: daily; w/ends for rest of Aug. 🖬 **www**.muumimaailma.fi

Exploring the courtyard of the late 13th-century Turku Castle

Savonlinna ❸

🏘 29,000. 🚇 🚌 🚢 in summer. 🛈 Puistokatu 1 (015-517 510). 🗹 International Opera Festival (Jul). **www**.savonlinnatravel.com

A good base from which to make excursions into the Saimaa Lakelands, Savonlinna also has charms of its own. Spread over several islands, the town boasts the castle of **Olavinlinna** (St. Olav's Castle), one of the best-preserved medieval castles in Scandinavia. The castle is home to the world-renowned Savonlinna International Opera Festival.

Founded in 1475, the castle consists of three towers and a bailey with an encircling wall reinforced by more towers. There are two museums: the **Castle Museum** illustrates the history of the castle, while the **Orthodox Museum** displays items of Russian Orthodox iconography from both Finland and Russia.

⚓ Olavinlinna
Tel 015-531 164. ◯ daily. ● some public hols. 🗹 🖬 (free for children under 7). 🛈 (summer only).

Environs
From Savonlinna harbor, steamships make excursions on Haapavesi and Pihlajavesi lakes, widely considered Finland's most beautiful scenery.

Rauhalinna Villa, in the village of Lehtiniemi, is half an hour by boat from Savonlinna. Open as a hotel-restaurant in the summer, this wooden manor house was built in 1900 by a lieutenant general of Czar Nicholas II as a wedding gift to his wife.

Side Trip to St. Petersburg ❹

Russia's second city, St. Petersburg is situated at the meeting of the Neva river and the Gulf of Finland, and is easily accessible from Helsinki by air, train, and boat. Founded in 1703 by Peter the Great and dubbed the "Venice of the North", the city comprises a bewitching mix of grand Neoclassical and Baroque architecture, sparkling waterways, and majestic bridges. Nearby, the extravagant imperial palaces of Peterhof and Czarskoe Selo offer an insight into the excesses of Czarist days.

Exploring St. Petersburg

The southern bank of the Neva is lined with stately palaces, and opposite, over the Troitskiy Most, sits the Peter and Paul Fortress. To the west lies Sennaya Ploschad, an area of pretty tree-lined canals and to the east is the Gostinyy Dvor, where shops, bars, and cafés line Nevskiy prospekt. The center is easily explored by foot but a boat trip is one of the highlights of a visit.

Nevskiy Prospekt ①

Ⓜ *Nevskiy Prospekt, Gostinyy Dvor.*

Russia's most famous street, Nevskiy prospekt, is also St. Petersburg's commercial hub. Laid out in the early days of the city, today the street teems with people late into the night.

The western stretch contains a wealth of fine buildings including the Baroque Stroganov Palace. Farther east, there are growing numbers of cafés and bars as well as three historic shopping arcades.

The Church on Spilled Blood, covered in colorful mosaics

Russian Museum ②

Inzhenernaya ulitsa 4. *Tel 595 4248.* Ⓜ *Nevskiy Prospekt, Gostinyy Dvor.* 🚌 *3, 7, 22, K-128, K-129, K-169.* ◯ *Wed–Mon.* 🎟 ♿ *phone for details.* 🎫 *English (314 3448 to book).* **www**.rusmuseum.ru

One of Carlo Rossi's finest Neoclassical creations, the Mikhaylovskiy Palace is the splendid setting for a truly outstanding collection of Russian art, ranging from medieval icons to the latest painting, sculpture, and applied art. The palace was built in 1819–25 for Grand Duke Mikhail Pavlovich. Alexander III's plans to create a public museum were realized by his son Nicholas II when the Russian Museum opened here in 1898. The grand staircase and White Hall are original features.

Church on Spilled Blood ③

Konyushennaya ploshchad. *Tel 315 1636.* Ⓜ *Nevskiy Prospekt, Gostinyy Dvor.* ◯ *Thu–Tue.* 🎟 📷 🎫

The Church on Spilled Blood, also known as the Resurrection Church of Our Savior, was built on the spot where on March 1, 1881 Czar Alexander II was assassinated. His successor, Alexander III, launched a competition for a permanent memorial. The winning design, in the Russian Revival style, was by Alfred Parland and Ignatiy Malyshev.

A riot of color, the overall effect of the church is created by the imaginative juxtaposition of materials that are lavished on the building, including 7,000 sq m (75,300 sq ft) of mosaics.

The Hermitage ④

Dvortsovaya nab 30–8. *Tel 710 9079.* 🚌 *7, 10, T-228, K-147, K-209.* ◯ *Tue–Sun.* 🎟 ♿ 🎫 *English (571 8446 to book).*

Occupying a grand ensemble of imperial buildings including the impressive Winter Palace, the Hermitage houses one of the world's greatest collections of art and artifacts. Ranging from Egyptian mummies to a dazzling array of Old Master and Impressionist paintings, it is essential to be selective.

The golden dome of St Isaac's Cathedral, visible across the city

St. Isaac's Cathedral ⑤

Isaakievskaya ploshchad. *Tel 315 9732.* Ⓜ *Nevskiy Prospekt, Sadovaya.* 🚌 *3, 10, 22, 27, K-169, K-180, K-190, K-252, K-289.* ◯ *Thu–Tue.* 🎟 🎫

St. Isaac's, one of the world's largest cathedrals, was designed in 1818 by the then unknown architect Auguste de Montferrand. The construction of the colossal building was a major feat of engineering. Thousands of wooden piles were sunk into the marshy ground to support its 300,000 tonnes. The cathedral opened in 1858 but was designated a museum of atheism during the Soviet era. Officially still a museum today, the church is filled with hundreds of impressive 19th-century works of art.

For hotels and restaurants in this region see pp700–1

The Mariinskiy Theater, one of Russia's most important cultural institutions

Mariinskiy Theater ⑥

Teatralnaya ploshchad. **Tel** 346 4141.
🚌 3, 22, 27. ⚫ for re-construction until late 2008. 🎫 📷
www.mariinsky.ru

This theater has been home to the world-famous Mariinskiy (Kirov) Opera and Ballet Company since 1860. Hidden behind its imposing façade is the sumptuous auditorium where many of Russia's greatest dancers have performed. Named in honor of Czarina Maria Alexandrovna, wife of Alexander II, the building was erected in 1860 by the architect Albert Kavos who designed the Bolshoy Theatre in Moscow.

SS Peter and Paul Fortress ⑦

Petropavlovskaya krepost.
Ⓜ Gorkovskaya. **Cathedral Tel** 232 9454. ⚫ Thu–Tue. 🎫 📷
English. **www**.spbmuseum.ru.

The founding of the Peter and Paul Fortress on May 27, 1703, on the orders of Peter the Great, is considered to mark the founding of the city. Its history is a gruesome one, since hundreds of forced laborers died while building the fortress and its bastions were later used to guard and torture many political prisoners, including Peter's own son Aleksey. The cells where prisoners were kept are open to the public, alongside a couple of museums and the magnificent cathedral which houses the tombs of the Romanovs.

Environs

Just a 45-minute trip by hydrofoil from the Hermitage, Peter the Great's sprawling Baroque residence, **Peterhof**, is a must-see when staying in the city for a few days. Designed by Jean Baptiste Le Blond, and built 1714–23, the palace lies at the center of a magnificent landscaped park complete with ornamental ponds and spurting fountains. Altogether, a perfect expression of imperial triumphalism.

Tsarskoe Selo, the lavish palace built for Czarina Elizabeth also lies within easy reach. Designed by Rasterelli in 1752, the 300-m (980-ft) long blue, gold, and white façade is a glitteringly striking sight.

♠ **Peterhof**
Petrodvorets, 30 km (19 miles) W of St. Petersburg. **Tel** 420 0073. 📞 from Baltic Station to Novy Petergof then bus 348, 350, and others. ⛴ board outside the Hermitage (May–Oct). ⚫ Tue–Sun. ⚫ last Tue of month. 🎫♠ 📷

♠ **Tsarskoe Selo**
25 km (16 miles) S of St. Petersburg. **Tel** 465 2024. 📞 from Vitebsk Station to Detskoe Selo, then bus 371 or 382. ⚫ Wed–Mon. ⚫ last Mon of month. 🎫 📷

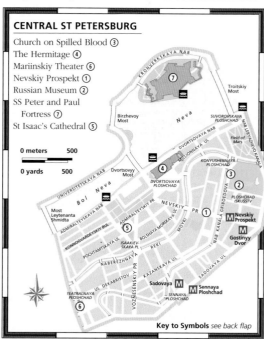

CENTRAL ST PETERSBURG

Church on Spilled Blood ③
The Hermitage ④
Mariinskiy Theater ⑥
Nevskiy Prospekt ①
Russian Museum ②
SS Peter and Paul Fortress ⑦
St Isaac's Cathedral ⑤

0 meters 500
0 yards 500

Key to Symbols see back flap

Practical & Travel Information

The Finnish are a practical people, and tourists can expect the local information services to be both accurate and helpful. Finland's main cities are all served by an efficient railroad system and regular, inexpensive internal flights. Finns take pride in their public transportation systems and promote environmentally-friendly modes of travel. Cycling and walking in summer and cross-country skiing in winter are an in-built part of the national psyche. The capital, Helsinki, is easy to navigate on foot, by bicycle, or using public transportation.

TOURIST INFORMATION

For general and location-specific information, get in touch with the **Finnish Tourist Board**, which has offices in major cities all over the world. The Finnish Tourist Board office in Helsinki has information about different parts of Finland in several languages. Helsinki, Turku, and Savonlinna all have a local tourist office.

The best time to visit Finland is between May and September, but winter in northern Finland has its own special, snow-laden charm. Many tourist attractions in Finland close on Mondays, and some have seasonal opening hours.

VISA REQUIREMENTS

Visitors who are not citizens of Norway, Denmark, Sweden, or Iceland must have a passport to enter Finland. Members of most EU countries may use an official EU identity card in lieu of their passport. Visas are not required for visitors from the UK, Ireland,

the United States, Canada, Australia, or New Zealand. At Finnish customs, there is a blue channel for citizens of EU countries.

SAFETY AND EMERGENCIES

Finland has very low crime statistics, although drunks (largely harmless) have been a common sight in Finnish towns and cities for years. Mosquitoes are very active during the summer months near water (which is just about everywhere), but their bites do not carry disease. Tap water is safe to drink.

In case of emergencies the appropriate number to call is listed in the Directory opposite.

LANGUAGE

Finland has two official languages – Finnish, which is spoken by 94 percent of the population, and Swedish, which is spoken by 6 percent. Road signs and maps are often in both languages and there are different national newspapers for each language,

too. Younger Finns invariably speak some English, and are very eager to practise it.

BANKING AND CURRENCY

The Finnish currency unit was the markka until 2002, when it was replaced by the euro, the common currency of the European Union *(see p15)*.

Banks usually open from 9:15am to 4:15pm Monday to Friday. Most international credit cards are accepted in many places all over Finland.

COMMUNICATIONS

Post offices in Finland usually open from 9am to 6pm Monday to Friday, although the main post office in Helsinki operates longer hours. You can buy stamps from kiosks and bookstores, as well as at post offices.

Public telephones are found in thousands of locations, and are usually always well maintained. Many take phonecards, available at kiosks and post offices.

SAUNAS

Many hotels have a sauna, but they are usually electric ones. For a memorable sauna experience, seek out a wood-fired sauna – preferably close to a lake or the sea – or a traditional "smoke sauna" *(savusauna)*. The sauna is a popular and family-friendly place in which to relax and unwind – there are over a million in Finland. Helsinki boasts the superb Kotiharjun wood-fired sauna (call 09-753 1535). The Finnish Sauna Society has two wood-fired saunas and three smoke saunas set beside the sea (call 09-686 0560 for more information).

FLYING TO FINLAND

Most international flights arrive at Helsinki's **Vantaa Airport**, which is 19 km (12 miles) north of Helsinki. **Finnair** and British Airways both operate daily scheduled services from London Heathrow to Helsinki. Some special "visit Father

THE CLIMATE OF FINLAND

In northern Finland (beyond the Arctic Circle), the sun remains above the horizon for a month in summer. This gives Finland its sobriquet "Land of the Midnight Sun." Even in Helsinki, there are almost 20 hours of daylight in summer. In winter, the average temperature falls well below 0° C (32° F), but low humidity makes the extreme cold less raw.

HELSINKI			
°C/F	21/70		
0°C	7/45	11/52	7/45
32°F	0/32		2/36
			-3/27
			-8/18
☼ 9	10	8	7
☂ 38 mm	74 mm	74 mm	41 mm
month Apr	Jul	Oct	Jan

Christmas" winter flights fly direct from the UK to Rovaniemi on the Arctic Circle. KLM and SAS operate regular flights from Amsterdam and Copenhagen respectively to Helsinki. Travel from North America to Helsinki usually involves connecting flights (changing in Greenland or in Europe) but Finnair flies direct from New York to Helsinki.

ARRIVING BY SEA

The luxury ferries that ply the waters between Stockholm in Sweden and the Finnish ports of Helsinki and Turku have a reputation for offering a state-of-the-art cruising experience. The superliners – operated by **Silja Line** and **Viking Line** – take about 13 hours to make the crossing, which allows plenty of time to enjoy shopping, entertainment, and the celebrated *smörgåsbord* buffets.

RAIL TRAVEL

Finland's national rail network is run by the State Railroads of Finland (Valtion Rautatiet or VR). Finnish trains are reliable and clean. Advance reservations are recommended for long-distance, intercity (IC), and some express (EP) trains. In Helsinki, tickets can be bought either at **Helsinki Central Station** or from **TourShop**, which is located at the Helsinki City Tourist Office.

TRAVELING BY BUS

Buses in rural areas are infrequent (but reliable), while intercity buses are fast and efficient. Long-distance journeys are very time-consuming, so it is worth considering the relatively inexpensive domestic flights.

TRAVELING BY CAR

Car rental has come down in cost since Finland joined the EU. Even so, car hire using the main inter-national agencies is still pricey. **Europcar** offers some of the more reasonable rates.

Laws about driving under the influence of alcohol are strict and rigidly enforced, as are speed restrictions. Elk and reindeer are a serious road danger, so do pay attention to animal hazard signs.

GETTING AROUND HELSINKI

Helsinki is manageable on foot or by bicycle, but buses, trams, and the metro provide easy alternatives. The 3T tram circles central Helsinki, stopping at several important sights. Cycle tours, city walks, and cruises are all available from the TourExpert office. Taxis are an expensive way of getting around; ask the driver for an idea of the cost before you embark on your journey.

Finland's island-hopping passenger motorcruisers are a fun form of transportation, giving a real taste of relaxed Finnish summer living.

If you plan to visit several attractions, it is worth investing in a Helsinki Card (available from the Helsinki City Tourist Office and from most hotels). Valid for one, two, or three days, the Card gives unlimited travel on public transportation and on some ferries, reductions on some theater, dance, and opera tickets, and free admission to all major Helsinki sights and nearly 50 museums. Other benefits include reductions on sightseeing tours and on goods in some shops.

Another option is the Helsinki City Transport tourist ticket, which entitles you to unlimited travel on all buses, trams, the metro, and local trains in Helsinki. The ticket is valid for one, three, or five days and is available at all Helsinki City Transport (HKL) points and tourist offices.

DIRECTORY

TOURIST INFORMATION

Finnish Tourist Board
www.mek.fi
www.visitfinland.com

In Finland:
Töölönkatu 11,
FIN-00101 Helsinki.
Tel 010-605 8000.

In the UK:
PO Box 33213,
London W6 8JX.
Tel 020-7365 2512.

In the US:
PO Box 4649, Grand Central Station, New York, NY 10163.
Tel 212-885 9700.

Helsinki City Tourist Office
Pohjoisesplanadi 19,
FIN-00099 Helsinki.
Tel 09-3101 3300.
www.hel.fi/tourism

EMBASSIES

Canada
Pohjoisesplanadi 25b,
Helsinki.
Tel 09-228 530.
www.dfait-maeci.gc.ca

UK
Itäinen Puistotie 17,
Helsinki. *Tel 09-2286 5100.*
www.
britishembassy.gov.uk

US
Itäinen Puistotie 14b,
Helsinki. *Tel 09-616 250.*
www.usembassy.fi

EMERGENCIES

Ambulance, Police, and Fire
Tel 112.

AIR TRAVEL

Finnair
Tel 09-818 8383
(Finland).
Tel 0870-241 4411 (UK).
Tel 800-950 5000 (US).
www.finnair.com

Vantaa Airport
Tel 0200-14636.
www.helsinkivantaa.fi

FERRY SERVICES

Silja Line
Tel 09-18041.
www.silja.fi

Viking Line
Tel 09-12 351.
www.vikingline.fi

RAIL TRAVEL

Helsinki Central Station
Tel 0600-41 902 or 0307-10. www.vr.fi

TourShop
Tel 09-2288 1500 (Finland).

CAR RENTAL

Avis
Tel 09-859 8333.

Budget
Tel 09-686 6500.

Europcar
Tel 040-306 2444.

Hertz
Tel 0200-11 22 33.

Where to Stay in Finland and St. Petersburg

PRICE CATEGORIES
Price categories are for a standard
double room per night in high season,
including breakfast, tax, and service.
Prices for St. Petersburg are in US dollars.
€ Under 65 euros (under $100)
€€ 65–135 euros ($100–$175)
€€€ 135–200 euros ($175–$250)
€€€€ 200–270 euros ($250–$325)
€€€€€ Over 270 euros (over $325)

Finns are very keen on sleek, modern hotels. As a result, Helsinki offers plenty of middle-range and upscale hotels. Prices often include a morning sauna and swim. In St. Petersburg, central hotels mainly fall into two categories: large and luxurious or smaller bed and breakfasts.

HELSINKI

CENTRAL HELSINKI Matkakoti Margarita   €
Itäinen Teatterikuja 3, 00100 **Tel** *09-622 4261* **Rooms** *15*   **Map** *C3*

This guesthouse is placed just behind the train station and a block from a verdant park great for a stroll. The rooms are quite small but completely adequate, and most have shared facilities. Rooms can be rented for the afternoon if you want to rest for a few hours before an evening train journey. **www.matkakoti-margarita.com**

CENTRAL HELSINKI Sokos Vaakuna   €€€
Asema-Aukio 2, 00100 **Tel** *020-1234 610* **Rooms** *270*   **Map** *C4*

Centrally located by the Central Railway Station, this lovely building, built in 1952, is one of the most stylish chain hotels in Finland. Rooms are furnished in dark woods and have very comfortable beds. The top floor restaurant, where breakfast is served, has great views of Helsinki's rooftops. **www.sokoshotels.fi**

CENTRAL HELSINKI Kämp   €€€€€
Pohjoisesplanadi 29, 00100 **Tel** *09-675 111* **Rooms** *179*   **Map** *C4*

Founded in 1887 and recently renovated, this Belle Epoque property is one of Helsinki's most outstanding hotels, and only one of two in the city with five stars. Many of the rooms are 19th-century style but with modern amenities and opulent marble bathrooms with separate bath and walk-in shower. The breakfasts here are divine. **www.hotelkamp.fi**

REST OF FINLAND

SAVONLINNA Seurahuone   €€
Kauppatori 4–6, 57130 **Tel** *015 5731* **Rooms** *84*

This modern establishment has rooms spread across two wings – one traditional, one more modern. The decor is a little bland but the hotel is reliable and the staff friendly and courteous. Rooms in the new wing have views over Lake Saimaa. **www.savonlinnanseurahuone.fi**

TURKU Omena Hotelli   €
Humalistonkatu 7, 20100 **Tel** *020-7716 555* **Rooms** *75*

Finland's new chain of self-service hotels has finally arrived in Turku. This unique establishment has no receptionist: bookings are made either online or at the kiosk downstairs. The ultra-modern rooms have all the necessary amenities and very comfortable beds. Easily the best hotel deal in the city. **www.omena.com**

ST. PETERSBURG

GOSTINYY DVOR Pushka Inn $$$
Naberezhnaya reki Moyki 14 **Tel** *312 0913* **Fax** *312 0913* **Rooms** *31*

This historic building, right on the river Moyka and next door to the Pushkin Museum, has been transformed into a comfortable, modern hotel. The decor is basic but you will struggle to find anything closer to the Hermitage. There are four apartments or family suites. **www.pushkainn.ru**

PALACE EMBANKMENT Astoria $$$$$
Isaakievskaya ploschad, Bolshaya Morskaya ulitsa 39 **Tel** *313 5750* **Fax** *313 5059* **Rooms** *223*

Fully renovated in 2002, the Astoria has managed to retain its historic charm. Rooms at the front offer outstanding views over St. Isaac's Cathedral and Square, and along the river Moyka. Those who cannot afford to stay here can still soak up the historic surroundings by taking tea in the lounge. **www.astoria.spb.ru**

Key to Symbols *see back cover flap*

Where to Eat in Finland and St. Petersburg

Eating out used to be a prohibitively expensive experience for toursits in Finland, but a wider range of restaurants means that even city-center dining now caters for all budgets. In St. Petersburg many restaurants serve a fixed-price "business lunch" that proves good value.

PRICE CATEGORIES
Price categories are for a three-course meal for one, including a glass of house wine, tax, and service. Prices for St. Petersburg are in US dollars.

€ Under 15 euros (under $25)
€€ 15–25 euros ($25–$40)
€€€ 25–35 euros ($40–$60)
€€€€ Over 55 euros (over $60)

HELSINKI

CENTRAL HELSINKI Zetor   €€€
Mannerheimintie 3, 00100 **Tel** *09-666 966*   **Map** *C4*

Owned by Finnish icons the Kaurismäki brothers, this quirky late-night restaurant complete with a rusty tractor is typified by sawdust on the floors and a meat-and-potato centric menu. Food is served until 3:30am, along with music and a late night bar.

CENTRAL HELSINKI Romanov   €€€€
Yrjönkatu 15, 00120 **Tel** *09-642 394*   **Map** *C4*

One of Helsinki's most respected Russian restaurants, the rooms here are decked out with portraits and photos of Csars and aristocrats. The food is rich with steak and fish dishes among the mains, as well as classic Russian dishes such as borscht and blini. A Helsinki classic well worth the price and dressing up for.

CENTRAL HELSINKI Strindberg   €€€€
Pohjoisesplanadi 33, 00130 **Tel** *09-681 2030*   **Map** *C4*

With its Parisian bistro feel, this café-restaurant is one of the best-loved and most central cafés in the capital – a perfect place for people-watching on weekend mornings. Downstairs, the café offers tasty pastries for breakfast, as well as very good coffee. Upstairs, the upscale restaurant features reindeer, Rydberg steak, and Baltic fish dishes.

REST OF FINLAND

SAVONLINNA Hilpeä Munkki   €€
Riihisaari, 57100 **Tel** *020-7291 760*

This summertime outdoor restaurant is located right next to the Olav castle, making it the perfect place to dine before or after an opera performance. The atmosphere is reminiscent of a medieval inn, with animal skins and candlelit tables. Food is traditional Finnish, with great broiled steak fillet, lamb and sausage dishes.

TURKU Viikinkiravintola Harald   €€€€
Aurakatu 3, 20100 **Tel** *022-765 050*

The decor here makes this restaurant one of the most interesting places to eat in Turku. A Viking theme reigns with wooden benches and animal heads on the wall. The food consists largely of hearty meat dishes such as venison braised in wine with garlic. There is a great and inexpensive lunch buffet.

ST. PETERSBURG

GOSTINYY DVOR Kavkaz-Bar $$$
Karavannaya ulitsa 18 **Tel** *312 1665*

Caucasian (Georgian and Armenian) cuisine, and excellent Georgian wines and brandies are on offer here – at a price. Kavkaz-Bar has a superb location close to Nevskiy prospekt, and an intimate atmosphere. It also serves the best vegetarian kebabs in town. A selection of dishes is available in the less formal outer café, overlooking a quiet square.

PALACE EMBANKMENT 1913 $$
Voznesenskiy prospekt 13 **Tel** *315 5148*

Named after the last year of Russian imperial greatness, 1913 prides itself on generous portions and outstanding regional dishes such as *draniki* (potato pancakes) with bacon, and sorrel soup, as well as lobster dishes. A warm atmosphere reigns with a singer and guitarist performing Russian songs from 8pm daily. Excellent service.

Map References *see map of Helsinki pp692–3*

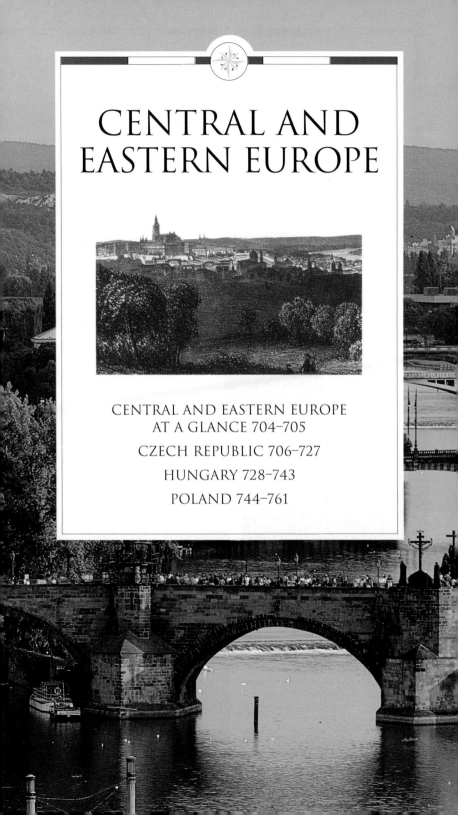

CENTRAL AND EASTERN EUROPE

CENTRAL AND EASTERN EUROPE
AT A GLANCE 704–705

CZECH REPUBLIC 706–727

HUNGARY 728–743

POLAND 744–761

Central and Eastern Europe at a Glance

At the geographical heart of mainland Europe, Hungary, Poland, and the Czech Republic have witnessed a huge surge in visitor numbers since the end of Communism in the late 1980s and early 1990s. Despite the widespread destruction caused by two world wars, their towns and cities retain a wealth of historic monuments, many of which have been painstakingly restored to their former glory. Fortunately, tourism has not destroyed the unique cultural identity of these once little-known countries.

Prague
(see pp710–21), *the capital of the Czech Republic, is a vibrant city with a rich architectural and cultural heritage. The hilltop castle complex is dominated by the magnificent St. Vitus's Cathedral, whose treasures include many royal tombs.*

Słupsk

Szczecin

Poznań

Wrocław

Karlsbad

PRAGUE • Kutná Hora

Plzeň

CZECH REPUBLIC
(See pp706 – 727)

Olomouc

Český Krumlov

Győr

Balatonfüred

Pécs

Bohemia (see pp722–3) *holds the greatest appeal for most foreign visitors to the Czech Republic. The region boasts elegant spas, fairy-tale castles perched high on thickly wooded hillsides, and many perfectly preserved medieval towns, such as Český Krumlov in the far south.*

Lake Balaton (see p738), *a huge freshwater lake in western Hungary, is the country's most popular summer vacation destination. Bordered by dozens of resorts, it offers beaches, safe bathing, and water sports, and also provides a habitat for a wide variety of flora and fauna.*

◁ **Charles Bridge and buildings of the Old Town in Prague, Czech Republic**

LOCATOR MAP

Warsaw (see pp748–53) *was largely rebuilt during the Communist era following complete destruction in World War II. Many of its grandest buildings date from the Baroque period, including the splendid Royal Castle.*

Cracow (see pp754–7), *in southern Poland, has historic monuments spanning hundreds of years, and has been declared a UNESCO World Heritage Site. Its skyline is dominated by dozens of churches, the most important being the Gothic St. Mary's Church in Market Square.*

Budapest (see pp732–7) *is rich in historical treasures, from medieval ruins to late 19th- and early 20th-century Secessionist buildings. Mátyás Church preserves some of its original Gothic features, such as the glorious stone carving on the Mary Portal.*

POLAND
(See pp744–761)

HUNGARY
(See pp728–743)

Gdańsk

Augustów

WARSAW

Cracow

BUDAPEST

Eger

0 km   75

0 miles   75

CZECH REPUBLIC

The Czech Republic is one of Europe's youngest states. In the years after World War II, foreign visitors to what was then Czechoslovakia rarely ventured farther than the capital, Prague. Today the country's beautifully preserved medieval towns and castles are attracting an ever-increasing number of tourists.

The Czech Republic is divided into two regions, Bohemia and Moravia. Rolling plains and lush, pine-clad mountains, dotted with medieval chateaux and 19th-century spa resorts, characterize the landscape of southern and western Bohemia. In spite of the recent influx of tourists, life here still proceeds at a gentle, relaxed pace. In contrast, much of northern Bohemia has been given over to mining and other heavy industry, with devastating effects on the local environment. Moravia has orchards and vineyards in the south, and a broad industrial belt in the north of the region.

Bohemia's largest city and the capital of the Czech Republic, Prague is a thriving cultural and commercial center that bears little relation to most people's expectations of an "Eastern" European city. Its wealth of magnificent architecture, spanning over a thousand years, has withstood two world wars in the last century.

Since the early 1990s the Czech Republic has emerged as a relatively healthy democratic state. Its economy has been boosted by tourism, and the country is now a member of both NATO and the EU.

HISTORY

From 500 BC the area now known as the Czech Republic was settled by Celtic tribes, who were later joined by Germanic peoples. The first Slavs, the forefathers of the Czechs, came to the region around 500 AD. Struggles for supremacy led to the emergence of a ruling dynasty, the Přemyslids, at the start of the 9th century. The Přemyslids were involved in many bloody family feuds. In 935 Prince Wenceslas was murdered by his brother, Boleslav. Later canonized, Wenceslas became Bohemia's best-known patron saint.

The reign of Holy Roman Emperor Charles IV in the 14th century heralded a Golden Age for Bohemia.

Rooftops of Prague's Malá Strana (Little Quarter), covered in snow

◁ The medieval Karlstein Castle, rising above picturesque wooded valleys in Bohemia

Charles chose Prague as his imperial residence and founded many prestigious institutions there, including central Europe's first university.

In the early 15th century, central Europe shook in fear of an incredible fighting force – the Hussites, followers of the reformer Jan Hus, who preached in Prague and attacked the corrupt practices of the Catholic Church. His execution for heresy in 1415 led to the Hussite wars. The radical wing of the Hussites, the Taborites, were finally defeated at the Battle of Lipany in 1434.

At the start of the 16th century the Austrian Habsburgs took over, beginning a period of rule that would last for almost 400 years. Religious turmoil led, in 1618, to the Protestant revolt and the 30 Years' War. The end of the war ushered in a period of persecution of all non-Catholics and a systematic Germanization of the country's institutions.

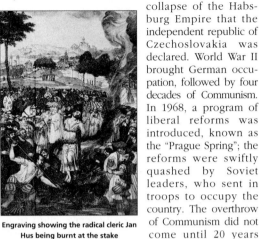

Engraving showing the radical cleric Jan Hus being burnt at the stake

KEY DATES IN CZECH HISTORY

500 BC Celts in Bohemia and Moravia. Joined by Germanic tribes in 1st century AD

AD 500–600 Slavs settle in the region

800 Dynasty of Pfemyslids founded

870 Pfemyslids build Prague Castle

1333 Charles IV makes Prague his home, marking the start of the city's Golden Age

1415 Jan Hus burnt at the stake for heresy; start of the Hussite Wars

1526 Habsburg rule begins with Ferdinand I

1583 Accession of Habsburg Emperor Rudolf II

1618 Protestant revolt leads to the 30 Years' War

1627 Beginning of Counter-Reformation committee in Prague

19th century Czech National Revival

1918 Foundation of Czechoslovakia

1948 Communist Party assumes power

1989 Year of the "Velvet Revolution"; Communist regime finally overthrown

1993 Czechoslovakia ceases to exist; creation of the new Czech Republic

2004 Czech Republic joins the EU

2007 New center-right coalition forms parliament

The 19th century saw a period of Czech national revival and the burgeoning of civic pride. But, a foreign power still ruled, and it was not until 1918 and the collapse of the Habsburg Empire that the independent republic of Czechoslovakia was declared. World War II brought German occupation, followed by four decades of Communism. In 1968, a program of liberal reforms was introduced, known as the "Prague Spring"; the reforms were swiftly quashed by Soviet leaders, who sent in troops to occupy the country. The overthrow of Communism did not come until 20 years later: in November 1989 a protest rally in Prague against police brutality led to the "Velvet Revolution" – a series of mass demonstrations and strikes that resulted in the resignation of the existing regime. The most recent chapter in Czech history was closed in 1993 with the peaceful division of Czechoslovakia into two independent states – Slovakia and the Czech Republic.

LANGUAGE AND CULTURE

Under the Habsburgs, Czech identity was largely suppressed and the Czech language became little more than a dialect, mainly spoken among the peasant population. In the 19th century, however, Austrian rule relaxed, and the Czechs began rediscovering their own culture. The first history of the Czech nation was written by the Moravian František Palacký, and Czech was re-established as an official language.

Since the Golden Age of the 14th century Prague has prided itself on its reputation as a flourishing cultural center. In the early 20th century the city had a Cubist movement to rival that of Paris. The Czech Republic has produced writers, artists, and musicians of world renown including Franz Kafka, Alfons Mucha, and Antonín Dvořák.

Exploring the Czech Republic

One of Europe's most beautiful capital cities, Prague is undoubtedly the highlight of a visit to the Czech Republic. Away from this bustling, cosmopolitan city, however, the tranquil Bohemian countryside is home to dozens of castles and historic towns, whose appearance has remained virtually unchanged for hundreds of years. Most of the main sights of interest can be visited on a day trip from Prague, and are easily reached from the capital by good public transportation and road networks. Slightly farther afield, Český Krumlov merits at least a couple of days' exploration.

Prague's Charles Bridge and the buildings of the Old Town

SIGHTS AT A GLANCE

Český Krumlov **5**
Karlsbad **4**
Karlstein **2**
Kutná Hora **3**
PRAGUE pp710–21 **1**

KEY

✈ Airport
— Highway
— Major road
— Railroad
--- International border

Prague ❶

Prague, capital of the Czech Republic, has a population of just over one million. In the late Middle Ages, during the reign of Charles IV, Prague's position as the crossroads of Europe aided its growth into a magnificent city, larger than Paris or London. In the 16th century the Austrian Habsburgs took over and built many of the Baroque palaces and gardens that delight visitors today. Some of these palaces now house important museums and galleries. Prague's Jewish Quarter has a handful of synagogues and a cemetery, which remarkably survived the Nazi occupation. Despite neglect under Communist rule, the historic center of the city has been preserved.

The Three Fiddles, an old house sign in Nerudova Street

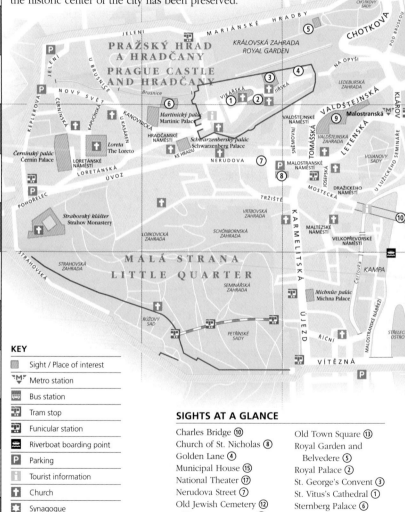

KEY

▢	Sight / Place of interest
Ⓜ	Metro station
🚌	Bus station
🚋	Tram stop
🚠	Funicular station
⛴	Riverboat boarding point
🅿	Parking
ℹ	Tourist information
✝	Church
✡	Synagogue
⸱⸱⸱	Pedestrian street

SIGHTS AT A GLANCE

Charles Bridge ⑩
Church of St. Nicholas ⑧
Golden Lane ④
Municipal House ⑮
National Theater ⑰
Nerudova Street ⑦
Old Jewish Cemetery ⑫
Old-New Synagogue ⑪
Old Town Hall ⑭

Old Town Square ⑬
Royal Garden and
  Belvedere ⑤
Royal Palace ②
St. George's Convent ③
St. Vitus's Cathedral ①
Sternberg Palace ⑥
Wallenstein Palace ⑨
Wenceslas Square ⑯

GETTING AROUND

Prague's subway, known as the
metro, is the fastest way of getting
around the city. It has three lines,
A, B, and C, and 54 stations. Line A
covers all the main areas of the city
center. Trams are the city's oldest
method of public transport. There are
also a number of night trams. Routes
14, 17, 22, and 23 pass many major
sights on both banks of the Vltava.

SEE ALSO

- **Where to Stay** p726

- **Where to Eat** p727

Corner of Old Town Square, with the Church of St. Nicholas

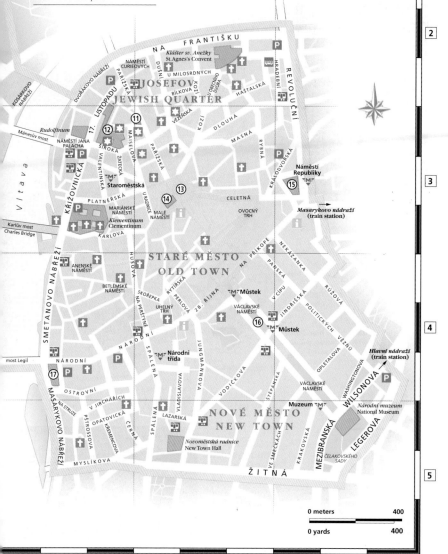

Street-by-Street: Prague Castle

The history of Prague begins with the castle, founded by Prince Bořivoj in the 9th century. Despite periodic fires and invasions, it has retained churches, chapels, halls, and towers from every period of its history, from the Gothic splendor of St. Vitus's Cathedral to the Renaissance additions of Rudolph II, the last Habsburg to use the castle as his principal residence. The courtyards date from 1753–75, when the whole area was rebuilt in Late Baroque and Neoclassical styles. The castle became the seat of the Czechoslovak president in 1918, and the current president of the Czech Republic has an office here.

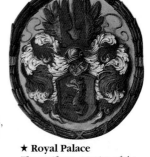

★ Royal Palace
The uniform exterior of the palace (see p714) conceals many fine Gothic and Renaissance halls. Coats of arms cover the walls and ceiling of the Room of the New Land Rolls.

The Powder Tower was used in the past for storing gunpowder and as a bell foundry. It is now a museum.

To Royal Garden

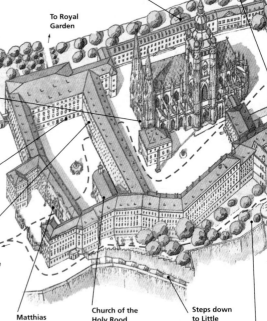

★ St. Vitus's Cathedral
This stained-glass window by Alfons Mucha is one of many 20th-century works of art added to the cathedral.

The Picture Gallery of Prague Castle, in the restored stables of the castle, has a good collection of Renaissance and Baroque paintings.

President's office

To Hradčanské náměstí (Castle Square)

KEY

– – – Suggested route

0 meters   60
0 yards   60

Matthias Gate (1614)

Church of the Holy Rood

Steps down to Little Quarter

STAR SIGHTS

★ St. Vitus's Cathedral

★ St. George's Basilica

★ Royal Palace

South Gardens
Various gardens have been laid out along the old ramparts overlooking the Little Quarter. These statues date from the 18th century.

Dalibor Tower
This grim 15th-century tower takes its name from the first man imprisoned in it, a young knight sentenced to death for harboring outlawed serfs.

Golden Lane *(see p714)* is lined with picturesque artisans' cottages, built in the late 16th century for the Castle's guards and gunners.

White Tower

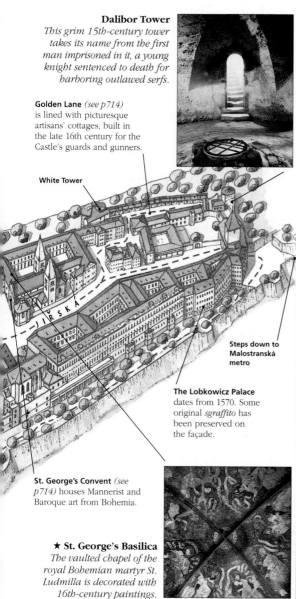

Steps down to Malostranská metro

The Lobkowicz Palace dates from 1570. Some original *sgraffito* has been preserved on the façade.

St. George's Convent *(see p714)* houses Mannerist and Baroque art from Bohemia.

★ **St. George's Basilica**
The vaulted chapel of the royal Bohemian martyr St. Ludmilla is decorated with 16th-century paintings.

THE DEFENESTRATION OF 1618

On May 23, 1618, more than 100 Protestant nobles stormed the Royal Palace to protest against the succession of the Habsburg Archduke Ferdinand. The two Catholic Governors, Jaroslav Martinic and Vilém Slavata, were confronted and thrown out of the eastern window along with their secretary, Philipp Fabricius. Falling some 15 m (50 ft), they landed in a dung heap. This event signaled the beginning of the Thirty Years' War. The Catholics attributed the survival of the Governors to the intervention of angels.

St. Vitus's Cathedral ①

Prague Castle, third courtyard.
Ⓜ *Hradčanská, Malostranská.*
🚊 *22, 23 to Prague Castle (Pražský hrad) or U Prašného mostu.* ☐ *daily (except during services).* ♿ *Steeple* ☐ *daily.* ● *in bad weather.* 📷

Work began on the city's most distinctive landmark in 1344 on the orders of John of Luxemburg. The Gothic cathedral replaced an earlier Romanesque basilica that stood on the site of a small rotunda dating back to the time of St. Wenceslas (c.925). The first architect of the new Gothic structure was the Frenchman Matthew of Arras. After his death, the Swabian Peter Parler took over. The eastern end of the cathedral dates from this period. The original entrance was the Golden Portal on the south side of the building. The present entrance, the western end of the nave, and the façade with its twin spires were added in 1872–1929.

The chapels house many saintly relics, the Bohemian crown jewels, and a number of royal tombs. The tomb of "Good King" Wenceslas stands in the St. Wenceslas Chapel, which is decorated with Gothic frescoes. Another spectacular memorial is the huge silver tomb (1736) of St. John Nepomuk, whose cult was encouraged during the Counter-Reformation.

Spectacularly vaulted chancel of St. Vitus's Cathedral

Royal Palace ②

Prague Castle, third courtyard. *Tel*
22-43 73 102. **www**.pribeh-hradv.cz
Ⓜ *Hradčanská, Malostranská.*
🚋 *22, 23.* ⏺ *daily.* 📷 ♿

From the time Prague Castle
was first fortified in stone in
the 11th century, the Royal
Palace was the seat of a long
line of Bohemian kings.

The building consists of
three different architectural
layers. A Romanesque palace,
built around 1135, forms the
basement of the present
structure. In the course of the
next 200 years, two further
palaces were built above this –
the first by Přemysl Otakar II
in 1253, and the second by
Charles IV in 1340. On the
top floor, and dominating the
entire palace structure, is the
massive Gothic Vladislav Hall,
with its splendid rib vaulting.
Designed by Benedikt Ried for
King Vladislav Jagiello, the
hall was completed in 1502.
The Riders' Staircase, just off
one side of the hall, is a flight
of wide sloping steps with a
magnificent Gothic rib-vaulted
ceiling. It was used by knights
on horseback to get to the
hall for jousting contests.

Under Habsburg rule, the
palace housed government
offices, courts, and the old
Bohemian Diet (seat of the
parliament). The Bohemian
Chancellery, the former royal
offices of the Habsburgs, is
the site of the famous 1618
defenestration *(see p713).* In
1619 the Bohemian nobles
deposed Emperor Ferdinand II

**The Riders' Staircase leading to the
Vladislav Hall, Royal Palace**

*Simeon and the Infant Jesus (1725) by the
Baroque painter Petr Brandl*

as King of Bohemia, electing
in his place Frederick of the
Palatinate. This led to the
Battle of the White Mountain
(1620), the first major battle of
the Thirty Years' War, fought
just outside Prague. The defeat
of the Bohemians ushered in
a period of persecution of all
non-Catholics and the
systematic Germanization of
the country's institutions.

Also worth seeing at the
Royal Palace are the New
Land Rolls, a set of rooms
decorated with the crests of
clerks who worked here from
1561 to 1774, and the All
Saints' Chapel, built by Peter
Parler for Charles IV.

St. George's Convent ③

Prague Castle, Jiřské náměstí.
Tel 25–75 31 644. Ⓜ *Hradčanská,
Malostranská.* 🚋 *22, 23.* ⏺ *daily.*
📷 **www**.ngprague.cz

Bohemia's first convent was
founded here in 973 by
Prince Boleslav II. Rebuilt
over the centuries, it was
finally abolished in 1782 when
it was converted into barracks.
Today, the convent holds a
fine collection of Bohemian
art dating from the era of the
Habsburg Emperor Rudolph II
to the end of the Baroque.

With his passion for the
unusual and the artificial,
Rudolph loved Mannerist

artists and invited
many to work at his
court in Prague. The
emperor's great
collection was
dispersed when
Prague Castle was
looted in 1648, but
the few works on
show here give an
idea of his tastes.
Among the best are
the paintings of the
German-born Hans
von Aachen and
the sculptures of the
Dutch-born
Adriaen de Vries.

The gallery of the
Baroque period
contains some
excellent religious
canvases by Petr
Brandl, including the
particularly moving painting
Simeon and the Infant Jesus,
as well as several masterly
portraits by Karel Škréta and
Jan Kupecký.

Adjoining the convent, **St.
George's Basilica** was founded
by Prince Vratislav in 920 and
is the best-preserved
Romanesque church in Prague.
The huge twin towers and
austere interior have been restored to give an idea of the
church's original appearance.
The rusty red façade was a
17th-century addition.

Golden Lane ④

Ⓜ *Hradčanská, Malostranská.*
🚋 *22, 23.* 📷

Named after the goldsmiths
who lived here in the 17th
century, this is one of the
most picturesque streets in
Prague. The tiny, brightly
painted houses that line one
side of it were built in the late
1500s for Rudolph II's castle
guards. A century later the
goldsmiths moved in. By the
19th century the area had
degenerated into a slum,
populated by Prague's poor
and the criminal community.
In the 1950s the area was
restored to something like its
original state, and most of the
houses were converted into
shops selling books, Bohemian
glass, and other souvenirs for
the tourists who flock here.

For hotels and restaurants in this region see p726 and p727

Golden Lane has been home to a number of well-known writers, including Franz Kafka (1883–1924), who stayed at No. 22 for a few months between 1916 and 1917.

Royal Garden and Belvedere ⑤

Prague Castle, U Prašného mostu.
🅼 *Hradčanská, Malostranská.*
🚋 *22, 23.* **Garden** ⬜ *May–Oct: daily.* 🎟 🔉 **Belvedere** ⬜ *only for exhibitions.* 🎟 🔉 www.hrad.cz

Prague's well-kept Royal Garden was created in 1535 for Ferdinand I. The garden contains some fine examples of 16th-century architecture, including the Belvedere, a beautiful arcaded summer-house with slender Ionic columns and a blue-green copper roof. Also known as the Royal Summer Palace (Královský letohrádek), the Italian Renaissance building was commissioned in the mid-16th century for Ferdinand's wife. It is now used as an art gallery. In front of it is the Singing Fountain, which owes its name to the musical sound the water makes as it hits the bronze bowl.

Also in the garden is the Ball Game Hall (Míčovna), built in 1569, and used primarily for playing a form of real tennis.

At the entrance to the garden, the Lion Court was where Rudolph II had his zoo (now a restaurant).

Artisans' cottages on Golden Lane, Prague Castle

Sternberg Palace ⑥

Hradčanské náměstí 15. **Tel** 22-05 14 598. 🅼 *Hradčanská, Malostranská.*
🚋 *22, 23 to Pohořelec or Prague Castle.* ⬜ *Tue–Sun.* 🎟 🔉
www.ngprague.cz

Franz Josef Sternberg founded the Society of Patriotic Friends of the Arts in Bohemia in 1796. Fellow noblemen would lend their finest pictures and sculpture to the society, which had its headquarters in the early 18th-century Sternberg Palace. Since 1949 the fine Baroque building has been used to house the National Gallery's collection of European art.

The palace has an impressive array of exhibits, including some particularly fine examples of Italian medieval art, Neapolitan works of the 17th and 18th centuries, Dutch and Flemish masterpieces, and German art of the 15th to 17th centuries. The 19th- and 20th-century exhibits, including works by Klimt, Picasso, and Miró, were moved to the Veletržní Palace, northeast of the city center, in 1996.

Among the highlights at the palace are Albrecht Dürer's *The Feast of the Rosary* (1506), *Head of Christ*, painted by El Greco in the 1590s, and Rembrandt's *Scholar in his Study* (1634).

Visitors can also see a collection of Renaissance bronzes, as well as the fascinating Chinese Cabinet. This richly decorated chamber, which combines the Baroque style with Far Eastern motifs, is now on display again after several years of restoration work.

The Belvedere, Emperor Ferdinand I's summer palace in the Royal Garden beside Prague Castle

Malá Strana

Malá Strana (the Little Quarter) is the part of Prague that has been least affected by recent history. Hardly any new building has taken place here since the 18th century, and the quarter is rich in splendid Baroque palaces and churches, and old houses with attractive signs. Founded in 1257, the area is built on the slopes below the castle, enjoying magnificent views across the river to the Old Town. The center of Malá Strana is Little Quarter Square, dominated by the impressive Church of St. Nicholas.

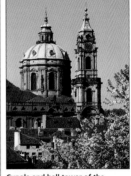

Cupola and bell tower of the Church of St. Nicholas

Sign of Jan Neruda's house, At the Two Suns, 47 Nerudova Street

Nerudova Street ⑦

Ⓜ *Malostranská.* 🚊 *12, 22, 23.*

This narrow picturesque street is named after the 19th-century writer Jan Neruda, who wrote many short stories set in this part of Prague. He lived in the house known as At the Two Suns (No. 47) between 1845 and 1857.

Before the introduction of house numbers in 1770, the city's houses were distinguished by signs. Nerudova's houses have a splendid selection of heraldic beasts and emblems. Ones to look for in particular

are the Red Eagle (No. 6), the Three Fiddles (No. 12), the Golden Horseshoe (No. 34), the Green Lobster (No. 43), and the White Swan (No. 49).

Nerudova Street also has a number of grand Baroque buildings, including the Thun-Hohenstein Palace (No. 20) – now the Italian embassy – and the Morzin Palace (No. 5) – home of the Romanian embassy. The latter has an interesting façade featuring two massive statues of Moors.

Church of St. Nicholas ⑧

Malostranské náměstí. *Tel 25-75 34 215.* Ⓜ *Malostranská.* 🚊 *12, 22, 23.* ◯ *daily.* 📷 ✓
www.psalterium.cz

Dominating Little Quarter Square, at the heart of Malá Strana, is the Church of St. Nicholas. Begun in 1703, it

is the acknowledged master-piece of architects Christoph and Kilian Ignaz Dientzenhofer, who were responsible for the greatest examples of Jesuit-influenced Baroque architecture in Prague. Neither lived to see the completion of the church – their work was finished in 1761 by Kilian's son-in-law, Anselmo Lurago.

Among the many works of art inside the church is Franz Palko's magnificent fresco, *The Celebration of the Holy Trinity*, which fills the 70-m (230-ft) high dome. A fresco of St. Cecilia, patron saint of music, watches over the church's splendid Baroque organ. Built in 1746, it was played by Mozart in 1787. Another star feature is the ornate 18th-century pulpit, lavishly adorned with golden cherubs. The impressive statues of the Church Fathers, which stand at the four corners of the crossing, are the work of Ignaz Platzer, as is the statue of St. Nicholas that graces the high altar.

Wallenstein Palace ⑨

Valdštejnský Palác, Valdštejnské nám-ěstí 4. *Tel 25-70 71 111.* Ⓜ *Malo-stranská.* 🚊 *12, 18, 22, 23.* **State Rooms** ◯ *10am–5pm Sat–Sun.* **Riding school** ◯ *for exhibitions.* ♿ **Garden** ◯ *Apr–Oct: daily.* ♿
www.senat.cz

The first large secular building of the Baroque era in Prague, this palace was commissioned by the imperial military

The superbly ornamented Baroque organ in the Church of St. Nicholas

commander Albrecht von Wallenstein (1581–1634). His victories in the 30 Years' War made him vital to Emperor Ferdinand II. Already showered with titles, Wallenstein started to covet the crown of Bohemia. He began to negotiate independently with the enemy, and in 1634 was killed on the Emperor's orders by mercenaries.

Wallenstein's intention was to overshadow even Prague Castle with his vast palace, built between 1624 and 1630. The magnificent main hall has a ceiling fresco of the commander portrayed as Mars, riding in a triumphal chariot. The palace is now used by the Czech Senate, but the State Rooms are open to the public.

Dotted with bronze statues and fountains, the gardens are laid out as they were when Wallenstein resided here. The Grotesquery is an unusual feature – an imitation of the walls of a cave, covered in stalactites. There is also a fine frescoed pavilion. The old Riding School is today used for National Gallery exhibitions.

Charles Bridge and the Little Quarter Bridge Tower

Charles Bridge ⑩

🚋 12, 22, 23 to Malostranské náměstí (for Little Quarter side); 17, 18 to Křížovnické náměstí (for Old Town side). **Little Quarter Bridge Tower** ☐ Apr–Oct: daily. 🖼 **Old Town Bridge Tower** ☐ daily. 🖼

One of the most familiar sights in Prague, the Charles Bridge (Karlův Most) connects the Old Town with the Little Quarter. Although it is now pedestrianized, at one time it took four carriages abreast. The bridge was commissioned by Charles IV in 1357 after the Judith Bridge was destroyed by floods.

The bridge's original decoration consisted of a simple wooden cross. In 1683 a statue of St. John Nepomuk – the first of the many Baroque statues that today line each side of the bridge – was added. The vicar general Jan Nepomucký was arrested in 1393 by Wenceslas IV for having displeased the king. He died under torture and his body was later thrown from the bridge. A number of finely worked reliefs depict the martyrdom of this saint, who was revered by the Jesuits as a rival to Jan Hus.

Between 1683 and the latter half of the 19th century several more statues were erected. Sculpted by Matthias Braun at the age of 26, the statue of St. Luitgard is regarded as one of the most artistically remarkable.

Another splendid piece of decoration, the 17th-century Crucifixion bears the Hebrew inscription "Holy, Holy, Holy Lord," paid for by a Jew as punishment for blasphemy.

At the Little Quarter end of the bridge stand two bridge towers. The shorter of these is the remains of the Judith Bridge and dates from 1188. The taller pinnacled tower was built in 1464. It offers a magnificent view of the city, as does the late 14th-century Gothic tower at the Old Town end of the bridge.

The vast 17th-century Wallenstein Palace and its gardens

Old-New Synagogue ⑪

Built around 1270, this is the oldest synagogue in
Europe, and one of the earliest Gothic buildings
in Prague. The synagogue has survived fires, the slum
clearances of the 19th century, and many Jewish
pogroms. Residents of the Jewish Quarter have often
had to seek refuge within its walls, and today it is still
the religious center for Prague's Jews. It was originally
called the New Synagogue, until another synagogue
was built nearby – this was later destroyed.

Right-hand Nave
*The glow from the bronze
chandeliers provides light
for worshippers using
the seats lining
the walls.*

**14th-century
stepped brick
gable**

★ Jewish Standard
*The historic banner of Prague's
Jews is decorated with a Star of
David, within which is depicted
the hat that had to be worn by
Jews in the 14th century.*

These windows
formed part of the
18th-century extension,
built to allow women
a view of the service.

Candlestick holder

★ Five-rib Vaulting
*Two massive octagonal
pillars inside the main hall
support the five-rib vaults.*

**The cantor's
platform** and
its lectern are
surrounded by
a wrought-iron
Gothic grille.

**Entrance to the
synagogue from
Červená Street**

Entrance Portal
*The tympanum above
the door in the south
vestibule is carved
with a vine, which
bears 12 bunches
of grapes, sym-
bolizing the
tribes of Israel.*

STAR FEATURES

★ Rabbi Löw's Chair

★ Five-rib Vaulting

★ Jewish Standard

VISITORS' CHECKLIST

Pařížská and Červená. **Tel** 22-23
19 002. **M** Staroměstská. **T** 17,
18. ◯ 9am–5pm Sun–Fri. ●
Jewish hols. 📷 ★ 8am Mon–Fri,
9am Sat. **www**.kehilaprag.cz

View across the Old Jewish Cemetery towards the Klausen Synagogue

The Ark is the holiest place
in the synagogue and holds
the sacred scrolls of the
Torah. The tympanum
above it is decorated
with 13th-century
leaf carvings.

Old Jewish
Cemetery ⑫

Široká 3 (main entrance). Tel 22-23
17 191 (reservations); 22-48 19 456
(Jewish museum). **M** Staroměstská.
T 17, 18. ◯ Sun–Fri. 📷 includes
entry to all Jewish sites except Old-
New Synagogue. ♿

Founded in 1478, for over 300
years this was the only burial
ground permitted to Jews.
Because of the lack of space,
people had to be buried on
top of each other, up to 12
layers deep. Today you can
see over 12,000 gravestones,
but around 100,000 people
are thought to have been
buried here – the last person,
Moses Beck, in 1787. The
most visited grave in the
cemetery is that of Rabbi Löw
(1520–1609). Visitors place
hundreds of pebbles and
wishes on his grave as a

mark of respect.
On the northern edge of the
cemetery, the **Klausen
Synagogue** (1694) stands on
the site of a number of small
Jewish schools and prayer
houses, known as klausen.
Today it is home to the **Jewish
Museum**, whose exhibits trace
the history of the Jews in
Central Europe back to the
Middle Ages. Next to the
synagogue is the former
ceremonial hall of the Jewish
Burial Society, built in 1906.
It now houses a permanent
exhibition of childrens'
drawings from the Terezín
concentration camp.
Also bordering the cemetery,
the **Pinkas Synagogue** was
founded in 1479, and now
serves as a memorial to all the
Jewish Czechoslovak citizens
who were imprisoned at
Terezín. Excavations at the
synagogue have turned up
fascinating relics of life in the
medieval ghetto, including a

★ **Rabbi Löw's Chair**
A Star of David marks
the chair of the Chief
Rabbi, placed where the
16th-century scholar,
Rabbi Löw, used to sit.

PRAGUE'S JEWISH QUARTER

In the Middle Ages Prague's Jewish
community was confined in an enclosed
ghetto. For centuries the Jews suffered
from oppressive laws – in the 16th
century they had to wear a yellow
circle as a mark of shame.
Discrimination was partially
relaxed in 1784 by Joseph II,
and the Jewish Quarter was
named Josefov after him. In
1850 the area was officially
incorporated as part of Prague. A
few years later the city authorities
razed the ghetto slums, but many
synagogues, the Town Hall, and the
Old Jewish Cemetery were saved.

**Ten Commandments motif
on the Spanish Synagogue**

The Old and New Towns

The heart of the city is the Old Town (Staré Město) and its central square. In the 11th century the settlements around the castle spread to the right bank of the Vltava. A marketplace in what is now Old Town Square was first mentioned in 1091, and houses and churches quickly sprang up around it. Founded in 1348 by Charles IV, the New Town (Nové Město) was mainly inhabited by tradesmen and craftsmen. In the late 19th century, much of it was demolished and completely redeveloped, giving it the appearance it has today.

Church of Our Lady before Týn in the Old Town Square

Old Town Square ⑬

Ⓜ *Staroměstská.*

Free of traffic, except for a handful of horse-drawn carriages, and ringed with historic buildings, Prague's enormous Old Town Square (Staroměstské náměstí) ranks among the finest public spaces of any European city.

Dominating the east side of the square is the **Church of Our Lady before Týn**, with its magnificent Gothic steeples. Begun in 1365, from the early 15th century until 1620 it was the main Hussite church in Prague.

Also on the east side of the square, the **House at the Stone Bell** has been restored to its former appearance as a Gothic town palace. The splendid 18th-century Rococo **Kinský Palace**, with its pretty pink and white stucco façade,

was designed by Kilian Ignaz Dientzenhofer. Today, it houses art exhibitions by the National Gallery.

At the northern end of the square, the **Church of St. Nicholas** stands on the site of a former church dating from the 12th century. The present building, completed by Kilian Ignaz Dientzenhofer in 1735, has a dramatic white façade, studded with statues by Antonín Braun. In summer, evening concerts are held here.

A colorful array of arcaded buildings of Romanesque or Gothic origin, with fascinating house signs, graces the south side of the square. Among the most attractive are the house called **At the Stone Ram** and the Neo-Renaissance **Štorch House**, also known as At the Stone Madonna.

At one end of the square stands the huge monument dedicated to the reformist Jan Hus, who was burnt at the stake for heresy in 1415.

In addition to historic buildings, there are also many shops, as well as restaurants and cafés, whose tables and chairs spill out onto the pavements of the square in summer.

Old Town Hall ⑭

Staroměstské náměstí 1. **Tel** *22-42 28 456.* Ⓜ *Staroměstská, Můstek.* 🚋 *17.* ⭕ *daily.* 📷 ♿ 🎫

Standing at the southwest corner of the Old Town Square, the Old Town Hall is one of the most striking buildings in Prague.

Established in 1338 after King John of Luxemburg agreed to set up a town

council, the Town Hall grew in the course of the next few centuries, and today consists of a row of colorful Gothic and Renaissance buildings.

The Old Town Hall Tower is one of the building's star features and dates from 1364. The gallery at the top provides a magnificent view of the city. Located on the first floor is the 14th-century Oriel Chapel, with its ornate, recently restored ceiling.

Another famous sight is the Astronomical Clock, built by the clockmaker Hanuš in 1490. The mechanism of the clock we see today was perfected by Jan Táborský between 1552 and 1572. The clock records three different kinds of time, Old Bohemian time, time as we know it, and so-called Babylonian time. It also shows the movement of the sun and moon through the 12 signs of the zodiac. Every time the clock strikes the hour, mechanical figures perform above the zodiac signs, drawing crowds of spectators. The lower section of the clock consists of the

Astronomical Clock and Calendar on the Old Town Hall Tower

Calendar. This beautifully decorated revolving dial, designed by celebrated artist Josef Mánes, dates from 1866.

Municipal House ⑮

Náměstí Republiky 5. **Tel** 22-20 02 101. Ⓜ Náměstí Republiky. ▓ 5, 8, 14, 26. **Gallery** ◯ daily. ▓ & www.obecnidum.cz

Prague's most prominent Art Nouveau building occupies the site of the former Royal Court palace, the king's residence between 1383 and 1485. The attractive exterior is embellished with allegorical statuary, and above the main entrance there is a mosaic entitled *Homage to Prague* by Karel Špillar.

Inside is Prague's principal concert venue, the Smetana Hall, which is also used as a ballroom. The interior is decorated with works by leading Czech artists of the early 20th century, including Alfons Mucha, one of the most successful exponents of the Art Nouveau style.

On October 28, 1918, Prague's Municipal House was the scene of the momentous proclamation of the new independent state of Czechoslovakia.

Wenceslas Square ⑯

Ⓜ Můstek, Muzeum. ▓ 3, 9, 14, 24.

Originally a medieval horse market, today Wenceslas Square remains an important commercial center, with shops, hotels, restaurants, and clubs.

At one end of the square is the **National Museum**. This grand building, with its monumental staircase and rich marbled interior, was completed in 1890 as a symbol of national prestige. The museum's collections are devoted mainly to mineralogy, archaeology, anthropology, and natural history.

View across the Vltava River to the National Theater

The huge equestrian statue of St. Wenceslas that stands in front of the National Museum was erected in 1912, the work of the 19th-century sculptor Josef Myslbek. At the foot of the pedestal there are smaller statues of Czech patron saints.

Also worth seeing are the Art Nouveau-style **Hotel Europa** (1906) and the **Church of Our Lady of the Snows**. This towering Gothic building is only part of a vast church planned in the 14th century but never completed.

Wenceslas Square has witnessed many important events in recent Czech history. In November 1989, a protest rally against police brutality took place here, leading to the Velvet Revolution

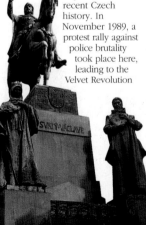

Statue of St. Wenceslas flanked by Czech patron saints in St. Wenceslas Square

National Theater ⑰

Národní divadlo, Národní 2. **Tel** 22-49 12 673. Ⓜ Národní třída. ▓ 17, 18, 22, 23 to Národní třída. ◯ for performances only or by arrangement (22-17 14 151). &
www.narodni-divadlo.cz

The National Theater has always been an important symbol of the Czech cultural revival. Work began on the building in 1868. The original Neo-Renaissance design was by the Czech architect Josef Zítek. After it was completely destroyed by fire – just days before the official opening – Josef Schulz was given the job of rebuilding the theater, and all the best Czech artists of the period contributed toward its lavish decoration. During the late 1970s and early 80s the theater underwent restoration work and the New Stage was built.

The theater's auditorium has an elaborately painted ceiling adorned with allegorical figures representing the arts. Equally impressive are the sumptuous gold and red stage curtain, and the ceiling fresco in the theater's lobby. The fresco is the final part of a triptych, painted by Frantíšeck Ženíšek in 1878, depicting the *Golden Age of Czech Art*.

The theater's vivid sky-blue roof, covered with stars, is said to symbolize the summit all artists should aim for.

Excursions in Bohemia

The sights that attract most visitors away from the capital are Bohemia's picturesque towns and castles, and its famous spa resorts. The castle at Karlstein, for example, stands in splendid isolation above wooded valleys that have changed little since Charles IV hunted here in the 14th century. Further south, the historic town of Český Krumlov retains a medieval atmosphere. Still popular as a therapeutic retreat, the spa town of Karlsbad is located in the leafy Teplá valley and offers a welcome respite from Prague's crowds.

Karlstein Castle, built by Emperor Charles IV in the 14th century

Karlstein ➋

Karlštejn, 25 km (16 miles) SW of Prague. **Tel** 311-68 16 95. 🚊 to Karlštejn (1.5 km/1 mile from castle). 🚌 to Karlštejn (1 km/0.6 miles from castle). ⬜ Mar–Nov: Tue–Sun. 🎦 obligatory. **Chapel of the Holy Rood** ⬜ Jun–Oct: Tue–Sun. 🎦 obligatory and by advance reservation only. **www**.hradkarlstejn.cz

Karlstein Castle was founded by Charles IV as a country retreat and a treasury for the imperial crown jewels. The present structure is largely a 19th-century reconstruction by Josef Mocker. The original building work took place between 1348 and 1367, supervised by the French master mason Matthew of Arras, and after him by Peter Parler. You can still see the audience hall and the bedchamber of Charles IV in the Royal Palace.

The central tower houses the Church of Our Lady, with its faded 14th-century wall paintings. A passage leads to the Chapel of St. Catherine, whose walls are adorned with semiprecious stones. The Chapel of the Holy Rood in the Great Tower, where the crown jewels were once kept, has gilded vaulting studded with glass stars. At one time the chapel held 127 panels painted by Master Theodoric (1357–65), one of the greatest painters of Charles IV's reign. Some panels have been restored and can now be seen in Prague's St. Agnes's Convent.

Kutná Hora ➌

70 km (45 miles) east of Prague. 🏠 20,000 🚊 🚌 ℹ️ Palackého náměstí 377 (327-51 23 78). **www**.kutnahora.cz

After deposits of silver were found here in the 13th century, Kutná Hora evolved from a small mining community into the second most important town in Bohemia after Prague. The Prague *groschen*, a silver coin that was in circulation all over Europe, was minted at the **Italian Court** (Vlašský dvůr), so-called because Florentine experts were employed to set up the mint. Strongly fortified, the Italian Court was also the ruler's seat in the town. In the late 14th century a palace was built, containing reception halls and the Chapel of St. Wenceslas and St. Ladislav. They can be visited by guided tour.

Kutná Hora's **Mining Museum**, housed in a former fort called the Hrádek, and the splendid 14th-century Gothic **Cathedral of St. Bar-**

Karlsbad ➍

Karlovy Vary, 140 km (85 miles) west of Prague. 🏠 60,000 🚊 🚌 ℹ️ Lázeňská 1 (353-22 40 97). **www**.karlovyvary.cz

Legend has it that Charles IV discovered one of the sources of mineral water that would make Karlsbad's fortune when one of his staghounds fell into

The three steeples of Kutná Hora's great Cathedral of St. Barbara

The spa town of Karlsbad with its 19th-century Mill Colonnade

CZECH BEERS

Czech beer-bottle cap

The best-known Czech beer is Pilsner, which is made by the lager method: top fermented and matured at low temperatures. The word "Pilsner" (now used as a generic name for similar lagers brewed all over the world) derives from Plzeň, a town 88 km (55 miles) southwest of Prague, where this type of beer was first brewed in 1842.

The brewery that developed the beer still makes Plzeňský pivo, as well as Plzeňský prazdroj (original source), better known by its German export name Pilsner Urquell. Guided tours of the brewery include a tasting. České Budějovice is Bohemia's other famous brewing town – home to the Czech Republic's biggest selling export beer, Budweiser Budvar.

Selection of Czech beers

a hot spring. By the end of the 16th century more than 200 spa buildings had been built in the town. Today there are 12 hot mineral springs. The best-known is the Vřídlo (Sprudel), which, at 72°C (162°F), is also the hottest.

Among the town's historic monuments are the 18th-century Baroque parish **church of Mary Magdalene**. The elegant 19th-century **Mill Colonnade** (Mlýnská kolonáda) is by Josef Zítek, architect of the National Theater *(see p721)* in Prague.

Karlsbad is also known for its Karlovy Vary china and Moser glass, and for summer concerts and cultural events.

Environs
Around 60 km (38 miles) southwest of Karlsbad is another of Bohemia's spa towns, **Marienbad** (Mariánské Lázně). Here the cast-iron colonnade, with frescoes by Josef Vyletěl, is an impressive sight. There are also many pleasant walks in the local countryside, especially in the protected Slavkov Forest.

Český Krumlov ❺

170 km (106 miles) south of Prague. 🏘 *15,000* 🚉 🚌 🛈 *náměstí Svornosti 2 (380-70 46 22).* **www**.ckrumlov.info

Of all the Czech Republic's medieval towns, Český Krumlov must rank as the finest. Almost entirely enclosed by a bend in the

River Vltava, the beautifully preserved Old Town (Staré Město) appears to have changed very little in the last few hundred years, although some buildings suffered severe flood damage in 2002. A maze of narrow cobbled streets radiates out from the main square (náměstí Svornosti), which is lined with elegant arcaded Renaissance buildings and the Gothic former town hall. On one of these streets – Horní – is the magnificent 16th-century sgraffitoed **Jesuit College** (now a hotel) and, opposite, a **museum** explaining the town's history. **Schiele Centrum** is housed in a 15th-century former brewery. The museum has an excellent collection of works by the Austrian painter Egon Schiele. Český Krumlov's most

famous sight is its 13th-century castle – the **Krumlovský Zámek** – in the Latrán quarter. In the older, lower part of the castle complex, the splendidly restored castle tower can be climbed for superb views of the whole town. Other highlights of the castle include a Rococo chapel, a lavishly decorated ballroom – the Maškarní sál – and the ornate 18th-century Rococo theater. The castle gardens provide a tranquil spot to sit and relax, while performances of opera and ballet take place in the gardens' open-air theater in July and August.

In summer, renting a canoe from one of a number of outlets in the town is a good way to enjoy the fine views of Český Krumlov from the river.

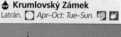

⚜ **Krumlovský Zámek**
Latrán. 🕐 Apr–Oct: Tue–Sun. 🖼 🚫

Český Krumlov's castle tower rising above the medieval Old Town

Practical & Travel Information

Since 1989 the Czech Republic has become far more open to visitors. The country has responded well to the huge influx of tourists, and facilities such as communications, banks, and information centers have improved considerably. The best way to explore Prague is on foot; if you are traveling to places of interest outside the capital, buses and trains are reliable and inexpensive.

WHEN TO VISIT

The busiest months are August and September, although Prague can be very crowded in June and at Easter also. The main sights are always packed at these times, but the crowds lend a carnival atmosphere, which can make a visit all the more enjoyable. Many sights are closed between the end of October and the beginning of April.

TOURIST INFORMATION

Tourist information offices in the Czech Republic range from private agencies to the state-owned **Čedok**. Many employ English speakers and offer a variety of English-language publications, maps, and guides. The efficient **Prague Information Service (PIS)** is the best source of tourist information for visitors to the capital. It has three offices in the city center, providing information in English, German, and Czech.

VISA REQUIREMENTS

Citizens of the US need a valid passport to enter the Czech Republic, and can stay for up to 90 days.

At present, New Zealand, Canadian, and Australian nationals require a visa, valid for three months.

SAFETY AND EMERGENCIES

Violent crime against tourists is rare in the Czech Republic. The main problem, especially in Prague, is petty theft from cars, hotel rooms, and pockets. At night, lone women are advised to avoid Prague's Wenceslas Square, which used to be a hangout for prostitutes.

It is an unwritten law that you should have your passport with you at all times in the Czech Republic. Although you are unlikely to be asked to produce it, having it could save a lot of problems.

In case of an emergency, the numbers to call are listed in the directory opposite.

HEALTH ISSUES

No inoculations are required for the Czech Republic. Visitors should take note that in winter sulphur dioxide levels in Prague often exceed the World Health Organization's safety levels. For prescription and non-prescription medicines, visit a pharmacy (lékárna).

FACILITIES FOR THE DISABLED

Disabled travelers seeking advice on transportation, accommodations, and sight-seeing tours should contact the **Czech Association of Persons with Disabilities** or, alternatively, the **Prague Wheelchair Association**.

BANKING AND CURRENCY

The Czech unit of currency is the Czech crown (Kč). Banking hours are generally 8am to 5pm Monday to Friday, with some branches closing at lunch. Bureaux de change in tourist spots are open every day, and some offer a 24-hour service. Although they give much better exchange rates than the banks, their commission charges are huge, often as high as 12 percent. Traveler's checks can only be changed in banks. Credit cards are becoming more widely accepted in the Czech Republic, but never assume that you can pay with them.

COMMUNICATIONS

Card-operated public phone booths are found all over the Czech Republic. You can buy phone- cards (telefonní karta) from most tobacconists and news-stands. It is possible to make international calls from a public phone, a post office or a hotel, although the latter option is usually highly expensive.

Most post offices are open from 8am until 6pm, Monday to Friday, and on Saturday mornings. Stamps (známky) can be purchased at most tobacconists and newsstands, as well as from post offices.

FLYING TO THE CZECH REPUBLIC

If you are traveling from the United States, **Czech Airlines (ČSA)** is the only airline that offers direct flights to Prague. A number of other carriers, including **Delta Air Lines**, **Air**

THE CLIMATE OF THE CZECH REPUBLIC

The Czech Republic enjoys long, warm days in summer, the hottest months being June, July, and August. The winter months can get bitterly cold; temperatures often drop below freezing and heavy snowfall is not uncommon. The wettest months are October and November but frequent light showers can occur in the summer months as well.

PRAGUE

°C/F	Apr	Jul	Oct	Jan
24/75 high	13/55	14/57	16/61	
low	3/37	5/41		0/32
0°C 32°F				-5/23
hrs	5.5 hrs	8.5 hrs	4 hrs	1.5 hrs
mm	73 mm	19 mm	95 mm	60 mm

Canada, **KLM**, and **Lufthansa** operate flights from the US and Canada to the Czech Republic, via another European city.

Carriers operating direct scheduled flights daily from the UK to Prague include **British Airways** and Czech Airlines (ČSA). The low-cost airline **easyJet** has flights to Prague from London Stansted.

Among a number of airlines flying from Australia and New Zealand to Prague are Lufthansa and KLM. Flights from Australasia require a stopover in Europe or Asia.

Čedaz runs an inexpensive and efficient minibus service from Prague's Ruzyně airport to the city center.

RAIL TRAVEL

Prague is connected by rail to all the major capitals of Europe, although it can be a rather slow way of getting to the Czech Republic. For example, the journey time from London to Prague is 19 hours. Nearly all international trains arrive at and depart from Hlavní nádraží, the city's biggest and busiest station.

The Czech Republic's state-run rail company, České Dráhy (ČD), operates two types of domestic routes. Express trains (*rychlík*) stop only at the major towns and cities and you pay a premium to travel on them. The slow trains, or *osobní*, stop at every station on the line.

For help with timetables and advice on fares in Prague, visit the local PIS or Information at Hlavní nádraží station.

TRAVELING BY BUS

Traveling by bus between Prague and other major European cities can be slow and tiring, but it is significantly less expensive than rail or air travel. Seats get booked up very quickly, especially in summer, so reserve well in advance. **Eurolines** is one of the main operators of international bus routes to Prague.

Within the Czech Republic, long-distance buses are run by Československá státní automobilová doprava (ČSAD). There is an extensive route network, and buses are often a less expensive way of traveling between towns than the trains. For popular routes you should buy your ticket in advance from the bus station.

The main bus terminal in Prague is Florenc, which serves all international and long-distance domestic routes.

TRAVELING BY CAR

There are few highways in the Czech Republic, which can make car travel slower than in other European countries. To travel on them you must purchase a tax disc (*dálniční známka*), valid for either 10 days or a month and available at the border or from post offices and gas stations.

Most of the major car rental firms have offices in Prague and at Ruzyně airport, but renting is relatively expensive.

DIRECTORY

CZECH TOURIST OFFICES ABROAD

UK
Czech Centre, 13 Harley Street, London W1G 9QG. *Tel* 020-7307 5180.
www.czechcentre. org.uk
Czech Tourism
www.czechtourism.com

US
1109 Madison Avenue, New York, NY 10028. *Tel* 212-288 0830.
www.czechcenter.com

TOURIST OFFICES IN PRAGUE

Čedok
Na příkopě 18, Prague. *Tel* 22-41 97 242.
www.cedok.cz

Prague Information Service
Na příkopě 20, Prague. *Tel* 22-17 141 38. *Tel* 22-44 825 62 (walking tours).
www.pis.cz

EMBASSIES AND CONSULATES

Australian Consulate
Klimentská 10, Prague. *Tel* 29-65 78 350.

Canadian Embassy
Muchova 6, Prague. *Tel* 27-21 01 800.
www.canada.cz

UK Embassy
Thunovská 14, Prague. *Tel* 25-74 02 111.
www.britain.cz

US Embassy
Tržiště 15, Prague. *Tel* 25-70 22 000.
www.usembassy.cz

EMERGENCY NUMBERS

Ambulance
Rychlá lékařská pomoc
Tel 155.
Tel 112 (English).

Fire
Tísňové volání hasičů
Tel 150 & 112 (Emglish).

Police
Tísňové volání policie
Tel 158 & 112 (English).

FACILITIES FOR THE DISABLED

Czech Association of Persons with Disabilities
Karlínské náměstí 12, Prague. *Tel* 22-48 15 914.
www.czechia.com/s2dp

Prague Wheelchair Association
Benediktská 6, Prague. *Tel* 22-48 26 078.

AIRLINES

Air Canada
Tel 888-247 2262 (Canada). *Tel* 22-48 10 181 (Czech Republic).
www.aircanada.ca

British Airways
Tel 0870-850 9850 (UK). *Tel* 1-800-AIRWAYS (US). *Tel* 22-21 14 444 (Czech Republic).
www.britishairways.com

Czech Airlines
Tel 870-4443 747 (UK). *Tel* 800-223 2365 (US). *Tel* 23-90 07 007 (Czech Republic). www.csa.cz

Delta Air Lines
Tel 800-241 4141 (US). *Tel* 22-49 46 733 (Czech Republic). www.delta-air.com

easyJet
Tel 0905-821 0905 (UK). www.easyjet.com

KLM
Tel 800-225 25 25 (US). *Tel* 2-33 09 09 33 (Czech Republic). www.klm.com

Lufthansa
Tel 800-399 LUFT (US). *Tel* 22-01 14 456 (Czech Republic). www.lufthansa.com

BUS COMPANIES

Eurolines
Tel 08705 -808 080 (UK). www.eurolines.co.uk

Where to Stay in the Czech Republic

Since the "Velvet Revolution" of 1989, tourism in the Czech Republic has boomed. As such, old hotels have been revamped and new establishments have sprung up. Top-range hotels equal those in the rest of Europe for quality and price. Budget hotels are sadly scarce.

PRICE CATEGORIES

Price categories for a double room per night including taxes and breakfast:

Ⓚ Under 3000 Kč
ⓀⓀ 3000–4500 Kč
ⓀⓀⓀ 4500–6000 Kč
ⓀⓀⓀⓀ 6000–8000 Kč
ⓀⓀⓀⓀⓀ Over 8000 Kč

PRAGUE

MALA STRANA (LITTLE QUARTER) Domus Henrici

Loretánská 11, Praha 1 **Tel** 22-05 11 369 **Fax** 22-05 11 502 **Rooms** 8 — **Map** A3

Part of the Hidden Places hotel group, you may have trouble finding this establishment. It's difficult to get much closer to the castle than this, so sightseers will love the location. Rooms are enormous and tastefully decorated. An excellent buffet breakfast is served on the terrace during the summer. **www.hidden-places.com**

MALA STRANA (LITTLE QUARTER) U Tří Pštrosů

Drazického náměstí 12, Praha 1 **Tel** 25-72 88 888 **Fax** 25-75 33 217 **Rooms** 18 — **Map** C3

Just beside Charles Bridge, the hotel "At The Three Ostriches" began life as the home of Jan Fux, an ostrich-feather dealer. It is one of the best-known hotel-restaurants in Prague. Family run, it has an intimate atmosphere, and children are especially welcome. The bedrooms have recently been refurbished. **www.utripstrosu.cz**

NEW TOWN Na Zlatém Kříži

Jungmannovo náměstí 2, Praha 1 **Tel** 22-42 19 501 **Fax** 22-22 45 418 **Rooms** 8 — **Map** E4

A challenger for the narrowest hotel in Prague award, the charming Golden Cross offers deceptively large, and rather luxurious double rooms and apartments, all with private bathrooms. A good buffet breakfast is served in the hotel's Gothic-style cellar. Transfers to and from the airport can be arranged. **www.goldencross.cz**

NEW TOWN Carlo IV

Senovážné náměstí 13, Praha 1 **Tel** 22-45 93 111 **Fax** 22-42 23 960 **Rooms** 152 — **Map** F3

This magnificently decorated hotel with shimmering marble floors, intricate hand-painted frescos in a Neoclassical building, is in the heart of the city. Part of the Boscolo Group, this hotel has some wonderful features, from the Box Block restaurant to the cigar bar, while the spa features Europe's best hotel swimming pool.

OLD TOWN Élite

Ostrovní 32, 110 00 Praha 1 **Tel** 22-49 32 250 **Fax** 22-49 30 787 **Rooms** 79 — **Map** 4D

The Élite is housed in a building which dates from the late-14th century. Its cosy atmosphere is aptly augmented by a stylish grill club on the ground floor, offering excellent Mediterranean and Argentinian cuisine, as well as a cocktail bar providing jazz and Latino music. An open atrium contains a day-bar with a small garden. **www.hotelelite.cz**

OLD TOWN Paříž

U Obecního domu 1, 110 00 Praha 1 **Tel** 22-21 95 195 **Fax** 22-42 25 475 **Rooms** 86 — **Map** F3

This Neo-Gothic building with a number of Art Nouveau elements was built by the celebrated architect Jan Vejrych, and was declared a historic monument in 1984. The rooms have been modernised in international style and everything is in pristine condition. **www.hotel-paris.cz**

REST OF THE CZECH REPUBLIC

ČESKY KRUMLOV Růže

Horní 154, 381 01, Česky Krumlov **Tel** 38-07 72 100 **Fax** 38-07 13 146 **Rooms** 70

The most luxurious hotel in Česky Krumlov. Housed in a former Jesuit monastery and furnished in Renaissance style, it also offers a superb range of facilities. The hotel hosts medieval feasts where guests can dress up in costume and sit down to a candlelit banquet accompanied by dancers, jugglers and musicians. **www.hotelruze.cz**

KARLSBAD (KARLOVY VARY) Grand Hotel Pupp

Mírové náměstí 2, 360 91, Karlovy Vary **Tel** 35-31 09 111 **Fax** 35-32 26 638 **Rooms** 112

One of the most famous Czech hotels, with traditions going back to the early 18th century. Luxuriously furnished rooms with minibar, safe, satellite TV, and dazzling bathrooms. The amenities include restaurant, casino, an impressive concert hall with Neo-Baroque interior, and of course a fabulous spa centre. **www.pupp.cz**

Key to Symbols see back cover flap

Where to Eat in the Czech Republic

New restaurants are constantly opening in the Czech Republic thanks to the thriving tourist industry. Many offer international cuisine but there are also plenty of traditional eateries offering local dishes. Compared to Western Europe, eating out is relatively inexpensive.

PRICE CATEGORIES
Price categories for an average three-course meal for one, including half a bottle of wine, and all unavoidable charges:

Ⓚ under 250 Kč
ⓀⓀ 250–450 Kč
ⓀⓀⓀ 450–650 Kč
ⓀⓀⓀⓀ over 650 Kč

PRAGUE

MALA STRANA (LITTLE QUARTER) Hungarian Grotto
Tomášská 12, Praha 1 **Tel** *25-75 32 344*
Map *C3*

The land of Tokay, Bull's Blood, goulash and paprika has inspired this reasonably priced, romantically rustic cellar restaurant with a pleasant outdoor courtyard. To add to the atmosphere, the premises are supposedly haunted by a cuckolded baker from the 17th century.

MALA STRANA (LITTLE QUARTER) U Malířů (At the Painter's)
Maltézské náměstí 11, Praha 1 **Tel** *25-75 30 318*
Map *C4*

There has been a restaurant on this spot since 1543. Even back then, U Malířůreceived high praise: King Rudolf II's foodtasters gave it three Royal stars. Today you can expect equally high quality, traditional and contemporary French cuisine in superb, sumptuous surroundings still fit for a king.

NEW TOWN U Fleků
Křemencova 11, Praha 1 **Tel** *22-49 34 019*
Map *D5*

This cavernous and often raucous brewery and restaurant with its many rooms and lounges is thought to have been founded in 1499, though nobody seems to know for sure. What's certain is that there's been an onsite brewery since the early 1900s, and the food is good, reliable upmarket Czech pub fare.

NEW TOWN La Perle de Prague
Rašín Building, Rašínovo nábřeži 80, Praha 1 **Tel** *22-19 84 160*
Map *D5*

Situated on the seventh floor of the Rasín Building (also known as the Dancing House), with views of the Vltava and Prague Castle, this is a reasonably priced, upscale French restaurant. The wine menu is quite extensive and the knowledgeable staff can help you choose. There's a well-stocked cocktail bar too.

OLD TOWN Klub Architekt
Betlémské náměstí 5A, Praha 1 **Tel** *22-44 01 214*
Map *D4*

This hidden jewel is tucked away in a warren of tunnels and arches, reached through a discreet courtyard close to the Bethlehem Chapel. The servings are hearty, and, unusual for an inexpensive Prague dining room. The menu includes a good, varied vegetarian selection.

OLD TOWN Chez Marcel
Haštalská 12, Praha 1 **Tel** *22-23 15 676*
Map *E3*

Chez Marcel is a touch of real France in the centre of Prague. This is where business people and students alike come for regional plats du jour, as well as steak *au poivre,* fresh mussels and probably the best French fries in the city. Surprisingly for such a good establishment, the food is reasonably priced.

REST OF THE CZECH REPUBLIC

ČESKY KRUMLOV Pivovar Eggenberg
Latrán 27, Česky Krumlov, 381 01 **Tel** *38-07 11 426*

Eggenberg is a brewery, and beer sets the tone in this restaurant, located in the former brewing coolrooms. There is a large, roomy restaurant with 150 seats as well as beer hall "Formanka" of 70 seats. Both offer Czech cuisine, light and dark beers on tap but you will find a good selection of Czech wine, too.

KARLSBAD (KARLOVY VARY) Alžbětiny lázně
Smetanovy sady 1145/1, Karlovy Vary, 360 01 **Tel** *77-50 57 762*

Situated on the first floor of the 19th-century Elisabeth´s Spa building, the restaurant offers traditional Czech as well as Mediterranean cuisine and is well renowned for their steaks. There is a wide selection of Moravian and international wines. The business lunch is good value for money.

Map References *see map of Prague pp710–11*

HUNGARY

Uniquely in central Europe, Hungary is peopled by descendants of the Magyars, a race from central Asia who settled here at the end of the 9th century. In more recent times the country has fought against Turkish, German, Austrian, and Russian occupiers, yet its rich indigenous culture remains intact. In 1989 Hungary became the first Soviet Bloc country to embrace Western-style democracy.

Hungary has an extremely varied landscape, with forests and mountains dominating the north and a vast plain covering the rest of the country. The Tisza river and its tributaries shape the eastern regions, while the west has Lake Balaton, one of the largest lakes in Europe. The Danube flows through the heart of the country, bisecting the capital, Budapest, where one-fifth of the population lives. Ethnically the country is 92 percent Magyar, 4 percent Romany, 2 percent German, and one percent Slovak, the final one percent being of Jewish origin.

HISTORY

In AD 100 the Romans established the town of Aquincum near modern-day Budapest, and ruled the area corresponding roughly to Hungary (then called Pannonia) for three centuries. The arrival of the Huns in the early 5th century led to the complete withdrawal of the Romans. After the death of Attila the Hun in 453, the area was ruled by the Goths, the Longobards, and the Avars. The ancestors of the modern Hungarians, the Magyars, migrated from the Urals in 896, under the leadership of Prince Árpád, whose dynasty ruled until 1301, when King András III died without leaving an heir.

The throne then passed to a series of foreign kings, including the French Angevins and the Lithuanian Jagiellos, but the country flourished, and during the reign of Mátyás Corvinus (1458–90) it became the greatest monarchy in Middle Europe. Mátyás's marriage to Beatrice, a Neapolitan princess, saw the Renaissance blossom throughout Hungary, but all was soon eclipsed by a series of Turkish invasions. The Turks won a major victory at the Battle of Mohács in 1526, then they returned in 1541 to take Buda, which

The Gellért monument in Budapest, dedicated to a martyred 11th-century bishop

◁ Neo-Gothic spires, flying buttresses, and stained-glass windows on Hungary's Parliament building

became the capital of Ottoman Hungary. To quell the Turkish advance, the Austrians, under Ferdinand of Habsburg, occupied western (or "Royal") Hungary, while the central plains stayed under Ottoman control; the eastern region, including Transylvania (now in Romania), became a semi-autonomous land, feudally tied to the Turks.

Christian armies led by the Habsburgs fought to recapture Buda, and finally defeated the Turks in 1686. Economic prosperity came with Austrian rule, but nationalism was cruelly suppressed, culminating in a major uprising in 1848. After crushing the rebellion, Emperor Franz Joseph I sought to unite the two nations, and so created the Dual Monarchy of Austro-Hungary in 1867.

Following World War I, the Habsburg Empire was dismantled, and Hungary lost two-thirds of its territory to the "successor states" of Yugoslavia, Czechoslovakia, and Romania. It was to

**Mátyás Corvinus,
King of Hungary (1458–90)**

regain these territories that Hungary backed Germany in World War II, but in 1945 Budapest was taken by the Russians. The subsequent Communist rule was ruthlessly upheld, most visibly in 1956 when demonstrations were crushed by Soviet tanks. Nevertheless, free elections finally took place in 1989, resulting in victory for the democratic opposition. Since then, the country has invested heavily in tourism, which is now a major source of income.

LANGUAGE AND CULTURE

Modern Hungarian, like Finnish, derives from a language originally spoken by the Finno-Ugric tribes of the Urals. It differs greatly from most other European languages, although Slavic, German, Caucasian, Latin, and Turkic words have been incorporated.

Traditional peasant culture was all but destroyed in the 20th century, but folk songs and dances still survive; Christmas and Easter are the best times to witness these, particularly in the countryside, where holy days are celebrated in style.

Exploring Hungary

Budapest has a pivotal location at the heart of central Europe, and it is also the perfect base for exploring Hungary itself. Szentendre, with its Serbian religious art, and Esztergom, where Hungary's first Christian king was crowned, are both only a short drive north, while Lake Balaton lies only a little further west. Pécs, a treasure trove of European history, lies to the south, while Eger and Tokaj stand in the wine-producing area to the east; the former, with its castle and Turkish minaret, is one of Hungary's most popular towns.

SIGHTS AT A GLANCE

BUDAPEST pp422–9 **❶**
Eger **❻**
Esztergom **❸**
Lake Balaton **❹**
Pécs **❺**
Szentendre **❷**
Tokaj **❼**

Chess-players in a bathhouse in Budapest

KEY DATES IN HUNGARIAN HISTORY

c.AD 100 Romans establish Aquincum

c.410 Huns overrun the region

896 Magyar tribes arrive

1001 Coronation of István I, Hungary's first king

1300s Angevin rule begins

1458–90 Reign of Mátyás Corvinus

1526 Turks win the Battle of Mohács

1526–41 Turks conquer Buda on three occasions

1541 The start of Ottoman rule

1686 Christian troops enter Buda, ending Turkish rule in Hungary

1848 Hungarian Nationalist uprising

1867 Compromise with Austria gives Hungary independence in internal affairs

1873 Buda and Pest become Budapest

1918 With the break-up of the Austro-Hungarian Empire, Hungary gains independence after nearly 400 years of foreign rule

1941 Hungary enters World War II

1945 Russian army takes Budapest

1956 Russia suppresses a nationalist uprising

1989 Hungary proclaimed a democratic republic

2003 Hungary becomes a member of EU

Musically, the country has always had much to be proud of, including composers Franz Liszt and Béla Bartók, while in literature the Communist years produced some very powerful voices, among them Tibor Déry and István Örkény. Otherwise the country is best known for its cuisine, which incorporates a wide range of beers and meat-based dishes (such as goulash), the latter invariably spiced with paprika, the country's most famous export.

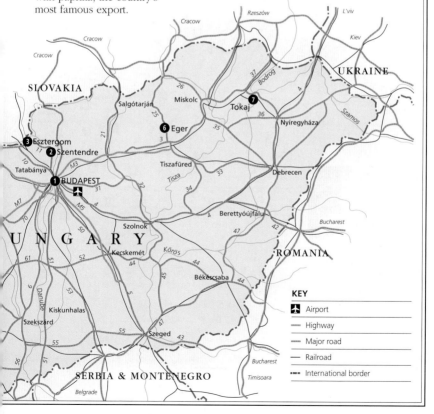

KEY

- ✈ Airport
- — Highway
- — Major road
- — Railroad
- ▪▪▪ International border

Budapest ❶

Budapest was founded in 1873 after the unification of three separate towns, Buda and Óbuda on the west bank of the Danube and Pest on the east. The city dates largely from the late 19th and early 20th centuries and is very much the creation of the nationalist enthusiasm of that era. All three towns had originally grown up in the second half of the twelfth century and Buda was the seat of Hungary's rulers from 1247. Turkish rule from 1541 to 1686, when it was recaptured by the Habsburgs, left little mark, except for the city's wonderful bathhouses.

SIGHTS AT A GLANCE

Gellért Hotel and Bath Complex ③
Hungarian National Museum ⑤
Inner City Parish Church ④
Mátyás Church ②
Museum of Fine Arts ⑨
Parliament ⑧
Royal Palace ①
St. Stephen's Basilica ⑦
State Opera House ⑥
Vajdahunyad Castle ⑩

Barrel-organist playing in the Castle district of Buda

0 meters   600

0 yards   600

GETTING AROUND

Trams are a convenient means of transportation for tourists, especially the 18, 19, and 61 on the Buda side and the 2, 4, and 6 in Pest. There are also some 200 bus routes. The three metro lines and the HÉV rail lines link the center with the suburbs. A new chipcard system has been introduced to cover all modes of public transportation.

Chain Bridge (Széchenyi lánchid), the first permanent bridge over the Danube, completed in 1849

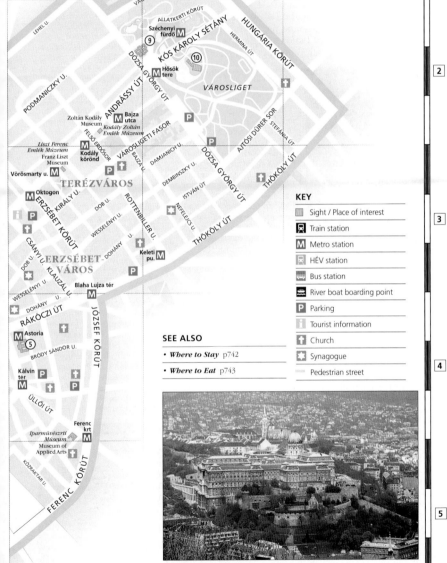

KEY

▦	Sight / Place of interest
🚉	Train station
Ⓜ	Metro station
🚈	HÉV station
🚌	Bus station
⛴	River boat boarding point
🅿	Parking
🛈	Tourist information
✝	Church
✡	Synagogue
—	Pedestrian street

SEE ALSO

- *Where to Stay* p742
- *Where to Eat* p743

Aerial view of Castle Hill and central Budapest

Buda

In 1247, Béla IV chose Buda, on the Danube's west bank, as his capital city. Its position, at 60 m (197 ft) above the river, made it a strategic choice. Buda expanded during Angevin rule, reaching a zenith under Mátyás Corvinus (1458–90), although further development was hindered by the Turkish occupation of 1541–1686. The Habsburgs' attempts to recover the city were devastating and by the time of its liberation, the city had been largely destroyed. In the 18th and 19th centuries, the Habsburgs set about rebuilding the palace and the old town, adding some magnificent buildings, but most had to be rebuilt again after the siege of 1945.

and Baroque art, and a wonderful selection of 19th- and 20th-century Hungarian works.

Notable early works include *The Madonna of Ba'rtfa* (1465–70), and the folding St. Anne Altarpiece (1510–20).

Among the 19th-century works, look out for the historical scenes by Bertalan Székely and the landscapes of Mihály Munkácsy, (1844–1900), widely held to be Hungary's greatest artist. The 20th-century works by Tivadar Kosztka Csontváry give a unique, idiosyncratic vision of the world.

The rebuilt Royal Palace with the heroic statue of Eugene of Savoy

Royal Palace ①

Szinház utca. 🚌 5, 16, 78, Várbusz.

King Béla IV (1235–70) built a royal castle in Buda, but its exact location is unknown. Around 1400 it was replaced by a Gothic palace, subsequently remodeled in Renaissance style by King Mátyás in 1458. Under Turkish rule, the palace was used to stable horses and store gunpowder, leading to its destruction in 1686 during the reconquest. A new palace, begun in 1719 by the Habsburgs, grew in size and grandeur under Maria Teresa, but this too was destroyed in the uprising of 1849 and had to be rebuilt in the second half of the 19th century.

When the Habsburg palace was again razed to the ground in February 1945, remains of the 15th-century Gothic palace were uncovered. These were

incorporated into the restored palace that visitors see today.

Various statues, gateways, and fountains have survived from the 19th-century palace. In the northwest courtyard stands the Mátyás Fountain (1904), depicting Mátyás Corvinus (1458–90) and his legendary love, the peasant girl, Ilonka. In front of the palace's rebuilt dome stands an equestrian statue (1900) of Prince Eugene of Savoy, victor of the Battle of Zenta against the Turks in 1697.

Today the palace houses a series of important national collections, including the Széchenyi National Library, with over five million books and manuscripts, the National Gallery, the Budapest History Museum, and the Museum of Contemporary History and Ludwig Collection.

🏛 Hungarian National Gallery

Royal Palace A-B-C-D Wings, Szent György tér 6. **Tel** (1) 375 5567. 🚌 5, 16, 78, Várbusz. ◯ Tue–Sun. 🈂 🖬 www.mng.hu
Established in 1957, the National Gallery has a superb collection of Hungarian art from medieval times to the 20th century. The permanent exhibits include a section of sculpture and stonework – the Lapidarium. There are also regular temporary exhibitions.

Highlights include a carved stone head of King Béla III, from c.1200, religious artifacts spanning several centuries, including many fine Gothic altarpieces, some Renaissance

St. Anne Altarpiece, National Gallery

🏛 Budapest History Museum

Royal Palace E Wing, Szent György tér 2. **Tel** (1) 487 8801. 🚌 5, 16, 78, Várbusz. ◯ Mon, Wed–Sun. 🈂 🖬 www.btm.hu
The city's history museum (*Budapesti Történeti Múzeum*), also known as the Castle Museum, illustrates the city's evolution from its origins under the Romans.

Damage to the palace in World War II led to chambers dating from the Middle Ages being uncovered in the south wing. These were recreated in the basement.

The ground floor exhibits cover the period from Roman times to the 15th century and include some Gothic statues, unearthed here in 1974. The first floor traces the history of the city from 1686 (the end of Turkish rule) to the present.

15th-century majolica floor in the Budapest History Museum

For hotels and restaurants in this region see p742 and p743

West front of the Mátyás Church, with tiled Béla Tower on the left

Mátyás Church ②

Szentháromság tér 2. **Tel** (1) 489 07 17. 🚌 Várbusz. ⬜ daily. ⬤ Sat pm, Sun am. 🖼 🎫 ♿ www.matyas-templom.hu

This church is mainly a Neo-Gothic reconstruction dating from 1874–96. Most of the original church (13th–15th centuries) was lost when the Turks turned it into their Great Mosque in 1541. The building had to be restored again after damage in World War II. The great rose window has been faithfully reproduced in its original Gothic style.

The tombs of King Béla III (13th century) and his wife can be seen in the Trinity Chapel, while the Mary Portal (near the main altar) is considered the finest example of Gothic stone carving in Hungary. Also fascinating is a Baroque statue of the Madonna: according to legend, the original was set into a wall during the Turkish occupation. When the church was virtually destroyed in 1686, the Madonna made a miraculous reappearance, which the Turks took as an omen of defeat.

Mátyás church stands in the heart of Buda's old town, which developed to the north of the Royal Palace from the 1200s onward.

In front of the church is Holy Trinity Square, with a memorial column to those who died in the plague of 1691. On the square stands the Old Town Hall, an elegant Baroque building with an onion-domed clock tower.

Baroque Madonna, Mátyás Church

Gellért Hotel and Bath Complex ③

Kelenhegyi út 4. **Tel** (1) 466 61 66. 🚌 7, 7A, 86. 🚋 18, 19, 47, 49. ⬜ daily. 🖼 ♿ www.budapestspas.hu

The earliest reference to the existence of healing waters at this site is found in the 13th century. In the later Middle Ages a hospital stood here and then, during the Turkish occupation, baths were built. The area takes its name from Bishop Gellért, whose monument on the hill is visible from many parts of the city. He was supposedly martyred here in 1046 by a group opposed to the introduction of Christianity. From the top of the hill one can admire a beautiful view of the whole of Budapest.

The Gellért Hotel, with its famous spa, was built between 1912 and 1918 in the Secession style, at the foot of the hill.

It boasts elaborate mosaics, stained-glass windows, statues, and fanciful balconies fronting the rooms. Its eastern-style towers and turrets offer superb views. The complex houses an institute of water therapy. The baths are separated into different areas for men and women. Each has plunge pools, a sauna, and a steam bath. The facilities have been modernized, but the glorious Secession interiors remain.

There is also an outdoor swimming pool with a wave machine, installed in 1927 and still in operation. The baths and health spa, with their sun terraces, restaurants, and cafés, are open to the public as well as to hotel guests.

OHER MUSEUMS IN BUDAPEST

Franz Liszt Museum
Vörösmarty utca 35. **Tel** (1) 322 98 04. Ⓜ Vörösmarty utca. ⬜ Mon–Sat. 🖼
www.lisztmuseum.hu
Museum in a house built in 1877 for Liszt (1811–86).

Museum of Applied Arts
Üllői út 33–37. **Tel** (1) 456 51 00. Ⓜ Ferenc körút. ⬜ Tue–Sun. 🖼 ♿ www.imm.hu
Fine collection of decorative arts, especially Art Nouveau artifacts.

Museum of Contemporary Art and Ludwig Museum
Komor Marcell utca 1. **Tel** (1) 555 34 44. 🚌 15, Csepeli HÉV. 🚋 2, 4, 6. ⬜ Tue–Sun. 🖼 ♿
www.ludwigmuseum.hu
A contemporary art museum with works by Warhol and Hockney.

Kodály Memorial Museum
Andrássy út 89. **Tel** (1) 352 7106. Ⓜ Kodály Körönd. ⬜ Tue, Wed, Sat, Sun. 🖼
The house in which the composer Kodály (1882–1967) lived and worked.

The men's section at the Gellért Baths

Pest

At the end of the 17th century, much of the walled city of Pest, on the east bank of the Danube, was in ruins and few residents remained. Gradually new residential districts began to be developed, extending beyond the medieval walls, and people started to return.

After a flood in 1838, which destroyed most of the rural dwellings in the areas around Pest, redevelopment schemes introduced grand houses and apartment blocks. The area of Városliget (City Park), once an expanse of marshland, was also developed in the 19th century.

The first bridge linking Pest and Buda was built in 1766. The two cities were united as Budapest in 1873.

The predominantly Baroque nave of the Inner City Parish Church

Inner City Parish Church ④

Március 15 tér 2. **Tel** (1) 318 3108. M *Ferenciek tere.* ◯ *daily.*

During the reign of István I (AD 1001–38), a small church stood on this site. St. Gellért was buried here after his martyrdom in 1046.

Work began on the Inner City Parish Church (*Belvárosi Plébánia templom*), adding to the existing building, in the 12th century. It is the oldest building in Pest. In the 14th century it was remodeled in Gothic style, and later used as a mosque by the Turks. After the fire of 1723, it was partly rebuilt in the Baroque style.

On the south side of the church is a Renaissance tabernacle bearing the Crest of Pest, created in the 16th century. Close to the main altar is a reminder of Turkish occupation: a *mihrab*, or prayer niche, indicating the direction of Mecca.

Hungarian National Museum ⑤

Múzeum körút 14–16. **Tel** (1) 338 21 22. ◯ *Tue–Sun.* M *Kálvin tér, Astoria.* ▦ *9, 15.* ▦ *47, 49.* ▨ *(temporary exhibitions only).* ▣ **www.**hnm.hu

The Hungarian National Museum was founded in 1802, when Count Ferenc Széchényi gave his personal collection to the nation. It is housed in an impressive Neoclassical edifice (1837–47).

In 1848, on the steps of the museum, poet Sándor Petőfi first read his *National Song*, which sparked the uprising against Habsburg rule. A reenactment is staged each year on March 15.

The museum's eclectic exhibits span the 11th century to the present day. Items on display include an 18th-century campaign chest, decorative weapons of Transylvanian princes, and a printing press used to print nationalist propaganda in 1848.

The museum is home to the Coronation Mantle donated by St. Stephen in 1031. It is made of Byzantine silks and is one of the oldest and best-preserved textile masterpieces in Europe.

Baroque campaign chest in the National Museum

Lavish interior of the 19th-century State Opera House

State Opera House ⑥

Andrássy út 22. **Tel** (1) 331 25 50. M *Opera.* ◯ *daily.* ▨ ▣ *at 3pm obligatory.* ♿ ▣ **www.**opera.hu

The State Opera House (*Magyar Állami Operaház*), opened in 1884, was the life's work of architect Miklós Ybl. The façade expresses musical themes, with statues of two of Hungary's most prominent composers, Ferenc Erkel and Franz Liszt. The opulence of the foyer, with its chandeliers, murals, and vaulted ceiling, is echoed in the grandeur of the sweeping main staircase and of the three-story auditorium.

St. Stephen's Basilica ⑦

Szent István tér 1. **Tel** (1) 317 28 59. M *Deák Ferenc tér.* **Treasury** ◯ *daily.* ▨ ♿ ▣ *daily.* **www.**basilica.hu

This Neoclassical church, dedicated to St. Stephen, or István, Hungary's first Christian king (1001–38), was built in 1851–1905 on a Greek cross floor plan. The church received the title Basilica Minor in 1938, the 900th anniversary of the king's death.

On the main altar is a marble statue of the saint; scenes from his life are depicted behind the altar. A painting to the right of the main entrance shows István dedicating Hungary to the Virgin Mary. His mummified forearm is kept in the Chapel of the Holy Right Hand.

The main entrance to the basilica is a massive door, decorated with carved heads of the 12 apostles. The dome reaches 96 m (315 ft) and is visible all over Budapest. Its interior is decorated with mosaics by Károly Lotz.

The basilica also has two distinctive towers. The one to the left of the main door houses a bell weighing 9 tons. This was funded by German Catholics to compensate for the loss of the original bell, which was looted by the Nazis in 1944.

Parliament ⑧

Kossuth Lajos tér 1–3. **Tel** *(1) 441 49 04*. **M** *Kossuth tér*. ▦ *70, 78*. ▦ *2, 2A*. ◯ *daily*. ● *during ceremonies*. ▨ *(free for EU citizens)*. ▮ *call (1) 441 49 04 to arrange*. ▤ ▯ **www**.parlament.hu

The Parliament (*Országház*) is Hungary's largest building – 268 m (880 ft) long, 96 m (315 ft) high, with 691 rooms. Built between 1884 and 1902, it was based on London's Houses of Parliament *(see p45)*. Although the façade is Neo-Gothic, the ground plan follows Baroque conventions, with a magnificent dome at the center. Beneath it is the Domed Hall, off which is the Gobelin Hall, with a Gobelin tapestry of Árpád

Tapestry of Árpád and Magyar chiefs in the Parliament building

(see p729) and fellow Magyar chiefs taking a blood oath. The greatest artists of the day decorated the interior of the building, and there are some spectacular ceiling frescoes by Károly Lotz and György Kiss.

Between the Domed Hall and the south wing is the National Assembly Hall. On the opposite side is the Congress Hall, a virtual mirror image of the National Assembly Hall. Both have public galleries.

Since 2000, the royal insignia have been displayed here.

Museum of Fine Arts ⑨

Hősök tere. **Tel** *(1) 469 71 00*. **M** *Hősök tere*. ▦ *4, 20, 30, 105*. ▦ *75, 79*. ◯ *Tue–Sun*. ▨ *(temporary exhibitions only)*. ▮ ▤ **www**.szepmuveszeti.hu

In 1870 the state bought a magnificent collection of paintings from the Esterházy family. Enriched by donations and acquisitions, the collection moved to its present location in 1906. As well as great

European paintings from every era from the Middle Ages to the 20th century, there are Egyptian, Greek, and Roman antiquities. Renaissance pieces include a wonderful unfinished Raphael known as the *Esterházy Madonna* and a small bronze by Leonardo da Vinci of François I of France. There are also paintings by Holbein and Dürer, seven works by El Greco, and a fabulous collection of old master drawings.

French 19th-century art is also very well represented, with works by Manet, Gauguin, and Toulouse-Lautrec.

Vajdahunyad Castle ⑩

Városliget. **Tel** *(1) 363 19 73*. **M** *Széchenyi Fürdő*. ◯ *daily*. ▨ *(temporary exhibitions only)*. ▮ ▤ **www**.mmgm.hu

This fantastical castle stands among trees at the edge of the lake in Városliget. It is in fact a complex of pavilions illustrating the evolution of Hungarian architecture. Created for the 1896 Millennium Celebrations as a temporary exhibit, it proved so popular that it was rebuilt permanently, in brick.

The pavilions are grouped in chronological order of style: Romanesque is followed by Gothic, Renaissance, Baroque, and so on, but the elements are linked to suggest a single, cohesive design. Details from more than 20 of Hungary's best-loved buildings are reproduced. The greatest emphasis is given to the medieval period, considered the most glorious in the country's history.

View across the lake of the Gothic *(left)* and Renaissance *(right)* sections of the Vajdahunyad Castle

Szentendre ❷

🏛 20,000. 🚗 🚌 🚆 from Budapest. 🚹 Dumtsa Jenő utca 22 **Tel**
(26) 317 965. **www**.szentendre.hu

Szentendre was settled by
Serbian refugees, who first
came here in the 14th century.
After the Turkish occupation
of Belgrade in 1690, more
Serbs arrived, ushering in a
period of great prosperity.
   The Slavic interiors of the
town's many churches are
filled with incense, icons, and
candlelight. **Blagovestenska
Church** on Fő tér, the main
square, has a magnificent
iconostasis, while other sites
worth visiting are **Belgrade
Cathedral**, for Sunday Mass,
and the bishop's palace. Next
door, the **Museum of Serbian
Art** contains displays of icons
and other religious artifacts.
   Many artists have made their
home in Szentendre, including
the Hungarian ceramic artist,
Margit Kovács (1902–77).
Her work can be seen at the
Margit Kovács Museum.

> 🏛 **Margit Kovács Museum**
> Vastag György utca 1. **Tel** (26) 310
> 244. ⬭ Tue–Sun. 📷 📹

Esztergom ❸

🏛 30,000. 🚗 🚌 🚆 from Budapest.

St. István, Hungary's first
Christian king, was baptized
in Esztergom and later
crowned here on Christmas
Day in AD 1000.
Dominating the city's skyline
is the huge **Catholic
Cathedral**, built in the early
19th century on the site of a
12th-century church. In the

The Tihany Peninsula, jutting out into Lake Balaton

treasury are religious artifacts
from the original church. The
16th-century marble Bakócz
burial chapel, next to the
southern entrance, was built
by Florentine craftsmen.
South of the cathedral, the
remains of Esztergom's **Castle**
date from the 10th century.
   In the picturesque old
town, Esztergom's central
square is bordered by many
lively pavement cafés.

> ⛪ **Castle**
> Szent István tér 1. **Tel** (33) 415 986.
> ⬭ Tue–Sun. 📷

Lake Balaton ❹

Siófok 🚗 🚌 🚆 to/from Balatonfüred. 🚹 Víztorony, Pf: 75 **Tel** (84)
315 355. **Balatonfüred** 🚗 🚌
🚢 to/from Siófok and Tihany.
🚹 Petőfi u 68 (87) 580 480.

Every summer Lake Balaton,
Europe's largest fresh-water
lake, attracts thousands of
vacationers. The southern

shore is the more developed,
with sandy beaches and a
wide choice of tourist
accommodations. The largest
resort is **Siófok**, characterized
by high-rise buildings, lively
bars, and noisy nightlife. By
day, windsurfing, sailing, and
pleasure cruises are available.
   Those in search of a more
peaceful atmosphere should
head for **Balatonvilágos**, set
atop attractive wooded cliffs,
or **Balatonberény**, which
has a nudist beach. Southwest
of Balatonberény, the tiny
lake known as **Kis-Balaton**
(Little Balaton) is a protected
nature reserve, home to over
80 species of birds.
   One of the most popular
destinations on Balaton's
northern shore is the spa
town of **Balatonfüred**,
whose mineral springs have
been used for curative
purposes since Roman times.
From here you can visit the
Tihany Peninsula, which
became Hungary's first
national park in 1957, and
boasts some of the most
beautiful scenery in the area.
   At the far northwestern tip
of the lake, the university
town of **Keszthely** has three
beaches, as well as a number
of other attractions, including
the Balaton Museum, which
covers the history and natural
history of the region, and the
imposing Festetics Palace. A
15-minute drive from Keszthely
brings you to **Hévíz**, an old
19th-century spa resort, where
you can bathe in the world's
second largest thermal lake.

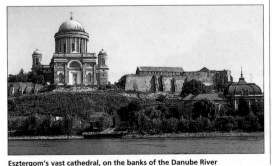

Esztergom's vast cathedral, on the banks of the Danube River

For hotels and restaurants in this region see p742 and p743

Pécs ❺

🏛 *180,000.* 🚊 🚌 ℹ️ *Széchenyi tér 9* **Tel** *(72) 213 315.*

First a Celtic, then a Roman settlement, Pécs was later ruled by the Turks from 1543 until 1686. Several monuments testify to these different periods of Pécs' history.

The city's main square, Széchenyi tér, is overlooked by the **Catholic Church**, formerly the Mosque of Gazi Kassim Pasha, built under Turkish occupation. Inside, a delicately decorated *mihrab* (prayer niche) serves as a reminder of the building's origins. Behind the church is the **Archaeological Museum**, whose exhibits date from prehistoric times to the Magyar conquest.

On Dom tér are Pécs' four-towered, Neo-Romanesque **Cathedral**, which stands on the foundations of an 11th-century basilica, and the Neo-Renaissance **Bishop's Palace** (1770). South of here, on Szent István tér, a stairway leads to the ruins of a 4th-century underground **chapel**, which contains a wonderful collection of frescoes. On nearby Apáca utca, recent excavations have unearthed a collection of **Roman tombs**. Remains of the city's **medieval walls**, erected after an invasion by the Mongols in the 13th century, include a 15th-century barbican.

Candlelit interior of Pécs' Neo-Romanesque cathedral

Pécs' museums include the **Csontváry Museum**, showing works by the artist Kosztka Tivadar Csontváry (1853–1919), and the **Vasarely Museum**, dedicated to Hungarian Op artist Victor Vasarely (1908–97).

🏛 **Archaeological Museum**
Széchenyi tér 12. **Tel** *(72) 312 719.*
⭕ *Tue–Sun.* ⬤ *Oct 1–Apr 1.* 📷

🏛 **Vasarely Museum**
Káptalan utca 3. **Tel** *(72) 514 044.*
⭕ *Tue–Sun.* 📷

Eger ❻

🏛 *60,000.* 🚊 🚌 ℹ️ *Bajcsy Zsilinsky u 9* **Tel** *(36) 517 715.*

One of the most popular tourist destinations in Hungary, Eger is also famous for its world-class wines.

At the heart of the town, on Eszterházy tér, are the Neoclassical **Cathedral** (1830s) and the **Lyceum**. A highlight of the latter is

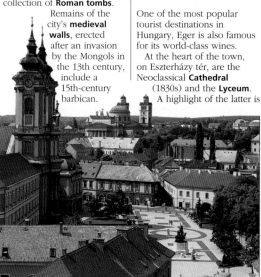

Eger's Baroque Minorite church, towering over Dobó István tér

the observatory, which affords stunning views of the town and surrounding vineyards.

Eger's 40-m (130-ft) **minaret** is a relic of 16th-century Turkish occupation, while the splendid Baroque **Minorite Church** on Dobó István tér dates from the 1770s.

Eger Castle was built in the 13th century following the Mongol invasion. The castle complex includes the Bishop's Palace (1470), which houses a museum of historical artifacts, and underground casemates.

♟ **Eger Castle**
Eger Vári. **Tel** *(36) 312 744.*
⭕ *daily.* 📷

Environs
Just west of the town, in the **Szépasszony Valley**, you can sample the region's wines, including the famous dry red, Egri Bikavér, or Bull's Blood.

Tokaj ❼

🏛 *20,000.* 🚊 🚌 ℹ️ *Serház utca 1* **Tel** *(47) 352 259.* **www**.tokaj.hu

Tokaj is located at the center of one of Hungary's most important wine-growing areas. Tokaji dessert wines range from sweet to dry and owe their distinctive full-bodied flavor to the volcanic soil in which the vines grow, and a type of mold peculiar to the region. The best cellars to visit for a tasting are the

Hungarian dessert wine Tokaji Aszú

Rákóczi Cellar, run by a foreign company, and the privately-owned **Hímesudvar** at No. 2 Bem utca.

Tokaj has a **synagogue** and a **Jewish cemetery**, relics of the period before World War I, when the town had a large Jewish population. The **Tokaj Museum** gives an interesting insight into the history of the town and its environs.

🍷 **Rákóczi Cellar**
Kossuth tér 15. **Tel** *(47) 352 408.* ⭕ *Apr–Oct: daily (call in advance).* 📷

Practical & Travel Information

In recent years, tourism has become an important part of the Hungarian national economy, and as a result, there have been vast improvements in communications, banking facilities, and public transportation. The biggest problem tourists face is the formidable language barrier. However, staff at many tourist offices, hotels, and other attractions, usually speak English or German.

WHEN TO VISIT

The most popular times to visit Hungary are between April and the end of June, and from the middle of August until October. July is usually extremely hot, and it is almost unbearable to stay in Budapest, although away from the capital the heat is less severe. From November until March, many museums have shorter opening hours or may close altogether.

TOURIST INFORMATION

Before leaving for Hungary, you can obtain various information leaflets and maps from the Hungarian National Tourist Office, which has branches worldwide.

Within Hungary, there are tourist information offices in most large towns. In Budapest, advice on sightseeing, accommodation, and cultural events is given by the offices of **Tourinform Budapest**. The **Vista Visitor Center** also offers these services, as well as a reduced-rate telephone center, left-luggage lockers, a bureau de change, and an internet café.

Visitors to the capital may wish to invest in the Budapest Card, which entitles cardholders, along with one child under 14, to unlimited use of the city's public transport system, free entry to 60 museums, the zoo and funfair, 50 per cent discount on guided tours, and 10 to 20 per cent discount on selected cultural events and at certain restaurants.

A new metro line in Budapest is under construction.

VISA REQUIREMENTS

Citizens of the US, Canada, Australia, New Zealand, and the European Union need only a valid passport to visit Hungary for up to 90 days.

For more information about visas and extended visits, see the Hungarian Ministry of Foreign Affairs' website (www.mfa.gov.hu).

PERSONAL SECURITY

Hungary is on the whole a safe country to travel in. As in most cities that attract large numbers of tourists, pickpockets operate in Budapest, targeting crowded metro stations, buses, and shopping malls. Rákóczi tér and Mátyás tér, in district VIII, are traditional hangouts for prostitutes; lone women should avoid these areas at night.

In the case of an emergency while on vacation, the relevant numbers to call are listed in the directory opposite.

HEALTH ISSUES

No special vaccinations are required for Hungary. Allergy sufferers and people with breathing difficulties who intend to visit Budapest should take account of the summer smog conditions, which are particulary acute in Pest. Those susceptible might consider staying in the castle district, where cars are banned, or retreating to the wooded Buda hills.

For treatments for minor ailments, visit a pharmacy (Gyógyszertár or Patika). If your nearest store is closed, it should display a list of 24-hour emergency pharmacies.

People with heart conditions who wish to use Hungary's thermal baths should seek a physician's advice beforehand.

FACILITIES FOR THE DISABLED

Hungary's public transportation systems, museums, and other attractions are gradually being renovated to make them wheelchair-friendly, but people with disabilities may still encounter problems. For more detailed information contact the **Hungarian Disabled Association**.

BANKING AND CURRENCY

The Hungarian currency is the forint (HUF or Ft). If you need to change money, the best rates of exchange are offered by banks and bureaux de change. Banks open from 8am to 5pm, Monday to Friday. While all banks are closed at the weekends, bureaux de change and ATMs remain open. Credit cards are more widely accepted now than before, but their use is still not as widespread as elsewhere in Europe and you shouldn't expect to be able to use them everywhere. It's wise to carry a little extra cash with you.

THE CLIMATE OF HUNGARY

Hungary enjoys some of the sunniest weather in Europe, with an average of eight hours of sunshine a day in summer. June, July, and August are the hottest months. In winter, temperatures can fall well below freezing and there may also be snowfall. Hungary has comparatively low rainfall. June usually gets the most rain, while the fall is the driest season.

BUDAPEST

°C/F	Apr	Jul	Oct	Jan
		26/79		
	15/59	15/59	15/59	
0°C 32°F	5/41		6/43	2/36
				-3/27
sunshine (hrs)	6 hrs	10 hrs	5 hrs	2 hrs
rainfall (mm)	42 mm	56 mm	40 mm	40 mm
month	Apr	Jul	Oct	Jan

COMMUNICATIONS

The Hungarian telephone system used to be notoriously bad, but improvements are now slowly being made. Phonecards, which are available from tobacconists, post offices, petrol stations, and some newspaper kiosks, are the best option when using public phones, although some booths still accept coins.

Post offices open from 8am to 6pm, Monday to Friday, and on Saturday mornings. Service can be slow and there are often long lines, so be prepared to wait.

FLYING TO HUNGARY

Direct scheduled flights between New York's JFK airport and Budapest's inter-national airport at Ferihegy are operated by **Malév**, the Hungarian national airline. Other major airlines flying from the US and Canada to Hungary include **Air France, British Airways, KLM, Lufthansa,** and **Northwest Airlines**, although services entail a transfer or touch-down at another European city. British Airways and Malév each operate three daily scheduled flights from London. Many low-cost airlines also operate daily flights from London.

Ferihegy airport is located 16 km (10 miles) from the center of Budapest. The efficient **Airport Minibus Shuttle** will take passengers from the airport to any address in the capital. Taxis are a quick and comfortable way of getting into the city.

RAIL TRAVEL

The Hungarian national rail network is very efficient, with trains invariably departing and arriving on time. Budapest has direct international rail links with 25 other capital cities, Keleti pu station handling the majority of the international traffic. High-speed trains to Vienna, the main communications hub for western Europe, depart approximately every three hours and take around 2 hours 25 minutes. There are also car-train services from Keleti pu to Thessaloníki in Greece.

Within Hungary, local trains are categorized according to speed: "slow" (*személy*), "speedy" (*sebes*), or "fast" (*gyors*). There are also modern intercity services between Budapest and the larger cities. A number of concessionary fares are available for those planning on doing a lot of rail travel in Hungary.

TRAVELING BY BUS

International buses to all European destinations, depart from Népliget station. Nationally, buses are run by Volánbusz, which operates routes to most cities and towns in Hungary.

TRAVELING BY CAR

To rent a car in Hungary you must be aged 21 years or over, and have held a full driver's license for at least a year. An international drivers' license helps also. Most of the big, international firms have offices at the airport in Budapest, or you can arrange rental at hotels and travel agencies throughout the country.

DIRECTORY

HUNGARIAN NATIONAL TOURIST OFFICES

www.hungary
tourism.hu

In the UK:
46 Eaton Place, London
SW1X 8AL. **Tel** 020-7823
1032. www.goto
hungary.co.uk

In the US:
150 East 58th Street,
33rd Floor, New York,
NY 10155-3398.
Tel 212-355 0240.
www.gotohungary.com

TOURIST INFORMATION

Tourinform Hotline (24 hrs)
Tel 06 80 630 800 (within
Hungary).
Tel +36 30 30 30 600
(abroad).

Tourinform Budapest
Sütö utca 2, Budapest V.
Tel (1) 438 80 80.

Vista Visitor Center
1061 Budapest,
Andrássy út 1.
Tel (1) 452 36 36.
www.vista.hu

EMBASSIES

Australia
1126 Királyhágó tér 8–9,
Budapest.
Tel (1) 457 97 77.
www.australia.hu

Canada
1027 Budapest,
Ganz út 12–14.
Tel (1) 392 33 60.
Fax (1) 392 33 90.

UK
1051 Harmincad utca 6,
Budapest.
Tel (1) 266 28 88.
www.britishembassy.hu

US
1054 Szabadság tér 12,
Budapest.
Tel (1) 475 44 00.
Fax (1) 475 47 64.
www.usembassy.hu

EMERGENCY NUMBERS

Ambulance
Tel 104
Fire
Tel 105
Police
Tel 107.

FACILITIES FOR THE DISABLED

Hungarian Disabled Association
1032 San Marco utca 76,
Budapest. **Tel** (1) 388 23
88. www.meosz.hu

AIR TRAVEL

Ferihegy Airport
Tel (1) 296 96 96.

Air France
Tel (1) 483 88 00 (Hungary).
Tel 800-237 2747 (US).

British Airways
Tel (1) 411 5555 (Hungary).
Tel 0845-773 3377 (UK).
Tel 877 428 2228 (US).

KLM
Tel (1) 373 77 37 (Hungary).
Tel 800-374 7747 (US).

Lufthansa
Tel (1) 411 99 00 (Hungary).
Tel 800-645 3880 (US).

Malév
Tel 06 40 212 121 (within
Hungary).
Tel 800-223 6884 (US).
Tel +36 12 35 53 88 88
(elsewhere).

Northwest Airlines
www.nwa.com

Where to Stay in Hungary

Hungary offers a range of accommodations, from top-class chain hotels to family-run pensions and hostels. In Budapest, bargain hunters can benefit from substantial weekend reductions offered by many luxury hotels in the low season. During the summer, when smog can prevail, it is best to opt for an air-conditioned hotel in Pest.

PRICE CATEGORIES
Price categories are for a standard double room with bathroom per night, including breakfast, tax, and service charges:

Ⓗ Under 15,000 HUF
ⒽⒽ 15,000–25,000 HUF
ⒽⒽⒽ 25,000–35,000 HUF
ⒽⒽⒽⒽ 35,000–50,000 HUF
ⒽⒽⒽⒽⒽ Over 50,000 HUF

BUDAPEST

BUDA Citadella

Citadella sétány, 1118 **Tel** *1-466 57 94* **Rooms** *14*   **Map** *C4*

This hostel-style hotel occupies the casements of the Citadel. It offers relatively inexpensive, neat, and clean double and multiple-occupancy rooms. A popular wine bar, restaurant, and nightclub are located in the Citadella complex. **www.citadella.hu**

BUDA Danubius Hotel Gellért

Szent Gellért tér 1, 1111 **Tel** *1-889 55 00* **Rooms** *233*   **Map** *C4*

This legendary spa hotel has both indoor and outdoor pools that provide an attractive environment in which to relax. Treatments such as massage are also available. Other facilities include two restaurants, a bar, café, nightclub, and banqueting halls. The rooms have probably seen grander days. **www.danubiusgroup.com/gellert**

BUDA Hilton

Hess Andrástér 1–3, 1014 **Tel** *1-889 66 00* **Rooms** *322*   **Map** *B3*

The Hilton, one of the most luxurious hotels in Budapest, is located in a building incorporating parts of a Gothic church and Jesuit monastery. In the heart of the Castle District, with magnificent views over the Danube and the Pest cityscape, the high prices here are more than justified. **www.budapest.hilton.com**

PEST Astoria

Kossuth Lajos utca 19–21, 1053 **Tel** *1-889 6000* **Rooms** *130*   **Map** *C3*

This old hotel, designed in the Secessionist style, but with a Neo-Baroque breakfast room, has been refurbished to recreate its original interior. Even for visitors not staying at the hotel, it is worth visiting the café to see the beautiful interior. Those staying at the hotel will find the bedrooms luxurious. **www.danubiusgroup.com/astoria**

PEST Kempinski Corvinus

Erzsébet tér 7–8, 1051 **Tel** *1-429 37 77* **Rooms** *369*   **Map** *D3*

This exclusive hotel – all glass and class – often welcomes heads of state and other notable personalities among its guests. The large and luxuriously furnished rooms are relaxing, and a perfect mix of luxury with modernity. The hotel has excellent fitness facilities, a pool, two good restaurants, bars, and a pub. **www.kempinski-budapest.com**

REST OF HUNGARY

BALATONFURED Annabella

Deák Ferenc utca 25, 8230 **Tel** *87-889 400* **Fax** *87-889 412* **Rooms** *388*

Close to the lake shore in the centre of Balatonfüred, the Annabella enjoys its own private beach. It also offers a number of smaller than standard double rooms, a bargain in a resort where these are hard to find. Pets are accepted at no extra cost, though not in the restaurants. Open only May–October. **www.danubiushotels.com/annabella**

EGER Senator-ház

Dobó tér 11, 3300 **Tel** *36-320 466* **Fax** *36-320 466* **Rooms** *14*

One of the oldest buildings in Eger, dating from 1753, the Senator-ház has a fantastic location on Dobó square in the shadow of Eger Castle. The rooms are on the small side but most have castle views. There is a good restaurant, café, and terrace. Guests have free admission to Eger's thermal baths at weekends. **www.senatorhaz.hu**

PECS Palatinus

Király utca 5, 7621 **Tel** *72-889 400* **Fax** *72-889 438* **Rooms** *94*

A mix of Secession and Art Deco styles, the façade and lobby of this hotel are tourist attractions in themselves. In addition, the hotel boasts sumptuous rooms and a first-class location on the elegant Király utca. Sauna, solarium, and steam bath are located in the basement. **www.danubiushotels.com/palatinus**

Key to Symbols *see back cover flap*

Where to Eat in Hungary

Hungary offers a variety of eateries at prices to suit most budgets. Two of the most common types are the *étterem*, a restaurant that offers Hungarian and international dishes, and the *csárda*, a taverna serving local specialties. Many ethnic venues have recently sprung up in Budapest, specializing in global cuisine.

PRICE CATEGORIES
Price categories are for a standard double room with bathroom per night, including breakfast, tax, and service charges:
Under 3,000 HUF
3,000–4,000 HUF
4,000–5,000 HUF
5,000–6,000 HUF
Over 6,000 HUF

BUDAPEST

BUDA Pest Buda Vendéglô

Fortuna utca 3 **Tel** *1-212 58 80*

Map *B2*

This is a small, elegant restaurant with arcaded walls in a listed building. Part of the former underground cave system gives space to its popular and extensive Hungarian and international wine cellar. The menu itself is not all that long but it is interesting nevertheless, and all the dishes are excellently prepared.

BUDA Rivalda Café & Restaurant

Színház utca 5–9 **Tel** *1-489 02 36*

Map *B3*

Next to the Castle Theater, the Rivalda's decor is theater-inspired yet not over-the-top. Its contemporary international cuisine, with a frequently changing menu, reflects the seasons, with most dishes based on local, fresh ingredients. Many dishes are inventive, and all are superbly presented. Live jazz piano music in the evenings.

PEST Károlyi Étterem és Kávéház

Károlyi Mihály utca 16 **Tel** *1-328 02 40*

Map *D4*

In the lovely courtyard of the Károlyi Palace is this elegant, sophisticated restaurant. Worth trying is the *borjúpaprikás lángosban* (veal paprika stew with potato pancakes). Its attractive gardens are uncommon in the city center. At weekends it is worth booking – the restaurant is often closed for weddings in summer.

PEST Maligán

Kossuth Lajos utca 38 **Tel** *1-240 90 10*

Map *D4*

Superb wine bar and bistro serving a fine selection of wine by the bottle and glass. The food is classically Hungarian with loads of goose dishes and other game such as pheasant and duck. Prices are terrific value and the service is superb: the staff are genuinely knowledgeable about food and wine.

PEST Belcanto

Dalszínház utca 8 **Tel** *1-269 31 01*

Map *C3*

Enjoy good international and Hungarian favorites while listening to the waiters and some customers or opera professionals sing popular opera pieces in the evening at this now legendary Hungarian restaurant, as famous for its good-time atmosphere as for its super food. There is also an orchestra playing dance music to really liven things up.

REST OF HUNGARY

BALATONFURED Stefánia Vitorlás

Tagore sétány 1 **Tel** *87-343 407*

On the shore of Lake Balaton with views out to Tihany Peninsula, this restaurant is situated in the refurbished clubhouse of the Balatonfüred Rowing and Sailing Club. Serving fish and game dishes to a buzzing crowd from morning until late, it is also the perfect spot to sample great local wine.

EGER Tulipánkert Vendéglô

Szépasszonyvölgy út 47 **Tel** *36-412 533*

Simple but perfect restaurant, terrace, garden and wine cellar up on Szépasszonyvölgy, a short drive southwest of the town. It is worth the trip to sample great Hungarian wines and superb cuisine. In high summer a Gypsy band creates a lively atmosphere as the barbecue sizzles with fine local pork and sausages.

ESZTERGOM Prímás Pince

Szent István tér 4 **Tel** *33-313 495*

What has long been an Esztergom favourite has become an international one thanks to countless happy diners who come here year after year. While the cuisine is standard Hungarian and the wine list less than worthy, the setting in the cellars of the castle is legendary. Disappointingly, it closes at 10pm, with last kitchen orders a little before.

Map References *see map of Budapest pp732–3*

POLAND

*L*ocated between Russia and Germany, Poland has always been a fiercely contested land. Released from the eastern bloc in 1989, the country is now developing rapidly, especially in the cities of Warsaw, Cracow, Gdańsk, and Wrocław. Monuments attest to a stormy history, but Poland is famed for its virtues, especially the generosity of its people and the excellence of its vodka.

Although situated on the plains of central Europe, Poland has an extremely varied landscape. Alpine scenery predominates in the Tatra Mountains to the south, while the north is dominated by lakes. Mountain lovers can make use of the well-developed infrastructure of hostels and shelters, such as those found in the Tatras. The countless lakes of Warmia and Mazuria, collectively known as the Land of a Thousand Lakes, are a haven for water-sports enthusiasts.

Poland's inhabitants, who number almost 39 million, all but constitute a single ethnic group, with minorities accounting for less than 4 percent of the population. The largest minorities are Belorussians and Ukrainians, who inhabit the east of the country, and Germans, who are concentrated mainly around the city of Opole in Silesia. The majority of Poles are Catholic, but large regions of the country, such as Cieszyn Silesia, have a substantial Protestant population. In the east there are also many Orthodox Christians. Religious denomination does not necessarily coincide with ethnic identity, although Belorussians tend to be Orthodox, while Ukrainians belong to the Greek Catholic (Uniate) Church.

HISTORY

Poland's borders have changed continually with the course of history. The origins of the Polish nation go back to the 10th century, when Slav tribes living in the area of Gniezno united under the Piast dynasty, which ruled Poland until 1370. Mieszko I converted to Christianity in 966, thus bringing his kingdom into Christian Europe, and made Poznań the seat of Poland's first bishop. The Piast dynasty ruled Poland with variable fortune and

Statue of the great 19th-century poet and patriot Adam Mickiewicz in Market Square, Cracow

◁ Altarpiece depicting the Assumption in St. Mary's Church, Cracow, carved by Veit Stoss (1447–1533)

Solidarity demonstrators staging a mass rally during a papal visit to Poland in 1987

embroiled the nation in domestic quarrels for 150 years. After this dynasty died out, the great Lithuanian prince Jagiełło took the Polish throne and founded a new dynasty. The treaty with Lithuania signed in 1385 initiated the long process of consolidation between these nations, culminating in 1569 with the signing of the Union of Lublin. Nevertheless, the so-called Republic of Two Nations (*Rzeczpospolita Obojga Narodów*) lasted until 1795. In 1572 the Jagiellonian dynasty died out, after which the Polish authorities introduced elective kings, with the nobility having the right to vote.

KEY DATES IN POLISH HISTORY

966 Adoption of Christianity under Mieszko I

1025 Coronation of Bolesław the Brave, first king of Poland

1320 The unification of the Polish state

1385 Poland and Lithuania unite under the Treaty of Krewo

1569 The Union of Lublin creates the Polish-Lithuanian Republic of Two Nations

1596 The capital moves from Cracow to Warsaw

1655 Beginning of the "Deluge" (the Swedish occupation), ending in 1660

1772–1918 Poland divided three times between Russia, Prussia, and Austria. The final partition (1795) is made after a Polish uprising led by Tadeusz Kościuszko

1918 Poland regains independence

1939 Soviet and German forces invade

1940 Auschwitz-Birkenau established; 1.5 million Poles and Jews are gassed during the war

1945 Communist government takes control

1980 Solidarity formed, led by Lech Wałęsa

1989 First free post-war elections are held. Lech Wałęsa wins the Presidency by a landslide

1999 Poland joins NATO

2004 Poland joins EU

The 17th century was dominated by wars with Sweden, Russia, and the Ottoman Empire, and although the country survived, it was considerably weakened, and its time of dominance was over. In 1795 it was partitioned by Russia, Prussia, and Austria, and was wiped off the map for more than 100 years. Attempts to wrest independence by insurrection were unsuccessful, and Poland did not regain its sovereignty until 1918. The arduous process of rebuilding and uniting the nation was still incomplete when, at the outbreak of World War II, a six-year period of German and Soviet occupation began. The price that Poland paid was very high: millions were murdered, including virtually its entire Jewish population. The country suffered devastation and there were huge territorial losses, which were only partly compensated by the Allies' decision to move the border westwards. After the war, Poland was subjugated by the Soviet Union, but the socialist economy proved ineffective. The formation of Solidarity (*Solidarność*) in 1980 accelerated the pace of change, which was completed when Poland regained its freedom after the June 1989 elections.

In 1999 Poland became a member of NATO, and in 2004 it joined the European Union.

LANGUAGE AND CULTURE

The legacy of more than 100 years of partition rule is still visible in Poland's cultural landscape. Russian, Prussian, and Austrian administrations left their mark not only on rural and urban architecture, but also on the customs and mentality of the people.

The Poles have a deep reverence for religious symbols and rituals, and the presence of the church can be seen everywhere, either in the form of lavish Baroque buildings or images of the Black Madonna. Wayside shrines are also a regular feature.

Polish is a West Slavic language closely related to Slovak and Czech. Many of its words (such as *Solidarność*) are borrowed from Latin, although German, Italian, and English words are also common.

Exploring Poland

Bordering the Baltic Sea, Poland is one of the largest countries of Central Europe, with a population of around 39 million. Warsaw, the capital, is located at the center of Poland, on the banks of the River Vistula (Wisła). Its location makes it an ideal base for visiting other cities, such as Cracow, the ancient royal capital; Gdańsk, the Hanseatic city whose shipyards gave birth to Solidarity; and Poznań, one of the oldest Polish cities. Cracow is one of the country's greatest treasures, offering excursions to the Polish mountains and the Cracow-Częstochowa Valley.

SIGHTS AT A GLANCE

Cracow pp754–7 **2**
WARSAW pp748–53 **1**

Children in traditional dress on a
Polish public holiday, Cracow

The Neoclassical entrance to
Warsaw's Wilanów Palace and Park

KEY

✈	Airport
⚓	Ferry port
—	Highway
---	Major road
—	Railroad
▪▪▪	International border

0 kilometers 100

0 miles 100

Warsaw ●

Warsaw is believed to have been founded in the late 13th century, when Duke Bolesław built a castle here overlooking the Vistula. It became capital of Poland in 1596, making it one of Europe's youngest capital cities. The present castle and other grand buildings of the Old Town date largely from the Renaissance and Baroque periods. By the end of World War II, some 80 percent of the buildings had been reduced to rubble. What you see today is the product of meticulous reconstruction undertaken during the Communist era. Warsaw is rich in museums and sights and the Varsovians are immensely proud of their history of resistance to oppression. The center has been declared a UNESCO World Heritage Site.

Wilanów Palace, a 17th-century royal retreat, which stands in a magnificent park on the outskirts of the city

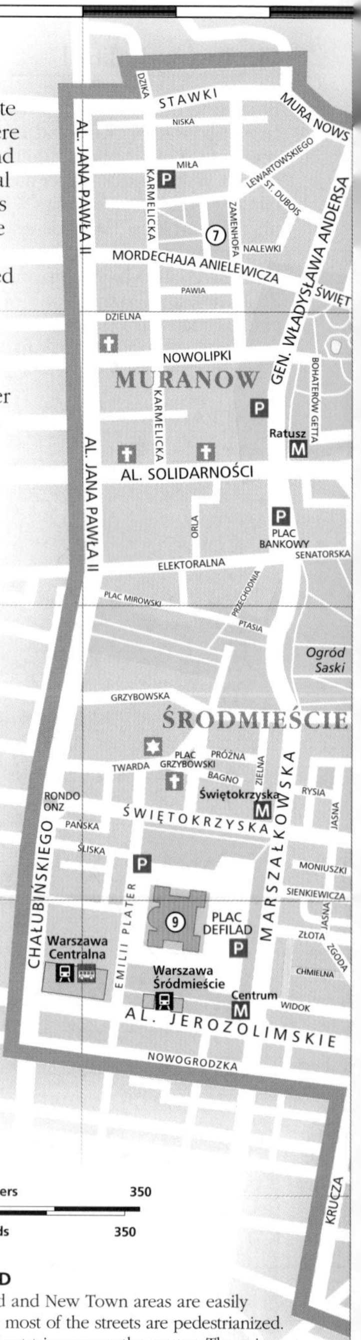

SIGHTS AT A GLANCE

Grand Theater ⑥
Monument to the Ghetto Heroes ⑦
Monument to those Fallen and
   Murdered in the East ⑧
National Museum ⑩
Old Town Market Square ①
Palace of Culture and
   Science ⑨
Royal Castle ③
Royal Route ⑤
St. Anna's Church ④
St. John's Cathedral ②

Greater Warsaw
(see inset map)
Łazienki Park ⑪
Wilanów Palace and Park ⑫

SEE ALSO

• *Where to Stay* p760

• *Where to Eat* p761

GETTING AROUND

The sights in the Old and New Town areas are easily visited on foot, since most of the streets are pedestrianized. Trams are best for short trips across the center. There is also an extensive bus service, but Warsaw's single metro line only serves suburbs to the south and is of little use to tourists. Taxis are reasonably priced, but use a reputable firm. Driving is getting more problematic, but the streets are still less crowded than in most European cities.

0 meters 350
0 yards 350

A   B   C

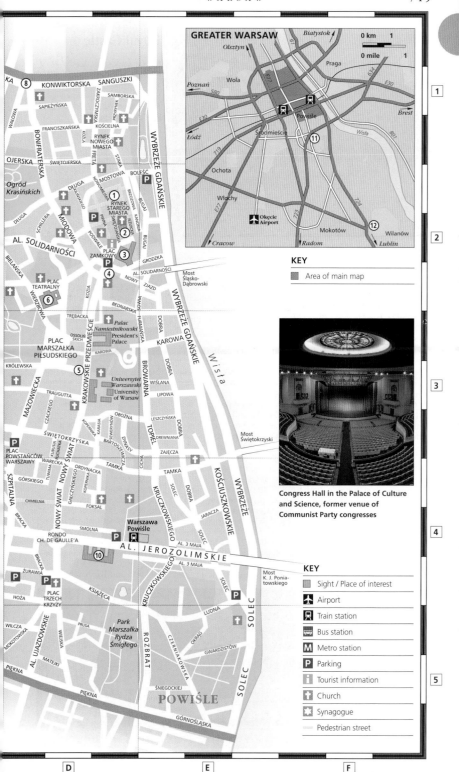

GREATER WARSAW

Białystok
Olsztyn
Poznań
Wola
Praga
Brest
Łódź
Powiśle
Śródmieście
Wisła
Ochota
Włochy
Okęcie Airport
Mokotów
Wilanów
Cracow
Radom
Lublin

0 km 1
0 mile 1

KONWIKTORSKA SANGUSZKI
KA
SAPIEŻYŃSKA
SAMBORSKA
MYŚLIWIECKA
PRZYRYNEK
FRANCISZKAŃSKA
KOŚCIELNA
KOŹLA
RYNEK NOWEGO MIASTA
FRETA
STARA
BONIFRATERSKA
ŚWIĘTOJERSKA
OJERSKA
MOSTOWA
BOLEŚĆ
WYBRZEŻE GDAŃSKIE
WALOWA
DŁUGA
NOWOMIEJSKA
BRZOZOWA
KANONIA
BUGAJ
Ogród Krasiński
DŁUGA
DUNAJEWSKIEGO
RYNEK STAREGO MIASTA
ŚWIĘTOJAŃSKA
BUGAJ
SCHILLERA
MIODOWA
PIWNA
PODWALE
PLAC ZAMKOWY
GRODZKA
AL. SOLIDARNOŚCI
NOWY ZJAZD
AL. SOLIDARNOŚCI
Most Śląsko-Dąbrowski
BIELAŃSKA
PLAC TEATRALNY
WIERZBOWA
KOZIA
BEDNARSKA
WYBRZEŻE GDAŃSKIE
TRĘBACKA
OSSOLIŃSKICH
Pałac Namiestnikowski President's Palace
FURMAŃSKA
DOBRA
KAROWA
PLAC MARSZAŁKA PIŁSUDSKIEGO
KRAKOWSKIE PRZEDMIEŚCIE
KAROWA
BROWARNA
KRÓLEWSKA
Uniwersytet Warszawski University of Warsaw
WIŚLANA
MAZOWIECKA
TRAUGUTTA
CZACKIEGO
OBOŻNA
LIPOWA
KOPERNIKA
SEWERYNÓW
DYNASY
LESZCZYŃSKA
DOBRA
ŚWIĘTOKRZYSKA
KUBUSIA
BARTOSZEWICZA
TOPIEL
DREWNIANA
Most Świętokrzyski
PLAC POWSTAŃCÓW WARSZAWY
KARASIA
PUCHATKA
ZAJĘCZA
GÓRSKIEGO
TUWIMA
WARECKA
ORDYNACKA
TAMKA
CICHA
TAMKA
SZPITALNA
GAŁCZYŃSKIEGO
KOPERNIKA
CHMIELNA
KRUCZKOWSKIEGO
SOLEC
DOBRA
FOKSAL
NOWY ŚWIAT
WYBRZEŻE KOŚCIUSZKOWSKIE
JARACZA
Warszawa Powiśle
BRACKA
RONDO CH. DE GAULLE'A
SMOLNA
AL. 3 MAJA
AL. JEROZOLIMSKIE
AL. 3 MAJA
Most K. J. Poniatowskiego
ŻURAWIA
SOLEC
HOŻA
PLAC TRZECH KRZYŻY
KSIĄŻĘCA
LUDNA
SOLEC
WILCZA
AL. UJAZDOWSKIE
PRUSA
WIEJSKA
MOKOTOWSKA
Park Marszałka Rydza Śmigłego
OKRĄG
ROZBRAT
CZERNIAKOWSKA
GWARDZISTÓW
MATEJKI
PIĘKNA
PIĘKNA
ŚNIEGOCKIEJ
SOLEC
POWIŚLE
GÓRNOŚLĄSKA

KEY

Area of main map

Congress Hall in the Palace of Culture and Science, former venue of Communist Party congresses

KEY

Sight / Place of interest
Airport
Train station
Bus station
M Metro station
P Parking
Tourist information
Church
Synagogue
Pedestrian street

D E F

Horse-drawn carriages in the colorful Old Town Market Square

Old Town Market Square ①

Rynek Starego Miasta. ▦ *E1, E2, E3, 116, 122, 160, 174, 175, 180, 192, 195, 303, 403, 503, 518.* **History Museum** *Tel 022-635 16 25.* ⬜ *Tue–Sun.*

Painstakingly restored after World War II, the Old Town Market Square was the center of Warsaw public life until the 19th century, when the focus of the growing, modern city moved. The tall, ornate, and colorful houses, which lend the square its unique character, were built by wealthy merchants in the 17th century.

The houses on one side form the **Warsaw History Museum** (Muzeum Historyczne m st Warszawy). This displays the city's history through paintings, photographs, sculpture, and archaeological finds. There is also a film show, with footage of the Nazis' systematic destruction of Warsaw in 1944. Today, café tables and stalls line the square, and horse-drawn carriages offer tours the of the Old Town.

St. John's Cathedral ②

Świętojańska 8. *Tel 022-831 02 89.* ▦ *E1, E2, E3, 116, 122, 160, 174, 175, 180, 192, 195, 303, 403, 503, 518.* ⬜ *daily (Sun: pm only).*

Completed in the early 15th century, St. John's Cathedral (katedra św Jana)

was originally a parish church. Gaining collegiate status in 1406, it was not until 1798 that St. John's became a cathedral. The coronation of Poland's last king, Stanisław August Poniatowski, in 1764, and the swearing of an oath by the deputies of the *Sejm* (Parliament) to uphold the 1791 Constitution took place here.

After World War II, various elaborate 19th-century additions were removed from the façade, and the cathedral was restored to its original Mazovian Gothic style. The interior features religious art, richly carved wooden stalls, and ornate tombs, including those of Gabriel Narutowicz (1865–1922), Poland's first president, assassinated two days after taking office, and Nobel prize-winning novelist Henryk Sienkiewicz (1846–1916). In a chapel founded by the Baryczka family hangs a 16th-century crucifix, which is credited with several miracles.

Royal Castle ③

Plac Zamkowy 4. *Tel 022-657 21 70.* ▦ *E1, E2, E3, 116, 122, 160, 174, 175, 180, 192, 195, 303, 403, 503, 518.* ⬜ *daily (separate tickets for Royal Apartments and Parliament).* ⬤ *Oct–Apr: Mon; public hols.* 🎫 *(free Sun).* 🎫

Warsaw's Royal Castle (Zamek Królewski) stands on the site of an original castle built here by the Mazovian dukes in the 14th century. It was transformed between 1598 and 1619 by King Zygmunt III Waza, who asked Italian architects to restyle the castle into a polygon. The king chose this castle as his royal residence in 1596, after the *Sejm* (Parliament) had moved here from Cracow in 1569. In the 18th century, King Augustus III remodeled the east wing in Baroque style and King Stanisław August Poniatowski added a library.

In 1939, the castle was burned, and then blown up by the Nazis in 1944. Reconstruction, which was funded by public donations, took from 1971 to 1988.

The castle's fascinating interiors are the result of its dual role: being a royal residence as well as the seat of parliament. Meticulously reconstructed, the castle has royal apartments, as well as the Chamber of Deputies and the Senate. Some of the woodwork and stucco is original, as are many of the furnishings and much of the art. Among the paintings are 18th-century works by Bellotto and Bacciarelli.

The opulent interior of the Marble Room in the Royal Castle

For hotels and restaurants in this region see p760 and p761

The magnificent Rococo organ loft of St. Anna's Church

St. Anna's Church ④

Krakowskie Przedmieście 68.
🚌 116, 122, 195, 503. ⬜ daily.

This imposing church on the Royal Route was founded by Anna, the widow of Duke Bolesław III, and built in the late 15th century, along with a Bernardine monastery. Extended between 1518 and 1533, the church was destroyed during the Swedish invasion of 1655, but later rebuilt in Baroque style. The Neoclassical façade was a subsequent addition, as was the free-standing bell tower, which dates from the 1820s.

The church has a magnificent interior, with several Rococo altars, a splendid organ, and frescoes by Walenty Żebrowski. A side chapel contains the relics of St. Władysław of Gielniów, Warsaw's patron saint. St. Anna's is a popular choice for weddings, partly due to the superstition that any marriage celebrated here will be a happy one.

Next to the church are the remains of the 16th-century Bernardine monastery, which was closed in 1864. The old cloisters in the monastery's east wing, however, have retained their original vaulted ceilings. Behind St. Anna's there is an attractive Neoclassical colonnade, known as Odwach. This is the city's best location for second-hand booksellers, and is an interesting place to browse.

Royal Route ⑤

Krakowskie Przedmieście and Nowy Świat. 🚌 116, 122, 195, 503.

The Royal Route (Trakt Królewski) is one of Warsaw's most historic and beautiful streets. Starting by Castle Square (Plac Zamkowy), and continuing all the way to the royal palace at Wilanów, the most interesting part of the route is along Krakowskie Przedmieście and Nowy Świat. These thoroughfares developed in the late Middle Ages, with their rural setting, by the banks of the Vistula river, attracting Warsaw's aristocracy and wealthy merchant class.

This social elite built grand summer residences and town houses here, while religious orders established lavish churches and monasteries. Krakowskie Przedmieście features many buildings from the 17th and 18th centuries, with several imposing palaces standing back from the road behind tree-lined squares and courtyards. Alongside, there are impressive town houses and some of the city's most interesting churches, including **St. Anna's, St. Joseph's,** and the **Church of the Assumption. Warsaw University** and the **Fine Arts Academy** are also located here, while various monuments pay tribute to eminent Poles.

Nowy Świat is lined with long rows of 18th- and 19th-century

Statue of Poland's most famous astronomer, Nicholas Copernicus (1473–1543), on the Royal Route

town houses. It is also one of the busiest shopping streets in the world, and full of large stores, fashionable boutiques, colorful sidewalk cafés, and a wide choice of restaurants.

Imposing Neoclassical façade of the Grand Theater

Grand Theater ⑥

Plac Teatralny. **Tel** 022-692 02 00. 🚌 100, 111, 310. **Ticket office** ⬜ daily.

One of the city's largest buildings before World War II, the Grand Theater was built in 1825–33, to a design by Antonio Corazzi and Ludwik Kozubowski. Many renowned craftsmen also contributed to the sublime, palatial interiors. Initially the building was to be named the National Theater, but the defeat of the 1830 November Uprising forced a change of name. The two statues that stand in front of the building are of the 19th-century composer Stanisław Moniuszko, known as the father of Polish opera, and of Wojciech Bogusławski, the man who instigated the construction of the theater.

The theater currently houses the National Opera and Ballet and a small theater museum. Severely damaged during World War II, the theater retained only its impressive Neoclassical façade and a few of its rooms. Greatly enlarged in the course of reconstruction, it acquired many modern interiors and far more extensive backstage facilities.

Monument to the Ghetto Heroes ⑦

Pomnik Bohaterów Getta, Zamenhofa. 🚌 *107, 111, 180.*

The Nazis created the Jewish ghetto in 1940 by driving the Jewish inhabitants of Warsaw and nearby villages into an area in the northwest of the city. The ghetto initially housed around 450,000 people, but by 1942 over 300,000 had been transported to death camps, and 100,000 others had died or been killed in the ghetto. The Ghetto Uprising of 1943 was an action of heroic defiance against the Nazis, planned not as a bid for liberty, but as an honorable way to die. Built to commemorate this action, the Monument to the Ghetto Heroes stands in the center of the former ghetto. It depicts men, women, and children struggling to flee the burning ghetto, together with a procession of Jews being driven to Nazi death camps.

A **Path of Remembrance**, lined with a series of granite blocks dedicated to events or heroes of the ghetto, links the ghetto memorial to the nearby Bunker Monument – on the site from where the uprising was co-ordinated – and the Umschlagplatz Monument. Engraved with hundreds of names, it marks the place from where many Jews were deported to the death camps, and represents the cattle trucks used for transportation.

Detail from the Monument to the Ghetto Heroes

Monument to Those Fallen and Murdered in the East ⑧

ul. Muranowska. 🚌 *116, 122, 127, 174, 175, 195, 303, 503, 518.* 🚊 *2, 4, 15, 18, 35, 36.*

This emotionally stirring monument, designed by Mirosław Biskupski, has the form of a typical railway wagon in which Poles were deported into the depths of the Soviet Union. It is filled with a pile of crosses symbolizing the hundreds of thousands of Poles carted off to the East in cattle vans and subsequently murdered in Soviet prison camps.

Palace of Culture and Science ⑨

Plac Defilad 1. **Tel** *022-656 76 00.* **Viewing Terrace** ☐ *daily.* 🖼

This monolithic building was a "gift" from Soviet Russia to the people of Warsaw, and intended as a monument to "the inventive spirit and social progress." Built in 1952–5 by the Russian architect, Lev Rudniev, it resembles Moscow's Socialist Realist tower blocks.

The palace still inspires extreme emotions among Varsovians, ranging from admiration to demands for its demolition. Since the end of Soviet domination, the building's role has changed. The tower itself now provides office space, and the Congress Hall, which once held Communist Party congresses, is now a venue for concerts and festivals. The palace remains a cultural center in other ways, with the Theater of Dramatic Art, a cinema, puppet theater, technology museum, and a sports complex.

The imposing Socialist Realist Palace of Culture and Science

National Museum ⑩

Aleje Jerozolimskie 3. **Tel** *022-629 30 93.* 🚌 *111, 117, 158, 507, 521.* 🚊 *7, 22, 24, 25.* ☐ *10am–4pm Tue–Sun (until 6pm Thu).* ● *public hols.* 🖼 *(free Sat).* **Military Museum** **Tel** *022-629 52 71.* ☐ *10am–5pm Wed, 10am–4pm Thu–Sun.* ● *some public hols.* 🖼 *(free Sat).* 📷

Originally established in 1862 as the Fine Art Museum, the National Museum (Muzeum Narodowe) was created in 1916. Its vast collection was started in 1862 with the purchase of 36 paintings. Subsequent acquisitions have turned the museum into one of the city's finest. Collections include ancient Greek, Roman, and Egyptian art, archaeological finds from Faras in present-day Sudan, and medieval Polish religious paintings, altarpieces, and sculptures.

The foreign art collection features Italian, French, Dutch, and Flemish works. There is a fine *Madonna and Child* by Sandro Botticelli. In the vast Polish art collection are works by Bernardo Bellotto (1720–80), nephew of Canaletto, who settled in Warsaw and painted fine views of the city. Of native Polish artists, Jan Matejko (1838–93) is one of the finest on display. He painted historical subjects such as *The Battle of Grunwald*. In an east wing of the museum, the **Military Museum** illustrates the history of Polish firearms and armor.

For hotels and restaurants in this region see p760 and p761

The impressive Neoclassical façade of Wilanów Palace, designed for King Jan III Sobieski

Łazienki Park ⑪

Łazienki Królewskie, Agrykola 1.
Tel 022-621 62 41. 📠 116, 195.
Park ◯ daily until dusk.
Palace on the Water ◯ 9am–4pm
Tue–Sun. ◑ days after public hols.
🅱

This huge park, studded with palaces, temples, and monuments, originally dates from the Middle Ages, when it belonged to the Mazovian dukes. By the early 17th century, it was owned by the Polish crown, and housed a royal menagerie. In 1674 the Grand Crown Marshal Stanisław Herakliusz Lubomirski acquired the park, and Tylman of Gameren designed its hermitage and bathing pavilion. The pavilion gave the park its name, as łazienki means "baths."

In the 18th century, the park was owned by King Stanisław August Poniatowski, and he commissioned Karol Agrykola, Karol Schultz, and Jan Schuch to lay it out as a formal garden. A number of new buildings were also completed during this time, and the pavilion was redesigned, by Dominik Merlini, as a royal summer residence. This became known as the **Palace on the Water**, and is one of the finest

examples of Neoclassical architecture in Poland. It now houses an architecture museum. Unfortunately the king was only able to enjoy the palace for a few years, as after the Third Partition of Poland he was forced to abdicate, and left Warsaw on January 7, 1795. The Nazis planned to blow it up but, lacking time on their withdrawal, set fire to it instead. It was rebuilt by 1965.

Solomon's Hall, reception room of Palace on the Water, Łazienki Park

Wilanów Palace and Park ⑫

S.K. Potockiego 10–16. **Tel** 022-842 07 95. 📠 E2, 116, 117, 130, 180, 519, 522. **Palace** ◯ 9am–4pm
Wed–Mon. ◑ Jan. 🅱 🅿 **Park** ◯
9:30am–dusk daily. 🅱 (free Thu). 🅿

Although it was a royal residence, Wilanów Palace, which is set within parkland

and beautiful formal gardens, was actually designed as a private retreat for King Jan III Sobieski, who valued family life above material splendor. The original property, known as Villa Nova, was purchased in 1677 and within two years had been rebuilt as a mansion, designed by royal architect Augustyn Locci. The elaborate façades were adorned with sculptures and murals, while the interiors were decorated by Europe's finest craftsmen.

Enlarged over subsequent years by its many different owners, the palace gained two large wings, a pair of towers, and a first-floor banqueting hall. The north wing comprises 19th-century rooms, formerly used as living quarters and as a gallery. The largest room, the Great Crimson Room, is used as a venue for entertaining VIPs. The south wing includes the late Baroque Great Dining Room, designed for King August II Mocny, as well as Princess Izabela Lubomirska's apartments, which feature a bathroom dating from 1775.

The most interesting rooms in the main part of the palace are the Neoclassical Great Hall, with marble detailing and allegorical friezes, and the ornate King's Bedchamber, with its 17th-century Turkish bed canopy. There are also apartments once occupied by King Jan III Sobieski and his wife Marysieńka, which retain many of their original 17th-century features, as well as an old nursery, governesses' rooms, and a fascinating portrait gallery. Outside the palace, in the old riding school building, there is an interesting poster museum.

The enchanting Palace on the Water, Łazienki Park

Cracow ❷

Head in Deputies' Hall, Royal Castle

For nearly six centuries Cracow was the capital of Poland and the country's largest city. Polish rulers resided at Wawel Castle until the court and parliament moved to Warsaw in 1596. Even then Cracow continued to be regarded as the official capital and rulers were still crowned and buried in the cathedral on Wawel Hill. The city still plays an important role in preserving the national identity. The prestigious Jagiellonian University is the oldest in the country and the city is full of memorials to illustrious Poles. Perhaps Cracow's greatest attraction lies in the fact that, unlike so many Polish cities, it was scarcely damaged in World War II. In recent years many buildings and monuments have been restored to their former glory.

Royal Castle
The Birds Hall, with its gilded coffered ceiling and marble fireplace, is one of the later 17th-century rooms in the castle's Royal Apartments.

WAWEL HILL

In about 1038 Kazimierz the Restorer made the citadel on Wawel Hill the seat of Polish political power. In the 16th century the Jagiellonian rulers transformed the Gothic castle into a magnificent Renaissance palace and endowed the cathedral with new chapels and works of art.

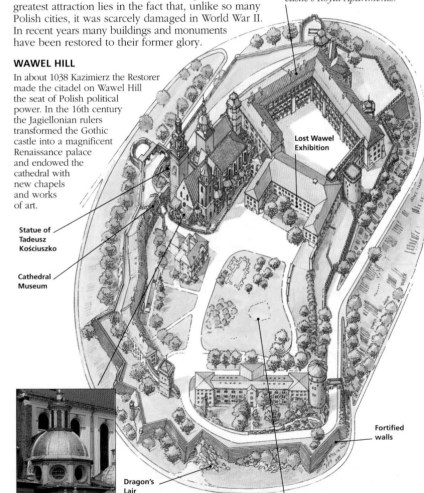

Lost Wawel Exhibition

Statue of Tadeusz Kościuszko

Cathedral Museum

Dragon's Lair

Fortified walls

Cracow Cathedral
The Zygmunt Chapel with its striking gilded dome was one of many additions to the cathedral made in the early 16th century.

The foundations of medieval houses that stood within the castle walls have been excavated here. The houses were razed by the Austrians in 1805–6 to create a parade ground.

⚓ Royal Castle

Wawel 5. *Tel 012-422 16 97.*
🚌 103, 124, 502. 🚋 7, 8, 18, 36.
Royal Apartments ◯ *daily.* ◉
Nov–Mar: Mon; public hols. **Orient in the Wawel** ◯ *Tue–Sun.* ◉ *Nov–Mar: Mon, Sun; public hols.* 📷 *(free Sun in winter, Mon in summer).* 📷

The present Renaissance castle was built in the first half of the 16th century. After the royal court moved from Cracow to Warsaw in 1596, the castle fell into decay. At the start of the 20th century it was given to the city of Cracow and work began to restore it to its former grandeur.

The richly decorated Royal Apartments are the main reason for visiting the castle. Most of the rooms reflect the tastes of the last Jagiellonian kings. They contain Italian paintings and furniture, painted friezes around the walls, and a fine collection of Flemish tapestries. The Hall of Deputies was where the lower house of the Polish parliament, the *Sejm*, met for debates. It is also known as the Hall of Heads because the ceiling is decorated with carved heads. On the top floor there is a suite of rooms from the 17th century, with portraits of the Waza kings, including one of Prince Władysław (later Władysław IV) by Rubens. The Crown Treasury and Armory are situated on the ground floor. The treasury's collection of royal jewels and regalia includes the coronation sword of the Polish kings.

The "Orient in the Wawel" collection on the first and second floors features Turkish tents and banners seized by the victorious Christian troops at the Siege of Vienna in 1683.

Turkish tent in the "Orient in the Wawel" exhibition in the castle

Royal Castle with the so-called Hen's Claw Wing on the right

🏛 Lost Wawel Exhibition

Wawel Hill. *Tel 012-422 16 97.* ◯ *daily.* ◉ *Nov–Mar: Tue; public hols.* 📷 *(free Sun in winter, Mon in summer).*

An exhibition in the castle basement includes the remains of an early church, thought to date from the 11th century. Computer models illustrate the development of Wawel Hill through the Middle Ages.

Baroque silver reliquary of St. Stanisław by Peter von der Rennen (1669–71), Cracow Cathedral

⛪ Cracow Cathedral

Wawel 3. *Tel 012-422 26 43.*
🚌 103, 124, 502. 🚋 7, 8, 18, 36.
◯ *daily (Sun: pm only).* **Cathedral Museum** *Tel 012-422 09 04.*
◯ *Tue–Sun.* 📷

Originally founded in 1020, the present cathedral is the third to stand on this site. It was completed in 1364 in the reign of Kazimierz the Great. The resting place of many Polish kings, the cathedral has always had great symbolic significance for the nation. It is dedicated to St. Stanisław, whose relics are housed in an ornate reliquary in the shape of a coffin beneath an eye-catching Baroque altar canopy in the center of the nave.

The original Gothic cathedral has seen many subsequent additions, notably the Baroque spire built in the early 18th century and the side chapels, which have been remodeled many times. There are many fine tombs of Polish rulers. The Renaissance Zygmunt Chapel was built in 1519–33 by the Italian Bartolomeo Berrecci. It contains an impressive double monument in red marble to Zygmunt the Old (reigned 1506–48) and his son Zygmunt August (reigned 1548–72). Look out too for the late Gothic canopied sarcophagus of Kazimierz Jagiellończyk carved by Veit Stoss (1492) in the Chapel of the Holy Cross. The marble tomb of Stefan Batory (reigned 1576–86), created by Santi Gucci in 1595, stands behind the altar.

The crypt is divided into sections containing the tombs and sarcophagi of other Polish rulers, leading poets, and national heroes, including Tadeusz Kościuszko, leader of the failed insurrection of 1794.

The Cathedral Museum houses a collection of sacred art and a selection of Polish royal regalia, including the coronation robe of the last Polish king, Stanisław August Poniatowski (reigned 1764–95).

🏛 Dragon's Lair

Wawel Hill. ◯ *Apr–Oct: daily.*
Beneath Wawel Hill is a series of caves associated with the legend of a dragon. In summer part of the cave system can be reached by a set of spiral steps. Children take delight in the bronze, fire-breathing statue of a dragon at the entrance.

Cracow: the Old Quarter

In 1257 Cracow was granted a charter by Duke Bolesław the Chaste. This was of key importance to the city, ensuring local government and trade privileges and stimulating the city's future development. The charter stipulated certain conditions: a large centrally located square, surrounded by a regular grid of streets, was to become the city center. The size of each plot determined the size of the houses. Although the architecture became ever more opulent over the centuries, this urban scheme has survived almost intact. To this day the Old Quarter remains the heart of modern Cracow. Many of the streets are pedestrianized, allowing visitors to enjoy the great concentration of historic sights.

The Slacker Crucifix (1496) by Veit Stoss in St. Mary's Church

The City Hall Tower in the western corner of Market Square

⊞ Market Square
Rynek Główny.

The Market Square is said to be the largest town square in Europe. In summer nearly 30 street cafés remain open here until the early hours. Flower stalls, street musicians, and artists selling their works all contribute to the lively atmosphere. The ornate Cloth Hall virtually divides the square in two. Two other buildings stand in the square: the small green-domed Church of St. Adalbert, below which is a museum of the history of the square, and the City Hall Tower, a relic of the original Gothic town hall. There is also a monumental statue of the great Polish poet Adam Mickiewicz (1798–1855).

Buildings around the square retain elements from every era in the history of the city. Many are decorated with an emblem that gives the house its name, for example the Palace of the Rams on the west side of the square, home of a famous cabaret since 1956. Christopher Palace takes its name from a 14th-century statue of St. Christopher. The house was remodeled in 1682–5 around a beautiful arcaded courtyard. It is home to the Museum of Cracow, where paintings, gold artifacts from local workshops, documents, and memorabilia are displayed in a series of grand stuccoed rooms.

⊞ Cloth Hall
Market Square 1/3. *Tel 012-422 11 66.* ⬜ *Tue–Sun.* 🏛 🎫

The Cloth Hall (Sukiennice) in the middle of Market Square originated in medieval times as a covered market. It was rebuilt after a fire in 1555 and then remodeled entirely in 1875 with arcades along the exterior that give it a Venetian look. Most of the stalls today sell souvenirs of various kinds and there is a gallery of 19th-century Polish painting on the upper floor. The Cloth Hall also contains a number of cafés – the Noworolski Café is one of the best in Cracow.

⛪ St. Mary's Church
Mariacki Square 5. *Tel 012-422 05 21.* ⬜ *Mon–Fri & during services.* 🏛 🎫

St. Mary's façade with its two impressive Gothic towers is set at an angle on the east side of Market Square. The left-hand tower is topped by a spire added in 1478. It served as the city's watch tower and still today a bugle call is played every hour. It is even broadcast on Polish radio at noon. The projecting porch between the towers was added in the Baroque period.

The church's greatest treasure is the huge altarpiece, 12 m (39 ft) high, by Veit Stoss, who lived in Cracow from 1477 to 1496. The outer panels show scenes from the lives of Christ and the Virgin. The middle shutters are opened each day at noon to reveal the huge carved centerpiece, *The Assumption of the Virgin* (see p742). There is also a fine crucifix by Veit Stoss, known as the Slacker Crucifix.

Horse-drawn cabs lined up in front of the Cloth Hall in Market Square

🏛 Czartoryski Museum

Św. Jana 19. *Tel 012-422 55 66.* 🚌 *124, 152, 192, 194.* 🚊 *3, 4, 5, 7, 12, 15, 19.* ⭘ *Tue–Sun.* ⬤ *Mon, one Sun a month.* 🖼 🎫 *(free Thu in winter).*
The core of the museum is the art collection assembled by Princess Isabella Czartoryska in the late 18th century. It contains some magnificent paintings, notably Leonardo da Vinci's *Lady with an Ermine* and Rembrandt's *Landscape with the Good Samaritan*. The museum also has decorative arts from all over Europe and a section on Polish history.

Leonardo's *Lady with an Ermine* in the Czartoryski Museum

🏛 Collegium Maius

Jagiellońska 15. *Tel 012-422 05 49.* 🚌 *124, 144, 152, 192.* 🚊 *14, 15, 18.* ⭘ *Mon–Sat.* 🖼 🎫 *obligatory (call to book visit).*
This is the oldest building of the Jagiellonian University. In the 15th century a number of houses were amalgamated to create lecture rooms and housing for professors. It was extensively remodeled in the mid-19th century. At the heart of the building is an attractive Gothic cloister. The University Museum moved here after World War II. Visitors can see the 16th-century Libraria and Great Hall, rooms still used by the Senate of the university, and the Treasury. There is also a Copernicus Room dedicated to the great astronomer, who studied here in 1491–95.

🌿 Planty

⭘ *daily.*
The Planty green belt follows the outline of Cracow's medieval walls, which were demolished in the early 19th century. A circuit through the park of about 5 km (3 miles) starting from Wawel leads along tree-lined paths and avenues, past fountains and statues. Only a small stretch of the city walls survives beside St. Florian's Gate at the north end of the Old Town. Nearby stands a well-preserved round barbican built in 1498–9, when Turkish incursions were a serious threat to the city.

✡ Old Synagogue

Szeroka 24. *Tel 012-422 09 62.* 🚌 *184, 198.* 🚊 *3, 9, 13.* ⭘ *daily.* ⬤ *Oct 16–Apr 15: Tue.*
In the late 15th century Cracow's Jewish quarter was established in the Kazimierz district, east of Wawel Hill. At the outbreak of World War II there was a community of some 70,000 Jews. The Nazis moved them all to a ghetto across the river, from where they were eventually deported to concentration camps.
Amazingly, a number of Jewish sites have survived. The Old Synagogue, carefully restored after the war, is not used for worship, but houses the Jewish Museum. The **Remu'h Synagogue** (c.1553), also on Szeroka Street, still functions. It is named after Rabbi Moses Remu'h, a 16th-century philosopher, whose tomb in the **Remu'h Cemetery** attracts pilgrims from all over the world. Most of the graves were destroyed by the Nazis, but fragments from them have been piled up to form a "wailing wall."

Hall of Prayers in Cracow's Old Synagogue

Entrance gate to the Auschwitz extermination camp

Environs

Although the name Oświęcim means little to most foreigners, its German form **Auschwitz** evokes fear and horror in people all round the world. It was here near the little town of Oświęcim, about 55 km (35 miles) west of Cracow, that the Nazis established their largest complex of concentration and extermination camps. The Auschwitz camp opened in June 1940, and in March 1941 a much larger camp was set up at nearby Birkenau (Brzezinka in Polish). In all, over 1,500,000 Jews and others were murdered here. The gas chambers, capable of killing thousands daily, were in use from 1942 to January 1945, when the camps were liberated by Soviet troops.
The area has been declared a UNESCO World Heritage Site and the two camps are preserved as the **Muzeum Oświęcim-Brzezinka** – a grim warning to future generations of mankind's capacity for inhumanity. Many structures were destroyed as the Nazis left, but the gate, with the chilling words "Arbeit macht frei" ("Work makes free") written above it, still stands.

🏛 Muzeum Oświęcim-Brzezinka

ul. Więzniów Oświęcimia 20. 📷 🚌 *Tel 033-843 21 33.* ⭘ *daily (closing time varies between 3pm in winter and 7pm in summer).* 🎫 **www.** auschwitz.org.pl

Practical & Travel Information

Since the fall of Communism in 1989, tourism has greatly increased in Poland. New shops and hotels have sprung up, and the quality of service has improved, especially in banks and post offices. Nevertheless, much of Poland's economy has yet to adjust to the post-Communist era; the health service has been reformed, but it lags behind the country's many developing sectors. In general, goods in Poland are much cheaper than in Western Europe.

VISAS AND CUSTOMS INFORMATION

A valid passport is required for admittance to Poland, but you may not need a visa; contact the Polish embassy in your country for details. Personal items may be brought into the country, but limits are imposed on the import and export of alcohol, tobacco, and cigarettes. Antiques exported from the country require a special permit. Gifts worth up to 175 Euros may be imported duty free.

PERSONAL SECURITY

Polish cities suffer from the same crime and security problems as most European capitals, so vigilance and care are needed. Security is provided by the state police, the highway police, and a number of private security organizations. The latter are often hired to protect public buildings and private houses, and to keep order at various events. In the city of Warsaw, it is advisable to avoid the Praga district after dusk, and in particular Ulica Brzeska.

MEDICAL EMERGENCIES

Citizens of the following countries are entitled to free medical treatment in Poland: EU members, Belarus, Tunisia, Ukraine, Mongolia, China, and the countries of the former Yugoslavia.

For visitors from other countries, first aid is provided free of charge at hospitals, but other types of treatment may incur a charge. Nevertheless, all visitors are advised to take out full medical insurance before arriving in Poland. Keep your policy documents with you at all times, as well as a passport for identifying yourself to hospital staff. An ambulance service is available 24 hours a day.

TOURIST INFORMATION

Information centers are generally found at train stations; these provide general regional information. For specific enquiries about accommodations, tickets, and trains, **Orbis** agencies are preferable. Hotel employees are also a good source of information.

CURRENCY AND BANKING

The official Polish currency is the złoty, each of which is divided into 100 grosze. In January 1995, four zeros were knocked off the złoty, so that 10,000 złoty became one Polish New Złoty (PLN). The old złoty banknotes were withdrawn and replaced with new notes, but they can still be exchanged in some banks. Money can also be changed at bureaux de change, many of which offer better rates than banks. The majority of banks are open from 8am to 6pm.

DISABLED TRAVELERS

Poland has a poor record for providing for disabled people, but things are rapidly changing. All renovated or new public buildings have ramps or lifts built into them, and there are also special taxis available. Nevertheless, many traditional sites of interest may prove difficult to enter. For general advice or for information about specific sites, contact the **Disabled People's National Council**.

COMMUNICATIONS

In recent years phonecard-operated telephones have been installed throughout Poland, replacing the older token-operated models. Phonecards can be bought at post offices and newsagents. Charges for long-distance national calls vary according to the time of day. The highest charges are for calls made between 8am and 6pm. Local calls are cheaper from 10pm to 6am. The charges for international calls do not vary with time of day. Poland has three mobile telephone networks, which operate on two wavelengths, 900 MHz and 1,800 MHz, and cover almost all of the country.

Poczta Polska, the Polish postal service, provides a wide range of services, and its offices are open from 8am to 8pm on weekdays; the main post office in Warsaw is open 24 hours a day, seven days a week. Letters to destinations within Poland usually arrive

THE CLIMATE OF POLAND

Poland's climate is influenced by cold polar air from Scandinavia, and subtropical air from the south. Polar-continental fronts dominate in winter, bringing crisp, frosty weather, while late summer and autumn (the most popular times to visit) enjoy plenty of warm sunny days. Winters, which always bring snow, can be very cold in the north.

WARSAW

°C/F	Apr	Jul	Oct	Jan
high	11/52	21/70	7/45	0/32
low	7/45	11/52	2/36	-3/27 / -8/18
sun hrs	5 hrs	7.5 hrs	3 hrs	1.5 hrs
rain mm	42 mm	56 mm	40 mm	40 mm

within 2 or 3 days of posting, while international mail may take up to a week; intercontinental mail can take up to three weeks to reach its destination. Local correspondence (within a town) should be posted in the green post boxes, and all other mail should be posted in the red boxes. For urgent mail, Poczta Polska provides both an express service and a courier service. The international DHL and UPS courier agencies also operate in Poland.

TRAVELING BY PLANE

Poland is well connected with the rest of the world. International flights from some 50 cities in 30 countries arrive in Warsaw. The airports at Gdańsk, Katowice, Szczecin, Poznań, Wrocław and Cracow also have international flights, linking Poland with much of Western Europe, as well as Prague, Budapest, Sofia, Bucharest, and the capitals of the former Soviet Union. Some 25 airlines, including British Airways, Air France, SAS (Scandinavia), and Lufthansa (Germany), operate from **Warsaw Okęcie** airport, which has direct connections with Canada, the US, Israel, and Thailand. **Cracow Balice,**

the second largest airport in Poland, offers a substantial number of domestic and international flights.

TRAVELING BY BUS

Most long-distance routes within Poland are served by Polish Motor Transport, Polska Komunikaja Samochodowa (PKS). A competitor is Polski Express, which offers cheaper fares, air-conditioned coaches, and pleasant staff, but the journeys tend to be longer, for the routes are rarely direct. Local buses are sometimes the only means of getting to minor towns and villages. The services are generally punctual, although before 8am and in the afternoon they may be crowded. Tickets for these are always bought from the driver.

TRAVELING BY TRAIN

International train services run between all major European and Polish cities. The journeys by fast train from Warsaw to Prague and Berlin take just six and nine hours respectively. The main rail route runs across Poland from east to west, connecting Russia with western Europe. Express lines connect almost all the big cities, and the trains

are fast and usually arrive on time. The most comfortable, and most expensive, are the InterCity trains, which also give passengers a snack. Euro and InterCity trains both provide compartments for mothers with children and for disabled people. Fares for ordinary and fast trains are very reasonable; express trains and sleeping cars are expensive, although not by the standards of the rest of Europe.
Suburban routes are served by electric trains, which sometimes consist of open-plan, double-decker cars.

TRAVELING BY CAR

Poland has few highways, and those that exist are generally in poor condition. An exception is the Cracow–Katowice highway, the first stretch of what promises to be a network of highways spanning the entire country.
Wherever you drive in Poland, always carry your passport, car insurance, license, green card, and rental contract with you, and if you are driving a foreign car, display the international symbol of its country of origin.
All the major international car rental companies operate in Warsaw and Cracow.

DIRECTORY

TOURIST OFFICES IN POLAND

Cracow
Rynek Główny 1–3.
Tel 012-421 77 06.

Warsaw
pl. Zamkowy 1/13.
Tel 022-635 18 81.

TOURIST OFFICES OUTSIDE POLAND

UK
First Floor, Remo House, 310–312 Regent Street, London W1B 3AX.
Tel 020-7580 8811 or 08700 675 012.
www.visitpoland.org

US
275 Madison Ave, New York 10016.

Tel 212-338 9412.
www.polandtour.org

EMERGENCY NUMBERS

Ambulance
Tel 999.

Fire Brigade
Tel 998.

Medical Advice
Tel 94 39.

Police
Tel 997.

EMBASSIES

Australia
Ul. Nowogrodzka 11, Warsaw.
Tel 022-521 34 44.

Canada
Ul. Matejki 1/5, Warsaw.
Tel 022-584 31 00.
www.canada.pl

UK
Al. Róż 1, Warsaw.
Tel 022-311 00 00.
www.britishembassy.pl

US
Al Ujazdowskie 29/31, Warsaw.
Tel 022-504 20 00.
http://poland.usembassy.gov

FACILITIES FOR THE DISABLED

Disabled People's National Council
ul. Zamenhofa 8, Warsaw.
Tel 022-831 40 40.

TRAIN STATIONS

Warsaw Central
Jerozolimskie 54.
Tel 022-9436.

AIRPORTS

Cracow John Paul II
Tel 012-639 30 00.

Warsaw Chopin
Tel 022-650 42 20.

CAR RENTAL

AVIS Poland
Cracow, ul. Lubicz 23.
Tel 012-629 61 08.
Warsaw Airport.
Tel 022-650 48 72.
www.avis.pl

Hertz Rent-a-Car
Cracow, al. Focha 1.
Tel 012-429 62 62.
Warsaw Airport.
Tel 022-650 28 96.
www.hertz.com.pl

Where to Stay in Poland

Poland has recently experienced a big improvement in hotel standards. Many new luxury hotels have been built, the majority of them part of international hotel chains. In Warsaw, good, moderately priced hotels are scarce. In central Cracow, however, a number of historic 19th-century hotels have been modernized.

PRICE CATEGORIES
Price categories are for a standard double room including breakfast, tax, and service:

ⓩ Under 270 złoty
ⓩⓩ 270–400 złoty
ⓩⓩⓩ 400–600 złoty
ⓩⓩⓩⓩ 600–800 złoty
ⓩⓩⓩⓩⓩ Over 800 złoty

WARSAW

CITY CENTER Nathan's Villa Hostel   ⓩ
ul. Piękna 24–26, 00-549 **Tel** *022-622 29 46* **Fax** *022-622 29 46* **Rooms** *10*   **Map** *C5*

Warsaw's best-loved hostel boasts brand-new dormitories, modern fittings, and a quiet courtyard location. Facilities on offer include fast Internet access, a fully equipped kitchen, and daily laundry. A range of private rooms has been added for those who do not wish to share a dormitory. **www.nathansvilla.com**

CITY CENTER Le Royal Meridien-Bristol   ⓩⓩⓩⓩ
ul. Krakowskie Przedmieście 42/44, 00-325 **Tel** *022-625 25 25* **Fax** *023-625 25 77* **Rooms** *205*   **Map** *D3*

A sumptuous Art Nouveau building and arguably the most famous hotel in Poland: the guest list runs from regents to rock stars. Rooms combine a pre-war aesthetic with 21st-century gadgetry, and the hotel has won countless awards for excellence. The Sunday brunches are renowned across the city. **www.lemeridien-bristol.com**

CITY CENTER Radisson SAS Centrum   ⓩⓩⓩⓩ
ul. Grzybowska 24, 00-132 **Tel** *022-321 88 88* **Fax** *022-321 88 89* **Rooms** *311*   **Map** *C2*

Chic five-star lodgings in the heart of Warsaw's financial quarter. The hotel's modern front conceals rooms designed in three separate styles: maritime, Scandinavian and Italian. Amenities include swimming pool and a gym, while those with less time on their hands will enjoy the addition of the "grab-and-run" breakfast. **www.radissonsas.com**

CITY CENTER InterContinental   ⓩⓩⓩⓩⓩ
ul. Emilii Plater 49, 00-125 **Tel** *022-328 88 88* **Fax** *022-328 88 89* **Rooms** *326*   **Map** *C3*

A three-legged futuristic tower with a 40th-floor swimming pool that stares on to the Palace of Culture and Science. immaculate rooms befit the hotel's ultra-modern style and offer internet access along with cable TV. Restaurants and bars can be found on the lower floors. **www.warsaw.intercontinental.com**

FARTHER AFIELD Premiere Classe   ⓩ
ul. Towarowa 2, 00-811 **Tel** *022-624 08 00* **Fax** *022-620 26 29* **Rooms** *126*

Basic rooms come with TVs and adjoining modern bathrooms in this building, which also houses Premiere Classe's sister hotels: the Campanile and Kyriad Prestige. The best one-star choice in Warsaw, and recommended for budget travelers who count themselves too old for hostels. Advance booking essential. **www.premiereclasse.com.pl**

CRACOW

OLD QUARTER Fortuna   ⓩⓩ
ul. Czapskich 5, 31-110 **Tel** *012-422 31 43* **Fax** *012-411 08 06* **Rooms** *25*

A newly renovated, historical hotel where service always comes with a smile. Set in a charming building, it has rooms that are larger than usual for this type of building, and the bathrooms are also well sized. Secure parking available on site. **www.hotel-fortuna.com.pl**

OLD QUARTER Pollera   ⓩⓩ
ul. Szpitalna 30, 31-024 **Tel** *042-210 44* **Fax** *042-213 89* **Rooms** *42*

An Art Nouveau gem in the heart of the Old Town, the Pollera was founded in 1834 and has welcomed its guests with flair and style ever since. During World War II, the Germans fell in love with the place and forbade anyone else (except staff) from entering. Today all are welcome, though you will need to book. **www.pollera.com.pl**

OLD QUARTER Elektor   ⓩⓩⓩⓩ
ul. Szpitalna 28, 31-024 **Tel** *042-323 17* **Fax** *042-323 27* **Rooms** *15*

In recent years, Prince and Princess Takamodo of Japan, King Harald V of Norway, and Grand Duke Jean of Luxembourg have all stayed at this outstanding hotel, widely regarded as the city's best. Nothing is too much trouble for the staff here, who make it their mission to please all guests, royalty or otherwise. **www.hotelelektor.com.pl**

Key to Symbols *see back cover flap*

Where to Eat in Poland

Polish food has seen a change of image with the opening of a new generation of restaurants all over Poland. Many take pride in updating traditional specialties, such as *pierogi* (ravioli) and dumplings. Good restaurants are plentiful in Warsaw and Cracow but watch out for high prices in the more touristy areas.

PRICE CATEGORIES
Price categories for a three-course meal per person, including half a bottle of wine and all unavoidable extra charges:
ⓩ Under 50 złoty
ⓩⓩ 50–70 złoty
ⓩⓩⓩ 70–90 złoty
ⓩⓩⓩⓩ 90–110 złoty
ⓩⓩⓩⓩⓩ Over 110 złoty

WARSAW

CITY CENTER Vino I Pasta
V ⓩ
ul. Sienkiewicza 4, 00-015 **Tel** *022-827 50 70* **Map** *C3*

Black-and-white photography hangs from exposed brick walls inside this minimalist restaurant, where diners have the choice of sitting at ground level or in the mezzanine. As the name suggests, wine and pasta are the main attractions here, with copious amounts of both served each day to the assembled crowds.

CITY CENTER Adler
ⓩⓩⓩ
ul. Mokotowska 69, 00-530 **Tel** *022-628 73 84* **Map** *D5*

Decked out with baskets of dried flowers and the odd *Pickelhaube* (spiked helmet), Adler embodies the atmosphere of a Bavarian beer hall, with staff in costume rushing around delivering gigantic portions of pig's neck and *Schnitzel*. The relatively high prices tend to draw in a corporate crowd, however.

CITY CENTER Papaya
V ⓩⓩⓩ
ul. Foksal 16, 00-372 **Tel** *022-826 48 51* **Map** *D4*

A great addition to Warsaw's booming fusion scene, Papaya features a *tepanyaki* grill and dishes like Kobe sirloin, and tuna steak with Thai basil and shrimps. The white color scheme creastes a hip, urbane atmosphere that attracts trendy young things. Expect a heavy bill at the end of your meal.

CITY CENTER U Fukiera
V ⓩⓩⓩⓩⓩ
Rynek Starego Miasta 27, 00-275 **Tel** *022-831 10 13* **Map** *D2*

A main-square location and a guest list that includes world leaders and royalty speak volumes for U Fukiera's reputation – and prices. Set inside a beautiful network of chambers, it is worth a visit for the interior alone, while the menu focuses on Polish classics cooked with ingenuity. The summer courtyard represents starlit dining at its finest.

FARTHER AFIELD Dom Polski
V ⓩⓩⓩⓩ
ul. Francuska 11, 03-906 **Tel** *022-616 24 32*

Having dinner at Dom Polski has long been a vital rite of passage for holiday-makers and expats alike, and this stands out as one of the classiest treats in Warsaw. The menu is seasonal but often includes fantastic game dishes, while the interiors of this pre-war villa are redolent of a country manor.

CRACOW

OLD QUARTER Pierogarnia
V ⓩ
ul. Sławkowska 32, 31-014 **Tel** *012-422 74 95*

No visitor to Cracow should leave the city without tasting the Polish specialty of *pierogi* (ravioli), and Pierogarnia is about the best place in town to enjoy that experience. Fillings are innumerable, and these tasty treats can be eaten as a snack or as part of a larger meal. The restaurant also serves other Polish delicacies.

OLD QUARTER Farina
V ⓩⓩⓩⓩ
ul. św. Marka 16, 31-017 **Tel** *012-422 16 80*

In this simple, uncluttered restaurant, the bare, highly polished wooden floors and white-washed walls are geared towards focusing the diner's attention on the excellent menu. A successful mix of Polish and Italian dishes attracts crowds of locals and visitors. Reservations are necessary in the evenings.

OLD QUARTER Cyrano de Bergerac
V ⓩⓩⓩⓩⓩ
ul. Sławkowska 26, 31-014 **Tel** *012-411 72 88*

Prices here may be high but they do not seem to deter diners from booking weeks in advance. This is a world-class French restaurant spread over two elegant rooms, with a quiet patio used in the summer months. The food is exquisite, cooked under the auspices of masterchef Pierre Gallard. Try the *garbure soupe béarnaise* (a thick soup).

Map References *see map of Warsaw pp748–9*

General Index

Page numbers in **bold** type refer
to main entries

A

Aachen, Hans von 714
Aalborg **683**
  hotels 686
  restaurants 687
Aalto, Alvar 690, 694
Abadie, Paul 166
Abbey Theatre (Dublin) 135
Abbeys
  Abbaye Royale de Fontevraud
  177
  Abbazia di San Fruttuoso 426
  Westminster Abbey
  (London) 44, **46–7**
  see also Monasteries
Abd al Rahman I, Caliph 326
ABEP (Lisbon) 377
Aberdeen **81**
  restaurants 107
  hotel 101
Absalon, Bishop of Copenhagen
  678, 682
Accademia (Venice) **441**
Accessories stores
  Italy **452**, 453
Accidents *see* Emergency services
Achílleion Palace (Corfu) 495
Acrocorinth 490
Acropolis (Athens) **478–80**
Acropolis Museum (Athens) **480**
ACTV Information Office
  (Venice) 451
ADAC 569
Adam, Robert 54, 63, 71
Adelcrantz, Carl Fredrik 647
Admiralty Arch (London) 50
Adolfo Domínguez 337
The Adoration of the Magi
  (Lochner) 563
The Adoration of the Shepherds
  (El Greco) 290
Aegean Aviation 505
Aertsen, Pieter 259
Aeschylus 447
Afonso IV, King of Portugal 367
Afonso Henriques,
  King of Portugal 353, 354
  Alcobaça 367
  Castelo de São Jorge
  (Lisbon) 359
  Coimbra 370
  Sé (Lisbon) 359
Agatha Ruiz de la Prada
  (Madrid) 337
Aggstein 587, 601
Agía Anna 497
Agios Ioánnis 485
  hotels 510
  restaurants 515
Agios Nikólaos 495, **501**
  hotels 513
  restaurants 517
Agnes, St. 400
Agnolo, Baccio d' 417
Agorakritos 480
Agricola, Mikael 694
Agrigento **447**
  hotels 461
  restaurants 467
Agrippa, Marcus 190, 400

Agrykola, Karol 753
Ahenny 124
Aigues-Mortes
  hotels 210
Aínos, Mount 495
Air Berlin 569
Air Canada 91, 201, 569, 725
Air Europa 335
Air France 17, 201, 741
Air Greece 505
Air New Zealand 91
Air travel **16–17**
  Austria **604**
  Belgium and Luxembourg **237**
  Czech Republic **724–5**
  Denmark **684**, 685
  Finland **698**, 699
  France **200**, 201
  Germany **568**, 569
  Great Britain **90**, 91
  Greece **504**, 505
  Hungary **741**
  Ireland **132**
  Italy **450**, 451
  Netherlands **264–5**
  Norway **668–9**
  Poland **759**
  Portugal **375**
  Spain **334**, 335
  St. Petersburg 697
  Sweden **652**, 653
  Switzerland **626**, 627
Aistulf, King 443
Aix-en-Provence **194**
  hotels 211
  restaurants 217
Aker Brygge (Oslo) **662**
Akershus Slott (Oslo) **661**
Akrotíri 497
Alabamahalle (Munich) 573
Albert, Prince Consort 55, 66
Albert Heijn (Amsterdam) 267
Alberti, Leon Battista 420, 430
Albertina (Vienna) 590, 592, 597
Albufeira 353, **373**
  hotels 378
  restaurants 381
Alcázar (Toledo) 297, **298**
Alcobaça **367**
  restaurants 380
Alcohol
  Beers of Germany **554**, 570
  Brugse Brouwerij-
  Mouterijmuseum (Bruges) **234**
  Czech Beers **723**
  Guinness Store House
  (Dublin) **121**
  Old Bushmills Distillery **131**
  port **371**
  The Wines of France **186–7**, 202
Aldobrandini family 400
Alentejo 372
Alexander I, Czar 594, 694
Alexander II, Czar 693, 696
Alexander III, Czar 696
Alexander VI, Pope 404
Alexander VII, Pope 394
Alexander the Great 27
  birthplace 488, **489**
  Greece 469, 470
Alexandrowka (Potsdam) **539**
Alfábia 319
Alfama (Lisbon) **358–9**
Alfonso V, King of Aragón 444

Alfonso VI, King of Castile 298
Alfonso IX, King of León 295
Alfonso XI, King of Spain 324
Alfonso XII, King of Spain 291
Alfonso XIII, King of Spain 285, 303
Algarve 372, 373
Alhambra (Granada) **322–3**
Alicante 319
  hotels 343
  restaurants 349
Alien (Rome) 455
Alitalia 17, 451
Alkamenes 480
Alkmaar **260**
  restaurants 271
All England Lawn Tennis and
  Croquet Club (Wimbledon) 95
Alps
  French Alps 183
  hotels **209–10**
  Jungfrau **619**
  restaurants **215–16**
  Swiss Alps 520, 613, **620–21**
Alt, Salome 603
Altauf, King 443
Alte Oper (Frankfurt) 573
Alte Pinakothek (Munich) **551**
Altea 319
  restaurants 349
Altes Museum (Berlin) **532**
Altmann & Kühne (Vienna) 607
Alto Jazz Café (Amsterdam) 267
Altomonte, Martino 599
Alykés 495
Amalfi 445
  hotels 461
  restaurants 467
Amalfi Coast **445**
Amalienborg (Copenhagen) **680**
Ambleside 77
Ambulances
  Austria 605
  Belgium and Luxembourg 237
  Czech Republic 725
  Denmark 685
  Finland 699
  France 199
  Germany 567
  Great Britain 89
  Greece 503
  Hungary 741
  Ireland 133
  Netherlands 265
  Norway 669
  Poland 759
  Portugal 375
  Spain 333
  Sweden 653
  Switzerland 627
Amélia, Queen of Portugal 362, 363
American Airlines 91, 201, 569
American Embassies *see* United
  States Embassies
American Express 17, 199, 505
Ammannati, Bartolommeo 405, 419
Amoopi 499
Amoreiras (Lisbon) 377
Amsterdam 143, 245, **248–59**
  hotels **268–9**
  map 248–9
  restaurants **270–71**
  Rijksmuseum **256–8**
Amsterdams Historisch
  Museum **252–3**

Amundsen, Roald 658, 664, 667
Ancienne Belgique (Brussels) 239
Ancient Agora (Athens) **477**
Andante Travels 507
Andersen, Hans Christian 674, **683**
 birthplace 682–3
 Little Mermaid (Copenhagen) **680**
Andersen, Hans Christian
 Nyhavn (Copenhagen) 680
András III, King of Hungary 729
Andratx 319
 hotels 345
 restaurants 351
Andronikos II, Emperor 492
Angelico, Fra 160
 The Annunciation 290, 415
Anglia English Bookshop
 (Munich) 571
Anna Amalia, Duchess
 of Weimar 543
Anne, Queen of England 54, 63, 74
Anne of Austria 153
Anne of Brittany 170, 176
Anne de Châtillon 735
Anne Frank Huis (Amsterdam) **253**
Annecy **183**
 hotels 209
The Annunciation (Fra Angelico)
 290, 415
Ano Merá 496
Anthonisz, Cornelis 253
Antibes 196
 hotels 211
Antico Martini (Venice) 455
Antik & Trödelmarkt (Berlin) 571
Antiques
 France **203**
 Great Britain **93**
Antony of Padua, St. 359, 431
Antwerp **230**
 hotels 241
 restaurants 243
Apeldoorn
 hotels 269
Apélla 499
Apollodorus of Damascus 402
Appel, Karel 259
Applied Arts Museum (Vienna) **597**
APT 449
Aquariums
 Oceanário de Lisboa (Lisbon) **358**
Aran Islands **129**
 restaurants 138
Áras an Uachtaráin (Dublin) 121
Arc de Triomphe (Paris) **165**
L'Arca de l'Avia (Barcelona) 337
Arch of Constantine (Rome) 403
Arch of Septimius Severus
 (Rome) 402
Arch of Titus (Rome) 402
Archángelos 499
Archelaos, King 489
Archer, A. 479
Archer, Colin 664
L'Archiduc (Brussels) 239
Architecture
 Greek temple architecture **482–3**
 Renaissance **421**
Archivo de Indias (Seville) 328
Arcimboldo, Giuseppe 596
Ardennes 235
Les Arènes (Arles) 193
Areópoli 492
 hotels 510

Argalastí 485
Argostóli 495
Århus **683**
 hotels 686
Aristotle 489
Arles
 hotels 211
 restaurants 217
 Street-by-Street map 192–3
Armand Basi (Barcelona) 337
Armani (Italy) 453
Arnolfo di Cambio 395
Arona 429
Árpád, Prince 729
Art Scene (Luxembourg City) 239
Art stores
 France **203**
 Great Britain **93**
Artis (Amsterdam) 255
Artois, Comte d' 167
*As the Old Sang, the Young Play
 Pipes* (Jordaens) 230
Asam, Cosmas Damian 550–51
Asam, Egid Quirin 551
Asamkirche (Munich) **550–51**
Ascona 625
Ashtown Castle (Dublin) 121
Assisi **406–7**
 Basilica di San Francesco **406–7**
 hotels 460
 restaurants 466
Association des Paralysés de
 France 199
Association of Pleasure Craft
 Operators 95
The Assumption (El Greco) 298
The Assumption of the Virgin
 (Rubens) 226–7
Assumption of the Virgin (Titian) 439
Atesa 335
Athanásios 486
Athens 385, **474–81**
 Acropolis **478–80**
 climate 502
 emergency services 503
 hotels **508–9**
 map 474–5
 restaurants **514–15**
 travel **504**, 505
Athos, Mount **489**
Athos Peninsula
 hotels 511
Atomic Café (Munich) 573
Atomium (Brussels) 229
Attalos, King of Pergamon 477
Attila the Hun 729, 731
AUB (Amsterdam) 267
Auditorio Nacional de Música
 (Madrid) 339
Auer Dult (Munich) 571
August II Mocny, King of Poland 753
Augustine, St. 64, 421
Augustinerkirche (Vienna) 592, **594**
Augustus, Emperor 27, 388, 398
 Palatine (Rome) 403
 Ravenna 443
 Trier 558
Augustus III, King of Poland 750
Augustus the Strong, Elector of
 Saxony 543
Aurelian, Emperor 399
Aurelius, Marcus, Emperor 401

Auschwitz **757**
Austen, Jane 70
Australian Embassies and
 Consulates
Australian Embassies and
 Austria 605
 Czech Republic 725
 Denmark 685
 France 199
 Germany 567
 Great Britain 89
 Greece 503
 Hungary 741
 Ireland 133
 Italy 449
 Netherlands 265
 Norway 669
 Poland 759
 Portugal 375
 Spain 333
 Sweden 653
 Switzerland 627
Austria **587–611**
 entertainment **606–7**
 history **587–9**
 hotels **608–9**
 language and culture **589**
 maps 520–21, 588–9
 practical information **604–5**
 restaurants **610–11**
 shopping **606**, 607
 travel **604**, 605
 Vienna **590–99**
Austria Tourism 607
Austrian Airlines 605
Auto Europe 19
Auto Jardim (Faro) 375
Autoworld (Brussels) 229
Avalanche bulletin
 (Switzerland) 627
AvD 569
Avercamp, Hendrick
 Winter Landscape with Skaters 256
Aviemore 87
 restaurants 107
Avignon **191**
 hotels 211
 restaurants 217
Ávila **295**
 hotels 343
 restaurants 349
Avis
 Finland 699
 France 201
 Germany 569
 Great Britain 91
 Greece 505
 Ireland 133
 Italy 451
 Poland 759
 Spain 335
Azéma 164
Aznar, Camón 318
Aznar, José María 279
Azulejos (tiles) **368**
Azulejos Santa Isabel
 (Seville) 337

B

B&W Café (Amsterdam) 267
Bmibaby 335
Babenberg dynasty 588
Bacciarelli 750

Bach, Johann Sebastian 525, 543
Bacharach 559
Il Baciccia 401
Bacon, Francis 39
Baden-Württemberg **556–7**
Baerze, Jacques de 184
Baiona 302
  hotels 342
  restaurants 348
Bairro Alto (Lisbon) **360–61**
Baixa (Lisbon) **360**
Balajo (Paris) 205
Balaton, Lake 704, **738**
Balatonberény 738
Balatonfüred 738
  hotels 742
  restaurants 743
Balatonvilágos 738
Balearic Islands 275, **319**
  ferries 335
  hotels **345**
  restaurants 351
Ballenberg 618
Ballet *see* Dance
Balthus 153
Balzac, Honoré de 167
Bamberg **544**
  hotels 576
  restaurants 582
Banco de España (Madrid) 286
La Bande des Six Nez (Brussels) 239
Bandinelli, Baccio 417
Bank notes (euros) **15**
Bank of Ireland (Dublin) 114
Banking
  Austria 604
  Belgium and Luxembourg 236
  Czech Republic 724
  Denmark 684
  France 199
  Germany 567
  Great Britain 89
  Greece 503
  Hungary 740
  Ireland 132
  Italy 449
  Netherlands 264
  Norway 668
  Poland 758
  Portugal 374–5
  Spain 333
  Sweden 652
Banqueting House (London) 45
Baptistry (Siena) 408
Barbican (London) 95
Barcelona 275, **306–15**
  Barri Gòtic 308–9
  hotels **341–2**
  map 306–7
  restaurants **347–8**
  Sagrada Família **312–13**
  tourist office 333
  travel **334**, 335
Bargello (Florence) **418**
Barnabas 486
Barocci, Federico 443
Barovier, Angelo 441
Barovier e Toso (Murano) 453
Barragem de Bravura 373
Barri Gòtic (Barcelona)
  Street-by-Street map 308–9
Barrie, J.M. 54
Barry, Sir Charles 45
Barry, E.M. 51

Bartók, Béla 731
Baryczka family 750
Basel **617**
  hotels 630
  restaurants 632
Basilica Aemilia (Rome) 402
Basilica of Constantine and
  Maxentius (Rome) 402
Basilica Julia (Rome) 402
Basílica de Santa Maria del Mar
  (Barcelona) **310**
Basilica di San Francesco
  (Assisi) **406–7**
Basilica di Superga 427
Basilique St-Denis (Paris) **170**
Basques 189, 279, **304**
Batalha **367**
Bath 35
  hotels 98–9
  restaurants 104
  Street-by-Street map 70–71
Bath Abbey 71
Bathers at Asnières (Seurat) 49
Baths
  Baths of Caracalla (Rome) 403
  Gellért Hill Baths (Budapest) **735**
Battlefields of Belgium **231**
Bauhaus 31, 543
Bavaria **544–5**
Bayerische Staatsoper (Munich) 573
Bayerisches Nationalmuseum
  (Munich) **552**
Bayeux **173**
  restaurants 214
Bayonne
  restaurants 216
Bayreuth **544**
  hotels 576
  restaurants 582
Beaches
  Costa Blanca 319
  Costa del Sol 321
  Côte d'Azur 196
  Lake Balaton 738
The Beatles 76
Beatrix, Queen of the
  Netherlands 262
Beaune **182**
  hotels 209
  restaurants 215
Beauvoir, Simone de 157
Beck, Moses 719
Becker, Harriet 663
Becket, Thomas à 64
Beckett, Samuel 116
Beddgelert 69
  hotels 99
Bede, Venerable 77
The Bedroom at Arles
  (Van Gogh) 259
Beer
  Beers of Germany **554**, 570
  Brugse Brouwerij-
  Mouterijmuseum (Bruges) **234**
  Czech Beers **723**
  Guinness Store House
  (Dublin) **121**
Beer Mania (Brussels) 239
Beethoven, Ludwig van
  525, 587, 594
  Beethovenhaus (Bonn) 561
  Secession Building (Vienna) 597
Begijnhof (Amsterdam) **253**
Begijnhof (Bruges) **234**

Behrens, Peter 557
Béla III, King of Hungary 734, 735
Béla IV, King of Hungary 734
Belém **362–5**
  map 357
Belfast **130**
  hotels 136–7
  restaurants 138
Belfast Cathedral 130
Belfort (Bruges) 232
Belgian National Railways 237
Belgium and Luxembourg **220–43**
  Battlefields of Belgium **231**
  Bruges: Street-by-Street map 232–3
  Brussels **222–9**
  entertainment **238–9**
  history **219–20**
  hotels **240–41**
  language and culture **220**
  Luxembourg **235**
  map 221
  practical information **236**
  restaurants **242–3**
  shopping **238**, 239
  travel **237**, 237
Bellagio 429
Belleek Pottery 135
Bellini, Giovanni
  Accademia (Venice) 441
  Ashmolean Museum (Oxford) 72
  Kunsthistorisches Museum
  (Vienna) 596
  Santa Maria Gloriosa dei Frari
  (Venice) 438–9
  Staatsgalerie (Stuttgart) 557
  Vatican Museums (Rome) 398
Bellinzona 625
  restaurants 633
Bellotto, Bernardo 750, 752
Belvedere (Prague) **715**
Belvedere (Vienna) **598–9**
Bemberg, Georges 189
Benáki Museum (Athens) **481**
Benákis, Antónios 481
Benedetto da Maiano 414
Benedict XI, Pope 407
Benedict XII, Pope 191
Benítses 495
Benz, Carl 552
Berenguer, Francesc 315
Bergen 636, 657, **666–7**
  hotels 670
  restaurants 671
Berggruen, Heinz 537
Berlin 521, **528–41**
  airports 569
  Berliner Dom **534–5**
  climate 566
  hotels **574–5**
  map 528–9
  Park Sanssouci **540–41**
  restaurants **580–81**
  shopping **570–71**
  tourist office 567
Berliner Ensemble (Berlin) 573
Bermejo, Bartolomé 290
Bern **618**
  restaurants 632
Bernhardt, Sarah 167
Bernini, Gian Lorenzo 29
  Museo e Galleria Borghese
  (Rome) 405
  Piazza Navona (Rome) 400
  St. Peter's (Rome) 394, 395

Bernini, Gian Lorenzo (cont.)
  Santa Maria del Popolo
    (Rome) 405
Berrecci, Bartolomeo 755
Berruguete, Pedro de 290
Bessarion, Cardinal 421
Betwys-y-Coed 69
BFI London IMAX (London) 95
Bianco, Bartolomeo 426
Biarritz 189
  hotels 210
  restaurants 216
Biblioteca Medicea-Laurenzia
  (Florence) 414
Bicycles *see* Cycling
Bienvenida, Antonio 292
Big Ben (London) 43
Bigarny, Philippe de 301
Bilbao **304**
  hotels 342
  restaurants 348
Bildergalerie (Potsdam) **541**
Billettzentrale BIZZ (Zürich) 629
Bimhuis (Amsterdam) 267
Bio-Bio (Athens) 507
Birger Jarl 643
Birka 648
Birmingham
  hotels 99
  restaurants 105
The Birth of Venus
  (Botticelli) 423, 424
Bismarck, Count Otto von 30, 524
Bjørnson, Bjørnsterne 662
Black Forest 526, **556**
Blaeu, Willem 252
Blake, William 49
Blanche de France 170
Blarney
  restaurants 139
Blarney Castle 126
Blarney Woollen Mills 135
Blenheim Palace **74–5**
Blind Donkey Alley (Bruges) 232
Blois **177**
  restaurants 214–15
Blom, Piet 263
Blue Caves (Zákynthos) 495
Boabdil 278, 323
Boats
  Finland **699**
  Frammuseet (Oslo) **664**
  Gondolas of Venice **439**
  Kon-Tiki Museum (Oslo) **664**
  Museu da Marinha (Lisbon) **363**
  Nederlands Scheepvaart Museum
    (Amsterdam) **255**
  Vasamuseet (Stockholm) **646**
  Vikings **665**
  Vikingsskipshuset (Oslo) **664**
  see also Ferries
Boboli Gardens (Florence) **425**
Boccaccio, Giovanni 414
Bode, Wilhelm von 532
Bodensee **555**
The Body Shop (London) 93
Bohemia 704, 707, **722–3**
Boileau, Louis-Auguste 164
Bois de Boulogne (Paris) **167**
Boitac, Diogo 364
Boleslav II, Prince 714
Bolesław the Brave, King of
  Poland 746
Bolesław the Chaste, Duke 756

Boleyn, Anne 60
Bologna **442**
  hotels 460
  restaurants 466
Bonaguida, Pacino di 415
Bonaparte, Louis 252
Boniface, St. 524, 555
Bon Marché store (Paris) 203
Bonn **561**
  hotels 577
  restaurants 583–4
  tourist office 567
The Book of Kells 116, **125**
Bookstores
  Belgium and Luxembourg
    238, 239
  Germany **571**
  Great Britain **92–3**
Boppard 559
La Boqueria (Barcelona) 337
Borca (Madrid) 337
Bordeaux **188**
  hotels 210
  restaurants 216
  wines 186, 187
Borders (London) 93
Borghese, Prince Camillo 405
Borghese, Pauline 405
Borghese, Cardinal Scipione 405
Borgia, Cesare 191
Borgund 657
Bofivoj, Prince 712
Borromeo, St. Charles (Carlo)
  429, 597
Borromini, Francesco 400
Borsalino 453
Børsen (Copenhagen) **679**
Bosch, Hieronymus 49, 227
  The Garden of Delights 288
  Groeninge Museum (Bruges) 234
  Museo del Prado (Madrid) 290
  Museu Nacional de Arte Antiga
    (Lisbon) 361
Botticelli, Sandro 420
  The Birth of Venus 423, 424
  Capilla Real (Granada) 320
  Galleria dell'Accademia
    (Florence) 415
  Kelvingrove Art Gallery
    (Glasgow) 80
  Museo del Prado (Madrid) 290
  Museo di Capodimonte
    (Naples) 444
  National Gallery (London) 49
  National Museum (Warsaw) 752
  Petit Palais (Avignon) 191
  Portrait of a Woman 560
  Vatican Museums (Rome) 398
Boulevard St-Michel (Paris) 156
Boulle, André Charles 160
Bouman, Elias 251
Bourbon family 314
Bowness 77
Boyle, Richard, Earl of Cork
  119
Brabo, Silvius 230
Brahms, Johannes 525
Bramante, Donato 396, 405
Brancusi, Constantin 153, 440
Brandenburg Gate (Berlin) **530**
Brandl, Petr 714
  St. Simeon 714
Branscombe
  hotels 99

Braque, Georges
  Centre Pompidou (Paris) 153
  Musée Picasso (Paris) 153
  Nasjonalgalleriet (Oslo) 663
  Peggy Guggenheim Collection
    (Venice) 440
  Sammlung Berggruen (Berlin) 537
Braun, Antonín 720
Braun, Matthias 717
Bremen **564–5**
  hotels 579
  restaurants 585
Brendan, St. 125
Brian Boru 110
Bricín 135
Bridges
  Charles Bridge (Prague) **717**
  Tower Bridge (London) **59**
Brighton 40, **64**
  hotels 98
  restaurants 104
Brione 625
Bristol **68**
  hotels 99
  restaurants 104
Britain *see* Great Britain
British Activity Holiday
  Association 95
British Airways 17
  Czech Republic 725
  France 201
  Germany 569
  Great Britain 91
  Hungary 741
  Italy 451
  Netherlands 265
  Spain 335
British Bookshop (Frankfurt am
  Main) 571
British Embassies
  Austria 605
  Belgium and Luxembourg 237
  Czech Republic 725
  Denmark 685
  Finland 699
  France 199
  Germany 567
  Greece 503
  Hungary 741
  Ireland 449
  Italy 449
  Netherlands 265
  Norway 669
  Poland 759
  Portugal 375
  Spain 333
  Sweden 653
  Switzerland 627
British Isles **33–139**
  Ireland **109–39**
  Great Britain **37–107**
  map **34–5**
  Scotland **80–87**
  Wales **69**
British Midland 91, 201, 569, 725
British Mountaineering Council 95
British Museum (London) 24, **52–3**
British Waterways 95
Brittany Ferries 201
Broederlam, Melchior 184
Bronzino
  Palazzo Vecchio (Florence) 419
  San Lorenzo (Florence) 414
  Uffizi (Florence) 424

Brotfabrik (Frankfurt) 573
Brown, Lancelot (Capability) 74, 75
Brown cafés
  Netherlands 266–7
Broxted
  hotels 98
Bruand, Libéral 162
Die Brücke 531
Brücke-Museum (Berlin) 538
Brueghel, Peter the Elder
  Alte Pinakothek (Munich) 551
  Hunters in the Snow 596
  Kunsthistorisches Museum
    (Vienna) 596
  Monasterio de las Descalzas
    Reales (Madrid) 285
  Musée Royaux des Beaux-Arts
    (Brussels) 226
  Museo del Prado (Madrid) 290
  National Gallery (London) 49
  The Tower of Babel 263
Brueghel, Peter the Younger
  234, 600
Bruges 221, **232–4**
  hotels 241
  restaurants 243
  Street-by-Street map 232–3
Brühl, Heinrich von 542
Brunel, Isambard Kingdom 68
Brunelleschi, Filippo 421
  Duomo (Florence) 417, 420
  Santa Croce (Florence) 418
Bruni, Leonardo 418
Bruparck (Brussels) **229**
Brussels 143, 219, **222–9**
  airport 237
  Brussels and the European
    Union **228**
  Hôtel de Ville **225**
  hotels **240**
  map 222–3
  restaurants **242**
Bruyn, Guillaume de 224
Bruyn, Sophia de 259
Buçaco
  restaurants 381
Buçaco National Forest 370
Buccellati 453
Bücherbogen (Berlin) 571
Buchexpress (Berlin) 571
Buckingham Palace (London) **48**
Budapest 705, 729, **732–7**
  climate 740
  hotels **742**
  map 732–3
  restaurants 743
Budapest History Museum
  (Budapest) **734**
Budapest Tourist 741
Budget (car rental)
  Finland 699
  France 201
  Great Britain 91
  Greece 505
  Ireland 133
  Portugal 375
Building of Bath Museum
  (Bath) 71
Bulbfields of the Netherlands **261**
Bulgari 453
The Bulldog (Amsterdam) 267
Bullfighting **293**
  Plaza de Toros de la Maestranza
    (Seville) **331**

Bullfighting (cont.)
  Plaza de Toros de las Ventas
    (Madrid) **292**
  Portugal **377**
  Spain **338**, 339
Bundestag (Berlin) 523
Bundestheaterkassen (Vienna) 607
Bunratty
  restaurants 139
Bunratty Castle **128**
Burberry (London) 93
Burges, William 69
Burggarten (Vienna) 592, **594**
Burghley, William Cecil,
  1st Lord 75
Burghley House 75
Burgkapelle (Vienna) 593, **594**
Burgos **299**
  Cathedral **300–301**
  hotels 343
  restaurants 349
Burgtheater (Vienna) **595**
Burgundy **182–5**
  hotels **209–10**
  restaurants **215–16**
  wines 187
Burgundy, Dukes of **182**, 184
Buring, J.G. 541
Burke, Edmund 116
Burns, Robert 84, 86
Bus Éireann 133
Buses **19**
  Austria **604**
  Belgium and Luxembourg **237**
  Czech Republic **725**
  Denmark **685**
  Finland **699**
  France **201**
  Germany **569**
  Great Britain **91**
  Greece **504**, 505
  Hungary **741**
  Ireland **133**
  Italy **451**
  Netherlands **265**
  Norway **669**
  Poland **759**
  Portugal **375**
  Spain **335**
  Sweden 653
  Switzerland **627**
Butler family 123
Bygdøy Peninsula **664**
Byron, Lord 484
Byzantine Italy **443**

C

Cabaret
  France **204**, 205
Cabinet War Rooms (London) 44
Cabo da Roca 366
Cabo de São Vicente 373
Cabral, Pedro Alvares 362
Cadenheads (Edinburgh) 93
Cádiz **325**
  restaurants 350
Caernarfon 69
Caesar, Julius 145, 182, 220, 402
Café de Chinitas (Madrid) 339
Cafés, Internet **14**
Cairngorms 85
La Caixa de Fang (Barcelona) 337
Calçats Sole (Barcelona) 337

Calle Mateos Gago (Seville) 329
Callejón del Agua (Seville) 329
Callixtus I, Pope 399
Calton Hill (Edinburgh) **86**
Calvin, Jean 614
Camargue **194**
Cambridge **73**
  hotels 99
  restaurants 105
Camden Lock (London) 93
Camões, Luís Vaz de 354
Camogli 426
Campen, Jacob van 252, 260
Canadian Airlines 451
Canadian Embassies
  Austria 605
  Czech Republic 725
  Denmark 685
  Finland 699
  France 199
  Germany 567
  Greece 503
  Hungary 741
  Ireland 133
  Italy 449
  Netherlands 265
  Norway 669
  Poland 759
  Portugal 375
  Spain 333
  Sweden 653
  Switzerland 627
Canadian High Commission
  (London) 89
Canal tours
  Netherlands 267
Canalejas, José 284
Canaletto 441
Cangas de Onís 303
  hotels 342
  restaurants 348
Cannes **196**, 196
  hotels 211
  restaurants 217
Canning House (London) 339
Canova, Antonio 405, 438, 439, 592
Cántaro (Madrid) 337
Canterbury **64**
  hotels 98
  restaurants 104
Il Cantuccio della Ceramica
  (Naples) 453
Canute, King 44
Cão, Diogo 362
Cap Ferrat 196
Capelle, Jan van de 258
Capitoline Museums (Rome) **401**
Capri 444
  hotels 461
  restaurants 467
Car rental **19**
Car travel **19**
  Austria **604**
  Belgium and Luxembourg **237**
  Czech Republic **725**
  Denmark **685**
  Finland **699**
  fly-drive **17**
  France **201**
  Germany **568**, 569
  Great Britain **91**
  Greece **504–5**
  Hungary **741**
  Ireland **133**

Car travel (cont.)
Italy **451**
Netherlands **265**
Norway **669**
Poland **759**
Portugal **375**
Spain **335**
Sweden **653**
Switzerland **627**
Caravaggio
Bildergalerie (Berlin) 541
Galleria Regionale di Palazzo
Bellomo (Syracuse) 447
Kunsthistorisches Museum
(Vienna) 596
Monte della Misericordia
(Naples) 444
National Gallery (London) 49
Santa Maria del Popolo (Rome) 405
The Taking of Christ 117
Uffizi (Florence) 424
Vatican Museums (Rome) 398
Carcassonne **190**
hotels 211
restaurants 217
Cardiff **69**
hotels 99
restaurants 105
Ca'Rezzonico (Venice) 455
Carl XVI Gustaf,
King of Sweden 644
Carl Augustus,
Duke of Weimar 543
Carlos I, King of Portugal
358, 360, 363
Carlos I, King of Spain 294
Carlos III, King of Spain
(Charles III of Naples) 284, 285,
286, 288, 444
Carlos IV, King of Spain 285
Carlos V, King of Spain 297
Carlu, Jacques 164
Carnac **173**
hotels 208
Caroline, Queen of England 54
Carpaccio, Vittore 191, 440, 441
*Portrait of a Young Man in a
Red Hat* 438
St. Augustine 421
Carpeaux, Jean Baptiste 162
Carracci, Annibale 49
Carson, Lord 130
Casa Bar (Zürich) 629
Casa de la Ciutat (Barcelona) 308
Casa Madrid (Madrid) 339
Casa-Museo de El Greco
(Toledo) **298**
Casa-Museu Gaudí (Barcelona) 315
Casa Patas (Madrid) 339
Cascais **366**
hotels 379
restaurants 381
Cascaishopping 377
Caserta 444
Cashel **126**
hotels 137
restaurants 139
Cassone Adimari
(Lo Scheggia) 415
Castell de Guadalest 319
Castel Sant' Angelo (Rome) **399**
Castelgrande 625
Castilho, João de 364, 365
Castle Howard 75

Castles
Acrocorinth 490
Akershus Slott (Oslo) **661**
Blarney Castle 126
Bunratty Castle **128**
Castell de Montjuïc
(Barcelona) 314
Castelo de São Jorge
(Lisbon) **359**
Dublin Castle **118–19**
Edinburgh Castle 83, **84**
Frederiksborg Slot 673, **682**
Karlstein Castle 707, **722**
Kastellet (Copenhagen) **681**
Neuschwanstein 523
Prague Castle 712–13
Rosenborg Slot
(Copenhagen) **681**
Royal Castle (Cracow) **755**
Royal Castle (Warsaw) **750**
SS Peter and Paul Fortress
(St. Petersburg) **697**
Suomenlinna Island Fortress
(Helsinki) **695**
Tower of London **60–61**
Vajdahunyad Castle
(Budapest) **737**
Windsor Castle **66–7**
see also Palaces
Castletown House **122**
Castro, Inês de 367, 370
Castro, Machado de 360
Castro, Ruiz de 444
Catalonia **305–17**
hotels **343**
restaurants **349**
Catamarans
Greece **505**
Catania
hotels 461
Catarina, Dona 365
Cathedrals
Barcelona 308, **309**
Berlin **534–5**
Brussels **226**
Burgos **300–301**
Chartres **180–81**
Cologne **562–3**
Cracow **755**
Dublin **118–19**
Florence 413, **416–17**
Helsinki **693–4**
Lisbon 359
London **58**
Paris **154–5**
Prague 712, **713**
Seville 328, **330**
Siena 408, **410**
Stockholm **643**
St. Petersburg **696**
Toledo 297, **298**
Warsaw **750**
see also Churches
Catherine, St. 408, 410
Catherine de' Medici 170,
178, 179
Catholic Church
St. Peter's (Rome) **394–5**
Spain 279
Cavallini, Pietro 399
Caves
Dachstein limestone caves 602
Dragon's Lair (Cracow) **755**
Lascaux **188**

Caves (cont.)
Lummelundagrottorna 649
CB Tours 239
Čedok (Prague) 725
Cellini, Benvenuto 160, 418, 419,
425, 596
Celtic Christianity **124–5**
Cenotaph (London) 45
Center of Hellenic Tradition
(Athens) 507
Central and Eastern
Europe **703–61**
Czech Republic **707–27**
Hungary **728–43**
map 704–5
Poland **744–61**
Central Fisheries Board
(Dublin) 135
Central Hall (London) 44
Central Holidays 17
Central Market (Athens) 507
Centre Belge de la Bande Dessinée
(Brussels) **226**
Centre des Renseignements des
Douanes (Paris) 203
Centre Excursionista de Catalunya
(Barcelona) 308
Centre Pompidou (Paris) **153**
Centro de Arte Reina Sofia
(Madrid) **291**
Centro Cultural de Belém
(Lisbon) 377
Centrum Judaicum (Berlin) **533**
Ceramics
Germany **571**
Portugal 376
Český Krumlov **723**
hotels 726
restaurants 727
Cézanne, Paul
Atelier Paul Cézanne
(Aix-en-Provence) 194
Musée de l'Orangerie
(Paris) 161
Chagall, Marc
Musée Chagall (Nice) 197
Peggy Guggenheim Collection
(Venice) 440
St. Peter's (Zürich) 623
Sprengel-Museum (Hanover) 564
Stedelijk Museum
(Amsterdam) 259
Chalgrin, Jean 165
Chalkí 497
Chambord
Château de Chambord **179**
hotels 209
Champagne 187
Champollion, Jean-François 52
Champs-Elysées (Paris) **165**
Chanel (Paris) 203
Chaniá **501**
hotels 513
restaurants 517
Channel Tunnel **91**, **200**, 201
Chanterène, Nicolau 364
Charlemagne, Emperor 28, 146,
388, 524, 588
Charles, Prince of Wales 58
Charles I, King of England 38
Banqueting House (London) 45
Greyfriars Kirk (Edinburgh) 85
Museum of London (London) 58
Richmond Park (London) 63

Charles II, King of England 48,
  60, 86
Charles III, King of Naples
  see Carlos III, King of Spain
Charles III, Prince of Monaco 197
Charles IV, Emperor 524, 545
  Charles Bridge (Prague) 717
  Karlsbad 722
  Karlstein Castle 722
  Prague 707–8, 720
  Royal Palace (Prague) 714
Charles V, Emperor (Carlos I
  of Spain) 29, 146, 220, 588
  Capitoline Museums (Rome) 401
  Louvre (Paris) 160
  Real Alcázar (Seville) 330
  Segovia 294
Charles V, King of France 159,
  160, 170
Charles VIII, King of France
  176, 421
Charles of Anjou 444
Charles the Bold, Duke of
  Burgundy 182, 614, 615
Charles Bridge (Prague) **717**
Charles Martel 176
Charlie, Bonnie Prince 86, 87
Charter flights **16–17**
  see also Air travel
Chartres
  Cathedral **180–81**
  hotels 209
  restaurants 215
Château Cheval Blanc 188
Château de Chambord **179**
Château de Chenonceau **178–9**
Château de Fontainebleau **171**
Château Latour 188
Château Margaux 188
Château de Saumur 145
Château de
  Vaux-le-Vicomte **170–71**
Château de Versailles **168–9**
Chatsworth House 75
Chaucer, Geoffrey 47, 64
Checkpoint Charlie (Berlin) 536
Chemins de Fer
  Luxembourgeois 237
Chenonceaux
  Château de Chenonceau
  178–9
  hotels 209
Chermayeff, Peter 358
Chersónisos 500
Chester **76**
  hotels 100
  restaurants 106
Chevrolet, Louis 617
Chichester, Francis 62
Chigi, Agostino 399, 405
Chillida, Eduardo 291, 304
Chinesisches Teehaus
  (Potsdam) 540
Chirac, Jacques 147
Chirico, Giorgio de 646
Chopin, Frédéric 167
Christ
  Heilig Bloed Basiliek
  (Bruges) 234
  Turin Shroud **427**
Christ Church Cathedral
  (Dublin) **119**
Christian III, King of
  Denmark 651

Christian IV, King of Denmark 661,
  674
  Børsen (Copenhagen) 679
  Frederiksborg Slot 682
  Kastellet (Copenhagen) 681
  Rosenborg Slot
  (Copenhagen) 681
Christian VI, King of Denmark
  678–9
Christian IX, King of Denmark 680
Christian Dior (Paris) 203
Christian Lacroix (Paris) 203
Christiania 676
Christianity, Early Celtic **124–5**
Christiansborg Palace
  (Copenhagen) **678–9**
Christo 564
Christus, Petrus 291
Chur **624**
  restaurants 633
Church on Spilled Blood (St
  Petersburg) **696**
Churches
  Asamkirche (Munich) **550–51**
  Augustinerkirche (Vienna) 592, **594**
  Basílica de Santa Maria del Mar
  (Barcelona) **310**
  Basilica di San Francesco
  (Assisi) **406–7**
  Basilique de St-Denis (Paris) **170**
  Church of St. Nicholas
  (Prague) **716**
  Church on Spilled Blood (St.
  Petersburg) **696**
  Frauenkirche (Munich) **550**
  Gesù (Rome) **401**
  Greyfriars Kirk (Edinburgh) **85**
  Heilig Bloed Basiliek
  (Bruges) **234**
  Inner City Paris Church
  (Budapest) **736**
  Kaiser-Wilhelm-Gedächtniskirche
  (Berlin) 527, **536**
  Karlskirche (Vienna) **597**
  Mátyás Church (Budapest) **735**
  Nieuwe Kerk (Amsterdam) **252**
  Oude Kerk (Amsterdam) **250**
  Panthéon (Paris) **157**
  Riddarholmskyrkan
  (Stockholm) **644**
  St. Anna's Church (Warsaw) **751**
  Sainte-Chapelle (Paris) **152**
  St-Germain-des-Prés (Paris) **157**
  St. Mark's (Venice) **434–5**
  St. Mary's Church (Cracow) **756**
  St. Stephen's Basilica
  (Budapest) **736–7**
  San Domenico (Siena) **410**
  San Lorenzo (Florence) **414**
  San Marco (Florence) **415**
  Santa Croce (Florence) **418**
  Santa Maria del Popolo
  (Rome) **405**
  Santa Maria della Salute
  (Venice) **440**
  Santa Maria Gloriosa dei Frari
  (Venice) **438–9**
  Santa Maria Maggiore (Rome) **404**
  Santa Maria Novella
  (Florence) **414**
  Santa Maria in Trastevere
  (Rome) **399**
  Santi Giovanni e Paolo
  (Venice) **439**

Churches (cont.)
  Stephansdom (Vienna) **595**
  Temppeliaukio Church
  (Helsinki) **696**
  see also Cathedrals
Churchill, Winston 44, 58, 74
El Cid 299, 318
  tomb of 300, 301
CIE Tours International 91
Cimabue 411, 418, 424
  St. Francis 406
Cimetière du Père Lachaise
  (Paris) **167**
Cinéaqua 164
Cinema *see* Film
Cione, Nardo di 414
Cipriani, Giovanni 48
The Circus (Bath) 70
Cité de l'Architecture et du
  Patrimoine 164
Cité de la Musique (Paris) 167,
  205
Cité des Sciences (Paris) 166–7
Ciutadella 319
  hotels 345
  restaurants 351
Clare, St. 407
Claude Lorrain 290, 401
Clement V, Pope 191
Clement VI, Pope 191
Clement VII, Pope 420
Clement XII, Pope 401
Clifden
  hotels 137
  restaurants 139
Climate **12, 13**
  Austria 604
  Belgium and Luxembourg 236
  Czech Republic 724
  Denmark 684
  Finland 698
  France 198
  Germany 566
  Great Britain 88
  Greece 502
  Hungary 740
  Ireland 132
  Italy 448
  Netherlands 264
  Norway 668
  Poland 758
  Portugal 374
  Spain 332
  Sweden 652
  Switzerland 626
Cloisters of St-Trophime
  (Arles) 193
Clonmacnoise 125
Cloth Hall (Cracow) **756**
The Clothed Maja (Goya) 289
Clothing stores
  France **202–3**
  Great Britain **92**, 93
  Italy **452**, 453
  Spain **336**, 337
Clovis, King of the Franks
  27, 146, 225
Club Alpino Italiano 455
Clubs
  France **204**, 205
  Italy **455**
Clusius, Carolus 261
Coastguards
  Great Britain 89

Coastguards (cont.)
Greece 503
COCEMFE 333
Coello, Claudio 284
Coffee shops
Austria **607**
Netherlands **266–7**
Coimbra **370**
hotels 379
restaurants 381
CO.IN.Sociale (Italy) 449
Coins, Euro **15**
Collegium Maius (Cracow) **757**
Collet, Charles 317
Cologne **561–3**
Cathedral **562–3**
hotels 577–8
restaurants 584
Colosseum (Rome) 392, **403**
Columba, St. 124
Columbanus, St. 124
Columbus, Christopher 29, 278
Barcelona 308, 310
Burgos 299
Santa Maria Maggiore
(Rome) 404
Seville 331
Combarro 302
Comédie des Champs-Elysées
(Paris) 205
Comédie Française (Paris) 205
Comhaltas Ceoltóirí Éireann 135
Comic strips
Centre Belge de la Bande
Dessinée (Brussels) **226**
Communications **14**
see also Mail services;
Telephones
Como 429
Como, Lake **429**
hotels 459
restaurants 465
Companys, Lluis 314
Comyn, John, Archbishop of
Dublin 118
Concertgebouw (Amsterdam) 267
Congreso de los Diputados
(Madrid) 286
Conímbriga 370
Connemara **129**
Conolly, William 122
Conran House (London) 93
Conservatoire de Musique de la
Ville de Luxembourg
(Luxembourg City) 239
Constable, John 49, 57
Constance, Lake *see* Bodensee
Constantine I, Emperor 27
Arch of Constantine (Rome) 403
Edict of Milan 428
St. Peter's (Rome) 394
Trier 558
Constantius, Emperor 435
Convents
Begijnhof (Amsterdam) **253**
Begijnhof (Bruges) **234**
St. George's Convent (Prague)
713, **714**
Conversion chart **13**
Copenhagen 636, **676–81**
hotels **686**
map 676–7
restaurants **687**
Copernicus, Nicolas 757

Coppet 616
Corazzi, Antonio 751
Corday, Charlotte 161
Córdoba **324**
hotels 344
The Mezquita **326–7**
restaurants 350
Corfu **494–5**
hotels **512**
restaurants **516**
Corfu Town **494**
Corinth, Ancient **490**
hotels 510
restaurants 515
Corippo 625
Cork **126**
hotels 137
restaurants 139
Cornejo, Pedro Duque 327
Cornwall **68**
Corot, Camille 166
Correggio 405
Correr, Teodoro 438
El Corte Inglés (Madrid) 337, 339
Cosmos Radio Taxi 451
Costa, Lorenzo 442
Costa Blanca **319**
Costa del Sol **321**
Côte d'Azur **196–7**
Cotral 451
Council Travel 17
Courbet, Gustave 165
Cousteau, Jacques 197
Coustou, Guillaume 159
Couture, Thomas 162
Covadonga 303
Covent Garden (London) **51**, 93
Coysevox, Antoine 159
Crabeth, Dirk
The Death of the Virgin Mary 250
Cracow 705, 745, **754–7**
hotels **760**
John Paul II Airport 759
map 754
restaurants **761**
tourist office 759
Crafts
Greece **506**, 507
Ireland **134**, 135
Italy **452**, 453
Spain **337**
Switzerland **628**, 629
Crafts Council of Ireland -
DESIGNyard 135
Cranach, Lucas the Elder
Alte Pinakothek (Munich) 551
Domkirche St. Jakob
(Innsbruck) 603
Germanisches Nationalmuseum
(Nuremberg) 545
Landesmuseum Joanneum
(Graz) 600
Musée du Louvre (Paris) 160
Sternberg Palace 715
Cranmer, Archbishop 72
Crawford Art Gallery (Cork) 135
Crete 385, **500–501**
hotels **513**
restaurants **517**
Crime *see* Security, personal
Cromwell, Oliver 129
Crosses
Ireland's High Crosses **124**
Crown Jewels (London) **60**

Cryptoporticus (Rome) 403
Csontváry, Tivadar
Kosztka 734, 739
Cubero, José 292
Cuchulainn 120
Curia (Rome) 402
Curie, Pierre and Marie 157
Currency **14–15**
Austria 604
Belgium and Luxembourg 236
Czech Republic 724
Denmark 684
Finland 698
France 199
Germany 567
Great Britain 89
Greece 503
Hungary 740
Ireland 132
Italy 449
Netherlands 264
Norway 668
Poland 758
Portugal 374–5
Spain 333
St. Petersburg 697
Sweden 652
Switzerland 626
Cusi (Milan) 453
Customs
customs and duty-free **12–13**
see also Passports and visas
Cuthbert, St. 77
Cutty Sark (London) 62
Cuvilliés, François de 549, 553
Cuvilliéstheater (Munich) 573
Cuypers, P.J.H. 256
Cyclades 469, **496–7**
hotels **512**
restaurants **516–17**
Cycletours Holland 267
Cycling
Denmark **685**
Germany 569
Netherlands 267
Switzerland 627
Czartoryski Museum (Cracow) **757**
Czech Airlines 725
Czech Association of Persons with
Disabilities 725
Czech Republic **707–27**
beers **723**
Bohemia **722–3**
climate 724
history **707–8**
hotels **726**
language and culture **708**
map 709
practical information **724–5**
Prague **710–21**
restaurants **727**
travel **724–5**

D

Da Gama, Vasco 354, 362, **363**
tomb of 364
Dachstein limestone caves 602
Dafní, Monastery of **484**
Dagobert 170
Dahl, Johann Christian 663
Dahlem (Berlin) **538**
Dalarna **649**
hotels 654

Dalí, Salvador 59, 291
  Espace Montmartre Salvador Dalí
    (Paris) 166
Dalibor Tower (Prague) 713
Dance
  Belgium and Luxembourg **238**,
    239
  flamenco **331**, **338–9**
  Germany **572**, 573
  Great Britain **94**, 95
  Greece 507
  Ireland **134**
  Portugal **376**, 377
Dandoy (Brussels) 239
Danish State Railways 685
Danish Tourist Board 685
Dansk Cyklist Førbund 685
Dante 388, 389, 414
  Duomo (Florence) 416
  tomb of 443
Danton, Georges Jacques 161
Danube, River 587, 601
Dardel, Nils 646
Darnley, Lord 81, 86
Dartmoor National Park 68
Dartmouth
  restaurants 105
Daumier, Honoré 162
David, Gerard 85
David, Jacques Louis 227
  The Oath of the Horatii 30
David (Donatello) 418
David (Michelangelo) 412,
  415, 419
Davos 621, 624
  hotels 631
De Bierkoning (Amsterdam) 267
De Bijenkorf (Amsterdam) 267
De Brakke Grond
  (Amsterdam) 267
De Gaulle, Charles 146, 147, 154
De Lijn 237
De Meervaart (Amsterdam) 267
De Melkweg (Amsterdam) 267
De Sica, Vittorio 389
De Vries, Adriaen 714
Deane, Sir Thomas 117
Dean's Yard (London) 44
The Death of the Virgin Mary
  (Crabeth) 250
Deerfield (Dublin) 121
Defenestration of Prague (1618)
  713, 714
La Défense (Paris) **167**
Degas, Edgar
  Gemäldegalerie Neue Meister
    (Dresden) 543
  Kelvingrove Art Gallery and
    Museum (Glasgow) 80
  Musée d'Orsay (Paris) 162
  Nasjonalgalleriet (Oslo) 663
  Ny Carlsberg Glyptotek
    (Copenhagen) 678
Delacroix, Eugène 162, 165
Delfi
  hotels 510
Delft **263**
  hotels 269
  restaurants 271
della Rovere family 400
Delos **496**
Delphi, Ancient **485**
Delta Airlines
  Austria 605

Delta Airlines (cont.)
  Czech Republic 725
  France 201
  Germany 569
  Great Britain 91
  Hungary 741
  Italy 451
  Netherlands 265
  Spain 335
Delvaux, Paul 234
Demoulin, Louis 231
Denia 319
  hotels 343
Denmark **673–87**
  Copenhagen **676–81**
  history **673–4**
  hotels **686**
  language and culture **674**
  map 675
  practical information **684–5**
  restaurants **687**
  travel **684–5**
Department stores
  Great Britain **92**, 93
  Italy **452**, 453
  Netherlands 267
  Spain **336**, 337
The Deposition (Lorenzetti) 406
Derain, André 161
Déry, Tibor 731
Descartes, René 157
Design stores
  Italy **452**, 453
Designer fashion
  France **202–3**
  Italy **452**, 453
Destination Gotland 653
Deutsche Bahn 569
Deutsche Oper (Berlin) 573
Deutsches Museum (Munich) **552**
Deutsches Theater (Berlin) 573
Deutsches Theater (Munich) 573
Devenish Island 125
Devon **68**
Devonshire, 4th Earl of 75
DFDS Seaways 653, 669, 685
Dialing codes **14**
Diamondland (Antwerp) 239
Diana, Princess of Wales 51, 54,
  58
Diane de Poitiers 178, **179**
Diderot, Denis 160
Dientzenhofer, Christoph 716
Dientzenhofer, Kilian Ignaz
  716, 720
Dietrich, Marlene 539
Dijon 143
  hotels 209
  restaurants 215
  Street-by-Street map 184–5
Dijver, River 232
Dimitsana
  hotels 510
Dingle 109, **127**
  hotels 137
  restaurants 139
Dinis, King of Portugal 367, 370
Diocletian, Emperor 435
Diogénis Palace (Athens) 507
Díon, Ancient 489
Disability Helpline
  (Great Britain) 89
Disabled People's National Council
  (Warsaw) 759

Disabled visitors
  Austria **604**
  Czech Republic 724
  France **198**, 199
  Germany **567**
  Great Britain **89**
  Greece **503**
  Hungary **740**
  Italy **449**
  Poland **758**, 759
  Portugal **374**
  Spain **333**
Discos
  Italy **455**
Discounts
  air travel **16**
  money-saving cards **12**
  rail passes 18
Disneyland Paris **170**
Distance charts **10**
  France 149
  Germany 527
  Great Britain 41
  Italy 391
  Spain 281
Dizzy (Rotterdam) 267
Dobson, William 48
Doctors *see* Medical care
Dodecanese 469, **498–9**
  hotels **513**
  restaurants **517**
Dodecanese Hydrofoils 505
Doge's Palace (Venice) **436–7**
Domäne Dahlem (Berlin) 538
Dominic, St. 442
Domitian, Emperor 400
Domus Augustana (Rome) 403
Domus Aurea (Rome) 403
Domus Flavia (Rome) 403
Doñana National Park
  see Parque Nacional de Doñana
Donatello 57, 420, 438
  David 418
  Duomo (Siena) 410
  Palazzo Vecchio (Florence) 419
  Piazza della Signoria
    (Florence) 419
  Pisa 411
  San Lorenzo (Florence) 414
Donner, Georg Raphael 599
Dóra Strátou Dance Theater
  (Athens) 507
Downing Street (London) 44
Dragon's Lair (Cracow) **755**
Dresden **542–3**
  hotels 575
  restaurants 581
Driving in Europe *see* Car travel
Drottningholm **647**
Drovetti, Bernardo 427
Druid Theatre (Galway) 135
DSB Ferries 685
Du Barry, Madame 161
Duarte, King of Portugal 367
Dublin 34, **112–21**
  Dublin Castle **118–19**
  hotels 136
  map 112–13
  restaurants 138
  Southeast Dublin: Street-by-
    Street map 114–15
Dublin City Gallery, The Hugh
  Lane 121
Dublin Literary Pub Crawl 135

Dublin Theatre Festival 135
Dublin Writers Museum (Dublin) 121
Dublinia (Dublin) **119**
Duccio, Agostino di 407, 410, 424
Duchêne, Achille 74
Duddon Valley 77
Dudley, Sir Robert 419
Dufy, Raoul 191, 197
Duncan I, King of Scotland 38
Duncan, David Douglas 622
Duncan, Isadora 167
Duomo (Florence) 413, **416–17**
Duomo (Siena) 408, **410**
Duquesnoy, Jérôme the Elder 224
Dürer, Albrecht 290, 424, 531
  Albrecht-Dürer-Haus (Würzburg) 545
  Four Apostles 551
  Kunsthistorisches Museum (Vienna) 596
Durham **77**
  hotels 100
  restaurants 106
Dürnstein 601
Dutch Tourist Information Office 265
Duty-free goods **12–13**
Dvořák, Antonín 708

E

Earthquakes, Lisbon **361**
Easter Rising (1916) 120
easyJet 17, 91, 201, 335, 569
Echternach **235**
  hotels 241
Ecstasy of St. Francis (Giotto) 406
Eden Project (St. Austell) 39, 68
Edinburgh 35, **82–6**
  climate 88
  Edinburgh Castle 83, **84**
  Edinburgh Festival 95
  hotels 101
  map 82–3
  restaurants 107
Edward I, King of England 60, 69
Edward III, King of England 66
Edward IV, King of England 60, 61
Edward the Confessor, King of England 44, 60
Effner, Joseph 553
Eger **739**
  hotels 742
  restaurants 743
Eggenberg, Johann Ulrich von 600
Eglise St-Etienne (Dijon) 185
Eglise St-Trophime (Arles) 192
Egmont, Count 227
Egyptian Obelisk (Arles) 192
Eiermann, Egon 536
Eiffel, Gustave 163, 371
Eiffel Tower (Paris) **163**
Eiger 618
Eisenhower, Dwight D. 172
Eisenstadt **600**
Eleanor of Aquitaine 177
Eleonora of Toledo 419, 424
Elevador de Santa Justa (Lisbon) 361
Elgin, Lord 53
Elgin Marbles **479**
Eliá 496
Eliot, T.S. 47

Elisabeth, Empress of Austria 495, 594, 599
Elizabeth, Czarina 697
Elizabeth I, Queen of England 38, 58, 116
Elizabeth II, Queen of England 39
  Buckingham Palace (London) 48
  coronation 46
  Holyrood Palace (Edinburgh) 86
Eloúnda 501
  hotels 513
Embassies
  Austria 605
  Belgium and Luxembourg 237
  Czech Republic 725
  Denmark 685
  Finland 699
  France 199
  Germany 567
  Great Britain 89
  Greece 503
  Hungary 741
  Ireland 133
  Italy 449
  Netherlands 265
  Norway 669
  Poland 759
  Portugal 375
  Spain 333
  Sweden 653
  Switzerland 627
Emerald Star 135
Emergency services
  Austria 605
  Belgium and Luxembourg 237
  Czech Republic 725
  Denmark 684, 685
  Finland 698, 699
  France 199
  Germany 566–7
  Great Britain 89
  Greece 502, 503
  Hungary 741
  Ireland 133
  Italy 448, 449
  Netherlands 265
  Norway 668, 669
  Poland 759
  Portugal 374, 375
  Spain 332–3
  Sweden 653
  Switzerland 626, 627
Emmental Valley 618
Emponas 499
Encants Vells (Barcelona) 337
Engel, Carl Ludwig 693, 694
England *see* Great Britain
Englischer Garten (Munich) **552–3**
English Golf Union 95
English Theatre (Frankfurt) 573
ENIT 449
Enlightenment 146
Ensor, John 116
Entertainment
  Austria **606–7**
  Belgium and Luxembourg **238–9**
  France **204–5**
  Germany **572–3**
  Great Britain **94–5**
  Greece **506–7**
  Ireland **134–5**
  Italy **454–5**
  Netherlands **266–7**

Entertainment (cont.)
  Portugal **376–7**
  Spain **338–9**
  Switzerland **628–9**
Epernay 172
Ephesos Museum (Vienna) 594
Epidaurus **491**
Erichsen, Edvard 680
Erik, St. 648
Erik XIV, King of Sweden 644
Erkel, Ferenc 736
Ermita del Cristo de la Luz (Toledo) 297
Ernst, Max 531, 683
El Escorial **294**
L'Espace Van Gogh (Arles) 192
Esplanadi (Helsinki) 693
Este, Borso d' 442
Este, Nicolò III d' 442
Este family 442
Estepona 321
  restaurants 350
Esterházy, Prince Paul 600
Esterházy family 600, 737
Estoril 366
  restaurants 381
Esztergom **738**
  restaurants 743
ET 335
ETA 279
Etiquette
  Austria 604
  Greece 503
  Italy 449
  Portugal 374
  Spain 333
Etna, Mount **447**
Eugene IV, Pope 415
Eugene of Savoy, Prince 593, 598–9, 734
Eulalia, St. 309
Eurail 18
Euro, currency **15**
Euro-Bike and Walking Tours 267
Eurofly 451
Eurolines 19, 201, 265, 335, 725
Europcar 19, 201, 335, 375, 451, 699
Europe, map 10–11
Europe by Car 19
European Parliament (Brussels) 219, **228**
European Union 31
  Brussels **228**
Europebyair 17
Eurostar **18**, 91, 201, 237
Eurotunnel **18**, 91, 201, 237
Evans, Sir Arthur 500
Everdingen, Cesar van 260
Évora **372**
  hotels 379
  restaurants 381
Exeter 68
  restaurants 105
Expedia 17
Expulsion of Heliodorus from the Temple (Raphael) 396

F

Fabriano, Gentile da 411
Fabricius, Philipp 713
Fado, Portugal **377**
Fainsilber, Adrien 167
Fairs, Germany **573**

Farnese, Cardinal Alessandro 403
Farnese, Isabel 294
Farnese family 399
Farnese Gardens (Rome) 403
Faro (Portugal) **372–3**
  hotels 379
  restaurants 381
Fårö (Sweden) 649
The Feast in the House of Levi
  (Veronese) 441
Federação Portuguesa
  de Golfe 377
Federación Española
  de Montaña y Escalada 339
Federación Hípica Española 339
Fédération Luxembourgeoisie
  de Canoë-Kayak
  (Luxembourg City) 239
Federazione Arrampicata
  Sportiva Italiana 455
Federazione Italiana
  Attività Subacquee 455
Feierwerk (Munich) 573
Feira da Ladra (Lisbon) 359
Felipe II, King of Spain *see* Philip II
Felipe III, King of Spain 284
Felipe IV, King of Spain 284, 291
Felipe V, King of Spain 284, 285, 295
Felix Meritis (Amsterdam) 267
Fellini, Federico 389
La Fenice (Venice) 455
Ferdinand, Archduke 713, 714
Ferdinand I, Emperor 708, 715
Ferdinand I, Grand
  Duke of Tuscany 425
Ferdinand II, Emperor 717
Ferdinand II, Grand
  Duke of Tuscany 419
Ferenc Rákóczi II, King of
  Hungary 736
Ferihegy Airport (Budapest) 741
Fernando I, King of Spain 292
Fernando III, King of Spain
  284, 300
Fernando V, King of Spain 278
Fernsehturm (Berlin) **533**
Ferragamo 453
Ferrara **442**
  hotels 460
  restaurants 466
Ferries **19**
  Belgium and Luxembourg **237**
  Denmark **684–5**
  Finland **699**
  France **200**, 201
  Great Britain **91**
  Greece **505**
  Ireland **133**
  Italy **451**
  Netherlands **265**
  Norway **669**
  Spain **335**
  Sweden **652–3**
Ferrovie dello Stato 451
Festivals
  Austria **607**
  Germany **573**
  Ireland **135**
  Italy **454**
  Switzerland **628–9**
FEVE 335
FGC 335
FGV 335
Filarete, Antonio 395

Film
  Belgium and Luxembourg **239**
  Filmpark Babelsberg
    (Potsdam) **539**
  France **204–5**
  Great Britain **94–5**
  Greece **506**
  Portugal **377**
  Switzerland **629**
Filóti 497
Filoxenia 507
Finbarr, St. 126
Findel Airport 237
Finland **689–701**
  Helsinki **692–5**
  history **689–90**
  hotels **700**
  language and culture **690**
  map **691**
  practical information **698–9**
  restaurants **701**
  travel **698–9**
Finlandia Hall (Helsinki) **694**
Finn MacCool 130
Finnair 653
Finnie Antiques (Glasgow) 93
Finnish Sauna Society 699
Finnish Tourist Board 699
Firá **497**
Fire services
  Austria 605
  Belgium and Luxembourg 237
  Czech Republic 725
  Denmark 685
  Finland 699
  France 199
  Germany 567
  Great Britain 89
  Greece 503
  Hungary 741
  Ireland 133
  Netherlands 265
  Norway 669
  Poland 759
  Portugal 375
  Spain 333
  Sweden 653
  Switzerland 627
First Travel Management 239
Fischer von Erlach, Johann
  Bernhard 597, 599, 603
Fischer von Erlach,
  Josef Emanuel 594
Fiskárdo 495
Fitzherbert, Mrs. 64
Fjord Line 669
Fjords, Norway 657, **666–7**
Flamenco **331**, **338–9**
Flanders, Counts of 230–31
Flaubert, Gustave 173
Flemish 219, 220
Fleury, Rohault de 166
Flight into Egypt (Tintoretto) 438
Florence 384, **412–25**
  Duomo **416–17**
  Florentine Renaissance **420–21**
  hotels **457–8**
  map 412–13
  restaurants **463–4**
  travel 450
  Uffizi **422–4**
Florentino, Nicolás 295
Floris V, Count of Holland 260,
  262

Flowers
  Bulbfields of the
    Netherlands **261**
  Flying *see* Air travel
  Flying Dolphin 505
FNAC (Paris) 205
Foch, Marshal 163
Focke & Meltzer
  (Amsterdam) 267
Folguera, Françesc 316
Folies-Bergère (Paris) 205
Folies Clubbing (Paris) 205
Fontainebleau
  Château de Fontainebleau **171**
  restaurants 213
Fontana della Barcaccia
  (Rome) 393
Fonte Gaia (Siena) 409
Fontevraud, Abbaye de **177**
  hotels 209
  restaurants 215
Food and drink
  Austria **606**, 607
  South of France **195**
  Great Britain **92**, 93
  Greece 506
  Italy **452–3**
  Portugal 376
  Spain **336–7**
  Switzerland **628**
  tapas **325**
  see also Restaurants
Forenede Danske Motorejere
  (FDM) 685
Forment, Damià 305
Formentera 318, **319**
  hotels 345
Forseth, Einar 645
Forsthaus Paulsborn (Berlin) 538
Fortezza Medicea (Siena) **410**
Fortnum and Mason
  (London) 93
Fortuny, Mariano 290
Forum of Trajan (Rome) 402
Foster, Sir Norman 31, 53, 530
Fountains
  Trevi Fountain (Rome) **404**
Fouquet, Nicolas 170
Four Apostles (Dürer) 551
Foyle's (London) 93
Fragonard, Jean Honoré 160
Frammuseet (Oslo) **664**
Frampton, George 54
France **141–217**
  Burgundy and the
    French Alps **182–5**
  climate 198
  distance chart 149
  entertainment **204–5**
  The Food of the South of
    France **195**
  history **145–6**
  hotels **206–11**
  landscape 22
  language and culture **147**
  Loire Valley **176–9**
  maps 142–3, 148–9
  Northern France **172–5**
  Paris **150–71**
  practical information **198–9**
  restaurants **212–17**
  shopping **202–3**
  South of France **190–97**
  Southwest France **188–9**

France (cont.)
 travel **200–201**
 wines **186–7**
Franchini, Gianfranco 31
Francini brothers 122
Francis, St. 406–7
Franco, General 278, 299, 304
François I, King of France 29,
 146, 596
 Blois 177
 Château de Chambord 179
 Château de Fontainebleau 171
 Les Invalides (Paris) 162
 Musée du Louvre (Paris) 158
 tomb of 170
François II, King of France 176
Frank, Anne
 Anne Frankhuis
 (Amsterdam) **253**
Frankfurt am Main **560**
 airport 569
 hotels 578
 restaurants 584
 shopping 571
 tourist office 567
Franz Joseph I, Emperor of
 Austria 730
 Hofburg (Vienna) 593, 594
 Schönbrunn Palace (Vienna) 599
Franz Liszt Museum (Budapest) 735
Frari (Venice) see Santa Maria
 Gloriosa dei Frari
Frauenkirche (Munich) **550**
Frederick I Barbarossa, Emperor
 28, 524, 563
Frederick II, Emperor 447
Frederik II, King of Denmark 682
Frederick II the Great, King of
 Prussia 29, 524
 Park Sanssouci
 (Potsdam) 540–41
 Schloss Charlottenburg
 (Berlin) 537
 Schloss Sanssouci (Potsdam) 539
Frederik V, King of Denmark 680
Frederik VI, King of Denmark
 674
Frederik VII, King of Denmark
 674, 679
Frederiksborg Slot 673, **682**
Freiburg im Breisgau **556**
 hotels 576
 restaurants 583
French Revolution 30, 153
Freud, Sigmund 589
 Freud Museum (Vienna) **596–7**
Friedrich I, King of Prussia 535
Friedrich II, King of Prussia
 see Frederick II the Great
Friedrich III, Emperor 595, 601
Friedrich, Caspar David 537, 543
Friedrich, Woldemar 535
Friedrich Wilhelm I, King of
 Prussia 539
Friedrich Wilhelm IV, King of
 Prussia 559
Frihedsmuseet (Copenhagen) **681**
Frink, Elisabeth 65
Froment, Nicolas 194
Frueauf, Rueland the Elder 599
Fuengirola 321
 restaurants 350
Fundação Calouste Gulbenkian
 (Lisbon) 377

Fundació Joan Miró
 (Barcelona) **314**
Fundação Serralves 371
Fundació Tàpies (Barcelona)
 311
Furtwangen 556
Futuroscope (Poitiers) 176

G

Gabriel, Jacques-Ange 161
Gaddi, Taddeo 418, 425
Gaelic language 110
Gainsborough, Thomas 48, 70,
 160
Galérie Bortier (Brussels) 239
Galéries d'Ixelles (Brussels) 239
Galeries Lafayette (Berlin) 571
Galeries Lafayette (Paris) 203
Galéries Saint-Hubert
 (Brussels) 239
Galerius, Emperor 488
Galileo 411, 418
 Museo di Storia della Scienza
 (Florence) 419
Gallarus Oratory 127
Gallego, Fernando 290
Gallen-Kallela, Akseli 694
Galleria dell'Accademia
 (Florence) **414–15**
Galleria d'Arte Rinascimento
 (Amsterdam) 267
Galleries
 see Museums and galleries
Galway **129**
 hotels 137
 restaurants 139
Galway Arts Festival 135
Galway Irish Crystal 135
Gandhi, Mahatma 53
Gandon, James 120
Gandria 625
Garbo, Greta 539
Garda, Lake **429**
 hotels 459
 restaurants 465
The Garden of Delights
 (Bosch) 288
Gardens see Parks and gardens
Gardermoen Airport (Oslo) 669
Gardone 429
Garibaldi, Giuseppe 388
Garter Lane Theatre
 (Waterford) 135
Gasteig (Munich) 573
Gate Theatre (Dublin) 121, 135
Gatti Francesco (Rome) 453
Gaudí, Antoni 30, 319
 Casa Milà "La Pedrera"
 (Barcelona) 311
 Casa-Museu Gaudí
 (Barcelona) 315
 Palau Güell (Barcelona) 310
 Parc Güell (Barcelona) **315**
 Sagrada Família
 (Barcelona) 275, **312–13**
Gauguin, Paul 259, 663, 737
Gehry, Frank 304
Gellért, St. 735, 736
Gellért Hotel and Bath Complex
 (Budapest) **735**
Gemäldegalerie (Berlin) 531
Geneva **616**
 hotels 630
 restaurants 632

Geneva, Lake **616–17**
 hotels 630
 restaurants 632
Geneviève, St. 157
Gennaro, San 444
Genoa **426**
 hotels 459
 restaurants 465
Genre painting **257**
Geobuch (Munich) 571
George II, King of England 44
George III, King of England 48, 63
George IV, King of England
 Brighton 64
 Buckingham Palace (London) 48
 National Gallery (London) 49
 Windsor Castle 66, 67
George V, King of England 66
Géricault, Théodore 166
Germany **522–65**
 Baden-Württemberg **556–7**
 Bavaria **544–55**
 beer **554**
 Berlin **528–41**
 climate 566
 Eastern Germany **542–3**
 entertainment **572–3**
 history **523–5**
 hotels **574–9**
 language and culture **525**
 maps 520–21, 526–7
 Northern Germany **564–5**
 practical information **566–7**
 restaurants **580–85**
 Rhine and Mosel Valleys **558–63**
 shopping **570–71**
 travel **568–9**
Gesù (Rome) **401**
Gesundbrunnen-Center (Berlin) 571
Gevrey-Chambertin
 hotels 209
Ghent **230–31**
 hotels 241
 restaurants 243
Ghiberti, Lorenzo 408, 416, 417
Ghirlandaio 361, 398, 414
Giambologna 415, 418, 419, 425
Giambono 441
Gian Nicola di Paolo 407
Gianni Versace (Paris) 203
Giant's Causeway **130–31**
Gibbons, Grinling 58, 63, 75
Gibbs, James 50
Gieves & Hawkes (London) 93
Gifts see Shopping
GIHP 199
Gilbert, Alfred 50
Gilbert of Hastings, Bishop of
 Lisbon 359
Gilda (Rome) 455
Gilles (Watteau) 24
Giò Moretti (Milan) 453
Giordano 290
Gioie (Rome) 453
Giorgio Armani (Paris) 203
Giorgione 80, 441
Giotto, 28, 398, 431
 Duomo (Florence) 416
 Ecstasy of St. Francis 406
 National Gallery (London) 49
 The Ognissanti Madonna 422, 424
 Santa Croce (Florence) 418
 Uffizi (Florence) 424
Gipsy Moth (London) 62

La Giralda (Seville) 328, **330**
Girard, Dominique 598
Giulio Romano 430
Glasgow **80**
  hotels 101
  restaurants 107
Glassware
  Germany **571**
Glendalough **123**, 124–5
Globe Theatre (London) **59**
Glyndebourne 95
Glyptothek (Munich) **551**
Godiva (Brussels) 239
Goethe, Johann Wolfgang von 524, 525, 531
  Goethehaus (Frankfurt) 560
  Weimar 543
Golden Bend (Amsterdam) **254**
Golden Lane (Prague) 713, **714–15**
Goldsmith, Oliver 116
Golf **81**
  Portugal **377**
Golfing Union of Ireland 135
Golz-Kinsky Palace (Prague) 720
Gonçalves, Nuno 361
Gondolas
  Venice **439**
Gonzaga family 430
González, Aníbal 331
González, Felipe 278
Gornostayev, A.M. 693
Gort, Lord 128
Górtys 493, 501
Gothenburg 641, **650**
  hotels 654
  restaurants 655
Gotland **649**
Göttweig Abbey 601
Goujon, Jean 159
Goya, Francisco 30
  The Clothed Maja 289
  Musée du Louvre (Paris) 160
  Museo de Bellas Artes (Valencia) 318
  Museo del Prado (Madrid) 290
  The Naked Maja 289
  Palacio Real (Madrid) 285
  Saturn Devouring One of his Sons 24
  statue of 275
Gozzoli, Benozzo 411
  The Procession of the Magi 420–21
Grachtengordel (Amsterdam) **254**
Grafton Street (Dublin) 114, **117**
Graham, James Gillespie 84
Graimberg, Count Charles de 557
Gran, Daniel 599
Gran Teatre del Liceu (Barcelona) 310, 339
Gran Vía (Madrid) **285**
Granada 275, **320**
  Alhambra **322–3**
  hotels 344
  restaurants 350
Grand Café Fashion (Milan) 455
Grand Canal (Venice) **439**
Grand Opera House (Belfast) 135
Grand Place (Brussels) **224**
Le Grand Rex (Paris) 205
Grand Theater (Warsaw) **751**
La Grande Arche (Paris) 167
Granet, François 194
Grant, Hugh 62

Grasmere 77
Grasser, Erasmus 550
Graubünden
  hotels **631**
  restaurants **633**
Graz **600**
  hotels 609
  restaurants 611
Great Britain **37–107**
  culture and the arts **39**
  entertainment **94–5**
  history **37–8**
  hotels **96–101**
  landscape 22
  London **42–63**
  map 40–41
  Northern Ireland **130–31**
  practical information **88–9**
  restaurants **102–7**
  Scotland **80–87**
  shopping **92–3**
  society and politics **38**
  travel **90–91**
  Wales **69**
Great Exhibition (1851) 55
Great North Eastern Railways 91
Great Western Trains 91
El Greco 160, 304, 715, 737
  The Adoration of the Shepherds 290
  The Assumption 298
  The Burial of the Count of Orgaz 296, 298
  Casa-Museo de El Greco (Toledo) **298**
Greece **469–517**
  Athens **474–81**
  Central Greece **484–7**
  Corfu and the Ionian Islands **494–5**
  Crete **500–501**
  Cyclades **496–7**
  entertainment **506–7**
  history **469–70**
  hotels **508–13**
  landscape 23
  language and culture **470–71**
  maps 385, 472–3
  Northern Greece **488–9**
  Peloponnese **490–93**
  practical information **502–3**
  restaurants **514–17**
  Rhodes and the Dodecanese **498–9**
  shopping **506**, 507
  Temple Architecture **482–3**
  travel **504–5**
Greek National Tourist Board 503
Greenwich **62**
Gregory VII, Pope 524
Gregory the Great, Pope 399
Grenoble **183**
  hotels 210
  restaurants 215–16
Greyfriars Kirk (Edinburgh) **85**
Grieg, Edvard 658, 666
Grimaldi family 197
Grimm, Wilhelm and Jakob 560
Grindelwald 618
  hotels 630
  restaurants 632
Gripsholms Slott 648
Groeninge Museum (Bruges) **234**
Grunewald (Berlin) **538**
Grünewald, Matthias 551

Gruppo Archeologico Romano 455
Gruuthuse Museum (Bruges) **234**
Gruyères 617
  hotels 630
Gualdo, Matteo da 407
Guaranteed Travel 507
Guardamar del Segura 319
Guardi, Francesco 361
Guarini, Guarino 427
Gucci, Santi 755
Güell, Count Eusebi 315
Guercino 401
Guernica (Picasso) 31
Guggenheim, Peggy 440
Guildhall (York) 78
Guincho 366
Guinness, Arthur 121
Guinness, Sir Benjamin 119
Guinness Storehouse (Dublin) **121**
Guise, Duc de 177
Guitarrería F. Manzanero (Madrid) 337
Gulbenkian, Calouste 361
Gustav II Adolf, King of Sweden 640, 644, 646
Gustav III, King of Sweden 640, 644, 648
Gustav III's Museum of Antiquities (Stockholm) 644
Gustav IV Adolf, King of Sweden 644
Gustav Vasa, King of Sweden 640, 647, 648
Gutach 556
Gutenberg, Johannes 559
Guy Laroche (Paris) 203
Gypsies
  flamenco 331
Gýtheio 492
  hotels 510
  restaurants 515

H

Haakon IV, King of Norway 658
Haarlem **260–61**
  hotels 269
  restaurants 271
Habsburg dynasty 524
  Bohemia 708
  Budapest 734
  Hofburg (Viena) 592
  Hungary 730
  Low Countries 219–20, 245
  Switzerland 614
  tombs of 594, 595
Hadrian, Emperor 160, 402, 493
  Castel Sant' Angelo (Rome) 399
  Pantheon (Rome) 400
  Temple of Olympian Zeus (Athens) 481
The Hague **262**
  hotels 269
  restaurants 271
Hague School 258
Haider, Jörg 589
al Hakam II, Caliph 326
Halles de Schaerbeek (Brussels) 239
Hallstatt **602**
  hotels 609
Hallstätter *See* 602
Hals, Frans
  Frans Hals Museum (Haarlem) 260–61

Hals, Frans (cont.)
  Musée Royaux des Beaux-Arts
    (Brussels) 227
  Rijksmuseum (Amsterdam) 258
  Wedding Portrait 24
Halspach, Jörg von 550
Ham House (London) 63
Hamburg **565**
  hotels 579
  restaurants 585
  shopping 571
Hamilton, James 80
Hammurabi, King 160
Hampton Court **63**
Hanau 560
Handel, George Frideric 260
Hankar, Paul 227
Hanover **564**
  hotels 579
  restaurants 585
Hanseatic League 639
Hanu 720
Harald Bluetooth, King of
  Denmark 674, 682
Harald the Fairhaired, King of
  Norway 657
Harald Hardrada, King of Norway
  658, 660
Hardangerfjord 666–7
Hardouin-Mansart, Jules
  162, 168, 169
Hardwick Hall 75
Harland, Sir Edward 130
Hårleman, Carl 644
Harrods (London) 93
Harvard, John 73
Harvey Nichols (London) 93
Hasenauer, Karl von 595
Hathaway, Anne 73
Haussmann, Baron Georges 30,
  164, 167
Havel, Václav 712
Hawksmoor, Nicholas 74, 75
Haydn, Joseph 589, 594, 600
Haydn Festspiele (Eisenstadt) 607
Hazelius, Artur 647
Health care *see* Medical care
Hector Russell (Glasgow) 93
Hedvig Eleonora, Queen of
  Sweden 647
Heidelberg **557**
  hotels 576
  restaurants 583
Heilig Bloed Basiliek (Bruges) **234**
Heinrich II, Count Palatine 559
Heinrich IV, Emperor 524
Hekticket Theaterkassen (Berlin) 573
Helicopter rescue
  Switzerland 627
Hellenic Holidays 505
Hellenic Ornithological Society 507
Hellenic Yachting Federation 507
Helsingør **682**
Helsinki 637, 689, **692–5**
  hotels **700**
  map 692–3
  restaurants **701**
  travel **699**
Helsinki Cathedral
  (Helsinki) **694**
Helsinki Central Station
  (Helsinki) 699
Helsinki City Tourist Office 699
Hemony, François 252

Henri II, King of France
  Basilique de St-Denis (Paris) 170
  Château de Chambord 179
  Château de Chenonceau 178
  Château de Fontainebleau 171
  Musée du Louvre (Paris) 159
Henri III, King of France 177
Henri IV, King of France
  Château de Fontainebleau 171
  Nantes 176
  Place des Vosges (Paris) 153
  Tours 177
Henrietta-Adelaide, Electress of
  Bavaria 553
Henry I, Duke of Brabant 226
Henry II, King of England 110
  Abbaye de Fontevraud 177
  Poitiers 176
  Windsor Castle 66
Henry III, King of England 47
Henry VI, King of England 73, 78
Henry VII, King of England 63
Henry VIII, King of England 38, 110
  Hampton Court 63
  Hyde Park (London) 54
  St. James's Park (London) 48
  Tower of London 60
Henry the Navigator, Prince 354, 361
  Monument to the Discoveries
    (Lisbon) 362–3
  tomb of 367
Hepworth, Barbara 39, 68
Herculano, Alexandre 365
Hercules 325
Hergé 226
Hermès (Paris) 203
The Hermitage (St. Petersburg) **696**
Hernán Ruiz family 327
Herodes Atticus 490
Herodes Atticus Theater (Athens) 507
Herrera, Juan de 294
Hertz
  Finland 699
  France 201
  Germany 569
  Great Britain 91
  Greece 505
  Ireland 133
  Italy 451
  Poland 759
  Portugal 375
  Spain 335
Het Hollands Kaasmuseum 260
Het Loo *see* Paleis Het Loo
Het Muziektheater (Amsterdam) 267
Heurige
  Austria **607**
Hévíz 738
Heyerdahl, Thor 664
High Crosses
  Ireland **124**
Highlands (Scotland) 34, **87**
Hildebrandt, Johann Lukas von 598
Hilliard, Nicholas 48
Hilmer, Heinz 531
Hire For Lower 91
Historiska Museet (Stockholm) **647**
History of Europe **26–31**
Hitler, Adolf 31, 220, 524, 525, 589
Hittorf, Jacques 165
Hjemmefrontmuseet (Oslo) **661**
Hockney, David 39, 49
Hodler, Ferdinand 531
Hofburg (Viena) **592–4**

Hoffman, Josef 597
Hoffmann, Ludwig 532
Hofjagd und Rüstkammer
  (Vienna) 594
Hogarth, William 48
Höger, Fritz 565
Hohenzollern family 534, 539
Holbein, Hans 160, 531, 560
Holge Danske 682
Holiday Autos 133
Holiday Care Service
  (Great Britain) 89
Holl, Steven 694
Holland *see* Netherlands
Holländisches Viertel
  (Potsdam) **539**
Hollandse Schouwburg
  (Amsterdam) 255
Hollywood (Milan) 455
The Holy Family (Michelangelo) 423
Holy Roman Empire 588
Holyroodhouse, Palace of
  (Edinburgh) **86**
Homem, Lopo 419
Honthorst, Gerard van 257
Hoorn, Count 227
Hopper, Edward 291
Horses
  Winter Riding School
    (Vienna) 592, **594**
Horta, Victor 226
  Musée Horta (Brussels) **229**
Hortus Botanicus Amsterdam 255
Hospital de los Venerables
  (Seville) 329, **330**
Hospitals *see* Medical care
Hôtel de Ville (Arles) 192
Hôtel de Ville (Brussels) **225**
Hôtel de Vogüé (Dijon) 184
Hotel Ritz (Madrid) 287
Hotels
  Austria **608–9**
  Belgium and
    Luxembourg **240–41**
  Czech Republic **726**
  Denmark **686**
  Finland **700**
  France **206–11**
  Germany **574–9**
  Great Britain **96–101**
  Greece **508–13**
  Hungary **742**
  Ireland **136–7**
  Italy **456–61**
  Netherlands **268–9**
  Norway **670**
  Poland **760**
  Portugal **378–9**
  Spain **340–45**
  St. Petersburg **700**
  Sweden **654**
  Switzerland **630–31**
Houdon, Jean-Antoine 160
Houishbrouwerij de Halve Maan
  (Bruges) 234
House of Augustus (Rome) 403
House of Livia (Rome) 403
House of the Vestal Virgins
  (Rome) 402
Household and kitchen goods
  Spain **337**
Houses of Parliament (London) **45**
Hoverspeed City Sprint 265
Howard, Catherine 60

Hughes, John Joseph 131
Hugo, Victor 153, 157
Huguet, Jaume 309
Humboldt Universität (Berlin) 530
Hume, David 86
Hungarian Disabled
  Association 741
Hungarian National Gallery
  (Budapest) **734**
Hungarian National Museum
  (Budapest) **736**
Hungary **729–43**
  Budapest **732–7**
  history **729–30**
  hotels **742**
  landscape 23
  language and culture **730–31**
  map 730–31
  practical information **740–41**
  restaurants **743**
  travel **741**
Hunters in the Snow (Brueghel) 596
Hus, Jan 708, 717, 720
Hussites 708
Huts of Romulus (Rome) 403
Huysum, Jan van 258
Hyde, Douglas 119
Hyde Park (London) **54**
Hydrofoils
  Greece **505**

I
Iberian Peninsula **273–381**
  map 274–5
  Portugal **353–81**
  Spain **277–351**
Iberrail 335
Ibiza 318, **319**
  hotels 345
  restaurants 351
Ibsen, Henrik 658, **662**, 664
ICA (London) 95
Iglesia de San Miguel de Escalada
  (León) 299
Iglesia de San Román
  (Toledo) 296
Iglesia de Santo Tomé
  (Toledo) 296, **298**
Ignatius Loyola, St. 401
Igreja do Carmo (Lisbon) 361
Iktinos 480
Ile de la Cité (Paris) **152**
Ilías Lalaoúnis Jewelry Museum
  (Athens) 507
Illa de la Discòrdia (Barcelona) 311
Immigration *see* Passports and visas
Imperial College (London) 55
Ingres, Jean 162, 165
Inishmore 129
Inner City Paris Church
  (Budapest) **736**
Innocent VIII, Pope 396
Innocent X, Pope 400, 401
Innsbruck **603**
  hotels 609
  restaurants 611
Instituto Cervantes 339
Insurance **13**
InterRail 18
Interjet 505
Interlaken **619**
  hotels 630
  restaurants 632

International Red Cross 615
International Student and Youth
  Travel Service 505
Internet
  booking air tickets **17**
  Internet cafés **14**
InterRent-Europcar 505
Inurria, Mateo 324
Les Invalides (Paris) **162–3**
Inverness **87**
  hotels 101
  restaurants 107
Ionian Islands **494–5**
  hotels **512**
  restaurants **516**
Irákleio **500**
  hotels 513
  restaurants 517
Ireland **109–39**
  climate 132
  Dublin **112–21**
  Early Celtic Christianity **124–5**
  entertainment **134–5**
  history **109–10**
  hotels **136–7**
  language and culture **110**
  map 111
  Northern Ireland **130–31**
  practical information **132–3**
  restaurants **138–9**
  shopping **134**, 135
  Southeast Ireland **122–3**
  Southwest Ireland **126–9**
  travel **132–3**
Irish Embassies
  Denmark 685
  Finland 699
  Greece 503
  Netherlands 265
  Norway 669
  Portugal 375
  Sweden 653
  Switzerland 627
Irish Ferries 133
Irish Film Institute 118
Irish Rail 133
Irish Tourist Board 133
Irving, Washington 323
Isabel, Santa 370
Isabel I, Queen of Castile 278, 330
Isabel II, Queen of Spain 292
Isabella Czartoryska, Princess 757
Ischia 444
Isidore, St. 284
Isla Mágica (Seville) 331
Isle of Skye 41, **87**
  hotels 101
  restaurants 107
Ismail I, Caliph 322
Isozaki, Arata 531
István, St. 736–7, 738
István I, King of Hungary 731, 736
Ital Reding Hofstatt (Schwyz) 622
Italian Birds Protection League
  (LIPU) 455
Italy **383–67**
  entertainment **454–5**
  Florentine Renaissance **420–21**
  history **387–8**
  hotels **456–61**
  language and culture **389**
  maps 384–5, 390–91
  practical information **448–9**
  restaurants **462–7**

Italy (cont.)
  Rome **392–405**
  shopping **452–3**
  Sicily **446–7**
  travel **450–51**
Ithaca 495
Izabela Lubomirska, Princess 753

J
JJacobsen, Arne 674, 683
Jacobsen, Carl 678
Jagdschloss Grunewald (Berlin) 538
Jagdzeumagazin (Berlin) 538
Jagiello, Prince 746
Jagiellończyk, Kazimierz 755
Jagiellonian dynasty 746, 754, 755
Jahn, Helmut 531
Jahrhunderthalle (Frankfurt) 573
Jaime I, King of Aragón 318
Jaime II, King of Aragón 309
James, St. 302
James I, King of England 38, 54, 84
James II, King of England 110
James II, King of Scotland 81
James IV, King of Scotland 86
James V, King of Scotland 86
James, Henry 438
Jan III Sobieski, King of
  Poland 753
Jank, Christian 555
Jansson, Tove 695
Jardin du Luxembourg (Paris) **157**
Jardin des Tuileries (Paris) **161**
La Java (Paris) 205
Jazz
  Belgium and Luxembourg **239**
  Germany **572–3**
Jazzkeller (Frankfurt) 573
Jelinek, Elfriede 589
Jensen, Georg 674
Jerez de la Frontera **325**
  restaurants 350
Jerpoint Glass 135
Jewelry
  Crown Jewels (London) **60**
  Greece 507
  Italy **452**, 453
The Jewish Bride (Rembrandt) 258
Jewish sights
  Anne Frankhuis (Amsterdam) **253**
  Centrum Judaicum & Neue
    Synagoge (Berlin) **533**
  Hollandse Schouwburg
    (Amsterdam) 255
  Jewish Museum (Prague) 719
  Joods Historisch Museum
    (Amsterdam) **251**
  Jüdisches Museum (Berlin) 536
  Monument to the Ghetto Heroes
    (Budapest) **752**
  Old Jewish Cemetery (Prague) **719**
  Old-New Synagogue
    (Prague) **718–19**
  Old Synagogue (Cracow) **757**
  Oswiecim (Auschwitz) **757**
  Prague's Jewish Quarter **719**
Joachim I, Elector of
  Brandenburg 534
Joachim II, Elector of
  Brandenburg 538
Joan of Arc 173, 176, 179
João I, King of Portugal 354, 367, 368
João II, King of Portugal 361
João III, King of Portugal 363, 366

João IV, King of Portugal 354, 358
João V, King of Portugal 358, 370
Johann Cicero, Elector of
    Brandenburg 534
John of Luxemburg, King of
    Bohemia 713, 720
John Lewis (London) 93
Johnson, Ester 119
Jonathon Markson Tennis 377
Jones, Inigo 45, 51, 62
Joods Historisch Museum
    (Amsterdam) 251
Jordaan (Amsterdam) 254
Jordaens, Jacob 231
    *As the Old Sang, the Young Play
    Pipes* 230
Jorvik (York) 79
José I, King of Portugal 360
Joselito 293
Joseph II, Emperor 598, 719
Joseph of Arimathea 234
Josephine, Empress 197
Jospin, Lionel 147
Joyce, James 115
Juan Carlos I, King of Spain 278
Juan-les-Pins 196
Juana, Doña 284
Jüdisches Museum (Berlin) 536
Jujol, Josep 315
Juliá Tours 335
Juliana, Queen of the
    Netherlands 255
Julius II, Pope
    St. Peter's (Rome) 394
    Santa Maria del Popolo
    (Rome) 405
    Sistine Chapel (Rome) 398
    Vatican Museums
    (Rome) 396, 398
Julius III, Pope 405
Junction Bar (Berlin) 573
Jungfrau 619
Jura mountains 613
Justinian, Emperor 443

K

KaDeWe (Berlin) 571
Kafka, Franz 708, 715
Kaiser-Wilhelm-Gedächtniskirche
    (Berlin) 527, 536
Kalampaka
    hotels 510
    restaurants 515
Kallikrates 480
Kamári (Kos) 499
Kamári (Santoríni) 497
Kámeiros, Ancient 499
Kammerspiele (Munich) 572
Kant Centrum Lace Shop (Bruges)
    239
Kant, Immanuel 525
Karamanlís, Konstantínos 471
Kardámaina 499
Kardamýli 492
    hotels 510
Karl VI, Emperor of Austria 597
Karl XII, King of Sweden 640, 645
Karl Johan, King of Norway 662
Karl Theodor, Elector of Bavaria 552
Karlsbad 722–3
    hotels 726
    restaurants 727
Karlskirche (Vienna) 597

Karlstein Castle 707, 722
Kárpathos 499
    hotels 513
    restaurants 517
Kassandros, King 488
Kassiópi 495
Kastellet (Copenhagen) 681
Kastráki 497
Kastrup Airport (Copenhagen) 685
Katarina Kyrka (Stockholm) 639
Katholikón (Metéora) 487
Kavos, Albert 697
Kazimierz the Great,
    King of Poland 755
Kazimierz the Restorer 754
Keats, John
    Keats-Shelley Memorial House
    (Rome) 404
Kefalloniá 495
    hotels 512
    restaurants 516
Kelefá Castle 492
Kemwel Holiday Autos 19
Kendal 77
Kenwood House (London) 95
Keswick 77
Keszthely 738
Kevin, St. 123
Kew (London) 63
Kew Bridge Steam Museum
    (London) 63
Kiasma, Museum of Contemporary
    Art (Helsinki) 694
Kierkegaard, Søren 674
Kilkenny 123
    hotels 137
    restaurants 139
Kilkenny Arts Week 135
Kilkenny Design Centre 135
Killarney 34, 127
    hotels 137
    restaurants 139
Kincraig Highland Wildlife Park 87
King, Martin Luther 662
Kinsale 127
    hotels 137
    restaurants 139
Kirchner, Ernst Ludwig 531
Kis-Balaton 738
Kiss, György 737
The Kiss (Rodin) 162
The Kitchen Maid (Vermeer) 256
Kitzbühel 588
Kjelland, Gabriel 667
Klausen Synagogue (Prague) 719
Klee, Paul 227, 537
Klenze, Leo von 548, 551, 552
Klimt, Gustav 597, 599, 601, 715
KLM 17, 265, 725, 741
Klosters 624
    hotels 631
    restaurants 633
Knights of St. John 498, 499
Knossos, Palace of 500
Knox, John 84
Kobenhavens Cyklebors
    (Copenhagen) 685
Koblenz 559
    hotels 578
    restaurants 584
Kodály Memorial Museum
    (Budapest) 735
Kohlbecker, Christoph 531
Komische Oper (Berlin) 573

Kon-Tiki Museum (Oslo) 664
Kongelige Slottet (Oslo) 662
Koninklijk Paleis
    (Amsterdam) 252
Koninklijk Theater Carré
    (Amsterdam) 267
Konstanz 555
Konzerthaus (Vienna) 607
Korisíon Lagoon 495
Kos 499
    hotels 513
    restaurants 517
Kościuszko, Tadeusz 746, 755
Kotiharjan 699
Kovács, Margit 738
Kozubowski, Ludwik 751
KPM (Berlin) 571
Krems 601
Kresilas 532
Kreuzberg (Berlin) 536
Kristina, Queen of Sweden 644, 645
Krohg, Christian 663
Krumpper, Hans 550
Küchel, Jakob Michael 544
Kulturforum (Berlin) 531
Kungliga Operan (Stockholm) 645
Kungsträdgården (Stockholm) 645
Kunstgewerbemuseum (Berlin) 531
Kunsthistorisches Museum
    (Vienna) 25, 596
Kupecký, Jan 714
Kurfürstendamm (Berlin) 537
Kutná Hora 722
Kylemore Abbey 129

L

La Chaux-de-Fonds 617
La Géode (Paris) 205
La Granja 319
Labatt's Apollo (London) 95
Ladislas, King of Naples 444
Ladulås, Magnus 644
Lady with an Ermine (Leonardo
    da Vinci) 757
Ładysław of Gielniów, St. 751
Laganás 495
Lagos 373
    hotels 379
    restaurants 381
Laguerre, Louis 75
Lake District (Great Britain) 77
    hotels 100
    restaurants 106
Lakes of Killarney 127
Lalique, René 162, 361
Laloux, Victor 162
Lamb and Flag (London) 51
Land's End 68
Landscapes of Europe 22–3
Landseer, Edwin 50
Lane, Sir Hugh 121
Lang, Fritz 539
Langhans, Carl Gotthard 530
Langlois, Henri 164
Languages
    Austria 589
    Belgium and Luxembourg
    220, 236
    Czech Republic 708
    Finland 690, 698
    Greece 470–71
    Hungary 730
    Ireland 110

Languages (cont.)
 Italy 389
 Netherlands 246
 Norway 658, 674
 Poland 746
 Portugal 354, 374
 Spain 279, 333
 St. Petersburg 697
 Sweden 640
 Switzerland 615
Lanvin (Paris) 203
Lanyon, Sir Charles 115
Lapin Agile (Paris) 166
Larsen, Henning 678
Larsson, Carl 645, 649
Larsson, Karin 649
Lascaux **188**
Lássi 495
Latimer, Bishop 72
Latin Quarter (Paris)
 Street-by-Street map 156–7
Lauda Air 605
Lauderdale family 63
Laura Ashley (London) 93
Laurana, Luciano 443
Lausanne 616
 hotels 630
 restaurants 632
Lawrence of Arabia 58
Łazienki Park (Budapest) **753**
Lazzi 451
Le Blond, Jean Baptiste 697
Le Brun, Charles 168, 169, 170–71
Le Corbusier 557, 617
Le Corte, Giusto 440
Le Nôtre, André
 Champs-Elysées (Paris) 165
 Jardin des Tuileries (Paris) 161
 Vaux-le-Vicomte 171
 Versailles 168
Le Vau, Louis 159, 168, 170
Leach, Bernard 57
Leather goods
 Spain **336**, 337
Lee, River 126
Leeds
 hotels 100
 restaurants 106
Lefkáda 495
Lefkós 499
Legentil, Alexandre 166
Léger, Fernand 531
Legoland **683**
Legros, Pierre
 Triumph of Faith over Heresy 401
Leiden **262**
 hotels 269
 restaurants 271
Leinster House (Dublin) 115
Leipzig **543**
 hotels 575
 restaurants 581
Leksand 649
Lenné, Peter Joseph 531, 539
Lennox, Lady Louisa 122
Lentos Kunstmuseum (Linz) 601
Leo X, Pope 398, 420, 421
León **299**
 hotels 343
 restaurants 349
Leonardo da Vinci 29, 420
 Château de Chambord 179
 Lady with an Ermine 757
 Last Supper 429, 560

Leonardo da Vinci (cont.)
 Mona Lisa 160
 Museum of Fine Arts
  (Budapest) 737
 National Gallery (London) 49
 Uffizi (Florence) 424
 Vatican Museums (Rome) 398
Leonor, Dona 358
Leopold I, Emperor of Austria 599
Leopold I, King of the Belgians 220
Léopold II, King of the
 Belgians 227, 228
Leopold III, Duke 600
L'Espluga de Francolí
 hotels 343
Letterfrack
 hotels 137
Liberty (London) 93
Librarie de Rome (Brussels) 239
Lichtenstein, Roy 560
Liebermann, Max 561
The Liffey (Dublin) **120**
Ligorio, Pirro 397
Limosa Holidays 507
Lindau 555
Líndos 499
Linz **601**
 hotels 609
 restaurants 611
Lippi, Filippino 411, 414
Lippi, Fra Filippo 424, 426
Lisbon 274, **356–65**
 climate 374
 earthquake of 1755 **361**
 entertainment **376–7**
 hotels **378**
 map 356–7
 Mosteiro dos Jerónimos 353,
  356, **364–5**
 restaurants **380**
 tourist office 375
Liszt, Franz 544, 731, 736
 Franz Liszt Museum
  (Budapest) 735
Litóchoro 489
 hotels 510
 restaurants 515
Little Athens (Paris) 156
Little Mermaid (Copenhagen) **680**
Little Nemo (Brussels) 239
Liverpool **76**
 restaurants 106
Llanberis 69
Llewelyn ap Gruffydd 69
Lobkowicz Palace (Prague) 713
Locarno 625
 restaurants 633
Locarno International Film
 Festival 625, 629
Locci, Augustyn 753
Loch Garten Nature Reserve 87
Lochner, Stephan
 The Adoration of the Magi 563
La Locomotive (Paris) 205
Loewe (Madrid) 337
Loggia della Mercanzia (Siena) 409
Loire Valley 142, **176–9**
 hotels **209**
 restaurants **214–15**
Lombardi family 439
London 35, 37, **42–63**
 British Museum **52–3**
 City and Southwark **58–61**

London (cont.)
 climate 88
 hotels **96–8**
 map 42–3
 restaurants **102–4**
 South Kensington: Street-by-
  Street map 55
 tourist office 89
 travel **90**
 West End **50–51**
 Westminster Abbey 44, **46–7**
 Whitehall and Westminster:
  Street-by-Street map 44–5
London Coliseum (London) 95
London Eye (London) **45**
London Planetarium (London) **54**
London Transport Museum
 (London) 51
London Underground (London) **90**
Longhena, Baldassare 440
Lorca, Federico García 293
Lorelei 559
Lorenzetti, Ambrogio 409, 424
Lorenzetti, Pietro 424
 The Deposition 406
L'Orme, Philibert de 179
Lost Wawel Exhibition (Cracow) **755**
Lotz, Károly 737
Louis IX, King of France 152, 157
Louis XI, King of France 177
Louis XII, King of France 170,
 176, 177
Louis XIII, King of France 153, 168
Louis XIV, King of France 29,
 146, 170, 231
 Avignon 191
 Château de Chambord 179
 Château de Versailles 168–9
 Les Invalides (Paris) 162, 163
 St-Jean-de-Luz 189
Louis XV, King of France 160
Louis XVI, King of France 30,
 161, 170
Louis-Philippe, King of France 161
Louise, Queen of Denmark 680
Louise de Lorraine 178
Lourdes **189**
Loúsios Gorge **493**
 hotels 510, 511
Louvre (Paris) *see* Musée du Louvre
Le Louvre des Antiquaires
 (Paris) 203
Lovers (Amsterdam) 267
Lovisa Ulrika, Queen of Sweden 647
Low Countries
 Belgium and Luxembourg **220–43**
 map 142–3
 Netherlands **245–71**
Löw, Rabbi 719
Lübeck **565**
 hotels 579
 restaurants 585
Lubomirski, Stanisław Herakliusz 753
Lucas van Leyden 258, 262
Lucca **411**
 hotels 460
 restaurants 466
Lucerne **622**
 hotels **631**
 restaurants **633**
Ludwig I, King of Bavaria 551, 553
Ludwig II, King of Bavaria 523, 555
Ludwig IV the Bavarian,
 Emperor 550

Ludwig Beck am Rathauseck
(Munich) 571
Lufthansa 17, 569, 725, 741
Lugano 625
hotels 631
restaurants 633
Luís I, King of Portugal 366
Luís Felipe, Prince of Portugal 360
Luke, St. 317
Lummelundagrottorna 649
Lunatheater (Brussels) 239
Lurago, Anselmo 716
Luther, Martin 29, 524, 694
Lutyens, Sir Edwin 45, 67
Luxembourg see Belgium
and Luxembourg
Luxembourg City **235**
hotels 241
restaurants 243
Lykourgos 479
Lyon **182–3**
hotels 210
restaurants 216
Lyric Theatre (Belfast) 135
Lyrikí Skiní Olympia
Theater (Athens) 507

M

Maas Gallery (London) 93
MacDonald, Flora 86
MacDonald, Ramsay 86
Macedonian royal family **488**
Machiavelli, Niccolò 418, 421
Machuca, Pedro 290
Mackintosh, Charles Rennie 80
McQueen, Alexander 39
Madame Tussaud's (London) **54**
Maderno, Carlo 395
Madonna (Riemenschneider) 25
Madonna of the Goldfinch
(Raphael) 424
Madonna of the Long Neck
(Parmigianino) 424
Madrid 275, **282–93**
climate 332
hotels **340–41**
map 282–3
Museo del Prado **288–90**
Paseo del Prado: Street-by-Street
map 286–7
restaurants **346–7**
tourist office 333
travel **334**, 335
Magalhães (Magellan), Fernão 362
Magasin Anglais
(Luxembourg City) 239
Magee and Co 135
Maggiore, Lake **429**
hotels 459
Maggiore Budget 451
Magritte, René 227, 234, 440
Mahler, Gustav 589
Mail services **14**
Austria 604–5
Belgium and Luxembourg 236
Czech Republic 724
Denmark 684
Finland 698
France 199
Germany 567
Great Britain 89
Greece 503
Hungary 741

Mail services (cont.)
Ireland 132
Italy 449
Netherlands 264
Norway 668
Poland 758–9
Portugal 375
Spain 333
Sweden 652
Switzerland 626
Mainau 555
Maintenon, Madame de 169
Mainz **558–9**
hotels 578
restaurants 584
Maison de Bonneterie
(Amsterdam) 267
Maison F. Rubbrecht (Brussels) 239
MAK (Applied Arts Museum,
Vienna) **597**
Malá Strana (Prague) **716–17**
Málaga **321**
hotels 344
restaurants 350
Mälaren, Lake **648**
Male, Emile 180
Malév 741
Malevich, Kazimir 259
Mália 500
Mallorca 318, **319**
hotels 345
restaurants 351
Malmö **651**
hotels 654
restaurants 655
Malmö Aviation 653
Manchester **76–7**
hotels 100
restaurants 106
Mánes, Josef 721
Manet, Edouard 162, 737
Máni Peninsula **492**
hotels 510
restaurants 515
Mann, Heinrich 565
Mann, Thomas 565
Manneken Pis (Brussels) **224**
Mannelli family 425
Mannerheim, General Carl Gustaf
Emil 690
Manolete 293, 324
Mansfield, Isaac 74
Mansion House (Dublin) 114
al Mansur, Caliph 326
Mantegna, Andrea 428–9
Mantova see Mantua
Mantua **430**
hotels 459
restaurants 465
Manuel I, King of Portugal 354
Batalha 367
Belém 362
Castelo de São Jorge (Lisbon) 359
Mosteiro dos Jerónimos
(Lisbon) 364
Palácio Nacional de Sintra
368, 369
Praça do Comércio (Lisbon) 360
Tomar 366
tomb of 365
Torre de Belém (Lisbon) 363
Manuel II, King of Portugal 354,
358
Manuel, Niklaus 618

Maó 319
hotels 345
restaurants 351
Maps
Amsterdam 248–9
Arles 192–3
Athens 474–5
Austria 588–9
Barcelona 306–7
Barcelona: Barri Gòtic 308–9
Bath 70–71
Beaches of the Côte d'Azur 196
Belém 357
Belgium and Luxembourg 221
Berlin 528–9
British Isles 34–5
Bruges 232–3
Brussels 222–3
Budapest 732–3
Central and Eastern Europe 704–5
Copenhagen 676–7
Corfu and the Ionian Islands 494
Cracow 754
Cyclades 496
Czech Republic 709
Denmark 675
Dijon 184–5
Dublin 112–13
Dublin: Southeast Dublin 114–15
Edinburgh 82–3
Europe 10–11
Finland 691
Florence 412–13
France 148–9
France and the Low
Countries 142–3
Germany 526–7
Germany, Austria and
Switzerland 520–21
Great Britain 40–41
Great Museums
and Galleries 24–5
Greece 385, 472–3, 500
Helsinki 692–3
Hungary 730–31
Iberian Peninsula 274–5
Ireland 111
Italy 384–5, 390–91
Landscapes of Europe 22–3
Lisbon 356–7
London 42–3, 44–5
London: South Kensington 55
Madrid 282–3
Madrid: Paseo del Prado 286–7
Metéora 486
Munich 546–7
Netherlands 247
Norway 659
Oslo 660–61
Paris 150–51
Paris: Latin Quarter 156–7
Park Sanssouci (Potsdam) 540–41
Poland 747
Portugal 355
Prague 710–11
Prague Castle 712–13
Rail network *inside back cover*
Rhodes and the Dodecanese 498
Rome 392–3
Scandinavia 636–7
Seville 328–9
Siena 408–9
Spain 280–81
Stockholm 642–3

Maps (cont.)
St. Petersburg 697
Sweden 641
Switzerland 614–15
Toledo 296–7
Venice 432–3
Vienna 590–91
Warsaw 748–9
Wines of France 186–7
York 78–9
Marbella 321
hotels 344
restaurants 351
Marble Hill House (London) 63
Marché aux Puces de St-Ouen
(St-Ouen) 203
Marconi, Guglielmo 442
Margaret, St. 84
Margaux
hotels 210
Margrethe I, Queen of
Denmark 674
Margrethe II, Queen of Denmark 680
Maria I, Queen of Portugal 358
Maria Alexandrovna, Czarina 697
Maria Christina, Princess 592
María Cristina, Queen of Spain 304
Maria Eleonora, Queen of
Sweden 644
Maria Laach 559
restaurants 584
Maria Louisa, Princess of Austria 599
María Luisa, Princess of Spain 331
Maria Stransky (Vienna) 607
Maria Teresa, Queen of France 189
Maria Theresa, Empress 588
Innsbruck 603
Royal Palace (Budapest) 734
Schönbrunn Palace (Vienna) 599
Marie-Antoinette, Queen of France
Bois de Boulogne (Paris) 167
Ile de la Cité (Paris) 152
Musée du Louvre (Paris) 160
Place de la Concorde (Paris) 161
tomb of 170
Versailles 169
Marie de Médicis,
Queen of France 157
Marienbad 723
Marienplatz (Munich) **550**
Mariinskiy Theater (St. Petersburg)
697
Marinella (Naples) 453
Marini, Marino 440
Maris, Matthijs 80
Mark, St. 434, 435
Marken **260**
Market Square (Cracow) **756**
Market Square (Helsinki) **693**
Markets
Belgium and Luxembourg **238**
France **202**
Germany **570**, 571
Great Britain **92**, 93
Greece **506**, 507
Italy **453**
Mercat de Sant Josep
(Barcelona) 310
Monastiráki (Athens) **476**, 507
Netherlands 266
Portugal 376
El Rastro (Madrid) **285**
Spain **336**, 337
Switzerland 628

Marks & Spencer (London) 93
Markt (Bruges) 231
Marlborough, John Churchill, 1st
Duke of 74
Marmorpalais (Potsdam) **539**
Marseille **194**
restaurants 217
Martí the Humane 309
Martin, St. 177
Martin V, Pope 420
Martin, Misses 130
Martinair 265
Martini, Simone 191, 424
The Martyrdom of St. Philip
(Ribera) 289
Martinic, Jaroslav 713
Marx, Karl 53, 525
Mary, Queen of Scots 81, 84, 86
Mary II, Queen of England 63
Mary of Burgundy 219
Mary of Guise 86
Mary Magdalene 182
Masaccio 49, 411, 414
Master of Alkmar 258
Master of Flémalle 226
Master of Koudewater
St. Catherine 257
Matejko, Jan 752
Matisse, Henri 153, 162
Musée Matisse (Nice) 197
Matterhorn 618, 620
Matthew of Arras 713, 722
Mátyás Church (Budapest) **735**
Mátyás (Matthias) Corvinus, King
of Hungary 29, 729, 730, 734
Mauricio, Bishop of Burgos 300
Mauve, Anton 258
Max Linder Panorama (Paris) 205
Maxentius, Emperor 403
Maximian, Emperor 435
Maximilian I, Elector of Bavaria 548
Maximilian I, Emperor 219, 225, 603
Maximilian II, King of Bavaria
552, 555
Maximilian Emmanuel, Elector of
Bavaria 552
Mazovian dukes 750, 753
Medical care and health issues
13
Austria 604, 605
Czech Republic 724
Denmark 684
France 198–9
Great Britain 89
Greece 502, 503
Hungary 740
Italy 448
Netherlands 264
Poland 758, 759
Portugal 374
Sweden 652
Medici, Anna Maria Lodovica de'
424
Medici, Cosimo I
Fortezza Medicea (Siena) 410
Palazzo Vecchio (Florence) 419
statue of 418, 419
Uffizi (Florence) 422
Medici, Cosimo il Vecchio
414, 415, 420
Medici, Francesco I 422
Medici, Lorenzo the Magnificent
420, 421
Medici, Piero de' 420

Medici family
Florentine Renaissance 420
Palazzo Pitti (Florence) 425
San Lorenzo (Florence) 414
Uffizi (Florence) 424
Meersburg 555
Megálo Metéoro (Metéora) 486
Meglinger, Kaspar 622
Meia Praia 373
Meinl am Graben (Vienna) 607
Meissen 543
restaurants 581
Meit, Conrad 552
Melanchthon, Philipp 694
Melissaní Cave-Lake 495
Melk **601**
restaurants 611
Mellon, Judge Thomas 131
Melusina (Luxembourg City) 239
Memling, Hans 234, 551, 596
Menabuoi, Giusto de' 431
Mengs, Anton Raffael 290
Menorca 318, **319**
hotels 345
restaurants 351
Menton 196
Mercator, Gerhard 227
Merlini, Dominik 753
Merrion Square (Dublin) **116–17**
Messel, Alfred 532
Messerschmidt, Franz Xavier 599
Metéora 469, **486–7**
hotels 510
restaurants 515
Metz & Co. (Amsterdam) 267
The Mezquita (Córdoba) **326–7**
Michelangelo 29, 420
Ashmolean Museum (Oxford) 72
Bargello (Florence) 418
Capitoline Museums (Rome) 401
Castello Sforzesco (Milan) 428
Christ 67
David 412, 415, 419
Duomo (Siena) 410
Galleria dell'Accademia
(Florence) 414–15
The Holy Family 423
Musée du Louvre (Paris) 160
Original Sin 398
Palazzo Vecchio (Florence) 419
Pietà 395
Quattro Prigioni 415, 421
Royal Academy (London) 50
St. Peter's (Rome) 394
San Domenico (Bologna) 442
San Lorenzo (Florence) 414
Sistine Chapel (Rome) 398
tomb of 418
Uffizi (Florence) 424
Villa Giulia (Rome) 405
Michelozzo 415
Mickiewicz, Adam 745, 756
Mies van der Rohe, Ludwig 557
Milan **428–9**
hotels 459
restaurants 465
transport 450
Mildert, William van, Bishop of
Durham 77
Miliés 485
Millais, John Everett 49, 61
Millennium Dome (London) (
Milles, Carl 647, 650
Millet, Jean François 80

Minoans 500–501
Minot, Archbishop of Dublin 118
Miradouro de Santa Luzia
(Lisbon) 359
Miró, Joan 153, 291, 319
Fundació Joan Miró
(Barcelona) **314**
Missiaglia (Venice) 453
Mistral, Frédéric 192
Miszko I, King of Poland 745, 746
Mitterand, François 147
Mobility International 89, 567
Mocker, Josef 722
Moda y Ole (Madrid) 337
Moderna Museet (Stockholm) **646**
Modigliani, Amedeo 161, 557
Molière 167
Molin, J.P. 645
Moller, Erik 683
Mona Lisa (Leonardo da Vinci) 160
Monaco 196, **197**
restaurants 217
Monasterboice 124
Monasteries
Glendalough **123**, 124–5
Metéora **486–7**
Monasteri de Lluc (Mallorca) 319
Monasterio de las Descalzas
Reales (Madrid) **284–5**
Monasterio de Santa María de las
Cuevas (Seville) **331**
Monastery of Dafní **484**
Monastery of Osios Loukás **484–5**
Monestir de Montserrat **316–17**
Mosteiro dos Jerónimos (Lisbon)
353, 356, **364–5**
Mount Athos **489**
Poblet **305**
Monastiráki (Athens) **476**, 507
Mönch 618
Mondrian, Piet
Haags Gemeentemuseum
(The Hague) 262
Peggy Guggenheim Collection
(Venice) 440
Stedelijk Museum
(Amsterdam) 259
Monemvasía **492**
hotels 510
restaurants 515
Monet, Claude 30, 49
Albertinum (Dresden) 543
Kelvingrove Art Gallery
(Glasgow) 80
Musée des Beaux Arts (Nice) 197
Musée de l'Orangerie (Paris) 161
Nasjonalgalleriet (Oslo) 663
Ny Carlsberg Glyptotek
(Copenhagen) 678
Rouen 173
Staatsgalerie (Stuttgart) 557
Stedelijk Museum
(Amsterdam) 259
Money *see* Currency
Money-saving cards **12**
Moní Filerímou 499
Moní Theotókou 495
La Monnaie (Brussels) 239
Monreale 446
Mont-St-Michel **174–5**
restaurants 214
Montand, Yves 167
Monte Carlo 197
hotels 211

Monte Mottarone 429
Montefeltro, Federico da 443
Montferrand, Auguste de 696
Montjuïc (Barcelona) **314**
Montmartre (Paris) **166**
Montreux 617
restaurants 632
Montreux International Jazz
Festival 629
Montserrat, Monestir de *see*
Monestir de Montserrat
Monument to the Discoveries
(Lisbon) **362–3**
Monument to the Ghetto Heroes
(Budapest) **752**
Monument to Those Fallen and
Murdered in the East 748, 752
Monumento del Dos de Mayo
(Madrid) 287
Moominworld 695
Moore, Henry 39, 49, 551
Moorish Spain **321**
Mora 649
Mora, Juan Gómez de la 284
Morales, Luis de 290, 321
Moravia 707
Morris, William 57
Morrison, Jim 167
Mosel Valley **558**
Moser, Koloman 597
Mosques
The Mezquita (Córdoba) **326–7**
Mosteiro dos Jerónimos (Lisbon)
353, 356, **364–5**
Motorways *see* Car travel
Moulin Rouge (Paris) 166, 205
Mountains
Pyrenees **189**
see also Alps
Mousikís Mégaron Concert Hall
(Athens) 507
Mozart, Wolfgang Amadeus 589,
602, 716
Grote Kerk (Haarlem) 260
Mozart Memorial (Vienna) 593
Salzburg 602, 603
Staatsoper (Vienna) 587
Mucha, Alfons 31, 708, 712, 721
Muckross House (Killarney) 127
Muhammad V, Caliph 322, 323
Muller, Daniel 235
Munch, Edvard 658
Munch-museet (Oslo) **663**
Nasjonalgalleriet (Oslo) 663
Neue Nationalgalerie (Berlin) 531
Sprengel-Museum (Hanover) 564
Wallraf-Richartz-Museum
(Cologne) 561
Young Woman on the Shore 663
Mungo, St. 80
Munich 521, **546–53**
airport 569
climate 566
hotels **575–6**
map 546–7
Oktoberfest 554
Residenz **548–9**
restaurants **582**
shopping 571
tourist office 567
Municipal House (Prague) **721**
Munkácsy, Mihály 734
Münster **564**
hotels 579

Münster (cont.)
restaurants 585
Murano **441**
Murillo, Bartolomé Esteban
Monasterio de las Descalzas
Reales (Madrid) 285
Museo de Bellas Artes
(Córdoba) 324
Museo de Bellas Artes
(Málaga) 321
Museo de Bellas Artes (Seville) 331
Mürren 618
Museums and galleries **24–5**
Accademia (Venice) **441**
Acropolis Museum (Athens) **480**
Alte Pinakothek (Munich) **551**
Altes Museum (Berlin) **532**
Amalienborg (Copenhagen) **680**
Amsterdams Historisch
Museum **252–3**
Anne Frankhuis (Amsterdam) **253**
Applied Arts Museum
(Vienna) **597**
Autoworld (Brussels) 229
Bargello (Florence) **414**
Bayerisches Nationalmuseum
(Munich) **552**
Belvedere (Vienna) **598–9**
Benáki Museum (Athens) **481**
Bildergalerie (Potsdam) **541**
British Museum (London) **52–3**
Brücke-Museum (Berlin) 538
Brugse Brouwerij-
Mouterijmuseum (Bruges) **234**
Budapest History Museum
(Budapest) **734**
Capitoline Museums (Rome) **401**
Casa-Museo de El Greco
(Toledo) **298**
Casa-Museu Gaudí
(Barcelona) 315
Centre Pompidou (Paris) **153**
Centro de Arte Reina Sofia
(Madrid) **291**
Cité des Sciences et de
l'Industrie (Paris) 166–7
Czartoryski Museum
(Cracow) **757**
Deutsches Museum
(Munich) **552**
Domäne Dahlem (Berlin) 538
Dublin Writers Museum
(Dublin) 121
Dublinia (Dublin) **119**
Ephesos Museum (Vienna) 594
Espace Montmartre Salvador
Dalí (Paris) 166
L'Espace Van Gogh (Arles) 192
Frammuseet (Oslo) **664**
Frans Hals Museum
(Haarlem) 260–61
Franz Liszt Museum
(Budapest) 735
Freud Museum (Vienna) **596–7**
Frihedsmuseet (Copenhagen) **681**
Fundació Joan Miró
(Barcelona) **314**
Fundació Tàpies (Barcelona) 311
Galleria dell'Accademia
(Florence) **414–15**
Gemäldegalerie (Berlin) 531
Glyptothek (Munich) **551**
Groeninge Museum (Bruges) **234**
Gruuthuse Museum (Bruges) **234**

Museums and galleries (cont.)
Guinness Storehouse
(Dublin) **121**
Gustav III's Museum of
Antiquities (Stockholm) 644
The Hermitage (St. Petersburg)
696
Historiska Museet (Stockholm)**647**
Hjemmerfrontmuseet
(Oslo) **661**
Hofjagd und Rüstkammer
(Vienna) 594
Hugh Lane Municipal Gallery of
Modern Art (Dublin) 121
Hungarian National Gallery
(Budapest) **734**
Hungarian National Museum
(Budapest) **736**
Jagdmuseum (Berlin) 538
Jewish Museum (Prague) 719
Joods Historisch Museum
(Amsterdam) **251**
Jüdisches Museum (Berlin) 536
Kew Bridge Steam Museum
(London) 63
Kiasma, Museum of
Contemporary Art (Helsinki) **694**
Kon-Tiki Museum (Oslo) **664**
Kunstgewerbemuseum
(Berlin) 531
Kunsthistorisches Museum
(Vienna) **596**
London Transport Museum
(London) 51
Lost Wawel Exhibition
(Cracow) **755**
Madame Tussaud's (London) **54**
Moderna Museet (Stockholm) **646**
Munch-museet (Oslo) **663**
Musée de l'Armée (Paris) 162
Musée d'Art et d'Histoire
(Geneva) 616
Musée d'Art Naïf Max Fourny
(Paris) 166
Musée des Beaux Arts (Dijon) 184
Musée du Costume et de la
Dentelle (Brussels) **224**
Musée de l'Homme (Paris) 164
Musée Horta (Brussels) **229**
Musée du Louvre
(Paris) 24,**158–60**
Musée Magnin (Dijon) 185
Musée de la Marine (Paris) 164
Musée de Montmartre (Paris) 166
Musée des Monuments Français
(Paris) 164
Musée de l'Orangerie (Paris) **161**
Musée de l'Ordre de la
Libération (Paris) 162
Musée d'Orsay (Paris) **162**
Musée Picasso (Paris) **153**
Musée des Plans-Reliefs
(Paris) 162
Musée du Quai Branly (Paris) 164
Musée Réattu (Arles) 192
Musée Rodin (Paris) **162**
Musée Royal de l'Armée et
d'Histoire Militaire (Brussels) 229
Musée Royaux d'Art et d'Histoire
(Brussels) 229
Musée Royaux des Beaux-Arts
(Brussels) **226–7**
Museo de América (Madrid) **292**
Museo Arqueológico (Seville) 331

Museums and galleries (cont.)
Museo Arqueológico Nacional
(Madrid) **292**
Museo de Arte Contemporáneo
(Seville) 331
Museo de Artes y Costumbres
Populares (Seville) 331
Museo de Artes Decorativas
(Lisbon) 359
Museo de Bellas Artes (Seville) **331**
Museo Correr (Venice) **438**
Museo e Galleria Borghese
(Rome) **405**
Museo Marítimo (Seville) 331
Museo Nacional de Artes
Decorativas (Madrid) 287
Museo Nazionale Romano
(Rome) 403
Museo dell'Opera del Duomo
(Siena) 408, 410
Museo del Prado (Madrid) 24,
288–90
Museo de Santa Cruz (Toledo)
297, **298**
Museo di Sant' Agostini 426
Museo di Storia della Scienza
(Florence) **419**
Museo Thyssen-Bornemisza
(Madrid) 286, **291**
Museon Arlaten (Arles) 192
Museu Arquelògic (Barcelona) 314
Museu d'Automates
(Barcelona) 315
Museu Calouste Gulbenkian
(Lisbon) **361**
Museu de Cera (Barcelona) 310
Museu do Chiado (Lisbon) 361
Museu Etnològic (Barcelona) 314
Museu Frederic Marès
(Barcelona) 309
Museu d'Història de la Ciutat
(Barcelona) 309
Museu da Marinha (Lisbon) **363**
Museu de la Música (Barcelona) 311
Museu Nacional d'Art de
Catalunya (Barcelona) **314–15**
Museu Nacional de Arte Antiga
(Lisbon) **361**
Museu Nacional do Azulejo
(Lisbon) **358**
Museu Nacional dos Coches
(Lisbon) **362**
Musée National du Moyen Age
(Paris) **156**
Museu Picasso (Barcelona) **311**
Museum Amstelkring
(Amsterdam) **250**
Museum of Applied Arts
(Budapest) 735
Museum of Contemporary
History and Ludwig Museum
(Budapest) 735
Museum of Cycladic Art
(Athens) **481**
Museum Europäischer Kulturen
(Berlin) 538
Museum of Fine Arts
(Budapest) **737**
Museum Het Rembrandthuis
(Amsterdam) **251**
Museum of London (London) **58**
Museum of Scotland (Edinburgh)
85
Museum Tinguely (Basel) 617

Museums and galleries (cont.)
Museum voor Volkskunde
(Bruges) **234**
Museum für Vor- und
Frühgeschichte (Berlin) 537
MuseumsQuartier Wien
(Vienna) **596**
Museumszentrum (Berlin) 538
Nasjonalgalleriet (Oslo) **663**
National Archaeological Museum
(Athens) **476**
National Gallery (Dublin) **117**
National Gallery (London) **49**
National Gallery of Art
(Athens) **481**
National Gallery of Scotland
(Edinburgh) **85**
National Maritime Museum
(London) 62
National Museum (Budapest) **752**
National Museum
(Copenhagen) **678**
National Museum of Ireland
Archaeology and History
(Dublin) 115, **117**
National Museum (Helsinki) **694**
National Museum (Prague) 721
National Portrait Gallery
(London) 50
Nationalmuseum (Stockholm) **645**
Natural History Museum
(London) 55, **56–7**
Naturhistorisches Museum
(Vienna) **595**
Nederlands Scheepvaart Museum
(Amsterdam) **255**
Nemo **255**
Neue Burg (Vienna) 593, **594**
Neue Nationalgalerie (Berlin) 531
Neue Pinakothek (Munich) **551**
Nordiska Museet (Stockholm) **647**
Norsk Folkemuseum (Oslo) **664**
Ny Carlsberg Glyptotek
(Copenhagen) **678**
Old Midleton Distillery
(Midleton) 126
Old Royal Observatory
(London) 62
Palazzo Pitti (Florence) **425**
Peggy Guggenheim Collection
(Venice) **440**
Pergamonmuseum (Berlin) **532**
Petit Palais (Paris) 165
Pinacoteca Nazionale (Siena) **410**
Pinatothek der Moderne 546, 552
Queen's Gallery (London) 48
Richard Wagner Museum
(Lucerne) 622
Rijksmuseum (Amsterdam) **256–8**
Royal Museum of Scotland
(Edinburgh) **85**
Russian Museum (St. Petersburg)
696
Sammlung alter
Musikinstrumente (Vienna) 594
Sammlung Berggruen (Berlin) **537**
Schatzkammer (Vienna) 592, **594**
Science Museum (London) 55, **56**
Scottish National Portrait Gallery
(Edinburgh) **86**
Skansen (Stockholm) **646**
Stadtmuseum (Munich) **550**
Statens Museum for Kunst
(Copenhagen) **681**

Museums and galleries (cont.)
  Stedelijk Museum
    (Amsterdam) **259**
  Sternberg Palace (Prague) **715**
  Tate Britain (London) **48–9**
  Tate Modern (London) 42, **59**
  Thorvaldsen's Museum
    (Copenhagen) 679
  Tower Bridge Experience
    (London) 59
  Tre Kronor Museum
    (Stockholm) 644
  Uffizi (Florence) **422–4**
  Ulster-American Folk Park **131**
  Van Gogh Museum
    (Amsterdam) **259**
  Vasamuseet (Stockholm) **646**
  Vatican Museums (Rome) **396–8**
  Victoria and Albert Museum
    (London) 55, **57**
  Vikingsskipshuset (Oslo) **664**
  Völkerkundemuseum
    (Vienna) 594
  Warsaw History Museum
    (Warsaw) 750
  Zoltán Kodály Museum
    (Budapest) 735
Music
  Austria **606–7**
  Belgium and Luxembourg
    238, 239
  France **204**, 205
  Germany **572**, 573
  Great Britain **94**, 95
  Greece **506–7**
  Ireland **134**
  Italy **454**, 455
  Portugal **376**, 377
  Spain **338**, 339
  Switzerland **629**
Music Festival in Great Irish
  Houses 135
Musikverein (Vienna) 607
Mussolini, Benito 388
Mycenae **491**
  hotels 510
Mýkonos **496**
  hotels 512
  restaurants 516
Myslbek, Josef 721
Mystery Park (Interlaken) 619
Mystrás **492–3**

N

Naantali 695
Náfplio **491**
  hotels 511
  restaurants 515
The Naked Maja (Goya) 289
Nantes **176**
  hotels 209
  restaurants 214, 215
Naples **444**
  hotels 461
  restaurants 467
Napoleon I, Emperor of France 30,
  67, 146, 524, 599
  Accademia (Venice) 441
  Alhambra (Granada) 322
  Arc de Triomphe du Carrousel
    (Paris) 158
  Arc de Triomphe (Paris) 165
  Battle of Waterloo 231

Napoleon I, Emperor of France
  (cont.)
  Château de Fontainebleau 171
  Cimetière du Père Lachaise
    (Paris) 167
  coronation 154, 160
  Helvetic Republic 614, 615
  Musée de la Marine (Paris) 164
  occupation of Vienna 588, 594
  Peninsular War 278, 354
  La Sorbonne 157
  tomb of 163
Napoleon III, Emperor of France
  30, 146, 164
  Bois de Boulogne (Paris) 167
  Windsor Castle 67
Nardi (Venice) 453
Narutowicz, Gabriel 750
Nash, John 50, 54, 64
Nasjonalgalleriet (Oslo) **663**
Nasmyth, Alexander 86
Nasrid dynasty 320, 322, 323
National Archaeological Museum
  (Athens) **476**
National Citer 201
National Concert Hall (Dublin) 135
National Express 91
National Gallery (Dublin) **117**
National Gallery (London) **49**
National Gallery of Art (Athens) **481**
National Gallery of Scotland
  (Edinburgh) **85**
National Library (Dublin) 115
National Maritime Museum
  (London) 62
National Museum (Budapest) **752**
National Museum
  (Copenhagen) **678**
National Museum (Dublin) 115, **117**
National Museum (Helsinki) **694**
National Museum (Prague) **721**
National Portrait Gallery (London) 50
National Theater (Athens) 507
National Theater (Lisbon) 360
National Theater (Prague) **721**
National Theatre (London) 95
National Trust (Britain) 84
National Welfare Organization
  (Athens) 507
Nationalmuseum (Stockholm) **645**
Nationaltheatret (Oslo) **662**
Natural History Museum
  (London) 55, **56–7**
Naturetrek 507
Naturhistorisches Museum
  (Vienna) **595**
Náxos **497**
  hotels 512
  restaurants 516
Nazarenes 543
Nederlands Scheepvaart Museum
  (Amsterdam) **255**
Nederlandse Spoorwegen
  Internationaal 265
Neílos 486
Nelson, Admiral Horatio 58, 447, 674
Nelson's Column (London) 50
Nemo **255**
Néos Mystrás
  hotels 511
  restaurants 515
Nepomuk, St. John 550, 713, 717
Nering, Johann Arnold 537
Nero, Emperor 403

Neruda, Jan 716
Nerudova Street (Prague) **716**
Ness, Loch 87
Netherlands **245–71**
  Amsterdam **248–59**
  bulbfields **261**
  entertainment **266–7**
  history **245–6**
  hotels **268–9**
  map 247
  practical information **264**
  restaurants **270–71**
  shopping **266**, 267
  travel **264–5**
Netherlands Board of Tourism
  (NBT) 265
Neuchâtel **617**
Neue Burg (Vienna) 593, **594**
Neue Kammern (Potsdam) **541**
Neue Nationalgalerie (Berlin) 531
Neue Pinakothek (Munich) **551**
Neue Synagoge (Berlin) **533**
Neue Wache (Berlin) 530
Neues Palais (Potsdam) 540, **541**
Neumann, Balthasar 544
Neuschwanstein 523, **555**
Nevskiy prospekt (St. Petersburg)
  696
New Morning (Paris) 205
New Town (Edinburgh) **84**
New Town (Prague) **720–21**
New Zealand Embassies
  Finland 699
  Germany 567
  Greece 503
  Norway 669
New Zealand High Commission
  (London) 89
Newgrange **122**
Newspapers
  Denmark 684
  Switzerland 626
Nice 148, **196–7**
  hotels 211
  restaurants 217
Nicholas II, Czar 690, 696
Nietzsche, Friedrich Wilhelm 543
Nieuwe Kerk (Amsterdam) **252**
The Night Watch (Rembrandt) 257
Nikolaiviertel (Berlin) **533**
Nîmes **190**
  hotels 211
  restaurants 217
Nina Ricci (Paris) 203
Nobel, Alfred 662
Nobile, Peter 593
Nor-Way Bussekspress (Oslo) 669
Nordiska Museet (Stockholm) **647**
Norges Statsbaner 669
Norman Shaw Buildings (London) 45
Norse Irish Ferries 133
Norsk Folkemuseum (Oslo) **664**
Den Norske Turistforening 669
North Sea Ferries 265
Northern Ireland 109, 110, **130–31**
Northern Ireland Railways 133
Northern Ireland Tourist
  Board 133
Northumberland, Dukes of 63
Norway **657–71**
  Bygdøy Peninsula **664**
  history **657–8**
  hotels **670**
  landscape 22

Norway (cont.)
  map 659
  Oslo **660–64**
  practical information **668–9**
  restaurants **671**
  travel **668–9**
  Vikings **665**
Norwegian Tourist Board 669
Nost, John 63
Notke, Bernt 643
Notre-Dame (Dijon) 184
Notre-Dame (Paris) **154–5**
Notre-Dame-de-la-Major (Arles)
  193
Notting Hill (London) **62**
Nuremberg **545**
  hotels 576–7
  restaurants 583
Ny Carlsberg Glyptotek
  (Copenhagen) **678**
Nyhavn (Copenhagen) **680**
Nymphenburger Porzellan
  Manufaktur (Munich) 571
Nyon 616

O

The Oath of the Horatii (David) 30
O'Brien family 128
O'Carolan, Turlough 119
Oceanário de Lisboa (Lisbon) **358**
O'Connell, Daniel 116–17, 120
O'Connell Street (Dublin) **120–21**
Oddbins (London) 93
Oddi e Seghetti (Rome) 453
Odense **682–3**
  hotels 686
  restaurants 687
Odo, Bishop of Bayeux 173
Oeder, G.C. 631
The Ognissanti Madonna (Giotto)
  422, 424
Oítylo 492
Olaf, St., King of Norway 78
Olbrich, Joseph Maria 597
Old Bushmills Distillery **131**
Old Jewish Cemetery (Prague) **719**
Old Midleton Distillery
  (Midleton) 126
Old-New Synagogue (Prague)
  718–19
Old Synagogue (Cracow) **757**
Old Town (Prague) **720–21**
Old Town Hall (Prague) **720–21**
Old Town Market Square
  (Warsaw) **750**
Old Town Square (Prague) **720**
An Old Woman Cooking Eggs
  (Velázquez) 85
Olsen, Jens 678
Olympia, Ancient **493**
  hotels 511
  restaurants 515
Olympia (Paris) 205
Olympiapark (Munich) **553**
Olympic Airlines 505
Olympos, Mount **489**
  hotels 510
  restaurants 515
Olympos (Kárpathos) 499
Onze Lieve Vrouwekerk
  (Bruges) 232
Open-air entertainment
  Italy **454**

Opening hours
  Austria 606
  Belgium and Luxembourg 236
  Denmark 684
  Finland 698
  France 198, 202
  Germany 567
  Great Britain 88, 92
  Greece 503
  Italy 449, 452
  Netherlands 264, 266
  Norway 668
  Spain 333, 336
  Switzerland 626
Opera
  Austria **606**, 607
  Belgium and Luxembourg
    238, 239
  Italy **454**, 455
  Opéra Comique (Paris) 205
  Opéra de Paris Bastille (Paris) 205
  Portugal **376**, 377
  Spain **338**, 339
  Staatsoper (Vienna) 587, **595**
  State Opera House (Budapest) **736**
Opera House (Cork) 135
Operetta
  Austria **606**, 607
  Opernhaus (Zürich) 629
Oporto **371**
  hotels 379
  restaurants 381
  tourist office 375
Orangerie (Potsdam) **541**
Orcagna, Andrea 414
Order of the Templars 366
Öresund Link **651**
Orféas (Athens) 507
Oriente station (Lisbon) 375
Original Sin (Michelangelo)
  398
Örkény, István 731
Orléans **179**
  restaurants 215
Ormonde, Duke of 121
Osios Loukás, Monastery of
  484–5
Oslo 636, **660–64**
  Bygdøy Peninsula **664**
  climate 668
  hotels **670**
  map 660–61
  restaurants **671**
Oslo Turistinformasjon 669
Östberg, Ragnar 645
Osterfjord 666
Ostia Antica (Rome) 455
Oświęcim (Auschwitz) **757**
O'Toole, Laurence, Archbishop of
  Dublin 119
Ottica Nuova di Malizia Michela
  (Milan) 453
Otto, King of the Saxons 28
Otto I, Emperor 524
Otto I, King of Greece 470
Oude Kerk (Amsterdam) **250**
Ouranoúpoli 489
  hotels 511
Outward Bound 95
OVDS 669
Oviedo **303**
  hotels 342
  restaurants 348
OVR 265

Oxford 37, **72**
  hotels 100
  restaurants 105

P

P&O European Ferries 19, 91,
  133, 201, 237, 335
P. Kooij (Amsterdam) 267
Pacassi, Nikolaus 599
Package deals, air travel **17**
Padua **431**
  hotels 459
  restaurants 465
Pais, Gualdim 366
Palace of Culture and Science
  (Budapest) **752**
Palaces
  Amalienborg (Copenhagen) **680**
  Belvedere (Vienna) **598–9**
  Blenheim Palace **74–5**
  Buckingham Palace (London) **48**
  Château de Chambord **179**
  Château de Chenonceau **178–9**
  Château de Vaux-le-Vicomte
    170–71
  Château de Versailles **168–9**
  Christiansborg Palace
    (Copenhagen) **678–9**
  Doge's Palace (Venice) **436–7**
  Drottningholm **647**
  El Escorial **294**
  Hampton Court **63**
  Hofburg (Viena) **592–4**
  Holyrood Palace (Edinburgh) **86**
  Jagdschloss Grunewald
    (Berlin) 538
  Knossos **500**
  Kongelige Slottet (Oslo) **662**
  Koninklijk Paleis
    (Amsterdam) **252**
  Marmorpalais (Potsdam) **539**
  Neues Palais (Potsdam) 540, **541**
  Palacio Arzobispal (Seville) 328
  Palacio de Linares (Madrid) 287
  Palácio Nacional de Sintra
    (Sintra) **368–9**
  Palacio Real (Madrid) **285**
  Palais des Ducs (Dijon) 184
  Palais Royal (Brussels) **227**
  Palau Reial Major (Barcelona) **309**
  Palazzo Altemps (Rome) 403
  Palazzo Doria Pamphilj
    (Rome) **400–401**
  Palazzo Piccolomini (Siena) 409
  Palazzo Pitti (Florence) **425**
  Palazzo Vecchio (Florence) **419**
  Paleis Het Loo **261**
  Peterhof (St. Petersburg) **697**
  Praça do Comércio (Lisbon) **360**
  Real Alcázar (Seville) 329, **330**
  Residenz (Munich) **548–9**
  Royal Palace (Budapest) **734**
  Royal Palace (Prague) 712, **714**
  Royal Palace (Stockholm) **644**
  St. James's Palace (London) 51
  Schloss Cecilienhof (Potsdam) **539**
  Schloss Charlottenburg
    (Berlin) **537**
  Schloss Charlottenhof
    (Potsdam) 540, **541**
  Schloss Eggenberg 600
  Schloss Nymphenburg
    (Munich) **553**
  Schloss Sanssouci (Potsdam)

Palaces (cont.)
528, 539, **541**
Schönbrunn Palace (Vienna) **599**
Sternberg Palace (Prague) **715**
Tsarskoe Selo (St. Petersburg)
697
Wallenstein Palace (Prague)
716–17
Wilanów Palace (Budapest)
748, **753**
see also Castles
Palácio Foz (Lisbon) 360
Palacký, František 708
Palaiokastrítsa 495
Palais des Beaux-Arts
(Brussels) 239
Palais de Chaillot (Paris) **164**
Palais Constantine (Arles) 192
Palais Omnisports de Paris-Bercy
(Paris) 205
Palais des Papes (Avignon) **191**
Palais Royal (Paris) 205
Palamino, Antonio 320
Palatine (Rome) **403**
Palau de la Generalitat
(Barcelona) 308
Palau Güell (Barcelona) 310
Palau de la Música Catalana
(Barcelona) 339
Palau Reial & Museu d'Historia de
la Ciutat (Barcelona) 309
Palavobis (Milan) 455
Palazzo Pubblico (Siena) **409**
Palé Music Festival 629
Palermo **446**
hotels 461
restaurants 467
Palio (Siena) **410**
Palko, Franz 716
Palladio, Andrea 431, 441
Palma de Mallorca 319
hotels 345
restaurants 351
Pamphilj family 400–401
Pamplona **304**
hotels 342
restaurants 348
Panthéon (Paris) **157**
Pantheon (Rome) **400**
Pantokrátor, Mount 495
Panxón 302
Papal Cross (Dublin) 121
Papandréou, Andréas 471
Parade Grounds (Bath) 71
Paradise beach (Mýkonos) 496
Paradiso (Amsterdam) 267
Parága 496
Parc d'Atraccions
(Barcelona) 315
Parc Nacional d'Aigüestortes **305**
Parc Ornithologique du
Pont-du-Gau 194
Parc des Princes (Paris) 205
Paris 142, **150–71**
Baron Haussmann **164**
Eiffel Tower **163**
hotels **206–8**
Latin Quarter: Street-by-Street
map **156–7**
map 150–51
Musée du Louvre **158–60**
Notre-Dame **154–5**
restaurants **212–13**
travel 200

Parks and gardens
Blenheim Palace 74
Boboli Gardens (Florence) **425**
Bois de Boulogne (Paris) **167**
Burggarten and Volksgarten
(Vienna) **594**
Château de Chenonceau 178
Château de Fontainebleau 171
Château de Vaux-le-Vicomte 171
Château de Versailles **169**
Eighteenth-century Gardens **75**
Englischer Garten (Munich) **552–3**
Hortus Botanicus Amsterdam 255
Hyde Park (London) **54**
Jardin du Luxembourg (Paris) **157**
Jardin des Tuileries (Paris) **161**
Jardins de Trocadéro (Paris) 164
Kew Gardens (London) 63
Kungsträdgården (Stockholm) **645**
Łazienki Park (Budapest) **753**
Museo e Galleria Borghese
(Rome) 405
Parc du Cinquantenaire
(Brussels) **228–9**
Parc Güell (Barcelona) **315**
Parc de la Villette (Paris) **166**
Park Sanssouci (Potsdam) **540–41**
Parque María Luisa (Seville) **331**
Parque del Retiro (Madrid) **291**
Phoenix Park (Dublin) **121**
Planty (Cracow) **757**
Regent's Park (London) **54**
Richmond Park (London) 63
Royal Garden (Prague) **715**
Schloss Charlottenburg
(Berlin) 537
Schönbrunn Palace and Gardens
(Vienna) **599**
Tiergarten (Berlin) **531**
Tivoli Gardens (Copenhagen)
673, **677**
Vigelandsparken (Oslo) **663**
Wilanów Park (Budapest) **753**
Parler, Peter 713, 714, 722
Parliament (Budapest) 729, **737**
Parliament Quarter (Brussels) **228**
Parmigianino
Madonna of the Long Neck 424
Parnell, Charles Stewart 121
Parnell Square (Dublin) **121**
Parodi 426
Parque Nacional de Doñana **325**
Parreirinha de Alfama (Lisbon) 377
Parthenon (Athens) 479, **480**, **482–3**
Paseo del Prado (Madrid)
Street-by-Street map 286–7
Passau **555**
hotels 577
restaurants 583
Passports and visas **12**
Austria 604
Belgium and Luxembourg 236
Czech Republic 724
Denmark 684
Finland 698
France 198
Germany 566
Great Britain 88
Greece 502
Hungary 740
Ireland 132
Italy 448
Netherlands 264
Norway 668

Passports and visas (cont.)
Poland 758
Portugal 374
Russia 697
Spain 332
Sweden 652
Switzerland 626
Past Times (London) 93
Pátmos 499
Patrick, St. 110, 118, 124, 126
Pau 189
hotels 210
restaurants 216
Paul, St. 470, 490
Paul III, Pope 401
Paul, Bruno 538
Pavarotti, Luciano 54
Pearse, Patrick 120
Pécs **739**
hotels 742
Pedro I, King of Castile 330, 367
Pedro IV, King of Portugal 358
Peggy Guggenheim Collection
(Venice) **440**
Pei, I.M. 159
Peisistratos 481
Pelayo 303
Pélekas 495
Pélla, Ancient **488–9**
Peloponnese 385, **490–93**
Penyal d'Ifach 319
Penzance
restaurants 105
Pepys, Samuel 51
Pergamonmuseum (Berlin) 25, **532**
Perikles 26, 470, 478, 480
Períssa 497
Perrault, Claude 159
Persius, Ludwig 541
Perugia **407**
hotels 460
restaurants 466
Perugino
Perugia 407
Pinacoteca Nazionale (Bologna)
442
Uffizi (Florence) 424
Vatican Museums (Rome) 398
Peruzzi, Baldassare 399
Pesne, Antoine 541
Pest **736–7**
hotels 742
restaurants 743
Petaloúdes 499
Peter the Great 696–7
Peter and Paul Fortress
see SS Peter and Paul Fortress
Peter, St. 317, 394–5
Peterhof (St. Petersburg) **696–7**
Le Petit Journal St-Michel (Paris) 205
Petit Point (Vienna) 607
Petőfi, Sándor 736
Petrarch 389
Petri, Olaus 643
Pfalzgrafenstein 559
Phaestos **501**
Pharmacies
Germany 566
Greece **502**, 503
Italy 448
Portugal 374
Spain 333
Pheidias 480, 481
Philharmonic Hall (Liverpool) 95

Philharmonie (Berlin) 573
Philip II, King of Macedon 27, 469,
 470, 488, 489
Philip (Felipe) II, King of Spain 227
 coach 362
 Dutch Revolt 263
 El Escorial 294
 Madrid 284
 and the Netherlands 246
 Pamplona 304
 and Portugal 354
Philip the Bold, Duke of Burgundy
 182, 219
Philip the Good, Duke of
 Burgundy 246
Philip the Magnanimous,
 Landgrave of Hesse 534
Philippa of Lancaster 367
Philippe-Auguste, King of France
 146, 158
Phoenix Column (Dublin) 121
Phoenix Park (Dublin) **121**
Photographers' Gallery (London) 93
Photography, in Greece 503
Piaf, Edith 167
Piamonte (Madrid) 337
Piano, Renzo 31, 531
Pianta, Francesco 438
Piast dynasty 745–6
Piazza del Campo (Siena) **409**
Piazza Navona (Rome) 387, **400**
Piazza della Signoria (Florence)
 418–19
Piazzetta, Giovanni Battista 441
Picasso, Pablo 31, 57, 59, 440
 Antibes 196
 Ashmolean Museum (Oxford) 72
 Casa Natal de Picasso (Málaga) 321
 Guernica 31, 291
 Kunstmuseum (Basel) 617
 Musée de Grenoble (Grenoble) 183
 Musée de l'Orangerie (Paris) 161
 Musée Picasso (Paris) **153**
 Musée Réattu (Arles) 192
 Museu Picasso (Barcelona) **311**
 Nasjonalgalleriet (Oslo) 663
 National Gallery of Art
  (Athens) 481
 Neue Nationalgalerie (Berlin) 531
 Picasso Museum (Lucerne) 622
 Sammlung Berggruen (Berlin) 537
 Sprengel-Museum (Hanover) 564
 Staatsgalerie (Stuttgart) 557
 Statens Museum for Kunst
  (Copenhagen) 681
 Stedelijk Museum
  (Amsterdam) 259
 Sternberg Palace (Prague) 715
Piccadilly (London) **50–51**
Picos de Europa **303**
Piero della Francesca
 The Duke and Duchess of Urbino
  423, 424
 Museu Nacional de Arte Antiga
  (Lisbon) 361
 National Gallery (London) 49
 Palazzo Ducale (Urbino) 443
Pierre Cardin (Paris) 203
Pierre Marcolini (Brussels) 239
Pietà (Michelangelo) 395
La Pietà (Venice) 455
Pilatus, Mount 622
Pílio **485**
 hotels 510, 511

Pinacoteca Nazionale (Siena) **410**
Pinatothek der Moderne 546, 552
 Pinkas Synagogue (Prague) 719
Pinturicchio
 Duomo (Siena) 410
 Museo Civico
  (San Gimignano) 411
 Museo e Galleria Borghese
  (Rome) 405
 Santa Maria del Popolo
  (Rome) 405
 Vatican Museums (Rome) 396
Pisa **411**
 hotels 460
 restaurants 466
Pisanello 431
Pisano, Andrea 416
Pisano, Giovanni 411
Pisano, Nicola 410, 411, 442
Pissarro, Camille 678
Pit Stop (Tinguely) 617
Pitti, Luca 425
Place de la Bastille (Paris) **153**
Place de la Concorde (Paris) **161**
Place du Grand Sablon
 (Brussels) **227**
Place Theatre (London) 95
Place des Vosges (Paris) **153**
Placidia, Galla 443
Pláka (Athens) **477**
Pláka (Náxos) 497
Planetarium (London) **54**
Plantage (Amsterdam) **255**
Plantin, Christopher 230
Planty (Cracow) **757**
Plataniás 485
Plato 421
Platys Gialós 496
Platzer, Ignaz 716
Playfair, William Henry 85, 86
Plaza Cánovas del Castillo
 (Madrid) 286
Plaza de Cibeles (Madrid) 287
Plaza Mayor (Madrid) **284**
Plaza Santa Cruz (Seville) 329
Plaza de Toros de la Maestranza
 (Seville) **331**, 339
Plaza de Toros de las Ventas
 (Madrid) **292**, 339
Plaza del Triunfo (Seville) 328
Plaza Virgen de los Reyes
 (Seville) 328
Plaza de Zocodover (Toledo) 297
Poble Espanyol (Barcelona) 314
Poblet **305**
Point Theatre (Dublin) 135
Poitiers **176**
 hotels 209
 restaurants 215
Polak, Jan 550
Poland **745–61**
 history **745–6**
 hotels **760**
 map 747
 practical information **758–9**
 restaurants **761**
 travel **759**
 Warsaw **748–53**
Police
 Austria 605
 Belgium and Luxembourg 237
 Czech Republic 725
 Denmark 685
 Finland 699

Police (cont.)
 France 198, 199
 Germany 566
 Great Britain 88, 89
 Greece **502**, 503
 Hungary 741
 Ireland 133
 Italy **448**, 449
 Netherlands 265
 Norway 669
 Poland 759
 Portugal 375
 Spain 332
 Sweden 653
 Switzerland 627
Pollença 319
 hotels 345
 restaurants 351
Pollock, Jackson 153, 440
Pombal, Marquês de 354, 360
 Évora 372
 Lisbon earthquake 361
Pomis, Pietro de 600
Pompadour, Madame de 169
Pompeii **445**
 restaurants 467
Pompey 304
Pont du Gard (Nîmes) 190
Pont-de-Gau 194
Ponta da Piedade 373
Ponte Vecchio (Florence) **425**
Pontevedra 302
 hotels 342
 restaurants 348
Pontormo, Jacopo 415, 424
Port **371**
Porta, Giacomo della 401
Porthkerry
 hotels 99
Portimão **373**
 hotels 379
 restaurants 381
Portmeirion
 hotels 99
Porto, Luigi da 430
Portobello Road (London) **62**, 93
Portofino Peninsula **426**
 hotels 459
 restaurants 465
Portovenere 426
Portrait of a Woman (Botticelli) 560
*Portrait of a Young Man in a Red
 Hat* (Carpaccio) 438
Portree 87
Portugal **353–81**
 entertainment **376–7**
 history **353–4**
 hotels **378–9**
 landscape 22
 Lisbon **356–65**
 map 355
 practical information **374–5**
 restaurants **380–81**
 shopping **376**, 377
 Southern Portugal **372–3**
 travel **375**
Portugália 375
Positano 445
 hotels 461
 restaurants 467
Postal services *see* Mail services
Potes 303
Potsdam **539–41**
Potsdamer Platz (Berlin) **531**

Potsdamer Platz Arkaden
(Berlin) 571
Potter, Beatrix 77
Poussin, Nicolas 85, 290, 596
Praça do Comércio (Lisbon) **360**
Prado (Madrid) *see* Museo del Prado
Prague 704, 707, 709, **710–21**
climate 724
hotels **726**
Jewish Quarter **719**
Malá Strana **716–17**
map 710–11
Old and New Towns **720–21**
Old-New Synagogue **718–19**
Prague Castle: Street-by-Street
map 712–13
restaurants **727**
Prague Information Service 725
Prague Wheelchair Association 725
Praia do Camilo 373
Praia de Dona Ana 373
Praia de Oura 373
Praia da Rocha 373
Praia de São Rafael 373
Praiano 445
Prater (Vienna) **598**
Prehistoric sites
Carnac **173**
Hallstatt 602
Lascaux **188**
Mycenae **491**
Newgrange **122**
Stonehenge **65**
Přemysl Otakar II, King of
Bohemia 714
Premyslid dynasty 707
Primaticcio 171
Printemps (Paris) 203
Prinzregententheater (Munich) 573
The Procession of the Magi
(Gozzoli) 420–21
Procida 444
Prostitution
Red Light District (Amsterdam)
250–51
Provence, Comte de 157
Prunksaal (Vienna) 592
Public holidays
Switzerland 628
Pubs, Irish **135**
Puerta Antigua de Bisagra
(Toledo) **298**
Puerta del Sol (Madrid) **284**
Puerto de Alcalá (Madrid) 287
El Puerto de Sta María
hotels 344
Puget, Pierre 160
Puig i Cadafalch, Josep 311
Pulteney Bridge (Bath) 71
Pump Rooms (Bath) 70
Punta Chiappa 426
Pyrenees **189**
Pyrgos Diroú 492

Q

Qantas 91, 201, 451, 569
Quadrat d'Or (Barcelona) **311**
Quarton, Enguerrand 160
Quasimodo (Berlin) 573
Quattro Prigioni (Michelangelo)
415, 421
Queen's Chapel (London) 51
Queen's Gallery (London) 48

Queen's House (London) 62
Quellien, Artus 252
Quercia, Jacopo della 408, 409, 442

R

RADAR 89
Rådhus (Oslo) **662**
Rådhuset (Copenhagen) **678**
Radio Taxi 451
Raeburn, Henry 85
Rail Europe 18, 91, 201, 505
Rail travel **18**
Austria **604**
Belgium and Luxembourg **237**
Czech Republic **725**
Denmark **685**
Finland **699**
France **200–201**
Germany **569**
Great Britain **90–91**
Greece **504**, 505
Hungary **741**
Ireland **133**
Italy **450**, 451
map *inside back cover*
Netherlands **265**
Norway **669**
Poland **759**
Portugal **375**
Spain **334–5**
Sweden **653**
Switzerland **626–7**
Raimund Theater (Vienna) 607
Rainaldi, Carlo 400, 401
Rainaldi, Girolamo 400, 401
Raiteneau, Wolf Dietrich von,
Archbishop of Salzburg
602, 603
Las Ramblas (Barcelona) **310**
Ramblers Holidays 507
Ramiro I, King of Aragón 303
Ramsay, Allan 85
Ranc, Jean 290
Rapallo 426
Raphael 29, 85, 421, 442
Alte Pinakothek (Munich) 551
Ashmolean Museum (Oxford) 72
birthplace 443
*Expulsion of Heliodorus from the
Temple* 396
Gemäldegalerie (Berlin) 531
Gemäldegalerie Alte Meister
(Dresden) 542
Madonna of the Goldfinch 424
Museo di Capodimonte
(Naples) 444
Museo del Prado (Madrid) 290
Museu Nacional de Arte Antiga
(Lisbon) 361
Museum of Fine Arts
(Budapest) 737
Orangerie (Potsdam) 541
Palazzo Pitti (Florence) 425
Pantheon (Rome) 400
Pinacoteca di Brera (Milan) 428–9
Santa Maria del Popolo
(Rome) 405
Vatican Museums (Rome)
396, **398**
Villa Farnesina (Rome) 399
Raschdorff, Julius 534
Rasmussen, Louise 679
Rasper & Söhne (Vienna) 607
Rastrelli 695

El Rastro (Madrid) **285**, 337
Rättvik 649
Rauhalinna Villa 697
Rauschenberg, Robert 646
Ravello 445
Ravenna **443**
hotels 460
restaurants 466
Ravy, Jean 155
Ray, Man 259
Real Alcázar (Seville) 329, **330**
Real Federación Española
de Golf 339
Real Federación Española
de Tenis 339
Real Federación Española
de Vela 339
Réattu, Jacques 192
Rebull, Joan
Three Gypsy Boys 308
Red Light District
(Amsterdam) **250–51**
Reformation 146, 524
Regent's Park (London) **54**
Rehn, Jean Eric 647
Reichstadt, Duke of 599
Reichstag (Berlin) **530**
Reims **172**
hotels 208
restaurants 214
Reisebüro Mondial (Vienna) 607
Reitschule (Bern) 629
Religion
Early Celtic Christianity **124–5**
Spain 279
The Miracle of Lourdes **189**
Vikings 665
Rembrandt 29, 49
Alte Pinakothek (Munich) 551
Amsterdams Historisch
Museum 252, 253
Ashmolean Museum (Oxford) 72
Czartoryski Museum (Cracow) 757
Gemäldegalerie (Berlin) 531
Gemäldegalerie Alte Meister
(Dresden) 542
The Jewish Bride 258
Kelvingrove Art Gallery
(Glasgow) 80
Kunsthistorisches Museum
(Vienna) 596
Mauritshuis (The Hague) 262
Museo del Prado (Madrid) 290
Museu Calouste Gulbenkian
(Lisbon) 361
Musée du Louvre (Paris) 160
Museum Boijmans-van
Beuningen (Rotterdam) 263
Museum Het Rembrandthuis
(Amsterdam) **251**
National Gallery of Art (Athens) 481
National Gallery of Scotland
(Edinburgh) 85
Nationalmuseum (Stockholm) 645
Niedersächsisches
Landesmuseum (Hanover) 564
The Night Watch 257
Rijksmuseum (Amsterdam) 258
St. Paul in Prison 556
Staatsgalerie (Stuttgart) 557
Städelsches Kunstinstitut
(Frankfurt) 560
Statens Museum for Kunst
(Copenhagen) 681

Rembrandt (cont.)
  Sternberg Palace (Prague) 715
  Uffizi (Florence) 424
Rempétiki Istoria (Athens) 507
Remu'h, Rabbi Moses 757
Renaissance, Florentine **420–21**
RENFE 335
Reni, Guido 541
Rennen, Peter von der 755
Renoir, Pierre Auguste 30
  Musée des Beaux Arts (Nice) 197
  Musée de l'Orangerie (Paris) 161
  Musée d'Orsay (Paris) 162
  Musée Picasso (Paris) 153
  Museu Calouste Gulbenkian
   (Lisbon) 361
  National Gallery (London) 49
Rental, car **19**
Residenz (Munich) **548–9**
Restaurants
  Austria **610–11**
  Belgium and Luxembourg **242–3**
  Czech Republic **727**
  Denmark **687**
  Finland **701**
  France **212–17**
  Germany **580–85**
  Great Britain **102–7**
  Greece **514–17**
  Hungary **743**
  Ireland **138–9**
  Italy **462–7**
  Netherlands **270–71**
  Norway **671**
  Poland **761**
  Portugal **380–81**
  Spain **346–51**
  St. Petersburg **701**
  Sweden **655**
  Switzerland **632–3**
  see also Food and drink
Réthymno **501**
  hotels 513
  restaurants 517
Reynolds, Sir Joshua 85, 160
Rhine Valley 520, 558, **559**
Rhodes **498–9**
  hotels **513**
  restaurants 517
Rías Baixas **302**
Ribera, José de
  The Martyrdom of St. Philip 289
  Monasterio de las Descalzas
   Reales (Madrid) 285
  Museo de Bellas Artes
   (Málaga) 321
  Museo del Prado (Madrid) 290
Richard I the Lionheart, King of
  England 44, 176, 177
Richard III, King of England 61
Richelieu, Cardinal 153
Richmond (Greater London) **63**
Riddarholmskyrkan (Stockholm) **644**
Ridley, Bishop 72
Ried, Benedikt 714
Riemenschneider, Tilman
  Bayerisches Nationalmuseum
   (Munich) 552
  Germanisches Nationalmuseum
   (Nuremberg) 545
  Kunsthistorisches Museum
   (Vienna) 596
  Madonna 25
  Würzburg 544

Rietveld, Gerrit 261
Rigaud, Hyacinthe 169
Rigi, Mount 622
Rijksmuseum (Amsterdam) 24,
  256–8
La Rinascente 453
Ring of Kerry 127
Riofrío 294
Rítsos, Giánnis 492
Riviera **196–7**
Rivièra Maison (Amsterdam) 267
Rizzio, David 86
Roads *see* Car travel
Robbia, Luca della 418
Robert the Bruce 38, 81
Roberts, John 123
Roberts, Julia 62
Robespierre, Maximilien de 161, 188
Robinson, Sir William 118
Roche, Otto de la 484
Rock of Cashel 109, **126**
Rock music
  Belgium and Luxembourg **239**
  Germany **572–3**
Rodin, Auguste
  The Burghers of Calais 44
  The Kiss 162
  Musée Calvet (Avignon) 191
  Musée Rodin (Paris) **162**
  Museum der Bildenden Künste
   (Leipzig) 543
  Victoria and Albert Museum
   (London) 57
Roentgen, David 597
Roger, King of Naples 445
Rogers, Richard 31
Roldán, Pedro 330
Roman remains
  Ancient Corinth **490**
  Ancient Rome **402–3**
  Arles 193
  Barcelona 308
  Nîmes 190
  Pompeii **445**
  Roman Baths (Bath) 71
  Roman Forum (Rome) 392, **402**
  Tarragona 305
Romanós, Emperor 484
Rome 384, 387, **392–405**
  Ancient Rome **402–3**
  climate 13, 448
  hotels **456–7**
  map 392–3
  restaurants **462–3**
  St. Peter's **394–5**
  transport 387
  Vatican Museums **396–8**
Römische Bäder (Potsdam) 540
Romney, George 75
Romulus and Remus 403, 408
Ronda **324**
  hotels 345
  restaurants 351
Roos, Fredrik 651
Roselli 398
Rosenborg Slot (Copenhagen) **681**
Roskilde **682**
Roslin, Alexander 645
Rossellino 418
Rossi, Carlo 696
Rossi, Vincenzo de' 425
Rothenburg ob der Tauber **545**
  hotels 577
  restaurants 583

Rothiemurchus Estate 87
Rothko, Mark 617
Rothschild, Baron Ferdinand 52
Rottaler, Lukas 550
Rotterdam **263**
  hotels 269
  restaurants 271
Rottmayr, Johann Michael 597, 599
Rotunda Hospital (Dublin) 121
Rouen **172–3**
  hotels 208
  restaurants 214
Rousánou (Metéora) 486
Rousseau, Henri Le Douanier 49,
  153, 161
Rousseau, Jean Jacques 146, 157
Royal Academy (London) **50**, 51
Royal Albert Hall (London) 55, 95
Royal Castle (Cracow) **755**
Royal Castle (Warsaw) **750**
Royal College of Music (London) 55
Royal Crescent (Bath) 70
Royal Exchange (Manchester) 95
Royal Festival Hall (London) 95
Royal Garden (Prague) **715**
Royal Mile (Edinburgh) **84–5**
Royal Museum (Edinburgh) **85**
Royal Naval College (London) 62
Royal Observatory Greenwich
  (London) **62**
Royal Opera House (London) 51, 95
Royal Palace (Budapest) **734**
Royal Palace (Prague) 712, **714**
Royal Palace (Stockholm) **644**
Royal Route (Warsaw) **751**
Royal Shakespeare Theatre
  (Stratford-upon-Avon) 95
Royal Tara China 135
Rubens, Peter Paul 220
  Alte Pinakothek (Munich) 551
  Antwerp 230
  *The Assumption of the
   Virgin* 226–7
  Banqueting House (London) 45
  Cologne 561
  Kunsthistorisches Museum
   (Vienna) 596
  Musée Royaux des Beaux-Arts
   (Brussels) 226–7
  Museo del Prado (Madrid) 290
  Museo Thyssen-Bornemisza
   (Madrid) 291
  Royal Palace (Stockholm) 644
  The Three Graces 288
  Uffizi (Florence) 424
  Weimar Schloss 543
Rudniev, Lev 752
Rudolf I, Emperor 588
Rudolf II, Emperor 596
  Czech Republic 708
  Prague 712, 714, 715
Rue Verrerie (Dijon) 185
Ruisdael, Jacob van 258
Rumford, Count von 552
Ruprecht I, Count Palatine 557
Russian Museum (St. Petersburg)
  696
Russian Orthodox Church
  Uspenski Cathedral (Helsinki) **693**
Ruysbroeck, Jan van 225
Ruyter, Admiral Michiel de 252
Ryanair 17, 91, 133, 201, 335, 451,
  569, 605, 653
Rynhart, Jean 117

S

S-tog Information 685
Sabartes, Jaime 311
Sacré-Coeur (Paris) 166
Sadler's Wells (London) 95
Saenredam, Pieter 258
Safety *see* Security, personal
Sagnier, Enric 315
Sagrada Família (Barcelona)
  275, **312–13**
Sagres 373
Saimaa, Lake 691
St. Andrews **81**
  restaurants 107
St. Ann's Church (Dublin) 114
St. Anna's Church (Warsaw) **751**
St-Bertrand-de-Comminges 189
St. Blasien 556
Sainte-Chapelle (Paris) **152**
St. Elizabeth's Day Flood 256
St. Francis (Cimabue) 406
St. George's Basilica (Prague) 713
St. George's Convent
  (Prague) 713, **714**
St-Germain-des-Prés (Paris) **157**
St. Goar 559
St. Isaac's Cathedral (St.
  Petersburg) **696**
St. Ives 68
  hotels 99
  restaurants 105
St. James Church (London) 50
St. James's Palace (London) 51
St. Janshospitaal (Bruges) 232
St-Jean-Cap-Ferrat
  hotels 211
St-Jean-de-Luz 189
  hotels 210
St-Julien-le-Pauvre (Paris) 157
St. John's Cathedral (Warsaw) **750**
St-Malo **173**
  hotels 208
  restaurants 214
St. Margaret's Church (London) 44
Saintes-Maries-de-la-Mer 194
St. Mark's (Venice) **434–5**
St. Martin-in-the-Fields
  (London) 37, 50
St. Martin's Theatre (London) 51
St. Mary's Church (Cracow) **756**
St. Michael's Mount 68
St-Michel (Dijon) 185
St. Olave's Church (York) 78
St. Patrick's Cathedral
  (Dublin) **118–19**
St. Paul in Prison (Rembrandt) 556
St. Paul's Cathedral (London) **58**
St. Paul's Church, Covent Garden
  (London) 51
St. Peter's (Rome) **394–5**
St. Petersburg (Russia) **696–7**
  hotels 700
  restaurants701
St-Raphaël 196
St-Séverin (Paris) 156
St. Simeon (Brandl) 714
St. Stephen's Basilica
  (Budapest) **736–7**
St. Stephen's Green (Dublin) 114
St-Tropez 196
  hotels 211
St. Vitus's Cathedral (Prague) 712,
  713

Salamanca **295**
  hotels 344
  restaurants 349
Salazar, António 354, 359
Salisbury **65**
  restaurants 104
Salle Pleyel (Paris) 205
Salò 429
Salón de Reinos 287
Salonica *see* Thessaloníki
Salvi, Nicola 404
Salzburg 520, **602–3**
  hotels 609
  restaurants 611
Salzburg Festival 607
Salzkammergut 602
Samariá Gorge **501**
La Samaritaine (Paris) 203
Sambin, Hugues 184
Sami 689–90
Sammlung alter Musikinstrumente
  (Vienna) 594
Sammlung Berggruen (Berlin) **537**
San Domenico (Siena) **410**
San Gimignano **411**
  hotels 460
  restaurants 466
San Lorenzo (Florence) **414**
San Lorenzo de El Escorial
  hotels 344
  restaurants 349
San Marco (Florence) **415**
San Sebastián **304**
  hotels 343
  restaurants 348
San Siro (Milan) 455
Sancha, Doña 292
Sansovino 436
Santa Apolónia station (Lisbon) 375
Santa Croce (Florence) **418**
Sant Francesc 319
Santa Francesca Romana (Rome) 402
Santi Giovanni e Paolo (Venice) **439**
Santa Margherita Ligure 426
Santa Maria Capua Vetere 444
Santa Maria Gloriosa dei Frari
  (Venice) **438–9**
Santa Maria Maggiore (Rome) **404**
Santa Maria Novella (Florence) **414**
Santa Maria del Popolo (Rome) **405**
Santa Maria della Salute
  (Venice) **440**
Santa Maria in Trastevere
  (Rome) **399**
Santander **303**
  hotels 343
  restaurants 348
Santiago de Compostela **302**
  hotels 343
  restaurants 348
Santoríni **497**
  hotels 512
  restaurants 517
Sanxenxo 302
São Roque (Lisbon) 361
São Vicente de Fora (Lisbon) **358**
El Sardinero 303
Sartre, Jean-Paul 157
SAS 17, 653, 669, 685
Sasso del Madonna 625
SATA 373
Sattler, Christopher 531
Saturn Devouring One of his Sons
  (Goya) 24

Sauer, Wilhelm 534
Saunas **698**, 699
Savonarola, Girolamo 415, 421
Savonlinna **695**
  hotels 700
  restaurants 701
Savoy, Dukes of 617
Scaglieri family 430
Scamozzi, Vincenzo 431
Scandinavia **635–701**
  Denmark **673–87**
  Finland **689–701**
  map 636–7
  Norway **657–71**
  Sweden **639–55**
Scandinavian Seaways 653
Scarpagnino 438
Schadow, Johann Gottfried 530
Schangau im Emmental
  hotels 630
Scharoun, Hans 531, 557
Schatzkammer (Vienna) 592, **594**
Schauspielfrankfurt (Frankfurt) 573
Lo Scheggia
  Cassone Adimari 415
Scheveningen 262
  restaurants 271
Schiele, Egon 601, 723
Schiller, Johann Christoph Friedrich
  von 524, 525, 543
Schilthorn 618
Schinkel, Karl Friedrich 532, 537
  Altes Museum (Berlin) 532
  Berliner Dom (Berlin) 534
  Galerie der Romantik (Berlin) 537
  Schloss Charlottenhof (Berlin) 541
Schloss Augarten (Vienna) 607
Schloss Cecilienhof
  (Potsdam) **539**
Schloss Charlottenburg (Berlin) **537**
Schloss Charlottenhof
  (Potsdam) 540, **541**
Schloss Eggenberg 600
Schloss Nymphenburg (Munich) **553**
Schloss Sanssouci (Potsdam)
  528, 539, **541**
Schloss Stolzenfels 559
Schlot (Berlin) 573
Schlüter, Andreas 535
Schmidt-Rottluff, Karl 531
Schnitger, Arp 565
Schönbrunn Palace and Gardens
  (Vienna) **599**
Schönbühel 601
Schott, Walter 534
Schubert, Franz 589, 594
Schuch, Jan 753
Schultz, Karol 753
Schulz, Josef 721
Schumann, Robert 525
Schützen im Gebirge
  restaurants 611
Schweizer Heimatwerk 629
Schweizertor (Vienna) 593
Schwyz 622
Science Museum (London) 55, **56**
Scorel, Jan van 258, 261
The Scotch House (London) 93
Scotland **80–87**
  Edinburgh **82–6**
  hotels **101**
  maps 34–5, 40
  restaurants **107**
  Tourist Board 89

Scott, Sir Giles Gilbert 59, 76
Scott, Sir Walter 84, 86
Scottish Citylink 91
Scottish Gallery (Edinburgh) 93
Scottish National Portrait Gallery
    (Edinburgh) 86
Scuola di San Giorgio degli
    Schiavoni (Venice) 440
Scuola Grande di San Rocco
    (Venice) 438
Sé (Lisbon) 359
Sea travel see Ferries
Sebastião, King of Portugal 354, 365
Secession 589, 597
Secession Building (Vienna) 597
Security, personal 13
    Austria 604
    Belgium and Luxembourg 236
    Czech Republic 724
    Denmark 684
    Finland 698
    France 198
    Germany 566
    Great Britain 88
    Greece 502
    Hungary 740
    Ireland 132
    Italy 448
    Netherlands 264
    Norway 668
    Poland 758
    Portugal 374
    Spain 332
    Sweden 652
    Switzerland 626
Sederholm House (Helsinki) 693
Segovia 294
    hotels 344
    restaurants 349
Seidel, Gabriel von 552
Seion Llanddeiniolen
    hotels 99
Selfridges (London) 93
Semper, Gottfried 595
Senate Square (Helsinki) 693
Serpotta, Giacomo 447
Sert, Josep Lluís 314
Sert, Josep Maria 304
Seurat, Georges
    Bathers at Asnières 49
Severus, Septimius, Emperor 402
Sévigné, Madame de 153
Seville 274, 328–31
    climate 332
    hotels 345
    restaurants 351
    Street-by-Street map 328–9
    tourist office 333
Sforza, Francesco 428
Sforza family 428
Shaftesbury, Earl of 50
Shakespeare, William 39, 430, 682
    Shakespeare's Globe (London) 59
    Stratford-upon-Avon 73
    Westminster Abbey (London) 47
Shaw, George Bernard 53, 117
Shelbourne Hotel (Dublin) 115
Shopping
    Austria 606, 607
    Belgium and Luxembourg
        238, 239
    France 202–3
    Germany 570–71
    Great Britain 92–3

Shopping (cont.)
    Greece 506, 507
    Ireland 134, 135
    Italy 452–3
    Netherlands 266, 267
    Portugal 376, 377
    Spain 336–7
    Switzerland 628, 629
Shrewsbury, Bess of Hardwick,
    Countess of 75
Le Shuttle 18
Sibelius, Jean 690
Siberië (Amsterdam) 267
Sicily 446–7
    hotels 461
    restaurants 467
Sidári 495
Siegfried, Count 220
Siena 408–10
    hotels 460–61
    Palio 410
    restaurants 466
    Street-by-Street map 408–9
Sienkiewicz, Henryk 750
Signorelli, Luca 398
Signoret, Simone 167
Silbermann, Gottfried 542
Silja Line 653, 699
Siloé, Diego de 300, 321
Siloé, Gil de 299, 300
Silves 373
Silvia, Queen of Sweden 644
Simone Martini 406, 410
Sinagoga del Tránsito (Toledo) 298
Sinn Fein 120
Sintra 355, 366
    hotels 379
    Palácio Nacional de Sintra 368–9
    restaurants 381
Siófok 738
Siracusa
    restaurants 467
Sirmione 429
Sisley, Alfred 161, 197, 678
Sistine Chapel (Rome) 398
Sita 451
Sixt Rent-a-Car 375, 451, 569
Sixtus IV, Pope 396, 398, 405
Skansen (Stockholm) 646
Ski Club of Great Britain 95, 629
Škréta, Karel 714
Sky Road 129
Skye, Isle of see Isle of Skye
Slacker Crucifix (Stoss) 756
Slavata, Vilém 713
Sloane, Sir Hans 52
Smirke, Robert 52
Smyth, Edward 120
Smyth's Irish Linen 135
SNCF 201
Snowdonia 69
Società Dante Alighieri 455
Sodoma 410
Sognefjord 667
Soirée bei Prinz Orlofsky
    (Schönbrunn) 607
Solari, Santino 603
Sombrerería Hermanos de J.
    Russi (Córdoba) 337
Sonogno 625
Sophie Charlotte, Electress
    of Brandenburg 537
Sophie Charlotte, Queen of
    Prussia 535

Sorbon, Robert de 157
La Sorbonne (Paris) 157
Sorolla, Joaquín 290
Sorrento 445
Sotogrande 321
Soubirous, Bernadette 189
Soúnio 484
    hotels 511
South African Embassy
    Germany 567
South Kensington (London)
    Street-by-Street map 55
Southey, Robert 77
Southwark (London) 58–9
Soutine, Chaim 161
Souvenirs see Shopping
Spain 277–351
    The Art of Bullfighting 293
    Catalonia 305–17
    Central Spain 294–301
    distance chart 281
    Eastern Spain and the Balearic
        Islands 318–19
    entertainment 338–9
    history 277–9
    hotels 340–45
    Madrid 282–93
    map 280–81
    Moorish Spain 321
    Northern Spain 302–4
    practical information 332–3
    restaurants 346–51
    shopping 336–7
    Southern Spain 320–31
    travel 334–5
Spanair 335
Spanish Steps (Rome) 393, 404
Special interest vacations
    France 205
    Great Britain 95
    Greece 507
    Italy 455
Specialty stores
    Spain 336
Spedale degli Innocenti
    (Florence) 421
Spencer House (London) 51
Špillar, Karel 721
Sports
    Austria 607
    France 205
    Germany 573
    Great Britain 95
    Greece 507
    Italy 455
    Portugal 377
    Switzerland 629
    Belgium and Luxembourg 239
    France 205
    Germany 573
    Great Britain 95
    Greece 507
    Ireland 135
    Spain 339
Sprecklesen, Otto von 167
SS Peter and Paul Fortress (St.
    Petersburg) 697
STA Travel 17
Staatliche Porzellanmanufaktur
    (Meissen) 571
Staatsoper (Berlin) 573
Staatsoper (Vienna) 587, 595
Stade de France (Paris) 205
Stadhuis (Bruges) 232

Stadshuset (Stockholm) 642, **644–5**
Stadsschouwburg (Amsterdam) 267
Stadtmuseum (Munich) **550**
Staël, Madame de 616
Stained glass
   Chartres Cathedral 181
Stanisław, St. 755
Stanisław August Poniatowski,
   King of Poland 750, 753, 755
State Apartments (Vienna) 593, **594**
State Opera House (Budapest) **736**
Statens Museum for Kunst
   (Copenhagen) **681**
Stavanger **666**
   hotels 670
   restaurants 671
Stávros Melissinós (Athens) 507
Stedelijk Museum
   (Amsterdam) **259**
Steen, Jan 258, 262
   Woman at her Toilet 257
Stefan Batory, King of Poland 755
Stein-am-Rhein 623
Stemnitsa
   hotels 511
Sten Sture the Elder 643
Stena Line 265, 653
Stena Sealink Line 133
Stephansdom (Vienna) **595**
Stephenson, George 30
Sternberg, Franz Josef 715
Sternberg Palace (Prague) **715**
Stevenson, Robert Louis 84
De Stijl 259, 261, 262
Stirling **81**
   restaurants 107
Stockholm 637, 639, **642–7**
   climate 652
   hotels **654**
   map 642–3
   restaurants **655**
   tourist office 653
   travel **653**
Stoeltie Diamonds (Amsterdam) 267
Stonehenge **65**
Stoppard, Tom 39
Storkyrkan (Stockholm) **643**
Stoss, Veit 745, 755
   Slacker Crucifix 756
Stoúpa 492
Stoúpa 492
Strachan, Douglas 81
Strasbourg **172**
   hotels 208–9
   restaurants 214
Stratford-upon-Avon **73**
   hotels 100
   restaurants 105–6
Strauss, Johann 589
Strauss, Richard 542
Street, George 119
Stresa 429
Strindberg, August 647
Strøget (Copenhagen) **679**
Strömma Kanalbolaget 653
Strongbow (Richard de Clare) 119
Stubbs, George 48
Stüler, Friedrich August 535, 645
Stupinigi 427
Stureplan and Sturegallerian
   (Stockholm) **645**
Stuttgart **556–7**
   hotels 577
   restaurants 583
   tourist office 567

Subirachs, Josep Maria 312
Subways
   Germany 569
   Italy 450
Suleimann the Magnificent, Sultan 498
Sully, Bishop de 154
Sundborn 639, 649
Suomalainen, Timo and
   Tuomo 694
Suomenlinna Island Fortress
   (Helsinki) **695**
Super Paradise beach
   (Mýkonos) 496
Superfast Ferries (Athens) 505
Surrealism 227
Swan Hellenic Cruises 507
Sweden **639–55**
   history **639–40**
   hotels **654**
   map 641
   practical information **652–3**
   restaurants **655**
   Stockholm **642–7**
   travel **652–3**
Swedish Travel & Tourism
   Council 653
Swift, Jonathan 119
Swiss Alpine Club 629
Swiss Federal Railways 627
Swiss Hiking Federation 629
Swiss International Airlines 627
Swiss National Park **624**
Switzerland **613–33**
   Alps **620–21**
   entertainment **628–9**
   history **613–15**
   hotels **630–31**
   landscape 23
   maps 520–21, 614–15
   practical information **626–7**
   restaurants **632–3**
   shopping **628**, 629
   travel **626–7**
Symphony Hall (Birmingham) 95
Synagogues
   Centrum Judaicum & Neue
      Synagoge (Berlin) **533**
   Old-New Synagogue (Prague)
      718–19
   Old Synagogue (Cracow) **757**
Syon House (London) 63
Syracuse **447**
Széchényi, Count Ferenc 736
Székely, Bertalan 734
Szentendre **738**
Szépasszony Valley 739

T

't Doktertje (Amsterdam) 267
Táborsky, Jan 720
The Taking of Christ
   (Caravaggio) 117
Taksími (Athens) 507
Taller del Moro (Toledo) 296
Talloires 183
Taormina **446**
   hotels 461
   restaurants 467
TAP Air Portugal 375
Tapas **325**
Tàpies, Antoni
   Fundació Tàpies
      (Barcelona) 311

Tarragona **305**
   hotels 343
   restaurants 349
Tasting Places 455
Tate, Sir Henry 48
Tate Britain (London) **48–9**
Tate Modern (London) 42, **59**
Taxes, sales **13**
   France 203
   Norway 668
   Portugal 376
Taxis
   Denmark **685**
   Finland **699**
   Ireland **133**
   Italy 451
   Norway **669**
   Switzerland 627
Taÿgetos, Mount 492
Teatre Nacional de Catalunya
   (Barcelona) 339
Teatro Albéniz (Madrid) 339
Teatro de la Comedia (Madrid) 339
Teatro María Guerrero (Madrid) 339
Teatro Muñoz Seca (Madrid) 339
Teatro Nacional Dona Maria II
   (Lisbon) 377
Teatro Nacional de São Carlos
   (Lisbon) 377
Teatro dell'Opera (Rome) 455
Teatro Príncipe - Palacio de las
   Variedades (Madrid) 339
Teatro Real de Madrid 339
Teatro Reina Victoria (Madrid) 339
Teatro San Carlo (Naples) 455
Teatro alla Scala (Milan) 455
Teatro de la Zarzuela (Madrid) 339
TEC 237
Tel-Entrada (Madrid) 339
Telephones **14**
   Austria 604
   Belgium and Luxembourg 236
   Czech Republic 724
   Denmark 684
   Finland 698
   France 199
   Germany 567
   Great Britain 89
   Greece 503
   Hungary 740–41
   Ireland 132
   Italy 449
   Netherlands 264
   Norway 668
   Poland 758
   Portugal 375
   Spain 333
   Sweden 652
   Switzerland 626
Temple, Sir William 118
Temple Bar (Dublin) **118**
Temples
   Greek temple architecture **482–3**
   Parthenon (Athens) 479, **480**,
      482–3
   Temple Expiatori del Sagrat Cor
      (Barcelona) 315
   Temple of Olympian Zeus
      (Athens) **481**
   Temple of Romulus (Rome)
      402
   Temple of Venus and Rome
      (Rome) 402
   Temple of Vesta (Rome) 402

Temples (cont.)
Temples of the Forum Boarium
(Rome) 403
Temppeliaukio Church
(Helsinki) **694**
Tennis
Portugal **377**
ter Borch, Gerard 257
Teresa, Mother 662
Teresa, St. 295
Tessin, Nicodemus the Elder 647
Tessin, Nicodemus the Younger
643, 644, 647
TEYCI (Madrid) 339
TFDS 669
Thalys 237, 265
Theater
Austria **606**, 607
Burgtheater (Vienna) **595**
France **204**, 205
Germany **572**, 573
Grand Theater (Warsaw) **751**
Great Britain **94**, 95
Greece **506**, 507
Mariinskiy Theater (St.
Petersburg) **697**
National Theater (Prague) **721**
Nationaltheatret (Oslo) **662**
Portugal **377**
Shakespeare's Globe (London) **59**
Spain **338**, 339
Switzerland **629**
Theater an der Wien (Vienna) 607
Theater Bellevue (Amsterdam) 267
Théâtre Antique (Arles) 193
Théâtre de l'Usine (Geneva) 629
Théâtre Municipal (Luxembourg
City) 239
Théâtre National de Chaillot
(Paris) 205
Théâtre National de la Colline
(Paris) 205
Theatre Royal (Bristol) 95
Theatre Royal (London) 51
Theme parks
Bruparck (Brussels) **229**
Disneyland Paris, **170**
Legoland **683**
Moominworld (Turku) 695
Theodoric, Master 722
Theodoric the Ostrogoth 27
Theodosius I, Emperor 493
Thessaloníki **488**
hotels 511
restaurants 516
Thienen, Jacques van 225
Thierry, Alexandre 163
Thíra, Ancient 497
Thomas Cook 199
Thomond, Earls of 128
Thornhill, Sir James 58, 75
Thorvaldsen, Bertel
Thorvaldsen's Museum
(Copenhagen) 679
The Three Graces (Rubens) 288
Three Gypsy Boys (Rebull) 308
Thurman, Uma 196
Thyssen-Bornemisza, Baron
Heinrich 291
Tibaldi 294
Tibidabo (Barcelona) **315**
Ticino **625**
hotels **631**
restaurants **633**

Ticketcorner (Zürich) 629
Tiepolo, Giambattista 290, 441, 544
Tiergarten (Berlin) **531**
Tigkáki 499
Tihany Peninsula 738
Tijou, Jean 58
Tiles, *azulejos* **368**
Tilgner, Viktor 593
Time zones **12**
Tinguely, Jean 259
Pit Stop 617
Tintoretto, Jacopo
Accademia (Venice) 441
Alte Pinakothek (Munich) 551
Capitoline Museums (Rome) 401
Doge's Palace (Venice) 437
Flight into Egypt 438
Kunsthistorisches Museum
(Vienna) 596
Museo del Prado (Madrid) 290
National Gallery of Scotland
(Edinburgh) 85
Scuola Grande di San Rocco
(Venice) 438
Scuola di San Giorgio degli
Schiavoni (Venice) 440
Tipping, Italy 449
Titian (Tiziano)
Alte Pinakothek (Munich) 551
Assumption of the Virgin 439
Capitoline Museums (Rome) 401
Duomo (Verona) 431
Fitzwilliam Museum
(Cambridge) 73
Gemäldegalerie Alte Meister
(Dresden) 542
Kunsthistorisches Museum
(Vienna) 596
Monasterio de las Descalzas
Reales (Madrid) 285
Museo di Capodimonte
(Naples) 444
Museo e Galleria Borghese
(Rome) 405
Museo del Prado (Madrid) 290
Museo Thyssen-Bornemisza
(Madrid) 291
National Gallery of Scotland
(Edinburgh) 85
Palazzo Pitti (Florence) 425
Scuola di San Giorgio degli
Schiavoni (Venice) 440
Statens Museum for Kunst
(Copenhagen) 681
Vatican Museums (Rome) 398
The Venus of Urbino 422, 424
Titus, Emperor 402
Tivoli Gardens (Copenhagen)
673, **677**
Todtmoos 556
Todtnau 556
Tokaj **739**
Toledo 274, **296–8**
hotels 344
restaurants 350
Street-by-Street map 296–7
Tomar **366–7**
restaurants 381
Tomé, Narciso 298
Torino *see* Turin
Torquay
restaurants 105
Torquemada, Tomás de 295
Torre de Belém (Lisbon) **363**

Torre del Oro (Seville) **330–31**
Torremolinos 321
hotels 345
restaurants 351
Torrevieja 319
Torriti, Jacopo 404
Toulouse **188–9**
hotels 210
restaurants 216–17
Toulouse-Lautrec, Henri de 737
TourExpert 699
Tourinform Budapest 741
Tourist offices
Austria **604**, 605
Belgium and Luxembourg
236, 237
Czech Republic **724**, 725
Denmark **684**, 685
Finland **698**, 699
France **198**, 199
Germany **567**
Great Britain **88**, 89
Greece **502**, 503
Hungary **740**, 741
Ireland **132**, 133
Italy **448–9**
Netherlands **264**, 265
Norway **668**, 669
Poland **758**, 759
Portugal **374**, 375
Spain **332**, 333
Sweden **652**, 653
Switzerland **626**, 627
Touristik Union International
(TUI) 567
Tours **177**
hotels 209
restaurants 215
The Tower of Babel (Brueghel) 263
Tower Bridge (London) **59**
Tower of London (London) **60–61**
Trafalgar Square (London) **50**
Tragicomica (Venice) 453
Trailfinders 17
Trains *see* Rail travel
Trajan, Emperor 27, 403
Trajan's Column (Rome) 402
Trajan's Markets (Rome) **402**
Trams
Germany 569
Italy 450
Trasmediterránea 335
Travel **16–19**
Austria **604**
Belgium and Luxembourg **237**
Czech Republic **724–5**
Denmark **684–5**
Finland **698–9**
France **200–201**
Germany **568–9**
Great Britain **90–91**
Greece **504–5**
Hungary **741**
Ireland **132–3**
Italy **450–51**
Netherlands **264–5**
Norway **668–9**
Poland **759**
Portugal **375**
Spain **334–5**
St. Petersburg 697
Sweden **652–3**
Switzerland **626–7**
Travel agents, air travel 17

Travers (Brussels) 239
Traverse (Edinburgh) 95
Tre Kronor Museum
  (Stockholm) 644
Trekking Hellas 507
Tremezzo 429
Trevi Fountain (Rome) **404**
Trier **558**
  hotels 578
  restaurants 584
Trinity College (Dublin) 115, **116**
Tristán, Luis 298
The Triumph of Bacchus
  (Velázquez) 288
Triumph of Faith over Heresy
  (Legros) 401
Troger, Paul 599
Troldhaugen 666, 667
Tromsø **667**
  hotels 670
Trondheim **667**
  hotels 670
  restaurants 671
Troost, Cornelis 258
Troupákis family 492
Truro 68
Tsarskoe Selo (St. Petersburg)
  696–7
Tschumi, Bernard 166
Tsiliví 495
Tunnel Club (Athens) 507
Tura, Cosmè 442
Turin **427**
  hotels 459
  restaurants 465
Turin Shroud **427**
Turku **695**
  hotels 700
  restaurants 701
Turner, J.M.W.
  Ashmolean Museum (Oxford) 72
  Musée du Louvre (Paris) 160
  Museu Calouste Gulbenkian
    (Lisbon) 361
  Tate Britain (London) 49
  Whitworth Art Gallery
    (Manchester) 77
Turpin, Dick 79
Tuscany 387
Tussaud, Madame 54
TWA 265, 335, 451
Tylman of Gameren 753

U

Uccello, Paolo 414, 424
Uffizi (Florence) 25, **422–4**
UK Embassies *see* British
  Embassies
Ulster *see* Northern Ireland
Ulster-American Folk Park **131**
Ulster Hall (Belfast) 135
Ulsterbus 133
UNESCO World Heritage Sites
  Alcobaça 367
  Batalha 367
  Bern 618
  Burgos 299, 300
  Cracow 705
  Drottningholm **647**
  Évora 372
  Graz 600
  Oswiecim (Auschwitz) **757**
  Parc Güell (Barcelona) **315**

UNESCO World Heritage Sites (cont.)
  Sintra 366
  Suomenlinna Island Fortress
    (Helsinki) **695**
  Warsaw 748
United Airlines 201, 265, 451, 569
United States Embassies
  Austria 605
  Belgium and Luxembourg 237
  Czech Republic 725
  Denmark 685
  Finland 699
  France 199
  Germany 567
  Great Britain 89
  Greece 503
  Hungary 741
  Norway 669
  Ireland 133
  Italy 449
  Netherlands 265
  Poland 759
  Portugal 375
  Spain 333
  Sweden 653
  Switzerland 627
Universities
  Cambridge 73
  Helsinki 693
  Oxford 72
  Trinity College (Dublin) 115, **116**
Unter den Linden (Berlin) **530**
Uppsala **648–9**
  restaurants 655
Urban VIII, Pope 394
Urbino **443**
  hotels 461
  restaurants 467
Urbino, Duke and Duchess of
  423, 424
Ursula, St. 561
Uspenski Cathedral (Helsinki) **693**
Utrecht **261**
  hotels 269
  restaurants 271
Utrillo, Maurice 161, 166

V

Vaccinations *see* Medical care
Vajdahunyad Castle
  (Budapest) **737**
Valdemar IV, King of Denmark 673
Valdés, Lucas 330
Valdés Leal, Juan de 330, 331
Valencia **318–19**
  hotels 343
  restaurants 349
Valentino 453
Valerian, Emperor 435
Valéry, Paul 164
Valley of Temples (Agrigento) 447
Vallgren, Ville 693
Value Added Tax **13**
Valvassori, Gabriele 401
Van Dyck, Sir Anthony 220
  Antwerp 230
  Bildergalerie (Berlin) 541
  Capitoline Museums (Rome) 401
  Gemäldegalerie (Berlin) 531
  Jagdschloss Grunewald
    (Grunewald) 538
  Musée Royaux des Beaux-Arts
    (Brussels) 227

Van Dyck, Sir Anthony (cont.)
  Museum voor Schone Kunsten
    (Ghent) 231
  National Gallery of Art (Athens) 481
  National Gallery of Scotland
    (Edinburgh) 85
  Niedersächsische Landesmuseum
    (Hanover) 564
  Palazzo Real (Genoa) 426
  Tate Britain (London) 48
  Uffizi (Florence) 424
Van Eyck, Jan 29
  Groeninge Museum (Bruges) 234
  Musée du Louvre (Paris) 160
  Museo Thyssen-Bornemisza
    (Madrid) 291
  Museum der Bildenden Künste
    (Leipzig) 543
  National Gallery (London) 49
  St. Baafskathedraal (Ghent) 231
Van Gogh, Theo 259
Van Gogh, Vincent 30
  The Bedroom at Arles 259
  Belvedere (Vienna) 599
  L'Espace Van Gogh (Arles) 192
  Gemäldegalerie Neue Meister
    (Dresden) 543
  Museo Thyssen-Bornemisza
    (Madrid) 291
  National Gallery (London) 49
  Sammlung Berggruen (Berlin) 537
  Van Gogh Museum
    (Amsterdam) **259**
Vanbrugh, Sir John 74, 75
Vanni, Andrea 410
Vantaa Airport (Helsinki) 699
Vanvitelli, Luigi 411
Vaporetti, Venice 451
Varlaam (Metéora) 486–7
Vasamuseet (Stockholm) **646**
Vasarely, Victor 739
Vasari, Giorgio
  Palazzo Vecchio (Florence) 419
  Uffizi (Florence) 422
  Villa Giulia (Rome) 405
Vátheia 492
Vatican Museums (Rome) 25,
  396–8
Vátos 495
Vaux-le-Vicomte, Château de
  170–71
Växjö **650**
Velázquez, Diego
  Gemäldegalerie (Berlin) 531
  Gemäldegalerie Alte Meister
    (Dresden) 542
  Kunsthistorisches Museum
    (Vienna) 596
  Museo del Prado (Madrid) 290
  Museu Nacional d'Art de
    Catalunya (Barcelona) 315
  National Gallery (London) 49
  An Old Woman Cooking Eggs 85
  Palazzo Doria Pamphilj
    (Rome) 401
  The Triumph of Bacchus 288
Velázquez Bosco 291
Veneziano, Paolo 441
Venice **432–41**
  climate 448
  Doge's Palace **436–7**
  gondolas **439**
  hotels **458**
  map 432–3

Venice (cont.)
　restaurants **464**
　St. Mark's **434–5**
　travel **451**
Venini (Venice) 453
The Venus of Urbino (Titian)
　422, 424
Verbruggen, Henri-Françoise 226
Verdi, Giuseppe 430
Verdun, Nikolaus von 563
Verhulst, Rombout 252
Vermeer, Jan
　Buckingham Palace (London) 48
　Gemäldegalerie Alte Meister
　　(Dresden) 542
　The Kitchen Maid 256
　Kunsthistorisches Museum
　　(Vienna) 596
　Mauritshuis (The Hague) 262
　Rijksmuseum (Amsterdam) 258
　Städelsches Kunstinstitut
　　(Frankfurt) 560
　tomb of 263
Verne, Jules 176
Verona **430–31**
　hotels 460
　restaurants 465
Verona Arena (Verona) 455
Veronese, Paolo
　Capitoline Museums (Rome) 401
　The Feast in the House of Levi 441
　Museo del Prado (Madrid) 290
　Vatican Museums (Rome) 398
Verrio, Antonio 63
Verrocchio, Andrea del 419
Versailles
　Château de Versailles **168–9**
　hotels 208
　restaurants 213
Veryan
　hotels 99
Vespasian, Emperor 403
Vesuvius, Mount 444
Vézelay **182**
　hotels 210
Via della Galluzza (Siena) 408
Viajes 2000　333
Vianden **235**
　hotels 241
Vicenza **431**
　hotels 460
　restaurants 466
Victor, St. 194
Victor Emanuel Monument
　(Rome) 388
Victoria, Queen of England
　30, 38, 79
　Buckingham Palace (London) 48
　Crown Jewels 60
　Killarney 127
Victoria and Albert Museum
　(London) 55, **57**
Victoria Coach Station (London) 91
Vienna 521, **590–99**
　climate 604
　Hofburg **592–4**
　hotels 608
　map 590–91
　restaurants 610
Vienna Boys Choir 593, 594
Vigeland, Gustav 636, 663
　Vigelandsparken (Oslo) **663**
Vignola, Giacomo Barozzi da 405
Viking Line 653, 699

Vikings 110, 639, **665**
　history 657
Vikingsskipshuset (Oslo) **664**
　York 79
Viktualienmarkt (Munich) 571
Vila Olímpica (Barcelona) **311**
Vilagarcia de Arousa
　restaurants 348
Vilamoura 373
Villa Farnesina (Rome) **399**
Villa Floridiana 444
Villa Giulia (Rome) **405**
Villaneuva, Juan de 288
Villar i Lozano, Francesc
　de Paula 313
Villeroy & Boch
　(Luxembourg City) 239
Vincent, St. 358, 359
Vinckenbrinck, Albert 252
Viollet-le-Duc, Eugène
　Carcassonne 190
　Musée des Monuments Français
　　(Paris) 164
　Notre-Dame (Paris) 154, 155
　Sainte-Chapelle (Paris) 152
Virgil 430
Virgin Atlantic 91
Virgin Megastore (Paris) 205
Virgin of Montserrat **317**
Virgin Trains 91
Visas *see* Passports and visas
Visby 637, **649**
Vischer studio 534
Visconti, Luchino 389
Visconti family 428, 625
VisitBritain Australia 89
VisitBritain Canada 89
VisitBritain Ireland 89
VisitBritain New Zealand 89
VisitBritain United States 89
Vista Visitor Center
　(Budapest) 741
Vittorio & Lucchino (Seville) 337
Vivienne Westwood (London) 93
Vladislav Jagiello, King of
　Bohemia 714
Volendam **260**
　hotels 269
Völkerkundemuseum (Vienna) 594
Volksbühne (Berlin) 573
Volksgarten (Vienna) **594**
Volkstheater (Vienna) 607
Vólos 485
　hotels 511
Voltaire 146, 157, 160
Vomero 444
Vratislav, Prince 714
Vries, Adrian de 160
Vroukoúnda 499
VVV Centraal Station
　(Amsterdam) 265
Vyletěl, Josef 723
Vyrós Gorge 492
Vyzítsa 485
　hotels 511

W

Wachau 587, **601**
Wagner, Richard 531
　Bayreuth **544**
　Deutsches Nationaltheater
　　(Weimar) 543
　Richard Wagner Museum

Wagner, Richard (cont.)
　(Lucerne) 622
　Ring cycle 525
　Sächsische Staatsoper
　　(Dresden) 542
Waldbühne (Berlin) 573
Waldmüller, Ferdinand Georg 599
Wales **69**
　hotels **98–9**
　maps 34, 40
　restaurants **104–5**
　Tourist Board 89
Wałęsa, Lech 746
Walker, The (Liverpool) 76
Wallenstein, Albrecht von 716–17
Wallenstein Palace (Prague)
　716–17
Walloons 219, 220
Wallot, Paul 530
Walpole, Sir Robert 38, 44
Warhol, Andy 59, 560, 683
Warsaw 705, **748–53**
　climate 758
　Fredric Chopin Airport 759
　hotels **760**
　map 748–9
　restaurants **761**
　tourist office 759
　train station 759
Warsaw History Museum
　(Warsaw) 750
Water buses
　Venice 451
Water sports
　Italy **455**
　Portugal **377**
Waterford **123**
　hotels 137
　restaurants 139
Waterford Crystal 135
Waterford Festival of Light Opera
　135
Waterhouse, Alfred 56
Waterkeyn, André 229
Waterloo **231**
　restaurants 243
Waterstone's (Brussels) 239
Waterstone's (Edinburgh) 93
Watteau, Antoine
　Gemäldegalerie Alte Meister
　　(Dresden) 542
　Gilles 24
　Museo del Prado (Madrid) 290
　Schloss Sanssouci (Berlin) 541
Weather *see* Climate
Webb, Sir Aston 48, 57
Wedding Portrait (Hals) 24
Weil, Daniel 57
Weimar **543**
　hotels 575
　restaurants 581–2
Weissenbruch, Hendrik 258
Welles, Orson 521
Wellington, Duke of 54, 231
Wellington Testimonial (Dublin) 121
Wembley Arena (London) 95
Wenceslas, St. 707, 713, 721
Wenceslas IV, King of Bohemia 717
Wenceslas Square (Prague) **721**
Wererskiold, Erik 663
Werff, Adriaan van der 258
Werner, Anton von 535
Wertheim (Berlin) 571
Westerman, Jan 250

Westminster (London)
Street-by-Street map 44–5
Westminster Abbey (London) 43,
44, **46–7**
Westwood, Vivienne 39
Wexford Opera Festival 135
Weyden, Rogier van der
Alte Pinakothek (Munich) 551
Groeninge Museum (Bruges) 234
Hôtel-Dieu (Beaune) 182
Kunsthistorisches Museum
(Vienna) 596
Musée Royaux des Beaux-Arts
(Brussels) 226
Museo del Prado (Madrid) 290
Museu Calouste Gulbenkian
(Lisbon) 361
Wheelchair access see Disabled
visitors
Whisky/whiskey
Old Bushmills Distillery **131**
The Whisky Shop (Glasgow) 93
Whitehall (London)
Street-by-Street map 44–5
Whymper, Edward **621**
Widder Bar (Zürich) 629
Wien Tourismus 605
Wiener Kammeroper (Vienna) 607
Wiener Philharmoniker (Vienna) 607
Wiener Volksoper (Vienna) 607
Wiener Werkstätte 597
Wigmore Hall (London) 95
Wilanów Palace and Park
(Budapest) 748, **753**
Wilde, Oscar 116, 117, 167
Wildlife
Alps 620
Camargue **194**
Parc Nacional d'Aigüestortes 305
Wilhelm I, Kaiser 524, 559
Wilhelm I, King of Württemberg 557
Wilhelm II, Kaiser 524
Wilhelm IV the Steadfast, Duke of
Bavaria 551
Wilhelmine, Margravine of
Bayreuth 544
Willendorf 601
William I the Conqueror, King of
England 78
Battle of Hastings 38
Bayeux Tapestry 173
Tower of London 60
Winchester 64
Windsor Castle 66
William I of Orange, King of the
Netherlands 220, 255
William III of Orange, King of
England 51, 117
Battle of the Boyne 110
Dublin Castle 118
Hampton Court 63
Hyde Park (London) 54
Paleis Het Loo 261
William V of Orange 246
William the Silent, Prince of
Orange 245, 262, 263
Willibrord, St. 235
Wilmcote
hotels 100
Winchester **64–5**
hotels 98
Windsor Castle **66–7**
Wines
France 186–7, **202**

Wines (cont.)
port **371**
Winter Landscape with Skaters
(Avercamp) 256
Winter Riding School
(Vienna) 592, **594**
Winter sports
Alps 621
Austria **607**
Switzerland **629**
Winterhalter, Franz Xaver
*Portrait of the Empress
Elisabeth* 594
Winterthur 623
Wit, Jacob de 250, 252
Wittamer (Brussels) 239
Wittelsbach family 548, 549, 551,
553, 555
Władysław IV, King of Poland 755
Wolf, Hugo 525
Wölfel, Carl 544
Wolsey, Cardinal 63, 72
Woman at her Toilet (Steen)
257
Wonderful Copenhagen 685
Wood, John the Elder 68, 70
Wood, John the Younger 70
Wordsworth, William 73, 77
Words'worth (Munich) 571
World War I 31
Battlefields of Belgium **231**
World War II 31
Anne Frankhuis (Amsterdam) **253**
Oswiecim (Auschwitz) **757**
Wouters, Rik 227, 230
Wren, Sir Christopher
Greenwich 62
Hampton Court 63
St. James Church (London) 50
St. Paul's Cathedral
(London) 29, 58
Sheldonian Theatre (Oxford)
72
Wright brothers 552
Würzburg **544**
hotels 577
restaurants 583
Wyatville, Sir Jeffry 67

X

Xabia 319
hotels 343

Y

Yáñez de la Almedina,
Fernando 290
Ybl, Miklós 736
Yeats, Jack B 117, 126
Yeats, W.B. 117
Yellow Bike (Amsterdam) 267
Yevele, Henry 46
York 35, **78–9**
hotels 101
restaurants 106–7
Street-by-Street map 78–9
York Castle Museum (York) 79
York Minster 78, 79
Yorkshire Museum (York) 78
Young Woman on the Shore
(Munch) 663
Yusuf I, Caliph 322
Yves Saint Laurent (Paris) 203

Z

Zadkine, Ossip 192
Zähringen, Counts von 556, 614
Zähringen, Duke of 618
Zákynthos **495**
hotels 512
restaurants 516
Zaragoza **318**
hotels 343
restaurants 349
Zarzuela, Spain **338**, 339
Żebrowski, Walenty 751
Ženíšek, Frantíšeck 721
Zénith (Paris) 205
Zermatt **619**
hotels 631
Zeughaus (Berlin) 530
Zimmermann, Franz 553
Zimmermann, Johann Baptiste
549, 553
Zítek, Josef 721, 723
Zoos
Artis (Amsterdam) 255
Dublin Zoo 121
Zoologischer Garten (Berlin) **536**
Zorn, Anders 649
Zum Schwarzen Kameel (Vienna)
607
Zurbarán, Francisco de 303
Monasterio de las Descalzas
Reales (Madrid) 285
Musée du Louvre (Paris) 160
Museo de Bellas Artes (Córdoba)
324
Museo de Bellas Artes (Málaga)
321
Museo de Bellas Artes (Seville) 331
Museo del Prado (Madrid) 290
Museu Nacional d'Art de
Catalunya (Barcelona) 315
The Sleeping Girl 325
Zürich **623**
hotels **631**
restaurants **633**
tourist office 627
Zwingli, Ulrich 614, 623
Zygmunt August, King of Poland
755
Zygmunt the Old, King of Poland
755
Zygmunt III Waza, King of Poland
750

Acknowledgments

Dorling Kindersley would like to thank the following people whose contributions and assistance have made the preparation of this book possible.

Main Contributors
Amy Brown, Nina Hathway, Vivien Stone, Kristina Woolnough.

Additional Contributors
John Ardagh, Rosemary Bailey, David Baird, Josie Barnard, Rosemary Barron, Gretel Beer, Ros Belford, Susie Boulton, Gerhard Bruschke, Caroline Bugler, Christopher Catling, Juliet Clough, Deidre Coffey, Marc Dubin, Paul Duncan, Joanna Egert-Romanowska, Olivia Ercoli, Judith Fayard, Stephanie Ferguson, Lisa Gerard-Sharp, Mike Gerrard, Andrew Gumbel, Andy Harris, Vicky Hayward, Zöe Hewetson, Adam Hopkins, Lindsay Hunt, Nick Inman, Tim Jepson, Colin Jones, Emma Jones, Marion Kaplan, Alister Kershaw, Michael Leapman, Philip Lee, Alec Lobrano, Sarah McAlister, Jerzy S. Majewski, Fred Mawer, Lynette Mitchell, Colin Nicholson, Roger Norum, Tadeusz Olsański, Małgorzata Omilanowska, Robin Osborne, Robin Pascoe, Alice Peebles, Tim Perry, Polly Phillimore, Paul Richardson, Anthony Roberts, Barnaby Rogerson, Zöe Ross, Kaj Sandell, Jane Shaw, Vladimír Soukup, Robert Strauss, Martin Symington, Allan Tillier, Nigel Tisdall, Roger Thomas, Tanya Tsikas, Roger Williams, Timothy Wright.

Illustrators
Acanto Arquitectura y Urbanismo S.L., Stephen Conlin, Gary Cross, Richard Draper, Nick Gibbard, Paul Guest, Stephen Gyapay, Studio Illibill, Kevin Jones Associates, Paweł Marczak, Maltings Partnership, Chris Orr and Associates, Otakar Pok, Robbie Polley, Jaroslav Staněk, Paul Weston, Andrzej Wielgosz, Ann Winterbotham, John Woodcock, Martin Woodward, Piotr Zubrzycki.

Design and Editorial Assistance
Douglas Amrine, Sonal Bhatt, Julie Bond, Lucinda Hawksley, Matthew Ibbotson, Jacky Jackson, Michelle de Larrabeiti, Delphine Lawrance, Helen Partington, Dave Pugh, Pete Quinlan, Marisa Renzullo, Simon Ryder, Sands Publishing Solutions, Sadie Smith, Leah Tether, Hugh Thompson, Conrad van Dyk, Karen Villabona, Simon Wilder, Dora Whitaker.

Factchecker
Jessica Hughes.

Proofreader
Stewart J. Wild.

Index
Hilary Bird.

Additional Picture Research
Nicole Kaczynski.

Additional DTP
Vinod Harish, Vincent Kurien, Azeem Siddiqui.

Additional Cartography
Uma Bhattacharya, Mohammad Hassan, Jasneet Kaur.

Production
Joanna Bull, Sarah Dodd, Marie Ingledew.

Publishing Manager
Helen Townsend.

Managing Art Editor
Jane Ewart.

Director of Publishing
Gilllian Allan.

Additional Photography
Max Alexander, Peter Anderson, Gabor Barka, Steve Bere, Clive Bournsnell, Maciej Bronarski, Demetrio Carrasco, Andrzej Chec, Krzysztof Chojnacki, Stephen Conlin, Joe Cornish, Andy Crawford, Michael Crocket, Wojciech Czerniewicz, Tim Daly, Jiří Doležal, Philip Dowell, Mike Dunning, Philip Enticknap, Jane Ewart, Foto Carfagna + Associati, Philip Gatward, Steve Gorton, A. Hayder, Heidi Grassley, John Heseltine, Gabriel Hilderbrandt, Roger Hilton, Rupert Horrox, Ed Ironside, Dorota Jarymowicz, Mariusz Jarymowicz, Piotr Jamski, Colin Keates, Paul Kenward, Alan Keohand, Dave King, Jiří Kopřiva, Mariusz Kowalewski, Vladimír Kozlík, Adrian Lascom, Cyril Laubscher, Neil Lukas, Eric Meacher, Wojciech Mędrzak, Neil Mersh, John Miller, John

Moss, Roger Moss, David Murray, Hanna Musiał, Maciej Musiał, Tomasz Myśluk, Stephen Oliver, John Parker, Agencja "Piękna," Milan Posselt, František Přeučil, Rob Reichenfeld, Tim Ridley, Kim Sayer, Jules Selmes, Anthony Souter, Clive Streeter, Stanislav Tereba, Matthew Ward, Alan Williams, Peter Wilson, Jeremy Whitaker, Linda Whitwam, Stephen Whitehorn, Paweł Wójcik, Stephen Wooster, Francesca Yorke, Jan Zych.

Additional Assistance
Dorling Kindersley would like to give special thanks to Britt Lightbody of the Danish Tourist Board, Henrik Thierlein, International Press Officer for Wonderful Copenhagen, Petter Ree of the Norwegian Embassy in London, Riitta Balza at the Finnish Tourist Board, London, and journalist Tone Sendberg.

Photography Permissions
Dorling Kindersley would like to thank all the churches, museums, galleries, and other sights that kindly gave their permission for us to photograph their establishments and works of art.

Picture Credits
t = top; tl = top left; tlc = top left center; tc = top center; tr = top right; cla = center left above; ca = center above; cra = center right above; cl = center left; c = center; cr = center right; clb = center left below; cb = center below; crb = center right below; bl = bottom left; b = bottom; bc = bottom center; bcl = bottom center left; br = bottom right; d = detail.

Every effort has been made to trace the copyright holders and we apologize in advance for any unintentional omissions. We would be pleased to insert the appropriate acknowledgments in any subsequent edition of this publication.

Works of art have been reproduced with the permission of the following copyright holders:
Maman Louise Bourgeois © DACS, London/VAGA, New York 2006 59tl; *Young Woman on the Shore* Edvard Munch © Munch Museum/Munch – Ellingsen Group, BONO, Oslo/DACS, London 2006, 663bl; *Guernica* Pablo Picasso © Succession Picasso/DACS, London 2006,

31bc; Pit Stop (1984) Jean Tinguely © ADAGP, Paris and DACS, London 2006 617tr.

The publisher would like to thank the following individuals, companies, and picture libraries for permission to reproduce their photographs:

AKG LONDON: *Cosimo de Medici* 420b, *St. Augustine* by Carpaccio 421crb, *Niccolò Machiavelli* 421br; Museo Archeologico Nazionale, *Farnese Hercules* 444c; Collection Archiv für Kunst und Geschichte, Berlin 718cla, 470t; Staatliche Kunstsammlungen, Kassel, *William I of Orange* by Anthonis Mor (1556) 246t; Museum Boijmans-van Beuningen, Rotterdam, *The Tower of Babel* (c.1525) by Peter Brueghel the Elder 263br; Naturhistorisches Museum/Eric Lessing 595brc; Niedersächsisches Landesmuseum, Hanover, *Friedrich II* by Antoine Pesne 524t; Rijksmuseum, *Winter Landscape with Skaters* (1618) by Hendrick Avercamp 256tc; San Francesco, Assisi/ Stefan Diller, *St. Francis Appears to the Monks at Arles* by Giotto (c.1295) 28br; Staatliche Kunstsammlungen, Dresden/ Gemäldegalerie Alte Meister, *Girl Reading a Letter* by Vermeer 542tr; Vatican Museums, Rome 27tl; ALAMY IMAGES: Brendan Hoffman 696bl; ALVEY AND TOWERS: 147br; MUSEUM AMSTELKRING: 250tr; AMSTERDAMS HISTORISCH MUSEUM: 252br, 253cl; ANCIENT EGYPT PICTURE LIBRARY: The Trustees of the British Museum 24cla; APEX PHOTO AGENCY: 39t; ARENAS FOTOGRAFIA ARTISTICA: 325cr; ARQUIVO ICONOGRAFICO S.A., BARCELONA: Museo del Prado, *The Triumph of Bacchus* by Velázquez 288tl; THE ART ARCHIVE: The Imperial War Museum 231bl; The British Library 125bl; ART DIRECTORS & TRIP: C. Rennie 639bc, 641b, 649b; ARTOTHEK SPECIALARCHIV FÜR GEMÄLDEFOTOGRAFIE, PEISSENBERG: *Four Apostles* (1526) by Albrecht Dürer 551tr; JAMES AUSTIN: 152b; AUSTRIAN NATIONAL TOURIST BOARD: 592bc.

JAUME BALAYNA: 313crb; C.H. BASTIN & J. EVRARD: 232bc; BAYERISCHES NATIONAL-MUSEUM, MUNICH: 552t; LA BELLE AURORE: 193b; BERLINER DOM: 534br; BETHNAL

GREEN MUSEUM OF CHILDHOOD/VICTORIA & ALBERT MUSEUM, LONDON: 57b; BILDARCHIV PREUSSISCHER KULTURBESITZ: 532t; Kunstgewerbemuseum, Berlin 531c; Pergamon Museum, Berlin 25t; GÉRARD BOULLAY: 155c, 155bl; THE BRIDGEMAN ART LIBRARY: Basilica di San Francesco, Assisi, *The Ecstasy of St. Francis* by Giotto 406tr; The British Museum 52c, 53tl, *The Festival of Sekhtet* 52br, *The Young Prince with his Parents* 53c; Lauros-Giraudon/ Chateau de Versailles, France, *Equestrian Portrait of Louis XIV* (c.1692) by Pierre Mignard 29tr; Crown Institute/Institute of Directors, London, UK, *Field Marshal King Leopold I of Belgium* by Nicholas Pieneman 220t; Galleria degli Uffizi, Firenze, *The Venus of Urbino* (1538) by Titian 422b, *The Duke of Urbino* (1460) by Piero della Francesca 423tr, *The Duchess of Urbino* (1460) by Piero della Francesca 423tl, *Madonna of the Gold-finch* (1506) by Raphael 424b; Kunst-historisches Museum, Vienna, *Matthias I, Hunyadi* (1440–90) 730t; Louvre, Paris, *Virgin of the Rocks* (c.1478) by Leonardo da Vinci 29bl, *The Oath of the Horatii* (1784) by Jacques-Louis David 30clb; Munch-Museet, Oslo, *Young Woman on the Shore* (1896) by Edvard Munch 663bl; Musée Carnavalet, Paris 30cla; Museo del Prado, Madrid, *The Three Graces* (1635) by Rubens 288cr, *The Clothed Maja* (c.1800) by Goya 289tr, *The Naked Maja* (c.1800) by Goya 289cra, *The Martyrdom of St. Philip* (c.1639) by José de Ribera 289cr, *The Annunciation* by Fra Angelico (c.1387–1455) 290cr, *The Santo Domingo el Antiguo Altarpiece*, depicting *The Adoration of the Shepherds*, by El Greco (1541–1614) 290bl; Museo Nacional Centro de Arte Reina Sofia, Madrid, *Guernica* (1937) by Pablo Picasso 31bc; Private Collection, *Queen Elizabeth I* by Marcus Gheeraerts the Younger 38t; Royal Holloway & Bedford New College, *Princes Edward and Richard in the Tower* by Sir John Everett Millais 61b; St. Peter's, Vatican, *Pietà* by Michelangelo 2r; THE BRITISH MUSEUM: 26br, 53br, 479br; BRITSTOCK-IFA: F. Aberham 619br; Erich Bach 623bl; S. Bohnacker 600t; Bernd Ducke 600bl; Torsten Fleer 235br; P. Graf 650t; G. Grafenhain 235cla, 601bl, 620cla, 651tr, 683br; S. Gräfenwhain 622tl; B. Moller 648b; 624bl; AP&F/Thomas Ulrich 621bc; BUDAPESTI TORTENETI MUZEUM: 734br; BUDAPESTI TURISZTIKAI HIVATAL: 735bl; INTERNATIONAL BULBFLOWER CENTRE: 261tc; MICHAEL BUSSELLE: 140–141.

CAMERA PRESS: Cecil Beaton 46cb; GIUSEPPE CARFAGNA & ASSOCIATI: 427bc; BIÈRES DE CHIMAY S.A: 220b; CHUR TOURISMUS: 624tc; COLLECTIONS DU MUSÉE INTERNATIONAL D'HORLOGERIE, LA CHAUX-DE-FONDS, SUISSE: Photo Institut l'homme et le Temps 617c; COLOGNE CATHEDRAL DOMBAUARCHIV: 562tl, 562cl, 562bl, 563tl, 563cra, 563crb, 563bl; ALAN COPSON PHOTOGRAPHY: 228cl; CORBIS: Archivo Iconografico, S.A., *An Old Woman Cooking Eggs* by Velázquez 85b; Arte & Immagini srl, *The Annunciation* by Fra Angelico 415tr; Yann Arthus-Betrand 304tl; Bettman Archive 525bl, 658t; Ric Ergenbright 522; Macduff Everton 650c; Historical Picture Archive 31bl; Hulton-Deutsch Collection 331cr; JAI/Alan Copson 371tr; Bob Krist 588t; Dennis Marsico 407tc; National Gallery London *Bathers at Asnières* by Seurat 49br; Richard T. Nowitz 623tr; José F. Poblete 625tl; Michael St. Maur Sheil 757tr; Gregor Schmid 523c; Ted Spiegel 665cl; Adam Woolfitt 143crb; JOE CORNISH: 77b, 78br, 79bl, 80b, 84t, 85t, 86b, 86t, 108c, 109b, 111tr, 124tr, 124bl, 126cl, 126cr, 126bl, 127tl, 127cr, 127br, 128cl, 128cr, 128bl, 128bl, 128br, 157t, 280t, 300tr, 319br, 366c, 367tr, 367cl, 367b, 471tr, 490t, 491br, 492b, 492t, 493b, 493t, 157t, 157t, 700–701; COVER ARCHIVO: Ilenas Quim 304br; CZARTORYSKI MUSEUM, CRACOW: *Lady with an Ermine* by Leonardo da Vinci 757cl.

IL DAGHERROTIPO: Riccardo D'Errico 443t; DEAN AND CHAPTER OF WESTMINSTER: 47bl; DEUTSCHES MUSEUM, MUNICH: 552b; C.M. DIXON: Vatican Museums, Rome 25br; JURGEN DRENTH: 244c; DUCHAS, THE HERITAGE SERVICE: 122b; DEUTSCHE PRESSE-AGENTUR GMBH: 542br, 554cla.

EMPICS LTD: Tony Marshall 389bl; ENGLISH HERITAGE: by kind permission of the Provost and Fellows of King's College, Cambridge 73tr; MARY EVANS PICTURE LIBRARY: 8r, 9c, 21c, 28tr, 30tr, 33c, 75bl, 81b, 110tl, 141c, *Napoleon Bonaparte* (c.1804) by Jacques-Louis David 146t, 273c, 278cr, 383c, 579c, 602bc, 635c, 640t, 674t, 701c; EYE UBIQUITOUS: James Davis 316br.

SIGMUND FREUD MUSEUM, VIENNA: 596br. GETTY IMAGES/STONE: Hideo Kuihara 2; Hugh Sitton 65t; James Strachan 704clb; GODO-FOTO: 318br; NICHOLAS P. GOULANDRIS FOUNDATION MUSEUM OF CYCLADIC AND

ANCIENT GREEK ART: 474bl; MICHAEL GRYCHOWSKI: 754tr; ©FMBG GUGGENHEIM BILBAO MUSEOA: London 2001. Erica Barahona Ede (All rights reserved. Total or partial reproduction is prohibited) 31bra; GUINNESS IRELAND ARCHIVES, DUBLIN: 121c.

SONIA HALLIDAY PHOTOGRAPHS: 35ca; ROBERT HARDING PICTURE LIBRARY: 23c, 23t, 27br, 159br, 171t, 279tr, 395b, 603tc, 620tr, 621tr, 621bla, 623cl, 637b, 649t, 682tl, 689bc, G. Hellier 603b, 739bl; K. Gillam 691b; Simon Harris 602t; John Miller 23c; The Picture Store 651b; Roy Rainford 520br; Chris Rennie 279tr; Adina Tovy 38b; Adam Woolfitt 637cla, 675t, 683cl; GORDON HENDERSON 81t; HISTORIC ROYAL PALACES 1999 (CROWN COPYRIGHT): 63t; ANGELO HORNAK LIBRARY: 78cla; HULTON ARCHIVE: 29tc, 30b, 146b, 228br, 253cr, 471c, 662bl, 708t; Imperial War Museum 31tl; HUNGARIAN NATIONAL GALLERY: 734tr; HUNGARIAN TOURIST BOARD: 739tr.

IDEAL PHOTO S.A.: T. Passios 489t; IMAGES COLOUR LIBRARY: 293ca, 293cb; IMPACT PHOTOS: Brian Harris 387b; INDEX FOTOTECA: 323c; INSTITUTO PORTUGUÊS DE MUSEUS: Museu Grão Vasco 362tr; ISTITUTO E MUSEO DI STORIA DELLA SCIENZA, FLORENCE: 419br.

STANISŁAWA JABŁOŃSKA: 744, 755bl; PAUL JACKSON 49tl; JARROLD PUBLISHING: ©2001 His Grace Duke of Marlborough 75c; MICHAEL JENNER PHOTOGRAPHY: 124bc; JOODS HISTORISCH MUSEUM, AMSTERDAM: 251tr; JORVIK, YORK: 79tl.

OLDRICK KARASEK: 706, 722b, 722t, 723tl, 723b; KENNEDY PR: 114cla; KONINKLIJK MUSEUM VOOR SCHONE KUNSTEN, ANTWERP: *As the Old Sang, The Young Play Pipes* (1638) by Jacob Jordaen 230bl; KUNSTHISTORISCHES MUSEUM, VIENNA: 594tr, 596c, *Empress Elisabeth* (1865) by Winterhalter 594tl, *Hunters in the Snow* (1565) by Peter Brueghel the Elder 596t.

LOCARNO FILM FESTIVAL: 625bl; LUXEMBOURG TOURIST OFFICE: pictures by kind permission of the Luxembourg Tourist Office, London 221b.

TOM MACKIE: 32–33; MADAME TUSSAUD'S, LONDON: 54bla; MAGYAR NEMZETI MUZEUM: 736bc; MARIA LAACH KUNSTVERLAG: 559c; MAK – ÖSTERREICHISCHE MUSEUM FÜR ANGEWANDTE

KUNST: 597cl; MARKGRÄFLICHES OPERNHAUS, BAYREUTH: 557t; MERCEDES-BENZ MUSEUM, STUTTGART: 557t; MUSEI CAPITOLINI, ROME: 27bl; MUSEI VATICANI E CAPELLA SISTINA, ROME: 394c, 394bl, 394t, 395tl, 395cr, 395ca, 396t, 396cl, 397tc, 397cr, 397cb, 398t; MUSEU DA CIDADE, LISBON: Portrait of *Marquês de Pombal* 361t; MUSEUM HUIS LAMBERT VAN MEERTEN, RBK: 263cl; MUSEUM JEAN TINGUELY BASEL: © ADAGP, Paris and DACS, London 2006 617tr; MUSEUM OF LONDON: 58b; MUSEU DA MARINHA, LISBON: *Manuel I* by Alberto Cutileiro 354t, *Vasco da Gama* 363br; MUSÉE NATIONAL DU CHÂTEAU DE VERSAILLES: 168tr, 168cl, 168bl, 169tr, 169tlb, 169bc; MUSÉES ROYAUX DES BEAUX-ARTS DE BELGIQUE: 226bc; MUSEO NACIONAL DEL PRADO, MADRID: *The Garden of Delights* (1505) by Hieronymus Bosch 288crb; MUSEO THYSSEN-BORNEMISZA, MADRID: *Our Lady of the Dry Tree* (c.1450) by Petrus Christus 286bl.

NÁRODNÍ GALERIE V PRAZE, PRAGUE: *Simeon and the Infant Jesus* by Petr Brandl 714t; NATIONAL GALLERY OF IRELAND, DUBLIN: *The Taking of Christ* (1602) by Caravaggio (Reproduction courtesy of the National Gallery of Ireland, Dublin) 117b; NATIONAL TRUST PHOTOGRAPHIC LIBRARY: 130b; Nick Meers 77c; TRUSTEES OF THE NATIONAL MUSEUMS OF SCOTLAND: 28tr; NIPPON TELEVISION NETWORK CORPORATION: *Original Sin* by Michelangelo, detail from the Sistine Chapel ceiling, Vatican, Rome 398br.

ORONOZ ARCHIVO FOTOGRÁFICO: 293cla, 299c, 326c; J.A Fernandez 304tr.

PA PHOTOS: DPA 31tr; EPA 525tr; PALACE OF CULTURE AND SCIENCE, WARSAW: 749cr; PALAIS HET LOOS: E. Boeijinga 261bl; PICTURES COLOUR LIBRARY: 682b, 738tr; ROBBIE POLLEY: 232bla; POWERSTOCK/ZEFA LTD: 750tl; Mauritius Gallery 598bc; PRISMA ARCHIVO FOTOGRÁFICO, BARCELONA: Palacio del Senado, *The Fall of Granada* by Francisco Pradilla 278tl.

REX FEATURES: 66c, 67br, 71c; Denis Cameron 325tr; Pertti Jenytin 688c; Sipa Press 196tr; RIJKSMUSEUM AMSTERDAM: 257c; *The Wedding Portrait* (c.1622) by Frans Hals 24tr; *The Kitchen Maid* (1658) by Jan Vermeer 256cl; *St. Elizabeth's Day Flood* (1500) 256bc; *The Night Watch* (1642) by Rembrandt 257tl; *Woman at her Toilet* (1660) by Jan Steen

257br; *The Jewish Bride* by Rembrandt 258br; RÉUNION DES MUSÉES NATIONAUX AGENCE PHOTOGRAPHIQUE: Louvre/ Lewandowski/LeMage *Mona Lisa (La Joconde)* by Leonardo da Vinci 160t; Louvre/Herve Lewandowski 160c; *Gilles* or *Pierrot* (c.1717) by Watteau 24clb; THE ROYAL COLLECTION: ©2001 Her Majesty Queen Elizabeth II: 60br, 60b, 61tl, 66tr, 67tl, 67tr, 67bl.

SCALA GROUP S.P.A: 394br, 394bla, 396b; Basilica di San Francesco, *St. Francis* (1280) by Cimabue 406cl, *The Deposition* (1323) by Lorenzetti 406bl, *The Life of St. Martin* (1315) by Simone Martini 406br; *Pope Leo X* 420clb; Palazzo Medici Riccardi, Firenze, *The Procession of the Magi* by Gozzoli 420–421; 421tl, 421ca, 443bla; Accademia, Venice, *The Feast in the House of Levi* by Veronese 441b; Bargello, Firenze, *David* by Donatello 418cl; Galleria degli Uffizi, Firenze 423cb; *The Ognissanti Madonna* (1310) by Giotto 422c, *The Birth of Venus* (1485) by Botticelli 423c, *The Holy Family* (1507) by Michelangelo, *Madonna of the Long Neck* (c.1534) by Parmigianino 424t; *The Annunciation* by Leonardo da Vinci 25crb; Galleria dell'Accademia: *Cassone Adimari* by Lo Scheggia 415b; SCHLOSSVERWALTUNG, MUNICH: 544b, 549t, 555c; HERMAN SCHOLTEN: 245b; SCIENCE MUSEUM, LONDON: 56tl, 56bl; SCIENCE PHOTO LIBRARY: M-SAT Ltd 10c; SCOPE: 186tr, 187c, 187br; SPECTRUM COLOUR LIBRARY: 8; STAATSGALERIE, STUTTGART: *St. Paul in Prison* (1627) by Rembrandt 556tr; STAD BRUGGE STEDLIJKE MUSEA: 234tc; STÄDELSCHES KUNSTINSTITUT UND STÄDTISCHE GALERIE, FRANKFURT AM MAIN: *Portrait of a Woman* (1480) by Sandro Botticelli 560c; STATENS HISTORISKA MUSEUM: 647c, 665tc, 665cr; STIFTUNG PREUSSISCHE SCHLÖSSER UND GÄRTEN

BERLIN-BRANDENBURG: 541br; STOCKPHOTOS: David Hornback 277b; SWISS NATIONAL MUSEUM, ZÜRICH: 614c; SWISS NATIONAL PARK: 620clb, 620cb, 620bl; SWISS TOURIST OFFICE: 622b.

TATE, LONDON 2001: Marcus Lee, *Maman* (1999) by Louise Bourgeois © DACS, London/VAGA, New York 2006 59t; TOPHAM PICTUREPOINT: 621cr; TOROS MAGAZINE: 293cr; THE TRAVEL LIBRARY: Galleria dell'Accademia 412bl; TRINITY COLLEGE, DUBLIN: Courtesy of the Board of Trinity College, Dublin 115t, 116tl, *Portrait of St. Matthew* from *The Book of Kells* 116c, 125t.

VAN GOGH MUSEUM, AMSTERDAM: Courtesy of the Vincent van Gogh Foundation 259c; *The Bedroom at Arles* by Vincent van Gogh 259t; VASA MUSEUM, STOCKHOLM: Hans Hammarskiold 646bl.

JEREMY WHITAKER: 75bl; CHRISTOPHER WILSON: 78bl; PETER WILSON: 468; JEPPE WIKSTRÖM: 20–21, 638c, 642b, 644b, 645t; WONDERFUL COPENHAGEN: 672c, 673bc, 679tr, 681bl, 683tr; WORLD PICTURES: 588b.

YORK CASTLE MUSEUM: 79c.

ZEFA, WARSAW: 520cla, 555b, 556br, 561b.

Jacket:
Front – ALAMY IMAGES: nagelestock.com main image; DK IMAGES: Peter Wilson clb. Back – ALAMY IMAGES: travelstock44.de.tl; DK IMAGES: clb; Joe Cornish cla; John Miller bl. Spine – ALAMY IMAGES: nagelestock.com t; DK Images: b.

All other images © Dorling Kindersley. For further information see: www.dkimages.com

---

SPECIAL EDITIONS OF DK TRAVEL GUIDES

DK Travel Guides can be purchased in bulk quantities at discounted prices for use in promotions or as premiums. We are also able to offer special editions and personalized jackets, corporate imprints, and excerpts from all of our books, tailored specifically to meet your own needs.

To find out more, please contact:
(in the United States) **SpecialSales@dk.com**
(in the UK) **Sarah.Burgess@dk.com**
(in Canada) DK Special Sales at **general@tourmaline.ca**
(in Australia) **business.development@pearson.com.au**